T0137011

Lecture Notes in Computer Science 11213

Commenced Publication in 1973
Founding and Former Series Editors:
Gerhard Goos, Juris Hartmanis, and Jan van Leeuwen

More information about this series at http://www.springer.com/series/7412

Lecture Notes in Computer Science 11213

Commenced Publication in 1973
Founding and Former Series Editors:
Gerhard Goos, Juris Hartmanis, and Jan van Leeuwen

More information about this series at http://www.springer.com/series/7412

Vittorio Ferrari · Martial Hebert
Cristian Sminchisescu · Yair Weiss (Eds.)

Computer Vision – ECCV 2018

15th European Conference
Munich, Germany, September 8–14, 2018
Proceedings, Part IX

 Springer

Editors
Vittorio Ferrari
Google Research
Zurich
Switzerland

Martial Hebert
Carnegie Mellon University
Pittsburgh, PA
USA

Cristian Sminchisescu
Google Research
Zurich
Switzerland

Yair Weiss
Hebrew University of Jerusalem
Jerusalem
Israel

ISSN 0302-9743   ISSN 1611-3349 (electronic)
Lecture Notes in Computer Science
ISBN 978-3-030-01239-7   ISBN 978-3-030-01240-3 (eBook)
https://doi.org/10.1007/978-3-030-01240-3

Library of Congress Control Number: 2018955489

LNCS Sublibrary: SL6 – Image Processing, Computer Vision, Pattern Recognition, and Graphics

This Springer imprint is published by the registered company Springer Nature Switzerland AG
The registered company address is: Gewerbestrasse 11, 6330 Cham, Switzerland

Foreword

It was our great pleasure to host the European Conference on Computer Vision 2018 in Munich, Germany. This constituted by far the largest ECCV event ever. With close to 2,900 registered participants and another 600 on the waiting list one month before the conference, participation more than doubled since the last ECCV in Amsterdam. We believe that this is due to a dramatic growth of the computer vision community combined with the popularity of Munich as a major European hub of culture, science, and industry. The conference took place in the heart of Munich in the concert hall Gasteig with workshops and tutorials held at the downtown campus of the Technical University of Munich.

One of the major innovations for ECCV 2018 was the free perpetual availability of all conference and workshop papers, which is often referred to as open access. We note that this is not precisely the same use of the term as in the Budapest declaration. Since 2013, CVPR and ICCV have had their papers hosted by the Computer Vision Foundation (CVF), in parallel with the IEEE Xplore version. This has proved highly beneficial to the computer vision community.

We are delighted to announce that for ECCV 2018 a very similar arrangement was put in place with the cooperation of Springer. In particular, the author's final version will be freely available in perpetuity on a CVF page, while SpringerLink will continue to host a version with further improvements, such as activating reference links and including video. We believe that this will give readers the best of both worlds; researchers who are focused on the technical content will have a freely available version in an easily accessible place, while subscribers to SpringerLink will continue to have the additional benefits that this provides. We thank Alfred Hofmann from Springer for helping to negotiate this agreement, which we expect will continue for future versions of ECCV.

September 2018

Horst Bischof
Daniel Cremers
Bernt Schiele
Ramin Zabih

Preface

Welcome to the proceedings of the 2018 European Conference on Computer Vision (ECCV 2018) held in Munich, Germany. We are delighted to present this volume reflecting a strong and exciting program, the result of an extensive review process. In total, we received 2,439 valid paper submissions. Of these, 776 were accepted (31.8%): 717 as posters (29.4%) and 59 as oral presentations (2.4%). All oral presentations were presented as posters as well. The program selection process was complicated this year by the large increase in the number of submitted papers, +65% over ECCV 2016, and the use of CMT3 for the first time for a computer vision conference. The program selection process was supported by four program co-chairs (PCs), 126 area chairs (ACs), and 1,199 reviewers with reviews assigned.

We were primarily responsible for the design and execution of the review process. Beyond administrative rejections, we were involved in acceptance decisions only in the very few cases where the ACs were not able to agree on a decision. As PCs, and as is customary in the field, we were not allowed to co-author a submission. General co-chairs and other co-organizers who played no role in the review process were permitted to submit papers, and were treated as any other author is.

Acceptance decisions were made by two independent ACs. The ACs also made a joint recommendation for promoting papers to oral status. We decided on the final selection of oral presentations based on the ACs' recommendations. There were 126 ACs, selected according to their technical expertise, experience, and geographical diversity (63 from European, nine from Asian/Australian, and 54 from North American institutions). Indeed, 126 ACs is a substantial increase in the number of ACs due to the natural increase in the number of papers and to our desire to maintain the number of papers assigned to each AC to a manageable number so as to ensure quality. The ACs were aided by the 1,199 reviewers to whom papers were assigned for reviewing. The Program Committee was selected from committees of previous ECCV, ICCV, and CVPR conferences and was extended on the basis of suggestions from the ACs. Having a large pool of Program Committee members for reviewing allowed us to match expertise while reducing reviewer loads. No more than eight papers were assigned to a reviewer, maintaining the reviewers' load at the same level as ECCV 2016 despite the increase in the number of submitted papers.

Conflicts of interest between ACs, Program Committee members, and papers were identified based on the home institutions, and on previous collaborations of all researchers involved. To find institutional conflicts, all authors, Program Committee members, and ACs were asked to list the Internet domains of their current institutions. We assigned on average approximately 18 papers to each AC. The papers were assigned using the affinity scores from the Toronto Paper Matching System (TPMS) and additional data from the OpenReview system, managed by a UMass group. OpenReview used additional information from ACs' and authors' records to identify collaborations and to generate matches. OpenReview was invaluable in refining conflict definitions and in generating quality matches. The only glitch is that, once the matches were generated, a small percentage of papers were unassigned because of discrepancies between the OpenReview conflicts and the conflicts entered in CMT3. We manually assigned these papers. This glitch is revealing of the challenge of using multiple systems at once (CMT3 and OpenReview in this case), which needs to be addressed in future.

After assignment of papers to ACs, the ACs suggested seven reviewers per paper from the Program Committee pool. The selection and rank ordering were facilitated by the TPMS affinity scores visible to the ACs for each paper/reviewer pair. The final assignment of papers to reviewers was generated again through OpenReview in order to account for refined conflict definitions. This required new features in the OpenReview matching system to accommodate the ECCV workflow, in particular to incorporate selection ranking, and maximum reviewer load. Very few papers received fewer than three reviewers after matching and were handled through manual assignment. Reviewers were then asked to comment on the merit of each paper and to make an initial recommendation ranging from definitely reject to definitely accept, including a borderline rating. The reviewers were also asked to suggest explicit questions they wanted to see answered in the authors' rebuttal. The initial review period was five weeks. Because of the delay in getting all the reviews in, we had to delay the final release of the reviews by four days. However, because of the slack included at the tail end of the schedule, we were able to maintain the decision target date with sufficient time for all the phases. We reassigned over 100 reviews from 40 reviewers during the review period. Unfortunately, the main reason for these reassignments was reviewers declining to review, after having accepted to do so. Other reasons included technical relevance and occasional unidentified conflicts. We express our thanks to the emergency reviewers who generously accepted to perform these reviews under short notice. In addition, a substantial number of manual corrections had to do with reviewers using a different email address than the one that was used at the time of the reviewer invitation. This is revealing of a broader issue with identifying users by email addresses that change frequently enough to cause significant problems during the timespan of the conference process.

The authors were then given the opportunity to rebut the reviews, to identify factual errors, and to address the specific questions raised by the reviewers over a seven-day rebuttal period. The exact format of the rebuttal was the object of considerable debate among the organizers, as well as with prior organizers. At issue is to balance giving the author the opportunity to respond completely and precisely to the reviewers, e.g., by including graphs of experiments, while avoiding requests for completely new material or experimental results not included in the original paper. In the end, we decided on the two-page PDF document in conference format. Following this rebuttal period, reviewers and ACs discussed papers at length, after which reviewers finalized their evaluation and gave a final recommendation to the ACs. A significant percentage of the reviewers did enter their final recommendation if it did not differ from their initial recommendation. Given the tight schedule, we did not wait until all were entered.

After this discussion period, each paper was assigned to a second AC. The AC/paper matching was again run through OpenReview. Again, the OpenReview team worked quickly to implement the features specific to this process, in this case accounting for the existing AC assignment, as well as minimizing the fragmentation across ACs, so that each AC had on average only 5.5 buddy ACs to communicate with. The largest number was 11. Given the complexity of the conflicts, this was a very efficient set of assignments from OpenReview. Each paper was then evaluated by its assigned pair of ACs. For each paper, we required each of the two ACs assigned to certify both the final recommendation and the metareview (aka consolidation report). In all cases, after extensive discussions, the two ACs arrived at a common acceptance decision. We maintained these decisions, with the caveat that we did evaluate, sometimes going back to the ACs, a few papers for which the final acceptance decision substantially deviated from the consensus from the reviewers, amending three decisions in the process.

We want to thank everyone involved in making ECCV 2018 possible. The success of ECCV 2018 depended on the quality of papers submitted by the authors, and on the very hard work of the ACs and the Program Committee members. We are particularly grateful to the OpenReview team (Melisa Bok, Ari Kobren, Andrew McCallum, Michael Spector) for their support, in particular their willingness to implement new features, often on a tight schedule, to Laurent Charlin for the use of the Toronto Paper Matching System, to the CMT3 team, in particular in dealing with all the issues that arise when using a new system, to Friedrich Fraundorfer and Quirin Lohr for maintaining the online version of the program, and to the CMU staff (Keyla Cook, Lynnetta Miller, Ashley Song, Nora Kazour) for assisting with data entry/editing in CMT3. Finally, the preparation of these proceedings would not have been possible without the diligent effort of the publication chairs, Albert Ali Salah and Hamdi Dibeklioğlu, and of Anna Kramer and Alfred Hofmann from Springer.

September 2018   Vittorio Ferrari
                                                            Martial Hebert
                                                     Cristian Sminchisescu
                                                               Yair Weiss

Organization

General Chairs

Horst Bischof — Graz University of Technology, Austria
Daniel Cremers — Technical University of Munich, Germany
Bernt Schiele — Saarland University, Max Planck Institute for Informatics, Germany
Ramin Zabih — CornellNYCTech, USA

Program Committee Co-chairs

Vittorio Ferrari — University of Edinburgh, UK
Martial Hebert — Carnegie Mellon University, USA
Cristian Sminchisescu — Lund University, Sweden
Yair Weiss — Hebrew University, Israel

Local Arrangements Chairs

Björn Menze — Technical University of Munich, Germany
Matthias Niessner — Technical University of Munich, Germany

Workshop Chairs

Stefan Roth — TU Darmstadt, Germany
Laura Leal-Taixé — Technical University of Munich, Germany

Tutorial Chairs

Michael Bronstein — Università della Svizzera Italiana, Switzerland
Laura Leal-Taixé — Technical University of Munich, Germany

Website Chair

Friedrich Fraundorfer — Graz University of Technology, Austria

Demo Chairs

Federico Tombari — Technical University of Munich, Germany
Joerg Stueckler — Technical University of Munich, Germany

Publicity Chair

Giovanni Maria
  Farinella
University of Catania, Italy

Industrial Liaison Chairs

Florent Perronnin   Naver Labs, France
Yunchao Gong   Snap, USA
Helmut Grabner   Logitech, Switzerland

Finance Chair

Gerard Medioni   Amazon, University of Southern California, USA

Publication Chairs

Albert Ali Salah   Boğaziçi University, Turkey
Hamdi Dibeklioğlu   Bilkent University, Turkey

Area Chairs

Kalle Åström   Lund University, Sweden
Zeynep Akata   University of Amsterdam, The Netherlands
Joao Barreto   University of Coimbra, Portugal
Ronen Basri   Weizmann Institute of Science, Israel
Dhruv Batra   Georgia Tech and Facebook AI Research, USA
Serge Belongie   Cornell University, USA
Rodrigo Benenson   Google, Switzerland
Hakan Bilen   University of Edinburgh, UK
Matthew Blaschko   KU Leuven, Belgium
Edmond Boyer   Inria, France
Gabriel Brostow   University College London, UK
Thomas Brox   University of Freiburg, Germany
Marcus Brubaker   York University, Canada
Barbara Caputo   Politecnico di Torino and the Italian Institute
                            of Technology, Italy
Tim Cootes   University of Manchester, UK
Trevor Darrell   University of California, Berkeley, USA
Larry Davis   University of Maryland at College Park, USA
Andrew Davison   Imperial College London, UK
Fernando de la Torre   Carnegie Mellon University, USA
Irfan Essa   GeorgiaTech, USA
Ali Farhadi   University of Washington, USA
Paolo Favaro   University of Bern, Switzerland
Michael Felsberg   Linköping University, Sweden

Sanja Fidler	University of Toronto, Canada
Andrew Fitzgibbon	Microsoft, Cambridge, UK
David Forsyth	University of Illinois at Urbana-Champaign, USA
Charless Fowlkes	University of California, Irvine, USA
Bill Freeman	MIT, USA
Mario Fritz	MPII, Germany
Jürgen Gall	University of Bonn, Germany
Dariu Gavrila	TU Delft, The Netherlands
Andreas Geiger	MPI-IS and University of Tübingen, Germany
Theo Gevers	University of Amsterdam, The Netherlands
Ross Girshick	Facebook AI Research, USA
Kristen Grauman	Facebook AI Research and UT Austin, USA
Abhinav Gupta	Carnegie Mellon University, USA
Kaiming He	Facebook AI Research, USA
Martial Hebert	Carnegie Mellon University, USA
Anders Heyden	Lund University, Sweden
Timothy Hospedales	University of Edinburgh, UK
Michal Irani	Weizmann Institute of Science, Israel
Phillip Isola	University of California, Berkeley, USA
Hervé Jégou	Facebook AI Research, France
David Jacobs	University of Maryland, College Park, USA
Allan Jepson	University of Toronto, Canada
Jiaya Jia	Chinese University of Hong Kong, SAR China
Fredrik Kahl	Chalmers University, USA
Hedvig Kjellström	KTH Royal Institute of Technology, Sweden
Iasonas Kokkinos	University College London and Facebook, UK
Vladlen Koltun	Intel Labs, USA
Philipp Krähenbühl	UT Austin, USA
M. Pawan Kumar	University of Oxford, UK
Kyros Kutulakos	University of Toronto, Canada
In Kweon	KAIST, South Korea
Ivan Laptev	Inria, France
Svetlana Lazebnik	University of Illinois at Urbana-Champaign, USA
Laura Leal-Taixé	Technical University of Munich, Germany
Erik Learned-Miller	University of Massachusetts, Amherst, USA
Kyoung Mu Lee	Seoul National University, South Korea
Bastian Leibe	RWTH Aachen University, Germany
Aleš Leonardis	University of Birmingham, UK
Vincent Lepetit	University of Bordeaux, France and Graz University of Technology, Austria
Fuxin Li	Oregon State University, USA
Dahua Lin	Chinese University of Hong Kong, SAR China
Jim Little	University of British Columbia, Canada
Ce Liu	Google, USA
Chen Change Loy	Nanyang Technological University, Singapore
Jiri Matas	Czech Technical University in Prague, Czechia

Yasuyuki Matsushita	Osaka University, Japan
Dimitris Metaxas	Rutgers University, USA
Greg Mori	Simon Fraser University, Canada
Vittorio Murino	Istituto Italiano di Tecnologia, Italy
Richard Newcombe	Oculus Research, USA
Minh Hoai Nguyen	Stony Brook University, USA
Sebastian Nowozin	Microsoft Research Cambridge, UK
Aude Oliva	MIT, USA
Bjorn Ommer	Heidelberg University, Germany
Tomas Pajdla	Czech Technical University in Prague, Czechia
Maja Pantic	Imperial College London and Samsung AI Research Centre Cambridge, UK
Caroline Pantofaru	Google, USA
Devi Parikh	Georgia Tech and Facebook AI Research, USA
Sylvain Paris	Adobe Research, USA
Vladimir Pavlovic	Rutgers University, USA
Marcello Pelillo	University of Venice, Italy
Patrick Pérez	Valeo, France
Robert Pless	George Washington University, USA
Thomas Pock	Graz University of Technology, Austria
Jean Ponce	Inria, France
Gerard Pons-Moll	MPII, Saarland Informatics Campus, Germany
Long Quan	Hong Kong University of Science and Technology, SAR China
Stefan Roth	TU Darmstadt, Germany
Carsten Rother	University of Heidelberg, Germany
Bryan Russell	Adobe Research, USA
Kate Saenko	Boston University, USA
Mathieu Salzmann	EPFL, Switzerland
Dimitris Samaras	Stony Brook University, USA
Yoichi Sato	University of Tokyo, Japan
Silvio Savarese	Stanford University, USA
Konrad Schindler	ETH Zurich, Switzerland
Cordelia Schmid	Inria, France and Google, France
Nicu Sebe	University of Trento, Italy
Fei Sha	University of Southern California, USA
Greg Shakhnarovich	TTI Chicago, USA
Jianbo Shi	University of Pennsylvania, USA
Abhinav Shrivastava	UMD and Google, USA
Yan Shuicheng	National University of Singapore, Singapore
Leonid Sigal	University of British Columbia, Canada
Josef Sivic	Czech Technical University in Prague, Czechia
Arnold Smeulders	University of Amsterdam, The Netherlands
Deqing Sun	NVIDIA, USA
Antonio Torralba	MIT, USA
Zhuowen Tu	University of California, San Diego, USA

Tinne Tuytelaars	KU Leuven, Belgium
Jasper Uijlings	Google, Switzerland
Joost van de Weijer	Computer Vision Center, Spain
Nuno Vasconcelos	University of California, San Diego, USA
Andrea Vedaldi	University of Oxford, UK
Olga Veksler	University of Western Ontario, Canada
Jakob Verbeek	Inria, France
Rene Vidal	Johns Hopkins University, USA
Daphna Weinshall	Hebrew University, Israel
Chris Williams	University of Edinburgh, UK
Lior Wolf	Tel Aviv University, Israel
Ming-Hsuan Yang	University of California at Merced, USA
Todd Zickler	Harvard University, USA
Andrew Zisserman	University of Oxford, UK

Technical Program Committee

Hassan Abu Alhaija	Peter Anderson	Arunava Banerjee
Radhakrishna Achanta	Juan Andrade-Cetto	Atsuhiko Banno
Hanno Ackermann	Mykhaylo Andriluka	Aayush Bansal
Ehsan Adeli	Anelia Angelova	Yingze Bao
Lourdes Agapito	Michel Antunes	Md Jawadul Bappy
Aishwarya Agrawal	Pablo Arbelaez	Pierre Baqué
Antonio Agudo	Vasileios Argyriou	Dániel Baráth
Eirikur Agustsson	Chetan Arora	Adrian Barbu
Karim Ahmed	Federica Arrigoni	Kobus Barnard
Byeongjoo Ahn	Vassilis Athitsos	Nick Barnes
Unaiza Ahsan	Mathieu Aubry	Francisco Barranco
Emre Akbaş	Shai Avidan	Adrien Bartoli
Eren Aksoy	Yannis Avrithis	E. Bayro-Corrochano
Yağız Aksoy	Samaneh Azadi	Paul Beardlsey
Alexandre Alahi	Hossein Azizpour	Vasileios Belagiannis
Jean-Baptiste Alayrac	Artem Babenko	Sean Bell
Samuel Albanie	Timur Bagautdinov	Ismail Ben
Cenek Albl	Andrew Bagdanov	Boulbaba Ben Amor
Saad Ali	Hessam Bagherinezhad	Gil Ben-Artzi
Rahaf Aljundi	Yuval Bahat	Ohad Ben-Shahar
Jose M. Alvarez	Min Bai	Abhijit Bendale
Humam Alwassel	Qinxun Bai	Rodrigo Benenson
Toshiyuki Amano	Song Bai	Fabian Benitez-Quiroz
Mitsuru Ambai	Xiang Bai	Fethallah Benmansour
Mohamed Amer	Peter Bajcsy	Ryad Benosman
Senjian An	Amr Bakry	Filippo Bergamasco
Cosmin Ancuti	Kavita Bala	David Bermudez

Jesus Bermudez-Cameo
Leonard Berrada
Gedas Bertasius
Ross Beveridge
Lucas Beyer
Bir Bhanu
S. Bhattacharya
Binod Bhattarai
Arnav Bhavsar
Simone Bianco
Adel Bibi
Pia Bideau
Josef Bigun
Arijit Biswas
Soma Biswas
Marten Bjoerkman
Volker Blanz
Vishnu Boddeti
Piotr Bojanowski
Terrance Boult
Yuri Boykov
Hakan Boyraz
Eric Brachmann
Samarth Brahmbhatt
Mathieu Bredif
Francois Bremond
Michael Brown
Luc Brun
Shyamal Buch
Pradeep Buddharaju
Aurelie Bugeau
Rudy Bunel
Xavier Burgos Artizzu
Darius Burschka
Andrei Bursuc
Zoya Bylinskii
Fabian Caba
Daniel Cabrini Hauagge
Cesar Cadena Lerma
Holger Caesar
Jianfei Cai
Junjie Cai
Zhaowei Cai
Simone Calderara
Neill Campbell
Octavia Camps

Xun Cao
Yanshuai Cao
Joao Carreira
Dan Casas
Daniel Castro
Jan Cech
M. Emre Celebi
Duygu Ceylan
Menglei Chai
Ayan Chakrabarti
Rudrasis Chakraborty
Shayok Chakraborty
Tat-Jen Cham
Antonin Chambolle
Antoni Chan
Sharat Chandran
Hyun Sung Chang
Ju Yong Chang
Xiaojun Chang
Soravit Changpinyo
Wei-Lun Chao
Yu-Wei Chao
Visesh Chari
Rizwan Chaudhry
Siddhartha Chaudhuri
Rama Chellappa
Chao Chen
Chen Chen
Cheng Chen
Chu-Song Chen
Guang Chen
Hsin-I Chen
Hwann-Tzong Chen
Kai Chen
Kan Chen
Kevin Chen
Liang-Chieh Chen
Lin Chen
Qifeng Chen
Ting Chen
Wei Chen
Xi Chen
Xilin Chen
Xinlei Chen
Yingcong Chen
Yixin Chen

Erkang Cheng
Jingchun Cheng
Ming-Ming Cheng
Wen-Huang Cheng
Yuan Cheng
Anoop Cherian
Liang-Tien Chia
Naoki Chiba
Shao-Yi Chien
Han-Pang Chiu
Wei-Chen Chiu
Nam Ik Cho
Sunghyun Cho
TaeEun Choe
Jongmoo Choi
Christopher Choy
Wen-Sheng Chu
Yung-Yu Chuang
Ondrej Chum
Joon Son Chung
Gökberk Cinbis
James Clark
Andrea Cohen
Forrester Cole
Toby Collins
John Collomosse
Camille Couprie
David Crandall
Marco Cristani
Canton Cristian
James Crowley
Yin Cui
Zhaopeng Cui
Bo Dai
Jifeng Dai
Qieyun Dai
Shengyang Dai
Yuchao Dai
Carlo Dal Mutto
Dima Damen
Zachary Daniels
Kostas Daniilidis
Donald Dansereau
Mohamed Daoudi
Abhishek Das
Samyak Datta

Achal Dave	Aykut Erdem	Ryo Furukawa
Shalini De Mello	Erkut Erdem	Yasutaka Furukawa
Teofilo deCampos	Hugo Jair Escalante	Andrea Fusiello
Joseph DeGol	Sergio Escalera	Fatma Güney
Koichiro Deguchi	Victor Escorcia	Raghudeep Gadde
Alessio Del Bue	Francisco Estrada	Silvano Galliani
Stefanie Demirci	Davide Eynard	Orazio Gallo
Jia Deng	Bin Fan	Chuang Gan
Zhiwei Deng	Jialue Fan	Bin-Bin Gao
Joachim Denzler	Quanfu Fan	Jin Gao
Konstantinos Derpanis	Chen Fang	Junbin Gao
Aditya Deshpande	Tian Fang	Ruohan Gao
Alban Desmaison	Yi Fang	Shenghua Gao
Frédéric Devernay	Hany Farid	Animesh Garg
Abhinav Dhall	Giovanni Farinella	Ravi Garg
Michel Dhome	Ryan Farrell	Erik Gartner
Hamdi Dibeklioğlu	Alireza Fathi	Simone Gasparin
Mert Dikmen	Christoph Feichtenhofer	Jochen Gast
Cosimo Distante	Wenxin Feng	Leon A. Gatys
Ajay Divakaran	Martin Fergie	Stratis Gavves
Mandar Dixit	Cornelia Fermuller	Liuhao Ge
Carl Doersch	Basura Fernando	Timnit Gebru
Piotr Dollar	Michael Firman	James Gee
Bo Dong	Bob Fisher	Peter Gehler
Chao Dong	John Fisher	Xin Geng
Huang Dong	Mathew Fisher	Guido Gerig
Jian Dong	Boris Flach	David Geronimo
Jiangxin Dong	Matt Flagg	Bernard Ghanem
Weisheng Dong	Francois Fleuret	Michael Gharbi
Simon Donné	David Fofi	Golnaz Ghiasi
Gianfranco Doretto	Ruth Fong	Spyros Gidaris
Alexey Dosovitskiy	Gian Luca Foresti	Andrew Gilbert
Matthijs Douze	Per-Erik Forssén	Rohit Girdhar
Bruce Draper	David Fouhey	Ioannis Gkioulekas
Bertram Drost	Katerina Fragkiadaki	Georgia Gkioxari
Liang Du	Victor Fragoso	Guy Godin
Shichuan Du	Jan-Michael Frahm	Roland Goecke
Gregory Dudek	Jean-Sebastien Franco	Michael Goesele
Zoran Duric	Ohad Fried	Nuno Goncalves
Pınar Duygulu	Simone Frintrop	Boqing Gong
Hazım Ekenel	Huazhu Fu	Minglun Gong
Tarek El-Gaaly	Yun Fu	Yunchao Gong
Ehsan Elhamifar	Olac Fuentes	Abel Gonzalez-Garcia
Mohamed Elhoseiny	Christopher Funk	Daniel Gordon
Sabu Emmanuel	Thomas Funkhouser	Paulo Gotardo
Ian Endres	Brian Funt	Stephen Gould

Venu Govindu
Helmut Grabner
Petr Gronat
Steve Gu
Josechu Guerrero
Anupam Guha
Jean-Yves Guillemaut
Alp Güler
Erhan Gündoğdu
Guodong Guo
Xinqing Guo
Ankush Gupta
Mohit Gupta
Saurabh Gupta
Tanmay Gupta
Abner Guzman Rivera
Timo Hackel
Sunil Hadap
Christian Haene
Ralf Haeusler
Levente Hajder
David Hall
Peter Hall
Stefan Haller
Ghassan Hamarneh
Fred Hamprecht
Onur Hamsici
Bohyung Han
Junwei Han
Xufeng Han
Yahong Han
Ankur Handa
Albert Haque
Tatsuya Harada
Mehrtash Harandi
Bharath Hariharan
Mahmudul Hasan
Tal Hassner
Kenji Hata
Soren Hauberg
Michal Havlena
Zeeshan Hayder
Junfeng He
Lei He
Varsha Hedau
Felix Heide

Wolfgang Heidrich
Janne Heikkila
Jared Heinly
Mattias Heinrich
Lisa Anne Hendricks
Dan Hendrycks
Stephane Herbin
Alexander Hermans
Luis Herranz
Aaron Hertzmann
Adrian Hilton
Michael Hirsch
Steven Hoi
Seunghoon Hong
Wei Hong
Anthony Hoogs
Radu Horaud
Yedid Hoshen
Omid Hosseini Jafari
Kuang-Jui Hsu
Winston Hsu
Yinlin Hu
Zhe Hu
Gang Hua
Chen Huang
De-An Huang
Dong Huang
Gary Huang
Heng Huang
Jia-Bin Huang
Qixing Huang
Rui Huang
Sheng Huang
Weilin Huang
Xiaolei Huang
Xinyu Huang
Zhiwu Huang
Tak-Wai Hui
Wei-Chih Hung
Junhwa Hur
Mohamed Hussein
Wonjun Hwang
Anders Hyden
Satoshi Ikehata
Nazlı Ikizler-Cinbis
Viorela Ila

Evren Imre
Eldar Insafutdinov
Go Irie
Hossam Isack
Ahmet Işcen
Daisuke Iwai
Hamid Izadinia
Nathan Jacobs
Suyog Jain
Varun Jampani
C. V. Jawahar
Dinesh Jayaraman
Sadeep Jayasumana
Laszlo Jeni
Hueihan Jhuang
Dinghuang Ji
Hui Ji
Qiang Ji
Fan Jia
Kui Jia
Xu Jia
Huaizu Jiang
Jiayan Jiang
Nianjuan Jiang
Tingting Jiang
Xiaoyi Jiang
Yu-Gang Jiang
Long Jin
Suo Jinli
Justin Johnson
Nebojsa Jojic
Michael Jones
Hanbyul Joo
Jungseock Joo
Ajjen Joshi
Amin Jourabloo
Frederic Jurie
Achuta Kadambi
Samuel Kadoury
Ioannis Kakadiaris
Zdenek Kalal
Yannis Kalantidis
Sinan Kalkan
Vicky Kalogeiton
Sunkavalli Kalyan
J.-K. Kamarainen

Martin Kampel
Kenichi Kanatani
Angjoo Kanazawa
Melih Kandemir
Sing Bing Kang
Zhuoliang Kang
Mohan Kankanhalli
Juho Kannala
Abhishek Kar
Amlan Kar
Svebor Karaman
Leonid Karlinsky
Zoltan Kato
Parneet Kaur
Hiroshi Kawasaki
Misha Kazhdan
Margret Keuper
Sameh Khamis
Naeemullah Khan
Salman Khan
Hadi Kiapour
Joe Kileel
Chanho Kim
Gunhee Kim
Hansung Kim
Junmo Kim
Junsik Kim
Kihwan Kim
Minyoung Kim
Tae Hyun Kim
Tae-Kyun Kim
Akisato Kimura
Zsolt Kira
Alexander Kirillov
Kris Kitani
Maria Klodt
Patrick Knöbelreiter
Jan Knopp
Reinhard Koch
Alexander Kolesnikov
Chen Kong
Naejin Kong
Shu Kong
Piotr Koniusz
Simon Korman
Andreas Koschan

Dimitrios Kosmopoulos
Satwik Kottur
Balazs Kovacs
Adarsh Kowdle
Mike Krainin
Gregory Kramida
Ranjay Krishna
Ravi Krishnan
Matej Kristan
Pavel Krsek
Volker Krueger
Alexander Krull
Hilde Kuehne
Andreas Kuhn
Arjan Kuijper
Zuzana Kukelova
Kuldeep Kulkarni
Shiro Kumano
Avinash Kumar
Vijay Kumar
Abhijit Kundu
Sebastian Kurtek
Junseok Kwon
Jan Kybic
Alexander Ladikos
Shang-Hong Lai
Wei-Sheng Lai
Jean-Francois Lalonde
John Lambert
Zhenzhong Lan
Charis Lanaras
Oswald Lanz
Dong Lao
Longin Jan Latecki
Justin Lazarow
Huu Le
Chen-Yu Lee
Gim Hee Lee
Honglak Lee
Hsin-Ying Lee
Joon-Young Lee
Seungyong Lee
Stefan Lee
Yong Jae Lee
Zhen Lei
Ido Leichter

Victor Lempitsky
Spyridon Leonardos
Marius Leordeanu
Matt Leotta
Thomas Leung
Stefan Leutenegger
Gil Levi
Aviad Levis
Jose Lezama
Ang Li
Dingzeyu Li
Dong Li
Haoxiang Li
Hongdong Li
Hongsheng Li
Hongyang Li
Jianguo Li
Kai Li
Ruiyu Li
Wei Li
Wen Li
Xi Li
Xiaoxiao Li
Xin Li
Xirong Li
Xuelong Li
Xueting Li
Yeqing Li
Yijun Li
Yin Li
Yingwei Li
Yining Li
Yongjie Li
Yu-Feng Li
Zechao Li
Zhengqi Li
Zhenyang Li
Zhizhong Li
Xiaodan Liang
Renjie Liao
Zicheng Liao
Bee Lim
Jongwoo Lim
Joseph Lim
Ser-Nam Lim
Chen-Hsuan Lin

Shih-Yao Lin
Tsung-Yi Lin
Weiyao Lin
Yen-Yu Lin
Haibin Ling
Or Litany
Roee Litman
Anan Liu
Changsong Liu
Chen Liu
Ding Liu
Dong Liu
Feng Liu
Guangcan Liu
Luoqi Liu
Miaomiao Liu
Nian Liu
Risheng Liu
Shu Liu
Shuaicheng Liu
Sifei Liu
Tyng-Luh Liu
Wanquan Liu
Weiwei Liu
Xialei Liu
Xiaoming Liu
Yebin Liu
Yiming Liu
Ziwei Liu
Zongyi Liu
Liliana Lo Presti
Edgar Lobaton
Chengjiang Long
Mingsheng Long
Roberto Lopez-Sastre
Amy Loufti
Brian Lovell
Canyi Lu
Cewu Lu
Feng Lu
Huchuan Lu
Jiajun Lu
Jiasen Lu
Jiwen Lu
Yang Lu
Yujuan Lu

Simon Lucey
Jian-Hao Luo
Jiebo Luo
Pablo Márquez-Neila
Matthias Müller
Chao Ma
Chih-Yao Ma
Lin Ma
Shugao Ma
Wei-Chiu Ma
Zhanyu Ma
Oisin Mac Aodha
Will Maddern
Ludovic Magerand
Marcus Magnor
Vijay Mahadevan
Mohammad Mahoor
Michael Maire
Subhransu Maji
Ameesh Makadia
Atsuto Maki
Yasushi Makihara
Mateusz Malinowski
Tomasz Malisiewicz
Arun Mallya
Roberto Manduchi
Junhua Mao
Dmitrii Marin
Joe Marino
Kenneth Marino
Elisabeta Marinoiu
Ricardo Martin
Aleix Martinez
Julieta Martinez
Aaron Maschinot
Jonathan Masci
Bogdan Matei
Diana Mateus
Stefan Mathe
Kevin Matzen
Bruce Maxwell
Steve Maybank
Walterio Mayol-Cuevas
Mason McGill
Stephen Mckenna
Roey Mechrez

Christopher Mei
Heydi Mendez-Vazquez
Deyu Meng
Thomas Mensink
Bjoern Menze
Domingo Mery
Qiguang Miao
Tomer Michaeli
Antoine Miech
Ondrej Miksik
Anton Milan
Gregor Miller
Cai Minjie
Majid Mirmehdi
Ishan Misra
Niloy Mitra
Anurag Mittal
Nirbhay Modhe
Davide Modolo
Pritish Mohapatra
Pascal Monasse
Mathew Monfort
Taesup Moon
Sandino Morales
Vlad Morariu
Philippos Mordohai
Francesc Moreno
Henrique Morimitsu
Yael Moses
Ben-Ezra Moshe
Roozbeh Mottaghi
Yadong Mu
Lopamudra Mukherjee
Mario Munich
Ana Murillo
Damien Muselet
Armin Mustafa
Siva Karthik Mustikovela
Moin Nabi
Sobhan Naderi
Hajime Nagahara
Varun Nagaraja
Tushar Nagarajan
Arsha Nagrani
Nikhil Naik
Atsushi Nakazawa

P. J. Narayanan
Charlie Nash
Lakshmanan Nataraj
Fabian Nater
Lukáš Neumann
Natalia Neverova
Alejandro Newell
Phuc Nguyen
Xiaohan Nie
David Nilsson
Ko Nishino
Zhenxing Niu
Shohei Nobuhara
Klas Nordberg
Mohammed Norouzi
David Novotny
Ifeoma Nwogu
Matthew O'Toole
Guillaume Obozinski
Jean-Marc Odobez
Eyal Ofek
Ferda Ofli
Tae-Hyun Oh
Iason Oikonomidis
Takeshi Oishi
Takahiro Okabe
Takayuki Okatani
Vlad Olaru
Michael Opitz
Jose Oramas
Vicente Ordonez
Ivan Oseledets
Aljosa Osep
Magnus Oskarsson
Martin R. Oswald
Wanli Ouyang
Andrew Owens
Mustafa Özuysal
Jinshan Pan
Xingang Pan
Rameswar Panda
Sharath Pankanti
Julien Pansiot
Nicolas Papadakis
George Papandreou
N. Papanikolopoulos

Hyun Soo Park
In Kyu Park
Jaesik Park
Omkar Parkhi
Alvaro Parra Bustos
C. Alejandro Parraga
Vishal Patel
Deepak Pathak
Ioannis Patras
Viorica Patraucean
Genevieve Patterson
Kim Pedersen
Robert Peharz
Selen Pehlivan
Xi Peng
Bojan Pepik
Talita Perciano
Federico Pernici
Adrian Peter
Stavros Petridis
Vladimir Petrovic
Henning Petzka
Tomas Pfister
Trung Pham
Justus Piater
Massimo Piccardi
Sudeep Pillai
Pedro Pinheiro
Lerrel Pinto
Bernardo Pires
Aleksis Pirinen
Fiora Pirri
Leonid Pischulin
Tobias Ploetz
Bryan Plummer
Yair Poleg
Jean Ponce
Gerard Pons-Moll
Jordi Pont-Tuset
Alin Popa
Fatih Porikli
Horst Possegger
Viraj Prabhu
Andrea Prati
Maria Priisalu
Véronique Prinet

Victor Prisacariu
Jan Prokaj
Nicolas Pugeault
Luis Puig
Ali Punjani
Senthil Purushwalkam
Guido Pusiol
Guo-Jun Qi
Xiaojuan Qi
Hongwei Qin
Shi Qiu
Faisal Qureshi
Matthias Rüther
Petia Radeva
Umer Rafi
Rahul Raguram
Swaminathan Rahul
Varun Ramakrishna
Kandan Ramakrishnan
Ravi Ramamoorthi
Vignesh Ramanathan
Vasili Ramanishka
R. Ramasamy Selvaraju
Rene Ranftl
Carolina Raposo
Nikhil Rasiwasia
Nalini Ratha
Sai Ravela
Avinash Ravichandran
Ramin Raziperchikolaei
Sylvestre-Alvise Rebuffi
Adria Recasens
Joe Redmon
Timo Rehfeld
Michal Reinstein
Konstantinos Rematas
Haibing Ren
Shaoqing Ren
Wenqi Ren
Zhile Ren
Hamid Rezatofighi
Nicholas Rhinehart
Helge Rhodin
Elisa Ricci
Eitan Richardson
Stephan Richter

Qing Sun
Zhaohui Sun
David Suter
Eran Swears
Raza Syed Hussain
T. Syeda-Mahmood
Christian Szegedy
Duy-Nguyen Ta
Tolga Taşdizen
Hemant Tagare
Yuichi Taguchi
Ying Tai
Yu-Wing Tai
Jun Takamatsu
Hugues Talbot
Toru Tamak
Robert Tamburo
Chaowei Tan
Meng Tang
Peng Tang
Siyu Tang
Wei Tang
Junli Tao
Ran Tao
Xin Tao
Makarand Tapaswi
Jean-Philippe Tarel
Maxim Tatarchenko
Bugra Tekin
Demetri Terzopoulos
Christian Theobalt
Diego Thomas
Rajat Thomas
Qi Tian
Xinmei Tian
YingLi Tian
Yonghong Tian
Yonglong Tian
Joseph Tighe
Radu Timofte
Massimo Tistarelli
Sinisa Todorovic
Pavel Tokmakov
Giorgos Tolias
Federico Tombari
Tatiana Tommasi

Chetan Tonde
Xin Tong
Akihiko Torii
Andrea Torsello
Florian Trammer
Du Tran
Quoc-Huy Tran
Rudolph Triebel
Alejandro Troccoli
Leonardo Trujillo
Tomasz Trzcinski
Sam Tsai
Yi-Hsuan Tsai
Hung-Yu Tseng
Vagia Tsiminaki
Aggeliki Tsoli
Wei-Chih Tu
Shubham Tulsiani
Fred Tung
Tony Tung
Matt Turek
Oncel Tuzel
Georgios Tzimiropoulos
Ilkay Ulusoy
Osman Ulusoy
Dmitry Ulyanov
Paul Upchurch
Ben Usman
Evgeniya Ustinova
Himanshu Vajaria
Alexander Vakhitov
Jack Valmadre
Ernest Valveny
Jan van Gemert
Grant Van Horn
Jagannadan Varadarajan
Gul Varol
Sebastiano Vascon
Francisco Vasconcelos
Mayank Vatsa
Javier Vazquez-Corral
Ramakrishna Vedantam
Ashok Veeraraghavan
Andreas Veit
Raviteja Vemulapalli
Jonathan Ventura

Matthias Vestner
Minh Vo
Christoph Vogel
Michele Volpi
Carl Vondrick
Sven Wachsmuth
Toshikazu Wada
Michael Waechter
Catherine Wah
Jacob Walker
Jun Wan
Boyu Wang
Chen Wang
Chunyu Wang
De Wang
Fang Wang
Hongxing Wang
Hua Wang
Jiang Wang
Jingdong Wang
Jinglu Wang
Jue Wang
Le Wang
Lei Wang
Lezi Wang
Liang Wang
Lichao Wang
Lijun Wang
Limin Wang
Liwei Wang
Naiyan Wang
Oliver Wang
Qi Wang
Ruiping Wang
Shenlong Wang
Shu Wang
Song Wang
Tao Wang
Xiaofang Wang
Xiaolong Wang
Xinchao Wang
Xinggang Wang
Xintao Wang
Yang Wang
Yu-Chiang Frank Wang
Yu-Xiong Wang

Zhaowen Wang
Zhe Wang
Anne Wannenwetsch
Simon Warfield
Scott Wehrwein
Donglai Wei
Ping Wei
Shih-En Wei
Xiu-Shen Wei
Yichen Wei
Xie Weidi
Philippe Weinzaepfel
Longyin Wen
Eric Wengrowski
Tomas Werner
Michael Wilber
Rick Wildes
Olivia Wiles
Kyle Wilson
David Wipf
Kwan-Yee Wong
Daniel Worrall
John Wright
Baoyuan Wu
Chao-Yuan Wu
Jiajun Wu
Jianxin Wu
Tianfu Wu
Xiaodong Wu
Xiaohe Wu
Xinxiao Wu
Yang Wu
Yi Wu
Ying Wu
Yuxin Wu
Zheng Wu
Stefanie Wuhrer
Yin Xia
Tao Xiang
Yu Xiang
Lei Xiao
Tong Xiao
Yang Xiao
Cihang Xie
Dan Xie
Jianwen Xie

Jin Xie
Lingxi Xie
Pengtao Xie
Saining Xie
Wenxuan Xie
Yuchen Xie
Bo Xin
Junliang Xing
Peng Xingchao
Bo Xiong
Fei Xiong
Xuehan Xiong
Yuanjun Xiong
Chenliang Xu
Danfei Xu
Huijuan Xu
Jia Xu
Weipeng Xu
Xiangyu Xu
Yan Xu
Yuanlu Xu
Jia Xue
Tianfan Xue
Erdem Yörük
Abhay Yadav
Deshraj Yadav
Payman Yadollahpour
Yasushi Yagi
Toshihiko Yamasaki
Fei Yan
Hang Yan
Junchi Yan
Junjie Yan
Sijie Yan
Keiji Yanai
Bin Yang
Chih-Yuan Yang
Dong Yang
Herb Yang
Jianchao Yang
Jianwei Yang
Jiaolong Yang
Jie Yang
Jimei Yang
Jufeng Yang
Linjie Yang

Michael Ying Yang
Ming Yang
Ruiduo Yang
Ruigang Yang
Shuo Yang
Wei Yang
Xiaodong Yang
Yanchao Yang
Yi Yang
Angela Yao
Bangpeng Yao
Cong Yao
Jian Yao
Ting Yao
Julian Yarkony
Mark Yatskar
Jinwei Ye
Mao Ye
Mei-Chen Yeh
Raymond Yeh
Serena Yeung
Kwang Moo Yi
Shuai Yi
Alper Yılmaz
Lijun Yin
Xi Yin
Zhaozheng Yin
Xianghua Ying
Ryo Yonetani
Donghyun Yoo
Ju Hong Yoon
Kuk-Jin Yoon
Chong You
Shaodi You
Aron Yu
Fisher Yu
Gang Yu
Jingyi Yu
Ke Yu
Licheng Yu
Pei Yu
Qian Yu
Rong Yu
Shoou-I Yu
Stella Yu
Xiang Yu

Yang Yu
Zhiding Yu
Ganzhao Yuan
Jing Yuan
Junsong Yuan
Lu Yuan
Stefanos Zafeiriou
Sergey Zagoruyko
Amir Zamir
K. Zampogiannis
Andrei Zanfir
Mihai Zanfir
Pablo Zegers
Eyasu Zemene
Andy Zeng
Xingyu Zeng
Yun Zeng
De-Chuan Zhan
Cheng Zhang
Dong Zhang
Guofeng Zhang
Han Zhang
Hang Zhang
Hanwang Zhang
Jian Zhang
Jianguo Zhang
Jianming Zhang
Jiawei Zhang
Junping Zhang
Lei Zhang
Linguang Zhang
Ning Zhang
Qing Zhang

Quanshi Zhang
Richard Zhang
Runze Zhang
Shanshan Zhang
Shiliang Zhang
Shu Zhang
Ting Zhang
Xiangyu Zhang
Xiaofan Zhang
Xu Zhang
Yimin Zhang
Yinda Zhang
Yongqiang Zhang
Yuting Zhang
Zhanpeng Zhang
Ziyu Zhang
Bin Zhao
Chen Zhao
Hang Zhao
Hengshuang Zhao
Qijun Zhao
Rui Zhao
Yue Zhao
Enliang Zheng
Liang Zheng
Stephan Zheng
Wei-Shi Zheng
Wenming Zheng
Yin Zheng
Yinqiang Zheng
Yuanjie Zheng
Guangyu Zhong
Bolei Zhou

Guang-Tong Zhou
Huiyu Zhou
Jiahuan Zhou
S. Kevin Zhou
Tinghui Zhou
Wengang Zhou
Xiaowei Zhou
Xingyi Zhou
Yin Zhou
Zihan Zhou
Fan Zhu
Guangming Zhu
Ji Zhu
Jiejie Zhu
Jun-Yan Zhu
Shizhan Zhu
Siyu Zhu
Xiangxin Zhu
Xiatian Zhu
Yan Zhu
Yingying Zhu
Yixin Zhu
Yuke Zhu
Zhenyao Zhu
Liansheng Zhuang
Zeeshan Zia
Karel Zimmermann
Daniel Zoran
Danping Zou
Qi Zou
Silvia Zuffi
Wangmeng Zuo
Xinxin Zuo

Contents – Part IX

Poster Session

PS-FCN: A Flexible Learning Framework for Photometric Stereo

Guanying Chen[1(✉)], Kai Han[2], and Kwan-Yee K. Wong[1]

[1] The University of Hong Kong, Pokfulam, Hong Kong
{gychen,kykwong}@cs.hku.hk
[2] University of Oxford, Oxford, UK
khan@robots.ox.ac.uk

Abstract. This paper addresses the problem of photometric stereo for non-Lambertian surfaces. Existing approaches often adopt simplified reflectance models to make the problem more tractable, but this greatly hinders their applications on real-world objects. In this paper, we propose a deep fully convolutional network, called PS-FCN, that takes an arbitrary number of images of a static object captured under different light directions with a fixed camera as input, and predicts a normal map of the object in a fast feed-forward pass. Unlike the recently proposed learning based method, PS-FCN does not require a pre-defined set of light directions during training and testing, and can handle multiple images and light directions in an order-agnostic manner. Although we train PS-FCN on synthetic data, it can generalize well on real datasets. We further show that PS-FCN can be easily extended to handle the problem of uncalibrated photometric stereo. Extensive experiments on public real datasets show that PS-FCN outperforms existing approaches in calibrated photometric stereo, and promising results are achieved in uncalibrated scenario, clearly demonstrating its effectiveness.

Keywords: Photometric stereo · Convolutional neural network

1 Introduction

Given multiple images of a static object captured under different light directions with a fixed camera, the surface normals of the object can be estimated using photometric stereo techniques. Early photometric stereo algorithms often assumed an ideal Lambertian reflectance model [1,2]. Unfortunately, most of the real-world objects are non-Lambertian, and therefore more general models are needed to make photometric stereo methods more practical. Bidirectional reflectance distribution function (BRDF) is a general form for describing the reflectance property of a surface. However, it is difficult to handle general non-parametric BRDFs in non-Lambertian photometric stereo. Many researchers therefore adopted analytical reflectance models [3–5] to simplify the problem. However, a specific analytical model is only valid for a small set of materials.

© Springer Nature Switzerland AG 2018
V. Ferrari et al. (Eds.): ECCV 2018, LNCS 11213, pp. 3–19, 2018.
https://doi.org/10.1007/978-3-030-01240-3_1

Besides, fitting an analytical model to all the captured data requires solving a complex optimization problem. Hence, it remains an open and challenging problem to develop a computationally efficient photometric stereo method that can handle materials with diverse BRDFs.

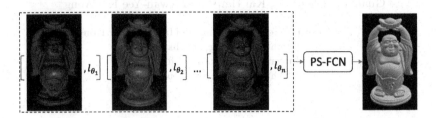

Fig. 1. Given an arbitrary number of images and their associated light directions as input, our model estimates a normal map of the object in a fast feed-forward pass.

Deep learning frameworks [6,7] have shown great success in both high-level and low-level computer vision tasks. In the context of photometric stereo, Santo *et al.* [8] recently proposed a deep fully-connected network, called DPSN, to learn the mapping between reflectance observations and surface normals in a per-pixel manner. For each pixel, DPSN takes observations under 96 pre-defined light directions as input and predicts a normal vector. Note that since DPSN depends on a pre-defined set of light directions during training and testing, its practical use is sort of limited. Besides, DPSN predicts a normal vector based solely on the reflectance observations of a single pixel, it cannot take full advantage of the information embedded in the neighborhood of a surface point.

In this paper, we propose a flexible fully convolutional network [9], called PS-FCN, for estimating a normal map of an object (see Fig. 1). Convolutional network inherently takes observations in a neighborhood into account in computing the feature map, making it possible for PS-FCN to take advantage of local context information (e.g., surface smoothness prior). PS-FCN is composed of three components, namely a *shared-weight feature extractor* for extracting feature representations from the input images, a *fusion layer* for aggregating features from multiple input images, and a *normal regression network* for inferring the normal map (see Fig. 3).

Unlike [8], PS-FCN does not depend on a pre-defined set of light directions during training and testing, and allows the light directions used in testing different from those used in training. It takes an arbitrary number of images with their associated light directions as input, and predicts a normal map of the object in a fast feed-forward pass. It can handle multiple images and light directions in an order-agnostic manner. To simulate real-world complex non-Lambertian surfaces for training PS-FCN, we create two synthetic datasets using shapes from the blobby shape dataset [10] and the sculpture shape dataset [11], and BRDFs from the MERL BRDF dataset [12]. After training on synthetic data, we show that PS-FCN can generalize well on real datasets, including the

DiLiGenT benchmark [13], the Gourd&Apple dataset [14], and the Light Stage Data Gallery [15]. We further demonstrate that PS-FCN can be easily extended to handle the problem of uncalibrated photometric stereo, which reiterates the flexibility of our model. Extensive experiments on public real datasets show that PS-FCN outperforms existing approaches in calibrated photometric stereo, and promising results are achieved in uncalibrated scenario, clearly demonstrating its effectiveness.

2 Related Work

In this section, we briefly review representative non-Lambertian photometric stereo techniques. More comprehensive surveys of photometric stereo algorithms can be found in [13,16]. Non-Lambertian photometric stereo methods can be broadly divided into four categories, namely outlier rejection based methods, sophisticated reflectance model based methods, exemplar based methods, and learning based methods.

Outlier rejection based methods assume non-Lambertian observations to be local and sparse such that they can be treated as outliers. Various outlier rejection methods have been proposed based on rank minimization [17], RANSAC [18], taking median values [19], expectation maximization [20], sparse Bayesian regression [21], etc. Outlier rejection methods generally require lots of input images and have difficulty in handling objects with dense non-Lambertian observations (e.g., materials with broad and soft specular highlights).

Many sophisticated reflectance models have been proposed to approximate the non-Lambertian model, including analytical models like Torrance-Sparrow model [3], Ward model [4], Cook-Torrance model [5], etc. Instead of rejecting specular observations as outliers, sophisticated reflectance model based methods fit an analytical model to all observations. These methods require solving complex optimization problems, and can only handle limited classes of materials. Recently, bivariate BRDF representations [22,23] were adopted to approximate isotropic BRDF, and a symmetry-based approach [24] was proposed to handle anisotropic reflectance without explicitly estimating a reflectance model.

Exemplar based methods usually require the observation of an additional reference object. Using a reference sphere, Hertzmann and Seitz [25] subtly transformed the non-Lambertian photometric stereo problem to a point matching problem. Exemplar based methods can deal with objects with spatially-varying BRDFs without knowing the light directions, but the requirement of known shape and material of the reference object(s) limits their applications. As an extension, Hui and Sankaranarayanan [26] introduced a BRDF dictionary to render virtual spheres without using a real reference object, but at the cost of requiring light calibration and longer processing time.

Recently, Santo et al. [8] proposed a deep fully-connected network, called DPSN, to regress per-pixel normal given a fixed number of observations (e.g., 96) captured under a pre-defined set of light directions. For each image point of the object, all its observations are concatenated to form a fixed-length vector, which is fed into a fully-connected network to regress a single normal vector. DPSN can handle diverse BRDFs without solving a complex optimization problem or requiring any reference objects. However, it requires a pre-defined set of light directions during training and testing, which limits its practical uses. In contrast, our PS-FCN does not depend on a pre-defined set of light directions during training and testing, and allows the light directions used in testing to be different from those used in training. It takes an arbitrary number of images with their light directions as input, and predicts a normal map of the object in a fast feed-forward pass. It can handle multiple images and light directions in an order-agnostic manner.

Typically, photometric stereo methods require calibrated light directions, and the calibration process is often very tedious. A few works have been devoted to handle uncalibrated photometric stereo (e.g., [27–32]). These methods can infer surface normals in the absence of calibrated light directions. Our PS-FCN can be easily extended to handle uncalibrated photometric stereo, by simply removing the light directions during training. Afterwards, it can solely rely on the input images without known light directions to predict the normal map of an object.

3   Problem Formulation

In this paper, we follow the conventional practice by assuming orthographic projection, directional lights, and the viewing direction pointing towards the viewer. Given q color images of an object with p pixels captured under different light directions[1], a normal matrix $\mathbf{N}_{3\times p}$, a light direction matrix $\mathbf{L}_{3\times q}$, and an observation matrix $\mathbf{I}_{3\times p\times q}$ can be constructed. We further denote the BRDFs for all observations as $\boldsymbol{\Theta}_{3\times p\times q}$, where each 3-vector $\boldsymbol{\Theta}_{:,i,j}$ is a function of the normal, light direction, and viewing direction at (i,j). The image formation equation can be written as

$$\mathbf{I} = \boldsymbol{\Theta} \circ \mathrm{repmat}(\mathbf{N}^{\top}\mathbf{L}, 3), \tag{1}$$

where $\circ$ represents element-wise multiplication, and $\mathrm{repmat}(\mathbf{X}, 3)$ repeats the matrix $\mathbf{X}$ three times along the first dimension.

For a Lambertian surface, the BRDF for a surface point degenerates to an unknown constant vector. Theoretically, with three or more independent observations, the albedo scaled surface normal can be solved using linear least squares [1]. However, pure Lambertian surfaces barely exist. We therefore have to consider a more complex problem of non-Lambertian photometric stereo, in which we estimate the normal matrix $\mathbf{N}$ from an observation matrix $\mathbf{I}$ and light direction matrix $\mathbf{L}$ under unknown general BRDFs $\boldsymbol{\Theta}$.

We design a learning framework based on (1) to tackle the problem of non-Lambertian photometric stereo. Different from previous methods which approximate $\boldsymbol{\Theta}$ with some sophisticated reflectance models, our method directly learns the mapping from $(\mathbf{I}, \mathbf{L})$ to $\mathbf{N}$ without explicitly modeling $\boldsymbol{\Theta}$.

---

[1] Images are normalized by light intensities, and each light direction is represented by a unit 3-vector.

4   Learning Photometric Stereo

In this section, we first introduce our strategy for adapting CNNs to handle a variable number of inputs, and then present a flexible fully convolutional network, called PS-FCN, for learning photometric stereo.

4.1   Max-Pooling for Multi-feature Fusion

CNNs have been successfully applied to dense regression problems like depth estimation [33] and surface normal estimation [34], where the number of input images is fixed and identical during training and testing. Note that adapting CNNs to handle a variable number of inputs during testing is not straightforward, as convolutional layers require the input to have a fixed number of channels during training and testing. Given a variable number of inputs, a shared-weight feature extractor can be used to extract features from each of the inputs (e.g., siamese networks), but an additional fusion layer is required to aggregate such features into a representation with a fixed number of channels. A convolutional layer is applicable for multi-feature fusion only when the number of inputs is fixed. Unfortunately, this is not practical for photometric stereo where the number of inputs often varies.

One possible way to tackle a variable number of inputs is to arrange the inputs sequentially and adopt a recurrent neural network (RNN) to fuse them. For example, [35] introduced a RNN framework to unify single- and multi-image 3D voxel prediction. The memory mechanism of RNN enables it to handle sequential inputs, but at the same time also makes it sensitive to the order of inputs. This order sensitive characteristic is not desirable for photometric stereo as it will restrict the illumination changes to follow a specific pattern, making the model less general.

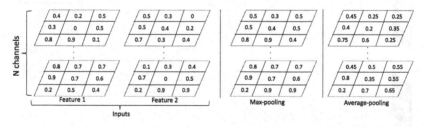

Fig. 2. A toy example for max-pooling and average-pooling mechanisms on multi-feature fusion.

More recently, order-agnostic operations (e.g., pooling layers) have been exploited in CNNs to aggregate multi-image information. Wiles and Zisserman [11] used max-pooling to fuse features of silhouettes from different views for novel view synthesis and 3D voxel prediction. Hartmann *et al.* [36] adopted average-pooling to aggregate features of multiple patches for learning multi-patch similarity. In general, max-pooling operation can extract the most salient information from all the features, while average-pooling can smooth out the salient and non-activated features. Figure 2 illustrates how max-pooling and average-pooling operations aggregate two features with a toy example.

For photometric stereo, we argue that max-pooling is a better choice for aggregating features from multiple inputs. Our motivation is that, under a certain light direction, regions with high intensities or specular highlights provide strong clues for surface normal inference (e.g., for a surface point with a sharp specular highlight, its normal is close to the bisector of the viewing and light directions). Max-pooling can naturally aggregate such strong features from images captured under different light directions. Besides, max-pooling can ignore non-activated features during training, making it robust to cast shadow. As will be seen in Sect. 6, our experimental results do validate our arguments. We observe from experiments that each channel of the feature map fused by max-pooling is highly correlated to the response of the surface to a certain light direction. Strong responses in each channel are found in regions with surface normals having similar directions. The feature map can therefore be interpreted as a decomposition of the images under different light directions (see Fig. 5).

4.2 Network Architecture

PS-FCN is a multi-branch siamese network [37] consisting of three components, namely a *shared-weight feature extractor*, a *fusion layer*, and a *normal regression network* (see Fig. 3). It can be trained and tested using an arbitrary number of images with their associated light directions as input.

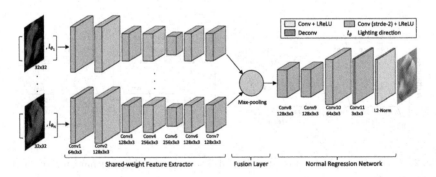

Fig. 3. Network architecture of PS-FCN.

For an object captured under q distinct light directions, we repeat each light direction (i.e., a 3-vector) to form a 3-channel image having the same spatial dimension as the input image ($3 \times h \times w$), and concatenate it with the input image. Hence, the input to our model has a dimension of $q \times 6 \times h \times w$. We separately feed the image-light pairs to the shared-weight feature extractor to extract a feature map from each of the inputs, and apply a max-pooling operation in the fusion layer to aggregate these feature maps. Finally, the normal regression network takes the fused feature map as input and estimates a normal map of the object.

The shared-weight feature extractor has seven convolutional layers, where the feature map is down-sampled twice and then up-sampled once, resulting in a down-sample factor of two. This design can increase the receptive field and preserve spatial information with a small memory consumption. The normal regression network has four convolutional layers and up-samples the fused feature map to the same spatial dimension as the input images. An L2-normalization layer is appended at the end of the normal regression network to produce the normal map.

PS-FCN is a fully convolutional network, and it can be applied to datasets with different image scales. Thanks to the max-pooling operation in the fusion layer, it possesses the order-agnostic property. Besides, PS-FCN can be easily extended to handle uncalibrated photometric stereo, where the light directions are not known, by simply removing the light directions during training.

4.3 Loss Function

The learning of our PS-FCN is supervised by the estimation error between the predicted and the ground-truth normal maps. We formulate our loss function using the commonly used cosine similarity loss

$$L_{normal} = \frac{1}{hw} \sum_{i,j} (1 - \mathbf{N}_{ij} \cdot \tilde{\mathbf{N}}_{ij}), \tag{2}$$

where $\mathbf{N}_{ij}$ and $\tilde{\mathbf{N}}_{ij}$ denote the predicted normal and the ground truth, respectively, at the point (i, j). If the predicted normal has a similar orientation as the ground truth, the dot-product $\mathbf{N}_{ij} \cdot \tilde{\mathbf{N}}_{ij}$ will be close to 1 and the loss will be small, and vice versa. Other losses like mean square error can also be adopted.

5 Dataset

The training of PS-FCN requires the ground-truth normal maps of the objects. However, obtaining ground-truth normal maps of real objects is a difficult and time-consuming task. Hence, we create two synthetic datasets for training and one synthetic dataset for testing. The publicly available real photometric stereo datasets are reserved to validate the generalization ability of our model. Experimental results show that our PS-FCN trained on the synthetic datasets generalizes well on the challenging real datasets.

5.1   Synthetic Data for Training

We used shapes from two existing 3D datasets, namely the blobby shape dataset [10] and the sculpture shape dataset [11], to generate our training data using the physically based raytracer Mitsuba [38]. Following DPSN [8], we employed the MERL dataset [12], which contains 100 different BRDFs of real-world materials, to define a diverse set of surface materials for rendering these shapes. Note that our datasets explicitly consider cast shadows during rendering. For the sake of data loading efficiency, we stored our training data in 8-bit PNG format.

(a) Blobby shape.   (b) Sculpture shape.

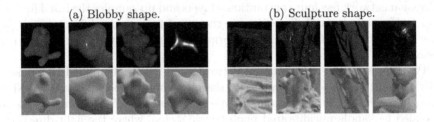

Fig. 4. Examples of the synthetic training data.

Blobby Dataset. We first followed [8] to render our training data using the blobby shape dataset [10], which contains 10 blobby shapes with various normal distributions. For each blobby shape, 1,296 regularly-sampled views (36 azimuth angles × 36 elevation angles) were used, and for each view, 2 out of 100 BRDFs were randomly selected, leading to 25,920 samples ($10 \times 36 \times 36 \times 2$). For each sample, we rendered 64 images with a spatial resolution of 128×128 under light directions randomly sampled from a range of $180° \times 180°$, which is more general than the range ($74.6° \times 51.4°$) used in the real data benchmark [13]. We randomly split this dataset into 99 : 1 for training and validation (see Fig. 4(a)).

Sculpture Dataset. The surfaces in the blobby shape dataset are usually largely smooth and lack of details. To provide more complex (realistic) normal distributions for training, we employed 8 complicated 3D models from the sculpture shape dataset introduced in [11]. We generated samples for the sculpture dataset in exactly the same way we did for the blobby shape dataset, except that we discarded views containing holes or showing uniform normals (e.g., flat facets). The rendered images are with a size of 512×512 when a whole sculpture shape is in the field of view. We then regularly cropped patches of size 128×128 from the rendered images and discarded those with a foreground ratio less than 50%. This gave us a dataset of 59,292 samples, where each sample contains 64 images rendered under different light directions. Finally, we randomly split this dataset into 99 : 1 for training and validation (see Fig. 4(b)).

Data Augmentation. To narrow the gap between real and synthetic data, data augmentation was carried out on-the-fly during training. Given an image of size

128×128, we randomly performed image rescaling (with the rescaled width and height within the range of [32, 128], without preserving the original aspect ratio) and noise perturbation (in a range of [−0.05, 0.05]). Image patches of size 32×32 were then randomly cropped for training.

5.2 Synthetic Data for Testing

To quantitatively evaluate the performance of our model on different materials and shapes, we rendered a synthetic test dataset using a *Sphere* shape and a *Bunny* shape. Each shape was rendered with all of the 100 BRDFs from MERL dataset under 100 randomly sampled light directions. Similarly, the light directions were sampled from a range of $180° \times 180°$. As a result, we obtained 200 testing samples, and each sample contains 100 images.

5.3 Real Data for Testing

We employed three challenging real non-Lambertian photometric stereo datasets for testing, namely the DiLiGenT benchmark [13], the Gourd&Apple dataset [14], and the Light Stage Data Gallery [15]. Note that none of these datasets were used during training.

The DiLiGenT benchmark [13] contains 10 objects of various shapes with complex materials. For each object, 96 images captured under different predefined light directions and its ground-truth normal map are provided. We quantitatively evaluated our model on both the main and test datasets of this benchmark.

The Gourd&Apple dataset [14] and the Light Stage Data Gallery [15] are two other challenging datasets that without ground-truth normal maps. The Gourd&Apple dataset is composed of three objects, namely *Gourd1*, *Gourd2*, and *Apple*. They provide 102, 98 and 112 image-light pairs, respectively. The Light Stage Data Gallery [15] is composed of six objects, and 253 image-light pairs are provided for each object.[2] We qualitatively evaluated our model on these two datasets to further demonstrate the transferability of our model.

6 Experimental Evaluation

In this section, we present experimental results and analysis. We carried out network analysis for PS-FCN on the synthetic test dataset, and compared our method with the previous state-of-the-art methods on the DiLiGenT benchmark [13]. Mean angular error (MAE) in degree was used to measure the accuracy of the predicted normal maps. We further provided qualitative results on the Gourd&Apple dataset [14] and the Light Stage Data Gallery [15].

---

[2] In our experiment, for each object in the Light Stage Data Gallery, we only used the 133 pairs with the front side of the object under illumination.

6.1 Implementation Details

Our framework was implemented in PyTorch [39] with 2.2 million learnable parameters. We trained our model using a batch size of 32 for 30 epochs, and it only took a few hours for training to converge using a single NVIDIA Titan X Pascal GPU (e.g., about 1 hour for 8 image-light pairs per sample on the blobby dataset, and about 9 hours for 32 image-light pairs per sample on both the blobby and sculpture datasets). Adam optimizer [40] was used with default parameters ($\beta_1 = 0.9$ and $\beta_2 = 0.999$), where the learning rate was initially set to 0.001 and divided by 2 every 5 epochs. Our code, model and datasets are available at https://guanyingc.github.io/PS-FCN.

Table 1. Results of network analysis on the synthetic test dataset. The numbers represent the average MAE of all the objects (the lower the better). B and S stand for the blobby and sculpture training datasets respectively. († indicates the number of per-sample image-light pairs used is identical during training and testing.)

		Variants		Tested with # images				
ID	Data	Fusion Type	Train #	1	8	16	32	100
0	B	Avg-p	16	38.60	8.96	6.70	6.13	5.61
1	B	Avg-p	32	45.04	10.94	7.28	6.00	5.52
2	B	Conv	†	-	-	7.09	6.49	-
3	B	Max-p	1	22.47	14.58	13.95	13.88	13.67
4	B	Max-p	8	27.96	7.40	6.24	5.87	5.82
5	B	Max-p	16	46.85	8.44	6.24	5.64	5.43
6	B	Max-p	32	45.17	11.84	6.64	5.50	5.30
7	B + S	Max-p	8	26.65	7.20	6.17	5.71	5.66
8	B + S	Max-p	16	36.07	7.71	5.94	5.29	5.03
9	B + S	Max-p	32	51.18	9.12	6.01	4.91	4.55

6.2 Network Analysis

We quantitatively analyzed PS-FCN on the synthetic test dataset. In particular, we first validated the effectiveness of max-pooling in multi-feature fusion by comparing it with average-pooling and convolutional layers. We then investigated the influence of per-sample input number during training and testing. Besides, we investigated the influence of the complexity of training data. Last, we evaluated the performance of PS-FCN on different materials. For all the experiments in network analysis, we performed 100 random trials (save for the experiments using all 100 image-light pairs per sample during testing) and reported the average results which are summarized in Table 1.

Effectiveness of Max-Pooling. Experiments with IDs 0, 1, 5 & 6 in Table 1 compared the performance of average-pooling and max-pooling for multi-feature fusion. It can be seen that max-pooling performed consistently better than

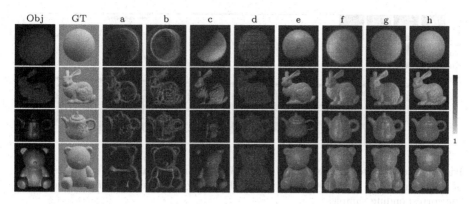

Fig. 5. Visualization of the learned feature map after fusion. The first two columns show the images and ground-truth normal maps. Each of the subsequent columns (a–h) shows one particular channel of the fused feature map. 8 out of the 128 channels of the feature map are presented. Note that different regions with similar normal directions are fired in different channels. Each channel can therefore be interpreted as the probability of the normal belonging to a certain direction (or alternatively as the object shading rendered under a certain light direction). Accurate normal maps can then be inferred from these probability distributions.

average-pooling, when the per-sample input number during testing was ≥ 16. Similarly, experiments with IDs 2, 5 & 6 showed that fusion by convolutional layers on the concatenated features was sub-optimal. This could be explained by the fact that the weights of the convolutional layers are related to the order of the concatenated features, while the orders of the input image-light pairs are random in our case, thus increasing the difficulty for the convolutional layers to find the relations among multiple features. Figure 5 visualizes the fused features (by max-pooling) of *Sphere* (blue-rubber) & *Bunny* (dark-red-paint) in synthetic test dataset, and *pot2* & *bear* in DiLiGenT main dataset. Note that all the image-light pairs were used as input and the features were normalized to $[0, 1]$.

Effects of Input Number. Referring to the experiments with IDs 3–6 in Table 1, for a fixed number of inputs during training, the performance of PS-FCN increased with the number of inputs during testing. For a fixed number of inputs during testing, PS-FCN performed better when the number of inputs during training was close to that during testing.

Effects of Training Ddata. By comparing experiments with IDs 4–6 (where the models were trained only on the blobby dataset) with experiments with IDs 7–9 (where the models were trained on both the blobby dataset and the sculpture dataset), we can see that the additional sculpture dataset with a more complex normal distribution helped to boost the performance. This suggests that the performance of PS-FCN could be further improved by introducing more complex and realistic training data.

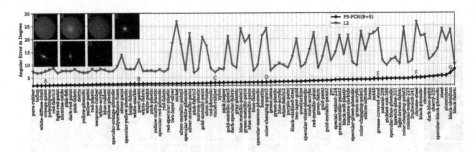

Fig. 6. Quantitative comparison between PS-FCN and L2 Baseline [1] on the samples of *Sphere* rendered with 100 different BRDFs. Images in the upper-left corner show the corresponding samples.

Results on Different Materials. Fig. 6 compares PS-FCN (trained with 32 per-sample inputs on both synthetic datasets) with L2 Baseline [1] on samples of *Sphere* that were rendered with 100 different BRDFs. It can be seen that PS-FCN significantly outperformed L2 Baseline. Note that PS-FCN generally performed better on materials with a light color than those with a dark color. This might be explained by the fact that max-pooling always tries to aggregate the most salient features for normal inference, and the image intensities of objects with a dark color are mostly very small. As a result, fewer useful features could be extracted to infer normals for objects of dark materials.

Table 2. Comparison of results on the DiLiGenT benchmark main dataset. The numbers represent the MAE (the lower the better). Results of PS-FCN under two different testing settings are reported, e.g., PS-FCN (B+S+32, 16) indicates the model trained on both the blobby dataset and the sculpture dataset with a per-sample input number of 32, and tested with a per-sample input number of 16. (Note that the result of PS-FCN (B+S+32, 16) is the average of 100 random trials.)

Method	ball	cat	pot1	bear	pot2	buddha	goblet	reading	cow	harvest	Avg.
L2 [1]	4.10	8.41	8.89	8.39	14.65	14.92	18.50	19.80	25.60	30.62	15.39
AZ08 [14]	2.71	6.53	7.23	**5.96**	11.03	12.54	13.93	14.17	21.48	30.50	12.61
WG10 [17]	2.06	6.73	7.18	6.50	13.12	10.91	15.70	15.39	25.89	30.01	13.35
IA14 [23]	3.34	6.74	6.64	7.11	8.77	10.47	9.71	14.19	13.05	25.95	10.60
ST14 [22]	**1.74**	**6.12**	**6.51**	6.12	8.78	10.60	10.09	13.63	13.93	25.44	10.30
DPSN [8]	2.02	6.54	7.05	6.31	7.86	12.68	11.28	15.51	8.01	16.86	9.41
PS-FCN (B+S+32, 16)	3.31	7.64	8.14	7.47	8.22	8.76	9.81	14.09	8.78	17.48	9.37
PS-FCN (B+S+32, 96)	2.82	6.16	7.13	7.55	**7.25**	**7.91**	**8.60**	**13.33**	**7.33**	15.85	**8.39**

6.3   Benchmark Comparisons

DiLiGenT Benchmark Main Dataset. We compared PS-FCN against the recently proposed learning based method DPSN [8] and other previous

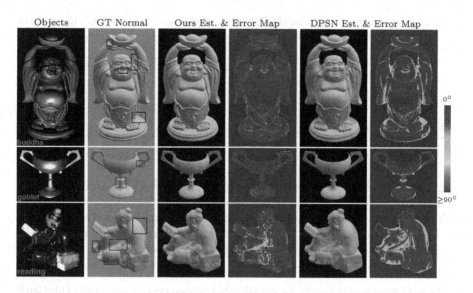

Fig. 7. Qualitative results on the DiLiGenT benchmark main dataset. The black boxes in the ground-truth normal maps are regions with cast shadows. Our method can produce more robust estimations in those regions compared with DPSN [8].

state-of-the-art methods. Quantitative results on the main dataset of the DiLi-GenT benchmark are shown in Table 2. Compared with other methods, PS-FCN performed particularly well on objects with complicated shapes (e.g., *buddha*, *reading*, and *harvest*) and/or spatially varying materials (e.g., *pot2*, *goblet* and *cow*). Our best performer, which achieved an average MAE of 8.39°, was trained with 32 per-sample inputs on both synthetic datasets and tested with all 96 inputs for each object. With only 16 inputs per object during testing, PS-FCN still outperformed the previous methods in terms of the average MAE. Figure 7 presents the qualitative comparison between PS-FCN and DPSN. It can be seen that PS-FCN is more robust in regions with cast shadows.

DiLiGenT Benchmark Test Dataset. We further evaluated our model on the test dataset of the DiLiGenT benchmark, with the ground-truth normal maps withheld by the original authors (see. Table 3). Similar to the results on the main dataset, PS-FCN outperformed other methods on the test dataset. More results of the other methods can be found on the benchmark website[3] for comparison.

Uncalibrated Photometric Stereo Extension. PS-FCN can be easily extended to handle uncalibrated photometric stereo by simply removing the light directions from the input. To verify the potential of our framework towards uncalibrated photometric stereo, we trained an uncalibrated variant of our model, denoted as UPS-FCN, taking only images as input (note that we assume the

---

[3] https://sites.google.com/site/photometricstereodata/home/summary-of-benchmarking-results.

Table 3. Comparison of results on the DiLiGenT benchmark test dataset. The numbers represent the MAE (the lower the better).

Method	cat	pot1	bear	pot2	buddha	goblet	reading	cow	harvest	Avg.
IA14 [23]	5.61	6.33	5.12	8.83	11.00	10.54	13.27	11.18	24.82	10.74
ST14 [22]	6.43	6.64	6.09	8.94	10.92	10.33	14.16	10.82	25.43	11.08
DPSN [8]	5.82	8.26	6.32	9.02	12.80	12.04	16.11	8.00	17.78	10.68
PS-FCN (B+S+32, 96)	6.24	7.59	5.42	7.11	8.30	8.62	13.43	7.98	15.93	8.96

images were normalized by the light intensities). UPS-FCN was trained on both synthetic datasets using 32 image-light pairs as input. We compared our UPS-FCN with the existing uncalibrated methods. The results are reported in Table 4, our UPS-FCN outperformed existing methods in terms of the average MAE, which demonstrates the effectiveness and flexibility of our model.

Table 4. Comparison of results for uncalibrated photometric stereo on the DiLiGenT benchmark main dataset. The numbers represent the MAE (the lower the better).

Method	ball	cat	pot1	bear	pot2	buddha	goblet	reading	cow	harvest	Avg.
AM07 [27]	7.27	31.45	18.37	16.81	49.16	32.81	46.54	53.65	54.72	61.70	37.25
SM10 [28]	8.90	19.84	16.68	11.98	50.68	15.54	48.79	26.93	22.73	73.86	29.59
WT13 [29]	4.39	36.55	9.39	6.42	14.52	13.19	20.57	58.96	19.75	55.51	23.93
PF14 [30]	4.77	9.54	9.51	9.07	15.90	14.92	29.93	24.18	19.53	29.21	16.66
LC18 [32]	9.30	12.60	12.40	10.90	15.70	19.00	18.30	22.30	15.00	28.00	16.30
UPS-FCN	6.62	14.68	13.98	11.23	14.19	15.87	20.72	23.26	11.91	27.79	16.02

6.4   Testing on Other Real Datasets

Due to absence of ground-truth normal maps, we qualitatively evaluated our best-performing model PS-FCN (B+S+32) on the Gourd&Apple dataset [14] and the Light Stage Data Gallery [15]. Figure 8 shows the estimated normal maps and surfaces reconstructed using [41]. The reconstructed surfaces convincingly reflect the shapes of the objects, demonstrating the accuracy of the normal maps predicted by PS-FCN.

7   Conclusions

In this paper, we have proposed a flexible deep fully convolutional network, called PS-FCN, that accepts an arbitrary number of images and their associated light directions as input and regresses an accurate normal map. Our PS-FCN does not require a pre-defined set of light directions during training and testing, and

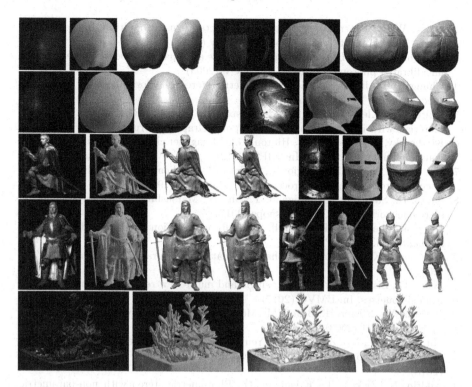

Fig. 8. Qualitative results for the Gourd&Apple dataset and Light Stage Data Gallery. For each shape, a sample input image, the estimated normal map, and two views of the reconstructed surfaces are shown. (Best viewed in PDF with zoom.)

allows the light directions used in testing different from that used in training. It can handle multiple images and light directions in an order-agnostic manner. In order to train PS-FCN, two synthetic datasets with various realistic shapes and materials have been created. After training, PS-FCN can generalize well on challenging real datasets. In addition, PS-FCN can be easily extended to handle uncalibrated photometric stereo. Results on diverse real datasets have clearly shown that PS-FCN outperforms previous calibrated photometric stereo methods, and promising results have been achieved in uncalibrated scenario.

Acknowledgments. We thank Hiroaki Santo for his help with the comparison to DPSN. We also thank Boxin Shi and Zhipeng Mo for their help with the evaluation on the DiLiGenT benchmark. We gratefully acknowledge the support of NVIDIA Corporation with the donation of the Titan X Pascal GPU used for this research. Kai Han is supported by EPSRC Programme Grant Seebibyte EP/M013774/1.

References

1. Woodham, R.J.: Photometric method for determining surface orientation from multiple images. Opt. Eng. **19**, 191130 (1980)

2. Silver, W.M.: Determining shape and reflectance using multiple images. Ph.D. thesis, Massachusetts Institute of Technology (1980)
3. Georghiades, A.S.: Incorporating the torrance and sparrow model of reflectance in uncalibrated photometric stereo. In: ICCV (2003)
4. Chung, H.S., Jia, J.: Efficient photometric stereo on glossy surfaces with wide specular lobes. In: CVPR (2008)
5. Ruiters, R., Klein, R.: Heightfield and spatially varying BRDF reconstruction for materials with interreflections. In: Computer Graphics Forum (2009)
6. Krizhevsky, A., Sutskever, I., Hinton, G.E.: Imagenet classification with deep convolutional neural networks. In: NIPS (2012)
7. LeCun, Y., Bottou, L., Bengio, Y., Haffner, P.: Gradient-based learning applied to document recognition. In: Proceedings of the IEEE (1998)
8. Santo, H., Samejima, M., Sugano, Y., Shi, B., Matsushita, Y.: Deep photometric stereo network. In: ICCV Workshops (2017)
9. Long, J., Shelhamer, E., Darrell, T.: Fully convolutional networks for semantic segmentation. In: CVPR (2015)
10. Johnson, M.K., Adelson, E.H.: Shape estimation in natural illumination. In: CVPR (2011)
11. Wiles, O., Zisserman, A.: SilNet: single-and multi-view reconstruction by learning from silhouettes. In: BMVC (2017)
12. Matusik, W., Pfister, H., Brand, M., McMillan, L.: A data-driven reflectance model. In: SIGGRAPH (2003)
13. Shi, B., Wu, Z., Mo, Z., Duan, D., Yeung, S.K., Tan, P.: A benchmark dataset and evaluation for non-lambertian and uncalibrated photometric stereo. IEEE TPAMI (2018)
14. Alldrin, N., Zickler, T., Kriegman, D.: Photometric stereo with non-parametric and spatially-varying reflectance. In: CVPR (2008)
15. Einarsson, P., et al.: Relighting human locomotion with flowed reflectance fields. In: EGSR (2006)
16. Herbort, S., Wöhler, C.: An introduction to image-based 3D surface reconstruction and a survey of photometric stereo methods. 3D Res. **2**, 4 (2011)
17. Wu, L., Ganesh, A., Shi, B., Matsushita, Y., Wang, Y., Ma, Y.: Robust photometric stereo via low-rank matrix completion and recovery. In: Kimmel, R., Klette, R., Sugimoto, A. (eds.) ACCV 2010 Part III. LNCS, vol. 6494, pp. 703–717. Springer, Heidelberg (2011). https://doi.org/10.1007/978-3-642-19318-7_55
18. Mukaigawa, Y., Ishii, Y., Shakunaga, T.: Analysis of photometric factors based on photometric linearization. JOSA A **24**, 3326–3334 (2007)
19. Miyazaki, D., Hara, K., Ikeuchi, K.: Median photometric stereo as applied to the segonko tumulus and museum objects. IJCV **86**, 229 (2010)
20. Wu, T.P., Tang, C.K.: Photometric stereo via expectation maximization. IEEE TPAMI **32**, 546–560 (2010)
21. Ikehata, S., Wipf, D., Matsushita, Y., Aizawa, K.: Robust photometric stereo using sparse regression. In: CVPR (2012)
22. Shi, B., Tan, P., Matsushita, Y., Ikeuchi, K.: Bi-polynomial modeling of low-frequency reflectances. IEEE TPAMI (2014)
23. Ikehata, S., Aizawa, K.: Photometric stereo using constrained bivariate regression for general isotropic surfaces. In: CVPR (2014)
24. Holroyd, M., Lawrence, J., Humphreys, G., Zickler, T.: A photometric approach for estimating normals and tangents. In: ACM TOG (2008)
25. Hertzmann, A., Seitz, S.M.: Example-based photometric stereo: shape reconstruction with general, varying BRDFs. IEEE TPAMI **27**, 1254–1264 (2005)

26. Hui, Z., Sankaranarayanan, A.C.: A dictionary-based approach for estimating shape and spatially-varying reflectance. In: ICCP (2015)
27. Alldrin, N.G., Mallick, S.P., Kriegman, D.J.: Resolving the generalized bas-relief ambiguity by entropy minimization. In: CVPR (2007)
28. Shi, B., Matsushita, Y., Wei, Y., Xu, C., Tan, P.: Self-calibrating photometric stereo. In: CVPR (2010)
29. Wu, Z., Tan, P.: Calibrating photometric stereo by holistic reflectance symmetry analysis. In: CVPR (2013)
30. Papadhimitri, T., Favaro, P.: A closed-form, consistent and robust solution to uncalibrated photometric stereo via local diffuse reflectance maxima. IJCV **107**, 139–154 (2014)
31. Lu, F., Matsushita, Y., Sato, I., Okabe, T., Sato, Y.: From intensity profile to surface normal: photometric stereo for unknown light sources and isotropic reflectances. IEEE TPAMI **37**, 1999–2012 (2015)
32. Lu, F., Chen, X., Sato, I., Sato, Y.: SymPS: BRDF symmetry guided photometric stereo for shape and light source estimation. IEEE TPAMI **40**, 221–234 (2018)
33. Eigen, D., Puhrsch, C., Fergus, R.: Depth map prediction from a single image using a multi-scale deep network. In: NIPS (2014)
34. Wang, X., Fouhey, D., Gupta, A.: Designing deep networks for surface normal estimation. In: CVPR (2015)
35. Choy, C.B., Xu, D., Gwak, J., Chen, K., Savarese, S.: 3D–R2N2: a unified approach for single and multi-view 3D object reconstruction. In: ECCV (2016)
36. Hartmann, W., Galliani, S., Havlena, M., Van Gool, L., Schindler, K.: Learned multi-patch similarity. In: ICCV (2017)
37. Bromley, J., Guyon, I., LeCun, Y., Säckinger, E., Shah, R.: Signature verification using a "siamese" time delay neural network. Int.J. Pattern Recogn. Artif. Intell. (1993)
38. Jakob, W.: Mitsuba renderer (2010)
39. Paszke, A., Gross, S., Chintala, S., Chanan, G.: PyTorch: tensors and dynamic neural networks in python with strong GPU acceleration (2017)
40. Kingma, D., Ba, J.: Adam: a method for stochastic optimization. In: ICLR (2015)
41. Frankot, R.T., Chellappa, R.: A method for enforcing integrability in shape from shading algorithms. IEEE TPAMI **10**, 439–451 (1988)

Ask, Acquire, and Attack: Data-Free UAP Generation Using Class Impressions

Konda Reddy Mopuri$^{(\boxtimes)}$ (iD), Phani Krishna Uppala (iD),
and R. Venkatesh Babu (iD)

Video Analytics Lab, Indian Institute of Science, Bangalore, India
kondamopuri@iisc.ac.in

Abstract. Deep learning models are susceptible to input specific noise, called adversarial perturbations. Moreover, there exist input-agnostic noise, called Universal Adversarial Perturbations (UAP) that can affect inference of the models over most input samples. Given a model, there exist broadly two approaches to craft UAPs: (i) data-driven: that require data, and (ii) data-free: that do not require data samples. Data-driven approaches require actual samples from the underlying data distribution and craft UAPs with high success (fooling) rate. However, data-free approaches craft UAPs without utilizing any data samples and therefore result in lesser success rates. In this paper, for data-free scenarios, we propose a novel approach that emulates the effect of data samples with class impressions in order to craft UAPs using data-driven objectives. Class impression for a given pair of category and model is a generic representation (in the input space) of the samples belonging to that category. Further, we present a neural network based generative model that utilizes the acquired class impressions to learn crafting UAPs. Experimental evaluation demonstrates that the learned generative model, (i) readily crafts UAPs via simple feed-forwarding through neural network layers, and (ii) achieves state-of-the-art success rates for data-free scenario and closer to that for data-driven setting without actually utilizing any data samples.

Keywords: Adversarial attacks · Attacks on ML systems
Data-free attacks · Image-agnostic perturbations · Class impressions

1 Introduction

Machine learning models are pregnable (e.g. [3,4,9]) at test time to specially learned, mild noise in the input space, commonly known as adversarial perturbations. Data samples created via adding these perturbations to clean samples are known as adversarial samples. Lately, the Deep Neural Networks (DNN) based object classifiers are also observed [7,11,14,28] to be drastically affected by the adversarial attacks with quasi imperceptible perturbations. Further, it

---

K. R. Mopuri and P. K. Uppala—Equal contribution

© Springer Nature Switzerland AG 2018
V. Ferrari et al. (Eds.): ECCV 2018, LNCS 11213, pp. 20–35, 2018.
https://doi.org/10.1007/978-3-030-01240-3_2

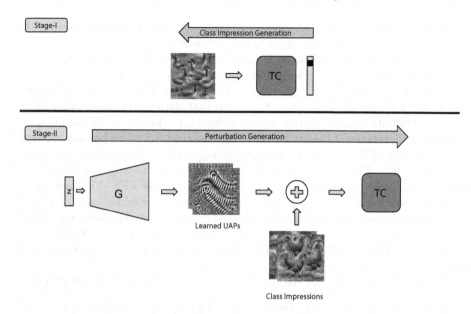

Fig. 1. Overview of the proposed approach. Stage-I, "Ask and Acquire" generates the "class impressions" to mimic the effect of actual data samples. Stage-II, "Attack" learns a neural network based generative model G which crafts UAPs from random vectors z sampled from a latent space.

is observed (e.g. [28]) that these adversarial perturbations exhibit cross model generalizability (transferability). This means, often same adversarial sample gets incorrectly classified by multiple models in spite of having different architectures and trained with disjoint training datasets. It enables attackers to launch simple black-box attacks [12,21] on the deployed models without any knowledge about their architecture and parameters.

However, most of the existing works (e.g. [14,28]) craft input-specific perturbations, i.e., perturbations are functions of input and they may not transfer across data samples. In other words, perturbation crafted for one data sample most often fails to fool the model when used to corrupt other clean data samples. However, recent findings by Moosavi-Dezfooli *et al.* [13] and Mopuri *et al.* [15,17] demonstrated that there exist input-agnostic (or image-agnostic) perturbations that when added, most of the data samples can fool the target classifier. Such perturbations are known as "Universal Adversarial Perturbations (UAP)", since a single noise can adversarially perturb samples from multiple categories. Furthermore, it is observed that similar to image-specific perturbations, UAPs also exhibit cross model generalizability enabling easy black-box attacks. Thus, UAPs pose a severe threat to the deployment of the vision models and require a meticulous study. Especially for applications which involve safety (e.g. autonomous driving) and privacy of the users (e.g. access granting), it is indispensable to develop robust models against such adversarial attacks.

Approaches that craft UAPs can be broadly categorized into two classes: (i) data-driven, and (ii) data-free approaches. Data-driven approaches such as [13] require access to samples of the underlying data distribution to craft UAPs using a fooling objective (e.g. confidence reduction as in Eq. (2)). Thus, UAPs crafted via data-driven approaches typically result in higher success rate (or fooling rate), i.e., fool the models more often. Note that data-driven approaches have access to the data samples and the model architecture along with the parameters. Further, performance of the crafted UAPs is observed [15,17] to be proportional to the number of data samples available during crafting. However the data-free approaches (e.g. FFF [17]), with a goal to understand the true stability of the the models, indirectly craft UAPs (e.g. activation loss of FFF [17]) instead of using a direct fooling objective. Note that data-free approaches have access to only the model architecture and parameters but not to any data samples. Thus, it is a challenging problem to craft UAPs in data-free scenarios and therefore the success rate of these UAPs would typically be lesser compared to that achieved by the data-driven ones.

In spite of being difficult, data-free approaches have important advantages:

- When compared to their data-driven counter parts, data-free approaches reveal accurate vulnerability of the learned representations and in turn the models. On the other hand, success rates reported by data-driven approaches act as a sort of upper bounds on the achievable rates. Also, it is observed [15,17] that their performance is proportional to the amount of data available for crafting UAPs.
- Because of the strong association of the data-driven UAPs to the target data, they suffer poor transferability across datasets. On the other hand, data-free UAPs transfer better across datasets [15,17].
- Data-free approaches are typically faster [17] to craft UAPs.

Thus, in this paper, we attempt to achieve best of both worlds, i.e., effectiveness of the data-driven objectives and efficiency, transferability of the data-free approaches. We present a novel approach for the data-free scenarios that emulates the effect of actual data samples with *"class impressions"* of the model and crafts UAPs via learning a feed-forward neural network. Class impressions are the reconstructed images from the model's memory which is the set of learned parameters. In other words, they are generic representations of the object categories in the input space (as shown in Fig. 2). In the first part of our approach, we acquire class impressions via simple optimization (Sect. 3.2) that can serve as representative samples from the underlying data distribution. After acquiring multiple class impressions for each of the categories, we perform the second part, which is learning a generative model (a feed-forward neural network) for efficiently generating UAPs. Thus, unlike the existing works [13,17] that solve complex optimizations to generate UAPs, our approach crafts via a simple feed-forward operation through the learned neural network. The major contributions of our work can be listed as:

- We propose a novel approach to handle the absence of data (via class impressions, Sect. 3.2) for crafting UAPs and achieve state-of-the-art success (fooling) rates.
- We present a generative network (Sect. 3.3) that learns to efficiently generate UAPs utilizing the class impressions.

The paper is organized as followed: Sect. 2 describes the relevant existing works, Sect. 3 presents the proposed framework in detail, Sect. 4 reports comprehensive experimental evaluation of our approach and finally Sect. 5 concludes the paper.

2   Related Works

Adversarial perturbations (e.g. [7,14,28]) reveal the vulnerability of the learning models to specific noise. Further, these perturbations can be input agnostic [13, 17] called "Universal Adversarial Perturbations (UAP)" and can pose severe threat to the deployability of these models. Existing approaches to craft the UAPs [13,15,17] perform complex optimizations every time we wish to craft a UAP. Differing from the previous works, we present a neural network that readily crafts UAPs. Only similar work by Baluja *et al.* [2] presents a neural network that transforms a clean image into an adversarial sample by passing through a series of layers. However, we learn a generative model which maps a latent space to that of UAPs. A concurrent work by Mopuri *et al.* [18] presents a similar generative model approach to craft perturbations but for data-driven case.

Also, existing data-free method [17] to craft UAPs achieves significantly less success rates compared to the data-driven methods such as UAP [13] and NAG [18]. In this paper, we attempted to reduce the gap between them by emulating the effect of data with the proposed class impressions. Our class impressions are obtained via simple optimization similar to visualization works such as [26,27]. Feature visualizations [16,25–27,29–31] are introduced to (i) understand what input patterns each neuron responds to, and (ii) gain intuitions into neural networks in order to alleviate the black-box nature of the neural networks. Two slightly different approaches exist for feature visualizations. In the first approach, a random input is optimized in order to maximize the activation of a chosen neuron (or set of neurons) in the architecture. This enables to generate visializations for a given neuron (as in [26]) in the input space.

In other approaches such as the Deep Dream [19] instead of choosing a neuron to activate, arbitrary natural image is passed as an input, and the network enhances the activations that are detected. This way of visualization finds the subtle patterns in the input and amplify them. Since our task is to generate class impressions that emulate the behaviour of real samples, we follow the former approach.

Since the objective is to generate class impressions that can be used to craft UAPs with the fooling objective, softmax probability neuron seems like the obvious choice to activate. However, this intuition is misleading, [20,26] have shown that directly optimizing at softmax leads to increase in the class probability by reducing the pre-softmax logits of other classes. Also, often it does not increase the pre-softmax value of the desired class, thus giving poor visualizations. In order to make the desired class more likely, we optimize the pre-softmax logits and our observations are in agreement with that of [20,26].

3   Proposed Approach

In this section we present the proposed approach to craft efficient UAPs for data-free scenarios. It is understood [13,17,18] that, because of data availability and a more direct optimization, data-driven approaches can craft UAPs that are effective in fooling. On the other hand, the data-free approaches can quickly craft generalizable UAPs by solving relatively simple and indirect optimizations. In this paper we aim to achieve the effectiveness of the data-driven approaches in the data-free setup. For this, first we create representative data samples called, *class impressions* (Fig. 2) to mimic the actual data samples of the underlying distribution. Later, we learn a neural network based generative model to craft UAPs using the generated class impressions and a direct fooling objective (Eq. (2)). Figure 1 shows the overview of our approach. Stage-I, "Ask and Acquire" is about the class impression generation from the target CNN model and Stage-II, "Attack" is training the generative model that learns to craft UAPs using the class impressions obtained in the first stage. In the following subsections, we will discuss these two stages in detail.

3.1   Notation

We first define the notations followed throughout this paper:

- f: target classifier (TC) under attack, which is a trained model with frozen parameters
- f_k^i: k^{th} activation in i^{th} layer of the target classifier
- $f^{ps/m}$: output of the pre-softmax layer
- $f^{s/m}$: output of the softmax (probability) layer
- v: additive universal adversarial perturbation (UAP)
- x: clean input to the target classifier, typically either data sample or class impression
- ξ: max-norm (l_1) constraint on the UAPs, i.e., maximum allowed strength of perturbation that can be added or subtracted at each pixel in the image.

3.2   Ask and Acquire the Class Impressions

Availability of the actual data samples can enable to solve for a direct fooling objective thus craft UAPs that can achieve high success rates [13]. Hence in the data-free scenarios we generate samples that act as proxy for data. Note that the attacker has access to only the model architecture and the learned parameters of the target classifier (CNN). The learned parameters are a function of training data and procedure. They can be treated as model's memory in which the essence

| Goldfish | Cock | Wolf spider | Lakeland terrier | Monarch |

Fig. 2. Sample class impressions generated for VGG-F [5] model. The name of the corresponding categories are mentioned below the images. Note that the impressions have several natural looking patterns located in various spatial locations and in multiple orientations.

of training has been encoded and saved. The objective of our first stage, "Ask and Acquire" is to tap the model's memory and acquire representative samples of the training data. We can then use only these representative samples to craft UAPs to fool the target classifier.

Note that we do not aim to generate natural looking data samples. Instead, our approach creates samples for which the target classifier predicts strong confidence. That is, we create samples such that the target classifier strongly believes them to be actual samples that belong to categories in the underlying data distribution. In other words, these are impressions of the actual training data that we try to reconstruct from model's memory. Therefore we name them *Class Impressions*. The motivation to generate these class impression is that, for the purpose of optimizing a fooling objective (e.g. Eq. 2) it is sufficient to have samples that behave like natural data samples, which is, to be predicted with high confidence. Thus, the ability of the learned UAPs to act as adversarial noise to these samples with respect to the target classifier generalizes to the actual samples.

Top panel of Fig. 1 shows the first stage of our approach to generate the class impressions. We begin with a random noisy image sampled from $\mathcal{U}[0, 255]$ and update it till the target classifier predicts a chosen category with high confidence. We achieve this via performing the optimization shown in Eq. (1). Note that we can create impression (CI_c) for any chosen class (c) by maximizing the predicted confidence to that class. In other words, we modify the random (noisy) image till the target network believes it to be an input from a chosen class c with high confidence. We consider the activations in the pre-softmax layer $f_c^{ps/m}$ (before we apply the softmax non-linearity) and maximize the model's confidence.

$$CI_c = \underset{x}{\operatorname{argmax}} \ f_c^{ps/m}(x) \tag{1}$$

While learning the class impressions, we perform typical data augmentations such as (i) random rotation in $[-5°, 5°]$, (ii) scaling by a factor randomly selected from $\{0.95, 0.975, 1.0, 1.025\}$, (iii) RGB jittering, and (iv) random cropping. Along with the above typical augmentations, we also add random uniform noise in $\mathcal{U}[-10, 10]$. Purpose of this augmentation is to generate robust impressions that behave similar to natural samples with respect to the augmentations and random noise. We can generate multiple impressions for a single category by varying the initialization, i.e., multiple initializations result in multiple class impressions. Note that the dimensions of the generated impressions would be same as that required by the model's input (e.g., $224 \times 224 \times 3$). We have implemented the optimization given in Eq. (1) in TensorFlow [1] framework. We used Adam [10] optimizer with a learning rate of 0.1 with other parameters set to their default values. In order to mimic the variety in terms of the difficulty of recognition (from easy to difficult samples), we have devised a stopping criterion for the optimization. We presume that the difficulty is inversely related to the confidence predicted by the classifier. Before we start the optimization in Eq. (1), we randomly sample a confidence value uniformly in $[0.55, 0.99]$ range and stop our optimization after the predicted confidence by the target classifier reaches that. Thus, the generated class impressions will have samples of varied difficulty.

Figure 2 shows sample class impressions generated for VGG-F [5] model. The corresponding category labels are mentioned below the impressions. Note that the generated class impressions clearly show several natural looking patterns located in various spatial locations and in multiple orientations. Figure 3 shows multiple class impressions generated by our method starting from different initializations for "Squirrel Monkey" category. Note that the impressions have different visual patterns relevant to the chosen category. We have generated 10 class impressions for each of the 1000 categories in ILSVRC dataset resulting in a total of 10000 class impressions. These samples will be used to learn a neural network based generative model that can craft UAPs through a feed-forward operation.

Fig. 3. Multiple class impressions for "Squirrel Monkey" category generated from different initializations for VGG-F [5] target classifier.

3.3 Attack: Craft the Data-Free Perturbations

After generating the class impressions in the first stage of our approach, we treat them as training data for learning a generator to craft the UAPs. Bottom panel of Fig. 1 shows the overview of our generative model. In the following subsections we present the architecture of our model along with the objectives that drive the learning.

3.4   Fooling Loss

We learn a neural network (G) similar to the generator part of a Generative Adversarial network (GAN) [6]. G takes a random vector z whose components are sampled from a simple distribution (e.g. $\mathcal{U}[-1,1]$) and transforms it into a UAP via a series of deconvolution layers. Note that in practice a mini-batch of vectors is processed. We train G in order to be able to generate the UAPs that can fool the target classifier over the underlying data distribution. To be specific, we train with a fooling loss computed over the generated class impressions (from Stage-I, Sect. 3.2) as the training data. Let us denote the predicted label on clean sample (x) as 'clean label' and that of a perturbed sample ($x + v$) as 'perturbed label'. The objective is to make the 'clean' and 'perturbed' labels different. To ensure this to happen, our training loss reduces the confidence predicted to the 'clean label' on the perturbed sample. Because of the softmax nonlinearity, confidence predicted to some other label increases and eventually causes a label flip, which is fooling the target classifier. Hence, we formulate our fooling loss as

$$L_f = -log(1 - f_c^{s/m}(x + v)) \qquad (2)$$

where c is the clean label predicted on x and $f_c^{s/m}$ is the probability (soft-max output) predicted to category c. Note that this objective is similar to most of the adversarial attacking methods (e.g. FGSM [7,21]) in spirit.

3.5   Diversity Loss

Fooling loss L_f (Eq. (2)) only trains G to learn UAPs that can fool the target classifier. In order to avoid learning a degenerate G which can only generate a single strong UAP, we enforce diversity in the generated UAPs. We enforce that the crafted UAPs within a mini-batch are diverse via maximizing the pairwise distance between their embeddings $f^l(x + v_i)$ and $f^l(x + v_j)$, where v_i and v_j belong to generations within a mini-batch. We consider the layers of the target CNN for projecting ($x + v$). Thus our training objective is comprised of a diversity loss given by

$$L_d = - \sum_{i,j=1, i \neq j}^{K} d(f^l(x + v_i), f^l(x + v_j)) \qquad (3)$$

where K is the mini-batch size, and d is a suitable distance metric (e.g., Euclidean or cosine distance) computed between the features extracted between a pair of adversarial samples. Note that the class impression x present in the two embeddings $f(x + v_i)$ and $f(x + v_j)$ is same. Therefore, pushing them apart via minimizing L_d will make the UAPs v_i and v_j dissimilar.

Therefore the loss we optimize for training our generative model for crafting UAPs is given by

$$Loss = L_f + \lambda L_d \qquad (4)$$

Note that this objective is similar in spirit to that presented in the concurrent work [18].

4   Experiments

In this section we present our experimental setup and the effectiveness of the proposed method in terms the success rates achieved by the crafted UAPs. For all our experiments we have considered ILSVRC [23] dataset and recognition models trained on it as the target CNNs. Note that, since we have considered data-free scenario, we extract class impressions to serve as data samples. Similar to the existing data-driven approach [13] that uses 10 data samples per class, we also extract 10 impressions for each class which makes a training data of 10000 samples.

4.1   Implementation Details

The dimension of the latent space is chosen as 10, i.e, z is random $10D$ vector sampled from $\mathcal{U}[-1, 1]$. We have investigated with other dimensions (e.g. 50, 100, etc.) for the latent space and found that 10 is efficient with respect to the number of parameters though the success rates are not very different. We used a mini-batch size of 32. All our experiments are implemented in TensorFlow [1] using Adam optimizer and the implementations are made available at https://github. com/val-iisc/aaa. The generator part (G) of the network maps the latent space Z to the UAPs for a given target classifier. The architecture of our generator consists of 5 deconv layers. The final deconv layer is followed by a $tanh$ non-linearity and scaling by ξ. Doing so limits the perturbations to $[-\xi, \xi]$. Similar to [13,17], the value of ξ is chosen to be 10 in order to add negligible adversarial noise. The architecture of G is adapted from [24]. We experimented on a variety of CNN architectures trained to perform object recognition on the ILSVRC [23] dataset. The generator (G) architecture is unchanged for different target CNN architectures and separately learned with the corresponding class impressions.

While computing the diversity loss (Eq. 3), for each of the class impressions in the mini-batch (x), we select a pair of generated UAPs (v_1 and v_2) and compute the distance between $f^l(x + v_1)$ and $f^l(x + v_2)$. The diversity loss would be sum of all such distances computed over the mini-batch members. We typically consider the softmax layer of the target CNN for extracting the embeddings. Also, since the embeddings are probability vectors, we use cosine distance between the extracted embeddings. Note that, we can use any other intermediate layer for embedding and Euclidean distance for measuring their separation.

Since our objective is to generate diverse UAPs that can fool effectively, we give equal weight to both the components of the loss, i.e., we keep $\lambda = 1$ in Eq. (4).

4.2   UAPs and the Success Rates

Similar to [13,15,17,18] we measure the effectiveness of the crafted UAPs in terms of their "success rate". It is the percentage of data samples (x) for which the target CNN predicts a different label upon adding the UAP (v). Note that we compute the success rates over the 50000 validation images from ILSVRC

Table 1. Success rates of the perturbations modelled by our generative network, compared against the data-free approach FFF [17]. Rows indicate the target net for which perturbations are modelled and columns indicate the net under attack. Note that, in each row, entry where the target CNN matches with the network under attack represents white-box attack and the rest represent the black-box attacks. The mean fooling rate achieved by the Generator (G) trained for each of the target CNNs is shown in the rightmost column.

		VGG-F	CaffeNet	GoogLeNet	VGG-16	VGG-19	ResNet-152	Mean FR
VGG-F	Ours	**92.37**	**70.12**	**58.51**	**47.01**	**52.19**	**43.22**	**60.56**
	FFF	81.59	48.20	38.56	39.31	39.19	29.67	46.08
CaffeNet	Ours	**74.68**	**89.04**	**52.74**	**50.39**	**53.87**	**44.63**	**60.89**
	FFF	56.18	80.92	39.38	37.22	37.62	26.45	46.29
GoogLeNet	Ours	**57.90**	**62.72**	**75.28**	**59.12**	**48.61**	**47.81**	**58.57**
	FFF	49.73	46.84	56.44	40.91	40.17	25.31	43.23
VGG-16	Ours	**58.27**	**56.31**	**60.74**	**71.59**	**65.64**	**45.33**	**59.64**
	FFF	46.49	43.31	34.33	47.10	41.98	27.82	40.17
VGG-19	Ours	**62.49**	**59.62**	**68.79**	**69.45**	**72.84**	**51.74**	**64.15**
	FFF	39.91	37.95	30.71	38.19	43.62	26.34	36.12
ResNet-152	Ours	**52.11**	**57.16**	**56.41**	**47.21**	**48.78**	**60.72**	**53.73**
	FFF	28.31	29.67	23.48	19.23	17.15	29.78	24.60

CaffeNet   VGG-F   GoogLeNet   VGG-19   ResNet-152

Fig. 4. Sample universal adversarial perturbations (UAP), learned by the proposed framework for different networks, the corresponding target CNN is mentioned below the UAP. Note that images shown are one sample for each of the target networks, and across different samplings the perturbations vary visually as shown in Fig. 6.

dataset. Table 1 reports the obtained success rates of the UAPs crafted by our generative model G on various networks. Each row denotes the target model for which we train G and the columns indicate the model we attack to fool. Thus, we report the transfer rates on the unseen models also, which is referred to as "black-box attacking" (off-diagonal entries). Similarly, when the target CNN over which we learn G matches with the model under attack, it is referred to as "white-box attacking" (diagonal entries). Note that the right most column shows the mean success rates achieved by the individual generator networks (G) obtained across all the 6 CNN models. Proposed method can craft UAPs that have on an average 20.18% higher mean success rate compared to the existing data-free method to craft UAPs (FFF [17]).

Figure 4 shows example UAPs learned by our approach for different target CNN models. Note that the pixel values in those perturbations lie in $[-10, 10]$. Also the UAPs for different models look different. Figure 5 shows a clean and corresponding perturbed samples after adding UAPs learned for different target CNNs. Note that each of the target CNNs misclassify them differently.

For the sake of completeness, we compare our approach with the data-driven counterpart also. Table 2 presents the white-box success rates for both data-free and data-driven methods to craft UAPs. We also show the fooling ability of random noise sampled in $[-10, 10]$ as a baseline. Note that the success rates obtained by random noise is very less compared to the learned UAPs. Thus the adversarial perturbations are highly structured and very effective compared to the performance of random noise as perturbation.

On the other hand, the proposed method of acquiring class impressions from the target model's memory increases the mean success rate by an absolute 20% from that of current state-of-the-art data-free approach (FFF [17]). Also, note that our approach performs close to the data-driven approach UAP [13] with a gap of 8%. These observations suggest that the class impressions are effective to serve the purpose of the actual data samples in the context of learning to craft the UAPs.

Table 2. Effectiveness of the proposed approach to handle the data absence. We compare the success rates against the data-driven approach UAP [13], data-free approach FFF [17] and random noise baseline.

	VGG-F	CaffeNet	GoogLeNet	VGG-16	VGG-19	ResNet-152	Mean
Baseline	12.62	12.9	10.29	8.62	8.40	8.99	10.30
FFF (w/o Data)	81.59	80.92	56.44	47.10	43.62	29.78	56.58
Ours (w/o Data)	92.37	89.04	75.28	71.59	69.45	60.72	76.41
UAP (w Data)	93.8	93.1	78.5	77.8	80.8	84.0	84.67

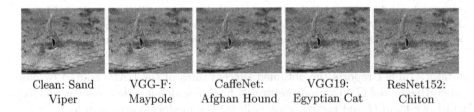

Clean: Sand Viper	VGG-F: Maypole	CaffeNet: Afghan Hound	VGG19: Egyptian Cat	ResNet152: Chiton

Fig. 5. Clean image (leftmost) of class "Sand Viper", followed by adversarial images generated by adding UAPs crafted for various target CNNs. Note that the perturbations while remaining imperceptible are leading to different misclassifications.

4.3   Comparison with Data Dependent Approaches

Table 3 presents the transfer rates achieved by the image-agnostic perturbations crafted by the proposed approach. Each row denotes the target model on which the generative model (G) is learned and columns denotes the models under attack. Hence, diagonal entries denote the white-box adversarial attacks and the off diagonal entries denote the black-box attacks. Note that the main draft presents only the white-box success rates, for completeness we present both here. Also note that, in spite of being a data-free approach the mean SR (extreme right column) obtained by our method is very close to that achieved by the state-of-the-art data-driven approach to craft UAPs.

Table 3. Success rates (SR) for the perturbations crafted by the proposed approach compared against the state-of-the-art data driven approach for crafting the UAPs.

		VGG-F	CaffeNet	GoogLeNet	VGG-16	VGG-19	ResNet-152	Mean SR
VGG-F	Ours	92.37	70.12	58.51	47.01	52.19	43.22	60.56
	UAP	93.7	71.8	48.4	42.1	42.1	47.4	57.58
CaffeNet	Ours	74.68	89.04	52.74	50.39	53.87	44.63	60.89
	UAP	74.0	93.3	47.7	39.9	39.9	48.0	56.71
GoogLeNet	Ours	57.90	62.72	75.28	59.12	48.61	47.81	58.57
	UAP	46.2	43.8	78.9	39.2	39.8	45.5	48.9
VGG-16	Ours	58.27	56.31	60.74	71.59	65.64	45.33	59.64
	UAP	63.4	55.8	56.5	78.3	73.1	63.4	65.08
VGG-19	Ours	62.49	59.62	68.79	69.45	72.84	51.74	64.15
	UAP	64.0	57.2	53.6	73.5	77.8	58.0	64.01
ResNet-152	Ours	52.11	57.16	56.41	47.21	48.78	60.72	53.73
	UAP	46.3	46.3	50.5	47.0	45.5	84.0	53.27

4.4   Diversity

The objective of having the diversity component (L_d) in the loss is to avoid learning a single UAP and to learn a generative model that can generate diverse set of UAPs for a given target CNN. We examine the distribution of predicted labels after adding the generated UAPs. This can reveal if there is a set of sink labels that attract most of the predictions. We have considered the G learned to fool VGG-F model and 50000 samples of ILSVRC validation set. We randomly select 10 UAPs generated by the G and compute the mean histogram of predicted labels. After sorting the histogram, most of the predicted labels (95%) for proposed approach spread over 212 labels out of the total 1000 target labels. Whereas the same number for UAP [13] is 173. The observed 22.5% higher diversity is attributed to our diversity component (L_d).

4.5   Simultaneous Targets

The ability of the adversarial perturbations to generalize across multiple models is observed with both image-specific [7,28] and agnostic perturbations [13,17]. It is an important issue to be investigated since it makes simple black-box attacks

Table 4. Generalizability of the UAPs crafted by the ensemble generator G_E learned on three target CNNs: CaffeNet, VGG-16 and ResNet-152. Note that because of the ensemble of the target CNNs, G_E learns to craft perturbations that have higher mean black-box success rates (MBBSR) compared to that of the individual generators.

	G_C	G_{V16}	G_{R152}	G_E
MBBSR	60.34	61.46	52.43	**68.52**

possible via transferring the perturbations to unknown models. In this subsection we investigate to learn a single G that can can craft UAPs to simultaneously fool multiple target CNNs.

We replace the single target CNN with an ensemble of three models: CaffeNet, VGG-16 and ResNet-152 and learn G_E using the fooling and diversity losses. Note that, since the class impressions vary from model to model, for this experiment we generate class impressions from multiple CNNs. Particularly, we simultaneously maximize the pre-softmax activation (Eq. (1)) of the desired class across individual target CNNs via optimizing their mean. We then investigate the generalizability of the generated perturbations. Table 4 presents the mean black-box success rate (MBBSR) for the UAPs generated by G_E on the remaining 3 models. For comparison, we present the MBBSR of the generators learned on the individual models. Because of the ensemble of the target CNNs G_E learns to craft more general UAPs and therefore achieves higher success rates than the individual generators.

4.6   Interpolating in the Latent Space

Our generator network (G) is similar to that in a typical GAN [6,22]. It maps the latent space to the space of UAPs for the given target classifier(s). In case of GANs, interpolating in the latent space can reveal signs of memorization. While traversing the latent space, smooth semantic change in the generations means the model has learned relevant representations. In our case, since we generate UAPs, we investigate if the interpolation has smooth visual changes and the intermediate UAPs can also fool the target CNN coherently.

Figure 6 shows the results of interpolating in the latent space for ResNet-152 as the target CNN. We sample a pair of points (z_1 and z_2) in the latent space and consider 5 intermediate points on the line joining them. We generate the UAPs corresponding to all these points by passing them through the learned generator architecture G. Figure 6 shows the generated UAPs and the corresponding success rates in fooling the target CNN. Note that the UAPs change visually smoothly between any pair of points and the success rate remains unchanged. This ensures that the representations learned are relevant and interesting.

4.7   Adversarial Training

We have performed adversarial training of target CNN with 50% mixture of clean and adversarial samples crafted using the learned generator (G). After 2

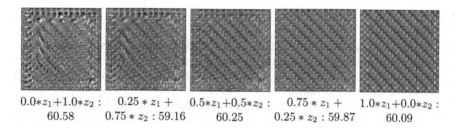

$0.0*z_1+1.0*z_2$: $0.25 * z_1 +$ $0.5*z_1+0.5*z_2$: $0.75 * z_1 +$ $1.0*z_1+0.0*z_2$:
        60.58 $0.75 * z_2 : 59.16$ 60.25 $0.25 * z_2 : 59.87$ 60.09

Fig. 6. Interpolation between a pair of points in Z space shows that the mapping learned by our generator has smooth transitions. The figure shows the perturbations corresponding to 5 points on the line joining a pair of points (z_1 and z_2) in the latent space. Note that these perturbations are learned to fool the ResNet-152 [8] architecture. Below each perturbation, the corresponding success rate obtained over 50000 images from ILSVRC 2014 validation images is mentioned. This shows the fooling capability of these intermediate perturbations is also high and remains same at different locations.

epochs, success rate of the G has dropped from 75.28 to 62.51. Note that the improvement is minor and the target CNN is still vulnerable. We then repeated the generator training for the finetuned network, resulting generator fools the finetuned network with an increased success rate of 68.72. After repeating this for multiple iterations, we observe that adversarial training does not make the target CNN significantly robust.

5   Discussion and Conclusions

In this paper we have presented a novel approach to mitigate the absence of data for crafting Universal Adversarial Perturbations (UAP). Class impressions are representative images that are easy to obtain via simple optimization from the target model. Using class impressions, our method drastically reduces the performance gap between the data-driven and data-free approaches to craft the UAPs. Success rates closer to that of data-driven UAPs demonstrate the effectiveness of class impressions in the context of crafting UAPs.

Another way to look at this observation is that it would be possible to extract useful information about the training data from the model parameters in a task specific manner. In this paper, we have extracted the class impressions as proxy data samples to train a generative model that can craft UAPs for the given target CNN classifier. It would be interesting to explore such feasibility for other applications as well.

The generative model presented in our approach is an efficient way to craft UAPs. Unlike the existing methods that perform complex optimizations, our approach constructs UAPs through a simple feed forward operation. Significant success rates, surprising cross model generalizability even in the absence of data reveal severe susceptibilities of the current deep learning models.

References

1. Abadi, M., et al.: TensorFlow: large-scale machine learning on heterogeneous systems. tensorflow.org (2015). http://tensorflow.org/
2. Baluja, S., Fischer, I.: Learning to attack: adversarial transformation networks. In: Proceedings of AAAI (2018)
3. Biggio, B., et al.: Evasion attacks against machine learning at test time. In: Blockeel, H., Kersting, K., Nijssen, S., Železný, F. (eds.) ECML PKDD 2013 Part III. LNCS (LNAI), vol. 8190, pp. 387–402. Springer, Heidelberg (2013). https://doi.org/10.1007/978-3-642-40994-3_25
4. Biggio, B., Fumera, G., Roli, F.: Pattern recognition systems under attack: design issues and research challenges. Int. J. Pattern Recogn. Artif. Intell. **28**(07) (2014)
5. Chatfield, K., Simonyan, K., Vedaldi, A., Zisserman, A.: Return of the devil in the details: delving deep into convolutional nets. In: Proceedings of the British Machine Vision Conference (BMVC) (2014)
6. Goodfellow, I.J., et al.: Generative adversarial nets. In: Advances in Neural Information Processing Systems (NIPS) (2014)
7. Goodfellow, I.J., Shlens, J., Szegedy, C.: Explaining and harnessing adversarial examples. In: International Conference on Learning Representations (ICLR) (2015)
8. He, K., Zhang, X., Ren, S., Sun, J.: Deep residual learning for image recognition. arXiv preprint arXiv:1512.03385 (2015)
9. Huang, L., Joseph, A.D., Nelson, B., Rubinstein, B.I., Tygar, J.D.: Adversarial machine learning. In: Proceedings of the 4th ACM Workshop on Security and Artificial Intelligence, AISec 2011 (2011)
10. Kingma, D., Ba, J.: Adam: a method for stochastic optimization. arXiv preprint arXiv:1412.6980 (2014)
11. Kurakin, A., Goodfellow, I., Bengio, S.: Adversarial examples in the physical world. In: International Conference on Learning Representations (ICLR) (2017)
12. Liu, Y., Chen, X., Liu, C., Song, D.: Delving into transferable adversarial examples and black-box attacks. In: International Conference on Learning Representations (ICLR) (2017)
13. Moosavi-Dezfooli, S., Fawzi, A., Fawzi, O., Frossard, P.: Universal adversarial perturbations. In: IEEE Conference on Computer Vision and Pattern Recognition (CVPR) (2017)
14. Moosavi-Dezfooli, S., Fawzi, A., Frossard, P.: DeepFool: a simple and accurate method to fool deep neural networks. In: IEEE Conference on Computer Vision and Pattern Recognition (CVPR) (2016)
15. Mopuri, K.R., Ganeshan, A., Babu, R.V.: Generalizable data-free objective for crafting universal adversarial perturbations. IEEE Trans. Pattern Anal. Mach. Intell. (2018)
16. Mopuri, K.R., Garg, U., Babu, R.V.: CNN fixations: an unraveling approach to visualize the discriminative image regions. arXiv preprint arXiv:1708.06670 (2017)
17. Mopuri, K.R., Garg, U., Babu, R.V.: Fast feature fool: a data independent approach to universal adversarial perturbations. In: Proceedings of the British Machine Vision Conference (BMVC) (2017)
18. Mopuri, K.R., Ojha, U., Garg, U., Babu, R.V.: NAG: network for adversary generation. In: Proceedings of the IEEE conference on Computer Vision and Pattern Recognition (CVPR) (2018)
19. Mordvintsev, A., Tyka, M., Olah, C.: Google deep dream (2015). https://research.googleblog.com/2015/06/inceptionism-going-deeper-into-neural.html

20. Olah, C., Mordvintsev, A., Schubert, L.: Feature visualization. Distill (2017). https://distill.pub/2017/feature-visualization
21. Papernot, N., McDaniel, P.D., Goodfellow, I.J., Jha, S., Celik, Z.B., Swami, A.: Practical black-box attacks against deep learning systems using adversarial examples. In: Asia Conference on Computer and Communications Security (ASIACCS) (2017)
22. Radford, A., Metz, L., Chintala, S.: Unsupervised representation learning with deep convolutional generative adversarial networks. arXiv preprint arXiv:1511.06434 (2015)
23. Russakovsky, O., et al.: ImageNet large scale visual recognition challenge. Int. J. Comput. Vis. (IJCV) **115**(3), 211–252 (2015)
24. Salimans, T., Goodfellow, I.J., Zaremba, W., Cheung, V., Radford, A., Chen, X.: Improved techniques for training GANs. In: Advances in Neural Information Processing Systems (NIPS) (2016)
25. Selvaraju, R.R., Cogswell, M., Das, A., Vedantam, R., Parikh, D., Batra, D.: Grad-CAM: visual explanations from deep networks via gradient-based localization. In: The IEEE International Conference on Computer Vision (ICCV) (2017)
26. Simonyan, K., Vedaldi, A., Zisserman, A.: Deep inside convolutional networks: visualising image classification models and saliency maps. In: International Conference on Learning Representations ICLR Workshops (2014)
27. Springenberg, J., Dosovitskiy, A., Brox, T., Riedmiller, M.: Striving for simplicity: the all convolutional net. In: International Conference on Learning Representations (ICLR) (workshop track) (2015)
28. Szegedy, C., et al.: Intriguing properties of neural networks. In: International Conference on Learning Representations (ICLR) (2013)
29. Zeiler, M.D., Fergus, R.: Visualizing and understanding convolutional networks. In: European Conference on Computer Vision (ECCV), pp. 818–833 (2014)
30. Zhang, J., Lin, Z., Brandt, J., Shen, X., Sclaroff, S.: Top-down neural attention by excitation backprop. In: European Conference on Computer Vision (ECCV) (2016)
31. Zhou, B., Khosla, A., Lapedriza, A., Oliva, A., Torralba, A.: Learning deep features for discriminative localization. In: Proceedings of Computer Vision and Pattern Recognition (CVPR) (2016)

Rendering Portraitures from Monocular Camera and Beyond

Xiangyu Xu[1,2(✉)], Deqing Sun[3], Sifei Liu[3], Wenqi Ren[4], Yu-Jin Zhang[1], Ming-Hsuan Yang[5,6], and Jian Sun[7]

[1] Tsinghua University, Beijing, China
xuxiangyu2014@gmail.com
[2] SenseTime, Beijing, China
[3] Nvidia, Santa Clara, USA
[4] Tencent AI Lab, Bellevue, USA
[5] UC Merced, Merced, USA
[6] Google, Menlo Park, USA
[7] Face++, Beijing, China

Abstract. Shallow Depth-of-Field (DoF) is a desirable effect in photography which renders artistic photos. Usually, it requires single-lens reflex cameras and certain photography skills to generate such effects. Recently, dual-lens on cellphones is used to estimate scene depth and simulate DoF effects for portrait shots. However, this technique cannot be applied to photos already taken and does not work well for whole-body scenes where the subject is at a distance from the cameras. In this work, we introduce an automatic system that achieves portrait DoF rendering for monocular cameras. Specifically, we first exploit Convolutional Neural Networks to estimate the relative depth and portrait segmentation maps from a single input image. Since these initial estimates from a single input are usually coarse and lack fine details, we further learn pixel affinities to refine the coarse estimation maps. With the refined estimation, we conduct depth and segmentation-aware blur rendering to the input image with a Conditional Random Field and image matting. In addition, we train a spatially-variant Recursive Neural Network to learn and accelerate this rendering process. We show that the proposed algorithm can effectively generate portraitures with realistic DoF effects using one single input. Experimental results also demonstrate that our depth and segmentation estimation modules perform favorably against the state-of-the-art methods both quantitatively and qualitatively.

1 Introduction

Shallow Depth of Field (DoF) shooting can enhance photos and render artistic images in which the region containing the main object at a certain distance to

Electronic supplementary material The online version of this chapter (https://doi.org/10.1007/978-3-030-01240-3_3) contains supplementary material, which is available to authorized users.

V. Ferrari et al. (Eds.): ECCV 2018, LNCS 11213, pp. 36–51, 2018.
https://doi.org/10.1007/978-3-030-01240-3_3

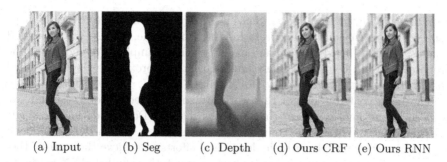

(a) Input   (b) Seg   (c) Depth   (d) Ours CRF   (e) Ours RNN

Fig. 1. The proposed method generates realistic DoF effects for whole-body portrait using a single RGB image (a) captured from a monocular camera. (b) and (c) are the segmentation and depth estimates of (a). (d) and (e) are our DoF results generated by the CRF based rendering system and the learned RNN filter, respectively.

the camera is well-focused, while other pixels are blurred [4]. Usually, a single-lens reflex (SLR) camera with a large aperture and certain photography skills are needed to render portraitures.

The portrait mode, which allows users to take DoF photos, is a major feature of the latest smart phones, *e.g.*, iPhone7+ and Google Pixel 2. Unlike SLR cameras, mobile phone cameras have a small, fixed-size aperture, which generates pictures with everything more or less in focus (Fig. 1(a)). Thus, generating DoF effects requires depth information, which has been obtained via specialized hardware in high-end phones. For example, iPhone 7+ relies on dual-lens to estimate depth, and Google Pixel2 uses Phase-Detect Auto-Focus (PDAF), which can also be regarded as two lenses on the left and right sides.

However, existing systems using specialized hardware have several limitations. First, they do not perform well for whole-body portraits which are at a relatively large distance to the lens. As the baseline between two lenses is small, it is challenging to estimate large depth fields. Second, it is impractical to implement these hardware solutions other than high-end phones. More importantly, there are billions of photos already taken that these systems cannot process.

In this paper, we introduce an automatic system that achieves DoF rendering for monocular cameras. Specifically, we use deep neural networks to estimate depth and segment portrait from a single image. While deep learning based methods have made significant progress in single image depth prediction and portrait segmentation, the results by state-of-the-art methods [7,9–11,20,23,25] are still too coarse for DoF rendering. To obtain more precise depth and segmentation, we improve the initial estimates using the Spatial Propagation Networks (SPN) [22]. With the refined depth and segmentation, our system applies depth and segmentation aware blurring to the background with Conditional Random Field (CRF) and image matting. Experimental results show that our system can achieve realistic DoF effects on a variety of half and full-body portrait images. To further accelerate this rendering process, we train a spatially-variant Recursive Neural Network (RNN) [21] filter with guidance from the depth and segmentation to learn to generate the DoF effects. Since it is extremely difficult to capture image pairs with and without DoF effects for the same scene, we use the generated results from the CRF-based system as our training samples. We show that the proposed network could effectively and efficiently approximate the CRF-based system and generate high-quality DoF results.

The main contributions of this work are summarized as follows. First, we propose an automatic system that achieves realistic DoF rendering for single portrait images. While some components of this system are known in the field, it requires meticulous algorithmic design and efforts to achieve the state-of-the-art results. Second, we train a depth and segmentation guided RNN model to approximate and accelerate the rendering process, which outperforms previous deep learning based filtering methods. In addition, we achieve the state-of-the-art performance on portrait segmentation using a SPN. We also demonstrate that sparse depth labels can be used for training a SPN, and that depth estimation can be improved by using additional portrait segmentation data.

2   Related Work

Portrait Segmentation. Deep learning achieves promising results on many applications [19,20,22,32,33]. For semantic segmentation, many recent works are based on CNNs. Long et al. [23] introduce fully convolutional neural network (FCNN), which convolutionalizes the classification networks, such as VGG [26], to directly output segmentation maps. Numerous segmentation methods have subsequently been developed. In particular, Shen et al. [25] adapt the FCNN to selfie portrait segmentation by using additional position and shape channels. Liu et al. [20] extend the FCNN by adding recurrent modules and use it on foreground segmentation. However, FCNN based methods do not explicitly model the pairwise relations (i.e. affinity) of pixels and their segmentation maps lack details and subtle structures. To remedy this problem, Chen et al. [5] and Zheng et al. [35] apply a dense CRF to model the affinity and refine the segmentation maps predicted by FCNNs. Liu et al. [22] propose the spatial propagation network with 2D propagation modules to learn pixel affinities in an end-to-end manner. As the fine structures and accurate segmentation boundaries are critical for rendering realistic DoF images, we apply SPNs to segment portraits and achieve the state-of-the-art results on a portrait segmentation dataset.

Depth Estimation with Single Image. Deep learning based models have been used to learn depth from a single image, both in supervised and unsupervised ways. For supervised depth learning, Eigen et al. [10] propose a CNN architecture that integrates coarse-scale depth prediction with fine-scale prediction. Furthermore, Eigen et al. [9] use a pre-trained classification network to improve depth accuracy, such as the AlexNet [16] and VGG [26] models. Recently, Laina et al. [17] use a ResNet-based encoder-decoder architecture to generate dense depth maps. These supervised-learning methods need densely-labeled RGB-D images which are limited to indoor scenes (e.g., NYU dataset [24]).

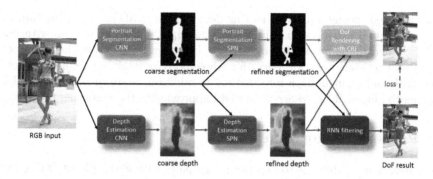

Fig. 2. Overview of the proposed algorithm. We first use off-the-shelf models for single image depth estimation and portrait segmentation. Then we further train SPNs to learn image affinities for refining the depth and segmentation. Finally, we generate the DoF result by exploiting both the refined depth and segmentation map, and learn a spatially-variant RNN to accelerate the rendering process.

On the other hand, several methods [11,13,30] learn depth map prediction in an unsupervised way using an image alignment loss that enforces left-right consistency of the training stereo pairs. However, these methods are still limited to specific scenarios (e.g., scenes in the KITTI [12] and Cityscape [8] datasets) and cannot handle portraits taken by cellphones in everyday life.

Chen *et al.* [7] propose the Depth in the Wild (DIW) dataset which consists of everyday images with relative depth labels between sparsely sampled point pairs. We show that SPN can be trained by sparse labels from the DIW dataset for accurate depth estimation. Moreover, the additional portrait segmentation dataset helps improve depth estimation for portraits, as we can enforce that the depth of different locations on the human body should be consistent.

DoF Rendering. The DoF effect is an important characteristic for realistic image synthesis in computer graphics. A number of DoF rendering methods have been proposed for image synthesis, such as rendering lightfield [27,34] and tracing rays [18,28]. All these image synthesis methods assume that the 3D information of the scene is known.

In contrast, generating DoF effects for RGB images captured from monocular cameras is more challenging. Some methods [14,36] rely on 3D cameras to capture the depth map as well as the RGB image, and generate DoF effects with the obtained depth. Barron *et al.* [2] recover depth with stereo pairs to render defocus images. Bae *et al.* [1] achieve desired DoF effects without using depth information by detecting and magnifying depth blur in a single image. However, their method needs the input images to have mild depth blur at first, which is not always accessible in real scenarios, such as small apertures of cellphones. Shen *et al.* [25] also generate DoF effects for single images by portrait segmentation. But their method is designed for selfies and cannot be used for whole-body images. In addition, the uniform blur kernel they use can bring boundary effects, as shown in Fig. 3(c). Different from the aforementioned methods, our method does not need special input or shooting devices such as 3D cameras. Instead, we use deep neural networks to obtain accurate depth and segmentation with fine details. Then we adopt a CRF model to split image layers using the estimated depth and generate the DoF effect for whole-body portraits by exploiting both the depth and segmentation information. In addition, we propose segmentation and depth guided RNN to accelerate and approximate the rendering process.

3   Proposed Algorithm

As it is extremely difficult to capture image pairs with and without DoF effect for the same scene, we do not take the elegant end-to-end approach for DoF rendering. Instead, we propose to integrate both learning-based and traditional vision algorithms into a novel system that does not require such a training set. Similar to Google Pixel2, our system simulates the real imaging process and applies depth-dependent blurring to an input image. While Google Pixel2 relies on hardware and lacks technical details, our software-based system works with any type of cellphone and can also process existing photos.

An overview of our system is shown in Fig. 2. Specifically, we first use off-the-shelf models for single image depth estimation [7] and portrait segmentation [20] to bootstrap our system. Since the initial estimation maps are coarse, we further train SPNs [22] to learn image affinity for refining the depth estimation and segmentation. With the refined depth and segmentation map, we split the background into layers of different depth using a CRF model and then perform segmentation and depth aware blur rendering to generate the DoF result. In the meanwhile, a spatially-variant RNN filter is learned with segmentation and depth as guidance map and the aforementioned DoF result as ground truth to accelerate the rendering process.

3.1   Portrait Segmentation

Spatial Propagation Network. The SPN [22] model consists of a deep CNN that learns the affinity entities of an input image I, and a spatial linear propagation module that refines a coarse mask M. The coarse mask is refined under the guidance of affinities, i.e., learned pairwise relationships for any pixel pairs. All modules are differentiable and can be jointly trained using backpropagation.

In this work, we adopt an encoder-decoder architecture with concatenation skip connections as the guidance network, where we use the VGG-16 [26] pre-trained network from the conv1 to pool5 as the downsampling part. The upsampling part has the exactly symmetric architecture and is learned from scratch. With the weights generated by the guidance network, the propagation module takes a coarse mask as input, and propagates the coarse information in four directions, i.e., left-to-right, top-to-bottom, and the other two with the reverse directions.

Loss Function. For portrait segmentation, the coarse mask of SPN for image I is generated by the foreground segmentation model [20]. We denote the output of SPN as v, and the final segmentation map is generated by a sigmoid function: $m = 1/(1 + \exp(-v))$. We use a pixel-wise cross-entropy loss for training, which is defined as:

$$L_1(m) = - \sum_{i \in \mathcal{F}} \log m_i - \sum_{j \in \mathcal{B}} \log(1 - m_j), \tag{1}$$

where the sets $\mathcal{F}$ and $\mathcal{B}$ contain pixels in the foreground and background masks of the ground truth, respectively.

3.2 Depth Estimation

The initial depth predicted by [7] is also refined by a SPN, which has the same network architecture as the one for segmentation. We use the Depth in the Wild dataset [7] that contains images from different scenes. As the images of this dataset are only sparsely annotated with relative depth between pairs of random point pairs, we use the ranking loss [7] for training. Consider a training image I and its annotation $\{i, j, \gamma\}$ where i and j are the two annotated points, and $\gamma \in \{+1, -1\}$ is the ground-truth depth relation between i and j: $\gamma = 1$ if i is further than j, and $\gamma = -1$ vice versa. Let z be the predicted depth map and z_i, z_j be the depths at point i and j. The ranking loss is defined as:

$$L_2(z) = \begin{cases} \log(1 + \exp(-z_i + z_j)), \gamma = +1, \\ \log(1 + \exp(z_i - z_j)), \gamma = -1, \end{cases} \tag{2}$$

which encourages the predicted depth difference between z_i and z_j to be consistent with the ground-truth ordinal relation.

In addition to the dataset with depth annotation, we also exploit the segmentation labels in the portrait segmentation dataset for better depth estimation of portrait images. As pixels at different locations of the portrait should have similar depth values, we use a loss function:

$$L_3(z) = \sum_{i,j \in \mathcal{F}} \max\{0, (z_i - z_j)^2 - \delta\}, \tag{3}$$

where $i, j \in \mathcal{F}$ are the pixels on the human body. As the depth values at different parts of the human body are not exactly the same, we adopt a soft constraint that allows small depth differences and only punishes the depth differences larger than a margin δ.

3.3 DoF Rendering

Most smartphones have two shooting modes that use the front and rear cameras respectively. For selfie images captured by a front camera, the background is always further than the person. To generate the DoF effect, we can simply blur

(a) Input   (b) Mask   (c) Uniform   (d) Guided

Fig. 3. Effectiveness of segmentation-guided blur kernel. A uniform blur causes boundary artifacts (c) while our method generates DoF effects with sharper boundaries (d).

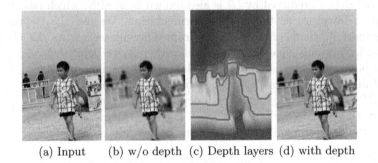

(a) Input   (b) w/o depth (c) Depth layers (d) with depth

Fig. 4. Comparison of the whole-body DoF results with and without using depth information. We generate more realistic result (d) by splitting depth layers (c).

the background with a disk blur kernel and keep the foreground clear. The blur process is formulated as:

$$B_i = m_i I_i + (1 - m_i) \sum_j w_{ij} I_j, \tag{4}$$

where I, B are the clear image and blurred result respectively; and m represents the portrait segmentation mask. The disk blur kernel w is defined as:

$$w_{ij} = \begin{cases} 1/C, \|p_i - p_j\| < r, \\ 0, \text{otherwise}, \end{cases} \tag{5}$$

where p_i is the coordinate of pixel i, and r is the radius of the disk blur kernel. The blur kernel is normalized by a constant C.

However, a uniform kernel may contaminate the background pixels with foreground pixels in the blurring process, and lead to boundary effect as shown in Fig. 3(c). To address this issue, we propose a new blur kernel $\hat{w}_{ij}$ which is guided by the segmentation mask m. The guided blur kernel is defined as:

$$\hat{w}_{ij}(m) = w_{ij}(1 - m_j)/\sum_j w_{ij}(1 - m_j), \tag{6}$$

where only the background pixels are used during the blurring process. Our method effectively removes the boundary effect as shown in Fig. 3(d).

Whole-Body Portraits. For whole-body portraits taken by a rear camera, naively blurring the background without considering the depth information cannot generate realistic results. As shown in Fig. 1(b), some parts of the background have similar depth with the human body and should also be kept clear. Thus, we exploit the depth estimation to generate better blurred portraitures.

As shown in Fig. 4(c), even with SPN refinement, the depth estimation from a single image is still imperfect and noisy. Thus we split the image into different depth layers using a CRF model which encourages depth smoothness in neighboring regions. The energy function for our depth labeling problem is formulated as:

$$E(l|z) = \sum_i u(l_i|z_i) + \lambda \sum_{(i,j)\in\mathcal{N}, i<j} e(l_i, l_j|z_i, z_j), \qquad (7)$$

where $\mathcal{N}$ is the 4-nearest-neighborhood system on pixels. In addition, λ is a hyper-parameter that balances the unary term $u(l_i|z_i)$ and the pairwise term $e(l_i, l_j|z_i, z_j)$. We derive the function $u(l_i|z_i)$ from the estimated depth z_i to measure the cost of assigning the layer label $l_i \in \{1, 2, ..., K\}$ to the pixel i. Specifically, we first find K clusters for the depth values using the K-means algorithm. We assume that the depth value in each cluster follows a Gaussian distribution, and $u(l_i|z_i)$ can be defined as the negative log-likelihood of the pixel i belonging to each cluster l_i:

$$u(l_i|z_i) = \|z_i - C_{l_i}\| / \sigma_{l_i}^2, \qquad (8)$$

where C_{l_i} and $\sigma_{l_i}^2$ are the cluster center and variance of the cluster l_i.

The pairwise term $e(l_i, l_j|z_i, z_j)$ measures the cost of assigning the labels l_i, l_j to the adjacent pixels i, j and imposes spatial smoothness:

$$e(l_i, l_j|z_i, z_j) = \mathbb{1}(l_i \neq l_j) \exp(-\|f_S(z)_{i\rightarrow j}\|), \qquad (9)$$

where $\mathbb{1}(\cdot)$ is the indicator function, and f_S is a Sobel operator which detects depth variations between the pixels i and j. We use the Graph Cut algorithm [15] to minimize the energy function $E(l|z)$.

After splitting the image I into K depth layers, we blur each layer l with a unique blur kernel $\hat{w}^l$ with different disk radius r^l. We assume that the human body should be kept clear and do not consider foreground blur. Thus, we set further layer with larger kernel size while closer layer with smaller one. The final result can be rendered by:

$$B_i = m_i I_i + (1 - m_i) \sum_{l=1}^{K} \sum_t g_{it} \mathbb{1}(l_t = l) \sum_j \hat{w}_{ij}^l(m) I_j, \qquad (10)$$

where g_{it} is a Gaussian kernel centered at pixel i which feathers and combines layers of different depth. $\sum_t g_{it} \mathbb{1}(l_t = l)$ measures to what degree pixel i belongs to layer l. Figure 4(d) shows a rendered DoF result.

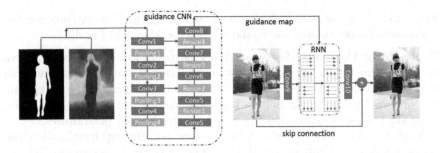

Fig. 5. Illustration of our spatially-variant RNN model. The proposed network contains two groups of RNNs for image filtering and a deep CNN to learn the guidance map with our refined depth and segmentation estimation. To simplify the network training, we add a skip connection from the input to output and learn the residual map instead of the RGB image.

3.4   RNN Filter Learning

While effective at generating high-quality DoF images, the CRF-based method is computationally expensive because of the CRF optimization, image matting and guided blurring. To reduce the computational cost, we train a deep neural network to approximate the rendering process. Since the DoF blur is spatially-variant, we adopt the RNN filters [21] instead of using a CNN which has the same convolutional kernel at different spatial locations. However, the original method [21] cannot be directly applied for our task, because it learns the the guidance map from RGB images and does not explicitly consider segmentation and depth information. To address this issue, we propose to use the refined segmentation and depth estimation to generate guidance for approximating DoF effects. To simplify the network training, we add a skip connection from the clear image input to the RNN output, because the generated DoF results resemble the original inputs. We use an encoder-decoder CNN to generate the guidance map for the following RNN which combines two groups of recursive filters in a cascaded scheme. The pipeline of our RNN model is shown in Fig. 5.

4   Experimental Results

We show the main results in this section and present more analysis and evaluations in the supplementary material.

4.1   Implementation Details

Network Training. To train the segmentation network for front camera, we use the selfie image dataset from [25] which is composed of 1428 training and 283 test images. For rear cameras, we use the Baidu human segmentation dataset which has 5387 densely labeled images [29] of which 500 are used for testing and the

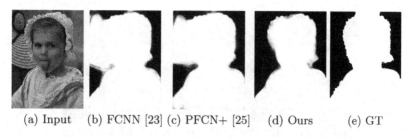

(a) Input   (b) FCNN [23] (c) PFCN+ [25]   (d) Ours   (e) GT

Fig. 6. Visual comparison of different segmentation methods on a selfie image.

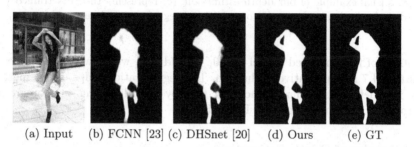

(a) Input   (b) FCNN [23] (c) DHSnet [20]   (d) Ours   (e) GT

Fig. 7. Visual comparison of different segmentation methods on a whole-body image.

rest for training. During training, we randomly change the aspect ratio and flip the image for data augmentation. To train the depth network, we use the Depth in the Wild [7] dataset which consists of 421K training and 74K test images. For the RNN training, we conduct our CRF-based DoF rendering method on the Baidu human dataset to generate 5K training image pairs and collect another 100 portrait images for evaluation. For all the networks, we use the standard SGD for training with momentum as 0.9 and learning rate as 0.0001.

DoF Rendering. Instead of using the segmentation map from SPN directly, we use the KNN matting method [6] to composite clear foreground and blurry background images. Our estimated segmentation result provides a good trimap initialization for image matting. We generate a trimap by setting the pixels within a 10-pixel radius of the segmentation boundary as the "unknown". This matting scheme performs well as our segmentation provides accurate initial segmentation boundaries. For the CRF model, we empirically split the image into $K = 6$ layers and set the hyper-parameter in (7) as $\lambda = 10$.

4.2 Results of Portrait Segmentation

We quantitatively evaluate our segmentation results on the selfie image dataset [25] and Baidu human segmentation dataset [29]. The segmentation performance is measured by the Interaction-over-Union (IoU) metric. As shown in Table 1, our algorithm achieves the state-of-the-art on selfies. For whole-body images [29], the proposed method achieves an IoU of 93.22 which outperforms

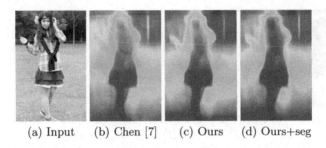

(a) Input   (b) Chen [7]   (c) Ours   (d) Ours+seg

Fig. 8. Visual example of our depth estimation. (c) represents the SPN trained with (2). (d) is further trained with (3) on additional segmentation data.

the 91.43 of the finetuned model of [20]. In addition, we show two examples in Figs. 6 and 7 for qualitative evaluation. The segmentation maps of our method have fine details and small structures, thereby providing accurate foreground information for generating good DoF effects.

4.3 Results of Depth Estimation

Similar to [7], we use the Weighted Human Disagreement Rate (WHDR) between the predicted ordinal relations and ground-truth ordinal relations to evaluate our method on the DIW test set. Although our result 14.35 on the DIW dataset is only slightly better than the 14.39 of [7], it shows that our SPN can estimate depth properly, and training SPN with sparse labels is effective. As the WHDR only measures ordinal relations of sparse point pairs (one pair each image), it does not evaluate the depth estimation performance well. We present visual examples for qualitative comparison in Fig. 8. Refinement with SPN removes noise in the background and generates sharper boundaries (*e.g.*, the background on the left side in Fig. 8(c)). As shown in Fig. 8(d), using additional segmentation data and our new depth loss (3) further improves the depth consistency on the human body and leads to better depth estimation for portraits.

4.4 Results of CRF-Based DoF Rendering

User Study. Since there is no ground truth for DoF images to perform a quantitative evaluation, we conduct the following user study on the generated DoF

Table 1. Quantitative comparison of different segmentation methods on the selfie image dataset [25]. GC represents graph cut. FCNN has been finetuned on the selfie training set for fair comparisons.

Methods	GC [3]	FCNN [23]	PFCN+ [25]	Ours
Mean IoU (%)	80.02	94.97	95.52	**96.40**

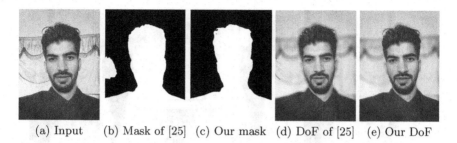

(a) Input   (b) Mask of [25]   (c) Our mask   (d) DoF of [25]   (e) Our DoF

Fig. 9. DoF results on a selfie image. Our method generates better segmentation mask and DoF result without boundary effect (note the glowing boundary in (d)).

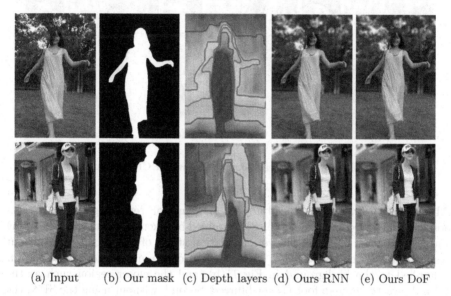

(a) Input   (b) Our mask   (c) Depth layers   (d) Ours RNN   (e) Ours DoF

Fig. 10. Visual example of our DoF results on whole-body images. Our method generates realistic DoF results.

results. This study uses 30 whole-body portrait images where: (a) 10 images are captured by single-lens reflex (SLR) camera, (b) 10 are generated by our algorithm, and (c) 10 images are generated by naively blurring the background without considering depth. These images are presented in a random order to 22 subjects, who are asked to decide if a presented image is generated by a computer or captured by a real SLR. 79.1% users regard (b) as real captured, while the numbers are 81.8% for (a) and 13.2% for (c). The user study shows that the proposed method can effectively generate realistic DoF results, while naively blurring without considering depth cannot generate convincing results. We show several visual examples for selfie and whole-body images in Figs. 9 and 10.

(a) input   (b) w/o depth   (c) w/o SPN

(d) w/o CRF   (e) w/o guided kernel   (f) final result

Fig. 11. Ablation study of each component in our CRF-based method.

Ablation Study. As introduced in Sect. 3.3, our DoF rendering system is composed of different components, $i.e.$, SPN, guided blur kernel, depth aware filtering and CRF model. Figure 11 shows an ablation study of each component of our system in rendering DoF images. First, without depth information, uniform blur is applied to the background in Fig. 11(b), and the closer region such as the ground near the human foot is over-blurred. Second, without using the SPN, the coarse segmentation map leads to incorrectly blurred foreground regions such as the top part of the hat in Fig. 11(c). Third, using a naive thresholding scheme to split depth layers instead of the CRF model generates unrealistic boundaries between the clear and blurry regions as shown in the middle part of Fig. 11(d). In addition, removing the guided blur kernel results in noticeable boundary artifacts around the trousers in Fig. 11(e). By contrast, our system effectively integrates different components and generates high-quality DoF results (Fig. 11(e)).

4.5 Results of RNN Filter

We evaluate the proposed RNN filter against the state-of-the-art deep filtering approaches [31] and [21]. We also train a CNN network with refined depth and segmentation maps as additional input to compare with our spatially-variant RNN design. This CNN has the same encoder-decoder structure as the guidance network in Sect. 3.4. For fair comparisons, we use the same settings and training data for all these methods as introduced in Sect. 4.1. As shown in Table 2,

Table 2. Quantitative comparison of different deep networks for learning DoF effects on the Baidu human test set [29].

Methods	Xu *et al.* [31]	Liu *et al.* [21]	Ours CNN	Ours RNN
PSNR (dB)	31.55	33.55	37.35	**40.74**
SSIM	0.9235	0.9432	0.9723	**0.9868**

the proposed filtering algorithm outperforms state-of-the-art methods for approximating DoF effects in terms of PSNR and SSIM. For qualitative evaluation, we show a visual example in Fig. 12. The CNN-based methods (Fig. 12(b) and (d)) incorrectly blur the foreground, such as the textures of the clothes, because CNN uses uniform kernel at different spatial locations and cannot well handle the spatially-variant DoF case. The result by Liu *et al.* contains significant artifacts on the background due to the lack of effective guidance. In contrast, the proposed RNN model explicitly uses the depth and segmentation as guidance to learn a spatially-variant image filter. Thus, we can effectively approximate the CRF-based rendering system and generate realistic DoF results (Fig. 12(e)).

(a) Input   (b) Xu [31]   (c) Liu [21]   (d) Ours CNN   (e) Ours RNN   (f) Ours CRF

Fig. 12. Visual example of our RNN filtering result. Our method generates realistic DoF result while others wrongly blur the foreground or contain significant artifacts.

Running Time. We implement the proposed algorithm on a desktop with an Intel i7 CPU, 8 GB RAM and an Nvidia GTX 1060 GPU. It takes about 8 s for the CRF-based method to process a 500 × 300 image. By contrast, the learned RNN filter takes only 1.12 s, which significantly accelerates the rendering process and makes it more practical for real applications.

5   Conclusions

In this work, we propose a deep learning and CRF based system that can automatically render realistic DoF results for single portrait images. A spatially-variant RNN filter is trained to accelerate the rendering process with guidance from depth and segmentation. In addition, we achieve the state-of-the-art performance on portrait segmentation using SPN. Furthermore, we demonstrate that sparse depth labels can be used for SPN training. We also show that depth estimation can be improved by enforcing depth consistency on human body with additional portrait segmentation data.

Acknowledgement. This work is supported in part by National Nature Science Foundation of P.R. China (No. 611711184, 61673234, U1636124), the NSF CAREER Grant (No. 1149783), and gifts from Adobe and Nvidia.

References

1. Bae, S., Durand, F.: Defocus magnification. Comput. Graph. Forum **26**, 571–579 (2007)
2. Barron, J.T., Adams, A., Shih, Y., Hernández, C.: Fast bilateral-space stereo for synthetic defocus. In: CVPR (2015)
3. Boykov, Y., Jolly, M.P.: Interactive graph cuts for optimal boundary & region segmentation of objects in N-D images. In: ICCV (2001)
4. Campbell, F.: The depth of field of the human eye. Optica Acta: Int. J. Opt. **4**, 157–164 (1957)
5. Chen, L., Papandreou, G., Kokkinos, I., Murphy, K., Yuille, A.L.: Semantic image segmentation with deep convolutional nets and fully connected CRFs. In: ICLR (2015)
6. Chen, Q., Li, D., Tang, C.: KNN matting. PAMI **25**, 2175–2188 (2013)
7. Chen, W., Fu, Z., Yang, D., Deng, J.: Single-image depth perception in the wild. In: NIPS (2016)
8. Cordts, M., et al.: The cityscapes dataset for semantic urban scene understanding. In: CVPR (2016)
9. Eigen, D., Fergus, R.: Predicting depth, surface normals and semantic labels with a common multi-scale convolutional architecture. In: ICCV (2015)
10. Eigen, D., Puhrsch, C., Fergus, R.: Depth map prediction from a single image using a multi-scale deep network. In: NIPS (2014)
11. Garg, R., B.G., V.K., Carneiro, G., Reid, I.: Unsupervised CNN for single view depth estimation: geometry to the rescue. In: Leibe, B., Matas, J., Sebe, N., Welling, M. (eds.) ECCV 2016 Part VIII. LNCS, vol. 9912, pp. 740–756. Springer, Cham (2016). https://doi.org/10.1007/978-3-319-46484-8_45
12. Geiger, A., Lenz, P., Urtasun, R.: Are we ready for autonomous driving? The KITTI vision benchmark suite. In: CVPR (2012)
13. Godard, C., Aodha, O.M., Brostow, G.J.: Unsupervised monocular depth estimation with left-right consistency. In: CVPR (2017)
14. Huhle, B., Schairer, T., Jenke, P., Straßer, W.: Realistic depth blur for images with range data. In: Kolb, A., Koch, R. (eds.) Dyn3D 2009. LNCS, vol. 5742, pp. 84–95. Springer, Heidelberg (2009). https://doi.org/10.1007/978-3-642-03778-8_7
15. Kolmogorov, V., Zabih, R.: What energy functions can be minimized via graph cuts? In: ECCV (2002)
16. Krizhevsky, A., Sutskever, I., Hinton, G.E.: ImageNet classification with deep convolutional neural networks. In: NIPS (2012)
17. Laina, I., Rupprecht, C., Belagiannis, V., Tombari, F., Navab, N.: Deeper depth prediction with fully convolutional residual networks. In: 3DV (2016)
18. Lee, S., Eisemann, E., Seidel, H.: Real-time lens blur effects and focus control. ACM Trans. Graph. (SIGGRAPH) **29**, 1–7 (2010)

19. Liu, C., Xu, X., Zhang, Y.J.: Temporal attention network for action proposal. In: ICIP (2018)
20. Liu, N., Han, J.: DHSNet: deep hierarchical saliency network for salient object detection. In: CVPR (2016)
21. Liu, S., Pan, J., Yang, M.: Learning recursive filters for low-level vision via a hybrid neural network. In: ECCV (2016)
22. Liu, S., De Mello, S., Gu, J., Zhong, G., Yang, M.-H., Kautz, J.: Learning affinity via spatial propagation networks. In: NIPS (2017)
23. Long, J., Shelhamer, E., Darrell, T.: Fully convolutional networks for semantic segmentation. In: CVPR (2015)
24. Silberman, N., Hoiem, D., Kohli, P., Fergus, R.: Indoor segmentation and Support inference from RGBD images. In: Fitzgibbon, A., Lazebnik, S., Perona, P., Sato, Y., Schmid, C. (eds.) ECCV 2012 Part V. LNCS, vol. 7576, pp. 746–760. Springer, Heidelberg (2012). https://doi.org/10.1007/978-3-642-33715-4_54
25. Shen, X., et al.: Automatic portrait segmentation for image stylization. Comput. Graph. Forum (Eurographics) **35**, 93–102 (2016)
26. Simonyan, K., Zisserman, A.: Very deep convolutional networks for large-scale image recognition. In: ICLR (2015)
27. Soler, C., Subr, K., Durand, F., Holzschuch, N., Sillion, F.X.: Fourier depth of field. ACM Trans. Graph. **28**, 18 (2009)
28. Wu, J., Zheng, C., Hu, X., Wang, Y., Zhang, L.: Realistic rendering of bokeh effect based on optical aberrations. Vis. Comput. **26**, 555–563 (2010)
29. Wu, Z., Huang, Y., Yu, Y., Wang, L., Tan, T.: Early hierarchical contexts learned by convolutional networks for image segmentation. In: ICPR (2014)
30. Xie, J., Girshick, R.B., Farhadi, A.: Deep3D: fully automatic 2D-to-3D video conversion with deep convolutional neural networks. In: ECCV (2016)
31. Xu, L., Ren, J., Yan, Q., Liao, R., Jia, J.: Deep edge-aware filters. In: ICML (2015)
32. Xu, X., Pan, J., Zhang, Y.J., Yang, M.H.: Motion blur kernel estimation via deep learning. TIP **27**, 194–205 (2018)
33. Xu, X., Sun, D., Pan, J., Zhang, Y., Pfister, H., Yang, M.H.: Learning to super-resolve blurry face and text images. In: ICCV (2017)
34. Yu, X., Wang, R., Yu, J.: Real-time depth of field rendering via dynamic light field generation and filtering. Comput. Graph. Forum **29**, 2099–2107 (2010)
35. Zheng, S., et al.: Conditional random fields as recurrent neural networks. In: ICCV (2015)
36. Zhou, T., Chen, J.X., Pullen, J.M.: Accurate depth of field simulation in real time. Comput. Graph. Forum **26**, 15–23 (2007)

Learning to Zoom: A Saliency-Based Sampling Layer for Neural Networks

Adrià Recasens[1(✉)], Petr Kellnhofer[1(✉)], Simon Stent[2], Wojciech Matusik[1], and Antonio Torralba[1]

[1] Massachusetts Institute of Technology, Cambridge, MA 02139, USA
{recasens,pkellnho,wojciech,torralba}@csail.mit.edu
[2] Toyota Research Institute, Cambridge, MA 02139, USA
simon.stent@tri.global

Abstract. We introduce a saliency-based distortion layer for convolutional neural networks that helps to improve the spatial sampling of input data for a given task. Our differentiable layer can be added as a preprocessing block to existing task networks and trained altogether in an end-to-end fashion. The effect of the layer is to efficiently estimate how to sample from the original data in order to boost task performance. For example, for an image classification task in which the original data might range in size up to several megapixels, but where the desired input images to the task network are much smaller, our layer learns how best to sample from the underlying high resolution data in a manner which preserves task-relevant information better than uniform downsampling. This has the effect of creating distorted, caricature-like intermediate images, in which idiosyncratic elements of the image that improve task performance are zoomed and exaggerated. Unlike alternative approaches such as spatial transformer networks, our proposed layer is inspired by image saliency, computed efficiently from uniformly downsampled data, and degrades gracefully to a uniform sampling strategy under uncertainty. We apply our layer to improve existing networks for the tasks of human gaze estimation and fine-grained object classification. Code for our method is available in: http://github.com/recasens/Saliency-Sampler.

Keywords: Task saliency · Image sampling · Attention
Spatial transformer · Convolutional neural networks · Deep learning

1 Introduction

Many modern neural network models used in computer vision have input size constraints [1–4]. These constraints exist for various reasons. By restricting the input resolution, one can control the time and computation required during both training and testing, and benefit from efficient batch training on GPU. On certain datasets, limiting the input feature dimensionality can also empirically increase performance by improving training sample coverage over the input space.

© Springer Nature Switzerland AG 2018
V. Ferrari et al. (Eds.): ECCV 2018, LNCS 11213, pp. 52–67, 2018.
https://doi.org/10.1007/978-3-030-01240-3_4

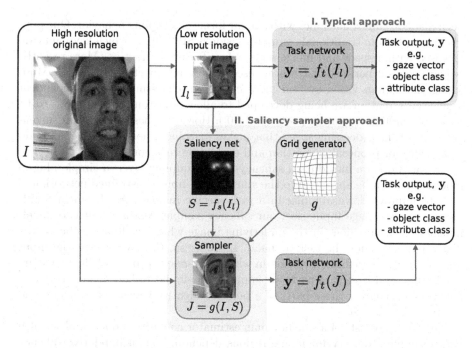

Fig. 1. Outline of our proposed saliency-based sampling layer. Numerous tasks in computer vision are solved by a task network (shown in green), operating on an image I_l which has been downsampled (for performance reasons) from a much larger original image I. For such tasks, where I is available but unused, we show that using a saliency sampler to downsample the image (rather than uniform downsampling) can lead to significant improvement in the task network performance for an identical architecture, as well as beating alternative sampling approaches such as bounding box proposals or spatial transformer networks. Our sampler is differentiable and can be trained end-to-end. The effect of the sampler is to discover and zoom in on (or sample more densely) those regions which are particularly informative to the task. In the case of gaze estimation, as seen here, the sampler locates the eyes as task-salient regions (S) and enlarges them in the resampled image (J). (Color figure online)

When the target input size is smaller than the images in the original dataset, the standard approach is to uniformly downsample the input images. Perhaps the best-known example is the commonly used 224×224 pixel input when training classifiers on the ImageNet Large Scale Visual Recognition Challenge [5], despite the presence of a range of image sizes – up to several megapixels – within the original dataset.

While uniform downsampling is simple and effective in many situations, it can be lossy for tasks which require information from different spatial resolutions and locations. In such cases, sampling the salient regions at the necessary (and possibly diverse) scales and locations is essential. Humans perform such tasks by saccading their gaze in order to gather the necessary information with a mixture of high-acuity foveal vision and coarser peripheral vision. Attempts have also been made to endow machines with similar forms of sampling behavior. One popular example from traditional computer vision is SIFT [6], in which keypoints are localised within space and image scale before feature extraction. More recently, region proposal networks have been used widely in object detection [7]. Mimicking the human vision system more closely, mechanisms for task-dependent sequential attention are being developed to allow numerous scene regions to be processed in high resolution (see e.g. [8–10]). However, these approaches surrender some of the processing speed that makes machine vision attractive, and add complexity for proposal generation and evaluating task completion.

In this work we introduce a saliency-based sampling layer: a simple plug-in module that can be appended to the start of any input-constrained network and used to improve downsampling in a task-specific manner. As shown in Fig. 1, given a target image input size, our saliency sampler learns to allocate pixels in that target to regions in the underlying image which are found to be particularly important for the task at hand. In doing so, the layer warps the input image, creating a deformed version in which task-relevant parts of the image are emphasized and irrelevant parts are suppressed, similar to how a caricature of a face tries to magnify those parts of a person's identity which make them stand out from the average.

Our layer consists of a saliency map estimator connected to a sampler which varies sampling density for image regions depending on their relative saliency values. Since the layer is designed to be fully differentiable, it can be inserted before any conventional network and trained end-to-end. Unlike sequential attention models [9–12], the computation is performed in a single pass of the saliency sampler at constant computational cost.

We apply our approach to tasks where the discovery of small objects or fine-grained details is important (see Fig. 2), and consistently find that adding our layer results in performance improvements over baseline networks.

2   Related Work

We divide the related work into three main categories: attention mechanisms, saliency-based methods, and adaptive image sampling methods.

Attention Mechanisms: Attention has been extensively used to improve the performance of CNNs. Jaderberg et al. [13] introduced the Spatial Transformer Network (STN), a layer that estimates a parametrized transformation from an input image in an effort to undo nuisance image variation (such as from object pose in the task of rigid object classification) and thereby improve model generalization. In their work, the authors proposed three types of transformation that could be learned: affine, projective and thin plate spline (TPS). Although our method also applies a transformation to the input image, our application is quite different: we do not attempt to undo variation such as local translation or rotation; rather we try to vary the resolution dynamically to favor regions of the input image which are more task salient. While our method could be

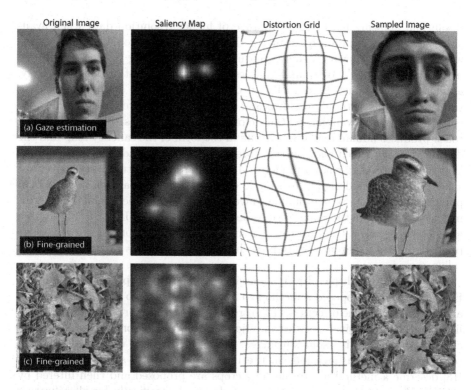

Fig. 2. Examples of resampled input images for various tasks using our proposed saliency sampler. Our module is able to discover saliency according to the task: for gaze estimation in (a), the sampler learns to zoom in on the subject's eyes to allow for higher precision gaze estimation; for fine-grained classification in (b), the sampler zooms in important parts of the bird's anatomy while cropping out much of the empty image; in (c), when no clear salient area is detected, the sampler defaults to a near-uniform sampling.

encapsulated within the TPS approach of [13], we implicitly prevent extreme transformations and fold-overs, which can easily occur for a TPS-based spatial transformer (and which also makes direct estimation of a non-parametrized sampling map intractable). We believe that this helps to prevent dramatic failures and therefore helps to make the module easier to learn.

Deformable convolutional networks (DCNs), introduced by Dai et al. [14], follow a similar motivation to STNs. They show that convolutional layers can learn to dynamically adjust their receptive fields to adapt to the input features and improve invariance to nuisance factors. Their proposal involves the replacement of any standard convolutional layer in a CNN with a deformable layer which learns to estimate offsets to the standard kernel sampling locations, conditioned on the input. We note four main differences with our work. First, while their method samples from the same low-resolution input as the original CNN architecture, our saliency sampler is designed to sample from any available resolution, allowing it to take advantage of higher resolution data when available. Second, our approach estimates the sample field through saliency maps which have been shown to emerge naturally when training fully convolutional neural networks [15]. We found that estimating local spatial offsets directly, as in a DCN, is much harder. Third, our method can be applied to existing trained networks without modification, while DCNs require changing network configurations by swapping in the deformable convolutions. Finally, our approach produces human readable outputs in the form of the saliency map and the deformed image which allow for easy visual inspection and debugging. We note that our proposed saliency sampler and DCNs are not mutually exclusive: our saliency sampler is designed to sample efficiently across scale space and could potentially make use of deformable convolutional layers to help model local geometric variations. In the same spirit as deformable networks, Li et al. [16] propose an encoder-decoder structure to use non-squared convolutions. As in [13], they predict directly a parametrization of these transformations instead of using a saliency map.

Attending to multiple objects recursively has also been previously explored. Eslami et al. [11] proposed a method to iteratively attend to multiple objects in an image. In the same direction, [12] introduced a method for fine-grained classification which recursively locates an object in a low-resolution image followed by cropping from a high-resolution image. More recently, [17] expanded this idea to multiple attention locations in the image, instead of a single one. Finally, [18] describe a method where multiple crops are proposed and then filtered by a CNN. We note that these methods are designed specifically for classification and are not as general as our proposed sampling layer.

Saliency-Based Methods: CNNs have been shown to naturally direct attention to task-salient regions of the input data. Zhou et al. [15] found that CNNs use a restricted portion of the image to inform their decision in a classification task. They proposed the use of Class Activation Maps (CAM) as a mechanism for localizing objects in images without explicit location feedback during training. Rosendfeld et al. [19] proposed an iterative method to crop the relevant regions of the image for fine-grained classification. They generate a CAM to highlight the regions most used by the network to make the final decision. These regions are used to crop a part of the image and generate a new CAM, which then highlights the regions of the image used by the network to inform the final prediction. As presented in [15], the CAM requires the use of a particular fully convolutional architecture. To overcome this limitation, [20] introduces a gradient-based method to generate CAMs. Their method can be used to understand a wide variety of networks. In our work, we take advantage of the ability of CNNs to naturally localise task-salient regions, by encouraging the network to attend more to those regions.

Adaptive Image Sampling Methods: Another possible approach to our problem is to pre-design certain feature detectors in a multi-scale strategy. This approach is usually taken when solving a particular problem where the features to use are very clear for humans. For instance, to solve the problem of gaze-tracking on a mobile device display, Khosla et al. [21] proposed the iTracker method, a gaze estimation system based on RGB images. Their system uses the image from the device's front-facing camera, and extracts high resolution crops of both eyes and face using separate detectors. Another example along this line was presented by Wang et al. [22], who generate the features of the input image at different scales to then select the best features and produce the final output.

Adaptive image sampling is also used for image retargeting in computer graphics [23]. Unlike in our case where the sampled image only serves as an intermediate representation for solving another problem, the goal of retargeting is to deform an image to fit a new shape and preserve content important for human observer as well as avoid visible deformations. Similarly to our concept, this can be driven by saliency [24] and formulated as an energy minimization [25] or Finite Element Method [26] problem.

3 Saliency Sampler

Let I be a high-resolution image of an arbitrary size and let I_l be a low-resolution image bounded by size $M \times N$ pixels suitable for a task network f_t (Fig. 1). Typically, CNNs rescale the input image I to I_l without exploiting the relative importance of I's pixels. However, if our task requires information from a certain image region more than others, it may be advantageous to sample this region more densely. The saliency sampler executes this by first analyzing I_l before sampling areas of I proportionally to their perceived importance. In doing so, the model can capture some of the benefit of increased resolution without significant additional computational burden or risk of overfitting.

The sampling process can be divided into two stages. In the first stage, a CNN is used to produce a saliency map. This map is task specific, since different tasks may require focus on different image regions. In the second stage, the most important image regions are sampled according to the saliency map.

3.1 Saliency Network

The saliency network f_s produces a saliency map S from the low resolution image: $S = f_s(I_l)$. The choice of network for this stage is flexible and may be changed depending on the task. For all choices of f_s, we apply a softmax operation in the final layer to normalize the output map.

3.2 Sampling Approach

Next, a sampler g takes as input the saliency map S along with the full resolution image I and computes $J = g(I, S)$ – that is, an image with the same dimensions as I_l, that has been sampled from I such that highly weighted areas in S are represented by a larger image extent (see Fig. 3). In this section, we will discuss the possible forms that g can take, and which one is more suitable for CNNs.

In all cases, we compute a mapping between the sampled image and the original image and then use the grid sampler introduced in [13]. This mapping can be written in the standard form as two functions $u(x, y)$ and $v(x, y)$ such that $J(x, y) = I(u(x, y), v(x, y))$.

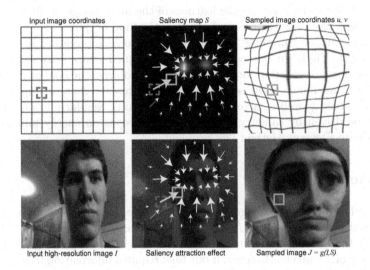

Input image coordinates   Saliency map S Sampled image coordinates u, v

Input high-resolution image I Saliency attraction effect   Sampled image $J = g(I, S)$

Fig. 3. Saliency sampler. The saliency map S (center, top) describes saliency as a mass attracting neighboring pixels (arrows). Each pixel (red square) of the output low-resolution image J samples from a location (cyan square) in the input high-resolution image I which is offset by this attraction (yellow arrow) as defined by the Saliency Sampler $g(I, S)$. This distorts the coordinate system of the image and magnifies important regions which get sampled more often than others.

The main goal for the design of u and v is to map pixels proportionally to the normalized weight assigned to them by the saliency map. Assuming that $u(x, y)$, $v(x, y)$, x and y range from 0 to 1, an exact approximation to this problem would be to find u and v such that:

$$\int_0^{u(x,y)} \int_0^{v(x,y)} S(x', y') dx' dy' = xy \tag{1}$$

However, finding u and v is equivalent to finding the change of variables that transforms the distribution set by $S(x, y)$ to a uniform distribution. This problem has been extensively explored and the usual solutions are computationally very costly [27]. For this reason, we need to take an alternative approach that is suitable for use in CNNs.

Our approach is inspired by the idea that each pixel (x', y') is pulling other pixels with a force $S(x', y')$ (see Fig. 3). If we add a distance kernel $k((x, y), (x', y'))$, this can be described as:

$$u(x, y) = \frac{\sum_{x',y'} S(x', y')k((x, y), (x', y'))x'}{\sum_{x',y'} S(x', y')k((x, y), (x', y'))} \qquad (2)$$

$$v(x, y) = \frac{\sum_{x',y'} S(x', y')k((x, y), (x', y'))y'}{\sum_{x',y'} S(x', y')k((x, y), (x', y'))} \qquad (3)$$

This formulation holds certain desirable properties for our functions u and v, notably:

Sampled Areas: Areas of higher saliency are sampled more densely, since those pixels with higher saliency mass will attract other pixels to them. Note that kernel k can act as a regularizer to avoid corner cases where all the pixels converge to the same value. In all our experiments, we use a Gaussian kernel with σ set to one third of the width of the saliency map, which we found to work well in various settings.

Convolutional Form: This formulation allows us to compute u and v with simple convolutions, which is key for the efficiency of the full system. This layer can be easily added in a standard CNN and preserve differentiability needed for training by backpropagation.

Note that the formulation in Eqs. 2 and 3 has an undesirable bias to sample towards the image center. We avoid this effect by padding the saliency map with its border values.

3.3   Training with the Saliency Sampler

The saliency sampler can be plugged into any convolutional neural network f_t where more informative subsampling of a higher resolution input is desired. Since the module is end-to-end differentiable, we can train the full pipeline with standard optimization techniques. Our complete pipeline consists of four steps (see Fig. 1):

1. We obtain a low resolution version I_l of the image I.
2. This image is used by the saliency network f_s to compute a saliency map $S = f_s(I_l)$, where task-relevant areas of the image are assigned higher weights.
3. We use the deterministic grid sampler g to sample the high resolution image I according to the saliency map, obtaining the resampled image $J = g(I, S)$ which has the same resolution as I_l.
4. The original task network f_t is used to compute our final output $y = f(J)$.

Both f_s and f_t have learnable parameters and so can be trained jointly for a particular task. We found helpful to blur the resampled input image of the task network for some epochs at the beginning of the training procedure. It forces the saliency sampler to zoom deeper into the image in order to further magnify small details otherwise destroyed by the consequent blur. This is beneficial even for the final performance of the model with the blur removed.

4   Experiments

In this section we apply the saliency sampler to two important problems in computer vision: gaze-tracking and fine-grained object recognition. In each case, we examine the benefit of augmenting standard methods on commonly used datasets with our sampling module. We also compare against the closest comparable methods. As an architecture for the saliency network f_s, in all the tasks we use ablations of ResNet-18 [4] pretrained on the ImageNet Dataset [28] and one final 1×1 convolutional layer to reduce the dimensionality of the saliency map S. We found this network to work particularly well for classification and regression problems.

4.1   Gaze Tracking

Gaze tracking systems typically focus, for obvious reasons, on the eyes. Most of the state-of-the-art methods for gaze tracking rely on eye detection, with eye patches provided to the model at the highest possible resolution. However, in this experiment we show how with fewer inputs we are able to achieve similar performance to more complex engineered systems that aim to only solve the gaze-tracking task. We benchmark our model against the iTracker dataset [21], and show how their original model can be simplified by using the saliency sampler.

As the task network f_t we use a standard AlexNet [1] with the final layer changed to regress two outputs and a sigmoid function as the final activation.

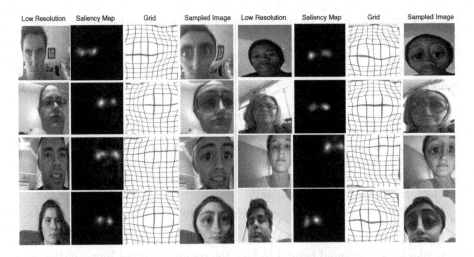

Fig. 4. Visualization of sampler behavior for iTracker gaze-tracking task. We show the low-resolution input image I_l, the saliency map S estimated by f_s, the sampling grid g, and the resampled image J. Note that the saliency network naturally discovers the eyes to be the most informative regions in the image to infer subject gaze, but also learns to preserve the approximate position of the head in the image, which is a further useful cue for estimating gaze position on a mobile device.

Table 1. Performance comparison on GazeCapture dataset. The table reports distance errors in cm for our models and benchmarks on the GazeCapture dataset.

Model	iPad (cm)	iPhone (cm)
iTracker	3.31	2.04
Plain AlexNet (AN)	5.44	2.63
AN + Deformable Convolutions	5.21	2.62
AN + STN TPS	4.44	2.39
AN + STN	4.33	2.25
AN + Grid Estimator	3.91	2.20
AN + Saliency Sampler (ours)	**3.29**	**2.03**

We choose AlexNet in order to be directly comparable to the iTracker system of [21], which is one of the state-of-the-art models for gaze tracking. The model has four inputs: two crops for both eyes, one crop for the face and a coarse encoding for the location of the face in the image. As saliency network f_S we use the initial 10 layers of ResNet-18. We aim to prove that our simple saliency sampler can allow a normal network to deal with the complexity of the four-input iTracker model by just magnifying the correct parts of a single input image.

We compare our model to various competitive baselines. First, we replace the top three convolutional layers of an AlexNet network (pretrained in the ImageNet dataset [1]) with three deformable convolution layers [14] (Deformable Convolutions). Second, we test the Spatial Transformer Network baseline [13] with the affine parametrization (STN) and TPS parametrization (STN TPS). As a localization network, we use a network similar to f_s for fairness. Third, we modify the network f_s to directly estimate the sampling grid functions u and v without the saliency map (Grid Estimator). We also compare against the system in [21], which was engineered specifically for the task (iTracker). As an error metric, we take the average distance error of the predicted to ground truth gaze location in the screen space of the iPhone/iPad devices on which the dataset was captured.

In Table 1, we present the performance of our model and baselines. Our model achieves a performance similar to iTracker, which enjoys the advantage of four different inputs with 224×224 pixels for each, while our system compresses all the information into a single image of 227×227 pixels. Our approach also improves performance over the Deformable Convolutions, both of the STN variants and the Grid Estimator by a difference ranging from 0.62 to 1.92 cm for iPad and 0.17 cm to 0.59 cm for iPhone. The STNs as well as the Deformable Convolutions have a hard time finding a transformation useful for the task, while the grid estimator is not able to find the functions u and v directly without the aid of a saliency map. The intermediate outputs of our method are shown in Fig. 4.

4.2   Fine-Grained Classification

Fine-grained classification problems pose a very particular challenge: the information to distinguish between two classes is usually hidden in a very small part of the image, sometimes unresolvable at low resolution. In this scenario, the saliency sampler can play an important role: magnify the important parts of the image to preserve as many of their pixels as possible and to help the final decision network. In this experiment, we study the problem using the iNaturalist dataset that contains 5,089 animal species [29]. Our evaluation was performed using the validation set, since the test set is private and reserved for a challenge (Fig. 5).

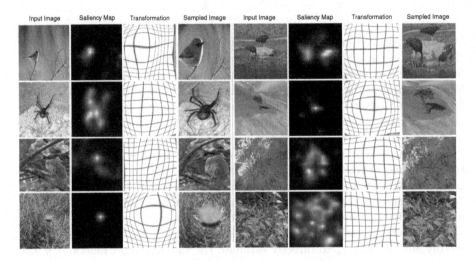

Fig. 5. Visualization of sampler behavior for iNat fine-grained classification task. Similarly to Fig. 4, the saliency network naturally discovers and zooms in on the most informative regions in the image, which tend to correspond to object parts.

In this experiment, we used the ResNet-101 [4] model pretrained on the ImageNet dataset [28] for the task network f_t as it has shown a very good performance in image classification. We used an input resolution of 227×227 for both the task and saliency networks, f_t and f_s. As saliency network f_S we use the initial 14 layers of ResNet-18, although the performance for other saliency networks can be found in Table 3.

As baselines for this task, we used the same methods as before, again with ResNet-101 as the base model. For the deformable convolutional network, we made the network modifications according to instructions in the original paper [14]. We also tested both the affine and the TPS version of STN (STN Affine and STN TPS) along with the direct grid estimator. Identically to our method, these baselines were allowed access to the original 800×800 pixel images in training time. In test time, the method had access to a center crop

Table 2. iNaturalist fine-grained classification results: top-1 and top-5 accuracy comparison on the validation set of the iNaturalist Challenge 2017 dataset.

Model	Top-1 (%)	[diff]	Top-5 (%)	[diff]
ResNet-101 227 (RN)	60	[-]	83	[-]
RN + Deformable Convolutions	44	[-16]	69	[-14]
RN + STN Affine	60	[0]	83	[0]
RN + Grid Estimator	61	[1]	83	[0]
RN + STN TPS	62	[2]	84	[1]
RN + CAM [15]	62	[2]	84	[1]
RN + Saliency Sampler (ours)	**65**	**[5]**	**86**	**[3]**

of 512×512 pixels. The localization networks were similar to f_s for fairness. To test whether a high-resolution input alone could improve the performance of the baseline Resnet-101 network, we also provided crops from the maximum activated regions for the ResNet-101 227 network, using the Class Activation Map method of [15] (`CAM`). We selected the class with the largest maximal activation, and computed the bounding box as in the original paper. We then cropped this region from the original input image and rescaled it to 227×227 resolution. These crops were used as inputs for the ResNet-101 227×227 network for the final classification.

Table 2 shows the classification accuracy for the various models compared. Our model is able to significantly outperform the ResNet-101 baseline by 5% and 3% for top-1 and top-5 accuracies respectively. The performance of the CAM-based method is closer to our method which is expected as it benefits from the same idea of emphasizing image details. However, our method still performs several points better, perhaps because of its greater flexibility to focus on local image regions non-uniformly and selectively zoom-in on certain features more than others. It also has a major benefit of being able to zoom in on an arbitrary number of non-collocated image locations, whereas doing so with crops involves determining the number of crops beforehand or having a proposal mechanism.

The spatial transformers and the grid estimator perform similar or a bit better than the ResNet-101 baseline. Like our method, those methods benefit from the ability to focus attention on a particular region of the image. However, the affine version of the spatial transformers applies a uniform deformation across the whole image, which may not be particularly well suited to the task, while the more flexible TPS version and the grid estimator, which in theory could more closely mimic the sampling introduced by our method, were found to be harder to optimize and were consistently found to perform worse.

Finally, the deformable convolutions method performs significantly worse than the ResNet-101 architecture. Despite our best efforts, we were not able to make the model converge to a competitive performance. This could be attributed to the difficulty of training the complex parametrization utilized in its design, which usually end up in a local minima. In contrast, our method benefits from

Table 3. Saliency network ablation: we measure the effect of different depths of saliency network f_s on the iNaturalist fine-grained classification task.

	None (no f_s)	6-layer	10-layer	14-layer
Top-1 (%)	60	62	64	**65**
Top-5 (%)	83	84	85	**86**

the fact that neural networks have a natural ability to predict salient image elements [30] and thus the optimization may be significantly easier.

To justify our claim that the saliency sampler can benefit different task network architectures, we repeat our experiment using a Inception V3 architecture [31]. The original performance is already very high (64% and 86% for top-1 and top-5 respectively) as it uses higher resolution (299) and a deeper network, but our sampler still results in a performance of 66% in top-1 and 87% in top-5.

Saliency Network Importance: In Table 3, we retrained ResNet-101 with different depths of saliency network f_s. We used different ablations of ResNet-18 with 6, 10 or 14 layers (which corresponds to adding one block at a time to build ResNet-18) for the experiment. The performance of the overall network increases with the complexity of the saliency model but with diminishing returns.

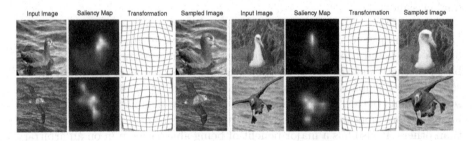

Fig. 6. Visualization of sampler behavior for the CUB-200 dataset: We show the sampled images for a ResNet-50 trained with the saliency sampler in the CUB-200 dataset. The saliency amplifies relevant image regions such as the bird's head.

4.3   CUB-200

To further prove that our model is useful across different datasets, we evaluated it in the CUB-200 dataset [32] (Table 4). Although the CUB-200 is also a fine-grained recognition dataset, it is significantly smaller and the images are better framed around subjects than in the iNaturalist dataset (see Fig. 6).

We used ResNet-50 as our task network and the initial 14 layers of ResNet-18 as our saliency network. By adding our sampling layer we achieve a 2.9% accuracy boost, which is less than the boost in iNaturalist, perhaps because

Table 4. Performance improvements from the addition of our sampling layer on the CUB-200 dataset [32]. **Res. (px)** refers to the input image resolution to the model.

	RN-50	RN-50+SS	DT-RAM	DT-RAM
Res. (px)	227	**227**	224	448
Top-1(%)	81.6	**84.5**	82.8	86.0

objects of interest are more tightly cropped in CUB-200. Compared to DT-RAM [33], one of the top performing models in CUB-200, our approach outperforms the comparable 224×224 version of RN-50 DT-RAM by 1.7%, using a simpler model. Our method is not as accurate as the 448×448 resolution version of DT-RAM, but the latter uses approximately 2 passes through a RN-50 on average and a larger input size leading to a higher computational cost.

5   Discussion

Adding our saliency sampler is most beneficial for image tasks where the important features are small and sparse, or appear across multiple image scales. The deformation introduced in the vicinity of the magnified regions could potentially discourage the network from strong deformations if another point of interest would be affected. This could be harmful for tasks such as text recognition. In practice, we observed that the learning process is able to deal with such situations well as it was capable of magnifying both collocated eyes without hindering the gaze prediction performance. That is particularly interesting as this task requires preservation of geometric information in the image. The method proved to be easier to train than other approaches which modify spatial sampling, such as Spatial Transformer Networks [13] or Deformable Convolutional Networks [14]. These methods ofter performed closer to the baseline as they failed to find suitable parameters for their sampling strategy. The non-uniform approach to the magnification introduced by our saliency map also enables variability of zoom over the spatial domain. This together with the end-to-end optimization results in a performance benefit over uniformly magnified area-of-interest crops as observed in our fine-grained classification task. Unlike in the case of the iTracker [21], we do not require prior knowledge about the relevant image features in the task.

6   Conclusion

We have presented the saliency sampler – a novel layer for CNNs that can adapt the image sampling strategy to improve task performance while preserving memory allocation and computational efficiency for a given image processing task. We have shown our technique's effectiveness in locating and focusing on image features important for the tasks of gaze tracking and fine-grained object recognition. The method is simple to integrate into existing models and can be efficiently trained in an end-to-end fashion. Unlike some of the other image transformation techniques, our method is not restricted to a predefined number or size of important regions and it can redistribute sampling density across the entire image domain. At the same time, the parametrization of our technique by a single scalar attention map makes it robust against irrecoverable image degradation due to fold-overs or singularities. This leads to a superior performance in problems that require the recovery of small image features such as eyes or subtle differences between related animal species.

Acknowledgment. This research was funded by Toyota Research Institute. We acknowledge NVIDIA Corporation for hardware donations.

References

1. Krizhevsky, A., Sutskever, I., Hinton, G.E.: ImageNet classification with deep convolutional neural networks. In: Conference on Neural Information Processing Systems (2012)
2. Iandola, F.N., Han, S., Moskewicz, M.W., Ashraf, K., Dally, W.J., Keutzer, K.: SqueezeNet: AlexNet-level accuracy with 50x fewer parameters and <0.5 mb model size. arXiv preprint arXiv:1602.07360 (2016)
3. Simonyan, K., Zisserman, A.: Very deep convolutional networks for large-scale image recognition. arXiv preprint arXiv:1409.1556 (2014)
4. He, K., Zhang, X., Ren, S., Sun, J.: Deep residual learning for image recognition. In: IEEE Conference on Computer Vision and Pattern Recognition, pp. 770–778 (2016)
5. Russakovsky, O., et al.: ImageNet large scale visual recognition challenge. Int. J. Comput. Vis. (IJCV) **115**(3), 211–252 (2015)
6. Lowe, D.G.: Distinctive image features from scale-invariant keypoints. Int. J. Comput. Vis. (IJCV) **60**(2), 91–110 (2004)
7. Ren, S., He, K., Girshick, R., Sun, J.: Faster R-CNN: towards real-time object detection with region proposal networks. In: Advances in Neural Information Processing System, pp. 91–99 (2015)
8. Itti, L., Koch, C., Niebur, E.: A model of saliency-based visual attention for rapid scene analysis. IEEE Trans. Pattern Anal. Mach. Intell. **20**(11), 1254–1259 (1998)
9. Mnih, V., Heess, N., Graves, A.: Recurrent models of visual attention. In: Advances in Neural Information Processing System, pp. 2204–2212 (2014)
10. Ba, J., Mnih, V., Kavukcuoglu, K.: Multiple object recognition with visual attention. arXiv preprint arXiv:1412.7755 (2014)
11. Eslami, S.A., Heess, N., Weber, T., Tassa, Y., Szepesvari, D., Hinton, G.E., et al.: Attend, infer, repeat: fast scene understanding with generative models. In: Advances in Neural Information Processing Systems, pp. 3225–3233 (2016)
12. Fu, J., Zheng, H., Mei, T.: Look closer to see better: recurrent attention convolutional neural network for fine-grained image recognition. In: Conference on Computer Vision and Pattern Recognition (2017)
13. Jaderberg, M., Simonyan, K., Zisserman, A., et al.: Spatial transformer networks. In: Advances in Neural Information Processing System, pp. 2017–2025 (2015)
14. Dai, J., et al.: Deformable convolutional networks. In: IEEE Conference on Computer Vision and Pattern Recognition, pp. 764–773 (2017)
15. Zhou, B., Khosla, A., Lapedriza, A., Oliva, A., Torralba, A.: Learning deep features for discriminative localization. In: IEEE Conference on Computer Vision and Pattern Recognition, pp. 2921–2929. IEEE (2016)

16. Li, J., Chen, Y., Cai, L., Davidson, I., Ji, S.: Dense transformer networks, May 2017. arXiv:1705.08881 [cs, stat] arXiv: 1705.08881

17. Zheng, H., Fu, J., Mei, T., Luo, J.: Learning multi-attention convolutional neural network for fine-grained image recognition. In: IEEE International Conference on Computer Vision (ICCV) (2017)

18. Xiao, T., Xu, Y., Yang, K., Zhang, J., Peng, Y., Zhang, Z.: The application of two-level attention models in deep convolutional neural network for fine-grained image classification. In: IEEE Conference on Computer Vision and Pattern Recognition, pp. 842–850. IEEE (2015)

19. Rosenfeld, A., Ullman, S.: Visual concept recognition and localization via iterative introspection. In: Lai, S.-H., Lepetit, V., Nishino, K., Sato, Y. (eds.) ACCV 2016. LNCS, vol. 10115, pp. 264–279. Springer, Cham (2017). https://doi.org/10.1007/978-3-319-54193-8_17

20. Selvaraju, R.R., Cogswell, M., Das, A., Vedantam, R., Parikh, D., Batra, D.: Grad-CAM: visual explanations from deep networks via gradient-based localization. In: IEEE Conference on Computer Vision and Pattern Recognition, pp. 618–626 (2017)

21. Khosla, A., et al.: Eye tracking for everyone. In: IEEE Conference on Computer Vision and Pattern Recognition, Las Vegas, June 2016

22. Wang, S., Luo, L., Zhang, N., Li, J.: AutoScaler: scale-attention networks for visual correspondence. In: British Machine Vision Conference (BMVC) (2017)

23. Rubinstein, M., Gutierrez, D., Sorkine, O., Shamir, A.: A comparative study of image retargeting. In: ACM Transactions on Graphics (TOG), vol. 29, p. 160. ACM (2010)

24. Wolf, L., Guttmann, M., Cohen-Or, D.: Non-homogeneous content-driven video-retargeting. In: IEEE International Conference on Computer Vision (ICCV), pp. 1–6. IEEE (2007)

25. Karni, Z., Freedman, D., Gotsman, C.: Energy-based image deformation. In: Computer Graphics Forum, vol. 28, pp. 1257–1268. Wiley Online Library (2009)

26. Kaufmann, P., Wang, O., Sorkine-Hornung, A., Sorkine-Hornung, O., Smolic, A., Gross, M.: Finite element image warping. In: Computer Graphics Forum, vol. 32, pp. 31–39. Wiley Online Library (2013)

27. Chen, R., Freedman, D., Karni, Z., Gotsman, C., Liu, L.: Content-aware image resizing by quadratic programming. In: Computer Vision and Pattern Recognition Workshops (CVPRW), pp. 1–8. IEEE (2010)

28. Deng, J., Dong, W., Socher, R., Li, L.J., Li, K., Fei-Fei, L.: ImageNet: a large-scale hierarchical image database. In: IEEE Conference on Computer Vision and Pattern Recognition, pp. 248–255. IEEE (2009)

29. Van Horn, G., et al.: The inaturalist challenge 2017 dataset. arXiv preprint arXiv:1707.06642 (2017)

30. Zhou, B., Khosla, A., Lapedriza, A., Oliva, A., Torralba, A.: Learning deep features for discriminative localization. In: IEEE Conference on Computer Vision and Pattern Recognition (2016)

31. Szegedy, C., Vanhoucke, V., Ioffe, S., Shlens, J., Wojna, Z.: Rethinking the inception architecture for computer vision. In: Proceedings of the IEEE Conference on Computer Vision and Pattern Recognition, pp. 2818–2826 (2016)

32. Wah, C., Branson, S., Welinder, P., Perona, P., Belongie, S.: The caltech-UCSD birds-200-2011 dataset (2011)

33. Li, Z., Yang, Y., Liu, X., Zhou, F., Wen, S., Xu, W.: Dynamic computational time for visual attention. arXiv preprint arXiv:1703.10332 (2017)

A Scalable Exemplar-Based Subspace Clustering Algorithm for Class-Imbalanced Data

Chong You$^{(\boxtimes)}$, Chi Li, Daniel P. Robinson, and René Vidal

Johns Hopkins University, Baltimore, MD, USA
cyou@cis.jhu.edu

Abstract. Subspace clustering methods based on expressing each data point as a linear combination of a few other data points (e.g., sparse subspace clustering) have become a popular tool for unsupervised learning due to their empirical success and theoretical guarantees. However, their performance can be affected by imbalanced data distributions and large-scale datasets. This paper presents an exemplar-based subspace clustering method to tackle the problem of imbalanced and large-scale datasets. The proposed method searches for a subset of the data that best represents all data points as measured by the ℓ_1 norm of the representation coefficients. To solve our model efficiently, we introduce a farthest first search algorithm which iteratively selects the least well-represented point as an exemplar. When data comes from a union of subspaces, we prove that the computed subset contains enough exemplars from each subspace for expressing all data points even if the data are imbalanced. Our experiments demonstrate that the proposed method outperforms state-of-the-art subspace clustering methods in two large-scale image datasets that are imbalanced. We also demonstrate the effectiveness of our method on unsupervised data subset selection for a face image classification task.

Keywords: Subspace clustering · Imbalanced data · Large-scale data

1 Introduction

The availability of large annotated datasets in computer vision, such as ImageNet, has led to many recent breakthroughs in object detection and classification using supervised learning techniques such as deep learning. However, as data size continues to grow, it has become increasingly difficult to annotate the data for training fully supervised algorithms. As a consequence, the development of unsupervised learning techniques that can learn from *unlabeled* datasets has become extremely important. Existing labeled databases, such as ImageNet, are manually organized to be class-balanced. On the other hand, the number of data samples in unlabeled datasets varies widely for different classes. Dealing with imbalanced data is hence a major challenge in unsupervised learning tasks.

© Springer Nature Switzerland AG 2018
V. Ferrari et al. (Eds.): ECCV 2018, LNCS 11213, pp. 68–85, 2018.
https://doi.org/10.1007/978-3-030-01240-3_5

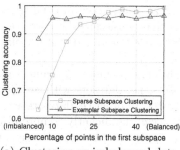
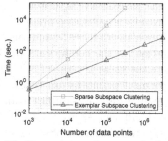

(a) Clustering on imbalanced data.   (b) Clustering on large-scale data.

Fig. 1. Subspace clustering on imbalanced data and large-scale data. (a) x and $100-x$ points (x is varied in the x-axis) are drawn uniformly at random from 2 subspaces of dimension 3 drawn uniformly at random in an ambient space of dimension 5. Note that the clustering accuracy of SSC decreases dramatically as the dataset becomes imbalanced. (b) 10 subspaces of dimension 5 are drawn uniformly at random in an ambient space of dimension 20. An equal number of points is drawn uniformly at random from each subspace. Note that the runtime of SSC increases dramatically with data size.

Traditional unsupervised learning methods exploit the fact that in many computer vision applications the underlying dimension of the data is much smaller than the ambient dimension. For example, it is well-known that the images of a face under varying illumination conditions can be well-approximated by a 9-dimensional subspace. In practice, computer vision datasets often contain multiple classes, hence they can be modeled by a union of low dimensional subspaces. *Subspace clustering* [1] is a popular approach for unsupervised learning from such data that jointly learns the union of subspaces and assigns each data point to its corresponding subspace.

Many recent subspace clustering methods follow a two-step approach: (1) learn an affinity graph among data points and (2) apply spectral clustering [2] to this graph. In particular, the state-of-the-art methods learn the affinity by exploiting the *self-expressiveness* property [3], which states that each data point in a union of subspaces can be written as a linear combination of other points from its own subspace. That is, given data $\mathcal{X} = \{x_1, \cdots, x_N\} \subseteq \mathbb{R}^D$, there exists $\{c_{ij}\}$ such that $x_j = \sum_{i \neq j} c_{ij} x_i$ and c_{ij} is nonzero only if x_i and x_j are from the same subspace. Such representations $\{c_{ij}\}$ are called *subspace-preserving*. In particular, if the subspace dimensions are small, then the representations can be taken to be sparse. Based on this observation, Sparse Subspace Clustering (SSC) [3,4] solves, for each $j \in \{1, 2, \ldots, N\}$, the sparse optimization problem

$$\min_{c_j \in \mathbb{R}^N} \|c_j\|_1 + \frac{\lambda}{2} \cdot \|x_j - \sum_{i \neq j} c_{ij} x_i\|_2^2, \tag{1}$$

where $\lambda > 0$ and $c_j = [c_{1j}, \cdots, c_{Nj}]^\top$. Subsequently, the affinity between any pair of points x_i and x_j is defined as $|c_{ij}| + |c_{ji}|$. Existing theoretical results

for noiseless as well as corrupted data show that, under certain conditions, the
solution to (1) is subspace-preserving [4–8], thus justifying the correctness of
SSC's affinity. Beyond SSC, many methods have been proposed that use different
regularization on the coefficients $\{c_{ij}\}$ [9–14].

Despite the great success of SSC and its variants, previous experimental evaluations focused primarily on balanced datasets, i.e. datasets with an approximately equal number of samples from each cluster. In practice, datasets are often
imbalanced and such skewed data distributions can significantly compromise the
clustering performance of SSC, as shown in Fig. 1(a). Theoretically, we conjecture that the solution to (1) for x_j in an under-represented class is more likely
to have nonzero entries corresponding to data points in over-represented classes,
which gives false connections in the graph affinity. A proof of this conjecture
will be the subject of future work. Another issue with many self-expressiveness
based subspace clustering methods is that they are limited to small or medium
scale datasets [15]. Figure 1(b) illustrates the running time of SSC as a function
of the number of data points N, which is roughly quadratic in N.

Paper Contributions. We propose an exemplar-based subspace clustering
approach to address the issues of imbalanced and large-scale data. Given a
dataset $\mathcal{X}$, the idea is to select a subset $\mathcal{X}_0$, which we call *exemplars*, and write
each data point as a linear combination of points in $\mathcal{X}_0$ (rather than $\mathcal{X}$ as in
SSC):

$$\min_{c_j \in \mathbb{R}^N} \|c_j\|_1 + \frac{\lambda}{2} \|x_j - \sum_{i:x_i \in \mathcal{X}_0} c_{ij} x_i\|_2^2. \tag{2}$$

Observe that (2) is potentially more robust to imbalanced data than (1) in
finding subspace-preserving representations when $\mathcal{X}_0$ is balanced across classes.
Moreover, (2) can potentially be solved more efficiently than (1) when $\mathcal{X}_0$ is
small relative to the original data $\mathcal{X}$. Thus, to achieve robustness to imbalanced
data and scalability to large datasets, we need an efficient algorithm for selecting
exemplars $\mathcal{X}_0$ that is more balanced across classes.

In this paper, we present a new model for selecting a set of exemplars $\mathcal{X}_0$
that is based on minimizing a maximum representation cost of the data $\mathcal{X}$. (The
proofs for results in this paper can be found in [16].) Moreover, we introduce an
efficient algorithm for solving the optimization problem that has linear time and
memory complexity. Compared to SSC, exemplar-based subspace clustering is
less sensitive to imbalanced data and more efficient for big data (see Fig. 1). In
addition, our work makes the following contributions:

– We present a geometric interpretation of our exemplar selection model and
  algorithm as one of finding a subset of the data that *best covers* the entire
  dataset as measured by the Minkowski functional of the subset.
– We prove that when the data lies in a union of independent subspaces, our
  method is guaranteed to select sufficiently many data points from each subspace and construct correct data affinities, even when the data is imbalanced.

- We evaluate our method on two imbalanced image datasets: the EMNIST handwritten letter dataset and the GTSRB street sign dataset. Experimental results show that our method outperforms the state-of-the-art in terms of clustering performance and running time.
- We demonstrate through experiments on the Extended Yale B face database that the exemplars selected by our model can be used for unsupervised subset selection tasks, where the goal is to select a subset from a big data set that may be used to train a classifier that incurs minimum performance loss.

2 Related Work

Sparse Dictionary Learning (SDL). Sparse representation of a given dataset is a well studied problem in signal processing and machine learning [17,18]. Given a set $\mathcal{X} \subseteq \mathbb{R}^D$ and an integer k, SDL computes a dictionary of atoms $\mathcal{D} \subseteq \mathbb{R}^D$ with $|\mathcal{D}| \leq k$ that minimizes the sparse representation cost. Based on SDL, [19] proposed a linear time subspace clustering algorithm that is guaranteed to be correct if the atoms in dictionary $\mathcal{D}$ lie in the same union of subspaces as the input data $\mathcal{X}$. However, there is little evidence that such a condition is satisfied in real data as the atoms of the dictionary $\mathcal{D}$ are not constrained to be a subset of $\mathcal{X}$. Another recent work [20], which used data-independent random matrices as dictionaries, also suffers from this issue and lacks correctness guarantees.

Sparse Dictionary Selection. Three variations of the SDL model that explicitly constrain the dictionary atoms to be taken from $\mathcal{X}$ are simultaneous sparse representation [21] and dictionary selection [22,23], which use greedy algorithms to solve their respective optimization problems, and group sparse representative selection [24–29], which uses a convex optimization based approach based on group sparsity. In particular, when the data is drawn from a union of independent subspaces, the method in [26] is shown to select a few representatives from each of the subspaces. However, these methods have quadratic complexity in the number of points in $\mathcal{X}$. Moreover, convex optimization based methods are not flexible in selecting a desired number of representatives since the size of the subset cannot be directly controlled by adjusting an algorithm parameter.

Subset Selection. Selecting a representative subset of the entire data has been studied in a wide range of contexts such as Determinantal Point Processes [30–32], Rank Revealing QR [33], Column subset selection [34,35], separable Nonnegative Matrix Factorization [36,37], and so on [38]. However, they do not model data as coming from a union of subspaces and there is no evidence that they can select good representatives from such data. Several recent works [39–41], which use different subset selection methods for subspace clustering, also lack justification that their selected exemplars are representative of the subspaces.

k-**Centers and** k-**Medoids.** The k-centers problem is a data clustering problem studied in theoretical computer science and operations research. Given a set $\mathcal{X}$

and an integer k, the goal is to find a set of centers $\mathcal{X}_0 \subseteq \mathcal{X}$ with $|\mathcal{X}_0| \leq k$ that minimizes the quantity $\max_{x \in \mathcal{X}} d^2(x, \mathcal{X}_0)$, where $d^2(x, \mathcal{X}_0) := \min_{v \in \mathcal{X}_0} \|x - v\|_2^2$ is the squared distance of x to the closest point in $\mathcal{X}_0$. A partition of $\mathcal{X}$ is given by the closest center to which each point $x \in \mathcal{X}$ belongs. The k-medoids is a variant of k-centers that minimizes the sum of the squared distances, i.e., minimizes $\sum_{x \in \mathcal{X}} d^2(x, \mathcal{X}_0)$ instead of the maximum distance. However, both k-centers and k-medoids model data as concentrating around several cluster centers, and do not generally apply to data lying in a union of subspaces.

3 Exemplar-Based Subspace Clustering (ESC)

In this section, we present our ESC method for clustering a given set of data points $\mathcal{X} = \{x_1, \cdots, x_N\}$. We first formulate the model for selecting a subset $\mathcal{X}_0$ of exemplars from $\mathcal{X}$. Since the model is a combinatorial optimization problem, we present an efficient algorithm for solving it approximately. Finally, we describe the procedure for generating the cluster assignments from the exemplars $\mathcal{X}_0$.

3.1 Exemplar Selection via Self-representation Cost

Without loss of generality, we assume that all data in $\mathcal{X}$ are normalized to have unit ℓ_2 norm. Recall that in SSC, each data point $x_j \in \mathcal{X}$ is written as a linear combination of all other data points with coefficient vector c_j. While the nonzero entries in each c_j determine a subset of $\mathcal{X}$ that can represent x_j with the minimum ℓ_1-norm on the coefficients, the collection of all x_j often needs the whole dataset $\mathcal{X}$. In ESC, the goal is to find a small subset $\mathcal{X}_0 \subseteq \mathcal{X}$ that represents all data points in $\mathcal{X}$. In particular, the set $\mathcal{X}_0$ should contain exemplars from each subspace such that the solution c_j to (2) for each data point $x_j \in \mathcal{X}$ is *subspace-preserving*, i.e. the nonzero entries of c_j correspond to points in the same subspace as x_j. In the following, we define a cost function from the optimization in (2) and then present our exemplar selection model.

Definition 1 (Self-representation cost function). *Given* $\mathcal{X} = \{x_1, \cdots, x_N\} \subseteq \mathbb{R}^D$, *we define the self-representation cost function* $F_\lambda : 2^{\mathcal{X}} \to \mathbb{R}$ *as*

$$F_\lambda(\mathcal{X}_0) := \sup_{x_j \in \mathcal{X}} f_\lambda(x_j, \mathcal{X}_0), \quad \text{where} \tag{3}$$

$$f_\lambda(x_j, \mathcal{X}_0) := \min_{c_j \in \mathbb{R}^N} \|c_j\|_1 + \frac{\lambda}{2}\|x_j - \sum_{i:x_i \in \mathcal{X}_0} c_{ij}x_i\|_2^2, \tag{4}$$

and $\lambda \in (1, \infty)$ *is a parameter. By convention, we assume* $f_\lambda(x_j, \emptyset) = \frac{\lambda}{2}$ *for all* $x_j \in \mathcal{X}$, *where* $\emptyset$ *denotes empty set.*

Geometrically, $f_\lambda(x, \mathcal{X}_0)$ measures how well data point $x \in \mathcal{X}$ is covered by the subset $\mathcal{X}_0$ (see Sect. 4). The function $f_\lambda(x, \mathcal{X}_0)$ has the following properties.

Lemma 1. *The function* $f_\lambda(x, \cdot)$ *is monotone with respect to the partial order defined by set inclusion, i.e.,* $f_\lambda(x, \mathcal{X}_0') \geq f_\lambda(x, \mathcal{X}_0'')$ *for any* $\emptyset \subseteq \mathcal{X}_0' \subseteq \mathcal{X}_0'' \subseteq \mathcal{X}$.

Lemma 2. *The value of $f_\lambda(x, \mathcal{X}_0)$ lies in $[1 - \frac{1}{2\lambda}, \frac{\lambda}{2}]$. The lower bound is achieved if and only if $x \in \mathcal{X}_0$ or $-x \in \mathcal{X}_0$, and the upper bound is achieved when $\mathcal{X}_0 = \emptyset$.*

Observe that if $\mathcal{X}_0$ contains enough exemplars from the subspace containing x_j and the optimal solution c_j to (4) is subspace-preserving, then it is expected that c_j will be sparse and that the residual $x_j - X_0 c_j$ will be close to zero. This suggests that we should select the subset $\mathcal{X}_0$ such that the value $f_\lambda(x_j, \mathcal{X}_0)$ is small. As the value $F_\lambda(\mathcal{X}_0)$ is achieved by the data point x_j that has the largest value $f(x_j, \mathcal{X}_0)$, we propose to perform exemplar selection by searching for a subset $\mathcal{X}_0^* \subseteq \mathcal{X}$ that minimizes the self-representation cost function, i.e.,

$$\mathcal{X}_0^* = \arg\min_{|\mathcal{X}_0| \leq k} F_\lambda(\mathcal{X}_0), \tag{5}$$

where $k \in \mathbb{Z}$ is the target number of exemplars. Note that the objective function $F_\lambda(\cdot)$ in (5) is monotone according to the following result.

Lemma 3. *For any $\emptyset \subseteq \mathcal{X}_0' \subseteq \mathcal{X}_0'' \subseteq \mathcal{X}$, we have $F_\lambda(\mathcal{X}_0') \geq F_\lambda(\mathcal{X}_0'')$.*

Solving the optimization problem (5) is NP-hard in general as it requires evaluating $F_\lambda(\mathcal{X}_0)$ for each subset $\mathcal{X}_0$ of size at most k. In the next section, we present an approximate algorithm that is computationally efficient.

3.2 A Farthest First Search (FFS) Algorithm for ESC

In Algorithm 1 we present an efficient algorithm for approximately solving (5). The algorithm progressively grows a candidate subset $\mathcal{X}_0$ (initialized as the empty set) until it reaches the desired size k. At each iteration i, step 3 of the algorithm selects the point $x \in \mathcal{X}$ that is worst represented by the current subset $\mathcal{X}_0^{(i)}$ as measured by $f_\lambda(x, \mathcal{X}_0^{(i)})$. A geometric interpretation of this step is presented in Sect. 4. In particular, it is shown in Lemma 2 that $f_\lambda(x, \mathcal{X}_0^{(i)}) = 1 - \frac{1}{2\lambda}$ for all $x \in \mathcal{X}_0^{(i)}$ and $f_\lambda(x, \mathcal{X}_0^{(i)}) > 1 - \frac{1}{2\lambda}$ if neither $x \in \mathcal{X}_0^{(i)}$ nor $-x \in \mathcal{X}_0^{(i)}$. Thus, $x \notin \mathcal{X}_0^{(i)}$ during every iteration of Algorithm 1.

We also note that the FFS algorithm can be viewed as an extension of the farthest first traversal algorithm (see, e.g. [42]), which is an approximation algorithm for the k-centers problem discussed in Sect. 2.

Algorithm 1. Farthest first search (FFS) for exemplar selection

---

Input: Data $\mathcal{X} = \{x_1, \ldots, x_N\} \subseteq \mathbb{R}^D$, parameters $\lambda > 1$ and $k \ll N$.
1: Select $x \in \mathcal{X}$ at random and set $\mathcal{X}_0^{(1)} \leftarrow \{x\}$.
2: **for** $i = 1, \cdots, k - 1$ **do**
3: $\quad \mathcal{X}_0^{(i+1)} = \mathcal{X}_0^{(i)} \cup \arg\max_{x \in \mathcal{X}} f_\lambda(x, \mathcal{X}_0^{(i)})$
4: **end for**
Output: $\mathcal{X}_0^{(k)}$

Efficient Implementation. Observe that each iteration of Algorithm 1 requires evaluating $f_\lambda(\boldsymbol{x}, \mathcal{X}_0^{(i)})$ for every $\boldsymbol{x} \in \mathcal{X}$. Therefore, the complexity of Algorithm 1 is linear in the total number of data points N assuming k is fixed and small. However, computing $f_\lambda(\boldsymbol{x}, \mathcal{X}_0^{(i)})$ itself is not easy as it requires solving a sparse optimization problem. In the following, we introduce an efficient implementation in which we skip the computation of $f_\lambda(\boldsymbol{x}, \mathcal{X}_0^{(i)})$ for some $\boldsymbol{x}$ in each iteration.

The idea underpinning this computational savings is the monotonicity of $f_\lambda(\boldsymbol{x}, \cdot)$ as discussed in Sect. 3.1. That is, for any $\emptyset \subseteq \mathcal{X}_0' \subseteq \mathcal{X}_0'' \subseteq \mathcal{X}$ we have $f_\lambda(\boldsymbol{x}_j, \mathcal{X}_0') \geq f_\lambda(\boldsymbol{x}_j, \mathcal{X}_0'')$. In the FFS algorithm where the set $\mathcal{X}_0^{(i)}$ is progressively increased, this implies that $f_\lambda(\boldsymbol{x}_j, \mathcal{X}_0^{(i)})$ is non-increasing in i. Using this result, our efficient implementation is outlined in Algorithm 2. In step 2 we initialize $b_j = f_\lambda(\boldsymbol{x}_j, \mathcal{X}_0^{(1)})$ for each $j \in \{1, \cdots, N\}$, which is an upper bound for $f_\lambda(\boldsymbol{x}_j, \mathcal{X}_0^{(i)})$ for $i \geq 1$. In each iteration i, our goal is to find a point $\boldsymbol{x} \in \mathcal{X}$ that maximizes $f_\lambda(\boldsymbol{x}, \mathcal{X}_0^{(i)})$. To do this, we first find an ordering $o_1, \cdots, o_N$ of $1, \cdots, N$ such that $b_{o_1} \geq \cdots \geq b_{o_N}$ (step 4). We then compute $f_\lambda(\cdot, \mathcal{X}_0^{(i)})$ sequentially for points in the list $\boldsymbol{x}_{o_1}, \cdots, \boldsymbol{x}_{o_N}$ (step 7) while keeping track of the highest value of $f_\lambda(\cdot, \mathcal{X}_0^{(i)})$ by the variable *max_cost* (step 9). Once the condition that $max\_cost \geq b_{o_{j+1}}$ is met (step 11), we can assert that for any $j' > j$ the point $\boldsymbol{x}_{o_{j'}}$ is not a maximizer of $f_\lambda(\boldsymbol{x}, \mathcal{X}_0^{(i)})$. This can be seen from $f_\lambda(\boldsymbol{x}_{o_{j'}}, \mathcal{X}_0^{(i)}) \leq b_{o_{j'}} \leq b_{o_{j+1}} \leq max\_cost$, where the first inequality follows from the monotonicity of $f_\lambda(\boldsymbol{x}_{o_{j'}}, \mathcal{X}_0^{(i)})$ as a function of i. Therefore, we can break the loop (step 12) and avoid computing $f_\lambda(\boldsymbol{x}_{o_j}, \mathcal{X}_0^{(i)})$ for the remaining j's.

3.3   Generating Cluster Assignments from Exemplars

After exemplars have been selected by Algorithm 2, we use them to compute a segmentation of $\mathcal{X}$. Specifically, for each $\boldsymbol{x}_j \in \mathcal{X}$ we compute $\boldsymbol{c}_j$ as a solution to the optimization problem (2). As we will see in Theorem 2, the vector $\boldsymbol{c}_j$ is expected to be subspace-preserving. As such, for any two points $\{\boldsymbol{x}_i, \boldsymbol{x}_j\} \subseteq \mathcal{X}$, one has $\langle \boldsymbol{c}_i, \boldsymbol{c}_j \rangle \neq 0$ only if $\boldsymbol{x}_i$ and $\boldsymbol{x}_j$ are from the same subspace.

Using this observation, we use a nearest neighbor approach to compute the segmentation of $\mathcal{X}$ (see Algorithm 3). First, the coefficient vectors $\{\boldsymbol{c}_j\}$ are normalized, i.e., we set $\tilde{\boldsymbol{c}}_j = \boldsymbol{c}_j / \|\boldsymbol{c}_j\|_2$. Then, for each $\tilde{\boldsymbol{c}}_j$ we find t-nearest neighbors with the largest positive inner product with $\tilde{\boldsymbol{c}}_j$. (Although it is natural to use the t largest inner-products in absolute value, that approach did not perform as well in our numerical experiments.) Finally, we compute an affinity matrix from the t-nearest neighbors and apply spectral clustering to get the segmentation.

Algorithm 2. An efficient implementation of FFS

Input: Data $\mathcal{X} = \{\boldsymbol{x}_1, \ldots, \boldsymbol{x}_N\} \subseteq \mathbb{R}^D$, parameters $\lambda > 1$ and k.
1: Select $\boldsymbol{x} \in \mathcal{X}$ at random and initialize $\mathcal{X}_0^{(1)} \leftarrow \{\boldsymbol{x}\}$.
2: Compute $b_j = f_\lambda(\boldsymbol{x}_j, \mathcal{X}_0^{(1)})$ for $j = 1, \cdots, N$.
3: **for** $i = 1, \cdots, k-1$ **do**
4:    Let $o_1, \cdots, o_N$ be an ordering of $1, \cdots, N$ such that $b_{o_p} \geq b_{o_q}$ when $p < q$.
5:    Initialize $max\_cost = 0$.
6:    **for** $j = 1, \cdots, N$ **do**
7:       Set $b_{o_j} = f_\lambda(\boldsymbol{x}_{o_j}, \mathcal{X}_0^{(i)})$.
8:       **if** $b_{o_j} > max\_cost$ **then**
9:          Set $max\_cost = b_{o_j}$, $new\_index = o_j$.
10:       **end if**
11:       **if** $j = N$ or $max\_cost \geq b_{o_{j+1}}$ **then**
12:          **break**
13:       **end if**
14:    **end for**
15:    $\mathcal{X}_0^{(i+1)} = \mathcal{X}_0^{(i)} \cup \{\boldsymbol{x}_{new\_index}\}$.
16: **end for**
Output: $\mathcal{X}_0^{(k)}$

---

4 Theoretical Analysis of ESC

In this section, we present a geometric interpretation of the exemplar selection model from Sect. 3.1 and the FFS algorithm from Sect. 3.2, and study their properties in the context of subspace clustering. To simplify the analysis, we assume that the self-representation $\boldsymbol{x}_j = \sum_{i \neq j} c_{ij} \boldsymbol{x}_i$ is strictly enforced by extending (4) to $\lambda = \infty$, i.e., we let

$$f_\infty(\boldsymbol{x}, \mathcal{X}_0) = \min_{\boldsymbol{c} \in \mathbb{R}^N} \|\boldsymbol{c}\|_1 \text{ s.t. } \boldsymbol{x} = \sum_{i:\boldsymbol{x}_i \in \mathcal{X}_0} c_{ij} \boldsymbol{x}_i. \tag{6}$$

By convention, we let $f_\infty(\boldsymbol{x}, \mathcal{X}_0) = \infty$ if the optimization problem is infeasible.

4.1 Geometric Interpretation

We first provide a geometric interpretation of the exemplars selected by (5). Given any $\mathcal{X}_0$, we denote the convex hull of the symmetrized data points in

---

Algorithm 3. Subspace clustering by ESC-FFS

Input: Data $\mathcal{X} = \{\boldsymbol{x}_1, \ldots, \boldsymbol{x}_N\} \subseteq \mathbb{R}^D$, parameters $\lambda > 1$, k and t.
1: Compute $\mathcal{X}_0$ from Algorithm 2, and then compute $\{\boldsymbol{c}_j\}$ from (2). Let $\tilde{\boldsymbol{c}}_j = \boldsymbol{c}_j / \|\boldsymbol{c}_j\|_2$.
2: Set $W_{ij} = 1$ if $\tilde{\boldsymbol{c}}_j$ is a t-nearest neighbor of $\tilde{\boldsymbol{c}}_i$ and 0 otherwise; Set $A = W + W^\top$.
3: Apply spectral clustering to A to obtain a segmentation of $\mathcal{X}$.
Output: Segmentation of $\mathcal{X}$.

$\mathcal{X}_0$ as $\mathcal{K}_0$, i.e., $\mathcal{K}_0 := \text{conv}(\pm\mathcal{X}_0)$ (see an example in Fig. 2). The Minkowski functional [43] associated with a set $\mathcal{K}_0$ is given by the following.

Definition 2 (Minkowski functional [43]). *The Minkowski functional associated with the set $\mathcal{K}_0 \subseteq \mathbb{R}^D$ is a map $\mathbb{R}^D \to R \cup \{+\infty\}$ given by*

$$\|\boldsymbol{x}\|_{\mathcal{K}_0} := \inf\{t > 0 : \boldsymbol{x}/t \in \mathcal{K}_0\}. \tag{7}$$

In particular, we define $\|\boldsymbol{x}\|_{\mathcal{K}_0} := \infty$ if the set $\{t > 0 : \boldsymbol{x}/t \in \mathcal{K}_0\}$ is empty.

Our geometric interpretation is characterized by the reciprocal of $\|\boldsymbol{x}\|_{\mathcal{K}_0}$. The Minkowski functional is a norm in $\text{span}(\mathcal{K}_0)$, the space spanned by $\mathcal{K}_0$, and its unit ball is $\mathcal{K}_0$. Thus, for any $\boldsymbol{x} \in \text{span}(\mathcal{K}_0)$, the point $\boldsymbol{x}/\|\boldsymbol{x}\|_{\mathcal{K}_0}$ is the intersection of the ray $\{t\boldsymbol{x} : t \geq 0\}$ and the boundary of $\mathcal{K}_0$. The green and red dots in Fig. 2 are examples of $\boldsymbol{x}$ and $\boldsymbol{x}/\|\boldsymbol{x}\|_{\mathcal{K}_0}$, respectively. It follows that the quantity $1/\|\boldsymbol{x}\|_{\mathcal{K}_0}$ is the length of the ray $\{t\boldsymbol{x} : t \geq 0\}$ inside the convex hull $\mathcal{K}_0$.

Using Definition 2, one can show that the following holds [5,44]:

$$\|\boldsymbol{x}\|_{\mathcal{K}_0} = f_\infty(\boldsymbol{x}, \mathcal{X}_0) \text{ for all } \boldsymbol{x} \in \mathbb{R}^D. \tag{8}$$

A combination of (8) and the interpretation of $1/\|\boldsymbol{x}\|_{\mathcal{K}_0}$ above provides a geometric interpretation of $f_\infty(\boldsymbol{x}, \mathcal{X}_0)$. That is, $f_\infty(\boldsymbol{x}, \mathcal{X}_0)$ is large if the length of the ray $\{t\boldsymbol{x} : t \geq 0\}$ inside $\mathcal{K}_0$ is small. In particular, $f_\infty(\boldsymbol{x}, \mathcal{X}_0)$ is infinity if $\boldsymbol{x}$ is not in the span of $\mathcal{X}_0$, i.e., $\boldsymbol{x}$ cannot be linearly represented by $\mathcal{X}_0$.

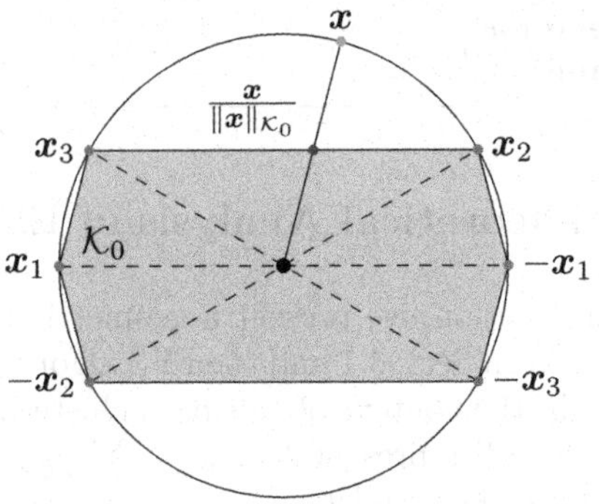

By using (8), the exemplar selection model in (5) is equivalent to computing

Fig. 2. A geometric illustration of the solution to (5) with $\mathcal{X}_0 = \{\boldsymbol{x}_1, \boldsymbol{x}_2, \boldsymbol{x}_3\}$. The shaded area is the convex hull $\mathcal{K}_0$. (Color figure online)

$$\mathcal{X}_0^* = \arg\max_{|\mathcal{X}_0|\leq k} \inf_{\boldsymbol{x}\in\mathcal{X}} 1/\|\boldsymbol{x}\|_{\mathcal{K}_0}. \tag{9}$$

Therefore, the solution to (5) is the subset $\mathcal{X}_0$ of $\mathcal{X}$ that maximizes the intersection of $\mathcal{K}_0$ and the ray $\{t\boldsymbol{x} : t \geq 0\}$ for every data $\boldsymbol{x} \in \mathcal{X}$ (i.e., maximizes the minimum of such intersections over all $\boldsymbol{x}$).

Furthermore, from (8) we can see that each iteration of Algorithm 1 selects the point $\boldsymbol{x} \in \mathcal{X}$ that minimizes $1/\|\boldsymbol{x}\|_{\mathcal{K}_0}$. Therefore, each iteration of FFS adds the point $\boldsymbol{x}$ that minimizes the intersection of the ray $\{t\boldsymbol{x} : t > 0\}$ with $\mathcal{K}_0$.

Relationship to the Sphere Covering Problem. Let us now consider the special case when the dataset $\mathcal{X}$ coincides with the unit sphere of $\mathbb{R}^D$, i.e., $\mathcal{X} = \mathbb{S}^{D-1}$. In this case, we establish that (5) is related to finding the minimum *covering radius*, which is defined in the following.

Definition 3 (Covering radius). *The covering radius of a set of points* $\mathcal{V} \subseteq \mathbb{S}^{D-1}$ *is defined as*

$$\gamma(\mathcal{V}) := \max_{\boldsymbol{w} \in \mathbb{S}^{D-1}} \min_{\boldsymbol{v} \in \mathcal{V}} \cos^{-1}(\langle \boldsymbol{v}, \boldsymbol{w} \rangle). \tag{10}$$

The covering radius of the set $\mathcal{V}$ can be interpreted as the minimum angle such that the union of spherical caps centered at each point in $\mathcal{V}$ with this radius covers the entire unit sphere $\mathbb{S}^{D-1}$. The following result establishes a relationship between the covering radius and our cost function.

Lemma 4. *For any finite* $\mathcal{X}_0 \subseteq \mathcal{X} = \mathbb{S}^{D-1}$ *we have* $F_\infty(\mathcal{X}_0) = 1/\cos\gamma(\pm\mathcal{X}_0)$.

It follows from Lemma 4 that $\arg\min_{|\mathcal{X}_0| \le k} F_\infty(\mathcal{X}_0) = \arg\min_{|\mathcal{X}_0| \le k} \gamma(\pm\mathcal{X}_0)$ when $\mathcal{X} = \mathbb{S}^{D-1}$, i.e., the exemplars $\mathcal{X}_0$ selected by (5) give the solution to the problem of finding a subset with minimum covering radius. Note that the covering radius $\gamma(\pm\mathcal{X}_0)$ of the subset $\mathcal{X}_0$ with $|\mathcal{X}_0| \le k$ is minimized when the points in the symmetrized set $\pm\mathcal{X}_0$ are as uniformly distributed on the sphere $\mathbb{S}^{D-1}$ as possible. The problem of equally distributing points on the sphere without symmetrizing them, i.e. $\min_{|\mathcal{X}_0| \le k} \gamma(\mathcal{X}_0)$, is known as the sphere covering problem. This problem was first studied by [45] and remains unsolved in geometry [46].

4.2 ESC on a Union of Subspaces

We now study the properties of our exemplar selection method when applied to data from a union of subspaces. Let $\mathcal{X}$ be drawn from a collection of subspaces $\{\mathcal{S}_\ell\}_{\ell=1}^n$ of dimensions $\{d_\ell\}_{\ell=1}^n$ with each subspace $\mathcal{S}_\ell$ containing at least d_ℓ samples that span $\mathcal{S}_\ell$. We assume that the subspaces are independent, which is commonly used in the analysis of subspace clustering methods [3,9,10,47,48].

Assumption 1. *The subspaces* $\{\mathcal{S}_\ell\}_{\ell=1}^n$ *are independent, i.e.,* $\sum_{\ell=1}^n d_\ell$ *is equal to the dimension of* $\sum_{\ell=1}^n \mathcal{S}_\ell$.

The next result shows that the solution to (5) contains enough exemplars from each subspace.

Theorem 1. *Under Assumption 1, for all* $k \ge \sum_{\ell=1}^n d_\ell$, *the solution* $\mathcal{X}_0^*$ *to the optimization problem in* (5) *contains at least* d_ℓ *linearly independent points from each subspace* $\mathcal{S}_\ell$. *Moreover, each point* $\boldsymbol{x} \in \mathcal{X}$ *is expressed as a linear combination of points in* $\mathcal{X}_0^*$ *that are from its own subspace.*

Theorem 1 shows that when k is set to be $\sum_{\ell=1}^n d_\ell$, then d_ℓ points are selected from subspace $\mathcal{S}_\ell$ regardless of the number of points in that subspace. Therefore, when the data is class imbalanced, (5) is able to select a subset that is more balanced provided that the dimensions of the subspaces do not differ dramatically. This discounts the effect that, when writing a data point as a linear combination of points from $\mathcal{X}$, it is more likely to choose points from oversampled subspaces. Theorem 1 also shows that only $\sum_{\ell=1}^n d_\ell$ points are needed to correctly represent all data points in $\mathcal{X}$. In other words, the required number of exemplars for representing the dataset does not scale with the size of the dataset $\mathcal{X}$.

Although the FFS algorithm in Sect. 3.2 is an approximation algorithm and does not necessarily give the solution to (5), the following result shows that it gives an approximate solution with attractive properties for subspace clustering.

Theorem 2. *The conclusion of Theorem 1 holds for $\mathcal{X}_0^{(k)}$ returned by Algorithm 1 provided $k \geq \sum_{\ell=1}^{n} d_\ell$.*

Theorem 2 shows that our algorithm FFS is able to select enough samples from each subspace even if the dataset is imbalanced. It also shows that for each data point in $\mathcal{X}$, the representation vector computed in step 1 of Algorithm 3 is subspace-preserving. Formally, we have established the following result.

Theorem 3. *Take any $k \geq \sum_{\ell=1}^{n} d_\ell$. Under Assumption 1, the representation vectors $\{c_j\}_{j=1}^{N}$ in step 1 of Algorithm 3 are subspace-preserving, i.e., c_{ij} is nonzero only if x_i and x_j are from the same subspace.*

5   Experiments

In this section, we demonstrate the performance of ESC for subspace clustering as well as for unsupervised subset selection tasks. The sparse optimization problem (4) in step 7 of Algorithm 2 and step 1 of Algorithm 3 are solved by the LASSO version of the LARS algorithm [49] implemented in the SPAMS package [50]. The nearest neighbors in step 2 of Algorithm 3 are computed by the k-d tree algorithm implemented in the VLFeat toolbox [51].

5.1   Subspace Clustering

We first demonstrate the performance of ESC for subspace clustering on large-scale class-imbalanced databases. These databases are described next.

Databases. We use two publicly available databases. The Extended MNIST (EMNIST) dataset [52] is an extension of the MNIST dataset that contains gray-scale handwritten digits and letters. We take all 190,998 images corresponding to 26 lower case letters, and use them as the data for a 26-class clustering problem. The size of each image in this dataset is 28 by 28. Following [48], each image is represented by a feature vector computed from a scattering convolutional network [53], which is translational invariant and deformation stable (i.e. it linearizes small deformations). Therefore, these features from EMNIST approximately follow a union of subspaces model.

The German Traffic Sign Recognition Benchmark (GTSRB) [54] contains 43 categories of street sign data with over 50,000 images in total. We remove categories associated with speed limit and triangle-shaped signs (except the yield sign) as they are difficult to distinguish from each other, which results in a final data set of 12,390 images in 14 categories. Each image is represented by a 1,568-dimensional HOG feature [55] provided with the database. The major intra-class variation in GTSRB is the illumination conditions, therefore the data can be well-approximated by a union of subspaces [56].

For both EMNIST and GTSRB, feature vectors are mean subtracted and projected to dimension 500 by PCA and normalized to have unit ℓ_2 norm. Both the EMNIST and GTSRB databases are imbalanced. In EMNIST, for example, the number of images for each letter ranges from 2,213 (letter "j") to 28,723 (letter "e"), and the number of samples for each letter is approximately equal to their frequencies in the English language. In Fig. 3 we show the number of instances for each class in both of these databases.

Baselines. We compare our approach with SSC [4] to show the effectiveness of exemplar selection in addressing imbalanced data. To handle large scale data, we use the efficient algorithm in [12] for solving the sparse recovery problem in SSC. For a fair comparison with ESC, we compute an affinity graph for SSC using the same procedure as that used for ESC, i.e., the procedure in Algorithm 3.

We also compare our method with k-means clustering and spectral clustering on the k-nearest neighbors graph, named "Spectral" in the following figures and tables. It is known [57] that Spectral is a provably correct method for subspace clustering. The k-means and k-d trees algorithms used to compute the k-nearest neighbor graph in Spectral are implemented using the VLFeat toolbox [51]. In addition, we compare with three other subspace clustering algorithms OMP [48], OLRSC [58] and SBC [19] that are able to handle large-scale data.

We compare these methods with ESC-FFS (Algorithm 3) with λ set to be 150 and 15 for EMNIST and GTSRB, respectively, and t set to be 3 for both databases. We also report the result of ESC-Rand when the exemplars are selected at random from $\mathcal{X}$, i.e., we replace the exemplar selection via FFS in step 1 of Algorithm 3 by selecting k atoms at random from $\mathcal{X}$ to form $\mathcal{X}_0$.

Fig. 3. Number of points in each class of EMNIST (left) and GTSRB (right) databases.

Evaluation Metrics. The first metric we use is the clustering accuracy. It measures the maximum proportion of points that are correctly labeled over all possible permutations of the labels. Concretely, let $\{C_1, \cdots, C_n\}$ be the ground-truth partition of the data, $\{G_1, \cdots, G_n\}$ be a clustering result of the same data, $n_{ij} = |C_i \cap G_j|$ be the number of common objects in C_i and G_j, and Π be the set of all permutations of $\{1, \cdots, n\}$. Clustering accuracy is defined as

$$\text{Accuracy} = \max_{\pi \in \Pi} \frac{100}{N} \sum_{i=1}^{n} n_{i,\pi(i)}. \tag{11}$$

In the context of classification, accuracy has been known to be biased when the dataset is class imbalanced [59]. For example, if a dataset is composed of 99% of samples from one particular class, then assigning all data points to the same label yields at least 99% accuracy. To address this issue, we also use the F-score averaged over all classes. Let $p_{ij} = n_{ij}/|G_j|$ be the precision and $r_{ij} = n_{ij}/|C_i|$ be the recall. The F-score between the clustering result G_i and the true class C_j is defined as $F_{ij} = \frac{2p_{ij}r_{ij}}{p_{ij}+r_{ij}}$. We report the average F-score given by

$$\text{F-score} = \max_{\pi \in \Pi} \frac{100}{n} \sum_{i=1}^{n} F_{i,\pi(i)}. \tag{12}$$

Results on EMNIST. Figure 4 shows the results on EMNIST. From left to right, the sub-figures show, respectively, the accuracy, the F-score and the running time (Y axis) as a function of the number of exemplars (X axis). We can see that ESC-FFS significantly outperforms all methods except SSC in terms of both accuracy and F-score when the number of exemplars is greater than 70.

Recall that in SSC each data point is expressed as a linear combination of all other points. By selecting a subset of exemplars and expressing points using these exemplars, ESC-FFS is able to outperform SSC when the number of exemplars reaches 200. In contrast, ESC-Rand does not outperform SSC by a significant amount, showing the importance of exemplar selection by FFS.

In terms of running time, we see that ESC-FFS is faster than SSC by a large margin. Specifically, ESC-FFS is almost as efficient as ESC-Rand, which indicates that the proposed FFS Algorithm 2 is efficient.

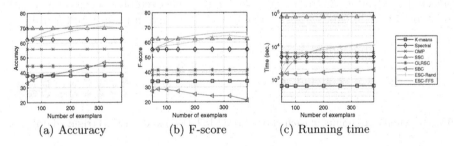

(a) Accuracy   (b) F-score   (c) Running time

Fig. 4. Subspace clustering on images of 26 lower case letters from EMNIST database.

Results on GTSRB. Table 1 reports the clustering performance on the GTSRB database. In addition to reporting average performance, we report the standard deviations. The variation in accuracy and F-score across trials is due to (1) random initializations of the k-means algorithm, which is used (trivially) in the K-means method, and in the spectral clustering step of all other methods, and (2) random dictionary initialization in OLRSC, SBC, ESC-Rand and ESC-FFS.

We observe that ESC-FFS outperforms all the other methods in terms of accuracy and F-score. In particular, ESC-FFS outperforms SSC, which in turn outperforms ESC-Rand, thus showing the importance of finding a representative set of exemplars and the effectiveness of FFS in achieving this. In addition, the standard deviation of accuracy and F-score for ESC-Rand are all larger than for ESC-FFS. This indicates that the set of exemplars given by FFS is more robust in giving reliable clustering results than the randomly selected exemplars in ESC-Rand. In terms of running time, ESC-FFS is also competitive.

Table 1. Subspace clustering on the GTSRB street sign database. The parameter k is fixed to be 160 for ESC-Rand and ESC-FFS. We report the mean and standard deviation for accuracy, F-score and running time (in sec.) from 10 trials.

	K-means	Spectral	OMP	SSC	OLRSC	SBC	ESC-Rand	ESC-FFS
Accuracy	63.7 ± 3.5	89.5 ± 1.3	82.8 ± 0.8	92.4 ± 1.1	71.6 ± 4.3	74.9 ± 5.2	89.7 ± 1.6	$\mathbf{93.0 \pm 1.3}$
F-score	54.4 ± 2.8	79.8 ± 2.5	67.8 ± 0.5	82.3 ± 2.8	66.7 ± 4.7	72.2 ± 8.5	75.5 ± 4.9	$\mathbf{85.3 \pm 2.5}$
Time (sec.)	$\mathbf{12.2 \pm 0.5}$	40.3 ± 0.7	22.0 ± 0.2	52.2 ± 0.7	64.9 ± 1.6	41.9 ± 0.4	21.5 ± 0.4	25.2 ± 1.2

5.2 Unsupervised Subset Selection

Given a large-scale unlabeled dataset, it is expensive to manually annotate all data. One solution is to select a small subset of data for manual labeling, and then infer the labels for the remaining data by training a model on the selected subset. In this section, we evaluate the performance of the FFS algorithm as a tool for selecting a subset of representatives for a given dataset. This subset is then subsequently exploited to classify the entire data set.

We use the Extended Yale B face database, which contains images of 38 faces and each of them is taken under 64 different illumination conditions. For this experiment, we create an imbalanced dataset by randomly selecting 10 classes and sampling a subset from each class. The number of images we sample for those 10 classes is 16 for the first 3 classes, 32 for the next 3 classes and 64 for the remaining 4 classes. We first apply FFS to select 100 images from this dataset. Note that during this phase we assume that the ground truth labeling is unknown. We then train three classifiers, the nearest neighbor (NN), sparse representation based classification (SRC) [60] and linear support vector machine (SVM) on the selected images, which is then used to classify all of the images.

We compare FFS with random sampling (Rand), k-centers, K-medoids [61], SMRS [26] and kDPP [32]. For k-centers, we implement the farthest first traversal algorithm (see, e.g. [42]). For K-medoids, we use the function provided by ®Matlab, which employs a variant of the algorithm in [61]. For SMRS and kDPP, we use the code provided by the authors. We set $\lambda = 100$ in FFS.

In Table 2 we report the classification accuracy averaged over 50 trials. We can see that the NN classifier works the best with K-medoids, but the performance of NN is worse than SRC and SVM. This is because images of the same face lie approximately in a subspace, and their pairwise distances may not be small. When SRC and SVM are used as classifiers, we can see that our method achieves the best performance.

Table 2. Classification from subsets on the Extended Yale B face database. We report the mean and standard deviation for classification accuracy and running time of the subset selection from 50 trials.

	Rand	k-centers	K-medoids	kDPP	SMRS	FFS
NN	69.4 ± 3.2	69.1 ± 3.7	**75.5 ± 2.8**	70.5 ± 3.2	69.0 ± 3.1	67.5 ± 4.0
SRC	84.7 ± 2.2	84.9 ± 2.6	86.0 ± 2.1	88.3 ± 2.3	83.4 ± 2.3	**91.4 ± 2.4**
SVM	83.7 ± 2.5	83.0 ± 2.8	85.3 ± 2.3	87.8 ± 2.1	82.1 ± 2.3	**91.0 ± 3.0**
Time (sec.)	**$<1e-3$**	0.26 ± 0.01	1.5 ± 0.1	0.57 ± 0.06	3.1 ± 0.2	0.70 ± 0.08

6   Conclusion

We presented a novel approach to subspace clustering for imbalanced and large-scale data. Our method searches for a set of exemplars from the given dataset, such that all data points can be well-represented by the exemplars in terms of a sparse representation cost. Analytically, we showed that the set of exemplars selected by our model has the property that its symmetrized convex hull covers as much of the rays $\{tx : t \geq 0\}$ as possible for all data points $x \in \mathcal{X}$. In the context of subspace clustering, we proved that our method selects a set of exemplars that is small and balanced, while being able to represent all data points. We also introduced an algorithm for approximately solving the exemplar selection optimization problem. Empirically we demonstrated that our method is effective for subspace clustering and unsupervised subset selection applications.

Acknowledgments. C. You, D. P. Robinson and R. Vidal are supported by NSF under grant 1618637. C. Li is supported by IARPA under grant 127228.

References

1. Vidal, R.: Subspace clustering. IEEE Signal Process. Mag. **28**(3), 52–68 (2011)
2. von Luxburg, U.: A tutorial on spectral clustering. Stat. Comput. **17**(4), 395–416 (2007)
3. Elhamifar, E., Vidal, R.: Sparse subspace clustering. In: IEEE Conference on Computer Vision and Pattern Recognition, pp. 2790–2797 (2009)
4. Elhamifar, E., Vidal, R.: Sparse subspace clustering: algorithm, theory, and applications. IEEE Trans. Pattern Anal. Mach. Intell. **35**(11), 2765–2781 (2013)
5. Soltanolkotabi, M., Candès, E.J.: A geometric analysis of subspace clustering with outliers. Ann. Stat. **40**(4), 2195–2238 (2012)
6. You, C., Vidal, R.: Geometric conditions for subspace-sparse recovery. In: International Conference on Machine Learning, pp. 1585–1593 (2015)

7. Wang, Y.X., Xu, H.: Noisy sparse subspace clustering. J. Mach. Learn. Res. **17**(12), 1–41 (2016)
8. You, C., Robinson, D., Vidal, R.: Provable self-representation based outlier detection in a union of subspaces. In: IEEE Conference on Computer Vision and Pattern Recognition (2017)
9. Liu, G., Lin, Z., Yu, Y.: Robust subspace segmentation by low-rank representation. In: International Conference on Machine Learning, pp. 663–670 (2010)
10. Lu, C.-Y., Min, H., Zhao, Z.-Q., Zhu, L., Huang, D.-S., Yan, S.: Robust and efficient subspace segmentation via least squares regression. In: Fitzgibbon, A., Lazebnik, S., Perona, P., Sato, Y., Schmid, C. (eds.) ECCV 2012. LNCS, vol. 7578, pp. 347–360. Springer, Heidelberg (2012). https://doi.org/10.1007/978-3-642-33786-4_26
11. Dyer, E.L., Sankaranarayanan, A.C., Baraniuk, R.G.: Greedy feature selection for subspace clustering. J. Mach. Learn. Res. **14**(1), 2487–2517 (2013)
12. You, C., Li, C.G., Robinson, D., Vidal, R.: Oracle based active set algorithm for scalable elastic net subspace clustering. In: IEEE Conference on Computer Vision and Pattern Recognition, pp. 3928–3937 (2016)
13. Yang, Y., Feng, J., Jojic, N., Yang, J., Huang, T.S.: ℓ^0-sparse subspace clustering. In: Leibe, B., Matas, J., Sebe, N., Welling, M. (eds.) ECCV 2016. LNCS, vol. 9906, pp. 731–747. Springer, Cham (2016). https://doi.org/10.1007/978-3-319-46475-6_45
14. Xin, B., Wang, Y., Gao, W., Wipf, D.: Building invariances into sparse subspace clustering. IEEE Trans. Signal Process. **66**(2), 449–462 (2018)
15. You, C., Donnat, C., Robinson, D., Vidal, R.: A divide-and-conquer framework for large-scale subspace clustering. In: Asilomar Conference on Signals, Systems and Computers (2016)
16. You, C., Li, C., Robinson, D., Vidal, R.: A scalable exemplar-based subspace clustering algorithm for class-imbalanced data (2018)
17. Aharon, M., Elad, M., Bruckstein, A.M.: K-SVD: an algorithm for designing overcomplete dictionaries for sparse representation. IEEE Trans. Signal Process. **54**(11), 4311–4322 (2006)
18. Bach, F., Jenatton, R., Mairal, J., Obozinski, G.: Optimization with sparsity-inducing penalties. J. Found. Trends Mach. Learn. **4**(1), 1–106 (2012)
19. Adler, A., Elad, M., Hel-Or, Y.: Linear-time subspace clustering via bipartite graph modeling. IEEE Trans. Neural Netw. Learn. Syst. **26**(10), 2234–2246 (2015)
20. Traganitis, P.A., Giannakis, G.B.: Sketched subspace clustering. IEEE Trans. Signal Process. **66**, 1663–1675 (2017)
21. Tropp, J.A., Gilbert, A.C., Strauss, M.J.: Algorithms for simultaneous sparse approximation. Part I: greedy pursuit. Signal Process. **86**(3), 572–588 (2006)
22. Cevher, V., Krause, A.: Greedy dictionary selection for sparse representation. IEEE J. Sel. Top. Signal Process. **5**(5), 979–988 (2011)
23. Das, A., Kempe, D.: Submodular meets spectral: greedy algorithms for subset selection, sparse approximation and dictionary selection. arXiv preprint arXiv:1102.3975 (2011)
24. Tropp, J.A.: Algorithms for simultaneous sparse approximation. Part II: convex relaxation. Signal Process. **86**, 589–602 (2006). Special Issue on Sparse approximations in signal and image processing
25. Cong, Y., Yuan, J., Liu, J.: Sparse reconstruction cost for abnormal event detection. In: The 24th IEEE Conference on Computer Vision and Pattern Recognition, CVPR 2011, Colorado Springs, CO, USA, 20–25 June 2011, pp. 3449–3456 (2011)

26. Elhamifar, E., Sapiro, G., Vidal, R.: See all by looking at a few: sparse modeling for finding representative objects. In: IEEE Conference on Computer Vision and Pattern Recognition (2012)

27. Meng, J., Wang, H., Yuan, J., Tan, Y.P.: From keyframes to key objects: video summarization by representative object proposal selection. In: CVPR, pp. 1039–1048 (2016)

28. Wang, H., Kawahara, Y., Weng, C., Yuan, J.: Representative selection with structured sparsity. Pattern Recognit. **63**, 268–278 (2017)

29. Cong, Y., Yuan, J., Luo, J.: Towards scalable summarization of consumer videos via sparse dictionary selection. IEEE Trans. Multimed. **14**(1), 66–75 (2012)

30. Borodin, A.: Determinantal point processes. arXiv preprint arXiv:0911.1153 (2009)

31. Gillenwater, J.A., Kulesza, A., Fox, E., Taskar, B.: Expectation-maximization for learning determinantal point processes. In: NIPS, pp. 3149–3157 (2014)

32. Kulesza, A., Taskar, B.: k-DPPs: Fixed-size determinantal point processes. In: ICML, pp. 1193–1200 (2011)

33. Chan, T.: Rank revealing QR factorizations. Linear Algebra Appl. **88–89**, 67–82 (1987)

34. Boutsidis, C., Mahoney, M.W., Drineas, P.: An improved approximation algorithm for the column subset selection problem. In: Proceedings of SODA, pp. 968–977 (2009)

35. Altschuler, J., Bhaskara, A., Fu, G., Mirrokni, V., Rostamizadeh, A., Zadimoghaddam, M.: Greedy column subset selection: new bounds and distributed algorithms. In: International Conference on Machine Learning, pp. 2539–2548 (2016)

36. Arora, S., Ge, R., Kannan, R., Moitra, A.: Computing a nonnegative matrix factorization–provably. In: Proceedings of the Forty-Fourth Annual ACM Symposium on Theory of Computing, pp. 145–162. ACM (2012)

37. Kumar, A., Sindhwani, V., Kambadur, P.: Fast conical hull algorithms for near-separable non-negative matrix factorization. In: Proceedings of the 30th International Conference on Machine Learning, ICML, pp. 231–239 (2013)

38. Elhamifar, E., Sapiro, G., Vidal, R.: Finding exemplars from pairwise dissimilarities via simultaneous sparse recovery. In: Neural Information Processing and Systems (2012)

39. Aldroubi, A., Sekmen, A., Koku, A.B., Cakmak, A.F.: Similarity matrix framework for data from union of subspaces. Appl. Comput. Harmon. Anal. **45**, 425–435 (2017)

40. Aldroubi, A., Hamm, K., Koku, A.B., Sekmen, A.: CUR decompositions, similarity matrices, and subspace clustering. arXiv preprint arXiv:1711.04178 (2017)

41. Abdolali, M., Gillis, N., Rahmati, M.: Scalable and robust sparse subspace clustering using randomized clustering and multilayer graphs. arXiv preprint arXiv:1802.07648 (2018)

42. Williamson, D.P., Shmoys, D.B.: The Design of Approximation Algorithms. Cambridge University Press, Cambridge (2011)

43. Vershynin, R.: Lectures in geometric functional analysis (2009)

44. Donoho, D.L.: Neighborly polytopes and sparse solution of underdetermined linear equations. Technical report. Stanford University (2005)

45. Toth, L.F.: On covering a spherical surface with equal spherical caps. Matematikai Fiz. Lapok **50**, 40–46 (1943). (in Hungarian)

46. Croft, H.T., Guy, R.K., Falconer, K.J.: Unsolved Problems in Geometry. Springer, New York (1991). https://doi.org/10.1007/978-1-4612-0963-8

47. Vidal, R., Tron, R., Hartley, R.: Multiframe motion segmentation with missing data using PowerFactorization, and GPCA. Int. J. Comput. Vis. **79**(1), 85–105 (2008)
48. You, C., Robinson, D., Vidal, R.: Scalable sparse subspace clustering by orthogonal matching pursuit. In: IEEE Conference on Computer Vision and Pattern Recognition, pp. 3918–3927 (2016)
49. Efron, B., Hastie, T., Johnstone, I., Tibshirani, R.: Least angle regression. Ann. Stat. **32**(2), 407–499 (2004)
50. Mairal, J., Bach, F., Ponce, J., Sapiro, G.: Online learning for matrix factorization and sparse coding. J. Mach. Learn. Res. **11**, 19–60 (2010)
51. Vedaldi, A., Fulkerson, B.: VLFeat: an open and portable library of computer vision algorithms (2008). http://www.vlfeat.org/
52. Cohen, G., Afshar, S., Tapson, J., van Schaik, A.: EMNIST: an extension of MNIST to handwritten letters. arXiv preprint arXiv:1702.05373 (2017)
53. Bruna, J., Mallat, S.: Invariant scattering convolution networks. IEEE Trans. Pattern Anal. Mach. Intell. **35**(8), 1872–1886 (2013)
54. Stallkamp, J., Schlipsing, M., Salmen, J., Igel, C.: Man vs. computer: benchmarking machine learning algorithms for traffic sign recognition. Neural Netw. **32**, 323–332 (2012)
55. Dalal, N., Triggs, B.: Histograms of oriented gradients for human detection. In: IEEE Conference on Computer Vision and Pattern Recognition (2005)
56. Basri, R., Jacobs, D.: Lambertian reflection and linear subspaces. IEEE Trans. Pattern Anal. Mach. Intell. **25**(2), 218–233 (2003)
57. Heckel, R., Bölcskei, H.: Robust subspace clustering via thresholding. IEEE Trans. Inf. Theory **61**(11), 6320–6342 (2015)
58. Shen, J., Li, P., Xu, H.: Online low-rank subspace clustering by basis dictionary pursuit. In: Proceedings of the 33rd International Conference on Machine Learning, pp. 622–631 (2016)
59. Brodersen, K.H., Ong, C.S., Stephan, K.E., Buhmann, J.M.: The balanced accuracy and its posterior distribution. In: 2010 20th International Conference on Pattern Recognition, ICPR, pp. 3121–3124. IEEE (2010)
60. Wright, S.J., Nowak, R.D., Figueiredo, M.A.T.: Sparse reconstruction by separable approximation. IEEE Trans. Signal Process. **57**, 2479–2493 (2009)
61. Park, H.S., Jun, C.H.: A simple and fast algorithm for K-medoids clustering. Expert Syst. Appl. **36**(2), 3336–3341 (2009)

RCAA: Relational Context-Aware Agents
for Person Search

Xiaojun Chang[1], Po-Yao Huang[1], Yi-Dong Shen[2(✉)], Xiaodan Liang[1],
Yi Yang[3], and Alexander G. Hauptmann[1]

[1] School of Computer Science, Carnegie Mellon University, Pittsburgh, USA
cxj273@gmail.com, berniebear@gmail.com, xdliang328@gmail.com,
alex@cs.cmu.edu
[2] Institute of Software, Chinese Academy of Sciences, Beijing, China
ydshen@ios.ac.cn
[3] Centre for Artificial Intelligence, University of Technology Sydney, Ultimo,
Australia
yee.i.yang@gmail.com

Abstract. We aim to search for a target person from a gallery of whole
scene images for which the annotations of pedestrian bounding boxes
are unavailable. Previous approaches to this problem have relied on a
pedestrian proposal net, which may generate redundant proposals and
increase the computational burden. In this paper, we address this problem by training relational context-aware agents which learn the actions
to localize the target person from the gallery of whole scene images. We
incorporate the relational spatial and temporal contexts into the framework. Specifically, we propose to use the target person as the query
in the query-dependent relational network. The agent determines the
best action to take at each time step by simultaneously considering the
local visual information, the relational and temporal contexts, together
with the target person. To validate the performance of our approach, we
conduct extensive experiments on the large-scale Person Search benchmark dataset and achieve significant improvements over the compared
approaches. It is also worth noting that the proposed model even performs better than traditional methods with perfect pedestrian detectors.

Keywords: Person search · Relational network

1 Introduction

Person re-identification (re-id) is an important research problem in which the
goal is to match the same person across different camera views or across time
within the same camera [1–5]. Its obvious applications include, but are not limited to, content-based video retrieval, video surveillance, and human-computer
interaction [6]. Due to its importance for these applications, it has attracted
increasing research attention in recent years. However, it remains challenging

© Springer Nature Switzerland AG 2018
V. Ferrari et al. (Eds.): ECCV 2018, LNCS 11213, pp. 86–102, 2018.
https://doi.org/10.1007/978-3-030-01240-3_6

and unsolved because of camera view changes, poor lighting conditions, severe background clutter and occlusion, and so on.

Despite the considerable progress that has been made, person re-id still cannot be directly applied to real-world applications. Most existing person re-id benchmark datasets and approaches focus on matching cropped person images from multiple non-overlapping cameras [7–9]. Although these approaches have achieved promising performance, they have major limitations for practical usage, since they are built upon the assumption of precise person detection. In real-world applications, precise bounding boxes are either unavailable or expensive to obtain. The off-the-shelf person detection algorithms would inevitably generate inaccurate proposals, thus deteriorating subsequent person re-id performance.

To close the gap between the research on person re-id and real-world applications, researchers have proposed the person search problem and several corresponding approaches [10–12]. We show the differences between person search and person re-id in Fig. 1. Xu *et al.* proposed to combine person detection and person matching scores using a sliding window search method [10]. Their method has several inherent drawbacks. Firstly, their algorithm is not scalable because of the sliding window algorithm. Secondly, they conduct person detection and search in two separate steps, which may lead to sub-optimal solution for person search. To address these problems, Xiao *et al.* proposed a new deep learning model to jointly conduct person detection and identification for person search [12]. However, their model also required to train a person proposal network for person candidate detection.

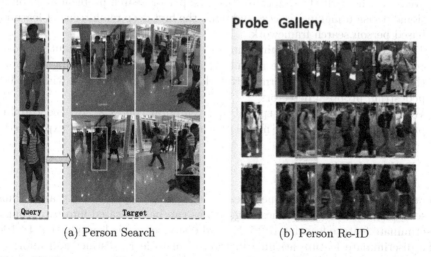

(a) Person Search   (b) Person Re-ID

Fig. 1. We show examples of person search and person re-identification. Person search aims at finding a specified person from whole scene images, while person re-id aims to match cropped person images from multiple non-overlapping cameras. From the comparison, we can see that person search problem setting is closer to real-world applications and more challenging.

Spatial and temporal context may provide additional crucial information but still remains under-explored for person search. Spatial context has been proved useful in tasks like visual question answering [13]. The target-person-dependent spatial relationships between objects in the whole scene image may contribute to more discriminative representations. Additionally, the success of sequential decision making in object detection [14] also sheds light for person re-id. An agent making multi-step inferences may better locate the target person with consideration of its temporal action and state memory.

In this work, we propose a top-down search strategy powered by a spatial and temporal context-aware agent to address the limitations and opportunities discussed above. Specifically, given the whole scene, its local image features, and the query image, we leverage a target-person-dependent relational network to extract the spatial context between objects. Then our deep reinforcement learning agent selects the best action to narrow down the precise location of the target person at each time step based on the spatial context and its temporal action and state memory. The selected action is expected to keep the target person within the target box while cutting off as much background as possible. In this paper, we define 14 actions to perform the transitions of the target box. This step is repeated until the optimal result is obtained (when the agent selects the action "Terminate"). The whole framework comprises no person proposal computing and is end-to-end trainable.

To summarize, we make the following contributions to the field of person search.

- We make the earliest attempt to solve the person search problem as a conditional decision-making process and build the first deep reinforcement learning based person search framework.
- The proposed model is trained in an end-to-end fashion without proposal computing, which could be redundant and noisy. It is interesting to notice that our model even perform better than traditional methods with perfect pedestrian proposal detectors.
- We incorporate relational spatial and temporal contexts into the training procedure, which guides the model to generate more informative "experience".

2   Related Works

Person Re-identification. Pioneer researchers have proposed many algorithms to solve the re-id problem. These algorithms can be separated into two groups, discriminate feature learning [7,15–17] and distance metric learning [1,3,18,19]. The discriminate feature learning methods aim to learn distinct and informative features from cropped pedestrian images, while the distance metric learning methods usually learn distance metrics that are robust to sample variance.

Inspired by the phenomenal results achieved by deep learning networks in many computer vision applications [20–22], many researchers have explored different deep convolutional neural network (DCNN) models to solve the person re-id problem. Some researchers have employed a Siamese convolutional network

[23] for person re-id. For example, Ahmed *et al.* [24] and Li *et al.* [8] proposed using pairs of cropped pedestrian images as input and training the network using a binary verification loss function. Other researchers have adopted a triplet framework to improve person re-id performance. Ding *et al.* [25] and Cheng *et al.* [2] trained networks with triplet samples to make the features from the same pedestrian close and the features from different pedestrians far apart. We also notice that Zheng *et al.* also contributed a benchmark dataset for person search [5]. However, they proposed separate detection and re-id methods with scores re-weighting to solve the problem, while we propose a reinforcement learning framework for joint detection and re-id.

Pedestrian Detection. Early works on pedestrian detectors were built upon hand-crafted features and linear classifiers. Representative works include DPM [26], ACF [27] and Checkerboards [28]. These off-the-shelf pedestrian detectors are widely used for a variety of computer vision applications. Recently, various deep learning models have been proposed to boost the performance of pedestrian detection. For example, Cai *et al.* [29] proposed to seek an algorithm for optimal cascade learning under a criterion that penalizes both detection errors and complexity. Tian *et al.* [30] sought to jointly optimize pedestrian detection with semantic tasks, including pedestrian attributes and scene attributes. Ouyang *et al.* [31] proposed to handle occlusion by jointly learning features and the visibility of different body parts. They could effectively estimate the visibility of parts at multiple layers and learn their relationship with the proposed discriminative deep model. Luo *et al.* [32] propose to automatically learn hierarchical features, salience maps, and mixture representations of different body parts. Their model is able to explicitly model the complex mixture of visual variations at multiple levels.

Deep Reinforcement Learning. Deep reinforcement learning (DRL) has attracted much research attention over the last few years. Its goal is to learn a policy function that determines sequential actions by maximizing the cumulative future rewards [33]. Many researchers have attempted to incorporate deep neural networks with RL algorithms [34,35]. A common method is to use deep neural networks to represent RL models. These researchers have achieved human-level performance while playing Atari games [34] or Go [35]. Concurrently, some researchers propose to apply DRL to computer vision tasks, such as action recognition [36], object localization [14] and visual tracking [37].

Two widely used DRL methods are discussed in the literature, Deep Q-Networks (DQN) and policy gradient. As an exemplar of Q-learning, DQN approximates the state-action value function with deep neural networks. The network is trained by minimizing the temporal-difference errors [34]. To obtain better performance and maintain stability, researchers have proposed different network architectures based on DQN, *i.e.* Double DQN [38], DDQN [39], *etc.*

The goal of policy gradient methods is to use gradient descent to directly learn the policy by optimizing the deep policy networks with respect to the expected future reward. Williams *et al.* [40] proposed using the immediate reward to obtain an estimation of the policy value. They called this method REINFORCE and applied it to detect actions in videos.

3   Relational Context-Aware Agents

3.1   Overview

Person search solves the problem of finding the precise position of the target person from a gallery of whole scene images. The system dynamically locates the target person by sequential actions that are determined by a spatial-temporal context-aware agent. Our agent accepts the spatial and temporal context, the local image feature and the query image as input, and predicts the best action to take. The bounding box is transformed from its current state by the predicted action, and the next action is predicted from the next state. This process is repeated until we reach an optimal result. We show structure of the proposed model in Fig. 2.

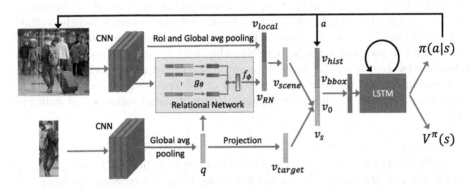

Fig. 2. The proposed relational spatial and temporal context-aware network. We adopt the relational network to compute the relational spatial context, and condition its processing on the target person. We encode the temporal context in the state of the LSTM. We use blue line to denote normal one-step feed-forward, and black line to denote action feedback loop.

3.2   Relational Decision Making

The proposed model follows Markov Decision Process (MDP), which is well suitable for modelling the sequential decision process. MDP is denoted as a tuple of states (S, A, R, γ), where $s \in S$ denotes a state of the environment, $a \in A$ denotes an action that the agent selects to transform the environment, $R : S \times A$ denotes the reward function that maps a state-action pair (s, a) to a reward $r \in \mathbb{R}$, and $\gamma \in (0,1]$ denotes a discount factor determining the decay rate in calculating the cumulative discounted reward of the entire trajectory. We represent the state and action as s_t and a_t, for $t = 1, \cdots, T$, where T denotes the termination step. We define the bounding box as $[x_t, y_t, w_t, h_t]$, where (x_t, y_t) is the center position, w_t and h_t are the width and the height of the bounding box, respectively.

Action. We show the 14 actions in Fig. 3. These actions can be grouped into three categories. The first category is for translating the current bounding box locally. The second category is for scaling the current bounding box to a smaller size (0.55 times as the original bounding box). The last category has only one action, namely "Terminate", which means the optimal result has been achieved. Similar to [14], the local translation group includes moving right/left horizontally, moving up/down vertically, making fatter/thinner horizontally and making fatter/thinner vertically. Each transformation action makes a discrete change to the current bounding box by a factor δ, where $\delta \in (0,1]$. For example, if the action "moving right horizontally" is selected, the bounding box will change from $[x_t, y_t, w_t, h_t]$ to $[x_t + \delta * w_t, y_t, w_t, h_t]$. δ is set as 0.2 in our experiments, since this value has been selected in the literature for its good trade-off between speed and localization accuracy.

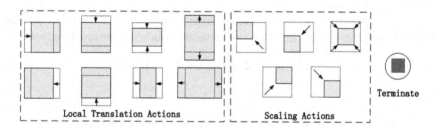

Fig. 3. Illustration of the 14 actions for the agent. The blue window with solid line denotes the bounding box after taking the corresponding action. The dashed line represents the bounding box before the action. The termination action means optimal result is reached

State. At each time step, we define the environment state as a combination of the whole image, the current bounding box, and the query person. In this paper, we initialize the bounding box as the whole image. We extract these features using the ResNet-50 [22] which is pre-trained on the large-scale ImageNet dataset [41]. Our framework utilizes the convolutional layers from the ResNet-50, followed by a ROI pooling layer [42,43] to extract a set of feature maps for the region proposal. We feed the whole image into the network, and obtain image feature maps after several convolutional layers. Then we feed these feature maps into a ROI pooling layer to extract the corresponding features for the object proposals.

Note that this is computationally efficient since we can share the computations in convolutional layers for all region proposals in one image. For the whole image and the query person image, we feed the feature maps into global average pooling layers [22] to obtain the feature vectors.

Reward. The reward function $R(s_t, a_t)$ is the improvement of localization performance when the action a_t is taken at the state s_t. In the literature [43], researchers employ the Intersection-over-Union (IoU) between the current bounding box and the ground-truth as the evaluation metric for its simplicity and effectiveness. However, as claimed in [44], this simple reward function tends to mislead the agent into learning suboptimal policies. It is essential to incorporate a shaping reward function into the original reward function. The shaping reward function is defined as:

$$F(s_t, a_t) = \gamma\Phi(s_{t+1}) - \Phi(s_t), \tag{1}$$
$$\Phi(s) = IoU(s_t) \tag{2}$$

where $\Phi(s)$ is a potential based reward. Following the literatures on deep reinforcement learning [43,45], we set the discount factor γ to 0.99. Ng *et al.* has proved that F is a necessary and sufficient condition to guarantee consistency with the optimal policy [44].

When the local translation action or scaling action is selected, by incorporating the shaping reward function, we have the following reward function:

$$R(s_t, a_t) = R'(s_t, a_t) + F(s_t, a_t), \tag{3}$$

where

$$R'(s_t, a_t) = \begin{cases} \text{IoU}(s_{t+1}), & \text{if IoU}(s_{t+1}) > \max \text{IoU}(s_k)|_{k=0}^t \\ -p, & \text{otherwise} \end{cases}. \tag{4}$$

The basic reward function $R'(s_t, a_t)$ will return $\text{IoU}(s_{t+1})$ when the new state s_{t+1} has higher IoU value than any previous states. Otherwise, we will give a penalty of $-p$ to the agent. Empirically, we set p as 0.05.

When the "Terminate" action is selected, the agent will receive a positive reward η if $\text{IoU}(s_T) > \tau$. Otherwise, a penalty will be given to the agent. The reward function $R(s_t, a_t)$ is defined as follows:

$$R(s_t, a_t) = \begin{cases} \eta & \text{if IoU}(s_t) > \tau \\ -\eta & \text{otherwise} \end{cases}. \tag{5}$$

In this paper, τ and η are empirically set as 0.5 and 1.0, respectively.

3.3   Network Structure

Following the traditional reinforcement learning setting, our agent interacts with the environment at each time step. We define a value function as $V^\pi(s) = \mathbb{E}[R_t | s_t = s]$, which measures the expected cumulative reward R_t for following a policy function π from any state s. The policy function $\pi(a|s)$ is used to select an action s from a set of actions given a state s. We approximate the value function and the policy function using a multi-layer neural network, which is a common practice in DRL. The network has two outputs, *i.e.* the distribution $\pi(a|s)$ over the possible actions and value estimation $V^\pi(s)$.

We employ the ResNet-50 [22] for feature extraction because it has demonstrated its superiority in terms of person re-id [46]. To encode the relational context information, we incorporate a Relational Network (RN) [13] to consider all the relations across all pairs of objects in the image. The RN can be simply defined as follows:

$$v_{\text{RN}} = f_\phi(\sum_{i,j} g_\theta(o_i, o_j)), \tag{6}$$

where $O = (o_1, \cdots, o_n)$ denote a set of "objects", o_i is the i-th object, and f_ϕ and g_θ are functions with parameters ϕ and θ. Santoro *et al.* have demonstrated that CNN embeddings can be used as a set of objects for an RN. We feed the image into the ResNet-50 and get the k feature maps of size $d \times d$ from the final convolutional layer, where k is the number of kernels in the final convolutional layer. We tag each of the d^2 k-dimensional cells in the $d \times d$ feature maps with an arbitrary coordinate indicating its relative spatial position, and treat it as an object for the RN. The existence and meaning of an object-object relation should be relevant to the query person. Hence, we make the function g_θ condition its processing on the query person:

$$v_{RN} = f_\phi(\sum_{i,j} g_\theta(o_i, o_j, q)). \tag{7}$$

We concatenate the whole scene image representation v_{RN} and the local representation v_{local}, resulting in the scene representation v_{scene}. We feed the feature maps of the target person to global average pooling and achieve the target person representation v_{target}. We project both features into a ℓ_2-normalized 256 dimensional subspace, and apply dot product and ℓ_2-norm to v'_{scene} and v'_{target}. For simplicity, we drop the apostrophe. Hence, we encode the observation of the current state as:

$$v_0 = \frac{v_{\text{scene}} \cdot v_{\text{target}}}{||v_{\text{scene}} \cdot v_{\text{target}}||}, \tag{8}$$

where $\cdot$ denotes element-wise dot product.

To step further, the temporal context is explored to track the states that the agent has encountered as well as all the actions that the agent has taken. In this work, we record 50 previous actions, resulting in a history vector $v_{\text{history}} \in \mathbb{R}^{700}$.

We encode the relative location and size of the region using a 5-dimensional vector:

$$v_{\text{bbox}} = \left[\frac{x_t - \frac{w_t}{2}}{w_t}, \frac{y_t - \frac{h_t}{2}}{h_t}, \frac{x_t + \frac{w_t}{2}}{w_t}, \frac{y_t + \frac{h_t}{2}}{h_t}, \frac{S_{\text{bbox}}}{S_{\text{image}}} \right], \tag{9}$$

where S_{bbox} is the size of bounding box and S_{image} is the size of the image. Then we represent the state as a vector $v_s = [v_0, v_{\text{history}}, v_{\text{bbox}}]$. We pass the vector representation of the state v_s to two FC layers with the same output size of 1,024, following by using a Long Short-Term Memory (LSTM) cell with Layer Normalization to track the past states. The temporal context for subsequent decision making is encoded by the state inside the LSTM cell.

3.4 Training

Although using a single agent to collect experiences may obtain promising results, it may achieve highly correlated data. Updating the system with these data would lead the agent to learn a suboptimal solution. To avoid the suboptimal solution, we employ the asynchronous advantage actor-critic (A3C) method [45] which asynchronously execute multiple agents in parallel, on multiple instances of the environment. A3C contains a policy function $\pi(a|s; \theta_\pi)$ and an estimate of the value function $V(s; \theta_v)$, where θ_π and θ_v are the parameters of the policy function and the value function, respectively. When we process one query, an agent interacts with the environment constructed by the query using the current network, and generates an episode $\{(s_t, a_t, r_t)\}_{t=0,\cdots,T}$ for training. The query is selected randomly during training. We update the network parameters asynchronously.

Following [45], we empirically group every N consecutive experiences in every episode. At each time step t, we convert the reward as

$$R'_t = \sum_{k=t}^{t_m(t)-1} \gamma^{k-t} r_k + \gamma^{t_m(t)-t} V(s_{t_m}(t)), \tag{10}$$

if the condition $t + N \le T$ is met. Note that $t_m(t) = \lceil \frac{t}{N} \rceil \cdot N$. Otherwise, we convert the reward according to $R'_t = \sum_{k=t}^{T} \gamma^{k-t} r_k$. We collect all the tuples in parallel, and use them to optimize in batch mode. We train the network by the ADAM optimizer [47], and optimize in batch mode as follows:

$$\theta_\pi \leftarrow \theta_\pi + \alpha((R'_t - V(s_t; \theta_v)) \nabla_{\theta_\pi} \log \pi(a_t|s_t; \theta_\pi) \tag{11}$$
$$+ \beta \nabla_{\theta_\pi} H(\pi(\cdot|s_t; \theta_\pi)))$$

$$\theta_v \leftarrow \theta_v - \alpha \nabla_{\pi_v} (R_t - V(s_t; \theta_v))^2, \tag{12}$$

where α denotes the learning rate, $H(\pi(\cdot|s_t; \theta_\pi))$ represents the entropy of the policy [45], β is the hyper parameter, $(R'_t - V(s_t; \theta_v)) \nabla_{\theta_\pi} \log \pi(a_t|s_t; \theta_\pi)$ is policy gradient which calculates the direction to update the policy such that the rewards of the agent will be improved.

4   Experiments

To evaluate the performance of the proposed model and study the impact of various factors on person search performance, we conduct extensive experiments on the large-scale person search dataset. In this section, we first describe the detailed experimental setup in Sect. 4.1. Then we compare the proposed model with the baseline algorithms in terms of Cumulative Matching Characteristics (CMC Top-K) and mean average precision (mAP). Afterwards, we conduct ablation study to analyze the effects of different components. Finally, we study the influence of gallery size.

4.1   Experimental Setup

Implementation Details: We use PyTorch to implement our model, and run the experiments on the NVIDIA TITAN Xp GPU. During training, 50 separate processes are used to run agents with environments, and one process to run policy and value network. When the training is finished, we fix the policy and value network for testing. A single agent is used to process each query for testing. For each query, we rank all the value V and retrieve the top ranked results.

Dataset Description: We test on the large-scale person search benchmark dataset provided by [12]. To the best of our knowledge, this is the only dataset available for person search. This dataset contains 8,432 labeled identities, who appear across different images. These people appear with full bodies and normal poses. Since person search problem mainly rely on body shapes and clothes rather than faces, the authors did not annotate people who change clothes and decorations in different video frames. This dataset has rich variations of pedestrian scales. The dataset is officially split into a training and a testing subset, without overlapping images between them. The test identity instances are divided into queries and galleries. We show the statistics of this dataset in Table 1.

Table 1. Statistics of the person search dataset with respect to training/test splits.

Split	# Images	# Pedestrians	# Identities
Training	11,206	55,272	5,532
Testing	6,978	40,871	2,900
Overall	18,184	96,143	8,432

Evaluation Protocols and Metrics: Following [12], we use two evaluation metrics to measure the performance, namely cumulative matching characteristics (CMC top-K) and mean averaged precision (mAP). The first metric has been widely used for the person re-id problem, where a matching is counted if there is at least one of the top-K predicted bounding boxes overlaps with the ground truths with intersection-over-union (IoU) greater or equal to 0.5. The second metric has been commonly used in the object detection tasks. The ILSVRC object detection criterion is used to judge the correctness of predicted bounding boxes. We calculate an averaged precision (AP) for each query based on the precision-recall curve, and then average the APs across all the queries to get the final result.

Compared Algorithms: To demonstrate the performance of our model, we first compare with the conventional methods for person search. These methods assume perfect pedestrian detection and break person search down into two separate tasks. We use two pedestrian detection methods and five pedestrian re-id approaches in the experiments. We use the off-the-shelf deep learning CCF detector [48] and Faster-RCNN (CNN) [49] with ResNet-50, specifically fine-tuned on the person search dataset. The ground truth (GT) bounding boxes are also used as the results a perfect detector. For pedestrian re-id, we used several well-known feature representations in the field, namely DenseSIFT-ColorHist (DSIFT) [16], Bag of Words (BoW) [50] and Local Maximal Occurrence (LOMO) [51]. We use each of the feature representation together with a specific distance metric learning algorithm, namely Euclidean, Cosine similarity, KISSME [52] and XQDA [51].

We also compare with a joint detection and identification feature learning algorithm [12], which jointly handles pedestrian detection and person re-id in a single CNN. To the best of our knowledge, this is the state-of-the-art person search algorithm in the literature. We drop the pedestrian proposal network, and train the remaining net to classify identities with Softmax loss from cropped pedestrian images, resulting another baseline method (IDNet), which has been exploited in [53].

4.2   Performance Comparison

We report the experimental results in Tables 2 and 3. We first compare the proposed framework with the conventional person search algorithms that break down the problem into two steps. From the experimental results shown in Tables 2 and 3, we can observe that our model performs much better than the compared baseline algorithms. The experimental results indicate that the pedestrian detector has a great impact on each person re-id algorithm. For example, for DSIFT + Euclidean, if an off-the-shelf detector (CCF) is used instead of a perfect detector (GT), the performance drops from 45.9% to 11.7%. This phenomenon confirms that it does not make sense to directly apply off-the-shelf pedestrian detector for the real-world person search problems. The incorrect detection result of the detector will deteriorate the subsequent re-id performance.

Table 2. Experimental comparisons for person search on the large-scale benchmark dataset. Cumulative matching characteristics (CMC top-K) is used as the evaluation metric. Results are shown in percentages. Larger CMC indicates better performance. The best results are marked in bold.

	CCF				CNN				GT			
	Top-1	Top-5	Top-10	Top-20	Top-1	Top-5	Top-10	Top-20	Top-1	Top-5	Top-10	Top-20
DSIFT + Euclidean	11.7	31.4	45.8	63.9	39.4	65.2	77.6	81.8	45.9	67.2	78.1	86.3
DSIFT + KISSME	13.9	34.2	48.7	66.4	53.6	68.8	78.5	86.4	61.9	74.2	83.5	88.7
BoW + Cosine	29.3	54.2	71.5	86.8	62.3	74.7	82.1	88.2	67.2	76.8	85.8	89.9
LOMO + XQDA	46.4	67.2	78.5	87.6	74.1	79.8	85.6	91.1	76.7	84.7	88.4	92.2
IDNet	57.1	80.2	90.1	95.6	74.8	80.7	87.9	93.0	78.3	85.6	89.1	94.3
Joint Detec. & Identifi.	–	–	–	–	78.7	83.6	90.5	95.2	80.5	87.8	91.2	96.3
RCAA	–	–	–	–	**81.3**	**88.2**	**92.4**	**97.6**	–	–	–	–

Table 3. Experimental comparisons for person search on the large-scale benchmark dataset. Mean average precision (mAP) is used as the evaluation metric. Results are shown in percentages. Larger mAP indicates better performance. The best results are marked in bold.

mAP (%)	CCF	CNN	GT
DSIFT + Euclidean	11.3	34.5	41.1
DSIFT + KISSME	13.4	47.8	56.2
BoW + Cosine	26.9	56.9	62.5
LOMO + XQDA	41.2	68.9	72.4
IDNet	50.9	68.6	73.1
Joint Detec. & Identifi.	–	75.7	77.9
RCAA	–	**79.3**	–

We can also find that the proposed model outperforms the joint detection and identification method by a large margin. For example, the proposed model outperforms Joint Detec. & Identifi. with mAP of 79.3 *vs* 75.7 on the benchmark dataset. We attribute this improvement to the end-to-end model and its ability to exploit relational context in the visual data. Also, since the proposed model is proposal-free, it is more efficient than the proposal-based methods.

Interestingly, we notice that the proposed model even outperforms the baseline algorithms using perfect pedestrian detectors (GT), which further confirms the superiority of our model for person search problem. For example, the proposed model outperforms Joint Detect. & Identifi. (with ground truth) with mAP of 79.3 *vs* 77.9.

We show some examples of our result on the benchmark dataset in Fig. 4. From the examples we can see that given a target person, the system can correctly retrieve and localize the required person from the gallery set.

Query   Results Retrieved from Gallery   Query   Results Retrieved from Gallery

Fig. 4. Example from the testing set of the benchmark dataset. The ground truth is the yellow bounding box. And the predicted box is the blue box. Best viewed in color.

4.3   Ablation Study

In this section, we conduct experiments to test the effect of the context, *i.e.* the relational spatial context and the temporal context, in the reinforcement learning algorithm. Note that the proposed model explores the relational context using a Relational Network, and the temporal context using an LSTM. We train two modified versions of the proposed model. The first one does not use the spatial and temporal context, which is denoted as "w/o spatial & temporal". The second does not consider the spatial context, which is denoted as "w/o spatial". The experimental results are reported in Table 4. From the experimental results we observe that both the spatial and temporal context plays a vital role in the proposed model.

We also compare with the global context proposed in [22]. We feed the feature maps into a RoI pooling layer, following by a global average pooling layer, resulting in global feature. We replaced the relational feature with the global feature, which is denoted as "w. global + temporal". The experimental results shown in Table 4 confirms that relational context achieves better performance than global context for person search problem.

4.4   The Influence of Gallery Size

Intuitively, the person search problem will become extremely challenging when the gallery size increases sharply. In this section, we vary the gallery size from 50 to full set of 6,978 images to test the influence of gallery size. We report the experimental results in terms of CMC top-1 and mAP in Fig. 5. When we

Table 4. Comparison between our model and other variants for person search problem. CMC Top-K and mAP are reported in this table. Performance is reported in percentages. Larger number indicates better performance. The best performance is marked in bold.

	CMC Top-K				mAP
	Top-1	Top-5	top-10	Top-20	
(w/o both)	72.5	79.4	83.2	86.9	69.8
(w/o relational spatial)	74.8	81.6	85.5	88.2	71.4
(w. global + temporal)	78.9	85.7	89.4	93.6	76.7
(Ours full)	**81.3**	**88.2**	**92.4**	**97.6**	**79.3**

process each query, we randomly select the corresponding gallery images from the full set.

From the experimental results, we have the following observations: (1) as the gallery size increases, the performance of all the compared algorithms decreases; (2) the proposed model outperforms the other compared algorithms by a large margin with right to different gallery sizes.

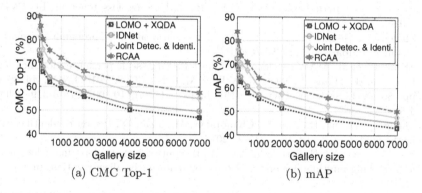

(a) CMC Top-1   (b) mAP

Fig. 5. The performance variance with right to different gallery sizes. The performance is reported in percentages.

5   Conclusions and Future Work

In this paper, we have made the earliest attempt to address the person search problem and built the first deep reinforcement learning based person search framework. Unlike previous works which rely on pedestrian proposal net, our approach leverages the relational context information and exploits the visual information and the query person a priori in a joint framework. We have conducted extensive experiments to evaluate the performance of our model. The experimental results confirm its superiority.

In the future we plan to exploit lenient learning [54] in our framework as stored transitions can become outdated due to agents updating their respective policies in parallel.

Acknowledgements. This work was supported in part by the Intelligence Advanced Research Projects Activity (IARPA) via Department of Interior/Interior Business Center (DOI/IBC) contract number D17PC00340, in part by China National 973 program 2014CB340301, and in part by the Data to Decisions CRC (D2D CRC) and the Cooperative Research Centres Programme. The U.S. Government is authorized to reproduce and distribute reprints for Governmental purposes notwithstanding any copyright annotation/herein. Disclaimer: The views and conclusions contained herein are those of the authors and should not be interpreted as necessarily representing the official policies or endorsements, either expressed or implied, of IARPA, DOI/IBC, or the U.S. Government.

References

1. Cheng, D., Chang, X., Liu, L., Hauptmann, A.G., Gong, Y., Zheng, N.: Discriminative dictionary learning with ranking metric embedded for person re-identification. In: IJCAI (2017)
2. Cheng, D., Gong, Y., Zhou, S., Wang, J., Zheng, N.: Person re-identification by multi-channel parts-based CNN with improved triplet loss function. In: CVPR (2016)
3. Zheng, W., Gong, S., Xiang, T.: Person re-identification by probabilistic relative distance comparison. In: CVPR (2011)
4. Zheng, L., et al.: MARS: a video benchmark for large-scale person re-identification. In: Leibe, B., Matas, J., Sebe, N., Welling, M. (eds.) ECCV 2016. LNCS, vol. 9910, pp. 868–884. Springer, Cham (2016). https://doi.org/10.1007/978-3-319-46466-4_52
5. Zheng, L., Zhang, H., Sun, S., Chandraker, M., Tian, Q.: Person re-identification in the wild. CoRR abs/1604.02531 (2016)
6. Yu, S., Yang, Y., Hauptmann, A.G.: Harry potter's marauder's map: localizing and tracking multiple persons-of-interest by nonnegative discretization. In: CVPR (2013)
7. Li, W., Wang, X.: Locally aligned feature transforms across views. In: CVPR (2013)
8. Li, W., Zhao, R., Xiao, T., Wang, X.: Deepreid: deep filter pairing neural network for person re-identification. In: CVPR (2014)
9. Zheng, W., Gong, S., Xiang, T.: Associating groups of people. In: BMVC (2009)
10. Xu, Y., Ma, B., Huang, R., Lin, L.: Person search in a scene by jointly modeling people commonness and person uniqueness. In: MM. ACM (2014)
11. Xiao, T., Li, S., Wang, B., Lin, L., Wang, X.: End-to-end deep learning for person search. CoRR abs/1604.01850 (2016)
12. Xiao, T., Li, S., Wang, B., Lin, L., Wang, X.: Joint detection and identification feature learning for person search. In: CVPR (2017)
13. Santoro, A., et al.: A simple neural network module for relational reasoning. CoRR abs/1706.01427 (2017)
14. Caicedo, J.C., Lazebnik, S.: Active object localization with deep reinforcement learning. In: ICCV (2015)

15. Wang, X., Doretto, G., Sebastian, T., Rittscher, J., Tu, P.H.: Shape and appearance context modeling. In: ICCV (2007)
16. Zhao, R., Ouyang, W., Wang, X.: Unsupervised salience learning for person re-identification. In: CVPR (2013)
17. Khamis, S., Kuo, C.-H., Singh, V.K., Shet, V.D., Davis, L.S.: Joint learning for attribute-consistent person re-identification. In: Agapito, L., Bronstein, M.M., Rother, C. (eds.) ECCV 2014. LNCS, vol. 8927, pp. 134–146. Springer, Cham (2015). https://doi.org/10.1007/978-3-319-16199-0_10
18. Liao, S., Li, S.Z.: Efficient PSD constrained asymmetric metric learning for person re-identification. In: ICCV (2015)
19. Pedagadi, S., Orwell, J., Velastin, S.A., Boghossian, B.A.: Local fisher discriminant analysis for pedestrian re-identification. In: CVPR (2013)
20. Krizhevsky, A., Sutskever, I., Hinton, G.E.: Imagenet classification with deep convolutional neural networks. In: NIPS (2012)
21. Simonyan, K., Zisserman, A.: Very deep convolutional networks for large-scale image recognition. In: ICLR (2015)
22. He, K., Zhang, X., Ren, S., Sun, J.: Deep residual learning for image recognition. In: CVPR (2016)
23. Yi, D., Lei, Z., Liao, S., Li, S.Z.: Deep metric learning for person re-identification. In: ICPR (2014)
24. Ahmed, E., Jones, M.J., Marks, T.K.: An improved deep learning architecture for person re-identification. In: CVPR (2015)
25. Ding, S., Lin, L., Wang, G., Chao, H.: Deep feature learning with relative distance comparison for person re-identification. Pattern Recogn. **48**(10), 2993–3003 (2015)
26. Felzenszwalb, P.F., Girshick, R.B., McAllester, D.A., Ramanan, D.: Object detection with discriminatively trained part-based models. IEEE Trans. Pattern Anal. Mach. Intell. **32**(9), 1627–1645 (2010)
27. Dollár, P., Appel, R., Belongie, S.J., Perona, P.: Fast feature pyramids for object detection. IEEE Trans. Pattern Anal. Mach. Intell. **36**(8), 1532–1545 (2014)
28. Zhang, S., Benenson, R., Schiele, B.: Filtered channel features for pedestrian detection. In: CVPR (2015)
29. Cai, Z., Saberian, M.J., Vasconcelos, N.: Learning complexity-aware cascades for deep pedestrian detection. In: ICCV (2015)
30. Tian, Y., Luo, P., Wang, X., Tang, X.: Pedestrian detection aided by deep learning semantic tasks. In: CVPR (2015)
31. Ouyang, W., Wang, X.: A discriminative deep model for pedestrian detection with occlusion handling. In: CVPR
32. Luo, P., Tian, Y., Wang, X., Tang, X.: Switchable deep network for pedestrian detection. In: CVPR (2014)
33. Sutton, R.S.: Introduction to Reinforcement Learning, vol. 135
34. Mnih, V., et al.: Playing atari with deep reinforcement learning. CoRR (2013)
35. Silver, D., Huang, A., Maddison, C.J., Guez, A., Sifre, L., van den Driessche, G., et al.: Mastering the game of go with deep neural networks and tree search. Nature **529**(7587), 484–489 (2016)
36. Jayaraman, D., Grauman, K.: Look-Ahead before you leap: end-to-end active recognition by forecasting the effect of motion. In: Leibe, B., Matas, J., Sebe, N., Welling, M. (eds.) ECCV 2016. LNCS, vol. 9909, pp. 489–505. Springer, Cham (2016). https://doi.org/10.1007/978-3-319-46454-1_30
37. Yun, S., Choi, J., Yoo, Y., Yun, K., Choi, J.Y.: Action-decision networks for visual tracking with deep reinforcement learning. In: ICCV (2017)

38. van Hasselt, H., Guez, A., Silver, D.: Deep reinforcement learning with double Q-learning. In: AAAI (2016)
39. Wang, Z., Schaul, T., Hessel, M., van Hasselt, H., Lanctot, M., de Freitas, N.: Dueling network architectures for deep reinforcement learning. In: ICML (2016)
40. Williams, R.J.: Simple statistical gradient-following algorithms for connectionist reinforcement learning. Mach. Learn. **8**, 229–256 (1992)
41. Russakovsky, O., Deng, J., Su, H., Krause, J., Satheesh, S., et al.: Imagenet large scale visual recognition challenge. Int. J. Comput. Vis. **115**(3), 211–252 (2015)
42. He, K., Zhang, X., Ren, S., Sun, J.: Spatial pyramid pooling in deep convolutional networks for visual recognition. IEEE Trans. Pattern Anal. Mach. Intell. **37**(9), 1904–1916 (2015)
43. Jie, Z., Liang, X., Feng, J., Jin, X., Lu, W., Yan, S.: Tree-structured reinforcement learning for sequential object localization. In: NIPS (2016)
44. Ng, A.Y., Harada, D., Russell, S.J.: Policy invariance under reward transformations: theory and application to reward shaping. In: Proceedings of the Sixteenth International Conference on Machine Learning (ICML 1999), Bled, Slovenia, 27–30 June 1999, pp. 278–287 (1999)
45. Mnih, V., et al.: Asynchronous methods for deep reinforcement learning. In: ICML (2016)
46. Geng, M., Wang, Y., Xiang, T., Tian, Y.: Deep transfer learning for person re-identification. CoRR abs/1611.05244 (2016)
47. Kingma, D.P., Ba, J.: Adam: a method for stochastic optimization. In: ICLR (2015)
48. Yang, B., Yan, J., Lei, Z., Li, S.Z.: Convolutional channel features. In: ICCV (2015)
49. Ren, S., He, K., Girshick, R.B., Sun, J.: Faster R-CNN: towards real-time object detection with region proposal networks. In: NIPS (2015)
50. Zheng, L., Shen, L., Tian, L., Wang, S., Wang, J., Tian, Q.: Scalable person re-identification: a benchmark. In: ICCV (2015)
51. Liao, S., Hu, Y., Zhu, X., Li, S.Z.: Person re-identification by local maximal occurrence representation and metric learning. In: CVPR (2015)
52. Köstinger, M., Hirzer, M., Wohlhart, P., Roth, P.M., Bischof, H.: Large scale metric learning from equivalence constraints. In: CVPR (2012)
53. Wang, Z., Li, H., Ouyang, W., Wang, X.: Learning deep representations for scene labeling with semantic context guided supervision. CoRR abs/1706.02493 (2017)
54. Potter, M.A., De Jong, K.A.: A cooperative coevolutionary approach to function optimization. In: Davidor, Y., Schwefel, H.-P., Männer, R. (eds.) PPSN 1994. LNCS, vol. 866, pp. 249–257. Springer, Heidelberg (1994). https://doi.org/10.1007/3-540-58484-6_269

Distractor-Aware Siamese Networks for Visual Object Tracking

Zheng Zhu[1,2] ⑮, Qiang Wang[1,2], Bo Li[3], Wei Wu[3(✉)], Junjie Yan[3], and Weiming Hu[1,2]

[1] University of Chinese Academy of Sciences, Beijing, China
[2] Institute of Automation, Chinese Academy of Sciences, Beijing, China
[3] SenseTime Group Limited, Beijing, China
wuwei@sensetime.com

Abstract. Recently, Siamese networks have drawn great attention in visual tracking community because of their balanced accuracy and speed. However, features used in most Siamese tracking approaches can only discriminate foreground from the non-semantic backgrounds. The semantic backgrounds are always considered as distractors, which hinders the robustness of Siamese trackers. In this paper, we focus on learning distractor-aware Siamese networks for accurate and long-term tracking. To this end, features used in traditional Siamese trackers are analyzed at first. We observe that the imbalanced distribution of training data makes the learned features less discriminative. During the off-line training phase, an effective sampling strategy is introduced to control this distribution and make the model focus on the semantic distractors. During inference, a novel distractor-aware module is designed to perform incremental learning, which can effectively transfer the general embedding to the current video domain. In addition, we extend the proposed approach for long-term tracking by introducing a simple yet effective local-to-global search region strategy. Extensive experiments on benchmarks show that our approach significantly outperforms the state-of-the-arts, yielding 9.6% relative gain in VOT2016 dataset and 35.9% relative gain in UAV20L dataset. The proposed tracker can perform at 160 FPS on short-term benchmarks and 110 FPS on long-term benchmarks.

Keywords: Visual tracking · Distractor-aware · Siamese networks

1 Introduction

Visual object tracking, which locates a specified target in a changing video sequence automatically, is a fundamental problem in many computer vision topics such as visual analysis, automatic driving and pose estimation. A core problem of tracking is how to detect and locate the object accurately and efficiently

---

The first three authors contributed equally to this work. This work is done when Zheng Zhu and Qiang Wang are interns at SenseTime Group Limited.

ⓒ Springer Nature Switzerland AG 2018
V. Ferrari et al. (Eds.): ECCV 2018, LNCS 11213, pp. 103–119, 2018.
https://doi.org/10.1007/978-3-030-01240-3_7

in challenging scenarios with occlusions, out-of-view, deformation, background cluttering and other variations [38].

Recently, Siamese networks, which follow a tracking by similarity comparison strategy, have drawn great attention in visual tracking community because of favorable performance [2,7,8,16,31,33,36,37]. SINT [31], GOTURN [8], SiamFC [2] and RASNet [36] learn a priori deep Siamese similarity function and use it in a run-time fixed way. CFNet [33] and DSiam [7] can online update the tracking model via a running average template and a fast transformation learning module, respectively. SiamRPN [16] introduces a region proposal network after the Siamese network, thus formulating the tracking as a one-shot local detection task.

Although these tracking approaches obtain balanced accuracy and speed, there are 3 problems that should be addressed: firstly, features used in most Siamese tracking approaches can only discriminate foreground from the non-semantic background. The semantic backgrounds are always considered as distractors, and the performance can not be guaranteed when the backgrounds are cluttered. Secondly, most Siamese trackers can not update the model [2,8,16,31,36]. Although their simplicity and fixed-model nature lead to high speed, these methods lose the ability to update the appearance model online which is often critical to account for drastic appearance changes in tracking scenarios. Thirdly, recent Siamese trackers employ a local search strategy, which can not handle the full occlusion and out-of-view challenges.

In this paper, we explore to learn Distractor-aware Siamese Region Proposal Networks (DaSiamRPN) for accurate and long-term tracking. SiamFC uses a weighted loss function to eliminate class imbalance of the positive and negative examples. However, it is inefficient as the training procedure is still dominated by easily classified background examples. In this paper, we identify that the imbalance of the *non-semantic* background and *semantic* distractor in the training data is the main obstacle for the representation learning. As shown in Fig. 1, the response maps on the SiamFC can not distinguish the people, even the athlete in the white dress can get a high similarity with the target person. High quality training data is crucial for the success of end-to-end learning tracker. We conclude that the quality of the representation network heavily depends on the distribution of training data. In addition to introducing positive pairs from existing large-scale detection datasets, we explicitly generate diverse semantic negative pairs in the training process. To further encourage discrimination, an effective data augmentation strategy customizing for visual tracking are developed.

After the offline training, the representation networks can generalize well to most categories of objects, which makes it possible to track general targets. During inference, classic Siamese trackers only use nearest neighbour search to match the positive templates, which might perform poorly when the target undergoes significant appearance changes and background clutters. Particularly, the presence of similar looking objects (distractors) in the context makes the tracking task more arduous. To address this problem, the surrounding contextual and temporal information can provide additional cues about the targets and help to maximize the discrimination abilities. In this paper, a novel distractor-aware module is designed, which can effectively transfer the general embedding to the current video domain and incrementally catch the target appearance variations during inference.

Besides, most recent trackers are tailored to short-term scenario, where the target object is always present. These works have focused exclusively on short sequences of a few tens of seconds, which is poorly representative of practitioners' needs. Except the challenging situations in short-term tracking, severe out-of-view and full occlusion introduce extra challenges in long-term tracking. Since conventional Siamese trackers lack discriminative features and adopt local search region, they are unable to handle these challenges. Benefiting from the learned distractor-aware features in DaSiamRPN, we extend the proposed approach for long-term tracking by introducing a simple yet effective local-to-global search region strategy. This significantly improves the performance of our tracker in out-of-view and full occlusion challenges.

We validate the effectiveness of proposed DaSiamRPN framework on extensive short-term and long-term tracking benchmarks: VOT2016 [14], VOT2017 [12], OTB2015 [38], UAV20L and UAV123 [22]. On short-term VOT2016 dataset, DaSiamRPN achieves a 9.6% relative gain in Expected Average Overlap compared to the top ranked method ECO [3]. On long-term UAV20L dataset, DaSiamRPN obtains 61.7% in Area Under Curve which outperforms the current best-performing tracker by relative 35.9%. Besides the favorable performance, our tracker can perform at far beyond real-time speed: 160 FPS on short-term datasets and 110 FPS on long-term datasets. All these consistent improvements demonstrate that the proposed approach establish a new state-of-the-art in visual tracking.

1.1   Contributions

The contributions of this paper can be summarized in three folds as follows:

1, The features used in conventional Siamese trackers are analyzed in detail. And we find that the imbalance of the *non-semantic* background and *semantic* distractor in the training data is the main obstacle for the learning.

2, We propose a novel Distractor-aware Siamese Region Proposal Networks (DaSiamRPN) framework to learn distractor-aware features in the off-line training, and explicitly suppress distractors during the inference of online tracking.

3, We extend the DaSiamRPN to perform long-term tracking by introducing a simple yet effective local-to-global search region strategy, which significantly improves the performance of our tracker in out-of-view and full occlusion challenges. In comprehensive experiments of short-term and long-term visual tracking benchmarks, the proposed DaSiamRPN framework obtains state-of-the-art accuracy while performing at far beyond real-time speed.

2   Related Work

Siamese Networks Based Tracking. Siamese trackers follow a tracking by similarity comparison strategy. The pioneering work is SINT [31], which simply searches for the candidate most similar to the exemplar given in the starting frame, using a run-time fixed but learns a priori deep Siamese similarity function. As a follow-up work, Bertinetto et.al [2] propose a fully convolutional Siamese network (SiamFC) to estimate the feature similarity region-wise between two frames. RASNet [36] advances this similarity metric by learning the attention mechanism with a Residual Attentional Network. Different from SiamFC and RASNet, in GOTURN tracker [8], the motion between successive frames is predicted using a deep regression network. These threee trackers are able to perform at 86 FPS, 83FPS and 100 FPS respectively on GPU because no fine-tuning is performed online. CFNet [33] interprets the correlation filters as a differentiable layer in a Siamese tracking framework, thus achieving an end-to-end representation learning. But the performance improvement is limited compared with SiamFC. FlowTrack [40] exploits motion information in Siamese architecture to improve the feature representation and the tracking accuracy. It is worth noting that CFNet and FlowTrack can efficiently online update the tracking model. Recently, SiamRPN [16] formulates the tracking as a one-shot local detection task by introducing a region proposal network after a Siamese network, which is end-to-end trained off-line with large-scale image pairs.

Features for Tracking. Visual features play a significant role in computer vision tasks including visual tracking. Possegger et.al [26] propose a distractor-aware model term to suppress visually distracting regions, while the color histograms features used in their framework are less robust than the deep features. DLT [35] is the seminal deep learning tracker which uses a multi-layer autoencoder network. The feature is pretrained on part of the 80M Tiny Image dataset [32] in an unsupervised fashion. Wang et al. [34] learn a two-layer neural network on a video repository, where temporally slowness constraints are imposed for feature learning. DeepTrack [17] learns two-layer CNN classifiers from binary samples and does not require a pre-training procedure. UCT [39] formulates the features learning and tracking process into a unified framework, enabling learned features are tightly coupled to tracking process.

Long-Term Tracking. Traditional long-term tracking frameworks can be divided into two groups: earlier methods regard tracking as local key point descriptors matching with a geometrical model [21, 24, 25], and recent approaches perform long-term tracking by combining a short-term tracker with a detector. The seminal work of latter categories is TLD [10], which proposes a memory-less flock of flows as a short-term tracker and a template-based detector run in parallel. Ma et al. [20]propose a combination of KCF tracker and a random ferns classifier as a detector that is used to correct the tracker. Similarly, MUSTer [9] is a long-term tracking framework that combines KCF tracker with a SIFT-based detector that is also used to detect occlusions. Fan and Ling [6] combines a DSST tracker [4] with a CNN detector [31] that verifies and potentially corrects proposals of the short-term tracker.

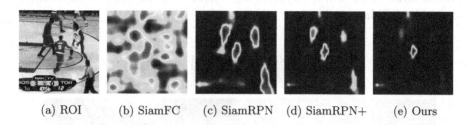

(a) ROI   (b) SiamFC   (c) SiamRPN   (d) SiamRPN+   (e) Ours

Fig. 1. Visualization of the response heatmaps of Siamese network trackers. (a) shows the search images. (b–e) show the heatmaps that produced by SiamFC, SiamRPN, SiamRPN+ (trained with distractors) and the DaSiamRPN.

3 Distractor-Aware Siamese Networks

3.1 Features and Drawbacks in Traditional Siamese Networks

Before the detailed discussion of our proposed framework, we first revisit the features of conventional Siamese network based tracking [2,16]. Siamese trackers use metric learning at their core. The goal is to learn an embedding space that can maximize the interclass inertia between different objects and minimize the intraclass inertia for the same object. The key contribution leading to the popularity and success of Siamese trackers is their balanced accuracy and speed.

Figure 1 visualizes of response maps of SiamFC and SiamRPN. It can be seen that for the targets, those with large differences in the background also achieve high scores, and even some extraneous objects get high scores. The representations obtained in SiamFC usually serve the discriminative learning of the categories in training data. In SiamFC and SiamRPN, pairs of training data come from different frames of the same video, and for each search area, the *non-semantic* background occupies the majority, while semantic entities and distractor occupy less. This imbalanced distribution makes the training model hard to learn instance-level representation, but tending to learn the differences between foreground and background.

During inference, nearest neighbor is used to search the most similar object in the search region, while the background information labelled in the first frame are omitted. The background information in the tracking sequences can be effectively utilized to increase the discriminative capability as shown in Fig. 1e.

To eliminate these issues, we propose to actively generate more semantics pairs in the offline training process and explicitly suppress the distractors in the online tracking.

3.2 Distractor-Aware Training

High quality training data is crucial for the success of end-to-end representation learning in visual tracking. We introduce series of strategies to improve the generalization of the learned features and eliminate the imbalanced distribution of the training data.

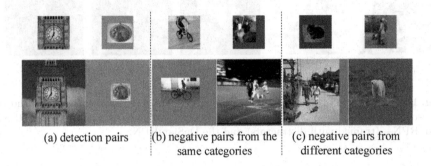

(a) detection pairs   (b) negative pairs from the   (c) negative pairs from
same categories   different categories

Fig. 2. (a) Positive pairs generated from detection datasets through augmenting still images. (b) negative pairs from the same category. (c) negative pairs from different categories.

Diverse Categories of Positive Pairs Can Promote the Generalization Ability. The original SiamFC is trained on the ILSVRC video detection datasets, which consists of only about 4,000 videos annotated frame-by-frame [28]. Recently, SiamRPN [16] explores to use sparsely labelled Youtube-BB [27] videos which consists of more than 200,000 videos annotated once in every 30 frames. In these two methods, target pairs of training data come from different frames in the same video. However, these video detection datasets only contain few categories (20 for VID [28], 30 for Youtube-BB [27]), which is not sufficient to train high-quality and generalized features for Siamese tracking. Besides, the bounding box regression branch in the SiamRPN may get inferior predictions when encountering new categories. Since labelling videos is time-consuming and expensive, in this paper, we greatly expand the categories of positive pairs by introducing large-scale ImageNet Detection [28] and COCO Detection [18] datasets. As shown in Fig. 2(a), through augmentation techniques (translation, resize, grayscale et.al), still images from detection datasets can be used to generate image pairs for training. The diversity of positive pairs is able to improve the tracker's discriminative ability and regression accuracy.

Semantic Negative Pairs Can Improve the Discriminative Ability. We attribute the less discriminative representation in SiamFC [2] and SiamRPN [16] to two level of imbalanced training data distribution. The first imbalance is the rare semantic negative pairs. Since the background occupies the majority in the training data of SiamFC and SiamRPN, most negative samples are non-semantic

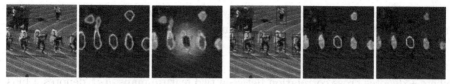

(a) General Siamese tracker   (b) Distractor-aware Siamese tracker

Fig. 3. Illustrations of our proposed Distractor-aware Siamese Region Proposal Networks (DaSiamRPN). The target and the background information are fully utilized in DaSiamRPN, which can suppress the influence of distractor during tracking.

(not real object, just background), and they can be easily classified. That is to say, SiamFC and SiamRPN learn the differences between foreground and background, and the losses between semantic objects are overwhelmed by the vast number of easy negatives. Another imbalance comes from the intraclass distractors, which usually perform as hard negative samples in the tracking process. In this paper, semantic negative pairs are added into the training process. The constructed negative pairs consist of labelled targets both in the same categories and different categories. The negative pairs from different categories can help tracker to avoid drifting to arbitrary objects in challenges such as out-of-view and full occlusion, while negative pairs from the same categories make the tracker focused on fine-grained representation. The negative examples are shown in Fig. 2(b) and (c).

Customizing Effective Data Augmentation for Visual Tracking. To unleash the full potential of the Siamese network, we customize several data augmentation strategies for training. Except the common translation, scale variations and illumination changes, we observe that the motion pattern can be easily modeled by the shallow layers in the network. We explicitly introduce motion blur in the data augmentation.

3.3 Distractor-Aware Incremental Learning

The training strategy in the last subsection can significantly improve the discrimination power on the offline training process. However, it is still hard to distinguish two objects with the similar attributes like Fig. 3a. SiamFC and SiamRPN use a cosine window to suppress the distractors. In this way, the performance is not guaranteed when the motion of objects are messy. Most existing Siamese network based approaches provide inferior performance when encountering with fast motion or background clutter. In summary, the potential flaw is mainly due to the misalignment of the general representation domain and the specific target domains. In this section, we propose a distractor-aware module to effectively transfer the general representation to the video domain.

The Siamese tracker learns a similarity metric $f(z, x)$ to compare an exemplar image z to a candidate image x in the embedding space φ:

$$f(z, x) = \varphi(z) \star \varphi(x) + b \cdot \mathbb{1} \tag{1}$$

where $\star$ denotes cross correlation between two feature maps, $b \cdot \mathbb{1}$ denotes a bias which is equated in every location. The most similar object of the exemplar will be selected as the target.

To make full use of the label information, we integrate the hard negative samples (distractors) in context of the target into the similarity metric. In DaSiamRPN, the Non Maximum Suppression (NMS) is adopted to select the potential distractors d_i in each frames, and then we collect a distractor set $\mathcal{D} := \{\forall d_i \in \mathcal{D}, f(z, d_i) > h \cap d_i \neq z_t\}$, where h is the predefined threshold, z_t is the selected target in frame t and the number of this set $|\mathcal{D}| = n$. Specifically, we get $17 * 17 * 5$ proposals in each frame at first, and then we use NMS to reduce redundant candidates. The proposal with highest score will be selected as the target z_t. For the remaining, the proposals with scores greater than a threshold are selected as distractors.

After that, we introduce a novel distractor-aware objective function to *re-rank* the proposals $\mathcal{P}$ which have *top-k* similarities with the exemplar. The final selected object is denoted as q:

$$q = \underset{p_k \in \mathcal{P}}{argmax} \ \ f(z, p_k) - \frac{\hat{\alpha} \sum_{i=1}^{n} \alpha_i f(d_i, p_k)}{\sum_{i=1}^{n} \alpha_i} \tag{2}$$

the weight factor $\hat{\alpha}$ control the influence of the distractor learning, the weight factor α_i is used to control the influence for each distractor d_i. It is worth noting that the computational complexity and memory usage increase n times by a direct calculation. Since cross correlation operation in the Eq. (1) is a linear operator, we utilize this property to speed up the distractor-aware objective:

$$q = \underset{p_k \in \mathcal{P}}{argmax} \ \ (\varphi(z) - \frac{\hat{\alpha} \sum_{i=1}^{n} \alpha_i \varphi(d_i)}{\sum_{i=1}^{n} \alpha_i}) \star \varphi(p_k) \tag{3}$$

it enables the tracker run in the comparable speed in comparisons with SiamRPN. This associative law also inspires us to incrementally learn the target templates and distractor templates with a learning rate β_t:

$$q_{T+1} = \underset{p_k \in \mathcal{P}}{argmax} \ \ (\frac{\sum_{t=1}^{T} \beta_t \varphi(z_t)}{\sum_{t=1}^{T} \beta_t} - \frac{\sum_{t=1}^{T} \beta_t \hat{\alpha} \sum_{i=1}^{n} \alpha_i \varphi(d_{i,t})}{\sum_{t=1}^{T} \beta_t \sum_{i=1}^{n} \alpha_i}) \star \varphi(p_k) \tag{4}$$

This distractor-aware tracker can adapt the existing similarity metric (general) to a similarity metric for a new domain (specific). The weight factor α_i can be viewed as the dual variables with sparse regularization, and the exemplars and distractors can be viewed as positive and negative samples in correlation filters. Actually, an online classifier is modeled in our framework. So the adopted classifier is expected to perform better than these only use general similarity metric.

3.4   DaSiamRPN for Long-Term Tracking

In this section, the DaSiamRPN framework is extended for long-term tracking. Besides the challenging situations in short-term tracking, severe out-of-view and full occlusion introduce extra challenges in long-term tracking, which are shown in Fig. 4. The search region in short-term tracking (SiamRPN) can not cover the target when it reappears, thus failing to track the following frames. We propose a simple yet effective switch method between short-term tracking phase and failure cases. In failure cases, an iterative local-to-global search strategy is designed to re-detect the target.

In order to perform switches, we need to identify the beginning and the end of failed tracking. Since the distractor-aware training and inference enable high-quality detection score, it can be adopted to indicate the quality of tracking results. Figure 4 shows the detection scores and according tracking overlaps in SiamRPN and DaSiamRPN. The detection scores of SiamRPN are not indicative, which can be still high even in out-of-view and full occlusion. That is to say, SiamRPN tends to find an arbitrary objectness in these challenges which causes drift in tracking. In DaSiamRPN, detection scores successfully indicate status of the tracking phase.

During failure cases, we gradually increase the search region by local-to-global strategy. Specifically, the size of search region is iteratively growing with a constant step when failed tracking is indicated. As shown in Fig. 4, the local-to-global search region covers the target to recover the normal tracking. It is worth noting that our tracker employs bounding box regression to detect the target, so the time-consuming image pyramids strategy can be discarded. In experiments, the proposed DaSiamRPN can perform at 110 FPS on long-term tracking benchmark.

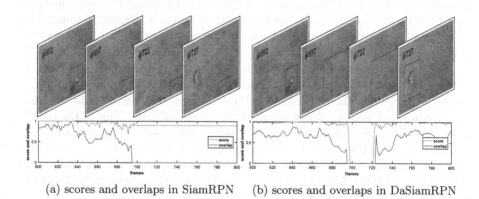

(a) scores and overlaps in SiamRPN   (b) scores and overlaps in DaSiamRPN

Fig. 4. The tracking results of video *person7* in out-of-view challenge. First row: tracking snapshots of SiamRPN and DaSiamRPN. Second row: detection scores and according overlaps of the two methods. The overlaps are defined as intersection-over-union (IOU) between tracking results and ground truth. Red: ground truth. Green: tracking box. Blue: Search region box. (Color figure online)

4   Experiments

Experiments are performed on extensive challenging tracking datasets, including VOT2015 [13], VOT2016 [14] and VOT2017 [12], each with 60 videos, UAV20L [22] with 20 long-term videos, UAV123 [22] with 123 videos and OTB2015 [38] with 100 videos. All the tracking results are provided by official implementations to ensure a fair comparison.

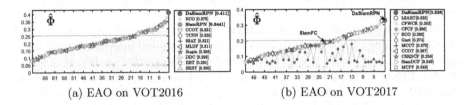

(a) EAO on VOT2016   (b) EAO on VOT2017

Fig. 5. Expected average overlap plot for VOT2016 (a) and VOT2017 (b).

4.1   Experimental Details

The modified AlexNet [15] pretrained using ImageNet [28] is used as described in SiamRPN [16]. The parameters of the first three convolution layers are fixed and only the last two convolution layers are fine-tuned. There are totally 50 epoches performed and the learning rate is decreased in log space from 10^{-2} to 10^{-4}. We extract image pairs from VID [28] and Youtube-BB [27] by choosing frames with interval less than 100 and performing crop procedure as described in Sect. 3.2. In ImageNet Detection [28] and COCO Detection [18] datasets, image pairs are generated for training by augmenting still images. To handle the gray videos in benchmarks, 25% of the pairs are converted to grayscale during training. The translation is randomly performed within 12 pixels, and the range of random resize varies from 0.85 to 1.15.

During inference phase, the distractor factor $\hat{\alpha}$ in Eq. (2) is set to 0.5, α_i is set to 1 for each distractor, and the incremental learning factor β_t in Eq. (4) is set to $\sum_{i=0}^{t-1}(\frac{\eta}{1-\eta})^i$, where $\eta = 0.01$. In the long-term tracking, we find that one step iteration of local-to-global is sufficient. Specifically, the sizes of the search region in short-term phase and defined failure cases are set to 255 and 767, respectively. The thresholds to enter and leave failure cases are set to 0.8 and 0.95. Our experiments are implemented using PyTorch on a PC with an Intel i7, 48G RAM, NVIDIA TITAN X. The proposed tracker can perform at 160 FPS on short-term benchmarks and 110 FPS on long-term benchmarks.

4.2   State-of-the-Art Comparisons on VOT Datasets

In this section the latest version of the Visual Object Tracking toolkit (*vot2017-challenge*) is used. The toolkit applies a reset-based methodology. Whenever a failure (zero overlap with the ground truth) is detected, the tracker is re-initialized five frames after the failure. The performance is measured in terms of accuracy (A), robustness (R), and expected average overlap (EAO). In addition, VOT2017 also introduces a real-time experiment. We report all these metrics compared with a number of the latest state-of-the-art trackers on VOT2015, VOT2016 and VOT2017.

The EAO curve evaluated on VOT2016 is presented in Fig. 5a and 70 other state-of-the-art trackers are compared. The EAO of our baseline tracker SiamRPN on VOT2016 is 0.3441, which already outperforms most of state-of-the-arts. However, there is still a gap compared with the top-ranked tracker ECO (0.375), which improves continuous convolution operators on multi-level feature maps. Most remarkably, the proposed DaSiamRPN obtains a EAO of 0.411, out-performing state-of-the-arts by relative 9.6%. Furthermore, our tracker runs at state-of-the-art speed with 160FPS, which is 500× faster than C-COT and 20× faster than ECO.

For the evaluation on VOT2017, Fig. 5b reports the results of ours against 51 other state-of-the-art trackers with respect to the EAO score. DaSiamRPN ranks first with an EAO score of 0.326. Among the top 5 trackers, CFWCR, CFCF, ECO, and Gnet apply continuous convolution operator as the baseline approach. The top performer LSART [30] decomposes the target into patches and applies a weighted combination of patch-wise similarities into a kernelized ridge regression. While our method is conceptually much simpler, powerful and is also easy to follow.

Figure 5b also reveals the EAO values in the real-time experiment denoted by red points. Our tracker obviously is the top-performer with a real-time EAO of 0.326 and outperforms the latest state-of-the-art real-time tracker CSRDCF++ by relative 53.8%.

Table 1 shows accuracy (A) and robustness (R), as well as expected average overlap (EAO) on VOT2015, VOT2016 and VOT2017. The baseline approach SiamRPN can process an astounding 200 frames per second while still getting an comparable performance with the state-of-the-arts. We find the performance gains of SiamRPN are mainly due to their accurate multi-anchors regression mechanism. We propose the distractor-aware module to improve the robustness, which can make our tracker much more harmonious. As a result, our approach, with the EAO of 0.446, 0.411 and 0.326 on three benchmarks, outperforms all the existing trackers by a large margin. We believe that the consistent improvements demonstrate that our approach makes real contributions by both the training process and online inference.

4.3   State-of-the-Art Comparisons on UAV Datasets

The UAV [22] videos are captured from low-altitude unmanned aerial vehicles. The dataset contains a long-term evaluation subset UAV20L and a short-term evaluation subset UAV123. The evaluation is based on two metrics: precision plot and success plot.

Table 1. Performance comparisons on public short-term benchmarks. OP: mean overlap precision at the threshold of 0.5; DP: mean distance precision of 20 pixels; EAO: expected average overlap, and mean speed (FPS). The red bold fonts and *blue italic* fonts indicate the best and the second best performance.

Trackers	OTB-2015		VOT2015			VOT2016			VOT2017			FPS
	OP	DP	A	R	EAO	A	R	EAO	A	R	EAO	
SiamFC	73.0	77.0	0.533	0.88	0.289	0.53	0.46	0.235	0.50	0.59	0.188	86
CFNet	69.9	74.7	-	-	-	-	-	-	-	-	-	75
Staple	70.9	78.4	0.57	1.39	0.300	0.54	0.38	0.295	*0.52*	0.69	0.169	80
CSRDCF	70.7	78.7	0.56	0.86	0.320	0.51	0.24	0.338	0.49	0.36	0.256	13
BACF	76.7	81.5	0.59	1.56	-	-	-	-	-	-	-	35
ECO-HC	78.4	85.6	-	-	-	0.54	0.30	0.322	0.49	0.44	0.238	60
CREST	77.5	83.7	-	-	-	0.51	0.25	0.283	-	-	-	1
MDNet	*85.4*	*90.9*	*0.60*	*0.69*	*0.378*	0.54	0.34	0.257	-	-	-	1
C-COT	82.0	89.8	0.54	0.82	0.303	0.54	0.24	0.331	0.49	*0.32*	0.267	0.3
ECO	84.9	91.0	-	-	-	0.55	0.20	*0.375*	0.48	0.27	*0.280*	8
SiamRPN	81.9	85.0	0.58	1.13	0.349	*0.56*	0.26	0.344	0.49	0.46	0.244	200
Ours	86.5	88.0	0.63	0.66	0.446	0.61	*0.22*	0.411	0.56	0.34	0.326	*160*

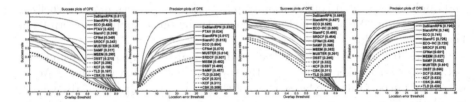

Fig. 6. Success and precision plots on UAV [22] dataset. First and second sub-figures are results of UAV20L, third and last sub-figures are results of UAV123.

Results on UAV20L. UAV20L is a long-term tracking benchmark that contains 20 sequences with average sequence length 2934 frames. Besides the challenging situations in short-term tracking, severe out-of-view and full occlusion introduce extra challenges. In this experiment, the proposed method is compared against recent trackers in [22]. Besides, ECO [3] (state-of-the-art short-term tracker), PTAV [6] (state-of-the-art long-term tracker), SiamRPN [16] (the baseline), SiamFC [2] and CFNet [33] (representative Siamese trackers) are added for comparison.

The results including success plots and precision plots are illustrated in Fig. 6. It clearly illustrates that our algorithm, denoted by DaSiamRPN, outperforms the state-of-the-art trackers significantly in both measures. In the success plot, our approach obtains an AUC score of 0.617, significantly outperforming state-of-the-art short-term trackers SiamRPN [16] and ECO [3]. The improvement ranges are relative 35.9% and 41.8%, respectively. Compared with PTAV [6],

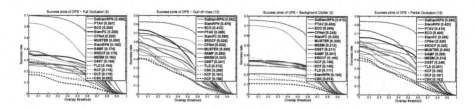

Fig. 7. Success plots with attributes on UAV20L. Best viewed on color display.

MUSTer [9] and TLD [10] which are qualified to perform long-term tracking, the proposed DaSiamRPN outperforms these trackers by relative 45.8%, 87.5% and 213.2%. In the precision plot, our approach obtains a score of 0.838, outperforming state-of-the-art long-term tracker (PTAV [6]) and short-term tracker (SiamRPN [16]) by relative 34.3% and 35.8%, respectively. The excellent performance of DaSiamRPN in this long-term tracking dataset can be attributed to the distractor-aware features and local-to-global search strategy.

For detailed performance analysis, we also report the results on various challenge attributes in UAV20L, i.e. full occlusion, out-of-view, background clutter and partial occlusion. Figure 7 demonstrates that our tracker effectively handles these challenging situations while other trackers obtain lower scores. Specially, in full occlusion and background clutter attributes, the proposed DaSiamRPN outperforms SiamRPN [16] by relative 153.1% and 393.2%.

Results on UAV123. UAV123 dataset includes 123 sequences with average sequence length of 915 frames. Besides the recent trackers in [22], ECO [3], PTAV [6], SiamRPN [16], SiamFC [2], CFNet [33] are added for comparison. Figure 6 illustrates the precision and success plots of the compared trackers. The proposed DaSiamRPN approach outperforms all the other trackers in terms of success and precision scores. Specifically, our method achieves a success score of 0.586, which outperforms the SiamRPN (0.527) and ECO (0.525) method with a large margin.

4.4 State-of-the-Art Comparisons on OTB Datasets

We evaluate the proposed algorithms with numerous fast and state-of-the-art trackers including SiamFC [2], CFNet [33], Staple [1], CSRDCF [19], BACF [11], ECO-HC [3], CREST [29], MDNet [23], CCOT [5], ECO [3], and the baseline tracker SiamRPN [16]. All the trackers are initialized with the ground-truth object state in the first frame. Mean overlap precision (OP) and mean distance precision (DP) are reported in Table 1.

Among the real-time trackers, SiamFC and CFNet are latest Siamese network based trackers while the accuracies is still left far behind the state-of-the-art BACF and ECO-HC with HOG features. The proposed DaSiamRPN tracker outperforms all these trackers by a large margin on both the accuracy and speed.

Table 2. Ablation analyses of our algorithm on VOT2016 [14] and UAV20L [22]

Component	SiamRPN	DaSiamRPN			
Positive pairs in detection data?		✓	✓	✓	✓
Semantic negative pairs?			✓	✓	✓
Distractor-aware updating?				✓	✓
Long-term tracking module?					✓
EAO in VOT2016	0.344	0.368	0.389	0.411	–
AUC in UAV20L(%)	45.4	47.2	48.6	49.8	61.7

For state-of-the-art comparisons on OTB, MDNet, trained on visual tracking datasets, performs the best against the other trackers at a speed of 1 FPS. C-COT and ECO achieve state-of-the-art performance, but their tracking speeds are not fast enough for real-time applications. The baseline tracker SiamRPN obtains an OP score of 81.9%, which is slightly less accurate than CCOT. The bottleneck of SiamRPN is its inferior robust performance. Since the distractor-aware mechanisms in both training and inference focus on improving the robustness, the proposed DaSiamRPN tracker achieves 3.0% improvement on DP and performs best OP score of 86.5% on OTB2015.

4.5   Ablation Analyses

To verify the contributions of each component in our algorithm, we implement and evaluate four variations of our approach. Analyses results include EAO on VOT2016 [14] and AUC on UAV20L [22].

As shown in Table 2, SiamRPN is our baseline algorithm. In VOT2016, the EAO criterion increases to 0.368 from 0.344 when detection data is added in training. Similarly, when negative pairs and distractor-aware learning are adopted in training and inference, both the performance increases by near 2%. In UAV20L, detection data, negative pairs in training and distractor-aware inference gain the performance by 1%–2%. The AUC criterion increases to 61.7% from 49.8% when long-term tracking module is adopted.

5   Conclusions

In this paper, we propose a distractor-aware Siamese framework for accurate and long-term tracking. During offline training, a distractor-aware feature learning scheme is proposed, which can significantly boost the discriminative power of the networks. During inference, a novel distractor-aware module is designed, effectively transferring the general embedding to the current video domain. In addition, we extend the proposed approach for long-term tracking by introducing a simple yet effective local-to-global search strategy. The proposed tracker obtains state-of-the-art accuracy in comprehensive experiments of short-term and long-term visual tracking benchmarks, while the overall system speed is still far from being real-time.

References

1. Bertinetto, L., Valmadre, J., Golodetz, S., Miksik, O., Torr, P.H.S.: Staple: complementary learners for real-time tracking. In: Proceedings of the IEEE Conference on Computer Vision and Pattern Recognition, June 2016
2. Bertinetto, L., Valmadre, J., Henriques, J.F., Vedaldi, A., Torr, P.H.S.: Fully-convolutional Siamese networks for object tracking. In: Hua, G., Jégou, H. (eds.) ECCV 2016. LNCS, vol. 9914, pp. 850–865. Springer, Cham (2016). https://doi.org/10.1007/978-3-319-48881-3_56
3. Danelljan, M., Bhat, G., Shahbaz Khan, F., Felsberg, M.: ECO: efficient convolution operators for tracking. In: Proceedings of the IEEE Conference on Computer Vision and Pattern Recognition, July 2017
4. Danelljan, M., Hger, G., Khan, F.S., Felsberg, M.: Accurate scale estimation for robust visual tracking. In: Proceedings of the British Machine Vision Conference, pp. 65.1–65.11 (2014)
5. Danelljan, M., Robinson, A., Shahbaz Khan, F., Felsberg, M.: Beyond correlation filters: learning continuous convolution operators for visual tracking. In: Leibe, B., Matas, J., Sebe, N., Welling, M. (eds.) ECCV 2016. LNCS, vol. 9909, pp. 472–488. Springer, Cham (2016). https://doi.org/10.1007/978-3-319-46454-1_29
6. Fan, H., Ling, H.: Parallel tracking and verifying: a framework for real-time and high accuracy visual tracking. In: Proceedings of the IEEE International Conference on Computer Vision (2017)
7. Guo, Q., Feng, W., Zhou, C., Huang, R., Wan, L., Wang, S.: Learning dynamic Siamese network for visual object tracking. In: Proceedings of the IEEE International Conference on Computer Vision, October 2017
8. Held, D., Thrun, S., Savarese, S.: Learning to track at 100 fps with deep regression networks. In: Leibe, B., Matas, J., Sebe, N., Welling, M. (eds.) ECCV 2016. LNCS, vol. 9905, pp. 749–765. Springer, Cham (2016). https://doi.org/10.1007/978-3-319-46448-0_45
9. Hong, Z., Chen, Z., Wang, C., Mei, X., Prokhorov, D., Tao, D.: MUlti-Store Tracker (MUSTer): a cognitive psychology inspired approach to object tracking. In: Proceedings of the IEEE Conference on Computer Vision and Pattern Recognition, pp. 749–758 (2015)
10. Kalal, Z., Mikolajczyk, K., Matas, J.: Tracking-learning-detection. IEEE Trans. Pattern Anal. Mach. Intell. 34(7), 1409–1422 (2012)
11. Kiani Galoogahi, H., Fagg, A., Lucey, S.: Learning background-aware correlation filters for visual tracking. In: Proceedings of the IEEE International Conference on Computer Vision, October 2017
12. Kristan, M., et al.: The visual object tracking VOT2017 challenge results. In: Proceedings of the The IEEE International Conference on Computer Vision Workshop, October 2017
13. Kristan, M., Matas, J., Leonardis, A., Felsberg, M.: The visual object tracking VOT2015 challenge results. In: Proceedings of the IEEE International Conference on Computer Vision Workshop, pp. 564–586 (2015)
14. Kristan, M., et al.: The visual object tracking VOT2016 challenge results. In: Hua, G., Jégou, H. (eds.) ECCV 2016. LNCS, vol. 9914, pp. 777–823. Springer, Cham (2016). https://doi.org/10.1007/978-3-319-48881-3_54
15. Krizhevsky, A., Sutskever, I., Hinton, G.E.: ImageNet classification with deep convolutional neural networks. In: Proceedings of the Advances in Neural Information Processing Systems, pp. 1097–1105 (2012)

16. Li, B., Yan, J., Wu, W., Zhu, Z., Hu, X.: High performance visual tracking with Siamese region proposal network. In: Proceedings of the IEEE Conference on Computer Vision and Pattern Recognition, pp. 8971–8980 (2018)
17. Li, H., Li, Y., Porikli, F.: DeepTrack: learning discriminative feature representations online for robust visual tracking. IEEE Trans. Image Process. **25**(4), 1834–1848 (2016)
18. Lin, T.-Y., et al.: Microsoft COCO: common objects in context. In: Fleet, D., Pajdla, T., Schiele, B., Tuytelaars, T. (eds.) ECCV 2014. LNCS, vol. 8693, pp. 740–755. Springer, Cham (2014). https://doi.org/10.1007/978-3-319-10602-1_48
19. Lukezic, A., Vojir, T., Zajc, L.C., Matas, J., Kristan, M.: Discriminative correlation filter with channel and spatial reliability. In: Proceedings of the IEEE Conference on Computer Vision and Pattern Recognition (2017)
20. Ma, C., Yang, X., Zhang, C., Yang, M.H.: Long-term correlation tracking. In: Proceedings of the IEEE Conference on Computer Vision and Pattern Recognition, pp. 5388–5396 (2015)
21. Maresca, M.E., Petrosino, A.: MATRIOSKA: a multi-level approach to fast tracking by learning. In: Petrosino, A. (ed.) ICIAP 2013. LNCS, vol. 8157, pp. 419–428. Springer, Heidelberg (2013). https://doi.org/10.1007/978-3-642-41184-7_43
22. Mueller, M., Smith, N., Ghanem, B.: A benchmark and simulator for UAV tracking. In: Leibe, B., Matas, J., Sebe, N., Welling, M. (eds.) ECCV 2016. LNCS, vol. 9905, pp. 445–461. Springer, Cham (2016). https://doi.org/10.1007/978-3-319-46448-0_27
23. Nam, H., Han, B.: Learning multi-domain convolutional neural networks for visual tracking. In: Proceedings of the IEEE Conference on Computer Vision and Pattern Recognition, June 2016
24. Nebehay, G., Pflugfelder, R.: Clustering of static-adaptive correspondences for deformable object tracking. In: Proceedings of the IEEE Conference on Computer Vision and Pattern Recognition, pp. 2784–2791 (2015)
25. Pernici, F., Del Bimbo, A.: Object tracking by oversampling local features. IEEE Trans. Pattern Anal. Mach. Intell. **36**(12), 2538–2551 (2014)
26. Possegger, H., Mauthner, T., Bischof, H.: In defense of color-based model-free tracking. In: Proceedings of the IEEE Conference on Computer Vision and Pattern Recognition, pp. 2113–2120 (2015)
27. Real, E., Shlens, J., Mazzocchi, S., Pan, X., Vanhoucke, V.: YouTube-BoundingBoxes: a large high-precision human-annotated data set for object detection in video. arXiv preprint arXiv:1702.00824 (2017)
28. Russakovsky, O., et al.: ImageNet large scale visual recognition challenge. Int. J. Comput. Vis. (IJCV) **115**(3), 211–252 (2015)
29. Song, Y., Ma, C., Gong, L., Zhang, J., Lau, R., Yang, M.H.: CREST: convolutional residual learning for visual tracking. In: Proceedings of the IEEE International Conference on Computer Vision (2017)
30. Sun, C., Lu, H., Yang, M.H.: Learning spatial-aware regressions for visual tracking. arXiv preprint arXiv:1706.07457 (2017)
31. Tao, R., Gavves, E., Smeulders, A.W.M.: Siamese instance search for tracking. In: Proceedings of the IEEE Conference on Computer Vision and Pattern Recognition, pp. 1420–1429 (2016)
32. Torralba, A., Fergus, R., Freeman, W.T.: 80 million tiny images: a large data set for nonparametric object and scene recognition. IEEE Trans. Pattern Anal. Mach. Intell. **30**(11), 1958–1970 (2008)

33. Valmadre, J., Bertinetto, L., Henriques, J.F., Vedaldi, A., Torr, P.H.S.: End-to-end representation learning for correlation filter based tracking. In: Proceedings of the IEEE Conference on Computer Vision and Pattern Recognition (2017)

34. Wang, L., Liu, T., Wang, G., Chan, K.L., Yang, Q.: Video tracking using learned hierarchical features. IEEE Trans. Image Process. **24**(4), 1424–1435 (2015)

35. Wang, N., Yeung, D.Y.: Learning a deep compact image representation for visual tracking. In: Proceedings of the Advances in Neural Information Processing Systems, pp. 809–817 (2013)

36. Wang, Q., Teng, Z., Xing, J., Gao, J., Hu, W., Maybank, S.: Learning attentions: Residual attentional Siamese network for high performance online visual tracking. In: The IEEE Conference on Computer Vision and Pattern Recognition, June 2018

37. Wang, Q., Zhang, M., Xing, J., Gao, J., Hu, W., Maybank, S.: Do not lose the details: reinforced representation learning for high performance visual tracking. In: 27th International Joint Conference on Artificial Intelligence

38. Wu, Y., Lim, J., Yang, M.H.: Object tracking benchmark. IEEE Trans. Pattern Anal. Mach. Intell. **37**(9), 1834–1848 (2015)

39. Zhu, Z., Huang, G., Zou, W., Du, D., Huang, C.: UCT: learning unified convolutional networks for real-time visual tracking. In: Proceedings of the IEEE International Conference on Computer Vision Workshops, October 2017

40. Zhu, Z., Wu, W., Zou, W., Yan, J.: End-to-end flow correlation tracking with spatial-temporal attention. arXiv preprint arXiv:1711.01124 (2017)

Face Recognition with Contrastive Convolution

Chunrui Han[1,2]📷, Shiguang Shan[1,3(✉)]📷, Meina Kan[1,3]📷, Shuzhe Wu[1,2]📷, and Xilin Chen[1]📷

[1] Key Lab of Intelligent Information Processing of Chinese Academy of Sciences, Institute of Computing Technology, CAS, Beijing 100190, China
{chunrui.han,shuzhe.wu}@vipl.ict.ac.cn,
{sgshan,kanmeina, xlchen}@ict.ac.cn
[2] University of Chinese Academy of Sciences, Beijing 100049, China
[3] CAS Center for Excellence in Brain Science and Intelligence Technology, Beijing, China

Abstract. In current face recognition approaches with convolutional neural network (CNN), a pair of faces to compare are independently fed into the CNN for feature extraction. For both faces the same kernels are applied and hence the representation of a face stays fixed regardless of whom it is compared with. As for us humans, however, one generally focuses on varied characteristics of a face when comparing it with distinct persons as shown in Fig. 1. Inspired, we propose a novel CNN structure with what we referred to as contrastive convolution, which specifically focuses on the distinct characteristics between the two faces to compare, i.e., those contrastive characteristics. Extensive experiments on the challenging LFW, and IJB-A show that our proposed contrastive convolution significantly improves the vanilla CNN and achieves quite promising performance in face verification task.

Keywords: Face recognition · Convolutional neural networks
Contrastive convolution · Kernel generator

1 Introduction

Face recognition is of great practical values as an effective approach for biometric authentication. The task of face recognition includes two categories, face identification which classifies a given face to a specific identity, and face verification which determines whether a pair of faces are of the same identity. The face verification task appears in a wide range of practical scenarios, e.g., phone unlocking with faces, remote bank account opening that uses faces for identity check, electronic payment with face, criminal tracking from surveillance cameras and etc. Though it has been studied for a long time, there still exist a great many challenges for accurate face verification, which is the focus of this work.

The most effective solutions for the face verification at present are employing the powerful CNN models. To verify whether a given pair of faces A and B are

© Springer Nature Switzerland AG 2018
V. Ferrari et al. (Eds.): ECCV 2018, LNCS 11213, pp. 120–135, 2018.
https://doi.org/10.1007/978-3-030-01240-3_8

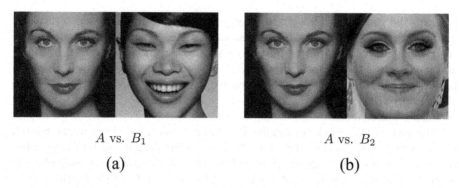

A vs. B_1 A vs. B_2

(a)   (b)

Fig. 1. Illustration of how we humans do face verification by focusing on distinct face characteristics when the same face A is compared with different persons. (a) When comparing A with B_1 who features small eyes, our focus is attracted to regions around the eyes of A; (b) when comparing A with B_2 whose face is round, we pay more attention to the contour of A. This reveals that a face should be described differently by using contrastive charateristics for example, when being compared with different persons.

of the same identity, most CNN-based methods generally first feed the two faces into a CNN to obtain their feature representations. Then, the similarity of the two features is calculated to determine whether they are the same person. Since the parameters of convolutional kernels are fixed once the training of CNN is completed, all faces are processed with identical kernels and thus mapped into a common discriminative feature space. This means that the representation of A stays unchanged regardless of who it is compared with, and this representation has to be discriminative enough to distinguish A from all other persons, which is quite challenging. By contrast, when we humans compare two faces, the observation of one face is guided by that of the other, i.e., finding the differences and putting more attention on them for better distinguishing of the two faces. Taking Fig. 1 for example, the same face A is compared with two different faces B_1 and B_2. When comparing with B_1 who features small eyes relative to A's big eyes, our focus on A will be attracted to regions around the eyes. When comparing with B_2 whose face is round relative to A's oval face, we will tend to pay more attention to the contour of face A during the observation. Naturally, we depict a face differently when comparing it with different persons so as to distinguish them more accurately.

Inspired by this observation, we propose a novel CNN structure with what we referred to as contrastive convolution, whose kernels are carefully designed and mainly focus on those distinct characteristics, i.e., contrastive features, between the two faces for better verification of them. Specifically, a kernel generator module is designed to generate personalized kernels of a face first. As personalized kernels of a specific person often have high correlation with its own features, the difference of the personalized kernels of the two faces are exploited as the contrastive convolutional kernels, which are expected to focus on the difference between the two faces. This contrastive convolution can be embedded into any kind of convolutional neural networks, and in this work it is embedded into the popular CNN, forming an novel face verification model as shown in Fig. 2, which is referred to as *Contrastive CNN*. To demonstrate the effectiveness of the proposed contrastive convolution, extensive experiments are performed on the challenging LFW and IJB-A dataset, and our contrastive CNN achieves quite promising performance.

The rest of this work is organized as follows: Sect. 2 reviews works related to face recognition in the wild and adaptative convolution. Section 3 describes the proposed deep convolutional neural network with contrastive convolution. Section 4 presents experimental results, and finally Sect. 5 concludes this work.

2   Related Work

Face Recognition. Face recognition is an important and classical topic in computer vision, in which face feature learning plays a significant role. An expressive feature descriptor can substantially improve the accuracy of face recognition. Some early works mainly focus on hand-crafted features, such as the well-known Local Binary Pattern (LBP) [2] and Gabor [34,36] which achieved favorable results in controlled environment. The discrimination ability of hand-crafted features heavily depends on the design principal which may be not beneficial for classification. Go a step further, a few learning-based approaches are proposed to learn more informative but mostly linear feature representation, including the famous Eigenfaces [28] and Fisherfaces [3,6]. Recently, deep convolutional neural networks (CNNs) arise with great performance improvement [13,16] benefitted from its excellent non-linear modeling capability. In [27], a CNN is proposed to extract deep features of the faces that are aligned to frontal through a general 3D shape model and performs better than many traditional face recognition methods. Afterwards, the performance of face recognition is further improved in quick succession by Deep ID2 [7], Deep ID2+ [26], which even surpass the human's performance for face verification on the Labeled Face in the Wild (LFW). Several recent works mainly focus on exploring better loss functions to imporve the performance of face recognition. In [9], a method named FaceNet is proposed to employ triplet loss for training on large-scale face images without alignment, and it achieves state-of-the-art on multiple challenging benchmarks including LFW [9] and YouTubeFaces [30]. In [18], Large-Margin softmax (L-Softmax) loss is proposed to explicitly reduce the intra-personal variations while enlarging the inter-personal differences. In SphereFace [17], a new loss of angular softmax (A-Softmax) is proposed and achieves excellent results on MageFace challenge [21]. Although the performance of face recognition on LFW and YTF datasets has reached human level [22,25–27], there still is a gap between human performance and automatic face recognition with extreme pose, illumination, expression, age, resolution variation in unconstrained environment [23] such as the challenging IJB-A [14], mainly due to the different perception mechanism. Therefore in this work, inspired by the human perception mechanism, we propose a new contrastive convolution for better face recognition.

Adaptive Convolution. There are some works exploring adaptive convolution to further improve the performance of CNN. In [4], kernels corresponding to an objective style can transform a given image from the original style to the objective style when convolving with the given image. In [38], scale-adaptive convolution is proposed to acquire flexible-size receptive fields during scene parsing for tackling the issue of inconsistent predictions of large objects and invisibility of small objects in conventional CNN. Most related to our work is those of dynamic input conditioned kernel generation, which includes, as far as we konw, dynamic convolution [15], dynamic filter network [11], and adaptive convolution [12]. Our work is fundamentally different from those works in two folds. First, the purpose of creating conditioned kernels is different. [11,15] focus on image prediction task, and the dynamically-generated filters are mainly used to predict the movement of pixels between frames. [12] focuses on the supervised learning, and the dynamically-generated kernels aim at incorporating the given side information (e.g., camera tilt angle and camera height) into image features. Differently, our dynamically-generated kernels attempt to highlight the difference between two images for better face verification. Second, the mechanism of kernel generation is different. In [11,12,15], kernels are generated only according to one input, which thus characterize the specific feature of input relative to common or general feature, while our contrastive kernels are created according to a pair of images, which characterize the specific feature of an image relative to another.

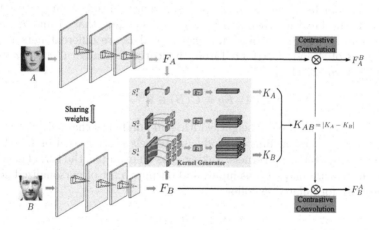

Fig. 2. The pipeline of our contrastive CNN. Given a pair of face images, A and B, a common feature extractor C consisting of several cascaded convolution layers is firstly used to obtain expressive feature representations F_A and F_B of them. Then, the kernel generator G consisting of several sub-generators generates personalized kernels for A and B respectively, based on which the contrastive kernels are achieved as $|K_A - K_B|$. Finally, with those contrastive kernels, the contrastive features of A and B are extracted via convolution operations respectively for the final similarity calculation. Note the subscript $*$ of S in kernel generator can be A or B.

3   Contrastive CNN

As mentioned above, the conventional CNN-based methods use the same feature of a face image no matter who it is compared with, while our proposed CNNs extract contrastive features of a face image based on who it is compared with. Contrastive features mainly describe those distinct characteristics between two faces which are extracted by the contrastive convolution proposed in this work. An overview of our method can be seen in Fig. 2.

Specifically, the whole verification model, referred to as *Contrastive CNN*, consists of a trunk CNN and a kernel generator, forming a successive architecture. The truck CNN C is designed for base feature representation, which is shared between the two images for efficiency although it can be generally different. Based on these base feature representation, the kernel generator G produces personalized kernels for a face image, attempting to highlight those salient features of a face relative to the mean face. And the contrastive kernels are designed as the difference of personalized kernels of two faces, attempting to focus on those contrastive characteristics between them. By performing convolution with those contrastive kernels, contrastive features of two faces are extracted respectively for the similarity calculation.

3.1   Kernel Generator

Denote a pair of face images as (A, B, L_{AB}), where A and B are face images, and L_{AB} is the label for them, with $L_{AB} = 1$ meaning that A and B are the same person, and $L_{AB} = 0$ meaning that A and B are different persons. The feature maps of A and B extracted from the feature extractor C are denoted as F_A and F_B respectively, i.e.

$$F_A = C(A), F_B = C(B) \in \mathbb{R}^{h_F \times w_F \times c_F} \tag{1}$$

where h_F, w_F and c_F are the height, width, and number of channels respectively.

The kernel generator aims at producing kernels specific to A or B, which is referred to as personalized kernels. Taking A as an example, the kernel generator G takes the feature maps F_A as input, and outputs a set of personalized kernels K_A, generally formulated as follows:

$$K_A = G(F_A) \tag{2}$$

Given only one face image A, i.e. with no reference face, it is impossible to obtain kernels depicting contrastive characteristics. So here, the generated kernels K_A is expected to highlight those intrinsic and salient features of A, which is the foundation of constructing contrastive convolutional kernels.

What's more, the kernel generator is designed with a hierarchical structure, allowing the personalized kernels to capture face characteristics at various scales, which can further effect on contrastive kernels K_{AB}. As shown in Fig. 2, there are multiple layers in kernel generator network, one sub-generator for each layer, obtaining kernels with different receptive field as different layers are usually with feature map in different scale. Generally, the generator G consists of multiple layers, e.g. T layers, and on each layer a sub-generator is designed, forming T sub-generators in total:

$$G = \{g_1, g_2, \cdots, g_T\}. \tag{3}$$

Specifically, the feature maps from i^{th} layer are denoted as $S_A^i|_{i=1}^T$, which are usually obtained by using the convolving or fully connected operations on the feature maps of $(i-1)^{th}$ layer, i.e., S_A^{i-1} with $S^0 = F_A$.

On each layer, the sub-generator g_i is constructed to generate a group of kernels in the same scale as below:

$$K_A^i = \{k_A^{i1}, k_A^{i2}, \ldots, k_A^{iN_i}\}, \tag{4}$$

where N_i is the number of kernels generated from g_i. Each kernel k_A^{ij} is expected to portray the characteristics of a local component of face image A, achieved by using a local patch as input:

$$k_A^{ij} = g_i(p_A^{ij}), \tag{5}$$

$$p_A^{ij} = R(S_A^i, c_{ij}, h_K, w_K), \tag{6}$$

where p_A^{ij} is a local patch cropped from S_A^i with the center at c_{ij}, height of h_K, and width of w_K. Here, R denotes the image crop operation. Generally, these patches can be taken at regular grid for easy implementation. The sub-generator g_i can be any kind of deep network structure, such as convolution layer or full connection layer, and a small one is preferable. In all our experiments, the g_i consists of only one fully connected layer.

The kernels from one sub-generator share similar receptive field but focus on different components. Kernels from different sub-generators have different receptive fields paying attention to characteristics in different scales. Altogether, a set of personalized kernels can be obtained as the union of kernels from all the sub-generators as below:

$$K_A = \{k_A^{11}, \ldots, k_A^{1N_1}, \ldots, k_A^{ij}, \ldots, k_A^{T1}, \ldots, k_A^{TN_T}\}. \tag{7}$$

The personalized kernels generated from the generator G are expected to capture the intrinsic characteristics of an image, regardless of pose, illuminations, expression and etc., leading to a loss in Eq. (15). The personalized kernels K_B of B can be generated similarly.

Finally, the contrastive kernels are achieved as the difference of personalized kernels of two face images, attempting to only focus on those distinct characteristics between two faces and subtract the commonality, formulated as follows:

$$K_{AB} = |K_A - K_B|. \tag{8}$$

The contrastive kernels are dynamically generated by considering the two faces to compare in testing stage, which is flexible and adaptive to the testing faces, resulting in more accurate feature representation. As shown in Fig. 4, the contrastive kernels created by Eq. (8) have high response to those different features, while low response to those common features between of the two faces as expected.

3.2 Contrastive Convolution

The contrastive convolution is very similar to conventional convolution, except that kernels used in contrastive convolution are dynamically generated according to different pairs being compared in the process of testing, while kernels used in conventional convolution are learned by large scale data and are fixed after training.

When comparing a pair of face images A and B, the contrastive features between A and B are extracted by convolving F_A and F_B with the contrastive kernels K_{AB} as follows:

$$F_A^B = K_{AB} \bigotimes F_A = [k_{AB}^{11} \otimes F_A; \cdots; k_{AB}^{ij} \otimes F_A; \cdots, k_{AB}^{T N_T} \otimes F_A] \qquad (9)$$

$$F_B^A = K_{AB} \bigotimes F_B = [k_{AB}^{11} \otimes F_B; \cdots; k_{AB}^{ij} \otimes F_B; \cdots, k_{AB}^{T N_T} \otimes F_B] \qquad (10)$$

where $\bigotimes$ means element-wise convolution. $K_{AB} \bigotimes F_A$ means each contrastive kernel in set K_{AB} is convolved with F_A.

With the contrastive feature representation of A and B, a simple linear regression followed by sigmoid activation is used to calculate the similarity S_A^B and S_B^A between A and B as follows:

$$S_A^B = \sigma(F_A^B \cdot W) \qquad (11)$$

$$S_B^A = \sigma(F_B^A \cdot W) \qquad (12)$$

Here, σ is sigmoid function with $\sigma(x) = \frac{e^x}{1+e^x}$, and $\cdot$ means dot product.

The final similarity S_{AB} between A and B is calculated as the average of the two similarities, i.e.

$$S_{AB} = \frac{1}{2}(S_A^B + S_B^A). \qquad (13)$$

3.3 Overall Objective

With the contrastive convolution, the similarity between a pair of images from the same person is expect to be 1, i.e. $s_{AB} = 1$ and that from different persons is expect to be 0, i.e. $s_{AB} = 0$. The cross entropy loss is used to maximize the similarity of same face pairs, while minimize the similarity of different face pairs as follows:

$$\min_{C,G,W} L_1 = -\frac{1}{N} \sum_{A,B} [L_{AB} \log(S_{AB}) + (1 - L_{AB}) \log(1 - S_{AB})] \qquad (14)$$

Here, N means the number of face pairs, L_{AB} is the label of the face pair of A and B, in which $L_{AB} = 1$ means the positive face pair, and $L_{AB} = 0$ means the negative face pair.

Moreover, the personalized kernels is expected to capture the intrinsic characteristics of a face, which means that the personalized kernels of face images of the same person should have high similarity even if with various pose, illuminations or expressions, forming another cross entropy loss in the following:

$$L_2 = -\frac{1}{2N} \left[\sum_A l_A \log(H(K_A)) + \sum_B l_B \log(H(K_B)) \right] \tag{15}$$

where $l_A \in \{0,1\}^M$ and $l_B \in \{0,1\}^M$ are the identity coding of A and B respectively in the form of one-hot coding with the number of persons as M. Here, $H(K) \in R^{M \times 1}$ is a small network used to regress the kernels to a one-hot code for classification.

Overall, the objective function of our CNN with contrastive convolution can be formulated as follows:

$$\min_{C,G,W,H} L_1 + \alpha L_2 \tag{16}$$

The α is a balance parameter, and is set as 1 in our experiments in addition to special instructions. This objective can be easily optimized by using the gradient decent same as most CNN based methods.

4 Experiments

In this section, we will evaluated our proposed CNN with contrastive convolution w.r.t. different architectures and compare with the state-of-art methods for face verification task on two wild challenging datasets: Labeled Faces in the Wild (LFW) [10], and IARPA Janus Benchmark A (IJB-A) [14].

4.1 Experimental Settings

Datasets. Three datasets are used for evaluation. The CASIA-WebFace [35] dataset is used for training, the LFW [10], and IJB-A [14] datasets are used for testing. The details of each dataset are as follows.

The **CASIA-WebFace** [35] dataset is a large scale face dataset containing about 10,000 subjects and 500,000 images collected from the internet. This dataset is often used to develop a deep network for face recognition in the wild, such as in [8,17,18,35].

The **LFW** dataset [10] includes 13,233 face images from 5,749 different identities with large variations in pose, expression and illuminations. On this dataset, we follow the standard unrestricted protocol of with labeled outside data, i.e. training on the outside labeled CASIA-WebFace, and testing on 6,000 face pairs from LFW. Please refer to [10] for more details.

Table 1. Architectures of the CNN used in our method with 4, 10, 16 layers respectively. Conv1.x, Conv2.x, Conv3.x and Conv4.x mean convolution layers that contain multiple convolution units. For example, conv[256, 3, 1] denotes convolution with 256 filters of size 3 × 3, and stride 1. The max[3, 2] denotes the max pooling within a region of size 3 × 3, and stride 2. In CNNs with 10 and 16 layers, the residual network structure is used for better performance and the residual units are shown in the double-column brackets. In the last contrastive convolutional layer, the convolution is the same as conventional convolution except that its kernels are dynamically generated during testing.

Layer	4-layer CNN	10-layer CNN	16-layer CNN
Input	112 × 112 × 3		
Conv1.x	conv[64, 3, 1]	conv[64, 3, 1]	conv[64, 3, 1]
Pool1	max[3, 2]		
Conv2.x	conv[128, 3, 1]	conv[128, 3, 1] $\begin{bmatrix} \text{conv}[128,3,1] \\ \text{conv}[128,3,1] \end{bmatrix} \times 1$	conv[128, 3, 1] $\begin{bmatrix} \text{conv}[128,3,1] \\ \text{conv}[128,3,1] \end{bmatrix} \times 2$
Pool2	max[3, 2]		
Conv3.x	conv[256, 3, 1]	conv[256, 3, 1] $\begin{bmatrix} \text{conv}[256,3,1] \\ \text{conv}[256,3,1] \end{bmatrix} \times 2$	conv[256, 3, 1] $\begin{bmatrix} \text{conv}[256,3,1] \\ \text{conv}[256,3,1] \end{bmatrix} \times 3$
Pool3	max[3, 2]		
Conv4.x	conv[512, 3, 1]	conv[512, 3, 1]	conv[512, 3, 1] $\begin{bmatrix} \text{conv}[512,3,1] \\ \text{conv}[512,3,1] \end{bmatrix} \times 1$
Pool4	max[3, 2]		
Contrastive Conv	conv[14, 3, 1]	conv[14, 3, 1]	conv[14, 3, 1]
Features	686 dimensions		

Fig. 3. Examplar images of a person from IJB-A dataset. Note the extreme variations of head poses, expression and image resolutions.

The **IJB-A** dataset [14] contains 5,712 images and 2,085 videos from 500 subjects captured from the wild environment. Because of the extreme variation in head pose, illumination, expression and resolution, so far IJB-A is regarded as the most challenging dataset for both verification and identification. A few example images of a subject from IJB-A can be seen in Fig. 3. The standard protocol on this dataset performs evaluations by using template-based manner, instead of image-based or video-based. A template may include images and/or videos of a subject.

Preprocessing. For all three datasets, [31] is firstly used to detect the faces, then each detected face is aligned to a canonical one according to the five landmarks (2 eyes centers, 1 nose tip, and 2 mouth corners) obtained from CFAN [37], and finally all aligned images are resized into 128×128 for training or testing.

Settings of CNNs. Tensorflow is used to implement all our experiments. For extensive investigation of our method, the proposed contrastive CNNs with base layers of 4, 10, and 16 are evaluated respectively. The detailed settings of the three CNNs are given in Table 1. Note that kernels in the last convolutional layer of our contrastive CNNs are dynamically generated in the testing stage with the kernel generator learnt in the training stage. We also compare our contrastive CNN with the conventional CNN, which is constructed by adding additional layer to the base CNN (referred to as L-Vanilla CNN) so that it has the same network structure as ours for fair comparison. The batch size is 128 for both methods, i.e. 128 images for baseline models and 64 pairs for our models. The face image pairs used in our method are randomly chosen from CASIA-WebFace with the same possibility between positive pairs and negative pairs when training. The length of personalized kernels are normalized to be 1 before they are used to calculate contrastive kernel. All models are trained with iterations as 200K, with learning rate as 0.1, 0.01 and 0.001 at the beginning, 100K iterations, and 160K iterations. Our contrastive CNN is designed with 3 sub-generators which generate 9, 4, and 1 contrastive kernels respectively, i.e. $T = 3, N_1 = 9, N_2 = 4, N_3 = 1$.

Table 2. Comparion between the vanilla CNN and our contrastive CNN. They share the same architecture for fair comparison.

Method	Loss	mAcc on LFW (%)	TAR(%)@FAR on IJB-A		
			0.1	0.01	0.001
L-VanillaCNN	Pairwise Loss	91.80	64.13	22.43	5.88
Contrastive CNN		95.20	78.73	52.51	31.37
L-VanillaCNN	Pairwise Loss	97.50	88.43	71.51	52.72
Contrastive CNN	+Softmax Loss	98.20	90.24	74.55	58.04

Table 3. Performance of our Contrastive CNN with different number of sub-generators on LFW in terms of mean accuracy (mAcc) and IJB-A in terms of TAR (%) at FAR = 0.1, 0.01, and 0.001.

# sub-generator	mAcc on LFW	TAR(%)@FAR on IJB-A		
		0.1	0.01	0.001
1	97.83	87.06	64.95	37.32
2	98.17	89.92	75.08	57.08
3	98.20	90.24	74.55	58.04

Table 4. Results of our Contrastive CNN with different base CNNs on LFW in terms of mean accuracy (mAcc) and IJB-A in terms of TAR at FAR = 0.1, 0.01, 0.001. Three base CNN structures with layers 4, 10, 16 are evaluated respectively, with architecture detailed in Table 1.

# Layers of base CNN	mAcc on LFW(%)	TAR(%)@FAR on IJB-A		
		0.1	0.01	0.001
4	98.20	90.24	74.55	58.04
10	98.93	93.17	80.35	61.83
16	99.12	95.31	84.01	63.91

4.2 Ablation Study of Contrastive Convolution

Effectiveness of Contrastive Convolution. To show the improvement of our contrastive convolution, we compare our contrastive CNN with what we referred to as L-Vanilla CNN, which is constructed by adding additional layers that have similar structure with our kernel generator to the base CNN so that it has the same network structure as ours. In our contrastive CNN, a kernel classification loss in Eq. (15) is used to make the personalized kernels of a specific face image capture the intrinsic characteristics regardless of pose, illumination or expression. Therefore, the comparison is conducted on two cases that one is with pairwise loss + softmax loss, and the other is with only pairwise loss. The results are shown in Table 2. As can be seen, for both vanilla CNN and our contrastive CNN, the results with softmax loss+pairwise loss are better than that only with pairwise loss, demonstrating the superiority of the softmax loss as that in [33]. More importantly, for both cases with softmax loss+pairwise loss and pairwise loss only, our proposed contrastive convolution performs much better than the conventional convolution, with an improvement up to 30% at FAR = 0.01. These comparison clearly and convincingly show that our contrastive CNN can significantly improve the conventional CNN.

Contrastive Convolution w.r.t. Number of Sub-generator. Our kernel generator is organized with a hierarchical structure consisting of several sub-generators, where kernels created from different sub-generators are equipped with different scales. Here, we investigate the influence of the number of sub-generator, i.e. three contrastive CNNs of which the number of sub-generator is 1, 2, 3, respectively and accordingly there are 9, 13, 14 contrastive kernels orderly in the 4-layer CNN shown in Table 1. The performance of Contrastive CNN with different number of sub-generator can be found in Table 3, where the performance is constantly improved with the increasing of number of sub-generator.

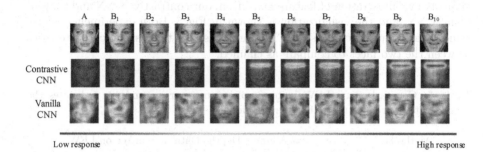

Fig. 4. Feature maps from our Contrastive CNN and Vanilla CNN for a given image A when comparing to images B_1–B_{10}. These feature maps for contrastive CNN mainly focus on the region of eyes and eyebrows.

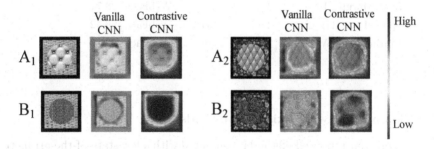

Fig. 5. Illustration of feature maps from contrastive CNN and vanilla CNN on the toy data for A_1 comparing with B_1, and A_2 comparing with B_2.

Contrastive Convolution w.r.t. Different Architectures. To further investigation, we demonstrate our contrastive convolution with different base CNNs. Three types of architecture with 4, 10, and 16 layers are used for evaluation, and the results are shown in Table 4. As can be seen, performance of our contrastive CNNs is constantly improved with the increasing of the depth of base CNN.

Visualization Comparison of Contrastive Features and Vanilla Features. To further verify that those contrastive kernels can capture the differences between the two faces being compared. We visualize those feature maps from our contrastive CNN and vanilla CNN in Fig. 4. Specifically, an image A is compared to 10 images from B_1 to B_{10}. As can be seen, the high response of our contrastive CNN only lies in the area where A differs from the compared image, while the high response of conventional CNN scatters over the whole image. Moreover, a toy experiment with images filled in simple geometry patterns is designed for more obvious illustration of feature maps from our contrastive CNN and conventional CNN, and the visualization is shown in Fig. 5. Both experiments clearly demonstrate that our contrastive CNN can focuses on the distinct characteristics between the two faces to compare as claimed.

Table 5. Comparison on LFW in terms of mean accuracy (mAcc). * denotes the outside data is private (not publicly available).

Methods	# Models	Depth	Data	mAcc on LFW
DeepFace [27]	3	7	4M*	97.35
DeepID2+ [26]	1	5	300K*	98.70
Deep FR [22]	1	15	2.6M	98.95
FaceNet [25]	1	14	200M*	99.65
Yi et al. [35]	1	10	WebFace	97.73
Ding et al. [8]	1	14	WebFace	98.43
LargeMargin [18]	1	17	WebFace	98.71
SphereFace [17]	1	64	WebFace	99.42
Contrastive CNN (ours)	1	16	WebFace	99.12

4.3   Comparison with Existing Methods

Furthermore, our proposed method is compared with a few state-of-the-art methods. In this experiment, contrastive CNN with 16 layers is used for fair comparison as most existing methods are equipped with large architectures. All methods are tested on the LFW and IJB-A datasets as shown in Tables 5 and 6. In Table 5, the proposed contrastive convolution outperforms all methods that are trained on WebFace with reasonable number of layer. In Table 6, our method achieves the best results of TAR = 63.91% for FAR = 0.001 on IJB-A, which demonstrates the effectiveness of our contrastive CNN.

5   Conclusion

In this work, we propose a novel CNN architecture with what we referred to as contrastive convolution for face verification. Instead of extracting the same features of a face no matter who it is compared in conventional CNN, our method

Table 6. Comparison on IJB-A in terms of TAR (%) at FAR = 0.1, 0.01, and 0.001. Results of GOTS and OPENBR are from [14]. It is worth noting that our Contrastive CNN is not finetuned on the training splits of IJB-A, while some of those methods, such as [5,24] are finetuned on the training splits of IJB-A for better performance.

Methods	TAR(%)@FAR on IJB-A		
	0.1	0.01	0.001
OPENBR	43.3	23.6	10.4
GOTS	62.7	40.6	19.8
ReST [32]	-	63.0	54.8
FastSearch [29]	89.3	72.9	51.0
PAM [20]	-	73.3	55.2
DR-GAN [19]	-	75.5	51.8
Deep Multi-pose [1]	91.1	78.7	-
Triplet Similarity [24]	94.5	79.0	59.0
Joint Bayesian [5]	96.1	81.8	-
Contrastive CNN (ours)	95.31	84.01	63.91

extracts contrastive features of a given face according to who it is compared with. The contrastive convolution is beneficial owing to its dynamitic generation of contrastive kernels based on the pair of faces being compared. The proposed contrastive convolution can be incorporated into any kind of CNN architecture. As evaluated on two wild benchmarks of LFW and IJB-A, the contrastive CNN achieves promising performance with significant improvement, demonstrating its effectiveness.

Acknowledgement. This work was partially supported by National Key Research and Development Program of China Grant 2017YFA0700804, Natural Science Foundation of China under contracts Nos. 61390511, 61650202, and 61772496.

References

1. AbdAlmageed, W., et al.: Face recognition using deep multi-pose representations. In: IEEE Winter Conference on Applications of Computer Vision (WACV) (2016)
2. Ahonen, T., Hadid, A., Pietikainen, M.: Face description with local binary patterns: application to face recognition. IEEE Trans. Pattern Anal. Mach. Intell. (TPAMI) **28**, 2037–2041 (2006)
3. Belhumeur, P.N., Hespanha, J.P., Kriegman, D.J.: Eigenfaces vs. Fisherfaces: recognition using class specific linear projection. IEEE Trans. Pattern Anal. Mach. Intell. (TPAMI) **19**, 711–720 (2002)
4. Chen, D., Yuan, L., Liao, J., Yu, N., Hua, G.: StyleBank: an explicit representation for neural image style transfer. In: The IEEE Conference on Computer Vision and Pattern Recognition (CVPR) (2017)

5. Chen, J.C., Patel, V.M., Chellappa, R.: Unconstrained face verification using deep CNN features. In: IEEE Winter Conference on Applications of Computer Vision (WACV) (2016)
6. Chen, J.C., Patel, V., Chellappa, R.: Landmark-based fisher vector representation for video-based face verification. In: IEEE International Conference on Image Processing (ICIP) (2015)
7. Chen, Y., Chen, Y., Wang, X., Tang, X.: Deep learning face representation by joint identification-verification. In: Advances in Neural Information Processing Systems (NIPS) (2014)
8. Ding, C., Tao, D.: Robust face recognition via multimodal deep face representation. IEEE Trans. Multimedia (TMM) **17**, 2049–2058 (2015)
9. Huang, G.B., Learned-Miller, E.: Labeled faces in the wild: updates and new reporting procedures. In: Department Computer Science, University Massachusetts Amherst, Amherst, MA, USA, Technical report (2014)
10. Huang, G.B., Mattar, M., Berg, T., Learned-Miller, E.: Labeled faces in the wild: a database for studying face recognition in unconstrained environments (2007)
11. Jia, X., De Brabandere, B., Tuytelaars, T., Gool, L.V.: Dynamic filter networks. In: NIPS (2016)
12. Kang, D., Dhar, D., Chan, A.: Incorporating side information by adaptive convolution. In: NIPS (2017)
13. Karpathy, A., Toderici, G., Shetty, S., Leung, T., Sukthankar, R., Fei-Fei, L.: Large-scale video classification with convolutional neural networks. In: IEEE Conference on Computer Vision and Pattern Recognition (CVPR) (2014)
14. Klare, B.F., Klein, B., Taborsky, E., Blanton, A.: Pushing the frontiers of unconstrained face detection and recognition: Iarpa Janus benchmark a. In: IEEE Conference on Computer Vision and Pattern Recognition (CVPR) (2015)
15. Klein, B., Wolf, L., Afek, Y.: A dynamic convolutional layer for short range weather prediction. In: CVPR (2015)
16. Krizhevsky, A., Sutskever, I., Hinton, G.E.: ImageNet classification with deep convolutional neural networks. In: Advances in Neural Information Processing Systems (NIPS) (2012)
17. Liu, W., Wen, Y., Yu, Z., Li, M., Raj, B., Song, L.: SphereFace: deep hypersphere embedding for face recognition. In: The IEEE Conference on Computer Vision and Pattern Recognition (CVPR) (2017)
18. Liu, W., Wen, Y., Yu, Z., Yang, M.: Large-margin softmax loss for convolutional neural networks. In: International Conference on Machine Learning (ICML) (2016)
19. Luan, T., Yin, X., Liu, X.: Disentangled representation learning GAN for pose-invariant face recognition. In: IEEE Conference on Computer Vision and Pattern Recognition (CVPR) (2017)
20. Masi, I., Rawls, S., Medioni, G., Natarajan, P.: Pose-aware face recognition in the wild. In: IEEE Conference on Computer Vision and Pattern Recognition (CVPR) (2016)
21. Miller, D., Brossard, E., Seitz, S., Kemelmachershlizerman, I.: MegaFace: a million faces for recognition at scale. arXiv preprint arXiv:1505.02108 (2015)
22. Parkhi, O.M., Vedaldi, A., Zisserman, A.: Deep face recognition. In: British Machine Vision Conference (BMVC) (2015)
23. Phillips, P.J., Hill, M.Q., Swindle, J.A., O'Toole, A.J.: Human and algorithm performance on the PaSC face recognition challenge. In: Biometrics Theory, Applications and Systems (BTAS) (2015)
24. Sankaranarayanan, S., Alavi, A., Chellappa, R.: Triplet similarity embedding for face verification. arXiv preprint arXiv:1602.03418 (2016)

25. Schroff, F., Kalenichenko, D., Philbin, J.: FaceNet: a unified embedding for face recognition and clustering. In: IEEE Conference on Computer Vision and Pattern Recognition (CVPR) (2015)
26. Sun, Y., Wang, X., Tang, X.: Deeply learned face representations are sparse, selective, and robust. In: IEEE Conference on Computer Vision and Pattern Recognition (CVPR) (2015)
27. Taigman, Y., Yang, M., Ranzato, M., Wolf, L.: DeepFace: closing the gap to human-level performance in face verification. In: IEEE Conference on Computer Vision and Pattern Recognition (CVPR) (2014)
28. Turk, M.A., Pentland, A.P.: Face recognition using eigenfaces. In: IEEE Conference on Computer Vision and Pattern Recognition (CVPR) (2002)
29. Wang, D., Otto, C., Jain, A.K.: Face search at scale. IEEE Trans. Pattern Anal. Mach. Intell. (TPAMI) (2017)
30. Wolf, L., Hassner, T., Maoz, I.: Face recognition in unconstrained videos with matched background similarity. In: IEEE Conference on Computer Vision and Pattern Recognition (CVPR) (2011)
31. Wu, S., Kan, M., He, Z., Shan, S., Chen, X.: Funnel-structured cascade for multi-view face detection with alignment-awareness. Neurocomputing **221**, 138–145 (2017)
32. Wu, W., Kan, M., Liu, X., Yang, Y., Shan, S., Chen, X.: Recursive spatial transformer (ReST) for alignment-free face recognition. In: IEEE International Conference on Computer Vision (ICCV) (2017)
33. Wu, Y., Liu, H., Li, J., Fu, Y.: Deep face recognition with center invariant loss. In: ACM Multimedia ThematicWorkshops (2017)
34. Xie, S., Shan, S., Chen, X., Chen, J.: Fusing local patterns of Gabor magnitude and phase for face recognition. IEEE Trans. Image Process. (TIP) (2010)
35. Yi, D., Lei, Z., Liao, S., Li, S.Z.: Learning face representation from scratch. arXiv preprint arXiv:1411.7923 (2014)
36. Zhang, B., Shan, S., Chen, X., Gao, W.: Histogram of Gabor phase patterns (HGPP): a novel object representation approach for face recognition. IEEE Trans. Image Process. (TIP) (2007)
37. Zhang, J., Kan, M., Shan, S., Chen, X.: Leveraging datasets with varying annotations for face alignment via deep regression network. In: IEEE International Conference on Computer Vision (ICCV) (2015)
38. Zhang, R., Tang, S., Zhang, Y., Li, J., Yan, S.: Scale-adaptive convolutions for scene parsing. In: IEEE International Conference on Computer Vision (ICCV) (2017)

Adding Attentiveness to the Neurons in Recurrent Neural Networks

Pengfei Zhang[1] [iD], Jianru Xue[1(✉)] [iD], Cuiling Lan[2(✉)] [iD], Wenjun Zeng[2] [iD], Zhanning Gao[1] [iD], and Nanning Zheng[1] [iD]

[1] Institute of Artificial Intelligence and Robotics, Xi'an Jiaotong University,
Xi'an, China
zpengfei@stu.xjtu.edu.cn, {jrxue,nnzheng}@mail.xjtu.edu.cn,
zhanninggao@gmail.com
[2] Microsoft Reserach Asia, Beijing, China
{culan,wezeng}@microsoft.com

Abstract. Recurrent neural networks (RNNs) are capable of modeling the temporal dynamics of complex sequential information. However,
the structures of existing RNN neurons mainly focus on controlling the
contributions of current and historical information but do not explore
the different importance levels of different elements in an input vector
of a time slot. We propose adding a simple yet effective Element-wise-
Attention Gate (EleAttG) to an RNN block (e.g., all RNN neurons in
a network layer) that empowers the RNN neurons to have the attentiveness capability. For an RNN block, an EleAttG is added to adaptively modulate the input by assigning different levels of importance,
i.e., attention, to each element/dimension of the input. We refer to an
RNN block equipped with an EleAttG as an EleAtt-RNN block. Specifically, the modulation of the input is content adaptive and is performed
at fine granularity, being element-wise rather than input-wise. The proposed EleAttG, as an additional fundamental unit, is general and can be
applied to any RNN structures, *e.g.*, standard RNN, Long Short-Term
Memory (LSTM), or Gated Recurrent Unit (GRU). We demonstrate the
effectiveness of the proposed EleAtt-RNN by applying it to the action
recognition tasks on both 3D human skeleton data and RGB videos.
Experiments show that adding attentiveness through EleAttGs to RNN
blocks significantly boosts the power of RNNs.

Keywords: Element-wise-Attention Gate (EleAttG)
Recurrent neural networks · Action recognition · Skeleton · RGB video

1 Introduction

In recent years, recurrent neural networks [25], such as standard RNN (sRNN),
its variant Long Short-Term Memory (LSTM) [15], and Gated Recurrent Unit
(GRU) [3], have been adopted to address many challenging problems with
sequential time-series data, such as action recognition [9], machine translation [2],

© Springer Nature Switzerland AG 2018
V. Ferrari et al. (Eds.): ECCV 2018, LNCS 11213, pp. 136–152, 2018.
https://doi.org/10.1007/978-3-030-01240-3_9

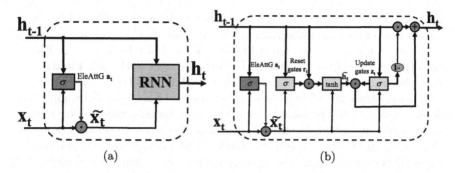

Fig. 1. Illustration of Element-wise-Attention Gate (EleAttG) (marked in red) for (a) a generic RNN block, where the RNN structure could be the standard RNN, LSTM, or GRU and (b) a GRU block which consists of a group of (*e.g.*, N) GRU neurons. In the diagram, each line carries a vector. The brown circles denote element-wise operation, *e.g.*, element-wise vector product or vector addition. The yellow boxes denote the units of the original GRU with the output dimension of N. The red box denotes the EleAttG with an output dimension of D, which is the same as the dimension of the input $\mathbf{x}_t$. (Color figure online)

and image caption [39]. They are powerful in exploring temporal dynamics and learning appropriate feature representations.

The structure of recurrent neural networks facilitates the processing of sequential data. RNN neurons perform the same task at each step, with the output being dependent on the previous output, *i.e.*, some historical information is memorized. Standard RNNs have difficulties in learning long-range dependencies due to the vanishing gradient problem [19]. The LSTM [15] or GRU [3] architectures combat vanishing gradients through a gating mechanism. Gates provide a way to optionally let information through or stop softly, which balances the contributions of the information of the current time slot and historical information. There are some variants of RNNs with slightly different designs [19]. Note a gate applies a single scaling factor to control the flow of the embedded information (as a whole) of the input rather than imposing controls on each element of the input. They are not designed to explore the potential different characteristics of the input elements.

Attention mechanisms which selectively focus on different parts of the data have been demonstrated to be effective for many tasks [23,28,31,36,46,49]. These inspire us to develop an Element-wise-Attention Gate (EleAttG) to augment the capability of RNN neurons. More specifically, for an RNN block, an EleAttG is designed to output an attention vector, with the same dimension as the input, which is then used to modulate the input elements. Note that similar to [29], we use an RNN block to represent an ensemble of N RNN neurons, which for example could be all the RNN neurons in an RNN layer. Figure 1(a) illustrates the EleAttG within a generic RNN block. Figure 1(b) shows a specific case when the RNN structure of GRU is used. The input $\mathbf{x}_t$ is first modulated by the response of the EleAttG to output $\tilde{\mathbf{x}}_t$ before other operations are applied to the

RNN block. We refer to an RNN block equipped with an EleAttG as EleAtt-RNN block. Depending on the underlying RNN structure used (*e.g.*, standard RNN, LSTM, GRU), the newly developed EleAtt-RNN will also be denoted as EleAtt-sRNN, EleAtt-LSTM, or EleAtt-GRU. An RNN layer with such EleAttG can replace the original RNN layer and multiple EleAtt-RNN layers can be stacked.

We demonstrate the effectiveness of the proposed EleAtt-RNN by applying it to action recognition. Specifically, for 3D skeleton-based human action recognition, we build our systems by stacking several EleAtt-RNN layers, using standard RNN, LSTM and GRU, respectively. EleAtt-RNNs consistently outperform the original RNNs for all the three types of RNNs. Our scheme based on EleAtt-GRU achieves state-of-the-art performance on three challenging datasets, *i.e.*, the NTU [30], N-UCLA [43], and SYSU [16] datasets. For RGB-based action recognition, we design our system by applying an EleAtt-GRU network to the sequence of frame-level CNN features. Experiments on both the JHMDB [18] and NTU [30] datasets show that adding EleAttGs brings significant gain.

The proposed EleAttG has the following merits. First, EleAttG is capable of adaptively modulating the input at a fine granularity, paying different levels of attention to different elements of the input, resulting in faster convergence in training and higher performance. Second, the design is very simple. For an RNN layer, only one line of code needs to be added in implementation. Third, the EleAttG is general and can be added to any underlying RNN structure, *e.g.*, standard RNN, LSTM, GRU, and to any layer.

2   Related Work

2.1   Recurrent Neural Networks

Recurrent neural networks have many different structures. In 1997, to address the vanishing gradient problem of standard RNN, Hochreiter *et al.* proposed LSTM, which introduces a memory cell that allows "constant error carrousels" and multiplicative gate units that learn to open and close access to the constant error flow [15]. Gers *et al.* made improvement by adding the "forget gate" that enables an LSTM cell to learn to reset itself (historical information) at appropriate times to prohibit the growth of the state indefinitely [11]. A variant of LSTM is the peephole LSTM, which allows the gates to access the cell [12]. GRU, which was proposed in 2014, is a simpler variant of LSTM. A GRU has a reset gate and an update gate which control the memory and the new input information. Between the LSTMs and GRUs, there is no clear winner [6,19]. For LSTM, a differential gating scheme is proposed in [37] which leverages the derivative of the cell state to gate the information flow. Its effectiveness is demonstrated on action recognition.

In this work, we address the capability of RNNs from a new perspective. We propose a simple yet effective Element-wise-Attention Gate which adaptively modulates the input elements to explore their different importances for an RNN block.

2.2   Attention Mechanisms

Attention mechanisms which selectively focus on different parts of the data have been proven effective for many tasks such as machine translation [28,36], image caption [49], object detection [23], and action recognition [31,46].

Luong *et al.* examine some simple attention mechanisms for neural machine translation. At each time step, the model infers the attention weights and uses them to average the embedding vectors of the source words [28]. For image caption, Xu *et al.* split an image into L parts with each part described by a feature vector. To allow the decoder which is built by LSTM blocks to selectively focus on certain parts of the image, the weighted average of all the feature vectors using learned attention weights is fed to the LSTM network at every time step [49]. A similar idea is used for RGB-based action recognition in [31]. The above attention models focus on how to average a set of feature vectors with suitable weights to generate a pooled vector of the same dimension as the input of RNN. They do not consider the fine-grained adjustment based on different levels of importance across the input dimensions. In addition, they address attention at the network level, but not RNN block level.

For skeleton-based action recognition, a global context-aware attention is proposed to allocate different levels of importance to different joints of different input frames [27]. Since the global information of a sequence is required to learn the attention, the system suffers from time delay. Song *et al.* propose a spatio-temporal attention model without requiring global information [33]. Before the main recognition network, a spatial attention subnetwork is added which modulates the skeleton input to selectively focus on discriminative joints at each time slot. However, their design is not general and has not been extended to higher RNN layers. In contrast, our proposed enhanced RNN, with EleAttG embedded as a fundamental unit of RNN block, is general, simple yet effective, which can be applied to any RNN block/layer.

2.3   Action Recognition

For action recognition, many studies focus on recognition from RGB videos [8, 32,40,44,50]. In recent years, 3D skeleton based human action recognition has been extensively studied and has been attracting increasing attention, thanks to its high level representation [13]. Many traditional approaches focus on how to design efficient features to solve the problems of small inter-class variation, large view variations, and the modeling of complicated spatial and temporal evolution [38,40,42,43,45,47].

For 3D skeleton based human action recognition, RNN-based approaches have been attractive due to their powerful spatio-temporal dynamic modeling ability. Du *et al.* propose a hierarchical RNN model with the hierarchical body partitions as input to different RNN layers [9]. To exploit the co-occurrence of discriminative joints of skeletons, Zhu *et al.* propose a deep regularized LSTM networks with group sparse regularization [52]. Shahroudy *et al.* propose a part-aware LSTM network by separating the original LSTM cell into five sub-cells corresponding to five major groups of human body [30]. Liu *et al.* propose a spatio-temporal LSTM structure to explore the contextual dependency of joints in spatio-temporal domains [26]. Li *et al.* propose an RNN tree network with a hierarchical structure which classifies the action classes that are easier to distinguish at the lower layers and the action classes that are harder to distinguish at higher layers [24]. To address the large view variation of the captured data, Zhang *et al.* propose a view adaptive subnetwork which automatically selects the best observation viewpoints within an end-to-end network for recognition [51].

For RGB-based action recognition, to exploit the spatial correlations, convolutional neural networks are usually used to learn the features [8,32,44,50]. Some approaches explore the temporal dynamics of the sequential frames by simply averaging/multiplying the scores/features of the frames for fusion [7,32,44]. Some other approaches leverage RNNs to model temporal correlations, with frame-wise CNN features as input at every time slot [8,50].

Our proposed EleAttG is a fundamental unit that aims to enhance the capability of an RNN block. We will demonstrate its effectiveness in both 3D skeleton based action recognition and RGB-based action recognition.

3   Overview of Standard RNN, LSTM, and GRU

Recurrent neural networks are capable of modeling temporal dynamics of a time sequence. They have a "memory" which captures historical information accumulated from previous time steps. To better understand the proposed EleAttG and its generalization capability, we briefly review the popular RNN structures, *i.e.*, standard RNN, Long Short Term Memory (LSTM) [15], and Gated Recurrent Unit (GRU) [3].

For a standard RNN layer, the output response $\mathbf{h_t}$ at time t is calculated based on the input $\mathbf{x_t}$ to this layer and the output $\mathbf{h_{t-1}}$ from the previous time slot

$$\mathbf{h}_t = \tanh\left(\mathbf{W}_{xh}\mathbf{x}_t + \mathbf{W}_{hh}\mathbf{h}_{t-1} + \mathbf{b}_h\right), \tag{1}$$

where $\mathbf{W}_{\alpha\beta}$ denotes the matrix of weights between α and β, $\mathbf{b_h}$ is the bias vector.

The standard RNN suffers from the gradient vanishing problem due to insufficient, decaying error back flow [15]. LSTM alleviates this problem by enforcing constant error flow through "constant error carrousels" within the cell unit c_t. The input gate i_t, forget gate f_t and output gate o_t learn to open and close access to the constant error flow. For an LSTM layer, the recursive computations of activations of the units are

$$\begin{aligned}
\mathbf{i}_t &= \sigma\left(\mathbf{W}_{xi}\mathbf{x}_t + \mathbf{W}_{hi}\mathbf{h}_{t-1} + \mathbf{b}_i\right), \\
\mathbf{f}_t &= \sigma\left(\mathbf{W}_{xf}\mathbf{x}_t + \mathbf{W}_{hf}\mathbf{h}_{t-1} + \mathbf{b}_f\right), \\
\mathbf{c}_t &= \mathbf{f}_t \odot \mathbf{c}_{t-1} + \mathbf{i}_t \odot \tanh(\mathbf{W}_{xc}\mathbf{x}_t + \mathbf{W}_{hc}\mathbf{h}_{t-1} + \mathbf{b}_c), \\
\mathbf{o}_t &= \sigma\left(\mathbf{W}_{xo}\mathbf{x}_t + \mathbf{W}_{ho}\mathbf{h}_{t-1} + \mathbf{b}_o\right), \\
\mathbf{h}_t &= \mathbf{o}_t \odot \tanh\left(\mathbf{c}_t\right),
\end{aligned} \tag{2}$$

where $\odot$ denotes an element-wise product. Note that $\mathbf{i_t}$ is a vector denoting the responses of a set of input gates of all the LSTM neurons in the layer.

GRU is an architecture that is similar to but much simpler than that of LSTM. A GRU has two gates, reset gate r_t and update gate z_t. When the response of the reset gate is close to 0, the hidden state h'_t is forced to ignore the previous hidden state and reset with the current input only. The update gate controls how much information from the previous hidden state will be carried over to the current hidden state h_t. The hidden state acts in a way similar to the memory cell in LSTM. For a GRU layer, the recursive computations of activations of the units are

$$
\begin{aligned}
\mathbf{r}_t &= \sigma\left(\mathbf{W}_{xr}\mathbf{x}_t + \mathbf{W}_{hr}\mathbf{h}_{t-1} + \mathbf{b}_r\right), \\
\mathbf{z}_t &= \sigma\left(\mathbf{W}_{xz}\mathbf{x}_t + \mathbf{W}_{hz}\mathbf{h}_{t-1} + \mathbf{b}_z\right), \\
\mathbf{h}'_t &= \tanh\left(\mathbf{W}_{xh}\mathbf{x}_t + \mathbf{W}_{hh}(\mathbf{r}_t \odot \mathbf{h}_{t-1}) + \mathbf{b}_h\right), \\
\mathbf{h}_t &= \mathbf{z_t} \odot \mathbf{h}_{t-1} + (\mathbf{1} - \mathbf{z_t}) \odot \mathbf{h}'_t.
\end{aligned}
\tag{3}
$$

For all the above designs, we note that the gates can control the information flow. However, the controlling of the flow takes the input $\mathbf{x_t}$ as a whole without adaptively treating different elements of the input differently.

4   Element-wise-Attention Gate for an RNN Block

For an RNN block, we propose an Element-wise-Attention Gate (EleAttG) to enable the RNN neurons to have the attentiveness capability. The response of an EleAttG is a vector $\mathbf{a_t}$ with the same dimension as the input $\mathbf{x_t}$ of the RNNs, which is calculated as

$$
\mathbf{a_t} = \phi\left(\mathbf{W_{xa}}\mathbf{x_t} + \mathbf{W_{ha}}\mathbf{h}_{t-1} + \mathbf{b_a}\right),
\tag{4}
$$

where ϕ denotes the activation function of Sigmoid, i.e., $\phi(s) = 1/(1 + e^{-s})$. $\mathbf{W}_{\alpha\beta}$ denotes the matrix of weights between α and β, and $\mathbf{b_a}$ denotes the bias vector. The current input $\mathbf{x_t}$ and the hidden states $\mathbf{h}_{t-1}$ are used to determine the levels of importance of each element of the input $\mathbf{x_t}$.

The attention response modulates the input to have an updated input $\widetilde{\mathbf{x}}_t$ as

$$
\widetilde{\mathbf{x}}_t = \mathbf{a_t} \odot \mathbf{x_t}.
\tag{5}
$$

The recursive computations of activations of the other units in the RNN block are then based on the updated input $\widetilde{\mathbf{x}}_t$, instead of the original input $\mathbf{x_t}$, as illustrated in Fig. 1.

For a standard RNN block with EleAttG (denoted as EleAtt-sRNN), the output responses $\mathbf{h}_t$ at time t are calculated as

$$
\mathbf{h}_t = \tanh\left(\mathbf{W}_{xh}\widetilde{\mathbf{x}}_t + \mathbf{W}_{hh}\mathbf{h}_{t-1} + \mathbf{b}_h\right).
\tag{6}
$$

Similarly, for an EleAtt-GRU block, the recursive computations of activations of the units are

$$
\begin{aligned}
\mathbf{r}_t &= \sigma\left(\mathbf{W}_{xr}\widetilde{\mathbf{x}}_\mathbf{t} + \mathbf{W}_{hr}\mathbf{h}_{t-1} + \mathbf{b}_r\right), \\
\mathbf{z}_t &= \sigma\left(\mathbf{W}_{xz}\widetilde{\mathbf{x}}_\mathbf{t} + \mathbf{W}_{hz}\mathbf{h}_{t-1} + \mathbf{b}_z\right), \\
\mathbf{h}'_t &= \tanh\left(\mathbf{W}_{xh}\widetilde{\mathbf{x}}_\mathbf{t} + \mathbf{W}_{hh}(\mathbf{r}_t \odot \mathbf{h}_{t-1}) + \mathbf{b}_h\right), \\
\mathbf{h}_t &= \mathbf{z}_\mathbf{t} \odot \mathbf{h}_{t-1} + (1 - \mathbf{z}_\mathbf{t}) \odot \mathbf{h}'_t.
\end{aligned}
\tag{7}
$$

The computations for an EleAtt-LSTM block can be obtained similarly.

Most attention designs use Softmax as the activation function such that the sum of the attention values is 1 [23,28,31,33,36,46,49]. In our design, we relax this sum-to-1 constraint by using the Sigmoid activation function, with response values ranging from 0 to 1. If the sum-to-1 constraint is not relaxed, the attention responses of the kth element will be affected by the changes of other elements' response values even when the levels of importance of this element are the same over consecutive time slots.

Note that in our design, an EleAttG is shared by all neurons in an RNN block/layer (see (5) and (6) for the standard RNN block, (5) and (7) for the GRU block). Theoretically, each RNN neuron (instead of block) can have its own attention gate at the cost of increased computation complexity and a larger number of parameters. We focus on the shared design in this work.

5   Experiments

We perform comprehensive studies to evaluate the effectiveness of our proposed EleAtt-RNN with EleAttG by applying it to action recognition from 3D skeleton data and RGB video, respectively.

To demonstrate the generalization capability of EleAttG, we add EleAttG to the standard RNN, LSTM, and GRU structures, respectively.

For 3D skeleton based action recognition, we use three challenging datasets, i.e., the NTU RGB+D dataset (NTU) [30], the Northwestern-UCLA dataset (N-UCLA) [43], and the SYSU Human-Object Interaction dataset (SYSU) [16]. The NTU is currently the largest dataset with diverse subjects, various viewpoints and small inter-class differences. Therefore, in-depth analyses are performed on the NTU dataset. For RGB-based action recognition, we take the CNN features extracted from existing, pre-trained models without finetuning on our datasets as the input to the RNN based recognition networks and evaluate the effectiveness of EleAttG on the NTU and the JHMDB datasets [18]. We conduct most of our experiments based on GRU here, as it has simpler structure than LSTM and better performance than standard RNN.

5.1   Datasets

NTU RGB+D Dataset (NTU) [30]. NTU is currently the largest RGB+D+Skeleton dataset for action recognition, including 56880 videos of in total more than 4 million frames. There are 60 action classes performed by different subjects. Each subject has 25 body joints and each joint has 3D coordinates. Three cameras placed in different positions are used to capture the data at the same time. We follow the standard protocols proposed in [30] including the Cross Subject (CS) and Cross View (CV) settings. For the CS setting, 40 subjects are equally split into training and testing groups. For the CV setting, the samples of cameras 2 and 3 are used for training while those of camera 1 are for testing.

Northwestern-UCLA Dataset (N-UCLA) [43]. N-UCLA is a small RGB+D+Skeleton dataset including 1494 sequences which records 10 actions performed by 10 subjects. 20 joints with 3D coordinates are provided in this dataset. Following [43], we use samples from the first two cameras as training data, and the samples from the third camera as testing data.

SYSU Human-Object Interaction Dataset (SYSU) [16]. SYSU is a small RGB+D+Skeleton dataset, including 480 sequences performed by 40 different subjects. It contains 12 actions. A subject has 20 joints with 3D coordinates. We follow the standard protocols proposed in [16] for evaluation. They include two settings. For the Cross Subject (CS) setting, half of the subjects are used for training and the others for testing. For the Same Subject (SS) setting, half of the sequences of each subject are used for training and others for testing. The average performance of 30-fold cross validation is reported.

JHMDB Dataset (JHMDB) [18]. JHMDB is an RGB-based dataset which has 928 RGB videos with each video containing about 15–40 frames. It contains 21 actions performed by different actors. This dataset is challenging where the videos are collected on the Internet which also includes outdoor activities.

5.2   Implementation Details

We perform our experiments on the deep learning platform of Keras [4] with Theano [1] as the backend. For the RNN networks, Dropout [34] with the probability of 0.5 is used to alleviate overfitting. Gradient clipping similar to [35] is used by constraining the maximum amplitude of the gradient to 1. Adam [21] is used to train the networks from end-to-end. The initial learning rate is set to 0.005 for 3D skeleton-based action recognition and 0.001 for RGB-based action recognition. During training, the learning rate will be reduced by a factor of 10 when the training accuracy does not increase. We use cross-entropy as the loss function.

For 3D skeleton-based action recognition, similar to the classification network design in [51], we build our systems by stacking three RNN layers with EleAttGs and one fully connected (FC) layer for classification. We use 100 RNN neurons in each layer. Considering the large difference on the sizes of the datasets, we set the batch size for the NTU, N-UCLA, and SYSU datasets to 256, 32, and 32, respectively. We use the sequence-level pre-processing method in [51] by setting the body center in the first frame as the coordinate origin to make the system

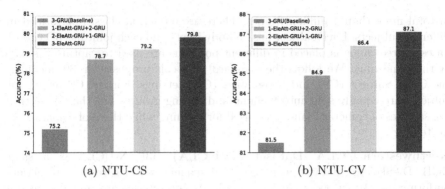

(a) NTU-CS   (b) NTU-CV

Fig. 2. Effectiveness of proposed EleAttGs on the three layered GRU network for 3D skeleton based human action recognition on the NTU dataset. "m-EleAtt-GRU+n-GRU" denotes that the first m layers are EleAtt-GRU layers and the remaining n layers are the original GRU layers.

invariant to the initial position of human body. To improve the robustness to view variations at the sequence level, we can perform data augmentation by randomly rotating the skeleton around the X, Y and Z axes by various degrees ranging from -35 to 35 during training. For the N-UCLA and SYSU datasets, we use the RNN models pre-trained on the NTU dataset to initialize the baseline schemes and the proposed schemes.

For RGB-based action recognition, we feed an RNN network with the features to further explore temporal dynamics. Since our purpose is to evaluate whether the proposed EleAttG can generally improve recognition accuracy, we extract CNN features using some available pre-trained models without finetuning for the specific dataset or task. For the JHMDB dataset, we use the TSN model from [44,48] which was trained on the HMDB dataset [22] to extract a 1024 dimensional feature for each frame. For the NTU dataset which has more videos, we take the ResNet50 model [5,14] which has been pre-trained on ImageNet as our feature extractor (2048 dimensional feature for each frame) considering the ResNet50 model is much faster than the TSN model. The implementation details of the RNN networks are similar to that discussed above. For the NTU dataset, we stack three EleAtt-GRU layers, with each layer consisting of 512 GRU neurons. For the JHMDB dataset, we use only one GRU layer (512 GRU neurons) with EleAttG to avoid overfitting, considering that the number of video samples is much smaller than that of the NTU dataset. The batch size is set to 256 for the NTU dataset and 32 for the JHMDB dataset.

5.3   Effectiveness of Element-Wise-Attention-Gates

Effectiveness on GRU Network. Figure 2 shows the effectiveness of EleAttG on the GRU network. Our final scheme with three EleAtt-GRU layers ("3-EleAtt-GRU") outperforms the baseline scheme "3-GRU(Baseline)" significantly,

Table 1. Effectiveness of proposed EleAttGs in the GRU network for RGB-based action recognition on the NTU and JHMDB datasets.

Dataset	NTU		JHMDB			
	CS	CV	Split1	Split2	Split3	Average
Baseline-GRU	61.3	66.8	60.6	59.2	62.9	60.9
EleAtt-GRU	63.3	70.6	64.5	59.2	65.0	62.9

Table 2. Effectiveness of EleAttGs on three types of RNN structures on the NTU dataset. "EleAtt-X" denotes the scheme with EleAttGs based on the RNN structure of X.

RNN structure	Scheme	CS	CV
Standard RNN	Baseline(1-sRNN)	51.6	57.6
	EleAtt-sRNN	**61.6**	**67.2**
LSTM	Baseline(3-LSTM)	77.2	83.0
	EleAtt-LSTM	**78.4**	**85.0**
GRU	Baseline(3-GRU)	75.2	81.5
	EleAtt-GRU	**79.8**	**87.1**

by **4.6%** and **5.6%** for the CS and CV settings, respectively. The performance increases as more GRU layers are replaced by the EleAtt-GRU layers.

Generalization to Other Input Signals. The proposed RNN block with EleAttG is generic and can be applied to different types of source data. To demonstrate this, we use CNN features extracted from RGB frames as the input of the RNNs for RGB based action recognition. Table 1 shows the performance comparisons on the NTU and JHMDB dataset respectively. The implementation details have been described in Sect. 5.2. We can see that the "EleAtt-GRU" outperform the "Baseline-GRU" by about 2–4% on the NTU dataset, and 2% on the JHMDB dataset. Note that the performance is not optimized since we have not used the fine-tuned CNN model on this dataset for this task.

Generalization on Various RNN Structures. The proposed EleAttG is generic and can be applied to various RNN structures. We evaluate the effects of EleAttGs on three representative RNN structures, *i.e.*, the standard RNN (sRNN), LSTM, GRU respectively and show the results in Table 2. Compared with LSTM and GRU, the standard RNN neurons do not have the gating designs which control the contributions of the current input to the network. The EleAttG can element-wise control the contribution of the current input, which remedies the lack of gate designs to some extent. The gate designs in LSTM and GRU can only control the information flow input-wise. In contrast, the proposed EleAttGs are capable of controlling the input element-wise, adding the attentiveness capability to RNNs. We can see that the adding of EleAttGs enhances performance significantly. Note that for sRNN, we build both the Baseline

Table 3. Performance comparisons on the NTU dataset in accuracy (%).

Method	CS	CV
Skeleton Quads [10]	38.6	41.4
Lie Group [38]	50.1	52.8
Dynamic Skeletons [16]	60.2	65.2
HBRNN-L [9]	59.1	64.0
Part-aware LSTM [30]	62.9	70.3
ST-LSTM + Trust Gate [26]	69.2	77.7
STA-LSTM [33]	73.4	81.2
GCA-LSTM [27]	74.4	82.8
URNN-2L-T [24]	74.6	83.2
Clips+CNN+MTLN [20]	79.6	84.8
VA-LSTM [51]	79.4	87.2
Baseline-GRU	75.2	81.5
EleAtt-GRU	79.8	87.1
EleAtt-GRU(aug.)	**80.7**	**88.4**

(1-sRNN) and our scheme using one sRNN layer rather than three as those for LSTM and GRU, in considering that the three layered sRNN baseline converges to a poorer performance, i.e., 33.6% and 42.8% for the CS and CV settings, which may be caused by the gradient vanishing of sRNN.

Comparisons with State-of-the-Arts on Skeleton Based Action Recognition. Tables 3, 4 and 5 show the performance comparisons with state-of-the-art approaches for the NTU, N-UCLA and SYSU datasets, respectively. "Baseline-GRU" denotes our baseline scheme which is built by stacking three GRU layers while "EleAtt-GRU" denotes our proposed scheme which replaces the GRU layers by the proposed GRU layers with EleAttGs. Implementation details can be found in Sect. 5.2. "EleAtt-GRU(aug.)" denotes that data argumentation by rotating skeleton sequences is performed during training. We achieve the best performances in comparison with other state-of-the-art approaches on all the three datasets. Our scheme "EleAtt-GRU" achieves significant gains over the baseline scheme "Baseline-GRU", of 4.6-5.6%, 4.7%, and 2.4-2.8% on the NTU, N-UCLA, and SYSU datasets, respectively.

Visualization of the Responses of EleAttGn. To better understand the learned element-wise attention, we observe the responses of the EleAttG in the first GRU layer for the skeleton based action recognition. In the first layer, the input (with dimension of $3 \times J$) at a time slot corresponds to the J joints with each joint represented by the X, Y, and Z coordinate values. The physical meaning of the attention responses is clear. However, in a higher layer, the EleAttG modulates the input features on each element which is more difficult to interpret and visualize. Thus, we perform visualization based on the attention

Table 4. Performance comparisons on the N-UCLA dataset in acc. (%).

Method	Accuracy
HOJ3D [47]	54.5
AE [41]	76.0
VA-LSTM [51]	70.7
HBRNN-L [9]	78.5
Baseline-GRU	84.3
EleAtt-GRU	89.0
EleAtt-GRU(aug.)	**90.7**

Table 5. Performance comparisons on the SYSU dataset in acc. (%).

Method	CS	SS
LAFF [17]	54.2	-
DS [16]	75.5	76.9
ST-LSTM [26]	76.5	-
VA-LSTM [51]	76.9	77.5
Baseline-GRU	82.1	82.1
EleAtt-GRU	84.9	84.5
EleAtt-GRU(aug.)	**85.7**	**85.7**

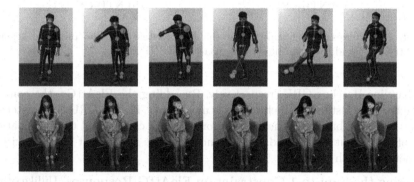

Fig. 3. Visualization based on the attention responses of the first GRU layer for the actions of *kicking* and *touching neck*. For each joint, the size of the yellow circle indicates the learned level of importance.

responses of the first GRU layer in Fig. 3 for the actions of *kicking* and *touching the neck*. Actually, the absolute response values cannot represent the relative importances across dimensions very well. The statistical energies of the different elements of the original input are different. For example, the foot joint which is in general far away from the body center has a higher average energy than that of the body center joint. We can imagine that there is a static modulation $\overline{a_i}$ on the ith element of the input, which can be calculated by the average energy before and after the modulation. For the ith element of an sample j with attention value $a_{i,j}$, we use the relative response value $\widehat{a_{i,j}} = a_{i,j}/\overline{a_i}$ for visualization to better reflect the importances among joints. Note that the sum of the relative responses for the X, Y, and Z of a joint is utilized for visualization. For the action of *touching neck* which is highly concerned with the joints on the arms and heads, the relative attention on those joints are larger. For *kicking*, the relative attention on the legs is large. These are consistent with a human's perception.

5.4   Discussions

Convergence of Learning. Figure 4 shows the loss curves for the training set and validation set during the training process for the proposed EleAtt-GRU and

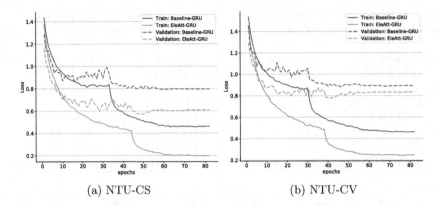

(a) NTU-CS   (b) NTU-CV

Fig. 4. Loss curves during training on the NTU dataset for the proposed scheme "EleAtt-GRU" and the baseline scheme "Baseline-GRU".

the baseline Baseline-GRU, respectively. By adding the EleAttGs, the convergence becomes faster and the final loss is much lower. EleAtt-GRU is consistently better than the baseline. The modulation of input can control the information flow of each input element adaptively and make the subsequent learning within the neurons much easier.

Relaxing the Sum-to-1 Constraint on EleAttG Responses. Unlike other works [27,33,49], we do not use Softmax, which enforces the sum of attention responses to be 1, as the activation function of EleAttG. Instead, we use the Sigmoid activation function to avoid introducing mutual influence of elements. We show the experimental comparisons between the cases with the sum-to-1 constraint ($w/constraint$) by using Softmax, and our case without such constraint ($wo/constraint$) by using Sigmoid in Table 6. "EleAttG-n^{th}" denotes that the nth GRU layer uses the GRU with EleAttG while the other layers still use the original GRU. "Baseline" denotes the baseline scheme with three GRU layers. We can see $wo/constraint$ always performs better than that with constraint $w/constraint$. Adding EleAttG with constraint on the second or the third layer even decreases the accuracy by about 2.4-3.2% in comparison with the baselines.

Number of Parameters Versus Performance. For an RNN block, the adding of an EleAttG increases the number of parameters. Taking a GRU block of N neurons with the input dimension of D as an example, the numbers of parameters for the original GRU block and the proposed EleAttG-GRU block are $3N(D + N + 1)$, and $3N(D + N + 1) + D(D + N + 1)$, respectively. We calculate the computational complexity by counting the number of floating-point operations (FLOPs) including all multiplication and addition operations. At a time slot, adding attention to the layer as in 4 and 5 takes $D(D + N + 1)$ multiplication operations and $D(D + N)$ addition operations. Then the complexity increases from $N(6D + 6N + 5)$ to $N(6D + 6N + 5) + D(2D + 2N + 1)$, which is approximately proportional to the number of parameters.

Table 6. Performance comparisons about relaxing the constraint to EleAttG on the NTU dataset in terms of accuracy (%).

Protocols	Method	Baseline	EleAttG-1st	EleAttG-2nd	EleAttG-3rd
CS	w/constraint	75.2	75.0	72.7	72.0
	wo/constrain	75.2	**78.7**	**77.3**	**76.4**
CV	w/constraint	81.5	83.7	79.1	78.8
	wo/constrain	81.5	**84.9**	**83.5**	**82.5**

Table 7. Effect of the number of parameters on the NTU dataset.

Scheme	# parameters	CS	CV
2-GRU(100)	0.14M	75.5	81.4
2-GRU(128)	0.21M	75.8	81.7
3-GRU(100)	0.20M	75.2	81.5
3-GRU(128)	0.31M	76.5	81.3
2-EleAtt-GRU(100)	0.20M	78.6	85.5
3-EleAtt-GRU(100)	0.28M	79.8	87.1

Table 7 shows the effect of the number of parameters under different experimental settings on the NTU dataset. Note that "m-GRU(n)" denotes the baseline scheme which is built by m GRU blocks (layers) with each layer composed of n neurons. "m-EleAtt-GRU(100)" denotes our scheme which includes m EleAtt-GRU layers with each layer composed of 100 neurons. We can see that the performance increases only a little when more neurons ("2-GRU(128)") or more layers ("3-GRU(100)") are used in comparison with the baseline "2-GRU(100)". In contrast, our scheme "2-EleAtt-GRU(100)", achieves significant gains of 3.1–4.1%. Similar observation can be found for three-layer case. With the similar number of parameters, adding EleAttG is much more effective than increasing the number of neurons or the number of layers.

6   Conclusions

In this paper, we propose to empower the neurons in recurrent neural networks to have the attentiveness capability by adding the proposed EleAttG. It can explore the varying importance of different elements of the inputs. The EleAttG is simple yet effective. Experiments show that our proposed EleAttG can be used in any RNN structures (*e.g* standard RNN, LSTM and GRU) and any layers of the multi-layer RNN networks. In addition, for both human skeleton-based and RGB-based action recognitions, EleAttG boosts performance significantly. We expect that, as a fundamental unit, the proposed EleAttG will be effective for improving many RNN-based learning tasks.

Acknowledgment. This work is supported by National Key Research and Development Program of China under Grant 2016YFB1001004, Natural Science Foundation of China under Grant 61773311 and Grant 61751308.

References

1. Al-Rfou, R., et al.: Theano: a python framework for fast computation of mathematical expressions. arXiv preprint arXiv:1605.02688, vol. 472, p. 473 (2016)
2. Cho, K., et al.: Learning phrase representations using RNN encoder-decoder for statistical machine translation. In: EMNLP, pp. 1724–1734. Association for Computational Linguistics, October 2014
3. Cho, K., et al.: Learning phrase representations using RNN encoder-decoder for statistical machine translation. arXiv preprint arXiv:1406.1078 (2014)
4. Chollet, F.: Keras (2015). https://github.com/fchollet/keras
5. Chollet, F.: Resnet50 model. https://github.com/fchollet/deep-learning-models/releases/download/v0.2/resnet50_weights_tf_dim_ordering_tf_kernels.h5
6. Chung, J., Gulcehre, C., Cho, K., Bengio, Y.: Empirical evaluation of gated recurrent neural networks on sequence modeling. arXiv preprint arXiv:1412.3555 (2014)
7. Diba, A., Sharma, V., Van Gool, L.: Deep temporal linear encoding networks. In: CVPR, pp. 2329–2338 (2017)
8. Donahue, J., et al.: Long-term recurrent convolutional networks for visual recognition and description. In: CVPR, pp. 2625–2634 (2015)
9. Du, Y., Wang, W., Wang, L.: Hierarchical recurrent neural network for skeleton based action recognition. In: Computer Vision and Pattern Recognition (CVPR), pp. 1110–1118 (2015)
10. Evangelidis, G., Singh, G., Horaud, R.: Skeletal quads: human action recognition using joint quadruples. In: ICPR, pp. 4513–4518. IEEE (2014)
11. Gers, F.A., Schmidhuber, J., Cummins, F.: Learning to forget: continual prediction with LSTM (1999)
12. Gers, F.A., Schraudolph, N.N., Schmidhuber, J.: Learning precise timing with LSTM recurrent networks. JMLR **3**(Aug), 115–143 (2002)
13. Han, F., Reily, B., Hoff, W., Zhang, H.: Space-time representation of people based on 3D skeletal data: a review. CVIU **158**, 85–105 (2017)
14. He, K., Zhang, X., Ren, S., Sun, J.: Deep residual learning for image recognition. In: CVPR, pp. 770–778 (2016)
15. Hochreiter, S., Schmidhuber, J.: Long short-term memory. Neural Comput. **9**(8), 1735–1780 (1997)
16. Hu, J.F., Zheng, W.S., Lai, J., Zhang, J.: Jointly learning heterogeneous features for RGB-D activity recognition. In: CVPR, pp. 5344–5352. IEEE (2015)
17. Hu, J.-F., Zheng, W.-S., Ma, L., Wang, G., Lai, J.: Real-time RGB-D activity prediction by soft regression. In: Leibe, B., Matas, J., Sebe, N., Welling, M. (eds.) ECCV 2016. LNCS, vol. 9905, pp. 280–296. Springer, Cham (2016). https://doi.org/10.1007/978-3-319-46448-0_17
18. Jhuang, H., Gall, J., Zuffi, S., Schmid, C., Black, M.J.: Towards understanding action recognition. In: ICCV, pp. 3192–3199. IEEE (2013)
19. Jozefowicz, R., Zaremba, W., Sutskever, I.: An empirical exploration of recurrent network architectures. In: ICML, pp. 2342–2350 (2015)
20. Ke, Q., Bennamoun, M., An, S., Sohel, F., Boussaid, F.: A new representation of skeleton sequences for 3D action recognition. In: CVPR, pp. 4570–4579. IEEE (2017)

21. Kingma, D.P., Ba, J.: Adam: a method for stochastic optimization. arXiv preprint arXiv:1412.6980 (2014)
22. Kuehne, H., Jhuang, H., Garrote, E., Poggio, T., Serre, T.: HMDB: a large video database for human motion recognition. In: ICCV, pp. 2556–2563. IEEE (2011)
23. Li, J., et al.: Attentive contexts for object detection. TMM **19**(5), 944–954 (2017)
24. Li, W., Wen, L., Chang, M.C., Lim, S.N., Lyu, S.: Adaptive RNN tree for large-scale human action recognition. In: Computer Vision and Pattern Recognition (CVPR), pp. 1444–1452 (2017)
25. Lipton, Z.C., Berkowitz, J., Elkan, C.: A critical review of recurrent neural networks for sequence learning. arXiv preprint arXiv:1506.00019 (2015)
26. Liu, J., Shahroudy, A., Xu, D., Wang, G.: Spatio-temporal LSTM with trust gates for 3D human action recognition. In: Leibe, B., Matas, J., Sebe, N., Welling, M. (eds.) ECCV 2016. LNCS, vol. 9907, pp. 816–833. Springer, Cham (2016). https://doi.org/10.1007/978-3-319-46487-9_50
27. Liu, J., Wang, G., Hu, P., Duan, L.Y., Kot, A.C.: Global context-aware attention LSTM networks for 3D action recognition. In: CVPR (2017)
28. Luong, M.T., Pham, H., Manning, C.D.: Effective approaches to attention-based neural machine translation. arXiv preprint arXiv:1508.04025 (2015)
29. Olah, C.: LSTM (2015). http://colah.github.io/posts/2015-08-Understanding-LSTMs/
30. Shahroudy, A., Liu, J., Ng, T.T., Wang, G.: NTU RGB+D: a large scale dataset for 3D human activity analysis. In: CVPR, June 2016
31. Sharma, S., Kiros, R., Salakhutdinov, R.: Action recognition using visual attention. arXiv preprint arXiv:1511.04119 (2015)
32. Simonyan, K., Zisserman, A.: Two-stream convolutional networks for action recognition in videos. In: NIPS, pp. 568–576 (2014)
33. Song, S., Lan, C., Xing, J., Zeng, W., Liu, J.: An end-to-end spatio-temporal attention model for human action recognition from skeleton data. In: AAAI, vol. 1, p. 7 (2017)
34. Srivastava, N., Hinton, G., Krizhevsky, A., Sutskever, I., Salakhutdinov, R.: Dropout: a simple way to prevent neural networks from overfitting. JMLR **15**(1), 1929–1958 (2014)
35. Sutskever, I., Vinyals, O., Le, Q.V.: Sequence to sequence learning with neural networks. In: NIPS, pp. 3104–3112 (2014)
36. Vaswani, A., et al.: Attention is all you need. In: NIPS, pp. 6000–6010 (2017)
37. Veeriah, V., Zhuang, N., Qi, G.J.: Differential recurrent neural networks for action recognition. In: ICCV, pp. 4041–4049. IEEE (2015)
38. Vemulapalli, R., Arrate, F., Chellappa, R.: Human action recognition by representing 3D skeletons as points in a lie group. In: CVPR, pp. 588–595 (2014)
39. Vinyals, O., Toshev, A., Bengio, S., Erhan, D.: Show and tell: a neural image caption generator. In: CVPR, pp. 3156–3164. IEEE (2015)
40. Wang, H., Schmid, C.: Action recognition with improved trajectories. In: ICCV, pp. 3551–3558 (2013)
41. Wang, J., Liu, Z., Wu, Y.: Learning actionlet ensemble for 3D human action recognition. Human Action Recognition with Depth Cameras. SCS, pp. 11–40. Springer, Cham (2014). https://doi.org/10.1007/978-3-319-04561-0_2
42. Wang, J., Liu, Z., Wu, Y., Yuan, J.: Mining actionlet ensemble for action recognition with depth cameras. In: CVPR, pp. 1290–1297. IEEE (2012)
43. Wang, J., Nie, X., Xia, Y., Wu, Y., Zhu, S.C.: Cross-view action modeling, learning and recognition. In: CVPR, pp. 2649–2656 (2014)

44. Wang, L., et al.: Temporal segment networks: towards good practices for deep action recognition. In: Leibe, B., Matas, J., Sebe, N., Welling, M. (eds.) ECCV 2016. LNCS, vol. 9912, pp. 20–36. Springer, Cham (2016). https://doi.org/10.1007/978-3-319-46484-8_2

45. Wang, P., Yuan, C., Hu, W., Li, B., Zhang, Y.: Graph based skeleton motion representation and similarity measurement for action recognition. In: Leibe, B., Matas, J., Sebe, N., Welling, M. (eds.) ECCV 2016. LNCS, vol. 9911, pp. 370–385. Springer, Cham (2016). https://doi.org/10.1007/978-3-319-46478-7_23

46. Wang, Y., Wang, S., Tang, J., O'Hare, N., Chang, Y., Li, B.: Hierarchical attention network for action recognition in videos. arXiv preprint arXiv:1607.06416 (2016)

47. Xia, L., Chen, C.C., Aggarwal, J.: View invariant human action recognition using histograms of 3D joints. In: Computer Vision and Pattern Recognition Workshop (CVPRW), pp. 20–27. IEEE (2012)

48. Xiong, Y.: TSN model (2016). https://github.com/yjxiong/temporal-segment-networks

49. Xu, K., et al.: Show, attend and tell: neural image caption generation with visual attention. In: ICML, pp. 2048–2057 (2015)

50. Yue-Hei Ng, J., Hausknecht, M., Vijayanarasimhan, S., Vinyals, O., Monga, R., Toderici, G.: Beyond short snippets: deep networks for video classification. In: CVPR, pp. 4694–4702 (2015)

51. Zhang, P., Lan, C., Xing, J., Zeng, W., Xue, J., Zheng, N.: View adaptive recurrent neural networks for high performance human action recognition from skeleton data. In: ICCV (2017)

52. Zhu, W., et al.: Co-occurrence feature learning for skeleton based action recognition using regularized deep LSTM networks. In: AAAI, vol. 2, p. 8 (2016)

Learning Dynamic Memory Networks for Object Tracking

Tianyu Yang$^{(\boxtimes)}$ ⓘ and Antoni B. Chan ⓘ

Department of Computer Science, City University of Hong Kong, Hong Kong, China
tianyyang8-c@my.cityu.edu.hk, abchan@cityu.edu.hk

Abstract. Template-matching methods for visual tracking have gained popularity recently due to their comparable performance and fast speed. However, they lack effective ways to adapt to changes in the target object's appearance, making their tracking accuracy still far from state-of-the-art. In this paper, we propose a dynamic memory network to adapt the template to the target's appearance variations during tracking. An LSTM is used as a memory controller, where the input is the search feature map and the outputs are the control signals for the reading and writing process of the memory block. As the location of the target is at first unknown in the search feature map, an attention mechanism is applied to concentrate the LSTM input on the potential target. To prevent aggressive model adaptivity, we apply gated residual template learning to control the amount of retrieved memory that is used to combine with the initial template. Unlike tracking-by-detection methods where the object's information is maintained by the weight parameters of neural networks, which requires expensive online fine-tuning to be adaptable, our tracker runs completely feed-forward and adapts to the target's appearance changes by updating the external memory. Moreover, unlike other tracking methods where the model capacity is fixed after offline training – the capacity of our tracker can be easily enlarged as the memory requirements of a task increase, which is favorable for memorizing long-term object information. Extensive experiments on OTB and VOT demonstrates that our tracker MemTrack performs favorably against state-of-the-art tracking methods while retaining real-time speed of 50 fps.

Keywords: Addressable memory · Gated residual template learning

1 Introduction

Along with the success of convolution neural networks in object recognition and detection, an increasing number of trackers [4,13,22,26,31] have adopted

Electronic supplementary material The online version of this chapter (https://doi.org/10.1007/978-3-030-01240-3_10) contains supplementary material, which is available to authorized users.

ⓒ Springer Nature Switzerland AG 2018
V. Ferrari et al. (Eds.): ECCV 2018, LNCS 11213, pp. 153–169, 2018.
https://doi.org/10.1007/978-3-030-01240-3_10

deep learning models for visual object tracking. Among them are two dominant tracking strategies. One is the *tracking-by-detection* scheme that online trains an object appearance classifier [22,26] to distinguish the target from the background. The model is first learned using the initial frame, and then fine-tuned using the training samples generated in the subsequent frames based on the newly predicted bounding box. The other scheme is *template matching*, which adopts either the target patch in the first frame [4,29] or the previous frame [14] to construct the matching model. To handle changes in target appearance, the template built in the first frame may be interpolated by the recently generated object template with a small learning rate [30].

The main difference between these two strategies is that tracking-by-detection maintains the target's appearance information in the weights of the deep neural network, thus requiring online fine-tuning with stochastic gradient descent (SGD) to make the model adaptable, while in contrast, template matching stores the target's appearance in the object template, which is generated by a feed forward computation. Due to the computationally expensive model updating required in tracking-by-detection, the speed of such methods are usually slow, e.g. [21,22,26] run at about 1 fps, although they do achieve state-of-the-art tracking accuracy. Template matching methods, however, are fast because there is no need to update the parameters of the neural networks. Recently, several trackers [4,13,36] adopt fully convolutional Siamese networks as the matching model, which demonstrate promising results and real-time speed. However, there is still a large performance gap between template-matching models and tracking-by-detection, due to the lack of an effective method for adapting to appearance variations online.

In this paper, we propose a dynamic memory network, where the target information is stored and recalled from external memory, to maintain the variations of object appearance for template-matching. Unlike tracking-by-detection where the target's information is stored in the weights of neural networks and therefore the capacity of the model is fixed after offline training, the model capacity of our memory networks can be easily enlarged by increasing the size of external memory, which is useful for memorizing long-term appearance variations. Since aggressive template updating is prone to overfit recent frames and the initial template is the most reliable one, we use the initial template as a conservative reference of the object and a residual template, obtained from retrieved memory, to adapt to the appearance variations. During tracking, the residual template is gated channel-wise and combined with the initial template to form the final matching template, which is then convolved with the search image features to get the response map. The channel-wise gating of the residual template controls how much each channel of the retrieved template should be added to the initial template, which can be interpreted as a feature/part selector for adapting the template. An LSTM (Long Short-Term Memory) is used to control the reading and writing process of external memory, as well as the channel-wise gate vector for the residual template. In addition, as the target position is at first unknown in the search image, we adopt an attention mechanism to locate the object roughly in the search image, thus leading to a soft representation of the target for the input to the LSTM controller. This helps to retrieve the most-related template in the memory. The whole framework is differentiable and therefore can be trained end-to-end with SGD. In summary, the contributions of our work are:

- We design a dynamic memory network for visual tracking. An external memory block, which is controlled by an LSTM with attention mechanism, allows adaptation to appearance variations.
- We propose gated residual template learning to generate the final matching template, which effectively controls the amount of appearance variations in retrieved memory that is added to each channel of the initial matching template. This prevents excessive model updating, while retaining the conservative information of the target.
- We extensively evaluate our algorithm on large scale datasets OTB and VOT. Our tracker performs favorably against state-of-the-art tracking methods while possessing real-time speed of 50 fps.

2 Related Work

Template-Matching Trackers. Matching-based methods have recently gained popularity due to its fast speed and comparable performance. The most notable is the fully convolutional Siamese networks (SiamFC) [4]. Although it only uses the first frame as the template, SiamFC achieves competitive results and fast speed. The key deficiency of SiamFC is that it lacks an effective model for online updating. To address this, [30] proposes model updating using linear interpolation of new templates with a small learning rate, but does only sees modest improvements in accuracy. Recently, the RFL (Recurrent Filter Learning) tracker [36] adopts a convolutional LSTM for model updating, where the forget and input gates control the linear combination of historical target information, i.e., memory states of LSTM, and incoming object's template automatically. Guo et al. [13] propose a dynamic Siamese network with two general transformations for target appearance variation and background suppression. To further improve the speed of SiamFC, [16] reduces the feature computation cost for easy frames, by using deep reinforcement learning to train policies for early stopping the feed-forward calculations of the CNN when the response confidence is high enough. SINT [29] also uses Siamese networks for visual tracking and has higher accuracy, but runs much slower than SiamFC (2 fps vs 86 fps) due to the use of deeper CNN (VGG16) for feature extraction, and optical flow for its candidate sampling strategy. Unlike other template-matching models that use sliding windows or random sampling to generate candidate image patches for testing, GOTURN [14] directly regresses the coordinates of the target's bounding box by comparing the previous and current image patches. Despite its advantage on handling scale and aspect ratio changes and fast speed, its tracking accuracy is much lower than other state-of-the-art trackers.

Different from existing matching-based trackers where the capacity of adaptivity is limited by the size of neural networks, we use SiamFC [4] as the baseline feature extractor and extend it to use an addressable memory, whose memory size is independent of neural networks and thus can be easily enlarged as memory requirements of a task increase, to adapt to variations of object appearance.

Memory Networks. Recent use of convolutional LSTM for visual tracking [36] shows that memory states are useful for object template management over long timescales. Memory networks are typically used to solve simple logical reasoning problem in natural language processing like question answering and sentiment analysis. The pioneering works include NTM (Neural Turing Machine) [11] and MemNN (Memory Neural Networks) [33]. They both propose an addressable external memory with reading and writing mechanism – NTM focuses on problems of sorting, copying and recall, while MemNN aims at language and reasoning task. MemN2N [28] further improves MemNN by removing the supervision of supporting facts, which makes it trainable in an end-to-end fashion. Based on their predecessor NTM, [12] proposes a new framework called DNC (Differentiable Neural Computer), which uses a different access mechanism to alleviate the memory overlap and interference problem. Recently, NTM is also applied to one-shot learning [25] by redesigning the method for reading and writing memory, and has shown promising results at encoding and retrieving new information quickly.

Our proposed memory model differs from the aforementioned memory networks in the following aspects. Firstly, for question answering problem, the input of each time step is a sentence, *i.e.*, a sequence of feature vectors (each word corresponds to one vector) which needs an embedding layer (usually RNN) to obtain an internal state. While for object tracking, the input is a search image which needs a feature extraction process (usually CNN) to get a more abstract representation. Furthermore, for object tracking, the target's position in the search image patch is unknown, and here we propose an attention mechanism to highlight the target's information when generating the read key for memory retrieval. Secondly, the dimension of feature vector stored in memory for natural language processing is relatively small (50 in MemN2N vs $6\times6\times256=9216$ in our case). Directly using the original template for address calculation is time-consuming. Therefore we apply an average pooling on the feature map to generate a template key for addressing, which is efficient and effective experimentally. Furthermore, we apply channel-wise gated residual template learning for model updating, and redesign the memory writing operation to be more suitable for visual tracking.

3   Dynamic Memory Networks for Tracking

In this section we propose a dynamic memory network with reading and writing mechanisms for visual tracking. The whole framework is shown in Fig. 1. Given the search image, first features are extracted with a CNN. The image features are input into an attentional LSTM, which controls the memory reading and writing. A residual templates is read from the memory and combined with the initial template learned from the first frame, forming the final template. The final template is convolved with the search image features to obtain

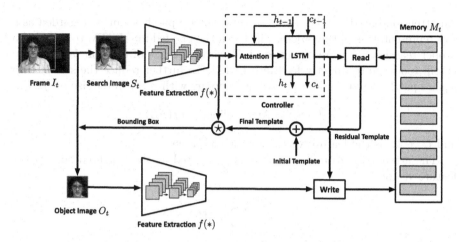

Fig. 1. The pipeline of our tracking algorithm. The green rectangle are the candidate region for target searching. The *Feature Extractions* for object image and search image share the same architecture and parameters. An attentional LSTM extracts the target's information on the search feature map, which guides the memory reading process to retrieve a matching template. The residual template is combined with the initial template, to obtain a final template for generating the response score. The newly predicted bounding box is then used to crop the object's image patch for memory writing. (Color figure online)

the response map, and the target bounding box is predicted. The new target's template is cropped using the predicted bounding box, features are extracted and then written into memory for model updating.

3.1 Feature Extraction

Given an input image I_t at time t, we first crop the frame into a search image patch S_t with a rectangle that is computed by the previous predicted bounding box. Then it is encoded into a high level representation $f(S_t)$, which is a spatial feature map, via a fully convolutional neural networks (FCNN). In this work we use the FCNN structure from SiamFC [4]. After getting the predicted bounding box, we use the same feature extractor to compute the new object template for memory writing.

3.2 Attention Scheme

Since the object information in the search image is needed to retrieve the related template for matching, but the object location is unknown at first, we apply an attention mechanism to make the input of LSTM concentrate more on the target. We define $\mathbf{f}_{t,i} \in \mathbb{R}^{n \times n \times c}$ as the i-th $n \times n \times c$ square patch on $f(S_t)$ in a sliding window fashion.[1] Each square patch covers a certain part of the search image.

---
[1] We use $6 \times 6 \times 256$, which is the same size of the matching template.

An attention-based weighted sum of these square patches can be regarded as a soft representation of the object, which can then be fed into LSTM to generate a proper read key for memory retrieval. However the size of this soft feature map is still too large to directly feed into LSTM. To further reduce the size of each square patch, we first adopt an average pooling with $n \times n$ filter size on $f(S_t)$,

$$f^*(S_t) = \text{AvgPooling}_{n \times n}(f(S_t)) \tag{1}$$

and $\mathbf{f}^*_{t,i} \in \mathbb{R}^c$ is the feature vector for the ith patch.

The attended feature vector is then computed as the weighted sum of the feature vectors,

$$\mathbf{a}_t = \sum_{i=1}^{L} \alpha_{t,i} \mathbf{f}^*_{t,i} \tag{2}$$

where L is the number of square patches, and the attention weights $\alpha_{t,i}$ is calculated by a softmax,

$$\alpha_{t,i} = \frac{\exp(r_{t,i})}{\sum_{k=1}^{L} \exp(r_{t,k})} \tag{3}$$

where

$$r_{t,i} = W^a \tanh(W^h \mathbf{h}_{t-1} + W^f \mathbf{f}^*_{t,i} + b) \tag{4}$$

is an attention network which takes the previous hidden state $\mathbf{h}_{t-1}$ of the LSTM controller and a square patch $\mathbf{f}^*_{t,i}$ as input. W^a, W^h, W^f and b are weight matrices and biases for the network.

By comparing the target's historical information in the previous hidden state with each square patch, the attention network can generate attentional weights that have higher values on the target and smaller values for surrounding regions. Figure 2 shows example search images with attention weight maps. We can see that our attention network can always focus on the target which is beneficial when retrieving memory for template matching.

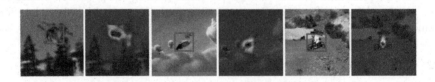

Fig. 2. Visualization of attentional weights map: for each pair, (left) search images and ground-truth target box, and (right) attention maps over search image. For visualization, the attention maps are resized using bicubic interpolation to match the size of the original image.

3.3 LSTM Memory Controller

For each time step, the LSTM controller takes the attended feature vector $\mathbf{a}_t$, obtained in the attention module, and the previous hidden state $\mathbf{h}_{t-1}$ as input, and outputs the new hidden state $\mathbf{h}_t$ to calculate the memory control signals, including read key, read strength, bias gates, and decay rate (discussed later). The internal architecture of the LSTM uses the standard model (details in the Supplemental), while the output layer is modified to generate the control signals. In addition, we also use layer normalization [2] and dropout regularization [27] for the LSTM. The initial hidden state $\mathbf{h}_0$ and cell state $\mathbf{c}_0$ are obtained by passing the initial target's feature map through one $n \times n$ average pooling layer and two separate fully-connected layer with tanh activation functions, respectively.

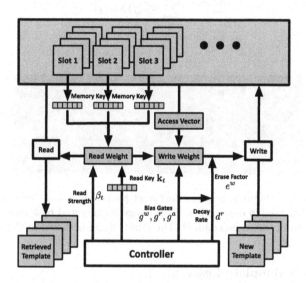

Fig. 3. Diagram of memory access mechanism.

3.4 Memory Reading

Memory is retrieved by computing a weighted summation of all memory slots with a read weight vector, which is determined by the cosine similarity between a read key and the memory keys. This aims at retrieving the most related template stored in memory. Suppose $\mathbf{M}_t \in \mathbb{R}^{N \times n \times n \times c}$ represents the memory module, such that $\mathbf{M}_t(j) \in \mathbb{R}^{n \times n \times c}$ is the template stored in the jth memory slot and N is the number of memory slots. The LSTM controller outputs the read key $\mathbf{k}_t \in \mathbb{R}^c$ and read strength $\beta_t \in [1, \infty]$,

$$\mathbf{k}_t = W^k \mathbf{h}_t + b^k \tag{5}$$

$$\beta_t = 1 + \log(1 + \exp(W^\beta \mathbf{h}_t + b^\beta)) \tag{6}$$

where $W^k, W^\beta, b^k, b^\beta$ are corresponding weight matrices and biases. The read key $\mathbf{k}_t$ is used for matching the contents in the memory, while the read strength β_t indicates the reliability of the generated read key. Given the read key and read strength, a *read weight* $\mathbf{w}_t^r \in \mathbb{R}^N$ is computed for memory retrieval,

$$\mathbf{w}_t^r(j) = \frac{\exp\left\{C(\mathbf{k}_t, \mathbf{k}_{\mathbf{M}_t(j)})\beta_t\right\}}{\sum_{j'} \exp\left\{C(\mathbf{k}_t, \mathbf{k}_{\mathbf{M}_t(j')})\beta_t\right\}} \tag{7}$$

where $\mathbf{k}_{\mathbf{M}_t(j)} \in \mathbb{R}^c$ is the memory key generated by a $n \times n$ average pooling on $\mathbf{M}_t(j)$. $C(\mathbf{x}, \mathbf{y})$ is the cosine similarity between vectors, $C(\mathbf{x}, \mathbf{y}) = \frac{\mathbf{x} \cdot \mathbf{y}}{\|\mathbf{x}\|\|\mathbf{y}\|}$. Finally, the template is retrieved from memory as a weighted sum,

$$\mathbf{T}_t^{\text{retr}} = \sum_{j=1}^{N} \mathbf{w}_t^r(j)\mathbf{M}_t(j). \tag{8}$$

Fig. 4. The feature channels respond to target parts: images are reconstructed from conv5 of the CNN used in our tracker. Each image is generated by accumulating reconstructed pixels from the same channel. The input image is shown in the top-left.

3.5   Residual Template Learning

Directly using the retrieved template for similarity matching is prone to overfit recent frames. Instead, we learn a residual template by multiplying the retrieved template with a channel-wise gate vector and add it to the initial template to capture the appearance changes. Therefore, our final template is formulated as,

$$\mathbf{T}_t^{\text{final}} = \mathbf{T}_0 + \mathbf{r}_t \odot \mathbf{T}_t^{\text{retr}}, \tag{9}$$

where $\mathbf{T}_0$ is the initial template and $\odot$ is channel-wise multiplication. $\mathbf{r}_t \in \mathbb{R}^c$ is the *residual gate* produced by LSTM controller,

$$\mathbf{r}_t = \sigma(W^r \mathbf{h}_t + b^r), \tag{10}$$

where W^r, b^r are corresponding weights and biases, and σ represents sigmoid function. The *residual gate* controls how much each channel of the retrieved template is added to the initial one, which can be regarded as a form of feature selection.

By projecting different channels of a target feature map to pixel-space using deconvolution, as in [37], we find that the channels focus on different object parts (see Fig. 4). Thus, the channel-wise feature residual learning has the advantage of updating different object parts separately. Experiments in Sect. 5.1 show that this yields a big performance improvement.

3.6   Memory Writing

The image patch with the new position of the target is used for model updating, *i.e.*, memory writing. The new object template $\mathbf{T}_t^{\text{new}}$ is computed using the feature extraction CNN. There are three cases for memory writing: (1) when the new object template is not reliable (e.g. contains a lot of background), there is no need to write new information into memory; (2) when the new object appearance does not change much compared with the previous frame, the memory slot that was previously read should be updated; (3) when the new target has a large appearance change, a new memory slot should be overwritten. To handle these three cases, we define the *write weight* as

$$\mathbf{w}_t^w = g^w \mathbf{0} + g^r \mathbf{w}_t^r + g^a \mathbf{w}_t^a, \tag{11}$$

where $\mathbf{0}$ is the zero vector, $\mathbf{w}_t^r$ is the read weight, and $\mathbf{w}_t^a$ is the allocation weight, which is responsible for allocating a new position for memory writing. The write gate g^w, read gate g^r and allocation gate g^a, are produced by the LSTM controller with a softmax function,

$$[g^w, g^r, g^a] = \text{softmax}(W^g \mathbf{h}_t + b^g), \tag{12}$$

where W^g, b^g are the weights and biases. Since $g^w + g^r + g^a = 1$, these three gates govern the interpolation between the three cases. If $g^w = 1$, then $\mathbf{w}_t^w = \mathbf{0}$ and nothing is written. If g^r or g^a have higher value, then the new template is either used to update the old template (using $\mathbf{w}_t^r$) or written into newly allocated position (using $\mathbf{w}_t^a$). The *allocation weight* is calculated by,

$$\mathbf{w}_t^a(i) = \begin{cases} 1, & \text{if } i = \underset{i}{\text{argmin}} \, \mathbf{w}_{t-1}^u(i) \\ 0, & \text{otherwise} \end{cases} \tag{13}$$

where $\mathbf{w}_t^u$ is the *access vector*,

$$\mathbf{w}_t^u = \lambda \mathbf{w}_{t-1}^u + \mathbf{w}_t^r + \mathbf{w}_t^w, \tag{14}$$

which indicates the frequency of memory access (both reading and writing), and λ is a decay factor. Memory slots that are accessed infrequently will be assigned new templates.

The writing process is performed with a *write weight* in conjunction with an *erase factor* for clearing the memory,

$$\mathbf{M}_{t+1}(i) = \mathbf{M}_t(i)(\mathbf{1} - \mathbf{w}_t^w(i)e^w) + \mathbf{w}_t(i)^w e^w \mathbf{T}_t^{\text{new}}, \tag{15}$$

where e^w is the *erase factor* computed by

$$e^w = d^r g^r + g^a, \tag{16}$$

and $d^r \in [0,1]$ is the *decay rate* produced by the LSTM controller,

$$d^r = \sigma(W^d \mathbf{h}_t + b^d), \tag{17}$$

where σ is sigmoid function. W^d and b^d are corresponding weights and biases. If $g^r = 1$ (and thus $g^a = 0$), then d^r serves as the decay rate for updating the template in the memory slot (case 2). If $g^a = 1$ (and $g^r = 0$), d^r has no effect on e^w, and thus the memory slot will be erased before writing the new template (case 3). Figure 3 shows the detailed diagram of the memory reading and writing process.

4   Implementation Details

We adopt an Alex-like CNN as in SiamFC [4] for feature extraction, where the input image sizes of the object and search images are $127 \times 127 \times 3$ and $255 \times 255 \times 3$ respectively. We use the same strategy for cropping search and object images as in [4], where some context margins around the target are added when cropping the object image. The whole network is trained offline on the VID dataset (object detection from video) of ILSVRC [24] from scratch, and takes about a day. Adam [17] optimization is used with a mini-batches of 8 video clips of length 16. The initial learning rate is 1e-4 and is multiplied by 0.8 every 10k iterations. The video clip is constructed by uniformly sampling frames (keeping the temporal order) from each video. This aims to diversify the appearance variations in one episode for training, which can simulate fast motion, fast background change, jittering object, low frame rate. We use data augmentation, including small image stretch and translation for the target image and search image. The dimension of memory states in the LSTM controller is 512 and the retain probability used in dropout for LSTM is 0.8. The number of memory slots is $N = 8$. The decay factor used for calculating the access vector is $\lambda = 0.99$. At test time, the tracker runs completely feed-forward and no online fine-tuning is needed. We locate the target based on the upsampled response map as in SiamFC [4], and handle the scale changes by searching for the target over three scales $1.05^{[-1,0,1]}$. To smoothen scale estimation and penalize large displacements, we update the object scale with the new one by exponential smoothing $s_t = (1 - \gamma) * s_{t-1} + \gamma s_{new}$, where s is the scale value and the exponential factor $\gamma = 0.6$. Similarly, we dampen the response map with a cosine window by an exponential factor of 0.15.

Our algorithm is implemented in Python with the TensorFlow toolbox [1]. It runs at about 50 fps on a computer with four Intel(R) Core(TM) i7-7700 CPU @ 3.60 GHz and a single NVIDIA GTX 1080 Ti with 11 GB RAM.

5 Experiments

We evaluate our proposed tracker, denoted as MemTrack, on three challenging datasets: OTB-2013 [34], OTB-2015 [35] and VOT-2016 [18]. We follow the standard protocols, and evaluate using precision and success plots, as well as area-under-the-curve (AUC).

5.1 Ablation Studies

Our MemTrack tracker contains three important components: (1) an attention mechanism, which calculates the attended feature vector for memory reading; (2) a dynamic memory network, which maintains the target's appearance variations; and (3) residual template learning, which controls the amount of model updating for each channel of the template. To evaluate their separate contributions to our tracker, we implement several variants of our method and verify them on OTB-2015 dataset.

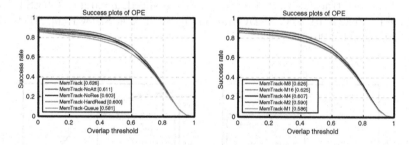

Fig. 5. Ablation studies: (left) success plots of different variants of our tracker on OTB-2015; (right) success plots for different memory sizes {1, 2, 4, 8, 16} on OTB-2015.

We first design a variant of MemTrack without attention mechanism (MemTrack-NoAtt), which averages all L feature vectors to get the feature vector $\mathbf{a}_t$ for the LSTM input. Mathematically, it changes (2) to $\mathbf{a}_t = \frac{1}{L} \sum_{i=1}^{L} \mathbf{f}_{t,i}^*$. As we can see in Fig. 5 (left), Memtrack without attention decreases performance, which shows the benefit of using attention to roughly localize the target in the search image. We also design a naive strategy that simply writes the new target template sequentially into the memory slots as a queue (MemTrack-Queue). When the memory is fully occupied, the oldest template will be replaced with the new template. The retrieved template is generated by averaging all templates stored in the memory slots. As seen in Fig. 5 (left), such simple approach cannot produce good performance, which shows the necessity of our dynamic memory network. We next devise a hard template reading scheme (MemTrack-HardRead), i.e., retrieving a single template by max cosine distance, to replace the soft weighted sum reading scheme. Figure 5 (left) shows that hard-templates decrease performance possibly due to its non-differentiability To verify the effectiveness of gated residual template learning, we design another variant of MemTrack— removing channel-wise residual gates (MemTrack-NoRes), *i.e.* directly adding the retrieved and initial templates to get the final template. From Fig. 5 (left), our gated residual template learning mechanism boosts the performance as it helps to select correct residual channel features for template updating.

We also investigate the effect of memory size on tracking performance. Figure 5 (right) shows success plots on OTB-2015 using different numbers of memory slots. Tracking accuracy increases along with the memory size and saturates at 8 memory slots. Considering the runtime and memory usage, we choose 8 as the default number.

5.2   Comparison Results

We compare our method MemTrack with 9 recent *real-time* trackers ($\geq$15 fps), including CFNet [30], LMCF [32], ACFN [5], RFL [36], SiamFC [4], SiamFC_U [30], Staple [3], DSST [7], and KCF [15] on both OTB-2013 and OTB-2015. To further show our tracking accuracy, we also compared with another 8 recent state-of-the art trackers that are *not* real-time speed, including CREST [26], CSR-DCF [19], MCPF [38], SRDCFdecon [9], SINT [29], SRDCF [6], HDT [23], HCF [20] on OTB-2015.

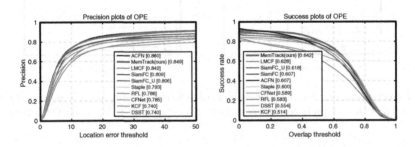

Fig. 6. Precision and success plot on OTB-2013 for recent real-time trackers.

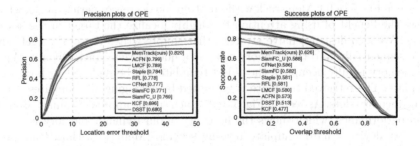

Fig. 7. Precision and success plot on OTB-2015 for recent real-time trackers.

OTB-2013 Results: OTB-2013 [34] dataset contains 51 sequences with 11 video attributes and two evaluation metrics, which are center location error and overlap ratio. Figure 6 shows the one-pass comparison results with recent real-time trackers on OTB-2013. Our tracker achieves the best AUC on the success plot and second place on precision plot. Compared with SiamFC [4], which is the baseline for matching-based methods without online updating, our tracker achieves an improvement of 4.9% on precision plot and 5.8% on success plot. Our method also outperforms SiamFC_U, the improved version of SiamFC [30] that uses simple linear interpolation of the old and new filters with a small learning rate for online updating. This indicates that our dynamic memory networks can handle object appearance changes better than simply interpolating new templates with old ones.

OTB-2015 Results: The OTB-2015 [35] dataset is the extension of OTB-2013 to 100 sequences, and is thus more challenging. Figure 7 presents the precision plot and success plot for recent real-time trackers. Our tracker outperforms all other methods in both measures. Specifically, our method performs much better than RFL [36], which uses the memory states of LSTM to maintain the object appearance variations. This demonstrates the effectiveness of using an external addressable memory to manage object appearance changes, compared with using LSTM memory which is limited by the size of the hidden states. Furthermore, MemTrack improves the baseline of template-based method SiamFC [4] with 6.4% on precision plot and 7.6% on success plot respectively. Our tracker also outperforms the most recently proposed two trackers, LMCF [32] and ACFN [5], on AUC score with a large margin. Figure 8 presents the comparison results of 8 recent state-of-the-art *non-real time* trackers for AUC score (left plot), and the AUC score vs speed (right plot) of all trackers. Our MemTrack, which runs in real-time, has similar AUC performance to CREST [26], MCPF [38] and SRDCFdecon [9], which all run at about 1 fps. Moreover, our MemTrack also surpasses SINT, which is another matching-based method with optical flow as motion information, in terms of both accuracy and speed. Figure 9 further shows the AUC scores of real-time trackers on OTB-2015 under different video attributes including illumination variation, out-of-plane rotation, scale variation,

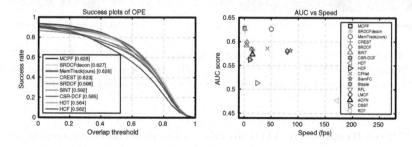

Fig. 8. (left) Success plot on OTB-2015 comparing our real-time MemTrack with recent *non-real-time* trackers. (right) AUC score vs speed with recent trackers.

occlusion, motion blur, fast motion, in-plane rotation, and low resolution. Our tracker outperforms all other trackers on these attributes. In particular, for the low-resolution attribute, our MemTrack surpasses the second place (SiamFC) with a 10.7% improvement on AUC score. In addition, our tracker also works well under out-of-plane rotation and scale variation. Figure 10 shows some qualitative results of our tracker compared with 6 real-time trackers.

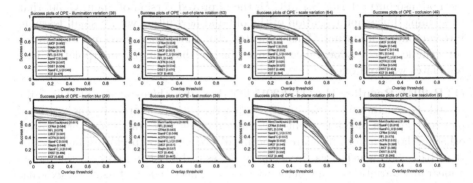

Fig. 9. The success plot of OTB-2015 on eight challenging attributes: illumination variation, out-of-plane rotation, scale variation, occlusion, motion blur, fast motion, in-plane rotation and low resolution

Fig. 10. Qualitative results of our MemTrack, along with SiamFC [4], RFL [36], CFNet [30], Staple [3], LMCF [32], ACFN [5] on eight challenge sequences. From left to right, top to bottom: *board, bolt2, dragonbaby, lemming, matrix, skiing, biker, girl2.*

VOT-2016 Results: The VOT-2016 dataset contains 60 video sequences with per-frame annotated visual attributes. Objects are marked with rotated bounding boxes to better fit their shapes. We compare our tracker with 8 trackers (four real-time and four top-performing)on the benchmark, including SiamFC

Table 1. Comparison results on VOT-2016 with top performers. The evaluation metrics include expected average overlap (EAO), accuracy and robustness value (A and R), accuracy and robustness rank (Ar and Rr). Best results are bolded, and second best is underlined. The up arrows indicate higher values are better for that metric, while down arrows mean lower values are better.

Trackers	MemTrack	SiamFC	RFL	HCF	KCF	CCOT	TCNN	DeepSRDCF	MDNet
EAO (↑)	0.2729	0.2352	0.2230	0.2203	0.1924	0.3310	0.3249	0.2763	0.2572
A (↑)	0.53	0.53	0.52	0.44	0.48	0.54	0.55	0.52	0.54
R (↓)	1.44	1.91	2.51	1.45	1.95	0.89	0.83	1.23	0.91
fps (↑)	50	86	15	11	172	0.3	1	1	1

[4], RFL [36], HCF [20], KCF [15], CCOT [10], TCNN [21], DeepSRDCF [8], and MDNet [22]. Table 1 summarizes results. Although our MemTrack performs worse than CCOT, TCNN and DeepSRDCF over EAO, it runs at 50 fps while others runs at 1 fps or below. Our tracker consistently outperforms the baseline SiamFC and RFL, as well as other real-time trackers. As reported in VOT2016, the SOTA bound is EAO 0.251, which MemTrack exceeds (0.273).

6 Conclusion

In this paper, we propose a dynamic memory network with an external addressable memory block for visual tracking, aiming to adapt matching templates to object appearance variations. An LSTM with attention scheme controls the memory access by parameterizing the memory interactions. We develop channelwise gated residual template learning to form the final matching model, which preserves the conservative information present in the initial target, while providing online adapability of each feature channel. Once the offline training process is finished, no online fine-tuning is needed, which leads to real-time speed of 50 fps. Extensive experiments on standard tracking benchmark demonstrates the effectiveness of our MemTrack.

Acknowledgments. This work was supported by grants from the Research Grants Council of the Hong Kong Special Administrative Region, China (Project No. [T32-101/15-R] and CityU 11212518), and by a Strategic Research Grant from City University of Hong Kong (Project No. 7004887). We are grateful for the support of NVIDIA Corporation with the donation of the Tesla K40 GPU used for this research.

References

1. Abadi, M., et al.: TensorFlow: large-scale machine learning on heterogeneous distributed systems. arXiv (2016)
2. Ba, J.L., Kiros, J.R., Hinton, G.E.: Layer normalization. arXiv (2016)
3. Bertinetto, L., Valmadre, J., Golodetz, S., Miksik, O., Torr, P.: Staple: complementary learners for real-time tracking. In: CVPR (2016)

4. Bertinetto, L., Valmadre, J., Henriques, J.F., Vedaldi, A., Torr, P.H.S.: Fully-convolutional siamese networks for object tracking. In: Hua, G., Jégou, H. (eds.) ECCV 2016. LNCS, vol. 9914, pp. 850–865. Springer, Cham (2016). https://doi.org/10.1007/978-3-319-48881-3_56

5. Choi, J., Chang, H.J., Yun, S., Fischer, T., Demiris, Y., Choi, J.Y.: Attentional correlation filter network for adaptive visual tracking. In: CVPR (2017)

6. Danelljan, M., Gustav, H., Khan, F.S., Felsberg, M.: Learning spatially regularized correlation filters for visual tracking. In: ICCV (2015)

7. Danelljan, M., Häger, G., Khan, F., Felsberg, M.: Accurate scale estimation for robust visual tracking. In: BMVC (2014)

8. Danelljan, M., Hager, G., Khan, F.S., Felsberg, M.: Convolutional features for correlation filter based visual tracking. In: ICCV Workshop on Visual Object Challenge (2015)

9. Danelljan, M., Häger, G., Khan, F.S., Felsberg, M.: Adaptive decontamination of the training set: a unified formulation for discriminative visual tracking. In: CVPR (2016)

10. Danelljan, M., Robinson, A., Shahbaz Khan, F., Felsberg, M.: Beyond correlation filters: learning continuous convolution operators for visual tracking. In: Leibe, B., Matas, J., Sebe, N., Welling, M. (eds.) ECCV 2016. LNCS, vol. 9909, pp. 472–488. Springer, Cham (2016). https://doi.org/10.1007/978-3-319-46454-1_29

11. Graves, A., Wayne, G., Danihelka, I.: Neural turing machines. arXiv (2014)

12. Graves, A., et al.: Hybrid computing using a neural network with dynamic external memory. Nature (2016)

13. Guo, Q., Feng, W., Zhou, C., Huang, R., Wan, L., Wang, S.: Learning dynamic siamese network for visual object tracking. In: ICCV (2017)

14. Held, D., Thrun, S., Savarese, S.: Learning to track at 100 FPS with deep regression networks. In: Leibe, B., Matas, J., Sebe, N., Welling, M. (eds.) ECCV 2016. LNCS, vol. 9905, pp. 749–765. Springer, Cham (2016). https://doi.org/10.1007/978-3-319-46448-0_45

15. Henriques, J.F., Caseiro, R., Martins, P., Batista, J.: High-speed tracking with kernelized correlation filters. TPAMI (2015)

16. Huang, C., Lucey, S., Ramanan, D.: Learning policies for adaptive tracking with deep feature cascades. In: ICCV (2017)

17. Kingma, D., Ba, J.: Adam: a method for stochastic optimization. arXiv (2014)

18. Kristan, M., et al.: The visual object tracking VOT2016 challenge results. In: Hua, G., Jégou, H. (eds.) ECCV 2016. LNCS, vol. 9914, pp. 777–823. Springer, Cham (2016). https://doi.org/10.1007/978-3-319-48881-3_54

19. Lukežič, A., Vojí, T., Čehovin, L., Matas, J., Kristan, M.: Discriminative correlation filter with channel and spatial reliability. In: CVPR (2017)

20. Ma, C., Huang, J.B., Yang, X., Yang, M.H.: Hierarchical convolutional features for visual tracking. In: ICCV (2015)

21. Nam, H., Baek, M., Han, B.: Modeling and propagating CNNs in a tree structure for visual tracking. In: ECCV (2016)

22. Nam, H., Han, B.: Learning multi-domain convolutional neural networks for visual tracking. In: CVPR (2016)

23. Qi, Y., et al.: Hedged deep tracking. In: CVPR (2016)

24. Russakovsky, O., et al.: ImageNet large scale visual recognition challenge. Int. J. Comput. Vis. (IJCV) **115**, 211–252 (2015)

25. Santoro, A., Bartunov, S., Botvinick, M., Wierstra, D., Lillicrap, T.: One-shot learning with memory-augmented neural networks. In: ICML (2016)

26. Song, Y., Ma, C., Gong, L., Zhang, J., Lau, R., Yang, M.H.: CREST: convolutional residual learning for visual tracking. In: ICCV (2017)
27. Srivastava, N., Hinton, G.E., Krizhevsky, A., Sutskever, I., Salakhutdinov, R.: Dropout: a simple way to prevent neural networks from overfitting. JMLR (2014)
28. Sukhbaatar, S., Szlam, A., Weston, J., Fergus, R.: End-to-end memory networks. In: NIPS (2015)
29. Tao, R., Gavves, E., Smeulders, A.W.M.: Siamese instance search for tracking. In: CVPR (2016)
30. Valmadre, J., Bertinetto, L., Henriques, F., Vedaldi, A., Torr, P.H.S.: End-to-end representation learning for correlation filter based tracking. In: CVPR (2017)
31. Wang, L., Ouyang, W., Wang, X., Lu, H.: Visual tracking with fully convolutional networks. In: ICCV (2015)
32. Wang, M., Liu, Y., Huang, Z.: Large margin object tracking with circulant feature maps. In: CVPR (2017)
33. Weston, J., Chopra, S., Bordes, A.: Memory networks. In: ICLR (2015)
34. Wu, Y., Lim, J., Yang, M.H.: Online object tracking: a benchmark. In: CVPR (2013)
35. Wu, Y., Lim, J., Yang, M.H.: Object tracking benchmark. PAMI (2015)
36. Yang, T., Chan, A.B.: Recurrent filter learning for visual tracking. In: ICCV Workshop on Visual Object Challenge (2017)
37. Zeiler, M.D., Fergus, R.: Visualizing and understanding convolutional networks. In: Fleet, D., Pajdla, T., Schiele, B., Tuytelaars, T. (eds.) ECCV 2014. LNCS, vol. 8689, pp. 818–833. Springer, Cham (2014). https://doi.org/10.1007/978-3-319-10590-1_53
38. Zhang, T., Xu, C., Yang, M.H.: Multi-task correlation particle filter for robust object tracking. In: CVPR (2017)

GeoDesc: Learning Local Descriptors by Integrating Geometry Constraints

Zixin Luo[1], Tianwei Shen[1], Lei Zhou[1], Siyu Zhu[1], Runze Zhang[1]([✉]),
Yao Yao[1], Tian Fang[2], and Long Quan[1]

[1] Hong Kong University of Science and Technology, Clear Water Bay, Hong Kong
{zluoag,tshenaa,lzhouai,szhu,rzhangaj,yyaoag,quan}@cse.ust.hk
[2] Shenzhen Zhuke Innovation Technology (Altizure), Shenzhen, China
fangtian@altizure.com

Abstract. Learned local descriptors based on Convolutional Neural Networks (CNNs) have achieved significant improvements on patch-based benchmarks, whereas not having demonstrated strong generalization ability on recent benchmarks of image-based 3D reconstruction. In this paper, we mitigate this limitation by proposing a novel local descriptor learning approach that integrates geometry constraints from multi-view reconstructions, which benefits the learning process in terms of data generation, data sampling and loss computation. We refer to the proposed descriptor as GeoDesc, and demonstrate its superior performance on various large-scale benchmarks, and in particular show its great success on challenging reconstruction tasks. Moreover, we provide guidelines towards practical integration of learned descriptors in Structure-from-Motion (SfM) pipelines, showing the good trade-off that GeoDesc delivers to 3D reconstruction tasks between accuracy and efficiency.

Keywords: Local features · Feature descriptors · Deep learning

1 Introduction

Computing local descriptors on interest regions serves as the subroutine of various computer vision applications such as panorama stitching [12], wide baseline matching [18], image retrieval [22], and Structure-from-Motion (SfM) [26,37, 40,41]. A powerful descriptor is expected to be invariant to both photometric and geometric changes, such as illumination, blur, rotation, scale and perspective changes. Due to the reliability, efficiency and portability, hand-crafted

---

Z. Luo, L. Zhou and Y. Yao were summer interns, T. Shen and R. Zhang were interns at Everest Innovation Technology (Altizure).
S. Zhu is with Alibaba A.I. Labs since Oct. 2017.

Electronic supplementary material The online version of this chapter (https://doi.org/10.1007/978-3-030-01240-3_11) contains supplementary material, which is available to authorized users.

V. Ferrari et al. (Eds.): ECCV 2018, LNCS 11213, pp. 170–185, 2018.
https://doi.org/10.1007/978-3-030-01240-3_11

descriptors such as SIFT [14] have been influentially dominating this field for more than a decade. Until recently, great efforts have been made on developing learned descriptors based on Convolutional Neural Networks (CNNs), which have achieved surprising results on patch-based benchmarks such as HPatches dataset [3]. However, on image-based datasets such as ETH local features benchmark [25], learned descriptors are found to underperform advanced variants of hand-crafted descriptors. The contradictory findings raise the concern of integrating those purportedly better descriptors in real applications, and show significant room of improvement for developing more powerful descriptors that generalize to a wider range of scenarios.

One possible cause of above contradictions, as demonstrated in [25], is the lack of generalization ability as a consequence of data insufficiency. Although previous research [4,27,28] discusses several effective sampling methods that produce seemingly large amount of training data, the generalization ability is still bounded to limited data sources, e.g., the widely-used Brown dataset [6] with only 3 image sets. Hence, it is not surprising that resulting descriptors tend to overfit to particular scenarios. To overcome it, research such as [29,38] applies extra regularization for compact feature learning. Meanwhile, LIFT [33] and [19] seek to enhance data diversity and generate training data from reconstructions of Internet tourism data. However, the existing limitation has not yet been fully mitigated, while intermediate geometric information is overlooked in the learning process despite the robust geometric property that local patch preserves, e.g., the well approximation of local deformations [20].

Besides, we lack guidelines for integrating learned descriptors in practical pipelines such as SfM. In particular, the *ratio criterion*, as suggested in [14] and justified in [10], has received almost no individual attention or was considered inapplicable for learned descriptors [25], whereas it delivers excellent matching efficiency and accuracy improvements, and serves as the necessity for pipelines such as SfM to reject false matches and seed feasible initialization. A general method to apply ratio criterion for learned descriptors is in need in practice.

In this paper, we tackle above issues by presenting a novel learning framework that takes advantage of geometry constraints from multi-view reconstructed data. In particular, we address the importance of data sampling for descriptor learning and summarize our contributions threefold. (i) We propose a novel batch construction method that simulates the pair-wise matching and effectively samples useful data for learning process. (ii) Collaboratively, we propose a loss formulation to reduce overfitting and improve the performance with geometry constraints. (iii) We provide guidelines about ratio criterion, compactness and scalability towards practical portability of learned descriptors.

We evaluate the proposed descriptor, referred to as GeoDesc, on traditional [9] and recent two large-scale datasets [3,25]. Superior performance is shown over the state-of-the-art hand-crafted and learned descriptors. We mitigate previous limitations by showing consistent improvements on both patch-based and image-based datasets, and further demonstrate its success on challenging 3D reconstructions.

2   Related Works

Networks Design. Due to weak semantics and efficiency requirements, existing descriptor learning often relies on shallow and thin networks, e.g., three-layer networks in DDesc [27] with 128-dimensional output features. Moreover, although widely-used in high-level computer vision tasks, max pooling is found to be unsuitable for descriptor learning, which is then replaced by L2 pooling in DDesc [27] or even removed in L2-Net [29]. To further incorporate scale information, DeepCompare [35] and L2-Net [29] use a two-stream central-surround structure which delivers consistent improvements at extra computational cost. To improve the rotational invariance, an orientation estimator is proposed in [34]. Besides of feature learning, previous efforts are also made on joint metric learning as in [7,8,35], whereas comparison in Euclidean space is more preferable by recent works [4,5,27,29,33] in order to guarantee its efficiency.

Loss Formulation. Various of loss formulations have been explored for effective descriptor learning. Initially, networks with a learned metric use softmax loss [8,35] and cast the descriptor learning to a binary classification problem (similar/dissimilar). With weakly annotated data, [15] formulates the loss on keypoint bags. More generally, pair-wise loss [27,33] and triplet loss [4,5,7] are used by networks without a learned metric. Both loss formulations encourage matching patches to be close whereas non-matching patches to be far-away in some measure space. In particular, triplet loss delivers better results [4,7] as it suffers less overfitting [13]. For effective training, recent L2-Net [29] and Hard-Net [17] use the structured loss for data sampling which drastically improves the performance. To further boost the performance, extra regularizations are introduced for learning compact representation in [29,38].

Evaluation Protocol. Previous works often evaluate on datasets such as [9, 16,31]. However, those datasets either are small, or lack diversity to generalize well to various applications of descriptors. As a result, the evaluation results are commonly inconsistent or even contradictory to each other as pointed out in [3], which limits the application of learned descriptors. Two novel benchmarks, HPatches [3] and ETH local descriptor benchmark [25] have been recently introduced with clearly defined protocols and better generalization properties. However, inconsistency still exists in the two benchmarks, where HPatches [3] benchmark demonstrates the significant outperformance from learned descriptors over the handcrafted, whereas the ETH local descriptor benchmark [25] finds that the advanced variants of the traditional descriptor are at least on par with the learning-based. The inconclusive results indicate that there is still significant room for improvement to learn more powerful feature descriptors.

3   Method

3.1   Network Architecture

We borrow the network in L2-Net [29], where the feature tower is constructed by eschewing pooling layers and using strided convolutional layers for in-network downsampling. Each convolutional layer except the last one is followed by a batch normalization (BN) layer whose weighting and bias parameters are fixed to 1 and 0. The L2-normalization layer after the last convolution produces the final 128-dimensional feature vector.

3.2 Training Data Generation

Acquiring high quality training data is important in learning tasks. In this section, we discuss a practical pipeline that automatically produces well-annotated data suitable for descriptor learning.

2D Correspondence Generation. Similar to LIFT [33], we rely on successful 3D reconstructions to generate ground truth 2D correspondences in an automatic manner. First, sparse reconstructions are obtained from standard SfM pipeline [24]. Then, 2D correspondences are generated by projecting 3D point clouds. In general, SfM is used to filter out most mismatches among images.

Although verified by SfM, the generated correspondences are still outlier-contaminated from image noise and wrongly registered cameras. It happens particularly often on Internet tourism datasets such as [23,30] (illustrated in Fig. 1(a)), and usually not likely to be filtered by simply limiting reprojection error. To improve data quality, we take one step further than LIFT by computing the visibility check based on 3D Delaunay triangulation [11] which is widely-used for outlier filtering in dense stereo. Empirically, 30% of 3D points will be discarded after the filtering while only points with high precision are kept for ground truth generation. Figure 1(b) gives an example to illustrate its effect.

(a)   (b)

Fig. 1. (a) Outlier matches after SfM verification (by COLMAP [24]) on *Gendarmenmarkt* dataset [30]. The reprojection error (next to the image) cannot be used to identify false matches. (b) Reconstructed sparse point cloud (top), where points in red (bottom) indicate being filtered by Delaunay triangulation and only reliable points in green are kept. The number of points decreases from 75k to 53k after the filtering. (Color figure online)

Matching Patch Generation. Next, the interest region of a 2D projection is cropped similar to LIFT, which is formulated by an similarity transformation

$$\begin{pmatrix} x_i^s \\ y_i^s \end{pmatrix} = \begin{bmatrix} \frac{k\sigma}{2}cos(\theta) & \frac{k\sigma}{2}sin(\theta) & x \\ -\frac{k\sigma}{2}sin(\theta) & \frac{k\sigma'}{2}cos(\theta) & y \end{bmatrix} \begin{pmatrix} x_i^t \\ y_i^t \end{pmatrix}, \tag{1}$$

where $(x_i^s, y_i^s), (x_i^t, y_i^t)$ are input and output regular sampling grids, and (x, y, σ, θ) are keypoint parameters (x, y coordinates, scale and orientation) from SIFT detector. The constant k is set to 12 as in LIFT, resulting in $12\sigma \times 12\sigma$ patches.

Due to the robust estimation of scale (σ) and orientation (θ) parameters of SIFT even in extreme cases [39], the resulting patches are mostly free of scale and rotation differences, thus suitable for training. In later experiments of image matching or SfM, we rely on the same cropping method to achieve scale and rotation invariance for learned descriptors.

3.3   Geometric Similarity Estimation

Geometries at a 3D point are robust and provide rich information. Inspired by the MVS (Multi-View Stereo) accuracy measurement in [36], we define two types of geometric similarity: patch similarity and image similarity, which will facilitate later data sampling and loss formulation.

Patch Similarity. We define patch similarity S_{patch} to measure the difficulty to have a patch pair matched with respect to perspective changes. Formally, given a patch pair, we relate it to its corresponding 3D track P which is seen by cameras centering at C_i and C_j. Next, we compute the vertex normal P_n at P from the surface model. The geometric relationship is illustrated in Fig. 2(a). Finally, we formulate S_{patch} as

$$S_{patch} = s_1 s_2 = g(\angle C_i P C_j, \sigma_1) g(\angle C_i P P_n - \angle C_j P P_n, \sigma_2), \qquad (2)$$

where s_1 measures the intersection angle between two viewing rays from the 3D track ($\angle C_i P C_j$), while s_2 measures the difference of incidence angles between a viewing ray and the vertex normal from the 3D track ($\angle C_i P P_n, \angle C_j P P_n$). The angle metric is defined as $g(\alpha, \sigma) = \exp(-\frac{\alpha^2}{2\sigma^2})$. As an interpretation, s_1 and s_2 measure the perspective change regarding a *3D point* and local *3D surface*, respectively. The effect of S_{patch} is illustrated in Fig. 2(b).

The accuracy of s_1 and s_2 depends on sparse and mesh reconstructions, respectively, and is generally sufficient for its use as shown in [36]. The similarity does not consider scale and rotation changes as already resolved from Eq. 1. Empirically, we choose $\sigma_1 = 15$ and $\sigma_2 = 20$ (in degree).

Image Similarity. Based on the patch similarity, we define the image similarity S_{image} as the average patch similarity of the correspondences between an image pair. The image similarity measures the difficulty to match an image pair and can be interpreted as a measurement of perspective change. Examples are given in Fig. 2(c). The image similarity will be beneficial for data sampling in Sect. 3.4.

3.4   Batch Construction

For descriptor learning, most existing frameworks take patch pairs (matching/non-matching) or patch triplets (reference, matching and non-matching) as input. As in previous studies, the convergence rate is highly dependent on being able to see useful data [21]. Here, "useful" data often refers to patch

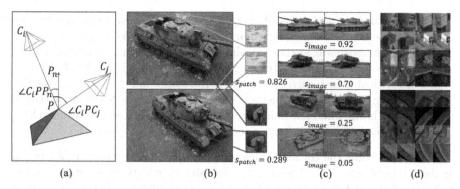

Fig. 2. (a) The patch similarity relies on the geometric relationship between cameras, tracks and surface normal. (b) The effect of patch similarity, which measures the difficulty to have a patch pair matched with respect to the perspective change. (c) The effect of image similarity, which measures the perspective change between an image pairs. (d) Batch data constructed by L2-Net [29] and HardNet [17] (top), whose in-batch patch pairs are often distinctive to each other and thus contribute nothing to the loss in the late learning (e.g., the margin-based loss). However, the batch data from the proposed batch construction method (bottom) consists of similar patch pairs due to the spatially close keypoints or repetitive patterns, which are considered harder to distinguish and thus raise greater challenges for learning

pairs/triplets that produce meaningful loss for learning. However, the effective sampling of such data is generally challenging due to the intractably large number of patch pair/triplet combination in the database. Hence, on one hand, sampling strategies such as hard negative mining [27] and anchor swap [4] are proposed, while on the other hand, effective batch construction is used in [7,17,29] to compare the reference patch against all the in-batch samples in the loss computation.

Inspired by previous works, we propose a novel batch construction method that effectively samples "useful" data by relying on geometry constraints from SfM, including the image matching results and image similarity S_{image}, to simulate the pair-wise image matching and sample data. Formally, given one image pair, we extract a *match set* $X = \{(x_1, x_1^+), (x_2, x_2^+), ..., (x_{N_1}, x_{N_1}^+)\}$, where N_1 is the set size and (x_i, x_i^+) is a matching patch pair surviving the SfM verification. A training batch is then constructed on N_2 match sets. Hence, the learning objective becomes to improve the matching quality for each match set. In Sect. 3.5, we will discuss the loss computation on each match set and batch data.

Compared with L2-Net [29] and HardNet [17] whose training batches are random sampled from the whole database, the proposed method produces harder samples and thus raises greater challenges for learning. As an example shown in Fig. 2(d), the training batch constructed by the proposed method consists of many similar patterns, due to the spatially close keypoints or repetitive textures. In general, such training batch has two major advantages for descriptor learning:

– It reflects the in-practice complexity. In real applications, image patches are often extracted between image pairs for matching. The proposed method simulates this scenario so that training and testing become more consistent.
– It generates hard samples for training. As observed in [4,17,21,27], hard samples are critical to fast convergence and performance improvement for descriptor learning. The proposed method effectively generates batch data that is sufficiently hard, while not being overfitting as constructed on real matching results instead of model inference results [27].

To further boost the training efficiency, we exclude image pairs that are too similar to contribute to the learning. Those pairs are effectively identified by the image similarity defined in Sect. 3.3. In practice, we discard image pairs whose S_{image} are larger than 0.85 (e.g., the toppest pair in Fig. 2(c)), which results in a 30% shrink of training samples.

3.5   Loss Formulation

We formulate the loss with two terms: structured loss and geometric loss.

Structured Loss. The structured loss used in L2-Net [29] and HardNet [17] is essentially suitable to consume the batch samples constructed in Sect. 3.4. In particular, the formulation in HardNet based on the "hardest-in-batch" strategy and a distance margin shows to be more effective than the log-likelihood formulation in L2-Net. However, we observe successive overfitting when applying the HardNet loss to our batch data, which we ascribe to the too strong constraint of "hardest-in-batch" strategy. In this strategy, the loss is computed on the data sample that produces the largest loss, and a margin with a large value (1.0 in HardNet) is set to push the non-matching pairs away from matching pairs. In our batch data, we already effectively sample the "hard" data which is often visually similar, thus forcing a large margin is inapplicable and stalls the learning. One simple solution is to decrease the margin value, whereas the performance drops significantly in our experiments.

To avoid above limitation and better take advantage of our batch data, we propose the loss formulation as follows. First, we compute the structured loss for one match set. Given normalized features $\mathbf{F}_1, \mathbf{F}_2 \in \mathbb{R}^{N_1 \times 128}$ computed on match set X for all (x_i, x_i^+), the cosine similarity matrix is derived by $\mathbf{S} = \mathbf{F}_1 \mathbf{F}_2^T$. Next, we compute $\mathbf{L} = \mathbf{S} - \alpha\mathbf{diag}(\mathbf{S})$ and formulate the loss as

$$E_1 = \frac{1}{N_1(N_1 - 1)} \sum_{i,j} (\max(0, l_{i,j} - l_{i,i}) + \max(0, l_{i,j} - l_{j,j})), \qquad (3)$$

where $l_{i,j}$ is the element in $\mathbf{L}$, and $\alpha \in (0, 1)$ is the distance ratio mimicking the behavior of ratio test [14] and pushing away non-matching pairs from matching pairs. Finally, we take the average of the loss on each match set to derive the final loss for one training batch.

The proposed formulation is distinctive from HardNet in three aspects. First, we compute the cosine similarity instead of Euclidean distance for computational efficiency. Second, we apply a *distance ratio margin* instead of a *fixed distance margin* as an adaptive margin to reduce overfitting. Finally, we compute the *mean* value of each loss element instead of the maximum ("hardest-in-batch") in order to cooperate the proposed batch construction.

Geometric Loss. Although E_1 ensures matching patch pairs to be distant from the non-matching, it does not explicitly encourage matching pairs to be close in its measure space. One simple solution is to apply a typical pair-wise loss in [27], whereas taking a risk of positive collapse and overfitting as observed in [13]. To overcome it, we adaptively set up the margin regarding the patch similarity defined in Sect. 3.3, serving as a soft constraint for maximizing the positive similarity. We refer to this term as *geometric loss* and formulate it as

$$E_2 = \sum_i \max(0, \beta - s_{i,i}), \beta = \begin{cases} 0.7 & s_{patch} \geq 0.5 \\ 0.5 & 0.2 \leq s_{patch} < 0.5 \\ 0.2 & \text{otherwise} \end{cases} \quad (4)$$

where β is the adaptive margin, $s_{i,i}$ is the element in S, namely, the cosine similarity of patch pair (x_i, x_i^+), while s_{patch} is the patch similarity for (x_i, x_i^+). We use $E_1 + \lambda E_2$ as the final loss, and empirically set α and λ to 0.4 and 0.2.

3.6 Training

We use image sets [30] as in LIFT [33], the SfM data in [23], and further collect several image sets to form the training database. Based on COLMAP [24], we run 3D reconstructions to establish necessary geometry constraints. Image sets that are overlapping with the benchmark data are manually excluded. We train the networks from scratch using Adam with a base learning rate of 0.001 and weight decay of 0.0001. The learning rate decays by 0.9 every 10,000 steps. Data augmentation includes randomly flipping, 90 degrees rotation and brightness and contrast adjustment. The match set size N_1 and batch size N_2 are 64 and 12, respectively. Input patches are standardized to have zero mean and unit norm.

4 Experiments

We evaluate the proposed descriptor on three datasets: the patch-based HPatches [3] benchmark, the image-based Heinly benchmark [9] and ETH local features benchmark [25]. We further demonstrate on challenging SfM examples.

4.1 HPatches Benchmark

HPatches benchmark [3] defines three complementary tasks: patch verification, patch matching, and patch retrieval. Different levels of geometrical perturbations are imposed to form EASY, HARD and TOUGH patch groups. In the task of verification, two subtasks are defined based on whether negative pairs are sampled from images within the same (SAMESEQ) or different sequences (DIFFSEQ). In the task of matching, two subtasks are defined based on whether the principle variance is viewpoint (VIEW) or illumination (ILLUM). Following [3], we use mean average precision (mAP) to measure the performance for all three tasks on HPatches split 'full'.

We select five descriptors to compare: SIFT as the baseline, RSIFT [2] and DDesc [27] as the best-performing hand-crafted and learned descriptors concluded in [3]. Moreoever, we experiment with recent learned descriptors L2-Net [29] and HardNet [17]. The proposed descriptor is referred to as GeoDesc.

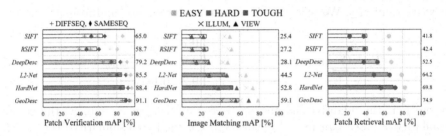

Fig. 3. Left to right: verification, matching and retrieval results on HPatches dataset, split 'full'. Results on different patch groups are colorized, while DIFFSEQ/SAMESEQ and ILLUM/VIEW denote the subtasks of verification and matching, respectively

As shown in Fig. 3, GeoDesc surpasses all the other descriptors on all three tasks by a large margin. In particular, the performance on TOUGH patch group is significantly improved, which indicates the superior invariance to large image changes of GeoDesc. Interestingly, comparing GeoDesc with HardNet, we observe some performance drop on EASY groups especially for illumination changes, which can be ascribed to the data bias for SfM data. Though applying randomness such as illumination during the training, we cannot fully mitigate this limitation which asks more diverse real data in descriptor learning.

In addition, we evaluate different configurations of GeoDesc on HPatches as shown in Table 1 to demonstrate the effect of each part of our method.

- *Config. 1*: the HardNet framework as the baseline.
- *Config. 2*: trained with the SfM data in Sect. 3.2. Compared with *Config. 1*, it is shown that crowd-sourced training data essentially improves the generalization ability. Meanwhile, on the other hand, *Config. 2* can be regarded as an extension of LIFT [33] with more advanced loss formulation.
- *Config. 3*: equipped with the proposed batch construction in Sect. 3.4. As discussed in Sect. 3.5, the "hardest-in-batch" strategy in HardNet is inapplicable to hard batch data and thus leads to performance drop compared with *Config. 2*. In practice, we need to adjust the margin value from 1.0 in HardNet to 0.6, otherwise the training will not even converge. Though trainable, the smaller margin value harms the final performance.

- *Config. 4*: equipped with the modified structured loss in Sect. 3.5. Notable performance improvements are achieved over *Config. 2* due to the collaborative use of proposed methods, showing the effectiveness of simulating pairwise matching and sampling hard data. Besides, replacing the *distance margin* with *distance ratio* can improve the training efficiency, as shown in Fig. 4.
- *Config. 5*: equipped with the geometric loss in Sect. 3.5. Further improvements are obtained over *Config. 4* as E_2 constrains the solution space and enhances the training efficiency.

To sum up, the "hardest-in-batch" strategy is beneficial when no other sampling is applied and most in-batch samples do not contribute to the loss. However, with harder batch data effectively constructed, it is advantageous to replace the "hardest-in-batch" and further boost the descriptor performance.

Table 1. Evaluation of different configurations of GeoDesc on HPatches. Modules are enabled if marked with "Y" otherwise with "-". *SfM Data* denotes the training with our SfM data, *Batch Construct.* denotes the equipment of proposed batch construction, while E_1 and E_2 denote the use of proposed structured loss and geometric loss, respectively. The last configuration (*Config. 5*) is our best model with GeoDesc

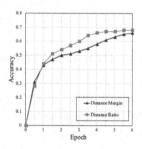

No.	GeoDesc configuration				HPatches benchmark tasks		
	SfM Data	*Batch Construct.*	E_1	E_2	*Verification*	*Matching*	*Retrieval*
1	-	-	-	-	88.4	52.8	69.8
2	Y	-	-	-	90.1	57.0	73.2
3	Y	Y	-	-	89.9	50.2	70.4
4	Y	Y	Y	-	90.9	58.5	74.5
5	Y	Y	Y	Y	**91.1**	**59.1**	**74.9**

Fig. 4. Effect of taking *distance ratio* in loss computation. The metric is the validation accuracy of patch triplets with a margin of 0.5 by cosine similarity.

4.2   Heinly Benchmark

Different from HPatches which experiments on image patches, the benchmark by Heinly et al. [9] evaluates pair-wise image matching regarding different types of photometric or geometric changes, targeting to provide practical insights for strengths and weaknesses of descriptors. We use two standard metrics as in [9] to quantify the matching quality. First, the *Matching Score = #Inlier Matches/#Features*. Second, the *Recall = #Inlier Matches/#True Matches*. Four descriptor are selected to compare: SIFT, the baseline hand-crafted descriptor; DSP-SIFT, the best hand-crafted descriptor even superior to the previous learning-based as evaluated in [25]; L2-Net and HardNet, the recent advanced learned descriptors. For fairness comparison, no ratio test and only cross check (mutual test) is applied for all descriptors.

Evaluation results are shown in Table 2. Compared with DSP-SIFT, GeoDesc performs comparably regarding image quality changes (compression, blur), while

Table 2. Evaluation results on pair-wise image matching on benchmark by Heinly *et al.* [9] with respect to different types of image changes

	Matching Score in %					Recall in %				
	SIFT	DSP-SIFT	L2-Net	HardNet	GeoDesc	SIFT	DSP-SIFT	L2-Net	HardNet	GeoDesc
JPEG	31.9	**35.1**	25.7	27.0	34.7	60.7	**66.9**	49.0	51.5	66.1
Blur	12.4	14.3	9.1	11.3	**14.4**	41.0	47.3	30.1	37.4	**47.7**
Exposure	32.9	34.8	33.9	34.9	**36.3**	78.2	82.6	80.4	82.8	**86.4**
Day-Night	5.6	5.7	6.8	7.4	**7.5**	29.2	29.7	35.6	38.9	**39.6**
Scale	35.8	34.7	32.6	34.8	**37.8**	81.2	78.8	73.6	79.0	**85.8**
Rotation	56.3	49.1	55.9	57.4	**59.8**	82.4	71.8	81.9	84.0	**87.6**
Scale-rotation	12.6	12.0	10.7	12.1	**14.3**	29.6	28.1	25.0	28.5	**33.7**
Planar	23.8	24.8	25.6	27.4	**29.1**	48.2	50.4	51.9	55.6	**59.1**

notably better for illumination and geometric changes (rotation, scale, viewpoint). On the other hand, GeoDesc delivers significant improvements on L2-Net and HardNet and particularly narrows the gap in terms of photometric changes, which makes GeoDesc applicable to different scenarios in real applications.

4.3   ETH Local Features Benchmark

The ETH local features benchmark [25] focuses on image-based 3D reconstruction tasks. We compare GeoDesc with SIFT, DSP-SIFT and L2-Net, and follow the same protocols in [25] to quantify the SfM quality, including the number of registered images (*# Registered*), reconstructed sparse points (*# Sparse Points*), image observations (*# Observations*), mean track length (*Track Length*) and mean reprojection error (*Reproj. Error*). For fairness comparison, we apply no distance ratio test for descriptor matching and extract features at the same keypoints as in [25].

As observed in Table 3, first, GeoDesc performs best on *# Registered*, which is generally considered as the most important SfM metric that directly quantifies the reconstruction completeness. Second, GeoDesc achieves best results on *# Sparse Points* and *# Observations*, which indicates the superior matching quality in the early step of SfM. However, GeoDesc fails to get best statistics about *Track Length* and *Reproj. Error* as GeoDesc computes the two metrics on significantly larger *# Sparse Points*. In terms of datasets whose scale is small and have similar track number (*Fountain, Herzjesu*), GeoDesc gives the longest *Track Length*.

To sum up, GeoDesc surpasses both the previous best-performing DSP-SIFT and recent advanced L2-Net by a notable margin. In addition, it is noted that L2-Net also shows consistent improvements over DSP-SIFT, which demonstrates the power of taking structured loss for learned descriptors.

4.4   Challenging 3D Reconstructions

To further demonstrate the effect of the proposed descriptor in a context of 3D reconstruction, we showcase selective image sets whose reconstructions fail or are in low quality with a typical SIFT-based 3D reconstruction pipeline but get significantly improved by integrating GeoDesc.

Table 3. Evaluation results on ETH local features benchmark [25] for SfM tasks

		# Images	# Registered	# Sparse Points	# Observations	Track Length	Reproj. Error
Fountain	SIFT	11	11	10,004	44K	4.49	**0.30px**
	DSP-SIFT		11	14,785	71K	4.80	0.41px
	L2-Net		11	16,119	78K	4.86	0.43px
	GeoDesc		11	**16,687**	**83K**	**4.99**	0.46px
Herzjesu	SIFT	8	8	4,916	19K	4.00	**0.32px**
	DSP-SIFT		8	7,760	32K	4.19	0.45px
	L2-Net		8	8,473	36K	4.27	0.47px
	GeoDesc		8	**8,720**	**38K**	**4.34**	0.55px
South Building	SIFT	128	128	62,780	353K	5.64	**0.42px**
	DSP-SIFT		128	110,394	664K	**6.02**	0.57px
	L2-Net		128	155,780	798K	5.13	0.58px
	GeoDesc		128	**170,306**	**887K**	5.21	0.64px
Madrid Metropolis	SIFT	1,344	440	62,729	416K	**6.64**	**0.53px**
	DSP-SIFT		476	107,028	681K	6.36	0.64px
	L2-Net		692	254,142	1,067K	4.20	0.69px
	GeoDesc		**809**	**306,976**	**1,200K**	3.91	0.66px
Gendarmenmarkt	SIFT	1,463	950	169,900	1,010K	**5.95**	**0.64px**
	DSP-SIFT		975	321,846	1,732K	5.38	0.74px
	L2-Net		1,168	667,392	2,611K	3.91	0.73px
	GeoDesc		**1,208**	**779,814**	**2,903K**	3.72	0.74px
Tower of London	SIFT	1,576	702	142,746	963K	6.75	**0.53px**
	DSP-SIFT		755	236,598	1,761K	**7.44**	0.64px
	L2-Net		1,049	558,673	2,617K	4.68	0.67px
	GeoDesc		**1,081**	**622,076**	**2,852K**	4.58	0.69px
Alamo	SIFT	2,915	743	120,713	1,384K	11.47	**0.54px**
	DSP-SIFT		754	144,341	1,815K	**12.58**	0.66px
	L2-Net		882	318,787	2,932K	9.17	0.76px
	GeoDesc		**893**	**353,329**	**3,159K**	8.94	0.84px
Roman Forum	SIFT	2,364	1,407	242,192	1,805K	7.45	**0.61px**
	DSP-SIFT		**1,583**	372,573	2,879K	**7.73**	0.71px
	L2-Net		1,537	708,794	4,530K	6.39	0.69px
	GeoDesc		1,566	**770,363**	**5,051K**	6.56	0.73px
Cornell	SIFT	6,514	4,999	1,010,544	6,317K	**6.25**	**0.53px**
	DSP-SIFT		4,946	1,177,916	7,233K	6.14	0.67px
	L2-Net		5,557	2,706,215	15,710K	5.81	0.72px
	GeoDesc		**5,823**	**3,076,476**	**17,550K**	5.70	0.96px

Fig. 5. Testing cases of challenging image sets, where a traditional SIFT-based reconstruction pipeline fails to apply but GeoDesc delivers significant improvement.

From examples shown in Fig. 5, it is clear to see the benefit of deploying GeoDesc in a reconstruction pipeline. First, by robust matching resistant to photometric and geometric changes, a complete sparse reconstruction registered with more cameras can be obtained. Second, due to more accurate camera pose estimation, the final fined mesh reconstruction is then derived.

5   Practical Guidelines

In this section, we discuss several practical guidelines to complement the performance evaluation and provide insights towards real applications. Following experiments are conducted with 231 extra high-resolution image pairs, whose keypoints are downsampled to ~10k per image. We use a single NVIDIA GTX 1080 GPU with TensorFlow [1], and forward each batch with 256 patches.

5.1   Ratio Criterion

The ratio criterion [14] compares the distance between the first and the second nearest neighbor, and establishes a match if the former is smaller than the latter to some ratio. For SfM tasks, the ratio criterion improves overall matching quality, RANSAC efficiency, and seeds robust initialization. Despite those benefits, the ratio criterion has received little attention, or even been considered inapplicable to learned descriptors in previous studies [25]. Here, we propose a general method to determine the ratio that well cooperates with existing SfM pipelines.

The general idea is simple: the new ratio should function similarly as SIFT's, as most SfM pipelines are parameterized for SIFT. To quantify the effect of the ratio criterion, we use the metric *Precision* = *#Inlier Matches/#Putative matches*, and determine the ratio that achieves similar *Precision* as SIFT's. As an example in Fig. 6, we compute the *Precision* of SIFT and GeoDesc on our experimental dataset, and find the best ratio for GeoDesc is 0.89 at which it gives similar *Precision* (0.70) as SIFT (0.69). This ratio is applied to experiments in Sect. 4.4 and shows robust results and compatibility in the practical SfM pipeline.

5.2   Compactness Study

A compact feature representation generally indicates better performance with respective to discriminativeness and scalability. To quantify the compactness, we reply on the intermediate result in Principal Component Analysis (PCA). First, we compute the explained variance v_i which is stored in increasing order for each feature dimension indexed by i. Then we estimate the compact dimensionality (denoted as Compact-Dim) by finding the minimal k that satisfies $\sum_i^k v_i / \sum_i^D v_i \geq t$, where t is a given threshold and D is the original feature dimensionality. In this experiment, we set $t = 0.9$, so that the Compact-Dim can be interpreted as the minimal dimensionality required to convey more than 90% information of the original feature. Obviously, larger Compact-Dim indicates less redundancy, namely greater compactness.

As a result, the Compact-Dim estimated on 4 millions feature vectors for SIFT, DSP-SIFT, L2-Net and GeoDesc is 56, 63, 75 and 100, respectively. The ranking of Compact-Dim effectively responds to previous performance evaluations, where descriptors with larger Compact-Dim yield better results.

5.3   Scalability Study

Computational Cost. As evaluated in [3, 25], the efficiency of learned descriptors is on par with traditional descriptors such as CPU-based SIFT. Here, we further compare with GPU-based SIFT [32] to provide insights about practicability. We evaluate the running time in three steps. First, keypoint detection and canonical orientation estimation by SIFT-GPU. Next, patches cropping by Eq. 1. Finally, feature inference of image patches. The computational cost and memory demand are shown in Table 4, indicating that with GPU support, not surprisingly, SIFT ($0.20s$) is still faster than the learned descriptor ($0.31s$), with a narrow gap due to the parallel implementation. For applications heavily relying on matching quality (e.g., 3D reconstruction), the proposed descriptor achieves a good trade-off to replace SIFT.

Quantization. To conserve disk space, I/O and memory, we linearly map feature vectors of GeoDesc from $[-1, 1]$ to $[0, 255]$ and round each element to unsigned-char value. The quantization does not affect the performance as evaluated on HPatches benchmark.

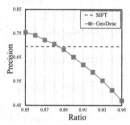

Fig. 6. Determine the ratio criterion of GeoDesc so that it has the same *Precision* as SIFT (at 0.89)

Table 4. Computational cost and memory demand of feature extraction of GeoDesc in three steps: SIFT-GPU extraction, patch cropping and feature inference. The total time cost is evaluated with three steps implemented in a parallel fashion

	SIFT	Crop.	Infer.	Total
Device	GPU	CPU	GPU	-
Memory (GB)	3.3	2.7	0.3	-
Time (s)	0.20	0.28	0.31	0.31

6   Conclusions

In contrast to prior work, we have addressed the advantages of integrating geometry constraints for descriptor learning, which benefits the learning process in terms of ground truth data generation, data sampling and loss computation. Also, we have discussed several guidelines, in particular, the *ratio criterion*, towards practical portability. Finally, we have demonstrated the superior performance and generalization ability of the proposed descriptor, GeoDesc, on three benchmark datasets in different scenarios, We have further shown the significant improvement of GeoDesc on challenging reconstructions, and the good trade-off between efficiency and accuracy to deploy GeoDesc in real applications.

Acknowledgment. This work is supported by T22-603/15N, Hong Kong ITC PSKL12EG02 and the Special Project of International Scientific and Technological Cooperation in Guangzhou Development District (No. 2017GH24).

References

1. Abadi, M., et al.: TensorFlow: large-scale machine learning on heterogeneous distributed systems. arXiv (2016)
2. Arandjelovic, R., Zisserman, A.: Three things everyone should know to improve object retrieval. In: CVPR (2012)
3. Balntas, V., Lenc, K., Vedaldi, A., Mikolajczyk, K.: HPatches: a benchmark and evaluation of handcrafted and learned local lescriptors. In: CVPR (2017)
4. Balntas, V., Riba, E., Ponsa, D., Mikolajczyk, K.: Learning local feature descriptors with triplets and shallow convolutional neural networks. In: BMVC (2016)
5. Balntas, V., Johns, E., Tang, L., Mikolajczyk, K.: PN-net: conjoined triple deep network for learning local image descriptors. arXiv (2016)
6. Brown, M.A., Hua, G., Winder, S.A.J.: Discriminative learning of local image descriptors. PAMI **33**, 43–57 (2011)
7. Vijay Kumar, B.G., Carneiro, G., Reid, I.: Learning local image descriptors with deep siamese and triplet convolutional networks by minimizing global loss functions. In: CVPR (2016)
8. Han, X., Leung, T., Jia, Y., Sukthankar, R., Berg, A.C.: MatchNet - unifying feature and metric learning for patch-based matching. In: CVPR (2015)
9. Heinly, J., Dunn, E., Frahm, J.-M.: Comparative evaluation of binary features. In: Fitzgibbon, A., Lazebnik, S., Perona, P., Sato, Y., Schmid, C. (eds.) ECCV 2012. LNCS, pp. 759–773. Springer, Heidelberg (2012). https://doi.org/10.1007/978-3-642-33709-3_54
10. Kaplan, A., Avraham, T., Lindenbaum, M.: Interpreting the ratio criterion for matching SIFT descriptors. In: Leibe, B., Matas, J., Sebe, N., Welling, M. (eds.) ECCV 2016. LNCS, vol. 9909, pp. 697–712. Springer, Cham (2016). https://doi.org/10.1007/978-3-319-46454-1_42
11. Labatut, P., Pons, J.P., Keriven, R.: Efficient multi-view reconstruction of large-scale scenes using interest points, delaunay triangulation and graph cuts. In: ICCV (2007)
12. Li, S., Yuan, L., Sun, J., Quan, L.: Dual-feature warping-based motion model estimation. In: ICCV (2015)
13. Lin, J., Morere, O., Chandrasekhar, V., Veillard, A., Goh, H.: DeepHash: getting regularization, depth and fine-tuning right. arXiv (2015)
14. Lowe, D.G.: Distinctive image features from scale-invariant keypoints. In: IJCV (2004)
15. Markuš, N., Pandžić, I.S., Ahlberg, J.: Learning local descriptors by optimizing the keypoint-correspondence criterion. In: ICPR (2016)
16. Mikolajczyk, K., Schmid, C.: A performance evaluation of local descriptors. PAMI **27**, 1615–1630 (2005)
17. Mishchuk, A., Mishkin, D., Radenovic, F.: Working hard to know your neighbor's margins: local descriptor learning loss. In: NIPS (2017)
18. Mishkin, D., Matas, J., Perdoch, M., Lenc, K.: WxBS: wide baseline stereo generalizations. In: BMVC (2015)
19. Mitra, R., et al.: A large dataset for improving patch matching. arXiv (2018)
20. Morel, J.M., Yu, G.: ASIFT: a new framework for fully affine invariant image comparison. SIAM J. Imaging Sci. **2**, 438–469 (2009)
21. Movshovitz-Attias, Y., Toshev, A., Leung, T.K., Ioffe, S., Singh, S.: No Fuss Distance Metric Learning using Proxies. In: ICCV (2017)

22. Philbin, J., Chum, O., Isard, M., Sivic, J., Zisserman, A.: Object retrieval with large vocabularies and fast spatial matching. In: CVPR (2007)
23. Radenović, F., Tolias, G., Chum, O.: CNN image retrieval learns from BoW: unsupervised fine-tuning with hard examples. In: Leibe, B., Matas, J., Sebe, N., Welling, M. (eds.) ECCV 2016. LNCS, vol. 9905, pp. 3–20. Springer, Cham (2016). https://doi.org/10.1007/978-3-319-46448-0_1
24. Schnberger, J.L., Frahm, J.M.: Structure-from-motion revisited. In: CVPR (2016)
25. Schönberger, J.L., Hardmeier, H., Sattler, T., Pollefeys, M.: Comparative evaluation of hand-crafted and learned local features. In: CVPR (2017)
26. Shen, T., Zhu, S., Fang, T., Zhang, R., Quan, L.: Graph-based consistent matching for structure-from-motion. In: Leibe, B., Matas, J., Sebe, N., Welling, M. (eds.) ECCV 2016. LNCS, vol. 9907, pp. 139–155. Springer, Cham (2016). https://doi.org/10.1007/978-3-319-46487-9_9
27. Simo-Serra, E., Trulls, E., Ferraz, L., Kokkinos, I., Fua, P., Moreno-Noguer, F.: Discriminative learning of deep convolutional feature point descriptors. In: CVPR (2015)
28. Sohn, K.: Improved deep metric learning with multi-class n-pair loss objective. In: NIPS (2016)
29. Tian, B.F.Y., Wu, F: L2-net: deep learning of discriminative patch descriptor in Euclidean space. In: CVPR (2017)
30. Wilson, K., Snavely, N.: Robust global translations with 1DSfM. In: Fleet, D., Pajdla, T., Schiele, B., Tuytelaars, T. (eds.) ECCV 2014. LNCS, vol. 8691, pp. 61–75. Springer, Cham (2014). https://doi.org/10.1007/978-3-319-10578-9_5
31. Winder, S., Hua, G., Brown, M.: Picking the best daisy. In: CVPR (2009)
32. Wu, C.: SiftGPU: a GPU implementation of sift (2007). http://cs.unc.edu/~ccwu/siftgpu
33. Yi, K.M., Trulls, E., Lepetit, V., Fua, P.: LIFT: learned invariant feature transform. In: Leibe, B., Matas, J., Sebe, N., Welling, M. (eds.) ECCV 2016. LNCS, vol. 9910, pp. 467–483. Springer, Cham (2016). https://doi.org/10.1007/978-3-319-46466-4_28
34. Yi, K.M., Verdie, Y., Fua, P., Lepetit, V.: Learning to assign orientations to feature points. In: CVPR (2015)
35. Zagoruyko, S., Komodakis, N.: Learning to compare image patches via convolutional neural networks. In: CVPR (2015)
36. Zhang, R., Li, S., Fang, T., Zhu, S., Quan, L.: Joint camera clustering and surface segmentation for large-scale multi-view stereo. In: ICCV (2015)
37. Zhang, R., Zhu, S., Fang, T., Quan, L.: Distributed very large scale bundle adjustment by global camera consensus. In: ICCV (2017)
38. Zhang, X., Yu, F.X., Kumar, S., Chang, S.F.: Learning spread-out local feature descriptors. In: CVPR (2017)
39. Zhou, L., Zhu, S., Shen, T., Wang, J., Fang, T., Quan, L.: Progressive large scale-invariant image matching in scale space. In: ICCV (2017)
40. Zhu, S., Fang, T., Xiao, J., Quan, L.: Local readjustment for high-resolution 3D reconstruction. In: CVPR (2014)
41. Zhu, S., et al.: Very large-scale global SFM by distributed motion averaging. In: CVPR (2018)

Unsupervised Image-to-Image Translation with Stacked Cycle-Consistent Adversarial Networks

Minjun Li[1,2], Haozhi Huang[2], Lin Ma[2], Wei Liu[2], Tong Zhang[2], and Yugang Jiang[1(✉)]

[1] Shanghai Key Lab of Intelligent Information Processing,
School of Computer Science, Fudan University, Shanghai, China
[2] Tencent AI Lab, Bellevue, USA
me@minjun.li, huanghz08@gmail.com, forest.linma@gmail.com,
wl2223@columbia.edu, tongzhang@tongzhang-ml.org, ygj@fudan.edu.cn

Abstract. Recent studies on unsupervised image-to-image translation have made remarkable progress by training a pair of generative adversarial networks with a cycle-consistent loss. However, such unsupervised methods may generate inferior results when the image resolution is high or the two image domains are of significant appearance differences, such as the translations between semantic layouts and natural images in the Cityscapes dataset. In this paper, we propose novel Stacked Cycle-Consistent Adversarial Networks (SCANs) by decomposing a single translation into multi-stage transformations, which not only boost the image translation quality but also enable higher resolution image-to-image translation in a coarse-to-fine fashion. Moreover, to properly exploit the information from the previous stage, an adaptive fusion block is devised to learn a dynamic integration of the current stage's output and the previous stage's output. Experiments on multiple datasets demonstrate that our proposed approach can improve the translation quality compared with previous single-stage unsupervised methods.

Keywords: Image-to-image translation · Unsupervised learning Genearative adverserial network (GAN)

1 Introduction

Image-to-image translation attempts to convert the image appearance from one domain to another while preserving the intrinsic image content. Many computer vision problems can be formalized as the image-to-image translation problem, such as super-resolution [14,20], image colorization [6,30,31], image segmentation [4,17], and image synthesis [1,13,21,26,33]. However, conventional image-to-image translation methods are all task specific. A common framework for universal image-to-image translation remains as an emerging research subject in the literature, which has gained considerable attention in recent studies [7,10,16,27,34].

© Springer Nature Switzerland AG 2018
V. Ferrari et al. (Eds.): ECCV 2018, LNCS 11213, pp. 186–201, 2018.
https://doi.org/10.1007/978-3-030-01240-3_12

Fig. 1. Given unpaired images from two domains, our proposed SCAN learns the image-to-image translation by a stacked structure in a coarse-to-fine manner. For the Cityscapes *Labels* → *Photo* task in 512 × 512 resolution, the result of SCAN (left) appears more realistic and includes finer details compared with the result of Cycle-GAN [34] (right).

Isola *et al.* [7] leveraged the power of generative adversarial networks (GANs) [5,18,28,32], which encourage the translation results to be indistinguishable from the real images in the target domain, to learn supervised image-to-image translation from image pairs. However, obtaining pairwise training data is time-consuming and heavily relies on human labor. Recent works [10,16,27,34] explore tackling the image-to-image translation problem without using pairwise data. In the unsupervised setting, besides the traditional adversarial loss used in supervised image-to-image translation, a cycle-consistent loss is introduced to restrain the two cross-domain transformations G and F to be the inverses of each other (*i.e.*, $G(F(x)) \approx x$ and $G(F(y)) \approx y$). By constraining both the adversarial loss and the cycle-consistent loss, the networks learn how to accomplish cross-domain transformations without using pairwise training data.

Despite the progress mentioned above, existing unsupervised image-to-image translation methods may generate inferior results when two image domains are of significant appearance differences or the image resolution is high. As shown in Fig. 1, the result of CycleGAN [34] in translating Cityscapes semantic layout to realistic picture lacks details and remains visually unsatisfactory. The reason for this phenomenon lies in the significant visual gap between the two distinct image domains, which makes the cross-domain transformation too complicated to be learned by using a single-stage unsupervised approach.

Jumping out of the scope of unsupervised image-to-image translation, many methods leveraged the power of multi-stage refinements to tackle image generation from latent vectors [3,9], caption-to-image [29] and supervised image-to-image translation [1,4,23]. By generating an image in a coarse to fine manner, a complicated transformation is broken down into easy-to-solve pieces. Wang *et al.* [23] successfully tackle the high-resolution image-to-image translation problem in such a coarse-to-fine manner with multi-scale discriminators. However, their method relies on pairwise training images, therefore cannot be directly applied to our unsupervised image-to-image translation task. To the best of our knowledge, there exists no attempt to exploit stacked networks to overcome the difficulties of learning unsupervised image-to-image translation.

In this paper, we propose the stacked cycle-consistent adversarial networks (SCANs) for the unsupervised learning of image-to-image translation. We decompose a complex image translation into multi-stage transformations, including a coarse translation followed by multiple refinement processes. The coarse translation learns to sketch a primary result in low-resolution. The refinement processes improve the translation by adding details into the previous results to produce higher resolution outputs. We use a conjunction of an adversarial loss and a cycle-consistent loss in all stages to learn translations from unpaired image data. To benefit more from multi-stage learning, we also introduce an adaptive fusion block in the refinement process to learn the dynamic integration of the current stage's output and the previous stage's output. Extensive experiments demonstrate that our proposed model can not only generate results with realistic details, but also enable learning unsupervised image-to-image translation in higher resolution.

In summary, our contributions are mainly two-fold. Firstly, we propose SCANs to model the unsupervised image-to-image translation problem in a coarse to fine manner for generating results with finer details in higher resolution. Secondly, we introduce a novel adaptive fusion block to dynamically integrate the current stage's output and the previous stage's output, which outperforms directly stacking multiple stages.

2 Related Work

Image-to-Image Translation. GANs [5] have shown impressive results in a wide range of image-to-image translation tasks including super-resolution [14,20], image colorization [7], and image style transfer [34]. The essential part of GANs is the idea of using an adversarial loss that encourages the translated results to be indistinguishable from real target images. Among the existing image-to-image translation works using GANs, perhaps the most well-known one would be Pix2Pix [7], in which Isola *et al.* applied GANs with a regression loss to learn pairwise image-to-image translation. Due to the fact that pairwise image data is difficult to obtain, image-to-image translation using unpaired data has drawn rising attention in recent studies. Recent works by Zhu *et al.* [34], Yi *et al.* [27], and Kim *et al.* [10] have tackled the image translation problem using a combination of adversarial and cycle-consistent losses. Taigman *et al.* [22] applied cycle-consistency in the feature level with the adversarial loss to learn a one side translation from unpaired images. Liu *et al.* [16] used a GAN combined with Variational Auto Encoder (VAE) to learn a shared latent space of two given image domains. Liang *et al.* [15] combined the ideas of adversarial and contrastive losses, using a contrastive GAN with cycle-consistency to learn the semantic transform of two given image domains with labels. Instead of trying to translate one image to another domain directly, our proposed approach focuses on using refining processes of multiple steps to generate a more realistic output with finer details by using unpaired image data.

Multi-stage Learning. Extensive works have proposed to use multiple stages to tackle complex generation or transformation problems. Eigen *et al.* [4] proposed a multi-scale network to predict depth, surface, and segmentation, which learns to refine the prediction result from coarse to fine. S2GAN introduced by Wang *et al.* [24] utilizes two networks arranged sequentially to first generate a structure image and then transform it into a natural scene. Zhang *et al.* [29] proposed StackGAN to generate high-resolution images from texts, which consists of two stages: Stage-I network generates coarse, low-resolution result, while the Stage-II network refines the result into high-resolution, realistic image. Chen *et al.* [1] applied a stacked refinement network to generate scenes from segmentation layouts. To accomplish generating high-resolution images from latent vectors, Kerras *et al.* [9] started from generating a 4×4 resolution output, then progressively stacked up both generator and discriminator to generate a 1024×1024 realistic image. Wang *et al.* [23] applied a coarse-to-fine generator with a multi-scale discriminator to tackle the supervised image-to-image translation problem. Different form the existing works, this work exploits stacked image-to-image translation networks combined with a novel adaptive fusion block to tackle the unsupervised image-to-image translation problem.

3   Proposed Approach

3.1   Formulation

Given two image domains X and Y, the mutual translations between them can be denoted as two mappings $G : X \to Y$ and $F : Y \to X$, each of which takes an image from one domain and translates it to the corresponding representation in the other domain. Existing unsupervised image-to-image translation approaches [10, 16, 22, 27, 34] finish the learning of G and F in a single stage, which generate results lacking details and are unable to handle complex translations.

In this paper, we decompose translations G and F into multi-stage mappings. For simplicity, now we describe our method in a two-stage setting. Specifically, we decompose $G = G_2 \circ G_1$ and $F = F_2 \circ F_1$. G_1 and F_1 (**Stage-1**) perform the cross-domain translation in a coarse scale, while G_2 and F_2 (**Stage-2**) serve as refinements on the top of the outputs from the previous stage. We first finish the training of Stage-1 in low-resolution and then train Stage-2 to learn refinement in higher resolution based on a fixed Stage-1.

Training two stages in the same resolution would make Stage-2 difficult to bring further improvement, as Stage-1 has already been optimized with the same objective function (see Sect. 4.5). On the other hand, we find that learning in a lower resolution allows the model to generate visually more natural results, since the manifold underlying the low-resolution images is easier to model. Therefore, first, we constrain Stage-1 to train on 2x down-sampled image samples, denoted by $X_\downarrow$ and $Y_\downarrow$, to learn a base transformation. Second, based on the outputs of Stage-1, we train Stage-2 with image samples X and Y in the original resolution. Such a formulation exploits the preliminary low-resolution results of Stage-1 and guides Stage-2 to focus on up-sampling and adding finer details, which helps improve the overall translation quality.

In summary, to learn cross-domain translations $G : X \to Y$ and $F : Y \to X$ on given domains X and Y, we first learn preliminary translations $G_1 : X_\downarrow \to Y_\downarrow$ and $F_1 : Y_\downarrow \to X_\downarrow$ at the 2x down-sampled scale. Then we use $G_2 : X_\downarrow \to X$ and $F_2 : Y_\downarrow \to Y$ to obtain the final output with finer details in the original resolution. Notice that we can iteratively decompose G_2 and F_2 into more stages.

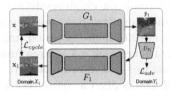

Fig. 2. Illustration of an overview of Stage-1 for learning coarse translations in low-resolution under an unsupervised setting. Solid arrow denotes input-outputs, the dashed arrow denotes the loss.

3.2   Stage-1: Basic Translation

In general, our Stage-1 module adopts a similar architecture of CycleGAN [34], which consists of two image translation networks G_1 and F_1 and two discriminators D_{X_1}, D_{Y_1}. Note that Stage-1 is trained in low-resolution image domains $X_\downarrow$ and $Y_\downarrow$. Figure 2 shows an overview of the Stage-1 architecture.

Given a sample $\mathbf{x}_1 \in X_\downarrow$, G_1 translates it to a sample $\hat{\mathbf{y}}_1 = G_1(\mathbf{x}_1)$ in the other domain $Y_\downarrow$. On the one hand, the discriminator D_{Y_1} learns to classify the generated sample $\hat{\mathbf{y}}_1$ to class 0 and the real image $\mathbf{y}$ to class 1. On the other hand, G_1 learns to deceive D_{Y_1} by generating more and more realistic samples. This can be formulated as an adversarial loss:

$$\mathcal{L}_{adv}(G_1, D_{Y_1}, X_\downarrow, Y_\downarrow) = \mathbb{E}_{\mathbf{y} \sim Y_\downarrow}[\log(D_{Y_1}(\mathbf{y}))] \\ + \mathbb{E}_{\mathbf{x} \sim X_\downarrow}[\log(1 - D_{Y_1}(G_1(\mathbf{x})))]. \tag{1}$$

While D_{Y_1} tries to maximize $\mathcal{L}_{adv}$, G_1 tries to minimize it. Afterward, we use F_1 to translate $\hat{\mathbf{y}}_1$ back to domain $X_\downarrow$, and constrain $F_1(G_1(\mathbf{x}))$ to be close to the input $\mathbf{x}$. This can be formulated as a cycle-consistent loss:

$$\mathcal{L}_{cycle}(G_1, F_1, X_\downarrow) = \mathbb{E}_{\mathbf{x} \sim X_\downarrow} \|\mathbf{x} - F_1(G_1(\mathbf{x}))\|_1. \tag{2}$$

Similarly, for a sample $\mathbf{y}_1 \in Y_\downarrow$, we use F_1 to perform translation, use D_{X_1} to calculate the adversarial loss, and then use G_1 to translate backward to calculate the cycle-consistent loss. Our full objective function for Stage-1 is a combination of the adversarial loss and the cycle-consistent loss:

$$\mathcal{L}_{Stage1} = \mathcal{L}_{adv}(G_1, D_{Y_1}, X_\downarrow, Y_\downarrow) + \mathcal{L}_{adv}(F_1, D_{X_1}, Y_\downarrow, X_\downarrow) \\ + \lambda[\mathcal{L}_{cycle}(G_1, F_1, X_\downarrow) + \mathcal{L}_{cycle}(F_1, G_1, Y_\downarrow)], \tag{3}$$

where λ denotes the weight of the cycle-consistent loss. We obtain the translations G_1 and F_1 by optimizing the following objective function:

$$G_1, F_1 = \arg\min_{G_1, F_1} \max_{D_{X_1}, D_{Y_1}} \mathcal{L}_{Stage1}, \tag{4}$$

which encourages these translations to transform the results to another domain while preserving the intrinsic image content. As a result, the optimized translations G_1 and F_1 can perform a basic cross-domain translation in low resolution.

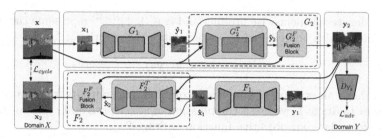

Fig. 3. Illustration of an overview of our Stage-2 for learning refining processes on the top of Stage-1 outputs. G_1 and F_1 are the translation networks learned in Stage-1. In the training process, we keep the weights of G_1 and F_1 fixed. Solid arrow denotes input-output, and the dashed arrow denotes the loss.

3.3 Stage-2: Refinement

Since it is difficult to learn a complicated translation with the limited ability of a single stage, the translated output of Stage-1 may seem plausible but still leaves us much room for improvement. To refine the output of Stage-1, we employ Stage-2 with a stacked structure built on the top of the trained Stage-1 to complete the full translation to generate higher resolution results with finer details.

Stage-2 consists of two translation networks G_2, F_2 and two discriminator network D_{X_2}, D_{Y_2}, as shown in Fig. 3. We only describe the architecture of G_2, since F_2 shares the same design (see Fig. 3).

G_2 consists of two parts: a newly initialized image translation network G_2^T and an adaptive fusion block G_2^F. Given the output of Stage-1 ($\hat{\mathbf{y}}_1 = G_1(\mathbf{x}_1)$), we use nearest up-sampling to resize it to match the original resolution. Different from the image translation network in Stage-1, which only takes $\mathbf{x} \in X$ as input, in Stage-2 we use both the current stage's input $\mathbf{x}$ and the previous stage's output $\hat{\mathbf{y}}_1$. Specifically, we concatenate $\hat{\mathbf{y}}_1$ and $\mathbf{x}$ along the channel dimension, and utilize G_2^T to obtain the refined result $\hat{\mathbf{y}}_2 = G_2^T(\hat{\mathbf{y}}_1, \mathbf{x})$.

Besides simply using $\hat{\mathbf{y}}_2$ as the final output, we introduce an adaptive fusion block G_2^F to learn a dynamic combination of $\hat{\mathbf{y}}_2$ and $\hat{\mathbf{y}}_1$ to fully utilize the entire two-stage structure. Specifically, the adaptive fusion block learns a pixel-wise linear combination of the previous results:

$$G_2^F(\hat{\mathbf{y}}_1, \hat{\mathbf{y}}_2) = \hat{\mathbf{y}}_1 \odot (1 - \boldsymbol{\alpha}_x) + \hat{\mathbf{y}}_2 \odot \boldsymbol{\alpha}_x, \tag{5}$$

Fig. 4. Illustration of the linear combination in an adaptive fusion block. The fusion block applies the fusion weight map α to find defects in the previous result $\hat{\mathbf{y}}_1$ and correct it precisely using $\hat{\mathbf{y}}_2$ to produce a refined output $\mathbf{y}_2$.

where $\odot$ denotes element-wise product and $\boldsymbol{\alpha} \in (0,1)^{H \times W}$ represents the fusion weight map, which is predicted by a convolutional network h_x:

$$\boldsymbol{\alpha}_x = h_x(\mathbf{x}, \hat{\mathbf{y}}_1, \hat{\mathbf{y}}_2). \tag{6}$$

Figure 4 shows an example of adaptively combining the outputs from two stages.

Similar to Stage-1, we use a combination of adversarial and cycle-consistent losses to formulate our objective function of Stage-2:

$$\mathcal{L}_{Stage2} = \mathcal{L}_{adv}(G_2 \circ G_1, D_{Y_2}, X, Y) + \mathcal{L}_{adv}(F_2 \circ F_1, D_{X_2}, Y, X)$$
$$+ \lambda[\mathcal{L}_{cycle}(G_2 \circ G_1, F_2 \circ F_1, X) + \mathcal{L}_{cycle}(F_2 \circ F_1, G_2 \circ G_1, Y)].\tag{7}$$

Optimizing this objective is similar to solving Eq. 4. The translation networks G_2 and F_2 are learned to refine the previous results by correcting defects and adding details on them.

Finally, we complete our desired translations G and F by combining the transformations in Stage-1 and Stage-2, which are capable of tackling a complex image-to-image translation problem under the unsupervised setting.

4   Experiments

The proposed approach is named *SCAN* or *SCAN Stage-N* if it has N stages in the following experiments. We explore several variants of our model to evaluate the effectiveness of our design in Sect. 4.7. In all experiments, we decompose the target translation into two stages, except for exploring the ability of the three-stage architecture in high-resolution tasks in Sect. 4.5.

We used the official released model of CycleGAN [34] and Pix2Pix [7] for 256×256 image translation comparisions. For 512×512 tasks, we train the CycleGAN with the official code since there is no available pre-trained model.

4.1   Network Architecture

For the image translation network, we follow the settings of [15,34], adopting the encoder-decoder architecture from Johnson *et al.* [8]. The network consists of two down-sample layers implemented by stride-2 convolution, six residual blocks and two up-sample layers implemented by sub-pixel convolution [20]. Note that different from [34], which used the fractionally strided convolution as the up-sample block, we use the sub-pixel convolution [20], for avoiding checkerboard artifacts [19]. The adaptive fusion block is a simple 3-layer convolutional network, which calculates the fusion weight map α using two Convolution-InstanceNorm-ReLU blocks followed by a Convolution-Sigmoid block. For the discriminator, we use the PatchGAN structure introduced in [7].

4.2   Datasets

To demonstrate the capability of our proposed method for tackling the complex image-to-image translation problem under unsupervised settings, we first conduct experiments on the Cityscapes dataset [2]. We compare with the state-of-the-art approaches in the *Labels* ↔ *Photo* task in 256 × 256 resolution. To further show the effectiveness of our method to learn complex translations, we also extended the input size to a challenging 512 × 512 resolution, namely the high-resolution Cityscapes *Labels* → *Photo* task.

Besides the *Labels* ↔ *Photo* task, we also select eight image-to-image translation tasks from [34], including *Map* ↔ *Aerial*, *Facades* ↔ *Labels* and *Horse* ↔ *Zebra*. We compare our method with the CycleGAN [34] in these tasks in 256 × 256 resolution.

4.3   Training Details

Networks in Stage-1 are trained from scratch, while networks in Stage-N are trained with the {Stage-1, · · · , Stage-(N − 1)} networks fixed. For the GAN loss, Different from the previous works [7,34], we adopt a gradient penalty term $\lambda_{gp}(||\nabla D(x)||_2 - 1)^2$ in the discriminator loss to achieve a more stable training process [12]. For all datasets, the Stage-1 networks are trained in 128 × 128 resolution, the Stage-2 networks are trained in 256 × 256 resolution. For the three-stage architecture in Sect. 4.5, the Stage-3 networks are trained in 512 × 512 resolution. We set batch size to 1, $\lambda = 10$ and $\lambda_{gp} = 10$ in all experiments. All stages are trained with 100 epochs for all datasets. We use Adam [11] to optimize our networks with an initial learning rate as 0.0002, and decrease it linearly to zero in the last 50 epochs.

4.4   Evaluation Metrics

FCN Score and Segmentation Score. For the Cityscapes dataset, we adopt the FCN Score and the Segmentation Score as evaluation metrics from [7] for the *Labels* → *Photo* task and the *Photo* → *Labels* task, respectively. The FCN Score employs an off-the-shelf FCN segmentation network [17] to estimate the realism of the translated images. The Segmentation Score includes three standard segmentation metrics, which are the per-pixel accuracy, the per-class accuracy, and the mean class accuracy, as defined in [17].

PSNR and SSIM. Besides using the FCN Score and the Segmentation Score, we also calculate the PSNR and the SSIM [25] for a quantitative evaluation. We apply the above metrics on the *Map ↔ Aerial* task and the *Facades ↔ Labels* task to measure both the color similarity and the structural similarity between the translated outputs and the ground truth images.

User Preference. We run user preference tests in the high-resolution Cityscapes *Labels → Photos* task and the *Horse → Zebra* tasks for evaluating the realism of our generated photos. In the user preference test, each time a user is presented with a pair of results from our proposed SCAN and the CycleGAN [34], and asked which one is more realistic. Each pair of the results is translated from the same image. Images are all shown in randomized order. In total, 30 images from the Cityscapes test set and 10 images from the Horse2Zebra test set are used in the user preference tests. As a result, 20 participates make a total of 600 and 200 preference choices, respectively.

Fig. 5. Comparisons on the Cityscapes dataset of 256 × 256 resolution. The left subfigure are *Labels → Photo* results and the right are *Photo → Labels* results. In the *Labels → Photo* task, our proposed SCAN generates more natural photographs than CycleGAN; in the *Photo → Labels* task, SCAN produces an accurate segmentation map while CycleGAN's results are blurry and suffer from deformation. SCAN also generates results that are visually closer to the supervised approach Pix2Pix than results of CycleGAN. Zoom in for better view.

4.5   Comparisons

Cityscapes *Labels ↔ Photo*. Table 1 shows the comparison of our proposed method SCAN and its variants with state-of-the-art methods in the Cityscapes *Labels ↔ Photo* tasks. The same unsupervised settings are adopted by all methods except Pix2Pix, which is trained under a supervised setting.

On the FCN Scores, our proposed SCAN Stage-2 128-256 outperforms the state-of-the-art approaches considering the pixel accuracy, while being competitive considering the class accuracy and the class IoU. On the Segmentation Scores, SCAN Stage-2 128-256 outperforms state-of-the-art approaches in all metrics. Comparing SCAN Stage-1 256 with CycleGAN, our modified network yields improved results, which, however, still perform inferiorly to SCAN Stage-2

Table 1. FCN Scores in Labels → Photo task and Segmentation Scores in Photo → Labels task on the Cityscapes dataset. The proposed methods are named after *SCAN (Stage-1 resolution)-(Stage-2 resolution)*. *FT* means we also *fine-tune* the Stage-1 model instead of fixing its weight. *FS* means directly train Stage-2 *from-scratch* without training Stage-1 model.

Method	Labels → Photo			Photo → Labels		
	Pixel acc.	Class acc.	Class IoU	Pixel acc.	Class acc.	Class IoU
CycleGAN [34]	0.52	0.17	0.11	0.58	0.22	0.16
Contrast-GAN [15]	0.58	**0.21**	**0.16**	0.61	0.23	0.18
SCAN Stage-1 128	0.46	0.19	0.12	0.71	0.24	0.20
SCAN Stage-1 256	0.57	0.15	0.11	0.63	0.18	0.14
SCAN Stage-2 256-256	0.52	0.15	0.11	0.64	0.18	0.14
SCAN Stage-2 128-256 *FS*	0.59	0.15	0.10	0.36	0.10	0.05
SCAN Stage-2 128-256 *FT*	0.61	0.18	0.13	0.62	0.19	0.13
SCAN Stage-2 128-256	**0.64**	0.20	**0.16**	**0.72**	**0.25**	**0.20**
Pix2Pix [7]	0.71	0.25	0.18	0.85	0.40	0.32

128-256. Also, we can find that SCAN Stage-2 128-256 achieves a much closer performance to the supervised approach Pix2Pix [7] than others.

We also compare our SCAN Stage-2 128-256 with different variants of SCAN. Comparing SCAN Stage-2 128-256 with SCAN Stage-1 approaches, we can find a substantial improvement on the FCN Scores, which indicates that adding the Stage-2 refinement helps to improve the realism of the output images. On the Segmentation Score, comparison of the SCAN Stage-1 128 and SCAN Stage-1 256 shows that learning from low-resolution yields better performance. Comparison between the SCAN Stage-2 128-256 and SCAN Stage-1 128 shows that adding Stage-2 can further improve from the Stage-1 results. To experimentally prove that the performance gain does not come from merely adding model capacity, we conducted a SCAN Stage-2 256-256 experiments, which perform inferiorly to the SCAN Stage-2 128-256.

To further analyze various experimental settings, we also conducted our SCAN Stage-2 128-256 in two additional settings, including *leaning two stages from-scratch* and *fine-tuning Stage-1*. We add supervision signals to both stages for these two settings. Learning two stages from scratch shows poor performance in both tasks, which indicates joint training two stages together does not guarantee performance gain. The reason for this may lie in directly training a high-capacity generator is difficult. Also, fine-tuning Stage-1 does not resolve this problem and has smaller improvement compared with fixing weights of Stage-1.

To examine the effectiveness of the proposed fusion block, we compare it with several variants: (1) *Learned Pixel Weight* (LPW), which is our proposed fusion block; (2) *Uniform Weight* (UW), in which the two stages are fused with the same weight at different pixel locations $\hat{y}_1(1-w) + \hat{y}_2 w$, and during training w gradually increases from 0 to 1; (3) *Learned Uniform Weight* (LUW), which is similar to *UW*, but w is a learnable parameter instead; (4) *Residual Fusion* (RF), which uses a simple residual fusion $\hat{y}_1 + \hat{y}_2$. The results are illustrated in Table 2. It can be observed that our proposed LPW fusion yields the best performance among all alternatives, which indicates that the LPW approach can learn better fusion of the outputs from two stages than approaches with uniform weights.

Table 2. FCN Scores and Segmentation Scores of several variants of the fusion block on the Cityscapes dataset.

Method	Labels → Photo			Photo → Labels		
	Pixel acc.	Class acc.	Class IoU	Pixel acc.	Class acc.	Class IoU
CycleGAN	0.52	0.17	0.11	0.58	0.22	0.16
SCAN 128-256 LPW	0.64	0.20	0.16	0.72	0.25	0.20
SCAN 128-256 UW	0.59	0.19	0.14	0.66	0.22	0.17
SCAN 128-256 LUW	0.59	0.18	0.12	0.70	0.24	0.19
SCAN 128-256 RF	0.60	0.19	0.13	0.68	0.23	0.18

In Fig. 5, we visually compare our results with those of the CycleGAN and the Pix2Pix. In the *Labels* →*Photo* task, SCAN generates more realistic and vivid photos compared to the CycleGAN. Also, the details in our results appear closer to those of the supervised approach Pix2Pix. In the *Photo* → *Labels* task, while SCAN can generate more accurate semantic layouts that are closer to the ground truth, the results of the CycleGAN suffer from distortion and blur.

Fig. 6. Translation results in the *Labels* → *Photo* task on the Cityscapes datasets of 512 × 512 resolution. Our proposed SCAN produces realistic images that even look at a glance like the ground truths. Zoom in for best view.

High-Resolution Cityscapes *Labels* → *Photo*. The CycleGAN only considers images in 256 × 256 resolution, and results of training CycleGAN directly in 512 × 512 resolution are not satisfactory, as shown in Figs. 1 and 6.

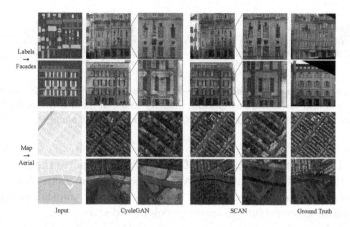

Fig. 7. Translation results in the Labels → Facades task and the Aerial → Map task. Results of our proposed SCAN shows finer details in both tasks comparing with Cycle-GAN's results.

By iteratively decomposing the Stage-2 into a Stage-2 and a Stage-3, we obtain a three-stage SCAN. During the translation process, the resolution of the output is growing from 128 × 128 to 256 × 256 and to 512 × 512, as shown in Fig. 1. Figure 6 shows the comparison between our SCAN and the CycleGAN in the high-resolution Cityscapes *Labels → Photo* task. We can clearly see that our proposed SCAN generates more realistic photos compared with the results of CycleGAN, and SCAN's outputs are visually closer to the ground truth images. The first row shows that our results contain realistic trees with plenty of details, while the CycleGAN only generates repeated patterns. For the second row, we can observe that the CycleGAN tends to simply ignore the cars by filling it with a plain grey color, while cars in our results have more details.

Also, we run a user preference study comparing SCAN with the CycleGAN with the setting described in Sect. 4.4. As a result, 74.9% of the queries prefer our SCAN's results, 10.9% prefer the CycleGAN's results, and 14.9% suggest that the two methods are equal. This result shows that our SCAN can generate overall more realistic translation results against the CycleGAN in the high-resolution translation task.

Table 3. PSNR and SSIM values in *Map ↔ Aerial* and *Facades ↔ Labels* tasks.

Method	Aerial → Map		Map → Aerial		Facades → Labels		Labels → Facades	
	PSNR	SSIM	PSNR	SSIM	PSNR	SSIM	PSNR	SSIM
CycleGAN [34]	21.59	0.50	12.67	0.06	6.68	0.08	7.61	0.11
SCAN	**25.15**	**0.67**	**14.93**	**0.23**	**8.28**	**0.29**	**10.67**	**0.17**

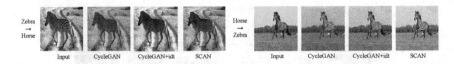

Fig. 8. Translation results in the Horse ↔ Zebra tasks. The CycleGAN changes both desired objects and backgrounds. Adding identity loss can fix this problem, but tends to be blurry compared with those from SCAN, which without using the identity loss.

Map ↔ Aerial and Facades ↔ Labels. Table 3 reports the performances regarding the PSNR/SSIM metrics. We can see that our methods outperform the CycleGAN in both metrics, which indicates that our translation results are more similar to ground truth in terms of colors and structures.

Figure 7 shows some of the sample results in the Aerial → Map task and the Labels → Facades task. We can observe that our results contain finer details while the CycleGAN results tend to be blurry.

Horse ↔ Zebra. Figure 8 compares the results of SCAN against those of the CycleGAN in the Horse ↔ Zebra task. We can observe that both SCAN and the CycleGAN successfully translate the input images to the other domain. As the Fig. 8 shows, the CycleGAN changes not only the desired objects in input images but also the backgrounds of the images. Adding the identity loss [34] can fix this problem, but the results still tend to be blurry compared with those from our proposed SCAN. A user preference study on Horse → Zebra translation is performed with the setting described in Sect. 4.4. As a result, 76.3% of the subjects prefer our SCAN's results against CycleGAN's, while 68.9% prefer SCAN's results against CycleGAN+idt's.

4.6   Visualization of Fusion Weight Distributions

To illustrate the role of the adaptive fusion block, we visualize the three average distributions of fusion weights (α_x in Eq. 5) over 1000 samples from Cityscapes dataset in epoch 1, 10, and 100, as shown in Fig. 9. We observed that the distribution of the fusion weights gradually shifts from left to right. It indicates a consistent increase of the weight values in the fusion maps, which implies more and more details of the second stage are bought to the final output.

4.7   Ablation Study

In Sect. 4.5, we report the evaluation results of SCAN and its variants, here we further explore SCAN by removing modules from it:

- SCAN w/o *Skip* Connection: remove the skip connection from the input to the translation network in the Stage-2 model, denoted by *SCAN w/o Skip*.
- SCAN w/o Adaptive *Fusion* Block: remove the final adaptive fusion block in the Stage-2 model, denoted by *SCAN w/o Fusion*.

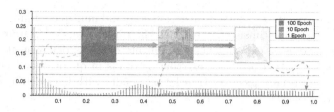

Fig. 9. Distributions of fusion weights over all pixels in different epochs. Each distribution is an average result over 1000 sample images from Cityscapes dataset. Dashed arrows indicate the average weights of fusion maps.

– SCAN w/o *Skip* Connection and Adaptive *Fusion* Block: remove both the skip connection from the input to the translation network and the adaptive fusion block in the Stage-2 model, denoted by *SCAN w/o Skip, Fusion*.

Table 4. FCN Scores in the Cityscapes dataset for ablation study, evaluated on the *Labels → Photo* task with different variants of the proposed SCAN.

Method	Pixel acc.	Class acc.	Class IoU
SCAN Stage-1 128	0.457	0.188	0.124
SCAN Stage-2 128-256 w/o Skip,Fusion	0.513	0.186	0.125
SCAN Stage-2 128-256 w/o Skip	0.593	0.184	0.136
SCAN Stage-2 128-256 w/o Fusion	0.613	0.194	0.137
SCAN Stage-2 128-256	**0.637**	**0.201**	**0.157**

Table 4 shows the results of the ablation study, in which we can observe that removing the adaptive fusion block as well as removing the skip connection both downgrade the performance. With both of the components removed, the stacked networks obtain marginal performance gain compared with Stage-1. Note that the fusion block only consists of three convolution layers, which have a relatively small size compared to the whole network. Refer to Table 1, in SCAN Stage-2 256-256 experiment, we double the network parameters compared to SCAN Stage-1 256, resulting in no improvement in the Label → Photo task. Thus, the improvement of the fusion block does not simply come from the added capacity.

Therefore, we can conclude that using our proposed SCAN structure, which consists of the skip connection and the adaptive fusion block, is critical for improving the overall translation performance.

5   Conclusions

In this paper, we proposed a novel approach to tackle the unsupervised image-to-image translation problem using a stacked network structure with cycle-consistency, namely SCAN. The proposed SCAN decomposes a complex image translation process into a coarse translation step and multiple refining steps, and then applies the cycle-consistency to learn the target translation from unpaired image data. Extensive experiments on multiple datasets demonstrate that our proposed SCAN outperforms the existing methods in quantitative metrics and generates more visually pleasant translation results with finer details compared to existing approaches.

Acknowledgement. This work was supported by two projects from NSFC (#61622204 and #61572134) and two projects from STCSM (#16JC1420401 and #16QA1400500).

References

1. Chen, Q., Koltun, V.: Photographic image synthesis with cascaded refinement networks. In: Proceedings of ICCV (2017)
2. Cordts, M., et al.: The cityscapes dataset for semantic urban scene understanding. In: Proceedings of CVPR (2016)
3. Denton, E.L., Chintala, S., Fergus, R., et al.: Deep generative image models using a laplacian pyramid of adversarial networks. In: Proceedings of NIPS (2015)
4. Eigen, D., Fergus, R.: Predicting depth, surface normals and semantic labels with a common multi-scale convolutional architecture. In: Proceedings of ICCV (2015)
5. Goodfellow, I., et al.: Generative adversarial nets. In: Proceedings of NIPS (2014)
6. Iizuka, S., Simo-Serra, E., Ishikawa, H.: Let there be color!: joint end-to-end learning of global and local image priors for automatic image colorization with simultaneous classification. ACM Trans. Graph. (TOG) **35**, 110 (2016)
7. Isola, P., Zhu, J.Y., Zhou, T., Efros, A.A.: Image-to-image translation with conditional adversarial networks. In: Proceedings of CVPR (2017)
8. Johnson, J., Alahi, A., Fei-Fei, L.: Perceptual losses for real-time style transfer and super-resolution. In: Leibe, B., Matas, J., Sebe, N., Welling, M. (eds.) ECCV 2016. LNCS, vol. 9906, pp. 694–711. Springer, Cham (2016). https://doi.org/10.1007/978-3-319-46475-6_43
9. Karras, T., Aila, T., Laine, S., Lehtinen, J.: Progressive growing of GANs for improved quality, stability, and variation. arXiv preprint arXiv:1710.10196 (2017)
10. Kim, T., Cha, M., Kim, H., Lee, J., Kim, J.: Learning to discover cross-domain relations with generative adversarial networks. In: Proceedings of ICML (2017)
11. Kingma, D., Ba, J.: Adam: A method for stochastic optimization. In: Proceedings of ICLR (2014)
12. Kodali, N., Abernethy, J., Hays, J., Kira, Z.: On convergence and stability of GANs. arXiv preprint arXiv:1705.07215 (2017)
13. Laffont, P.Y., Ren, Z., Tao, X., Qian, C., Hays, J.: Transient attributes for high-level understanding and editing of outdoor scenes. ACM Trans. Graph. (TOG) **33**, 149 (2014)
14. Ledig, C., et al.: Photo-realistic single image super-resolution using a generative adversarial network. In: Proceedings of CVPR (2017)
15. Liang, X., Zhang, H., Xing, E.P.: Generative semantic manipulation with contrasting GAN. In: Proceedings of NIPS (2017)
16. Liu, M.Y., Breuel, T., Kautz, J.: Unsupervised image-to-image translation networks. In: Proceedings of NIPS (2017)

17. Long, J., Shelhamer, E., Darrell, T.: Fully convolutional networks for semantic segmentation. In: Proceedings of CVPR (2015)
18. Mirza, M., Osindero, S.: Conditional generative adversarial nets. arXiv preprint arXiv:1411.1784 (2014)
19. Odena, A., Dumoulin, V., Olah, C.: Deconvolution and checkerboard artifacts. Distill 1(10), e3 (2016)
20. Shi, W., et al.: Real-time single image and video super-resolution using an efficient sub-pixel convolutional neural network. In: Proceedings of CVPR (2016)
21. Simo-Serra, E., Iizuka, S., Sasaki, K., Ishikawa, H.: Learning to simplify: fully convolutional networks for rough sketch cleanup. ACM Trans. Graph. (TOG) 35(4), 121 (2016)
22. Taigman, Y., Polyak, A., Wolf, L.: Unsupervised cross-domain image generation. In: Proceedings of ICLR (2016)
23. Wang, T.C., Liu, M.Y., Zhu, J.Y., Tao, A., Kautz, J., Catanzaro, B.: High-resolution image synthesis and semantic manipulation with conditional GANs. In: Proceedings of CVPR (2018)
24. Wang, X., Gupta, A.: Generative image modeling using style and structure adversarial networks. In: Leibe, B., Matas, J., Sebe, N., Welling, M. (eds.) ECCV 2016. LNCS, vol. 9908, pp. 318–335. Springer, Cham (2016). https://doi.org/10.1007/978-3-319-46493-0_20
25. Wang, Z., Bovik, A.C., Sheikh, H.R., Simoncelli, E.P.: Image quality assessment: from error visibility to structural similarity. IEEE Trans. Image Process. (TIP) 13(4), 600–612 (2004)
26. Xie, S., Tu, Z.: Holistically-nested edge detection. In: Proceedings of ICCV (2015)
27. Yi, Z., Zhang, H., Gong, P.T., et al.: DualGAN: unsupervised dual learning for image-to-image translation. In: Proceedings of ICCV (2017)
28. Xiong, Z., Luo, W., Ma, L., Liu, W., Luo, J.: Learning to generate time-lapse videos using multi-stage dynamic generative adversarial networks. In: Proceedings of CVPR (2018)
29. Zhang, H., et al.: StackGAN: text to photo-realistic image synthesis with stacked generative adversarial networks. In: Proceedings of ICCV (2016)
30. Zhang, R., Isola, P., Efros, A.A.: Colorful image colorization. In: Leibe, B., Matas, J., Sebe, N., Welling, M. (eds.) ECCV 2016. LNCS, vol. 9907, pp. 649–666. Springer, Cham (2016). https://doi.org/10.1007/978-3-319-46487-9_40
31. Zhang, R., et al.: Real-time user-guided image colorization with learned deep priors. ACM Trans. Graph. (TOG) (2017)
32. Zhao, B., Chang, B., Jie, Z., Feng, J.: Modular generative adversarial networks. arXiv preprint arXiv:1804.03343 (2018)
33. Zhao, B., Wu, X., Cheng, Z.Q., Liu, H., Jie, Z., Feng, J.: Multi-view image generation from a single-view. arXiv preprint arXiv:1704.04886 (2017)
34. Zhu, J.Y., Park, T., Isola, P., Efros, A.A.: Unpaired image-to-image translation using cycle-consistent adversarial networks. In: Proceedings of ICCV (2017)

Find and Focus: Retrieve and Localize Video Events with Natural Language Queries

Dian Shao[1]([📧])[iD], Yu Xiong[1][iD], Yue Zhao[1][iD], Qingqiu Huang[1][iD], Yu Qiao[2][iD], and Dahua Lin[1][iD]

[1] CUHK-SenseTime Joint Lab, The Chinese University of Hong Kong, Shatin, Hong Kong
{sd017,xy017,zy317,hq016,dhlin}@ie.cuhk.edu.hk
[2] SIAT-SenseTime Joint Lab, Shenzhen Institutes of Advanced Technology, Chinese Academy of Sciences, Beijing, China
yu.qiao@siat.ac.cn

Abstract. The thriving of video sharing services brings new challenges to video retrieval, *e.g.* the rapid growth in video duration and content diversity. Meeting such challenges calls for new techniques that can effectively retrieve videos with natural language queries. Existing methods along this line, which mostly rely on embedding videos as a whole, remain far from satisfactory for real-world applications due to the limited expressive power. In this work, we aim to move beyond this limitation by delving into the internal structures of both sides, the queries and the videos. Specifically, we propose a new framework called *Find and Focus (FIFO)*, which not only performs top-level matching (paragraph vs. video), but also makes part-level associations, localizing a video clip for each sentence in the query with the help of a focusing guide. These levels are complementary – the top-level matching narrows the search while the part-level localization refines the results. On both ActivityNet Captions and modified LSMDC datasets, the proposed framework achieves remarkable performance gains (Project Page: https://ycxioooong.github.io/projects/fifo).

1 Introduction

Over the past few years, the explosive growth of video content brings unprecedented challenges to video retrieval. Retrieving a video that one really wants is sometimes like finding a needle in a haystack. For example, entering a short query *"dancing people"* on Youtube would result in tens of millions of video

---

D. Shao and Y. Xiong—Equal contribution.

Electronic supplementary material The online version of this chapter (https://doi.org/10.1007/978-3-030-01240-3_13) contains supplementary material, which is available to authorized users.

© Springer Nature Switzerland AG 2018
V. Ferrari et al. (Eds.): ECCV 2018, LNCS 11213, pp. 202–218, 2018.
https://doi.org/10.1007/978-3-030-01240-3_13

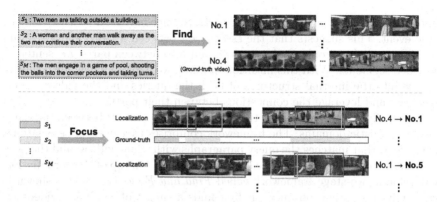

Fig. 1. An overview of our *Find and Focus* framework. Given a query paragraph, the system first retrieves a number of candidate videos in the Find stage, and then applies clip localization to each candidate video, to identify the associations between query sentences and video clips. The resulting localization scores can further refine the initial retrieval results. For example, the ground-truth video is ranked as No. 4 in the Find stage and promoted to No. 1 after the Focus stage.

entries, many of which are lengthy and filled with irrelevant fragments. To tackle such challenges, we aim to explore a new way to retrieve videos, one that can efficiently locate the relevant clips from a large and diverse collection.

Video retrieval is not new in computer vision. The research on this topic dates back to 1990s [26]. Classical content-based retrieval techniques [2,5,27,34,42] primarily rely on matching visual features with a fixed set of concepts. This approach can only work with a closed setting, where all videos belong to a pre-defined list of categories. The problem of *video retrieval in the wild* remains widely open. In recent years, an alternative approach, namely retrieving videos with natural language queries, emerges as a promising way to break the closed-set assumption. The efforts along this line are usually based on visual semantic embedding [6,7,13,16,20,30,36,38], where each image or video and its corresponding description are embedded into a common space and their representations are aligned.

It is noteworthy that both the classical techniques and visual semantic embedding share a common paradigm, namely, to encode each video as a whole into a feature vector and perform the retrieval simply by feature matching. This paradigm has two important limitations. First, a *single* vector representation lacks the expressive power to characterize a video with rich structures, and second, it lacks the capability of temporal localization, Note that these are not serious issues in conventional experimental settings where all video samples in the dataset are short clips. However, they become significant challenges in real-world applications where the videos are usually long and not trimmed.

In this work, we aim to move beyond such limits and develop an effective method that can retrieve complex events, *i.e.* those with rich temporal structures, based on natural language queries. We observe that people often describe a complex event with a paragraph, where each sentence may refer to a certain part of the event. This suggests that the association between a video and a relevant description exists not only at the top level but also between parts, *i.e.* sentences and video segments. With this intuition in mind, we explore a new idea, that is, to delve into the internal structures of both the queries and the videos, trying to identify and leverage the connections between their parts.

Specifically, we propose a structured framework to connect between the visual and the linguistic domains. The framework comprises two levels of associations, the *top-level* that matches the query paragraphs with whole videos, and the *part-level* that aligns individual sentences with video clips. On top of this formulation, we develop a two-stage framework called *Find and Focus* (*FIFO*), as shown in Fig. 1. Given a paragraph query, it first finds a subset of candidate videos via top-level matching. Then for each candidate, it localizes the clips for individual sentences in the query. Finally, the part-level associations are used to refine the ranking of retrieval results. In this way, the framework *jointly* accomplishes two tasks: retrieving videos and localizing relevant segments. Note that in our framework, these two tasks benefit each other. On one hand, the top-level matching narrows the search, thus reducing the overall cost, especially when working with a large database. On the other hand, the part-level localization refines the results, thus further improving the ranking accuracy. To facilitate clip localization, we develop a semantics-guided method to generate clip proposals, which allows the framework to focus on those clips with significant meanings.

Our main contributions are summarized as follows: (1) We propose a structured formulation that captures the associations between the visual and the linguistic domains at both top-level and part-level. (2) Leveraging the two-level associations, we develop a *Find and Focus* framework that jointly accomplishes video retrieval and clip localization. Particularly, the localization stage is supported by a new method, *Visual Semantic Similarity* (VSS), for proposing clip candidates, which helps to focus on the segments with significant meanings. (3) On two public datasets, ActivityNet Captions [17] and a modified version of Large Scale Movie Description Challenge (LSMDC) [23], the proposed framework obtains remarkable improvement.

2 Related Work

Visual Semantic Embedding. VSE [7,16] is a general approach to bridge visual and linguistic modalities. It has been adopted in various tasks, such as image question answering [22], image captioning [13,14], and image-text matching [6,16,31,36], etc. This approach was later extended to videos [19,21,24]. Plummer *et al.* [21] proposed to improve video summarization by learning a space for joint vision-language embedding. Zhu *et al.* [44] adopted the joint embedding method for aligning books to movies. In these works, each video is embedded as a whole, and its internal structures are not explicitly exploited.

Video Retrieval. Recent methods for video retrieval roughly fall into three categories: concept-based [2,5,27,34], graph-based [18], and those based on feature embeddings. Early works [27] often adopted the concept-based method, which involves detecting a list of visual concepts from the given videos. Recently, Yu *et al.* [41] proposed to improve this paradigm through end-to-end learning. A fundamental limitation of such methods is that they require a predefined list of concepts, which is difficult to provide sufficient coverage in real-world applications. Graph-based methods have also been widely used for matching images with text [11,12,37]. Lin *et al.* [18] explored a graph-based method which matches the objects in a video and the words in a description via bipartite matching. This method also requires a predefined list of objects and nouns.

Many works focused more on learning a joint embedding space for both videos and descriptions [20,30,38]. However, Otani *et al.* [20] embedded each video as a whole, therefore having difficulty in handling long videos that contain multiple events. It is not capable of temporal localization either. Also both [20] and [38] harness external resources through web search, while our framework only utilizes the video-text data in the training set. There are also works [3,4,29] aligning text and video based on character identities, discriminative clustering, or object discovery, without fully mining the semantic meaning of data.

Temporal Localization. Temporal localization, *i.e.* finding video segments for a query, is often explored in the context of action detection. Early methods mainly relied on sliding windows and hand-crafted features [8,10,28]. Recent works [25,40,43] improved the performance using convolutional networks. In these methods, *actionness* is a key factor to consider when evaluating proposals. However, in our settings, the query sentences can describe static scenes. Hence, we have to consider the *significance* of each proposal in a more general sense.

Retrieval in Video Captioning. We note that recent works on video captioning [17,39] often use video retrieval to assess the quality of generated captions. In their experiments, individual sentences and video clips are matched respectively. The temporal structures among video clips are not explicitly leveraged. Hence, these works essentially differ from our two-level structured framework.

3 Methodology

Our primary goal is to develop a framework that can retrieve videos with natural language descriptions and at the same time localize the relevant segments. For this task, it is crucial to model the temporal structures of the videos, for which only the top-level embeddings may not be sufficient. As mentioned, our basic idea is to delve into the internal structures, establishing the connections between the textual queries and the videos, not only at the top level, but also at the part level, *i.e.* sentences and video clips.

In this section, we formalize the intuition above into a two-level formulation in Sect. 3.1, which lays the conceptual foundation. We then proceed to describe how we identify the part-level associations between sentences and video clips in Sect. 3.2, which we refer to as *clip localization*. In Sect. 3.3, we put individual pieces together to form a new framework called *Find and Focus* (*FIFO*), which jointly accomplishes retrieval and localization.

3.1 Two-level Structured Formulation

Our task involves two domains: the query paragraphs in the linguistic domain and the videos in the visual domain. Both paragraphs and videos consist of internal structures. As shown in Fig. 2, a paragraph P is composed of a sequence of sentences $(s_1, \ldots, s_M)$; while a video V is composed of multiple clips $\{c_1, \ldots, c_N\}$, each capturing an event. When a paragraph P is describing a video V, each sentence s_i thereof may refer to a specific clip in V. We refer to such correspondences between sentences and clips as *part-level associations*. The part-level associations convey significant information about the relations between a video and a corresponding paragraph. As we will show in our experiments, leveraging such information can significantly improve the accuracy of retrieval.

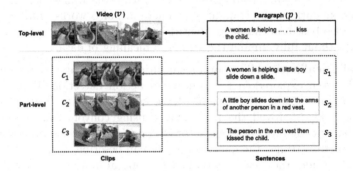

Fig. 2. This figure shows our two-level structured formulation. The upper half depicts the video-paragraph correspondence while the lower half represents the part-level associations between individual clips and sentences. Each individual pair of clip and sentence is denoted in different colors. (Color figure online)

3.2 Clip Localization

The part-level associations are identified via *clip localization*. Given a paragraph P and a video V, it first derives the features for the sentences in P and the snippets in V. Based on these features, it generates a collection of video clip candidates in a semantic-sensitive way, and then solves the correspondences between the sentences and the clips, via a robust matching method. The whole process of clip localization is illustrated in Fig. 3.

Feature Extraction. Given a video, it can be represented by a sequence of snippet-specific features as $V = (\mathbf{f}_1, \ldots, \mathbf{f}_T)$, where T is the number of snippets. The snippets are the units for video analysis. For every snippet (6 frames in our work), $\mathbf{f}_j$ is extracted with a two-stream CNN, trained following the TSN paradigm [35]. In a similar way, we can represent a query paragraph with a series of sentence-specific features as $P = (\mathbf{s}_1, \ldots, \mathbf{s}_M)$, where M is the number of sentences. Note that the visual features and the sentence features are in two *separate* spaces of different dimensions. To directly measure their similarities, we should first embed both features into a *common* semantic space as $\tilde{\mathbf{f}}_j$ and $\tilde{\mathbf{s}}_i$, where they are well aligned. The complete feature embedding process will be introduced in Sect. 3.3.

Clip Proposal. In our two-level formulation, each sentence corresponds to a video clip. A clip usually covers a range of snippets, and the duration of the clips for different sentences can vary significantly. Hence, to establish the part-level associations, we have to prepare a pool of clip candidates.

Inspired by the *Temporal Actionness Grouping* (TAG) method in [43], we develop a semantic-sensitive method for generating video clip proposals. The underlying idea is to find those continuous temporal regions, *i.e.* continuous ranges of snippets, that are semantically relevant to the queries. Specifically, given a sentence s_i, we can compute the *semantic relevance* of the j-th snippet by taking the cosine similarity between $\tilde{\mathbf{f}}_j$ and $\tilde{\mathbf{s}}_i$. Following the watershed scheme in TAG [43], we group the snippets into ranges of varying durations and thus obtain a collection of video clips[2]. For a query paragraph P, the entire clip pool is formed by the union of the collections derived for individual sentences.

Compared to TAG [43], the above method differs in how it evaluates the significance of a snippet. TAG is based on *actionness*, which is semantic-neutral and is only sensitive to those moments where certain actions happen; while our method uses semantic relevance, which is query-dependent and can respond to a much broader range of scenarios, including stationary scenes.

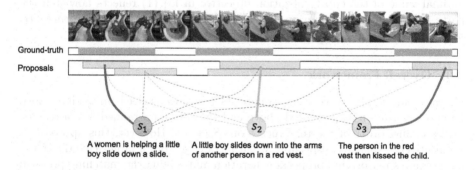

Fig. 3. This figure shows the clip localization process. Given a video with ground-truth clips in green bars, a number of clip proposals colored in blue are generated using a semantic sensitive method. Each sentence is possibly associated with multiple clips, which are represented by thin dash lines. The optimal correspondence, illustrated by the thick lines, is obtained by a robust cross-domain matching. (Color figure online)

Cross-Domain Matching. Given a set of sentences $\{s_1, \ldots, s_M\}$ from the query paragraph P and a set of clip proposals $\{c_1, \ldots, c_N\}$ derived by the proposal generation method, the next is to find the correspondences between them.

---

[2] The technical details of this scheme is provided in the supplemental materials.

In principle, this can be accomplished by *bipartite matching*. However, we found empirically that the one-to-one correspondence enforced by bipartite matching can sometimes lead to misleading results due to outliers. To improve the robustness of the matching, we propose a *robust bipartite matching scheme*, which allows each sentence to be associated with up to u_{max} clips.

We can formalize this modified matching problem as a linear programming problem as follows. We use a binary variable x_{ij} to indicate the association between c_j and s_i. Then the problem can be expressed as

$$\text{maximize} \sum_{i=1}^{M} \sum_{j=1}^{N} r_{ij} x_{ij}; \quad \text{s.t.} \quad \sum_{j=1}^{N} x_{ij} \leq u_{max}, \ \forall i; \quad \sum_{i=1}^{M} x_{ij} \leq 1, \ \forall j. \quad (1)$$

Here, r_{ij} is the *semantic relevance* between the sentence s_i the clip c_j, which is given by

$$r_{ij} \triangleq \frac{\tilde{\mathbf{s}}_i^T \tilde{\mathbf{g}}_j}{\|\tilde{\mathbf{s}}_i\| \cdot \|\tilde{\mathbf{g}}_j\|}, \quad \text{with} \quad \tilde{\mathbf{g}}_j = \frac{1}{|C_j|} \sum_{t \in C_j} \tilde{\mathbf{f}}_t. \quad (2)$$

Here, $\tilde{\mathbf{g}}_j$ is the visual feature that summarizes the video clip c_j, which is snippet-wise feature averaged over its temporal window C_j. Moreover, the two inequalities in Eq. (1) respectively enforce the following constraints: (1) each sentence s_j can be matched to *at most* u_{max} clips, and (2) each clip corresponds to *at most* one sentence, *i.e.* the associated clips for different sentences are disjoint.

The above problem can be solved efficiently by Hungarian algorithm. The optimal value of the clip localization objective in Eq. (1) reflects how well the parts in both modalities can be matched. We call this optimal value *part-level association score*, and denote it by $S_p(V, P)$.

3.3   Overall Framework

Given a paragraph P, we can evaluate its relevance to each individual video by clip localization as presented above and thus obtain a ranked list of results, in descending order of the relevance score $S_p(V, P)$. However, this approach is prohibitively expensive, especially when retrieving from a large-scale database, as it requires performing proposal generation and solving the matching problem *on the fly*.

To balance the retrieval performance and runtime efficiency, we propose a two-stage framework called *Find and Focus*, which is illustrated in Fig. 1. In the Find stage, we perform top-level matching based on the overall representations for both the videos and the query. We found that while top-level matching may not be very accurate for ranking the videos, it can effectively narrow down the search by filtering out a majority of the videos in the database that are clearly irrelevant, while retaining most relevant ones. Note that top-level matching can be done very efficiently, as the top-level representations of the videos can be precomputed and stored. In the Focus stage, we perform detailed clip localization for each video in the top-K list by looking into their internal structures.

The resultant localization scores will be used to refine the ranking. The detailed procedure is presented below.

Find: Top-Level Retrieval. Given the snippet-level features denoted in Sect. 3.2, both the top-level representation $\mathbf{v}$ for a video V and $\mathbf{p}$ for a paragraph P can be achieved by aggregating all their part-level features.

In order to establish the connections between $\mathbf{v}$ and $\mathbf{p}$, at first we have to learn two embedding networks F_{vis}^{top} and F_{text}^{top} respectively for the visual and the linguistic domains, through which we could project them into a common space, as $\tilde{\mathbf{v}} = F_{vis}^{top}(\mathbf{v}; \mathbf{W}_{vis}^{top})$ and $\tilde{\mathbf{p}} = F_{text}^{top}(\mathbf{p}; \mathbf{W}_{text}^{top})$. Here, the embedding networks F_{vis}^{top} and F_{text}^{top} for top-level data can be learned based on the ranking loss [6,16]. Then the top-level relevance between V and P, denoted by $S_t(V, P)$, is defined as the cosine similarity between $\tilde{\mathbf{v}}$ and $\tilde{\mathbf{p}}$.

Based on the top-level relevance scores, we can pick the top K videos given a query paragraph P. We found that with a small K, the initial search can already achieve a high recall. Particularly, for ActivityNet Captions [17], which comprises about 5000 videos, the initial search can retain over 90% of the ground-truth videos in the top-K list with $K = 100$ (about 2% of the database).

Focus: Part-Level Refinement. Recall that through the embeddings learned in the Find stage, both visual features and linguistic features have already been projected into a common space Ω. These preliminarily embedded features could be further refined for clip localization task. The refined features for a snippet-specific feature f_j and a sentence s_i are denoted as $\hat{\mathbf{f}}_j = F_{vis}^{ref}(F_{vis}^{top}(\mathbf{f}_j))$ and $\tilde{\mathbf{s}}_i = F_{text}^{ref}(F_{text}^{top}(\mathbf{s}_i))$, where F_{vis}^{ref} and F_{text}^{ref} represent the feature refinement networks. We will elaborate on how these feature embedding networks F^{top} and refinement networks F^{ref} are trained in Sect. 4.

For each of the K videos retained by the Find stage, we perform clip localization, in order to identify the associations between its clips and the sentences in the query. The localization process not only finds the clips that are relevant to a specific query sentence but also yields a part-level association score $S_p(V, P)$ for the video V at the same time.

Here, the part-level score $S_p(V, P)$, which is derived by aligning the internal structures, provides a more accurate assessment of how well the video V matches the query P and thus is a good complement to the top-level score $S_t(V, P)$. In this framework, we combine both scores into the *final* relevance score in a multiplicative way, as $S_r(V, P) = S_t(V, P) \cdot S_p(V, P)$. We use the final scores to re-rank the videos. Intuitively, this reflects the criterion that a truly relevant video should match the query at both the top level and the part level.

4   Learning the Embedding Networks

Our *Find and Focus* framework comprises two stages. In the first stage, a top-level embedding model is used to align the top-level features of both domains. In the second stage, the embedded features will be further refined for making part-level associations. Below we introduce how these models are trained.

Embedding for Top-Level Data. The objective of the first stage is to learn the networks F_{vis}^{top} and F_{text}^{top}, which respectively embed the original visual features $\{\mathbf{v}_j\}$ and the paragraph features $\{\mathbf{p}_i\}$ into a common space, as $\tilde{\mathbf{v}}_j = F_{vis}^{top}(\mathbf{v}_j; \mathbf{W}_{vis}^{top})$ and $\tilde{\mathbf{p}}_i = F_{text}^{top}(\mathbf{p}_i; \mathbf{W}_{text}^{top})$. These networks are learned jointly with the following margin-based ranking loss:

$$\mathcal{L}^{Find}(\mathbf{W}_{vis}^{top}, \mathbf{W}_{text}^{top}) = \sum_i \sum_{j \neq i} \max\left(0, S_t(V_j, P_i) - S_t(V_i, P_i) + \alpha\right). \quad (3)$$

Here, $S_t(V_j, P_i)$ is the top-level relevance between the video V_j and the paragraph P_i, which, as mentioned, is defined to be the cosine similarity between $\tilde{\mathbf{v}}_j$ and $\tilde{\mathbf{p}}_i$ in the learned space. Also, α is the margin which we set to 0.2. This objective encourages high relevance scores between each video and its corresponding paragraph, i.e. $S_t(V_i, P_i)$, and low relevance scores for mismatched pairs.

Refined Embedding for Part-Level Data. We use refined embeddings for identifying part-level associations. Specifically, given a clip c_j and a sentence s_i, their refined features, respectively denoted as $\tilde{\mathbf{g}}_j$ and $\tilde{\mathbf{s}}_i$, can be derived via refined embedding networks as follows:

$$\tilde{\mathbf{g}}_j = F_{vis}^{ref}(F_{vis}^{top}(\mathbf{g}_j; \mathbf{W}_{vis}^{top}); \mathbf{W}_{vis}^{ref}); \quad \tilde{\mathbf{s}}_i = F_{text}^{ref}(F_{text}^{top}(\mathbf{s}_i; \mathbf{W}_{text}^{top}); \mathbf{W}_{text}^{ref}). \quad (4)$$

Given s in a paragraph, we randomly pick one positive clip c^+ whose temporal IoU (tIoU) is greater than 0.7 out of all clip proposals from the corresponding video, and L negative proposals with tIoU below 0.3. The refined embedding networks F_{vis}^{ref} and F_{text}^{ref} are then trained with a ranking loss defined as below:

$$\mathcal{L}^{Ref}(\mathbf{W}_{vis}^{ref}, \mathbf{W}_{text}^{ref}) = \sum_{j=1}^{L} \max\left(0, s_r(c_j, s) - s_r(c^+, s) + \beta\right). \quad (5)$$

Here, $s_r(c_j, s)$ is the cosine similarity between the refined features as $s_r(c_j, s) = \cos(\tilde{\mathbf{g}}_j, \tilde{\mathbf{s}})$; and the margin β is set to 0.1. This loss function encourages high similarity between the embedded feature of the positive proposal c^+ and that of the query sentence s, while trying to reduce those between negative pairs.

5 Experiments

5.1 Dataset

ActivityNet Captions. ActivityNet Captions [17] consists of $20K$ videos with $100K$ sentences, which are aligned to localized clips. On average, each paragraph has 3.65 sentences, The number of annotated clips in one video ranges from 2 to 27, and the temporal extent of each video clip ranges from 0.05 s to 407 s. About 10% of the clips overlap with others. The complete dataset is divided into three disjoint subsets (training, validation, and test) by 2:1:1. We train models on the training set. Since the test set is not released, we test the learned models on the validation set `val_1`.

Modified LSMDC. LSMDC [23] consists of more than $128k$ clip-description pairs collected from 200 movies. However, for a considerable fraction of these movies, the provided clip descriptions are not well aligned with our acquired film videos possibly due to different versions. Excluding such videos and those kept for blind test, we retain 74 movies in our experiments. Besides, if we treat each movie as a video, we only have 74 video samples, which are not enough for training the top-level embedding. To circumvent this issue, we divide each movie into 3-min chunks, each serving as a whole video. In this way, 1677 videos are obtained and partitioned into two disjoint sets, 1188 videos from 49 movies for training and 489 videos from the other 25 movies for testing.

5.2   Implementation Details

For ActivityNet Captions, we extract a 1024-dimensional vector for every snippet of a video as its raw feature, using a TSN [35] with BN-Inception as its backbone architecture. We also extract word frequency histogram (Bag of Words weighted with tf-idf) as the raw representation for each paragraph or sentence. For the modified LSMDC, we use the feature from the pool5 layer of ResNet101 [9] as the raw feature for video data, and the sum of word embeddings for text.

We set the dimension of the common embedding space to be 512. We train both the top-level embedding networks in the Find stage and the refinement network in the Focus stage using Adam [15] with the momentum set to 0.9.

5.3   Whole Video Retrieval

We first compare our framework with the following methods on the task of whole video retrieval: (1) LSTM-YT [33] uses the latent states in the LSTM for cross-modality matching. (2) S2VT [32] uses several LSTMs to encode video frames and associate videos with text data. (3) Krishna *et al.* [17] encode each paragraph using the captioning model and each clip with a proposal model.

For performance evaluation, we employ the following metrics: (1) Recall@K, the percentage of ground truth videos that appear in the resultant top-K list, and (2) MedR, the median rank of the ground truth videos. These metrics are commonly used in retrieval tasks [17,20].

Table 1 shows the results of whole video retrieval on ActivityNet Captions dataset. From the results, we observe: (1) The VSE model trained in the Find stage is already able to achieve a substantial improvement over previous methods in terms of Recall@50, which shows that it is suitable for top-level matching. (2) Our proposed FIFO framework achieves the best performance consistently on all metrics. With a further refinement in the Focus stage by localizing clips in the selected top 20 candidate videos, all recall rates with different settings of K are boosted considerably. For example, Recall@1 is improved by about 20%, and Recall@5 is improved by about 8%.

We also evaluate our framework on the modified LSMDC dataset. From the results shown in Table 2, we observe similar trends, but more obvious.

Table 1. Results for whole video retrieval on ActivityNet Captions.

	R@1	R@5	R@10	R@50	MedR
Random	0.02	0.10	0.20	1.02	2458
LSTM-YT [33]	0	4	-	24	102
S2VT [32]	5	14	-	32	78
Krishna *et al.* [17]	14	32	-	65	34
VSE (Find)	11.69	34.66	50.03	85.66	10
Ours (Find + refine in Top 20)	**14.11**	37.12	52.13	-	10
Ours (Find + refine in Top 100)	14.05	**37.40**	**52.94**	**86.72**	9

Table 2. Results for whole video retrieval on modified LSMDC dataset.

	R@1	R@5	R@10	R@50	MedR
Random	0.20	1.02	2.04	10.22	244
VSE (Find)	2.66	10.63	16.36	52.97	45
Ours (Find + refine in Top 20)	**3.89**	**13.70**	20.04	-	45
Ours (Find + refine in Top 70)	**3.89**	13.50	**20.25**	**56.65**	40

Compared to VSE, our method improves Recall@1 by about 46% (from 2.66 to 3.89) and Recall@5 by about 29% (from 10.63 to 13.70).

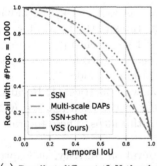
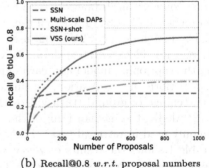

(a) Recall at different tIoU thresholds   (b) Recall@0.8 *w.r.t.* proposal numbers

Fig. 4. Comparison of different proposal generation methods on ActivityNet Captions.

5.4   Proposal Generation and Clip Localization

We evaluate the performance of our proposal generation method, *visual semantic similarity* (VSS), in comparison with previous methods on ActivityNet Captions dataset. The performance is measured in terms of the recall rate at different tIoU thresholds. From the results shown in Fig. 4(a), we can see that our method outperforms all the other methods consistently across all tIoU thresholds. Particularly, with the tIoU threshold set to 0.5, our method can achieve a high recall 95.09% with 1000 proposals, significantly outperforming SSN+shot, a state-of-the-art method for video clip proposal, which achieves recall 84.35% with 1000 proposals. The performance gain is primarily thanks to our design that employs semantic significance instead of actionness in proposal rating.

Figure 4(b) shows that when we increase the number of proposals, the recall improves consistently and significantly. This suggests that our method tends to produce new proposals covering different temporal regions.

Table 3. Comparison of clip localization performance for different proposal methods.

ActivityNet, clip localization Recall@tIoU			
	Recall@0.3	Recall@0.5	Recall@0.7
SSN [43]	15.85	7.33	3.20
SSN [43]+shot [1]	16.71	8.74	4.30
Ours (VSS)	**28.52**	**13.46**	**5.21**

Furthermore, we compare the quality of temporal proposals generated by different methods in the task of clip localization. The performance is measured by the recall rate with different tIoU thresholds. Table 3 shows the results. Again, our proposal generation method outperforms others by a large margin.

5.5   Ablation Studies

Different Language Representations. We compare the performance of different ways to represent text on ActivityNet Captions dataset. The first two rows in Table 4 show the filtering effect of TF-IDF. The bottom two rows demonstrate that using a better word aggregation method will lead to a performance promotion, as Fisher vector [10] models a distribution over words.

Table 4. Different word representations for video retrieval on ActivityNet caption.

		R@1	R@5	R@10	R@50	MedR
BoW with tf-idf	(Find)	11.69	34.66	50.03	85.66	10
	(Find + refine in Top 100)	14.05	37.40	52.94	86.72	9
BoW without tf-idf	(Find)	11.57	33.03	49.89	85.66	11
	(Find + refine in Top 100)	13.46	36.67	52.09	86.26	9
word2vec	(Find)	9.05	27.96	42.95	81.55	14
	(Find + refine in Top 100)	10.92	32.38	46.55	82.06	12
word2vec + Fisher Vec	(Find)	11.80	34.35	50.07	85.93	10
	(Find + refine in Top 100)	13.75	37.93	53.41	86.30	9

Choice of K in Video Selection. Here, K is the number of videos retained in the initial Find stage. We compare the influence of K on the final retrieval performance, with the results reported in Table 5. The results demonstrate that the Focus stage can significantly improve the retrieval results. Generally, increasing K can lead to better performance. However, on ActivityNet Captions, as K goes beyond 20, the performance gradually saturates. Note that when K is set to a very large number ($K = 1000$), we can get almost 100% recall in Find stage. But the results are close to $K = 100$ with high computational cost.

Table 5. Retrieval performance on ActivityNet Captions with different settings of K.

	Recall@1	Recall@5	Recall@10	Recall@15	Recall@20	Recall@50
No refinement	11.69	34.66	50.03	59.90	67.34	85.66
$K = 10$	13.93	36.65	-	-	-	-
$K = 20$	**14.11**	37.12	52.13	61.62	-	-
$K = 50$	14.05	37.40	52.90	**63.29**	70.53	-
$K = 100$	14.05	37.40	52.94	63.27	**70.75**	**86.72**
$K = 1000$	14.01	**37.44**	**53.06**	63.11	70.34	86.62

Table 6. The influence caused by feature refinement under the task of clip localization.

Dataset	ActivityNet Captions			Modified LSMDC		
Clip localization Recall@tIoU	R@0.3	R@0.5	R@0.7	R@0.3	R@0.5	R@0.7
VSS (not refined feature)	27.04	12.74	4.72	5.00	2.48	0.75
VSS (refined feature)	**28.52**	**13.46**	**5.21**	**5.25**	**2.49**	**0.86**

Table 7. Comparison of the performance between different settings of the bipartite matching algorithm in the focus stage.

$u_{max} = 1$		$u_{max} = 2$		$u_{max} = 3$	
Recall@1	Recall@5	Recall@1	Recall@5	Recall@1	Recall@5
13.87	36.61	**13.93**	**36.65**	13.75	36.59

Feature Refinement. Recall that the embedded features in the Find stage can be further refined during the Focus stage. Here, we compare the performance in the task of clip localization, with or without feature refinement. The performance is measured by the recall rate of clip localization at different tIoU thresholds. The results in Table 6 show that the feature refinement in the Focus stage leads to more favorable features, which could better capture the semantic relevance across modalities.

Bipartite Matching. We try different settings for bipartite matching in the Focus stage, by varying u_{max}, the maximum number of clips allowed to be

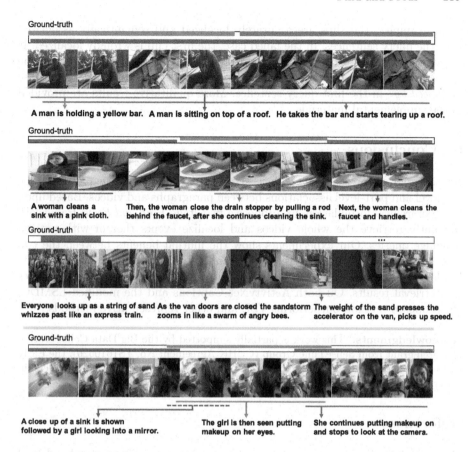

Ground-truth

A man is holding a yellow bar. A man is sitting on top of a roof. He takes the bar and starts tearing up a roof.

Ground-truth

A woman cleans a sink with a pink cloth.   Then, the woman close the drain stopper by pulling a rod behind the faucet, after she continues cleaning the sink.   Next, the woman cleans the faucet and handles.

Ground-truth

Everyone looks up as a string of sand whizzes past like an express train.   As the van doors are closed the sandstorm zooms in like a swarm of angry bees.   The weight of the sand presses the accelerator on the van, picks up speed.

Ground-truth

A close up of a sink is shown followed by a girl looking into a mirror.   The girl is then seen putting makeup on her eyes.   She continues putting makeup on and stops to look at the camera.

Fig. 5. Qualitative results of video retrieval and clip localization on ActivityNet Captions and modified LSMDC datasets. For every video with several representative frames, the ground-truth video clip is denoted in colored bars above. The localized clips associated with the query sentences are illustrated below each video. (Color figure online)

matched to a sentence. Table 7 shows that slightly increasing u_{max} can moderately improve the retrieval results, as it makes the matching process more resilient to outliers. However, the performance gain diminishes when u_{max} is too large due to the confusion brought by the increased matching clips. We observe that on ActivityNet Captions, the bipartite matching achieves the best performance when u_{max} is set to 2, and this setting is also adopted in our experiments.

5.6 Qualitative Results

We present the qualitative results of the joint video retrieval and clip localization on both ActivityNet Captions and modified LSMDC datasets in Fig. 5. We visualize three successful cases plus one failed case. We can see that in the above three examples, the clips are accurately localized and semantically associated with the query sentences. In the failed case, the first clip is wrongly localized. It reveals that although being able to capture information about objects and the static scenes, our method sometimes ignores complex relations, *e.g.* the phrase *"followed by"* in the first query sentence. More qualitative results are provided in the supplemental materials.

6   Conclusions

In this paper, we presented a two-level structured formulation to exploit both the top-level and part-level associations between paragraphs and videos. Based upon this hierarchical formulation, we propose a two-stage *Find and Focus* framework to jointly retrieve the whole videos and localize events therein with natural language queries. Our experiments show the mutual benefits between the two stages. In particular, the top-level retrieval in the Find stage helps to alleviate the burden of clip localization; while the clip localization in the Focus stage refines the retrieval results. On both ActivtyNet Captions and the modified LSMDC, the proposed method outperforms VSE and other representative methods.

Acknowledgments. This work is partially supported by the Big Data Collaboration Research grant from SenseTime Group (CUHK Agreement No. TS1610626), the Early Career Scheme (ECS) of Hong Kong (No. 24204215), and International Partnership Program of Chinese Academy of Sciences (172644KYSB20160033).

References

1. Apostolidis, E., Mezaris, V.: Fast shot segmentation combining global and local visual descriptors. In: IEEE International Conference on Acoustics, Speech and Signal Processing (ICASSP), pp. 6583–6587. IEEE (2014)
2. Aytar, Y., Shah, M., Luo, J.: Utilizing semantic word similarity measures for video retrieval. In: IEEE Conference on Computer Vision and Pattern Recognition (CVPR), pp. 1–8. IEEE (2008)
3. Bojanowski, P., et al.: Weakly-supervised alignment of video with text. In: IEEE International Conference on Computer Vision (ICCV), pp. 4462–4470 (2015)
4. Chen, K., Song, H., Loy, C.C., Lin, D.: Discover and learn new objects from documentaries. In: 2017 IEEE Conference on Computer Vision and Pattern Recognition (CVPR), pp. 1111–1120. IEEE (2017)
5. Dalton, J., Allan, J., Mirajkar, P.: Zero-shot video retrieval using content and concepts. In: the 22nd ACM International Conference on Information and Knowledge Management (CIKM), pp. 1857–1860. ACM (2013)
6. Faghri, F., Fleet, D.J., Kiros, J.R., Fidler, S.: VSE++: improved visual-semantic embeddings. arXiv preprint arXiv:1707.05612 (2017)
7. Frome, A., Corrado, G.S., Shlens, J., Bengio, S., Dean, J., Mikolov, T., et al.: Devise: a deep visual-semantic embedding model. In: Advances in Neural Information Processing Systems (NIPS), pp. 2121–2129 (2013)
8. Gaidon, A., Harchaoui, Z., Schmid, C.: Temporal localization of actions with actoms. IEEE Trans. Pattern Anal. Mach. Intell. **35**(11), 2782–2795 (2013)

9. He, K., Zhang, X., Ren, S., Sun, J.: Deep residual learning for image recognition. In: IEEE Conference on Computer Vision and Pattern Recognition (CVPR), pp. 770–778 (2016)

10. Jain, M., Van Gemert, J., Jégou, H., Bouthemy, P., Snoek, C.: Action localization with tubelets from motion. In: IEEE International Conference on Computer Vision and Pattern Recognition (CVPR) (2014)

11. Johnson, J., et al.: Image retrieval using scene graphs. In: IEEE Conference on Computer vision and Pattern Recognition (CVPR), pp. 3668–3678 (2015)

12. Jouili, S., Tabbone, S.: Hypergraph-based image retrieval for graph-based representation. Pattern Recognit. **45**(11), 4054–4068 (2012)

13. Karpathy, A., Fei-Fei, L.: Deep visual-semantic alignments for generating image descriptions. In: IEEE Conference on Computer Vision and Pattern Recognition (CVPR), pp. 3128–3137 (2015)

14. Karpathy, A., Joulin, A., Fei-Fei, L.: Deep fragment embeddings for bidirectional image sentence mapping. In: Advances in Neural Information Processing Systems (NIPS), pp. 1889–1897 (2014)

15. Kingma, D.P., Ba, J.: Adam: a method for stochastic optimization. arXiv preprint arXiv:1412.6980 (2014)

16. Kiros, R., Salakhutdinov, R., Zemel, R.S.: Unifying visual-semantic embeddings with multimodal neural language models. arXiv preprint arXiv:1411.2539 (2014)

17. Krishna, R., Hata, K., Ren, F., Fei-Fei, L., Niebles, J.C.: Dense-captioning events in videos. In: IEEE International Conference on Computer Vision (ICCV) (2017)

18. Lin, D., Fidler, S., Kong, C., Urtasun, R.: Visual semantic search: retrieving videos via complex textual queries. In: IEEE Conference on Computer Vision and Pattern Recognition (CVPR), pp. 2657–2664 (2014)

19. Liu, W., Mei, T., Zhang, Y., Che, C., Luo, J.: Multi-task deep visual-semantic embedding for video thumbnail selection. In: IEEE Conference on Computer Vision and Pattern Recognition (CVPR), pp. 3707–3715 (2015)

20. Otani, M., Nakashima, Y., Rahtu, E., Heikkilä, J., Yokoya, N.: Learning joint representations of videos and sentences with web image search. In: Hua, G., Jégou, H. (eds.) ECCV 2016. LNCS, vol. 9913, pp. 651–667. Springer, Cham (2016). https://doi.org/10.1007/978-3-319-46604-0_46

21. Plummer, B.A., Brown, M., Lazebnik, S.: Enhancing video summarization via vision-language embedding. In: IEEE Conference on Computer Vision and Pattern Recognition (CVPR) (2017)

22. Ren, M., Kiros, R., Zemel, R.: Image question answering: a visual semantic embedding model and a new dataset. Adv. Neural Inf. Process. Systems (NIPS) **1**(2), 5 (2015)

23. Rohrbach, A., et al.: Movie description. Int. J. Comput. Vis. **123**(1), 94–120 (2017)

24. Sharghi, A., Gong, B., Shah, M.: Query-focused extractive video summarization. In: Leibe, B., Matas, J., Sebe, N., Welling, M. (eds.) ECCV 2016. LNCS, vol. 9912, pp. 3–19. Springer, Cham (2016). https://doi.org/10.1007/978-3-319-46484-8_1

25. Shou, Z., Wang, D., Chang, S.F.: Temporal action localization in untrimmed videos via multi-stage CNNs. In: IEEE Conference on Computer Vision and Pattern Recognition (CVPR), pp. 1049–1058 (2016)

26. Smoliar, S.W., Zhang, H.: Content based video indexing and retrieval. IEEE Multimed. **1**(2), 62–72 (1994)

27. Snoek, C.G., Worring, M.: Concept-based video retrieval. Found. Trends Inf. Retrieval **2**(4), 215–322 (2008)

28. Tang, K., Yao, B., Fei-Fei, L., Koller, D.: Combining the right features for complex event recognition. In: IEEE International Conference on Computer Vision (ICCV), pp. 2696–2703. IEEE (2013)

29. Tapaswi, M., Bäuml, M., Stiefelhagen, R.: Aligning plot synopses to videos for story-based retrieval. Int. J. Multimed. Inf. Retrieval **4**(1), 3–16 (2015)

30. Torabi, A., Tandon, N., Sigal, L.: Learning language-visual embedding for movie understanding with natural-language. arXiv preprint arXiv:1609.08124 (2016)

31. Vendrov, I., Kiros, R., Fidler, S., Urtasun, R.: Order-embeddings of images and language. In: International Conference on Representation Learning (ICLR) (2016)

32. Venugopalan, S., Rohrbach, M., Donahue, J., Mooney, R., Darrell, T., Saenko, K.: Sequence to sequence-video to text. In: IEEE International Conference on Computer Vision (ICCV), pp. 4534–4542 (2015)

33. Venugopalan, S., Xu, H., Donahue, J., Rohrbach, M., Mooney, R., Saenko, K.: Translating videos to natural language using deep recurrent neural networks. arXiv preprint arXiv:1412.4729 (2014)

34. Wang, D., Li, X., Li, J., Zhang, B.: The importance of query-concept-mapping for automatic video retrieval. In: the 15th ACM International Conference on Multimedia, pp. 285–288. ACM (2007)

35. Wang, L., et al.: Temporal segment networks: towards good practices for deep action recognition. In: Leibe, B., Matas, J., Sebe, N., Welling, M. (eds.) ECCV 2016. LNCS, vol. 9912, pp. 20–36. Springer, Cham (2016). https://doi.org/10.1007/978-3-319-46484-8_2

36. Wang, L., Li, Y., Lazebnik, S.: Learning deep structure-preserving image-text embeddings. In: IEEE Conference on Computer Vision and Pattern Recognition (CVPR), pp. 5005–5013 (2016)

37. Wu, B., Lang, B., Liu, Y.: GKSH: graph based image retrieval using supervised kernel hashing. In: International Conference on Internet Multimedia Computing and Service, pp. 88–93. ACM (2016)

38. Xu, R., Xiong, C., Chen, W., Corso, J.J.: Jointly modeling deep video and compositional text to bridge vision and language in a unified framework. In: AAAI Conference on Artificial Intelligence (AAAI), vol. 5, p. 6 (2015)

39. Yao, L., et al.: Describing videos by exploiting temporal structure. In: IEEE International Conference on Computer Vision (ICCV), pp. 4507–4515 (2015)

40. Yeung, S., Russakovsky, O., Mori, G., Fei-Fei, L.: End-to-end learning of action detection from frame glimpses in videos. In: Proceedings of the IEEE Conference on Computer Vision and Pattern Recognition, pp. 2678–2687 (2016)

41. Yu, Y., Ko, H., Choi, J., Kim, G.: End-to-end concept word detection for video captioning, retrieval, and question answering. In: IEEE Conference on Computer Vision and Pattern Recognition (CVPR) (2017)

42. Zhang, H.J., Wu, J., Zhong, D., Smoliar, S.W.: An integrated system for content-based video retrieval and browsing. Pattern Recognit. **30**(4), 643–658 (1997)

43. Zhao, Y., Xiong, Y., Wang, L., Wu, Z., Tang, X., Lin, D.: Temporal action detection with structured segment networks. In: IEEE International Conference on Computer Vision (ICCV), vol. 8 (2017)

44. Zhu, Y., et al.: Aligning books and movies: towards story-like visual explanations by watching movies and reading books. In: IEEE International Conference on Computer Vision (ICCV), pp. 19–27 (2015)

Face Super-Resolution Guided by Facial Component Heatmaps

Xin Yu[1(✉)], Basura Fernando[1], Bernard Ghanem[2], Fatih Porikli[1],
and Richard Hartley[1]

[1] Australian National University, Canberra, Australia
{xin.yu,fatih.porikli,richard.hartley}@anu.edu.au, Basuraf@gmail.com
[2] King Abdullah University of Science and Technology, Thuwal, Saudi Arabia
Bernard.Ghanem@kaust.edu.sa

Abstract. State-of-the-art face super-resolution methods leverage deep convolutional neural networks to learn a mapping between low-resolution (LR) facial patterns and their corresponding high-resolution (HR) counterparts by exploring local appearance information. However, most of these methods do not account for facial structure and suffer from degradations due to large pose variations and misalignments. In this paper, we propose a method that explicitly incorporates structural information of faces into the face super-resolution process by using a multi-task convolutional neural network (CNN). Our CNN has two branches: one for super-resolving face images and the other branch for predicting salient regions of a face coined *facial component heatmaps*. These heatmaps encourage the upsampling stream to generate super-resolved faces with higher-quality details. Our method not only uses low-level information (*i.e.*, intensity similarity), but also middle-level information (*i.e.*, face structure) to further explore spatial constraints of facial components from LR inputs images. Therefore, we are able to super-resolve very small unaligned face images (16 × 16 pixels) with a large upscaling factor of 8×, while preserving face structure. Extensive experiments demonstrate that our network achieves superior face hallucination results and outperforms the state-of-the-art.

Keywords: Face · Super-resolution · Hallucination
Facial component localization · Multi-task neural networks

1 Introduction

Face images provide crucial clues for human observation as well as computer analysis [1,2]. However, the performance of most existing facial analysis techniques, such as face alignment [3,4] and identification [5], degrades dramatically when the resolution of a face is adversely low. Face super-resolution (FSR) [8],

Electronic supplementary material The online version of this chapter (https://doi.org/10.1007/978-3-030-01240-3_14) contains supplementary material, which is available to authorized users.

© Springer Nature Switzerland AG 2018
V. Ferrari et al. (Eds.): ECCV 2018, LNCS 11213, pp. 219–235, 2018.
https://doi.org/10.1007/978-3-030-01240-3_14

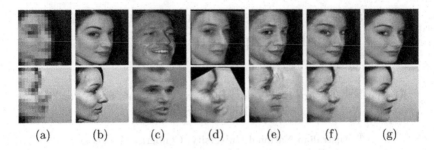

(a)   (b)   (c)   (d)   (e)   (f)   (g)

Fig. 1. Comparison of state-of-the-art face super-resolution methods on very low-resolution (LR) face images. Columns: (a) unaligned LR inputs. (b) Original HR images. (c) Nearest Neighbors (NN) of aligned LR faces. Note that image intensities are used to find NN. (d) CBN [6]. (e) TDAE [7]. (f) TDAE†. We retrain the original TDAE with our training dataset. (g) Our results.

also known as face hallucination, provides a viable way to recover a high-resolution (HR) face image from its low-resolution (LR) counterpart and has attracted increasing interest in recent years. Modern face hallucination methods employ deep learning [6,7,9–16] and achieve state-of-the-art performance. These methods explore image intensity correspondences between LR and HR faces from large-scale face datasets. Since near-frontal faces prevail in popular large-scale face datasets [17,18], deep learning based FSR methods may fail to super-resolve LR faces under large pose variations, as seen in the examples of Fig. 1. In fact, in these examples, the face structure has been distorted and facial details are not fully recovered by state-of-the-art super-resolution methods.

A naive idea to remedy this issue is to augment training data with large pose variations (*i.e.*, [19]) and then retrain the neural networks. As shown in Fig. 1(f), this strategy still leads to suboptimal results where facial details are missing or distorted due to erroneous localization of LR facial patterns. This limitation is common in intensity-based FSR methods that only exploit local intensity information in super-resolution and do not take face structure or poses into account. We postulate that methods that explicitly exploit information about the locations of facial components in LR faces have the capacity to improve super-resolution performance.

Another approach to super-resolve LR face images is to localize facial components in advance and then upsample them [6,20] progressively. However, localizing these facial components with high accuracy is generally a difficult task in very LR images, especially under large pose variations. As shown in Fig. 1(e), the method of Zhu *et al.* [6] fails to localize facial components accurately and produces an HR face with severe distortions. Therefore, directly detecting facial components or landmarks in LR faces is suboptimal and may lead to ghosting artifacts in the final result.

In contrast to previous methods, we propose a method that super-resolves LR face images while predicting face structure in a collaborative manner. Our intuition is that, although it is difficult to accurately detect facial landmarks in

LR face images, it is possible to localize facial components (not landmarks) and identify the visibility of the components on the super-resolved faces or the intermediate upsampled feature maps because they can provide enough resolution for localization. Obtaining the locations of facial components can in turn facilitate face super-resolution.

Driven by this idea, we propose a multi-task deep neural network to upsample LR images. In contrast to the state-of-the-art FSR methods [6,7,12,13], our network not only super-resolves LR images but also estimates the spatial positions of their facial components. Then the estimated locations of the facial components are regarded as a guidance map which provides the face structure in super-resolution. Here, face structure refers to the locations and visibility of facial components as well as the relationship between them and we use heatmaps to represent the probability of the appearance of each component. Since the resolution of the input faces is small, (*i.e.*, 16 × 16 pixels), localizing facial components is also very challenging. Instead of detecting facial components in LR images, we opt to localize facial components on super-resolved feature maps. Specifically, we first super-resolve features of input LR images, and then employ a spatial transformer network [21] to align the feature maps. The upsampled feature maps are used to estimate the heatmaps of facial components. Since the feature maps are aligned, the same facial components may appear at the corresponding positions closely. This also provides an initial estimation for the component localization. Furthermore, we can also largely reduce the training examples for localizing facial components when input faces or feature maps are pre-aligned. For instance, we only use $30K$ LR/HR face image pairs for training our network, while a state-of-the-art face alignment method [4] requires about $230K$ images to train a landmark localization network.

After obtaining the estimated heatmaps of facial components, we concatenate them with the upsampled feature maps to infuse the spatial and visibility information of facial components into the super-resolution procedure. In this fashion, higher-level information beyond pixel-wise intensity similarity is explored and used as an additional prior in FSR. As shown in Fig. 1(g), our presented network is able to upsample LR faces in large poses while preserving the spatial structure of upsampled face images.

Overall, the contributions of our work can be summarized as:

- We present a novel multi-task framework to super-resolve LR face images of size 16 × 16 pixels by an upscaling factor of 8×, which not only exploits image intensity similarity but also explores the face structure prior in face super-resolution.
- We not only upsample LR faces but also estimate the face structure in the framework. Our estimated facial component heatmaps provide not only spatial information of facial components but also their visibility information, which cannot be deduced from pixel-level information.
- We demonstrate that the proposed two branches, *i.e.*, upsampling and facial component estimation branches, collaborate with each other in super-resolution, thus achieving better face hallucination performance.

– Due to the design of our network architecture, we are able to estimate facial component heatmaps from the upsampled feature maps, which provides enough resolutions and details for estimation. Furthermore, since the feature maps are aligned before heatmap estimation, we can largely reduce the number of training images to train the heatmap estimation branch.

To the best of our knowledge, our method is the first attempt to use a multi-task framework to super-resolve very LR face images. We not only focus on learning the intensity similarity mappings between LR and HR facial patterns, similar to [7,13,22], but also explore the face structure information from images themselves and employ it as an additional prior for super-resolution.

2   Related Work

Exploiting facial priors, such as spatial configuration of facial components, in face hallucination is the key factor different from generic super-resolution tasks. Based on the usage of the priors, face hallucination methods can be roughly grouped into global model based and part based approaches.

Global model based approaches aim at super-resolving an LR input image by learning a holistic appearance mapping such as PCA. Wang and Tang [23] learn subspaces from LR and HR face images respectively, and then reconstruct an HR output from the PCA coefficients of the LR input. Liu et al. [24] employ a global model for the super-resolution of LR face images but also develop a markov random field (MRF) to reduce ghosting artifacts caused by the misalignments in LR images. Kolouri and Rohde [25] employ optimal transport techniques to morph an HR output by interpolating exemplar HR faces. In order to learn a good global model, LR inputs are required to be precisely aligned and to share similar poses to the exemplar HR images. When large pose variations and misalignments exit in LR inputs, these methods are prone to produce severe artifacts.

Part based methods are proposed to super-resolve individual facial regions separately. They reconstruct the HR counterparts of LR inputs based on either reference patches or facial components in the training dataset. Baker and Kanade [26] search the best mapping between LR and HR patches and then use the matched HR patches to recover high-frequency details of aligned LR face images. Motivated by this idea, [22,27–29] average weighted position patches extracted from multiple aligned HR images to upsample aligned LR face images in either the image intensity domain or sparse coding domain. However, patch based methods also require LR inputs to be aligned in advance and may produce blocky artifacts when the upscaling factor is too large. Instead of using position patches, Tappen and Liu [30] super-resolve HR facial components by warping the reference HR images. Yang et al. [20] localize facial components in the LR images by a facial landmark detector and then reconstruct missing high-frequency details from similar HR reference components. Because facial component based methods need to extract facial parts in LR images and then align them to exemplar images accurately, their performance degrades dramatically when the resolutions of input faces become unfavorably small.

Recently, deep learning techniques have been applied to the face hallucination field and achieved significant progress. Yu and Porikli [10] present a discriminative generative network to hallucinate aligned LR face images. Their follow-up works [7,31] interweave multiple spatial transformer networks [21] with the deconvolutional layers to handle unaligned LR faces. Xu et al. [32] employ the framework of generative adversarial networks [33,34] to recover blurry LR face images by a multi-class discriminative loss. Dahl et al. [13] leverage the framework of PixelCNN [35] to super-resolve very low-resolution faces. Since the above deep convolutional networks only consider local information in super-resolution without taking the holistic face structure into account, they may distort face structure when super-resolving non-frontal LR faces. Zhu et al. [6] present a cascade bi-network, dubbed CBN, to localize LR facial components first and then upsample the facial components, but CBN may produce ghosting faces when localization errors occur. Concurrent to our work, the algorithms [14,15] also employ facial structure in face hallucination. In contrast to their works, we propose a multi-task network which can be trained in an end-to-end manner. In particular, our network not only estimates the facial heatmaps but also employs them for achieving high-quality super-resolved results.

3 Our Proposed Method

Our network mainly consists of two parts: a multi-task upsampling network and a discriminative network. Our multi-task upsampling network (MTUN) is composed of two branches: an upsampling branch and a facial component heatmap estimation branch (HEB). Figure 2 illustrates the overall architecture of our proposed network. The entire network is trained in an end-to-end fashion.

3.1 Facial Component Heatmap Estimation

When the resolution of input images is too small, facial components will be even smaller. Thus, it is very difficult for state-of-the-art facial landmark detectors to localize facial landmarks in very low-resolution images accurately. However, we propose to predict facial component heatmaps from super-resolved feature maps rather than localizing landmarks in LR input images, because the upsampled feature maps contain more details and their resolutions are large enough for estimating facial component heatmaps. Moreover, since 2D faces may exhibit a wide range of poses, such as in-plane rotations, out-of-plane rotations and scale changes, we may need a large number of images for training HEB. For example, Bulat and Tzimiropoulos [4] require over $200K$ training images to train a landmark detector, and there is still a gap between the accuracy of [4] and human labeling. To mitigate this problem, our intuition is that when the faces are roughly aligned, the same facial components lie in the corresponding positions closely. Thus, we employ a spatial transformer network (STN) to align

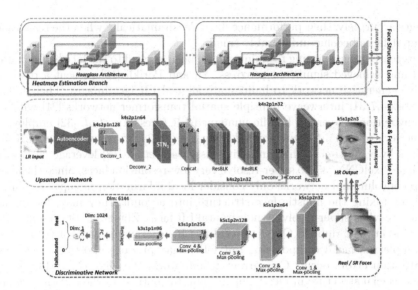

Fig. 2. The pipeline of our multi-task upsampling network. In the testing phase, the upsampling branch (blue block) and the heatmap estimation branch (green block) are used. (Color figure online)

the upsampled features before estimating heatmaps. In this way, we not only ease the heatmap estimation but also significantly reduce the number of training images used for learning HEB.

We use heatmaps instead of landmarks based on three reasons: (i) localizing each facial landmark individually is difficult in LR faces even for humans and erroneous landmarks would lead to distortions in the final results. On the contrary, it is much easier to localize each facial components as a whole. (ii) Even state-of-the-art landmark detectors may fail to output accurate positions in high-resolution images, such as in large pose cases. However, it is not difficult to estimate a region represented by a heatmap in those cases. (iii) Furthermore, our goal is to provide clues of the spatial positions and visibility of each component rather than the exact shape of each component. Using heatmaps as a probability map is more suitable for our purpose.

In this paper, we use four heatmaps to represent four components of a face, i.e., eyes, nose, mouth and chain, respectively. We exploit 68 point facial landmarks to generate the ground-truth heatmaps. Specifically, each landmark is represented by a Gaussian kernel and the center of the kernel is the location of the landmark. By adjusting the standard variance of Gaussian kernels in accordance with the resolutions of feature maps or images, we can generate a heatmap for each component. The generated ground-truth heatmaps are shown in Fig. 3(c). Note that, when self-occlusions appear, some components are not visible and they will not appear in the heatmaps. In this way, heatmaps not only provides the locations of components but also their visibility in the original LR input images.

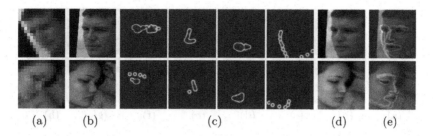

(a)   (b)   (c)   (d)   (e)

Fig. 3. Visualization of estimated facial component heatmaps. Columns: (a) unaligned LR inputs. (b) HR images. (c) Ground-truth heatmaps generated from the landmarks of HR face images. (d) Our results. (e) The estimated heatmaps overlying over our super-resolved results. Note that, we overlap four estimated heatmaps together and upsample the heatmaps to fit our upsampled results

In order to estimate facial component heatmaps, we employ the stacked hourglass network architecture [36]. It exploits a repeated bottom-up and top-down fashion to process features across multiple scales and is able to capture various spatial relationships among different parts. As suggested in [36], we also use the intermediate supervision to improve the performance. The green block in Fig. 2 illustrates our facial component heatmap estimation branch. We feed the aligned feature maps to HEB and then concatenate the estimated heatmaps with the upsampled feature maps for super-resolving facial details. In order to illustrate the effectiveness of HEB, we resize and then overlay the estimated heatmaps over the output images as visible in Fig. 3(e). The ground-truth heatmaps are shown in Fig. 3(c) for comparison.

3.2   Network Architecture

Multi-task Upsampling Network: Figure 2 illustrates the architecture of our proposed multi-task upsampling network (MTUN) in the blue and green blocks. MTUN consists of two branches: an upsampling branch (blue block) and a facial component heatmap estimation branch (green block). The upsampling branch firstly super-resolves features of LR input images and then aligns the feature maps. When the resolution of the feature maps is large enough, the upsampled feature maps are fed into HEB to estimate the locations and visibility of facial components. Thus we obtain the heatmaps of the facial components of LR inputs. The estimated heatmaps are then concatenated with the upsampled feature maps to provide the spatial positions and visibility information of facial components for super-resolution.

In the upsampling branch, the network is composed of a convolutional autoencoder, deconvolutional layers and an STN. The convolutional autoencoder is designed to extract high-frequency details from input images while removing image noise before upsampling and alignment, thus increasing the super-resolution performance. The deconvolutional layers are employed to super-resolve the feature maps. Since input LR faces undergo in-plane rotations, translations

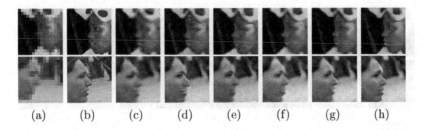

(a)   (b)   (c)   (d)   (e)   (f)   (g)   (h)

Fig. 4. Comparisons of different losses for the super-resolution. Columns: (a) unaligned LR inputs. (b) Original HR images. (c) $\mathcal{L}_p$. (d) $\mathcal{L}_p + \mathcal{L}_f$. (e) $\mathcal{L}_p + \mathcal{L}_f + \mathcal{L}_\mathcal{U}$. (f) $\mathcal{L}_p + \mathcal{L}_h$. (g) $\mathcal{L}_p + \mathcal{L}_f + \mathcal{L}_h$. (h) $\mathcal{L}_p + \mathcal{L}_f + \mathcal{L}_\mathcal{U} + \mathcal{L}_h$. For simplicity, we omit the trade-off weights.

and scale changes, STN is employed to compensate for those affine transformations, thus facilitating facial component heatmap estimation.

After obtaining aligned upsampled feature maps, those feature maps are used to estimate facial component heatmaps by an HEB. We construct our HEB by a stacked hourglass architecture [36], which consists of residual blocks and upsampling layers, as shown in the green block of Fig. 2.

Our multi-task network aims at super-resolving input face images as well as predicting heatmaps of facial components in the images. As seen in Fig. 4(c), when we only use the upsampling branch to super-resolve faces without using HEB, the facial details are blurred and some facial components, *e.g.*, mouth and nose, are distorted in large poses. Furthermore, the heatmap supervision also forces STN to align the upsampled features more accurately, thus improving super-resolution performance. Therefore, these two tasks collaborate with each other and benefit from each other as well. As shown in Fig. 4(f), our multi-task network achieves better super-resolved results.

Discriminative Network: Recent works [7,10,32,37] demonstrate that only using Euclidean distance (ℓ_2 loss) between the upsampled faces and the ground-truth HR faces tends to output over-smoothed results. Therefore, we incorporate a discriminative objective into our network to force super-resolved HR face images to lie on the manifold of real face images.

As shown in the red block of Fig. 2, the discriminative network is constructed by convolutional layers and fully connected layers similar to [34]. It is employed to determine whether an image is sampled from real face images or hallucinated ones. The discriminative loss, also known as adversarial loss, is back-propagated to update our upsampling network. In this manner, we can super-resolve more authentic HR faces, as shown in Fig. 4(h).

3.3 Loss Function

Pixel-Wise Loss: Since the upsampled HR faces should be similar to the input LR faces in terms of image intensities, we employ the Euclidean distance, also known as pixel-wise ℓ_2 loss, to enforce this similarity as follows:

$$\mathcal{L}_p(w) = \mathbb{E}_{(\hat{h}_i, h_i) \sim p(\hat{h}, h)} \|\hat{h}_i - h_i\|_F^2 = \mathbb{E}_{(l_i, h_i) \sim p(l, h)} \|\mathcal{U}_w(l_i) - h_i\|_F^2, \quad (1)$$

where $\hat{h}_i$ and $\mathcal{U}_w(l_i)$ both represent the upsampled faces by our MTUN, w is the parameters of MTUN, l_i and h_i denote the LR input image and its HR ground-truth counterpart respectively, $p(l, h)$ represents the joint distribution of the LR and HR face images in the training dataset, and $p(\hat{h}, h)$ indicates the joint distribution of the upsampled HR faces and their corresponding HR ground-truths.

Feature-Wise Loss: As mentioned in [10,32,37], only using pixel-wise ℓ_2 loss will produce over-smoothed super-resolved results. In order to achieve high-quality visual results, we also constrain the upsampled faces to share the same features as their HR counterparts. The objective function is expressed as:

$$\mathcal{L}_f(w) = \mathbb{E}_{(\hat{h}_i, h_i) \sim p(\hat{h}, h)} \|\psi(\hat{h}_i) - \psi(h_i)\|_F^2 = \mathbb{E}_{(l_i, h_i) \sim p(l, h)} \|\psi(\mathcal{U}_w(l_i)) - \psi(h_i)\|_F^2, \quad (2)$$

where $\psi(\cdot)$ denotes feature maps of a layer in VGG-19 [38]. We use the layer ReLU32, which gives good empirical results in our experiments.

Discriminative Loss: Since super-resolution is inherently an under-determined problem, there would be many possible mappings between LR and HR images. Even imposing intensity and feature similarities may not guarantee that the upsampling network can output realistic HR face images. We employ a discriminative network to force the hallucinated faces to lie on the same manifold of real face images, and our goal is to make the discriminative network fail to distinguish the upsampled faces from real ones. Therefore, the objective function for the discriminative network $\mathcal{D}$ is formulated as:

$$\mathcal{L}_\mathcal{D}(d) = \mathbb{E}_{(\hat{h}_i, h_i) \sim p(\hat{h}, h)} \left[\log \mathcal{D}_d(h_i) + \log(1 - \mathcal{D}_d(\hat{h}_i)) \right] \quad (3)$$

where d represents the parameters of the discriminative network $\mathcal{D}$, $p(h)$, $p(l)$ and $p(\hat{h})$ indicate the distributions of the real HR, LR and super-resolved faces respectively, and $\mathcal{D}_d(h_i)$ and $\mathcal{D}_d(\hat{h}_i)$ are the outputs of $\mathcal{D}$. To make our discriminative network distinguish the real faces from the upsampled ones, we maximize the loss $\mathcal{L}_\mathcal{D}(d)$ and the loss is back-propagated to update the parameters d.

In order to fool the discriminative network, our upsampling network should produce faces as much similar as real faces. Thus, the objective function of the upsampling network is written as:

$$\mathcal{L}_\mathcal{U}(w) = \mathbb{E}_{(\hat{h}_i) \sim p(\hat{h})} \left[\log \mathcal{D}_d(\hat{h}_i) \right] = \mathbb{E}_{l_i \sim p(l)} \left[\log \mathcal{D}_d(\mathcal{U}_w(l_i)) \right]. \quad (4)$$

We minimize Eq. 4 to make our upsampling network generate realistic HR face images. The loss $\mathcal{L}_\mathcal{U}(w)$ is back-propagated to update the parameters w.

Face Structure Loss: Unlike previous works [7,10,32], we not only employ image pixel information (*i.e.*, pixel-wise and feature-wise losses) but also explore the face structure information during super-resolution. In order to achieve spatial relationships between facial components and their visibility, we estimate the heatmaps of facial components from the upsampled features as follows:

$$\mathcal{L}_h(w) = \mathbb{E}_{(l_i, h_i) \sim p(l, h)} \frac{1}{M} \sum_{k=1}^{M} \frac{1}{N} \sum_{j=1}^{N} \|\mathcal{H}_j^k(h_i) - \mathcal{H}_j^k(\tilde{\mathcal{U}}_w(l_i))\|_2^2, \quad (5)$$

where M is the number of the facial components, N indicates the number of Gaussian kernels in each component, $\tilde{\mathcal{U}}_w(l_i)$ is the intermediate upsampled feature maps by $\mathcal{U}$, $\mathcal{H}_j^k$ represents the j-th kernel in the k-th heatmap, and $\mathcal{H}_j^k(h_i)$ and $\mathcal{H}_j^k(\tilde{\mathcal{U}}_w(l_i))$ denote the ground-truth and estimated kernel positions in the heatmaps. Due to self-occlusions, some parts of facial components are invisible and thus N varies according to the visibility of those kernels in the heatmaps. Note that, the parameters w not only refer to the parameters in the upsampling branch but also those in the heatmap estimation branch.

Training Details: In training our discriminative network $\mathcal{D}$, we only use the loss $\mathcal{L}_\mathcal{D}(d)$ in Eq. 3 to update the parameters d. Since the discriminative network aims at distinguishing upsampled faces from real ones, we maximize $\mathcal{L}_\mathcal{D}(d)$ by stochastic gradient ascent.

In training our multi-task upsampling network $\mathcal{U}$, multiple losses, *i.e.*, $\mathcal{L}_p$, $\mathcal{L}_f$, $\mathcal{L}_\mathcal{U}$ and $\mathcal{L}_h$, are involved to update the parameters w. Therefore, in order to achieve authentic super-resolved HR face images, the objective function $\mathcal{L}_\mathcal{T}$ for training the upsampling network $\mathcal{U}$ is expressed as:

$$\mathcal{L}_\mathcal{T} = \mathcal{L}_p + \alpha\mathcal{L}_f + \beta\mathcal{L}_\mathcal{U} + \mathcal{L}_h, \tag{6}$$

where α, β are the trade-off weights. Since our goal is to recover HR faces in terms of appearance similarity, we set α and β to 0.01. We minimize $\mathcal{L}_\mathcal{T}$ by stochastic gradient descent. Specifically, we use RMSprop optimization algorithm [39] to update the parameters w and d. The discriminative network and upsampling network are trained in an alternating fashion. The learning rate r is set to 0.001 and multiplied by 0.99 after each epoch. We use the decay rate 0.01 in RMSprop.

3.4   Implementation Details

In our multi-task upsampling network, we employ similarity transformation estimated by STN to compensate for in-plane misalignments. In Fig. 2, STN is built by convolutional and ReLU layers (Conv+ReLU), max-pooling layers with a stride 2 (MP2) and fully connected layers (FC). Specifically, our STN is composed of MP2, Conv+ReLU (k5s1p0n20), MP2, Conv+ReLU (k5s1p0n20), MP2, FC+ReLU (from 80 to 20 dimensions) and FC (from 20 to 4 dimensions), where k, s and p indicate the sizes of filters, strides and paddings respectively, and n represents the channel number of the output feature maps. Our HEB is constructed by stacking four hourglass networks and we also apply intermediate supervision to the output of each hourglass network. The residual block is constructed by BN, ReLU, Conv (k3s1p1nN$_i$), BN, ReLU and Conv (k1s1p0nN$_o$), where N$_i$ and N$_o$ indicate the channel numbers of input and output feature maps.

In the experimental part, some algorithms require alignment of LR inputs, *e.g.*, [22]. Hence, we employ an STN$_0$ to align the LR face images to the upright position. STN$_0$ is composed of Conv+ReLU (k5s1p0n64), MP2, Conv+ReLU (k5s1p0n20), FC+ReLU (from 80 to 20 dimensions), and FC (from 20 to 4 dimensions).

4   Experimental Results

In order to evaluate the performance of our proposed network, we compare with the state-of-the-art methods [6,7,22,37,40] qualitatively and quantitatively. Kim *et al.* [40] employ a very deep convolutional network to super-resolve generic images, known as VDSR. Ledig *et al.*'s method [37], dubbed SRGAN, is a generic super-resolution method, which employs the framework of generative adversarial networks and is trained with pixel-wise and adversarial losses. Ma *et al.*'s method [22] exploits position patches in the dataset to reconstruct HR images. Zhu *et al.*'s method [6], known as CBN, first localizes facial components in LR input images and then super-resolves the localized facial parts. Yu and Porikli [7] upsample very low-resolution unaligned face images by a transformative discriminative autoencoder (TDAE).

4.1   Dataset

Although there are large-scale face datasets [17,18], they do not provide structural information, *i.e.*, facial landmarks, for generating ground-truth heatmaps. In addition, we found that most of faces in the celebrity face attributes (CelebA) dataset [17], as one of the largest face datasets, are near-frontal. Hence, we use images from the Menpo facial landmark localization challenges (Menpo) [19] as well as images from CelebA to generate our training dataset. Menpo [19] provides face images in different poses and their corresponding 68 point landmarks or 39 point landmarks when some facial parts are invisible. Because Menpo only contains about $8K$ images, we also collect another $22K$ images from CelebA. We crop the aligned faces and then resize them to 128×128 pixels as our HR ground-truth images h_i. Our LR face images l_i are generated by transforming and downsampling the HR faces to 16×16 pixels. We choose 80% of image pairs for training and 20% of image pairs for testing.

4.2   Qualitative Comparisons with SoA

Since [22] needs to align input LR faces before super-resolution and [7] automatically outputs upright HR face images, we align LR faces by a spatial transformer network STN_0 for a fair comparison and better illustration. The upright HR ground-truth images are also shown for comparison.

Bicubic interpolation only upsamples image intensities from neighboring pixels instead of generating new contents for new pixels. As shown in Fig. 5(c), bicubic interpolation fails to generate facial details.

VDSR only employs a pixel-wise ℓ_2 loss in training and does not provide an upscaling factor 8×. We apply VDSR to an LR face three times by an upscaling factor 2×. As shown in Fig. 5(d), VDSR fails to generate authentic facial details and the super-resolved faces are still blurry.

SRGAN is able to super-resolve an image by an upscaling factor of 8× directly and employs an adversarial loss to enhance details. However, SRGAN does not

Table 1. Quantitative comparisons on the entire test dataset

Methods	Bicubic	VDSR [40]	SRGAN [37]	Ma [22]	CBN [6]	TDAE [7]	TDAE†	Ours†	Ours‡	Ours
PSNR	18.83	18.65	18.57	18.66	18.49	18.87	21.39	22.69	22.83	**23.14**
SSIM	0.57	0.57	0.55	0.53	0.55	0.52	0.62	0.66	0.65	**0.68**

take the entire face structure into consideration and thus outputs ringing artifacts around facial components, such as eyes and mouth, as shown in Fig. 5(e).

Ma *et al.*'s method is sensitive to misalignments in LR inputs because it
hallucinates HR faces by position-patches. As seen in Fig. 5(f), obvious blur
artifacts and ghosting facial components appear in the hallucinated faces. As
the upscaling factor increases, the correspondences between LR and HR patches
become inconsistent. Thus, the super-resolved face images suffer severe blocky
artifacts.

CBN first localizes facial components in LR faces and then super-resolves
facial details and entire face images by two branches. As shown in Fig. 5(g), CBN
generates facial components inconsistent with the HR ground-truth images in
near-frontal faces and fails to generate realistic facial details in large poses. This
indicates that it is difficult to localize facial components in LR faces accurately.

TDAE employs ℓ_2 and adversarial losses and is trained with near-frontal
faces. Due to various poses in our testing dataset, TDAE fails to align faces in
large poses. For a fair comparison, we retrain the decoder of TDAE with our
training dataset. As visible in Fig. 5(h), TDAE still fails to realistic facial details
due to various poses and misalignments.

Our method reconstructs authentic facial details as shown in Fig. 5(i). Our
facial component heatmaps not only facilitate alignment but also provide spatial configuration of facial components. Therefore, our method is able to produce
visually pleasing HR facial details similar to the ground-truth faces while preserving face structure. (More results are shown in the supplementary materials.)

4.3   Quantitative Comparisons with SoA

We also evaluate the performance of all methods quantitatively on the entire
test dataset by the average PSNR and the structural similarity (SSIM) scores.
Table 1 indicates that our method achieves superior performance compared to
other methods, *i.e.*, outperforming the second best with a large margin of **1.75**
dB in PSNR. Note that, the average PSNR of TDAE for its released model is
only 18.87 dB because it is trained with near-frontal faces. Even after retaining
TDAE, indicated by TDAE†, its performance is still inferior to our results. It
also implies that our method localizes facial components and aligns LR faces
more accurately with the help of our estimated heatmaps.

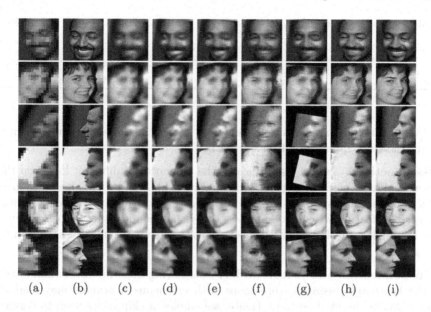

(a)   (b)   (c)   (d)   (e)   (f)   (g)   (h)   (i)

Fig. 5. Comparisons with the state-of-the-art methods. (a) Unaligned LR inputs. (b) Original HR images. (c) Bicubic interpolation. (d) Kim *et al.*'s method [40] (VDSR). (e) Ledig *et al.*'s method [37] (SRGAN). (f) Ma *et al.*'s method [22]. (g) Zhu *et al.*'s method [6] (CBN). (h) Yu and Porikli's method [7] (TDAE). Since TDAE is not trained with near-frontal face images, we retrain it with our training dataset. (i) Our method.

5   Analysis and Discussion

Effectiveness of HEB: As shown in Fig. 4(c), (d) and (e), we demonstrate that the visual results without HEB suffer from distortion and blur artifacts. By employing HEB, we can localize the facial components as seen in Fig. 3, and then recover realistic facial details. Furthermore, HEB provides the spatial locations of facial components and an additional constraint for face alignments. Thus we achieve higher reconstruction performance as shown in Table 3.

Feature Sizes for HEB: In our network, there are several layers which can be used to estimate facial component heatmaps, *i.e.*, feature maps of sizes 16, 32, 64 and 128, respectively. We employ HEB at different layers and demonstrate the influence of the sizes of feature maps. Due to GPU memory limitations, we only compare the super-resolution performance of using features of sizes 16 ($\mathcal{R}16$), 32 ($\mathcal{R}32$) and 64 ($\mathcal{S}4$) to estimate heatmaps. As shown in Table 2, as the resolution of feature maps increases, we obtain better super-resolution performance. Therefore, we employ the upsampled feature maps of size 64×64 to estimate heatmaps.

Depths of HEB: Table 2 demonstrates the performance influenced by the stack number of hourglass networks. Due to the limitation of GPU memory, we only conduct our experiments on the stack number ranging from 1 to 4. As indicated

Table 2. Ablation study of HEB

	Position		Depth			
	$\mathcal{R}16$	$\mathcal{R}32$	$S1$	$S2$	$S3$	$S4$
PSNR	21.97	21.98	22.32	22.91	22.93	**23.14**
SSIM	0.63	0.64	0.64	0.67	0.67	**0.68**

Table 3. Ablation study on the loss

	w/o $\mathcal{L}_h$			w/ $\mathcal{L}_h$		
	$\mathcal{L}_p$	$\mathcal{L}_{p+f}$	$\mathcal{L}_{p+f+u}$	$\mathcal{L}_p$	$\mathcal{L}_{p+f}$	$\mathcal{L}_{p+f+u}$
PSNR	21.43	21.57	21.55	23.23	23.35	23.14
SSIM	0.66	0.66	0.65	0.69	0.69	0.68

in Table 2, the final performance improves as the stack number increases. Hence, we set the stack number to 4 for our HEB.

Loss Functions: Table 3 also indicates the influences of different losses on the super-resolution performance. As indicated in Table 3 and Fig. 4, using the face structure loss improves the super-resolved results qualitatively and quantitatively. The feature-wise loss improves the visual quality and the discriminative loss makes the hallucinated faces sharper and more realistic, as shown in Fig. 4(h).

Skip Connection and Autoencoder: Considering there are estimation errors in the heatmaps, fusing feature maps with erroneous heatmaps may lead to distortions in the final outputs. Hence, we employ a skip connection to correct the errors in Fig. 2. As indicated in Table 1, using the skip connection, we can improve the final quantitative result by 0.45 dB in PSNR. The result without using skip connection is indicated by Ours[†]. We also remove our autoencoder and upsample LR inputs directly and the result is denoted as Ours[‡]. As shown in Table 1, we achieve 0.31 dB improvement with the help of the autoencoder.

6   Conclusion

We present a novel multi-task upsampling network to super-resolve very small LR face images. We not only employ the image appearance similarity but also exploit the face structure information estimated from LR input images themselves in the super-resolution. With the help of our facial component heatmap estimation branch, our method super-resolves faces in different poses without distortions caused by erroneous facial component localization in LR inputs.

Acknowledgement. This work was supported by Australian Research Council Centre of Excellence for Robotic Vision (project number CE140100016), the Australian Research Council's Discovery Projects funding scheme (project DP150104645) and the King Abdullah University of Science and Technology (KAUST) Office of Sponsored Research.

References

1. Fasel, B., Luettin, J.: Automatic facial expression analysis: a survey. Pattern Recognit. **36**(1), 259–275 (2003)
2. Zhao, W., Chellappa, R., Phillips, P.J., Rosenfeld, A.: Face recognition: a literature survey. ACM Comput. Surv. (CSUR) **35**(4), 399–458 (2003)

3. Xiong, X., De la Torre, F.: Supervised descent method and its applications to face alignment. In: Proceedings of the IEEE Conference on Computer Vision and Pattern Recognition (CVPR), pp. 532–539 (2013)
4. Bulat, A., Tzimiropoulos, G.: How far are we from solving the 2D & 3D face alignment problem? (and a dataset of 230,000 3D facial landmarks). In: International Conference on Computer Vision (ICCV) (2017)
5. Taigman, Y., Yang, M., Ranzato, M., Wolf, L.: Deepface: closing the gap to human-level performance in face verification. In: Proceedings of the IEEE Conference on Computer Vision and Pattern Recognition (CVPR), pp. 1701–1708 (2014)
6. Zhu, S., Liu, S., Loy, C.C., Tang, X.: Deep cascaded bi-network for face hallucination. In: Proceedings of European Conference on Computer Vision (ECCV), pp. 614–630 (2016)
7. Yu, X., Porikli, F.: Hallucinating very low-resolution unaligned and noisy face images by transformative discriminative autoencoders. In: Proceedings of the IEEE Conference on Computer Vision and Pattern Recognition (CVPR), pp. 3760–3768 (2017)
8. Baker, S., Kanade, T.: Hallucinating faces. In: Proceedings of 4th IEEE International Conference on Automatic Face and Gesture Recognition, FG 2000, pp. 83–88 (2000)
9. Zhou, E., Fan, H.: Learning face hallucination in the wild. In: Twenty-Ninth AAAI Conference on Artificial Intelligence, pp. 3871–3877 (2015)
10. Yu, X., Porikli, F.: Ultra-resolving face images by discriminative generative networks. In: Leibe, B., Matas, J., Sebe, N., Welling, M. (eds.) ECCV 2016. LNCS, vol. 9909, pp. 318–333. Springer, Cham (2016). https://doi.org/10.1007/978-3-319-46454-1_20
11. Yu, X., Porikli, F.: Imagining the unimaginable faces by deconvolutional networks. IEEE Trans. Image Process. **27**, 2747–2761 (2018)
12. Cao, Q., Lin, L., Shi, Y., Liang, X., Li, G.: Attention-aware face hallucination via deep reinforcement learning. In: Proceedings of the IEEE Computer Society Conference on Computer Vision and Pattern Recognition (CVPR), pp. 690–698 (2017)
13. Dahl, R., Norouzi, M., Shlens, J.: Pixel recursive super resolution. In: International Conference on Computer Vision (ICCV), pp. 5439–5448 (2017)
14. Bulat, A., Tzimiropoulos, G.: Super-FAN: integrated facial landmark localization and super-resolution of real-world low resolution faces in arbitrary poses with GANs. arXiv preprint arXiv:1712.02765 (2017)
15. Chen, Y., Tai, Y., Liu, X., Shen, C., Yang, J.: FSRNet: end-to-end learning face super-resolution with facial priors. arXiv preprint arXiv:1711.10703 (2017)
16. Yu, X., Fernando, B., Hartley, R., Porikli, F.: Super-resolving very low-resolution face images with supplementary attributes. In: Proceedings of the IEEE Conference on Computer Vision and Pattern Recognition (CVPR), pp. 908–917 (2018)
17. Liu, Z., Luo, P., Wang, X., Tang, X.: Deep learning face attributes in the wild. In: Proceedings of International Conference on Computer Vision (ICCV), pp. 3730–3738 (2015)
18. Huang, G.B., Ramesh, M., Berg, T., Learned-Miller, E.: Labeled faces in the wild: a database for studying face recognition in unconstrained environments. Technical report 07–49, University of Massachusetts, Amherst (2007)
19. Zafeiriou, S., Trigeorgis, G., Chrysos, G., Deng, J., Shen, J.: The menpo facial landmark localisation challenge: a step towards the solution. In: Proceedings of the IEEE Conference on Computer Vision and Pattern Recognition Workshops (CVPRW), pp. 2116–2125 (2017)

20. Yang, C.Y., Liu, S., Yang, M.H.: Structured face hallucination. In: Proceedings of the IEEE Computer Society Conference on Computer Vision and Pattern Recognition (CVPR), pp. 1099–1106 (2013)
21. Jaderberg, M., Simonyan, K., Zisserman, A., et al.: Spatial transformer networks. In: Advances in Neural Information Processing Systems (NIPS), pp. 2017–2025 (2015)
22. Ma, X., Zhang, J., Qi, C.: Hallucinating face by position-patch. Pattern Recogn. **43**(6), 2224–2236 (2010)
23. Wang, X., Tang, X.: Hallucinating face by eigen transformation. IEEE Trans. Syst. Man Cybern. Part C: Appl. Rev. **35**(3), 425–434 (2005)
24. Liu, C., Shum, H.Y., Freeman, W.T.: Face hallucination: theory and practice. Int. J. Comput. Vis. **75**(1), 115–134 (2007)
25. Kolouri, S., Rohde, G.K.: Transport-based single frame super resolution of very low resolution face images. In: Proceedings of the IEEE Computer Society Conference on Computer Vision and Pattern Recognition (CVPR), pp. 4876–4884 (2015)
26. Baker, S., Kanade, T.: Limits on super-resolution and how to break them. IEEE Trans. Pattern Anal. Mach. Intell. **24**(9), 1167–1183 (2002)
27. Yang, J., Wright, J., Huang, T.S., Ma, Y.: Image super-resolution via sparse representation. IEEE Trans. Image Process. **19**(11), 2861–2873 (2010)
28. Li, Y., Cai, C., Qiu, G., Lam, K.M.: Face hallucination based on sparse local-pixel structure. Pattern Recogn. **47**(3), 1261–1270 (2014)
29. Jin, Y., Bouganis, C.S.: Robust multi-image based blind face hallucination. In: Proceedings of the IEEE Computer Society Conference on Computer Vision and Pattern Recognition (CVPR), pp. 5252–5260 (2015)
30. Tappen, M.F., Liu, C.: A bayesian approach to alignment-based image hallucination. In: Fitzgibbon, A., Lazebnik, S., Perona, P., Sato, Y., Schmid, C. (eds.) ECCV 2012. LNCS, vol. 7578, pp. 236–249. Springer, Heidelberg (2012). https://doi.org/10.1007/978-3-642-33786-4_18
31. Yu, X., Porikli, F.: Face hallucination with tiny unaligned images by transformative discriminative neural networks. In: Thirty-First AAAI Conference on Artificial Intelligence (2017)
32. Xu, X., Sun, D., Pan, J., Zhang, Y., Pfister, H., Yang, M.H.: Learning to super-resolve blurry face and text images. In: Proceedings of the IEEE Conference on Computer Vision and Pattern Recognition (ICCV), pp. 251–260 (2017)
33. Goodfellow, I., Pouget-Abadie, J., Mirza, M.: Generative adversarial networks. In: Advances in Neural Information Processing Systems (NIPS), pp. 2672–2680 (2014)
34. Radford, A., Metz, L., Chintala, S.: Unsupervised representation learning with deep convolutional generative adversarial networks, pp. 1–15. arXiv:1511.06434 (2015)
35. Van Den Oord, A., Kalchbrenner, N., Kavukcuoglu, K.: Pixel recurrent neural networks. In: Proceedings of International Conference on International Conference on Machine Learning (ICML), pp. 1747–1756 (2016)
36. Newell, A., Yang, K., Deng, J.: Stacked hourglass networks for human pose estimation. In: Leibe, B., Matas, J., Sebe, N., Welling, M. (eds.) ECCV 2016. LNCS, vol. 9912, pp. 483–499. Springer, Cham (2016). https://doi.org/10.1007/978-3-319-46484-8_29
37. Ledig, C., et al.: Photo-realistic single image super-resolution using a generative adversarial network. In: Proceedings of the IEEE Computer Society Conference on Computer Vision and Pattern Recognition (CVPR), pp. 4681–4690 (2017)
38. Simonyan, K., Zisserman, A.: Very deep convolutional networks for large-scale image recognition. arXiv preprint arXiv:1409.1556 (2014)

39. Hinton, G.: Neural networks for machine learning lecture 6a: overview of mini-batch gradient descent reminder: the error surface for a linear neuron (2012)
40. Kim, J., Kwon Lee, J., Mu Lee, K.: Accurate image super-resolution using very deep convolutional networks. In: Proceedings of the IEEE Computer Society Conference on Computer Vision and Pattern Recognition (CVPR), pp. 1646–1654 (2016)

Reverse Attention for Salient Object Detection

Shuhan Chen$^{(\boxtimes)}$, Xiuli Tan, Ben Wang, and Xuelong Hu

School of Information Engineering, Yangzhou University, Yangzhou, China
c.shuhan@gmail.com, t.xiuli0214@gmail.com, wangben9503@163.com,
xlhu@yzu.edu.cn

Abstract. Benefit from the quick development of deep learning techniques, salient object detection has achieved remarkable progresses recently. However, there still exists following two major challenges that hinder its application in embedded devices, low resolution output and heavy model weight. To this end, this paper presents an accurate yet compact deep network for efficient salient object detection. More specifically, given a coarse saliency prediction in the deepest layer, we first employ residual learning to learn side-output residual features for saliency refinement, which can be achieved with very limited convolutional parameters while keep accuracy. Secondly, we further propose reverse attention to guide such side-output residual learning in a top-down manner. By erasing the current predicted salient regions from side-output features, the network can eventually explore the missing object parts and details which results in high resolution and accuracy. Experiments on six benchmark datasets demonstrate that the proposed approach compares favorably against state-of-the-art methods, and with advantages in terms of simplicity, efficiency (**45 FPS**) and model size (**81 MB**).

Keywords: Salient object detection · Reverse attention
Side-output residual learning

1 Introduction

Salient object detection, also known as saliency detection, aims to localize and segment the most conspicuous and eye-attracting objects or regions in an image. It is usually served as a pre-processing step to facilitate various subsequent high-level vision tasks, such as image segmentation [1], image captioning [2], and so on. Recently, with the quick development of deep convolutional neural networks (CNNs), salient object detection has achieved significant improvements over conventional hand-crafted feature based approaches. The emergence of fully convolutional neural networks (FCNs) [3] further pushed it to a new state-of-the-art due to its efficiency and end-to-end training. Such architecture also benefits other applications, *e.g.*, semantic segmentation [4], edge detection [5].

Albeit profound progresses have been made, there still exists two major challenges that hinder its applications in real-world, *e.g.*, embedded devices. One is

© Springer Nature Switzerland AG 2018
V. Ferrari et al. (Eds.): ECCV 2018, LNCS 11213, pp. 236–252, 2018.
https://doi.org/10.1007/978-3-030-01240-3_15

the low resolution of the saliency maps produced by FCNs based saliency models. Due to the repeated stride and pooling operations in CNN architectures, it is inevitable to lose resolution and difficult to refine, making it infeasible to locate salient objects accurately, especially for the object boundaries and small objects. The other is the heavy weight and large redundancy of the existing deep saliency models. As can be seen in Fig. 1, all the listed deep models are larger than 100 MB, which is too heavy for a pre-processing step to apply in subsequent high-level tasks, and also not memory efficient for embedded devices.

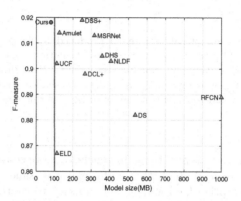

Fig. 1. Maximum F-Measure of recent deep CNN-based saliency detection models on ECSSD, including DS [6], ELD [7], DCL$^+$ [8], DHS [8], RFCN [9], NLDF [10], DSS$^+$ [11], MSRNet [12], Amulet [13], UCF [14], and ours (red circle). As can be seen that the proposed model is the only one less than 100 MB while achieves comparable performance with state-of-the-art methods. (Color figure online)

Diverse solutions have been explored to improve the resolution of the FCNs based prediction. Early works [8,15,16] usually combined it with an extra region or superpixel based stream to fuse their respective advantages at the expense of high time cost. Then, some simple yet effective structures are constructed to combine the complementary cues of shallow and deep CNN features, which capture low-level spatial details and high-level semantic information respectively, such as skip connections [12], short connections [11], dense connections [17], adaptive aggregation [13]. Such multi-level feature fusion schemes also play an important role in semantic segmentation [18,19], edge detection [20], skeleton detection [21,22]. Nevertheless, the existing archaic fusions are still incompetent for saliency detection under complex real-world scenarios, especially when dealing with multiple salient objects with diverse scales. In addition, some time consuming post-processing skills are also applied for refinement, *e.g.*, superpixel-based filter [23], fully connected conditional random field (CRF) [8,11,24]. However, to the best of our knowledge, there are no saliency detection networks explored considering both lightweight model and high accuracy.

To this end, we present an accurate yet compact deep salient object detection network which achieved comparable performance with state-of-the-art methods,

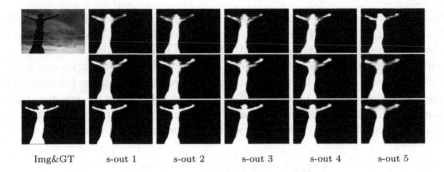

Img&GT   s-out 1   s-out 2   s-out 3   s-out 4   s-out 5

Fig. 2. Visual comparison of saliency maps produced by DSS [11] (top row), our method without (middle row) and with reverse attention (bottom row) in different side-outputs, respectively. As can be seen clearly that the resolutions of the saliency maps are improved gradually from deep to shallow side-outputs, and our reverse attention based side-output residual learning performs much better than short connections [11].

thus enables for real-time applications. In generally, more convolutional channels with large kernel size leads to better performance in salient object detection due to the large receptive field and model capacity to capture more semantic information, *e.g.*, there are 512 channels with kernel size 7×7 in the last side-output of DSS [11]. In a different way, we introduce residual learning [25] into the architecture of HED [5], and regard salient object detection as a super-resolution reconstruction problem [26]. Given the low resolution prediction of FCNs, side-output residual features are learned to refine it step by step. Note that it can be achieved only using convolution with 64 channels and kernel size 3×3 in each side-output, whose parameters are significant fewer than DSS.

Similar residual learning was also utilized in skeleton detection [21] and image super-resolution [27]. However, the performance is not satisfactory enough if we directly apply it for salient object detection due to its challenging. Since most of the existing deep saliency models are fine-tuned from image classification network, the fine-tuned network will unconsciously focus on the regions with high response values during residual learning as can be seen in Fig. 5, thus struggling to capture the residual details, *e.g.*, object boundaries and other undetected object parts. To solve it, we propose reverse attention to guide side-output residual learning in a top-down manner. Specifically, prediction of deep layer is upsampled then reversed to weight its neighbor shallow side-output feature, which quickly guides the network to focus on the undetected regions for residual capture, thus leads to better performance as seen in Fig. 2.

In summary, the contributions of this paper can be concluded as: (1) We introduce residual learning into the architecture of HED for salient object detection. With the help of the learned side-output residual features, the resolution of the saliency map can be improved gradually with much fewer parameters compared to the existing deep saliency networks. (2) We further propose reverse attention to guide side-output residual learning. By erasing the current prediction, the network can disscover the missing object parts and residual details effectively and quickly, which leads to significant performance improvement. (3) Benefit from the above two components, our approach consistently achieves comparable performance with state-of-the-art methods, and with advantages in terms of simplicity, efficiency (45 FPS) and model size (81 MB).

2   Related Work

There are plenty of saliency detection methods proposed in the past two deceads. Here, we only focus on the recent state-of-the-art methods. Almost all of them are FCNs based and try to solve the common problem: how to produce saliency map with high resolution by using FCNs? Kuen *et al.* [28] applied recurrent unit into FCNs to iteratively refine each salient region. Hu *et al.* [23] entended a superpixel-based guided filter to be a layer in the network for boundary refinement. Hou *et al.* [11] designed short connections for multi-scale feature fusion, while in Amulet [13], multi-level convolutional features were aggregated adaptively. Luo *et al.* [10] proposed a multi-resolution grid structure to capture both local and global cues. In addition, a new loss function was introduced to penalize errors on the boundaries. Zhang *et al.* [14] further proposed a novel upsampling method to reduce the artifacts produced in deconvolution. Recently, dilated convolution [23] and dense connections [17] are further incorporated to obtain high resolution saliency map. There are also some progressive works to address the above issue in semantic segmentation. In [19], skip connections was proposed to refine object instances, while in [29], it was used to build a Laplacian pyramid reconstruction network for object boundary refinement.

Instead of fusing multi-level convolutional features as the above works, we try to learn residual feature for low resolution refinement. The idea of residual learning was first proposed by He *et al.* [25] for image classification. After that, it was widely applied in various applications. Ke *et al.* [21] leraned side-output residual feature for accurate object symmetry detection. Kim *et al.* [27] built a very deep convolutional network based on residual learning for accurate image super-resolution.

Although it is natural to apply it for salient object detection, the performance is not satisfactory enough. To solve it, we introduce attention mechanism which is inspired from human perception process. By using top information to efficiently guide bottom-up feedforward process, it has achieved great success in many tasks. Attention model was designed to weight multi-scale features in [12,30]. Residual attention module was stacted to generate deep attention-aware features for image classification in [31]. In ILSVRC 2017 Image Classification Challenge, Hu *et al.* [32] won the 1st place by constructing Squeeze-and-Excitation block for channel attention. Huang *et al.* [33] designed an attention mask to highlight the prediction of the reverse object class, which then be subtracted from the original prediction to correct the mistakes in the confusion area for semantic segmentation. Inspired but differed from it, we employ reverse attention in a top-down manner to guide side-output residual learning. Benefit from it, we can learn more accurate residual details which leads to significant improvement.

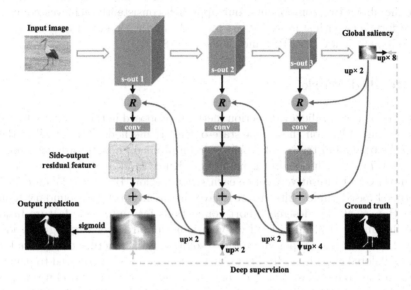

Fig. 3. The overall architecture of the proposed network. Here, only three side-outputs are listed for illustration. "*R*" denotes the proposed reverse attention block that is illustrated in Fig. 4. As can be seen, the residual error decreases along the stacking orientation with the supervision both on the input and output of the residual unit (yellow circle). (Color figure online)

3   Proposed Method

In this section, we first describe the overall architecture of the proposed deep salient object detection network, and then present the details of the main components one by one, which are corresponding to side-output residual learning and top-down reverse attention respectively.

3.1   Architecture

The proposed network is built upon the HED [5] architecture and choses VGG-16 [34] as backbone. We use the layers up to "pool5" and select {conv1_2, conv2_2, conv3_3, conv4_3, conv5_3} as side-outputs, which have strides of {1, 2, 4, 8, 16} pixels with respect to the input image repectively. We first reduce the dimension of "pool5" into 256 by convolution with kernel size 1×1, and then add three convolutional layers with 5×5 kernels to capture global saliency. Since the resolution of the global saliency map is only 1/32 of the input image, we further learn residual feature in each side-output to improve its resolution gradually. In specifically, D convolutional layers with 3×3 kernels and 64 channels are stacked for residual learning. The reverse attention block is embedded before side-output residual learning. The prediction of the shallowest side-output is fed into a sigmoid layer for final output. The overall architecture is shown in Fig. 3 and complete configurations are outlined in Table 1.

Table 1. The configurations of the proposed network. $(n, k \times k) \times D$ denotes stacking D convolutional layers with channel number (n) and kernel size (k), and ReLU layer is added for nonlinear transformation.

Side output 1–5	Global saliency
$(64, 1 \times 1)$	$(256, 1 \times 1)$
$\{(64, 3 \times 3), \text{ReLU}\} \times D$	$\{(256, 5 \times 5), \text{ReLU}\} \times 3$
$(1, 3 \times 3)$	$(1, 1 \times 1)$

3.2   Side-Output Residual Learning

As we know, deep layers of network capture high-level semantic information but messy details, while it is opposite for shallow ones. Based on this observation, multi-level features fusion is a common choice to capture their complementary cues, however, it will degrade the confident prediction of deep layers when combining with shallow ones. In this paper, we implement it in a different yet more efficient way by employing residual learning to remedy the errors between the predicted saliency maps and the ground truth. Specifically, the residual feature is learned by applying deep supervision both on the input and output of the designed residual unit, which is illustrated in Fig. 3. Formally, given the upsampled input saliency map S_{i+1}^{up} by a factor 2 in side-output stage $i + 1$, and the residual feature R_i learned in side-output stage i, then the deep supervision can be formulated as:

$$
\begin{cases}
\{S_{i+1}\}^{up \times 2^{i+1}} \approx G \\
\{S_{i+1}^{up} + R_i\}^{up \times 2^i} = \{S_i\}^{up \times 2^i} \approx G
\end{cases}
, \tag{1}
$$

where S_i is the output of the residual unit and G is ground truth, $up \times 2^i$ denotes the upsample operation by a factor 2^i, which is implemented by the same bilinear interpolation with HED [5].

Such a learning objective inherits the following good property. The residual units establish shortcut connections between the predictions from different scales and the ground truth, which makes it easier to remedy their errors with higher scale adaptability. Generally, the error between the input and output of the residual unit is fairly small based on the same supervision, thus can be learned more easily with fewer parameters and iterations. To the extreme, the error is approximately equal to zero if the prediction is close enough to the ground truth. As a result, the constructed network can be very efficient and lightweight.

3.3   Top-Down Reverse Attention

Although it is natural and straightforward to learn residual details for saliency refinement, it is not easy for the network to capture them accurately without extra supervision, which will result in unsatisfactory detection. Since most of the existing saliency detection networks are fine-tuned from image classification networks which are only responsive to small and sparse discriminative object parts, it obviously deviates from the requirement of the saliency detection task that needs to explore dense and integral regions for pixel-wise prediction. To mitigate this gap, we propose a reverse attention based side-output residual learning approach for expanding object regions progressively. Starting with a coarse saliency map generated in the deepest layer with high semantic confidence but low resolution, our proposed approach guides the whole network to sequentially discover complement object regions and details by erasing the current predicted salient regions from side-output features, where the current prediction is upsampled from its deeper layer. Such a top-down erasing manner can eventually refine the coarse and low resolution prediction into a complete and high resolution saliency map with these explored regions and details, see Fig. 4 for illustration.

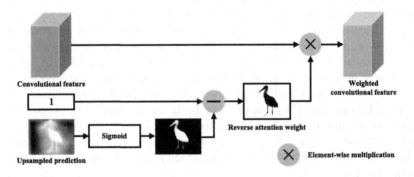

Fig. 4. Illustration of the proposed reverse attention block, whose input and output are highlighted in blue and green respectively. (Color figure online)

Given the side-output feature T and reverse attention weight A, then the output attentive feature can be produced by their element-wise multiplication, which can be formulated as:

$$F_{z,c} = A_z \cdot T_{z,c}, \tag{2}$$

where z and c denote the spatial position of the feature map and the index of the feature channel, respectively. And the reverse attention weight in side-output stage i is simply generated by subtracting the upsampled prediction of side-output $i+1$ from one, which is computed as below:

$$A_i = 1 - \mathrm{Sigmoid}(S_{i+1}^{up}). \tag{3}$$

Figure 5 shows some visual examples of the learned residual feature to illustrate the effectiveness of the proposed revrse attention. As can be seen, the proposed network well captured the residual details near object boundaries with the help of reverse attention. While without reverse attention, it learned some redundant features inside object which is helpless for saliency refinement.

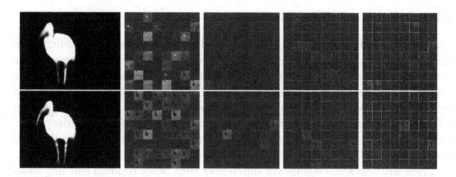

Fig. 5. Visualization of residual features in different side-outputs of the proposed network without (the first row) and with reverse attention (the second row). From left to right are saliency map, the last convolutional feature from side output 1 to 4, respectively. After appling our reverse attention, the proposed network well captured spatial details near object boundaries which is beneficial for saliency refinement, especially in shallow layers. Best viewed in color. (Color figure online)

3.4   Supervision

As shown in Fig. 3, deep supervision is applied to each side-output stage as did in [5,11]. Each side-output produces a loss term $\mathcal{L}_{side}$ which is defined as below:

$$\mathcal{L}_{\text{side}}(I, G, W, w) = \sum_{m=1}^{M} \ell_{\text{side}}^{(m)}(I, G, W, w^{(m)}), \tag{4}$$

where M regards to the total side-output numbers including global saliency, W denotes the collection of all standard network layer parameters, I and G refer to the input image and the corresponding ground truth respectively. Each side-output layer is regarded as a pixel-wise classifier with the corresponding weights w which is represented by

$$w = (w^{(1)}, w^{(2)}, ..., w^{(M)}). \tag{5}$$

Here, $\ell_{\text{side}}^{(m)}$ represents the image-level class-balanced cross-entropy loss function [5] of the mth side output, which is computed by the following formulation:

$$\ell_{\text{side}}^{(m)}(I, G, W, w^{(m)}) = -\sum_{z=1}^{|I|} G(z) log Pr(G(z) = 1|I(z); W, w^{(m)})$$
$$+ (1 - G(z)) log Pr(G(z) = 0|I(z); W, w^{(m)}), \tag{6}$$

where $Pr(G(z) = 1|I(z); W, w^{(m)})$ represents the probability of the activation value at location z in the mth side output, z is the saptial coordinate. Different with HED [5] and DSS [11], there is no fusion layer included in our approach. The output of the first side-output is used as our final prediction after a sigmoid layer in the testing stage.

3.5   Difference to Other Networks

Though shares the same name, the proposed network significantly differs from reverse attention network [33], which applied reverse attention to weight the prediction that is not associated with a target class, in this way to amplify the reverse-class response in the confused region, thus can help the original branch make correct prediction. While in our approach, the usage of reverse attention is totally different. It is used to erase the confident prediction from deep layer, which can guide the network to explore the missing object regions and details effectively.

There are also some significant differences with other residual learning based architectures, *e.g.*, side-output residual network (SRN) [21], and Laplacian reconstruction network (LRN) [29]. In SRN, the residual feature is learned from each side-output of VGG-16 directly, while in this paper, it is learned after reverse attention that is applied to guide residual learning. The main difference with LRN lies in the usage of the wight mask, which is used to weight the learned side-output features for boundary refinement in LRN, in contrast, we apply it before side-output feature learning for guidance. In addition, the weight mask in LRN is generated from the edge of deep prediction which will miss some object regions due to its low resolution, while in this paper, we apply it to focus on all the undetected regions for saliency refinement, which not only refines object boundaries well but also highlights object regions more completely.

4   Experiments

4.1   Experimental Setup

The proposed network is built on the top of the implementations of HED [5] and DSS [11], and trained though the publicly available Caffe [35] library. The whole network is trained end-to-end using full-resolution images and optimized by stochastic gradient descent method. The hyper-parameters are set as below: batch size (1), iter_size (10), the momentum (0.9), the weight decay (5e-4), learning rate is initialized as 1e−8 and decreased by 10% when the training loss reaches a flat, the training iteration number (10K). All these parameters were fixed during the following experiments. The source code will be released[1].

We comprehensively evaluated our method on six representative datasets, including MSRA-B [36], HKU-IS [37], ECSSD [38], PASCAL-S [39], SOD [40], and DUT-OMRON [41], which contain 5000, 4447, 1000, 850, 300, 5168 well

---

[1] http://shuhanchen.net.

annotated images, respectively. Among them, PASCAL-S and DUT-OMRON are more challenging than the others. To guarantee a fair comparison with the existing approaches, we utilize the same training sets as in [8,10,11,42] and test all of the datasets with the same model. Data augmentation is also implemented the same with [10,11] to reduce the over-fitting risk, which increased by 2 times through horizontal flipping.

Three standard and widely agreed metrics are used to evaluate the performance, including Precision-Recall (PR) curve, F-measure, and the Mean Absolute Error (MAE). Pairs of precision and recall values are calculated by comparing the binary saliency maps with the ground truth to plot the PR curve, where the thresholds are in the range of [0, 255]. The F-measure is adopted to measure the overall performance, which is defined as the weighted harmonic mean of precision and recall:

$$F_\beta = (1 + \beta^2) \frac{\text{Precision} \times \text{Recall}}{\beta^2 \text{Precision} + \text{Recall}}, \tag{7}$$

where β^2 is set to 2 to emphasize the precision over recall as suggested in [43]. Only the maximum F-Measure is reported here to to show the best performance a detector can achieve. Given the normalized saliency map S and ground truth G, the MAE score is calculated by their average per-pixel difference:

$$\text{MAE} = \frac{1}{H \times W} \sum_{x=1}^{H} \sum_{y=1}^{W} |S(x,y) - G(x,y)|, \tag{8}$$

where W and H are the width and height of the saliency map, respectively.

4.2   Ablation Studies

Before comparing with the state-of-the-art methods, we first evaluate the influence of different design options (the depth D), the effectiveness of the proposed side-output residual learning and reverse attention in this section.

Depth D. We make a experiment to see how the depth D affects the performance by varying it from 1 to 3. The results on PASCAL-S and DUT-OMRON are shown in Table 2. As can be seen that the best performance is obtained when $D = 2$. Therefore, we set it as 2 in the following experiments.

Side-Output Residual Learning. To investigate the effectiveness of the side-output residual learning, we separately evaluate the performance of each side-output prediction and show in Table 3. We can find that the performance is gradually improved by combing more side-output residual features.

Table 2. Performance comparison with different numbers of D.

	PASCAL-S		DUT-OMRON	
	F_β	MAE	F_β	MAE
$D = 1$	0.830	**0.100**	0.776	0.067
$D = 2$	**0.834**	0.104	**0.786**	**0.062**
$D = 3$	0.824	0.106	0.778	0.064

Table 3. Performance comparison with different side-output predictions.

	PASCAL-S		DUT-OMRON	
	F_β	MAE	F_β	MAE
Side-output 5	0.817	0.111	0.755	0.071
Side-output 4	0.827	0.106	0.776	0.065
Side-output 3	0.831	**0.104**	0.785	**0.062**
Side-output 2	0.832	**0.104**	0.786	**0.062**
Side-output 1	**0.834**	0.104	**0.786**	**0.062**

Reverse Attention. As illustrated in Fig. 5, the network well located at the object boundaries with the help of reverse attention. Here, we perform a detailed comparison using F-measure and MAE scores which are reported in Table 4. From the results, we can get the following observations: (1) Without reverse attention, our performance is similiar to the state-of-the-art method DSS (without CRF-based post-processing), which indicates its large redundancy. (2) After applying reverse attention, the performance is improved by a large margin, specifically, we obtained an average of 1.4% gain in terms of F-measure and 0.5% decrease for MAE score, which clearly demonstrates its effectiveness.

4.3   Performance Comparison with State-of-the-art

We compare the proposed method with 10 state-of-the-art ones, including 9 recent CNN-based approaches, DCL$^+$ [8], DHS [44], SSD [45], RFCN [9], DLS [23], NLDF [10], DSS and DSS$^+$ [11], Amulet [13], UCF [14], and one conventional top approach, DRFI [42], where symbol "+" indicates that the network includes CRF-based post-processing. Note that all the saliency maps of the above methods are produced by running source codes or pre-computed by the authors, and ResNet based methods are not included for fair comparison.

Quantitative Evaluation. The results of quantitative comparison with state-of-the-art methods are reported in Table 4 and Fig. 7. We can clearly observe that our approach significantly outperforms the competing methods both in terms of F-measure and MAE scores, expecially on the challenging datasets (*e.g.*, DUT-OMRON). For PR curves, we also achieved comparable performance with state-of-the-arts except at high level of recall (recall > 0.9). In comparison to the top method, DSS$^+$, which uses a CRF-based post-processing step to

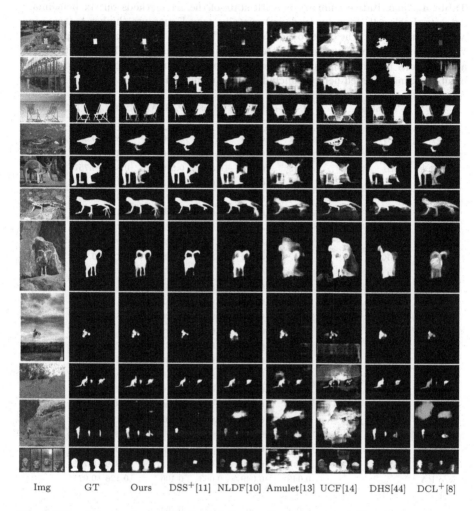

Img   GT   Ours   DSS+[11]   NLDF[10]   Amulet[13]   UCF[14]   DHS[44]   DCL+[8]

Fig. 6. Visual comparisons with the existing methods in some challenging cases: complex scenes, low contrast, and multiple (small) salient objects. (Color figure online)

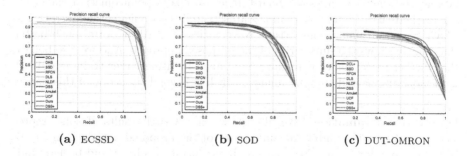

(a) ECSSD   (b) SOD   (c) DUT-OMRON

Fig. 7. Comparison of precision-recall curves on different datasets.

Table 4. Quantitative comparison with state-of-the-art methods on six benchmark datasets. Each cell (from up to down) contains max F-measure (higher better), and MAE (lower better). The top two results are highlighted in red and green respectively. "RA" denotes the proposed reverse attention, and "MK" is MSRA-10K [46], the other abbreviations are the initials of each dataset metioned in the paper. Note that the number of images listed here are including the augmented ones.

	Training		MSRA-B	HKU-IS	ECSSD	PASCAL-S	SOD	DUT-OMRON
	Dataset	#Images						
DRFI [42]	MB	2.5k	0.851	0.775	0.784	0.690	0.699	0.664
			0.123	0.146	0.172	0.210	0.223	0.150
DCL$^+$ [8]	MB	2.5k	0.918	0.907	0.898	0.810	0.831	0.757
			0.047	0.048	0.071	0.115	0.131	0.080
DHS [44]	MK+D	9.5k × 12	-	0.892	0.905	0.824	0.823	-
			-	0.052	0.061	0.094	0.127	-
SSD [45]	MB	2.5k	0.902	-	0.865	0.774	0.793	0.754
			0.160	-	0.193	0.220	0.222	0.193
RFCN [9]	MK	10k	-	0.894	0.889	0.829	0.799	0.744
			-	0.088	0.109	0.133	0.169	0.111
DLS [23]	MK	10k	-	0.835	0.852	0.753	-	0.687
			-	0.070	0.088	0.132	-	0.090
NLDF [10]	MB	2.5k × 2	0.911	0.902	0.903	0.826	0.837	0.753
			0.048	0.048	0.065	0.099	0.123	0.080
Amulet [13]	MK	10k × 8	-	0.899	0.914	0.832	0.795	0.743
			-	0.050	0.061	0.100	0.144	0.098
UCF [14]	MK	10k × 8	-	0.888	0.902	0.818	0.805	0.730
			-	0.061	0.071	0.116	0.148	0.120
DSS [11]	MB	2.5k × 2	0.920	0.900	0.908	0.826	0.834	0.764
			0.043	0.050	0.063	0.102	0.126	0.072
DSS$^+$ [11]	MB	2.5k × 2	0.929	0.916	0.919	0.835	0.843	0.781
			0.034	0.040	0.055	0.095	0.122	0.063
Ours w/o RA	MB	2.5k × 2	0.919	0.898	0.905	0.818	0.839	0.762
			0.042	0.049	0.063	0.106	0.126	0.071
Ours	MB	2.5k × 2	0.931	0.913	0.918	0.834	0.844	0.786
			0.036	0.045	0.059	0.104	0.124	0.062

refine the resolution, nevertheless, our approach still attains nearly identical (or better) performance across the board. It also needs to point out that the existing methods used different training datasets and data augmentaion strategies, which caused an unfair comparison. Nevertheless, we still perform much better that clearly shows the superiority of the proposed approach. And we also believe that further performance gain can be obtained by using larger training dataset with more augmented training images, which is beyond the scope of this paper.

Qualitative Evaluation. We also show some visual results of some representative images to exhibit the superiority of the proposed approach in Fig. 6, including complex scenes, low contrast between salient object and background, multiple (small) salient objects with diverse characteristics (*e.g.*, size, color).

Table 5. Average execution time comparison with other methods on ECSSD.

	DHS	DSS	NLDF	UCF	Amulet	Ours
Times(s)	0.026	0.048	0.048	0.168	0.080	**0.022**

Taking all the cases into account, it can be observed clearly that our approach not only highlights the salient regions correctly with less false detection but also produces sharp boundaries and coherent details (*e.g.*, the *mouth* of the bird in the 4th row of Fig. 6). It is also interesting to note that the proposed method even corrected some false labeling in the ground truth, *e.g.*, the left *horn* in the 7th row of Fig. 6. Nevertheless, we still obtain unsatisfactory results in some challenging cases, taking the last row of Fig. 6 for example, to segment all the salient objects completely is still very difficult for the existing methods.

Execution Time. Finally, we investigate the efficiency of our method, and conduct all the experiments on a single NVIDIA TITAN Xp GPU for fair comparison. It only takes less than 2 h to train our model, for comparison, DSS needs about 6 h. We also compared the average execution time with other five leading CNN-based methods on ECSSD. As can be seen from Table 5, our approach is much faster than all the competing methods. Therefore, considering both in visual quality and efficiency, our approach is the best choice for real-time applications up to now.

5 Conclusions

As a low-level pre-processing step, salient object detection has great applicability in various high-level tasks yet remains not being well solved, which mainly lies on the following two aspects: low resolution output and heavy model weight. In this paper, we presented an accurate yet compact deep network for efficient salient object detection. Instead of directly learning multi-scale saliency features in different side-output stages, we employ residual learning to learn side-output residual features for saliency refinement. Based on it, the resolution of the global saliency map generated by the deepest convolutional layer was improved gradually with very limited parameters. We further propose reverse attention to guide such side-output residual learning in a top-down manner. Benefit from it, our network learned more accurate residual features, which leads to significant performance improvement. Extensive experimental resutls demonstrate that the proposed approach performs favorably against state-of-the-art ones both in quantitative and qualitative comparisons, which enables it a better choice for further real-world applications, and also makes it a great potential to apply in other end-to-end pixel-level prediction tasks. Nevertheless, the global saliency branch and backbone (VGG-16) network still contain large redundancy, which will be further explored by introducing handcrafted saliency prior and learning from scratch in our future work.

Acknowledgments. This work was supported by the Natural Science Foundation of China (No. 61502412), Natural Science Foundation for Youths of Jiangsu Province (No. BK20150459), Foundation of Yangzhou University (No. 2017CXJ026).

References

1. Wei, Y., et al.: STC: a simple to complex framework for weakly-supervised semantic segmentation. IEEE Trans. Pattern Anal. Mach. Intell. **39**(11), 2314–2320 (2017)
2. Xu, K., et al.: Show, attend and tell: neural image caption generation with visual attention. In: ICML, pp. 2048–2057 (2015)
3. Long, J., Shelhamer, E., Darrell, T.: Fully convolutional networks for semantic segmentation. In: CVPR, pp. 3431–3440 (2015)
4. Dai, J., He, K., Li, Y., Ren, S., Sun, J.: Instance-sensitive fully convolutional networks. In: Leibe, B., Matas, J., Sebe, N., Welling, M. (eds.) ECCV 2016 Part VI. LNCS, vol. 9910, pp. 534–549. Springer, Cham (2016). https://doi.org/10.1007/978-3-319-46466-4_32
5. Xie, S., Tu, Z.: Holistically-nested edge detection. In: ICCV, pp. 1395–1403 (2015)
6. Li, X., et al.: DeepSaliency: multi-task deep neural network model for salient object detection. IEEE Trans. Image Proc. **25**(8), 3919–3930 (2016)
7. Lee, G., Tai, Y.W., Kim, J.: Deep saliency with encoded low level distance map and high level features. In: CVPR, pp. 660–668 (2016)
8. Li, G., Yu, Y.: Deep contrast learning for salient object detection. In: CVPR, pp. 478–487 (2016)
9. Wang, L., Wang, L., Lu, H., Zhang, P., Ruan, X.: Saliency detection with recurrent fully convolutional networks. In: Leibe, B., Matas, J., Sebe, N., Welling, M. (eds.) ECCV 2016 Part IV. LNCS, vol. 9908, pp. 825–841. Springer, Cham (2016). https://doi.org/10.1007/978-3-319-46493-0_50
10. Luo, Z., Mishra, A., Achkar, A., Eichel, J., Li, S., Jodoin, P.M.: Non-local deep features for salient object detection. In: CVPR, pp. 6593–6601 (2017)
11. Hou, Q., Cheng, M.M., Hu, X., Borji, A., Tu, Z., Torr, P.: Deeply supervised salient object detection with short connections. In: CVPR, pp. 5300–5309 (2017)
12. Li, G., Xie, Y., Lin, L., Yu, Y.: Instance-level salient object segmentation. In: CVPR, pp. 247–256 (2017)
13. Zhang, P., Wang, D., Lu, H., Wang, H., Ruan, X.: Amulet: aggregating multi-level convolutional features for salient object detection. In: ICCV, pp. 202–211 (2017)
14. Zhang, P., Wang, D., Lu, H., Wang, H., Yin, B.: Learning uncertain convolutional features for accurate saliency detection. In: ICCV, pp. 212–221 (2017)
15. Chen, T., Lin, L., Liu, L., Luo, X., Li, X.: DISC: deep image saliency computing via progressive representation learning. IEEE Trans. Neural Netw. Learn. Syst. **27**(6), 1135–1149 (2016)
16. Tang, Y., Wu, X.: Saliency detection via combining region-level and pixel-level predictions with CNNs. In: Leibe, B., Matas, J., Sebe, N., Welling, M. (eds.) ECCV 2016 Part VIII. LNCS, vol. 9912, pp. 809–825. Springer, Cham (2016). https://doi.org/10.1007/978-3-319-46484-8_49
17. Xiao, H., Feng, J., Wei, Y., Zhang, M.: Deep salient object detection with dense connections and distraction diagnosis. IEEE Trans. Multimedia (2018)
18. Olaf, R., Philipp, F., Thomas, B.: U-net: convolutional networks for biomedical image segmentation. In: MICCAI, pp. 234–241 (2015)

19. Pinheiro, P.O., Lin, T.-Y., Collobert, R., Dollár, P.: Learning to refine object segments. In: Leibe, B., Matas, J., Sebe, N., Welling, M. (eds.) ECCV 2016 Part I. LNCS, vol. 9905, pp. 75–91. Springer, Cham (2016). https://doi.org/10.1007/978-3-319-46448-0_5

20. Liu, Y., Yao, J., Li, L., Lu, X., Han, J.: Learning to refine object contours with a top-down fully convolutional encoder-decoder network. In: ArXiv e-prints (2017)

21. Ke, W., Chen, J., Jiao, J., Zhao, G., Ye, Q.: SRN: side-output residual network for object symmetry detection in the wild. In: CVPR, pp. 302–310 (2017)

22. Shen, W., Zhao, K., Jiang, Y., Wang, Y., Bai, X., Yuille, A.: DeepSkeleton: learning multi-task scale-associated deep side outputs for object skeleton extraction in natural images. IEEE Trans. Image Proc. **26**(11), 5298–5311 (2017)

23. Hu, P., Shuai, B., Liu, J., Wang, G.: Deep level sets for salient object detection. In: CVPR, pp. 2300–2309 (2017)

24. Krähenbühl, P., Koltun, V.: Efficient inference in fully connected CRFs with Gaussian edge potentials. In: NIPS, pp. 109–117 (2011)

25. He, K., Zhang, X., Ren, S., Sun, J.: Deep residual learning for image recognition. In: CVPR, pp. 770–778 (2016)

26. Lai, W.S., Huang, J.B., Ahuja, N., Yang, M.H.: Deep Laplacian pyramid networks for fast and accurate super-resolution. In: CVPR, pp. 624–632 (2017)

27. Kim, J., Kwon Lee, J., Mu Lee, K.: Accurate image super-resolution using very deep convolutional networks. In: CVPR, pp. 1646–1654 (2016)

28. Kuen, J., Wang, Z., Wang, G.: Recurrent attentional networks for saliency detection. In: CVPR, pp. 3668–3677 (2016)

29. Ghiasi, G., Fowlkes, C.C.: Laplacian pyramid reconstruction and refinement for semantic segmentation. In: Leibe, B., Matas, J., Sebe, N., Welling, M. (eds.) ECCV 2016 Part III. LNCS, vol. 9907, pp. 519–534. Springer, Cham (2016). https://doi.org/10.1007/978-3-319-46487-9_32

30. Chen, L.C., Yang, Y., Wang, J., Xu, W., Yuille, A.L.: Attention to scale: Scale-aware semantic image segmentation. In: CVPR, pp. 3640–3649 (2016)

31. Wang, F., et al.: Residual attention network for image classification. In: CVPR, pp. 6450–6458 (2017)

32. Hu, J., Shen, L., Sun, G.: Squeeze-and-excitation networks. In: ArXiv e-prints (2017)

33. Huang, Q., et al.: Semantic segmentation with reverse attention. In: BMVC (2017)

34. Simonyan, K., Zisserman, A.: Very deep convolutional networks for large-scale image recognition. In: ArXiv e-prints (2014)

35. Jia, Y., Shelhamer, E., et al.: Caffe: convolutional architecture for fast feature embedding. In: ACM Multimedia, pp. 675–678 (2014)

36. Liu, T., et al.: Learning to detect a salient object. IEEE Trans. Pattern Anal. Mach. Intell. **33**(2), 353–367 (2011)

37. Li, G., Yu, Y.: Visual saliency detection based on multiscale deep cnn features. IEEE Trans. Image Proc. **25**(11), 5012–5024 (2016)

38. Shi, J., Yan, Q., Xu, L., Jia, J.: Hierarchical image saliency detection on extended CSSD. IEEE Trans. Pattern Anal. Mach. Intell. **38**(4), 717–729 (2016)

39. Li, Y., Hou, X., Koch, C., Rehg, J.M., Yuille, A.L.: The secrets of salient object segmentation. In: CVPR, pp. 280–287 (2014)

40. Martin, D., Fowlkes, C., Tal, D., Malik, J.: A database of human segmented natural images and its application to evaluating segmentation algorithms and measuring ecological statistics. In: ICCV, pp. 416–423 (2001)

41. Yang, C., Zhang, L., Lu, H., Ruan, X., Yang, M.H.: Saliency detection via graph-based manifold ranking. In: CVPR, pp. 3166–3173 (2013)

42. Jiang, H., Wang, J., Yuan, Z., Wu, Y., Zheng, N., Li, S.: Salient object detection: A discriminative regional feature integration approach. In: CVPR. 2083–2090 (2013)
43. Borji, A., Cheng, M.M., Jiang, H., Li, J.: Salient object detection: a benchmark. IEEE Trans. Image Proc. 24(12), 5706–5722 (2015)
44. Liu, N., Han, J.: DHSNet: deep hierarchical saliency network for salient object detection. In: CVPR, pp. 678-686 (2016)
45. Kim, J., Pavlovic, V.: A shape-based approach for salient object detection using deep learning. In: Leibe, B., Matas, J., Sebe, N., Welling, M. (eds.) ECCV 2016 Part IV. LNCS, vol. 9908, pp. 455–470. Springer, Cham (2016). https://doi.org/10.1007/978-3-319-46493-0_28
46. Cheng, M.M., Mitra, N.J., Huang, X., Torr, P.H., Hu, S.M.: Global contrast based salient region detection. IEEE Trans. Pattern Anal. Mach. Intell. 37(3), 569–582 (2015)

Action Search: Spotting Actions in Videos and Its Application to Temporal Action Localization

Humam Alwassel[(✉)], Fabian Caba Heilbron, and Bernard Ghanem

King Abdullah University of Science and Technology (KAUST),
Thuwal, Saudi Arabia
{humam.alwassel,fabian.caba,bernard.ghanem}@kaust.edu.sa
http://www.humamalwassel.com/publication/action-search/

Abstract. State-of-the-art temporal action detectors inefficiently search the entire video for specific actions. Despite the encouraging progress these methods achieve, it is crucial to design automated approaches that only explore parts of the video which are the most relevant to the actions being searched for. To address this need, we propose the new problem of *action spotting* in video, which we define as finding a specific action in a video while observing a small portion of that video. Inspired by the observation that humans are extremely efficient and accurate in spotting and finding action instances in video, we propose *Action Search*, a novel Recurrent Neural Network approach that mimics the way humans spot actions. Moreover, to address the absence of data recording the behavior of human annotators, we put forward the *Human Searches* dataset, which compiles the search sequences employed by human annotators spotting actions in the AVA and THUMOS14 datasets. We consider temporal action localization as an application of the *action spotting* problem. Experiments on the THUMOS14 dataset reveal that our model is not only able to explore the video efficiently (observing on average **17.3%** of the video) but it also accurately finds human activities with **30.8%** mAP.

Keywords: Video understanding · Action localization
Action spotting

1 Introduction

Similar to many video-related applications, such as video object detection and video surveillance, temporal action localization requires an efficient search for

---

The first two authors contributed equally to this work. Authors ordering was determined by three coin flips.

Electronic supplementary material The online version of this chapter (https://doi.org/10.1007/978-3-030-01240-3_16) contains supplementary material, which is available to authorized users.

© Springer Nature Switzerland AG 2018
V. Ferrari et al. (Eds.): ECCV 2018, LNCS 11213, pp. 253–269, 2018.
https://doi.org/10.1007/978-3-030-01240-3_16

different visual targets in videos. With the recent exponential growth in the number videos online (*e.g.* over 400 video hours are uploaded to YouTube every minute), it is crucial today to develop methods that can simultaneously search this large volume of videos efficiently and spot actions accurately. Thus, we propose the new problem of *action spotting* in video, which we define as finding a specific action in a video sequence while observing a small portion of that video. Since the computational cost is directly impacted by the number of observations made in a video, this spotting problem brings search efficiency to the forefront. Obviously, the overall computational cost of such an action search can be reduced by making the per-observation computation faster, as done in many previous work; however, as the video becomes long and the action instances sparse in the video, the number of observations needed dominates this cost.

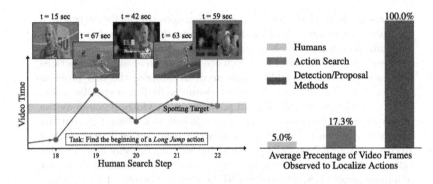

Fig. 1. Left: A partial search sequence a human performed to find the start of a *Long Jump* action (the shaded green area). Notably, humans are efficient in spotting actions without observing a large portion of the video. **Right:** An efficiency comparison between humans, *Action Search*, and other detection/proposal methods on THUMOS14 [24]. Our model is 5.8x more efficient than other methods. (Color figure online)

To get intuitions on how to automatically perform an efficient action search in video, we take notice of how humans approach the problem. In Fig. 1 (left), we show part of a search sequence a human observer carries out when asked to find the beginning of a *Long Jump* action in a long video. This sequence reveals that the person can quickly find the spotting target (in 22 search steps) without observing the entire video, which indicates the possible role temporal context plays in searching for actions. In this case, only a very small portion of the video is observed before the search successfully terminates. In fact, we observe a similar search pattern for different action targets and across different annotators.

Early approaches for temporal action localization rely on trimmed data to learn sophisticated models [29,41,46]. These methods achieve great success at detecting human actions. Despite the encouraging progress in action localization and the attention it is recently attracting, the goal of accurate detection remains elusive to automated systems. A main drawback of current detection methods is that they do not exploit (and totally discard) the search process human annotators follow to produce the final temporal annotations, which are inherently the only information from the annotation process used to train these detection models. As such, these methods need to scan the whole video in an exhaustive manner (either by observing all video frames or a uniform temporal subsampling of them) to detect human actions. This is inefficient; thus, it is crucial to investigate methods that observe the smallest percentage of the video and maintain a state-of-the-art mAP. This naturally leads to faster, more efficient methods, which implies that *action spotting* is essential for temporal action localization.

In this paper, we focus on *action spotting* as a precursor to temporal action localization, since one can reformulate action localization as an *action spotting* problem followed by a regression task to define the action length. Based on observations drawn from the user study in Sect. 3, we believe that *action spotting* is an effective precursor that departs from the focus of the traditional action proposal precursor. Action proposal generation aims to localize the temporal bounds of actions as tightly as possible, while the goal of *action spotting* is to search for action instances as efficiently as possible. Moreover, action proposal generation is class-agnostic, while *action spotting* is class-specific. Figure 1 (right) compares the efficiency of action localization using traditional approaches (*e.g.* proposals) against using our *action spotting*-based method.

Recent temporal action localization datasets [6,24,37] use human annotators to label the action boundaries in a video. Although these datasets are opening new and exciting challenges in the field, they lack an important component: the sequence of steps the human annotator follows to produce the final annotation. These search sequences can be collected for *free* when creating new datasets or extending current ones, and they are a valuable resource for *action spotting*.

Inspired by the observation that humans are extremely efficient and accurate in finding individual action instances in a video, we aim to solve the *action spotting* problem in this paper by imitating how humans search in videos.

Contributions. **(i)** To address the lack of data on the behavior of human annotators, we put forward the *Human Searches* dataset, a new dataset composed of the search sequences of human annotators for the AVA [21] and THUMOS14 [24] datasets (Sect. 3). **(ii)** We propose *Action Search*, a novel Recurrent Neural Network approach that mimics the way humans spot actions in untrimmed videos (Sect. 4). **(iii)** We validate *Action Search* in the *action spotting* problem by demonstrating it requires on average **16.6%** and **22.3%** fewer observations to successfully spot an action than two baseline models (Sect. 5.1). Moreover, when our model is used in the domain of temporal action localization, it achieves state-of-the-art detection results on the THUMOS14 [24] dataset with **30.8%** mAP while only observing on average **17.3%** of the video (Sect. 5.2).

2   Related Work

Datasets. Recognizing and localizing human activities in video often require an extensive collection of annotated data. In recent years, several datasets for temporal action localization have become available. For instance, Jiang *et al.* [24] introduce THUMOS14, a large-scale dataset of untrimmed video sequences with 20 different sports categories. Concurrently, ActivityNet [6] establishes a large benchmark of long YouTube videos with 200 annotated daily activities. Later, Sigurdsson *et al.* [37] release *Charades*, a day-to-day indoor actions database captured in a crowdsourced manner. More recently, Google introduced AVA [21], short for *atomic visual actions*, a densely annotated dataset localizing human actions in space and time. All four datasets use human annotators to localize intended activities in a video. Although these datasets are opening new challenges in the field, they all miss an important component: the search sequence the human annotator follows to produce the final annotation, which is a form of supervised annotation that can be collected for *free* during the annotation process. In Sect. 3, we introduce the *Human Searches* dataset, which allows us to disrupt the current paradigm on how action datasets are structured/collected and how action spotting/localization models can potentially be trained.

Temporal Action Localization. A large number of works have successfully tackled the task of action recognition [8,9,28,38,42] and spatio-temporal localization [10,18,27,30,33,39]. Here, we briefly review some of the influential works in the realm of temporal action localization. Early methods have relied on the sliding-window-plus-classifier combination to produce the actions temporal boundaries [13,15,23,29]. Recently, a series of works have explored the idea of action proposals to reduce the computational complexity incurred by sliding window-based approaches. Notably, Shou *et al.* [35] introduce a multi-stage system that finds and classifies interest regions to produce temporal action locations. Meanwhile, Caba Heilbron *et al.* [7] propose a sparse learning framework to rank a segment based on its similarity to training samples. In the same spirit, contemporary works [4,14,17] produce action proposals by exploiting the effectiveness of deep neural networks. More recently, end-to-end methods have proven to boost the performance of two-stage approaches, demonstrating the importance of jointly optimizing the feature extraction and detection process [3,41,43,46]. Other researchers have used language models [32], action progression analysis [26,34], and high-level semantics [5] to produce high-fidelity action detections.

The large body of work on temporal action localization has mostly focused on improvements in detection performance and/or speed, while very few works have targeted the development of efficient search mechanisms. The dominant search strategy in prior work has focused on exhaustively observing the entire video (either by observing all frames or a uniform temporal subsampling of them) at least once. The pioneering approach of Yeung *et al.* [44] comes as a departure from this paradigm, whereby they introduce the *Frame Glimpses* method to predict the temporal bounds of an action by observing very few frames. Their reinforcement learning-based method tries to learn a policy to intelligently jump through the video for the immediate purpose of detection. While it shares a similar goal, our model avoids the subtleties of learning such policies by exploiting ground truth data depicting how humans sequentially annotate actions. Using such information for action localization, our method outperforms *Frame*

Glimpses and achieves state-of-the-art detection results on THUMOS14 [24] (see Sect. 5.2).

Sequence Prediction. Recurrent Neural Networks (RNNs) and specifically Long Short Term Memory (LSTM) networks have successfully tackled several sequence prediction problems [1,2,19,20]. For instance, Alahi *et al.* [1] introduce an LSTM based model to predict human motion trajectories in crowded scenes. Graves *et al.* [19] propose an RNN that learns to predict the next stroke in online handwriting prediction. Motivated by the success of these approaches, Sect. 4 introduces our novel Learning-to-Search strategy, which formulates the problem of *action spotting* as a sequence prediction problem.

3 Action Spotting: What Do Humans Do?

In this section and motivated by how well humans spot and localize actions in videos, we investigate some factors that intuitively seem to play a role in this process. Specifically, we address the following questions: are humans distracted when they are asked to find multiple action classes? and is spotting an action easier than finding its temporal boundaries? Finally, we describe our key idea.

Single vs. Multiple Class Search. To investigate whether humans are distracted when asked to find multiple action classes, we conduct an online user study on Amazon Mechanical Turk. We ask participants to find an instance of a particular action class in a 15 min video. We design a user interface that includes a time bar, which allows Turkers to navigate over the video quickly until the action is found. Typically, the action instances last three seconds, are sparsely localized, and at least one occurs in the video.

We investigate two variants of the task: (i) a *single class search* to find one instance of a given action class and (ii) a *multiple class search*, which asks Turkers to find one instance from a larger set of action classes. By logging Turker interactions with the user interface, we measure the number of observed frames they require to find an action instance. As compared to *single class search*, we find that Turkers observe 190% and 210% more frames when asked to find an action instance among 10 and 20 action classes, respectively. This observation motivates our intuition that action search can be performed more efficiently when the target task is "simpler" (*i.e.* it incorporates a smaller number of action classes). See the **supplementary material** for more details about this experiment.

Spotting vs. Localization. *Action spotting* is the process of finding any temporal occurrence of an action (*e.g.* any frame inside a *Long Jump* instance) while observing as little as possible from a video. In contrast, action localization focuses on pinpointing precise temporal extents of an action (*i.e.* the exact start and end of a *Long Jump* instance), which usually leads to fine-grained and exhaustive search mechanisms. To measure the effects of searching for fine-grained targets, we ask Turkers to find the starting time of a single target action in a video. We note that Turkers tend to first spot the action and then refine its temporal boundaries. Interestingly, while searching, Turkers perform *three times* more search steps to refine the temporal boundaries of an action, as compared to the number of search steps needed for spotting the same action. This observation motivates our intuition that *action spotting* can be performed more efficiently than action localization, especially when action instances are short in duration and sparse in frequency within a video. We partially attribute this behavior to the fact that determining precise temporal extents of some actions is ambiguous [36]. See the **supplementary material** for more details about this experiment.

Key Idea. Searching for and localizing actions in video is a task humans can do efficiently. However, current automatic methods lack such ability. This shortcoming arises primarily from the fact that existing models are trained without an intelligent search mechanism. This is in part due to the limitations of existing datasets which only provide supervision about the action's temporal location in the video, while ignoring the entire process the annotator follows to find this action. To address these limitations, we collect two novel datasets of *Human Searches*, where videos are annotated with the search steps a human follows to temporally spot/localize actions. We refer to such step sequences as *search sequences*. Below, we describe these collected datasets (refer to the **supplementary material** for the annotation process details and additional statistics).

(i) AVA searches (targets are actions): We collect search sequences from the AVA v1.0 dataset [21], which is composed of feature films and contains 192 15-min-long videos. We select 15 action classes (out of the original 80 actions) based on the two conditions: (1) the average action coverage is relatively small; and (2) the action class has at least 10 videos in the training set. Based on these two conditions, actions such as *talk to, stand*, or *watch (a person)* are discarded due to their extremely large coverage. Moreover, actions like *shovel, kick*, or *exit* are discarded because they only have a few training samples. To gather the search sequences, we assign Turkers the task of spotting action instances in the AVA training videos. In other words, the Turker's task is to spot *any* frame inside the temporal bounds of a given action. We only accept workers with more than 1000 HITs submitted. In addition, we use the existing AVA dataset ground truth to filter out noisy annotations. We use a total of 139 AVA training videos and collect 3988 search sequences. Notably, humans only observe a very small portion of the video (less than 1%) before spotting the action.

(ii) THUMOS14 searches (targets are actions starting times): We collect 1761 search sequences from the training videos of THUMOS14 [24], a large-scale dataset of untrimmed videos with 20 different sports categories. We aim to use this searches dataset for *action spotting* with the purpose of *action localization*. Using the same collection process as in the *AVA searches*, we ask Turkers to find an action's *starting time*. We choose to define the Turkers' task this way because defining the action's starting time is easier than defining its end time [36]. Analyzing the collected data, we observe that humans find the actions in 6 steps on average and define the starting points with an additional 16 steps. This translates into observing only 5% of the video. Figure 2 shows two examples from the collected dataset. With its release, we hope *Human Searches* will enable new research directions in the video understanding field.

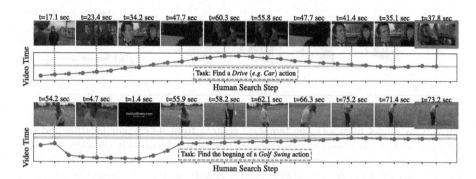

Fig. 2. Illustration of two human search sequences from our *Human Searches* dataset for an AVA [21] training video (first row) and a THUMOS14 [24] training video (second row). The shaded green areas are where the search targets occur. (Color figure online)

4 Proposed Action Search Model

In this section, we discuss the *Action Search* model architecture, the approach used to train it, and some specific implementation details. Figure 3 gives an overview of the main architecture of our approach.

4.1 Model Architecture

The input to *Action Search* is a sequence of visual observations $(\mathbf{X}_1, \mathbf{X}_2, \ldots, \mathbf{X}_n)$ and the output is a sequence of temporal locations $(f(\mathbf{X}_1), f(\mathbf{X}_2), \ldots, f(\mathbf{X}_n))$, *i.e.* a search sequence, produced by the search process. For a given video and at the ith search step, a visual encoder represents the observation $\mathbf{X}_i$ extracted from the model's current temporal location in the video by a feature vector $\mathbf{v}_i$. We cast the search mechanism as a sequential decision making process modeled by an LSTM search network. This LSTM takes three inputs $(\mathbf{h}_{i-1}, f(\mathbf{X}_{i-1}), \mathbf{v}_i)$, where $\mathbf{h}_{i-1}$ is the LSTM state from the previous step (an aggregation of information from previous steps), $f(\mathbf{X}_{i-1})$ is the predicted temporal location from the previous step (the model's current location), and $\mathbf{v}_i$ is the feature vector representing the current visual observation. Finally, a fully-connected layer transforms $\mathbf{h}_i$ (the updated state) to produce $f(\mathbf{X}_i)$, the next location to search in the video.

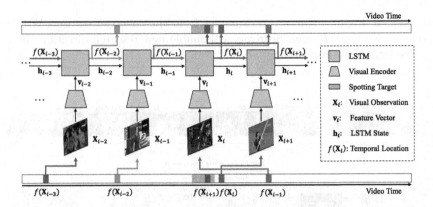

Fig. 3. Our model harnesses the temporal context from its current location and the history of what it has observed to predict the next search location in the video. At each step, (i) a visual encoder transforms the visual observation extracted from the model's current temporal location to a representative feature vector; (ii) an LSTM consumes this feature vector plus the state and temporal location produced in the previous step; (iii) the LSTM outputs its updated state and the next search location; (iv) the model moves to the new temporal location.

4.2 Learning to Search

We employ a multi-layer LSTM network in training *Action Search* to produce search sequences that align with human search sequences in the same video. Following the observations from the user study in Sect. 3, *action spotting* should be class-driven, and thus we train a separate LSTM for each action class.

For a training video and at each search step, the network consumes visual observations at its current temporal location, along with the temporal location from the previous step. After running for n steps, the network produces a search sequence $(f(\mathbf{X}_1), f(\mathbf{X}_2), \ldots, f(\mathbf{X}_n))$. Given the search sequence of a human annotator $(y_1, y_2, \ldots, y_n)$ for the same video in our *Human Searches* dataset, we compute the loss L as the average Huber loss at each search step

$$L = \frac{1}{n} \sum_{i=1}^{n} H_\delta(y_i, f(\mathbf{X}_i)), \tag{1}$$

$$H_\delta(y, f(\mathbf{X})) = \begin{cases} \frac{1}{2}(y - f(\mathbf{X}))^2 & \text{if } |y - f(\mathbf{X})| \le \delta, \\ \delta |y - f(\mathbf{X})| - \frac{1}{2}\delta^2 & \text{otherwise.} \end{cases} \tag{2}$$

where $\delta > 0$. We choose the mean Huber loss over the mean squared loss, $\frac{1}{n} \sum_{i=1}^{n}(y_i - f(\mathbf{X}_i))^2$, in order to overcome the effects of outliers that might arise from the different Turkers searching the same video. Moreover, the mean Huber loss is convex and differentiable in a local neighborhood around its minimum, giving it an advantage over the mean absolute loss, $\frac{1}{n} \sum_{i=1}^{n} |y_i - f(\mathbf{X}_i)|$.

4.3   Implementation Details

Training Stage. Although our pipeline is differentiable and can be trained end-to-end, we simplify and expedite training by fixing the visual encoder to precomputed ResNet-152 [22] features (pretrained on ImageNet [12]) extracted from the average-pooling layer. We reduce the feature dimensionality to 512 using PCA. We employ teacher forcing for training the LSTMs. For a stable training process, we represent each $f(\mathbf{X}_i)$ and y_i as relative steps to the previous search location and normalize the ground truth output search sequence in a per-class fashion. Each LSTM network is trained using the Adam optimizer [25] with an exponential learning rate decay. We unroll the LSTM for a fixed number of steps, ranging from 2^2 to 2^5, for the backpropagation computation. To regularize the multi-layer LSTM network, we follow the RNN dropout techniques introduced by Pham *et al.* [31] and Zaremba *et al.* [45]. We set $\delta = 1$ in the Huber loss.

Inference Stage. Since videos typically contain multiple instances of the same action class, we initialize our model at multiple random points. Each search is run for a fixed number of steps. The number of initial points and the search sequence length are cross-validated per class using the validation subset. However, we prefer to launch many short search sequences as opposed to few long ones, since LSTM states tend to saturate and become unstable after a large number of iterations [40]. Thus, one may view the *Action Search* model as a random sampler with a smart local search: the first search steps are a random sampling of the video (exploration), while the later search steps are fine-grained steps (local search) that rely on the temporal context accumulated throughout the search.

4.4   Model Variants

Here, we present different variants of *Action Search* network structure and training. Experiments using these flavors show minimal effects on the final results.

Training with Weighted Loss. In order to put more emphasis on learning the steps towards the end of the ground truth search sequence, each term in the loss L is weighted inversely proportional to how close the search step is to the target action instance. We consider this variant to give less weight to learning the first search steps a human annotator makes (seemingly random) before accumulating enough temporal context knowledge to guide subsequent search steps.

Early Stopping Confidence Score. Another flavor integrates a new module that consumes the LSTM state $\mathbf{h}$ along with the feature vector $\mathbf{v}$ at each step and produces a probability p to determine if the search sequence has reached the spotting target. To train this model variant, we assign a probability $p = 1$ to all frames inside the spotting targets and $p = 0$ elsewhere. We add to L a new term that computes the softmax cross-entropy loss of this confidence score.

5 Experiments

5.1 Action Search for Action Spotting

In this subsection, we demonstrate that our model is able to mimic the human search process when spotting actions in the AVA dataset [21]. We first introduce our experimental protocol including a brief description of the dataset and metric used. Then, we compare *Action Search* against two spotting baseline models.

Dataset. We conduct this experiment using the AVA v1.0 dataset [21], which is among the largest annotated action datasets and is composed of feature films. We pick 15 action categories out of the original 80 set of actions. We train our model using the collected *AVA searches* from our *Human Searches* dataset. However, we prune off the search sequences with less than 8 steps. Refer to Sect. 3 for a description of the *AVA searches* and details about the action categories selection criteria. We evaluate our model on 35 testing videos. We use AVA 3-s annotations to define temporal boundaries for each action instance.

Metric. We compare our model against other approaches according to the *action spotting* metric, which we define to be the expected number of unique observations made per video until spotting an action. An action is spotted if the model lands *anywhere* between its ground truth temporal bounds.

Baseline Methods. To demonstrate the effectiveness of our approach in learning to search efficiently, we consider two baseline models, *Random Baseline* and *Direction Baseline* (refer to the **supplementary material** for more baselines).

Random Baseline: This model picks both the search direction and step size randomly. In particular, if the current search step is at time t of the video, it randomly picks between searching before t in the interval $[0, t]$ or after t in the interval $[t, d]$, where d is the duration of the video. The model then picks the next search location randomly from a uniform distribution on the selected interval.

Direction Baseline: This model picks the search direction using a trained *direction network* and chooses the search step size randomly. In particular, if the current search step is at time t of the video, its *direction network* uses the visual observation of the current frame to decide between searching before or after t, and then picks the next search location randomly from a uniform distribution on the selected interval. The *direction network* is based on a ResNet-152 [22] architecture with a binary softmax classifier. To train this network, we annotated each video frame with the search direction that leads to the nearest ground truth instance boundary. The *direction network* is class-specific and achieves an average of 95% training and 91% validation accuracy per class.

Results and Analysis. We run *Action Search* and the two baseline methods for 1000 independent search trials per test video to compute the *action spotting* metric. At each trial, we initialize each model at a random temporal location in the video, and we reinitialize the search model if it fails to spot an action after 500 steps. Figure 4 shows the cumulative performance of all three models over videos with different action coverage (*i.e.* the percentage of the video

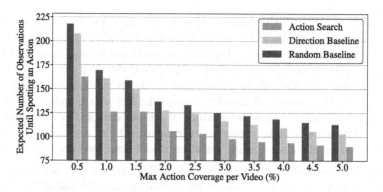

Fig. 4. *Action spotting* results for the AVA testing set for 1000 independent search trials per video. We report the cumulative spotting metric results on videos with action coverage (*i.e.* the percentage of video containing actions) ≤5%. *Action Search* takes 22%, 17%, and 13% fewer observations than the *Direction Baseline* on videos with at most 0.5%, 2.5%, and 5% action coverage, respectively.

length that contains action instances). Unlike both the *Direction Baseline* and *Random Baseline*, *Action Search* is able to harness temporal context to expedite the search process and, as a result, takes on average **16.6%** and **22.3%** less observations, respectively, before successfully spotting actions. Notably, there is a great performance difference between our model and the two baselines in videos with very sparse actions (*i.e.* action coverage ≤1%). We attribute this to the importance of temporal context when searching for sparse actions in video.

5.2   Action Search for Action Localization

In this subsection, we combine *Action Search* with an off-the-shelf action classifier to temporally localize human actions. Our approach achieves state-of-the-art detection performance on THUMOS14 [24], one of the most challenging temporal action localization datasets, while observing only **17.3%** of the video frames on average. We first explain how *action spotting* is used as a precursor to temporal action localization, and then introduce our experimental protocol, including a brief description of the dataset and metric. Finally, we compare our method against state-of-the-art detectors and present an ablation study of our model.

From Action Spotting to Localization. We train *Action Search* to spot the *start* of actions using the *THUMOS14 searches* dataset described in Sect. 3. To define the spotted action length, we use a simple heuristic based on class-specific fixed prior lengths. Specifically, from an output search sequence $(f(\mathbf{X}_1), f(\mathbf{X}_2), \ldots, f(\mathbf{X}_n))$, produced by our model, we generate the temporal segments $\mathcal{Q} = \{ [f(\mathbf{X}_i), f(\mathbf{X}_i) + d] \mid i \in \{1, \ldots, n\};\ d \in \mathcal{D} \}$, where $\mathcal{D}$ is a set of class-specific fixed action duration priors precomputed from the validation videos. In pursuit of assigning a class label to each segment, we use a pretrained classifier to provide probabilistic action scores. Finally, we follow the standard practice of applying *non-maximum-suppression* to remove duplicate detections.

Prediction. To reduce the number of search models we apply on a video to obtain its temporal predictions, we perform the following steps. We uniformly sample a small random set of N fixed-length segments from a given test video. These N segments are then classified using an off-the-shelf action classifier in order to obtain the top-k likely global class labels for the test video. To reduce complexity, *Action Search* then only runs the LSTM search models associated with these k activity classes to produce a set of temporal search sequences. These sequences are then aggregated and transformed into a set of final temporal predictions using the class-specific duration priors described above.

Dataset. We conduct our experiment using THUMOS14 [24], one of the most popular datasets for temporal localization. It contains 200 and 213 videos for training and testing, respectively. To train our *Action Search* model, we use the *THUMOS14 searches* dataset described in Sect. 3 (discarding the search sequences with less than 8 search steps). Following the standard evaluation protocol, we evaluate our approach on the testing videos. We choose to do our experiments in THUMOS14 instead of other large-scale datasets such as Charades [37] or ActivityNet [6] due to the expensive costs of *re-annotating* such datasets with search sequences. However, we provide an experiment in the **supplementary material** where we evaluate *Action Search* (trained on THUMOS14) on the ActivityNet v1.2 validation videos with the same THUMOS14 classes.

Metric. We compare our model against other methods according to the mean Average Precision (mAP) and penalize duplicate detections. We report the mAP at multiple temporal Intersection-over-Union (tIoU) thresholds.

Implementation Details. We initialize *Action Search* at random temporal locations in the video. We use the Res3D (+ S-CNN) classifier [35,41] as an off-the-shelf pretrained action classifier to classify the N random fixed-length segments, as well as, to classify the temporal action segments generated by our method. After cross-validating on the validation subset, we set $N = 24$, as it achieves the highest average recall while maintaining a small number of segments. Empirically, we find setting $k = 4$ provides the best trade-off between global video classification accuracy and number of search models to run.

Results and Analysis. In Table 1a, we compare our localization approach with state-of-the-art techniques. We assess methods in terms of mAP and the average percentage of observed frames (**S**). Our approach achieves state-of-the-art detection performance while observing much less of the video. For instance, at 0.5 tIoU, we achieve a competitive 30.8% mAP (compared to [16]'s 31.0% mAP) and observe on average 17.3% of each video. To understand the strengths of our method, we break down the results and discuss the following findings:

(1) Our method outperforms its baseline (Res3D + S-CNN [41]) by 8.3% mAP (0.5 tIoU). This baseline uses the same classifier *Action Search* uses, but its action proposals are generated by a CNN. We attribute this improvement to our approach's ability to discard irrelevant portions of the video, which allows the detector to prune false positive detections. This finding indicates the importance of *Action Search* as a precursor to localization.

Table 1. Temporal localization results (mAP at tIoU) on the THUMOS14 testing set. We assign '–' to unavailable mAP values. We report the average percentage of observed frames (**S**) for each approach. (a) Comparison against state-of-the-art methods: Our method (*Action Search + Priors* + Res3D + S-CNN) achieves state-of-the-art results while observing only 17.3% of the video; (b) Video features effect: We compare C3D for *Action Search* visual encoder + the C3D-based classifier from [35] vs. ResNet for *Action Search* visual encoder + the Res3D-based classifier from [41]; (c) The trade-off between *Action Search* training size and performance: mAP and **S** score improve as we increase the training size.

(a)

Method	mAP at tIoU					S
	0.3	0.4	0.5	0.6	0.7	
Frame Glimpses [44]	36.0	26.4	17.1	–	–	40 *
Shou *et al.* [35]	36.3	28.7	19.0	–	–	100
Shou *et al.* [34]	40.1	29.4	23.3	13.1	7.9	100
Gao *et al.* [17]	44.1	34.9	25.6	–	–	100
Dai *et al.* [11]	–	33.3	25.6	15.9	9.0	100
Xu *et al.* [43]	44.8	35.6	28.9	–	–	100
Buch *et al.* [3]	45.7	–	29.2	–	9.6	100
Zhao *et al.* [46]	**51.9**	41.0	29.8	–	–	100
Gao *et al.* [16]	50.1	41.3	**31.0**	19.1	9.9	100
Res3D + S-CNN [41]	40.6	32.6	22.5	12.3	6.4	100
Our method	51.8	**42.4**	30.8	**20.2**	**11.1**	**17.3**

(b)

Backbone Arch.	mAP at tIoU					S
	0.3	0.4	0.5	0.6	0.7	
C3D	43.7	35.2	23.9	18.8	4.3	45.1
ResNet	51.8	42.4	30.8	20.2	11.1	17.3

(c)

Training Size	mAP at tIoU					S
	0.3	0.4	0.5	0.6	0.7	
0% [41]	40.6	32.6	22.5	12.3	6.4	100
25%	41.1	32.9	22.4	12.1	6.4	63.5
50%	47.5	38.3	26.1	16.6	8.1	34.4
75%	50.2	41.0	29.5	18.1	9.4	24.1
100%	51.8	42.4	30.8	20.2	11.1	17.3

*We assume each of the 20 *Frame Glimpses* [44] models observes 2% of the video and report an upper-bound of 40% frames observed.

(2) Our method outperforms *Frame Glimpses* [44] in both mAP and **S**. We observe a 13.7% mAP (0.5 tIoU) improvement and a 22.7% reduction in **S**. We attribute the improvement on **S** to the strategy we follow to train *Action Search*. Instead of relying on a reinforcement policy to explore the video, as *Frame Glimpses* does, we learn to search by imitating humans. Thus, we argue that their search policy is unable to learn temporal context reasoning as well as *Action Search*. This finding justifies the need for the *Human Searches* dataset (Sect. 3) and the supervised strategy we follow to train our model.

(3) Although it uses a naive approach to detect actions, our method surpasses state-of-the-art approaches [3,16,46]. Opting for simplicity, we build our detector by combining *Action Search* with a pretrained off-the-shelf classifier. This straightforward approach allows us to achieve state-of-the-art results while only observing 17.3% of video frames. We argue further improvements can be obtained by combining *Action Search* with sophisticated models such as [16,46].

Ablation Study. We investigate two aspects of our model: (**i**) the backbone architecture for the *Action Search* visual encoder and the off-the-shelf classifier (refer to Table 1b), and **(ii)** the trade-off between *Action Search* training set size and performance in terms of mAP and **S** (refer to Table 1c).

(i) Table 1b shows using a C3D architecture (*i.e.* C3D for *Action Search* visual encoder + the C3D-based classifier from [35]) improves the performance of the baseline [35] by 4.9% mAP (0.5 tIoU) while observing 54.9% less frames. However, a ResNet backbone architecture gives better results in both mAP and **S**. We attribute this to the facts that ResNet offers a richer feature space, the off-the-shelf classifier from [41] is more sophisticated compared to the classifier from [35], and ResNet uses 1 frame per observation while C3D needs 16 frames.

(ii) *Action Search* is trained on *THUMOS14 searches* dataset, which contains on average 8.8 human searches per video. Training on more human searches would lead to a better performing model, but collecting human searches for *existing* datasets is expensive (although *free* for new datasets). Nonetheless, we observe in Table 1c that training *Action Search* on half of the *THUMOS14 searches* dataset (*i.e.* 4.4 human searches per video), the model improves the detection performance of [41] by 3.6% mAP (0.5 tIoU) while observing only **S** = 34.4% of the frames. Notably, training on as little as 2.2 human searches per video cuts the percentage of observed frames by 36.5% while keeping a similar mAP performance. In general, as we decrease the training set size, the efficiency of the search degrades (**S** increases) since the model is

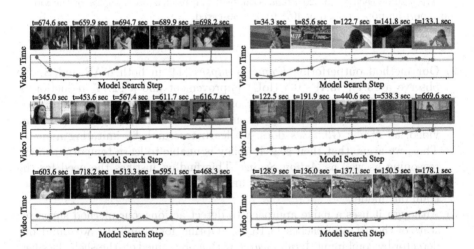

Fig. 5. Qualitative search sequences produced by *Action Search*. The left column corresponds to AVA [21] testing videos, and the right column corresponds to THUMOS14 [24] testing videos. The top two rows depict examples when our model successfully spots the target action location (in green). The last row illustrate failure cases, *i.e.* when the action location (in red) is not spotted exactly. We observe that *Action Search* uses temporal context to reason about where to search next. In failure cases, we notice that our model often oscillates around actions without spotting frames within the exact temporal location. (Color figure online)

not exposed to as many human searches variations. These findings further justify the need for the *Human Searches* dataset and the supervised strategy we follow to train our model.

5.3 Spotting at a Glance

Figure 5 depicts qualitative search sequences of our *Action Search* model, which exploits temporal context to spot the actions quickly. For example, it uses information about scenes/concepts such as gala dinner and fights to spot actions such as *clink glass* and *shoot*, respectively (top two rows, left column). Furthermore, when spotting the start times of actions, our model seems to understand the inherent temporal structures of actions. *Action Search* surprisingly understands when an action finishes and is able to rewind (jump back) and spot the beginning of the action (top row, right column). Typical failure cases (actions are not spotted) occur when the search sequences oscillate around the target action but they miss its exact location (last row, left column). Additionally, *Action Search* may fail when action boundaries are ambiguous. When our model finds content visually similar to the target action, it remains static for a few search steps and then decides to explore the video further (last row, right column).

6 Conclusion

In this paper, we introduced *Action Search*, a new learning model to imitate how humans search for actions in videos, and a new dataset called *Human Searches* to train such model. Extensive experiments demonstrated that *Action Search* produces reliable action detections. We plan to release our *Human Searches* dataset to the vision community and expect that further works can extend the use of search processes for action detection and other applications.

Acknowledgments. This publication is based upon work supported by the King Abdullah University of Science and Technology (KAUST) Office of Sponsored Research (OSR) under Award No. OSR-CRG2017-3405.

References

1. Alahi, A., Goel, K., Ramanathan, V., Robicquet, A., Fei-Fei, L., Savarese, S.: Social LSTM: human trajectory prediction in crowded spaces. In: CVPR (2016)
2. Bengio, S., Vinyals, O., Jaitly, N., Shazeer, N.: Scheduled sampling for sequence prediction with recurrent neural networks. In: NIPS (2015)
3. Buch, S., Escorcia, V., Ghanem, B., Fei-Fei, L., Niebles, J.C.: End-to-end, single-stream temporal action detection in untrimmed videos. In: BMVC (2017)
4. Buch, S., Escorcia, V., Shen, C., Ghanem, B., Carlos Niebles, J.: SST: single-stream temporal action proposals. In: CVPR, July 2017
5. Caba Heilbron, F., Barrios, W., Escorcia, V., Ghanem, B.: SCC: semantic context cascade for efficient action detection. In: CVPR (2017)

6. Caba Heilbron, F., Escorcia, V., Ghanem, B., Carlos Niebles, J.: ActivityNet: a large-scale video benchmark for human activity understanding. In: CVPR (2015)
7. Caba Heilbron, F., Carlos Niebles, J., Ghanem, B.: Fast temporal activity proposals for efficient detection of human actions in untrimmed videos. In: CVPR (2016)
8. Caba Heilbron, F., Thabet, A., Carlos Niebles, J., Ghanem, B.: Camera motion and surrounding scene appearance as context for action recognition. In: Cremers, D., Reid, I., Saito, H., Yang, M.-H. (eds.) ACCV 2014. LNCS, vol. 9006, pp. 583–597. Springer, Cham (2015). https://doi.org/10.1007/978-3-319-16817-3_38
9. Carreira, J., Zisserman, A.: Quo vadis, action recognition? A new model and the kinetics dataset. In: CVPR, July 2017
10. Chen, W., Xiong, C., Xu, R., Corso, J.J.: Actionness ranking with lattice conditional ordinal random fields. In: CVPR (2014)
11. Dai, X., Singh, B., Zhang, G., Davis, L.S., Chen, Y.Q.: Temporal context network for activity localization in videos. In: ICCV (2017)
12. Deng, J., Dong, W., Socher, R., Li, L.J., Li, K., Fei-Fei, L.: ImageNet: a large-scale hierarchical image database. In: CVPR (2009)
13. Duchenne, O., Laptev, I., Sivic, J., Bach, F., Ponce, J.: Automatic annotation of human actions in video. In: ICCV (2009)
14. Escorcia, V., Caba Heilbron, F., Carlos Niebles, J., Ghanem, B.: DAPs: deep action proposals for action understanding. In: ECCV (2016)
15. Gaidon, A., Harchaoui, Z., Schmid, C.: Actom sequence models for efficient action detection. In: CVPR (2011)
16. Gao, J., Yang, Z., Nevatia, R.: Cascaded boundary regression for temporal action detection. In: BMVC (2017)
17. Gao, J., Yang, Z., Sun, C., Chen, K., Nevatia, R.: TURN TAP: temporal unit regression network for temporal action proposals. In: ICCV (2017)
18. Gkioxari, G., Malik, J.: Finding action tubes. In: CVPR (2015)
19. Graves, A.: Generating sequences with recurrent neural networks. arXiv preprint arXiv:1308.0850 (2013)
20. Graves, A., Jaitly, N.: Towards end-to-end speech recognition with recurrent neural networks. In: International Conference on Machine Learning (2014)
21. Gu, C., et al.: AVA: a video dataset of spatio-temporally localized atomic visual actions. In: CVPR (2018)
22. He, K., Zhang, X., Ren, S., Sun, J.: Deep residual learning for image recognition. In: CVPR (2016)
23. Jain, M., van Gemert, J.C., Snoek, C.G.: What do 15,000 object categories tell us about classifying and localizing actions? In: CVPR (2015)
24. Jiang, Y.G., et al.: THUMOS challenge: action recognition with a large number of classes (2014). http://crcv.ucf.edu/THUMOS14/
25. Kingma, D.P., Ba, J.: Adam: a method for stochastic optimization. ArXiv e-prints, December 2014
26. Ma, S., Sigal, L., Sclaroff, S.: Learning activity progression in LSTMs for activity detection and early detection. In: CVPR (2016)
27. Mettes, P., van Gemert, J.C., Snoek, C.G.M.: Spot on: action localization from pointly-supervised proposals. In: Leibe, B., Matas, J., Sebe, N., Welling, M. (eds.) ECCV 2016. LNCS, vol. 9909, pp. 437–453. Springer, Cham (2016). https://doi.org/10.1007/978-3-319-46454-1_27
28. Carlos Niebles, J., Chen, C.W., Fei-Fei, L.: Modeling temporal structure of decomposable motion segments for activity classification. In: ECCV (2010)
29. Oneata, D., Verbeek, J., Schmid, C.: Efficient action localization with approximately normalized fisher vectors. In: CVPR (2014)

30. Peng, X., Schmid, C.: Multi-region two-stream R-CNN for action detection. In: Leibe, B., Matas, J., Sebe, N., Welling, M. (eds.) ECCV 2016. LNCS, vol. 9908, pp. 744–759. Springer, Cham (2016). https://doi.org/10.1007/978-3-319-46493-0_45

31. Pham, V., Bluche, T., Kermorvant, C., Louradour, J.: Dropout improves recurrent neural networks for handwriting recognition. ArXiv e-prints, November 2013

32. Richard, A., Gall, J.: Temporal action detection using a statistical language model. In: CVPR (2016)

33. Saha, S., Singh, G., Sapienza, M., Torr, P.H., Cuzzolin, F.: Deep learning for detecting multiple space-time action tubes in videos. In: BMVC (2016)

34. Shou, Z., Chan, J., Zareian, A., Miyazawa, K., Chang, S.F.: CDC: convolutional-de-convolutional networks for precise temporal action localization in untrimmed videos. In: CVPR (2017)

35. Shou, Z., Wang, D., Chang, S.F.: Temporal action localization in untrimmed videos via multi-stage CNNs. In: CVPR (2016)

36. Sigurdsson, G.A., Russakovsky, O., Gupta, A.: What actions are needed for understanding human actions in videos? In: ICCV, October 2017

37. Sigurdsson, G.A., Varol, G., Wang, X., Farhadi, A., Laptev, I., Gupta, A.: Hollywood in homes: crowdsourcing data collection for activity understanding. In: Leibe, B., Matas, J., Sebe, N., Welling, M. (eds.) ECCV 2016. LNCS, vol. 9905, pp. 510–526. Springer, Cham (2016). https://doi.org/10.1007/978-3-319-46448-0_31

38. Simonyan, K., Zisserman, A.: Two-stream convolutional networks for action recognition in videos. In: Advances in Neural Information Processing Systems, pp. 568–576 (2014)

39. Soomro, K., Idrees, H., Shah, M.: Predicting the where and what of actors and actions through online action localization. In: CVPR (2016)

40. Sukhbaatar, S., Weston, J., Fergus, R., et al.: End-to-end memory networks. In: Advances in Neural Information Processing Systems (2015)

41. Tran, D., Ray, J., Shou, Z., Chang, S., Paluri, M.: ConvNet architecture search for spatiotemporal feature learning. CoRR abs/1708.05038 (2017). http://arxiv.org/abs/1708.05038

42. Wang, H., Kläser, A., Schmid, C., Liu, C.L.: Action recognition by dense trajectories. In: CVPR (2011)

43. Xu, H., Das, A., Saenko, K.: R-C3D: region convolutional 3D network for temporal activity detection. In: ICCV (2017)

44. Yeung, S., Russakovsky, O., Mori, G., Fei-Fei, L.: End-to-end learning of action detection from frame glimpses in videos. In: CVPR (2016)

45. Zaremba, W., Sutskever, I., Vinyals, O.: Recurrent neural network regularization. ArXiv e-prints, September 2014

46. Zhao, Y., Xiong, Y., Wang, L., Wu, Z., Lin, D., Tang, X.: Temporal action detection with structured segment networks. In: ICCV (2017)

PSANet: Point-wise Spatial Attention Network for Scene Parsing

Hengshuang Zhao[1(✉)], Yi Zhang[2], Shu Liu[1], Jianping Shi[3],
Chen Change Loy[4], Dahua Lin[2], and Jiaya Jia[1,5]

[1] The Chinese University of Hong Kong, Shatin, Hong Kong
{hszhao,sliu,leojia}@cse.cuhk.edu.hk
[2] CUHK-Sensetime Joint Lab, The Chinese University of Hong Kong,
Shatin, Hong Kong
{zy217,dhlin}@ie.cuhk.edu.hk
[3] SenseTime Research, Beijing , China
shijianping@sensetime.com
[4] Nanyang Technological University, Singapore, Singapore
ccloy@ntu.edu.sg
[5] Tencent Youtu Lab, Shenzhen, China

Abstract. We notice information flow in convolutional neural networks is restricted inside local neighborhood regions due to the physical design of convolutional filters, which limits the overall understanding of complex scenes. In this paper, we propose the *point-wise spatial attention network* (PSANet) to relax the local neighborhood constraint. Each position on the feature map is connected to all the other ones through a self-adaptively learned attention mask. Moreover, information propagation in bi-direction for scene parsing is enabled. Information at other positions can be collected to help the prediction of the current position and vice versa, information at the current position can be distributed to assist the prediction of other ones. Our proposed approach achieves top performance on various competitive scene parsing datasets, including ADE20K, PASCAL VOC 2012 and Cityscapes, demonstrating its effectiveness and generality.

Keywords: Point-wise spatial attention
Bi-direction information flow · Adaptive context aggregation
Scene parsing · Semantic segmentation

1 Introduction

Scene parsing, a.k.a. semantic segmentation, is a fundamental and challenging problem in computer vision, in which each pixel is assigned with a category label.

H. Zhao and Y. Zhang—Equal contribution.

Electronic supplementary material The online version of this chapter (https:// doi.org/10.1007/978-3-030-01240-3_17) contains supplementary material, which is available to authorized users.

© Springer Nature Switzerland AG 2018
V. Ferrari et al. (Eds.): ECCV 2018, LNCS 11213, pp. 270–286, 2018.
https://doi.org/10.1007/978-3-030-01240-3_17

It is a key step towards visual scene understanding, and plays a crucial role in applications such as auto-driving and robot navigation.

The development of powerful deep *convolutional neural networks* (CNNs) has made remarkable progress in scene parsing [1,4,5,26,29,45]. Owing to the design of CNN structures, the receptive field of it is limited to local regions [27,47]. The limited receptive field imposes a great adverse effect on *fully convolutional networks* (FCNs) based scene parsing systems due to insufficient understanding of surrounded contextual information.

To address this issue, especially leveraging long-range dependency, several modifications have been made. Contextual information aggregation through dilated convolution is proposed by [4,42]. Dilations are introduced into the classical compact convolution module to expand the receptive field. Contextual information aggregation can also be achieved through pooling operation. Global pooling module in ParseNet [24], different-dilation based *atrous spatial pyramid pooling* (ASPP) module in DeepLab [5] and different-region based *pyramid pooling module* (PPM) in PSPNet [45] can help extract the context information to a certain degree. Different from these extensions, *conditional random field* (CRF) [2–4,46] and *Markov random field* (MRF) [25] are also utilized. Besides, *recurrent neural network* (RNN) is introduced in ReSeg [38] for its capability to capture long-range dependencies. However, these dilated-convolution-based [4,42] and pooling-based [5,24,45] extensions utilize homogeneous contextual dependencies for all image regions in a non-adaptive manner, ignoring the difference of local representation and contextual dependencies for different categories. The CRF/MRF-based [2–4,25,46] and RNN-based [38] extensions are less efficient than CNN-based frameworks.

In this paper, we propose the *point-wise spatial attention network* (PSANet) to aggregate long-range contextual information in a flexible and adaptive manner. Each position in the feature map is connected with all other ones through self-adaptively predicted attention maps, thus harvesting various information nearby and far away. Furthermore, we design the bi-directional information propagation path for a comprehensive understanding of complex scenes. Each position collects information from all others to help the prediction of itself and vice versa, the information at each position can be distributed globally, assisting the prediction of all other positions. Finally, the bi-directionally aggregated contextual information is fused with local features to form the final representation of complex scenes.

Our proposed PSANet achieves top performance on three most competitive semantic segmentation datasets, *i.e.*, ADE20K [48], PASCAL VOC 2012 [9] and Cityscapes [8]. We believe the proposed point-wise spatial attention module together with the bi-directional information propagation paradigm can also benefit other dense prediction tasks. We give all implementation details, and make the code and trained models publicly available to the community[1]. Our main contribution is three-fold:

---

[1] https://github.com/hszhao/PSANet.

- We achieve long-range context aggregation for scene parsing by a learned point-wise position-sensitive context dependency together with a bi-directional information propagation paradigm.
- We propose the *point-wise spatial attention network* (PSANet) to harvest contextual information from all positions in the feature map. Each position is connected with all others through a self-adaptively learned attention map.
- PSANet achieves top performance on various competitive scene parsing datasets, demonstrating its effectiveness and generality.

2   Related Work

Scene Parsing and Semantic Segmentation. Recently, CNN based methods [4–6,26,42,45] have achieved remarkable success in scene parsing and semantic segmentation tasks. FCN [26] is the first approach to replace the fully-connected layer in a classification network with convolution layers for semantic segmentation. DeconvNet [29] and SegNet [1] adopted encoder-decoder structures that utilize information in low-level layers to help refine the segmentation mask. Dilated convolution [4,42] applied skip convolution on feature map to enlarge network's receptive field. UNet [33] concatenated output from low-level layers with higher ones for information fusion. DeepLab [4] and CRF-RNN [46] utilized CRF for structure prediction in scene parsing. DPN [25] used MRF for semantic segmentation. LRR [11] and RefineNet [21] adopted step-wise reconstruction and refinement to get parsing results. PSPNet [45] achieved high performance though pyramid pooling strategy. There are also high efficiency frameworks like ENet [30] and ICNet [44] for real-time applications like automatic driving.

Context Information Aggregation. Context information plays a key role for image understanding. Dilated convolution [4,42] inserted dilation inside classical convolution kernels to enlarge the receptive field of CNN. Global pooling was widely adopted in various basic classification backbones [13,14,19,35,36] to harvest context information for global representations. Liu *et al.* proposed ParseNet [24] that utilizes global pooling to aggregate context information for scene parsing. Chen *et al.* developed ASPP [5] module and Zhao *et al.* proposed PPM [45] module to obtain different regions' contextual information. Visin *et al.* presented ReSeg [38] that utilizes RNN to capture long-range contextual dependency information.

Attention Mechanism. Attention mechanism is widely used in neural networks. Mnih *et al.* [28] learned an attention model that adaptively select a sequence of regions or locations for processing. Chen *et al.* [7] learned several attention masks to fuse feature maps or predictions from different branches. Vaswani *et al.* [37] learned a self-attention model for machine translation. Wang *et al.* [40] got attention masks by calculating the correlation matrix between each spatial point in the feature map. Our point-wise attention masks are different from the aforementioned studies. Specifically, masks learned through our PSA module are self-adaptive and sensitive to location and category information. PSA learns to aggregate contextual information for each individual point adaptively and specifically.

3   Framework

In order to capture contextual information, especially in the long range, information aggregation is of great importance for scene parsing [5, 24, 38, 45]. In this paper, we formulate the information aggregation step as a kind of information flow and propose to adaptively learn a pixel-wise global attention map for each position from two perspectives to aggregate contextual information over the entire feature map.

3.1   Formulation

General feature learning or information aggregation is modeled as

$$\mathbf{z}_i = \frac{1}{N} \sum_{\forall j \in \Omega(i)} F(\mathbf{x}_i, \mathbf{x}_j, \Delta_{ij}) \mathbf{x}_j \tag{1}$$

where $\mathbf{z}_i$ is the newly aggregated feature at position i, and $\mathbf{x}_i$ is the feature representation at position i in the input feature map $\mathbf{X}$. $\forall j \in \Omega(i)$ enumerates all positions in the region of interest associated with i, and Δ_{ij} represents the relative location of position i and j. $F(\mathbf{x}_i, \mathbf{x}_j, \Delta_{ij})$ can be any function or learned parameters according to the operation and it represents the information flow from j to i. Note that by taking relative location Δ_{ij} into account, $F(\mathbf{x}_i, \mathbf{x}_j, \Delta_{ij})$ is sensitive to different relative locations. Here N is for normalization.

Specifically, we simplify the formulation and design different functions F with respect to different relative locations. Equation (1) is updated to

$$\mathbf{z}_i = \frac{1}{N} \sum_{\forall j \in \Omega(i)} F_{\Delta_{ij}}(\mathbf{x}_i, \mathbf{x}_j) \mathbf{x}_j \tag{2}$$

where $\{F_{\Delta_{ij}}\}$ is a set of position-specific functions. It models the information flow from position j to position i. Note that the function $F_{\Delta_{ij}}(\cdot, \cdot)$ takes both the source and target information as input. When there are many positions in the feature map, the number of the combination $(\mathbf{x}_i, \mathbf{x}_j)$ is very large. In this paper, we simplify the formulation and make an approximation.

At first, we simplify the function $F_{\Delta_{ij}}(\cdot, \cdot)$ as

$$F_{\Delta_{ij}}(\mathbf{x}_i, \mathbf{x}_j) \approx F_{\Delta_{ij}}(\mathbf{x}_i) \tag{3}$$

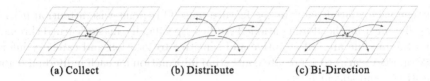

(a) Collect   (b) Distribute   (c) Bi-Direction

Fig. 1. Illustration of bi-direction information propagation model. Each position both 'collects' and 'distributes' information for more comprehensive information propagation.

In this approximation, the information flow from j to i is only related to the semantic feature at target position i and the relative location of i and j. Based on Eq. (3), we rewrite Eq. (2) as

$$\mathbf{z}_i = \frac{1}{N} \sum_{\forall j \in \Omega(i)} F_{\Delta_{ij}}(\mathbf{x}_i)\mathbf{x}_j \tag{4}$$

Similarly, we simplify the function $F_{\Delta_{ij}}(\cdot, \cdot)$ as

$$F_{\Delta_{ij}}(\mathbf{x}_i, \mathbf{x}_j) \approx F_{\Delta_{ij}}(\mathbf{x}_j) \tag{5}$$

in which the information flow from j to i is only related to the semantic feature at source position j and the relative location of position i and j.

We finally decompose and simplify the function as a bi-direction information propagation path. Combining Eqs. (3) and (5), we get

$$F_{\Delta_{ij}}(\mathbf{x}_i, \mathbf{x}_j) \approx F_{\Delta_{ij}}(\mathbf{x}_i) + F_{\Delta_{ij}}(\mathbf{x}_j) \tag{6}$$

Formally, we model this bi-direction information propagation as

$$\mathbf{z}_i = \frac{1}{N} \sum_{\forall j \in \Omega(i)} F_{\Delta_{ij}}(\mathbf{x}_i)\mathbf{x}_j + \frac{1}{N} \sum_{\forall j \in \Omega(i)} F_{\Delta_{ij}}(\mathbf{x}_j)\mathbf{x}_j. \tag{7}$$

For the first term, $F_{\Delta_{ij}}(\mathbf{x}_i)$ encodes to what extent the features at other positions can help prediction. Each position 'collects' information from other positions. For the second term, the importance of the feature at one position to features at other positions is predicted by $F_{\Delta_{ij}}(\mathbf{x}_j)$. Each position 'distributes' information to others. This bi-directional information propagation path, shown in Fig. 1, enables the network to learn more comprehensive representations, evidenced in our experimental section.

Specifically, our PSA module, aiming to adaptively predict the information flow over the entire feature map, takes all the positions in feature map as $\Omega(i)$ and utilizes the convolutional layer as the operation of $F_{\Delta_{ij}}(\mathbf{x}_i)$ and $F_{\Delta_{ij}}(\mathbf{x}_j)$. Both $F_{\Delta_{ij}}(\mathbf{x}_i)$ and $F_{\Delta_{ij}}(\mathbf{x}_j)$ can then be regarded as predicted attention values to aggregate feature $\mathbf{x}_j$. We further rewrite Eq. (7) as

$$\mathbf{z}_i = \frac{1}{N} \sum_{\forall j} \mathbf{a}_{i,j}^c \mathbf{x}_j + \frac{1}{N} \sum_{\forall j} \mathbf{a}_{i,j}^d \mathbf{x}_j, \tag{8}$$

where $\mathbf{a}_{i,j}^c$ and $\mathbf{a}_{i,j}^d$ denote the predicted attention values in the point-wise attention maps $\mathbf{A}^c$ and $\mathbf{A}^d$ from 'collect' and 'distribute' branches, respectively.

3.2 Overview

We show the framework of the PSA module in Fig. 2. The PSA module takes a spatial feature map $\mathbf{X}$ as input. We denote the spatial size of $\mathbf{X}$ as $H \times W$. Through the two branches as illustrated, we generate pixel-wise global attention maps for each position in feature map $\mathbf{X}$ through several convolutional layers. We aggregate input feature map based on attention maps following Eq. (8) to generate new feature representations with the long-range contextual information incorporated, $i.e.$, $\mathbf{Z}^c$ from the 'collect' branch and $\mathbf{Z}^d$ from the 'distribute' branch.

We concatenate the new representations $\mathbf{Z}^c$ and $\mathbf{Z}^d$ and apply a convolutional layer with batch normalization and activation layers for dimension reduction and feature fusion. Then we concatenate the new global contextual feature with the local representation feature $\mathbf{X}$. It is followed by one or several convolutional layers with batch normalization and activation layers to generate the final feature map for following subnetworks.

We note that all operations in our proposed PSA module are differentiable, and can be jointly trained with other parts of the network in an end-to-end manner. It can be flexibly attached to any feature maps in the network. By predicting contextual dependencies for each position, it adaptively aggregates suitable contextual information. In the following subsections, we detail the process of generating the two attention maps, $i.e.$, $\mathbf{A}^c$ and $\mathbf{A}^d$.

3.3 Point-wise Spatial Attention

Network Structure. PSA module firstly produces two point-wise spatial attention maps, $i.e.$, $\mathbf{A}^c$ and $\mathbf{A}^d$ by two parallel branches. Although they represent different information propagation directions, network structures are just the same. As shown in Fig. 2, in each branch, we firstly apply a convolutional layer with 1×1 filters to reduce the number of channels of input feature map $\mathbf{X}$ to reduce computational overhead ($i.e.$, $C_2 < C_1$ in Fig. 2). Then another

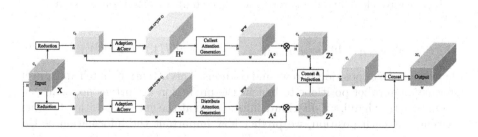

Fig. 2. Architecture of the proposed PSA module.

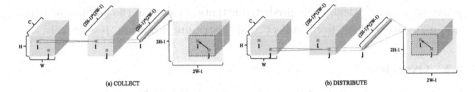

Fig. 3. Illustration of point-wise spatial attention.

convolutional layer with 1×1 filters is applied for feature adaption. These layers are accompanied with batch normalization and activation layers. Finally, one convolutional layer is responsible for generating the global attention map for each position.

Instead of predicting a map with size $H \times W$ for each position i, we predict an over-completed map $\mathbf{h}_i$, i.e., with size $(2H-1) \times (2W-1)$, covering the input feature map. As a result, for feature map $\mathbf{X}$, we get a temporary representation map $\mathbf{H}$ with spatial size $H \times W$ and $(2H-1) \times (2W-1)$ channels. As illustrated by Fig. 3, for each position i, $\mathbf{h}_i$ can be reshaped to a spatial map with $2H-1$ rows and $2W-1$ columns and centers on position i, of which only $H \times W$ values are useful for feature aggregation. The valid region is highlighted as the dashed bounding box in Fig. 3.

With our instantiation, the set of filters used to predict the attention maps at different positions are not the same. This enables the network to be sensitive to the relative positions by adapting weights. Another instantiation to achieve this goal is to utilize a fully-connected layer to connect the input feature map and the predicted pixel-wise attention map. But this will lead to an enormous number of parameters.

Attention Map Generation. Based on the predicted over-completed map $\mathbf{H}^c$ from the 'collect' branch and $\mathbf{H}^d$ from the 'distribute' branch, we further generate attention maps $\mathbf{A}^c$ and $\mathbf{A}^d$, respectively.

In the 'collect' branch, at each position i, with k_{th} row and l_{th} column, we predict how current position is related to other positions based on feature at position i. As a result, $\mathbf{a}_i^c$ corresponds to the region in $\mathbf{h}_i^c$ with H rows and W columns starting from $(H-k)_{th}$ row and $(W-l)_{th}$ column.

Specifically, element at s_{th} row and t_{th} column in attention mask $\mathbf{a}_i^c$, i.e., $\mathbf{a}_{[k,l]}^c$ is

$$\mathbf{a}_{[k,l],[s,t]}^c = \mathbf{h}_{[k,l],[H-k+s,W-l+t]}^c, \quad \forall s \in [0,H), \quad t \in [0,W) \tag{9}$$

where $[\cdot, \cdot]$ indexes position in rows and columns. This attention map helps collect informative in other positions to benefit the prediction at current position.

On the other hand, we distribute information at the current position to other positions. At each position, we predict how important the information at the current position to other positions is. The generation of $\mathbf{a}_i^d$ is similar to $\mathbf{a}_i^c$. This attention map helps to distribute information for better prediction.

These two maps encode the context dependency between different position pairs in a complementary way, leading to improved information propagation and enhanced utilization of long-range context. The benefits of utilizing those two different attentions are manifested in experiments.

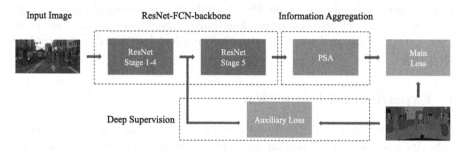

Fig. 4. Network structure of ResNet-FCN-backbone with PSA module incorporated. Deep supervision is also adopted for better performance.

3.4 PSA Module with FCN

Our PSA module is scalable and can be attached to any stage in the FCN structure. We show our instantiation in Fig. 4.

Given an input image $\mathbf{I}$, we acquire its local representation through FCN as feature map $\mathbf{X}$, which is the input of the PSA module. Same as that of [45], we take ResNet [13] as the FCN backbone. Our proposed PSA module is then used to aggregate long-range contextual information from the local representation. It follows stage-5 in ResNet, which is the final stage of the FCN backbone. Features in stage-5 are semantically stronger. Aggregating them together leads to a more comprehensive representation of long-range context. Moreover, the spatial size of the feature map at stage-5 is smaller and can reduce computation overhead and memory consumption. Referring to [45], we also utilize the same deep supervision technique. An auxiliary loss branch is applied apart from the main loss as illustrated in Fig. 4.

3.5 Discussion

There has been research making use of context information for scene parsing. However, the widely used dilated convolution [4,42] utilized a fixed sparse grid to operate the feature map, losing the ability to utilize information of the entire image. While pooling strategies [5,24,45] captures global context with fixed weight at each position, they can not adapt to the input data and are less flexible. Recently proposed non-local method [40] encodes global context by calculating the correlation of semantic features between each pair of positions on the input feature map, ignoring the relative location between these two positions.

Different from these solutions, our PSA module adaptively predicts global attention maps for each position on the input feature map by convolutional layers, taking the relative location into account. Moreover, the attention maps can be predicted from two perspectives, aiming at capturing different types of information flow between positions. The two attention maps actually build the bi-direction information propagation path as illustrated in Fig. 1. They collect and distribute information over the entire feature map. The global pooling technique is just a special case of our PSA module in this regard. As a result, our PSA module can effectively capture long-range context information, adapt to input data and utilize diverse attention information, leading to more accurate prediction.

4   Experimental Evaluation

The proposed PSANet is effective on scene parsing and semantic segmentation tasks. We evaluate our method on three challenging datasets, including complex scene understanding dataset ADE20K [48], object segmentation dataset PAS-CAL VOC 2012 [9] and urban-scene understanding dataset Cityscapes [8]. In the following, we first show the implementation details related to training strategy and hyper-parameters, then we show results on corresponding datasets and visualize the learned masks generated by the PSA module.

4.1   Implementation Details

We conduct our experiments based on Caffe [15]. During training, we set the mini-batch size as 16 with synchronized batch normalization and base learning rate as 0.01. Following prior works [5,45], we adopt 'poly' learning rate policy and the power is set to 0.9. We set maximum iteration number to 150 K for experiments on the ADE20K dataset, 30K for VOC 2012 and 90 K for Cityscapes. Momentum and weight decay are set to 0.9 and 0.0001 respectively. For data augmentation, we adopt random mirror and random resize between 0.5 and 2 for all datasets. We further add extra random rotation between $-10°$ and $10°$, and random Gaussian blur for ADE20K and VOC 2012 datasets.

4.2   ADE20K

The scene parsing dataset ADE20K [48] is challenging for up to 150 classes and diverse complex scenes up to 1,038 image-level categories. It is divided into 20K/2K/3K for training, validation and testing, respectively. Both objects and stuffs need to be parsed for the dataset. For evaluation metrics, both *mean of class-wise intersection over union* (Mean IoU) and *pixel-wise accuracy* (Pixel Acc.) are adopted.

Comparison of Information Aggregation Approaches. We compare the performance of several different information aggregation approaches on the validation set of ADE20K with two network backbones, *i.e.*, ResNet with 50 and

Table 1. Contextual information aggregation with different approaches. Results are reported on *validation* set of ADE20K dataset. 'SS' stands for single-scale testing and 'MS' means multi-scale testing strategy is utilized.

Method	Mean IoU(%) / Pixle Acc.(%)	
	SS	MS
ResNet50-Baseline	37.23/78.01	38.48/78.92
ResNet50+DenseCRF[a] [18]	37.97/78.51	38.86/79.32
ResNet50+GlobalPooling [24]	40.07/79.52	41.22/80.35
ResNet50+ASPP [5]	40.39/79.71	42.18/80.73
ResNet50+NonLocal [40]	40.93/79.97	41.94/80.71
ResNet50+PSP [45]	41.68/80.04	42.78/80.76
ResNet50+COLLECT(Compact)	41.07/79.61	41.99/80.32
ResNet50+COLLECT	41.27/79.74	42.56/80.56
ResNet50+DISTRIBUTE	41.46/80.12	42.63/80.90
ResNet50+COLLECT+DISTRIBUTE	41.92/80.17	42.97/80.92
ResNet101-Baseline	39.66/79.44	40.71/80.17
ResNet101+COLLECT	42.70/80.53	43.68/81.24
ResNet101+DISTRIBUTE	42.11/80.01	43.38/81.12
ResNet101+COLLECT+DISTRIBUTE	42.75/80.71	43.77/81.51

[a] CRF parameters: bi_w=3.5, bi_xy_std=55, bi_rgb_std=3, pos_w=2, pos_xy_std=1.

101 layers. The experimental results are listed in Table 1. Our baseline network is ResNet-based FCN with dilated convolution module incorporated at stage 4 and 5, *i.e.*, dilations are set to 2 and 4 for these two stages respectively.

Based on the feature map extracted by FCN, DenseCRF [18] only brings slight improvement. Global pooling [24] is a simple and intuitive attempt to harvest long-range contextual information, but it treats each position on the feature map equally. Pyramid structures [5,45] with several branches can capture contextual information at different scales. Another option is to use an attention mask for each position in the feature map. A non-local method was adopted in [40], in which attention mask for each position is generated by calculating the feature correlation between each paired positions. In our PSA module, apart from the uniqueness of the attention mask for each point, our point-wise masks are self-adaptively learned with convolutional operations instead of simply matrix multiplication adopted by non-local method [40]. Compared with these information aggregation methods, our method performs better, which shows that the PSA module is a better choice in terms of capturing long-range contextual information.

We further explore the two branches in our PSA module. Taking ResNet50 as an example with information flow in 'collect' mode (denoted as '+COLLECT') in Table 1, our single scale testing results get 41.27/79.74 in terms of Mean IoU and Pixel Acc. (%)., exceeding the baseline by 4.04/1.73. This significant improvement demonstrates the effectiveness of our proposed PSA module, even

Table 2. Methods comparison with results reported on ADE20K *validation* set.

Method	Mean IoU(%)	Pixel Acc.(%)
FCN-8s [26]	29.39	71.32
SegNet [1]	21.64	71.00
DilatedNet [42]	32.31	73.55
CascadeNet [48]	34.90	74.52
RefineNet101 [21]	40.20	-
RefineNet152 [21]	40.70	-
PSPNet50 [45]	42.78	80.76
PSPNet101 [45]	43.29	81.39
WiderNet [41]	43.73	81.17
PSANet50	42.97	80.92
PSANet101	43.77	81.51

Table 3. Methods comparison with results reported on VOC 2012 *test* set.

Method	mIoU(%)
LRR [11]	79.3
DeepLabv2 [5]	79.7
G-CRF [3]	80.4
SegModel [34]	81.8
LC [20]	82.7
DUC_HDC [39]	83.1
Large_Kernel_Matters [31]	83.6
RefineNet [21]	84.2
ResNet-38 [41]	84.9
PSPNet [45]	85.4
DeepLabv3 [6]	85.7
PSANet	85.7

with only uni-directional information flow in a simplified version. With our bi-direction information flow model (denoted as '+COLLECT +DISTRIBUTE'), the performance further increases to 41.92/80.17, outperforming the baseline model by 4.69/2.16 in terms of absolute improvement and 12.60/2.77 in terms of relative improvement. The improvement is just general to backbone networks. This manifests that both of the two information propagation paths are effective and complementary to each other. Also note that our location-sensitive mask generation strategy plays a key role for our high performance. Method denoted as '(compact)' means compact masks are generated with size $H \times W$ instead of the over-completed ones with doubled size, ignoring the relative location information. The performance is higher if the relative location is taken into account. However, the 'compact' method outperforms the 'non-local' method, which also indicates that the long-range dependency adaptively learned from the feature map as we propose is better than that calculated from the feature correlation.

Method Comparison. We show the comparison between our method and others in Table 2. With the same network backbone, PSANet gets higher performance than those of RefineNet [21] and PSPNet [45]. PSANet50 even outperforms RefineNet with much deeper ResNet-152 as the backbone. It is slightly better than WiderNet [41] that uses a powerful backbone called Wider ResNet.

Visual Improvements. We show the visual comparison of the parsing results in Fig. 5. PSANet much improves the segmentation quality, where more accurate and detailed predictions are generated compared to the one without the PSA module. We include more visual comparisons between PSANet and other approaches in the supplementary material.

4.3 PASCAL VOC 2012

PASCAL VOC 2012 segmentation dataset [9] is for object-centric segmentation and contains 20 object classes and one background. Following prior works

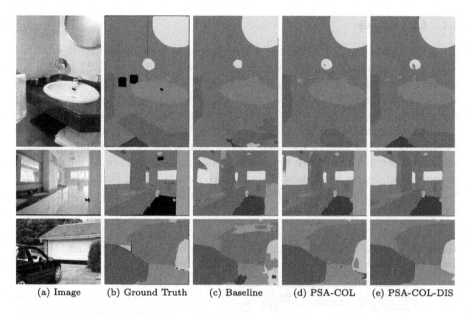

(a) Image   (b) Ground Truth   (c) Baseline   (d) PSA-COL   (e) PSA-COL-DIS

Fig. 5. Visual improvement on *validation* set of ADE20K. The proposed PSANet gets more accurate and detailed parsing results. 'PSA-COL' denotes PSANet with 'COL-LECT' branch and 'PSA-COL-DIS' stands for bi-direction information flow mode, which further enhances the prediction.

Table 4. Improvements introduced by PSA module. Results are reported with models trained on *train_aug* set and evaluated on *val* set of VOC 2012.

Method	Mean IoU(%) / Pixle Acc.(%) SS	MS
Res50-Baseline	67.12/92.83	67.57/92.98
+COL	76.96/94.79	78.00/95.01
+COL+DIS	77.24/94.88	78.14/95.12
Res101-Baseline	70.64/93.82	71.22/93.95
+COL	77.90/95.02	79.07/95.32
+COL+DIS	78.51/95.18	79.77/95.43

Table 5. Improvements introduced by PSA module. Results are reported with models trained on *fine_train* set and evaluated on *fine_val* set of Cityscapes.

Method	Mean IoU(%) / Pixle Acc.(%) SS	MS
Res50-Baseline	71.93/95.53	72.99/95.76
+COL	76.51/95.95	77.50/96.15
+COL+DIS	76.65/95.99	77.79/96.24
Res101-Baseline	74.83/96.03	75.89/96.23
+COL	77.06/96.18	78.05/96.39
+COL+DIS	77.94/96.10	79.05/96.30

[4,5,45], we utilize the augmented annotations from [12] resulting 10,582, 1,449 and 1,456 images for training, validation and testing. Our introduced PSA module is also very effective for object segmentation as shown in Table 4. It boosts the performance greatly, exceeding the baseline by a large margin.

Following methods of [4–6,45], we also pre-train on the MS-COCO [23] dataset and then finely tune the system on the VOC dataset. Table 3 lists the performance of different frameworks on VOC 2012 test set – PSANet achieves top performance. Visual improvement is clear as shown in the supplementary material. Similarly, better prediction is yielded with PSA module incorporated.

4.4   Cityscapes

Cityscapes dataset [8] is collected for urban scene understanding. It contains 5,000 finely annotated images divided into 2,975, 500, and 1,525 images for training, validation and testing. 30 common classes of road, person, car, etc. are annotated and 19 of them are used for semantic segmentation evaluation. Besides, another 20,000 coarsely annotated images are also provided.

We first show the improvement brought by our PSA module based on the baseline method in Table 5 and then list the comparison between different methods on test set in Table 6 with two settings, *i.e.*, training with only *fine* data and training with *coarse+fine* data. PSANet achieves the best performance under both settings. Several visual predictions are included in the supplementary material.

Table 6. Methods comparison with results reported on Cityscapes *test* set. Methods trained using both *fine* and *coarse* data are marked with †.

Method	mIoU(%)
DeepLabv2 [5]	70.4
LC [20]	71.1
Adelaide [22]	71.6
FRRN [32]	71.8
RefineNet [21]	73.6
PEARL [16]	75.4
DUC_HDC [39]	77.6
SAC [43]	78.1
PSPNet^a [45]	78.4
ResNet-38 [41]	78.5
SegModel [34]	78.5
Multitask Learning [17]	78.5
PSANet^a	78.6
PSANet^b	80.1

Method	mIoU(%)
LRR-4x† [11]	71.8
SegModel† [34]	79.2
DUC_HDC† [39]	80.1
Netwarp† [10]	80.5
ResNet-38† [41]	80.6
PSPNet† [45]	81.2
DeepLabv3† [6]	81.3
PSANet†	81.4

^{a} Trained with *fine_train* set only
^{b} Trained with *fine_train* + *fine_val* set

4.5   Mask Visualization

To get a deeper understanding of our PSA module, we visualize the learned attention masks as shown in Fig. 6. The images are from the validation set of ADE20k. For each input image, we show masks at two points (red and blue ones), denoted as the red and blue ones. For each point, we show the mask generated by both 'COLLECT' and 'DISTRIBUTE' branches. We find that attention masks pay low attention at the current position. This is reasonable because the aggregated feature representation is concatenated with the original local feature, which already contains local information.

We find that our attention mask effectively focuses on related regions for better performance. For example in the first row, the mask for the red point, which locates on the beach, assigned a larger weight to the sea and beach which

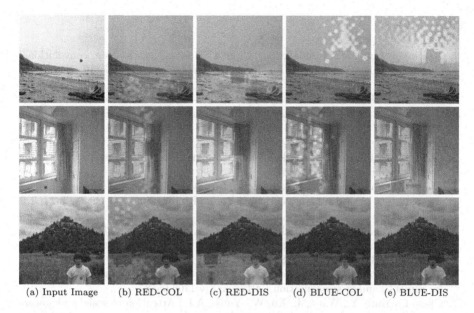

(a) Input Image   (b) RED-COL   (c) RED-DIS   (d) BLUE-COL   (e) BLUE-DIS

Fig. 6. Visualization of learned masks by PSANet. Masks are sensitive to location and category information that harvest different contextual information. (Color figure online)

is beneficial to the prediction of red point. While the attention mask for the blue point in the sky assigns a higher weight to other sky regions. A similar trend is also spotted in other images.

The visualized masks confirm the design intuition of our module, in which each position gather informative contextual information from regions both nearby and far away for better prediction.

5   Concluding Remarks

We have presented the PSA module for scene parsing. It adaptively predicts two global attention maps for each position in the feature map by convolutional layers. Position-specific bi-directional information propagation is enabled for better performance. By aggregating information with the global attention maps, long-range contextual information is effectively captured. Extensive experiments with top ranking scene parsing performance on three challenging datasets demonstrate the effectiveness and generality of the proposed approach. We believe the proposed module can advance related techniques in the community.

Acknowledgments. This work is partially supported by The Early Career Scheme (ECS) of Hong Kong (No. 24204215). We thank Sensetime Research for providing computing resources.

References

1. Badrinarayanan, V., Kendall, A., Cipolla, R.: SegNet: a deep convolutional encoder-decoder architecture for image segmentation. TPAMI **39**, 2481–2495 (2017)
2. Chandra, S., Kokkinos, I.: Fast, exact and multi-scale inference for semantic image segmentation with deep Gaussian CRFs. In: Leibe, B., Matas, J., Sebe, N., Welling, M. (eds.) ECCV 2016. LNCS, vol. 9911, pp. 402–418. Springer, Cham (2016). https://doi.org/10.1007/978-3-319-46478-7_25
3. Chandra, S., Usunier, N., Kokkinos, I.: Dense and low-rank Gaussian CRFs using deep embeddings. In: ICCV (2017)
4. Chen, L., Papandreou, G., Kokkinos, I., Murphy, K., Yuille, A.L.: Semantic image segmentation with deep convolutional nets and fully connected CRFs. In: ICLR (2015)
5. Chen, L., Papandreou, G., Kokkinos, I., Murphy, K., Yuille, A.L.: DeepLab: semantic image segmentation with deep convolutional nets, atrous convolution, and fully connected CRFs. TPAMI **40**, 834–848 (2018)
6. Chen, L.C., Papandreou, G., Schroff, F., Adam, H.: Rethinking atrous convolution for semantic image segmentation (2017). arXiv:1706.05587
7. Chen, L., Yang, Y., Wang, J., Xu, W., Yuille, A.L.: Attention to scale: scale-aware semantic image segmentation. In: CVPR (2016)
8. Cordts, M., et al.: The cityscapes dataset for semantic urban scene understanding. In: CVPR (2016)
9. Everingham, M., Gool, L.J.V., Williams, C.K.I., Winn, J.M., Zisserman, A.: The Pascal visual object classes VOC challenge. IJCV **88**, 303–338 (2010)
10. Gadde, R., Jampani, V., Gehler, P.V.: Semantic video CNNs through representation warping. In: ICCV (2017)
11. Ghiasi, G., Fowlkes, C.C.: Laplacian pyramid reconstruction and refinement for semantic segmentation. In: Leibe, B., Matas, J., Sebe, N., Welling, M. (eds.) ECCV 2016. LNCS, vol. 9907, pp. 519–534. Springer, Cham (2016). https://doi.org/10.1007/978-3-319-46487-9_32
12. Hariharan, B., Arbelaez, P., Bourdev, L.D., Maji, S., Malik, J.: Semantic contours from inverse detectors. In: ICCV (2011)
13. He, K., Zhang, X., Ren, S., Sun, J.: Deep residual learning for image recognition. In: CVPR (2016)
14. Huang, G., Liu, Z., Weinberger, K.Q., van der Maaten, L.: Densely connected convolutional networks. In: CVPR (2017)
15. Jia, Y., et al.: Caffe: convolutional architecture for fast feature embedding. In: ACM MM (2014)
16. Jin, X., et al.: Video scene parsing with predictive feature learning. In: ICCV (2017)
17. Kendall, A., Gal, Y., Cipolla, R.: Multi-task learning using uncertainty to weigh losses for scene geometry and semantics. In: CVPR (2018)
18. Krähenbühl, P., Koltun, V.: Efficient inference in fully connected CRFs with Gaussian edge potentials. In: NIPS (2011)
19. Krizhevsky, A., Sutskever, I., Hinton, G.E.: Imagenet classification with deep convolutional neural networks. In: NIPS (2012)
20. Li, X., Liu, Z., Luo, P., Loy, C.C., Tang, X.: Not all pixels are equal: difficulty-aware semantic segmentation via deep layer cascade. In: CVPR (2017)

21. Lin, G., Milan, A., Shen, C., Reid, I.D.: RefineNet: multi-path refinement networks for high-resolution semantic segmentation. In: CVPR (2017)
22. Lin, G., Shen, C., Reid, I.D., van den Hengel, A.: Efficient piecewise training of deep structured models for semantic segmentation. In: CVPR (2016)
23. Lin, T.Y., et al.: Microsoft COCO: common objects in context. In: Fleet, D., Pajdla, T., Schiele, B., Tuytelaars, T. (eds.) ECCV 2014. LNCS, vol. 8693, pp. 740–755. Springer, Cham (2014). https://doi.org/10.1007/978-3-319-10602-1_48
24. Liu, W., Rabinovich, A., Berg, A.C.: ParseNet: looking wider to see better (2015). arXiv:1506.04579
25. Liu, Z., Li, X., Luo, P., Loy, C.C., Tang, X.: Semantic image segmentation via deep parsing network. In: ICCV (2015)
26. Long, J., Shelhamer, E., Darrell, T.: Fully convolutional networks for semantic segmentation. In: CVPR (2015)
27. Luo, W., Li, Y., Urtasun, R., Zemel, R.: Understanding the effective receptive field in deep convolutional neural networks. In: NIPS (2016)
28. Mnih, V., Heess, N., Graves, A., et al.: Recurrent models of visual attention. In: NIPS (2014)
29. Noh, H., Hong, S., Han, B.: Learning deconvolution network for semantic segmentation. In: ICCV (2015)
30. Paszke, A., Chaurasia, A., Kim, S., Culurciello, E.: ENet: a deep neural network architecture for real-time semantic segmentation (2016). arXiv:1606.02147
31. Peng, C., Zhang, X., Yu, G., Luo, G., Sun, J.: Large kernel matters-improve semantic segmentation by global convolutional network. In: CVPR (2017)
32. Pohlen, T., Hermans, A., Mathias, M., Leibe, B.: Full-resolution residual networks for semantic segmentation in street scenes. In: CVPR (2017)
33. Ronneberger, O., Fischer, P., Brox, T.: U-Net: convolutional networks for biomedical image segmentation. In: Navab, N., Hornegger, J., Wells, W.M., Frangi, A.F. (eds.) MICCAI 2015. LNCS, vol. 9351, pp. 234–241. Springer, Cham (2015). https://doi.org/10.1007/978-3-319-24574-4_28
34. Shen, F., Gan, R., Yan, S., Zeng, G.: Semantic segmentation via structured patch prediction, context CRF and guidance CRF. In: CVPR (2017)
35. Simonyan, K., Zisserman, A.: Very deep convolutional networks for large-scale image recognition. In: ICLR (2015)
36. Szegedy, C., et al.: Going deeper with convolutions. In: CVPR (2015)
37. Vaswani, A., et al.: Attention is all you need. In: NIPS (2017)
38. Visin, F., et al.: ReSeg: a recurrent neural network-based model for semantic segmentation. In: CVPR Workshop (2016)
39. Wang, P., et al.: Understanding convolution for semantic segmentation. In: WACV (2018)
40. Wang, X., Girshick, R., Gupta, A., He, K.: Non-local neural networks. In: CVPR (2018)
41. Wu, Z., Shen, C., van den Hengel, A.: Wider or deeper: revisiting the ResNet model for visual recognition (2016). arXiv:1611.10080
42. Yu, F., Koltun, V.: Multi-scale context aggregation by dilated convolutions. In: ICLR (2016)
43. Zhang, R., Tang, S., Zhang, Y., Li, J., Yan, S.: Scale-adaptive convolutions for scene parsing. In: ICCV (2017)
44. Zhao, H., Qi, X., Shen, X., Shi, J., Jia, J.: ICNet for real-time semantic segmentation on high-resolution images. In: ECCV (2018)
45. Zhao, H., Shi, J., Qi, X., Wang, X., Jia, J.: Pyramid scene parsing network. In: CVPR (2017)

46. Zheng, S., et al.: Conditional random fields as recurrent neural networks. In: ICCV (2015)
47. Zhou, B., Khosla, A., Lapedriza, À., Oliva, A., Torralba, A.: Object detectors emerge in deep scene CNNs. In: ICLR (2015)
48. Zhou, B., Zhao, H., Puig, X., Fidler, S., Barriuso, A., Torralba, A.: Scene parsing through ADE20K dataset. In: CVPR (2017)

Repeatability Is Not Enough: Learning Affine Regions via Discriminability

Dmytro Mishkin[✉], Filip Radenović, and Jiři Matas

Visual Recognition Group, Center for Machine Perception, FEE,
CTU in Prague, Prague, Czech Republic
{mishkdmy,filip.radenovic,matas}@cmp.felk.cvut.cz

Abstract. A method for learning local affine-covariant regions is presented. We show that maximizing geometric repeatability does not lead to local regions, a.k.a features, that are reliably matched and this necessitates descriptor-based learning. We explore factors that influence such learning and registration: the loss function, descriptor type, geometric parametrization and the trade-off between matchability and geometric accuracy and propose a novel hard negative-constant loss function for learning of affine regions. The affine shape estimator – AffNet – trained with the hard negative-constant loss outperforms the state-of-the-art in bag-of-words image retrieval and wide baseline stereo. The proposed training process does not require precisely geometrically aligned patches. The source codes and trained weights are available at https://github.com/ducha-aiki/affnet.

Keywords: Local features · Affine shape · Loss function
Image retrieval

1 Introduction

Local features, forming correspondences, are exploited in state of the art pipelines for 3D reconstruction [1,2], two-view matching [3], 6DOF image localization [4]. Classical local features have also been successfully used for providing supervision for CNN-based image retrieval [5].

Affine-convariance [6] is a desirable property of local features since it allows robust matching of images separated by a wide baseline [3,7], unlike scale-covariant features like ORB [8] or difference of Gaussian (DoG) [9] that rely on tests carried out on circular neighborhoods. This is the reason why the Hessian-Affine detector [6] combined with the RootSIFT descriptor [9,10] is the gold standard for local feature in image retrieval [11,12]. Affine covariant features also provide stronger geometric constraints, e.g., for image rectification [13].

On the other hand, the classical affine adaptation procedure [14] fails in 20%–40% [7,15] cases, thus reducing the number and repeatability of detected local

© Springer Nature Switzerland AG 2018
V. Ferrari et al. (Eds.): ECCV 2018, LNCS 11213, pp. 287–304, 2018.
https://doi.org/10.1007/978-3-030-01240-3_18

features. It is also not robust to significant illumination change [15]. Applications where the number of detected features is important, *e.g.*, large scale 3D reconstruction [2], therefore use the DoG detector. Alleviating the problem of the drop in the number of correspondences caused by the non-repeatability of the affine adaptation procedure, may lead to connected 3D reconstructions and improved image retrieval engines [16,18].

This paper makes four contributions towards robust estimation of the local affine shape. First, we experimentally show that geometric repeatability of a local feature is not a sufficient condition for successful matching. The learning of affine shape increases the number of corrected matches if it steers the estimators towards discriminative regions and therefore must involve optimization of a descriptor-related loss.

Second, we propose a novel loss function for descriptor-based registration and learning, named the *hard negative-constant loss*. It combines the advantages of the triplet and contrastive positive losses. Third, we propose a method for learning the affine shape, orientation and potentially other parameters related to geometric and appearance properties of local features. The learning method does not require a precise ground truth which reduces the need for manual annotation.

Last but not least, the learned AffNet itself significantly outperforms prior methods for affine shape estimation and improves the state of art in image retrieval by a large margin. Importantly, unlike the de-facto standard [14], AffNet does not significantly reduce the number of detected features, it is thus suitable even for pipelines where affine invariance is needed only occasionally.

1.1   Related Work

The area of learning local features has been active recently, but the attention has focused dominantly on learning descriptors [19–25] and translation-covariant detectors [26–29]. The authors are not aware of any recent work on learning or improvement of local feature affine shape estimation. The most closely related work is thus the following.

Hartmann *et al.* [30] train random forest classifier for predicting feature matchability based on a local descriptor. "Bad" points are discarded, thus speeding up the matching process in a 3D reconstruction pipeline. Yi *et al.* [31] proposed to learn feature orientation by minimizing descriptor distance between positive patches, i.e. those corresponding to the same point on the 3D surface. This allows to avoid hand-picking a "canonical" orientation, thus learning the one which is the most suitable for descriptor matching. We have observed that direct application of the method [31] for affine shape estimation leads to learning degenerate shapes collapsed to single line. Yi *et al.* [32] proposed a multi-stage framework for learning the descriptor, orientation and translation-covariant detector. The detector was trained by maximizing the intersection-over-union and the reprojection error between corresponding regions.

Lenc and Vedaldi [28] introduced the "covariant constraint" for learning various types of local feature detectors. The proposed covariant loss is the Frobenius norm of the difference between the local affine frames. The disadvantage of such approach is that it could lead to features that are, while being repeatable, not necessarily suited for the matching task (see Sect. 2.2). On top of that, the common drawback of the Yi *et al.* [32] and Lenc and Vedaldi [28] methods is that they require to know the exact geometric relationship between patches which increases the amount of work needed to prepare the training dataset. Zhang *et al.* [27] proposed to "anchor" the detected features to some pre-defined features with known good discriminability like TILDE [26]. We remark that despite showing images of affine-covariant features, the results presented in the paper are for translation-covariant features only. Savinov *et al.* [29] proposed a ranking approach for unsupervised learning of a feature detector. While this is natural and efficient for learning the coordinates of the center of the feature, it is problematic to apply it for the affine shape estimation. The reason is that it requires sampling and scoring of many possible shapes.

Finally, Choy *et al.* [33] trained a "Universal correspondence network" (UCN) for a direct correspondence estimation with contrastive loss on a patch descriptor distance. This approach is related to the current work, yet the two methods differ in several important aspects. First, UCN used an ImageNet-pretrained network which is subsequently fine-tuned. We learn the affine shape estimation from scratch. Second, UCN uses dense feature extraction and negative examples extracted from the same image. While this could be a good setup for short baseline stereo, it does not work well for wide baseline, where affine features are usually sought. Finally, we propose the hard negative-constant loss instead of the contrastive one.

2   Learning Affine Shape and Orientation

2.1   Affine Shape Parametrization

A local affine frame is defined by 6 parameters of the affine matrix. Two form a translation vector (x, y) which is given by the keypoint detector and in the rest of the paper we omit it and focus on the *affine transformation* matrix A,

$$A = \begin{pmatrix} a_{11} & a_{12} \\ a_{21} & a_{22} \end{pmatrix}. \tag{1}$$

Among many possible decompositions of matrix A, we use the following

$$A = \lambda R(\alpha) A' = \det A \begin{pmatrix} \cos\alpha & \sin\alpha \\ -\sin\alpha & \cos\alpha \end{pmatrix} \begin{pmatrix} a'_{11} & 0 \\ a'_{21} & a'_{22} \end{pmatrix}, \tag{2}$$

where $\lambda = \det A$ is the scale, $R(\alpha)$ the *orientation* matrix and A'^1 is the *affine shape* matrix with $\det A' = 1$. A' is decomposed into identity matrix I and *residual shape* A'':

$$A' = I + A'' = \begin{pmatrix} a'_{11} & 0 \\ a'_{21} & a'_{22} \end{pmatrix} = \begin{pmatrix} 1 & 0 \\ 0 & 1 \end{pmatrix} + \begin{pmatrix} a''_{11} & 0 \\ a''_{21} & a''_{22} \end{pmatrix} \tag{3}$$

---

[1] A' has a (0,1) eigenvector, preserving the vertical direction.

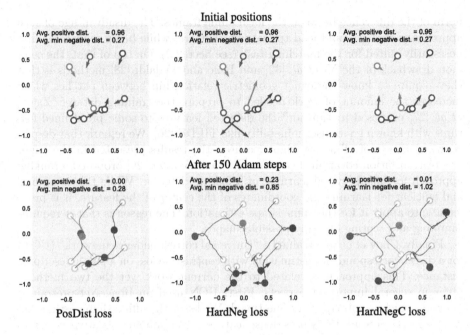

Fig. 1. A toy example optimization problem illustrating the proposed hard negative-constant (HardNegC) loss. Five pairs of points, representing 2D descriptors, are generated and the losses are minimized by Adam [34]: the positive descriptor distance (PosDist) [31] – left, the hard negative (HardNeg) margin loss [23] – center, HardNegC– right. Top row: identical initial positions of five pairs of matching points. Arrows show the gradient direction and relative magnitude. Bottom row: points after 150 steps of Adam optimization, trajectories are shown by dots. HardNeg loss has a difficulty with the green and magenta point pairs, because the negative example lies between two positives. Minimization of the positive distance only leads to a small distance to the negative examples. The proposed HardNegC loss first pushes same class points close to each other and then distributes them to increase distance to the negative pairs.

We show that the different parameterizations of the affine transformation significantly influence the performance of CNN-based estimators of local geometry, see Table 2.

2.2   The Hard Negative-Constant Loss

We propose a loss function called hard negative-constant loss (HardNegC). It is based on the hard negative triplet margin loss [23] (HardNeg), but the distance to the hardest (i.e. closest) negative example is treated as constant and the respective derivative of L is set to zero:

$$L = \frac{1}{n} \sum_{i=1,n} \max\left(0, 1 + d(s_i, \dot{s}_i) - d(s_i, N)\right), \quad \frac{\partial L}{\partial N} := 0, \qquad (4)$$

where $d(s_i, \dot{s}_i)$ is the distance between the matching descriptors, $d(s_i, N)$ is a distance to the hardest negative example N in the mini-batch for i^{th} pair.

$$d(s_i, N) = \min\left(\min_{j \neq i} d(s_i, \dot{s}_j), \min_{j \neq i} d(s_j, \dot{s}_i)\right)$$

The difference between the Positive descriptor distance loss (PosDist) used for learning local feature orientation in [31] and the HardNegC and HardNeg losses is shown on a toy example in Fig. 1. Five pairs of points in the 2D space are generated and their positions are updated by the Adam optimizer [34] for the three loss functions. PosDist converges the first, but the different class points end up near each other, because the distance to the negative classes is not incorporated in the loss. The HardNeg margin loss has trouble when the points from different classes lie between each other. The HardNegC loss behavior first resembles the PosDist loss, bringing positive points together and then distributes them in the space, satisfying the triplet margin criterion.

2.3   Descriptor Losses for Shape Registration

Exploring how local feature repeatability is connected with descriptor similarity, we conducted an shape registration experiment (Fig. 2). Hessian features are detected in reference HSequences [35] illumination images and reprojected by (identity) homography to another image in the sequence. Thus, the repeatability is 1 and reprojection error is 0. Then, the local descriptors (HardNet [23], SIFT [9], TFeat [21] and raw pixels) are extracted and features are matched by first-to-second-nearest neighbor ratio [9] with threshold 0.8. This threshold was suggested by Lowe [9] as a good trade-off between false positives and false negatives. For SIFT, 22% of the geometrically correct correspondences are not the nearest SIFTs and they cannot be matched, regardless of the threshold. In our experiments, the 0.8 threshold worked well for all descriptors and we used it, in line with previous papers, in all experiments.

Notice that for all descriptors, the percentage of correct matches even for the *perfect* geometrical registration is only about 50%.

Adam optimizer is used to update affine region A to minimize the descriptor-based losses: PosDist, HardNeg and HardNegC. The top two rows show the results for A matrices coupled for both images, bottom – the descriptor difference optimization is allowed to deform A and $\dot{A}$ in both images independently, which leads to a pair of affine regions that are not in perfect geometric correspondence, yet they are more matchable. Note, that no training of any kind is involved.

Such descriptor-driven optimization, not maintaining perfect registration, produces a descriptor that is matched successfully up to 90% of the detections under illumination changes.

For most of the unmatched regions, the affine shapes become a degenerate lines – shown in top graphs, and the number of degenerate ellipses is high for PosDist loss; HardNeg and HardNegC perform better.

The bottom row of Fig. 2 shows results for experiments where affine shapes pairs are independent in each image. Optimization of descriptor losses lead to an increase of the geometric error on the affine shape. Error E is defined as the mean square error on A matrix difference:

$$E = \sum_{i=1}^{n} \frac{2(A_i - \dot{A}_i)^2}{\det A + \det \dot{A}} \tag{5}$$

Again, PosDist loss leads to a larger error. CNN-based descriptors, HardNet and TFeat lead to relative small geometric error when reaching matchability plateau, while for SIFT and raw pixels the shapes diverge. Figure 3 shows the case when the initialized shapes include a small amount of the reprojection error.

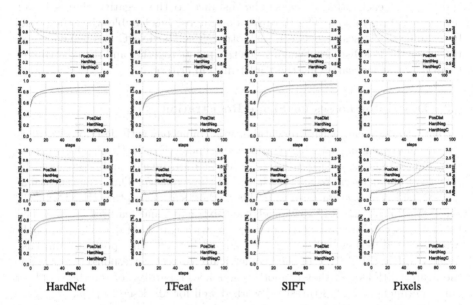

| HardNet | TFeat | SIFT | Pixels |

Fig. 2. Matching score versus geometric repeatability experiment. Affine shape registration by a minimization of descriptor losses of corresponding features. Descriptor losses: green – L2- descriptor distance (PosDist) [31], red – hard triplet margin Hard-Neg [23], blue – proposed HardNegC. Average over HSequences, illumination subset. *All features are initially perfectly registered.* First two rows: single feature geometry for both images, second two rows: feature geometries are independent in each image. Top row: geometric error of corresponding features (solid) and percentage of non-collapsed, i.e. elongation ≤ 6, features (dashed). Bottom row: the percentage of correct matches. This experiment shows that even perfectly initially registered feature might not be matched with any of descriptors – initial matching score is roughly ≈30...50%. But it is possibly to find measurement region, which offers both discriminativity and repeatability. PosDist loss squashes most of the features, leading to the largest geometrical error. HardNeg loss produces the best results in the number of survived feature and geometrical error. HardNegC performs slightly worse than HardNeg, slightly outperforming it on matching score. However, HardNegC is easier to optimize for AffNet learning – see Table 1. (Color figure online)

2.4 AffNet Training Procedure

The main blocks of the proposed training procedure are shown in Fig. 5. First, a batch of matching patch pairs $(P_i, \dot{P}_i)_{i=1..n}$ is generated, where P_i and $\dot{P}_i$ correspond to the same point on a 3D surface. Rotation and skew transformation matrices (T_i, T'_i) are randomly and independently generated. The patches P_i and $\dot{P}_i$ are warped by $(T_i, \dot{P}_i)$ respectively into A-transformed patches. Then, a 32×32 center patch is cropped and a pair of transformed patches is fed into the convolutional neural network AffNet, which predicts a pair of affine transformations $A_i, \dot{P}_i$, that are applied to the T_i-transformed patches via spatial transformers ST [36].

Thus, geometrically normalized patches are cropped to 32×32 pixels and fed into the descriptor network, e.g. HardNet, SIFT or raw patch pixels, obtaining descriptors $(s_i, \dot{s}_i)$. Descriptors $(s_i, \dot{s}_i)$ are then used to form triplets by the procedure proposed in [23], followed by our newly proposed hard negative-constant loss (Eq. 4).

More formally, we are finding affine transformation model parameters θ such that estimated affine transformation A minimizes descriptor HardNegC loss:

$$A(\theta|(P, \dot{P})) = \arg \min_{\theta} L(s, \dot{s}) \qquad (6)$$

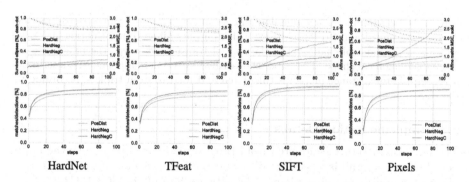

Fig. 3. Minimization of descriptor loss by optimization of affine parameters of corresponding features. Average over HPatchesSeq, illumination subset. Top row: geometric error of corresponding features (full line) and percentage of non-collapsed, *i.e.* elongation ≤ 6, features (dashed line). Bottom row: the fraction correct matches. All features initially have the same medium amount of reprojection noise. Left to right: HardNet, SIFT, TFeat, mean-normalized pixels descriptors.

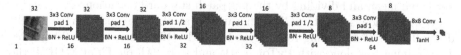

Fig. 4. AffNet. Feature map spatial size – top, # channels – bottom. /2 stands for stride 2.

2.5   Training Dataset and Data Preprocessing

UBC Phototour [37] dataset is used for training. It consists of three subsets: *Liberty, Notre Dame* and *Yosemite* with about $2 \times 400\text{k}$ normalized 64×64 patches in each, detected by DoG and Harris detectors. Patches are verified by 3D reconstruction model. We randomly sample 10M pairs for training.

Although positive point corresponds to roughly the same point on the 3D surface, they are not perfectly aligned, having position, scale, rotation and affine noise. We have randomly generated affine transformations, which consist in random rotation – tied for pair of corresponding patches, and anisotropic scaling t in random direction by magnitude t_m, which is gradually increased during the training from the initial value of 3 to 5.8 at the middle of the training. The tilt is uniformly sampled from range $[0, t_m]$.

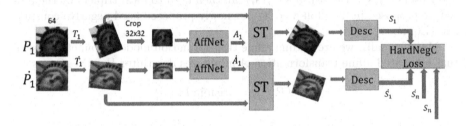

Fig. 5. AffNet training. Corresponding patches undergo random affine transformation $T_i, \dot{T}_i$, are cropped and fed into AffNet, which outputs affine transformation $A_i, \dot{A}_i$ to an unknown canonical shape. ST – the spatial transformer warps the patch into an estimated canonical shape. The patch is described by a differentiable CNN descriptor. $n \times n$ descriptor distance matrix is calculated and used to form triplets, according to the HardNegC loss.

2.6   Implementation Details

The CNN architecture is adopted from HardNet [23], see Fig. 4, with the number of channels in all layers reduced 2x and the last 128D output replaced by a 3D output predicting ellipse shape. The network formula is 16C3-16C3-32C3/2-32C3-64C3/2-64C3-3C8, where 32C3/2 stands for 3x3 kernel with 32 filters and stride 2. Zero-padding is applied in all convolutional layers to preserve the size, except the last one. BatchNorm [38] layer followed by ReLU [39] is added after each convolutional layer, except the last one, which is followed by hyperbolic tangent activation. Dropout [40] with 0.25 rate is applied before the last convolution layer. Grayscale input patches 32×32 pixels are normalized by subtracting the per-patch mean and dividing by the per-patch standard deviation.

Optimization is done by SGD with learning rate 0.005, momentum 0.9, weight decay 0.0001. The learning rate decayed linearly [42] to zero within 20 epochs. The training was done with PyTorch [41] and took 24 h on Titan X GPU; the bottleneck is the data augmentation procedure. The inference time is 0.1 ms per patch on Titan X, including patch sampling done on CPU and Baumberg iteration – 0.05 ms per patch on CPU.

3   Empirical Evaluation

3.1   Loss Functions and Descriptors for Learning Measurement Region

We trained different versions of the AffNet and orientation networks, with different combinations affine transformation parameterizations and descriptors with the procedure described above. The results of the comparison based on the number of correct matches (reprojection error ≤ 3 pixel) on the hardest pair for each of the 116 sequences from the HSequences [35] dataset are shown in Tables 1 and 2.

The proposed HardNetC loss is the only loss function with no "not converged" results. In the case of convergence, all tested descriptors and loss functions lead to comparable performance, unlike registration experiments in the previous section. We believe it is because now the CNN always outputs the same affine transformation for a patch, unlike in the previous experiment, where repeated features may end up with different shapes.

Affine transformation parameterizations are compared in Table 2. All attempts to learn affine shape and orientation jointly in one network fail completely, or perform significantly worse than the two-stage procedure, when affine shape is learned first and orientation is estimated on an affine-shape-normalized patch. Learning residual shape A'' (Eq. 3) leads to the best results overall. Note, that such parameterization does not contain enough parameters to include feature orientation, thus "joint" learning is not possible. Slightly worse performance is obtained by using an identity matrix prior for learnable biases in the output layer.

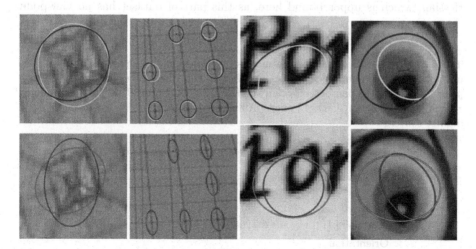

Fig. 6. AffNet (top) and Baumberg (bottom) estimated affine shape. One ellipse is detected in the reference image, the other is a reprojected closest match from the second image. Baumberg ellipses tend to be more elongated, average axis ratio is 1.99 vs. 1.63 for AffNet, median: Baumberg 1.72 vs 1.39 AffNet. The statistics are calculated over 16M features on Oxford5k.

3.2   Repeatability

Repeatability of affine detectors: Hessian detector + affine shape estimator was benchmarked, following classical work by Mikolajczyk *et al.* [7], but on recently introduced larger HSequences [35] dataset by VLBenchmarks toolbox [43].

HSequences consists of two subsets. *Illumination* part contains 57 image sixplets with illumination changes, both natural and artificial. There is no difference is viewpoint in this subset, geometrical relation between images in sixplets is identity.Second part is *Viewpoint*, where 59 image sixplets vary in scale, rotation, but mostly in horizontal tilt. The average viewpoint change is a bit smaller than in well-known *graffiti* sequence from Oxford-Affine dataset [7].

Local features are detected in pairs of images, reprojected by ground truth homography to the reference image and closest reprojected region is found for each region from reference image. The correspondence is considered correct, when overlap error of the pair is less than 40%. The repeatability score for a given pair of images is a ratio between number of correct correspondences and the smaller number of detected regions in common part of scene among two images.

Results are shown in Fig. 7. Original affine shape estimation procedure, implemented in [11] is denoted Baum SS 19, as 19×19 patches are sampled from scale space. AffNet takes 32×32 patches, which are sampled from original image. So for fair comparison, we also tested Baum versions, where patches are sampled from original image, with 19 and 33 pixels patch size.

AffNet slightly outperforms all the variants of Baumberg procedure for images with viewpoint change in terms of repeatability and more significant – in number of correspondences. The difference is even bigger for them image with illumination change only, where AffNet performs almost the same as plain Hessian, which is upper bound here, as this part of dataset has no viewpoint changes.

Table 1. Learning the affine transform: loss functions and descriptor comparison. The median of average number of correct matches on the HSequences [35] hardest image pairs 1–6 for the Hessian detector and the HardNet descriptor. The match considered correct for reprojection error ≤ 3 pixels. Affine shape is parametrized as in Eq. 3. n/c – did not converge.

Training descriptor/loss	PosDist	HardNeg	HardNegC
Affine shape			
SIFT	n/c	385	386
HardNet	n/c	n/c	**388**
Baumberg [14]	298		
Orientation			
SIFT	**387**	379	382
HardNet	386	383	380
Dominant orientation [9]	339		

We have also tested AffNet with other detectors on the Viewpoint subset of the HPatches. The repeatabilities are the following (no affine adaptation/Baumberg/AffNet): DoG: 0.46/0.51/0.52, Harris: 0.41/0.44/0.47, Hessian: 0.47/0.52/0.56 The proposed methods outperforms the standard (Baumberg) for all detectors.

One reason for such difference is the feature-rejection strategy. Baumberg iterative procedure rejects feature in one of three cases. First, elongated ellipses with long-to-short axis ratio more than six are rejected. Second, features touching boundary of the image are rejected. This is true for the AffNet post-processing procedure as well, but AffNet produces less elongated shapes: average axis ratio on Oxford5k 16M features is 1.63 vs. 1.99 for Baumberg. Both cases happen less often for AffNet, increasing the number of surviving features by 25%.

Table 2. Learning the affine transform: parameterization comparison. The average number of correct matches on the HPatchesSeq [35] hardest image pairs 1–6 for the Hessian detector and the HardNet descriptor. Cases compared, affine shape combined with the de-facto handcrafted standard dominant orientation, affine shape and orientation learnt separately or jointly. The match considered correct for reprojection error ≤ 3 pixels. The HardNegC loss and HardNet descriptor used for learning. n/c – did not converge.

Eq.	Matrix	Estimated parameters		Orientation		
			Biases	Learned		Dominant
			init	Jointly	Separately	gradient [9]
(1)	A	$(a_{11}, a_{12}, a_{21}, a_{22})$	0	n/c	n/c	n/c
(1)	A	$(a_{11}, a_{12}, a_{21}, a_{22})$	1	n/c	360	320
(2)	A', $R(\alpha)$	$(a'_{11}, 0, a'_{21}, a'_{22})$, $(\sin\alpha, \cos\alpha)$	1	250	327	286
(3)	A''	$(a''_{11}, a''_{21}, a''_{22})$	1	-	370	340
(3)	A''	$(1 + a''_{11}, a''_{21}, 1 + a''_{22})$	0	-	**388**	349

Table 3. AffNet vs. Baumberg affine shape estimators on wide baseline stereo datasets, with Hessian and adaptive Hessian detectors, following the protocol [15]. The number of matched image pairs and the average number of inliers. The ⎡numbers⎤ of image pairs in a dataset are boxed. Best results are in **bold**.

Detector	EF [44]		EVD [3]		OxAff [7]		SymB [45]		GDB [46]		LTLL [47]	
	33	inl.	15	inl.	40	inl.	46	inl.	22	inl.	172	inl.
HesAff [6]	**33**	78	2	38	**40**	1008	34	153	17	199	26	34
HesAffNet	**33**	112	2	48	**40**	1181	**37**	203	19	222	46	36
AdHesAff [15]	**33**	111	3	33	**40**	1330	35	190	19	286	28	35
AdHesAffNet	**33**	**165**	**4**	**42**	**40**	**1567**	**37**	**275**	**21**	**336**	**48**	**39**

We compared performance of the Baumberg vs. AffNet on the same number of features in Sect. 3.4. Finally, features whose shape did not converge within sixteen iteration are removed. This is quite rare, it happens in approximately 1% cases. Example of shapes estimated by AffNet and the Baumberg procedure are shown in Fig. 6.

3.3   Wide Baseline Stereo

We conducted an experiment on wide baseline stereo, following local feature detector benchmark protocol, defined in [15] on the set of two-view matching datasets [44–47]. The local features are detected by benchmarked detector, described by HardNet++ [23] and HalfRootSIFT [48] and geometrically verified by RANSAC [49]. Two following metrics are reported: the number of successfully matched image pairs and average number of correct inliers per matched pair. We have replaced original affine shape estimator in Hessian-Affine with AffNet in Hessian and Adaptive threshold Hessian (AdHess).

The results are shown in Table 3. AffNet outperforms Baumberg in both number of registered image pairs and/or number of correct inliers in all datasets, including painting-to-photo pairs in SymB [45] and multimodal pairs in GDB [46], despite it was not trained for that domains.

The total runtimes per image are the following (average for 800×600 images). Baseline HesAff + dominant gradient orientation + SIFT: no CNN components – 0.4 s. HesAffNet (CNN) + dominant gradient orientation + SIFT – 0.8 s, 3 CNN components: HesAffNet + OriNet + HardNet – 1.2 s. Now the data is naively transferred from CPU to GPU and back each of the stages, which generates the major bottleneck.

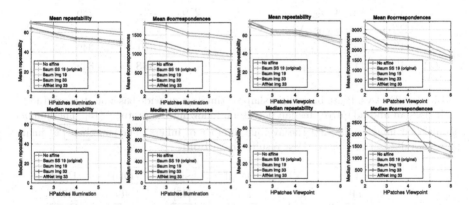

Fig. 7. Repeatability and the number of correspondences (mean top, median bottom row) on the HSequences [35]. AffNet is compared with the de facto standard Baumberg iteration [14] according to the Mikolajczyk protocol [7]. Left – images with illumination differences, right – with viewpoint and scale changes. SS – patch is sampled from the scale-space pyramid at the level of the detection, image – from the original image; 19 and 33 – patch sizes. Hessian-Affine is from [11]. For illumination subset, performance of Hessian with no adaptation is an upper bound, and AffNet performs close to it.

3.4   Image Retrieval

We evaluate the proposed approach on standard image retrieval datasets Oxford5k [54] and Paris6k [55]. Each dataset contains images (5062 for Oxford5k and 6391 for Paris6k) depicting 11 different landmarks and distractors. The performance is reported as mean average precision (mAP) [54]. Recently, these benchmarks have been revisited, annotation errors fixed and new, more challenging sets of queries added [17]. The revisited datasets define new test protocols: *Easy*, *Medium*, and *Hard*.

We use the multi-scale Hessian-affine detector [7] with the Baumberg method for affine shape estimation. The proposed AffNet replaces Baumberg, which we denote HessAffNet. The use of HessAffNet increased the number of used feature, from 12.5M to 17.5M for Oxford5k and from 15.6M to 21.2M for Paris6k, because more features survive the affine shape adaptions, as explained in Sect. 3.2. We also performed additional experiment by restricting number of AffNet features to same as in Baumberg – HesAffNetLess in Table 4. We evaluated HesAffNet

Table 4. Performance (mAP) evaluation of the bag-of-words (BoW) image retrieval on the Oxford5k and Paris6k benchmarks. Vocabulary consisting of 1M visual words is learned on independent dataset: Oxford5k vocabulary for Paris6k evaluation and *vice versa*. SV: spatial verification. QE(t): query expansion with t inliers threshold. The best results are in **bold**.

Detector–Descriptor	Oxford5k				Paris6k			
	BoW	+SV	+SV+QE(15)	+SV+QE(8)	BoW	+SV	+SV+QE(15)	+SV+QE(8)
HesAff–RootSIFT [10]	55.1	63.0	78.4	80.1	59.3	63.7	76.4	77.4
HesAffNet–RootSIFT	61.6	72.8	86.5	88.0	63.5	71.2	81.7	83.5
HesAff–TFeat-M* [21]	46.7	55.6	72.2	73.8	43.8	51.8	65.3	69.7
HesAffNet–TFeat-M*	45.5	57.3	75.2	77.5	50.6	58.1	72.0	74.8
HesAff–HardNet++ [23]	60.8	69.6	84.5	85.1	65.0	70.3	79.1	79.9
HesAffNetLess–HardNet++	64.3	73.3	86.1	87.3	62.0	68.7	79.1	79.2
HesAffNet–HardNet++	**68.3**	**77.8**	**89.0**	**91.1**	**65.7**	**73.4**	**83.3**	**83.3**

Table 5. Performance (mAP) comparison with the state-of-the-art in local feature-based image retrieval. Vocabulary is learned on independent dataset: Oxford5k vocabulary for Paris6k evaluation and *vice versa*. All results are with spatial verification and query expansion. VS: vocabulary size. SA: single assignment. MA: multiple assignments. The best results are in **bold**.

Method	VS	Oxford5k		Paris6k	
		SA	MA	SA	MA
HesAff–SIFT–BoW-fVocab [50]	16M	74.0	84.9	73.6	82.4
HesAff–RootSIFT–HQE [12]	65k	85.3	88.0	81.3	82.8
HesAff–HardNet++–HQE [23]	65k	86.8	88.3	82.8	84.9
HesAffNet–HardNet++–HQE	65k	**87.9**	**89.5**	**84.2**	**85.9**

Table 6. Performance (mAP, mP@10) comparison with the state-of-the-art in image retrieval on the R-Oxford and R-Paris benchmarks [17]. SV: spatial verification. HQE: hamming query expansion. αQE: α query expansion. DFS: global diffusion. The best results are in **bold**.

Method	Medium				Hard			
	R-Oxford		R-Paris		R-Oxford		R-Paris	
	mAP	mP@10	mAP	mP@10	mAP	mP@10	mAP	mP@10
ResNet101–GeM+αQE [51]	67.2	86.0	80.7	**98.9**	40.7	54.9	61.8	90.6
ResNet101–GeM[51]+DFS [52]	69.8	84.0	88.9	96.9	40.5	54.4	78.5	**94.6**
ResNet101–R-MAC[53]+DFS [52]	69.0	82.3	**89.5**	96.7	44.7	60.5	**80.0**	94.1
ResNet50–DELF[60]–HQE+SV	73.4	88.2	84.0	98.3	50.3	67.2	69.3	93.7
HesAff–RootSIFT–HQE [12]	66.3	85.6	68.9	97.3	41.3	60.0	44.7	79.9
HesAff–RootSIFT–HQE+SV [12]	71.3	88.1	70.2	98.6	49.7	69.6	45.1	83.9
HesAffNet–HardNet++–HQE	71.7	89.4	72.6	98.1	47.5	66.3	48.9	85.9
HesAffNet–HardNet++–HQE+SV	**75.2**	**90.9**	73.1	98.1	**53.3**	**72.6**	48.9	89.1

with both hand-crafted descriptor RootSIFT [10] and state-of-the-art learned descriptors [21,23].

First, HesAffNet is tested within the traditional bag-of-words (BoW) [56] image retrieval pipeline. A flat vocabulary with 1M centroids is created with the k-means algorithm and approximate nearest neighbor search [57]. All descriptors of an image are assigned to a respective centroid of the vocabulary, and then they are aggregated with a histogram of occurrences into a BoW image representation.

We also apply spatial verification (SV) [54] and standard query expansion (QE) [55]. QE is performed with images that have either 15 (typically used) or 8 inliers after the spatial verification. The results of the comparison are presented in Table 4.

AffNet achieves the best results on both Oxford5k and Paris6k datasets, in most of the cases it outperforms the second best approach by a large margin. This experiment clearly shows the benefit of using AffNet in the local feature detection pipeline.

Additionally, we compare with state-of-the-art local-feature-based image retrieval methods. A visual vocabulary of 65k words is learned, with Hamming embedding (HE) [58] technique added that further refines descriptor assignments with a 128 bits binary signature. We follow the same procedure as HesAff–RootSIFT–HQE [12] method. All parameters are set as in [12]. The performance of AffNet methods is the best reported on both Oxford5k and Paris6k for local features (Table 5).

Finally, on the revisited R-Oxford and R-Paris, we compare with state-of-the-art methods in image retrieval, both local and global feature based: the best-performing fine-tuned networks [59], ResNet101 with generalized-mean pooling (ResNet101–GeM) [51] and ResNet101 with regional maximum activations pooling (ResNet101–R-MAC) [53]. Deep methods use re-ranking methods: α query expansion (αQE) [51], and global diffusion (DFS) [52]. Results are in Table 6.

HesAffNet performs best on the R-Oxford. It is consistently the best performing local-feature method, yet is worse than deep methods on R-Paris. A possible explanation is that deep networks (ResNet and DELF) were finetuned from ImageNet, which contains Paris-related images, e.g. Sacre-Coeur and Notre Dame Basilica in the "church" category. Therefore global deep nets are partially evaluated on the training set.

4 Conclusions

We presented a method for learning affine shape of local features in a weakly-supervised manner. The proposed HardNegC loss function might find other application domains as well. Our intuition is that the distance to the hard-negative estimates the local density of all points and provides a scale for the positive distance. The resulting AffNet regressor bridges the gap between performance of the similarity-covariant and affine-covariant detectors on images with short baseline and big illumination differences and it improves performance of affine-covariant detectors in the wide baseline setup. AffNet applied to the output of the Hessian detector improves the state-of-the art in wide baseline matching, affine detector repeatability and image retrieval.

We experimentally show that descriptor matchability, not only repeatability should be taken into account when learning a feature detector.

Acknowledgements. The authors were supported by the Czech Science Foundation Project GACR P103/12/G084, the Austrian Ministry for Transport, Innovation and Technology, the Federal Ministry of Science, Research and Economy, and the Province of Upper Austria in the frame of the COMET center SCCH, the CTU student grant SGS17/185/OHK3/3T/13, and the MSMT LL1303 ERC-CZ grant.

References

1. Schonberger, J.L., Frahm, J.M.: Structure-from-motion revisited. In: Conference on Computer Vision and Pattern Recognition (CVPR), pp. 4104–4113 (2016)
2. Schonberger, J.L., Hardmeier, H., Sattler, T., Pollefeys, M.: Comparative evaluation of hand-crafted and learned local features. In: Conference on Computer Vision and Pattern Recognition (CVPR) (2017)
3. Mishkin, D., Matas, J., Perdoch, M.: Mods: Fast and robust method for two-view matching. Comput. Vis. Image Underst. **141**, 81–93 (2015)
4. Sattler, T., et al.: Benchmarking 6DOF Urban Visual Localization in Changing Conditions. ArXiv e-prints, July 2017
5. Radenović, F., Tolias, G., Chum, O.: CNN Image retrieval learns from BoW: unsupervised fine-tuning with hard examples. In: Leibe, B., Matas, J., Sebe, N., Welling, M. (eds.) ECCV 2016. LNCS, vol. 9905, pp. 3–20. Springer, Cham (2016). https://doi.org/10.1007/978-3-319-46448-0_1
6. Mikolajczyk, K., Schmid, C.: Scale and affine invariant interest point detectors. Int. J. Comput. Vis. (IJCV) **60**(1), 63–86 (2004)
7. Mikolajczyk, K., et al.: A comparison of affine region detectors. Int. J. Comput. Vis. (IJCV) **65**(1), 43–72 (2005)

8. Rublee, E., Rabaud, V., Konolige, K., Bradski, G.: ORB: an efficient alternative to SIFT or SURF. In: International Conference on Computer Vision (ICCV), pp. 2564–2571 (2011)

9. Lowe, D.G.: Distinctive image features from scale-invariant keypoints. Int. J. Comput. Vis. (IJCV) **60**(2), 91–110 (2004)

10. Arandjelovic, R., Zisserman, A.: Three things everyone should know to improve object retrieval. In: Conference on Computer Vision and Pattern Recognition (CVPR), pp. 2911–2918 (2012)

11. Perdoch, M., Chum, O., Matas, J.: Efficient representation of local geometry for large scale object retrieval. In: Conference on Computer Vision and Pattern Recognition (CVPR), pp. 9–16 (2009)

12. Tolias, G., Jegou, H.: Visual query expansion with or without geometry: refining local descriptors by feature aggregation. Pattern Recognit. **47**(10), 3466–3476 (2014)

13. Pritts, J., Kukelova, Z., Larsson, V., Chum, O.: Radially-distorted conjugate translations. In: CVPR (2018)

14. Baumberg, A.: Reliable feature matching across widely separated views. In: CVPR, pp. 1774–1781. IEEE Computer Society (2000)

15. Mishkin, D., Matas, J., Perdoch, M., Lenc, K.: Wxbs: wide baseline stereo generalizations. arXiv:1504.06603 (2015)

16. Schonberger, J.L., Radenovic, F., Chum, O., Frahm, J.M.: From single image query to detailed 3D reconstruction. In: Conference on Computer Vision and Pattern Recognition (CVPR), pp. 5126–5134 (2015)

17. Radenovic, F., Iscen, A., Tolias, G., Avrithis, Y., Chum, O.: Revisiting Oxford and Paris: large-scale image retrieval benchmarking. In: Conference on Computer Vision and Pattern Recognition (CVPR) (2018)

18. Radenovic, F., Schonberger, J.L., Ji, D., Frahm, J.M., Chum, O., Matas, J.: From dusk till dawn: modeling in the dark. In: Proceedings of the IEEE Conference on Computer Vision and Pattern Recognition, pp. 5488–5496 (2016)

19. Zagoruyko, S., Komodakis, N.: Learning to compare image patches via convolutional neural networks. In: Conference on Computer Vision and Pattern Recognition (CVPR) (2015)

20. Han, X., Leung, T., Jia, Y., Sukthankar, R., Berg, A.C.: MatchNet: unifying feature and metric learning for patch-based matching. In: Conference on Computer Vision and Pattern Recognition (CVPR), pp. 3279–3286 (2015)

21. Balntas, V., Riba, E., Ponsa, D., Mikolajczyk, K.: Learning local feature descriptors with triplets and shallow convolutional neural networks. In: British Machine Vision Conference (BMVC) (2016)

22. Tian, Y., Fan, B., Wu, F.: L2-net: deep learning of discriminative patch descriptor in euclidean space. In: Conference on Computer Vision and Pattern Recognition (CVPR) (2017)

23. Mishchuk, A., Mishkin, D., Radenovic, F., Matas, J.: Working hard to know your neighbor's margins: local descriptor learning loss. In: Proceedings of NIPS, December 2017

24. Zhang, X., Felix, X.Y., Kumar, S., Chang, S.F.: Learning spread-out local feature descriptors. ArXiv e-prints (August 2017)

25. Dosovitskiy, A., Fischer, P., Springenberg, J.T., Riedmiller, M.A., Brox, T.: Discriminative unsupervised feature learning with exemplar convolutional neural networks. IEEE Trans. Pattern Anal. Mach. Intell. **38**(9), 1734–1747 (2016)

26. Verdie, Y., Yi, K., Fua, P., Lepetit, V.: TILDE: a temporally invariant learned detector. In: Proceedings of the IEEE Conference on Computer Vision and Pattern Recognition, pp. 5279–5288 (2015)
27. Zhang, X., Felix, Y., Karaman, S., Chang, S.F.: Learning discriminative and transformation covariant local feature detectors. In: CVPR (2017)
28. Lenc, K., Vedaldi, A.: Learning covariant feature detectors. In: Hua, G., Jégou, H. (eds.) ECCV 2016. LNCS, vol. 9915, pp. 100–117. Springer, Cham (2016). https://doi.org/10.1007/978-3-319-49409-8_11
29. Savinov, N., Seki, A., Ladicky, L., Sattler, T., Pollefeys, M.: Quad-networks: unsupervised learning to rank for interest point detection. ArXiv e-prints, November 2016
30. Hartmann, W., Havlena, M., Schindler, K.: Predicting matchability. In: CVPR, pp. 9–16. IEEE Computer Society (2014)
31. Yi, K.M., Verdie, Y., Fua, P., Lepetit, V.: Learning to assign orientations to feature points. In: Proceedings of the Computer Vision and Pattern Recognition (2016)
32. Yi, K.M., Trulls, E., Lepetit, V., Fua, P.: LIFT: learned invariant feature transform. In: Leibe, B., Matas, J., Sebe, N., Welling, M. (eds.) ECCV 2016. LNCS, vol. 9910, pp. 467–483. Springer, Cham (2016). https://doi.org/10.1007/978-3-319-46466-4_28
33. Choy, C.B., Gwak, J., Savarese, S., Chandraker, M.: Universal correspondence network. In: Advances in Neural Information Processing Systems, pp. 2414–2422 (2016)
34. Kingma, D.P., Ba, J.: Adam: a method for stochastic optimization. In: ICLR (2015)
35. Balntas, V., Lenc, K., Vedaldi, A., Mikolajczyk, K.: HPatches: a benchmark and evaluation of handcrafted and learned local descriptors. In: Conference on Computer Vision and Pattern Recognition (CVPR) (2017)
36. Jaderberg, M., Simonyan, K., Zisserman, A., Kavukcuoglu, K.: Spatial transformer networks. ArXiv e-prints, June 2015
37. Brown, M., Lowe, D.G.: Automatic panoramic image stitching using invariant features. Int. J. Comput. Vis. (IJCV) **74**(1), 59–73 (2007)
38. Ioffe, S., Szegedy, C.: Batch normalization: accelerating deep network training by reducing internal covariate shift. arXiv:1502.03167 (2015)
39. Nair, V., Hinton, G.E.: Rectified linear units improve restricted Boltzmann machines. In: International Conference on Machine Learning (ICML), pp. 807–814 (2010)
40. Srivastava, N., Hinton, G.E., Krizhevsky, A., Sutskever, I., Salakhutdinov, R.: Dropout: a simple way to prevent neural networks from overfitting. J. Mach. Learn. Res. (JMLR) **15**(1), 1929–1958 (2014)
41. Paszke, A., et al.: Automatic differentiation in PyTorch. In: Proceedings of NIPS Workshop, December 2017
42. Mishkin, D., Sergievskiy, N., Matas, J.: Systematic evaluation of convolution neural network advances on the Imagenet. Comput. Vis. Image Underst. **161**, 11–19 (2017)
43. Lenc, K., Gulshan, V., Vedaldi, A.: Vlbenchmarks (2012)
44. Zitnick, C.L., Ramnath, K.: Edge foci interest points. In: International Conference on Computer Vision (ICCV), pp. 359–366 (2011)
45. Hauagge, D.C., Snavely, N.: Image matching using local symmetry features. In: Computer Vision and Pattern Recognition (CVPR), pp. 206–213 (2012)
46. Yang, G., Stewart, C.V., Sofka, M., Tsai, C.L.: Registration of challenging image pairs: initialization, estimation, and decision. Pattern Anal. Mach. Intell. (PAMI) **29**(11), 1973–1989 (2007)

47. Fernando, B., Tommasi, T., Tuytelaars, T.: Location recognition over large time lags. Comput. Vis. Image Underst. **139**, 21–28 (2015)

48. Kelman, A., Sofka, M., Stewart, C.V.: Keypoint descriptors for matching across multiple image modalities and non-linear intensity variations. In: CVPR (2007)

49. Lebeda, K., Matas, J., Chum, O.: Fixing the locally optimized RANSAC. In: BMVC (2012)

50. Mikulik, A., Perdoch, M., Chum, O., Matas, J.: Learning vocabularies over a fine quantization. Int. J. Comput. Vis. (IJCV) **103**(1), 163–175 (2013)

51. Radenović, F., Tolias, G., Chum, O.: Fine-tuning CNN image retrieval with no human annotation. arXiv:1711.02512 (2017)

52. Iscen, A., Tolias, G., Avrithis, Y., Furon, T., Chum, O.: Efficient diffusion on region manifolds: recovering small objects with compact CNN representations. In: CVPR (2017)

53. Gordo, A., Almazan, J., Revaud, J., Larlus, D.: End-to-end learning of deep visual representations for image retrieval. IJCV **124**, 237–254 (2017)

54. Philbin, J., Chum, O., Isard, M., Sivic, J., Zisserman, A.: Object retrieval with large vocabularies and fast spatial matching. In: Conference on Computer Vision and Pattern Recognition (CVPR), pp. 1–8 (2007)

55. Philbin, J., Chum, O., Isard, M., Sivic, J., Zisserman, A.: Lost in quantization: improving particular object retrieval in large scale image databases. In: Conference on Computer Vision and Pattern Recognition (CVPR), pp. 1–8 (2008)

56. Sivic, J., Zisserman, A.: Video Google: a text retrieval approach to object matching in videos. In: International Conference on Computer Vision (ICCV), pp. 1470–1477 (2003)

57. Muja, M., Lowe, D.G.: Fast approximate nearest neighbors with automatic algorithm configuration. In: International Conference on Computer Vision Theory and Application (VISSAPP), pp. 331–340 (2009)

58. Jegou, H., Douze, M., Schmid, C.: Improving bag-of-features for large scale image search. Int. J. Comput. Vis. (IJCV) **87**(3), 316–336 (2010)

59. He, K., Zhang, X., Ren, S., Sun, J.: Deep residual learning for image recognition. In: CVPR (2016)

60. Noh, H., Araujo, A., Sim, J., Weyand, T., Han, B.: Large-scale image retrieval with attentive deep local features. In: ICCV (2017)

Compressing the Input for CNNs with the First-Order Scattering Transform

Edouard Oyallon[1,4,5][✉], Eugene Belilovsky[2], Sergey Zagoruyko[3],
and Michal Valko[4]

[1] CentraleSupelec, Université Paris-Saclay, Gif-sur-Yvette, France
edouard.oyallon@centralesupelec.fr
[2] MILA, University of Montreal, Montreal, Canada
[3] WILLOW – Inria Paris, Paris, France
[4] SequeL – Inria Lille, Lille, France
[5] GALEN – Inria Saclay, Palaiseau, France

Abstract. We study the *first-order* scattering transform as a candidate for reducing the signal processed by a *convolutional neural network* (CNN). We show theoretical and empirical evidence that in the case of natural images and sufficiently small translation invariance, this transform preserves most of the signal information needed for classification while *substantially reducing* the spatial resolution and total signal size. We demonstrate that cascading a CNN with this representation performs on par with ImageNet classification models, commonly used in downstream tasks, such as the ResNet-50. We subsequently apply our trained hybrid ImageNet model as a base model on a detection system, which has typically larger image inputs. On Pascal VOC and COCO detection tasks we demonstrate improvements in the inference speed and training memory consumption compared to models trained directly on the input image.

Keywords: CNN · SIFT · Image descriptors · First-order scattering

1 Introduction

Convolutional neural networks (CNNs) for supervised vision tasks learn often from raw images [1] that could be arbitrarily large. Effective reduction of the spatial dimension and total signal size for CNN processing is difficult. One way is to learn this dimensionality reduction during the training of a supervised CNN. Indeed, the very first layers of standard CNNs play often this role and reduce the spatial resolution of an image via *pooling* or *stride operators*. Yet, they generally maintain the input layer sizes and even increase it by expanding the number of channels. These pooling functions can correspond to a linear pooling such as wavelet pooling [2], a spectral pooling [3], an average pooling, or a non-linear pooling such as ℓ^2-pooling [4], or max-pooling. For example, the two first layers of an AlexNet [5], a VGG [6] or a ResNet [7] reduce the resolution

© Springer Nature Switzerland AG 2018
V. Ferrari et al. (Eds.): ECCV 2018, LNCS 11213, pp. 305–320, 2018.
https://doi.org/10.1007/978-3-030-01240-3_19

respectively by 2^3, 2^1, and 2^2, while the dimensionality of the layer is increased by a factor 1.2, 5.3, and 1.3 respectively. This spatial size reduction is important for computational reasons because the complexity of convolutions is quadratic in spatial size while being linear in the number of channels. This suggests that reducing the input size to subsequent CNN layers calls for a careful design. In this work, we (a) analyze a generic method that, *without learning*, reduces *input size* as well as *resolution* and (b) show that it *retains enough information* and structure that permits applying a CNN to obtain competitive performance on classification and detection.

Natural images have a lot of redundancy, that can be exploited by finding a frame to obtain a sparse representation [8,9]. For example, a wavelet transform of piece-wise smooth signals (e.g., natural images) leads to a multi-scale and sparse representation [10]. This fact can be used for a compression algorithm [11]. Since in this case the most of the information corresponds to just a few wavelet coefficients, a transform coding can be applied to select them and finally quantize the signal, which is consequently a more compact representation. Yet, this leads to variable signal size and thus this method is not amenable for CNNs that require a constant-size input. Another approach is to select a subset of these coefficients, which would be a linear projection. Yet, a linear projection would imply an unavoidable loss of significant discriminative information which is not desirable for vision applications. Thus, we propose to use a *non-linear* operator to reduce the signal size and we justify such construction.

Prior work has proposed to input predefined features into CNNs or neural networks. For example, [12] proposed to apply a deep neural network on Fisher vectors. This approach relies on the extraction of overlapping descriptors, such as SIFT, at irregular spatial locations and thus does not permit a fixed size output. Moreover, the features used in these models increase the signal size. In [13], wavelets representations are combined at different layer stages, similarly to DenseNet [14]. [15] proposes to apply a 2D Haar transform that leads to subsampled representation by a factor of 2^1 but is limited to this resolution. Concurrent to our work, [16] proposed to train CNNs on top of raw DCT to improve inference speed by reducing the spatial resolution, yet this transformation is orthogonal and thus preserves the input size. Moreover, [17] proposes to input *second-order* scattering coefficients to a CNN, that are named *hybrid scattering networks*, which lead to a competitive performance on datasets such as ImageNet. The scattering transform is a *non-linear* operator based on a cascade of wavelet transforms and modulus non-linearity which are spatially averaged. This leads to a reduction in the spatial resolution of the signal. However, although the second-order scattering representation is more discriminative, it produces a larger signal than the original input size.

In this work, we also input predefined features into CNNs, *but* with the explicit goal of an initial stage producing a compressed representation that is still amenable to processing by a CNN. In particular, we show that the first-order scattering representation is a natural candidate for several vision tasks. This descriptor leads to high accuracy on large-scale classification and detection while it can be computed much faster than its second-order counterpart because it requires fewer convolutions. As explained in [18], this descriptor is similar to SIFT and DAISY descriptors that have been used as feature extractors in many classical image classification and detection systems [19,20]. In this paper, we show that in the case of hybrid networks [12,17], using the *first-order scattering only* can have favorable properties with respect to the second-order ones and possibly higher-order ones.

The core of our paper it the analysis and justification of the combination of first-order scattering and CNNs. We support it both with theoretical and numerical arguments. In Sect. 2, we justify that first-order scattering with small-scale invariance reduces the spatial resolution and signal while preserving important attributes. First, we motivate the first-order scattering from a dimensionality reduction view in Sect. 2.1. Then, in Sect. 2.2, we illustrate the negligible loss of information via a good reconstruction of synthetic signals and natural images using only a first-order scattering. Next, in Sect. 3 we present our experiments[1] on challenging datasets. We demonstrate competitive performance with ImageNet models commonly used in transfer learning in Sect. 3.1. In Sect. 3.2 we show on COCO and Pascal VOC detection tasks that these base networks can lead to improvements in terms of inference speed and memory consumption versus accuracy.

2   First-Order Scattering

In this section, we motivate the construction of a first-order *scattering transform* from a compression perspective. Indeed, a scattering transform is traditionally built as a representation that preserves high-frequency information, while building stable invariants w.r.t. translations and deformations. While using the same tools, we adopt a rather different take. We show theoretically and numerically that a first-order *scattering transform* builds limited invariance to translation, reduces the size of an input signal, preserves most of the information needed to discriminate and reconstruct a natural image. Note also that this representation is able to discriminate *spatial* and *frequency variations* of natural images. In this section, we deal with *Gábor wavelets* [21] since their analysis is simpler, while for the experiments we will use modified Gábor wavelets, namely *Morlet wavelets* [17] for the sake of comparison. We show that the first-order scattering transform does not lose significant signal characteristics of natural images, by providing reconstruction examples obtained via a mean-square error minimization. In particular, we demonstrate this property on *Gaussian blobs* as a simplified proxy for natural images.

2.1   A Reduction of the Spatial Resolution

Definition. A scattering first-order transform [22] is defined from a *mother wavelet* ψ and a *low-pass filter* ϕ. An input signal x is filtered by a collection of

---

[1] Code available at https://github.com/edouardoyallon/pyscatlight.

dilated band-pass wavelets obtained from ψ, followed by a *modulus* and finally averaged by a *dilation* of ϕ. The wavelets we chose decompose the signal in a basis in which transient structure of a signal is represented more compactly. We describe the construction of each filter and justify the necessity of each operator. First, let us fix an integer J that specifies the window length of the low-pass filter. For the sake of simplicity, we consider Gábor filters [21]. These filters provide a good localization tradeoff between *frequency* and *space planes*, due to Heisenberg uncertainty principle [9]. Thus, having

$$\kappa(\omega) \triangleq e^{-2\sigma_0^2 \|\omega\|^2}$$

for a fixed bandwidth σ_0 and a slant s that discriminates angles, we set for $\omega = (\omega_1, \omega_2)$,

$$\widehat{\psi}(\omega) \triangleq \kappa\left(\left(\omega_1, \frac{\omega_2}{s}\right) - \omega_0\right) \quad \text{and} \quad \widehat{\phi}(\omega) \triangleq \kappa(\omega).$$

The frequency plane (and in particular the image frequency circle of radius π) needs to be covered by the support of the filters to avoid an information loss. This issue is solved by the action of the Euclidean group on ψ via rotation $r_{-\theta}$ and dilation by $j \leq J$,

$$\psi_{j,\theta}(u) = \frac{1}{2^{2j}} \psi\left(r_{-\theta} \frac{u}{2^j}\right) \quad \text{and} \quad \phi_J(u) = \frac{1}{2^{2J}} \phi\left(\frac{u}{2^J}\right).$$

In this case, each wavelet $\psi_{j,\theta}$ has a bandwidth of $1/(2^j \sigma_0)$ and its central frequency is $2^j r_{-\theta} \omega_0$. If a filter has a compact support in the frequency domain, then due to Nyquist principle, we can reduce the spatial sampling of the resulting convolution. We do this approximation in the case of Gábor filters. As we shall see, this localization in frequency is also fundamental because it permits to obtain a *smooth envelope*. The parameters $j \leq J$ and $\theta \in \Theta$ are discretized and σ_0 is adjusted such that a wavelet transform preserves all the energy of $\widehat{x}$, characterized by

$$\exists \varepsilon_0 \geq 0, \forall \omega, \|\omega\| < \pi : \ 1 - \varepsilon_0 \leq \sum_{j \leq J, \theta \in \Theta} \left|\widehat{\psi}_{j,\theta}(\omega)\right|^2 + \left|\widehat{\phi}_J(\omega)\right|^2 \leq 1 + \varepsilon_0.$$

As a result, the transform is bi-Lipschitz and the magnitude of ε_0 determines the conditioning of the wavelet transform. An ideal setting is $\varepsilon_0 = 0$, for which the transform is an isometry which gives a one-to-one mapping of the signal while preserving its ℓ^2-norm. Applying a convolution with these wavelets followed by a modulus removes the phase of a signal and thus should lead to a loss of information.

In fact, [23] proves that it is possible to reconstruct a signal from the modulus of its wavelet transform up to a global translation with *Cauchy wavelets*. Furthermore, there exists an algorithm of reconstruction [24], with stability guarantees and extension to other class of wavelets. Consequently, the modulus of a wavelet transform does not lead to a significant loss if applied appropriately.

Additionally, [22] demonstrates that this representation is stable to deformations, which permits building invariants to deformations, convenient in many vision applications. We now explain how the dimensionality reduction occurs. The scattering first-order transform S [22] parametrized by J is[2] defined as

$$Sx(u) = \left\{ |x \star \psi_{j,\theta}| \star \phi_J(2^J u), x \star \phi_J(2^J u) \right\}_{\theta \in \Theta, j \leq J}.$$

The low-pass filter ϕ_J builds a transformation that is locally invariant to translation up to 2^J. Therefore, it reduces the spatial sampling of the signal by a factor of 2^J. This also means that when discretized image of length N represented by N^2 coefficients, is filtered by the low-pass filter ϕ_J, the signal is represented by $N^2/2^{2J}$ coefficients. Consequently, the number of coefficients used to represent Sx is

$$(1 + |\Theta| J) \frac{N^2}{2^{2J}}.$$

In our case, we use $|\Theta| = 8$, because it permits obtaining a good covering of the frequency plane, and thus, the input signal x is compressed via Sx if $J \geq 3$. The low-pass filtering implies a necessary loss of information because it discards some high-frequency structure and only retains low frequencies which are more invariant to translation. It is fundamental to evaluate the quality of this compressed representation in order to validate that enough information is available for supervised classifier such as CNNs, which is what we do next.

Preserving Signal Information via Modulus. We evaluate the loss of information due to the low-pass filtering, which captures signal attributes located in the low-frequency domain. Notice that there would be no loss of information if the Fourier transform of the wavelet-modulus representation was located in a compact domain included in the bandwidth of ϕ_J. Unfortunately, this property is not guaranteed in practice.

Nonetheless, Gábor wavelets are *approximately analytic* which implies that when convolved with a signal x, the resulting envelope is smoother [9,22,25–27]. A smooth envelope of the signal implies that a significant part of its energy can be captured and preserved by a low-pass filter [22]. Furthermore, under limited assumptions of point-wise regularity on x, if the signal does not vanish, it is possible to quantify this smoothness, as done in [27]. Informally, for a translation $x_a(u) \triangleq x(u - a)$ by a of x, it means that if $\|a\| \ll 1$, then we imply that

$$|x_a \star \psi|(u) \approx |x \star \psi|(u).$$

Here, we simply give some explicit constant w.r.t. the stability to translation, that we relate to the envelope of ψ. Indeed, the Gábor filter ψ concentrates its energy around a central frequency ω_0,

$$\exists \eta_0 > 0, \exists \omega_0, \varepsilon \geq 0, \forall \omega, \quad \|\omega - \omega_0\|_2 > \eta_0 \implies |\hat{\psi}(\omega)| \leq \varepsilon.$$

---

[2] In the following, we omit the dependence w.r.t. the scale J.

First-order scattering incorporates more information if the modulus operator has smoothed the signal. To this end, we characterize the stability w.r.t. translations in the case of Gábor wavelets. In particular, we provide the following Lipschitz bound w.r.t. translations.

Proposition 1. *For any signal $x \in \ell^2$,*

$$\|x_a \star \psi - e^{-i\omega_0^\mathsf{T} a} x \star \psi\| \le \|x\| \left(\|\eta_0\| \|a\| + \widetilde{\varepsilon}(\|a\|) \right),$$

where $\widetilde{\varepsilon}$ is a term of the order of ε.

Proof. Observe that

$$\|x_a \star \psi - e^{-i\omega_0^\mathsf{T} a} x \star \psi\|^2 = \int \left| \left(e^{-i\omega^\mathsf{T} a} - e^{-i\omega_0^\mathsf{T} a} \right) \widehat{\psi}(\omega) \widehat{x}(\omega) \right|^2 d\omega \ \textit{via Parseval identity}$$

$$\le 4\varepsilon^2 \|x\|^2 + \int_{\|\omega - \omega_0\| < \eta_0} \left| (e^{-i\omega^\mathsf{T} a} - e^{-i\omega_0^\mathsf{T} a}) \widehat{\psi}(\omega) \right|^2 |\widehat{x}(\omega)|^2 \, d\omega.$$

(note that $x \mapsto e^{ix}$ is 1-Lipschitz, thus we apply the Cauchy-Schwartz inequality)

$$\le \|x\|^2 \left(4\varepsilon^2 + \|a\|^2 \eta_0^2 \right).$$

Taking the square root finishes the proof.

We note that this inequality is near-optimal, for Gábor wavelets, if $x(u) = \delta_0$ is a Dirac in 0, then $|e^{i\omega_0^\mathsf{T} a} \psi(a) - \psi(0)| \sim \|x\| \|a\| \eta_0$. Observe that dilating the mother wavelet ψ to ψ_j is equivalent to dilating the bandwidth η_0 to $2^{-j}\eta_0$. Following the reasoning, low-frequency Gábor wavelets are more likely to be invariant to a translation.

Proposition 1 characterizes the Lipschitz stability w.r.t. translations and indicates that the more localized a Gábor wavelet is, the more translation-stable is the resulting signal. This way, we justify Gábor wavelets as a great candidate for a wavelet transform with a smooth modulus with limited assumptions on x.

Note that using only small-bandwidth Gábor wavelets instead of dilated ones should be avoided because it would lead to significantly more filters. Furthermore, [22] shows that those filters will be more unstable to deformations, such as dilation, which is not desirable for vision applications.

Despite the stability to translation, there is no guarantee that the first-order scattering preserves the complete energy of the signal. The next section characterizes this energy loss via an image model based on Gaussian blobs and a reconstruction algorithm for natural images.

2.2   Information Loss

We now characterize the information loss for natural images in two ways. First, we perform an empirical reconstruction of an image from its first-order scattering coefficients, as done for the second order in [28,29] and observe that for

(a) **middle**: PSNR $\approx 26dB$, right: PSNR $\approx 20dB$

(b) **middle**: PSNR $\approx 23dB$, right: PSNR $\approx 19dB$

Fig. 1. Reconstructed images from first-order scattering coefficients, $J = 3, 4$ and their PSNR. Color channels can be slightly translated leading to artifacts. (**left**) Original image x (**middle**) reconstruction $\widetilde{x}_3$ from Sx, $J = 3$ (**right**) reconstruction $\widetilde{x}_4$ from Sx, $J = 4$. This demonstrates that even complex images can be reconstructed for $J = 3$, while dividing the spatial resolution by 2^3.

natural images, we can indeed obtain an effective reconstruction of the first-order scattering. This is a strong indication that the relevant signal information is preserved. Second, we consider a generic signal model and show that for relatively low-scale factors J, the reconstruction is practically achieved.

Reconstruction. Following [28, 29], we propose to reconstruct an input image x from its first-order scattering Sx coefficient of scales J, via a ℓ^2-norm minimization

$$\widetilde{x}_J = \inf_y \|Sx - Sy\|. \tag{1}$$

We use a gradient descent as all the operators are weakly differentiable and we analyze the reconstructed signal. Figure 1 compares the reconstruction of a natural image with the first-order scattering for the scales $J = 3$ and $J = 4$. In our experiments, we optimize for this reconstruction with ADAM with an initial learning rate of 10 during 10^3 iterations, reducing by 10 the learning rate every

2×10^2 iterations. We measure the reconstruction error of $\widetilde{x}_J$ from an original image x in terms of relative error, defined as

$$\mathrm{err}_J(x) = \frac{\|S\widetilde{x}_J - Sx\|}{\|Sx\|}.$$

In other words, we evaluate how close the scattering representation of an image is to its reconstruction. We stop the optimization procedure as soon as we get $\mathrm{err}_J(x) \sim 2 \times 10^{-3}$. In the case $J = 3$, observe that the important and high-frequency structure of the signals, as well as their spatial localization, are preserved. On the contrary, when $J = 4$, the fine-scale structure is neither well reconstructed nor correctly located, which tends to indicate that $J \geq 4$ might not be a good-scale candidate for S. We now characterize this loss more precisely on a model based on blobs.

Gaussian Blob Model. Explicit computation of scattering coefficients for general signals is difficult because a modulus is a non-linear operator that usually leads to non-analytic expressions. Therefore, we consider a simplified class of signals [30] for which computations are exact and analytical. For a symmetric matrix Σ, we consider the unnormalized signal

$$\widehat{x}_\Sigma(\omega) \triangleq e^{-\omega^\mathsf{T} \Sigma \omega}.$$

Figure 2 shows several signals belonging to this class. Such signals correspond to blobs or lines as on Fig. 2, which are frequent in natural images [31]. We apply our reconstruction algorithm and we explain why the reconstructions is challenging.

In particular, we prove the following proposition that is derived from convolutions between Gaussians and permits to compute their first-order scattering coefficients. Intuitively, this proposition says that for a particular class of signals, we can get their exact reconstruction from their first-order scattering coefficients. Note that for large values of J, the reconstruction is numerically infeasible.

Proposition 2. *For any symmetric Σ, j, and θ,*

$$|x_\Sigma \star \psi_{j,\theta}|(u) \propto \bigl(x_\Sigma \star |\psi_{j,\theta}|\bigr)(u).$$

Proof. Without loss of generality, we prove the result for $\widehat{\psi}(\omega) \triangleq e^{-\|\Gamma\omega - b\|^2}$, where Γ is invertible and $b \in \mathbb{R}^2$. Then, $\widehat{|\psi|}(\omega) \propto e^{-\|\Gamma\omega\|^2}$. Let $\Delta(u) \triangleq x_\Sigma \star \psi(u)$. Then by definition,

$$\widehat{\Delta}(\omega) \propto e^{-\omega^\mathsf{T}(\Sigma + \Gamma^\mathsf{T}\Gamma)\omega + 2\omega^\mathsf{T}\Gamma b}.$$

As $\Gamma^\mathsf{T}\Gamma \succ 0$, we can set $\widetilde{b} \triangleq \bigl(\Sigma + \Gamma^\mathsf{T}\Gamma\bigr)^{-1}\Gamma b$. Then, the result comes from an inverse Fourier transform applied to

$$\widehat{\Delta}(\omega) \propto e^{-(\omega - \widetilde{b})^\mathsf{T}(\Sigma + \Gamma^\mathsf{T}\Gamma)(\omega - \widetilde{b})}.$$

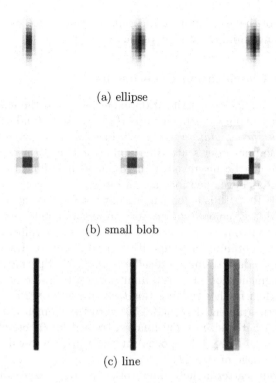

(a) ellipse

(b) small blob

(c) line

Fig. 2. Reconstruction of different signals of type x_Σ. (**left**) original image (**middle**) reconstruction via for $J = 3$ (**right**) reconstruction for $J = 4$

Therefore, the first-order scattering coefficients are given by

$$Sx_\Sigma \propto \{x_\Sigma \star (|\psi_{j,\theta}| \star \phi_J), x_\Sigma \star \phi_J\}_{\theta \in \Theta, j \leq J}.$$

A naïve inversion of the first-order scattering coefficients would be an inversion of the convolution with $|\psi_{j,\theta}| \star \phi_J$ which is unfortunately poorly conditioned for large values of J since this filter is a low-pass one. However, solving the optimization (1) leads to a different solution due to the presence of the modulus during the gradient computation. For $J \leq 3$, it is possible to recover the original signal as shown in Fig. 2. Nevertheless, there is a lack of spatial localization for $J \geq 4$ due to the averaging ϕ_J, that we observe during our reconstruction experiment. This confirms our choice of $J = 3$ for the remainder of the paper.

3   Numerical Experiments

We perform numerical experiments using first-order scattering output as the input to a CNN. Our experiments aim to both validate that the first-order scattering can preserve the key signal information and highlight the practical importance of it. In particular, we find that we obtain performance close to some of the state-of-the-art systems *while improving inference speed* and memory consumption during training by light years.

3.1 ImageNet Classification Experiments

We first describe our image classification experiments on the challenging ImageNet dataset. Each of our experiments is performed using standard hyperparameters *without a specific adaptation* to our hybrid architecture. Extensive architecture search for the first-order scattering input is not performed and we believe that these results can be improved with resources matching the architectures and hyperparameters developed for natural images.

ImageNet ILSVRC2012 is a challenging dataset for classification. It consists of 1k classes, 1.2M large colored images for training and 400k images for testing. We demonstrate that our representation does not lose significant information for classification by obtaining a competitive performance on ImageNet. We follow a standard procedure training procedures [7,17,32]. Specifically, we applied standard data augmentation and crop input images to a size of 224^2. The first order scattering then further reduces this to a size of 28×28. We trained our CNNs by stochastic gradient descent (SGD) with the momentum of 0.9, weight decay of 10^{-4} and batch size of 256 images, trained for 90 epochs. We reduce the learning rate by 0.1 every 30 epochs. At test time, we rescale the images to 256^2 and crop an image of size 224^2.

To construct our scattering hybrid networks, we stay close to an original CNN reference model. In particular, we build our models out of the ResNets [7] and WideResNets [32] models. A typical ResNet consists of an initial layer followed by $K = 4$ so-called layer groups that in turn consist of $[n_1, \ldots, n_K]$ residual blocks, where n_i specifies the number of blocks in each layer group. Furthermore, the width in each blocks is a constant and equal to $[w_1, \ldots, w_K]$. Similarly to [17], an initial convolutional layer is applied to increase the number of channels from $3 \times (1 + 8J) = 75$ to w_1. A stride of 2 is applied at the initial layer of the blocks $k \geq 2$, to reduce the spatial resolution. Each of the residual blocks contains two convolutional operators, except when a stride of 2 is applied in order to replace the identity mapping, in which case there are three convolutional operators, as done in [7]. In the following, we refer to ScatResNet-L as the architecture with L convolutional operators. As discussed we used $J = 3$, as done in [17].

In our first experiment, we aim to directly compare to the results of [17] which use the second-order scattering. Thus we use the same structure that applies $K = 2$ layer groups on the scattering input instead of the typical 4. This architecture was called the ScatResNet-10 [17], and has $[2, 2]$ layers of width $[256, 512]$. The number of parameters is about 12M in both cases. Notice that the number of parameters varies only since the initial number of input channels change. Table 1 reports similar accuracy for order 1 and order 2 scattering, which indicates that if enough data is available and there is a small invariance to translation J, then for natural image classification, the order 2 does not provide significantly more information that can be exploited by a CNN.

Now we demonstrate that the scattering first-order transform continues to scale further when applying more sophisticated networks. Note that this would not have been possible with a second-order scattering in a reasonable time. In our case, we avoid computing many convolutions. Scaling to these modern networks permits us to apply the scattering in the subsequent section to common computer vision tasks that require a base network from ImageNet, and where the smaller input size leads to gains in speed and memory.

The models we construct are the ScatResNet-50, based on the ResNet50 architecture, and the WideScatResNet-50-2 based on the wide ResNet that expands the channel width and leads to competitive performance [32]. Since the scattering input starts at a much lower resolution, we bypass the first group of the typical ResNet, which normally consists of $K = 4$ layer groups and reduce the number of groups to $K = 3$. A typical ResNet50 has 16 residual blocks distributed among the 4 layer groups. We maintain the same number of total residual blocks and thereby layers as in the ResNet50, redistributing them among the three groups using [5, 8, 3] blocks. As in their non-scattering analogue we apply bottleneck blocks [7]. The width of the blocks for ScatResNet-50 and WideScatResNet-50-2 are [128, 256, 512] and [256, 512, 1024], which matches the widths of groups 2 through 4 of their non-scattering counterparts.

Table 1. Accuracy on ImageNet. Note that scattering based models have input sizes of $28 \times 28 \times 75$ while the normal ImageNet models are trained on $224 \times 224 \times 3$.

Architecture	Top 1	Top 5	#params
Order 1,2 + ScatResNet-10 [17]	68.7	88.6	12.8M
Order 1 + ScatResNet-10	67.7	87.7	11.4M
Order 1 + ScatResNet-50	74.5	92.0	27.8M
Order 1 + WideScatResNet-50-2	76.2	92.8	107.2M
ResNet-50 (pytorch)	76.1	92.9	25.6M
ResNet-101(pytorch)	77.4	93.6	45.4M
VGG-16 [6]	68.5	88.7	138M
ResNet-50 [7]	75.3	92.2	25.6M
ResNet-101	76.4	92.9	45.4M
WideResNet50-2 [32]	77.9	94.0	68.9M
ResNet-152	77.0	93.3	60.2M

Table 1 indicates that the performance obtained by those architectures can be competitive with their respective reference architectures for classification. We compare to the reference models trained using the same procedures as ours[3]. We additionally compare to published results of these models and several

---

[3] http://pytorch.org/docs/0.3.0/torchvision/models.html.

related ones. We evaluate the memory and speed of the ScatResNet-50 model and compare it to the reference models ResNet-50 and the next biggest ResNet model ResNet-101 in the first two rows of Table 2. Our comparisons are done on a single GPU. As in [16,33], we evaluate the inference time of the CNN from the encoding. For memory, we consider memory usage during training as we believe the scattering models are useful for training with fewer resources. We find that our scattering model has favorable properties in memory and speed usage compared to its non-scattering analogues. In fact, as the next step, we demonstrate large improvements in accuracy, speed, and memory on detection tasks using the ScatResNet-50 network, which indicates that ScatResNet-50 features are also generic for detection.

Table 2. Speed and memory consumption for ImageNet classification sizes (224×224) and detection scale 800px. We compare the inference speed of the learned CNN between the different models and for the detection models the inference speed of feature extraction. To evaluate memory we determine the maximum batch size possible for training on a single GPU. We use a single 11GB Ti 1080 GPU for all comparisons.

Architecture	Classification models		Detection models	
	Speed	Max im.	Speed	Max im.
	(64 images)	ImageNet	(4 images)	COCO
Order 1 + ScatResNet-50	0.072	175	0.073	9
ResNet-50	0.095	120	0.104	7
ResNet-101	0.158	70	0.182	2

3.2   Detection Experiments

Finally, we apply our hybrid architectures to detection. We base our experiments and hyperparameters on those indicated by the Faster-RCNN implementation of [34] without any specific adaptation to the dataset. We consider both the VOC07 and COCO and adopt the ScatResNet-50 network as the basis of our model. We shared the output of the second layer across a region proposal network and a detection network, which are kept fixed. The receptive field of each output neuron corresponds to 16^2, which is similar to [7,35,36]. The next layers will be fine-tuned for the detection tasks and fed to classification and box-regression layers, as in [35], and a *region proposal network* as done in [36]. Similarly to [7,36], we fixed all the batch normalization [37] layers, including the running means and biases.

Pascal VOC07. Pascal VOC2007 [38] consists of 10k images split equally for training ("train+val") and testing, with about 25k annotations. We chose the same hyperparameters as used in [34]. We used an initial learning rate of 10^{-3} that we dropped by 10 in epoch 5 and we report the accuracy of the epoch 6

Table 3. Mean average precision on Pascal VOC7 dataset. First-order scattering permits outperforms the related models.

Architecture	mAP
Faster-RCNN Order 1 + ScatResNet-50 (ours)	73.3
Faster-RCNN ResNet-50 (ours)	70.5
Faster-RCNN ResNet-101 (ours)	72.5
Faster-RCNN VGG-16 [34]	70.2

in Table 3 on the test set. During training, the images are flipped and rescaled with a ratio between 0.5 and 2, such that the smaller size is 600px as [7,36].

The training procedures used for detection often vary substantially. This includes batch size, weight decay for different parameters, and the number of training epochs among others. Due to this inconsistency, we train our own baseline models. We use the trained base networks for ResNet-50 and ResNet-101 provided as part of the `torchvision` package in `pytorch` [39] and train the detection models in exactly the same way as described above for ScatResNet50, ResNet-50, and ResNet-101. Table 3 reports a comparison of our ScatResNet model and the ResNet50 and ResNet101 model on this task. The results clearly show that our architecture and base network leads to a substantially better performance in terms of the mAP. On this particular dataset, perhaps due to its smaller size, we find the hybrid model can outperform even models with substantially stronger base networks [17] i.e the performance of ScatResNet-50 is above that of the ResNet101 based model. In the second two rows of Table 2, we show the memory and speed of the different models. The inference speed of the base network feature extractor is shown and for memory, we show the maximum batch size that one can train with. The tradeoff in mAP vs. speed and mAP vs. memory consumption here clearly favors the scattering based models. We now consider a larger scale version of this task on the COCO dataset.

Table 4. Mean average precision on COCO 2015 minival. Our method obtains competitive performance with respect to popular methods.

Architecture	mAP
Faster-RCNN Order 1 + ScatResNet-50	32.2
Faster-RCNN ResNet-50 (ours)	31.0
Faster-RCNN ResNet-101 (ours)	34.5
Faster-RCNN VGG-16 [34]	29.2
Detectron [40]	41.8

COCO. We likewise deploy the ScatResNet-50 on the COCO dataset [41]. This detection dataset is more difficult than than PASCAL VOC07. It has 120k images, out of which we use 115k for training and 5k for validation (minival), with 80 different categories. We again follow the implementation of [34] and their training and evaluation protocol. Specifically, we train the Faster-RCNN networks for 6 epochs with an initial learning rate of 8×10^{-3}, multiplying by a factor 0.1 at epoch 4. We use a minimal size of 800px, and similar scale augmentation w.r.t. Pascal VOC07. We use a batch size of 8 on 4 GPUs and train again all 3 models ScatResNet-50, ResNet-50, and ResNet-101. At test time, we restrict the maximum size to be 1200px as in [34] to permit an evaluation on a single GPU.

Table 4 reports the mAP of our model compared to its non-hybrid counterparts. This score is computed via the standard averaged over IoU thresholds $[0.5, 0.95]$. Our architecture accuracy falls between the one of a ResNet-50 and a ResNet-101. Observing Table 2 the tradeoff in mAP vs. speed and mAP vs. memory consumption here still favors the scattering based models. The results indicate that scattering based models can be favorable even in sophisticated *near*-state-of-the-art models. We encourage future work on combining scattering based models with the *most*-state-of-the-art architectures and pipelines.

4   Conclusion

We consider the problem of compressing an input image while retaining the information and structure necessary to allow a typical CNN to be applied. To the best of our knowledge, this problem has not been directly tackled with an effective solution. We motivate the use of the *first-order scattering* as a candidate for performing the *signal reduction*. We first refine several theoretical results regarding the stability with respect to translation of the first-order scattering. This motivates the use of Gábor wavelets that capture many signal attributes. We then show both on an analytical model and experimentally that reconstruction is possible. We perform experiments on challenging image classification and detection datasets ImageNet and COCO, showing that CNNs approaching the state-of-the-art performance can be built on top of the first-order scattering. This work opens the way to a research on transformations that build compressed input representations. Finally, we incite research on families of wavelets that could increase the resolution reduction and on determining whether our result generalizes to other classes of signals.

Acknowledgements. E. Oyallon was supported by a GPU donation from NVIDIA and partially supported by a grant from the DPEI of Inria (AAR 2017POD057) for the collaboration with CWI. S. Zagoruyko was supported by the DGA RAPID project DRAAF. The research presented was also supported by European CHIST-ERA project DELTA, French Ministry of Higher Education and Research, Nord-Pas-de-Calais Regional Council, Inria and Otto-von-Guericke-Universität Magdeburg associated-team north-European project Allocate, and French National Research Agency projects ExTra-Learn (n.ANR-14-CE24-0010-01) and BoB (n.ANR-16-CE23-0003).

References

1. LeCun, Y., Kavukcuoglu, K., Farabet, C., et al.: Convolutional networks and applications in vision. In: International Symposium on Circuits and Systems, pp. 253–256 (2010)
2. Williams, T., Li, R.: Wavelet pooling for convolutional neural networks. In: International Conference on Learning Representations (2018)
3. Rippel, O., Snoek, J., Adams, R.P.: Spectral representations for convolutional neural networks. In: Neural Information Processing Systems, pp. 2449–2457 (2015)
4. Le, Q.V.: Building high-level features using large scale unsupervised learning. In: International Conference on Acoustics, Speech and Signal Processing, pp. 8595–8598 (2013)
5. Krizhevsky, A., Sutskever, I., Hinton, G.E.: ImageNet classification with deep convolutional neural networks. In: Neural Information Processing Systems, pp. 1097–1105 (2012)
6. Simonyan, K., Zisserman, A.: Very deep convolutional networks for large-scale image recognition. arXiv:1409.1556 (2014)
7. He, K., Zhang, X., Ren, S., Sun, J.: Deep residual learning for image recognition. In: Computer Vision and Pattern Recognition, pp. 770–778 (2016)
8. Forsyth, D.A., Ponce, J.: Computer Vision: A Modern Approach. Prentice Hall Professional Technical Reference, Upper Saddle River (2002)
9. Mallat, S.: A Wavelet Tour of Signal Processing. Academic Press, Cambridge (1999)
10. Mallat, S., Hwang, W.L.: Singularity detection and processing with wavelets. Trans. Inf. Theory **38**(2), 617–643 (1992)
11. Skodras, A., Christopoulos, C., Ebrahimi, T.: The JPEG 2000 still image compression standard. Signal Process. Mag. **18**(5), 36–58 (2001)
12. Perronnin, F., Larlus, D.: Fisher vectors meet neural networks: a hybrid classification architecture. In: Computer Vision and Pattern Recognition, pp. 3743–3752 (2015)
13. Fujieda, S., Takayama, K., Hachisuka, T.: Wavelet convolutional neural networks for texture classification. arXiv:1707.07394 (2017)
14. Huang, G., Liu, Z., Weinberger, K.Q., van der Maaten, L.: Densely connected convolutional networks. In: Computer Vision and Pattern Recognition (2017)
15. Levinskis, A.: Convolutional neural network feature reduction using wavelet transform. Elektronika ir Elektrotech. **19**(3), 61–64 (2013)
16. Gueguen, L., Sergeev, A., Liu, R., Yosinski, J.: Faster neural networks straight from JPEG. In: International Conference on Learning Representations Workshop (2018)
17. Oyallon, E., Belilovsky, E., Zagoruyko, S.: Scaling the scattering transform: deep hybrid networks. In: International Conference on Computer Vision (2017)
18. Bruna, J., Mallat, S.: Invariant scattering convolution networks. Trans. Pattern Anal. Mach. Intell. **35**(8), 1872–1886 (2013)
19. Sánchez, J., Perronnin, F., Mensink, T., Verbeek, J.: Image classification with the fisher vector: theory and practice. Int. J. Comput. Vis. **105**(3), 222–245 (2013)
20. Morel, J.M., Yu, G.: ASIFT: a new framework for fully affine invariant image comparison. J. Imaging Sci. **2**(2), 438–469 (2009)
21. Olshausen, B.A., Field, D.J.: Emergence of simple-cell receptive field properties by learning a sparse code for natural images. Nature **381**(6583), 607 (1996)

22. Mallat, S.: Group invariant scattering. Commun. Pure Appl. Math. **65**(10), 1331–1398 (2012)
23. Mallat, S., Waldspurger, I.: Phase retrieval for the cauchy wavelet transform. J. Fourier Anal. Appl. **21**(6), 1251–1309 (2015)
24. Waldspurger, I., d'Aspremont, A., Mallat, S.: Phase recovery, maxcut and complex semidefinite programming. Math. Program. **149**(1–2), 47–81 (2015)
25. Krajsek, K., Mester, R.: A unified theory for steerable and quadrature filters. In: Braz, J., Ranchordas, A., Araújo, H., Jorge, J. (eds.) GRAPP/VISAPP-2006. CCIS, vol. 4, pp. 201–214. Springer, Heidelberg (2007). https://doi.org/10.1007/978-3-540-75274-5_13
26. Soulard, R.: Ondelettes analytiques et monogènes pour la représentation des images couleur. Ph.D. thesis, Université de Poitiers (2012)
27. Delprat, N., Escudié, B., Guillemain, P., Kronland-Martinet, R., Tchamitchian, P., Torresani, B.: Asymptotic wavelet and gabor analysis: extraction of instantaneous frequencies. Trans. Inf. Theory **38**(2), 644–664 (1992)
28. Bruna, J., Mallat, S.: Audio texture synthesis with scattering moments. arXiv:1311.0407 (2013)
29. Bruna, J.: Scattering representations for recognition. Ph.D. thesis, École Polytechnique (2013)
30. Lindeberg, T.: Feature detection with automatic scale selection. Int. J. Comput. Vis. **30**(2), 79–116 (1998)
31. Lowe, D.G.: Distinctive image features from scale-invariant keypoints. Int. J. Comput. Vis. **60**(2), 91–110 (2004)
32. Zagoruyko, S., Komodakis, N.: Wide residual networks. In: British Machine Vision Conference (2016)
33. Torfason, R., Mentzer, F., Agustsson, E., Tschannen, M., Timofte, R., Van Gool, L.: Towards image understanding from deep compression without decoding. arXiv:1803.06131 (2018)
34. Yang, J., Lu, J., Batra, D., Parikh, D.: A faster pytorch implementation of faster R-CNN. https://github.com/jwyang/faster-rcnn.pytorch (2017)
35. Girshick, R.B.: Fast R-CNN. In: International Conference on Computer Vision, pp. 1440–1448 (2015)
36. Ren, S., He, K., Girshick, R., Sun, J.: Faster R-CNN: towards real-time object detection with region proposal networks. Trans. Pattern Anal. Mach. Intell. **39**(6), 1137–1149 (2017)
37. Ioffe, S., Szegedy, C.: Batch normalization: accelerating deep network training by reducing internal covariate shift. arXiv:1502.03167 (2015)
38. Everingham, M., Van Gool, L., Williams, C.K., Winn, J., Zisserman, A.: The pascal visual object classes (VOC) challenge. Int. J. Comput. Vis. **88**(2), 303–338 (2010)
39. Paszke, A., et al.: Automatic differentiation in pytorch (2017)
40. He, K., Gkioxari, G., Dollár, P., Girshick, R.: Mask R-CNN. In: International Conference Computer Vision, pp. 2980–2988 (2017)
41. Lin, T.-Y.: Microsoft COCO: common objects in context. In: Fleet, D., Pajdla, T., Schiele, B., Tuytelaars, T. (eds.) ECCV 2014. LNCS, vol. 8693, pp. 740–755. Springer, Cham (2014). https://doi.org/10.1007/978-3-319-10602-1_48

Faces as Lighting Probes via Unsupervised Deep Highlight Extraction

Renjiao Yi[1,2(✉)], Chenyang Zhu[1,2], Ping Tan[1], and Stephen Lin[3]

[1] Simon Fraser University, Burnaby, Canada
{renjiaoy,cza68,pingtan}@sfu.ca
[2] National University of Defense Technology, Changsha, China
[3] Microsoft Research, Beijing, China
stevelin@microsoft.com

Abstract. We present a method for estimating detailed scene illumination using human faces in a single image. In contrast to previous works that estimate lighting in terms of low-order basis functions or distant point lights, our technique estimates illumination at a higher precision in the form of a non-parametric environment map. Based on the observation that faces can exhibit strong highlight reflections from a broad range of lighting directions, we propose a deep neural network for extracting highlights from faces, and then trace these reflections back to the scene to acquire the environment map. Since real training data for highlight extraction is very limited, we introduce an unsupervised scheme for finetuning the network on real images, based on the consistent diffuse chromaticity of a given face seen in multiple real images. In tracing the estimated highlights to the environment, we reduce the blurring effect of skin reflectance on reflected light through a deconvolution determined by prior knowledge on face material properties. Comparisons to previous techniques for highlight extraction and illumination estimation show the state-of-the-art performance of this approach on a variety of indoor and outdoor scenes.

Keywords: Illumination estimation · Unsupervised learning

1 Introduction

Spicing up selfies by inserting virtual hats, sunglasses or toys has become easy to do with mobile augmented reality (AR) apps like *Snapchat* [43]. But while the entertainment value of mobile AR is evident, it is just as clear to see that the generated results are usually far from realistic. A major reason is that virtual objects are typically not rendered under the same illumination conditions as in the imaged scene, which leads to inconsistency in appearance between the object

Electronic supplementary material The online version of this chapter (https:// doi.org/10.1007/978-3-030-01240-3_20) contains supplementary material, which is available to authorized users.

V. Ferrari et al. (Eds.): ECCV 2018, LNCS 11213, pp. 321–338, 2018.
https://doi.org/10.1007/978-3-030-01240-3_20

and its background. For high photorealism in AR, it is thus necessary to estimate the illumination in the image, and then use this estimate to render the inserted object compatibly with its surroundings.

Illumination estimation from a single image is a challenging problem because lighting is intertwined with geometry and reflectance in the appearance of a scene. To make this problem more manageable, most methods assume the geometry and/or reflectance to be known [18,19,27,30,32,36,37,48]. Such knowledge is generally unavailable in practice; however, there exist priors about the geometry and reflectance properties of human faces that have been exploited for illumination estimation [10,12,17,34]. Faces are a common occurrence in photographs and are the focus of many mobile AR applications. The previous works on face-based illumination estimation consider reflections to be diffuse and estimate only the low-frequency component of the environment lighting, as diffuse reflectance acts as a low-pass filter on the reflected illumination [32]. However, a low-frequency lighting estimate often does not provide the level of detail needed to accurately depict virtual objects, especially those with shiny surfaces.

In addressing this problem, we consider the parallels between human faces and mirrored spheres, which are conventionally used as lighting probes for acquiring ground truth illumination. What makes a mirrored sphere ideal for illumination recovery is its perfectly sharp specular reflections over a full range of known surface normals. Rays can be traced from the camera's sensor to the sphere and then to the surrounding environment to obtain a complete environment map that includes lighting from all directions and over all frequencies, subject to camera resolution. We observe that faces share these favorable properties to a large degree. They produce fairly sharp specular reflections (highlights) over its surface because of the oil content in skin. Moreover, faces cover a broad range of surface normals, and there exist various methods for recovering face geometry from a single image [2,10,34,38,51]. Unlike mirrored spheres, the specular reflections of faces are not perfectly sharp and are mixed with diffuse reflection. In this paper, we propose a method for dealing with these differences to facilitate the use of faces as lighting probes.

We first present a deep neural network for separating specular highlights from diffuse reflections in face images. The main challenge in this task is the lack of ground truth separation data on real face images for use in network training. Although ground truth separations can be generated synthetically using graphics models [41], it has become known that the mismatch between real and synthetic data can lead to significant reductions in performance [42]. We deal with this issue by pretraining our network with synthetic images and then finetuning the network using an unsupervised strategy with real photos. Since there is little real image data on ground truth separations, we instead take advantage of the property that the diffuse chromaticity values over a given person's face are relatively unchanged from image to image, aside from a global color rescaling due to different illumination colors and sensor attributes. From this property, we show that the diffuse chromaticity of multiple aligned images of the same face should form a low-rank matrix. We utilize this low-rank feature in place of ground truth separations to finetune the network using multiple real images of the same face, downloaded from the MS-celeb-1M database [7]. This unsupervised finetuning is shown to significantly improve highlight separation over the use of supervised learning on synthetic images alone.

With the extracted specular highlights, we then recover the environment illumination. This recovery is inspired by the frequency domain analysis of reflectance in [32], which concludes that reflected light is a convolved version of the environment map. Thus, we estimate illumination through a deconvolution of the specular reflection, in which the deconvolution kernel is determined from prior knowledge of face material properties. This approach enables recovery of higher-frequency details in the environment lighting.

This method is validated through experimental comparisons to previous techniques for highlight extraction and illumination estimation. On highlight extraction, our method is shown to produce results that more closely match the ground truth acquired by cross-polarization. For illumination estimation, greater precision is obtained over a variety of both indoor and outdoor scenes. We additionally show that the 3D positions of local point lights can be estimated using this method, by triangulating the light source positions from the environment maps of multiple faces in an image. With this 3D lighting information, the spatially variant illumination throughout a scene can be obtained. Recovering the detailed illumination in a scene not only benefits AR applications but also can promote scene understanding in general.

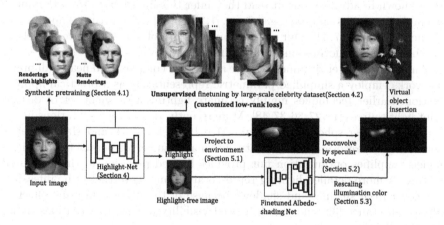

Fig. 1. Overview of our method. An input image is first separated into its highlight and diffuse layers. We trace the highlight reflections back to the scene according to facial geometry to recover a non-parametric environment map. A diffuse layer obtained through intrinsic component separation [24] is used to determine illumination color. With the estimated environment map, virtual objects can be inserted into the input image with consistent lighting.

2   Related Work

Highlight extraction involves separating the diffuse and specular reflection components in an image. This problem is most commonly addressed by removing highlights with the help of chromatic [11,46,47,52] as well as spatial [22,44,45] information from neighboring image areas, and then subtracting the resulting diffuse image from the original input to obtain the highlight component. These techniques are limited in the types of surface textures that can be handled, and they assume that the illumination color is uniform or known.

In recent work [16], these restrictions are avoided for the case of human faces by utilizing additional constraints derived from physical and statistical face priors. Our work also focuses on human faces but employs a deep learning approach instead of a physics-based solution for highlight extraction. While methods developed from physical models have a tangible basis, they might not account for all factors that influence image appearance, and analytical models often provide only a simplified approximation of natural mechanisms. In this work, we show that directly learning from real image data can lead to improved results that additionally surpass deep learning on synthetic training data [41].

Illumination estimation is often performed from a single image, as this is the only input available in many applications. The majority of single-image methods assume known geometry in the scene and estimate illumination from shading [18, 30,32,48] and shadows [18,26,27,36,37]. Some methods do not require geometry to be known in advance, but instead they infer this information from the image by employing priors on object geometry [1,20,25,33] or by fitting shape models for faces [6,10,12,17,34]. Our work also makes use of statistical face models to obtain geometric information for illumination estimation.

An illumination environment can be arbitrarily complex, and nearly all previous works employ a simplified parametric representation as a practical approximation. Earlier techniques mainly estimate lighting as a small set of distant point light sources [18,27,36,37,48]. More recently, denser representations in the form of low-order spherical harmonics [1,6,10,12,17,32,34] and Haar wavelets [26] have been recovered. The relatively small number of parameters in these models simplifies optimization but provides limited precision in the estimated lighting. A more detailed lighting representation may nevertheless be infeasible to recover from shading and shadows because of the lowpass filtering effect of diffuse reflectance [32] and the decreased visibility of shadow variations under extended lighting.

Greater precision has been obtained by utilizing lighting models specific to a certain type of scene. For outdoor environments, sky and sun models have been used for accurate recovery of illumination [3,9,13,14]. In research concurrent to ours, indoor illumination is predicted using a convolutional neural network trained on data from indoor environment maps [5]. Similar to our work, it estimates a non-parametric representation of the lighting environment with the help of deep learning. Our approach differs in that it uses human faces to determine the environment map, and employs deep learning to recover an intermediate quantity, namely highlight reflections, from which the lighting can be analytically solved. Though our method has the added requirement of having a face in the image, it is not limited to indoor scenes and it takes advantage of more direct evidence about the lighting environment. We later show that this more direct evidence can lead to higher precision in environment map estimates.

Highlight reflections have been used together with diffuse shading to jointly estimate non-parametric lighting and an object's reflectance distribution function [19]. In that work, priors on real-world reflectance and illumination are utilized as constraints to improve inference in an optimization-based approach. The method employs an object with known geometry, uniform color, and a shiny surface as a probe for the illumination. By contrast, our work uses arbitrary faces, which are a common occurrence in natural scenes. As shown later, the optimization-based approach can be sensitive to the complications presented by faces, such as surface texture, inexact geometry estimation, and spatially-variant reflectance. Our method reliably extracts a key component of illumination estimation – highlight reflections – despite these obstacles by using a proposed deep learning scheme.

3   Overview

As shown in Fig. 1, we train a deep neural network called *Highlight-Net* to extract the highlight component from a face image. This network is trained in two phases. First, pretraining is performed with synthetic data (Sect. 4.1). Subsequently, the network is finetuned in an unsupervised manner with real images from a celebrity dataset (Sect. 4.2).

For testing, the network takes an input image and estimates its highlight layer. Together with reconstructed facial geometry, the extracted highlights are used to obtain an initial environment map, by tracing the highlight reflections back towards the scene. This initial map is blurred due to the band-limiting effects of surface reflectance [32]. To mitigate this blur, our method performs deconvolution on the environment map using kernels determined from facial reflectance statistics (Sect. 5).

4   Face Highlight Removal

4.1   Pretraining with Synthetic Data

For Highlight-Net, we adopt a network structure used previously for intrinsic image decomposition [24], a related image separation task. To pretrain this network, we render synthetic data using generic face models [29] and real indoor and outdoor HDR environment maps collected from the Internet. Details on data preparation are presented in Sect. 6.1. With synthetic ground truth specular images, we minimize the L2 loss between the predicted and ground truth highlights for pretraining.

4.2   Unsupervised Finetuning on Real Images

With only pretraining on synthetic data, Highlight-Net performs inadequately on real images. This may be attributed to the limited variation of face shapes, textures, and environment maps in the synthetic data, as well as the gap in appearance between synthetic and real face images. Since producing a large-scale collection of real ground-truth highlight separation data is impractical, we present an unsupervised strategy for finetuning Highlight-Net that only requires real images of faces under varying illumination environments.

This strategy is based on the observation that the diffuse chromaticity over a given person's face should be consistent in different images, regardless of illumination changes, because a person's facial surface features should remain the same. Among images of the same face, the diffuse chromaticity map should differ only by global scaling factors determined by illumination color and sensor attributes, which we correct in a preprocessing step. Thus, a matrix constructed by stacking the aligned diffuse chromaticity maps of a person should be of low rank. In place of ground-truth highlight layers of real face images, we use this low-rank property of ground-truth diffuse layers to finetune our Highlight-Net.

This finetuning is implemented using the network structure shown in Fig. 2(a), where Highlight-Net is augmented with a low-rank loss. The images for training are taken from the MS-celeb-1M database [7], which contains 100 images for each of 100,000 celebrities. After some preprocessing described in Sect. 6.1, we have a set of aligned frontal face images under a consistent illumination color for each celebrity.

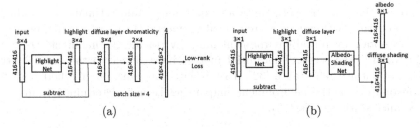

Fig. 2. (a) Network structure for finetuning Highlight-Net; (b) Testing network structure for separating an input face image into three layers: highlight, diffuse shading, and albedo.

From this dataset, four face images of the same celebrity are randomly selected for each batch. A batch is fed into Highlight-Net to produce the estimated highlight layers for the four images. These highlight layers are subtracted from the original images to obtain the corresponding diffuse layers. For a diffuse layer I_d, its diffuse chromaticity map is computed per-pixel as

$$chrom(I_d) = \frac{1}{(I_d(r) + I_d(g) + I_d(b))} (I_d(r), I_d(g)) \tag{1}$$

where r, g, and b denote the color channels. Each diffuse chromaticity map is then reshaped into a vector I^{dc}, and the vectors of the four images are stacked into a matrix $D = \left[I_1^{dc}, I_2^{dc}, I_3^{dc}, I_4^{dc} \right]^T$. With a low-rank loss enforced on D, Highlight-Net is finetuned through backpropagation.

Since the diffuse chromaticity of a face should be consistent among images, the rank of matrix D should ideally be one. So we define the low-rank loss as its second singular value, during backpropagation the partial derivative of σ_2 with respect to each matrix element is evaluated according to [28]:

$$D = U \Sigma V^T, \qquad \Sigma = diag(\sigma_1, \sigma_2, \sigma_3, \sigma_4),$$

$$loss_{lowrank} = \sigma_2, \qquad \frac{\partial \sigma_2}{\partial D_{i,j}} = U_{i,2} \times V_{j,2}. \tag{2}$$

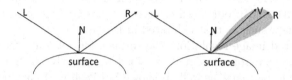

Fig. 3. Left: Mirror reflection. Right: Specular reflection of a rough surface.

5 Illumination Estimation

5.1 Environment Map Initialization

The specular reflections of a mirror are ideal for illumination estimation, because the observed highlights can be exactly traced back to the environment map when surface normals are known. This exact tracing is possible because a highlight reflection is directed along a single reflection direction R that mirrors the incident lighting direction L about the surface normal N, as shown on the left side of Fig. 3. This raytracing approach is widely used to capture environment maps with mirrored spheres in computer graphics applications.

For the specular reflections of a rough surface like human skin, the light energy is instead tightly distributed around the mirror reflection direction, as illustrated on the right side of Fig. 3. This specular lobe can be approximated by the specular term of the Phong model [31] as

$$I_s = k_s (R \cdot V)^\alpha, \qquad R = 2(L \cdot N)N - L \tag{3}$$

where k_s denotes the specular albedo, V is the viewing direction, and α represents the surface roughness. We specifically choose to use the Phong model to take advantage of statistics that have been compiled for it, as described later.

As rigorously derived in [32], reflection can be expressed as the environment map convolved with the surface BRDF (bidirectional reflectance distribution

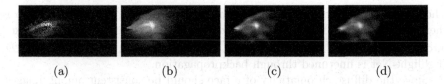

(a)   (b)   (c)   (d)

Fig. 4. Intermediate results of illumination estimation. (a) Traced environment map by forward warping; (b) Traced environment map by inverse warping; (c) Map after deconvolution; (d) Final environment map after illumination color rescaling. (Color figure online)

function), e.g., the model in Eq. 3. Therefore, if we trace the highlight component of a face back toward the scene, we obtain a convolved version of the environment map, where the convolution kernel is determined by the specular reflectance lobe. With surface normals computed using a single-image face reconstruction algorithm [51], our method performs this tracing to recover an initial environment map, such as that exhibited in Fig. 4(a).

Due to limited image resolution, the surface normals on a face are sparsely sampled, and an environment map obtained by directly tracing the highlight component would be sparse as well, as shown in Fig. 4(a). To avoid this problem, we employ inverse image warping where for each pixel p in the environment map, trace back to the face to get its corresponding normal N_p and use the available face normals nearest to N_p to interpolate a highlight value of N_p. In this way, we avoid the holes and overlaps caused by directly tracing (i.e., forward warping) highlights to the environment map. The result of this inverse warping is illustrated in Fig. 4(b).

5.2   Deconvolution by the Specular Lobe

Next, we use the specular lobe to deconvolve the filtered environment map. This deconvolution is applied in the spherical domain, rather than in the spatial domain parameterized by latitude and longitude which would introduce geometric distortions.

Consider the deconvolution kernel K_x centered at a point $\mathbf{x} = (\theta_x, \phi_y)$ on the environment map. At a nearby point $\mathbf{y} = (\theta_y, \phi_y)$, the value of K_x is

$$K_x(\mathbf{y}) = k_s^x (L_y \cdot L_x)^{\alpha_x} \tag{4}$$

where L_x and L_y are 3D unit vectors that point from the sphere center toward $\mathbf{x}$ and $\mathbf{y}$, respectively. The terms α_x and k_s^x denote the surface roughness and specular albedo at $\mathbf{x}$.

To determine α_x and k_s^x for each pixel in the environment map, we use statistics from the MERL/ETH Skin Reflectance Database [50]. In these statistics, faces are categorized by skin type, and every face is divided into ten regions, each with its own mean specular albedo and roughness because of differences in skin properties, e.g., the forehead and nose being relatively more oily. Using the mean albedo and roughness value of each face region for the face's skin type[1], our method performs deconvolution by the Richardson-Lucy algorithm [21,35]. Figure 4(c) shows an environment map after deconvolution.

5.3   Rescaling Illumination Color

The brightness of highlight reflections often leads to saturated pixels, which have color values clipped at the maximum image intensity. As a result, the highlight intensity in these color channels may be underestimated. This problem is illustrated in Fig. 5, where the predicted highlight layer appears blue because the light energy in the red and green channels is not fully recorded in the input image. To address this issue, we take advantage of diffuse shading, which is generally free of saturation and indicative of illumination color.

(a)	(b)	(c)	(d)

Fig. 5. (a) Input photo; (b) Automatically cropped face region by landmarks [53] (network input); (c) Predicted highlight layer (scaled by 2); (d) Highlight removal result. (Color figure online)

Diffuse reflection (i.e., the diffuse layer) is the product of albedo and diffuse shading, and the diffuse shading can be extracted from the diffuse layer through intrinsic image decomposition. To accomplish this decomposition, we finetune the intrinsic image network from [24] using synthetic face images to improve the network's effectiveness on faces. Specifically, 10,000 face images were synthesized from 50 face shapes randomly generated using the Basel Face Model [29], three different skin tones, diffuse reflectance, and environment maps randomly selected from 100 indoor and 100 outdoor real HDR environment maps. Adding this Albedo-Shading Net to our system as shown in Fig. 2(b) yields a highlight layer, albedo layer, and diffuse shading layer from an input face.

With the diffuse shading layer, we recolor the highlight layer H extracted via Highlight-Net by rescaling its channels. When the blue channel is not saturated, its value is correct and the other channels are rescaled relative to it as

$$[H'(r),\ H'(g),\ H'(b)] = [H(b) * c_d(r)/c_d(b),\ H(b) * c_d(g)/c_d(b),\ H(b)] \quad (5)$$

---

[1] Skin type is determined by the closest mean albedo to the mean value of the face's albedo layer. Extraction of the face's albedo layer is described in Sect. 5.3.

where c_d is the diffuse shading chromaticity. Rescaling can similarly be solved from the red or green channels if they are unsaturated. If all channels are saturated, we use the blue channel as it is likely to be the least underestimated based on common colors of illumination and skin. After recoloring the highlight layer, we compute its corresponding environment map following the procedure in Sects. 5.1 and 5.2 to produce the final result, such as shown in Fig. 4(d).

5.4 Triangulating Lights from Multiple Faces

In a scene where the light sources are nearby, the incoming light distribution can vary significantly at different locations. An advantage of our non-parametric illumination model is that when there are multiple faces in an image, we can recover this spatially variant illumination by inferring the environment map at each face and using them to triangulate the 3D light source positions.

As a simple scheme to demonstrate this idea, we first use a generic 3D face model (e.g., the Basel Face Model [29]) to solve for the 3D positions of each face in the camera's coordinate system, by matching 3D landmarks on the face model to 2D landmarks in the image using the method of [53]. Highlight-Net is then utilized to acquire the environment map at each of the faces. In the environment maps, strong light sources are detected as local maxima found through non-maximum suppression. To build correspondences among the lights detected from different faces, we first match them according to their colors. When there are multiple lights of the same color, their correspondence is determined by triangulating different combinations between two faces, with verification using a third face. In this way, the 3D light source positions can be recovered.

6 Experiments

6.1 Training Data

For the pretraining of Highlight-Net, we use the Basel Face Model [29] to randomly generate 50 3D faces. For each face shape, we adjust the texture map to simulate three different skin tones. These 150 faces are then rendered under 200 different HDR environment maps, including 100 from indoor scenes and 100 from outdoor scenes. The diffuse and specular components are rendered separately, where a spatially uniform specular albedo is randomly generated between [0, 1]. Some examples of these renderings are provided in the supplemental document. For training, we preprocessed each rendering by subtracting the mean image value and then normalizing to the range [0, 1].

In finetuning Highlight-Net, the image set for each celebrity undergoes a series of commonly-used preprocessing steps so that the faces are aligned, frontal, radiometrically calibrated, and under a consistent illumination color. For face frontalization, we apply the method in [8]. We then identify facial landmarks [53] to crop and align these frontal faces. The cropped images are radiometrically calibrated by the method in [15], and their color histograms are matched by the built-in histogram transfer function in MATLAB [23] to reduce illumination color differences. We note that in each celebrity's set, images were manually removed if the face exhibits a strong expression or multiple lighting colors, since these cases often lead to inaccurate spatial alignment or poor illumination color matching. Some examples of these preprocessed images are presented in the supplementary material.

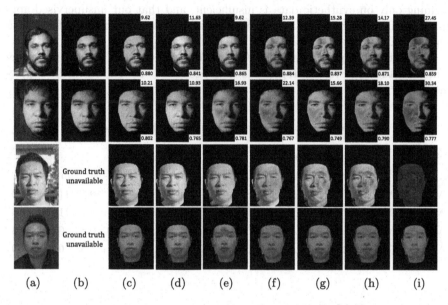

Fig. 6. Highlight removal comparisons on laboratory images with ground truth and on natural images. Face regions are cropped out automatically by landmark detection [53]. (a) Input photo. (b) Ground truth captured by cross-polarization for lab data. (c–h) Highlight removal results by (c) our finetuned Highlight-Net, (d) Highlight-Net without finetuning, (e) [41], (f) [16], (g) [40], (h) [52], and (i) [47]. For the lab images, RMSE values are given at the top-right, and SSIM [49] (larger is better) at the bottom-right.

6.2   Evaluation of Highlight Removal

To examine highlight extraction performance, we compare our highlight removal results to those of several previous techniques [16,40,41,47,52] in Fig. 6. The first two rows show results on faces with known ground truth captured by cross-polarization under an indoor directional light. In order to show fair comparisons for both absolute intensity errors and structural similarities, we use both RMSE and SSIM [49] as error/similarity metrics. The last two rows are qualitative comparisons on natural outdoor and indoor illuminations, where ground truth is unavailable due to the difficulty of cross-polarization in general settings. In all of these examples, our method outperforms the previous techniques, which generally have difficulty in dealing with the saturated pixels that commonly appear in highlight regions. We note that since most previous techniques are based on color analysis and the dichromatic reflection model [39], they cannot process grayscale images, unlike our CNN-based method. For results on grayscale images and additional color images, please refer to the supplement. The figure also illustrates the importance of training on real image data. Comparing our finetuning-based method in (c) to our method without finetuning in (d) and a CNN-based method trained on synthetic data [41] in (e) shows that training only on synthetic data is insufficient, and that our unsupervised approach for finetuning on real images substantially elevates the quality of highlight separation.

Quantitative comparisons over 100 synthetic faces and 30 real faces are presented in Table 1. Error histograms and image results are shown in the supplement.

Table 1. Quantitative highlight removal evaluation.

	Synthetic data					Real data					
	Ours	[41]	[16]	[40]	[52]	[47]	Ours	[41]	[16]	[40]	[52]	[47]
Mean RMSE	**3.37**	4.15	5.35	6.75	8.08	28.00	**7.61**	8.93	10.34	10.51	11.74	19.60
Median RMSE	**3.41**	3.54	4.68	6.41	7.82	29.50	**6.75**	8.71	10.54	9.76	11.53	22.96
Mean SSIM	**0.94**	**0.94**	0.92	0.91	0.91	0.87	0.89	0.89	**0.90**	0.86	0.88	0.88
Median SSIM	**0.95**	0.94	0.92	0.91	0.91	0.87	0.90	0.90	**0.91**	0.88	0.90	0.89

Table 2. Illumination estimation on synthetic data.

Relighting RMSE	Diffuse bunny					Glossy bunny				
	Ours	[9]	[5]	[19]	[12]	Ours	[9]	[5]	[19]	[12]
Mean (outdoor)	**10.78**	18.13	\	21.20	17.77	**11.02**	18.28	\	21.63	18.28
Median (outdoor)	**9.38**	17.03	\	19.95	15.91	**9.74**	17.67	\	20.49	16.30
Mean (indoor)	**13.18**	\	29.25	25.40	20.52	**13.69**	\	29.71	25.92	21.01
Median (indoor)	**11.68**	\	25.99	25.38	19.22	**11.98**	\	26.53	25.91	19.75

6.3 Evaluation of Illumination Estimation

Following [9], we evaluate illumination estimation by examining the relighting errors of a Stanford bunny under predicted environment maps and the ground truth. The lighting estimation is performed on synthetic faces rendered into captured outdoor and indoor scenes and their recorded HDR environment maps. Results are computed for both a diffuse and a glossy Stanford bunny (see the supplement for rendering parameters, visualization of rendered bunnies, and estimated environment maps). The comparison methods include the following:

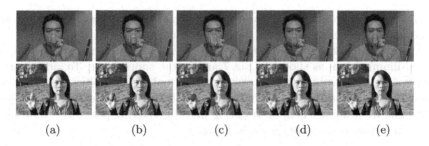

Fig. 7. Virtual object insertion results for indoor (first row) and outdoor (second row) scenes. (a) Photos with real object. Object insertion by (b) our method, (c) [5] for the first row and [9] for the second row, (d) [19], (e) [12]. More results in the supplement.

Fig. 8. Object insertion results by our method.

our implementation of [12] which uses a face to recover spherical harmonics (SH) lighting up to second order under the assumption that the face is diffuse; downloaded code for [19] which estimates illumination and reflectance given known surface normals that we estimate using [51]; online demo code for [9] which is designed for outdoor images; and author-provided results for [5] which is intended for indoor images.

The relighting errors are presented in Table 2. Except for [9] and [5], the errors were computed for 500 environment maps estimated from five synthetic faces under 100 real HDR environment maps (50 indoor and 50 outdoor). Since [9] and [5] are respectively for outdoor and indoor scenes and are not trained on faces, their results are each computed from LDR crops from the center of the 50 indoor/outdoor environment maps. We found [9] and [5] to be generally less precise in estimating light source directions, especially when light sources are out-of-view in the input crops, but they still provide reasonable approximations. For [5], the estimates of high frequency lighting become less precise when the indoor environment is more complicated. The experiments indicate that [19] may be relatively sensitive to surface textures and imprecise geometry in comparison to our method, which is purposely designed to deal with faces. For the Spherical Harmonics representation [12], estimates of a low-order SH model are seen to lack detail, and the estimated face albedo incorporates the illumination color, which leads to environment maps that are mostly white (see supplement for examples). Overall, the results indicate that our method provides the closest estimates to the ground truth. For a comparison of environment map estimation errors in real scenes, please refer to the supplement.

We additionally conducted comparisons on virtual object insertion using estimated illumination, as shown in Fig. 7 and in the supplement. To aid in verification, we also show images that contain the actual physical object (an Android robot). In some cases such as the bottom of (c), lighting from the side is estimated as coming from farther behind, resulting in a shadowed appearance. Additional object insertion results are shown in Fig. 8.

6.4   Demonstration of Light Source Triangulation

Using the simple scheme described in Sect. 5.4, we demonstrate the triangulation of two local light sources from an image with three faces, shown in Fig. 9(a). The estimated environment maps from the three faces are shown in Fig. 9(b). We triangulate the point lights from two of them, while using the third for validation. In order to provide a quantitative evaluation, we use the DSO SLAM system [4] to reconstruct the scene, including the faces and light sources. We manually mark the reconstructed faces and light sources in the 3D point clouds as ground truth. As shown in Fig. 9(c–d), the results of our method are close to this ground truth. The position errors are 0.19 m, 0.44 m and 0.29 m for the faces from left to right, and 0.41 m and 0.51 m for the two lamps respectively. If the ground truth face positions are used, the position errors of the lamps are reduced to 0.20 m and 0.49 m, respectively.

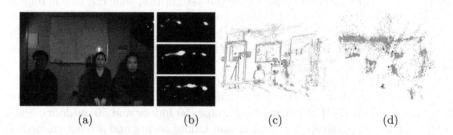

(a)   (b)   (c)   (d)

Fig. 9. (a) Input image with multiple faces; (b) their estimated environment maps (top to bottom are for faces from left to right); estimated 3D positions from (c) side view and (d) top view. Black dot: camera. Red dots: ground truth of faces and lights. Blue dots: estimated faces and lights. Orange dots: estimated lights using ground truth of face positions. (Color figure online)

7   Conclusion

We proposed a system for non-parametric illumination estimation based on an unsupervised finetuning approach for extracting highlight reflections from faces. In future work, we plan to examine more sophisticated schemes for recovering spatially variant illumination from the environment maps of multiple faces in an image. Using faces as lighting probes provides us with a better understanding of the surrounding environment not viewed by the camera, which can benefit a variety of vision applications.

Acknowledgments. This work is supported by Canada NSERC Discovery Grant 611664. Renjiao Yi is supported by scholarship from China Scholarship Council.

References

1. Barron, J.T., Malik, J.: Shape, illumination, and reflectance from shading. IEEE Trans. Pattern Anal. Mach. Intell. (PAMI) **37**(8), 1670–1687 (2015)
2. Blanz, V., Vetter, T.: A morphable model for the synthesis of 3D faces. In: ACM SIGGRAPH, pp. 187–194. ACM (1999)
3. Calian, D.A., Lalonde, J.F., Gotardo, P., Simon, T., Matthews, I., Mitchell, K.: From faces to outdoor light probes. In: Computer Graphics Forum, vol. 37, pp. 51–61. Wiley Online Library (2018)
4. Engel, J., Koltun, V., Cremers, D.: Direct sparse odometry. IEEE Trans. Pattern Anal. Mach. Intell. **40**, 611–625 (2017)
5. Gardner, M.A., et al.: Learning to predict indoor illumination from a single image. ACM Trans. Graph. (SIGGRAPH Asia) **9**(4) (2017)
6. Garrido, P., Valgaerts, L., Wu, C., Theobalt, C.: Reconstructing detailed dynamic face geometry from monocular video. ACM Trans. Graph. (TOG) **32**(6), 158:1–158:10 (2013)
7. Guo, Y., Zhang, L., Hu, Y., He, X., Gao, J.: MS-Celeb-1M: a dataset and benchmark for large-scale face recognition. In: Leibe, B., Matas, J., Sebe, N., Welling, M. (eds.) ECCV 2016. LNCS, vol. 9907, pp. 87–102. Springer, Cham (2016). https://doi.org/10.1007/978-3-319-46487-9_6
8. Hassner, T., Harel, S., Paz, E., Enbar, R.: Effective face frontalization in unconstrained images. In: Proceedings of the IEEE Conference on Computer Vision and Pattern Recognition, pp. 4295–4304 (2015)
9. Hold-Geoffroy, Y., Sunkavalli, K., Hadap, S., Gambaretto, E., Lalonde, J.F.: Deep outdoor illumination estimation. In: IEEE International Conference on Computer Vision and Pattern Recognition (2017)
10. Kemelmacher-Shlizerman, I., Basri, R.: 3D face reconstruction from a single image using a single reference face shape. IEEE Trans. Pattern Anal. Mach. Intell. (PAMI) **33**(2), 394–405 (2011)
11. Kim, H., Jin, H., Hadap, S., Kweon, I.: Specular reflection separation using dark channel prior. In: Proceedings of IEEE Conference on Computer Vision and Pattern Recognition, pp. 1460–1467 (2013)
12. Knorr, S.B., Kurz, D.: Real-time illumination estimation from faces for coherent rendering. In: 2014 IEEE International Symposium on Mixed and Augmented Reality, ISMAR, pp. 113–122. IEEE (2014)
13. Lalonde, J.-F., Narasimhan, S.G., Efros, A.A.: What does the sky tell us about the camera? In: Forsyth, D., Torr, P., Zisserman, A. (eds.) ECCV 2008. LNCS, vol. 5305, pp. 354–367. Springer, Heidelberg (2008). https://doi.org/10.1007/978-3-540-88693-8_26
14. Lalonde, J.F., Narasimhan, S.G., Efros, A.A.: What do the sun and the sky tell us about the camera? Int. J. Comput. Vis. **88**(1), 24–51 (2010)

15. Li, C., Lin, S., Zhou, K., Ikeuchi, K.: Radiometric calibration from faces in images. In: Proceedings of the IEEE Conference on Computer Vision and Pattern Recognition, pp. 3117–3126 (2017)
16. Li, C., Lin, S., Zhou, K., Ikeuchi, K.: Specular highlight removal in facial images. In: Proceedings of the IEEE Conference on Computer Vision and Pattern Recognition, pp. 3107–3116 (2017)
17. Li, C., Zhou, K., Lin, S.: Intrinsic face image decomposition with human face priors. In: Fleet, D., Pajdla, T., Schiele, B., Tuytelaars, T. (eds.) ECCV 2014. LNCS, vol. 8693, pp. 218–233. Springer, Cham (2014). https://doi.org/10.1007/978-3-319-10602-1_15
18. Li, Y., Lin, S., Lu, H., Shum, H.Y.: Multiple-cue illumination estimation in textured scenes. In: Proceedings of International Conference on Computer Vision, pp. 1366–1373 (2003)
19. Lombardi, S., Nishino, K.: Reflectance and illumination recovery in the wild. IEEE Trans. Pattern Anal. Mach. Intell. (PAMI) **38**(1), 129–141 (2016)
20. Lopez-Moreno, J., Hadap, S., Reinhard, E., Gutierrez, D.: Compositing images through light source detection. Comput. Graph. **34**(6), 698–707 (2010)
21. Lucy, L.B.: An iterative technique for the rectification of observed distributions. The Astron. J. **79**, 745 (1974)
22. Mallick, S.P., Zickler, T., Belhumeur, P.N., Kriegman, D.J.: Specularity removal in images and videos: a PDE approach. In: Leonardis, A., Bischof, H., Pinz, A. (eds.) ECCV 2006. LNCS, vol. 3951, pp. 550–563. Springer, Heidelberg (2006). https://doi.org/10.1007/11744023_43
23. Mathworks: MATLAB R2014b. https://www.mathworks.com/products/matlab.html
24. Narihira, T., Maire, M., Yu, S.X.: Direct intrinsics: learning albedo-shading decomposition by convolutional regression. In: Proceedings of the IEEE International Conference on Computer Vision, p. 2992 (2015)
25. Nishino, K., Nayar, S.K.: Eyes for relighting. In: ACM Transactions on Graphics, TOG, vol. 23, pp. 704–711. ACM (2004)
26. Okabe, T., Sato, I., Sato, Y.: Spherical harmonics vs. haar wavelets: basis for recovering illumination from cast shadows. In: Proceedings of IEEE Conference on Computer Vision and Pattern Recognition, vol. 1, pp. 50–57 (2004)
27. Panagopoulos, A., Wang, C., Samaras, D., Paragios, N.: Illumination estimation and cast shadow detection through a higher-order graphical model. In: Proceedings of IEEE Conference on Computer Vision and Pattern Recognition (2011)
28. Papadopoulo, T., Lourakis, M.I.A.: Estimating the Jacobian of the singular value decomposition: theory and applications. In: Vernon, D. (ed.) ECCV 2000. LNCS, vol. 1842, pp. 554–570. Springer, Heidelberg (2000). https://doi.org/10.1007/3-540-45054-8_36
29. Paysan, P., Knothe, R., Amberg, B., Romdhani, S., Vetter, T.: A 3D face model for pose and illumination invariant face recognition. In: Sixth IEEE International Conference on Advanced Video and Signal Based Surveillance, AVSS 2009, pp. 296–301. IEEE (2009)
30. Pessoa, S., Moura, G., Lima, J., Teichrieb, V., Kelner, J.: Photorealistic rendering for augmented reality: a global illumination and BRDF solution. In: 2010 IEEE Virtual Reality Conference, VR, pp. 3–10. IEEE (2010)
31. Phong, B.T.: Illumination for computer generated pictures. Commun. ACM **18**(6), 311–317 (1975)
32. Ramamoorthi, R., Hanrahan, P.: A signal-processing framework for inverse rendering. In: ACM SIGGRAPH, pp. 117–128. ACM (2001)

33. Rematas, K., Ritschel, T., Fritz, M., Gavves, E., Tuytelaars, T.: Deep reflectance maps. In: Proceedings of the IEEE Conference on Computer Vision and Pattern Recognition, pp. 4508–4516 (2016)
34. Richardson, E., Sela, M., Or-El, R., Kimmel, R.: Learning detailed face reconstruction from a single image. In: Proceedings of IEEE Conference on Computer Vision and Pattern Recognition (2017)
35. Richardson, W.H.: Bayesian-based iterative method of image restoration. JOSA **62**(1), 55–59 (1972)
36. Sato, I., Sato, Y., Ikeuchi, K.: Acquiring a radiance distribution to superimpose virtual objects onto a real scene. IEEE Trans. Vis. Comput. Graph. (TVCG) **5**, 1–12 (1999)
37. Sato, I., Sato, Y., Ikeuchi, K.: Illumination from shadows. IEEE Trans. Pattern Anal. Mach. Intell. (PAMI) **25**, 290–300 (2003)
38. Sela, M., Richardson, E., Kimmel, R.: Unrestricted facial geometry reconstruction using image-to-image translation. In: Proceedings of International Conference on Computer Vision (2017)
39. Shafer, S.: Using color to separate reflection components. Color Res. Appl. **10**(4), 210–218 (1985)
40. Shen, H.L., Zheng, Z.H.: Real-time highlight removal using intensity ratio. Appl. Opt. **52**(19), 4483–4493 (2013)
41. Shi, J., Dong, Y., Su, H., Yu, S.X.: Learning non-Lambertian object intrinsics across ShapeNet categories. In: Proceedings of IEEE Conference on Computer Vision and Pattern Recognition (2017)
42. Shrivastava, A., Pfister, T., Tuzel, O., Susskind, J., Wang, W., Webb, R.: Learning from simulated and unsupervised images through adversarial training. In: Proceedings of IEEE Conference on Computer Vision and Pattern Recognition (2017)
43. Snap Inc.: Snapchat. https://www.snapchat.com/
44. Tan, P., Lin, S., Quan, L.: Separation of highlight reflections on textured surfaces. In: Proceedings of IEEE Conference on Computer Vision and Pattern Recognition, vol. 2, pp. 1855–1860 (2006)
45. Tan, P., Lin, S., Quan, L., Shum, H.Y.: Highlight removal by illumination-constrained inpainting. In: Proceedings of International Conference on Computer Vision (2003)
46. Tan, R., Ikeuchi, K.: Reflection components decomposition of textured surfaces using linear basis functions. In: Proceedings of IEEE Conference on Computer Vision and Pattern Recognition, vol. 1, pp. 125–131 (2005)
47. Tan, R.T., Nishino, K., Ikeuchi, K.: Separating reflection components based on chromaticity and noise analysis. IEEE Trans. Pattern Anal. Mach. Intell. **26**(10), 1373–1379 (2004)
48. Wang, Y., Samaras, D.: Estimation of multiple illuminants from a single image of arbitrary known geometry. In: Heyden, A., Sparr, G., Nielsen, M., Johansen, P. (eds.) ECCV 2002. LNCS, vol. 2352, pp. 272–288. Springer, Heidelberg (2002). https://doi.org/10.1007/3-540-47977-5_18
49. Wang, Z., Bovik, A.C., Sheikh, H.R., Simoncelli, E.P.: Image quality assessment: from error visibility to structural similarity. IEEE Trans. Image Process. **13**(4), 600–612 (2004)
50. Weyrich, T., et al.: Analysis of human faces using a measurement-based skin reflectance model. In: ACM Transactions on Graphics, TOG, vol. 25, pp. 1013–1024. ACM (2006)

51. Yang, F., Wang, J., Shechtman, E., Bourdev, L., Metaxas, D.: Expression flow for 3D-aware face component transfer. In: ACM Transactions on Graphics, TOG, vol. 30, p. 60. ACM (2011)
52. Yang, Q., Wang, S., Ahuja, N.: Real-time specular highlight removal using bilateral filtering. In: Daniilidis, K., Maragos, P., Paragios, N. (eds.) ECCV 2010. LNCS, vol. 6314, pp. 87–100. Springer, Heidelberg (2010). https://doi.org/10.1007/978-3-642-15561-1_7
53. Zhu, X., Ramanan, D.: Face detection, pose estimation, and landmark localization in the wild. In: 2012 IEEE Conference on Computer Vision and Pattern Recognition CVPR, pp. 2879–2886. IEEE (2012)

DetNet: Design Backbone for Object Detection

Zeming Li[1]([✉])[iD], Chao Peng[2][iD], Gang Yu[2][iD], Xiangyu Zhang[2][iD],
Yangdong Deng[1][iD], and Jian Sun[2][iD]

[1] School of Software, Tsinghua University, Beijing, China
lizm15@mails.tsinghua.edu.cn, dengyd@tsinghua.edu.cn
[2] Megvii Inc. (Face++), Beijing, China
{pengchao,yugang,zhangxiangyu,sunjian}@megvii.com

Abstract. Recent CNN based object detectors, either one-stage methods like YOLO, SSD, and RetinaNet, or two-stage detectors like Faster R-CNN, R-FCN and FPN, are usually trying to directly finetune from ImageNet pre-trained models designed for the task of image classification. However, there has been little work discussing the backbone feature extractor specifically designed for the task of object detection. More importantly, there are several differences between the tasks of image classification and object detection. (i) Recent object detectors like FPN and RetinaNet usually involve extra stages against the task of image classification to handle the objects with various scales. (ii) Object detection not only needs to recognize the category of the object instances but also spatially locate them. Large downsampling factors bring large valid receptive field, which is good for image classification, but compromises the object location ability. Due to the gap between the image classification and object detection, we propose DetNet in this paper, which is a novel backbone network specifically designed for object detection. Moreover, DetNet includes the extra stages against traditional backbone network for image classification, while maintains high spatial resolution in deeper layers. Without any bells and whistles, state-of-the-art results have been obtained for both object detection and instance segmentation on the MSCOCO benchmark based on our DetNet (4.8G FLOPs) backbone. Codes will be released (https://github.com/zengarden/DetNet).

Keywords: Object detection · Convolutional neural network
Image classification

1 Introduction

Object detection is one of the most fundamental tasks in computer vision. Due to the rapid progress of deep convolutional neural networks (CNN) [10–12, 15–17, 35, 36, 38, 40], the performance of object detection has been significantly improved.

© Springer Nature Switzerland AG 2018
V. Ferrari et al. (Eds.): ECCV 2018, LNCS 11213, pp. 339–354, 2018.
https://doi.org/10.1007/978-3-030-01240-3_21

Recent CNN based object detectors can be categorized into one-stage detectors, like YOLO [29,30], SSD [24], and RetinaNet [22], and two-stage detectors, e.g. Faster R-CNN [31], R-FCN [18], FPN [21]. Both of them depend on the backbone network pretrained for the ImageNet classification task. However, there is a gap between the image classification and the object detection problem, which not only needs to recognize the category of the object instances but also spatially localize the bounding-boxes. More specifically, there are two problems using the classification backbone for object detection tasks. (i) Recent detectors, e.g., FPN, involve extra stages compared with the backbone network for ImageNet classification in order to detect objects with various sizes. (ii) Traditional backbones produce higher receptive field based on large downsampling factors, which is beneficial to the visual classification. However, the spatial resolution is compromised which will fail to accurately localize the large objects and recognize the small objects.

A well designed detection backbone should tackle all of the problems above. In this paper, we propose DetNet, which is a novel backbone designed for object detection. More specifically, to address the large scale variations of the object instances, DetNet involves additional stages which are utilized in the recent object detectors like FPN. Different from traditional pre-trained models for ImageNet classification, we maintain the spatial resolution of the features even though extra stages are included. However, high resolution feature maps bring more challenges to build a deep neural network due to the computational and memory cost. To keep the efficiency of our DetNet, we employ a low complexity dilated bottleneck structure. By integrating these improvements, our DetNet not only maintains high resolution feature maps but also keeps the large receptive field, both of which are important for the object detection task.

To summarize, we have the following contributions:

- We are the first to analyze the inherent drawbacks of traditional ImageNet pre-trained model for fine-tuning recent object detectors.
- We propose a novel backbone, called DetNet, which is specifically designed for the object detection task by maintaining the spatial resolution and enlarging the receptive field.
- We achieve new state-of-the-art results on MSCOCO object detection and instance segmentation track based on a low complexity DetNet59 backbone.

2   Related Works

Object detection is a heavily researched topic in computer vision. It aims at finding "where" and "what" each object instance is when given an image. Old detectors extract image features by using hand-engineered object component descriptors, such as HOG [5], SIFT [26], Selective Search [37], Edge Box [41]. For a long time, DPM [8] and its variants were the dominant methods among traditional object detectors. With the rapid progress of deep convolutional neural networks, CNN based object detectors have yielded remarkable results and become a new trend in the detection literature. In the network structure, recent

CNN based detectors are usually split into two parts. The one is the backbone network, and the other is the detection branch. We briefly introduce these two parts as follows.

2.1 Backbone Network

The backbone networks for object detection are usually borrowed from the ImageNet [32] classification. In the last few years, ImageNet has been regarded as the most authoritative datasets to evaluate the capability of deep convolution neural networks. Many novel networks are designed to get higher performance for ImageNet. AlexNet [17] is among the first to try to increase the depth of CNN. In order to reduce the network computation and increase the valid receptive field, AlexNet down-samples the feature map with 32 strides which is a standard setting for the following works. VGGNet [35] stacks 3×3 convolution operation to build a deeper network, while still involves 32 strides in feature maps. Most of the following researches adopt VGG like structure, and design a better component in each stage (split by stride). GoogleNet [36] proposes a novel inception block to involve more diverse features. ResNet [10] adopts "bottleneck" design with residual sum operation in each stage, which has been proved a simple and efficient way to build a deeper neural network. ResNext [38] and Xception [2] use group convolution layer to replace the traditional convolution. It reduces the parameters and increases the accuracy simultaneously. DenseNet [13] densely concat several layers, it further reduces parameters while keeping competitive accuracy. Another different research is Dilated Residual Network [39] which extracts features with less strides. DRN achieves notable results on segmentation, while has little discussion on object detection. There are still lots of research for efficient backbone, such as [11,15,40]. However they are usually designed for classification.

2.2 Object Detection Branch

Detection branch is usually attached to the base-model which is designed and trained for ImageNet classification dataset. There are two different design logic for object detection. The one is one-stage detector, which directly uses backbone for object instance prediction. For example, YOLO [29,30] uses a simple efficient backbone DarkNet [29], and then simplifies detection as a regression problem. SSD [24] adopts reduced VGGNet [35] and extracts features in multi-layers, which enables network more powerful to handle variant object scales. RetinaNet [22] uses ResNet as a basic feature extractor, then involves "Focal" loss [22] to address class imbalance issue caused by extreme foreground-background ratio. The other popular pipeline is the two-stage detector. Specifically, recent two-stage detector will predict lots of proposals first based on the backbone, then an additional classifier is involved for proposal classification and regression. Faster R-CNN [31] directly generates proposals from the backbone by using Region Proposal Network (RPN). R-FCN [18] proposes to generate a position sensitive feature map from the output of the backbone, then a novel pooling methods called position sensitive pooling is utilized for each proposal. Deformable convolution Networks [4] tries to enable convolution operation with geometric transformations by learning additional offsets without supervision. It is among the first to ameliorate backbone for object detection. Feature Pyramid Network [21] constructs feature pyramids by exploiting inherent multi-scale, pyramidal hierarchy of deep convolutional networks, specifically FPN combines multi-layer output by utilizing U-shape structure, and still borrows the traditional ResNet without further study. DSOD [33] first proposes to train detection from scratch, whose results are lower than pretrained methods.

In conclusion, traditional backbones are usually designed for ImageNet classification. What is the suitable backbone for object detection is still an unexplored field. Most of the recent object detectors, no matter one-stage or two-stage, follow the pipeline of ImageNet pre-trained models, which is not optimal for detection performance. In this paper, we propose DetNet. The key idea of DetNet is to design a better backbone for object detection.

3   DetNet: A Backbone Network for Object Detection

3.1   Motivation

Recent object detectors usually rely on a backbone network which is pretrained on the ImageNet classification dataset. As the task of ImageNet classification is different from the object detection which not only needs to recognize the category of the objects but also spatially localize the bounding-boxes. The design principles for the image classification is not good for the localization task as the spatial resolution of the feature maps is gradually decreased for the standard networks like VGG16 and Resnet. A few techniques like Feature Pyramid Network (FPN) as in Fig. 1A. [21] and dilation are applied to these networks to maintain the spatial resolution. However, there still exists the following three problems when trained with these backbone networks.

The Number of Network Stages Is Different. As shown in Fig. 1B, typical classification network involves 5 stages, with each stage down-sampling feature maps by pooling 2x or stride 2 convolution. Thus the spatial size of the output feature map is "32x" sub-sampled. Different from traditional classification network, feature pyramid detectors usually adopt more stages. For example, in Feature Pyramid Networks (FPN) [21], an additional stage $P6$ is added to handle larger objects. The stages of $P6$ and $P7$ are added in RetinaNet [22] in a similar way. Obviously, extra stages like $P6$ are not pre-trained in the ImageNet dataset.

Weak Visibility (Localization) of Large Objects. The feature map with strong semantic information has strides of 32 respect to the input image, which brings large valid receptive field and leads the success of ImageNet classification task. However, large stride factor is harmful for the object localization. In Feature Pyramid Networks, the large object is generated and predicted within the deeper

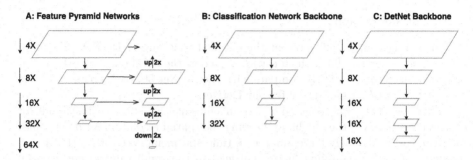

Fig. 1. Comparisons of different backbones used in FPN. Feature pyramid networks (FPN) with the traditional backbone is illustrated in (A). The traditional backbone for image classification is illustrated in (B). Our proposed backbone is illustrated in (C), which has higher spatial resolution and the same stages as FPN. We do not illustrate stage 1 (with stride 2) feature map due to the limitation of figure size.

layers, the boundary of these object may be too blurry to get an accurate regression. This case is even worse when more stages are involved into the classification network, since more down-sampling brings more strides to object.

Invisibility (Recall) of Small Objects. Another drawback of large stride is the missing of small objects. The information from the small objects will be easily weaken as the spatial resolution of the feature maps is decreased and the large context information is integrated. Therefore, Feature Pyramid Network predicts small object in shallower layers. However, shallow layers usually only have low semantic information which may be not sufficient to recognize the category of the object instances. Therefore the detectors usually enhance their classification capability by involving the context cues of high-level representations from the deeper layers. As Fig. 1A shows, Feature Pyramid Networks relieve it by adopting bottom-up pathway. However, if the small objects are missing in deeper layers, these context cues will be decreased simultaneously.

To address these problems, we propose DetNet which has following characteristics. (i) The number of stages is directly designed for Object Detection. (ii) Even though we involve more stages (such as 6 stages or 7 stages) than traditional classification network, we maintain high spatial resolution of the feature maps, while keeping large receptive field.

DetNet has several advantages over traditional backbone networks like ResNet for object detection. First, DetNet has exactly the same number of stages as the detector used, therefore extra stages like *P6* can be pre-trained in the ImageNet dataset. Second, benefited by high resolution feature maps in the last stage, DetNet is more powerful in locating the boundary of astronomical objects and finding the small objects. More detailed discussion can be referred to Sect. 4.

3.2 DetNet Design

In this subsection, we will present the detailed structure of DetNet. We adopt ResNet-50 as our baseline, which is widely used as the backbone network in a lot of object detectors. To fairly compare with the ResNet-50, we keep stage 1,2,3,4 the same as original ResNet-50 for our DetNet.

There are two challenges to make an efficient and effective backbone for object detection. On the one hand, keeping the spatial resolution for deep neural network costs extremely large amount of time and memory. On the other hand, reducing the down-sampling factor will lead to the small valid receptive field, which will be harmful to many vision tasks, such as image classification and semantic segmentation.

DetNet is carefully designed to address the two challenges. Specifically, DetNet follows the same setting for ResNet from the first stage to the fourth stage. The difference starts from the fifth stage and an overview of our DetNet for image classification can be found in Fig. 2D. Let us discuss the implementation details of DetNet59 derived from the ResNet50. Similarly, our DetNet can be easily extended with deep layers like ResNet101. The detailed design of our DetNet59 is illustrated as follows:

- We introduce the extra stage, e.g., *P6*, in the backbone which will be utilized for object detection as in FPN. Meanwhile, we fix the spatial resolution as 16x downsampling after stage 4.
- Since the spatial size is fixed after stage 4, in order to introduce a new stage, we employ a dilated [1, 25, 27] bottleneck with 1×1 convolution projection (Fig. 2B) in the beginning of the each stage. We find the model in Fig. 2B is important for multi-stage detectors like FPN.
- We apply bottleneck with dilation as a basic network block to efficiently enlarge the receptive field. Since dilated convolution is still time consuming, our stage 5 and stage 6 keep the same channels as stage 4 (256 input channels for bottleneck block). This is different from traditional backbone design, which will double channels in a later stage.

It is easy to integrate DetNet with any detectors with/without feature pyramid. Without losing representativeness, we adopt prominent detector FPN as our baselines to validate the effectiveness of DetNet. Since DetNet only changes the backbone of FPN, we fix the other structures in FPN except for backbone. Because we do not reduce spatial size after stage 4 of Resnet-50, we simply sum the output of these stages in top-down path way.

4   Experiments

In this section, we will evaluate our approach on the popular MS COCO benchmark, which has 80 objects categories. There are 80k images in the training set, and 40k images in the validation dataset. Following a common practice, we further split the 40k validation set into 35k *large-val* datasets and 5k *mini-val*

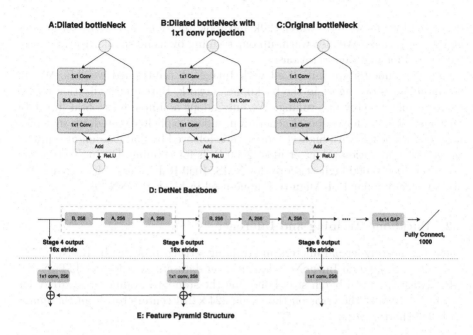

Fig. 2. Detail structure of DetNet (D) and DetNet based Feature Pyramid NetWork (E). Different bottleneck block used in DetNet is illustrated in (A, B). The original bottleneck is illustrated in (C). DetNet follows the same design as ResNet before stage 4, while keeps spatial size after stage 4 (e.g. stage 5 and 6).

datasets. All of our validation experiments involve training set and the *large-val* for training (about 115k images), then test on 5k *mini-val* datasets. We also report the final results of our approach on COCO *test-dev*, which has no disclosed labels.

We use standard coco metrics to evaluate our approach, including AP (averaged precision over intersection-over-union thresholds), AP_{50}, AP_{75} (AP at use different IoU thresholds), and AP_S, AP_M, AP_L (AP at different scales: small, middle, large).

4.1   Detector Training and Inference

Following training strategies provided by Detectron[1] repository [7], our detectors are end-to-end trained on 8 Pascal TITAN XP GPUs, optimized by synchronized SGD with a weight decay of 0.0001 and momentum of 0.9. Each mini-batch has 2 images, so the effective batch-size is 16. We resize the shorter edge of the image to 800 pixels, the longer edge is limited to 1333 pixels to avoid large memory cost. We pad the images within mini-batch to the same size by filling zeros into the right-bottom of the image. We use typical "2x" training settings used in Detectron [7]. Learning rate is set to 0.02 at the begin of the training, and then

---
[1] https://github.com/facebookresearch/Detectron.

decreased by a factor of 0.1 after 120k and 160k iterations and finally terminates at 180k iterations. We also warm-up our training by using smaller learning rate 0.02×0.3 for first 500 iterations.

All experiments are initialized with ImageNet pre-trained weights. We fix the parameters of stage 1 in the backbone network. Batch normalization is also fixed during detector fine-tuning. We only adopt a simple horizontal flip data augmentation. As for proposal generation, unless explicitly stated, we first pick up 12000 proposals with highest scores, then followed by non maximum suppression (NMS) operation to get at most 2000 RoIs for training. During testing, we use 6000/1000 (6000 highest scores for NMS, 1000 RoIs after NMS) setting. We also involve popular RoI-Align technique used in Mask R-CNN [9].

4.2 Backbone Training and Inference

Following most hyper-parameters and training settings provided by ResNext [38], we train backbone on ImageNet classification datasets by 8 Pascal TITAN XP GPUs with 256 total batch size. Following the standard evaluation strategy for testing, we report the error on the single 224×224 center crop from the image with 256 shorter sides.

4.3 Main Results

We adopt FPN with the ResNet-50 backbone as our baseline because FPN is a prominent detector for many other vision tasks, such as instance segmentation and skeleton [9]. To validate the effectiveness of DetNet for FPN, we propose DetNet-59 which involves an additional stage compared with ResNet-50. More design details can be found in Sect. 3. Then we replace ResNet-50 backbone with DetNet-59 and keep the other structures the same as the original FPN.

We first train DetNet-59 on ImageNet classification, results are shown in Table 1. DetNet-59 has 23.5% top-1 error at the cost of 4.8G FLOPs. Then we train FPN with DetNet-59, and compare it with ResNet-50 based FPN. From Table 1 we can see DetNet-59 has superior performance than ResNet-50 (over 2 points gains in mAP).

Since DetNet-59 has more parameters than ResNet-50 (because we involving additional stage for FPN *P6*), a natural hypothesis is that the improvement is mainly due to more parameters. To validate the effectiveness of DetNet-59, we also train FPN with ResNet-101 which has 7.6G FLOPs complexity, the results is 39.8 mAP. ResNet-101 has much more FLOPs than DetNet-59, and still yields lower mAP than DetNet-59. We further add the FPN experiments based on DetNet-101. Specifically, DetNet-101 has 20 (6 in DetNet-59) repeated bottleneck blocks in ResNet stage 4. As expected, DetNet-101 has superior results than ResNet-101, which validates that DetNet is more suitable than ResNet as a backbone network for object detection.

As DetNet is directly designed for object detection, to further validate the advantage of DetNet, we train FPN based on DetNet-59 and ResNet-50 from

Table 1. Results of different backbones used in FPN. We first report the standard Top-1 error on ImageNet classification (the lower error is, the better accuracy in classification). FLOPs means the computation complexity. We also illustrate FPN COCO results to investigate effectiveness of these backbone for object detection.

Backbone	Classification		FPN results					
	Top1 err	FLOPs	mAP	AP_{50}	AP_{75}	AP_s	AP_m	AP_l
ResNet-50	24.1	3.8G	37.9	60.0	41.2	22.9	40.6	49.2
DetNet-59	23.5	4.8G	**40.2**	61.7	43.7	23.9	43.2	52.0
ResNet-101	23.0	7.6G	39.8	62.0	43.5	24.1	43.4	51.7
DetNet-101	23.0	7.9G	41.8	62.8	45.7	25.4	45.2	55.1

scratch. The results are shown in Table 2. Noticing that we use multi-gpu synchronized batch normalization during training as in [28] in order to train from scratch. Concluding from the results, DetNet-59 still outperforms ResNet-50 by 1.8 points, which further validate that DetNet is more suitable for object detection.

Table 2. FPN results on different backbones, which is trained from scratch. Since we don't involve ImageNet pre-trained weights, we want to directly compare backbone capability for object detection.

Backbone	mAP	AP_{50}	AP_{75}	AP_s	AP_m	AP_l
ResNet-50 from scratch	34.5	55.2	37.7	20.4	36.7	44.5
DetNet-59 from scratch	**36.3**	56.5	39.3	22.0	38.4	46.9

4.4 Results Analysis

In this subsection, we will analyze how DetNet improves the object detection. There are two key-points in object detection evaluation: average precision (AP) and average recall (AR). AR means how much objects we can find out, AP means how much objects are correctly localized (right label for classification). AP and AR are usually evaluated on different IoU threshold to validate the regression capability for object location. The larger IoU is, the more accurate regression needs. AP and AR are also evaluated on different range of bounding box areas (small, middle, and large) to find the detail results on the various scales of the objects.

At first, we investigate the impact of DetNet on detection accuracy. We evaluate the performance on different IoU thresholds and object scales as shown in Table 3.

DetNet-59 has an impressive improvement in the performance of large object location, which brings 5.5 (40.0 vs 34.5) points gains in AP_{85}@large. The reason

Table 3. Comparison of Average Precision (AP) of FPN on different IoU thresholds and different bounding box scales. AP_{50} is a effective metric to evaluate classification capability. AP_{85} requires accurate location of the bounding box prediction. Therefore it validates the regression capability of our approaches. We also illustrate AP at different scales to capture the influence of high resolution feature maps in backbone.

Models	scales	mAP	AP_{50}	AP_{60}	AP_{70}	AP_{80}	AP_{85}
ResNet-50	over all scales	37.9	60.0	55.1	47.2	33.1	22.1
	small	22.9	40.1	35.5	28.0	17.5	10.4
	middle	40.6	63.9	59.0	51.2	35.7	23.3
	large	49.2	72.2	68.2	60.8	46.6	34.5
DetNet-59	over all scales	40.2	61.7	57.0	49.6	36.2	25. 8
	small	23.9	41.8	36.8	29.8	17.7	10.5
	middle	43.2	65.8	61.2	53.6	39.9	27.3
	large	52.0	73.1	69.5	63	51.4	40.0

Table 4. Comparison of Average Recall (AR) of FPN on different IoU thresholds and different bounding box scales. AR_{50} is a effective metric to show how many reasonable bounding boxes we find out (class agnostic). AR_{85} means how accurate of box location.

Models	scales	mAR	AR_{50}	AR_{60}	AR_{70}	AR_{80}	AR_{85}
ResNet-50	over all scales	52.8	80.5	74.7	64.3	46.8	34.2
	small	35.5	60.0	53.8	43.3	28.7	18.7
	middle	56.0	84.9	79.2	68.7	50.5	36.2
	large	67.0	95.0	90.9	80.3	63.1	50.2
DetNet-59	over all scales	56.1	83.1	77.8	67.6	51.0	38.9
	small	39.2	66.4	59.4	47.3	29.5	19.6
	middle	59.5	87.4	82.5	72.6	55.6	41.2
	large	70.1	95.4	91.8	82.9	69.1	56.3

is that original ResNet based FPN has a big stride in deeper feature map, large objects may be challenging to get an accurate regression.

We also investigate the influence of DetNet for finding the small objects. As shown in Table 4, we make the detail statistics on averaged recall at different IoU threshold and scales. We conclude the table as follows:

- Compared with ResNet-50, DetNet-59 is more powerful for finding missing small objects, which yields 6.4 points gain (66.4 vs 60.0) in AR_{50} for the small object. DetNet keeps the higher resolution in deeper stages than ResNet, thus we can find smaller objects in deeper stages. Since we use up-sampling pathway in Fig. 1A. Shallow layer can also involve context cues for finding small objects. However, AR_{85}@small is comparable (18.7 vs 19.6) between ResNet-50 and DetNet-59. This is reasonable. DetNet has no use for small object location, because ResNet based FPN has already used the large feature map for the small object.
- DetNet is good for large object localization, which has 56.3 (vs 50.2) in AR_{85} for large objects. However, AR_{50} in the large object does not change too

much (95.4 vs 95.0). In general, DetNet finds more accurate large objects rather than missing large objects.

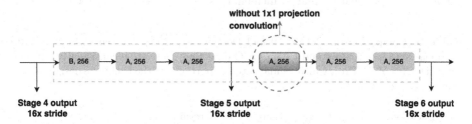

Fig. 3. The detail structure of DetNet-59-NoProj, which adopts module in Fig. 1A to split stage 6 (while original DetNet-59 adopts Fig. 1B to split stage 6). We design DetNet-59-NoProj to validate the importance of involving a new semantic stage as FPN for object detection. (Color figure online)

4.5 Discussion

As mentioned in Sect. 3, the key idea of DetNet is a novel designed backbone specifically for object detection. Based on a prominent object detector like Feature Pyramid Network, DetNet-59 follows exactly the same number of stages as FPN while maintaining high spatial resolution. To discuss the importance of the backbone for object detection, we first investigate the influence of stages.

Since the stage-6 of DetNet-59 has the same spatial size as stage-5, a natural hypothesis is that DetNet-59 simply involves a deeper stage-5 rather than producing a new stage-6. To prove DetNet-59 indeed involves an additional stage, we carefully analyze the details of DetNet-59 design. As shown in Fig. 2B. DetNet-59 adopts a dilated bottleneck with simple 1×1 convolution as the projection layer to split stage 6. It is much different from traditional ResNet, when spatial size of the feature map does not change, the projection will be simple identity in bottleneck structure(Fig. 2A) rather than 1×1 convolution(Fig. 2B). We break this convention. We claim the bottleneck with 1×1 convolution projection is effective to create a new stage even spatial size is unchanged.

To prove our idea, we involve DetNet-59-NoProj which is modified DetNet-59 by removing 1×1 projection convolution. Detail structure is shown in Fig. 3. There are only minor differences (red cell) between DetNet-59 (Fig. 2D) and DetNet-59-NoProj (Fig. 3).

First we train DetNet-59-NoProj in ImageNet classification, results are shown in Table 5. DetNet-59-NoProj has 0.5 higher Top1 error than DetNet-59. Then We train FPN based on DetNet-59-NoProj in Table 5. DetNet-59 outperforms DetNet-59-NoProj over 1 point for object detection.

The experimental results validate the importance of involving a new stage as FPN used for object detection. When we use module in Fig. 2A in our network, the output feature map is not much different from the input feature map, because output feature map is just sum of original input feature map and its transformation. Therefore, it is not easy to create a novel semantic stage for the network. While if we adopt module in Fig. 2B, it will be more divergent between input and output feature map, which enables us to create a new semantic stage.

Table 5. Comparison of DetNet-59 and DetNet-59-NoProj. We report both results on ImageNet classification and FPN COCO detection. DetNet-59 consistently outperforms DetNet-59-NoProj, which validates the importance of the backbone design (same semantic stage) as FPN.

Backbone	Classification		FPN results					
	Top1 err	FLOPs	mAP	AP_{50}	AP_{75}	AP_s	AP_m	AP_l
DetNet-59	23.5	4.8G	**40.2**	61.7	43.7	23.9	43.2	52.0
DetNet-59-NoProj	24.0	4.6G	39.1	61.3	42.1	23.6	42.0	50.1

Table 6. Comparison of FPN results on DetNet-59 and ResNet-50-dilated to validate the importance of pre-train backbone for detection. ResNet-50-dilated means that we fine-tune detection based on ResNet-50 weights, while involving dilated convolution in stage-5 of the ResNet-50. We don't illustrate Top-1 error of ResNet-50-dilated because it can not be directly used for image classification.

Backbone	Classification		FPN results					
	Top1 err	FLOPs,	mAP	AP_{50}	AP_{75}	AP_s	AP_m	AP_l
DetNet-59	23.5	4.8G	**40.2**	61.7	43.7	23.9	43.2	52.0
ResNet-50-dilated	–	6.1G	39.0	61.4	42.4	23.3	42.1	50.0

Another natural question is that "what is the result if we train FPN initialized with ResNet-50 parameters, and dilate stage 5 of the ResNet-50 during detector fine-tuning (for simplify, we denote it as ResNet-50-dilated)". To show the importance of pre-train backbone for detection, we compare DetNet-59 based FPN with ResNet-50-dilate based FPN in Table 6. ResNet-50-dilated has more FLOPs than DetNet-59, while gets lower performance than DetNet-59. Therefore, we have shown the importance of directly training base-model for object detection.

4.6   Comparison to State of the Art

We evaluate DetNet-59 based FPN on MSCOCO [20,23] detection test-dev dataset, and compare it with recent state-of-the-art methods listed in Table 7. Noticing that test-dev dataset is different from the mini-validation dataset used in ablation experiments. It has no disclosed labels and is evaluated on the server. Without any bells and whistles, our simple but efficient backbone achieves new

Fig. 4. Illustrative results of DetNet-59 based FPN.

Fig. 5. Illustrative results of DetNet-59 based Mask R-CNN.

state-of-the-art on COCO object detection, even outperforms strong competitors with ResNet-101 backbone. It is worth noting that DetNet-59 has only 4.8G FLOPs complexity while ResNet-101 has 7.6G FLOPs. We refer the original FPN results provided in Mask R-CNN [9]. It should be higher by using Detectron [7] repository, which will generate 39.8 mAP for FPN-ResNet-101.

To validate the generalization capability of our approach, we also evaluate DetNet-59 for MSCOCO instance segmentation based Mask R-CNN. Results are shown in Table 8 for test-dev. Thanks for the impressive ability of our DetNet59, we obtain a new state-of-the-art result on instance segmentation as well.

Some of the results are visualized in Figs. 4 and 5. Detection results of FPN with DetNet-59 backbone are shown in Fig. 4. Instance segmentation results of Mask R-CNN with DetNet-59 backbone are shown in Fig. 5. We only illustrate bounding boxes and instance segmentation no less than 0.5 classification scores.

Table 7. Comparison of object detection results between our approach and state-of-the-art on MSCOCO test-dev datasets. Based on our simple and effective backbone DetNet-59, our model outperforms all previous state-of-the-art. It is worth noting that DetNet-59 yields better results with much lower FLOPs.

Models	Backbone	mAP	AP_{50}	AP_{75}	AP_s	AP_m	AP_l
SSD513 [24]	ResNet-101	31.2	50.4	33.3	10.2	34.5	49.8
DSSD513 [6,24]	ResNet-101	33.2	53.3	35.2	13.0	35.4	51.1
Faster R-CNN+++ [10]	ResNet-101	34.9	55.7	37.4	15.6	38.7	50.9
Faster R-CNN G-RMI[a] [14]	Inception-ResNet-v2	34.7	55.5	36.7	13.5	38.1	52.0
RetinaNet [22]	ResNet-101	39.1	59.1	42.3	21.8	42.7	50.2
FPN [9]	ResNet-101	37.3	59.6	40.3	19.8	40.2	48.8
FPN	**DetNet-59**	**40.3**	62.1	43.8	23.6	42.6	50.0

[a]http://image-net.org/challenges/talks/2016/GRMI-COCO-slidedeck.pdf.

Table 8. Comparison of instance segmentation results between our approach and other state-of-the-art on MSCOCO test-dev datasets. Benefit from DetNet-59, we achieve a new state-of-the-art on instance segmentation task.

Models	Backbone	mAP	AP_{50}	AP_{75}	AP_s	AP_m	AP_l
MNC [3]	ResNet-101	24.6	44.3	24.8	4.7	25.9	43.6
FCIS [19] + OHEM [34]	ResNet-101-C5-dilated	29.2	49.5	-	7.1	31.3	50.0
FCIS+++ [19] + OHEM	ResNet-101-C5-dilated	33.6	54.5	-	-	-	-
Mask R-CNN [9]	ResNet-101	35.7	58.0	37.8	15.5	38.1	52.4
Mask R-CNN	**DetNet-59**	**37.1**	60.0	39.6	18.6	39.0	51.3

5   Conclusion

In this paper, we design a novel backbone network specifically for the object detection task. Traditionally, the backbone network is designed for the image classification task and there is a gap when transferred to the object detection task. To address this issue, we present a novel backbone structure called DetNet, which is not only optimized for the classification task but also localization friendly. Impressive results have been reported on the object detection and instance segmentation based on the COCO benchmark.

References

1. Chen, L.C., Papandreou, G., Kokkinos, I., Murphy, K., Yuille, A.L.: Semantic image segmentation with deep convolutional nets and fully connected CRFs. arXiv preprint arXiv:1412.7062 (2014)
2. Chollet, F.: Xception: deep learning with depthwise separable convolutions. arXiv preprint arXiv:1610.02357 (2016)
3. Dai, J., He, K., Sun, J.: Instance-aware semantic segmentation via multi-task network cascades. In: Proceedings of the IEEE Conference on Computer Vision and Pattern Recognition, pp. 3150–3158 (2016)

4. Dai, J., et al.: Deformable convolutional networks. arXiv preprint arXiv:1703.06211 (2017)
5. Dalal, N., Triggs, B.: Histograms of oriented gradients for human detection. In: IEEE Computer Society Conference on Computer Vision and Pattern Recognition, CVPR 2005, vol. 1, pp. 886–893. IEEE (2005)
6. Fu, C.Y., Liu, W., Ranga, A., Tyagi, A., Berg, A.C.: DSSD: deconvolutional single shot detector. arXiv preprint arXiv:1701.06659 (2017)
7. Girshick, R., Radosavovic, I., Gkioxari, G., Dollár, P., He, K.: Detectron (2018). https://github.com/facebookresearch/detectron
8. Girshick, R.B., Felzenszwalb, P.F., McAllester, D.: Discriminatively trained deformable part models, release 5 (2012)
9. He, K., Gkioxari, G., Dollár, P., Girshick, R.: Mask R-CNN. arXiv preprint arXiv:1703.06870 (2017)
10. He, K., Zhang, X., Ren, S., Sun, J.: Deep residual learning for image recognition. In: Proceedings of the IEEE Conference on Computer Vision and Pattern Recognition, pp. 770–778 (2016)
11. Howard, A.G., et al.: MobileNets: efficient convolutional neural networks for mobile vision applications. arXiv preprint arXiv:1704.04861 (2017)
12. Hu, J., Shen, L., Sun, G.: Squeeze-and-excitation networks. arXiv preprint arXiv:1709.01507 (2017)
13. Huang, G., Liu, Z.: Densely connected convolutional networks
14. Huang, J., et al.: Speed/accuracy trade-offs for modern convolutional object detectors. arXiv preprint arXiv:1611.10012 (2016)
15. Iandola, F.N., Han, S., Moskewicz, M.W., Ashraf, K., Dally, W.J., Keutzer, K.: SqueezeNet: AlexNet-level accuracy with 50x fewer parameters and <0.5 mb model size. arXiv preprint arXiv:1602.07360 (2016)
16. Ioffe, S., Szegedy, C.: Batch normalization: accelerating deep network training by reducing internal covariate shift. In: International Conference on Machine Learning, pp. 448–456 (2015)
17. Krizhevsky, A., Sutskever, I., Hinton, G.E.: ImageNet classification with deep convolutional neural networks. In: Advances in Neural Information Processing Systems, pp. 1097–1105 (2012)
18. Li, Y., He, K., Sun, J., et al.: R-FCN: object detection via region-based fully convolutional networks. In: Advances in Neural Information Processing Systems, pp. 379–387 (2016)
19. Li, Y., Qi, H., Dai, J., Ji, X., Wei, Y.: Fully convolutional instance-aware semantic segmentation. In: IEEE Conference on Computer Vision and Pattern Recognition, CVPR, pp. 2359–2367 (2017)
20. Lin, T.Y., Dollár, P.: MS COCO API (2016). https://github.com/pdollar/coco
21. Lin, T.Y., Dollár, P., Girshick, R., He, K., Hariharan, B., Belongie, S.: Feature pyramid networks for object detection. arXiv preprint arXiv:1612.03144 (2016)
22. Lin, T.Y., Goyal, P., Girshick, R., He, K., Dollár, P.: Focal loss for dense object detection. arXiv preprint arXiv:1708.02002 (2017)
23. Lin, T.-Y., et al.: Microsoft COCO: common objects in context. In: Fleet, D., Pajdla, T., Schiele, B., Tuytelaars, T. (eds.) ECCV 2014. LNCS, vol. 8693, pp. 740–755. Springer, Cham (2014). https://doi.org/10.1007/978-3-319-10602-1_48
24. Liu, W., et al.: SSD: single shot MultiBox detector. In: Leibe, B., Matas, J., Sebe, N., Welling, M. (eds.) ECCV 2016. LNCS, vol. 9905, pp. 21–37. Springer, Cham (2016). https://doi.org/10.1007/978-3-319-46448-0_2

25. Long, J., Shelhamer, E., Darrell, T.: Fully convolutional networks for semantic segmentation. In: Proceedings of the IEEE Conference on Computer Vision and Pattern Recognition, pp. 3431–3440 (2015)
26. Lowe, D.G.: Distinctive image features from scale-invariant keypoints. Int. J. Comput. Vis. **60**(2), 91–110 (2004)
27. Mallat, S.: A Wavelet Tour of Signal Processing. Academic Press, Cambridge (1999)
28. Peng, C., et al.: MegDet: a large mini-batch object detector. arXiv preprint arXiv:1711.07240 (2017)
29. Redmon, J., Divvala, S., Girshick, R., Farhadi, A.: You only look once: unified, real-time object detection. In: Proceedings of the IEEE Conference on Computer Vision and Pattern Recognition, pp. 779–788 (2016)
30. Redmon, J., Farhadi, A.: YOLO9000: better, faster, stronger. arXiv preprint arXiv:1612.08242 (2016)
31. Ren, S., He, K., Girshick, R., Sun, J.: Faster R-CNN: towards real-time object detection with region proposal networks. In: Advances in Neural Information Processing Systems, pp. 91–99 (2015)
32. Russakovsky, O., et al.: Imagenet large scale visual recognition challenge. Int. J. Comput. Vis. **115**(3), 211–252 (2015)
33. Shen, Z., Liu, Z., Li, J., Jiang, Y.G., Chen, Y., Xue, X.: DSOD: learning deeply supervised object detectors from scratch. In: The IEEE International Conference on Computer Vision, ICCV, vol. 3, p. 7 (2017)
34. Shrivastava, A., Gupta, A., Girshick, R.: Training region-based object detectors with online hard example mining. In: Proceedings of the IEEE Conference on Computer Vision and Pattern Recognition, pp. 761–769 (2016)
35. Simonyan, K., Zisserman, A.: Very deep convolutional networks for large-scale image recognition. arXiv preprint arXiv:1409.1556 (2014)
36. Szegedy, C., et al.: Going deeper with convolutions. In: Proceedings of the IEEE Conference on Computer Vision and Pattern Recognition, pp. 1–9 (2015)
37. Uijlings, J.R., Van De Sande, K.E., Gevers, T., Smeulders, A.W.: Selective search for object recognition. Int. J. Comput. Vis. **104**(2), 154–171 (2013)
38. Xie, S., Girshick, R., Dollár, P., Tu, Z., He, K.: Aggregated residual transformations for deep neural networks. In: 2017 IEEE Conference on Computer Vision and Pattern Recognition, CVPR, pp. 5987–5995. IEEE (2017)
39. Yu, F., Koltun, V., Funkhouser, T.: Dilated residual networks. In: Computer Vision and Pattern Recognition, vol. 1 (2017)
40. Zhang, X., Zhou, X., Lin, M., Sun, J.: ShuffleNet: an extremely efficient convolutional neural network for mobile devices. arXiv preprint arXiv:1707.01083 (2017)
41. Zitnick, C.L., Dollár, P.: Edge boxes: locating object proposals from edges. In: Fleet, D., Pajdla, T., Schiele, B., Tuytelaars, T. (eds.) ECCV 2014. LNCS, vol. 8693, pp. 391–405. Springer, Cham (2014). https://doi.org/10.1007/978-3-319-10602-1_26

Structured Siamese Network
for Real-Time Visual Tracking

Yunhua Zhang⬭, Lijun Wang⬭, Jinqing Qi$^{(\boxtimes)}$⬭, Dong Wang⬭,
Mengyang Feng⬭, and Huchuan Lu⬭

School of Information and Communication Engineering,
Dalian University of Technology, Dalian, China
{zhangyunhua,wlj,mengyang_feng}@mail.dlut.edu.cn,
{jinqing,wdice,lhchuan}@dlut.edu.cn

Abstract. Local structures of target objects are essential for robust tracking. However, existing methods based on deep neural networks mostly describe the target appearance from the global view, leading to high sensitivity to non-rigid appearance change and partial occlusion. In this paper, we circumvent this issue by proposing a local structure learning method, which simultaneously considers the local patterns of the target and their structural relationships for more accurate target tracking. To this end, a local pattern detection module is designed to automatically identify discriminative regions of the target objects. The detection results are further refined by a message passing module, which enforces the structural context among local patterns to construct local structures. We show that the message passing module can be formulated as the inference process of a conditional random field (CRF) and implemented by differentiable operations, allowing the entire model to be trained in an end-to-end manner. By considering various combinations of the local structures, our tracker is able to form various types of structure patterns. Target tracking is finally achieved by a matching procedure of the structure patterns between target template and candidates. Extensive evaluations on three benchmark data sets demonstrate that the proposed tracking algorithm performs favorably against state-of-the-art methods while running at a highly efficient speed of 45 fps.

Keywords: Tracking · Deep learning · Siamese network

1   Introduction

Single object tracking is a fundamental problem in computer vision, where the target object is identified in the first video frame and successively tracked in subsequent frames. Although much progress has been made in the past decades, tremendous challenges still exist in designing a robust tracker that can well handle significant appearance changes, pose variations, severe occlusions, and background clutters with real-time speed.

© Springer Nature Switzerland AG 2018
V. Ferrari et al. (Eds.): ECCV 2018, LNCS 11213, pp. 355–370, 2018.
https://doi.org/10.1007/978-3-030-01240-3_22

A survey [18] has investigated recent deep neural networks (DNNs) for visual tracking by either finetuning pre-trained deep models online [28,32,34,35] or directly utilizing pre-trained deep features to characterize the targets [7,10, 21,29,30]. Though promising performance has been reported, these methods only exploit the holistic model for target representation and ignore detailed information.

The above issues are mostly handled by part-based models in traditional methods [19,20]. Rather than describing the entire object with a single global model, the part-based approaches divide the target region into a number of fixed rectangular patches and are capable of capturing the local patterns of the target. As a consequence, they are more flexible in handling non-rigid appearance variations. Nonetheless, these methods have their own drawbacks. On the one hand, these methods process local patterns independently and fail to leverage their structure relationship, giving rise to noisy and inaccurate prediction. On the other hand, these methods mostly rely on hand-crafted features. It is still very rare to explore local models using deep learning techniques due to the high computational overhead involved in deep feature extraction for multiple local regions.

To address the above issues, this paper proposes a new structure constrained part-based model for visual tracking using DNNs. As opposed to prior part-based trackers, our method does not explicitly divide the target into parts. Instead, we identify object parts with discriminative patterns using a local pattern detection module, which are more computationally efficient. To enforce the structural relationship among local patterns, the predicted local patterns are further refined by considering contextual information from correlated patterns using a message passing module. For a more principled solution, we formulate the message passing module as the inference process of a CRF, which can be effectively implemented using differentiable operations and embedded into a neural network. As a result, the entire model can be trained in an end to end manner for online tracking, such that the local pattern detection module can learn to automatically identify the key object parts while the message passing module learns to encode the structure relationships among detected patterns. The target tracking is finally achieved through template-candidate matching over the detected local patterns using a Siamese network architecture.

Our method has three advantages over existing DNN based trackers. Firstly, our method performs on the object part level, and is therefore more flexible in handling non-rigid appearance change and partial occlusion. Meanwhile, owing to the local pattern detection module, our method is highly efficient and runs at a real time speed of 45 fps. In addition, our method can effectively leverage the structure context among local patterns, yielding more accurate target detection.

The Main Contribution of this Paper can be Summarized as Follows: (i) We propose a local pattern detection scheme, which can automatically identify discriminative local parts of target objects. (ii) We implement the message passing process via differentiable operations, and reformulate it via a neural network module. By doing this, our network can simultaneously learn the local patterns and the relationships among local patterns in an end-to-end manner. This yields more accurate tracking results. (iii) A new matching framework based on the Siamese network is proposed, which successively applies and ensembles the new techniques, and runs at a real time speed. Extensive evaluations performed on three widely adopted benchmarks show that the proposed method performs favorably against state-of-the-art methods in terms of both tracking accuracy and efficiency.

2 Related Work

This section reviews existing tracking methods that are mostly related to ours.

Tracking by Discriminative Appearance Modeling: One simple yet effective manner of using deep networks for visual tracking is to directly apply correlation filters on the multi-dimensional feature maps of deep Convolutional Neural Networks (CNNs), where the pre-trained CNN model is fixed. Recently, Danelljan et al. [10] have introduced a continuous spatial domain formulation named C-COT, allowing effective integration of multi-resolution deep features. C-COT and its improved version ECO [7] have achieved top performance in the VOT challenge [17], but they are not suitable for real-time applications as the tracking speed is rather slow. Another category of deep trackers [24,34,35] update a pre-trained CNN online to account for the target-specific appearance at test time. For instance, Wang et al. [34] proposes a feature map selection scheme and predicts a response map for the target with a heavily online updating schedule. However, these methods [24,34,35] rely on computationally inefficient search algorithms, such as sliding window or candidate sampling, which significantly reduce their applicability in real time scenarios. Meanwhile, they also highly rely on online updates, which are computationally inefficient and not desirable for real-time tasks.

Tracking by Siamese Network: Siamese network based trackers [3,31] select target from candidate patches through a matching function learned offline on image pairs. The matching function is usually implemented by two-branch CNNs with tied parameters, which takes the image pairs as input and predicts their similarity. Although SiamFC [3] can run beyond real-time, its tracking accuracy is still inferior to state-of-the-art trackers, due to the lack of online adaptation ability. Despite SINT [31] achieves higher tracking accuracy, it adopts optical flow to facilitate candidate sampling and is much slower (about 2 fps) than SiamFC. Recently, the DSiamM tracker [11] proposes to perform online update of siamese network by integrating correlation filters into the network. In [14], a policy is learned to decide whether to locate objects on early layers to speed up the tracking process. Though we also adopt the Siamese network architecture for tracking, our method significantly differs from existing methods in that ours is able to automatically detect local patterns of target appearance and models their structure relationships. Experiments confirm that our method can better handle challenge cases like drastic appearance change, partial occlusion, and rotation.

Part-Based Trackers: These days, the method to track non-rigid object has attracted great attention. Since common trackers can barely deal with extreme deformations, some trackers aim at this task try to exploit part information and achieve promising performance. In [27], an online gradient boosting decision tree operating on individual patches is intergraded. [38] uses Markov Chain on superpixel graph, but information propagation through a graph could be slow depending on the structure. Both Liu et al. [20] and Li et al. [19] propose the patch-based trackers based on correlation filter and combine the patches within a particle filter framework. However, these methods separately learn the correlation filter for each part and record the relative positions between each part and the target center. In addition, the existing patch based trackers rigidly divide the target object into fixed number of fragments. Discriminative local structure fails to be maintained by such rough rigid patch dividing, and features of such patches contain little semantic information. Reasonable updating strategies of such methods are hard to design and easy to drift due to drastic deformation changes.

Conditional Random Field for Image Segmentation: Conditional random field (CRF) has been widely used in image segmentation task [4,16,40]. They utilize CRF to establish pairwise potentials on all pairs of pixels in the image to exploit interactions of pixels. The method [16] develops a fully connected pairwise CRF with efficient computation to capture fine edge details while also catering for long range dependencies. This model was shown to largely improve the performance of a boosting-based pixel-level classifier. Chen et al. [4] uses a CRF to refine segmentation results obtained from a CNN and Zheng et al. [40] embeds the CRF inference procedure into the network and enables end-to-end training. They all use CRF to capture interactions of pixels and achieve state-of-the-art performance in image segmentation task. Inspired by their approaches, we adopt CRF inference to model the contextual information of local patterns by message passing, and capture the structure of object to enhance the robustness of the tracker. Contrary to adopt fixed Gaussian kernels to formulate pairwise terms as in their work, we use learnable convolution kernels to model pairwise terms, which can better encode object local patterns.

3 Structured Siamese Network

3.1 Overview

In this work, we propose a structured siamese network, which simultaneously performs discriminative pattern detection, local structure learning and integration in an end-to-end manner. Figure 1 overviews the pipeline of our tracking algorithm. The two-stream siamese network [3] is trained offline to locate a 127×127 template image z within a larger 255×255 search image x. A similarity function is learned to densely compare the template image z to each candidate region of the same size in the search image x, so as to predict a score map that highlights the target region. Specifically, a cross-correlation layer is proposed to compute the similarity for all translated sub-regions in x in one pass:

$$F(z, x) = \varphi(z) * \varphi(x) + v, \tag{1}$$

where φ is the convolutional feature embedding generated by each network stream; $v \in \mathbb{R}$ denotes the bias; and $F(.,.)$ represents the predicted confidence score map of size 17×17.

The two streams of the network share the same architecture and parameters, consisting of three components: local pattern detector, context modeling module and integration module. The details of these components are presented in details in the following sections.

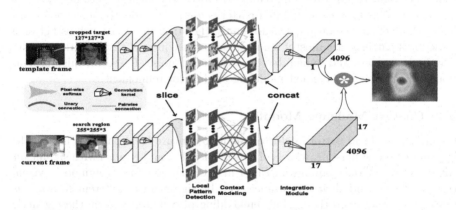

Fig. 1. The pipeline of our StructSiam algorithm.

The final cross-correlation operation is based on the obtained maps, which we call structure patterns.

Training the network adopts the logistic loss:

$$L = log(1 + e^{-yv}), \tag{2}$$

where v is the real-valued score of a single template-candidate pair and $y \in \{+1, -1\}$ is its ground-truth label as in [3].

3.2 Informative Local Pattern Detector

Informative local patterns are crucial cues to characterize target appearance. Instead of manually dividing the target region into pre-fixed parts, we design the local pattern detector to automatically identify discriminative patterns through end-to-end training.

The local pattern detector comprises two convolutional layers with kernel size of 11×11 and 5×5 respectively. Each of these convolutional layers is followed by a batch normalization layer [15], a ReLU layer [23], and a 3×3 max pooling layer. The module takes the image crop as input and detects local patterns of target appearance. The output feature map has 256 channels, each of which corresponds to a specific local pattern. Softmax layer is adopted to normalize the output feature map across channels.

As opposed to features in deeper layers that have low resolution and limited detailed information, the proposed local pattern detector, with only two convolutional layers and two max pooling layers, has a relatively small receptive field. Therefore, it can better focus on local regions of the target and preserve more detailed information (see the visualized results of the local pattern detector module in Fig. 1 as examples). This design is also consistent with recent findings [7,10] in visual tracking that detailed low level features are more discriminative and suitable for target matching. However, the local pattern detector has a major drawback. Since individual patterns are independently detected by different channels of the output feature maps, the structure relationships between these local patterns are mostly ignored. As a consequence, the detection results may be inaccurate and vulnerable to background noise. Based on this observation, we introduce the context modeling module for refinement.

3.3   Context Modeling Module

Generally, our local pattern detector tends to capture local patterns like heads, legs and torsos of persons, wheels of cars or bicycles, and regions with significant edges (we will show examples in Fig. 4 in Sect. 4). They are common in visual tracking tasks, and their appearances can be significantly different for various targets, sequences and time. Thus, embedding prior knowledge on these generic local patterns into the network is benefit for target recognition during tracking. We regard the prior knowledge as the relationships among local patterns. When the tracked object is undergoing cluttered background or drastic appearance change, the detection result of each single local pattern is not reliable. Thus the relationships between different local patterns (i.e., context information) should be considered to facilitate the detection process. The context information incorporation is achieved by message passing, which can enforce the responses of regions that are highly structural, and suppress the noisy background responses. To implement the message passing process efficiently, we introduce conditional random field (CRF) approximation into our network. We formulate the target's local pattern detection problem by using a graph and model the joint probability relationships among local patterns generated by previous stage through CRF.

Let X_i be the random variable associated to pixel i, which represents the type of local pattern assigned to the pixel i and can take any value from a pre-defined set $\mathcal{P} = \{p_1, p_2, ..., p_c\}$, and c is the channel size of feature maps. We regard each channel represents a specific local pattern. Let X be the vector formed by the random variables $X_1, X_2, ..., X_N$, where N is the number of pixels in the feature map. Given a graph $G = (V, E)$, where $V = \{X_1, X_2, ..., X_N\}$, and a global observation (image) I, the pair (I, X) can be modeled as a CRF characterized by a Gibbs distribution of the form $P(X = x|I) = \frac{1}{Z(I)} e^{-E(x|I)}$. Here $E(x)$ is called the energy of the configuration $x \in \mathcal{L}^N$ and $Z(I)$ is the partition function. From now on, we drop the conditioning on I in the notation for convenience.

The energy of a label assignment x is given by:

$$E(x) = \Sigma_i \psi_u(x_i) + \Sigma_i \Sigma_{j=max(0,i-R)}^{min(N-1,i+R)} \psi_p(x_i, x_j), \tag{3}$$

where the unary energy component $\psi_u(x_i)$ measures the inverse likelihood (and therefore, the cost) of the pixel i is subordinate to the local pattern x_i, and pairwise energy component $\psi_p(x_i, x_j)$ measures the cost of assigning local pattern types x_i, x_j to pixels i, j simultaneously, and R is the scope of the surrounding pixels taken into consideration for pairwise energy computation. In our model, unary energies are obtained from local pattern detector's output, which predict labels for pixels without considering the smoothness and the consistency of the local pattern type assignments. The pairwise energies serve as data-dependent smoothing terms and encourage assigning correlated types to pixels with similar features. Considering the translation invariance property of natural images, we implement the pairwise energy using convolutional operations as follows:

$$\psi_p(x_i, x_j) = \Sigma_{j=max(0,i-R)}^{min(N-1,i+R)} w_{i,j} * x_j + b_i, \tag{4}$$

where the kernels $w_{i,j}$ and biases b_i for $i = 1, ..., N$, are shared for all locations in the local patterns' maps and we set $w_{i,j=i} = 0$ to prevent message passing from x_i to itself.

Minimizing the above CRF energy $E(x)$ yields the most probable local structure distribution for the input image. Since the direct minimization is intractable, we adopt the mean-field variational inference to approximate the CRF distribution $P(z)$ with the product of independent marginal distributions, i.e., $Q(z) = \prod_i Q(z_i)$. To this end, we first consider individual steps of the mean-field algorithm summarized in Algorithm 1, and implement them using differentiable operations for end-to-end training. Let $U_i(p)$ denote the negative of the unary energy, i.e., $U_i(p) = -\psi_u(X_i = p)$, where p denotes the local pattern type. In our CRF, the unary energy ψ_u is obtained directly from the output of local pattern detector.

In the first step of Algorithm 1, we initialize $Q_i(p)$ with $Q_i(p) \leftarrow \frac{1}{Z_i} e^{U_i(p)}$, where $Z_i = \Sigma_p e^{U_i(p)}$. Note that this is equivalent to applying a softmax function over the unary potentials U across all the labels at each pixel. The message passing (step 4 in Algorithm 1) is then performed by applying two 3×3 convolutional kernels on Q as described in (4). The receptive field for each output pixel is 5×5, which is $\frac{5}{6}$ of the target object (considering the output size of the target template) and is enough to model target structure. Since there is no activation layer (e.g., ReLU) between the two convolution layers, they can be used to implement the linear mapping in (4) with less parameters than one 5×5 convolution layer. The kernels are learned to encode the context structural information among local patterns. The output from the message passing stage is subtracted element-wisely from the unary input U. Finally, the normalization step of the iteration can be implemented by another softmax operation with no parameters.

Algorithm 1. Mean-field approximation.

1: Initialize Q^0, $Q_i^0(p) = \frac{1}{Z_i}(U_i(p))$ for all i
2: Initialize the iteration times L.
3: **for** $t = 1 : L$ **do**
4:      $\tilde{Q}_i(p) = \Sigma_{j=max(0,i-R)}^{j=min(N-1,i+R)} w_{i,j} \times Q_j^{t-1} + b_i$
5:      $\hat{Q}_i \leftarrow U_i(p) - \tilde{Q}_i(p)$
6:      $Q_i^t \leftarrow \frac{1}{Z_i}e^{\hat{Q}_i(p)}$
7: **end for**

Given the above implementation, one iteration of the mean-field algorithm can be formulated as a stack of common neural network layers. Multiple mean-field iterations can be achieved by recurrently passing the estimated probability Q through the network multiple times. In practice, we find that three iterative steps are enough to obtain a satisfying performance.

Every local pattern receives message from other patterns, which can be seen as contextual information. The contextual information indicates the structure information of the input image inherently. Consequently, the local pattern maps are effectively refined after message passing stage. The final score map is less noisy when the tracking target is undergoing cluttered background and drastic deformation challenges.

In general, by message passing among local patterns, the CRF probability model describes the universal structure information of generic objects despite the category of the target. Since all operations of the context modeling module are differentiable, the whole network can be trained in an end-to-end manner.

3.4   Integration Module

The output maps of the context modeling module are capable of capturing precise local patterns' information. Since various local patterns correspond to different positions in the target region, directly correlating the template with the search region is vulnerable to deformation. In contrast to SiameseFC [3] using features with spatial layout for correlation, our integration module aggregates the local patterns (of both target and candidates) into a 1×1 feature map, with each channel acting as an attribute to indicate the existence of certain pattern regardless of its location. In our method, feature maps corresponding to the template and search region are fed into the 6×6 convolution layer, which leads to a $1 \times 1 \times 4096$ tensor representing the template and a $17 \times 17 \times 4096$ tensor **T** representing the search region. These two tensors are correlated to obtain the final response. Clearly, each spatial position (x, y) in the search region has a corresponding $1 \times 1 \times 4096$ tensor $\mathbf{T}(x, y, :)$ which is different from others. Each pixel in the final maps indicates the local pattern information for a region, and the final correlation finds the pixel (as the center of the target) that incorporates the same local patterns as the target's. The feature variation caused by drastic deformation changes can be reduced to some extent in this way, which will be proved in Sect. 4.

Table 1. The speed of trackers compared.

	Ours	ACFN	LCT	SCT	MEEM	CFNet-conv2	SiameseFC	Staple	KCF	DSST
Speed/fps	45	15	27	40	10	75	58	80	172	24

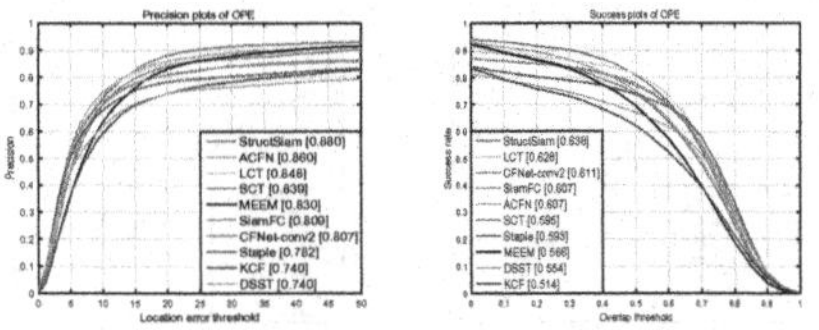

(a) Comparisons on OTB2013 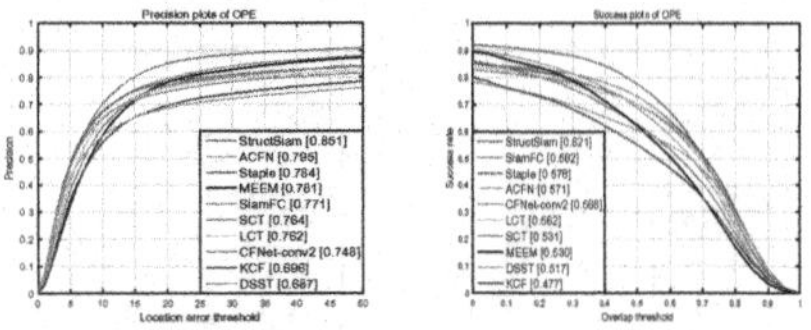   (b) Comparisons on OTB2015

Fig. 2. Comparison on OTB2013 and OTB2015 using distance precision rate (DPR) and overlap success rate (AUC).

4   Experiments

4.1   Implementation Details

Training Data. Since the motivation of our network is different from Siame-seFC, which aims to learn a matching function to perform metric learning, training only on ILSVRC2014 VID dataset is not suitable. Visual object tracking task is to track generic objects no matter what categories. The ILSVRC2014 VID dataset is more biased to animals contains head, limbs and torso, that will lead to ineffective learning of our structured network. And rotation objects are necessary for structure patterns learning, which aim to response to the center of structural regions. To model generic object inner structure, we use ILSVRC2014 VID dataset [25] and ALOV dataset [26]. We discard the common sequences appear in the testing datasets for a fair comparison.

Parameter Setting. We implement the proposed method in python with the Tensorflow library [1]. The parameters of the whole network are initialized randomly guided by a Gaussian distribution [12]. It is well known that softmax leads to vanishing of gradients which makes the network training inefficient. Thus, we multiply the feature maps with a constant β, which will make the network converge much faster. β is set to equal to the channel size of feature maps, i.e., $\beta = 256$. Training is performed over 50 epochs, each consisting of 60,000 sampled pairs. The gradients for each iteration are estimated using mini-batches of size 8, and the learning rate is annealed geometrically at each epoch from 10^{-2} to 10^{-5} as in [3]. We use the SGD method to conduct optimization and train the network with a single NVIDIA GeForce GTX 1080 and an Intel Core i7-4790 at 3.6 GHz.

Tracking Algorithm. With the learned StructSiam, we summarize our tracking algorithm as follows: given the target location at I_1, i.e., a bounding box $b_1 \in \mathbb{R}$, we crop the corresponding region to serve as the target template O_1 that is

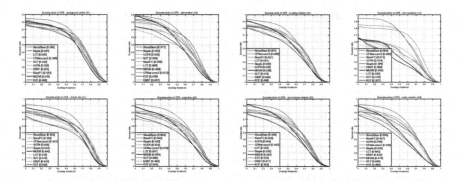

Fig. 3. The success plots over eight tracking challenges, including background clutter, deformation, in-plane rotation, low resolution, motion blur, occlusion, out-of-plane rotation and scale variation.

slightly larger than b_1 and centered at b_1. We then extract the deep features of O_1 to get F_1. When tracking at the tth frame, we crop search regions on three scales, i.e., $1.025^{\{-1,0,1\}} \times S_0$, where S_0 is the original scale, centering at b_{t-1}. Then, we get 3 response maps via (1). We search the maximum value among the three response maps and get its respective location and scale, which leads to b_t.

4.2 Experiments on OTB2013

OTB2013 [36] contains 50 fully annotated sequences that are collected from commonly used tracking sequences. We compare our tracker with other 9 state-of-art real-time trackers, including LCT [22], MEEM [39], SiameseFC [3], Staple [2], KCF [13], DSST [8], ACFN [6], SCT [5], CFNet [33]. Following the protocol in [36], we report the results in one-pass evaluation (OPE) using two metrics: precision and success plots, as shown in Fig. 2(a). The precision metric computes the rate of frames whose center location is within some certain distance with the ground truth location. The success metric computes the overlap ratio between the tracked and ground truth bounding boxes. In addition, we report the area under curve (AUC) score of success plots and distance precision score at 20 pixels threshold in the precision plots for each tracking method. Overall, StructSiam performs favorably against other real-time state-of-the-art trackers on this dataset. Our tracker achieves a distance precision rate (DPR) of 87.4% and AUC score of 0.638 with real-time speed of 45 fps. Besides, it outperforms other competing real-time ones in terms of accuracy.

4.3 Experiments on OTB2015

The OTB2015 [37] dataset is the extension of OTB2013 and is more challenging. The evaluation criteria of two benchmarks are identical. Compared to the same real-time trackers mentioned above, the result is shown in Fig. 2(b) and the comparison of speed is shown in Table 1. On the OTB2015 dataset, our tracker achieves a DPR of 85.1% and AUC of 62.1%. Considering both speed and accuracy, our method achieves a very competitive result.

Attribute-Based Evaluation. We further analyze the performance of Struct-Siam under different attributes in OTB2015 [37] to demonstrate the effectiveness of information passing between local structures on feature learning. Figure 3 shows the OPE plots for eight major attributes, including background clutter, deformation, in-plane rotation, low resolution, motion blur, occlusion, out-of-plane rotation and scale variation. From Fig. 3, we have the following observations. First, our method is effective in handling occlusion, owing to that the relationships among local structures are implicitly modeled through message passing. In contrast, the SiameseFC method pre-trains the network only using a single global feature model as the output, which is less effective in handling partial occlusion. Second, our method performs well in the presence of motion blur, since the noisy features extracted from blurred images can be refined by the CRF module. Other trackers based on correlation filters and SiameseFC are sensitive to motion blur, this phenomenon may result from the extracted feature is destroyed when motion blur occurs. Thus, this attribute also demonstrates the effectiveness of the CRF approximation. Besides, the proposed method achieves better performance for other challenging factor, which further demonstrates that our method has good generalization ability.

Qualitative Evaluation. In Fig. 4, we select three representative sequences (including the challenges of deformation, occlusion and rotation) to visualize the effectiveness of our algorithm compared to other real-time trackers. Each column of the responses maps in the top of Fig. 4 represents one typical channel's responses before the correlation layer across different frames and different sequences. As we can see, the selected channels are prone to response on regions around heads, legs, and torsos of persons and wheels of motorbikes. Their responses are stable with different inputs. To further compare our algorithm with global model, we show the responses of a global model (implemented with AlexNet) on the right. They are too noisy to distinguish target from background, and fail to consistently highlight the same local parts across frames after severe deformations. More results are shown in the bottom of Fig. 4. Overall, the visual evaluation indicates that our StructSiam tracker performs favorably against other real-time state-of-the-art trackers.

Ablation Study. Our algorithm contains local pattern detectors, message passing layers and integration layer. We conduct ablation analysis to compare each component's effect on the performance on OTB15 dataset. As shown in the Fig. 5a, b, and c denote the local pattern detectors, message passing module and integration layer respectively, and onlyVID denotes the network that trained with only ILSVRC VID dataset. Specially, we test the performance of the network without message passing layers by replacing them with simple 3×3 convolution layers. The results show that, all components proposed in this framework are essential and complementing each other. The performance of the proposed tracker will degrade drastically if any component is removed. Due to

Response maps on different frames   **Global model's response maps**

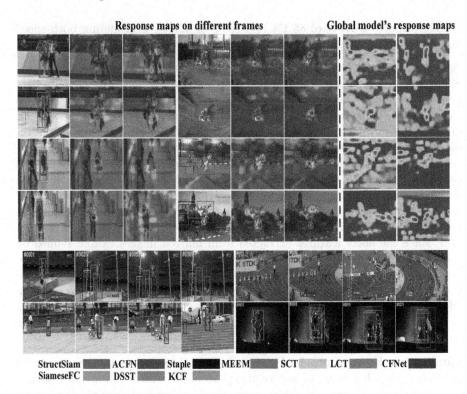

StructSiam ■■■ ACFN■■■ Staple ■■■ MEEM ■■■ SCT ■■■ LCT ■■■ CFNet ■■■
SiameseFC ■■■ DSST ■■■ KCF ■■■

Fig. 4. Qualitative evaluation of the proposed algorithm and other state-of-the-art real-time trackers on seven sequences (Skater2, Walking2, MotorRolling, Jump, Girl2, Bolt2 and Trans).

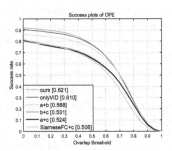

Fig. 5. Ablation study.

the relatively large performance gain through integration module, we further prove that the simply embedding integration module into SiameseFC (denoted as "SiameseFC+c") leads to an inferior performance. Therefore, our performance improvement does not mainly come from the integration layer. Since SiameseFC was trained with only ILSVRC VID dataset, we test the performance of our tracker without ALOV300 training dataset for a fair comparison. As we can see in the Fig. 5, in this condition, our tracker performs better than SiameseFC with a large margin, which illustrates the effectiveness of our algorithm.

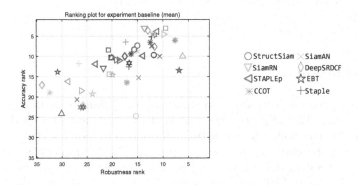

Fig. 6. Comparison on VOT2016 benchmark.

4.4   Experiments on VOT2016 Benchmark [17]

VOT-2016 has 60 sequences and re-initializes testing trackers when it misses the target. The expected average overlap (EAO) considering both bounding box overlap ratio (accuracy) and the re-initialization times (robustness) serves as the major evaluation metric on VOT-2016. We compare our StructSiam tracker with state-of-the-art trackers on the VOT 2016 benchmark, including CCOT [10], Staple [2], EBT [41], DeepSRDCF [9] and SiamFC [3]. As indicated in the VOT 2016 report [17], the strict state-of-the-art bound is 0.251 under the EAO metric. That is, the trackers are considered as state-of-the-art ones when their EAO values exceed 0.251.

Table 2 and Fig. 6 show the results from our StructSiam tracker and the state-of-the-art trackers. Among these methods, CCOT achieves the best results under the expected average overlap (EAO) metric. However, the top performance trackers are far from real-time requirements. CCOT and DeepSRDCF are less than 1 fps, and EBT only has 3 fps. Meanwhile, the performance of our Struct-Siam tracker is higher than SiamAN, which has the same depth of network with ours. SiamRN represents SiameseFC using ResNet as architecture and its performance is higher than ours but the speed is far more slower. It is likely to be due to the deeper network. StructSiam achieves the fastest speed and the lower speed of SiamAN may be credited to its hardware condition. According to the analysis of VOT report and the definition of the strict state-of-the-art bound, our StructSiam tracker can be regarded as a state-of-the-art method with real-time performance.

Table 2. Comparison with the state-of-the-art trackers on the VOT 2016 dataset with expected average overlap (EAO) measuring method.

	CCOT	Staple	EBT	DeepSRDCF	StructSiam	SiamAN	SiamRN
EAO	0.331	0.295	0.291	0.276	0.264	0.235	0.277
Speed	0.5	11	3	0.38	16	9	5

5   Conclusion

This work presents a powerful local structure-based siamese network for visual object tracking. The proposed network can detect discriminative local patterns automatically and model the contextual information to form the structure of the object in a probability way by message passing. The final matching procedure is based on the final structural patterns of the target object, which facilitates dealing with several challenges such as drastic appearance change, rotation, partial occlusion and motion blur. The experimental results demonstrate that our tracker achieves promising performance with a real-time speed. In the future, we will extend the proposed structured Siamese network to handle other vision tasks.

Acknowledgement. This work was supported by the Natural Science Foundation of China under Grant 61725202, 61751212, 61771088, 61632006 and 91538201.

References

1. Abadi, M., et al.: Tensorflow: large scale machine learning on heterogeneous distributed systems. In: arXiv preprint arXiv:1603.04467 (2016)
2. Bertinetto, L., Valmadre, J., Golodetz, S., Miksik, O., Torr, P.H.S.: Staple: complementary learners for real-time tracking. In: CVPR (2016)
3. Bertinetto, L., Valmadre, J., Henriques, J.F., Vedaldi, A., Torr, P.H.S.: Fully-convolutional siamese networks for object tracking. In: Hua, G., Jégou, H. (eds.) ECCV 2016. LNCS, vol. 9914, pp. 850–865. Springer, Cham (2016). https://doi.org/10.1007/978-3-319-48881-3_56
4. Chen, L.C., Papandreou, G., Kokkinos, I., Murphy, K., Yuille, A.L.: Semantic image segmentation with deep convolutional nets and fully connected CRFs. In: ICLR (2015)
5. Choi, J., Chang, H.J., Jeong, J., Demiris, Y., Jin, Y.C.: Visual tracking using attention-modulated disintegration and integration. In: CVPR (2016)
6. Choi, J., Chang, H.J., Yun, S., Fischer, T., Demiris, Y., Jin, Y.C.: Attentional correlation filter network for adaptive visual tracking. In: CVPR (2017)
7. Danelljan, M., Bhat, G., Khan, F.S., Felsberg, M.: ECO: efficient convolution operators for tracking. In: CVPR (2017)
8. Danelljan, M., Hger, G., Khan, F.S., Felsberg, M.: Accurate scale estimation for robust visual tracking. In: BMVC (2014)
9. Danelljan, M., Hger, G., Khan, F.S., Felsberg, M.: Convolutional features for correlation filter based visual tracking. In: ICCV Workshop (2015)

10. Danelljan, M., Robinson, A., Khan, F.S., Felsberg, M.: Beyond correlation filters: learning continuous convolution operators for visual tracking. In: ECCV (2016)
11. Guo, Q., Feng, W., Zhou, C., Huang, R., Wan, L., Wang, S.: Learning dynamic Siamese network for visual object tracking. In: ICCV (2017)
12. He, K., Zhang, X., Ren, S., Sun, J.: Delving deep into rectifiers: surpassing human-level performance on imagenet classification. In: ICCV (2015)
13. Henriques, J.F., Caseiro, R., Martins, P., Batista, J.: High-speed tracking with kernelized correlation filters. In: ICVS (2008)
14. Huang, C., Lucey, S., Ramanan, D.: Learning policies for adaptive tracking with deep feature cascades. In: ICCV (2017)
15. Ioffe, S., Szegedy, C.: Batch normalization: accelerating deep network training by reducing internal covariate shift. In: ICML (2015)
16. Krähenbühl, P., Koltun, V.: Efficient inference in fully connected CRFs with Gaussian edge potentials. In: NIPS, pp. 109–117 (2011)
17. Kristan, M., et al.: The visual object tracking VOT2016 challenge results. In: Hua, G., Jégou, H. (eds.) ECCV 2016. LNCS, vol. 9914, pp. 777–823. Springer, Cham (2016). https://doi.org/10.1007/978-3-319-48881-3_54
18. Li, P., Wang, D., Wang, L., Lu, H.: Deep visual tracking: review and experimental comparison. Pattern Recogn. **76**, 323–338 (2018)
19. Li, Y., Zhu, J., Hoi, S.C.H.: Reliable patch trackers: robust visual tracking by exploiting reliable patches. In: CVPR (2015)
20. Liu, T., Wang, G., Yang, Q.: Real-time part-based visual tracking via adaptive correlation filters. In: CVPR (2015)
21. Ma, C., Huang, J.B., Yang, X., Yang, M.H.: Hierarchical convolutional features for visual tracking. In: ICCV (2015)
22. Ma, C., Yang, X., Zhang, C., Yang, M.H.: Long-term correlation tracking. In: CVPR (2015)
23. Nair, V., Hinton, G.E.: Rectified linear units improve restricted boltzmann machines. In: ICML (2010)
24. Nam, H., Baek, M., Han, B.: Modeling and propagating CNNs in a tree structure for visual tracking. In: arXiv preprint arXiv:1608.07242 (2016)
25. Russakovsky, O., et al.: Imagenet large scale visual recognition challenge. Int. J. Comput. Vis. **115**(3), 211–252 (2014)
26. Smeulders, A.W.M., Chu, D.M., Cucchiara, R., Calderara, S., Dehghan, A., Shah, M.: Visual tracking: an experimental survey. IEEE Trans. Pattern Anal. Mach. Intell. **36**, 1442–1468 (2014)
27. Son, J., Jung, I., Park, K., Han, B.: Tracking-by-segmentation with online gradient boosting decision tree. In: ICCV, pp. 3056–3064 (2016)
28. Song, Y., Ma, C., Gong, L., Zhang, J., Lau, R., Yang, M.H.: Crest: convolutional residual learning for visual tracking. In: ICCV (2017)
29. Sun, C., Wang, D., Lu, H., Yang, M.H.: Correlation tracking via joint discrimination and reliability learning (2018)
30. Sun, C., Wang, D., Lu, H., Yang, M.H.: Learning spatial-aware regressions for visual tracking (2018)
31. Tao, R., Gavves, E., Smeulders, A.W.M.: Siamese instance search for tracking. In: CVPR (2016)
32. Teng, Z., Xing, J., Wang, Q., Lang, C., Feng, S., Jin, Y.: Robust object tracking based on temporal and spatial deep networks. In: ICCV (2017)
33. Valmadre, J., Bertinetto, L., Henriques, J.F., Vedaldi, A., Torr, P.H.S.: End-to-end representation learning for correlation filter based tracking. In: CVPR (2017)

34. Wang, L., Ouyang, W., Wang, X., Lu, H.: Visual tracking with fully convolutional networks. In: ICCV (2015)
35. Wang, L., Ouyang, W., Wang, X., Lu, H.: STCT: sequentially training convolutional networks for visual tracking. In: CVPR (2016)
36. Wu, Y., Lim, J., Yang, M.H.: Online object tracking: a benchmark. In: CVPR (2013)
37. Wu, Y., Lim, J., Yang, M.H.: Object tracking benchmark. IEEE Trans. Pattern Anal. Mach. Intell. **37**, 1834–1848 (2015)
38. Yeo, D., Son, J., Han, B., Han, J.H.: Superpixel-based tracking-by-segmentation using markov chains. In: CVPR, pp. 511–520 (2017)
39. Zhang, J., Ma, S., Sclaroff, S.: MEEM: robust tracking via multiple experts using entropy minimization. In: Fleet, D., Pajdla, T., Schiele, B., Tuytelaars, T. (eds.) ECCV 2014. LNCS, vol. 8694, pp. 188–203. Springer, Cham (2014). https://doi.org/10.1007/978-3-319-10599-4_13
40. Zheng, S., et al.: Conditional random fields as recurrent neural networks. In: ICCV (2015)
41. Zhu, G., Porikli, F., Li, H.: Beyond local search: tracking objects everywhere with instance-specific proposals. In: CVPR (2016)

Associating Inter-image Salient Instances for Weakly Supervised Semantic Segmentation

Ruochen Fan[1], Qibin Hou[2], Ming-Ming Cheng[2], Gang Yu[3], Ralph R. Martin[4], and Shi-Min Hu[1]($^{(\boxtimes)}$)

[1] Tsinghua University, Beijing, China
frc16@mails.tsinghua.edu.cn, shimin@tsinghua.edu.cn
[2] Nankai University, Tianjin, China
andrewhoux@gmail.com, cmm@nankai.edu.cn
[3] Megvii Inc., Beijing, China
yugang@megvii.com
[4] Cardiff University, Cardiff CF243AA, UK
ralph@cs.cardiff.ac.uk

Abstract. Effectively bridging between image level keyword annotations and corresponding image pixels is one of the main challenges in weakly supervised semantic segmentation. In this paper, we use an instance-level salient object detector to automatically generate salient instances (candidate objects) for training images. Using similarity features extracted from each salient instance in the whole training set, we build a similarity graph, then use a graph partitioning algorithm to separate it into multiple subgraphs, each of which is associated with a single keyword (tag). Our graph-partitioning-based clustering algorithm allows us to consider the relationships between all salient instances in the training set as well as the information within them. We further show that with the help of attention information, our clustering algorithm is able to correct certain wrong assignments, leading to more accurate results. The proposed framework is general, and any state-of-the-art fully-supervised network structure can be incorporated to learn the segmentation network. When working with DeepLab for semantic segmentation, our method outperforms state-of-the-art weakly supervised alternatives by a large margin, achieving 65.6% mIoU on the PASCAL VOC 2012 dataset. We also combine our method with Mask R-CNN for instance segmentation, and demonstrated for the first time the ability of weakly supervised instance segmentation using only keyword annotations.

Keywords: Semantic segmentation · Weak supervision · Graph partitioning

© Springer Nature Switzerland AG 2018
V. Ferrari et al. (Eds.): ECCV 2018, LNCS 11213, pp. 371–388, 2018.
https://doi.org/10.1007/978-3-030-01240-3_23

1   Introduction

Semantic segmentation, providing rich pixel level labeling of a scene, is one of the most important tasks in computer vision. The strong learning ability of convolutional neural networks (CNNs) has enabled significant progress in this field recently [5,26,28,45,46]. However, the performance of such CNN-based methods requires a large amount of training data annotated to pixel-level, *e.g.*, PASCAL VOC [11] and MS COCO [27]; such data are very expensive to collect. As an approach to alleviate the demand for pixel-accurate annotations, weakly supervised semantic segmentation has drawn great attention recently. Such methods merely require supervisions of one or more of the following kinds: keywords [18,21,22,41,42], bounding boxes [35], scribbles [25], points [2], *etc.*, making the collection of annotated data much easier. In this paper, we consider weakly supervised semantic segmentation using only image-level keyword annotations.

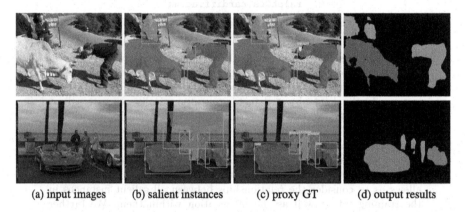

(a) input images   (b) salient instances   (c) proxy GT   (d) output results

Fig. 1. Input images (a) are fed into a salient instance detection method (*e.g.*, S⁴Net [12]) giving instances shown in colour in (b). Our system automatically generates proxy ground-truth data (c) by assigning correct tags to salient instances and rejecting noisy instances. Traditional fully supervised semantic/instance segmentation methods learn from these proxy ground-truth data; final generated segmentation results are shown in (d). (Color figure online)

In weakly supervised semantic segmentation, one of the main challenges is to effectively build a bridge between image-level keyword annotations and corresponding semantic objects. Most previous state-of-the-art methods focus on generating *proxy ground-truth* from the original images by utilizing low-level cue detectors to capture pixel-level information. This may be done using a saliency detector [4,19,21,41] or attention models [4,41], for example. Because these methods give only pixel-level saliency/attention information, it is difficult to distinguish different types of semantic objects from the heuristic cues produced. Thus, the ability to discriminate semantic instances is essential. With the rapid development of saliency detection algorithms, some saliency extractors, such as MSRNet [23] and S^{4}Net [12], are now not only able to predict gray-level salient objects but also instance-level masks. Inspired by the advantages of such instance-level salient object detectors, in this paper, we propose to carry out the instance distinguishing task in the early saliency detection stage, with the help of S^{4}Net, greatly simplifying the learning pipeline. Figure 1(b) shows some instance-level saliency maps predicted by S^{4}Net.

In order to make use of the salient instance masks with their bounding boxes, two main obstacles need to be overcome. **Firstly**, an image may be labeled with multiple keywords, so determining a correct keyword (tag) for each class-agnostic salient instance is essential. For example, see Fig. 1(b): the upper image is associated with two image-level labels: 'sheep' and 'person'. Allocating the correct tag to each detected instance is difficult. **Secondly**, not all salient instances generated by the salient instance detector are semantically meaningful; incorporating such noisy instances would degrade downstream operations. For example, in the lower image in Fig. 1(b), an obvious noisy instance occurs in the sky (shown in gray). Such instances and the associated noisy labels frequently arise using current algorithms. Therefore, recognizing and excluding such noisy salient instances is important in our approach. The two obstacles described above can be regarded as posing a tag-assignment problem, *i.e.,* associating salient instances, including both semantically meaningful and noisy ones, with correct tags.

In this paper, we take into consideration both the intrinsic properties of a salient instance and the semantic relationships between all salient instances in the whole training set. Here we use the term *intrinsic properties* of a salient instance to refer to the appearance information within its (single) region of interest. In fact, it is possible to predict a correct tag for a salient instance using only its intrinsic properties: see [18,21,41]. However, as well as the appearance information within each region of interest, there are also strong semantic relationships between all salient instances: salient instances in the same category typically share similar semantic features. We will show that taking this property into account is important in the tag-assignment operation in Sect. 5.2.

More specifically, our proposed framework contains an attention module to predict the probability of a salient instance belonging to a certain category, based on its intrinsic properties. On the other hand, to assess semantic relationships, we use a semantic feature extractor which can predict a semantic feature for each salient instance; salient instances sharing similar semantic information have close semantic feature vectors. Based on the semantic features, a similarity graph is built, in which the vertices represent salient instances and the edge weights record the semantic similarity between a pair of salient instances. We use a graph partitioning algorithm to divide the graph into subgraphs, each of which represents a specific category. The graph partitioning process is modelled as a mixed integer quadratic program (MIQP) problem [3], for which a globally optimal solution can be found. The aim is to make the vertices in each subgraph as similar as possible, while taking into account the intrinsic properties of the salient instances.

Our approach provides high-quality proxy-ground-truth data, which can be used to train any state-of-the-art fully-supervised semantic segmentation methods. When working with DeepLab [5] for semantic segmentation, our method obtains mean intersection-over-union (mIoU) of 65.6% for PASCAL VOC 2012 test set, beating the current state-of-the-art. In addition to pixel-level semantic segmentation, this paper demonstrated for the first time the ability of weakly supervised instance segmentation using only keyword annotations, by fitting our instance level proxy ground-truth data into latest instance segmentation network, *i.e.*, Mask R-CNN [14]. In summary, the main contributions of this paper are:

- the first use of salient instances in a weakly supervised segmentation framework, significantly simplifying object discrimination, and performing instance-level segmentation under weak supervision.
- a weakly supervised segmentation framework exploiting not only the information inside salient instances but also the relationships between all objects in the whole dataset.

2   Related Work

While longstanding research has considered fully supervised semantic segmentation, *e.g.*, [5,26,28,45,46], more recently, weakly-supervised semantic segmentation has come to the fore. Early work such as [40] relied on hand-crafted features, such as color, texture, and histogram information to build a graphical model. However, with the advent of convolutional neural network (CNN) methods, this conventional approach has been gradually replaced because of its lower performance on challenging benchmarks [11]. We thus only discuss weakly supervised semantic segmentation work based on CNNs.

In [31], Papandreou *et al.* use the expectation-maximization algorithm [8] to perform weakly-supervised semantic segmentation based on annotated bounding boxes and image-level labels. Similarly, Qi *et al.* [35] used proposals generated by Multiscale Combinatorial Grouping (MCG) [34] to help localize semantically meaningful objects. Scribbles and points are further used as additional supervision. In [25], Lin *et al.* made use of a region-based graphical model, with scribbles providing ground-truth annotations to train the segmentation network. Bearman *et al.* [2] likewise leveraged knowledge from human-annotated points as supervision.

Other works rely only on image-level labels. Pathak *et al.* [32] addressed the weakly-supervised semantic segmentation problem by introducing a series of constraints. Pinheiro *et al.* [33] treated this problem as a multiple instance learning problem. In [22], three loss functions are designed to gradually expand the areas located by an attention model [47]. Wei *et al.* [41] improved this approach using an adversarial erasing scheme to acquire more meaningful regions that provide more accurate heuristic cues for training. In [42], Wei *et al.* presented a simple-to-complex framework which used saliency maps produced by the methods in [6,20] as initial guides. Hou *et al.* [18] advanced this approach by combining the saliency maps [17] with attention maps [44]. More recently, Oh *et al.* [30] and Chaudhry *et al.* [4] considered linking saliency and attention cues together, but they adopted different strategies to acquire semantic objects. Roy and Todorovic [37] leveraged both bottom-up and top-down attention cues and fused them via a conditional random field as a recurrent network. Very recent work [16,21] tackles the weakly-supervised semantic segmentation problem using images or videos from the Internet. Nevertheless, the ideas used to obtain heuristic cues are similar to those in previous works.

In this paper, differently from all the aforementioned methods, we propose a weakly supervised segmentation framework using salient instances. We assign tags to salient instances to generate proxy ground-truth for fully supervised segmentation network. The tag-assignment problem is modeled as graph partitioning, in which both the relationships between all salient instances in the whole dataset, as well as the information within them are taken into consideration.

3   Overview and Network Structure

We now present an overview of our pipeline, then discuss our network structure and tag-assignment algorithm. Our proposed framework is shown in Fig. 2. Most previous work which relies on pixel level cues (such as saliency, edges and attention maps) regards instance discrimination as a key task. However, with the development of deep learning, saliency detectors are now available that can predict saliency maps along with instance bounding boxes. Given training images labelled only with keywords, we use an instance-level saliency segmentation network, S^4Net [12], to extract salient instances from every image. Each salient instance has a bounding box and a mask indicating a visually noticeable foreground object in an image. These salient instances are class-agnostic, so the extractor S^4Net does not need to be trained for our training set. Although salient instances contain ground-truth masks for training a segmentation mask, there are two major limitations in the use of such salient instances to train a segmentation network. The first is that an image may be labelled by multiple keywords. For example, a common type of scene involves *pedestrians* walking near *cars*. Determining the correct keyword associated with each salient instance is necessary. The second is that instances detected by S^4Net may not fall into the categories in the training set. We refer to such salient instances as noisy instances. Eliminating such noisy instances is a necessary part of our complete pipeline. Both limitations can be removed by solving a tag-assignment problem, in which we associate salient instances with correct tags based on image keywords, and tag others as noisy instances.

Our pipeline takes into consideration both the intrinsic characteristics of a single region, and the relationships between all salient instances. A classification network responds strongly to discriminative areas (pixels) of an object in the score map for the correct category of the object. Therefore, inspired by class activation mapping (CAM) [47], we use an attention module to identify the tags of salient instances directly from their intrinsic characteristics. One weakness

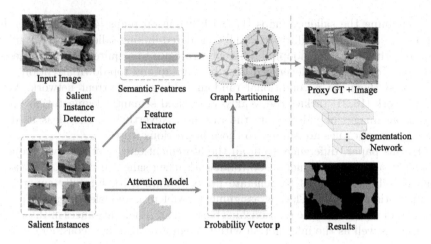

Fig. 2. Pipeline. Instances are extracted from the input images by a salient instance detector (*e.g.*, S^{4}Net [12]). An attention module predicts the probability of each salient instance belonging to a certain category using its intrinsic properties. Semantic features are obtained from the salient instances and used to build a similarity graph. Graph partitioning is used to determine the final tags of the salient instances. The fully supervised segmentation network (*e.g.*, DeepLab [5] or Mask R-CNN [14]) is trained using the proxy ground-truth generated.

of existing weakly supervised segmentation work is that it treats the training set image by image, ignoring the relationships between salient instances across the entire training set. However, salient instances belonging to the same category share similar contextual information which is of use in tag-assignment. Our architecture extracts *semantic features* for each salient instance; regions with similar semantic information have similar semantic features. These are used to construct a similarity graph. The tag-assignment problem now becomes one of graph partitioning, making use not only of the intrinsic properties of a single salient instance, but the global relationships between all salient instances.

3.1 Attention Module

The attention module in our pipeline is used to determine the correct tag for each salient instance from its intrinsic characteristics. Formally, let C be the number of categories (excluding the background) in the training set. Given an image I, the attention module predicts C attention maps. Each pixel in a map indicates the probability that the pixel belongs to the corresponding object category. Following FCAN [4], we make use of a fully convolutional network as our classifier. After prediction of C score maps by the backbone model, *e.g.*, off the shelf VGG16 [39] or ResNet101 [15], the classification result $\mathbf{y}$ is output by a sigmoid layer fed with the average of the score maps using a global average pooling (GAP) layer. Notice that $\mathbf{y}$ is not a probability distribution, as the input image may have multiple keywords. An attention map denoted by A_i can be produced by feeding the i-th score map into a sigmoid layer. As images may be associated with multiple keywords, we treat network optimization as C independent binary classification problems. Thus, the loss function is:

$$L_a = -\frac{1}{C} \sum_i^C (\bar{\mathbf{y}}_\mathbf{i} \log \mathbf{y}_\mathbf{i} + (1 - \bar{\mathbf{y}}_\mathbf{i}) \log(1 - \mathbf{y}_\mathbf{i})), \qquad (1)$$

where $\bar{\mathbf{y}}_\mathbf{i}$ denotes the keyword ground-truth. The dataset for weakly supervised semantic segmentation is used to train the classifier, after which the attention maps for the images in this dataset can be obtained.

Assuming that a salient instance has a bounding box (x_0, y_0, x_1, y_1) in image I, the probability of this salient instance belonging to the i-th category $\mathbf{p_i}$ is:

$$\mathbf{p_i} = -\frac{1}{(x_1 - x_0)(y_1 - y_0)} \sum_{x=x_0}^{x_1} \sum_{y=y_0}^{y_1} A_i(x, y), \qquad (2)$$

and the tag for this salient instance is given by $\arg\max(\mathbf{p})$.

3.2   Semantic Feature Extractor

The attention module introduced above assigns tags to salient instances from their intrinsic properties, but fails to take relationships between all salient instances into consideration. To discover such relationships, we use a semantic feature extractor to produce feature vectors for each input region of interest, such that regions of interest with similar semantic content share similar features. To avoid the need for additional data, we use ImageNet [9] to train this model.

The network architecture of the semantic feature extractor is very similar to that of a standard classifier. ResNet [15] is used as the backbone model. We add a GAP layer after the last layer of ResNet to obtain a 2048-channel semantic feature vector $\mathbf{f}$. During the training phase, a 1000-dimensional auxiliary classification vector $\mathbf{y}$ is predicted by feeding $\mathbf{f}$ into a 1×1 convolutional layer.

Our training objective is to maximize the distance between features from regions of interest with different semantic content and minimize the distance between features from the same category. To this end, in addition to the standard softmax-cross entropy classification loss, we employ center loss [43] to directly concentrate features on similar semantic content. For a specific category of ImageNet, the standard classification loss trains $\mathbf{y}$ to be the correct probabilistic distribution, and the center loss simultaneously learns a center $\mathbf{c}$ for the semantic features and penalizes the distance between $\mathbf{f}$ and $\mathbf{c}$. The overall loss function is formulated as:

$$L = L_{cls} + \lambda L_c, \qquad L_c = 1 - \frac{\mathbf{f} \cdot \mathbf{c}_{\bar{\mathbf{y}}}}{\|\mathbf{f}\| \, \|\mathbf{c}_{\bar{\mathbf{y}}}\|}, \qquad (3)$$

where L_{cls} is the softmax-crossentropy loss, $\bar{y}$ is the ground-truth label of a training sample and $\mathbf{c}_{\bar{\mathbf{y}}}$ is the center of the $\bar{y}$-th category.

In every training iteration, the center for the category of the input sample is updated using:

$$\mathbf{c}_{\tilde{y}}^{t+1} = \mathbf{c}_{\tilde{y}}^{t} + \alpha \cdot (\mathbf{f} - \mathbf{c}_{\tilde{y}}^{t}), \qquad (4)$$

4   Tag-Assignment Algorithm

In order to assign a correct keyword to every salient instance with or identify it as a noisy instance, we use a tag-assignment algorithm, exploiting both the intrinsic properties of a single salient instance, and the relationships between all salient instances in the whole dataset. The tag-assignment process is modeled as a graph partitioning problem. Although the purpose of graph partitioning can be considered as clustering, traditional clustering algorithms using a hierarchical approach [36], k-means [29], DBSCAN [10] or OPTICS [1], are unsuited to our task as they only consider relationships between input data points, and ignore the intrinsic properties of each data point.

In detail, assume that n salient instances have been produced from the training set by S^{4}Net, and n semantic features extracted for each salient instance, denoted as $\mathbf{f}_j$, $j = 1, \ldots, n$. As Sect. 3.1 described, we predict the probability of every salient instance j belonging to category i, written as $\mathbf{p}_{ij}$, $i = 0, \ldots, C, j = 1, \ldots, n$, where category 0 means the salient instance is a noisy one.

Let the image keywords for a salient instance j be the set K_j. The purpose of the tag-assignment algorithm is to predict the final tags of the salient instances $\mathbf{x}_{ij}, i = 0, \ldots, C, j = 1, \ldots, n$, such that $\mathbf{x}_{ij} \in \{0, 1\}$ if $i \in K_j$ and otherwise $\mathbf{x}_{ij} \in \{0\}$, and $\sum_i \mathbf{x}_{ij} = \mathbf{1}$, where $\mathbf{x}_{0j} = 1$ means that instance j is considered noisy.

We associate semantic similarity with the edges of a weighted undirected similarity graph having a vertex for each salient instance, and an edge for each pair of salient instances which are strongly similar. Edge weights give the similarity of a salient instance pair. Tag-assignment thus becomes a graph partitioning process. The vertices are partitioned into C subsets, each representing a specific category; their vertices are tagged accordingly. As salient instances in the same category have similar semantic content and semantic features, a graph partitioning algorithm should ensure the vertices inside a subset are strongly related while the vertices in different subsets should be as weakly related as possible. We define the cohesiveness of a specific subgraph as the sum of edge weights linking vertices inside the subgraph; the optimization target is to maximize the sum of cohesiveness over all categories. This graph partitioning problem can be modeled as a mixed integer quadratic program (MIQP) problem as described later.

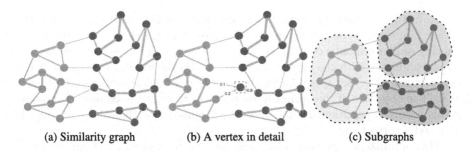

(a) Similarity graph   (b) A vertex in detail   (c) Subgraphs

Fig. 3. Graph partitioning. (a): Similarity graph, thickness of edges indicating edge weights; color shows the correct tags of the vertices. (b): Consider the vertex bounded by a dotted square—only by including it in the red subgraph can the objective be optimized. (c): Subgraphs after partitioning. (Color figure online)

4.1 Construction of the Similarity Graph

Let the similarity graph of vertices, edges and weights be $G = (V, E, W)$. Initially, we calculate the cosine similarity between every pair of features to determine W:

$$\begin{cases} W_{ij} = \frac{\mathbf{f_i} \cdot \mathbf{f_j}}{\|\mathbf{f_i}\| \|\mathbf{f_j}\|} + 1, & i \neq j, \\ W_{ij} = 0, & i = j, \end{cases} \tag{5}$$

If every pair of vertices is related by an edge, G would be a dense graph, the number of edges growing quadratically with the number of vertices, and in turn, cohesiveness would be dominated by the number of vertices in the subset. In order to eliminate the effect of the size of the subgraph, we turn G into a sparse graph by edge reduction, so that each vertex retains only those k linked edges with the largest weights. In our experiments, we set $k = 3$.

4.2 The Primary Graph Partitioning Algorithm

As described above, the cohesiveness of a subset i can be written in matrix form as $\mathbf{x}_i^T W \mathbf{x}_i$. As x_i is a binary vector with length n, this formula simply sums the weights of edges between all vertices in subgraph i. To maximize cohesiveness over all categories, we formulate the following optimization problem:

$$\max_{\mathbf{x}} \sum_{i=1}^{C} \mathbf{x}_i^T W \mathbf{x}_i, \qquad \text{such that}$$

$$\text{s.t.} \sum_{i=1}^{C} \mathbf{x}_i = 1, \tag{6}$$

$$\mathbf{x}_{ij} \in \begin{cases} \{0, 1\} & \text{if } i \in K_j \\ \{0\} & \text{otherwise.} \end{cases}$$

To further explain this formulation, consider a salient instance, such as the vertex bounded by dotted square in Fig. 3(b), which belongs to category i_a. Sharing similar semantic content, the vertex representing this salient instance has strong similarity with the vertices in subset i_a. So the weights of edges between this vertex and subset i_a are larger than between it and any other subset, such as i_b. The objective of the optimization problem reaches a maximum if and only if this vertex is partitioned into subset i_a, meaning that the salient instance is assigned a correct tag.

This optimization problem can easily be transformed into a standard mixed integer quadratic programing (MIQP) problem. Although this MIQP is non-convex because of its zero diagonal and nonnegative elements, it can easily be reformulated as a convex MIQP, since all the variables are constrained to be 0 or 1. It can be solved by a branch-and-bound method using IBM-CPLEX [3].

4.3 The Graph Partitioning with Attention and Noisy Vertices

The tag assignment problem in Sect. 4.2 identifies keywords for salient instances using semantic relationships between the salient instances. However, the intrinsic properties of a salient instance are also important in tag assignment. As explained in Sect. 3.1, the attention module predicts the probability $\mathbf{p}_{ij}$ that a salient instance j belongs to category i. In order to make use of the intrinsic characteristics of the salient instances, we reformulate the optimization problem as:

$$\max_{\mathbf{x}} \sum_{i=1}^{C} \mathbf{x}_i^T W \mathbf{x}_i + \beta \mathbf{p}_i \mathbf{x}_i, \qquad \text{such that}$$

$$\sum_{i=1}^{C} \mathbf{x}_i = 1, \tag{7}$$

$$\mathbf{x}_{ij} \in \begin{cases} \{0,1\} & \text{if } i \in K_j \\ \{0\} & \text{otherwise,} \end{cases}$$

where the hyper-parameter β balances intrinsic instance information and global object relationship information.

As the salient instances are obtained by the class-agnostic S^4Net, some salient instances may fall outside the categories of the training set. We should thus further adjust the optimization problem to reject such noisy vertices:

$$\max_{\mathbf{x}} \sum_{i=1}^{C} \mathbf{x}_i^T W \mathbf{x}_i + \beta \mathbf{p}_i \mathbf{x}_i, \qquad \text{such that}$$

$$\sum_{i=1}^{C} \mathbf{x}_i \leq 1,$$

$$\sum_{i=1j} \mathbf{x}_{ij} = \lfloor rn \rfloor, \tag{8}$$

$$\mathbf{x}_{ij} \in \begin{cases} \{0,1\} & \text{if } i \in K_j \\ \{0\} & \text{otherwise,} \end{cases}$$

where the retention ratio r determines the number of vertices recognized as non-noisy.

5   Experiments

In this section, we show the efficacy of our method on the challenging PASCAL VOC 2012 semantic segmentation benchmark and at the same time conduct comparisons with state-of-the-art methods. The results show that our proposed framework greatly outperforms all existing weakly-supervised methods. We also perform a series of experiments to analyze the importance of each component in our method and discuss limitations highlighted by the experiments. We furthermore present the first results of instance-level segmentation for MS COCO.

5.1   Methodology

Datasets. We consider two training sets widely used in other work, the PASCAL VOC 2012 semantic segmentation dataset [11] plus an augmented version of this set [13]. As it has been widely used as a main training set [4,22,41], we also do so. We also consider a simple dataset [18], all of whose images were automatically selected from the ImageNet dataset [38]. We show the results of training on both sets individually, as well as in combination. Details concerning the datasets can be found in Table 1b. We have tested our method on both the PASCAL VOC 2012 validation set and test set. For instance-level segmentation, the training process is performed on the standard COCO trainval set; all pixel-level masks in the ground-truth are removed. We evaluate the performance using the standard COCO evaluation metric. We use ImageNet as an auxiliary dataset to pretrain all backbone models and the feature extractor.

Hyper-parameters and Model Settings. In order to concentrate feature vectors for salient instances in the same category, we use center loss. As suggested in [43], we set $\lambda = 10^{-3}$ and $\alpha = 0.5$ to train center loss. However, unlike in the original version, center loss is calculated by cosine distance instead of Euclidean distance for consistency with the distance measure used in similarity graph construction. The semantic feature extractor is trained on ImageNet using input images cropped and resized to 224×224 pixels. The attention module is implemented as a standard classifier and ResNet-50 is used as the backbone model. We use all the training data (PASCAL VOC 2012 or simple ImageNet) to train this module. For the traditional fully supervised segmentation CNNs in our framework, we train DeepLab using the following hyper-parameters: initial learning rate $= 2.5 \times 10^{-4}$), divided by a factor of 10 after 20k iterations, weight decay $= 5 \times 10^{-4}$, and momentum $= 0.9$. The mask-RCNN for instance-level segmentation is trained using: initial learning rate $= 2 \times 10^{-3}$, divided by a factor of 10 after 5 epochs, weight decay $= 10^{-4}$, and momentum $= 0.9$.

Table 1. Ablation study for our proposed framework on three datasets. The best result in each column is highlighted in **bold**. Subscripts represent growth relative to the value above. Numbers of samples in the three datasets are also given.

Methods	mIoU (%)				dataset	size
	VOC	SI	VOC+SI			
random	56.4	–	61.3		VOC	10,582
attention	$62.0_{+5.6}$	–	$62.7_{+1.4}$		SI	24,000
GP w/o filtering	$64.0_{+2.0}$	62.8	$64.9_{+2.2}$		VOC + SI	34,582
GP + filtering	$\mathbf{64.5_{+0.5}}$	$\mathbf{63.9_{+1.1}}$	$\mathbf{65.6_{+0.7}}$			

(a) **Ablation results** 'Random' refers to keywords of an image being assigned randomly to the salient instances. 'Attention' stands for the framework using only the attention module. The results of the whole pipeline with or without noisy salient instance filtering are also given.

(b) **Size of each dataset** In the experiments, we use 10,582 images from the augmented PASCAL VOC 2012 dataset, and 24,000 from the simple ImageNet dataset.

Table 2. Influence of the hyper-parameters β and r on graph partitioning. The best result for each hyper-parameter is highlighted in **bold**. This experiment is conducted on the PASCAL VOC dataset.

β	0	3	10	30	90	300
mIoU (%)	63.2	63.9	64.1	**64.5**	63.6	62.9

r	1.00	0.95	0.90	0.85	0.80	0.75
mIoU (%)	63.8	**64.5**	64.1	63.4	62.3	60.9

(a) **Influence of β** The hyper-parameter β balances instance intrinsic information and global object relationship information in the optimization model. $\beta = 0$ means the graph is partitioned solely using global relationship information.

(b) **Influence of r** The retention ratio r determines the proportion of salient instances labeled as valid during graph partitioning. $r = 0$ means a tag-assignment algorithm without noisy instances filtering.

5.2   Sensitivity Analysis

To analyze the importance of each component of our proposed framework, we perform a series of ablation experiments using three datasets. Table 1a shows the results of the ablation study. As for existing works, the PASCAL VOC 2012 training set (VOC) [11] is used in our experiments. Also, the simple ImageNet (SI) used important dataset in our experiments. Unlike in PASCAL VOC 2012, in the simple ImageNet dataset every image has only one keyword. The results in Table 1a are evaluated on PASCAL VOC test set and the results in Table 2 are evaluated on PASCAL VOC val set.

Importance of Each Component of the Framework. Figure 1a shows that it is impossible to obtain reasonable results by assign the image keywords to instances randomly, indicating the necessity of tag assignment. One can observe from Table 1a that the proposed graph partitioning operation brings 2.2% improvement compared to the single attention module for the combined PASCAL VOC and simple ImageNet dataset. These results indicate that global object relationship information across the whole dataset is useful in tag-assignment and clearly contributes to the final segmentation performance. The results on the three datasets, especially for the simple ImageNet set which contains more noisy salient instances, show that the noise filtering mechanism further improves segmentation performance.

Balancing Ratio β. Graph partitioning depends on two key hyper-parameters: balancing ratio β and retention ratio r, and they have great impact on the final performance of the whole framework. The balancing ratio β balances information within salient instances to global object relationship information across the whole dataset. If β is set to 0, graph partitioning depends solely on the global relationship information; as β increases, the influence of the intrinsic properties of the salient instances also increases. Table 2a shows the influence of β. Even using only global relationship information ($\beta = 0$), reasonable results can still be obtained. This verifies the effectiveness and importance of the global relationship information. When $\beta = 30$, 1.3% performance gain is obtained as intrinsic properties of the salient instances are also taken into consideration during graph partitioning. Too large a value of β decreases use of global relationship information and may impair the final performance.

Retention Ratio r. The other key hyper-parameter, the retention ratio r, determines the proportion of salient instances to be regarded as valid in graph partitioning, as a proportion $(1 - r)$ of the instances are rejected as noise. Table 2b shows the influence of r on PASCAL VOC val set. Eliminating a proper number of salient instances having low confidence improves the quality of the proxy-ground-truth and benefits the final segmentation results, but too small a retention ratio leads to a performance decline.

5.3   Comparison with Existing Work

We compare our proposed method with existing state-of-the-art weakly super-vised semantic segmentation approaches. Table 3 shows results based on the PAS-CAL VOC 2012 'val' and 'test' sets. We can see that our framework achieves the best results for both 'val' and 'test' sets. Specifically, our approach improves on the baseline result presented in Mining Pixels [18] by 6.0% points for the 'test' set and 5.8% for the 'val' set. It is further worth noting that our framework even outperforms the methods with additional supervision in the form of scribbles and points.

In addition to the semantic segmentation results, we present results for instance-level segmentation under weak supervision using only keyword annotations. Table 4 compares our results to those from state-of-the-art fully supervised methods. Using only original RGB images with keywords, our method achieves results within 36.9% of the best fully supervised method.

Table 3. Pixel-level segmentation results on the PASCAL VOC 2012 'val' and 'test' sets compared to those from existing state-of-the-art approaches. The default training dataset is VOC 2012 for our proposed framework, while '†' indicates experiments using both VOC 2012 and the simple ImageNet dataset. The best keyword-based result in each column is highlighted in **bold**.

Method	Publication	Supervision			Dataset	
		Keywords	Scribbles	Points	val	test
CCNN [32]	ICCV'15	✓			35.3%	-
EM-Adapt [31]	ICCV'15	✓			38.2%	39.6%
MIL [33]	CVPR'15	✓			42.0%	-
SEC [22]	ECCV'16	✓			50.7%	51.7%
AugFeed [35]	ECCV'16	✓			54.3%	55.5%
STC [42]	PAMI'17	✓			49.8%	51.2%
Roy et al. [37]	CVPR'17	✓			52.8%	53.7%
Oh et al. [30]	CVPR'17	✓			55.7%	56.7%
AS-PSL [41]	CVPR'17	✓			55.0%	55.7%
WebS-i2 [21]	CVPR'17	✓			53.4%	55.3%
DCSP-VGG16 [4]	BMVC'17	✓			58.6%	59.2%
Mining Pixels [18]	EMMCVPR'17	✓			58.7%	59.6%
ours-VGG16 (Ours)	-	✓			61.3%	62.1%
ours-ResNet101	-	✓			63.6%	64.5%
ours-VGG16† (Ours)	-	✓			61.9%	63.1%
ours-ResNet101†	-	✓			**64.5%**	**65.6%**
ScribbleSup [25]	CVPR'16	✓	✓		63.1%	-
Bearman et al. [2]	ECCV'16	✓		✓	49.1%	-

Table 4. Instance segmentation results on the COCO test-dev set compared to those of existing approaches. The training set for our weakly supervised framework is the COCO training set without pixel level annotations (masks).

Method	Weakly	Fully	AP	AP_{50}	AP_{75}	AP_S	AP_M	AP_L
FCIS [24]		✓	29.2%	49.5%	-	7.1%	31.3%	50.0%
MNC [7]		✓	24.6%	44.3%	24.8%	4.7%	25.9%	43.6%
Mask-RCNN [14]		✓	37.1%	60.0%	39.6%	35.3%	35.3%	35.3%
Ours	✓		13.7%	25.5%	13.5%	00.7%	15.7%	26.1%

5.4 Efficiency Analysis

We use IBM-CPLEX [3] to solve the MIQP in graph partitioning process. Because our academic version CPLEX restricts the maximum number of variables to be optimized, we use batches of 400 salient instances in implementation. To assign tags for 18878 salient instances extracted from VOC dataset, $\lceil 18878/400 \rceil = 48$ batches are processed sequentially, which takes 226M memory and 22.14 s on an i7 4770HQ CPU.

6 Conclusions

We have proposed a novel weakly supervised segmentation framework, focusing on generating accurate proxy-ground-truth based on salient instances extracted from the training images and tags assigned to them. In this paper, we introduce salient instances to weakly supervised segmentation, significantly simplifying the object discrimination operation in existing work and enabling our framework to conduct instance-level segmentation. We regard the tag-assignment task as a network partitioning problem which can be solved by a standard approach. In order to improve the accuracy of tag-assignment, both the information from individual salient instances, and from the relationships between all objects in the whole dataset are taken into consideration. Experiments show that our method achieves new state-of-the art results on the PASCAL VOC 2012 semantic segmentation benchmark and demonstrated for the first time weakly supervised results on the MS COCO instance-level segmentation task using only keyword annotations.

Acknowledgments. This research was supported by the Natural Science Foundation of China (Project Number 61521002, 61620106008, 61572264) and the Joint NSFC-ISF Research Program (project number 61561146393), the national youth talent support program, Tianjin Natural Science Foundation for Distinguished Young Scholars (NO. 17JCJQJC43700), Huawei Innovation Research Program.

References

1. Ankerst, M., Breunig, M.M., Kriegel, H.P., Sander, J.: OPTICS: ordering points to identify the clustering structure. In: ACM Sigmod Record, vol. 28, pp. 49–60. ACM (1999)
2. Bearman, A., Russakovsky, O., Ferrari, V., Fei-Fei, L.: What's the point: semantic segmentation with point supervision. In: Leibe, B., Matas, J., Sebe, N., Welling, M. (eds.) ECCV 2016. LNCS, vol. 9911, pp. 549–565. Springer, Cham (2016). https://doi.org/10.1007/978-3-319-46478-7_34
3. Blieklú, C., Bonami, P., Lodi, A.: Solving mixed-integer quadratic programming problems with IBM-CPLEX: a progress report. In: Proceedings of the Twenty-Sixth RAMP Symposium, pp. 16–17 (2014)
4. Chaudhry, A., Dokania, P.K., Torr, P.H.: Discovering class-specific pixels for weakly-supervised semantic segmentation. BMVC (2017)
5. Chen, L.C., Papandreou, G., Kokkinos, I., Murphy, K., Yuille, A.L.: Deeplab: semantic image segmentation with deep convolutional nets, atrous convolution, and fully connected CRFs. IEEE TPAMI **40**, 834–848 (2017)
6. Cheng, M., Mitra, N.J., Huang, X., Torr, P.H., Hu, S.: Global contrast based salient region detection. IEEE TPAMI **37**, 569–582 (2015)
7. Dai, J., He, K., Sun, J.: Instance-aware semantic segmentation via multi-task network cascades. In: Proceedings of the IEEE Conference on Computer Vision and Pattern Recognition, pp. 3150–3158 (2016)
8. Dempster, A.P., Laird, N.M., Rubin, D.B.: Maximum likelihood from incomplete data via the EM algorithm. J. R. Stat. Soc. Ser. B (Methodol.) **39**, 1–38 (1977)
9. Deng, J., Dong, W., Socher, R., Li, L.J., Li, K., Fei-Fei, L.: Imagenet: a large-scale hierarchical image database. In: IEEE Conference on Computer Vision and Pattern Recognition, 2009. CVPR 2009, pp. 248–255. IEEE (2009)
10. Ester, M., Kriegel, H.P., Sander, J., Xu, X., et al.: A density-based algorithm for discovering clusters in large spatial databases with noise. In: Kdd, vol. 96, pp. 226–231 (1996)
11. Everingham, M., Eslami, S.A., Van Gool, L., Williams, C.K., Winn, J., Zisserman, A.: The PASCAL visual object classes challenge: a retrospective. IJCV **111**, 98–136 (2015)
12. Fan, R., Hou, Q., Cheng, M.M., Mu, T.J., Hu, S.M.: S^4Net: single stage salient-instance segmentation. arXiv preprint arXiv:1711.07618 (2017)
13. Hariharan, B., Arbeláez, P., Bourdev, L., Maji, S., Malik, J.: Semantic contours from inverse detectors. In: ICCV (2011)
14. He, K., Gkioxari, G., Dollár, P., Girshick, R.: Mask R-CNN. In: 2017 IEEE International Conference on Computer Vision (ICCV), pp. 2980–2988. IEEE (2017)
15. He, K., Zhang, X., Ren, S., Sun, J.: Deep residual learning for image recognition. In: Proceedings of the IEEE Conference on Computer Vision and Pattern Recognition, pp. 770–778 (2016)
16. Hong, S., Yeo, D., Kwak, S., Lee, H., Han, B.: Weakly supervised semantic segmentation using web-crawled videos. In: CVPR (2017)
17. Hou, Q., Cheng, M.M., Hu, X., Borji, A., Tu, Z., Torr, P.: Deeply supervised salient object detection with short connections. In: CVPR (2017)
18. Hou, Q., Massiceti, D., Dokania, P.K., Wei, Y., Cheng, M.-M., Torr, P.H.S.: Bottom-up top-down cues for weakly-supervised semantic segmentation. In: Pelillo, M., Hancock, E. (eds.) EMMCVPR 2017. LNCS, vol. 10746, pp. 263–277. Springer, Cham (2018). https://doi.org/10.1007/978-3-319-78199-0_18

19. Hou, Q., Dokania, P.K., Massiceti, D., Wei, Y., Cheng, M.M., Torr, P.: Bottom-up top-down cues for weakly-supervised semantic segmentation. arXiv preprint arXiv:1612.02101 (2016)
20. Jiang, H., Wang, J., Yuan, Z., Wu, Y., Zheng, N., Li, S.: Salient object detection: a discriminative regional feature integration approach. In: 2013 IEEE Conference on Computer Vision and Pattern Recognition (CVPR), pp. 2083–2090. IEEE (2013)
21. Jin, B., Ortiz Segovia, M.V., Susstrunk, S.: Webly supervised semantic segmentation. In: CVPR, pp. 3626–3635 (2017)
22. Kolesnikov, A., Lampert, C.H.: Seed, expand and constrain: three principles for weakly-supervised image segmentation. In: Leibe, B., Matas, J., Sebe, N., Welling, M. (eds.) ECCV 2016. LNCS, vol. 9908, pp. 695–711. Springer, Cham (2016). https://doi.org/10.1007/978-3-319-46493-0_42
23. Li, G., Xie, Y., Lin, L., Yu, Y.: Instance-level salient object segmentation. In: 2017 IEEE Conference on Computer Vision and Pattern Recognition (CVPR), pp. 247–256. IEEE (2017)
24. Li, Y., Qi, H., Dai, J., Ji, X., Wei, Y.: Fully convolutional instance-aware semantic segmentation. In: IEEE Conference on Computer Vision and Pattern Recognition (CVPR), pp. 2359–2367 (2017)
25. Lin, D., Dai, J., Jia, J., He, K., Sun, J.: Scribblesup: scribble-supervised convolutional networks for semantic segmentation. In: CVPR (2016)
26. Lin, G., Milan, A., Shen, C., Reid, I.: Refinenet: multi-path refinement networks with identity mappings for high-resolution semantic segmentation. In: CVPR (2017)
27. Lin, T.-Y., et al.: Microsoft COCO: common objects in context. In: Fleet, D., Pajdla, T., Schiele, B., Tuytelaars, T. (eds.) ECCV 2014. LNCS, vol. 8693, pp. 740–755. Springer, Cham (2014). https://doi.org/10.1007/978-3-319-10602-1_48
28. Long, J., Shelhamer, E., Darrell, T.: Fully convolutional networks for semantic segmentation. In: CVPR (2015)
29. MacQueen, J., et al.: Some methods for classification and analysis of multivariate observations. In: Proceedings of the Fifth Berkeley Symposium on Mathematical Statistics and Probability, vol. 1, pp. 281–297, Oakland, CA, USA (1967)
30. Oh, S.J., Benenson, R., Khoreva, A., Akata, Z., Fritz, M., Schiele, B.: Exploiting saliency for object segmentation from image level labels. In: CVPR (2017)
31. Papandreou, G., Chen, L.C., Murphy, K., Yuille, A.L.: Weakly-and semi-supervised learning of a DCNN for semantic image segmentation. arXiv preprint arXiv:1502.02734 (2015)
32. Pathak, D., Krahenbuhl, P., Darrell, T.: Constrained convolutional neural networks for weakly supervised segmentation. In: ICCV (2015)
33. Pinheiro, P.O., Collobert, R.: From image-level to pixel-level labeling with convolutional networks. In: CVPR (2015)
34. Pont-Tuset, J., Arbelaez, P., Barron, J.T., Marques, F., Malik, J.: Multiscale combinatorial grouping for image segmentation and object proposal generation. IEEE TPAMI (2017)
35. Qi, X., Liu, Z., Shi, J., Zhao, H., Jia, J.: Augmented feedback in semantic segmentation under image level supervision. In: Leibe, B., Matas, J., Sebe, N., Welling, M. (eds.) ECCV 2016. LNCS, vol. 9912, pp. 90–105. Springer, Cham (2016). https://doi.org/10.1007/978-3-319-46484-8_6
36. Rokach, L., Maimon, O.: Clustering methods. In: Maimon, O., Rokach, L. (eds.) Data Mining and Knowledge Discovery Handbook, pp. 321–352. Springer, Boston (2005). https://doi.org/10.1007/0-387-25465-X_15

37. Roy, A., Todorovic, S.: Combining bottom-up, top-down, and smoothness cues for weakly supervised image segmentation. In: CVPR (2017)
38. Russakovsky, O., et al.: Imagenet large scale visual recognition challenge. IJCV **115**, 211–252 (2015)
39. Simonyan, K., Zisserman, A.: Very deep convolutional networks for large-scale image recognition. In: ICLR (2015)
40. Vezhnevets, A., Ferrari, V., Buhmann, J.M.: Weakly supervised structured output learning for semantic segmentation. In: CVPR, pp. 845–852. IEEE (2012)
41. Wei, Y., Feng, J., Liang, X., Cheng, M.M., Zhao, Y., Yan, S.: Object region mining with adversarial erasing: a simple classification to semantic segmentation approach. In: CVPR (2017)
42. Wei, Y., et al.: STC: a simple to complex framework for weakly-supervised semantic segmentation. IEEE TPAMI **39**, 2314–2320 (2016)
43. Wen, Y., Zhang, K., Li, Z., Qiao, Y.: A discriminative feature learning approach for deep face recognition. In: Leibe, B., Matas, J., Sebe, N., Welling, M. (eds.) ECCV 2016. LNCS, vol. 9911, pp. 499–515. Springer, Cham (2016). https://doi.org/10.1007/978-3-319-46478-7_31
44. Zhang, J., Lin, Z., Brandt, J., Shen, X., Sclaroff, S.: Top-down neural attention by excitation backprop. In: ECCV (2016)
45. Zhao, H., Shi, J., Qi, X., Wang, X., Jia, J.: Pyramid scene parsing network. In: CVPR (2017)
46. Zheng, S., et al.: Conditional random fields as recurrent neural networks. In: ICCV (2015)
47. Zhou, B., Khosla, A., Lapedriza, A., Oliva, A., Torralba, A.: Learning deep features for discriminative localization. In: CVPR (2016)

HybridFusion: Real-Time Performance Capture Using a Single Depth Sensor and Sparse IMUs

Zerong Zheng[1], Tao Yu[1,2], Hao Li[3], Kaiwen Guo[4], Qionghai Dai[1],
Lu Fang[5], and Yebin Liu[1(✉)]

[1] Tsinghua University, Beijing, China
liuyebin@mail.tsinghua.edu.cn
[2] Beihang University, Beijing, China
[3] University of Southern California, Los Angeles, CA, USA
[4] Google Inc., Mountain View, CA, USA
[5] Tsinghua-Berkeley Shenzhen Institute, Tsinghua University, Shenzhen, China

Abstract. We propose a light-weight yet highly robust method for real-time human performance capture based on a single depth camera and sparse inertial measurement units (IMUs). Our method combines non-rigid surface tracking and volumetric fusion to simultaneously reconstruct challenging motions, detailed geometries and the inner human body of a clothed subject. The proposed hybrid motion tracking algorithm and efficient per-frame sensor calibration technique enable non-rigid surface reconstruction for fast motions and challenging poses with severe occlusions. Significant fusion artifacts are reduced using a new confidence measurement for our adaptive TSDF-based fusion. The above contributions are mutually beneficial in our reconstruction system, which enable practical human performance capture that is real-time, robust, low-cost and easy to deploy. Experiments show that extremely challenging performances and loop closure problems can be handled successfully.

Keywords: Performance capture · Real-time · Single-view · IMU

1 Introduction

The 3D acquisition of human performances has been a challenging topic for decades due to the shape and deformation complexity of dynamic surfaces, especially for clothed subjects. To ensure high-fidelity digitalization, sophisticated multi-camera array systems [4,5,7,8,14,17,24,29,43] are preferred for professional productions. TotalCapture [13], the state-of-the-art human performance capture system, uses more than 500 cameras to minimize occlusions during

Electronic supplementary material The online version of this chapter (https://doi.org/10.1007/978-3-030-01240-3_24) contains supplementary material, which is available to authorized users.

ⓒ Springer Nature Switzerland AG 2018
V. Ferrari et al. (Eds.): ECCV 2018, LNCS 11213, pp. 389–406, 2018.
https://doi.org/10.1007/978-3-030-01240-3_24

human-object interactions. Not only are these systems difficult to deploy and costly, they also come with a significant amount of synchronization, calibration, and data processing effort.

On the other end of the spectrum, the recent trend of using a single depth camera for dynamic scene reconstruction [10,12,25,31] provides a very convenient and real-time approach for performance capture combined with online non-rigid volumetric depth fusion. However, such monocular systems are limited to slow and controlled motions. While improvement has been demonstrated lately in systems like BodyFusion [44], DoubleFusion [45] and SobolevFusion [32], it is still impossible to reconstruct occluded limb motions (Fig. 1(b)) and ensure loop closure during online reconstruction. For practical deployment, such as gaming, where fast motion is expected and possibly interactions between multiple users, it is necessary to ensure continuously reliable performance capture.

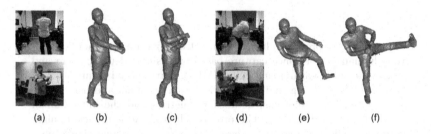

(a)   (b)   (c)   (d)   (e)   (f)

Fig. 1. The state-of-the-art methods easily get failed under severe occlusions. (a, d): color references captured from Kinect (up) and a 3rd person view (down). (b, e) and (c, f): results of DoubleFusion and our method rendered in the 3rd person view. (Color figure online)

We propose HybridFusion, a real-time dynamic surface reconstruction system that achieves high-quality reconstruction of extremely challenging performances using hybrid sensors, i.e., a single depth camera and several inertial measurement units (IMUs) sparsely located on the body. Intuitively, for the cases of extremely fast or highly occluded or self-rotating limb motions, which cannot be handled by the optical sensors alone, the IMUs can provide high frame rate orientation information that help infer better human motion estimations. Moreover, they are low cost and easy to wear. For other cases, a single depth camera owns sufficient capacity to achieve robust reconstruction, so as to maintain the light-weight and convenient property of the whole system compared to multi-camera ones.

Combining IMUs with depth sensors within a non-rigid depth fusion framework is non-trivial. First, we need to minimize the effort and experience required for mounting and calibrating each IMU. We, therefore, propose a per-frame sensor calibration algorithm integrated into the tracking procedure to get accurate IMU calibration without any additional extra steps. We also extend the non-rigid tracking optimization to a hybrid tracking optimization by adding the IMU constraints. Moreover, previous tracking&fusion methods [25,45] may generate seriously deteriorated reconstruction results for challenging motions and occlusions due to the wrongly fused geometry, which will further affect the tracking performance, and vice versa. We thus propose a simple yet effective scheme that jointly models the influence of body-camera distance, fast motions and occlusions in one metric, which guides the TSDF (Truncated Signed Distance Field) fusion to achieve robust and precise results even under challenging motions (see Fig. 1). Using such a light-weight hybrid setup, we believe HybridFusion presents the right sweet spot for practical performance capture system as it is real-time, robust and easy to deploy. Commodity users can capture high-quality body performances and 3D content for gaming, VR/AR applications at home.

Note that IMUs or even hybrid sensors have been adopted previously to improve the skeleton-based motion tracking [11,20,22,28]. Comparing with these state-of-the-art hybrid motion capture systems like [11], the superiority of HybridFusion is twofold: for one, our system can reconstruct the detailed outer surface of the subject and estimate the inner body shape simultaneously, while [11] needs a pre-defined model as input; for another, our system can track the non-rigid motion of the outer surface, while [11] outputs skeleton poses merely. By further examining the differences in the skeleton tracking solely, our system still demonstrates substantially higher accuracy. In [11] IMU readings are only used to query similar poses in a database, yet we integrate the inertial measurements into a hybrid tracking energy. The detailed model and non-rigid registration further improve the accuracy of pose estimation, since a detailed geometry model with an embedding deformation node graph better describes the motion of the user than a body model driven by a kinetic chain.

The main contributions of HybridFusion can be summarized as follows.

- **Hybrid motion tracking.** We propose a hybrid non-rigid tracking algorithm for accurate skeleton motion and non-rigid surface motion tracking in real-time. We introduce an IMU term that significantly improves the tracking performance even under severe occlusion.
- **Sensor calibration.** We introduce a per-frame sensor calibration method to optimize the relationship between each IMU and its attached body part during the capture process. Unlike other IMU-based methods [2,20,28], this method removes the requirement of explicit calibration and provides accurate calibration results along the sequence.
- **Adaptive Geometry fusion.** To address the problem that previous TSDF fusion methods are vulnerable in some challenging cases (far body-camera distance, fast motions, occlusions, etc.), we propose an adaptive TSDF fusion method that considers all the factors above in one tracking confidence measurement to get more robust and detailed TSDF fusion results.

2   Related Work

The related work can be classified into two categories: IMU-based human performance capture and volumetric dynamic reconstruction. We refer readers to overview of prior works including pre-scanned template based dynamic reconstruction [9,15,34,40,42,46], shape template based dynamic reconstruction [1,3,18,29,30] and free-form dynamic reconstruction [16,23,26,35,37] in [45].

IMU-Based Human Performance Capture. A line of research on combining vision and IMUs [11,20–22,27,28] or even using IMUs alone [41] targets at high quality human performance capture. Among all of those works, Malleson *et al.* [20] combined multi-view color inputs, sparse IMUs and SMPL model [18] in a real-time full-body skeleton motion capture system. Pons-moll *et al.* [28] used multi-view color inputs, sparse IMUs and pre-scanned user templates to perform full-body motion capture offline. The system is improved by using 6 IMUs alone [41] to reconstruct natural human skeleton motion using global optimization method, but still offline. Vlasic *et al.* [39] used the output of the inertial sensors for extended kalman filter to perform human skeleton motion capture. Tautges *et al.* [36] and Ronit *et al.* [33] both utilized sparse accelerometer data and data-driven methods to retrieve correct poses in the database. Helten *et al.* [11] used the most similar setup to our method (single-view depth information, sparse IMUs and parametric human body model). They combined generative tracker and discriminative tracker that retrieving closest poses in a dataset and perform real-time human motion tracking. However, the parametric body model cannot describe detailed surfaces of clothing.

Non-rigid Surface Integration. Starting from DynamicFusion [25], non-rigid surface integration methods get more and more popular [10,12,31] because of the single-view, real-time and template-free properties. It also inspires a branch of multi-view volumetric dynamic reconstruction methods [6,7] that achieved high quality reconstruction results. The basic idea of non-rigid surface integration is to perform non-rigid surface tracking and TSDF surface fusion iteratively, such that the surface information gets more and more complete along the scene motions when unseen surface parts get observed and tracked. To improve the reconstruction performance of DynamicFusion on human body motions, Body-Fusion [44] integrated articulated human motion prior (skeleton kinematic chain structure) and constraint the non-rigid deformation and skeleton motion to be similar. DoubleFusion [45] leveraged parametric body model (SMPL [18]) in non-rigid surface integration to improve the tracking, loop closure and fusion performance, and achieved the state-of-the-art single-view human performance capture results. However, all of these methods are still incompetent to handle fast and challenging motions, especially for occluded motions.

3   Overview

Initialization. We adopt 8 IMUs that sparsely located on the upper and lower limbs of the performer as shown in Fig. 2. It is worth mentioning that unlike [20, 41] which require IMUs to be specific to model vertices, the IMUs in our system are attached to bones as we merely trust and use the orientation measurements. Such strategy greatly relaxes users' efforts to wear the sensors since they only need to ensure the IMUs are attached to the correct bones and roughly aligned

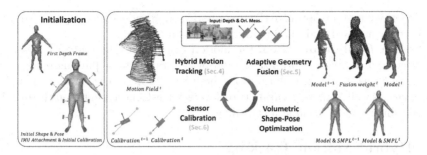

Fig. 2. Illustration of HybridFusion pipeline.

with their length directions. Here the number of IMUs is determined by the balance between performance and convenience, as further elaborated in Sect. 7.3.

The performer is required to start with a rough A-pose. After getting the first depth frame, we use it to initialize the TSDF volume by projecting the depth pixels into the volume, and then estimate the initial shape parameters β_0 and pose θ_0 using volumetric shape-pose optimization [45]. We construct a "double node graph" consisting of predefined on-body node graph and free-form sampled far-body node graph. We use θ_0 and the initial IMU readings to initialize sensor calibration. The triangle mesh is extracted from the TSDF volume with Marching Cube algorithm [19].

Main Pipeline. The lack of ground truth transformation between IMUs and their attached bones leads to unstable tracking performance in our hybrid motion tracking step. Therefore, we keep optimizing the sensor calibration frame by frame, and the calibration gets more and more accurate thanks to the increasing number of successfully tracked frames with different skeleton poses. Following [45], we also optimize the inner body shape and the canonical pose. In summary, our pipeline performs hybrid motion tracking, adaptive geometry fusion, volumetric shape-pose optimization and sensor calibration sequentially, as shown in Fig. 2. Below is a brief introduction of the main components of our pipeline.

- **Hybrid Motion Tracking.** Given the current depth map and the IMU measurements, we propose to jointly track the skeletal motion and the surface non-rigid deformation through a new hybrid motion tracking algorithm. We construct a new energy term to constrain the orientations of the skeleton bones using the orientation measurements of their corresponding IMUs.
- **Adaptive Geometry Fusion.** To improve the robustness of the fusion step, we propose an adaptive fusion method that utilizes tracking confidence to adjust the weight of TSDF fusion adaptively. The tracking confidence can be estimated according to the normal equations in the current procedure of hybrid motion tracking.
- **Volumetric Shape-Pose Optimization.** We perform volumetric shape-pose optimization after adaptive geometry fusion. Based on the updated

TSDF volume, we optimize the inner body shape and canonical pose to obtain better canonical body fitting and skeleton embedding.
- **Sensor Calibration.** Given the motion tracking results and IMU readings at current frame, we optimize the sensor calibration to acquire more accurate estimations of the transformations between IMUs and their corresponding bones, as well as more accurate transformation estimation between the inertial coordinate and the camera coordinate.

4   Hybrid Motion Tracking

Since our pipeline focuses on performance capture of human, we adopt a double-layer surface representation for motion tracking, which has been proved to be efficient and robust in [45]. Similar to [9,44,45], our motion tracking is under the assumption that human motion largely follows articulated structures. Therefore, we use two kinds of motion parameterizations, skeleton motions and non-rigid node deformation. Combining IMU orientation informations, we construct a energy function for hybrid motion tracking in order to solve the two motion components in a joint optimization scheme. Given the depth map $\mathfrak{D}_t$ and inertial measurements $\mathfrak{M}_t$ of current frame t, the energy function is:

$$E_{\text{mot}} = \lambda_{\text{IMU}} E_{\text{IMU}} + \lambda_{\text{depth}} E_{\text{depth}} + \lambda_{\text{bind}} E_{\text{bind}} + \lambda_{\text{reg}} E_{\text{reg}} + \lambda_{\text{pri}} E_{\text{pri}}, \qquad (1)$$

where E_{IMU}, E_{depth}, E_{bind}, E_{reg} and E_{prior} represent IMU, depth, binding, regularization and pose prior term respectively. E_{IMU} and E_{depth} are data terms that constrain the results to be consistant with IMU and depth input, E_{bind} regularizes the surface non-rigid deformation with articulated skeleton motion, E_{reg} constrains the locally as-rigid-as-possible property of the node graph and E_{prior} is used to penalize unnatural human poses. To simplify the notation, we claim that all variables in this section take their values at the current frame t, and drop their subscripts of frame index.

IMU Term. To bridge the sensors' measurements and hybrid motion tracking pipeline, we select $N = 8$ binding bones on the SMPL model (Fig. 2 Initialization) for the N inertial sensors, and these bones are denoted by b_i^{IMU}($i = 1, \ldots, N$). The IMU term penalizes the orientation difference between IMU readings and the estimated orientations of their attached binding bones:

$$E_{\text{IMU}} = \sum_{i \in \mathcal{S}} \left\| \mathbf{R}_{I2C} \widetilde{\mathbf{R}}_i \mathbf{R}_{S2B,i}^{-1} - \mathbf{R}\big(\mathbf{b}_i^{IMU}\big) \right\|_F^2, \qquad (2)$$

where $\mathcal{S}$ is the index set of IMUs; $\widetilde{\mathbf{R}}_i$ is the orientation measurement of i-th sensor in the inertial coordinate system. $\mathbf{R}_{I2C}$ is the rotation offset between the inertial coordinate and the camera coordinate system, while $\mathbf{R}_{S2B,i}$ is the offset between the i-th IMU and its corresponding bone; more details are elaborated in Sect. 5. $\mathbf{R}(\mathbf{b}_i^{IMU})$ is the rotational part of the skeleton skinning matrix $\mathbf{G}(\mathbf{b}_i^{IMU})$, which is defined as:

$$\mathbf{G}(\mathbf{b}_i^{IMU}) = \mathbf{G}_j = \prod_{k \in \mathcal{K}_j} \exp\left(\theta_k \hat{\xi}_k\right), \qquad (3)$$

where j is the index of $\mathbf{b}_i^{IMU}$ in the skeleton structure; $\mathbf{G}_j$ is the cascaded rigid transformation of jth bone; $\mathcal{K}_j$ represents parent bones indices of jth bone along the backward kinematic chain; $\exp(\theta_k \hat{\xi}_k)$ is the exponential map of the twist associated with kth bone.

Note that $\mathbf{R}_{I2C}$ and $\mathbf{R}_{B2S}$ are crucial parameters determining the effectiveness of the IMU term, and therefore they are continually optimized in our pipeline even though we can obtain sufficiently accurate estimations through initial calculation. We provide more details about calculating and optimizing $\mathbf{R}_{I2C}$ and $\mathbf{R}_{S2B}$ in Sect. 5.

The other energy terms in Eq. 1 are detailed in [44, 45], as well as the efficient GPU solver for motion tracking. Please refer to these two papers for more details.

5   Sensor Calibration

On one hand, an inertial sensor gives orientation measurements in the inertial coordinate system, which is typically defined by the gravity field and geomagnetic field. On the other hand, our performance capture system runs in the camera coordinate system, which is independent of the inertial coordinate. The relationship between these two coordinates can be described as a constant mapping denoted by $\mathbf{R}_{I2C}$. Based on the mapping, we can transform all IMU outputs from inertial coordinate to the camera coordinate system, as formulated in Eq. 2. As illustrated in Fig. 3, several coordinate systems are involved in order to estimate the mapping: (1) the i-th IMU sensor coordinate system $C_{\mathbf{S}_i}$, which is aligned with the ith sensor itself, and changes when the sensor moves, (2) the inertial coordinate system $C_{\mathbf{I}}$, which remains static all the time, (3) the i-th bone coordinate system $C_{\mathbf{B}_i}$, which is aligned with the bone associated with the ith IMU sensor, and changes when the subject acts or moves, (4) the camera coordinate system $C_{\mathbf{C}}$, which also remains static. Accordingly, R_{S2B} is the transformation from $C_{\mathbf{S}}$ to $C_{\mathbf{B}}$, R_{I2C} is from $C_{\mathbf{I}}$ to $C_{\mathbf{S}}$, and their inverse transformations are denoted as R_{B2S} and R_{C2I}.

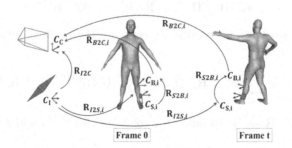

Fig. 3. Illustration of different coordinates and their relationship.

5.1 Initial Sensor Calibration

We calculate an approximation of $\mathbf{R}_{I2C}$ during the initialization of our pipeline. After fitting the SMPL model to the depth image, the mapping $\mathbf{R}_{B2C,i}$: $C_{\mathbf{B}_i} \rightarrow C_{\mathbf{C}}$ is available according to $\mathbf{R}_{B2C,i} = \mathbf{R}_{t_0}\left(\mathbf{b}_i^{IMU}\right)$, where the subscript t_0 is the index of the first frame. Besides, we can also obtain the mapping from $C_{\mathbf{I}}$ to $C_{\mathbf{S}_i}$ by assigning the inverse matrix of the sensor's reading at the first frame: $\mathbf{R}_{I2S,i} = \widetilde{\mathbf{R}}_{i,t_0}^{-1}$. To transform $C_{\mathbf{I}}$ into $C_{\mathbf{C}}$ through the path $C_{\mathbf{I}} \rightarrow C_{\mathbf{S}_i} \rightarrow C_{\mathbf{B}_i} \rightarrow C_{\mathbf{C}}$, we need to know the rotation offset between the IMUs and their corresponding bone coordinate systems $\mathbf{R}_{S2B,i}$: $C_{\mathbf{S}_i} \rightarrow C_{\mathbf{B}_i}$. We assume that they are constant as the sensors are tightly attached to the limbs and we then predefine them according to the placement of the sensors. Thus, we can compute $\mathbf{R}_{I2C}$ by

$$
\begin{aligned}
\mathbf{R}_{I2C} &= \operatorname*{SLERP}_{i=1,\ldots,N}\{(\mathbf{R}_{I2C,i}\,,\,w_i)\} = \operatorname*{SLERP}_{i=1,\ldots,N}\{(\mathbf{R}_{B2C,i}\mathbf{R}_{S2B,i}\mathbf{R}_{I2S,i}\,,\,w_i)\} \\
&= \operatorname*{SLERP}_{i=1,\ldots,N}\left\{\left(\mathbf{R}_{t_0}\left(\mathbf{b}_i^{IMU}\right)\mathbf{R}_{S2B,i}\widetilde{\mathbf{R}}_{i,t_0}^{-1}\,,\,w_i\right)\right\},
\end{aligned}
\tag{4}
$$

where SLERP $\{\cdot\}$ is the operator of spherical linear interpolation, and w_i is the interpolation weight, which is set to $1/N$ in our experiment.

5.2 Per-Frame Calibration Optimization

Even though the influence of measurement noises tends to be diminished by averaging $\mathbf{R}_{I2C,i}$ (Sect. 5.1), the solution of the initial sensor calibration is still prone to errors due to the sparse IMU setup and the rough assignments of $\mathbf{R}_{S2B,i}$. Therefore, we propose an efficient method to continuously optimize the sensor calibration. As formulated in Sect. 4, the orientation measurements and motion estimation are related by $\mathbf{R}_{I2C}$ and $\mathbf{R}_{B2S,i}$:

$$
\mathbf{R}_{I2C}\widetilde{\mathbf{R}}_i = \mathbf{R}\left(\mathbf{b}_i^{IMU}\right)\mathbf{R}_{B2S,i}^{-1},
\tag{5}
$$

thus we can compute the accumulated rotations from t_0 to t as:

$$
\mathbf{R}_{I2C}\widetilde{\mathbf{R}}_{i,t}\widetilde{\mathbf{R}}_{i,t_0}^{-1}\mathbf{R}_{I2C}^{-1} = \mathbf{R}_t\left(\mathbf{b}_i^{IMU}\right)\mathbf{R}_{t_0}^{-1}\left(\mathbf{b}_i^{IMU}\right).
\tag{6}
$$

Given the motion tracking results, we estimate the optimal rotation offset of frame t according to

$$
\hat{\mathbf{R}}_{I2C} = \arg\min_{\mathbf{R}_{I2C}}\sum_{i\in\mathcal{S}}\left\|\mathbf{R}_{I2C}\widetilde{\mathbf{R}}_{i,t}\widetilde{\mathbf{R}}_{i,t_0}^{-1}\mathbf{R}_{I2C}^{-1} - \mathbf{R}_t\left(\mathbf{b}_i^{IMU}\right)\mathbf{R}_{t_0}^{-1}\left(\mathbf{b}_i^{IMU}\right)\right\|_F^2,
\tag{7}
$$

and then update $\mathbf{R}_{I2C}$ by blending the solution with the original value:

$$
\mathbf{R}_{I2C} \leftarrow \operatorname{SLERP}\left\{(\mathbf{R}_{I2C},w)\,;\left(\hat{\mathbf{R}}_{I2C},\omega\right)\right\}
\tag{8}
$$

where w,ω are both interpolation weights. We set $w = 1 - \frac{1}{t}, \omega = \frac{1}{t}$ to make sure the final solution coverage to a stable global optimum. We optimize $\mathbf{R}_{S2B,i}$ in similar ways.

6 Adaptive Geometry Fusion

Similar to prior works [7,10,12,25,45], we integrate depth maps into a reference volume. To deal with the ambiguity caused by voxel collision, we follow [7,10,45] to detect collided voxels by voting the TSDF value at live frame and avoid integrating depth information into these voxels. Besides voxel collision, the surface fusion still suffers from inaccurate motion tracking, which is a factor that previous fusion methods do not consider. Inspired by previous works addressing the uncertainty of parameter estimation [38,47], we propose to fuse geometry adaptively according to the tracking confidence that measures the performance of hybrid motion tracking. Specifically, we denote x_t as the motion parameters being solved and assume it approximately follows a normal distribution:

$$p(x_t|\mathfrak{D}_t, \mathfrak{M}_t) \simeq \mathcal{N}(\mu_t, \Sigma_t), \tag{9}$$

where μ_t is the solution of motion tracking and the covariance Σ_t measures the tracking uncertainty. By assuming $p(x_t|\mathfrak{D}_t, \mathfrak{M}_t) \propto \exp(-E_{\mathrm{mot}})$, we can approximate the covariance as

$$\Sigma_t = \sigma^2 \left(\mathbf{J}^T \mathbf{J}\right)^{-1} \tag{10}$$

where $\mathbf{J}$ is the Jacobian of E_{mot}.

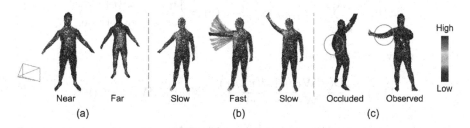

Fig. 4. Visualization of the estimated per-node tracking confidence in 3 scenarios: large body-camera distance (a), fast motions (b) and occlusions (c).

We regard the diagonal of Σ_t^{-1} as the confidence vector of the solution μ_t, which contains the confidence of both skeleton tracking and non-rigid tracking parameters calculated by our hybrid motion tracking algorithm. Since the TSDF fusion step only needs node graph to perform non-rigid deformation [25], we merge the two types of motion tracking confidence together to get a more accurate estimation of hybrid tracking confidence for each node. Therefore, the tracking confidence $C_{track}(\mathbf{x}_k)$ corresponding to a node $\mathbf{x}_k$ can be computed as

$$C_{track}(\mathbf{x}_k) = (1-\lambda) \min\left(\frac{\mathrm{diag}(\bar{\Sigma}_t^{-1})_{\mathbf{x}_k}}{\eta_{\mathbf{x}_k}}, 1\right) + \lambda \sum_{j \in \mathcal{B}} w_{j,x_k} \min\left(\frac{\mathrm{diag}(\bar{\Sigma}_t^{-1})_{\mathbf{b}_j}}{\eta_{\mathbf{b}_j}}, 1\right) \tag{11}$$

where $\mathcal{B}$ is the index set of bones; $\mathrm{diag}(\bar{\Sigma}_t^{-1})_{\mathbf{x}_k}$ and $\mathrm{diag}(\bar{\Sigma}_t^{-1})_{\mathbf{b}_j}$ are the averaged covariance values of all ICP iterations corresponding to the kth node and jth bone respectively. w_{j,x_k} is the skinning weight associated with $\mathbf{x}_k$.

To better illustrate the tracking confidence, we classify the performance capture scenarios that will adversely impact the tracking performance into 3 categories (far body-camera distance, fast motions and occlusions) and visualized the estimated tracking confidence of each node in these scenarios in Fig. 4. Since the quality of depth input is inversely proportional to body-camera distance and the low quality depth will significantly deteriorate the tracking and fusion performance, the tracking confidence of all nodes declines when the body is far from the camera (Fig. 4(a)); Moreover, the nodes under fast motions also have low tracking confidence (Fig. 4(b)), as the tracking performance for fast motions is usually worse than slow motions due to the blurred depth input and lack of correspondences; Last, for single-view capture system, occlusions will lead to lack of observations and worse tracking performance of corresponding body parts. Thus, the tracking confidence of occluded nodes decreases as in Fig. 4(c).

After calculating the tracking confidence, we perform adaptive geometry fusion as follows. For a voxel v, $\mathbf{D}(v)$ denotes the TSDF value of the voxel, $\mathbf{W}(v)$ denotes its accumulated fusion weight, $\mathbf{d}(v)$ is the projective signed distance function (PSDF) value, and $\omega(v)$ is the fusion weight of v at current frame:

$$\omega'(v) = \sum_{\mathbf{x}_k \in \mathcal{N}(v)} C_{track}(\mathbf{x}_k), \quad \omega(v) = \begin{cases} 0 & \omega'(v) < \tau, \\ \omega'(v) & \text{otherwise.} \end{cases} \quad (12)$$

Finally, the voxel is updated by

$$\mathbf{D}(v) \leftarrow \frac{\mathbf{D}(v)\mathbf{W}(v) + \mathbf{d}(v)\omega(v)}{\mathbf{W}(v) + \omega(v)}, \quad \mathbf{W}(v) \leftarrow \mathbf{W}(v) + \omega(v) \quad (13)$$

where $\mathcal{N}(v)$ is the collection of the KNN deformation nodes of voxel v, and τ is a threshold controlling the minimum integration weight.

7   Experiments

We evaluate the performance of our proposed method in this section. In Sect. 7.1 we present details on the setup of our system and report the main parameters of our pipeline. Then we compare our system with the state-of-the-art method both qualitatively and quantitatively in Sect. 7.2. We also provide evaluations of our main contributions in Sect. 7.3.

Figure 5 demonstrates the reconstructed dynamic geometries and the inner body shapes on several motion sequences, including sports, dancing and so on. From the results we can see that our system is able to reconstruct various kinds of challenging motions and inner body shapes using a single-view setup.

Fig. 5. Example results reconstructed by our system. In each grid, the left image is the color reference; the middle one is the fused surface geometry; and the right one is the inner body shape estimated by our system. (Color figure online)

7.1 System Setup

For the hard-ware setup, we use Kinect One and Noitom Legacy suite as the depth sensor and inertial sensors respectively. Our system runs in real-time (33 ms per frame) on a NVIDIA TITAN X GPU and an Intel Core i7-6700K CPU. The majority of the running time is spent on the joint motion tracking (23 ms) and the adaptive geometric fusion (6 ms). The sensor calibration optimization takes 1 ms while the shape-pose optimization takes 3 ms.

The weights of energy terms serve to balance the impact of different tracking cues, where the weight of IMU term is set to 5.0, while the other energy weights are identical to [16]. More specifically, the strategy of assigning λ_{IMU} is to ensure that (1) the IMU term can produce rough pose estimations, when there is a lack of correspondences (fast motion and/or occlusion), and (2) the IMU term does not affect the tracking adversely, when enough correspondences are available. Note that $\lambda_{depth} = 1.0$ and $\lambda_{bind} = 1.0$ initially, and the binding term will be gradually relaxed so as to capture the detailed non-rigd motion of the surface. The weights of the regularization term and prior term are fixed to 5.0 and 0.01 respectively, avoiding undesirable results.

7.2 Comparison

We compare against the state-of-the-art method, DoubleFusion [45] on 4 sequences, as shown in Fig. 6. The tracking performance of our system clearly outperforms DoubleFusion especially under severe occlusions. To make quantitative comparison, we capture several sequences using the Vicon and our system simultaneously. Both systems are synchronized by flashing the infrared LED. We calibrate these two systems spatially by manually selecting the corresponding point pairs and calculate their transformation. After that, we transform the marker positions from the Vicon coordinate into the camera coordinate at the first frame, followed by tracking their motions using the motion field and comparing the per-frame positions with the Vicon-detected ground-truth. We do the same tests on DoubleFusion. Figure 7 presents the curves of per-frame maximum error of DoubleFusion and our method on one sequence. We also list the average errors over the entire sequence in Table 1. From the numerical results we can see that our system achieve the higher tracking accuracy than DoubleFusion.

Table 1. Average numerical errors on the entire sequence.

Method	DoubleFusion	HybridFusion
Avg. of Max. Err. (m)	0.0854	0.0655

We also compare our skeleton tracking performance against the state-of-the-art hybrid tracker, [11], using its published dataset. As depicted in Table 2, our system maintains more accurate and stable performance for skeleton tracking, inducing much smaller tracking errors than [11].

Table 2. Average joint tracking error and standard deviation in millimeters (compared with [11]).

Sequence	D1	D2	D3	D4	D5	D6
Helten *et al.* [11]	35.7(24.9)	47.4(31.4)	44.4(33.8)	34.7(25.4)	59.1(45.3)	56.2(41.6)
Ours	20.9(15.2)	27.6(19.6)	27.0(17.6)	15.5(15.6)	43.5(33.6)	40.9(27.5)

7.3   Evaluation

Sensor Calibration. In Fig. 8, we evaluate the proposed per-frame sensor calibration on a simple sequence. Figure 8(c) is the surface reconstruction results only using initial calibration results as described in Sect. 5.1, without the per-frame calibration optimization step (Sect. 5.2). We can see that the joint motion tracking performance suffers from the inaccuracy of the initial calibration results. Moreover, the erroneous motion tracking performance will lead to erroneous surface fusion results (ghost hands and legs). With the per-frame calibration optimization algorithm, our system can generate accurate motion tracking and surface fusion results as shown in Fig. 8(d).

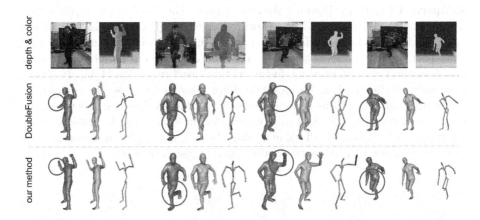

Fig. 6. Qualitative comparison against DoubleFusion. 1st row: Color and depth image as reference. 2nd and 3rd rows: The results reconstructed by DoubleFusion and our system respectively. (Color figure online)

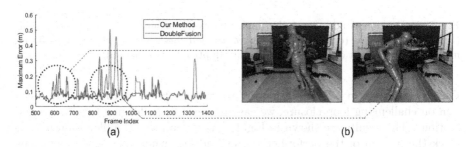

Fig. 7. Quantitative comparison on tracking accuracy against DoubleFusion. (a): The curves of maximum position error. (b): The results of our system on two time instances.

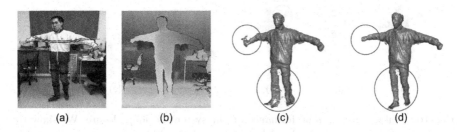

Fig. 8. Evaluation of per-frame sensor calibration optimization. (a), (b): Color and depth images as reference. (c): The reconstruction results without calibration optimization. (d): The reconstruction results with calibration optimization. (Color figure online)

Adaptive Geometry Fusion. We also evaluate the effectiveness of the adaptive geometric fusion method. We captured several sequences in three challenging scenarios for detailed surface fusion, which include far body-camera distance, body-part occlusion and fast motion. We then compare our adaptive geometry fusion method against previous fusion method used in [10,25,44,45]. In Fig. 9, the results of the previous fusion method are presented on the left side of each sub-figure, while the reconstruction results with adaptive fusion are shown on the right. As shown in Fig. 4, the fusion weights in our system can be automatically adjusted (set to a very small value or skip the fusion step) in all the situations, resulting in more plausible and detailed surface fusion results.

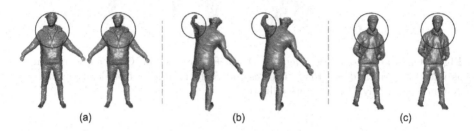

Fig. 9. Evaluation of adaptive fusion under far body-camera distance (a), occlusions (b) and fast motions (c). In each sub-figure, the left mesh is fused by previous fusion method and the right one is fused using our adaptive fusion method.

Challenging Loop Closure. In order to evaluate the performance of our system on challenging loop closure, we capture several challenging turning around motions. The results are shown in Fig. 10. As we can see, DoubleFusion fails to track the motion of the performer's arms and legs when they are occluded by the body and finally generates unsatisfactory loop closure results. In contrast, our system is able to track those motions under severe occlusions, generating complete and plausible models with such challenging turning around motions.

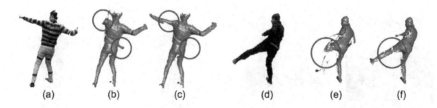

Fig. 10. Evaluation of the performance of our system on loop closure. We show the results in different frames. (a, d): Color reference. (b, e): The results reconstructed by DoubleFusion. (c, f): The results generated by our system. (Color figure online)

The Number of IMUs. To better evaluate our contributions, we also make experiments on the number of IMUs used in hybrid motion tracking. In Fig. 11, the performer wears the full set of Noitom Legacy suite containing 17 IMUs attached on different body parts and performs several challenging motion such as leapfrogging, punching and so on. Regarding the tracking results with 17 IMUs as the ground-truth, we can get an estimation of tracking errors using different sensor setups. In Fig. 11, we present the average position error of joints using different numbers of IMUs. This experiment proves that using 8 IMUs (less than a half of the full set) with a single depth camera can achieve accurate tracking while preserving the convenience for usage.

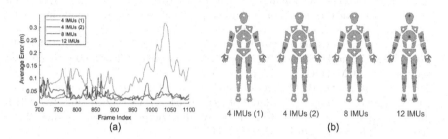

Fig. 11. Evaluation of the number of IMUs. (a): The curves of average position error of joints under different configurations. (b): Illustration of the 4 IMU configurations.

8 Discussion

Conclusion. In this paper, we have presented a practical and highly robust real-time human performance capture system that can simultaneously reconstruct challenging motions, detailed surface geometries and plausible inner body shapes using a single depth camera and sparse IMUs. We believe the practicability of our system enables light-weight, robust and real-time human performance capture, which makes it possible for users to capture high-quality 4D performances even at home. The real-time reconstructed results can be used in both AR/VR, gaming and virtual try-on applications.

Limitations. Our system cannot reconstruct very accurate surface mesh when people wearing very wide cloth because the cloth deformations are too complex for our sparse node-graph deformation model. Also, human-object interactions are very challenging, using divide-and-conquer scheme may provide plausible results. Although the IMUs we used are relatively small and easy to wear, it may still limit body motions. However, as the IMUs are getting more and more small and accurate, we believe the system setup can be even easier in the future.

Acknowledgement. This work is supported by the National Key Foundation for Exploring Scientific Instrument of China No. 2013YQ140517; the National NSF of China grant No. 61522111, No. 61531014, No. 61233005, No. 61722209 and No. 61331015. Hao Li was supported by the ONR YIP grant N00014-17-S-FO14, the CONIX Research Center, an SRC program sponsored by DARPA, the U.S. ARL under contract number W911NF-14-D-0005, Adobe, and Sony.

References

1. Anguelov, D., Srinivasan, P., Koller, D., Thrun, S., Rodgers, J., Davis, J.: Scape: shape completion and animation of people. ACM Trans. Graph. **24**(3), 408–416 (2005)
2. Baak, A., Helten, T., Müller, M., Pons-Moll, G., Rosenhahn, B., Seidel, H.-P.: Analyzing and evaluating markerless motion tracking using inertial sensors. In: Kutulakos, K.N. (ed.) ECCV 2010. LNCS, vol. 6553, pp. 139–152. Springer, Heidelberg (2012). https://doi.org/10.1007/978-3-642-35749-7_11
3. Bogo, F., Kanazawa, A., Lassner, C., Gehler, P., Romero, J., Black, M.J.: Keep it SMPL: automatic estimation of 3D human pose and shape from a single image. In: Leibe, B., Matas, J., Sebe, N., Welling, M. (eds.) ECCV 2016. LNCS, vol. 9909, pp. 561–578. Springer, Cham (2016). https://doi.org/10.1007/978-3-319-46454-1_34
4. Bradley, D., Popa, T., Sheffer, A., Heidrich, W., Boubekeur, T.: Markerless garment capture. In: ACM TOG. vol. 27, p. 99. ACM (2008)
5. Brox, T., Rosenhahn, B., Gall, J., Cremers, D.: Combined region and motion-based 3D tracking of rigid and articulated objects. IEEE TPAMI **32**(3), 402–415 (2010)
6. Dou, M., et al.: Motion2fusion: real-time volumetric performance capture. ACM Trans. Graph. **36**(6), 246:1–246:16 (2017)
7. Dou, M., et al.: Fusion4D: real-time performance capture of challenging scenes. ACM TOG **35**(4), 114 (2016)
8. Gall, J., Stoll, C., De Aguiar, E., Theobalt, C., Rosenhahn, B., Seidel, H.P.: Motion capture using joint skeleton tracking and surface estimation. In: CVPR, pp. 1746–1753. IEEE (2009)
9. Guo, K., Xu, F., Wang, Y., Liu, Y., Dai, Q.: Robust non-rigid motion tracking and surface reconstruction using l0 regularization. In: ICCV, pp. 3083–3091 (2015)
10. Guo, K., Xu, F., Yu, T., Liu, X., Dai, Q., Liu, Y.: Real-time geometry, Albedo and motion reconstruction using a single RGBD camera. ACM Trans. Graph. (TOG) **36**(3) (2017)
11. Helten, T., Muller, M., Seidel, H.P., Theobalt, C.: Real-time body tracking with one depth camera and inertial sensors. In: The IEEE International Conference on Computer Vision (ICCV), December 2013
12. Innmann, M., Zollhöfer, M., Nießner, M., Theobalt, C., Stamminger, M.: Volumedeform: real-time volumetric non-rigid reconstruction. In: ECCV (2016)
13. Joo, H., Simon, T., Sheikh, Y.: Total capture: a 3D deformation model for tracking faces, hands, and bodies. In: CVPR. IEEE (2018)
14. Leroy, V., Franco, J.S., Boyer, E.: Multi-view dynamic shape refinement using local temporal integration. In: ICCV. IEEE (2017)
15. Li, H., Adams, B., Guibas, L.J., Pauly, M.: Robust single-view geometry and motion reconstruction. In: ACM TOG. vol. 28, p. 175. ACM (2009)
16. Liao, M., Zhang, Q., Wang, H., Yang, R., Gong, M.: Modeling deformable objects from a single depth camera. In: ICCV (2009)
17. Liu, Y., Gall, J., Stoll, C., Dai, Q., Seidel, H., Theobalt, C.: Markerless motion capture of multiple characters using multiview image segmentation. IEEE Trans. Pattern Anal. Mach. Intell. **35**(11), 2720–2735 (2013)
18. Loper, M., Mahmood, N., Romero, J., Pons-Moll, G., Black, M.J.: SMPL: a skinned multi-person linear model. ACM Trans. Graph. (Proc. SIGGRAPH Asia) **34**(6), 248:1–248:16 (2015)

19. Lorensen, W.E., Cline, H.E.: Marching cubes: a high resolution 3D surface construction algorithm. In: Proceedings of the 14th Annual Conference on Computer Graphics and Interactive Techniques, SIGGRAPH 1987, pp. 163–169. ACM, New York, NY, USA (1987)

20. Malleson, C., Volino, M., Gilbert, A., Trumble, M., Collomosse, J., Hilton, A.: Realtime full-body motion capture from video and IMUs. In: 2017 Fifth International Conference on 3D Vision (3DV) (2017)

21. von Marcard, T., Henschel, R., Black, M., Rosenhahn, B., Pons-Moll, G.: Recovering accurate 3D human pose in the wild using IMUs and a moving camera. In: European Conference on Computer Vision, September 2018

22. von Marcard, T., Pons-Moll, G., Rosenhahn, B.: Human pose estimation from video and IMUs. Trans. Pattern Anal. Mach. Intell. PAMI **38**(8) (2016)

23. Mitra, N.J., Flöry, S., Ovsjanikov, M., Gelfand, N., Guibas, L.J., Pottmann, H.: Dynamic geometry registration. In: SGP, pp. 173–182 (2007)

24. Mustafa, A., Kim, H., Guillemaut, J., Hilton, A.: General dynamic scene reconstruction from multiple view video. In: 2015 IEEE International Conference on Computer Vision, ICCV 2015, Santiago, Chile, 7–13 December 2015, pp. 900–908 (2015)

25. Newcombe, R.A., Fox, D., Seitz, S.M.: DynamicFusion: reconstruction and tracking of non-rigid scenes in real-time. In: The IEEE Conference on Computer Vision and Pattern Recognition (CVPR), June 2015

26. Pekelny, Y., Gotsman, C.: Articulated object reconstruction and markerless motion capture from depth video. In: CGF. vol. 27, pp. 399–408. Wiley Online Library (2008)

27. Pons-Moll, G., et al.: Outdoor human motion capture using inverse kinematics and von mises-fisher sampling. In: IEEE International Conference on Computer Vision (ICCV), pp. 1243–1250, November 2011

28. Pons-Moll, G., Baak, A., Helten, T., Müller, M., Seidel, H.P., Rosenhahn, B.: Multisensor-fusion for 3D full-body human motion capture. In: IEEE Conference on Computer Vision and Pattern Recognition (CVPR), June 2010

29. Pons-Moll, G., Pujades, S., Hu, S., Black, M.: ClothCap: seamless 4D clothing capture and retargeting. ACM Trans. Graph. (Proc. SIGGRAPH) **36**(4), 73:1–73:15 (2017). Two first authors contributed equally

30. Pons-Moll, G., Romero, J., Mahmood, N., Black, M.J.: Dyna: a model of dynamic human shape in motion. ACM Trans. Graph. (Proc. SIGGRAPH) **34**(4), 120:1–120:14 (2015)

31. Slavcheva, M., Baust, M., Cremers, D., Ilic, S.: KillingFusion: Non-rigid 3D reconstruction without correspondences. In: IEEE Conference on Computer Vision and Pattern Recognition (CVPR) (2017)

32. Slavcheva, M., Baust, M., Ilic, S.: SobolevFusion: 3D reconstruction of scenes undergoing free non-rigid motion. In: IEEE/CVF Conference on Computer Vision and Pattern Recognition (CVPR) (2018)

33. Slyper, R., Hodgins, J.: Action capture with accelerometers. In: Gross, M., James, D. (eds.) Eurographics/SIGGRAPH Symposium on Computer Animation. The Eurographics Association (2008)

34. Sumner, R.W., Schmid, J., Pauly, M.: Embedded deformation for shape manipulation. In: SIGGRAPH, SIGGRAPH 2007. ACM, New York (2007)

35. Süßmuth, J., Winter, M., Greiner, G.: Reconstructing animated meshes from time-varying point clouds. In: CGF. vol. 27, pp. 1469–1476. Blackwell Publishing Ltd. (2008)

36. Tautges, J., et al.: Motion reconstruction using sparse accelerometer data. ACM Trans. Graph. **30**(3), 18:1–18:12 (2011)
37. Tevs, A., et al.: Animation cartography-intrinsic reconstruction of shape and motion. ACM TOG **31**(2), 12 (2012)
38. Tkach, A., Tagliasacchi, A., Remelli, E., Pauly, M., Fitzgibbon, A.: Online generative model personalization for hand tracking. ACM Trans. Graph. **36**(6), 243:1–243:11 (2017)
39. Vlasic, D., et al.: Practical motion capture in everyday surroundings. In: Proceedings of SIGGRAPH 2007. ACM (2007)
40. Vlasic, D., Baran, I., Matusik, W., Popović, J.: Articulated mesh animation from multi-view silhouettes. In: ACM TOG. vol. 27, p. 97. ACM (2008)
41. von Marcard, T., Rosenhahn, B., Black, M., Pons-Moll, G.: Sparse inertial poser: automatic 3D human pose estimation from sparse IMUs. Computer Graphics Forum, Proceedings of the 38th Annual Conference of the European Association for Computer Graphics (Eurographics), pp. 349–360 (2017)
42. Xu, W., et al.: MonoPerfCap: human performance capture from monocular video. ACM TOG **37**, 27 (2017)
43. Ye, G., Liu, Y., Hasler, N., Ji, X., Dai, Q., Theobalt, C.: Performance capture of interacting characters with handheld kinects. In: Fitzgibbon, A., Lazebnik, S., Perona, P., Sato, Y., Schmid, C. (eds.) ECCV 2012. LNCS, pp. 828–841. Springer, Heidelberg (2012). https://doi.org/10.1007/978-3-642-33709-3_59
44. Yu, T., et al.: BodyFusion: real-time capture of human motion and surface geometry using a single depth camera. In: The IEEE International Conference on Computer Vision (ICCV). ACM, October 2017
45. Yu, T., et al.: DoubleFusion: real-time capture of human performance with inner body shape from a depth sensor. In: IEEE Conference on Computer Vision and Pattern Recognition (CVPR) (2018)
46. Zollhöfer, M., et al.: Real-time non-rigid reconstruction using an RGB-D camera. ACM TOG **33**(4), 156 (2014)
47. Zou, D., Tan, P.: CoSLAM: collaborative visual slam in dynamic environments. IEEE Trans. Pattern Anal. Mach. Intell. **35**(2), 354–366 (2013)

Learning Human-Object Interactions by Graph Parsing Neural Networks

Siyuan Qi[1,2], Wenguan Wang[1,3], Baoxiong Jia[1,4], Jianbing Shen[3,5(✉)], and Song-Chun Zhu[1,2]

[1] University of California, Los Angeles, Los Angeles, USA
syqi@cs.ucla.edu, wenguanwang.ai@gmail.com, baoxiongjia@ucla.edu,
sczhu@stat.ucla.edu
[2] International Center for AI and Robot Autonomy (CARA), Los Angeles, USA
[3] Beijing Institute of Technology, Beijing, China
shenjianbing@bit.edu.cn
[4] Peking University, Beijing, China
[5] Inception Institute of Artificial Intelligence, Abu Dhabi, United Arab Emirates

Abstract. This paper addresses the task of detecting and recognizing human-object interactions (HOI) in images and videos. We introduce the Graph Parsing Neural Network (GPNN), a framework that incorporates structural knowledge while being differentiable end-to-end. For a given scene, GPNN infers a parse graph that includes (i) the HOI graph structure represented by an adjacency matrix, and (ii) the node labels. Within a message passing inference framework, GPNN iteratively computes the adjacency matrices and node labels. We extensively evaluate our model on three HOI detection benchmarks on images and videos: HICO-DET, V-COCO, and CAD-120 datasets. Our approach significantly outperforms state-of-art methods, verifying that GPNN is scalable to large datasets and applies to spatial-temporal settings.

Keywords: Human-object interaction · Message passing
Graph parsing · Neural networks

1 Introduction

The task of human-object interaction (HOI) understanding aims to infer the relationships between human and objects, such as "riding a bike" or "washing a bike". Beyond traditional visual recognition of individual instances, *e.g.*, human pose estimation, action recognition, and object detection, recognizing HOIs requires a deeper semantic understanding of image contents. Recently, deep neural networks (DNNs) have shown impressive progress on above individual tasks of instance recognition, while relatively few methods [1,2,14,38] were proposed for HOI recognition. This is mainly because it requires *reasoning* beyond *perception*, by integrating information from human, objects, and their complex relationships.

S. Qi and W. Wang—Equal contribution.

© Springer Nature Switzerland AG 2018
V. Ferrari et al. (Eds.): ECCV 2018, LNCS 11213, pp. 407–423, 2018.
https://doi.org/10.1007/978-3-030-01240-3_25

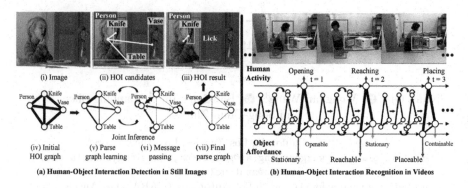

Fig. 1. Illustration of the proposed GPNN for learning HOI. GPNN offers a generic HOI representation that applies to (a) HOI detection in images and (b) HOI recognition in videos. With the integration of graphical model and neural network, GPNN can iteratively learn/infer the graph structures (a.v) and message passing (a.vi). The final parse graph explains a given scene with the graph structure (*e.g.*, the link between the person and the knife) and the node labels (*e.g.*, lick). A thicker edge corresponds to stronger information flow between nodes in the graph.

In this paper, we propose a novel model, Graph Parsing Neural Network (GPNN), for HOI recognition. The proposed GPNN offers a general framework that explicitly represents HOI structures with graphs and automatically parses the optimal graph structures in an end-to-end manner. In principle, it is an generalization of Message Passing Neural Network (MPNN) [12]. An overview of GPNN is shown in Fig. 1. The following two aspects motivate our design.

First, we seek a unified framework that utilizes the learning capability of neural networks and the power of graphical representations. Recent deep learning based HOI models showed promising results, but few touched how to interpret well and explicitly leverage spatial and temporal dependencies and human-object relations in such structured task. Aiming for this, we introduce GPNN. It inherits the complementary strengths of neural networks and graphical models, for forming a coherent HOI representation with strong learning ability. Specifically, with the structured representation of an HOI graph, the rich relations are explicitly utilized, and the information from individual elements can be efficiently integrated and broadcasted over the structures. The whole model and message passing operations are well-defined and fully differentiable. Thus it can be efficiently learned from data in an end-to-end manner.

Second, based on our efficient HOI representation and learning power, GPNN applies to diverse HOI tasks in both static and dynamic scenes. Previous studies for HOI achieved good performance in their specific domains (spatial [1,14] or temporal [20,34,35]). However, none of them addresses a generic framework for representing and learning HOI in both images and videos. The key difficulty lies in the diverse relations between components. Given a set of human and objects candidates, there may exist an uncertain number of human-object interaction pairs (see Fig. 1 (a.ii) as an example). The relations become more complex after taking temporal factors into consideration. Thus pre-fixed graph structures, as adopted by most previous graphical or structured DNN models [11,20,22,43], are not an optimal choice. Seeking a better generalization ability, GPNN incorporates an essential *link function* for addressing the problem of graph structure learning. It learns to infer the adjacency matrix in an end-to-end manner and thus can infer a parse graph that explicitly explains the HOI relations. With such learnable graph structure, GPNN could also limit the information flow from irrelevant nodes while encouraging message to propagate between related nodes, thus improving graph parsing.

We extensively evaluate the proposed GPNN on three HOI datasets, namely HICO-DET [1], V-COCO [17] and CAD-120 [22], for HOI detection from images (HICO-DET, V-COCO) and HOI recognition and anticipation in spatial-temporal settings (CAD-120). The experimental results verify the generality and scalability of our GPNN based HOI representation and show substantial improvements over state-of-the-art approaches, including pure graphical models and pure neural networks. We also demonstrate GPNN outperforms its variants and other graph neural networks with pre-fixed structures.

This paper makes three major contributions. **First**, we propose the GPNN that incorporates structural knowledge and DNNs for learning and inference. **Second**, with a set of well defined modular functions, GPNN addresses the HOI problem by jointly performing graph structure inference and message passing. **Third**, we empirically show that GPNN offers a scalable and generic HOI representation that applies to both static and dynamic settings.

2   Related Work

Human-Object Interaction. Reasoning human actions with objects (like "playing baseball", "playing guitar"), rather than recognizing individual actions ("playing") or object instances ("baseball", "guitar"), is essential for a more comprehensive understanding of what is happening in the scene. Early work in HOI understanding studied Bayesian model [15,16], utilized contextual relationship between human and objects [47–49], learned structured representations with spatial interaction and context [8], exploited compositional models [9], or referred to a set of HOI exemplars [19]. They were mainly based on handcrafted features (*e.g.*, color, HOG, and SIFT) with object and human detectors. More recently, inspired by the notable success of deep learning and the availability of large-scale HOI datasets [1,2], several deep learning based HOI models were then proposed. Specifically, Mallya *et al.*[29] modified Fast RCNN model [13] for HOI recognition, with the assistance of Visual Question Answering (VQA). In [38], zero-shot learning was applied for addressing the long-tail problem in HOI recognition. In [1], the human proposals, object regions, and their combinations were fed into a multi-stream network for tackling the HOI detection problem. Gkioxari *et al.* [14] estimated an action-type specific density map for identifying the interacted object locations, with a modified Faster RCNN architecture [36].

Although promising results were achieved by above deep HOI models, we still observe two unsolved issues. First, they lack a powerful tool to represent the structures in HOI tasks explicitly and encodes them into modern network architectures efficiently. Second, despite the successes in specific tasks, a complete and generic HOI representation is missing. These approaches can not be easily extended to HOI recognition from videos. Aiming to address those issues, we introduce GPNN for imposing high-level relations into DNN, leading to a powerful HOI representation that is applicable in both static and dynamic settings.

Neural Networks with Graphs/Graphical Models. In the literature, some approaches were proposed to combine graphical models and neural networks. The most intuitive approach is to build graphical models upon DNN, where the network that generates features is trained first, and its output is used to compute potential functions for the graphical predictor. Typical methods were used in human pose estimation [42], human part parsing [33,45], and semantic image segmentation [3,4]. These methods lack a deep integration in the sense that the computation process of graphical models cannot be learned end-to-end. Some attempts [7,21,31,32,37,40,44,51] were made to generalize neural network operations (*e.g.*, convolutions) directly from regular grids (*e.g.*, images) to graphs. For the HOI problem, however, a structured representation is needed to capture the high-level spatial-temporal relations between humans and objects. Some other work integrated network architectures with graphical models [12,20] and gained promising results on applications such as scene understanding [24,30, 46], object detection and parsing [27,50], and VQA [41]. However, these methods only apply to problems that have pre-fixed graph structures. Liang *et al.*[26] merged graph nodes using Long Short-Term Memory (LSTM) for human parsing problem, under the assumption that the nodes are mergeable.

Those methods achieved promising results in their specific tasks and well demonstrated the benefit in completing deep architectures with domain-specific structures. However, most of them are based on pre-fixed graph structures, and they have not yet been studied in HOI recognition. In this work, we extend previous graphical neural networks with learnable graph structures, which well addresses the rich and high-level relations in HOI problems. The proposed GPNN can automatically infer the graph structure and utilize that structure for enhancing information propagation and further inference. It offers a generic HOI representation for both spatial and spatial-temporal settings. To the best of our knowledge, this is a first attempt to integrate graph models with neural networks in a unified framework to achieve state-of-art results in HOI recognition.

3   Graph Parsing Neural Network for HOI

3.1   Formulation

For HOI understanding, human and objects are represented by nodes, and their relations are defined as edges. Given a complete HOI graph that includes all the possible relationships among human and objects, we want to automatically infer a parse graph by keeping the meaningful edges and labeling the nodes.

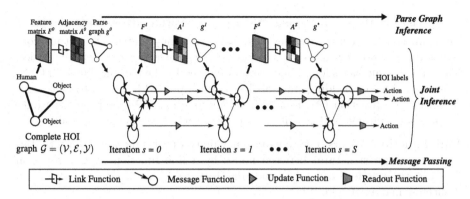

Fig. 2. Illustration of the forward pass of GPNN. GPNN takes node and edge features as input, and outputs a parse graph in a message passing fasion. The structure of the parse graph is given by a soft adjacency matrix. It is computed by the *link function* based on the features (or hidden node states). The darker the color in the adjacency matrix, the stronger the connectivity is. Then *message functions* compute incoming messages for each node as a weighted sum of the messages from other nodes. Thicker edges indicate larger information flows. The *update functions* update the hidden internal states of each node. Above process is repeated for several steps, iteratively and jointly learning the computation of graph structures and message passing. Finally, for each node, the *readout functions* output HOI action or object labels from the hidden node states. See Sect. 3 for more details.

Formally, let $\mathcal{G} = (\mathcal{V}, \mathcal{E}, \mathcal{Y})$ denote the complete HOI graph. Nodes $v \in \mathcal{V}$ take unique values from $\{1, \cdots, |\mathcal{V}|\}$. Edges $e \in \mathcal{E}$ are two-tuples $e = (v, w) \in \mathcal{V} \times \mathcal{V}$. Each node v has a output state $y_v \in \mathcal{Y}$ that takes a value from a set of labels $\{1, \cdots, Y_v\}$ (*e.g.*, actions). A parse graph $g = (\mathcal{V}_g, \mathcal{E}_g, \mathcal{Y}_g)$ is a sub-graph of $\mathcal{G}$, where $\mathcal{V}_g \subseteq \mathcal{V}$ and $\mathcal{E}_g \subseteq \mathcal{E}$. Given the node features $\Gamma^{\mathcal{V}}$ and edge features $\Gamma^{\mathcal{E}}$, we want to infer the optimal parse graph g^* that best explains the data according to a probability distribution p:

$$g^* = \underset{g}{\text{argmax}} \; p(g|\Gamma, \mathcal{G}) = \underset{g}{\text{argmax}} \; p(\mathcal{V}_g, \mathcal{E}_g, \mathcal{Y}_g|\Gamma, \mathcal{G})$$
$$= \underset{g}{\text{argmax}} \; p(\mathcal{Y}_g|\mathcal{V}_g, \mathcal{E}_g, \Gamma)p(\mathcal{V}_g, \mathcal{E}_g|\Gamma, \mathcal{G}) \quad (1)$$

where $\Gamma = \{\Gamma^{\mathcal{V}}, \Gamma^{\mathcal{E}}\}$. Here $p(\mathcal{V}_g, \mathcal{E}_g|\Gamma, \mathcal{G})$ evaluates the graph structure, and $p(\mathcal{Y}_g|\mathcal{V}_g, \mathcal{E}_g, \Gamma)$ is the labeling probability for the nodes in the parse graph.

This formulation provides us a principled guideline for designing the GPNN. We design the network to approximate the computations of $\text{argmax}_g \, p(\mathcal{V}_g, \mathcal{E}_g|\Gamma, \mathcal{G})$ and $\text{argmax}_g \, p(\mathcal{Y}_g|\mathcal{V}_g, \mathcal{E}_g, \Gamma)$. We introduce four types of functions as individual modules in the forward pass of a GPNN: *link functions*, *message functions*, *update functions*, and *readout functions* (as illustrated in Fig. 2). The link functions $L(\cdot)$ estimate the graph structure, giving an approximation of $p(\mathcal{V}_g, \mathcal{E}_g|\Gamma, \mathcal{G})$. The message, update and readout functions together resemble the belief propagation process and approximate $\text{argmax}_{\mathcal{Y}_g} \, p(\mathcal{Y}_g|\mathcal{V}_g, \mathcal{E}_g, \Gamma)$.

Specifically, the link function (⊕) takes edge features (▌) as input and infers the connectivities between nodes. The soft adjacency matrix (▌) is thus constructed and used as weights for messages passing through edges between nodes. The incoming messages for a node are summarized by the message function (↷), then the hidden embedding state of the node is updated based on the messages by an update function (▶). Finally, readout functions (▶) compute the target outputs for each nodes. Those four types of functions are defined as follows:

Link Function. We first infer an adjacency matrix that represents connectivities (*i.e.*, the graph structure) between nodes by a link function. A link function $L(\cdot)$ takes the node features $\Gamma^{\mathcal{V}}$, and edge features $\Gamma^{\mathcal{E}}$ as input and outputs an adjacency matrix $A \in [0,1]^{|\mathcal{V}| \times |\mathcal{V}|}$:

$$A_{vw} = L(\Gamma_v, \Gamma_w, \Gamma_{vw}) \tag{2}$$

where A_{vw} denotes the (v, w)-th entry of the matrix A. Here we overload the notation and let Γ_v denote node features and Γ_{vw} denote edge features. In this way, the structure of a parse graph g can be approximated by the adjacency matrix. Then we start to propagate messages over the parse graph, where the soft adjacency matrix controls the information to be passed through edges.

Message and Update Functions. Based on the learned graph structure, the message passing algorithm is adopted for inference of node labels. During belief propagation, the hidden states of the nodes are iteratively updated by communicating with other nodes. Specially, message functions $M(\cdot)$ summarize messages to nodes coming from other nodes, and update functions $U(\cdot)$ update the hidden node states according to the incoming messages. At each iteration step s, the two functions computes:

$$m_v^s = \sum_w A_{vw} M(h_v^{s-1}, h_w^{s-1}, \Gamma_{vw}) \tag{3}$$

$$h_v^s = U(h_v^{s-1}, m_v^s) \tag{4}$$

where m_v^s is the summarized incoming message for node v at s-th iteration and h_v^s is the hidden state for node v. The node connectivity A encourages the information flow between nodes in the parse graph. The message passing phase runs for S steps towards convergence. At the first step, the node hidden states h_v^0 are initialized by node features Γ_v.

Readout Function. Finally, for each node, hidden state is fed into a readout function to output a label:

$$y_v = R(h_v^S). \tag{5}$$

Here the readout function $R(\cdot)$ computes output y_v for node v by activating its hidden state h_v^S (node embeddings).

Iterative Parsing. Based on the above four functions, the messages are passed along the graph and weighted by the learned adjacency matrix A. We further extend above process into a joint learning framework that iteratively infers the graph structure and propagates the information to infer node labels. In particular, instead of learning A only at the beginning, we iteratively infer A with the updated node information and edge features at each step s:

$$A_{vw}^s = L(h_v^{s-1}, h_w^{s-1}, m_{vw}^{s-1}). \tag{6}$$

Then the messages in Eq. 3 are redefined as:

$$m_v^s = \sum_w A_{vw}^s M(h_v^{s-1}, h_w^{s-1}, \Gamma_{vw}). \tag{7}$$

In this way, both the graph structure and the message update can be jointly and iteratively learned in a unified framework. In practice, we find such a strategy would bring better performance (detailed in Sect. 4.3).

In next section, we show that by implementing each function by neural networks, the entire system is differentiable end-to-end. Hence all the parameters can be learned using gradient-based optimization.

3.2 Network Architecture

Link Function. Given the complete HOI graph $\mathcal{G} = (\mathcal{V}, \mathcal{E}, \mathcal{Y})$, we use d_V and d_E to denote the dimension of the node features and the edge features, respectively. In a message passing step s, we first concatenate all the node features (hidden states) $\{h_v^s \in \mathbb{R}^{d_V}\}_v$ and all the edge features (messages) $\{m_{vw}^s \in \mathbb{R}^{d_E}\}_{v,w}$ to form a feature matrix $F^s \in \mathbb{R}^{|V| \times |V| \times (2d_V + d_E)}$ (see ▮ in Fig. 2). The link function is defined as a small neural network with one or several convolutional layer(s) (with $1 \times 1 \times (2d_V + d_E)$ kernels) and a *sigmoid* activation. Then the adjacency matrix $A^s \in [0, 1]^{|\mathcal{V}| \times |\mathcal{V}|}$ can be computed as:

$$A^s = \sigma(\mathbf{W}^L * F^s), \tag{8}$$

where $\mathbf{W}^L$ is the learnable parameters of the link function network $L(\cdot)$ and $*$ denotes conv operation. The *sigmoid* operation $\sigma(\cdot)$ is for normalizing the values of the elements of A^s into $[0, 1]$. The essential effect of multiple convolutional layers with 1×1 kernels is similar to fully connected layers applied to each individual edge features, except that the filter weights are shared by all the edges. In practice, we find such operation generates good enough results and leads to a high computation efficiency.

For spatial-temporal problems where the adjacency matrices should account for the previous states, we use convolutional LSTMs [39] for modeling $L(\cdot)$ in temporal domain. At time t, the link function takes $F^{s,t}$ as input features and the previous adjacency matrix $A^{s,t-1}$ as hidden state: $A^{s,t} = convLSTM(F^{s,t}, A^{s,t-1})$. Again, the kernel size for the conv layer in convLSTM is $1 \times 1 \times (2d_V + d_E)$.

Message Function. In our implementation, the message function $M(\cdot)$ in Eq. 3 is computed by:

$$M(h_v, h_w, \Gamma_{vw}) = [\mathbf{W}_V^M h_v, \mathbf{W}_V^M h_w, \mathbf{W}_E^M \Gamma_{vw}], \tag{9}$$

where $[.,.]$ denotes concatenation. It concatenates the outputs of linear transforms (*i.e.*, fully connected layers parametrized by $\mathbf{W}_V^M$ and $\mathbf{W}_E^M$) that takes node hidden states h_v or edge features Γ_{vw} as input.

Update Function. Recurrent neural networks [10,18] are natural choices for simulating the iterative update process, as done by previous works [12]. Here we apply Gated Recurrent Unit (GRU) [5] as the update function, because of its recurrent nature and smaller amount of parameters. Thus the update function in Eq. 4 is implemented as:

$$h_v^s = U(h_v^{s-1}, m_v^s) = GRU(h_v^{s-1}, m_v^s), \tag{10}$$

where h_v^s is the hidden state and m_v^s is used as input features. As demonstrated in [25], the GRU is more effective than vanilla recurrent neural networks.

Readout Function. A typical implementation of readout functions is combining several fully connected layers (parameterized by $\mathbf{W}^R$) followed by an activation function:

$$y_v = R(h_v^S) = \varphi(\mathbf{W}^R h_v^S). \tag{11}$$

Here the activation function $\varphi(\cdot)$ can be used as *softmax* (one-class outputs) or *sigmoid* (multi-class outputs) according to different HOI tasks.

In this way, the entire GPNN is implemented to be fully differentiable and end-to-end trainable. The loss for specific HOI task can be computed for the outputs of readout functions, and the error can propagate back according to chain rule. In next section, we will offer more details for implementing GPNN for HOI tasks on spatial and spatial-temporal settings and present qualitative as well as quantitative results.

4 Experiments

To verify the effectiveness and generic applicability of GPNN, we perform experiments on two HOI problems: (i) HOI detection in images [1,17], and (ii) HOI recognition and anticipation from videos [22]. The first experiment is performed on HICO-DET [1] and V-COCO [17] datasets, showing that our approach is scalable to large datasets (about 60 K images in total) and achieves a good detection accuracy over a large number of classes (more than 600 classes of HOIs). The second experiment is reported on CAD-120 dataset [22], showing that our method is well applicable to spatial-temporal domains.

4.1 Human-Object Interaction Detection in Images

For HOI detection in an image, the goal is to detect pairs of a human and an object bounding box with an interaction class label connecting them.

Datasets. We use HICO-DET [1] and V-COCO [17] datasets for benchmarking our GPNN model. HICO-DET provides more than 150 K annotated instances of human-object pairs in 47,051 images (37,536 training and 9,515 testing).

Table 1. HOI detection results (mAP) on HICO-DET dataset [1]. Higher values are better. The best scores are marked in **bold**.

Methods	Full (mAP %) ↑	Rare (mAP %) ↑	Non-rare (mAP %) ↑
Random	1.35×10^{-3}	5.72×10^{-4}	1.62×10^{-3}
Fast-RCNN(union) [13]	1.75	0.58	2.10
Fast-RCNN(score) [13]	2.85	1.55	3.23
HO-RCNN [1]	5.73	3.21	6.48
HO-RCNN+IP [1]	7.30	4.68	8.08
HO-RCNN+IP+S [1]	7.81	5.37	8.54
Gupta *et al.*[17]	9.09	7.02	9.71
Shen *et al.*[38]	6.46	4.24	7.12
InteractNet [14]	9.94	7.16	10.77
GPNN	**13.11**	**9.34**	**14.23**
Performance gain(%)	31.89	30.45	32.13

Fig. 3. HOI detection results on HICO-DET [1] **test images.** Human and objects are shown in red and green rectangles, respectively. Best viewed in color.

It has the same 80 object categories as MS-COCO [28] and 117 action categories. V-COCO is a subset of MS-COCO [28]. It consists of a total of 10,346 images with 16,199 people instances, where ∼2.5K images in the train set, ∼2.8K images for validation and ∼4.9K images for testing. Each annotated person has binary labels for 26 different action classes. Note that three actions (*i.e.*, *cut*, *eat*, and *hit*) are annotated with two types of targets: *instrument* and *direct object*.

Implementation Details. Humans and objects are represented by nodes in the graph, while human-object interactions are represented by edges. In this experiment, we use a pre-trained deformable convolutional network [6] for object detection and features extraction. Based on the detected bounding boxes, we extract node features ($7 \times 7 \times 80$) from the position-sensitive region of interest (PS RoI) pooling layer from the deformable ConvNet. We extract the edge feature from a combined bounding box, *i.e.*, the smallest bounding box that contains both two nodes' bounding boxes. The functions of GPNN are implemented as follows. We use a convolutional network (128-128-1)-Sigmoid($\cdot$) with 1×1 kernels for the link function. The message functions are composed of a fully connected layer,

Table 2. HOI detection results (mAP) on V-COCO [17] dataset. Legend: *Set 1* indicates 18 HOI actions with one object, and *Set 2* corresponds to 3 HOI actions (*i.e., cut, eat, hit*) with two objects (*instrument* and *object*).

Method	Set 1 (mAP %) ↑	Set 2 (mAP %) ↑	Ave. (mAP %) ↑
Gupta *et al.* [17]	33.5	26.7	31.8
InteractNet [14]	42.2	33.2	40.0
GPNN	**44.5**	**42.8**	**44.0**
Performance gain (%)	5.5	28.9	10.0

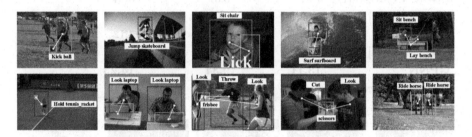

Fig. 4. HOI detection results on V-COCO [17] test images. Human and objects are shown in red and green rectangles, respectively. Best viewed in color. (Color figure online)

concatenation, and summation. For a node v, the neighboring node feature Γ_w and edge feature Γ_{vw} are passed through a fully connected layer and concatenated. The final incoming message is a weighted sum of messages from all neighboring nodes. Specifically, the message for node v coming from node w through edge $e = (v, w)$ is the concatenation of output from FC(d_V-d_V) and FC(d_E-d_E). A GRU(d_V) is used for the update function. The propagation step number S is set to be 3. For the readout function, we use a FC(d_V-117)-Sigmoid($\cdot$) and FC(d_V-26)-Sigmoid($\cdot$) for HICO-DET and V-COCO, respectively.

The probability of an HOI label of a human-object pair is given by the product of the final output probabilities from the human node and the object node. We employ an L1 loss for the adjacency matrix. For the node outputs, we use a weighted multi-class multi-label hinge loss. The reasons are two-folds: the training examples are not balanced, and it is essentially a multi-label problem for each node (there might not even exist a meaningful human-object interaction for detected humans and objects).

Our model is implemented using PyTorch and trained with a machine with a single Nvidia Titan Xp GPU. We start with a learning rate of 1e-3, and the rate decays every 5 epochs by 0.8. The training process takes about 20 epochs ($\sim$15 h) to roughly converge with a batch size of 32.

Comparative Methods. We compare our method with eight baselines: (1) Fast-RCNN (union) [13]: for each human-object proposal from detection results, their attention windows are used as the region proposal for Fast-RCNN. (2) Fast-RCNN (score) [13]: given human-object proposals, HOI is predicted by linearly combining the human and object detection scores. (3) HO-RCNN [1]: a multi-stream architecture with a ConvNet to classify human, object and human-object proposals, respectively. The final output is computed by combining the scores from all the three streams. (4) HO-RCNN+IP [1] and (5) HO-RCNN+IP+S [1]: HO-RCNN with additional components. Interaction Patterns (IP) acts as a attention filter to images. S is an extra path with a single neuron that uses the raw object detection score to produce an offset for the final detection. More detailed descriptions of above five baselines can be found in [1]. (6) Gupta *et al.*[17]: trained based on Fast-RCNN [13]. We use the scores reported in [14]. (7) Shen *et al.*[38]: final predictions are from two Faster RCNN [36] based networks which are trained for predicting verb and object classes, respectively. (8) InteractNet [14]: a modified Faster RCNN [36] with an additional human-centric branch that estimates an action-specific density map for locating objects.

Experiment Results. Following the standard settings in HICO-DET and V-COCO benchmarks, we evaluate HOI detection using mean average precision (mAP). An HOI detection is considered as a true positive when the human detection, the object detection, and the interaction class are all correct. The human and object bounding boxes are considered as true positives if they overlap with a ground truth bounding boxes of the same class with an intersection over union (IoU) greater than 0.5. For HICO-DET dataset, we report the mAP over three different HOI category sets: (i) all 600 HOI categories in HICO (Full); (ii) 138 HOI categories with less than 10 training instances (Rare); and (iii) 462 HOI categories with 10 or more training instances (Non-Rare). For V-COCO dataset, since we concentrate on HOI detection, we report the mAP on three groups: (i) 18 HOI action classes with one target object; (ii) 3 HOI categories with two types of objects; (iii) all 24 ($=18 + 3 \times 2$) HOI classes. Results are evaluated on the test sets and reported in Tables 1 and 2.

As shown in Table 1, the proposed GPNN substantially outperforms the comparative methods, achieving **31.89%**, **30.45%**, and **32.13%** improvement over the second best methods on the three HOI category sets on the HICO-DET dataset. The results on V-COCO dataset (in Table 2) also consistently demonstrate the superior performance of the proposed GPNN. Two important **conclusions** can be drawn from the results: **(i)** our method is scalable to large datasets; **(ii)** and our method performs better than pure neural network. Some visual results can be found in Figs. 3 and 4.

4.2   Human-Object Interaction Recognition in Videos

The goal of this experiment is to detect and predict the human sub-activity labels and object affordance labels as the human-object interaction progresses in videos. The problem is challenging since it involves complex interactions that humans make with multiple objects, and objects also interact with each other.

Table 3. Human activity detection and future anticipation results on CAD-120 [22] dataset, measured via F1-score.

Method	Detection (F1-score) ↑		Anticipation (F1-score) ↑	
	Sub-activity(%)	Object Affordance(%)	Sub-activity(%)	Object Affordance(%)
ATCRF [22]	80.4	81.5	37.9	36.7
S-RNN [20]	83.2	88.7	62.3	80.7
S-RNN (multi-task) [20]	82.4	**91.1**	65.6	80.9
GPNN	**88.9**	88.8	**75.6**	**81.9**
Performance gain(%)	8.1	-	15.2	1.2

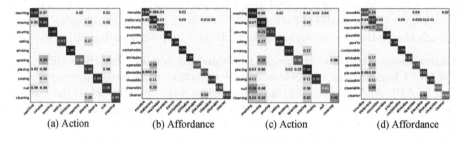

| (a) Action | (b) Affordance | (c) Action | (d) Affordance |

Fig. 5. Confusion matrices of HOI detection (a)(b) and anticipation (c)(d) results on CAD-120 [22] dataset. Zoom in for more details.

CAD-120 Dataset [22]. It has 120 RGB-D videos of 4 subjects performing 10 activities, each of which is a sequence of sub-activities involving 10 actions (*e.g.*, reaching, opening), and 12 object affordances (*e.g.*, reachable, openable) in total.

Implementation Details. The link function is implemented as: convLSTM (1024-1024-1024-1)-Sigmoid(·) (*i.e.*, a four-layer convLSTM). We use the same architecture as the previous experiment for message functions and update functions: [FC(d_V-d_V), FC(d_E-d_E)] for message function and GRU(d_V) for update function. The propagation step number S is set to be 3. We use a FC(d_V-10)-Softmax(·) and a FC(d_V-12)-Softmax(·) for readout functions of sub-activity and object affordance detection/anticipation, respectively. We employ an L1 loss for the adjacency matrix and a cross entropy loss for the node outputs. We use the publicly available node and edge features from [23].

Comparative Methods. We compare our method with two baselines: anticipatory temporal CRF (ATCRF) [22] and structural RNN (S-RNN) [20]. ATCRF is a top-performing graphical model approach for this problem, while S-RNN is the state-of-art method using structured neural networks. ATCRF models the human activities through a spatial-temporal conditional random field. S-RNN casts a pre-defined spatial-temporal graph as an RNN mixture by representing nodes and edges as LSTMs.

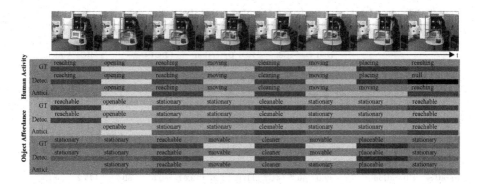

Fig. 6. HOI detection results on a "cleaning objects" activity on CAD-120 [22] dataset. Human are shown in red rectangle. Two objects are shown in green and blue rectangles, respectively. Detection and anticipation results are shown by different bars. For anticipation task, the label of the sub-activity at time t is anticipated at time t-1. (Color figure online)

Experiment Results. In Table 3 we show the quantitative comparison of our method with other competitors. It shows the F1-scores averaged over all classes on detection and activity anticipation tasks. GPNN greatly improves over ATCRF and S-RNN, especially on anticipation task. Our method outperforms the other two for the following reasons. (i) Comparing to ATCRF limited to the Markov assumption, our method allows arbitrary graph structures with improved representation ability. (ii) Our method enjoys the benefit of deep integration of graphical models and neural networks and can be learned in an end-to-end manner. (iii) Rather than relying on a pre-fixed graph structure as in S-RNN, we infer the graph structure via learning an adjacency matrix and thus be able to control the information flow between nodes during massage passing. Figure 5 show the confusion matrices for detecting and predicting the sub-activities and object affordances, respectively. From above results we can draw two important **conclusions**: **(i)** our method is well applicable to the spatio-temporal domain; and **(ii)** our method outperforms pure graphical models (*e.g.*, ATCRF) and deep networks with pre-fixed graph structures (*e.g.*, S-RNN). Figure 6 shows a qualitative visualization of "cleaning objects". We show one representative frame for each sub-activity as well as the corresponding detections and anticipations.

4.3 Ablation Study

In this section, we analyze the contributions of different model components to the final performance and examine the effectiveness of our main assumptions. Table 4 shows the detailed results on all three datasets.

Integration of DNN with Graphical Model. We first examine the influence of integrating DNN with a graphical model. We directly feed the features, which are originally used for GPNN, into different fully connected networks for

Table 4. Ablation study of GPNN model. Higher values are better.

Aspect	Method	V-COCO [17]			HICO-DET [1]			CAD-120 [22]			
		HOI Detection mAP(%) ↑			HOI Detection mAP(%) ↑			HOI Detec. F1-score(%) ↑		HOI Antici. F1-score(%) ↑	
		Set 1	Set 2	Ave.	Full	Rare	Non-rare	Sub-activity	Object Aff.(%)	Sub-activity	Object Aff.(%)
	GPNN (3 iterations)	**44.5**	**42.8**	**44.0**	**13.11**	**9.34**	**14.23**	**88.9**	**88.8**	75.6	**81.9**
Graph structure	w/o graph	27.4	30.0	28.1	7.88	2.04	9.62	50.2	20.8	32.3	19.6
	constant graph	34.6	33.3	34.3	8.75	1.94	10.79	85.3	85.6	73.8	79.1
	w/o graph loss	37.7	40.5	38.4	8.15	6.24	8.72	85.2	85.8	74.7	79.2
	w/o joint parsing	43.6	39.4	42.5	10.17	5.81	11.47	79.3	79.2	74.7	80.3
Iterative learning	1 iteration	42.0	40.7	41.7	11.38	7.27	12.61	80.5	80.7	75.2	81.1
	2 iterations	44.1	42.2	43.6	12.37	9.01	13.38	87.9	86.1	**76.1**	81.5
	4 iterations	43.6	40.9	42.9	12.39	8.95	13.41	87.9	85.7	75.5	80.6

predicting HOI action or object classes. From Table 4, we can observe the performance of *w/o graph* is significantly worse than GPNN model over various HOI datasets. This supports our view that modeling high-level structures and leveraging learning capabilities of DNNs together is essential for HOI tasks.

GPNN with Fixed Graph Structures. In Sect. 3, GPNN automatically infers graph structures (*i.e.*, parse graph) via learning a soft adjacency matrix. To assess this strategy, we fix all the entries in the soft adjacency matrices to be constant 1. This way the graph structures are fixed and the information flow between nodes are not weighted. For *constant graph* baseline, we see obvious performance decrease, compared with the full GPNN model. This indicates that inferring graph structures is critical to get reasonable performance.

GPNN without Supervision on Link Functions. We perform experiments by turning off the L1 loss on adjacency matrices (*w/o graph loss* in Table 4). We can observe that the intermediate L1 loss is effective, further verifying our design to learn the graph structure. Another interesting observation is that training the model without this loss has a similar effect to training with constant graph. Hence supervision on the graph is fairly important.

Jointly Learning Parse Graph and Message Passing. We next study the effect of jointly learning graph structures and message passing. By isolating graph parsing from message passing, we obtain *w/o joint parsing*, where the adjacency matrices are directly computed by link functions from edge features at the beginning. We observe a performance decrease in Table 4, showing that learning graph structures and message passing together indeed boost the performance.

Iterative Learning Process. Next we examine the effect of iterative message passing, we report three baselines: *1 iteration*, *2 iterations*, and *4 iterations*, which correspond to the results from different message passing iterations. The baseline *GPNN* (first row in Table 4) are the results after three iterations. From the results we observe that the iterative learning process is able to gradually improve the performance in general. We also observe that when the iteration round is increased to a certain extent, the performance drops slightly.

5 Conclusion

In this paper, we propose Graph Parsing Neural Network (GPNN) for inferring a parse graph in an end-to-end manner. The network can be decomposed into four distinct functions, namely link functions, message functions, update functions and readout functions, for iterative graph inference and message passing. GPNN provides a generic HOI representation that is applicable in both spatial and spatial-temporal domains. We demonstrate a substantial performance gain on three HOI datasets, showing the effectiveness of the proposed framework.

Acknowledgments. The authors thank Prof. Ying Nian Wu from UCLA Statistics Department for helpful comments on this work. This research is supported by DARPA XAI N66001-17-2-4029, ONR MURI N00014-16-1-2007, ARO W911NF1810296, and N66001-17-2-3602.

References

1. Chao, Y.W., Liu, Y., Liu, X., Zeng, H., Deng, J.: Learning to detect human-object interactions (2018)
2. Chao, Y.W., Wang, Z., He, Y., Wang, J., Deng, J.: HICO: A benchmark for recognizing human-object interactions in images. In: ICCV (2015)
3. Chen, L.C., Papandreou, G., Kokkinos, I., Murphy, K., Yuille, A.L.: Deeplab: Semantic image segmentation with deep convolutional nets, atrous convolution, and fully connected CRFs. PAMI (2016)
4. Chen, L.C., Schwing, A., Yuille, A., Urtasun, R.: Learning deep structured models. In: ICML (2015)
5. Cho, K., Van Merriënboer, B., Bahdanau, D., Bengio, Y.: On the properties of neural machine translation: encoder-decoder approaches. In: Syntax, Semantics and Structure in Statistical Translation, p. 103 (2014)
6. Dai, J., et al.: Deformable convolutional networks. In: ICCV (2017)
7. Defferrard, M., Bresson, X., Vandergheynst, P.: Convolutional neural networks on graphs with fast localized spectral filtering. In: NIPS (2016)
8. Delaitre, V., Sivic, J., Laptev, I.: Learning person-object interactions for action recognition in still images. In: NIPS (2011)
9. Desai, C., Ramanan, D.: Detecting actions, poses, and objects with relational phraselets. In: Fitzgibbon, A., Lazebnik, S., Perona, P., Sato, Y., Schmid, C. (eds.) ECCV 2012. LNCS, vol. 7575, pp. 158–172. Springer, Heidelberg (2012). https://doi.org/10.1007/978-3-642-33765-9_12
10. Elman, J.L.: Finding structure in time. Cogn. Sci. (1990)
11. Fang, H.S., Xu, Y., Wang, W., Zhu, S.C.: Learning pose grammar to encode human body configuration for 3D pose estimation. In: AAAI (2018)
12. Gilmer, J., Schoenholz, S.S., Riley, P.F., Vinyals, O., Dahl, G.E.: Neural message passing for quantum chemistry. In: ICML (2017)
13. Girshick, R.: Fast R-CNN. In: ICCV (2015)
14. Gkioxari, G., Girshick, R., Dollár, P., He, K.: Detecting and recognizing human-object interactions. In: CVPR (2018)
15. Gupta, A., Davis, L.S.: Objects in action: an approach for combining action understanding and object perception. In: CVPR (2007)

16. Gupta, A., Kembhavi, A., Davis, L.S.: Observing human-object interactions: using spatial and functional compatibility for recognition. PAMI (2009)
17. Gupta, S., Malik, J.: Visual semantic role labeling. arXiv preprint arXiv:1505.04474 (2015)
18. Hochreiter, S., Schmidhuber, J.: Long short-term memory. Neural Comput. (1997)
19. Hu, J.F., Zheng, W.S., Lai, J., Gong, S., Xiang, T.: Recognising human-object interaction via exemplar based modelling. In: ICCV (2013)
20. Jain, A., Zamir, A.R., Savarese, S., Saxena, A.: Structural-RNN: deep learning on spatio-temporal graphs. In: CVPR (2016)
21. Kipf, T.N., Welling, M.: Semi-supervised classification with graph convolutional networks. In: ICLR (2017)
22. Koppula, H.S., Saxena, A.: Anticipating human activities using object affordances for reactive robotic response. PAMI (2016)
23. Koppula, H.S., Gupta, R., Saxena, A.: Learning human activities and object affordances from RGB-D videos. Int. J. Robot. Res. (2013)
24. Li, R., Tapaswi, M., Liao, R., Jia, J., Urtasun, R., Fidler, S.: Situation recognition with graph neural networks. In: ICCV (2017)
25. Li, Y., Tarlow, D., Brockschmidt, M., Zemel, R.: Gated graph sequence neural networks. In: ICLR (2016)
26. Liang, X., Lin, L., Shen, X., Feng, J., Yan, S., Xing, E.P.: Interpretable structure-evolving LSTM. In: ICCV (2017)
27. Liang, X., Shen, X., Feng, J., Lin, L., Yan, S.: Semantic object parsing with graph LSTM. In: Leibe, B., Matas, J., Sebe, N., Welling, M. (eds.) ECCV 2016. LNCS, vol. 9905, pp. 125–143. Springer, Cham (2016). https://doi.org/10.1007/978-3-319-46448-0_8
28. Lin, T.-Y., Maire, M., Belongie, S., Hays, J., Perona, P., Ramanan, D., Dollár, P., Zitnick, C.L.: Microsoft COCO: common objects in context. In: Fleet, D., Pajdla, T., Schiele, B., Tuytelaars, T. (eds.) ECCV 2014. LNCS, vol. 8693, pp. 740–755. Springer, Cham (2014). https://doi.org/10.1007/978-3-319-10602-1_48
29. Mallya, A., Lazebnik, S.: Learning models for actions and person-object interactions with transfer to question answering. In: Leibe, B., Matas, J., Sebe, N., Welling, M. (eds.) ECCV 2016. LNCS, vol. 9905, pp. 414–428. Springer, Cham (2016). https://doi.org/10.1007/978-3-319-46448-0_25
30. Marino, K., Salakhutdinov, R., Gupta, A.: The more you know: using knowledge graphs for image classification. In: CVPR (2016)
31. Monti, F., Boscaini, D., Masci, J., Rodolà, E., Svoboda, J., Bronstein, M.M.: Geometric deep learning on graphs and manifolds using mixture model CNNs. In: CVPR (2016)
32. Niepert, M., Ahmed, M., Kutzkov, K.: Learning convolutional neural networks for graphs. In: ICML (2016)
33. Park, S., Nie, X., Zhu, S.C.: Attribute and-or grammar for joint parsing of human pose, parts and attributes. PAMI (2017)
34. Qi, S., Huang, S., Wei, P., Zhu, S.C.: Predicting human activities using stochastic grammar. In: ICCV (2017)
35. Qi, S., Jia, B., Zhu, S.C.: Generalized earley parser: bridging symbolic grammars and sequence data for future prediction. In: ICML (2018)
36. Ren, S., He, K., Girshick, R., Sun, J.: Faster R-CNN: towards real-time object detection with region proposal networks. In: NIPS (2015)
37. Seo, Y., Defferrard, M., Vandergheynst, P., Bresson, X.: Structured sequence modeling with graph convolutional recurrent networks. arXiv preprint arXiv:1612.07659 (2016)

38. Shen, L., Yeung, S., Hoffman, J., Mori, G., Fei-Fei, L.: Scaling human-object interaction recognition through zero-shot learning (2018)
39. Shi, X., Chen, Z., Wang, H., Yeung, D.Y., Wong, W.K., Woo, W.c.: Convolutional LSTM network: a machine learning approach for precipitation nowcasting. In: NIPS (2015)
40. Simonovsky, M., Komodakis, N.: Dynamic edge-conditioned filters in convolutional neural networks on graphs. In: CVPR (2017)
41. Teney, D., Liu, L., van den Hengel, A.: Graph-structured representations for visual question answering. In: CVPR (2017)
42. Tompson, J.J., Jain, A., LeCun, Y., Bregler, C.: Joint training of a convolutional network and a graphical model for human pose estimation. In: NIPS (2014)
43. Wang, W., Xu, Y., Shen, J., Zhu, S.C.: Attentive fashion grammar network for fashion landmark detection and clothing category classification. In: CVPR (2018)
44. Wu, Z., Lin, D., Tang, X.: Deep Markov random field for image modeling. In: Leibe, B., Matas, J., Sebe, N., Welling, M. (eds.) ECCV 2016. LNCS, vol. 9912, pp. 295–312. Springer, Cham (2016). https://doi.org/10.1007/978-3-319-46484-8_18
45. Xia, F., Zhu, J., Wang, P., Yuille, A.L.: Pose-guided human parsing by an And/Or graph using pose-context features. In: AAAI (2016)
46. Xu, D., Zhu, Y., Choy, C.B., Fei-Fei, L.: Scene graph generation by iterative message passing. In: ICCV (2017)
47. Yao, B., Fei-Fei, L.: Grouplet: a structured image representation for recognizing human and object interactions. In: CVPR (2010)
48. Yao, B., Fei-Fei, L.: Modeling mutual context of object and human pose in human-object interaction activities. In: CVPR (2010)
49. Yao, B., Jiang, X., Khosla, A., Lin, A.L., Guibas, L., Fei-Fei, L.: Human action recognition by learning bases of action attributes and parts. In: ICCV (2011)
50. Yuan, Y., Liang, X., Wang, X., Yeung, D.Y., Gupta, A.: Temporal dynamic graph LSTM for action-driven video object detection. In: ICCV (2017)
51. Zheng, S., et al.: Conditional random fields as recurrent neural networks. In: ICCV (2015)

Macro-Micro Adversarial Network
for Human Parsing

Yawei Luo[1,2]([✉]), Zhedong Zheng[2], Liang Zheng[2,3], Tao Guan[1], Junqing Yu[1], and Yi Yang[2]

[1] School of Computer Science and Technology,
Huazhong University of Science and Technology, Wuhan, China
{royalvane,qd_gt,yjqing}@hust.edu.cn
[2] CAI, University of Technology Sydney, Sydney, Australia
zdzheng12@gmail.com, liangzheng06@gmail.com, yee.i.yang@gmail.com
[3] Singapore University of Technology and Design, Singapore, Singapore

Abstract. In human parsing, the pixel-wise classification loss has drawbacks in its low-level local inconsistency and high-level semantic inconsistency. The introduction of the adversarial network tackles the two problems using a single discriminator. However, the two types of parsing inconsistency are generated by distinct mechanisms, so it is difficult for a single discriminator to solve them both. To address the two kinds of inconsistencies, this paper proposes the Macro-Micro Adversarial Net (MMAN). It has two discriminators. One discriminator, Macro D, acts on the low-resolution label map and penalizes semantic inconsistency, *e.g.,* misplaced body parts. The other discriminator, Micro D, focuses on multiple patches of the high-resolution label map to address the local inconsistency, *e.g.,* blur and hole. Compared with traditional adversarial networks, MMAN not only enforces local and semantic consistency explicitly, but also avoids the poor convergence problem of adversarial networks when handling high resolution images. In our experiment, we validate that the two discriminators are complementary to each other in improving the human parsing accuracy. The proposed framework is capable of producing competitive parsing performance compared with the state-of-the-art methods, *i.e.,* mIoU = 46.81% and 59.91% on LIP and PASCAL-Person-Part, respectively. On a relatively small dataset PPSS, our pre-trained model demonstrates impressive generalization ability. The code is publicly available at https://github.com/RoyalVane/MMAN.

Keywords: Human parsing · Adversarial network · Inconsistency Macro-Micro

1 Introduction

Human parsing aims to segment a human image into multiple semantic parts. It is a pixel-level prediction task which requires to understand human images in

© Springer Nature Switzerland AG 2018
V. Ferrari et al. (Eds.): ECCV 2018, LNCS 11213, pp. 424–440, 2018.
https://doi.org/10.1007/978-3-030-01240-3_26

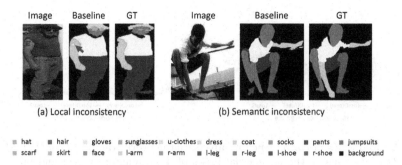

(a) Local inconsistency   (b) Semantic inconsistency

| | hat | | hair | | gloves | | sunglasses | | u-clothes | | dress | | coat | | socks | | pants | | jumpsuits |
| | scarf | | skirt | | face | | l-arm | | r-arm | | l-leg | | r-leg | | l-shoe | | r-shoe | | background |

Fig. 1. Drawbacks of the pixel-wise classification loss. (a) Local inconsistency, which leads to a hole on the arm. (b) semantic inconsistency, which causes unreasonable human poses. The inconsistencies are indicated by red arrows. (Color figure online)

both the global level and the local level. Human parsing can be widely applied to human behavior analysis [9], pose estimation [34] and fashion synthesis [40]. Recent advances in human parsing and semantic segmentation [10,19,23,34,36, 37] mostly explore the potential of the convolutional neural network (CNN).

Based on CNN architecture, the *pixel-wise classification loss* is usually used [10,19,34] which punishes the classification error for each pixel. Despite providing an effective baseline, the pixel-wise classification loss which is designed for per-pixel category prediction, has two drawbacks. First, the pixel-wise classification loss may lead to *local inconsistency*, such as holes and blur. The reason is that it merely penalizes the false prediction on every pixel without explicitly considering the correlation among the adjacent pixels. For illustration, we train a baseline model (see Sect. 3.2) with the pixel-wise classification loss. As shown in Fig. 1(a), some pixels which belongs to "arm" are incorrectly predicted as "upper-clothes" by the baseline. This is undesirable but is the consequence of local inconsistency of the baseline loss. Second, pixel-wise classification loss may lead to *semantic inconsistency* in the overall segmentation map, such as unreasonable human poses and incorrect spatial relationship of body parts. Compared to the local inconsistency, the semantic inconsistency is generated from deeper layers. When only looking at a local region, the learned model does not have an overall sense of the topology of body parts. As shown in Fig. 1(b), the "arm" is merged with an adjacent "leg", indicating incorrect part topology (three legs). Therefore, the pixel-wise classification loss does not explicitly consider the semantic consistency, so that long-range dependency may not be well captured.

In the attempt to address the inconsistency problems, the conditional random fields (CRFs) [17] can be employed as a post processing method. However, CRFs usually handle inconsistency in very limited scope (locally) due to the pairwise potentials, and may even generate worse label maps given poor initial segmentation result. As an alternative to CRFs, a recent work proposes the use of adversarial network [24]. Since the adversarial loss assesses whether a label map is real or fake by joint configuration of many label variables, it can enforce

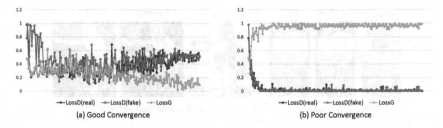

Fig. 2. Two types of convergence in adversarial network training. *LossD* (*real*) and *LossD* (*fake*) denote the adversarial losses of discriminator on real and fake image respectively, and *LossG* denotes the loss of generator. **(a)** Good convergence, where *LossD* (*real*) and *LossD* (*fake*) converge to 0.5 and *LossG* converges to 0. It indicates a successful adversarial network training, where *G* is able to fool *D*. **(b)** Poor convergence, where *LossD* (*real*) and *LossD* (*fake*) converge to 0 and *LossG* converges to 1. It stands for an unbalanced adversarial network training, where *D* can easily distinguish generated images from real images.

higher-level consistency, which cannot be achieved with pairwise terms or the per-pixel classification loss. Now, an increasing number of works adopt the routine of combining the cross entropy loss with an adversarial loss to produce label maps closer to the ground truth [5,12,27].

Nevertheless, the previous adversarial network also has its limitations. First, the single discriminator back propagates only one adversarial loss to the generator. However, the local inconsistency is generated from top layers and the semantic inconsistency is generated from deep layers. The two targeted layers can not be discretely trained with only one adversarial loss. Second, a single discriminator has to look at overall high-resolution image (or a large part of it) in order to supervise the global consistency. As mentioned by numbers of literatures [7,14], it is very difficult for a generator to fool the discriminator on a high-resolution image. As a result, the single discriminator back propagates a maximum adversarial loss invariably, which makes the training unbalanced. We call it *poor convergence problem*, as shown in Fig. 2.

In this paper, the basic objective is to improve the local and semantic consistency of label maps in human parsing. We adopt the idea of adversarial training and at the same time aim to addresses its limitations, *i.e.*, the inferior ability in improving parsing consistency with a single adversarial loss and the poor convergence problem. Specifically, we introduce the Macro-Micro Adversarial Nets (MMAN). MMAN consists of a dual-output generator (*G*) and two discriminators (*D*), named Macro *D* and Micro *D*. The three modules constitute two adversarial networks (Macro *AN*, Micro *AN*), addressing the semantic consistency and the local consistency, respectively. Given an input human image, the CNN-based generator outputs two segmentation maps with different resolution levels, *i.e.*, low resolution and high resolution. The input of Macro *D* is a low-resolution segmentation map, and the output is the confidence score of semantic consistency. The input of Micro *D* is the high-resolution segmentation result,

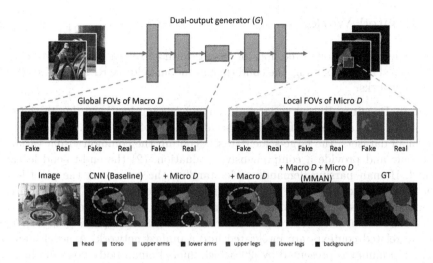

Fig. 3. Top: A brief pipeline of MMAN. Two discriminators are attached to a CNN-based generator (G). The Macro D works on the low-resolution label map and has a global receptive field, focusing on semantic consistency. Micro D focuses on multiple patches and has small receptive fields on high-resolution label map, thus supervising the local consistency. The Macro (Micro) discriminator yields "fake" if semantic (local) inconsistency is observed, otherwise it gives "real". **Bottom**: qualitative results of using Macro D, Micro D and MMAN, respectively. We observe that Macro D and Micro D correct semantic inconsistency (green dashed circle) and local inconsistency (orange dashed circle), respectively, and that MMAN possesses the merits of both. (Color figure online)

and its outputs is the confidence score of local consistency. A brief pipeline of the proposed framework is shown in Fig. 3. It is in two critical aspects that MMAN departs from previous works. First, our method explicitly copes with the local inconsistency and semantic inconsistency problem using two task-specific adversarial networks individually. Second, our method does not use large-sized FOVs on high-resolution image, so we can avoid the poor convergence problem. More detailed description of the merits of the proposed network is provided in Sect. 3.5.

Our contributions are summarized as follows:

- We propose a new framework called Macro-Micro Adversarial Network (MMAN) for human parsing. The Macro AN and Micro AN focus on semantic and local inconsistency respectively, and work in complementary way to improve the parsing quality.
- The two discriminators in our framework achieve local and global supervision on the label maps with small field of views (FOVs), which avoids the poor convergence problem caused by high-resolution images.
- The proposed adversarial net achieves very competitive mIoU on the LIP and PASCAL-Person-Part datasets, and can be well generalized on a relatively small dataset PPSS.

2 Related Works

Our review focuses on three lines of literature most relevant to our work, *i.e.*, CNN-based human parsing, the conditional random fields (CRFs) and the adversarial networks.

Human Parsing. Recent progress in human parsing has been due to the two factors: (1) the available of the large-scale datasets [4,10,19,25]. Comparing to the small datasets, the large-scale datasets contain the common visual variance of people and provide a comprehensive evaluation. (2) the end-to-end learned model. Human parsing demands understanding the person on the pixel level. The recent works apply the convolutional neural network (CNN) to learn the segmentation result in an end-to-end manner. In [34], human poses are extracted in advance and utilized as strong structural cues to guide the parsing. In [21], four human-related contexts are integrated into a unified network. A novel human-related grammar is presented by [29] which infers human body pose and human part segmentation jointly.

Conditional Random Fields. Using the pixel-wise classification loss, CNN usually ignores the micro context between pixels and the macro context between semantic parts. Conditional random fields (CRFs) [17,18,22] are one of the common methods to enforce spatial contiguity in the output label maps. Served as a post-process procedure for image segmentation, CRFs further fine-tune the output map. However, the most common used CRFs are with pair-wise potentials [2,26], which has very limited parameters and handles low-level inconsistencies with a small scope. Higher-order potentials [16,18] have also been observed to be effective in enforcing the semantic validity, but the corresponding energy pattern and the clique form are usually difficult to design. In summary, the utilization of context in CNN remains an open problem.

Adversarial Networks. Adversarial networks have demonstrated the effectiveness in image synthesis [13,28,30,38,39]. By minimizing the adversarial loss, the discriminator leads the generator to produce high-fidelity images. In [24], Luc *et al.* add the adversarial loss for training semantic segmentation and yield the competitive results. Similar idea then has been applied in street scene segmentation [12] and medical image segmentation [5,27]. Contemporarily, an increasing body of literature [7,14] report the difficulty of training the adversarial networks on the high-resolution images. Discriminator can easily recognize the fake high-resolution image, which leads to the training unbalance. The generator and discriminator are prone to stuck in a local minimum.

The main difference between MMAN and the adversarial learning methods above is that the we explicitly endow adversarial training with the macro and micro subtasks. We observe that the two subtasks are complementary to each other to achieve superior parsing accuracy to the baseline with a single adversarial loss and are able to reduce the risk of the training unbalance.

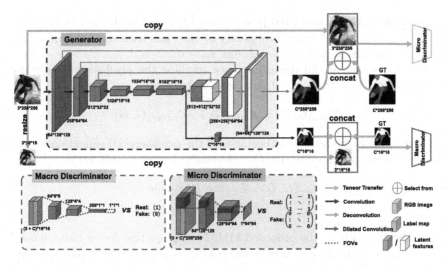

Fig. 4. MMAN has three components: a dual-output generator (blue dashed box), a Macro discriminator (green dashed box) and a Micro discriminator (orange dashed box). Given an input image of size $3 \times 256 \times 256$, the generator G first produces a low-resolution ($8192 \times 16 \times 16$) tensor, from which a low-resolution label map ($C \times 16 \times 16$) and a high-resolution label map ($C \times 256 \times 256$) are generated, where C is the number of classes. Finally, for the each label map (sized $C \times 16 \times 16$, for example), we concatenate it with an RGB image (sized $3 \times 16 \times 16$) along the 1st axis (number of channels), which is fed into the corresponding discriminator. (Color figure online)

3   Macro-Micro Adversarial Network

Figure 4 illustrates the architecture of the proposed Macro-Micro Adversarial Network. The network consists of three components, *i.e.,* a dual-output generator (G) and two task-specific discriminators (D_{Ma} and D_{Mi}). Given an input image of size $3 \times 256 \times 256$, G outputs two label maps of size $C \times 16 \times 16$ and $C \times 256 \times 256$, respectively. D_{Ma} supervises the entire label map of $C \times 16 \times 16$ and D_{Mi} focuses on patches of the label map of size $C \times 256 \times 256$, respectively, so that global and local inconsistencies are penalized. In Sect. 3.1, we illustrate the training objectives, followed by the structure illustration in Sects. 3.2, 3.3 and 3.4. The merits of the proposed network are discussed in Sect. 3.5.

3.1   Training Objectives

Given a human image x of shape $3 \times H \times W$ and a target label map y of shape $C \times H \times W$ where C is the number of classes including the background, the traditional pixel-wise classification loss (multi-class cross-entropy loss) can be formulated as:

$$\mathcal{L}_{mce}(G) = \sum_{i=1}^{H \times W} \sum_{c=1}^{C} -y_{ic} \log \hat{y}_{ic}, \tag{1}$$

where $\hat{y}_{ic}$ denotes the predicted probability of the class c on the i-th pixel. The y_{ic} denotes the ground truth probability of the class c on the i-th pixel. If the i-th pixel belongs to class c, $y_{ic} = 1$, else $y_{ic} = 0$.

To enforce the spatial consistency, we combine the pixel-wise classification loss with the adversarial loss. It can be formulated as:

$$\mathcal{L}_{mix}(G, D) = \mathcal{L}_{mce}(G) + \lambda \mathcal{L}_{adver}(G, D), \tag{2}$$

where λ controls the relative importance of the pixel-wise classification loss and the adversarial loss. Specifically, the adversarial loss $\mathcal{L}_{adver}(G, D)$ is:

$$\mathcal{L}_{adver}(G, D) = \mathbb{E}_{x,y}[\log D(x, y)] + \\ \mathbb{E}_x[\log(1 - D(x, G(x)))]. \tag{3}$$

As shown in Fig. 4, the proposed MMAN employs the *"cross-entropy loss + adversarial loss"* to supervise both the bottom and top output from the generator G:

$$\mathcal{L}_{MMAN}(G, D_{Ma}, D_{Mi}) = \mathcal{L}_{adver}(G, D_{Ma}) + \lambda_1 \mathcal{L}_{mce_l}(G) + \\ \lambda_2 \mathcal{L}_{adver}(G, D_{Mi}) + \lambda_3 \mathcal{L}_{mce_h}(G), \tag{4}$$

where $\mathcal{L}_{mce_l}(G)$ donates the cross-entropy loss between the low-resolution output and the small-sized target label map, while the $\mathcal{L}_{mce_h}(G)$ refers to the cross-entropy loss between the high-resolution output and the original ground-truth label map. Similarly, $\mathcal{L}_{adver}(G, D_{Ma})$ is the adversarial loss focusing on the low-resolution map, and $\mathcal{L}_{adver}(G, D_{Mi})$ is based on the high-resolution map. The hyper parameters λ_1, λ_2 and λ_3 control the relative importance of the four losses. The training objective of MMAN is:

$$G^*, D_{Ma}^*, D_{Mi}^* = \arg \min_G \max_{D_{Ma}, D_{Ma}} \mathcal{L}_{MMAN}(G, D_{Ma}, D_{Mi}). \tag{5}$$

We solve Eq. 5 by alternate between optimizing G, D_{Ma} and D_{Mi} until $\mathcal{L}_{MMAN}(G, D_{Ma}, D_{Mi})$ converges.

3.2 Dual-Output Generator

For the generator (G), we utilize DeepLab-ASPP [2] framework with ResNet-101 [11] model pre-trained on the ImageNet dataset [6] as our starting point due to its simplicity and effectiveness. We augment DeepLab-ASPP architecture with cascaded upsampling layers and skip connect them with early layers, which is similar with U-net [31]. Furthermore, we add a bypass to output the deep feature tensor from the bottom layers and transfer it to a label map with a convolution layer. The small-sized label map severs as the second output in parallel with the original sized label map from the top layer. We refer to the augmented dual-output architecture as Do-DeepLab-ASPP and adopt it as our baseline. For the dual output, we supervise the cross-entropy loss from top layers with ground truth label maps of original size, since it can retain visual details. Besides, we supervise the cross-entropy loss of bottom layers with a resized label map, *i.e.*, 1/16 times of the original size. The shrunken label map pays more attentions to the coarse-grained human structure. The same strategy is applied to adversarial loss. We concatenated the respect label map with RGB image of corresponding size along class channel as a strong condition to discriminators.

3.3   Macro Discriminator

Macro discriminator (D_{Ma}) aims to lead the generator to produce realistic label map that consist with high-level human characteristics, such as reasonable human poses and correct spatial relationship of body parts. D_{Ma} is attached to the bottom layer of G and focuses on an overall low-resolution label map. It consists of 4 convolution layers with kernel size of 4×4 and stride of 2. Each convolution layer follows by one instance-norm layer and one LeakyRelu function. Given a output label map from G, D_{Ma} downsamples it to 1×1 to achieve the global supervision on it. The output of D_{Ma} is the confidence score of semantic consistency.

3.4   Micro Discriminator

Micro discriminator (D_{Mi}) is designed to enforce the local consistency in label maps. We follow the idea of "PatchGAN" [13] in designing the D_{Mi}. Different from D_{Ma} that has a global receptive field on the (shrunken) label map, D_{Mi} only penalizes local error at the scale of image patches. The kernel size of D_{Mi} is 4×4 and the stride is 2. Micro D has a shallow structure of 3 convolution layers, each convolution layer follows by one instance-norm layer and one LeakyRelu function. D_{Mi} aims to classify if each 22×22 patch in an high-resolution image is real or fake, which is suitable for enforcing the local consistency. After running D_{Mi} convolutationally across the label map, we will obtain multiple response from every receptive field. We finally averages all responses to provide the ultimate output of D_{Mi}.

3.5   Discussions

In CNN-based human parsing, convolution layers go deep to extract part-level features, and deconvolution layers bring the in-depth features back to pixel-level locations. It seems intuitive to arrange the Macro D to deeper layers to supervise high-level semantic features and Micro D to top layers, focusing on low-level visual features. Besides the intuitive motivation, however, we can benefit more from such arrangement. The merits of MMAN are summarized in four aspects.

Functional Specialization of Macro D and Micro D. Compared with the single discriminator which attempts to solve two levels of inconsistency alone, Macro D and Micro D are specified in addressing one of the two consistency problems. Take Macro D as an example. First, Macro D is attached to the deep layer of G. Because the semantic inconsistency is originally generated from the deep layers, a such designed Macro D allows the loss to back propagated to G more directly. Second, Macro D acts on a low-resolution label map that retains the semantic-level human structure while filtering out the pixel-level details. It enforces Macro D to focus on the global inconsistency without disturbing by local errors. The same reasoning applies to Micro D. In Sect. 4.5, we validate that MMAN consistently outperforms the adversarial networks with a single adversarial loss [5,24].

Functional Complementarity of Macro D and Micro D. As mentioned in [35], supervising classification loss in early deep layers can offer a good coarse-grained initialization for later top layers. Correspondingly, decreasing the loss in top layers can remedy the coarse semantic feature with fine-grained visual details. We assume that the adversarial loss has the same characteristic to work in complementary pattern. We clarify our hypothesis in Sect. 4.4.

Small FOVs to Avoid Poor Convergence Problem. Reported by increasing literatures [7,14], the existing adversarial networks have drawbacks in coping with complex high-resolution images. In our framework, Macro D acts on a low-resolution label map and Micro D has multiple but small FOVs on a high-resolution label map. As a result, both Macro D and Micro D avoid using large FOVs as the actual input, which effectively reduce the convergence risk caused by high resolution. We show this benefit in Sect. 4.5.

Efficiency. Comparing with the single adversarial network [5,24], MMAN achieves the supervision across the overall images with two shallower discriminators, which have fewer parameters. It also owning to the small FOVs of the discriminators. The efficiency of MMAN is showed in variant study in Sect. 4.5.

4   Experiment

4.1   Dataset

LIP [10] is a recently introduced large-scale dataset, challenging in the severe pose complexity, heavy occlusions and body truncation. It contains 50,462 images in total, including 30,362 for training, 10,000 for testing and 10,000 for validation. LIP defines 19 human part (clothes) labels, including hat, hair, sunglasses, upperclothes, dress, coat, socks, pants, gloves, scarf, skirt, jumpsuits, face, right arm, left arm, right leg, left leg, right shoe and left shoe, and a background class.

PASCAL-Person-Part [4] annotates the human part segmentation labels and is a subset of PASCAL-VOC 2010 [8]. PASCAL-Person-Part includes 1,716 images for training and 1,817 for testing. In this dataset, an image may contain multiple persons with unconstrained poses and environment. Six human body part classes and the background class are annotated.

PPSS [25] includes 3,673 annotated samples, which are divided into a training set of 1,781 images and a testing set of 1,892 images. It defines seven human parts and a background class. Collected from 171 surveillance videos, the dataset can reflect the occlusion and illumination variation in real scene.

Evaluation Metric. The human parsing accuracy of each class is measured in terms of pixel intersection-over-union (IoU). The mean intersection-over-union (mIoU) is computed by averaging the IoU across all classes. We use both IoU for each class and mIoU as evaluation metrics for each dataset.

4.2 Implementation Details

In our implementation, input images are resized so that its shorter side is fixed to 288. A 256×256 crop is randomly sampled from the image or its horizontal flipped version. The per-pixel mean is subtracted from the cropped image. We adopt instance normalization [32] after each convolution. For the hyperparameters in Eq. 4, we set $\lambda_1 = 25$, $\lambda_2 = 1$ and $\lambda_3 = 100$. For the down-sampling network of the generator, we use the ImageNet [6] pretrained network as initialization. The weights of the rest of the network are initialized from scratch using Gaussian distribution with standard deviation as 0.001. We use Adam optimizer [15] with a mini-batch size of 1. We set $\beta 1 = 0.9$, $\beta 2 = 0.999$ and *weightdecay* = 0.0001. Learning rate starts from 0.0002. On the LIP dataset, learning rate is divided by 10 after 15 epochs, and the models are trained for 30 epochs. On the Pascal-Person-Part dataset, learning rate is divided by 10 after 25 epochs, and the models are trained for 50 epochs. We use dropout in the deconvolution layers, following the practice in [13]. We alternately optimize the D and G. During testing, we average the per-pixel classification scores at multiple scales, *i.e.*, testing images are resized to $\{0.8, 1, 1.2\}$ times of their original size.

4.3 Comparison with the State-of-the-Art Methods

In this section, we compare our result with the state-of-the-art methods on the three datasets. First, on the **LIP dataset**, we compare MMAN with five state-of-the-art methods in Table 1. The proposed MMAN yields an mIoU of 46.65%, while the mIoU of the five competing methods is 18.17% [1], 28.29% [23], 42.92% [3], 44.13% [2] and 44.73% [10], respectively. For a fair comparison, we further implement ASN [24] and SSL [10] on our baseline, *i.e*, Do-Deeplab-ASPP. On the same baseline, MMAN outperforms ASN [24] and SSL [10] by +1.40% and +0.62% in terms of mIoU, respectively. It clearly indicates that our method outperforms the state of the art. The comparison of per-class IoU indicates that improvement is mainly from classes which are closely related to human pose, such as arms, legs and shoes. In particular, MMAN is capable of distinguishing between "left" and "right", which gives a huge boost in following human parts: more than +2.5% improvement in left/right arm, more than +10% improvement in left/right leg and more than +5% improvement in left/right shoe. The comparison implies that MMAN is capable of enforcing the consistency of semantic-level features, *i.e.*, human pose.

Table 1. Method comparison of per-class IoU and mIoU on LIP validation set.

Method	hat	hair	glov	sung	clot	dress	coat	sock	pant	suit	scarf	skirt	face	l-arm	r-arm	l-leg	r-leg	l-sh	r-sh	bkg	avg
SegNet[1]	26.60	44.01	0.01	0.00	34.46	0.00	15.97	3.59	33.56	0.01	0.00	0.00	52.38	15.30	24.23	13.82	13.17	9.26	6.47	70.62	18.17
FCN-8s[23]	39.79	58.96	5.32	3.08	49.08	12.36	26.82	15.66	49.41	6.48	0.00	2.16	62.65	29.78	36.63	28.12	26.05	17.76	17.70	78.02	28.29
Attention[3]	58.87	66.78	23.32	19.48	63.20	29.63	49.70	35.23	66.04	24.73	12.84	20.41	70.58	50.17	54.03	38.35	37.70	26.20	27.09	84.00	42.92
DeepLab-ASPP[2]	56.48	65.33	29.98	19.67	62.44	30.33	51.03	40.51	69.00	22.38	11.29	20.56	70.11	49.25	52.88	42.37	35.78	33.81	32.89	84.53	44.03
Attention+SSL[10]	59.75	67.25	28.95	21.57	65.30	29.49	51.92	38.52	68.02	24.48	14.92	24.32	71.01	52.64	55.79	40.23	38.80	28.08	29.03	84.56	44.73
Do-DeepLab-ASPP	56.16	65.28	28.53	20.16	62.54	29.04	51.22	38.00	69.82	22.62	10.63	19.94	69.88	51.83	53.01	45.68	46.08	35.82	34.72	83.47	44.72
Macro AN	57.24	65.28	28.87	19.56	64.02	27.51	51.39	38.13	70.11	22.81	9.05	19.35	68.60	54.19	56.29	50.57	51.22	37.15	37.42	83.25	45.60
Micro AN	57.47	65.05	28.66	16.93	63.95	31.45	51.11	39.64	70.85	25.58	6.87	18.96	68.89	53.62	56.69	49.81	49.42	35.35	35.65	84.46	45.52
ASN [24]	56.92	64.34	28.07	17.78	64.90	30.85	51.90	39.75	71.78	25.57	7.97	17.63	70.77	53.53	56.70	49.58	48.21	34.57	33.31	84.01	45.41
SSL [10]	58.21	67.17	31.20	23.65	63.66	28.31	52.35	39.58	69.40	28.61	13.70	22.52	74.84	52.83	55.67	48.22	47.49	31.80	29.97	84.64	46.19
MMAN	57.66	65.63	30.07	20.02	64.15	28.39	51.98	41.46	71.03	23.61	9.65	23.20	69.54	55.30	58.13	51.90	52.17	38.58	39.05	84.75	46.81

Table 2. Performance comparison in terms of per-class IoU with five state-of-the-art methods on the PASCAL-Person-Part test set.

Method	head	torso	u-arms	l-arms	u-legs	l-legs	bkg	avg
Deeplab-ASPP [2]	81.33	60.06	41.16	40.95	37.49	32.56	92.81	55.19
HAZN [33]	80.79	59.11	43.05	42.76	38.99	34.46	93.59	56.11
Attention [3]	81.47	59.06	44.15	42.50	38.28	35.62	93.65	56.39
LG-LSTM [20]	82.72	60.99	45.40	47.76	42.33	37.96	88.63	57.97
Attention + SSL [10]	83.26	62.40	47.80	45.58	42.32	39.48	94.68	59.36
Do-Deeplab-ASPP	81.82	59.53	44.80	42.79	38.32	36.38	93.91	56.79
Macro AN	82.01	61.19	45.24	44.30	39.73	36.75	93.89	57.58
Micro AN	82.44	61.35	44.79	43.68	38.41	36.05	93.93	57.23
MMAN	82.46	61.41	46.05	45.17	40.93	38.83	94.30	58.45
Attention + MMAN	82.58	62.83	48.49	47.37	42.80	40.40	94.92	59.91

Second, on **PASCAL-Person-Part**, the comparison is shown in Table 2. We apply the same model structure used on the LIP dataset to train the PASCAL-Person-Part dataset. Our model yields an mIoU of 58.45% on the test set. It is higher than most of the compared methods and is only slightly inferior to "Attention+SSL" [10] by 0.91%. This is probably due to the human scale variance in this dataset, which can be addressed by the attention algorithm proposed in [3] and applied in [10].

Therefore, we add a plug-and-play module to our model, *i.e.*, attention network [3]. In particular, we employ multi-scale input and use the attention network to merge the results. The final model "Attention+MMAN" improves mIoU to 59.91%, which is higher than the current state-of-the-art method [10] by +0.55%. When we look into the per-class IoU scores, we have similar observations to the those on LIP. The largest improvement can be observed in arms and legs. The improvement over the state-of-the-art methods [3,10,20] is over +0.6% in upper arms, over +1.8% in lower arms, over +0.4% in upper legs and over +0.9% in lower legs, respectively. The comparisons indicate that our method is very competitive.

Third, we deploy the model trained on LIP to the testing set of the **PPSS dataset** without any fine-tuning. We aim to evaluate the generalization ability of the proposed model.

To make the labels in the LIP and PPSS datasets consistent, we merge the fine-grained labels of LIP into coarse-grained human part labels defined in PPSS.

Table 3. Comparison of human parsing accuracy on the PPSS dataset [25]. Best performance is highlighted in blue.

Method	head	face	up-cloth	arms	lo-cloth	legs	bkg	avg
DL [25]	22.0	29.1	57.3	10.6	46.1	12.9	68.6	35.2
DDN [25]	35.5	44.1	68.4	17.0	61.7	23.8	80.0	47.2
ASN [24]	51.7	51.0	65.9	29.5	52.8	20.3	83.8	50.7
MMAN	53.1	50.2	69.0	29.4	55.9	21.4	85.7	52.1

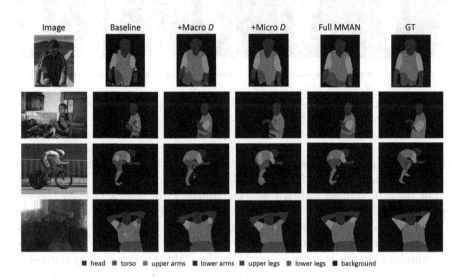

Fig. 5. Qualitative parsing results on the Pascal-Person-Part dataset.

The evaluation result is reported in Table 3. MMAN yields an mIoU of 52.11%, which significantly outperforms DL [25] DDN [25] and ASN [24] by +16.9%, +4.9% and +1.4%, respectively. Therefore, when directly tested on another dataset with different image styles, our model still yields good performance.

In Fig. 5, we provide some segmentation examples obtained by Baseline (Do-Deeplab-ASPP), Baseline+Macro D, Baseline+Micro D and full MMAN, respectively. The ground truth label maps are also shown. We observe that Baseline+Micro D reduces the blur and noise significantly and aids to generate sharp boundaries, and that Baseline+Macro D corrects the unreasonable human poses. The full MMAN method integrates the advantages of both Macro AN and Micro AN and achieves higher parsing accuracy. We also present qualitative results on the PPSS dataset in Fig. 6.

4.4 Ablation Study

This section presents ablation studies of our method. Since two components are involved, *i.e.,* Macro D and Micro D, we remove them one at a time to

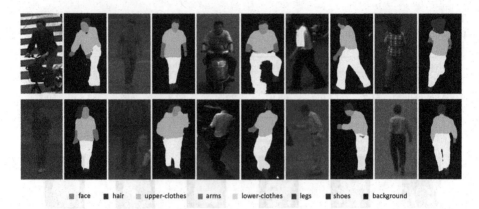

face ■ hair ▨ upper-clothes ▨ arms ▨ lower-clothes ■ legs ■ shoes ■ background

Fig. 6. Qualitative parsing results on the PPSS dataset. RGB image and the label map are showed in pairs. (Color figure online)

evaluate their contributions respectively. Results on LIP and PASCAL-Person-Part datasets are shown in Tables 1 and 2, respectively.

On the LIP dataset, when removing Macro D or Micro D from the system, mIoU will drop 1.21% and 1.29%, respectively, compared with the full MMAN system. Meanwhile, when compared with the baseline approach, employing Macro D or Micro D alone brings +0.88% and +0.80% improvement in mean IoU. Similar observations can be made on the PASCAL-Person-Part dataset as well.

To further evaluate the respective function of the two different discriminators, we add two external experiments: (1) For Macro D, we calculate another mIoU using the low-resolution segmentation maps, which filter out pixel-wise details and retain high-level human structures. So this new mIoU is more suitable for evaluating Macro D. (2) For Micro D, we count the "isolated pixels" in high-resolution segmentation maps, which reflects local inconsistency such as "holes". The "isolated pixel rate" (IPR) can be viewed as a better indicator for evaluating Micro D. We see from Table 4 that Macro D is better than Micro D at improving "mIoU (low-reso.)", proving that Macro D *specializes in preserving high-level human structures*. We also see that Micro D is better than Macro D at decreasing IPR, suggesting that Micro D *specializes in improving local consistency* of the result.

4.5 Variant Study

We further evaluate three different variants of MMAN, *i.e.*, Single AN, Double AN, and Multiple AN, on the LIP dataset. Table 5 details the numer of parameter, global FOV (g.FOV) and local FOV (l.FOV) sizes, as well as the architecture sketch of each variant. The result of original MMAN is also presented for a clear comparison.

Table 4. Comparison in IPR and mIOUs

method	IPR	mIoU (low-reso.)	mIoU (high-reso.)
baseline	5.62	50.66	44.72
+macro D	4.23	55.79	45.60
+micro D	2.81	53.60	45.52
+CRF	1.53	52.77	45.45
MMAN	2.47	56.95	46.81

Table 5. Variant study of MMAN.

variant	arch.	g.FOV	l.FOV	#par	pc.	mIoU
sAN	‖••••‖	256 × 256	-	3.2M	√	45.23
dAN	‖••••‖	256 × 256	22 × 22	3.8M	√	46.15
mAN	‖••••‖	16 × 16	22 × 22	1.8M	-	46.97
MMAN	‖••••‖	16 × 16	22 × 22	1.2M	-	46.81

Single AN refers to the traditional adversarial network with only one discriminator. The discriminator is attached to the top layer and has a global receptive field on a 256 × 256 label map. As the result shows, Single AN yields 45.23% in mean IoU, which is slightly higher than the baseline but lower than MMAN. This result suggests that employing Macro D and Micro D outperforms the single discriminator, which proves the correctness of the analysis in Sect. 3.5. What is more, we observe the poor convergence (pc) problem when training the Single AN. It is due to the employment of large FOVs on the high-resolution label map.

Double AN has the same number of discriminators with MMAN. The difference lies in that the Double AN attaches the Macro D to the top layer. Compared to Double AN, MMAN significantly improves the result by 0.82%. The result illustrates the complementary effects of Macro D and Micro D: Macro D acts on deep layers and offers a good coarse-grained initialization for later top layers and Micro D helps to remedies the coarse semantic feature with fine-grained visual details.

Multiple AN is designed to evaluate the parsing accuracy when employing more than two discriminators. To this end, we attach an extra discriminator to the 3rd deconvolution layer of G. In particular, the discriminator has the same architecture with micro D and focuses on 22 × 22 patches on a 64 × 64 label map. As the result shows in Table 5, employing three discriminators brings very slightly improvement (0.16%) in mean IoU, but results in more complex architecture and more parameters.

5 Conclusions

In this paper, we introduce a novel Macro-Micro adversarial network (MMAN) for human parsing, which significantly reduces the semantic inconsistency, e.g., misplaced human parts, and the local inconsistency, e.g., blur and holes, in the parsing results. Our model achieves comparative parsing accuracy with the state-of-the-art methods on two challenge human parsing datasets and has a good generalization ability on other datasets. The two adversarial losses are complementary and outperform previous methods that employ a single adversarial loss. Furthermore, MMAN achieves both global and local supervisions with small receptive fields, which effectively avoids the poor convergence problem of adversarial network in handling high-resolution images.

Acknowledgment. This work is partially supported by the National Natural Science Foundation of China (No. 61572211). We acknowledge the Data to Decisions CRC (D2D CRC) and the Cooperative Research Centers Programme for funding this research.

References

1. Badrinarayanan, V., Kendall, A., Cipolla, R.: SegNet: a deep convolutional encoder-decoder architecture for image segmentation. IEEE Trans. Pattern Anal. Mach. Intell. **39**(12), 2481–2495 (2017)
2. Chen, L.C., Papandreou, G., Kokkinos, I., Murphy, K., Yuille, A.L.: Deeplab: Semantic image segmentation with deep convolutional nets, atrous convolution, and fully connected CRFs. arXiv preprint arXiv:1606.00915 (2016)
3. Chen, L.C., Yang, Y., Wang, J., Xu, W., Yuille, A.L.: Attention to scale: scale-aware semantic image segmentation. In: Proceedings of the IEEE Conference on Computer Vision and Pattern Recognition, pp. 3640–3649 (2016)
4. Chen, X., Mottaghi, R., Liu, X., Fidler, S., Urtasun, R., Yuille, A.: Detect what you can: detecting and representing objects using holistic models and body parts. In: Proceedings of the IEEE Conference on Computer Vision and Pattern Recognition, pp. 1971–1978 (2014)
5. Dai, W., et al.: SCAN: Structure Correcting Adversarial Network for Chest X-rays Organ Segmentation. arXiv preprint arXiv:1703.08770 (2017)
6. Deng, J., Dong, W., Socher, R., Li, L.J., Li, K., Fei-Fei, L.: ImageNet: a large-scale hierarchical image database. In: IEEE Conference on Computer Vision and Pattern Recognition 2009, CVPR 2009, pp. 248–255. IEEE (2009)
7. Denton, E.L., Chintala, S., Fergus, R., et al.: Deep generative image models using a Laplacian pyramid of adversarial networks. In: Advances in Neural Information Processing Systems, pp. 1486–1494 (2015)
8. Everingham, M., Van Gool, L., Williams, C.K.I., Winn, J., Zisserman, A.: The PASCAL visual object classes challenge 2010 (VOC2010) results. http://www.pascal-network.org/challenges/VOC/voc2010/workshop/index.html
9. Gan, C., Lin, M., Yang, Y., de Melo, G., Hauptmann, A.G.: Concepts not alone: exploring pairwise relationships for zero-shot video activity recognition. In: AAAI, p. 3487 (2016)
10. Gong, K., Liang, X., Shen, X., Lin, L.: Look into person: self-supervised structure-sensitive learning and a new benchmark for human parsing (2017). arXiv preprint arXiv:1703.05446
11. He, K., Zhang, X., Ren, S., Sun, J.: Deep residual learning for image recognition. In: Proceedings of the IEEE Conference on Computer Vision and Pattern Recognition, pp. 770–778 (2016)
12. Hung, W.C., Tsai, Y.H., Liou, Y.T., Lin, Y.Y., Yang, M.H.: Adversarial learning for semi-supervised semantic segmentation (2018). arXiv preprint arXiv:1802.07934
13. Isola, P., Zhu, J.Y., Zhou, T., Efros, A.A.: Image-to-image translation with conditional adversarial networks. arXiv preprint (2017)
14. Karras, T., Aila, T., Laine, S., Lehtinen, J.: Progressive growing of GANS for improved quality, stability, and variation, In: ICLR (2018)
15. Kingma, D.P., Ba, J.: Adam: a method for stochastic optimization. arXiv preprint arXiv:1412.6980 (2014)
16. Kohli, P., Torr, P.H.: Robust higher order potentials for enforcing label consistency. Int. J. Comput. Vis. **82**(3), 302–324 (2009)

17. Krähenbühl, P., Koltun, V.: Efficient inference in fully connected CRFs with Gaussian edge potentials. In: Advances in Neural Information Processing Systems, pp. 109–117 (2011)

18. Li, Q., Arnab, A., Torr, P.H.: Holistic, instance-level human parsing. arXiv preprint arXiv:1709.03612 (2017)

19. Liang, X., et al.: Deep human parsing with active template regression. IEEE Trans. Pattern Anal. Mach. Intell. **37**(12), 2402–2414 (2015)

20. Liang, X., Shen, X., Xiang, D., Feng, J., Lin, L., Yan, S.: Semantic object parsing with local-global long short-term memory. In: Proceedings of the IEEE Conference on Computer Vision and Pattern Recognition, pp. 3185–3193 (2016)

21. Liang, X., Xu, C., Shen, X., Yang, J., Liu, S.: Human parsing with contextualized convolutional neural network. In: Proceedings of the IEEE International Conference on Computer Vision, pp. 1386–1394 (2015)

22. Liu, Z., Li, X., Luo, P., Loy, C.C., Tang, X.: Semantic image segmentation via deep parsing network. In: Computer Vision (ICCV), IEEE International Conference on 2015, pp. 1377–1385. IEEE (2015)

23. Long, J., Shelhamer, E., Darrell, T.: Fully convolutional networks for semantic segmentation. In: Proceedings of the IEEE Conference on Computer Vision and Pattern Recognition, pp. 3431–3440 (2015)

24. Luc, P., Couprie, C., Chintala, S., Verbeek, J.: Semantic segmentation using adversarial networks. arXiv preprint arXiv:1611.08408 (2016)

25. Luo, P., Wang, X., Tang, X.: Pedestrian parsing via deep decompositional network. In: Computer Vision (ICCV), IEEE International Conference on 2013, pp. 2648–2655, IEEE (2013)

26. Luo, Y., Guan, T., Pan, H., Wang, Y., Yu, J.: Accurate localization for mobile device using a multi-planar city model. In: Pattern Recognition (ICPR), 23rd International Conference on 2016, pp. 3733–3738. IEEE (2016)

27. Moeskops, P., Veta, M., Lafarge, M.W., Eppenhof, K.A.J., Pluim, J.P.W.: Adversarial training and dilated convolutions for brain MRI segmentation. In: Cardoso, M.J., et al. (eds.) DLMIA/ML-CDS -2017. LNCS, vol. 10553, pp. 56–64. Springer, Cham (2017). https://doi.org/10.1007/978-3-319-67558-9_7

28. Odena, A., Olah, C., Shlens, J.: Conditional image synthesis with auxiliary classifier Gans. arXiv preprint arXiv:1610.09585 (2016)

29. Park, S., Nie, X., Zhu, S.C.: Attribute and-or grammar for joint parsing of human pose, parts and attributes. IEEE Trans. Pattern Anal. Mach. Intell., 1555–1569 (2017)

30. Reed, S.E., Akata, Z., Mohan, S., Tenka, S., Schiele, B., Lee, H.: Learning what and where to draw. In: Advances in Neural Information Processing Systems, pp. 217–225 (2016)

31. Ronneberger, O., Fischer, P., Brox, T.: U-Net: convolutional networks for biomedical image segmentation. In: Navab, N., Hornegger, J., Wells, W.M., Frangi, A.F. (eds.) MICCAI 2015. LNCS, vol. 9351, pp. 234–241. Springer, Cham (2015). https://doi.org/10.1007/978-3-319-24574-4_28

32. Ulyanov, D., Vedaldi, A., Lempitsky, V.S.: Instance normalization: the missing ingredient for fast stylization (2016). CoRR abs/1607.08022. http://arxiv.org/abs/1607.08022

33. Xia, F., Wang, P., Chen, L.-C., Yuille, A.L.: Zoom better to see clearer: human and object parsing with hierarchical auto-zoom net. In: Leibe, B., Matas, J., Sebe, N., Welling, M. (eds.) ECCV 2016. LNCS, vol. 9909, pp. 648–663. Springer, Cham (2016). https://doi.org/10.1007/978-3-319-46454-1_39

34. Xia, F., Zhu, J., Wang, P., Yuille, A.L.: Pose-guided human parsing by an and/or graph using pose-context features. In: AAAI, pp. 3632–3640 (2016)
35. Xue, Y., Xu, T., Zhang, H., Long, R., Huang, X.: SegAN: adversarial network with multi-scale l-1 loss for medical image segmentation. arXiv preprint arXiv:1706.01805 (2017)
36. Zhang, X., Kang, G., Wei, Y., Yang, Y., Huang, T.: Self-produced guidance for weakly-supervised object localization. In: European Conference on Computer Vision. Springer (2018)
37. Zhang, X., Wei, Y., Feng, J., Yang, Y., Huang, T.: Adversarial complementary learning for weakly supervised object localization. In: IEEE CVPR (2018)
38. Zhong, Z., Zheng, L., Li, S., Yang, Y.: Generalizing a person retrieval model hetero- and homogeneously. In: ECCV (2018)
39. Zhong, Z., Zheng, L., Zheng, Z., Li, S., Yang, Y.: Camera style adaptation for person re-identification. In: CVPR (2018)
40. Zhu, S., Fidler, S., Urtasun, R., Lin, D., Loy, C.C.: Be your own prada: fashion synthesis with structural coherence. In: International Conference on Computer Vision (ICCV) (2017)

Stereo Computation for a Single Mixture Image

Yiran Zhong[1,3,4(✉)], Yuchao Dai[2], and Hongdong Li[1,4]

[1] Australian National University, Canberra, Australia
{yiran.zhong,hongdong.li}@anu.edu.au
[2] Northwestern Polytechnical University, Xi'an, China
daiyuchao@nwpu.edu.cn
[3] Data61 CSIRO, Canberra, Australia
[4] Australian Centre for Robotic Vision, Canberra, Australia

Abstract. This paper proposes an original problem of *stereo computation from a single mixture image* – a challenging problem that had not been researched before. The goal is to separate (*i.e.*, unmix) a single mixture image into two constitute image layers, such that the two layers form a left-right stereo image pair, from which a valid disparity map can be recovered. This is a severely illposed problem, from one input image one effectively aims to recover three (*i.e.*, left image, right image and a disparity map). In this work we give a novel deep-learning based solution, by jointly solving the two subtasks of image layer separation as well as stereo matching. Training our deep net is a simple task, as it does not need to have disparity maps. Extensive experiments demonstrate the efficacy of our method.

Keywords: Stereo computation · Image separation
Anaglyph · Monocular depth estimation · Double vision

1 Introduction

Stereo computation (stereo matching) is a well-known and fundamental vision problem, in which a dense depth map D is estimated from two images of the scene from slightly different viewpoints. Typically, one of the cameras is in the left (denoted by I_L) and the other in the right (denoted by I_R), just like we have left and right two eyes. Given a single image, it is generally impossible to infer a disparity map, unless using strong semantic-dependent image priors such as those single-image depth-map regression works powered by deep-learning [1–3]. Even though these learning based monocular depth estimation methods could predict a reasonable disparity map from a single image, they all assume the input image to be *an original color image.*

Electronic supplementary material The online version of this chapter (https://doi.org/10.1007/978-3-030-01240-3_27) contains supplementary material, which is available to authorized users.

© Springer Nature Switzerland AG 2018
V. Ferrari et al. (Eds.): ECCV 2018, LNCS 11213, pp. 441–456, 2018.
https://doi.org/10.1007/978-3-030-01240-3_27

In this paper, we propose a novel and original problem, assuming instead one is provided with one *single mixture image* (denoted by I) which is a composition of an original stereo image pair I_L and I_R, *i.e.* $I = f(I_L, I_R)$, and the task is to simultaneously recover both the stereo image pair I_L and I_R, and an accurate dense depth-map D. Under our problem definition, f denotes different image composition operators that generate the mixture image, which is to be defined in details later. This is a very challenging problem, due to the obvious ill-pose (under-constrained) nature of the task, namely, from one input mixture image I one effectively wants to recover three images (I_L, I_R, and D).

In theory it appears to be a blind signal separation (BSS) task, *i.e.*, separating an image into two different component images. However, conventional methods such as BSS using independent component analysis (ICA) [4] are unsuitable for this problem as they make strong assumptions on the statistical independence between the two components. Under our problem definition, I_L, I_R are highly correlated. In computer vision, image layer separation such as reflection and highlight removal [5,6] are also based on the difference in image statistics, again, unsuitable. Another related topic is image matting [7], which refers to the process of accurate foreground estimation from an image. However it either needs human interaction or depends on the difference between foreground object and background, which cannot be applied to our task.

In this paper, we advocate a novel deep-learning based solution to the above task, by using a simple network architecture. We could successfully solve for a stereo pair L, R and a dense depth map D from a single mixture image I. Our network consists of an image separation module and a stereo matching module, where the two modules are optimized jointly. Under our framework, the solution of one module benefits the solution of the other module. It is worth-noting that the training of our network does not require ground truth depth maps.

At a first glance, this problem while intrigue, has pure intellectual interest only, not perhaps no practical use. In contrast, we show this is not the case: in this paper, we show how to use it to solve for three very different vision problems: double vision, de-analygphy and even monocular depth estimation.

The requirement for de-anaglyph is still significant. If search on Youtube, there are hundreds if not thousands of thousands of anaglyph videos, where the original stereo images are not necessarily available. Our methods and the previous work [8,9] enable the recovery of the stereo images and the corresponding disparity map, which will significantly improve the users' *real 3D experience*. As evidenced in the experiments, our proposed method clearly outperforms the existing work with a wide gap. Last but not least, our model could also handle the task of monocular depth estimation and it comes as a surprise to us: Even with one single mixture image, trained on the KITTI benchmark, our method produces the state of the art depth estimation, with results more better than those traditional two images based methods.

2   Setup the Stage

In this paper we study two special cases of our novel problem of *joint image separation and stereo computation*, namely *anaglyph* (red-cyan stereo) and *diplopia* (double vision) (see Fig. 1), which have not been well-studied in the past.

Fig. 1. Examples of image separation for single image based stereo computation. **Left column:** A double-vision image is displayed here. **Right column:** A red-cyan stereo image contains channels from the left and right images. (Color figure online)

(1) **Double vision (aka. diplopia)**: *Double vision* is the simultaneous perception of two images (a stereo pair) of a single object in the form of a single mixture image. Specifically, under the double vision (diplopia) model (*c.f.* Fig. 1 (left column)), the perceived image $I = f(I_L, I_R) = (I_L + I_R)/2$, *i.e.*, the image composition is f a direct average of the left and the right images. Note that the above equation shares similarity with the linear additive model in layer separation [5,10,11] for reflection removal and raindrop removal, we will discuss the differences in details later.

(2) **Red-Cyan stereo (aka. anaglyph)**: An anaglyph (*c.f.* Fig. 1 (right column)) is a single image created by selecting chromatically opposite colors (typically red and cyan) from a stereo pair. Thus given a stereo pair I_L, I_R, the image composition operator f is defined as $I = f(I_L, I_R)$, where the red channel of I is extracted from the red channel of I_L while its green and blue channels are extracted from I_R. De-anaglyph [8,9] aims at estimating both the stereo pair I_L, I_R (color restoration) and computing its disparity maps.

At a first glance, the problem seems impossible as one has to generate two images plus a dense disparity map from *one single input*. However, since the two constitute images are not arbitrary but related by a valid disparity map. Therefore, they must be able to aligned well along the scanlines horizontally. For anaglyph stereo, existing methods [8,9] exploit both image separation constraint and disparity map computation to achieve color restoration and stereo computation. Joulin and Kang [9] reconstructed the original stereo pairs given the input anaglyph by using a modified SIFT-flow method [12]. Williem *et.al.* [8] presented a method to solve the problem within iterations of color restoration and stereo computation. These works suggest that by properly exploiting the image separation and stereo constraints, it is possible to restore the stereo pair images and compute the disparity map from a single mixture image.

There is little work in computer vision dealing with double vision (diplopia), which is nonetheless an important topic in ophthalmology and visual cognition. The most related works seem to be layer separation [5,10], where the task is to decompose an input image into two layers corresponding to the background image and the foreground image. However, there are significant differences between our problem and general layer separation. For layer separation, the two layers of the composited image are generally independent and statistically different. In contrast, the two component images are highly correlated for double vision.

Even though there have been remarkable progresses in monocular depth estimation, current state-of-the-art network architectures [1,2] and [13] cannot be directly applied to our problem. This is because that they depend on a single left/right image input, which is unable to handle image mixture case investigated in this work. Under our problem definition, the two tasks of image separation and stereo computation are tightly coupled: stereo computation is not possible without correct image separation; on the other hand, image separation will benefit from disparity computation.

In this paper, we present a unified framework to handle the problem of stereo computation for a single mixture image, which naturally unifies various geometric vision problems such as anaglyph, diplopia and even monocular depth estimation. Our network can be trained with the supervision of stereo pair images only without the need for ground truth disparity maps, which significantly reduces the requirements for training data. Extensive experiments demonstrate that our method achieves superior performances.

3   Our Method

In this paper, we propose an end-to-end deep neural network to simultaneously learn image separation and stereo computation from a single mixture image. It can handle a variety forms of problems such as anaglyph, de-diplopia and even monocular depth estimation. Note that existing work designed for either layer-separation or stereo-computation cannot be applied to our problem directly. This is because these two problems are deeply coupled, $i.e.$, the solution of one problem affects the solution of the other problem. By contrast, our formulation to be presented as below, jointly solves both problems.

3.1   Mathematical Formulation

Under our mixture model, quality of depth map estimation and image separation are evaluated jointly and therefore, the solution of each task can benefit from each other. Our network model ($c.f.$, Fig. 2) consists of two modules, $i.e.$ an image separation module and a stereo computation module. During network training, only the ground-truth stereo pairs are needed to provide supervisions for both image separation and stereo computation.

By considering both the image separation constraint and the stereo computation constraint in network learning, we define the overall loss function as:

$$\mathcal{L}(\theta_L, \theta_R, \theta_D) = \mathcal{L}_C(\theta_L, \theta_R) + \mathcal{L}_D(\theta_D), \tag{1}$$

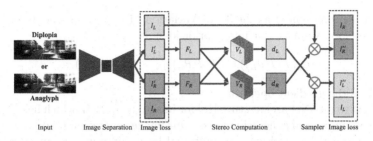

Fig. 2. Overview of our proposed stereo computation for a single mixture image framework. Our network consists of an image separation module and a stereo computation module. Take a single mixture image as input, our network simultaneously separates the image into a stereo image pair and computes a dense disparity map.

where $\theta_L, \theta_R, \theta_D$ denote the network parameters corresponding to the image separation module (left image prediction and right image prediction) and the stereo computation module. A joint optimization of $(\theta_L, \theta_R, \theta_D) = \arg\min \mathcal{L}(\theta_L, \theta_R, \theta_D)$ gives both the desired stereo image pair and the disparity map.

3.2 Image Separation

The input single mixture image $I \in \mathbb{R}^{H \times W \times 3}$ encodes the stereo pair image as $I = f(I_L, I_R)$, where f is the image composition operator known a prior. To learn the stereo image pair from the input single mixture image, we present a unified end-to-end network pipeline. Specifically, denote $\mathcal{F}$ as the learned mapping from the mixture image to the predicted left or right image parameterized by θ_L or θ_R. The objective function of our image separation module is defined as,

$$\alpha_c \mathcal{L}_c(\mathcal{F}(I; \theta_L), I_L) + \alpha_p \mathcal{L}_p(\mathcal{F}(I; \theta_L)), \tag{2}$$

where I is the input single mixture image, I_L, I_R are the ground truth stereo image pair. The loss function $\mathcal{L}$ measures the discrepancy between the predicted stereo images and the ground truth stereo images. The object function for the right image is defined similarly.

In evaluating the discrepancy between images, various loss functions such as ℓ_2 loss [14], classification loss [15] and adversarial loss [16] can be applied. Here, we leverage the pixel-wise ℓ_1 regression loss as the content loss of our image separation network,

$$\mathcal{L}_c(\mathcal{F}(I; \theta_L), I_L) = |\mathcal{F}(I; \theta_L) - I_L|. \tag{3}$$

This loss allows us to perform end-to-end learning as compatible with the stereo matching loss and do not need to consider class imbalance problem or add an extra network structure as a discriminator.

Researches on natural image statistics show that a typical real image obeys sparse spatial gradient distributions [17]. According to Yang *et.al.* [5], such a prior can be represented as the Total Variation (TV) term in energy minimization. Therefore, we have our image prior loss:

$$\mathcal{L}_p(\mathcal{F}(I;\theta_L)) = |\mathcal{F}(I;\theta_L)|_{\text{TV}} = |\nabla\mathcal{F}(I;\theta_L)|, \qquad (4)$$

where ∇ is the gradient operator.

We design a U-Net architecture [18] for image separation, which has been used in various conditional generation tasks. Our image separation module consists of 22 convolutional layers. Each convolutional layer contains one convolution-relu pair except for the last layer and we use element-wise add for each skip connection to accelerate the convergence. For the output layer, we utilize a "tanh" activation function to map the intensity value between -1 and 1. A detailed description of our network structure is provided in the supplemental material.

The output of our image separation module is a 6 channels image, where the first 3 channels represent the estimated left image $\mathcal{F}(I;\theta_L)$ and the rest 3 channels for the estimated right image $\mathcal{F}(I;\theta_R)$. When the network converges, we could directly use these images as the image separation results. However, for the de-anaglyph task, as there is extra constraint (the mixture happens at channel level), we could leverage the color prior of an anaglyph that the desired image separation (colorization) can be further improved by warping corresponding channels based on the estimated disparity maps.

For the monocular depth estimation task, only the right image will be needed as the left image has been provided as input.

3.3   Stereo Computation

The input to the stereo computation module is the separated stereo image pair from the image separation module. The supervision of this module is the ground truth stereo pairs rather than the inputs. The benefit of using ground truth stereo pairs for supervision is that it makes the network not only learn how to find the matching points, but also makes the network to extract features that are robust to the noise from the generated stereo images.

Figure 2 shows an overview of our stereo computation architecture, we adopt a similar stereo matching architecture from Zhong *et. al.* [19] without its consistency check module. The benefit for choosing such a structure is that their model can converge within 2000 iterations which makes it possible to train the entire network in an end-to-end fashion. Additionally, removing the need of ground truth disparity maps enables us to access much more accessible stereo images.

Our loss function for stereo computation is defined as:

$$\mathcal{L}_D = \omega_w(\mathcal{L}_w^l + \mathcal{L}_w^r) + \omega_s(\mathcal{L}_s^l + \mathcal{L}_s^r), \qquad (5)$$

where $\mathcal{L}_w^l, \mathcal{L}_w^r$ denote the image warping appearance loss, $\mathcal{L}_s^l, \mathcal{L}_s^r$ express the smoothness constraint on the disparity map.

Similar to $\mathcal{L}_c$, we form a loss in evaluating the image similarity by computing the pixel-wise ℓ_1 distance between images. We also add a structural similarity term SSIM [20] to improve the robustness against illumination changes across images. The appearance loss $\mathcal{L}_w^l$ is derived as:

$$\mathcal{L}_w^l(I_L, I_L'') = \frac{1}{N} \sum \lambda_1 \frac{1 - \mathcal{S}(I_L, I_L'')}{2} + \lambda_2 \left| I_L - I_L'' \right|, \tag{6}$$

where N is the total number of pixels and I_L'' is the reconstructed left image. λ_1, λ_2 balance between structural similarity and image appearance difference. According to [2], I_L'' can be fully differentially reconstructed from the right image I_R and the right disparity map d_R through bilinear sampling [21].

For the smoothness term, similar to [2], we leverage the Total Variation (TV) and weight it with image's gradients. Our smoothness loss for disparity field is:

$$\mathcal{L}_s^l = \frac{1}{N} \sum |\nabla_u d_L| \, e^{-|\nabla_u I_L|} + |\nabla_v d_L| \, e^{-|\nabla_v I_L|}. \tag{7}$$

3.4   Implementation Details

We implement our network in TensorFlow [22] with 17.1M trainable parameters. Our network can be trained from scratch in an end-to-end fashion with a supervision of stereo pairs and optimized using RMSProp [23] with an initial learning rate of 1×10^{-4}. Input images are normalized with pixel intensities level ranging from -1 to 1. For the KITTI dataset, the input images are randomly cropped to 256×512, while for the Middlebury dataset, we use 384×384. We set disparity level to 96 for the stereo computation module. For weighting loss components, we use $\alpha_c = 1, \alpha_p = 0.2, \omega_w = 1, \omega_s = 0.05$. We set $\lambda_1 = 0.85, \lambda_2 = 0.15$ throughout our experiments. Due to the hardware limitation (Nvidia Titan Xp), we only use batch size 1 during network training.

4   Experiments and Results

In this section, we validate our proposed method and present experimental evaluation for both de-anaglyph and de-diplopia (double vision). For experiments on anaglyph images, given a pair of stereo images, the corresponding anaglyph image can be generated by combining the red channel of the left image and the green/blue channels of the right image. Any stereo pairs can be used to quantitatively evaluate the performance of de-anaglyph. However, since we also need to quantitatively evaluate the performance of anaglyph stereo matching, we use two stereo matching benchmarking datasets for evaluation: Middlebury dataset [24] and KITTI stereo 2015 [25]. Our network is initially trained on the KITTI Raw dataset with 29000 stereo pairs that listed by [2] and further fine-tuned on Middlebury dataset. To highlight the generalization ability of our network, we also perform qualitative experiments on random images from Internet. For de-diplopia (double vision), we synthesize our inputs by averaging stereo pairs. Qualitative and quantitative results are reported on KITTI stereo 2015 benchmark [25] as well. Similar to the de-anaglyph experiment, we train our initial model on the KITTI raw dataset.

4.1   Advantages of Joint Optimization

Our framework consists of image separation and stereo computation, where the solution of one subtask benefits the solution of the other subtask. Direct stereo computation is impossible for a single mixture image. To analyze the advantage of joint optimization, we perform ablation study in image separation without stereo computation and the results are reported in Table 1. Through joint optimization, the average PSNR increases from 19.5009 to 20.0914, which demonstrates the benefit of introducing the stereo matching loss in image separation.

Table 1. Ablation study of image separation on KITTI.

Metric	Image separation only	Joint optimization
PSNR	19.5009	20.0914

4.2   Evaluation of Anaglyph Stereo

We compare the performance of our method with two state-of-the-art de-anaglyph methods: Joulin et.al. [9] and Williem et.al. [8]. Evaluations are performed on two subtasks: stereo computation and image separation (color restoration).

Stereo Computation. We present qualitative comparison of estimated disparity maps in Fig. 3 for Middlebury [24] and in Fig. 4 for KITTI 2015 [25]. Stereo pairs in Middlebury are indoor scenes with multiple handcrafted layouts and the ground truth disparities are captured by highly accurate structural light sensors. On the other hand, the KITTI stereo 2015 consists of 200 outdoor frames in their training set, which is more challenging than the Middlebury dataset. The ground truth disparity maps are generated by sparse LIDAR points and CAD models.

Fig. 3. Qualitative stereo computation results on the Middlebury dataset by our method. From left to right: input anaglyph image, ground truth disparity map, disparity map generated by Williem et.al. [8] and our method.

On both datasets, our method can generate more accurate disparity maps than previous ones from visual inspection. It can be further evidenced by the quantitative results of bad pixel percentage that shown in Table. 2 and Fig. 5. For the Middlebury dataset, our method achieves 32.55% performance leap than

Fig. 4. Qualitative disparity map recovery results on KITTI-2015 of our method. Top row: input anaglyph image and ground truth disparity map. Bottom row: result of Williem *et.al.* [8] and our result.

Williem *et.al.* [8] and 352.28% performance leap than Joulin *et.al.* [9]. This is reasonable as Joulin *et.al.* [9] did not add disparity into its optimization. For the KITTI dataset, we achieve an average bad pixel ratio (denoted as D1_all) of 5.96% with 3 pixel thresholding across 200 images in the training set as opposed to 13.66% by Joulin *et.al.* [9] and 14.40% by Williem *et.al.* [8].

Table 2. Performance comparison in disparity map estimation for de-anaglyph on the Middlebury dataset. We report the bad pixel ratio with a threshold of 1 pixel. Disparities are scaled according to the provided scaling factor on the Middlebury dataset.

Method	Tsukuba	Venus	Cones	Teddy	Mean
Joulin [9]	14.02	25.90	23.49	43.85	26.82
Williem [8]	12.53	2.24	8.00	8.68	7.86
Ours	**10.44**	**1.25**	**4.51**	**7.51**	**5.93**

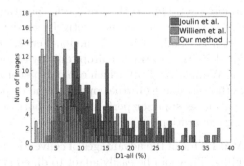

Fig. 5. Disparity map estimation results comparison on the KITTI stereo 2015 dataset.

Image Separation. As an anaglyph image is generated by concatenating the red channel from the left image and the green and blue channels from the right image, the original color can be found by warping the corresponding channels based on the estimated disparity maps. We leverage such a prior for de-anaglyph and adopt the post-processing step from Joulin *et.al.* [9] to handle occluded regions. Qualitative and quantitative comparison of image separation performance are conducted on the Middlebury and KITTI datasets. We employ the Peak Signal-to-Noise Ratio (PSNR) to measure the image restoration quality.

Qualitative results for both datasets are provided in Figs. 6 and 7. Our method is able to recover colors in the regions where ambiguous colorization options exist as those areas rely more on the correspondence estimation, while other methods tend to fail in this case.

Fig. 6. Qualitative image separation results on the KITTI-2015 dataset. Top to bottom: Input, ground truth, result from Williem *et.al.* [8], our result. Our method successfully recovers the correct color of the large textureless region on the right of the image while the other method fails.

Tables 3 and 4 report the performance comparison between our method and state-of-the-art de-anaglyph colorization methods: Joulin *et.al.* [9] and Williem *et.al.* [8] on the Middlebury dataset and on the KITTI dataset correspondingly. For the KITTI dataset, we calculated the mean PSNR throughout the total 200 images of the training set. Our method outperforms others with a notable margin. Joulin *et.al.* [9] is able to recover relatively good restoration results when the disparity level is small, such as Tsukuba, Venus, and KITTI. When the disparity level doubled, its performance drops quickly as for Cone and Teddy images. Different with Williem *et.al.* [8], which can only generate disparity maps at pixel level, our method is able to further optimize the disparity map to sub-pixel level, therefore achieves superior performance in both stereo computation and image restoration (separation).

Anaglyph in the Wild. One of the advantages of conventional methods is their generalization capability. They can be easily adapt to different scenarios with or without parameter changes. Deep learning based methods, on the other hand, are more likely to have a bias on specific dataset. In this section, we provide qualitative evaluation of our method on anaglyph images downloaded from the Internet to illustrate the generalization capability of our method. Our method, even though trained on the KITTI dataset which is quite different from all these

Table 3. Performance comparisons (PSNR) in image separation (restoration) for the task of de-anaglyph on the Middlebury dataset.

Method	Tsukuba		Venus		Cones		Teddy	
	Left	Right	Left	Right	Left	Right	Left	Right
Joulin [9]	30.83	32.88	29.66	31.97	21.52	24.54	21.16	24.59
Williem [8]	30.32	31.12	31.41	34.93	23.68	26.17	23.14	31.05
Ours	**32.99**	**35.31**	**35.05**	**37.74**	**26.31**	**30.17**	**28.44**	**35.53**

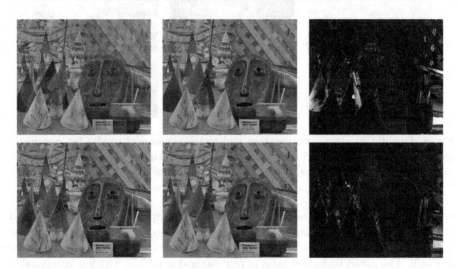

Fig. 7. Qualitative comparison in image separation (restoration) on the Middlebury dataset. The first column shows the input anaglyph image and the ground truth image. The results of Williem *et. al.* [8] (top) and our method (bottom) with their corresponding error maps are shown in the second and the third column.

Table 4. Performance comparisons (PSNR) in image separation (restoration) for the task of de-anaglyph on the KITTI dataset.

Dataset	View	Joulin [9]	Williem [8]	Ours
KITTI	Left	25.13	24.57	**26.30**
	Right	27.19	26.94	**28.76**

images, achieves reliable image separation results as demonstrated in Fig. 8. This further confirms the generalization ability of our network model.

4.3 Evaluation for Double-Vision Unmixing

Here, we evaluate our proposed method for unmixing of double-vision image, where the input image is the average of a stereo pair. Similar to anaglyph, we

Fig. 8. Qualitative stereo computation and image separation results for real world anaglyph images downloaded from the Internet. Left to right: input anaglyph images, disparity maps of our method, image separation results of our method.

evaluate our performance based on the estimated disparities and reconstructed stereo pair on the KITTI stereo 2015 dataset. For disparity evaluation, we use the oracle disparity maps (that are computed with clean stereo pairs) as a reference in Fig. 9. The mean bad pixel ratio of our method is 6.67%, which is comparable with the oracle's performance as 5.28%. For image separation, we take a layer separation method [26] as a reference. A quantitative comparison is shown in Table 5. Conventional layer separation methods tend to fail in this scenario as the statistic difference between the two mixed images is minor which violates the assumption of these methods. Qualitative results of our method are shown in Fig. 10.

Table 5. Performance comparison in term of PSNR for the task of image restoration from double-vision images on the KITTI dataset.

Dataset	View	Li *et.al.*[26]	Ours
KITTI	Left	17.03	**24.38**
	Right	7.67	**24.55**

5   Beyond Anaglyph and Double-Vision

Our problem definition also covers the problem of monocular depth estimation, which aims at estimating a depth map from a single image [2, 3, 27, 28]. Under

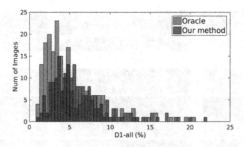

Fig. 9. Stereo computation results on the KITTI 2015 dataset. The oracle disparity map is computed with clean stereo images.

Fig. 10. Qualitative diplopia unmixing results by our proposed method. Top to bottom, left to right: input diplopia image, ground truth left image, restored left image by our method, and our estimated disparity map.

this setup, the image composition operator f is defined as $I = f(I_L, I_R) = I_L$ or $I = f(I_L, I_R) = I_R$, *i.e.*, the mixture image is the left image or the right image. Thus, monocular depth estimation is a special case of our problem definition.

We evaluated our framework for monocular depth estimation on the KITTI 2015 dataset. Quantitative results and qualitative results are provided in Table 6 and Fig. 11, where we compare our method with state-of-the-art methods [1], [29] and [2]. Our method, even designed for a much more general problem, outperforms both [1] and [29] and achieves quite comparable results with [2].

Table 6. Monocular depth estimation results on the KITTI 2015 dataset using the split of Eigen *et.al.* [27]. Our model is trained on 22,600 stereo pairs from the KITTI raw dataset listed by [2] by 10 epochs. Depth metrics are from Eigen *et.al.* [27]. Our performance is better than the state-of-the-art method [2].

Methods	Abs Rel	Sq Rel	RMSE	RMSE log	$\delta < 1.25$	$\delta < 1.25^2$	$\delta < 1.25^3$
Zhou *et.al.* [29]	0.183	1.595	6.709	0.270	0.734	0.902	0.959
Garg *et.al.* [1]	0.169	1.080	5.104	0.273	0.740	0.904	0.962
Godard *et.al.* [2]	0.140	0.976	4.471	0.232	0.818	0.931	0.969
Ours	0.126	0.835	3.971	0.207	0.845	0.942	0.975

Fig. 11. Qualitative monocular estimation evaluations on the KITTI-2015 dataset: Top to bottom: left image, ground truth, results from Zhou *et.al.*[29], results from Garg *et.al.*[1], results from Godard *et.al.*[2] and our results. Since the ground truth depth points are very sparse, we interpolated it with a color guided depth painting method [30] for better visualization.

6   Conclusion

This paper has defined a novel problem of stereo computation from a single mixture image, where the goal is to separate a single mixture image into a pair of stereo images–from which a legitimate disparity map can be estimated. This problem definition naturally unifies a family of challenging and practical problems such as anaglyph, diplopia and monocular depth estimation. The problem goes beyond the scope of conventional image separation and stereo computation. We have presented a deep convolutional neural network based framework that jointly optimizes the image separation module and the stereo computation module. It is worth noting that we do not need ground truth disparity maps in network learning. In the future, we will explore additional problem setups such as "alpha-matting". Other issues such as occlusion handling and extension to handle video should also be considered.

Acknowledgements. Y. Zhong's PhD scholarship is funded by Data61. Y. Dai is supported in part by National 1000 Young Talents Plan of China, Natural Science Foundation of China (61420106007, 61671387), and ARC grant (DE140100180). H. Li's work is funded in part by ACRV (CE140100016). The authors are very grateful to NVIDIA's generous gift of GPUs to ANU used in this research.

References

1. Garg, R., Vijay Kumar, B.G., Carneiro, G., Reid, I.: Unsupervised CNN for single view depth estimation: geometry to the rescue. In: Leibe, B., Matas, J., Sebe, N., Welling, M. (eds.) ECCV 2016. LNCS, vol. 9912, pp. 740–756. Springer, Cham (2016). https://doi.org/10.1007/978-3-319-46484-8_45
2. Godard, C., Mac Aodha, O., Brostow, G.J.: Unsupervised monocular depth estimation with left-right consistency. In: Proceeding IEEE Conference Computer Vision Pattern Recognition (2017)
3. Li, B., Shen, C., Dai, Y., van den Hengel, A., He, M.: Depth and surface normal estimation from monocular images using regression on deep features and hierarchical CRFs. In: Proceedings IEEE Conference Computer Vision Pattern Recognition, June 2015
4. Bronstein, A.M., Bronstein, M.M., Zibulevsky, M., Zeevi, Y.Y.: Sparse ICA for blind separation of transmitted and reflected images. Intl J. Imaging Sci. Technol. **15**(1), 84–91 (2005)
5. Yang, J., Li, H., Dai, Y., Tan, R.T.: Robust optical flow estimation of double-layer images under transparency or reflection. In: Proceedings IEEE Conference Computer Vision Pattern Recognition (June 2016)
6. Li, Z., Tan, P., Tan, R.T., Zou, D., Zhou, S.Z., Cheong, L.F.: Simultaneous video defogging and stereo reconstruction. In: Proceedings IEEE Conference Computer Vision Pattern Recognition (June 2015) 4988–4997
7. Levin, A., Lischinski, D., Weiss, Y.: A closed-form solution to natural image matting. IEEE Trans. Pattern Anal. Mach. Intell. **30**(2), 228–242 (2008)
8. Williem, W., Raskar, R., Park, I.K.: Depth map estimation and colorization of anaglyph images using local color prior and reverse intensity distribution. In: Proceedings IEEE International Conference Computer Vision, pp. 3460–3468 (Dec 2015)
9. Joulin, A., Kang, S.B.: Recovering stereo pairs from anaglyphs. In: Proceedings IEEE Conference Computer Vision Pattern Recognition, pp. 289–296 (2013)
10. Li, Y., Brown, M.S.: Single image layer separation using relative smoothness. In: Proceedings IEEE Conference Computer Vision Pattern Recognition (June 2014)
11. Fan, Q., Yang, J., Hua, G., Chen, B., Wipf, D.: A generic deep architecture for single image reflection removal and image smoothing. In: Proceedings IEEE International Conference Computer Vision (2017)
12. Liu, C., Yuen, J., Torralba, A.: Sift flow: dense correspondence across scenes and its applications. IEEE Trans. Pattern Anal. Mach. Intell. **33**(5), 978–994 (2011)
13. Xie, J., Girshick, R., Farhadi, A.: Deep3D: fully automatic 2D-to-3D video conversion with deep convolutional neural networks. In: Leibe, B., Matas, J., Sebe, N., Welling, M. (eds.) ECCV 2016. LNCS, vol. 9908, pp. 842–857. Springer, Cham (2016). https://doi.org/10.1007/978-3-319-46493-0_51
14. Iizuka, S., Simo-Serra, E., Ishikawa, H.: Let there be color!: Joint end-to-end learning of global and local image priors for automatic image colorization with simultaneous classification. ACM Trans. Graph. **35**(4), 110:1–110:11 (2016)
15. Zhang, R., Isola, P., Efros, A.A.: Colorful image colorization. In: Leibe, B., Matas, J., Sebe, N., Welling, M. (eds.) ECCV 2016. LNCS, vol. 9907, pp. 649–666. Springer, Cham (2016). https://doi.org/10.1007/978-3-319-46487-9_40
16. Isola, P., Zhu, J.Y., Zhou, T., Efros, A.A.: Image-to-image translation with conditional adversarial networks. In: Proceedings IEEE Conference Computer Vision Pattern Recognition (2017)

17. Levin, A., Weiss, Y.: User assisted separation of reflections from a single image using a sparsity prior. IEEE Trans. Pattern Anal. Mach. Intell. **29**(9), 1647–1654 (2007)

18. Ronneberger, O., Fischer, P., Brox, T.: U-Net: convolutional networks for biomedical image segmentation. In: Navab, N., Hornegger, J., Wells, W.M., Frangi, A.F. (eds.) MICCAI 2015. LNCS, vol. 9351, pp. 234–241. Springer, Cham (2015). https://doi.org/10.1007/978-3-319-24574-4_28

19. Zhong, Y., Dai, Y., Li, H.: Self-supervised learning for stereo matching with self-improving ability (2017). arXiv:1709.00930

20. Wang, Z., Bovik, A.C., Sheikh, H.R., Simoncelli, E.P.: Image quality assessment: from error visibility to structural similarity. IEEE Trans. Image Proc. **13**(4), 600–612 (2004)

21. Jaderberg, M., Simonyan, K., Zisserman, A., kavukcuoglu, k.: Spatial transformer networks. In: Proceedings Advances Neural Information Processing System, pp. 2017–2025 (2015)

22. Abadi, M., Agarwal, A., et al., P.B.: Tensorflow: Large-scale machine learning on heterogeneous distributed systems. CoRR arXiv:abs/1603.04467 (2016)

23. Tieleman, T., Hinton, G.: Lecture 6.5–RmsProp: divide the gradient by a running average of its recent magnitude. In: COURSERA: Neural Networks for Machine Learning (2012)

24. Scharstein, D., Szeliski, R.: A taxonomy and evaluation of dense two-frame stereo correspondence algorithms. Int. J. Comp. Vis. **47**(1–3), 7–42 (2002)

25. Menze, M., Geiger, A.: Object scene flow for autonomous vehicles. In: Proceedings IEEE Conference Computer Vision Pattern Recognition (2015)

26. Li, Y., Brown, M.S.: Single image layer separation using relative smoothness. In: Proceedings IEEE Conference Computer Vision Pattern Recognition, pp. 2752–2759 (2014)

27. Eigen, D., Puhrsch, C., Fergus, R.: Depth map prediction from a single image using a multi-scale deep network. In: Proceedings Advances Neural Information Processing System (2014)

28. Li, B., Dai, Y., He, M.: Monocular depth estimation with hierarchical fusion of dilated CNNS and soft-weighted-sum inference. Pattern Recogn. **83**, 328–339 (2018)

29. Zhou, T., Brown, M., Snavely, N., Lowe, D.G.: Unsupervised learning of depth and ego-motion from video. In: Proceedings IEEE Conference Computer Vision Pattern Recognition (2017)

30. Yang, J., Ye, X., Li, K., Hou, C., Wang, Y.: Color-guided depth recovery from RGB-D data using an adaptive autoregressive model. In: IEEE Transactions Image Proceedings, vol. 23, pp. 3443-3458 (Aug 2014)

Dividing and Aggregating Network for Multi-view Action Recognition

Dongang Wang[1] ID, Wanli Ouyang[1,2] ID, Wen Li[3] ID, and Dong Xu[1]([✉])

[1] School of Electrical and Information Engineering, The University of Sydney,
Camperdown, Australia
{dongang.wang,wanli.ouyang,dong.xu}@sydney.edu.au
[2] SenseTime Computer Vision Research Group, The University of Sydney,
Camperdown, Australia
[3] Computer Vision Laboratory, ETH Zurich, Zürich, Switzerland
liwen@vision.ee.ethz.ch

Abstract. In this paper, we propose a new Dividing and Aggregating Network (DA-Net) for multi-view action recognition. In our DA-Net, we learn view-independent representations shared by all views at lower layers, while we learn one view-specific representation for each view at higher layers. We then train view-specific action classifiers based on the view-specific representation for each view and a view classifier based on the shared representation at lower layers. The view classifier is used to predict how likely each video belongs to each view. Finally, the predicted view probabilities from multiple views are used as the weights when fusing the prediction scores of view-specific action classifiers. We also propose a new approach based on the conditional random field (CRF) formulation to pass message among view-specific representations from different branches to help each other. Comprehensive experiments on two benchmark datasets clearly demonstrate the effectiveness of our proposed DA-Net for multi-view action recognition.

Keywords: Dividing and Aggregating Network
Multi-view action recognition · Large-scale action recognition

1 Introduction

Action recognition is an important problem in computer vision due to its broad applications in video content analysis, security control, human-computer interface, etc. Recently, significant improvements have been achieved, especially with the deep learning approaches [23,24,27,35,40].

Multi-view action recognition is a more challenging task as action videos of the same person are captured by cameras from different viewpoints. It is well-known that failure in handling feature variations caused by viewpoints may yield poor recognition results [31,42,43].

One motivation of this paper is to learn view-specific deep representations. This is different from existing approaches for extracting view-invariant features

© Springer Nature Switzerland AG 2018
V. Ferrari et al. (Eds.): ECCV 2018, LNCS 11213, pp. 457–473, 2018.
https://doi.org/10.1007/978-3-030-01240-3_28

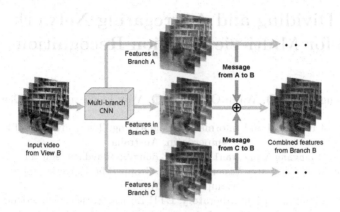

Fig. 1. The motivation of our work for learning view-specific deep representations and passing messages among them. The features extracted in different branches should focus on different regions related to the same action. Message passing from different branches will help each other and thus improve the final classification performance. We only show the message passing from other branches to Branch B for better illustration.

using global codebooks [18,19,28] or dictionaries [43]. Because of the large divergence in specific settings of viewpoint, the visible regions are different, which makes it difficult to learn invariant features among different views. Thus, it is more beneficial to learn view-specific feature representation to extract the most discriminative information for each view. For example, at camera view A, the visible region could be the upper part of human body, while the camera views B and C have more visible cues like hands and legs. As a result, we should encourage the features of videos captured from camera view A to focus on the upper body region, while the features of videos from camera view B to focus on other regions like hands and legs. In contrast, the existing approaches tend to discard such view-specific discriminative information.

Another motivation of this paper is that the view-specific features can be used to help each other. Since these features are specific to different views, they are naturally complementary to each other. This provides us with the opportunity to pass message among these features so that they can help each other through interaction. Take Fig. 1 as an example, for the same input image from View B, the features from branches A, B, C focus on different regions. By conducting well-defined message passing, the specific features from View A and View C can be used for refining the features for View B, leading to more accurate representations for action recognition.

Based on the above two motivations, we propose a *Dividing and Aggregating Network (DA-Net)* for multi-view action recognition. In our DA-Net, each branch learns a set of view-specific features. We also propose a new approach based on *conditional random field* (CRF) to learn better view-specific features by passing message to each other. Finally, we introduce a new fusion approach by using the predicted view probabilities as the weights for fusing the classification results from multiple view-specific classifiers to output the final prediction score for action classification.

To summarize, our contributions are three-fold:

(1) We propose a multi-branch network for multi-view action recognition. In this network, the lower CNN layers are shared to learn view-independent representations. Taking the shared features as the input, each view has its own CNN branch to learn its view-specific features.
(2) Conditional random field (CRF) is introduced to pass message among view-specific features from different branches. A feature in a specific view is considered as a continuous random variable and passes message to the feature in another view. In this way, view-specific features at different branches communicate and help each other.
(3) A new view-prediction-guided fusion method for combining action classification scores from multiple branches is proposed. In our approach, we simultaneously learn multiple view-specific classifiers and the view classifier. An action prediction score is obtained for each branch, and multiple action prediction scores are fused by using the view prediction probabilities as the weights.

2   Related Works

Action Recognition. Researchers have made significant contributions in designing effective features as well as classifiers for action recognition [17,26, 30,34,36]. Wang et al. [32] proposed the iDT feature to encode the information from edge, flow and trajectory. The iDT feature became dominant in the THUMOS 2014 and 2015 challenges [7]. In the deep learning community, Tran et al. proposed C3D [27], which designs a 3D CNN model for video datasets by combining appearance features with motion information. Sun et al. [25] applied the factorization methods to decompose 3D convolution kernels and used the spatio-temporal features in different layers of CNNs. The recent trend in action recognition follows two-stream CNNs. Simonyan and Zisserman [24] first proposed the two-stream CNN to extract features from the RGB key frames and the optical flow channel. Wang et al. [34] integrated the key factors from iDT and CNN and achieved significant performance improvement. Wang et al. also proposed the temporal segment network (TSN) [35] to utilize segments of videos under the two-stream CNN framework. Researchers also transform the two-stream structure to the multi-branch structure. In [6], Feichtenhofer et al. proposed a single CNN that fuses the spatial and temporal features before the final layers, which achieves excellent results. Wang et al. proposed a multi-branch neural network, where each branch deals with different level of features and then fuse them together [36]. However, these works did not take the multi-view action recognition into consideration. Therefore, they do not learn view-specific features or use view prediction probabilities as the prior when fusing the classification scores from multiple branches as in our work. They do not use message passing to improve their features, either.

Multi-view Action Recognition. For the multi-view action recognition tasks where the videos are from different viewpoints, the existing action recognition approaches may not achieve satisfactory recognition results [15,16,31,42]. The methods using view-invariant representations are popular for multi-view action recognition. Wu *et al.* [37] and Turaga *et al.* [28] proposed to construct the common space as the multi-view action feature space by using global GMM or Grassmann and Stiefel manifolds and achieved promising results. In recent works, Zheng *et al.* [43], Kong *et al.* [10] and Hossein *et al.* [19] designed different methods to learn the global codebook or dictionary to better extract view-invariant representations from action videos. By treating the problem as a domain adaptation problem, Li *et al.* [12] and Mancini *et al.* [14] proposed new approaches to learn robust classifiers or domain-invariant features. Different from these methods for learning view-invariant features in the common space, we directly learn view-specific features by using multi-branch CNNs. With these view-specific features, we exploit the relationship among them in order to effectively leverage multi-view features.

Conditional Random Field (CRF). CRF has been exploited for action recognition in [29] as it can connect features and outputs, especially for temporal signals like actions. Chen *et al.* proposed L-CORF [3] for locating actions in videos, where CRF was used for modeling spatial-temporal relationship in each single-view video. CRF could also exploit the relationship among spatial features. It has been successfully introduced for image segmentation in the deep learning community by Zheng *et al.* [44], which deals with the relationship among pixels. Xu *et al.* [38,39] modeled the relationship of pixels to learn the edges of objects in images. Recently, Chu *et al.* [4,5] have utilized discrete CRF in CNN for human pose estimation. Our work is the first for action recognition by exploiting the relationship among features from videos captured by cameras from different viewpoints. Our experiments demonstrate the effectiveness of our message passing approach for multi-view action recognition.

3 Multi-view Action Recognition

3.1 Problem Overview

In the multi-view action recognition task, each sample in the training or test set consists of multiple videos captured from different viewpoints. The task is to train a robust model by using those multi-view training videos, and perform action recognition on multi-view test videos.

Let us denote the training data as $\{(\mathbf{x}_{i,1}, \ldots, \mathbf{x}_{i,v}, \ldots, \mathbf{x}_{i,V})|_{i=1}^{N}\}$, where $\mathbf{x}_{i,v}$ is the i-th training sample/video from the v-th view, V is the total number of views, and N is the number of multi-view training videos. The label of the i-th multi-view training video $(\mathbf{x}_{i,1}, \ldots, \mathbf{x}_{i,V})$ is denoted as $y_i \in \{1, \ldots, K\}$ where K is the total number of action categories. For better presentation, we may use $\mathbf{x}_i$ to represent one video when we do not care about which specific view each video comes from, where $i = 1, \ldots, NV$.

To effectively cope with the multi-view training data, we design a new multi-branch neural network. As shown in Fig. 2, this network consists of three modules. (1) **Basic Multi-branch Module:** This network extracts the common features (*i.e.* view-independent features) for all videos by using one shared CNN, and then extracts view-specific features by using multiple CNN branches, which will be described in Sect. 3.2. (2) **Message Passing Module:** Based on the basic multi-branch module, we also propose a message passing approach to improve view-specific features from different branches, which will be introduced in Sect. 3.3. (3) **View-prediction-guided Fusion Module:** The refined view-specific features from different branches are passed through multiple view-specific action classifiers and the final scores are fused with the guidance of probabilities from the view classifier that is trained based on view-independent features.

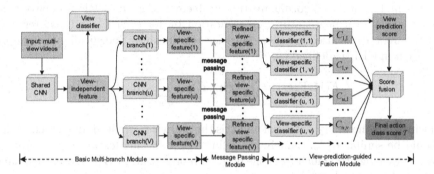

Fig. 2. Network structure of our newly proposed Dividing and Aggregating Network (DA-Net). (1) **Basic multi-branch module** is composed of one shared CNN and several view-specific CNN branches. (2) **Message passing module** is introduced between every two branches and generate the refined view-specific features. (3) In the **view-prediction-guided fusion module**, we design several view-specific action classifiers for each branch. The final scores are obtained by fusing the results from all action classifiers, in which the view prediction probabilities from the view classifier are used as the weights.

3.2   Basic Multi-branch Module

As shown in Fig. 2, the basic multi-branch module consists of two parts: (1) *shared CNN:* Most of the convolutional layers are shared to save computation and generate the common features (*i.e.* view-independent features); (2) *CNN branches:* Following the shared CNN, we define V view-specific branches, and view-specific features can be extracted from these branches.

In the initial training phase, each training video $\mathbf{x}_i$ first flows through the shared CNN, and then only goes to the v-th view-specific branch. Then, we build one view-specific classifier to predict the action label for the videos from each view. Since each branch is trained by using training videos from a specific viewpoint, each branch captures the most informative features for its corresponding view. Thus, it can be expected that the features from different views are complementary to each other for predicting the action classes. We refer to this structure as the *Basic Multi-branch Module*.

3.3 Message Passing Module

To effective integrate different view-specific branches for multi-view action recognition, we further exploit the inter-view relationship by using a *conditional random field (CRF)* model to pass message among features extracted from different branches.

Let us denote the multi-branch features for one training video as $\mathbf{F} = \{\mathbf{f}_v\}_{v=1}^V$, where each $\mathbf{f}_v$ is the view-specific feature vector extracted from the v-th branch. Our objective is to estimate the refined view-specific feature $\mathbf{H} = \{\mathbf{h}_v\}_{v=1}^V$. As shown in Fig. 3(a), we formulate this problem under the CRF framework, in which we learn a new feature representation $\mathbf{h}_v$ for each $\mathbf{f}_v$, and also regularize different $\mathbf{h}_v$'s based on their pairwise relationship. Specifically, the energy function in CRF is defined as,

$$E(\mathbf{H}, \mathbf{F}, \Theta) = \sum_v \phi(\mathbf{h}_v, \mathbf{f}_v) + \sum_{u,v} \psi(\mathbf{h}_u, \mathbf{h}_v), \tag{1}$$

in which ϕ is the unary potential and ψ is the pairwise potential. In particular, $\mathbf{h}_v$ should be similar to $\mathbf{f}_v$, namely the refined view-specific feature representation does not change too much from the original representation. Therefore, the unary potential is defined as follows,

$$\phi(\mathbf{h}_v, \mathbf{f}_v) = -\frac{\alpha_v}{2}\|\mathbf{h}_v - \mathbf{f}_v\|^2, \tag{2}$$

where α_v is a weight parameter that will be learnt during the training process. Moreover, we employ a bilinear potential function to model the correlation among features from different branches, which is defined as

$$\psi(\mathbf{h}_u, \mathbf{h}_v) = \mathbf{h}_v{}^\top \mathbf{W}_{u,v} \mathbf{h}_u, \tag{3}$$

where $\mathbf{W}_{u,v}$ is the matrix modeling the relationship among different features. $\mathbf{W}_{u,v}$ can be learnt during the training process.

Following [20], we use mean-field update to infer the mean vector of $\mathbf{h}_u$ as:

$$\mathbf{h}_v = \frac{1}{\alpha_v}(\alpha_v \mathbf{f}_v + \sum_{u \neq v}(\mathbf{W}_{u,v}\mathbf{h}_u)). \tag{4}$$

Thus, the refined view-specific feature representation $\{\mathbf{h}_v|_{v=1}^V\}$ can be obtained by iteratively applying the above equation.

From the definition of CRF, the first term in Eq. (4) serves as the unary term for receiving the information from the feature $\mathbf{f}_v$ for its own view v. The second term is the pair-wise term that receives the information from other views u for

$u \neq v$. The $\mathbf{W}_{u,v}$ in Eqs. (3) and (4) models the relationship between the feature vector $\mathbf{h}_u$ from the u-th view and the feature $\mathbf{h}_v$ from the v-th view.

The above CRF model can be implemented in neural networks as shown in [5,44], thus it can be naturally integrated in the basic multi-branch network, and optimized in the end-to-end training process based on the basic multi-branch module. The basic multi-branch module together with the message passing module is referred to as the *Cross-view Multi-branch Module* in the following sections. The message passing process can be conducted multiple times with the shared $\mathbf{W}_{u,v}$'s in each iteration. In our experiments, we perform only one iteration as it already provides good feature representations.

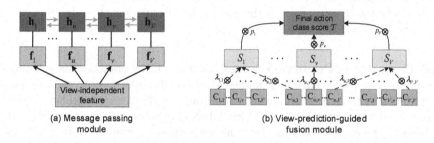

(a) Message passing module

(b) View-prediction-guided fusion module

Fig. 3. The details for (a) inter-view message passing module discussed in Sect. 3.3, and (b) view-prediction-guided fusion module described in Sect. 3.4. Please see the corresponding sections for the detailed definitions and descriptions.

3.4   View-Prediction-Guided Fusion

In multi-view action recognition, a body movement might be captured from more than one viewpoint and should be recognized from different aspects, which implies that different views contain certain complementary information for action recognition. To effectively capture such cross-view complementary information, we therefore propose a *View-prediction-guided Fusion Module* to automatically fuse the prediction scores from all view-specific classifiers for action recognition.

Learning View-Specific Classifiers. In the cross-view multi-branch module, instead of passing each training video into only one specific view as in the basic multi-branch module, we feed each video $\mathbf{x}_i$ into all V branches.

Given a training video $\mathbf{x}_i$, we will extract features from each branch individually, which will lead to V different representations. Considering we have training videos from V different views, there would be in total $V \times V$ types of cross-view information, each corresponding to a branch-view pair (u, v) for $u, v = 1, \ldots, V$, where u is the index of the branch and v is the index of the view that the videos belong to.

Then, we build view-specific action classifiers in each branch based on different types of visual information, which leads to $V \times V$ different classifiers. Let us denote $C_{u,v}$ as the score generated by using the v-th view-specific classifier from the u-th branch. Specifically, for the video $\mathbf{x}_i$, the score is denoted as $C_{u,v}^i$. As shown in Fig. 3(b), the fused score of all the results from the v-th view-specific classifiers in all branches is denoted as S_v. Specifically, for the video $\mathbf{x}_i$, the fused score S_v^i can be formulated as follows,

$$S_v^i = \sum_u \lambda_{u,v} C_{u,v}^i, \tag{5}$$

where $\lambda_{u,v}$'s are the weights for fusing $C_{u,v}$'s, which can be jointly learnt during the training procedure and shared by all videos. For the v-th value in the u-th branch, we initialize the value of $\lambda_{u,v}$ when $u = v$ twice as large as the value of $\lambda_{u,v}$ when $u \neq v$, as $C_{v,v}$ is the most related score for the v-th view when compared with other scores $C_{u,v}$'s $(u \neq v)$.

Soft Ensemble of Prediction Scores. Different CNN branches share common information and have each own refined view-specific information, so the combination of results from all branches should achieve better classification results. Besides, we do not want to use the view labels of input videos during the training or testing process. In that case, we further propose a strategy to fuse all view-specific action prediction scores $\{S_v|_{v=1}^V\}$ based on the view prediction probabilities of each video, instead of using only the one score from the known view as in the basic multi-branch module.

Let us assume each training video $\mathbf{x}_i$ is associated with V view prediction probabilities $\{p_v^i|_{v=1}^V\}$, where each p_v^i denotes the probability of $\mathbf{x}_i$ belonging to the v-th view and $\sum_v p_v^i = 1$. Then, the final prediction score T^i can be calculated as the weighted mean of all view-specific scores based on the corresponding view prediction probabilities,

$$T^i = \sum_{v=1}^V p_v^i S_v^i. \tag{6}$$

To obtain the view prediction probabilities, as shown in Fig. 2, we additionally train a *view classifier* by using the common features (*i.e.* view-independent feature) after the *shared CNN*. We use the cross entropy loss for the view classifier and the action classifier, denoted as $\mathcal{L}_{view}$ and $\mathcal{L}_{action}$ respectively.

The final model is learnt by jointly optimizing the above two losses, *i.e.*,

$$\mathcal{L} = \mathcal{L}_{action} + \mathcal{L}_{view}, \tag{7}$$

where we treat the two losses equally and this setting leads to satisfactory results.

The cross-view multi-branch module with view-prediction-guided fusion module forms our *Dividing and Aggregating Network (DA-Net)*. It is worth mentioning that we only use view labels for training the basic multi-branch module and the fine-tuning steps after the basic multi-branch module and the test stages do not require view labels of videos. Even the test video comes from an unseen view, our model can still automatically calculate its view prediction probabilities by using the view classifier, and ensemble the prediction scores from view-specific classifiers for final prediction (see our experiments on *cross-view* action recognition in Sect. 4.3).

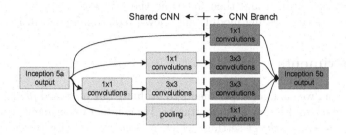

Fig. 4. The layers used in the shared CNN and CNN branches in the `inception_5b` block. The layers in yellow color are included in the shared CNN, while the layers in red color are duplicated for different branches. The layers after `inception_5b` are also duplicated. The `ReLU` and `BatchNormalization` layers after each convolutional layer are treated similarly as the corresponding convolutional layers. (Color figure online)

3.5   Network Architecture

We illustrate the architecture of our DA-Net in Fig. 2. The shared CNN can be any of the popular CNN architectures, which is followed with V view-specific branches, each corresponding to one view. Then, we build $V \times V$ view-specific classifiers on top of those view-specific branches, where each branch is connected to V classifiers. Those $V \times V$ view-specific classifiers are further ensembled to produce V branch-level scores using Eq. (5). Finally, those V branch-level scores are reweighed to obtain the final prediction score, where the weights are the view probabilities generated from the view classifier, which is trained after the shared CNN. Like other deep neural networks, our proposed model can be trained by using popular optimization approaches such as the stochastic gradient descent (SGD) algorithm. We first train the basic multi-branch module to learn view-specific feature in each branch, and then we fine-tune all the modules.

In our implementation, we build our network based on the temporal segment network (TSN) [35] with some modifications. In particular, we use the BN-Inception [9] as the backbone network. The shared CNN layers include the ones from the input to the block `inception_5a`. As shown in Fig. 4, for each path within the `inception_5b` block, we duplicate the last convolutional layer (shown in red in Fig. 4) for multiple times for multiple branches and the previous layers are shared in the shared CNN. The rest average pooling and fully connected layers after the `inception_5b` block are also duplicated for multiple branches. The corresponding parameters are also duplicated at initialization stage and learnt separately. Similarly as in TSN, we also train a two-stream network [24], where two streams are learnt separately using two modalities, RGB and dense optical flow, respectively. In the testing phase, given a test sample with multiple views of videos, $(\mathbf{x}_1, \ldots, \mathbf{x}_V)$, we pass each video $\mathbf{x}_v$ to two streams, and obtain its prediction by fusing the outputs from two streams.

The training of our DA-Net has the same starting point of TSN. We first train the network based on the basic multi-branch module to learn the basic features of each branch and then fine-tune the learnt network by additionally adding the message passing module and view-prediction-guided fusion module.

4   Experiments

In this section, we conduct experiments to evaluate our proposed model by using two benchmark multi-view action datasets. We conduct experiments on two settings: (1) the *cross-subject* setting, which is used to evaluate the effectiveness of our proposed model for learning from multi-view videos, and (2) the *cross-view* setting, which is used to evaluate the generalization ability of our proposed model to unseen views.

4.1   Datasets and Setup

NTU RGB+D (NTU). [21] is a large scale dataset for human action recognition, which contains 60 daily actions performed by 40 different subjects. The actions are captured by Kinect v2 in three viewpoints. The modalities of data including RGB videos, depth maps and 3D joint information, where only the RGB videos are used for our experiments. The total number of RGB videos is 56, 880 containing more than 4 million frames.

Northwestern-UCLA Multiview Action (NUMA). [33] is another popular multi-view action recognition benchmark dataset. In this dataset, 10 daily actions are performed by 10 subjects for several times, which are captured by three static cameras. In total, the dataset consists of 1, 475 RGB videos and the correlated depth frames and skeleton information, where only the RGB videos are used for our experiments.

4.2   Experiments on Multi-view Action Recognition

The *cross-subject* evaluation protocol is used in this experiment. All action videos of a few subjects from all views are selected as the training set, and the action videos of the remaining subjects are used for testing.

For the NTU dataset, we use the same cross-subject protocol as in [21]. We compare our proposed method with a wide range of baselines, among which the work in [1, 21, 22] include 3D joint information, and the work in [2, 13] used RGB videos only. We also include the TSN method [35] as a baseline for comparison, which can be treated as a special case of our DA-Net without explicitly exploiting the multi-view information in training videos. The results are shown in the third column of Table 1. We observe that the TSN method achieves much better results than the previous works using multi-modality data, which could be attributed to the usage of deep neural networks for learning effective video representations. Moreover, the recent works from Baradel *et al.* [2] and Luvizon *et al.* [13] reported the results using only RGB videos, where the work from Luvizon *et al.* [13] achieves similar performance as the TSN method. Our proposed DA-Net outperforms all existing state-of-the-art algorithms and the baseline TSN method.

Table 1. Accuracy comparison between our DA-Net and other state-of-the-art works on the NTU dataset. When using RGB videos, our DA-Net, TSN [35] and the work from Zolfaghari *et al.* [45] use optical flow generated from RGB videos while the rest works do not extract optical flow features. Four methods additionally utilize the pose modality. The best results are shown in bold.

Methods	Modalities	Cross-subject accuracy	Cross-view accuracy
DSSCA-SSLM [22]	Pose+RGB	74.9%	-
STA-Hands [1]	Pose+RGB	82.5%	88.6%
Zolfaghari *et al.* [45]	Pose+RGB	80.8%	-
Baradel *et al.* [2]	Pose+RGB	84.8%	90.6%
Luvizon *et al.* [13]	RGB	84.6%	-
TSN [35]	RGB	84.93%	85.36%
DA-Net (Ours)	RGB	**88.12%**	**91.96%**

Table 2. Average accuracy comparison (the cross-subject setting) between our DA-Net and other works on the NUMA dataset. The results are generated by averaging the accuracy of each subject. The best result is shown in bold.

Methods	Average accuracy
Li and Zickler [11]	50.7%
MST-AOG [33]	81.6%
Kong *et al.* [10]	81.1%
TSN [35]	90.3%
DA-Net (ours)	**92.1%**

For the NUMA dataset, we use the 10-fold evaluation protocol, where videos of each subject will be used as the test videos each time. To be consistent with other works, we report the video-level accuracy, in which the videos of each view are evaluated separately. The average accuracies are shown in Table 2, where our proposed DA-Net again outperforms all other baseline methods.

The results on both datasets clearly demonstrate the effectiveness of our DA-Net for learning deep models using multi-view RGB videos. By learning view-specific features as well as classifiers and conducting message passing, videos from multiple views are utilized more effectively. As a result, we can learn more discriminative features and our DA-Net can achieve better action classification results when compared with previous methods.

Table 3. Average accuracy comparison on the NUMA dataset [33] (the cross-view setting) when the videos from two views are used for training and the videos from the remaining view are used for testing. The best results are shown in bold. For fair comparison, we only report the results from the methods using RGB videos.

{Source}|Target	{1, 2}|3	{1, 3}|2	{2, 3}|1	Average accuracy
DVV [41]	58.5%	55.2%	39.3%	51.0%
nCTE [8]	68.6%	68.3%	52.1%	63.0%
MST-AOG [33]	-	-	-	73.3%
NKTM [18]	75.8%	73.3%	59.1%	69.4%
R-NKTM [19]	78.1%	-	-	-
Kong *et al.* [10]	-	-	-	77.2%
TSN [35]	84.5%	80.6%	76.8%	80.6%
DA-Net (ours)	**86.5%**	**82.7%**	**83.1%**	**84.2%**

4.3   Generalization to Unseen Views

Our DA-Net can also be readily used for generalization to unseen views, which is also known as the *cross-view* evaluation protocol. We employ the *leave-one-view-out* strategy in this setting, in which we use videos from one view as the test set, and employ videos from the remaining views for training our DA-Net.

Different from the training process under the cross-subject setting, the total number of branches in the network is set to the total number of views minus 1, since videos from one viewpoint are reserved for testing. During the testing stage, the videos from the target view (*i.e.* unseen view) will go through all the branches and the view classifier can still provide the prediction scores of each testing video belonging to a set of source views (*i.e.* seen views). The scores indicate the similarity between the videos from the target view and those from the source views, based on which we can still obtain the weighted fusion scores that can be used for classifying videos from the target view.

For the NTU dataset, we follow the original cross-view setting in [21], in which videos from view 2 and view 3 are used for training while videos from view 1 are used for testing. The results are shown in the fourth column of Table 1. On this cross-view setting, our DA-Net also outperforms the existing methods by a large margin.

For the NUMA dataset, we conduct three-fold cross validation. The videos from two views together with their action labels are used as the training data to learn the network and the videos from the remaining view are used for testing. The videos from the unseen view are not available during the training stage.

We report our results in Table 3, which shows our DA-Net achieves the best performance. Our results are even better than the methods that use the videos from the unseen view as unlabeled data in [10]. The detailed accuracy for each class is shown in Fig. 5. Again we observe that DA-Net is better than nCTE [8] and NKTM [18] in almost all the action classes.

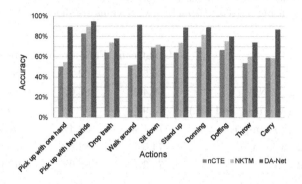

Fig. 5. Average recognition accuracy in each class on the NUMA dataset under the cross-view setting. All the three methods do not utilize the features from the unseen view during the training process.

From the results, we observe that our DA-Net is robust even without using videos from the target view during the training process. A possible explanation is as follows. Building upon the TSN architecture, our DA-Net further learns view-specific features, which produces better representations to capture information from each view. Second, the message passing module further improves the feature representation on different views. Finally, the newly proposed soft ensemble fusion scheme using view prediction probabilities as the weight also contributes to performance improvement. Although videos from the unseen view are not available in the training process, the view classifiers are still able to be used to predict probabilities of the given test video belonging to each seen view, which are useful to obtain the final prediction scores.

4.4 Component Analysis

To study the performance gain of different modules in our proposed DA-Net, we report the results of three variants of our DA-Net. In particular, in the first variant, we remove the view-prediction-guided fusion module, and only keep the basic multi-branch module and message passing module, which is referred to as *DA-Net (w/o fus.)*. Similarly in the second variant, we remove the message passing module, and only keep the basic multi-branch module and view-prediction-guided fusion module, which is referred to as *DA-Net (w/o msg.)*. In the third variant, we only keep the basic multi-branch module, which is referred to as *DA-Net (w/o msg. and fus.)*. Specially in *DA-Net (w/o msg. and fus.)* and *DA-Net (w/o fus.)*, since the fusion part is ablated, we only train one classifier for each branch, and we equally fuse the prediction scores from all branches for obtaining the action recognition results.

Table 4. Accuracy for cross-view setting on the NTU dataset. The second and third columns are the accuracies from the RGB-stream and flow-stream, respectively. The final results after fusing the scores from the two streams are shown in the fourth column.

Method	RGB-stream	Flow-stream	Two-stream
TSN [35]	66.5%	82.2%	85.4%
Ensemble TSN	69.4%	86.6%	87.8%
DA-Net (w/o msg. and fus.)	73.9%	87.7%	89.8%
DA-Net (w/o msg.)	74.1%	88.4%	90.7%
DA-Net (w/o fus.)	74.5%	88.6%	90.9%
DA-Net	75.3%	88.9%	**92.0%**

We take the NTU dataset under the cross-view setting as an example for component analysis. The baseline TSN method [35] is also included for comparison. Moreover, we further report the results from an ensemble version of TSN, in which we train two TSN's based on the videos from view 2 and the videos from view 3 individually, and then average their prediction scores on the test videos from view 1 for prediction results. We refer to it as *Ensemble TSN*.

The results of all methods are shown in Table 4. We observe that both Ensemble TSN and our *DA-Net (w/o msg. and fus.)* achieve better results than the baseline TSN method, which indicates that learning individual representation for each view helps to capture view-specific information, and thus improves the action recognition accuracy. Our *DA-Net (w/o msg. and fus.)* outperforms the Ensemble TSN method for both modalities and after two-stream fusion, which indicates that learning common features (*i.e.* view-independent features) shared by all branches for *DA-Net (w/o msg. and fus.)* will possibly lead to better performance.

Moreover, by additionally using the message passing module, *DA-Net (w/o fus.)* gains consistent improvement over *DA-Net (w/o msg. and fus.)*. A possible reason is that videos from different views share complementary information, and the message passing process could help refine the feature representation on each branch. The *DA-Net (w/o msg.)* is also better than *DA-Net (w/o msg. and fus.)*, which demonstrates the effectiveness of our view-prediction-guided fusion module. Our DA-Net effectively integrate the predictions from all view-specific classifiers in a soft ensemble manner. In the view-prediction-guided fusion module, all the view-specific classifiers integrate the total $V \times V$ types of cross-view information. Meanwhile, the view classifier softly ensembles the action prediction scores by using view prediction probabilities as the weights.

5   Conclusion

In this paper, we have proposed the Dividing and Aggregating Network (DA-Net) to address action recognition using multi-view videos. The comprehensive experiments have demonstrated that our newly proposed deep learning method outperforms the baseline methods for multi-view action recognition. Through the component analysis, we demonstrate that view-specific representations from different branches can help each other in an effective way by conducting message passing among them. It is also demonstrated that it is beneficial to fuse the prediction scores from multiple classifiers by using the view prediction probabilities as the weights.

Acknowledgement. This work is supported by SenseTime Group Limited.

References

1. Baradel, F., Wolf, C., Mille, J.: Human action recognition: pose-based attention draws focus to hands. In: The IEEE International Conference on Computer Vision (ICCV) Workshops, October 2017
2. Baradel, F., Wolf, C., Mille, J.: Pose-conditioned spatio-temporal attention for human action recognition. arXiv preprint arXiv:1703.10106 (2017)
3. Chen, W., Xiong, C., Xu, R., Corso, J.J.: Actionness ranking with lattice conditional ordinal random fields. In: Proceedings of the IEEE conference on computer vision and pattern recognition, pp. 748–755 (2014)
4. Chu, X., Ouyang, W., Li, H., Wang, X.: Structured feature learning for pose estimation. In: Proceedings of the IEEE Conference on Computer Vision and Pattern Recognition, pp. 4715–4723 (2016)
5. Chu, X., Ouyang, W., Wang, X., et al.: CRF-CNN: modeling structured information in human pose estimation. In: Advances in Neural Information Processing Systems, pp. 316–324 (2016)
6. Feichtenhofer, C., Pinz, A., Zisserman, A.: Convolutional two-stream network fusion for video action recognition. In: Proceedings of the IEEE Conference on Computer Vision and Pattern Recognition, pp. 1933–1941 (2016)
7. Gorban, A., et al.: THUMOS challenge: action recognition with a large number of classes (2015). http://www.thumos.info/
8. Gupta, A., Martinez, J., Little, J.J., Woodham, R.J.: 3D pose from motion for cross-view action recognition via non-linear circulant temporal encoding. In: Proceedings of the IEEE Conference on Computer Vision and Pattern Recognition, pp. 2601–2608 (2014)
9. Ioffe, S., Szegedy, C.: Batch normalization: accelerating deep network training by reducing internal covariate shift. In: International Conference on Machine Learning, pp. 448–456 (2015)
10. Kong, Y., Ding, Z., Li, J., Fu, Y.: Deeply learned view-invariant features for cross-view action recognition. IEEE Trans. Image Process. **26**(6), 3028–3037 (2017)
11. Li, R., Zickler, T.: Discriminative virtual views for cross-view action recognition. In: 2012 IEEE Conference on Computer Vision and Pattern Recognition (CVPR), pp. 2855–2862. IEEE (2012)

12. Li, W., Xu, Z., Xu, D., Dai, D., Van Gool, L.: Domain generalization and adaptation using low rank exemplar SVMs. IEEE Trans. Pattern Anal. Mach. Intell. **40**, 1114–1127 (2017)
13. Luvizon, D.C., Picard, D., Tabia, H.: 2D/3D pose estimation and action recognition using multitask deep learning. In: The IEEE Conference on Computer Vision and Pattern Recognition (CVPR), June 2018
14. Mancini, M., Porzi, L., Rota Bul, S., Caputo, B., Ricci, E.: Boosting domain adaptation by discovering latent domains. In: The IEEE Conference on Computer Vision and Pattern Recognition (CVPR), June 2018
15. Niu, L., Li, W., Xu, D.: Multi-view domain generalization for visual recognition. In: The IEEE International Conference on Computer Vision (ICCV), December 2015
16. Niu, L., Li, W., Xu, D., Cai, J.: An exemplar-based multi-view domain generalization framework for visual recognition. IEEE Trans. Neural Netw. Learn. Syst. **29**(2), 259–272 (2016)
17. Oneata, D., Verbeek, J., Schmid, C.: Action and event recognition with fisher vectors on a compact feature set. In: Proceedings of the IEEE International Conference on Computer Vision, pp. 1817–1824 (2013)
18. Rahmani, H., Mian, A.: Learning a non-linear knowledge transfer model for cross-view action recognition. In: Proceedings of the IEEE Conference on Computer Vision and Pattern Recognition, pp. 2458–2466 (2015)
19. Rahmani, H., Mian, A., Shah, M.: Learning a deep model for human action recognition from novel viewpoints. IEEE Trans. Pattern Anal. Mach. Intell. **40**(3), 667–681 (2017)
20. Ristovski, K., Radosavljevic, V., Vucetic, S., Obradovic, Z.: Continuous conditional random fields for efficient regression in large fully connected graphs. In: AAAI, pp. 840–846 (2013)
21. Shahroudy, A., Liu, J., Ng, T.T., Wang, G.: NTU RGB+D: a large scale dataset for 3D human activity analysis. In: Proceedings of the IEEE Conference on Computer Vision and Pattern Recognition, pp. 1010–1019 (2016)
22. Shahroudy, A., Ng, T.T., Gong, Y., Wang, G.: Deep multimodal feature analysis for action recognition in RGB+D videos. IEEE Trans. Pattern Anal. Mach. Intell. **40**(5), 1045–1058 (2017)
23. Shou, Z., Wang, D., Chang, S.F.: Temporal action localization in untrimmed videos via multi-stage CNNs. In: Proceedings of the IEEE Conference on Computer Vision and Pattern Recognition, pp. 1049–1058 (2016)
24. Simonyan, K., Zisserman, A.: Two-stream convolutional networks for action recognition in videos. In: Advances in Neural Information Processing Systems, pp. 568–576 (2014)
25. Sun, L., Jia, K., Yeung, D.Y., Shi, B.E.: Human action recognition using factorized spatio-temporal convolutional networks. In: Proceedings of the IEEE International Conference on Computer Vision, pp. 4597–4605 (2015)
26. Sun, S., Kuang, Z., Sheng, L., Ouyang, W., Zhang, W.: Optical flow guided feature: a fast and robust motion representation for video action recognition. In: The IEEE Conference on Computer Vision and Pattern Recognition (CVPR), June 2018
27. Tran, D., Bourdev, L., Fergus, R., Torresani, L., Paluri, M.: Learning spatiotemporal features with 3D convolutional networks. In: Proceedings of the IEEE International Conference on Computer Vision, pp. 4489–4497 (2015)
28. Turaga, P., Veeraraghavan, A., Srivastava, A., Chellappa, R.: Statistical computations on grassmann and stiefel manifolds for image and video-based recognition. Trans. Pattern Anal. Mach. Intell. **33**(11), 2273–2286 (2011)

29. Vail, D.L., Veloso, M.M., Lafferty, J.D.: Conditional random fields for activity recognition. In: Proceedings of the 6th International Joint Conference on Autonomous Agents and Multiagent Systems, p. 235. ACM (2007)
30. Wang, H., Kläser, A., Schmid, C., Liu, C.L.: Action recognition by dense trajectories. In: 2011 IEEE Conference on Computer Vision and Pattern Recognition (CVPR), pp. 3169–3176. IEEE (2011)
31. Wang, H., Kläser, A., Schmid, C., Liu, C.L.: Dense trajectories and motion boundary descriptors for action recognition. Int. J. Comput. Vis. **103**(1), 60–79 (2013)
32. Wang, H., Schmid, C.: Action recognition with improved trajectories. In: Proceedings of the IEEE International Conference on Computer Vision, pp. 3551–3558 (2013)
33. Wang, J., Nie, X., Xia, Y., Wu, Y., Zhu, S.C.: Cross-view action modeling, learning and recognition. In: Proceedings of the IEEE Conference on Computer Vision and Pattern Recognition, pp. 2649–2656 (2014)
34. Wang, L., Qiao, Y., Tang, X.: Action recognition with trajectory-pooled deep-convolutional descriptors. In: Proceedings of the IEEE Conference on Computer Vision And Pattern Recognition, pp. 4305–4314 (2015)
35. Wang, L., et al.: Temporal Segment Networks: Towards Good Practices for Deep Action Recognition. In: Leibe, B., Matas, J., Sebe, N., Welling, M. (eds.) ECCV 2016. LNCS, vol. 9912, pp. 20–36. Springer, Cham (2016). https://doi.org/10.1007/978-3-319-46484-8_2
36. Wang, Y., Song, J., Wang, L., Van Gool, L., Hilliges, O.: Two-stream SR-CNNs for action recognition in videos. In: BMVC (2016)
37. Wu, X., Xu, D., Duan, L., Luo, J.: Action recognition using context and appearance distribution features. In: 2011 IEEE Conference on Computer Vision and Pattern Recognition (CVPR), pp. 489–496. IEEE (2011)
38. Xu, D., Ouyang, W., Alameda-Pineda, X., Ricci, E., Wang, X., Sebe, N.: Learning deep structured multi-scale features using attention-gated CRFs for contour prediction. In: Advances in Neural Information Processing Systems 30, pp. 3961–3970. Curran Associates, Inc. (2017)
39. Xu, D., Ricci, E., Ouyang, W., Wang, X., Sebe, N.: Multi-scale continuous CRFs as sequential deep networks for monocular depth estimation. In: The IEEE Conference on Computer Vision and Pattern Recognition (CVPR), July 2017
40. Yang, Y., Krompass, D., Tresp, V.: Tensor-train recurrent neural networks for video classification. In: International Conference on Machine Learning, pp. 3891–3900 (2017)
41. Zhang, Z., Wang, C., Xiao, B., Zhou, W., Liu, S., Shi, C.: Cross-view action recognition via a continuous virtual path. In: Proceedings of the IEEE Conference on Computer Vision and Pattern Recognition, pp. 2690–2697 (2013)
42. Zheng, J., Jiang, Z.: Learning view-invariant sparse representations for cross-view action recognition. In: Proceedings of the IEEE International Conference on Computer Vision, pp. 3176–3183 (2013)
43. Zheng, J., Jiang, Z., Chellappa, R.: Cross-view action recognition via transferable dictionary learning. IEEE Trans. Image Process. **25**(6), 2542–2556 (2016)
44. Zheng, S., et al.: Conditional random fields as recurrent neural networks. In: Proceedings of the IEEE International Conference on Computer Vision, pp. 1529–1537 (2015)
45. Zolfaghari, M., Oliveira, G.L., Sedaghat, N., Brox, T.: Chained multi-stream networks exploiting pose, motion, and appearance for action classification and detection. In: The IEEE International Conference on Computer Vision (ICCV), October 2017

Selective Zero-Shot Classification with Augmented Attributes

Jie Song[1], Chengchao Shen[1], Jie Lei[1], An-Xiang Zeng[2], Kairi Ou[2],
Dacheng Tao[3], and Mingli Song[1]([✉]) [iD]

[1] College of Computer Science and Technology, Zhejiang University,
Hangzhou, China
{sjie,chengchaoshen,ljaylei,brooksong}@zju.edu.cn
[2] Alibaba Group, Hangzhou, China
{renzhong,suzhe.okr}@taobao.com
[3] UBTECH Sydney AI Centre, SIT, FEIT,
University of Sydney, Camperdown, Australia
dacheng.tao@sydney.edu.au

Abstract. In this paper, we introduce a selective zero-shot classification problem: how can the classifier avoid making dubious predictions? Existing attribute-based zero-shot classification methods are shown to work poorly in the selective classification scenario. We argue the undercomplete human defined attribute vocabulary accounts for the poor performance. We propose a selective zero-shot classifier based on both the human defined and the automatically discovered residual attributes. The proposed classifier is constructed by firstly learning the defined and the residual attributes jointly. Then the predictions are conducted within the subspace of the defined attributes. Finally, the prediction confidence is measured by both the defined and the residual attributes. Experiments conducted on several benchmarks demonstrate that our classifier produces a superior performance to other methods under the risk-coverage trade-off metric.

Keywords: Zero-shot classification · Selective classification
Defined attributes · Residual attributes · Risk-coverage trade-off

1 Introduction

Zero-Shot Classification (ZSC) addresses the problem of recognizing images from novel categories, *i.e.*, those categories which are not seen during the training phase. It has attracted much attention [1–6] in the last decade due to its importance in real-world applications, where the data collection and annotation are both laboriously difficult. Existing ZSC methods usually assume that both the seen and the unseen categories share a common semantic space (*e.g.*, attributes [1,2]) where both the images and the class names can be projected. Under this assumption, the recognition of images from unseen categories can be achieved by the nearest neighbor search in the shared semantic space.

© Springer Nature Switzerland AG 2018
V. Ferrari et al. (Eds.): ECCV 2018, LNCS 11213, pp. 474–490, 2018.
https://doi.org/10.1007/978-3-030-01240-3_29

Although there is a large literature on ZSC, the prediction of existing zero-shot classifiers remains quite unreliable compared to that of the fully supervised classifiers. This limits their deployment in real-world applications, especially where mistakes may cause severe risks. For example, in autonomous driving, a wrong decision can result in traffic accidents. In clinical trials, a misdiagnosis may make the patient suffer from great pain and loss.

To reduce the risk of misclassifications, selective classification improves classification accuracy by rejecting examples that fall below a confidence threshold [7,8]. Motivated by this, in this paper we introduce a Selective Zero-Shot Classification (Selective ZSC) problem: the zero-shot classifier can abstain from predicting when it is uncertainty about its predictions. It requires that the classifier not only makes accurate predictions given images from unseen categories but also be self-aware. In other words, the classifier should be able to know when it is confident (or uncertain) about their predictions. The confidence is typically quantified by a confidence score function. Equipped with this ability, the classifier can leave the classification of images when it is uncertain about its predictions to the external domain expert (*e.g.,* drivers in autonomous driving, or doctors in clinical trials).

Selective classification is an old topic in machine learning field. However, we highlight its importance in the context of ZSC in threefold. Firstly, the predictions of zero-shot classifiers are not so accurate compared with those of fully supervised classifiers, which poses large difficulty in Selective ZSC. Secondly, it is shown in our experiments (in Sect. 6.3) that most existing zero-shot classifiers exhibit poor self-awareness. This results in their inferior performance in the settings of Selective ZSC. Lastly, albeit its great importance in real-world applications, selective classification remains under-studied in the field of ZSC.

Typically, existing ZSC methods rely on human defined attributes for novel class recognition. Attributes are a type of mid-level semantic properties of visual objects that can be shared across different object categories. Manually defined attributes are often those nameable properties such as color, shape, and texture. However, the discriminative properties for the classification task are often not exhaustively defined and sometimes hard to be described in a few words or some semantic concepts. Thus, the under-complete defined attribute vocabulary results in inferior performance of attribute-based ZSC methods. We call the residual discriminative but not defined properties *residual attributes*. To make safer predictions for zero-shot classification, we argue both the defined and the residual attributes should be exploited. These two types of attributes together are named *augmented attributes* in this paper.

We propose a much safer selective classifier for zero-shot recognition based on augmented attributes. The proposed classifier is constructed by firstly learning the augmented attributes. Motivated by [9,10], we formulate the attribute learning task as a dictionary learning problem. After the learning of the augmented attributes, the defined attributes can be directly utilized to accomplish traditional zero-shot recognitions. The confidence function thus can be defined within the subspace of defined attributes. The residual attributes, however, can not be directly exploited for classification because there are no associations between the residual attributes and the unseen categories. Instead of conducting direct predictions, we leverage the residual attributes to improve the self-awareness of the classifier constructed on defined attributes. Specifically, we define another confidence function based on the consistency between the defined and the residual attributes. Combining the confidence obtained on the augmented attributes and confidence produced within the defined attributes, the proposed selective classifier significantly outperforms other methods in extensive experiments.

To sum up, we made the following contributions: (1) we introduce the selective zero-shot classification problem, which is important yet under-studied; (2) we propose a selective zero-shot classifier, which leverages both the manually defined and the automatically discovered residual attributes for safer predictions; (3) we propose a solution to the learning of residual discriminative properties in addition to the manually defined attributes; (4) experiments demonstrate our method significantly outperforms existing state-of-the-art methods.

2 Related Work

2.1 Zero-Shot Learning

Typically, existing ZSC methods consist of two steps. The first step is an embedding process, which maps both the image representations and the class names to a shared embedding space. This step can also be viewed as a kind of multi-modality matching problem [11,12]. The second step is a recognition process, which is usually accomplished by some form of nearest neighbor searches in the shared space learned from the first step. Existing ZSC approaches mainly differ in the choices for the embedding model and the recognition model. For example, DAP [1] adopts probabilistic attribute classifiers for embedding and Bayes classifier for recognition. Devise [13], Attribute Label Embedding (ALE) [14], Simple ZSC [3] and Structured Joint Embedding (SJE) [4] adopt linear projection and inner product for embedding and recognition, respectively. However, they exploit different objective functions for optimization. Embedding Model (LatEm) [15] and Cross Model Transfer (CMT) [16] employ nonlinear projection for embedding to overcome the limitations of linear models. Different from above methods, Semantic Similarity Embedding (SSE) [17], Convex Combination of Semantic Embeddings (CONSE) [18] and Synthesized Classifiers (SYNC) [19] build the shared embedding space by expressing images and semantic class embeddings as a mixture of seen class proportions. For a more comprehensive review about ZSC, please refer to [5,20].

2.2 Defined Attributes and Latent Attributes

Attributes are usually defined as the explainable properties such as color, shape, and parts. With manually defined attributes as a shared semantic vocabulary, novel classes can be easily defined such that zero-shot recognition can be accomplished via the association between the defined attributes and the categories.

However, manually finding a discriminative and meaningful set of attributes can sometimes be difficult. The method for learning discriminative latent attributes has been exploited [9,21–24]. Tamara *et al.* [21] propose to automatically identify attributes vocabulary from text descriptions of images sampled from the Internet. Viktoriia *et al.* [22] propose to augment defined attributes with latent attributes to facilitate few-shot learning. Mohammad *et al.* [23] propose to discover attributes by trading off between predictability and discrimination. Felix *et al.* [24] propose to design attributes without concise semantic terms for visual recognition by incorporating both the category-separability and the learnability into the learning criteria. Peixi *et al.* [9] propose a dictionary learning model to decompose the dictionary space into three parts corresponding to defined, latent discriminative and latent background attributes. Different from these works, in this paper we augment the manually defined attributes with residual attributes to improve the self-awareness of zero-shot classifier.

2.3   Selective Classification

Safety issues have attracted much attention in the AI research community in the last several years. For example, Szegedy *et al.* [25] find that deep neural networks are easily fooled by adversarial examples. Following their work, many methods are proposed to construct more robust classifiers.

To reduce the risk of misclassifications, selective classification [7,8] improve classification accuracy by rejecting examples that fall below a confidence threshold. For different classifiers, the confidence scores can be defined in various ways. Most generative classification models are probabilistic, therefore they provide such confidence scores in nature. However, most discriminative models do not have direct access to the probability of their predictions [26]. Instead, related non-probabilistic scores are used as proxies, such as the margin in the SVM classifier and the softmax output or MC-Dropout [27] in deep neural networks. In this paper, we propose to exploit the residual attributes to compensate the limitations of defined attributes and make the classifier more self-aware.

3   Problem Formulation of Selective Zero-Shot Classification

We summarize some key notations used in this paper in Table 1 for reference.

Let $\mathcal{X}$ be the feature space (e.g., raw image data or feature vectors) and $\mathcal{Y}$ be a finite label set. Let $P_{\mathcal{X},\mathcal{Y}}$ be a distribution over $\mathcal{X} \times \mathcal{Y}$. In a standard multi-class zero-shot classification problem, given training data $\mathbf{X}_s = [\mathbf{x}_1, \mathbf{x}_2, ..., \mathbf{x}_{N_s}]$ and corresponding defined attribute annotations $\mathbf{D}_s = [\mathbf{d}_1, \mathbf{d}_2, ..., \mathbf{d}_{N_s}]$ and label annotations $\mathbf{y}_s = [y_1, y_2, ..., y_{N_s}]^T, y_i \in \mathcal{Y}_s$, the goal is to learn a classifier $f \colon \mathcal{X} \to \mathcal{Y}$. The classifier is usually used to recognize test data $\mathbf{X}_u = [\mathbf{x}_1^u, \mathbf{x}_2^u, ..., \mathbf{x}_{N_u}^u]$ from $\mathcal{Y}_u \subset \mathcal{Y}$ which is unseen during training, *i.e.*, $\mathcal{Y}_s \cap \mathcal{Y}_u = \emptyset$.

In the proposed Selective ZSC problem, the learner should output a selective classifier defined to be a pair (f, g), where f is a standard zero-shot classifier,

Table 1. Some key notations used in this paper. Some of them are also explained in the main text.

Notations	Definition
$\mathcal{Y}_s, \mathcal{Y}_u$	Seen label set and unseen label set
N_s, N_u	Number of seen (unseen) images, N_s (N_u) $\in \mathbb{N}^+$
K_o	Number of dimensions of the feature space, $K_o \in \mathbb{N}^+$
$\mathbf{x}_i$	An instance in the feature space, $\mathbf{x}_i \in \mathbb{R}^{K_o}$
$\mathbf{X}_s, \mathbf{X}_u$	Seen/Unseen image representations, $\mathbf{X}_s \in \mathbb{R}^{K_o \times N_s}, \mathbf{X}_u \in \mathbb{R}^{K_o \times N_u}$
$\mathbf{y}_s$	Label annotations for the training data $\mathbf{X}_s$, $\mathbf{y}_s \in \mathbb{R}^{N_s}$
K_d, K_r	Number of dimensions of the defined and the residual attribute space
$\mathbf{D}_s$	Defined attribute annotations $\mathbf{D}_s \in \mathbb{R}^{K_d \times N_s}$ for the training data $\mathbf{X}_s$
$\mathbf{D}_o$	Defined attribute annotations $\mathbf{D}_o \in \mathbb{R}^{K_d \times |\mathcal{Y}_s|}$ for the seen classes
$\mathbf{R}_o$	Residual attribute representations $\mathbf{R}_o \in \mathbb{R}^{K_r \times |\mathcal{Y}_s|}$ for the seen classes
$[\mathbf{d}_i; \mathbf{r}_i]$	Augmented attribute representation of $\mathbf{x}_i$. $\mathbf{d}_i$ is the defined attributes, and $\mathbf{r}_i$ is the residual attributes
$[\mathbf{d}^j; \mathbf{r}^j]$	Augmented attribute representation of class j
$\mathbf{s}_d, \mathbf{s}_r$	Similarity vectors from the defined/residual attributes, $\mathbf{s}_d, \mathbf{s}_r \in \mathbb{R}^{|\mathcal{Y}_s|}$

and $g : \mathcal{X} \rightarrow \{0, 1\}$ is a selection function which is usually defined as $g(\mathbf{x}) = \mathbb{1}\{conf(\mathbf{x}) > \tau\}$. $conf$ is a confidence function, τ is a confidence threshold, and $\mathbb{1}$ is an indicator function. Given a test sample $\mathbf{x}$,

$$(f, g)(\mathbf{x}) \triangleq \begin{cases} f(\mathbf{x}), & g(\mathbf{x}) = 1 \\ reject, & g(\mathbf{x}) = 0 \end{cases} \tag{1}$$

The selective zero-shot classifier abstains from prediction when $g(\mathbf{x}) = 0$. Its performance is usually evaluated by the risk-coverage curve [8,28]. More details about the evaluation metric can be found in Sect. 6.1.

4   The Proposed Selective Zero-Shot Classifier

In this section, we assume the model for augmented attributes has been learned and introduce our proposed selective classifier (f, g) based on the augmented attributes. Then in the next section, we introduce how the augmented attributes are learned.

Let $\mathcal{D}$ be the defined attribute space and $\mathcal{R}$ be the residual attribute space. For each $\mathbf{x} \in \mathcal{X}$, we can obtain its augmented attribute prediction $[\mathbf{d}; \mathbf{r}] \in \mathcal{DR}$ by the trained attribute model, where $\mathcal{DR} = \mathcal{D} \times \mathcal{R}$. In zero-shot learning, for each seen category $y_s \in \mathcal{Y}_s$, an attribute annotation $\mathbf{d}^{y_s}$ of the defined attributes is given. $\mathbf{D}_o \in \mathbb{R}^{K_d \times |\mathcal{Y}_s|}$ is the class-level attribute annotation matrix, where the i-th column vector denotes the defined attribute annotation for the i-th seen category. Since no annotations of residual attributes are provided for the

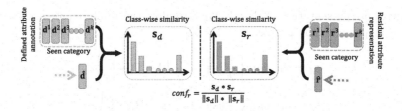

Fig. 1. The confidence defined with the aid of the residual attributes.

seen categories, we adopt the center of residual attribute predictions for each seen category as its residual attribute representation, denoted by $\mathbf{r}^{y_s}$. Let $\mathbf{R}_o \in \mathbb{R}^{K_r \times |\mathcal{Y}_s|}$ be the class-level residual attribute representation matrix. During the test phase, only the defined attributes are annotated for unseen categories ($\mathbf{d}^{y_u}$ for $y_u \in \mathcal{Y}_u$).

4.1 Zero-Shot Classifier f

The zero-shot classifier f is built on the defined attributes solely, as no annotations for residual attributes are provided. Given the defined attribute prediction $\hat{\mathbf{d}}$ of a test image, the classifier f is constructed by some form of nearest neighbor search

$$\hat{y} = \arg \max_{k \in \mathcal{Y}_u} sim(\hat{\mathbf{d}}, \mathbf{d}^k), \tag{2}$$

where sim is the similarity function. In fact, many ZSC approaches follow the above general formulation, even though they may differ in the concrete form of sim. In this paper, it is simply defined as the cosine similarity.

4.2 Confidence Function

With $sim(\cdot)$ defined within the subspace of the manually defined attributes, the prediction confidence can be defined as the similarity score:

$$conf_d = sim(\hat{\mathbf{d}}, \mathbf{d}^k). \tag{3}$$

However, as aforementioned, the defined attribute vocabulary alone is limited in its discriminative power. Thus the confidence score obtained within the defined attribute subspace is shortsighted. To tackle this issue, we propose to explore and exploit the residual attributes to overcome the shortcomings of the confidence produced by the defined attributes. Figure 1 illustrates the confidence score produced resorting to the residual attributes. Specifically, given a test image from an unseen class, we can obtain its augmented attribute presentation ($[\hat{\mathbf{d}}; \hat{\mathbf{r}}]$) by feeding the test image to the attribute prediction model. With this attribute presentation, two similarity vectors ($\mathbf{s}_d, \mathbf{s}_r$) can be computed: $\mathbf{s}_d$ for the defined attributes and $\mathbf{s}_r$ for the residual attributes. In these similarity vectors, the value of dimension k measures the similarity between the predicted attributes and attribute presentation of class k. We formulate the similarity vector learning task as a sparse coding problem:

$$\mathbf{s}_d = \arg\min_{\mathbf{s}} \left\{ \frac{\gamma}{2} \|\mathbf{s}\|^2 + \frac{1}{2} \left\| \hat{\mathbf{d}} - \mathbf{D}_o \mathbf{s} \right\|_F^2 \right\}, \tag{4}$$

$$\mathbf{s}_r = \arg\min_{\mathbf{s}} \left\{ \frac{\gamma}{2} \|\mathbf{s}\|^2 + \frac{1}{2} \|\hat{\mathbf{r}} - \mathbf{R}_o \mathbf{s}\|_F^2 \right\}. \tag{5}$$

Then the confidence score can then be defined as the consistency of these two vectors:

$$conf_r = sim(\mathbf{s}_d, \mathbf{s}_r). \tag{6}$$

The above confidence function is built on the intuition that the more consistent the defined and the residual attributes are, the less additional discriminative information the residual attributes provide for the current test image. Therefore, classification based on the defined attributes solely approximates classification based on the whole augmented attributes. Imagine that the residual attributes produce the same similarity vector as the defined attributes, then the residual attributes completely agree with the defined attribute on the prediction they made. However, if the residual attributes produce absolutely different similarity vector, then they do not reach a consensus. The defined attributes are short-sighted in this case and the produced prediction is more unreliable.

Combining the confidence function defined within the defined attribute subspace and that defined with the aid of residual attributes, the final confidence is

$$conf = (1 - \lambda)conf_d + \lambda conf_r, \tag{7}$$

where λ is a trade-off hyper-parameter which is set via cross-validation.

5   Augmented Attribute Learning

In this section, we introduce how the augmented attributes are learned. We formulate the augmented attribute learning task as a dictionary learning problem. The dictionary space is decomposed into two parts: (1) $\mathbf{Q}_d$ corresponding to the defined-attribute-correlated dictionary subspace part which is correlated to the defined attribute annotations and the class annotations, (2) $\mathbf{Q}_r$ corresponding to the residual attribute dictionary subspace which is correlated to the class annotations and thus also useful for the classification task. To learn the whole dictionary space, three criteria are incorporated: (1) the defined attributes alone should be able to accomplish the classification task as better as possible; (2) the residual attributes should complement the discriminative power of defined attributes for classification; (3) the residual attributes should not rediscover the patterns that exist in the defined attributes. With all the three criteria, the objective function is formulated as:

$$\arg \min_{\{\mathbf{Q}_d, \mathbf{L}, \mathbf{Q}_l, \mathbf{U}, \mathbf{Q}_r, \mathbf{R}_s, \mathbf{V}\}}$$

$$\|\mathbf{X}_s - \mathbf{Q}_d\mathbf{L}\|_F^2 + \alpha\|\mathbf{L} - \mathbf{Q}_l\mathbf{D}_s\|_F^2 + \beta\|\mathbf{H} - \mathbf{U}\mathbf{L}\|_F^2$$

$$+ \|\mathbf{X}_s - \mathbf{Q}_d\mathbf{L} - \mathbf{Q}_r\mathbf{R}_s\|_F^2 + \delta\|\mathbf{H} - \mathbf{U}\mathbf{L} - \mathbf{V}\mathbf{R}_s\|_F^2$$

$$- \eta\|\mathbf{R}_s - \mathbf{W}\mathbf{L}\|_F^2,$$

$$s.t. \ \mathbf{W} = \arg \min_{\mathbf{W}} \|\mathbf{R}_s - \mathbf{W}\mathbf{L}\|_2^2, \ \|\mathbf{w}_i\|_2^2 \le 1, \ \|\mathbf{q}_{di}\|_2^2 \le 1,$$

$$\|\mathbf{q}_{ri}\|_2^2 \le 1, \|\mathbf{q}_{li}\|_2^2 \le 1, \ \|\mathbf{u}_i\|_2^2 \le 1, \ \|\mathbf{v}_i\|_2^2 \le 1, \ \forall i.$$

(8)

In the above formulation, the second, the third, and the fourth lines are corresponding to the first, the second, and the third criteria, respectively. As the proposed classifier f makes predictions based on only the defined attributes, the first criterion protects f from being distracted from its classification task. However, defined attributes are usually not equally valuable for classification and some of them are highly correlated. Instead of adopting the defined attributes directly, we employ discriminative latent attributes proposed in [10] for zero-shot classification. $\mathbf{L}$ is latent attributes which are derived from the defined attributes and $\mathbf{H} = [\mathbf{h}_1, \mathbf{h}_2, ...]$ where $\mathbf{h}_i = [0, ..., 0, 1, 0, ..., 0]^T$ is a one hot vector which gives the label of sample i. Thus $\mathbf{U}$ can be regarded as the seen-class classifier in the latent attribute space. For the second criterion, we assume the learned residual attributes suffer little of the above problem and adopt them and the discriminative latent attributes jointly for the classification task. For the third criterion, as we expect the residual attributes discover non-redundant properties, the defined attributes should not be predictive for the residual attributes. $\mathbf{w}_i$ is the i-th column of $\mathbf{W}$.

Optimizing the three criteria simultaneously is challenging as there are several hyper-parameters which are set via cross-validation. Furthermore, it may degrade the performance of f, as f makes predictions based on the defined attributes solely. We divide the optimization problem in Eq. 8 into two subproblems which are optimized separately. In the first subproblem, only the first criterion is considered and we optimize $\mathbf{Q}_d, \mathbf{L}, \mathbf{Q}_l$ and $\mathbf{U}$ to strive for f with higher performance. In the second subproblem, $\mathbf{Q}_d, \mathbf{L}, \mathbf{Q}_l$ and $\mathbf{U}$ are fixed and we optimize $\mathbf{Q}_r, \mathbf{R}_s$ and $\mathbf{V}$ with taking the second and the third criteria into consideration. With our proposed optimization procedure, the cross validation work for hyper-parameters $\{\alpha, \beta, \delta, \eta\}$ is significantly reduced as $\{\alpha, \beta\}$ and $\{\delta, \eta\}$ are cross validated separately.

The First Subproblem. Taking only the first criterion into consideration, Eq. 8 is simplified to be

$$\arg \min_{\{\mathbf{Q}_d, \mathbf{L}, \mathbf{Q}_l, \mathbf{U}\}} \|\mathbf{X}_s - \mathbf{Q}_d\mathbf{L}\|_F^2 + \alpha\|\mathbf{L} - \mathbf{Q}_l\mathbf{D}_s\|_F^2 + \beta\|\mathbf{H} - \mathbf{U}\mathbf{L}\|_F^2,$$

$$s.t. \ \|\mathbf{q}_{di}\|_2^2 \le 1, \|\mathbf{q}_{li}\|_2^2 \le 1, \ \|\mathbf{u}_i\|_2^2 \le 1, \ \forall i.$$

(9)

This is the problem proposed in [10]. Equation 9 is not convex for $\mathbf{Q}_d, \mathbf{L}, \mathbf{Q}_l$ and $\mathbf{U}$ simultaneously, but it is convex for each of them separately. An alternating optimization method is adopted to solve it. Detailed optimization process can be found in [10].

The Second Subproblem. After solving the first subproblem, $\mathbf{Q}_d, \mathbf{L}, \mathbf{Q}_l$ and $\mathbf{U}$ are fixed and Eq. 8 is simplified to be

$$\arg\min_{\{\mathbf{Q}_r, \mathbf{R}_s, \mathbf{V}\}} \|\mathbf{X}_s - \mathbf{Q}_d\mathbf{L} - \mathbf{Q}_r\mathbf{R}_s\|_F^2 + \delta\|\mathbf{H} - \mathbf{U}\mathbf{L} - \mathbf{V}\mathbf{R}_s\|_F^2 - \eta\|\mathbf{R}_s - \mathbf{W}\mathbf{L}\|_F^2,$$

$$s.t. \ \mathbf{W} = \arg\min_{\mathbf{W}} \|\mathbf{R}_s - \mathbf{W}\mathbf{L}\|_2^2, \ \|\mathbf{w}_i\|_2^2 \le 1, \|\mathbf{q}_{ri}\|_2^2 \le 1, \ \|\mathbf{v}_i\|_2^2 \le 1, \ \forall i.$$
(10)

Similarly, $\mathbf{Q}_r, \mathbf{R}_s$ and $\mathbf{V}$ are optimized by the alternate optimization method. The optimization process is briefly described as follows.

(1) Fix $\mathbf{Q}_r, \mathbf{V}$ and update $\mathbf{R}_s$:

$$\arg\min_{\mathbf{R}_s} \left\|\tilde{\mathbf{X}} - \tilde{\mathbf{Q}}\mathbf{R}_s\right\|_F^2,$$
(11)

where

$$\tilde{\mathbf{X}} = \begin{bmatrix} \mathbf{X}_s - \mathbf{Q}_d\mathbf{L} \\ \delta(\mathbf{H} - \mathbf{U}\mathbf{L}) \\ -\eta(\mathbf{W}\mathbf{L}) \end{bmatrix}, \ \tilde{\mathbf{Q}} = \begin{bmatrix} \mathbf{Q}_r \\ \delta\mathbf{V} \\ -\eta\mathbf{I} \end{bmatrix},$$

and $\mathbf{I}$ is the identity matrix. $\mathbf{R}_s$ has the closed-form solution as

$$\mathbf{R}_s = (\tilde{\mathbf{Q}}^T\tilde{\mathbf{Q}})^{-1}\tilde{\mathbf{Q}}^T\tilde{\mathbf{X}}.$$
(12)

(2) Fix $\mathbf{R}_s, \mathbf{V}$ and update $\mathbf{Q}_r$:

$$\arg\min_{\mathbf{Q}_r} \|\mathbf{X}_s - \mathbf{Q}_d\mathbf{L} - \mathbf{Q}_r\mathbf{R}_s\|_F^2, \ s.t. \ \|\mathbf{q}_{ri}\|_2^2 \le 1, \ \forall i.$$
(13)

The above problem can be solved by the Lagrange dual and the analytical solution is

$$\mathbf{Q}_r = (\mathbf{X}_s - \mathbf{Q}_d\mathbf{L})\mathbf{R}_s^T(\mathbf{R}_s\mathbf{R}_s^T + \mathbf{\Lambda})^{-1},$$
(14)

where $\mathbf{\Lambda}$ is a diagonal matrix constructed by all the Lagrange dual variables.

(3) Fix $\mathbf{R}_s, \mathbf{Q}_r$ and update $\mathbf{V}$:

$$\arg\min_{\mathbf{V}} \|\mathbf{H} - \mathbf{U}\mathbf{L} - \mathbf{V}\mathbf{R}_s\|_F^2, \ s.t. \ \|\mathbf{v}_i\|_2^2 \le 1, \ \forall i.$$
(15)

The above problem can be solved in the same way as Eq. 13 and the solution is

$$\mathbf{V} = (\mathbf{H} - \mathbf{U}\mathbf{L})\mathbf{R}_s^T(\mathbf{R}_s\mathbf{R}_s^T + \mathbf{\Lambda})^{-1}.$$
(16)

(4) Computing $\mathbf{W}$:

$$\arg\min_{\mathbf{W}} \|\mathbf{R}_s - \mathbf{W}\mathbf{L}\|_F^2, \ s.t. \ \|\mathbf{w}_i\|_2^2 \le 1, \ \forall i.$$
(17)

Similar to Eqs. 14 and 16, we can get the solution

$$\mathbf{W} = \mathbf{R}_s\mathbf{L}^T(\mathbf{L}\mathbf{L}^T + \mathbf{\Lambda})^{-1}.$$
(18)

The complete algorithm is summarized in Algorithm 1. The optimization process usually converges quickly, after tens of iterations in our experiments.

Algorithm 1. Augmented Attribute Learning for Selective ZSC

Input: $\mathbf{X}_s, \mathbf{D}_s, \mathbf{H}, \alpha, \beta, \delta, \eta, K_r$

Output: $\mathbf{Q}_d, \mathbf{L}, \mathbf{Q}_l, \mathbf{U}, \mathbf{Q}_r, \mathbf{R}_s, \mathbf{V}$

1: Optimizing the first subproblem according to [10], obtaining $\mathbf{Q}_d, \mathbf{L}, \mathbf{Q}_l, \mathbf{U}$.
2: Fixing $\mathbf{Q}_d, \mathbf{L}, \mathbf{Q}_l, \mathbf{U}$ obtained from 1, and initializing $\mathbf{Q}_r, \mathbf{V}, \mathbf{W}$ randomly according to K_r.
3: **while** not converge **do**
4:     Optimizing $\mathbf{R}_s$ according to Eq. 12.
5:     Optimizing $\mathbf{Q}_r$ according to Eq. 14.
6:     Optimizing $\mathbf{V}$ according to Eq. 16.
7:     Optimizing $\mathbf{W}$ according to Eq. 18.
8: **return** $\mathbf{Q}_d, \mathbf{L}, \mathbf{Q}_l, \mathbf{U}, \mathbf{Q}_r, \mathbf{R}_s, \mathbf{V}$

6 Experiments

6.1 Datasets and Settings

Datasets. We conduct experiments on three benchmark image datasets for ZSC, including aPascal&aYahoo (**aP&Y**) [29], Animals with Attributes (**AwA**) [1] and Caltech-UCSD Birds-200-2011 (**CUB-200**) [30]. For all the datasets, we split the categories into seen and unseen sets in the same way as [10]: (1) There are two attribute datasets in **aP&Y**: aPascal and aYahoo. These two datasets contains images from disjoint object classes. The categories in aPascal dataset are used as seen classes and those in aYahoo as the unseen ones. (2) **AwA** contains 50 categories, 40 of which are used as seen categories, and the rest 10 are used as the unseen ones. (3) **CUB-200** is a bird dataset for fine-grained recognition. It contains 200 categories, of which 150 are used as seen categories and the rest 50 as the unseen ones. For all the datasets, we adopt the pre-trained VGG19 [31] to extract features.

Cross Validation. There are several hyper-parameters (including γ, $K_r, \alpha, \beta, \delta, \eta$) which are set via cross-validation. As aforementioned, our proposed optimization procedure relaxes the laborious cross-validation work by decomposing the original problem into two subproblems. α, β are firstly optimized on the validation data independent of the others. After that, to further relax the cross-validation work, we optimize δ, η, K_r independent of γ. Finally, γ is optimized. In this paper, we adopt five-fold cross-validation [17] for all these parameters.

Evaluation Metrics. The performance of the classifier is quantified using *coverage* and *risk*. The coverage is defined to be the probability mass of the non-rejected region in $\mathcal{X}_u$ (the feature space of unseen classes)

$$coverage(f, g) \triangleq E_p[g(\mathbf{x})], \tag{19}$$

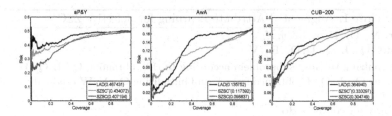

Fig. 2. Comparisons among different variants of the proposed method (best viewed in color). AURCC is given in brackets.

and the selective risk of (f, g) is

$$risk(f, g) \triangleq \frac{E_p[\ell(f(\mathbf{x}), y)g(\mathbf{x})]}{coverage(f, g)}, \tag{20}$$

where ℓ is defined to be $0/1$ loss. The risk can be traded off for coverage. Thus the overall performance of a selective classifier can be measured by its Risk-Coverage Curve (RCC), where risk is defined to be a function of the coverage [8, 28]. The Area Under Risk-Coverage Curve (AURCC) is usually adopted to quantify the performance.

6.2   Ablation Study

The Effectiveness of Three Criteria. We have incorporated three criteria into the learning of augmented attributes. In this section, we validate the effectiveness of them. We make comparisons among three variants of the proposed method. For the first one, only the first criterion is considered. In other words, no residual attributes are learned, and the classification model degrades to LAD [10] ($conf = conf_d$). For the second one (dubbed SZSC$^-$), the first and the second criteria are considered. For the third one (dubbed SZSC), all the three criteria are incorporated. For all the three variants, the dimensions of the residual attributes are kept the same as that of the defined attributes ($K_r = K_d$). Other hyper-parameters are set via cross-validation. The risk-coverage curves on all the three benchmark datasets are depicted in Fig. 2. It can be seen that on all the three datasets, the proposed method achieves the best performance when all the three criteria are involved.

Trade-Off Between Two Confidence Scores. The proposed confidence function is composed of two parts: the confidence defined within the defined attributes ($conf_d$) and the confidence defined with the aid of the residual attributes ($conf_r$). In this section, we test how the trade-off parameter λ affects the performance of SZSC. If $\lambda = 0$, the confidence depends entirely on the defined attributes. On the contrary, if $\lambda = 1$, the confidence is composed of $conf_r$ only. All other hyper-parameters are kept the same for fair comparisons.

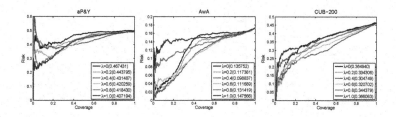

Fig. 3. Risk-coverage curves of the proposed method with varying λ.

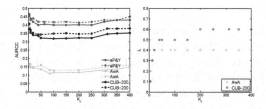

Fig. 4. How AURCC (left) and the optimal λ (right) change with varying K_r.

Experimental results on all the three benchmark datasets are shown in Fig. 3. It reveals that the appropriately combined confidence significantly improve the classifier's performance on all the three datasets. More surprisingly, on aP&Y the optimally combined confidence relies heavily on $conf_r$ ($\lambda = 1.0$). The undercomplete defined attribute vocabulary and the large difference between the seen and the unseen categories may account for that.

Dimensions of the Residual Attribute Space. In this section, we investigate how the performance changes with the varying K_r. Similarly, all other hyper-parameters are kept the same. For a more comprehensive view of the proposed method, both SZSC$^-$ and SZSC are evaluated. Experimental results are shown in Fig. 4 (left). It can be observed that the number of dimensions of the residual attribute space also makes unneglected impacts on the final performance. Too small K_r (< 50) will leave the residual discriminative properties not fully explored. Conversely, too large K_r (> 300) renders the optimization more challenging and time-consuming. Both these two cases degrade the performance. Furthermore, we test that how the cross-validated λ changes with K_r. Results are depicted in Fig. 4 (right). It can be seen that with small K_r, the confidence obtained via the residual attributes is unreliable and the optimally combined confidence relies heavily (small λ) on the $conf_d$. However, as K_r becomes larger, λ also becomes larger which indicates that $conf_r$ plays a more important role.

6.3 Benchmark Comparison

Competitors. Several existing ZSC models are selected for benchmark comparison, including SSE [17], SYNC [19], SCoRe [32], SAE [33] and LAD [10].

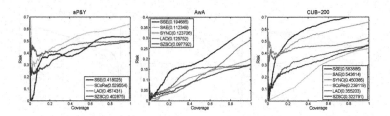

Fig. 5. Risk-coverage curves of existing methods and SZSC.

The selection criteria are (1) representativeness: they cover a wide range of models; (2) competitiveness: they clearly represent the state-of-the-art; (3) recent work: all of them are published in the past three years; (4) reproducibility: all of them are code available, so the provided results in this paper are reproducible. We briefly review them and introduce their typical confidence functions as follows. SSE adopts SVM as the classification model. The margin in SVM classifier is employed as the confidence. SCoRe utilizes deep neural networks integrated with a softmax classifier for ZSC. The softmax output is usually employed for misclassification or out-of-distribution example dection [34]. We also use it as the proxy of the confidence for SCoRe. For the other competitors, the classification task is usually accomplished via nearest neighbor searches in the shared embedding space. We take the cosine similarity as the confidence.

For fair comparisons, both the proposed method and the competitors are tested with features extracted by VGG19. Experimental results are provided in Fig. 5. From the figure, we can conclude that: (1) Many existing ZSC methods exhibit poor performance in Selective ZSC settings. With lower coverage, these classifiers are expected to yield higher accuracy (i.e., lower risk). However, many methods violate that regularity in many cases, especially on aP&Y and CUB. These experimental results give us a more comprehensive view of existing ZSC methods. (2) The proposed method outperforms most existing methods significantly on all the three benchmark datasets. One exception is that SCoRe which utilizes deep neural networks behaves better on CUB-200. However, it produces a much worse performance on aP&Y, as there is a large imbalance among the number of images in different categories (51–5071). (3) Although bringing some improvement, the proposed method remains far behind the ideal. It indicates that there still exists large space for further study.

Augmenting the Self-awareness of Existing Methods. The proposed method focuses on augmenting the defined attributes with residual properties to improve zero-shot performance in selective classification settings. It is orthogonal to how to exploit the defined attributes for ZSC. Thus the proposed method can be combined with most existing attribute-based methods to improve their performance in Selective ZSC settings. Here we propose a simple combining strategy: the confidence functions of existing ZSC methods are directly combined with the proposed confidence function defined with the aid of residual attributes.

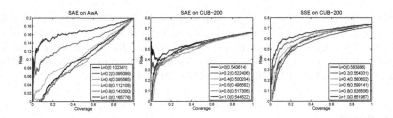

Fig. 6. Combining SZSC with SAE and SSE.

In other words, $conf_r$ is agnostic about the classification model which is used for recognition, and $conf_d$ in Eq. 7 is replaced with the confidence of existing ZSC methods. Experiments are conducted with SAE on AwA and CUB-200 and SSE on CUB-200. Results are shown in Fig. 6. We can see that with the simple proposed combining strategy, the performance of SAE and SSE can be further improved to some degree. These compelling results suggest that the confidence defined by the consistency between the defined and the residual attributes has some generalization ability across ZSC models. We believe learning the residual attributes adaptively with the specified ZSC model (*e.g.*, SCoRe) will further improve the performance, which is left for future research.

7 Conclusions and Future Work

In this paper, we introduce an important yet under-studied problem: zero-shot classifiers can abstain from prediction when in doubt. We empirically demonstrate that existing zero-shot classifiers behave poorly in this new settings, and propose a novel selective classifier to make safer predictions. The proposed classifier explores and exploits the residual properties beyond the defined attributes for defining confidence functions. Experiments show that the proposed classifier achieves significantly superior performance in selective classification settings. Furthermore, it is also shown that the proposed confidence can also augment existing ZSC methods for safer classification.

There are several research lines which are worthy of further study following our work. For example, we propose to learn residual attributes to improve the performance of attribute-based classifiers. Similar ideas may also work for zero-shot classifiers built on word vectors or text descriptions. Another example is that in this paper we propose a straightforward combing strategy to improve the performance of existing methods. We believe learning the residual attributes adaptively with the ZSC model can further improve the final performance. Finally, considering the importance of the proposed selective zero-shot classification problem, we encourage researchers to pay more attention to this new challenge.

Acknowledgements. This work is supported by National Key Research and Development Program (2016YFB1200203), National Natural Science Foundation of China (61572428, U1509206), Fundamental Research Funds for the Central Universities (2017FZA5014) and Key Research, Development Program of Zhejiang Province (2018C01004) and ARC FL-170100117, DP-180103424 of Australia.

References

1. Lampert, C.H., Nickisch, H., Harmeling, S.: Learning to detect unseen object classes by between-class attribute transfer. In: 2009 IEEE Conference on Computer Vision and Pattern Recognition, CVPR 2009, pp. 951–958. IEEE (2009)
2. Akata, Z., Perronnin, F., Harchaoui, Z., Schmid, C.: Label-embedding for attribute-based classification. In: Proceedings of the IEEE Conference on Computer Vision and Pattern Recognition, pp. 819–826 (2013)
3. Romera-Paredes, B., Torr, P.: An embarrassingly simple approach to zero-shot learning. In: International Conference on Machine Learning, pp. 2152–2161 (2015)
4. Akata, Z., Reed, S., Walter, D., Lee, H., Schiele, B.: Evaluation of output embeddings for fine-grained image classification. In: Proceedings of the IEEE Conference on Computer Vision and Pattern Recognition, pp. 2927–2936 (2015)
5. Xian, Y., Schiele, B., Akata, Z.: Zero-shot learning - the good, the bad and the ugly. In: The IEEE Conference on Computer Vision and Pattern Recognition (CVPR), July 2017
6. Song, J., Shen, C., Yang, Y., Liu, Y., Song, M.: Transductive unbiased embedding for zero-shot learning. In: The IEEE Conference on Computer Vision and Pattern Recognition (CVPR), June 2018
7. Chow, C.K.: An optimum character recognition system using decision functions. IRE Trans. Electron. Comput. EC **6**(4), 247–254 (1957)
8. El-Yaniv, R., Wiener, Y.: On the foundations of noise-free selective classification. J. Mach. Learn. Res. **11**, 1605–1641 (2010)
9. Peng, P., Tian, Y., Xiang, T., Wang, Y., Huang, T.: Joint learning of semantic and latent attributes. In: Leibe, B., Matas, J., Sebe, N., Welling, M. (eds.) ECCV 2016. LNCS, vol. 9908, pp. 336–353. Springer, Cham (2016). https://doi.org/10.1007/978-3-319-46493-0_21
10. Jiang, H., Wang, R., Shan, S., Yang, Y., Chen, X.: Learning discriminative latent attributes for zero-shot classification. In: The IEEE International Conference on Computer Vision (ICCV), October 2017
11. Kan, M., Shan, S., Chen, X.: Multi-view deep network for cross-view classification. In: The IEEE Conference on Computer Vision and Pattern Recognition (CVPR), June 2016
12. Fu, Y., Hospedales, T.M., Xiang, T., Fu, Z., Gong, S.: Transductive multi-view embedding for zero-shot recognition and annotation. In: Fleet, D., Pajdla, T., Schiele, B., Tuytelaars, T. (eds.) ECCV 2014. LNCS, vol. 8690, pp. 584–599. Springer, Cham (2014). https://doi.org/10.1007/978-3-319-10605-2_38
13. Frome, A., Corrado, G.S., Shlens, J., Bengio, S., Dean, J., Mikolov, T., et al.: Devise: a deep visual-semantic embedding model. In: Advances in neural information processing systems, pp. 2121–2129 (2013)
14. Akata, Z., Perronnin, F., Harchaoui, Z., Schmid, C.: Label-embedding for image classification. IEEE Trans. Pattern Anal. Mach. Intell. **38**(7), 1425–1438 (2016)

15. Xian, Y., Akata, Z., Sharma, G., Nguyen, Q., Hein, M., Schiele, B.: Latent embeddings for zero-shot classification. In: The IEEE Conference on Computer Vision and Pattern Recognition (CVPR), June 2016
16. Socher, R., Ganjoo, M., Manning, C.D., Ng, A.: Zero-shot learning through cross-modal transfer. In: Advances in Neural Information Processing Systems, pp. 935–943 (2013)
17. Zhang, Z., Saligrama, V.: Zero-shot learning via semantic similarity embedding. In: Proceedings of the IEEE International Conference on Computer Vision, pp. 4166–4174 (2015)
18. Norouzi, M., et al.: Zero-shot learning by convex combination of semantic embeddings. In: Proceedings of ICLR. Citeseer (2014)
19. Changpinyo, S., Chao, W.L., Gong, B., Sha, F.: Synthesized classifiers for zero-shot learning. In: Proceedings of the IEEE Conference on Computer Vision and Pattern Recognition, pp. 5327–5336 (2016)
20. Fu, Y., Xiang, T., Jiang, Y.G., Xue, X., Sigal, L., Gong, S.: Recent advances in zero-shot recognition: toward data-efficient understanding of visual content. IEEE Signal Process. Mag. 35(1), 112–125 (2018)
21. Berg, T.L., Berg, A.C., Shih, J.: Automatic attribute discovery and characterization from noisy web data. In: Daniilidis, K., Maragos, P., Paragios, N. (eds.) ECCV 2010. LNCS, vol. 6311, pp. 663–676. Springer, Heidelberg (2010). https://doi.org/10.1007/978-3-642-15549-9_48
22. Sharmanska, V., Quadrianto, N., Lampert, C.H.: Augmented attribute representations. In: Fitzgibbon, A., Lazebnik, S., Perona, P., Sato, Y., Schmid, C. (eds.) ECCV 2012. LNCS, vol. 7576, pp. 242–255. Springer, Heidelberg (2012). https://doi.org/10.1007/978-3-642-33715-4_18
23. Rastegari, M., Farhadi, A., Forsyth, D.: Attribute discovery via predictable discriminative binary codes. In: Fitzgibbon, A., Lazebnik, S., Perona, P., Sato, Y., Schmid, C. (eds.) ECCV 2012. LNCS, vol. 7577, pp. 876–889. Springer, Heidelberg (2012). https://doi.org/10.1007/978-3-642-33783-3_63
24. Yu, F.X., Cao, L., Feris, R.S., Smith, J.R., Chang, S.F.: Designing category-level attributes for discriminative visual recognition. In: 2013 IEEE Conference on Computer Vision and Pattern Recognition, June 2013
25. Szegedy, C., et al.: Intriguing properties of neural networks. In: International Conference on Learning Representations (2014)
26. Mandelbaum, A., Weinshall, D.: Distance-based confidence score for neural network classifiers. CoRR abs/1709.09844 (2017)
27. Gal, Y., Ghahramani, Z.: Dropout as a Bayesian approximation: representing model uncertainty in deep learning. In: Proceedings of the 33rd International Conference on Machine Learning (ICML2016) (2016)
28. Geifman, Y., El-Yaniv, R.: Selective classification for deep neural networks. In: Guyon, I., et al. (eds.) Advances in Neural Information Processing Systems 30, pp. 4885–4894. Curran Associates, Inc. (2017)
29. Farhadi, A., Endres, I., Hoiem, D., Forsyth, D.: Describing objects by their attributes. In: 2009 IEEE Conference on Computer Vision and Pattern Recognition, CVPR 2009, pp. 1778–1785. IEEE (2009)
30. Welinder, P., et al.: Caltech-UCSD Birds 200. Technical report CNS-TR-2010-001, California Institute of Technology (2010)
31. Simonyan, K., Zisserman, A.: Very deep convolutional networks for large-scale image recognition. arXiv preprint arXiv:1409.1556 (2014)

32. Morgado, P., Vasconcelos, N.: Semantically consistent regularization for zero-shot recognition. In: The IEEE Conference on Computer Vision and Pattern Recognition (CVPR), July 2017
33. Kodirov, E., Xiang, T., Gong, S.: Semantic autoencoder for zero-shot learning. In: The IEEE Conference on Computer Vision and Pattern Recognition (CVPR), July 2017
34. Hendrycks, D., Gimpel, K.: A baseline for detecting misclassified and out-of-distribution examples in neural networks. arXiv preprint arXiv:1610.02136 (2016)

Modeling Varying Camera-IMU Time Offset in Optimization-Based Visual-Inertial Odometry

Yonggen Ling[(✉)], Linchao Bao, Zequn Jie, Fengming Zhu, Ziyang Li, Shanmin Tang, Yongsheng Liu, Wei Liu, and Tong Zhang

Tencent AI Lab, Shenzhen, China
ylingaa@connect.ust.hk, linchaobao@gmail.com, zequn.nus@gmail.com,
fridazhu@gmail.com, {tzeyangli,mickeytang,kakarliu}@tencent.com,
wl2223@columbia.edu, tongzhang@tongzhang-ml.org

Abstract. Combining cameras and inertial measurement units (IMUs) has been proven effective in motion tracking, as these two sensing modalities offer complementary characteristics that are suitable for fusion. While most works focus on global-shutter cameras and synchronized sensor measurements, consumer-grade devices are mostly equipped with rolling-shutter cameras and suffer from imperfect sensor synchronization. In this work, we propose a nonlinear optimization-based monocular visual inertial odometry (VIO) with varying camera-IMU time offset modeled as an unknown variable. Our approach is able to handle the rolling-shutter effects and imperfect sensor synchronization in a unified way. Additionally, we introduce an efficient algorithm based on dynamic programming and red-black tree to speed up IMU integration over variable-length time intervals during the optimization. An uncertainty-aware initialization is also presented to launch the VIO robustly. Comparisons with state-of-the-art methods on the Euroc dataset and mobile phone data are shown to validate the effectiveness of our approach.

Keywords: Visual-inertial odometry
Online temporal camera-IMU calibration
Rolling shutter cameras

1 Introduction

Online, robust, and accurate localization is the foremost important component for many applications, such as autonomous navigation of mobile robots, online augmented reality, and real-time localization-based service. A monocular VIO that consists of one IMU and one camera is particularly suitable for this task as these two sensors are cheap, ubiquitous, and complementary. However, a VIO works only if both visual and inertial measurements are aligned spatially and temporally. This requires that both sensor measurements are synchronized and sensor extrinsics between sensors are known. While online sensor extrinsic

© Springer Nature Switzerland AG 2018
V. Ferrari et al. (Eds.): ECCV 2018, LNCS 11213, pp. 491–507, 2018.
https://doi.org/10.1007/978-3-030-01240-3_30

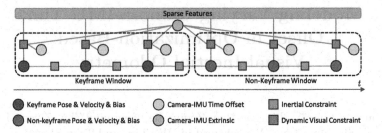

Fig. 1. The graph representation of our model. All variables (circles) and constraints (squares) in both the keyframe window and non-keyframe window are involved in the optimization. Note that modeling the camera-IMU time offset for each frame raises computational difficulties during the optimization, since the computation of visual constraints depends on the estimated time offset. In other words, the visual constraints in our model are "dynamic" due to the varying camera-IMU time offset. (Color figure online)

calibration has gained lots of discussions in recent works, VIO with inperfect synchronization is less explored. Historically, some works [12,14] calibrate the sensor time offsets offline, and assume that these parameters are not changed in next runs. In real cases, time offsets change over time due to the variation of the system processing payload and sensor jitter. Other works [10,18,21] calibrate sensor time offsets online in an extended Kalman filter (EKF) framework. However, these methods suffer from the inherent drawbacks of filtering based approaches. They require a good prior about the initial system state (such as poses, velocities, biases, the camera-IMU extrinsic/time offsets) such that the estimation at each update step converges close to the global minimum. In contrast to filtering based approaches, nonlinear optimization-based methods [4,13,17,40] iteratively re-linearize all nonlinear error costs from visual and inertial constraints to better treat the underlying nonlinearity, leading to increased tracking robustness and accuracy. However, introducing time offsets in a nonlinear optimization framework is non-trivial since the visual constraints are varying as they depend on the estimated time offsets that are varied between iterations. Another critical problem of VIO is the use of rolling-shutter cameras. Unlike global-shutter cameras that capture all rows of pixels at one time instant, rolling-shutter cameras capture each row of pixels at a different time instant. The rolling-shutter effect on captured images causes a significant geometry distortion if the system movement is fast. Without taking the rolling-shutter effect into account, the estimation performance degrades rapidly. Unfortunately, most consumer-grade cameras (such as cameras on mobile phones) are rolling-shutter cameras. If we optimize camera poses at every readout time of rolling-shutter cameras, the computational complexity will be intractable.

To the best of our knowledge, we are the first to propose a nonlinear optimization-based VIO to overcome the difficulties mentioned above. The graph representation of our model is shown in Fig. 1. Different from prior VIO algorithms based on nonlinear optimization, we incorporate an unknown, dynamically changing time offset for each camera image (shown as yellow circle in Fig. 1).

The time offset is jointly optimized together with other variables like poses, velocities, biases, and camera-IMU extrinsics. We show that by modeling the time offset as a time-varying variable, imperfect camera-IMU synchronization and rolling-shutter effects can be handled in a unified formulation (Sects. 4.1 and 4.2). We derive the Jacobians involved in the optimization after introducing the new variable (Sect. 4.3), and show that the varying time offset brings computational challenges of pose computation over variable-length time intervals. An efficient algorithm based on dynamic programming and red-black tree is proposed to ease these difficulties (Sect. 4.4). Finally, since the nonlinear optimization is based on linearization, an initial guess is required for optimization bootstrap. A poor initialization may lead to a decrease of VIO robustness and accuracy. To improve the robustness of the system bootstrap, we present an initialization scheme, which takes the uncertainty of sensor measurements into account and better models the underlying sensor noises. Main contributions of this paper are as follows:

- We propose a nonlinear optimization-based VIO with varying camera-IMU time offset modeled as an unknown variable, to deal with the rolling-shutter effects and online temporal camera-IMU calibration in a unified framework.
- We design an efficient algorithm based on dynamic programming and red-black tree to speed up the IMU integration over variable-length time intervals, which is needed during optimization.
- We introduce an uncertainty-aware initialization scheme to improve the robustness of the VIO bootstrap.

Qualitative and quantitative results on the Euroc dataset with simulated camera-IMU time offsets and real-world mobile phone data are shown to demonstrate the effectiveness of the proposed method.

2   Related Work

The idea of VIO goes back at least to the work [35] proposed by Roumeliotis *et al.* based on filtering and the work [13] proposed by Jung and Taylor based on nonlinear optimization. Subsequently, lots of work have been published based on an exemplar implementation of filtering based approaches, called EKF [11,19,27,33]. EKFs predict latest motions using IMU measurements and perform updates according to the reprojection errors from visual measurements. To bound the algorithmic complexity, many works follow a loosely coupled fashion [23–26,33,38]. Relative poses are firstly estimated by IMU propagations as well as vision-only structure from motion algorithms separately. They are then fused together for motion tracking. Alternatively, approaches in a tightly coupled fashion optimize for estimator states using raw measurements from IMUs and cameras [19,27]. They take the relations among internal states of different sensors into account, thus achieving higher estimation accuracy than loosely coupled methods at the cost of a higher computational complexity. Additionally, to benefit from increased accuracy offered by relinearization, nonlinear optimization-based methods iteratively minimize errors from both inertial measurements and visual measurements [4,17,40]. The main drawback of nonlinear optimization-based methods is their high computational complexity due to repeated linearizations, which can be lessened by limiting the variables to optimize and utilizing structural sparsity of the visual-inertial problem [17].

Recent approaches on VIOs consider the problem of spatial or temporal camera-IMU calibration. The camera-IMU relative transformation is calibrated offline [6] using batch optimization, or online by including it into the system state for optimization [19,38,39]. The temporal calibration between the camera and the IMU is a less-explored topic [10,12,14,18]. Jacovitti et al. [12] estimate the time-offset by searching the peak that maximizes the correlation of different sensor measurements. Kelly et al. [14] firstly estimated rotations from different sensors independently, and then temporally aligned these rotations in the rotation space. However, both [12,14] cannot estimate time-varying time offsets. Li et al. [18] adopted a different approach. They assume constant velocities around local trajectories. Time offsets are included in the estimator state vector, and optimized together with other state variables within an EKF framework. Instead of explicitly optimizing the time offset, Guo et al. [10] proposed an interpolation model to account for the pose displacements caused by time offsets.

While most works on VIOs use global-shutter cameras, deployments on consumer devices drive the need for using rolling-shutter cameras. A straightforward way to deal with rolling-shutter effects is to rectify images as if they are captured by global-shutter cameras, such as the work [15] proposed by Klein and Murray that assumes a constant velocity model and corrects distorted image measurements in an independent thread. For more accurate modeling, some approaches extend the camera projection function to take rolling-shutter effects into account. They represent local trajectories using zero order parameterizations [18,20] or higher order parameterizations [36]. Instead of modeling the trajectories, [22] predicts the trajectories using IMU propagation and models the prediction errors of the estimated trajectories. These errors are represented as a weighted sum of temporal basis functions.

3 Preliminaries

In this section we briefly review the preliminaries of the nonlinear optimization framework used in our model. For detailed derivations, please refer to [17,32].

We begin by giving notations. We consider $(\cdot)^w$ as the earth's inertial frame, and $(\cdot)^{b_k}$ and $(\cdot)^{c_k}$ as the IMU body frame and camera frame while taking the kth image, respectively. We use $\mathbf{p}_Y^X$, $\mathbf{v}_Y^X$, and $\mathbf{R}_Y^X$ to denote the 3D position, velocity, and rotation of frame Y w.r.t. frame X, respectively. The corresponding quaternion ($\mathbf{q}_Y^X = [q_x, q_y, q_z, q_w]$) for rotation is in Hamilton notation in our formulation. We assume that the intrinsic of the monocular camera is calibrated beforehand with known focal length and principle point. The relative translation and rotation between the monocular camera and the IMU are $\mathbf{p}_b^c$ and $\mathbf{q}_b^c$. The system-recorded time instant for taking the kth image is t_k, while the image is actually captured at $\tilde{t}_k = t_k + \Delta t_k^o$, with an unknown time offset Δt_k^o due to inaccurate timestamps. Note that the time offset Δt_k^o is generally treated as a known constant in other optimization-based VIO algorithms, whereas it is modeled as an unknown variable for each image in our model.

In a sliding-window nonlinear optimization framework, the full state is usually encoded as $\mathcal{X} = [\mathbf{x}_{b_0} \ldots \mathbf{x}_{b_k} \ldots \mathbf{x}_{b_n} \mathbf{f}_0^w \ldots \mathbf{f}_j^w \ldots \mathbf{f}_m^w \mathbf{p}_c^b \mathbf{q}_c^b]$, where a sub-state $\mathbf{x}_{b_k} = [\mathbf{p}_{b_k}^w, \mathbf{v}_{b_k}^w, \mathbf{q}_{b_k}^w, \mathbf{b}_a^{b_k}, \mathbf{b}_\omega^{b_k}]$ consists of the position, velocity, rotation, linear acceleration bias, and angular velocity bias at t_k, $\mathbf{f}_j^w$ is the 3D Euclidean position of feature j in the world coordinate, and $\mathbf{p}_c^b$ as well as $\mathbf{q}_c^b$ are the camera-IMU extrinsics. Finding the MAP estimate of state parameters is equivalent to minimizing the sum of the Mahalanobis norm of all measurement errors:

$$\min_{\mathcal{X}} \ ||\mathbf{b}_p - \mathbf{H}_p\mathcal{X}||^2 + \sum_{\hat{\mathbf{z}}_{k+1}^k \in S_i} ||r_i(\hat{\mathbf{z}}_{k+1}^k, \mathcal{X})||_{\mathbf{\Sigma}_{k+1}^k}^2 + \sum_{\hat{\mathbf{z}}_{ik} \in S_c} ||r_c(\hat{\mathbf{z}}_{ik}, \mathcal{X})||_{\mathbf{\Sigma}_c}^2, \quad (1)$$

where $\mathbf{b}_p$ and $\mathbf{H}_p$ are priors obtained via marginalization [17], S_i and S_c are the sets of IMU and camera measurements, with the corresponding inertial and visual constraints modeled by residual functions $r_i(\hat{\mathbf{z}}_{k+1}^k, \mathcal{X})$ and $r_c(\hat{\mathbf{z}}_{ik}, \mathcal{X})$, respectively. The corresponding covariance matrices are denoted as $\mathbf{\Sigma}_{k+1}^k$ and $\mathbf{\Sigma}_c$.

To derive the inertial residual term $r_i(\hat{\mathbf{z}}_{k+1}^k, \mathcal{X})$ in Eq. (1), the IMU propagation model needs to be derived from the kinematics equation first, that is

$$\mathbf{p}_{b_{k+1}}^w = \mathbf{p}_{b_k}^w + \mathbf{v}_{b_k}^w \Delta t_k - \frac{1}{2}\mathbf{g}^w \Delta t_k^2 + \mathbf{R}_{b_k}^w \hat{\boldsymbol{\alpha}}_{k+1}^k,$$

$$\mathbf{v}_{b_{k+1}}^w = \mathbf{v}_{b_k}^w - \mathbf{g}^w \Delta t_k + \mathbf{R}_{b_k}^w \hat{\boldsymbol{\beta}}_{k+1}^k, \quad (2)$$

$$\mathbf{q}_{k+1}^w = \mathbf{q}_k^w \otimes \hat{\mathbf{q}}_{k+1}^k,$$

where $\Delta t_k = t_{k+1} - t_k$, $\mathbf{g}^w = [0, 0, 9.8]^T$ is the gravity vector in the earth's inertial frame, and $\hat{\mathbf{z}}_{k+1}^k = \{\hat{\boldsymbol{\alpha}}_{k+1}^k, \hat{\boldsymbol{\beta}}_{k+1}^k, \hat{\mathbf{q}}_{k+1}^k\}$ as well as its covariance $\mathbf{\Sigma}_{k+1}^k$ can be obtained by integrating linear accelerations $\mathbf{a}^{b_t}$ and angular velocities $\boldsymbol{\omega}^{b_t}$ [5]. Then the inertial residual term can be derived as:

$$r_i(\hat{\mathbf{z}}_{k+1}^k, \mathcal{X}) = \begin{bmatrix} \mathbf{R}_w^{b_k}(\mathbf{p}_{b_{k+1}}^w - \mathbf{p}_{b_k}^w - \mathbf{v}_{b_k}^w \Delta t_k + \frac{1}{2}\mathbf{g}^w \Delta t_k^2) - \hat{\boldsymbol{\alpha}}_{k+1}^k \\ \mathbf{R}_w^{b_k}(\mathbf{v}_{b_{k+1}}^w - \mathbf{v}_{b_k}^w + \mathbf{g}^w \Delta t_k) - \hat{\boldsymbol{\beta}}_{k+1}^k \\ (\hat{\mathbf{q}}_{k+1}^k)^{-1}(\mathbf{q}_{b_k}^w)^{-1}\mathbf{q}_{b_{k+1}}^w \end{bmatrix}. \quad (3)$$

The visual residual term $r_c(\hat{\mathbf{z}}_{ik}, \mathcal{X})$ in Eq. (1) is defined by the projection errors of tracked sparse features, which can be obtained using ST corner detector [34] and tracked across sequential images using sparse optical flow [1]. Note that, to handle the rolling-shutter effect, the generalized epipolar geometry [3] can be adopted as the fitted model in the RANSAC outlier removal procedure during correspondences establishment. Suppose a feature $\mathbf{f}_i^w$ in the world coordinate, following the pinhole model, its projection $\mathbf{u}_i^k$ on the k frame is:

$$\mathbf{u}_i^k = \begin{bmatrix} x_i^{c_k}/z_i^{c_k} \\ y_i^{c_k}/z_i^{c_k} \end{bmatrix}, \text{ where } \mathbf{f}_i^{c_k} = \begin{bmatrix} x_i^{c_k} \\ y_i^{c_k} \\ z_i^{c_k} \end{bmatrix} = \mathbf{R}_b^c(\mathbf{R}_w^{b_k}(\mathbf{f}_i^w - \mathbf{p}_{b_k}^w) - \mathbf{p}_c^b). \quad (4)$$

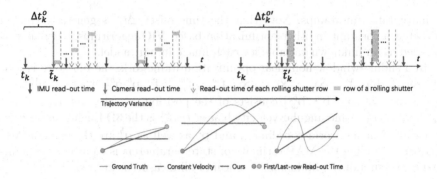

Fig. 2. The illustration of a camera-IMU sensor suite with a rolling-shutter camera and imperfect camera-IMU synchronization. We 'average' the rolling shutter readout time instants and approximate the rolling-shutter images (top-left) with global-shutter images captured at the 'middle-row' readout time of the rolling-shutter cameras (top-right). The position of this 'middle-row' is optimized to be the expected position of the local ground truth trajectory (bottom).

Then the projection error is $r_c(\hat{\mathbf{z}}_{ik}, \mathcal{X}) = \mathbf{u}_i^k - \hat{\mathbf{u}}_i^k$, where $\hat{\mathbf{u}}_i^k$ is the tracked feature location. The covariance matrix $\boldsymbol{\Sigma}_c$ is set according to the tracking accuracy of the feature tracker. By linearizing the cost function in Eq. (1) at the current best estimation $\hat{\mathcal{X}}$ with respect to error state $\delta\mathcal{X}$, the nonlinear optimization problem is solved via iteratively minimizing the following linear system over $\delta\mathcal{X}$ and updating the state estimation $\hat{\mathcal{X}}$ by $\hat{\mathcal{X}} \leftarrow \hat{\mathcal{X}} + \delta\mathcal{X}$ until convergence:

$$\min_{\delta\mathcal{X}} ||\mathbf{b}_p - \mathbf{H}_p(\hat{\mathcal{X}} + \delta\mathcal{X})||^2 + \sum_{\hat{\mathbf{z}}_{k+1}^k \in S_i} ||r_i(\hat{\mathbf{z}}_{k+1}^k, \hat{\mathcal{X}}) + \mathbf{H}_k\delta\mathcal{X}||^2_{\boldsymbol{\Sigma}_{k+1}^k}$$
$$+ \sum_{\hat{\mathbf{z}}_{ik} \in S_c} ||r_c(\hat{\mathbf{z}}_{ik}, \hat{\mathcal{X}}) + \mathbf{H}_k^i\delta\mathcal{X}||^2_{\boldsymbol{\Sigma}_c}, \tag{5}$$

where $\mathbf{H}_k$ and $\mathbf{H}_k^i$ are Jacobians of the inertial and visual residual functions.

4   Modeling Varying Camera-IMU Time Offset

In this section, we first show that rolling-shutter effects can be approximately compensated by modeling a camera-IMU time offset (Sect. 4.1). Then we present our time-varying model for the offset (Sect. 4.2) and the derivation of the Jacobian for optimization after introducing the time offset variable (Sect. 4.3). Finally, an efficient algorithm is described to accelerate the IMU integration over variable-length time intervals (Sect. 4.4), required by the optimization.

4.1   Approximate Compensation for Rolling-Shutter Effects

Figure 2(a) shows a camera-IMU suite with a rolling-shutter camera and imperfect camera-IMU synchronization. The system-recorded time instant for taking the kth image is t_k, which serves as our time reference for the retrieval of IMU data. Due to imperfect sensor synchronization (or inaccurate timestamps), the image is actually captured at $\tilde{t}_k = t_k + \Delta t_k^o$, with an unknown time offset Δt_k^o. With a rolling-shutter camera, this means that $\tilde{t}_k$ is the time instant when the camera starts to read out pixels row by row. Instead of modeling local trajectories using constant velocities [10,15,20], we model them with constant poses, which are expected poses of local trajectories (Fig. 2). With this approximation, a rolling-shutter image captured at $\tilde{t}_k$ with time offset Δt_k^o can be viewed as an global-shutter image captured at $\tilde{t}_k'$ with time offset $\Delta t_k^{o'}$. In the following, we slightly abuse notation by replacing $\Delta t_k^{o'}$ with Δt_k^o and $\tilde{t}_k'$ with $\tilde{t}_k$. We also replace $\mathbf{p}_{b_k}^w$ and $\mathbf{R}_w^{b_k}$ in Eq. (4) by $\tilde{\mathbf{p}}_{b_k}^w$ and $\tilde{\mathbf{R}}_w^{b_k}$ as they are now evaluated at time instant $\tilde{t}_k$. To calculate the pose at $\tilde{t}_k$, we use IMU propagation from the pose at t_k:

$$\tilde{\mathbf{p}}_{b_k}^w = \mathbf{p}_{b_k}^w + \mathbf{v}_{b_k}^w \Delta t_k^o - \frac{1}{2}\mathbf{g}^w(\Delta t_k^o)^2 + \mathbf{R}_{b_k}^w \hat{\boldsymbol{\alpha}}_{c_k}^{b_k},$$

$$\tilde{\mathbf{q}}_{b_k}^w = \mathbf{q}_{b_k}^w \otimes \hat{\mathbf{q}}_{c_k}^{b_k}, \tag{6}$$

$$\hat{\boldsymbol{\alpha}}_{c_k}^{b_k} = \iint_{t \in [t_k, \tilde{t}_k]} \mathbf{R}_t^{b_k}(\mathbf{a}^{b_t} - \mathbf{b}_a^{b_k})dt^2,$$

$$\hat{\mathbf{q}}_{c_k}^{b_k} = \int_{t \in [t_k, t_{c_k}]} \frac{1}{2}\begin{bmatrix} -\lfloor \boldsymbol{\omega}^{b_t} - \mathbf{b}_\omega^{b_k} \rfloor_\times & \boldsymbol{\omega}^{b_t} - \mathbf{b}_\omega^{b_k} \\ -(\boldsymbol{\omega}^{b_t} - \mathbf{b}_\omega^{b_k})^T & 0 \end{bmatrix} \mathbf{q}_{b_t}^{b_k} dt \tag{7}$$

where $\mathbf{a}^{b_t}/\boldsymbol{\omega}^{b_t}$ is the instant linear acceleration/angular velocity. Since only discrete IMU measurements are available on IMUs, $\hat{\boldsymbol{\alpha}}_{c_k}^{b_k}$ and $\hat{\mathbf{q}}_{c_k}^{b_k}$ in (7) are approximately computed using numerical integration (i.e. mid-point integration).

The benefit of our constant-pose approximation is that additional variables, i.e. velocities and the rolling-shutter row time, are not needed for estimation, which leads to a large reduction of computational complexity.

4.2 Modeling Camera-IMU Time Offset

From the previous subsection, we see that the time offset Δt_k^o is the addition of two parts. The first part is the camera-IMU time offset, which varies smoothly because of the system payload variation and sensor jitter. The second part is the compensated time offset caused by the rolling-shutter effect approximation, which varies smoothly according to the change of local trajectories. We see Δt_k^o as a slowly time-varying quantity and model it as a Gaussian random walk: $\dot{\Delta t_k^o} = \mathbf{n}_o$, where $\mathbf{n}_o$ is zero-mean Gaussian noise with covariance $\boldsymbol{\Sigma}_o$. Since time offsets we optimize are at discrete time instants, we integrate this noise over the time interval between two consecutive frames in the sliding window $[t_k, t_{k+1}]$: $\Delta t_{k+1}^o = \Delta t_k^o + \mathbf{n}_k^o, \boldsymbol{\Sigma}_k^o = \Delta t_k \boldsymbol{\Sigma}_o$, where $\mathbf{n}_k^o$ and $\boldsymbol{\Sigma}_k^o$ are discrete noise and covariance, respectively. Thus we add $\|\Delta t_{k+1}^o - \Delta t_k^o\|_{\boldsymbol{\Sigma}_k^o}$ into Eq. (1) for all consecutive frames. By including constraints between consecutive time offsets, we avoid "offset jumping" between consecutive frames.

4.3   Optimization with Unknown Camera-IMU Time Offset

Our state vector at time instant t_k reads as $\mathbf{x}_{b_k} = [\mathbf{p}_{b_k}^w, \mathbf{v}_{b_k}^w, \mathbf{q}_{b_k}^w, \mathbf{b}_a^{b_k}, \mathbf{b}_\omega^{b_k}, \Delta t_k^o]$, where Δt_k^o is the dynamically changing camera-IMU time offset modeling both the approximate compensation of rolling-shutter effects and imperfect sensor synchronization. With Δt_k^o, the error state $\delta\mathcal{X}$ for linearization becomes $\delta\mathcal{X} = [\delta\mathbf{p}_{b_k}^w \; \delta\mathbf{v}_{b_k}^w \; \delta\boldsymbol{\theta}_{b_k}^w \; \delta\mathbf{b}_a^{b_k} \; \delta\mathbf{b}_\omega^{b_k} \; \delta\mathbf{p}_b^c \; \delta\boldsymbol{\theta}_b^c \; \delta\mathbf{f}_i^w \; \delta\Delta t_k^o]$, where we adopt a minimal error representation for rotations $(\delta\boldsymbol{\theta}_{b_k}, \delta\boldsymbol{\theta}_b^c \in \mathbb{R}^3)$: $\mathbf{q}_{b_k}^w = \hat{\mathbf{q}}_{b_k}^w \otimes \begin{bmatrix} \frac{\delta\boldsymbol{\theta}_{b_k}^w}{2} \\ 1 \end{bmatrix}$, $\mathbf{q}_b^c = \hat{\mathbf{q}}_b^c \otimes \begin{bmatrix} \frac{\delta\boldsymbol{\theta}_b^c}{2} \\ 1 \end{bmatrix}$. Other error-state variables $\delta\mathbf{p}_{b_k}^w$, $\delta\mathbf{v}_{b_k}^w$, $\delta\mathbf{b}_a^{b_k}$, $\delta\mathbf{b}_\omega^{b_k}$, $\delta\mathbf{p}_b^c$, $\delta\mathbf{f}_i^w$, and $\delta\Delta t_k^o$ are standard additive errors. After introducing $\delta\Delta t_k^o$, the Jacobian $\mathbf{H}_k$ of the inertial residual function in Eq. (5) remains the same as before, while the Jacobian $\mathbf{H}_k^i$ of the visual residual function needs to be reformulated. Denoting $(\hat{\cdot})$ the states obtained from the last iteration of the nonlinear optimization, the Jacobian $\mathbf{H}_k^i$ can be written as

$$\mathbf{H}_k^i = \frac{\partial r_c}{\partial \delta\mathcal{X}} = \frac{\partial r_c}{\partial \mathbf{f}_i^{c_k}} \frac{\partial \mathbf{f}_i^{c_k}}{\partial \delta\mathcal{X}} = \begin{bmatrix} \frac{1}{\hat{z}_i^{c_k}} & 0 & -\frac{\hat{x}_i^{c_k}}{\hat{z}_i^{c_k}} \\ 0 & \frac{1}{\hat{z}_i^{c_k}} & -\frac{\hat{y}_i^{c_k}}{\hat{z}_i^{c_k}} \end{bmatrix} \mathbf{J},$$

$$\mathbf{J} = [-\hat{\mathbf{R}}_b^c \tilde{\mathbf{R}}_w^{b_k} \quad -\hat{\mathbf{R}}_b^c \tilde{\mathbf{R}}_w^{b_k} \Delta \hat{t}_k^o \quad \hat{\mathbf{R}}_b^c \tilde{\mathbf{R}}_w^{b_k} \lfloor \hat{\mathbf{f}}_i^w - \tilde{\mathbf{p}}_{b_k}^w \rfloor_\times \quad \mathbf{0}_{3\times6} \quad \hat{\mathbf{R}}_b^c \lfloor \hat{\mathbf{f}}_i^{c_k} \rfloor_\times \quad \hat{\mathbf{R}}_b^c \tilde{\mathbf{R}}_w^{b_k} \; \mathbf{J}_{\delta\Delta t}],$$

$$\mathbf{J}_{\delta\Delta t} = \hat{\mathbf{R}}_b^c (\lfloor \boldsymbol{\omega}^{b_k} \rfloor_\times \tilde{\mathbf{R}}_w^{b_k} (\hat{\mathbf{f}}_i^w - \tilde{\mathbf{p}}_{b_k}^w) + \tilde{\mathbf{R}}_w^{b_k} \mathbf{v}_{b_k}^w + \mathbf{g}^w \Delta \hat{t}_k^o),$$

where $\lfloor \cdot \rfloor_\times$ denotes the skew symmetric matrix of a vector. Recall that the position $\tilde{\mathbf{p}}_{b_k}^w$ and rotation $\tilde{\mathbf{R}}_w^{b_k}$ in the Jacobian is computed at time instant $\tilde{t}_k$ instead of t_k, which depends on variable $\Delta \hat{t}_k^o$ and varies in each iteration of the optimization. Besides, the computation of the feature position $\hat{\mathbf{f}}_i^{c_k}$ projected on the k-th frame depends on $\tilde{\mathbf{p}}_{b_k}^w$ and $\tilde{\mathbf{R}}_w^{b_k}$ as shown in Eq. (4), which also needs to be recomputed when $\Delta \hat{t}_k^o$ changes. We in the next section present a novel algorithm based on dynamic programming and red-black tree to efficiently compute $\tilde{\mathbf{p}}_{b_k}^w$ and $\tilde{\mathbf{R}}_w^{b_k}$ as the estimated time offset $\Delta \hat{t}_k^o$ varies during the iterations.

4.4   Efficient IMU Integration over Variable-Length Time Intervals

With a naive implementation, the computation of $\hat{\boldsymbol{\alpha}}_{c_k}^{b_k}$ and $\hat{\mathbf{q}}_{c_k}^{b_k}$ in Eq. (7) between t_k and $\tilde{t}_k$ needs to be recomputed each time the offset Δt_k^o changes during the optimization. In order to reuse the intermediate integration results, we decompose the integration into two steps (Fig. 3): firstly, compute the integration between t_k and t_i; secondly, compute the integration between t_i and $\tilde{t}_k$. Here, without loss of generality, we assume t_i is the closest IMU read-out time instant before $\tilde{t}_k$. The decomposition makes the results in the first step reusable since the integration is computed over variable yet regular time intervals. We design an algorithm based on discrete dynamic programming [16] and red-black tree [16] to perform efficient integration over the variable-length time intervals.

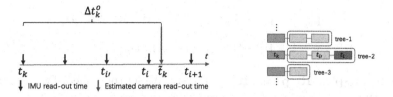

Fig. 3. Computing the pose at $\tilde{t}_k$ from the pose at t_k is decomposed into two steps (left): firstly, compute the pose at t_i, where t_i is the closest IMU measurement time instant to $\tilde{t}_k$ and smaller than $\tilde{t}_k$; secondly, compute the pose at $\tilde{t}_k$ based on the pose at t_i. We design an algorithm based on dynamic programming and red-black tree (right) for efficient indexing to accelerate the first step. (Color figure online)

Specifically, we build a table (implemented as a red-black tree [16]) for each time instant t_k to store the intermediate results of IMU integration starting from t_k (right part of Fig. 3). Each node in the tree stores a key-value pair, where the key is an IMU read-out time t_i and the value is the integration from t_k to t_i computed using Eq. (7). Note that this integration is independent of the pose and velocity at t_k, so the stored results do not need to be updated when the pose and velocity in Eq. (6) as t_k change. During the optimization, each time when we need to compute the integration from t_k to t_i (recall that t_i is variable according to $\tilde{t}_k$), we first try to search in the tree at t_k to query the integration results for t_i. If the query failed, we then instead search if there exists a record for another IMU read-out time $t_{i'}$ such that $t_{i'} < t_i$. If multiple records exist, we select the maximum $t_{i'}$ (which is closest to t_i), and compute the integration from t_k to t_i based on the retrieved record at $t_{i'}$ and IMU measurements from $t_{i'}$ to t_i. During the process, each time a new integration is computed, the result is stored into the tree for future retrieval.

5   Uncertainty-Aware Initialization

We initialize our VIO system by first running a vision-only bundle adjustment on K consecutive frames. Suppose that the K consecutive rotations and positions obtained from vision-only bundle adjustment are $[\mathbf{p}_{c_0}^{c_0} \mathbf{R}_{c_0}^{c_0} \dots \mathbf{p}_{c_{K-1}}^{c_0} \mathbf{R}_{c_{K-1}}^{c_0}]$. The goal of the initialization is to solve initial velocities $[\mathbf{v}_{b_k}^{b_0} \dots \mathbf{v}_{b_{K-1}}^{b_0}]$, gravity vector $\mathbf{g}^{c_0}$, and metric scale s. The initializations in [28,31] solve for the unknowns by minimizing the least squares of the L_2 errors between the poses obtained from vision-only bundle adjustment and the poses obtained from IMU integration. These methods do not take into account the uncertainties introduced by IMU noise during the IMU integration, which can cause failures of the initialization when the camera-IMU time offset is unknown (see Sect. 6.2).

We employ a different method to perform uncertainty-aware initialization by incorporating the covariances obtained during the IMU integration. The IMU propagation model for the K initialization images can be written as

$$\mathbf{p}_{b_{k+1}}^{co} = \mathbf{p}_{b_k}^{co} + \mathbf{R}_{b_k}^{co} \mathbf{v}_{b_k}^{b_k} \Delta t_k - \frac{1}{2} \mathbf{g}^{co} \Delta t_k^2 + \mathbf{R}_{b_k}^{co} \hat{\boldsymbol{\alpha}}_{k+1}^k,$$

$$\mathbf{R}_{b_{k+1}}^{co} \mathbf{v}_{b_{k+1}}^{b_{k+1}} = \mathbf{R}_{b_k}^{co} \mathbf{v}_{b_k}^{b_k} - \mathbf{g}^{co} \Delta t_k + \mathbf{R}_{b_k}^{co} \hat{\boldsymbol{\beta}}_{k+1}^k, \tag{8}$$

where $\mathbf{p}_{b_k}^{co} = s\mathbf{p}_{c_k}^{co} - \mathbf{R}_{b_k}^{co} \mathbf{p}_c^b$ and $\mathbf{R}_{b_k}^{co} = \mathbf{R}_{c_k}^{co} \mathbf{R}_b^c$. We set the camera-IMU extrinsics $\mathbf{p}_c^b$ and $\mathbf{R}_c^b$ to a zero vector and an identity matrix, respectively. Instead of minimizing the L_2 norm of the measurement errors, we minimize the Mahalanobis norm of the measurement errors as:

$$\min_{\mathcal{X}} \sum_{\hat{\mathbf{z}}_{k+1}^k \in S_i} \left\| \begin{bmatrix} \mathbf{R}_{c_0}^{b_k}(s\mathbf{p}_{c_{k+1}}^{co} - \mathbf{R}_{b_{k+1}}^{co}\mathbf{p}_c^b - s\mathbf{p}_{c_k}^{co} + \mathbf{R}_{b_k}^{co}\mathbf{p}_c^b + \frac{1}{2}\mathbf{g}^{co}\Delta t_k^2) - \mathbf{v}_{b_k}^{b_k}\Delta t_k - \hat{\boldsymbol{\alpha}}_{k+1}^k \\ \mathbf{R}_{c_0}^{b_k}(\mathbf{R}_{b_{k+1}}^{co}\mathbf{v}_{b_{k+1}}^{b_{k+1}} + \mathbf{g}^{co}\Delta t_k) - \mathbf{v}_{b_k}^{b_k} - \hat{\boldsymbol{\beta}}_{k+1}^k \end{bmatrix} \right\|_{\Sigma_{k+1}^k}^2,$$

where $\hat{\mathbf{z}}_{k+1}^k = \{\hat{\boldsymbol{\alpha}}_{k+1}^k, \hat{\boldsymbol{\beta}}_{k+1}^k\}$ and Σ_{k+1}^k is the covariance matrix computed during IMU integration [5]. Note that the covariance Σ_{k+1}^k in our formulation models the uncertainty of the IMU measurements. The resulting problem is a weighted least squares problem and can be solved efficiently. After solving the problem, we project the solved variables into the world coordinate. Other variables like accelerator biases, gyrocope biases, and time offsets are initialized as zeros.

6   Experiments

We compare our approach to state-of-the-art monocular VIO systems: OKVIS [17] and VINS-Mono [30]. Loop closure in VINS-Mono is disabled for a fair comparison. The number of keyframes and non-keyframes in the optimization window of OKVIS and our approach are set to be 8 and 3 respectively. The sliding window size in VINS-Mono is set to be 11.

6.1   Performance on the Euroc Dataset

Sequences of the Euroc dataset consist of synchronized global-shutter stereo images (only mono/left images are used) and IMU measurements. The complexity of these sequences varies regarding trajectory length, flight dynamics, and illumination conditions. Ground truth poses are obtained by Vicon motion capture system. For presentation, we use numbers to denote sequence names: 1-5 for MH_01_easy–MH_05_difficult, 6-8 for V1_01_easy–V1_03_difficult, 9-11 for V2_01_easy–V2_03_difficult.

Significance of Online Temporal Camera-IMU Calibration. Two error metrics are used for tracking accuracy evaluation: the average relative rotation error (deg) and the average relative translation error (m) [8]. Approaches are compared under different simulated time offsets between visual and inertial measurements: no time offsets; 30 ms offset; 60 ms offset. Figure 4 shows the comparison results. When visual measurements and inertial measurements are synchronized, the average relative rotation/translation error between VINS-Mono and our approach are similar, while OKVIS performs the worst. As the time

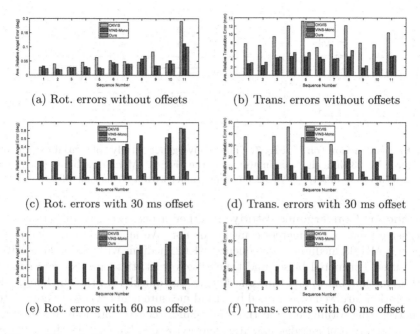

(a) Rot. errors without offsets   (b) Trans. errors without offsets

(c) Rot. errors with 30 ms offset   (d) Trans. errors with 30 ms offset

(e) Rot. errors with 60 ms offset   (f) Trans. errors with 60 ms offset

Fig. 4. The relative rot. and trans. errors with different time offsets on Euroc.

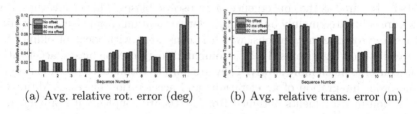

(a) Avg. relative rot. error (deg)   (b) Avg. relative trans. error (m)

Fig. 5. The average relative rot. and trans. errors of our approach with different time offsets on Euroc.

offset increases, VINS-Mono and OKVIS perform worse and worse due to the lack of camera-IMU time offset modeling. Our estimator achieves the smallest tracking error when there exists a time offset. OKVIS fails to track in sequence 2–5 when the time offset is set to be 60 ms. We have tested different approaches under larger time offsets, such as 90 ms. However, neither OKVIS or VINS-Mono provides reasonable estimates. We thus omit comparisons for larger time offsets. We also illustrate the tracking performance of our approach under different time offsets in Fig. 5. We see that, by modeling the time offset properly, there is no significant performance decrease as time offset increases. Figure 6 gives a visual comparison on trajectories estimated by our approach and VINS-Mono on the Euroc sequence V1_03_difficult with a 60 ms time offset. Noticeable 'jaggies' are found on the trajectory estimated by VINS-Mono.

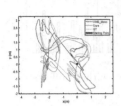

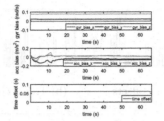

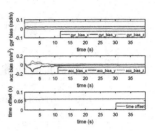

Fig. 6. Comparison on the Euroc V1_03_difficult with a 60 ms time offset.

Fig. 7. The convergence study of variables in our estimator on the Euroc MH_03_medium (left) and V1_02_medium (right) with a 60 ms time offset.

Parameter Convergence Study. Another aspect we pay attention to is whether estimator parameters converge or not. We analyze our results on the sequence MH_03_medium and sequence V1_02_medium with a simulated 60 ms time offset. Estimated biases and time offsets w.r.t. time are plotted in Fig. 7. Both gyroscope biases and time offsets converge quickly. On the one hand, relative rotations are well constrained by visual measurements. They are not related to metric scale estimation. On the other hand, relative rotations are the first-order integration of angular velocities and gyroscope biases, thus they are easy to estimate. Another interesting thing we found is that, the convergence of time offsets is the same as the convergence of gyroscope biases. This means that, time offsets are calibrated mainly by aligning relative rotations from visual constraints and from gyroscope integrations, which is consistent with ideas of offline time offset calibration algorithms [12,14]. Compared to gyroscope biases, acceleration biases converge much more slowly. They are hard to estimate as positions are the second-order integration of accelerations and acceleration biases. Additionally, acceleration measurements obtained from IMUs are coupled with gravity measurements. Abundant rotations collected across time are required to distinguish actual accelerations and gravity vector from measurements.

6.2   Performance on Mobile Phone Data

One of the applications of VIO is the motion tracking on mobile phones. We collect visual and inertial measurements using Samsung Galaxy S8 with a rolling-shutter camera and unsynchronized sensor measurements. Google developed ARCore [9] is also used for comparison. After recording the data, we run our system on the Samsung Galaxy S8. It takes 70 ± 10 ms for each nonlinear optimization.

Qualitative Comparison of Tracking Accuracy. We use AprilTag [37] to obtain time-synchronized and drift-free ground truths (Fig. 8(d)). We detect tags on captured images. If tags are detected, we calculate ground truth camera poses via P3P [7] using tag corners. Since VINS-Mono performs better than OKVIS, we only include tracking results from VINS-Mono for the following comparison. We test our approach with two conditions: (1) 'Ours-fix': the variable time-delay

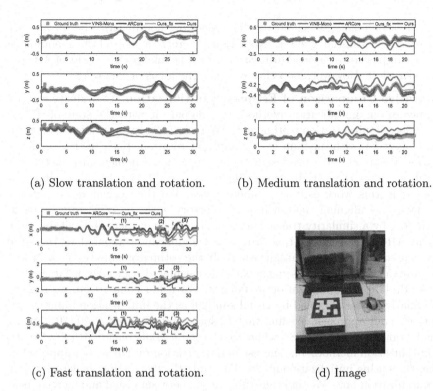

(a) Slow translation and rotation.   (b) Medium translation and rotation.

(c) Fast translation and rotation.   (d) Image

Fig. 8. The qualitative comparison of tracking accuracy. VINS-Mono fails to track on the fast translation and rotation sequence.

estimation is switched off, i.e. is replaced with a single time offset, to account for the camera-IMU synchronization; (2) 'Ours': the variable time-delay is enabled to account for both the camera-IMU synchronization and the rolling-shutter effect approximation. Three sequences are recorded around an office desk. These datasets are increasingly difficult to process in terms of motion dynamics: slow, medium, and fast translation and rotation (Fig. 8). To align coordinates of different approaches for comparison, we regularly move the mobile phone at the beginning of recorded sequences (see 0–5 s in (a), 0–4 s in (b), and 0–6 s in (c)). VINS-Mono performs worst among all datasets, as it does not model time offsets between visual and inertial measurements. Our approach with condition 'Ours-fix' performs worse than the one with condition 'Ours'. The tracking accuracy of our approach is comparable to that of ARCore in small and medium motion settings. While for the fast translation and rotation sequence, where part of captured images are blurred, our approach exhibits better tracking robustness compared to ARCore. ARCore loses tracks in time periods within dashed boxes (1) (2) (3). This is because ARCore is based on EKF [11], which requires good initial guesses about predicted states. If pose displacements are large and feature correspondences are not abundant because of image blur, ARCore may fail. Conversely, our nonlinear optimization approach iteratively minimizes errors from sensor measurements, which treats the underlying non-linearity better and are less sensitive to initial guesses. Note that, there is a loop closing module in ARCore for pose recovery and drift correction. The final position drift of ARCore is thus smallest. However, loop closing is not the focus of this work.

Qualitative Comparison of Estimator Initialization. To evaluate the significance of our initialization method, we compare it with the state-of-the-art visual-inertial initialization method [28]. We record 20 testing sequences on Samsung Galaxy S8 with medium translation and rotation. Each testing sequence lasts for about 30 s. We use the first 2-s sensor measurements to do the initialization. After the initialization is done, we use the visual-inertial estimator proposed in this work estimate camera poses. We then calculate an optimal scale factor by aligning the estimated trajectory with the trajectory reported by ARCore by a similarity transformation [2]. Although there is inevitably pose drift in ARCore estimates, this drift is not significant compared to the scale error caused by improper initializations. If the estimator fails to track in any time intervals of the testing sequences or the calculated scale error is larger than 5%, we declare the initialization as failures. For a fair comparison, we use the same relative poses obtained by visual sfm [29] as the initialization input of [28] and that of our approach. We find that 14 successful trials out of 20 (70%) using initialization proposed in [28], while 18 successful trials out of 20 (90%) using our initialization method. The successful initialization rate using our approach is higher than using initialization in [28]. We study the two testing sequences where our initialization fails. We find that time offsets between visual and inertial measurements in these two sequences are larger than 100 ms (this can be obtained by enumerating offsets and testing whether the following visual-inertial estimator outputs are close to that of ARCore or not after initialization), causing a big inconsistency when aligning the visual and inertial measurements. Since the main focus of this work is on the estimator, we are going to handle this failure case thoroughly in the future work.

7   Conclusions

In this work, we proposed a nonlinear optimization-based VIO that can deal with rolling-shutter effects and imperfect camera-IMU synchronization. We modeled the camera-IMU time offset as a time-varying variable to be estimated. An efficient algorithm for IMU integration over variable-length time intervals, which is required during the optimization, was also introduced. The VIO can be robustly launched with our uncertainty-aware initialization scheme. The experiments demonstrated the effectiveness of the proposed approach.

References

1. Baker, S., Matthews, I.: Lucas-Kanade 20 years on: a unifying framework. Int. J. Comput. Vis. **56**(3), 221–255 (2004)
2. Horn, B.K.P.: Closed-form solution of absolute orientation using unit quaternions. Opt. Soc. Am. **4**, 629–642 (1987)

3. Dai, Y., Li, H., Kneip, L.: Rolling shutter camera relative pose: generalized epipolar geometry. In: Proceedings of the IEEE International Conference on Computer Vision and Pattern Recognition (2016)
4. Dong-Si, T., Mourikis, A.I.: Estimator initialization in vision-aided inertial navigation with unknown camera-IMU calibration. In: Proceedings of the IEEE/RSJ International Conference on Intelligent Robots and System (2012)
5. Forster, C., Carlone, L., Dellaert, F., Scaramuzza, D.: IMU preintegration on manifold for efficient visual-inertial maximum-a-posteriori estimation. In: Proceedings of Robotics: Science and System (2015)
6. Furgale, P., Rehder, J., Siegwart, R.: Unified temporal and spatial calibration for multi-sensor systems. In: Proceedings of the IEEE/RSJ International Conference on Intelligent Robots and System (2013)
7. Gao, X.S., Hou, X.R., Tang, J., Cheng, H.F.: Complete solution classification for the perspective-three-point problem. IEEE Trans. Pattern Anal. Mach. Intell. **25**, 930–943 (2003)
8. Geiger, A., Lenz, P., Urtasun, R.: Are we ready for autonomous driving? The KITTI vision benchmark suite. In: Conference on Computer Vision and Pattern Recognition (CVPR) (2012)
9. Google: ARCore: https://developers.google.com/ar/
10. Guo, C., Kottas, D., DuToit, R., Ahmed, A., Li, R., Roumeliotis, S.: Efficient visual-inertial navigation using a rolling-shutter camera with inaccurate timestamps. In: Proceedings of Robotics: Science and Systems (2014)
11. Hesch, J.A., Kottas, D.G., Bowman, S.L., Roumeliotis, S.I.: Consistency analysis and improvement of vision-aided inertial navigation. IEEE Trans. Robot. **30**(1), 158–176 (2014)
12. Jacovitti, G., Scarano, G.: Discrete time techniques for time delay estimation. IEEE Trans. Signal Process. **41**, 525–533 (1993)
13. Jung, S.H., Taylor, C.J.: Camera trajectory estimation using inertial sensor measurements and structure from motion results. In: Proceedings of the IEEE International Conference on Computer Vision and Pattern Recognition (2001)
14. Kelly, J., Sukhatme, G.: A general framework for temporal calibration of multiple proprioceptive and exteroceptive sensors. In: Khatib, O., Kumar, V., Sukhatme, G. (eds.) Experimental Robotics. STAR, vol. 79, pp. 195–209. Springer, Heidelberg (2010). https://doi.org/10.1007/978-3-642-28572-1_14
15. Klein G., Murray D.: Parallel tracking and mapping on a camera phone. In: Proceedings of the Sixth IEEE and ACM International Symposium on Mixed and Augmented Reality (2009)
16. Knuth, D.: The Art of Computer Programming, vol. 1–3. Addison-Wesley Longman Publishing Co., Inc., Boston (1998)
17. Leutenegger, S., Furgale, P., Rabaud, V., Chli, M., Konolige, K., Siegwart, R.: Keyframe-based visual-inertial SLAM using nonlinear optimization. In: Proceedings of Robotics: Science and System (2013)
18. Li, M., Mourikis, A.I.: 3D motion estimation and online temporal calibration for camera- IMU systems. In: Proceedings of the IEEE International Conference on Robotics and Automation (2013)
19. Li, M., Mourikis, A.I.: High-precision, consistent EKF-based visual-inertial odometry. Intl. J. Robot. Res. **32**(6), 690–711 (2013)
20. Li, M., Mourikis, A.I.: Real-time motion tracking on a cellphone using inertial sensing and a rolling shutter camera. In: Proceedings of the IEEE International Conference on Robotics and Automation (2013)

21. Li, M., Mourikis, A.I.: Online temporal calibration for camera-IMU systems: theory and algorithms. Int. J. Robot. Res. **33**, 947–964 (2014)
22. Li, M., Mourikis, A.I.: Vision-aided inertial navigation with rolling-shutter cameras. Int. J. Robot. Res. **33**, 1490–1507 (2014)
23. Ling, Y., Kuse, M., Shen, S.: Edge alignment-based visual-inertial fusion for tracking of aggressive motions. Auton. Robot. **42**, 513–528 (2017)
24. Ling, Y., Shen, S.: Dense visual-inertial odometry for tracking of aggressive motions. In: Proceedings of the IEEE International Conference on Robotics and Biomimetics (2015)
25. Ling, Y., Shen, S.: Aggressive quadrotor flight using dense visual-inertial fusion. In: Proceedings of the IEEE International Conference on Robotics and Automation (2016)
26. Lynen, S., Achtelik, M., Weiss, S., Chli, M., Siegwart, R.: A robust and modular multi-sensor fusion approach applied to MAV navigation. In: Proceedings of the IEEE/RSJ International Conference on Intelligent Robots and System (2013)
27. Mourikis, A.I., Roumeliotis, S.I.: A multi-state constraint Kalman filter for vision-aided inertial navigation. In: Proceedings of the IEEE International Conference on Robotics and Automation (2007)
28. Mur-Artal, R., Tards, J.D.: Visual-inertial monocular slam with map reuse. IEEE Robot. Autom. Lett. **2**, 796–803 (2017)
29. Mur-Artal, R., Montiel, J.M.M., Tardós, J.D.: ORB-SLAM: a versatile and accurate monocular SLAM system. IEEE Trans. Robot. **31**(5), 1147–1163 (2015). https://doi.org/10.1109/TRO.2015.2463671
30. Qin, T., Li, P., Shen, S.: VINS-Mono: a robust and versatile monocular visual-inertial state estimator. arXiv preprint arXiv:1708.03852 (2017)
31. Qin, T., Shen, S.: Robust initialization of monocular visual-inertial estimation on aerial robots. In: Proceedings of the IEEE/RSJ International Conference on Intelligent Robots and System (2017)
32. Shen, S., Michael, N., Kumar, V.: Tightly-coupled monocular visual-inertial fusion for autonomous flight of rotorcraft MAVs. In: Proceedings of the IEEE International Conference on Robotics and Automation, Seattle, WA, May 2015
33. Shen, S., Mulgaonkar, Y., Michael, N., Kumar, V.: Vision-based state estimation for autonomous rotorcraft MAVs in complex environments. In: Proceedings of the IEEE International Conference on Robotics and Automation (2013)
34. Shi, J., Tomasi, C.: Good features to track. In: Proceedings of IEEE Conference on Computer Vision and Pattern Recognition (1994)
35. Roumeliotis, S.I., Johnson, A.E., Montgomery, J.F.: Augmenting inertial navigation with image-based motion estimation. In: Proceedings of the IEEE International Conference on Robotics and Automation (2002)
36. Lovegrove, S., Patron-Perez, A., Sibley, G.: Spline fusion: a continuous-time representation for visual-inertial fusion with application to rolling shutter cameras. In: British Machine Vision Conference (2013)
37. Wang, J., Olson, E.: AprilTag 2: efficient and robust fiducial detection. In: Proceedings of the IEEE/RSJ International Conference on Intelligent Robots and System (2016)
38. Weiss, S., Achtelik, M.W., Lynen, S., Chi, M., Siegwart, R.: Real-time onboard visual-inertial state estimation and self-calibration of MAVs in unknown environments. In: Proceedings of the IEEE International Conference on Robotics and Automation (2012)

39. Yang, Z., Shen, S.: Monocular visual-inertial fusion with online initialization and camera-IMU calibration. In: Proceedings of the IEEE/RSJ International Conference on Intelligent Robots and System (2015)
40. Yang, Z., Shen, S.: Tightly-coupled visual-inertial sensor fusion based on IMU pre-integration. Technical report, Hong Kong University of Science and Technology (2016). http://www.ece.ust.hk/~eeshaojie/vins2016zhenfei.pdf

An Adversarial Approach to Hard Triplet Generation

Yiru Zhao[1,2], Zhongming Jin[2], Guo-jun Qi[2,3], Hongtao Lu[1(✉)],
and Xian-sheng Hua[2(✉)]

[1] Key Laboratory of Shanghai Education Commission for Intelligent Interaction
and Cognitive Engineering, Shanghai Jiao Tong University, Shanghai, China
{yiru.zhao,htlu}@sjtu.edu.cn
[2] Alibaba Damo Academy, Alibaba Group, Hangzhou, China
{zhongming.jinzm,xiansheng.hxs}@alibaba-inc.com
[3] Laboratory for MAchine Perception and LEarning,
University of Central Florida, Orlando, USA
guojun.qi@ucf.edu

Abstract. While deep neural networks have demonstrated competitive
results for many visual recognition and image retrieval tasks, the major
challenge lies in distinguishing similar images from different categories
(i.e., hard negative examples) while clustering images with large variations from the same category (i.e., hard positive examples). The current state-of-the-art is to *mine* the most hard triplet examples from the
mini-batch to train the network. However, mining-based methods tend
to look into these triplets that are hard in terms of the current estimated network, rather than deliberately generating those hard triplets
that really matter in globally optimizing the network. For this purpose,
we propose an adversarial network for Hard Triplet Generation (HTG)
to optimize the network ability in distinguishing similar examples of
different categories as well as grouping varied examples of the same categories. We evaluate our method on the real-world challenging datasets,
such as CUB200-2011, CARS196, DeepFashion and VehicleID datasets,
and show that our method outperforms the state-of-the-art methods
significantly.

Keywords: Image retrieval · Hard examples · Adversarial nets

1 Introduction

Deep metric learning is of great practical importance and has shown promising
results in many tasks, such as image retrieval [20,31,32,44], face recognition [26,
34,40], person re-identification [1,28,46], etc. In spite of various forms of deep
metric learning in different tasks, it shares a common goal of learning an optimal

---

Y. Zhao—This work was done when the author was visiting Alibaba as a research
intern.

V. Ferrari et al. (Eds.): ECCV 2018, LNCS 11213, pp. 508–524, 2018.
https://doi.org/10.1007/978-3-030-01240-3_31

image representation that pulls semantically similar images close to each other while pushing dissimilar ones apart in a learned feature space.

Deep metric learning often considers images in triplets as its training units inside a mini-batch. A triplet contains a query along with a relevant and an irrelevant example. Then a deep metric learning algorithm seeks to push the relevant (irrelevant) example towards (away from) the query in the underlying embedding space. It is obvious that randomly choosing triplets can be very inefficient to train a deep embedding network, as not all triplets are equally informative [44]. Some triplets contain harder examples that cannot be well handled by the current embedding network, where the irrelevant example is closer to the query than the relevant counterpart. Using these harder triplets for training can not only result in faster convergence of the learning algorithm [31], but also better improve the global structure of the embedding space by learning sharper boundaries between relevant and irrelevant examples for given queries [32]. This leads to several recent works to *mine* hard examples for training [2,29].

However, mining-based methods aim to find those triplets from existing training examples that are hard in terms of the current network. This is essentially a greedy algorithm, which could make the trained feature embedding network vulnerable to a bad local optimum [20,44]. In this paper, we seek an approach that can deliberately generate hard triplets to optimize the network globally, instead of using a greedy strategy to explore existing samples only for the current network. The objective of generating hard triplets should also be integrated with the objective of learning an optimal feature embedding network for different tasks. For this purpose, we propose an adversarial learning algorithm, where a hard triplet generator and an embedding network are jointly optimized in an adversarial fashion to mutually benefit each other. Our overarching goal is to learn an optimal embedding of images that is adequate in distinguishing between the relevant and the irrelevant examples even for the most challenging queries in the hardest triplets.

2 Related Works

2.1 Metric Learning

The goal of distance metric learning is to learn an embedding representation such that similar samples are mapped to nearby points on a manifold and dissimilar ones are mapped apart from each other [41]. Thanks to the success of deep neural networks (DNNs) [14,30,35], deep metric learning has shown great superiority on many visual recognition tasks [1,9,20,26,34,42,44].

In a standard deep metric learning network, a DNN model f is trained to embed an input image x into a new representation $f(x)$ by minimizing triplet loss [27,39] that showed better performance than contrastive loss [6]. However, triplet loss is quite sensitive to a proper selection of triplets and often suffers from slow convergence and poor local optima. To address this, [16] proposed a coupled clusters loss to make the training more stable and achieved higher accuracy. [20] proposed a lifted structured embedding where each positive pair compared its distance against those of all negative pairs weighted by the margin constraint. [31] presented multi-class N-pairs loss to improve the triplet loss by pushing away multiple negative examples simultaneously at each iteration.

Indeed, not all triplets are equally informative to train a model. Hence mining hard triplet examples plays a very important role to effectively train deep metric networks [2,29]. The mining-based method is often performed by sampling hard triplets from existing training examples in a mini-batch. These hard triplets reflect the cases that cannot be well handled by the current model. Thus it is essentially a greedy algorithm that could be vulnerable to bad local minimum [20]. [44] presented a family of models with different levels of complexities in a cascaded manner to mine hard examples adaptively. These methods select hard examples only based on the absolute distances and are sensitive to the threshold set manually.

Inspired by the development of generative adversarial networks (GANs) [5], we propose to learn an adversarial network that can deliberately generate hard triplets in a principled fashion to improve the feature embedding network, instead of greedily mining from existing training examples.

2.2   Generative Adversarial Networks

Recently, generative adversarial networks (GANs) [5] have shown very promising results for many generative tasks such as image generation [3,24] and translation [11,43,47]. More important, the adversarial training and its ability of modeling data distributions have been utilized to improve many discriminative tasks as well.

For example, [33] combined neural network classifiers with an adversarial generative model to regularize a discriminatively trained classifiers, which yields classification performance compared with state-of-the-art results for semi-supervised learning. [15] proposed Perceptual GANs that generate super-resolution representations for small objects to boost detection accuracy by leveraging iteratively updated generator networks and discriminator networks. [22] presented a Lipschitz regularized GAN to explore the margin between different classes of examples and their generated counterparts in both supervised and semi-supervised settings, and it is extended to a loss-sensitive learning framework by pull-backing original full-dimensional data onto a latent manifold representation to explore the distribution of both labeled and unlabeled samples [4]. [23] instead localized GAN-based parameterization of data manifolds so that the Laplace-Beltrami operator for semi-supervised learning can be accurately formalized without resorting to Graph Laplacian approximation. [38] learned an adversarial network by generating examples with occlusions and deformations to challenge original object detectors. Such an adversarial learning strategy significantly boosts detection performance. In contrast, in this paper, we propose a generative network in the feature embedding space to produce challenging triplets by pulling negative pairs closer and pushing positive pairs apart. Through these generated hard triplets, we wish to boost the performance of the associated

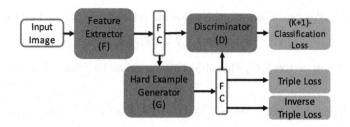

Fig. 1. Architecture of the adversarial training method.

feature embedding network so that it can correctly retrieve relevant examples even in adversarial cases.

3 Hard Triplet Generation

Our goal is to learn a feature embedding network to extract features from images. The obtained features ought to be resilient against inter-class similarity (i.e., hard negative examples) as well as intra-class variance (i.e., hard positive examples). In contrast to existing mining-based methods that merely rely on existing examples, we present an alternative approach by generating hard triplets to challenge the ability of feature embedding network correctly distinguishing relevant examples from irrelevant counterparts in these triplets. The architecture of the proposed method is shown in Fig. 1.

Formally, we denote the feature embedding network by F, whose output for an input image x is $F(x) \in \mathbb{R}^L$. Given a triplet $<a, p, n>$, $<a, p>$ is a positive (relevant) pair and $<a, n>$ is a negative (irrelevant) pair. The original objective function to train F is to minimize the following triplet loss,

$$\mathcal{L}'_{F,tri} = [d(F(a), F(p)) - d(F(a), F(n)) + m]_+ \tag{1}$$

where $d(x_1, x_2) = \|\frac{x_1}{\|x_1\|} - \frac{x_2}{\|x_2\|}\|^2$ is the squared Euclidean distance between two $l2$-normalized feature vectors, and $[\cdot]_+ \triangleq \max(\cdot, 0)$ takes the positive component of its input. Then, the network is trained to find an embedding where the distance between the negative pair ought to be larger than the distance between the positive pair by at least a margin m.

3.1 Adversarial Triplet Generator G

Now let us consider a hard example generator G that generates a new adversarial sample $G(F(x)) \in \mathbb{R}^L$ by manipulating the feature representation $F(x)$ of an input x. Specifically, G learns to produce challenging triplets of examples by pushing apart the vectors from the same category while pulling closer the vectors from different categories.

Formally, We can minimize the following adversarial triplet loss to train G,

$$\mathcal{L}_{G,tri} = [d(G(F(a)), G(F(n))) - d(G(F(a)), G(F(p))) + m]_+ \tag{2}$$

Then, given a fixed G, the objective function to train F in our method becomes

$$\mathcal{L}_{F,tri} = [d(G(F(a)), G(F(p))) - d(G(F(a)), G(F(n))) + m]_+ \tag{3}$$

Clearly, $\mathcal{L}_{F,tri}$ and $\mathcal{L}_{G,tri}$ constitute an adversarial loss pair. Compared with the original training loss (1), F is trained through hard triplets of examples generated by G by pulling the positive pair closer and pushing the negative pair apart to meet the margin m.

3.2 Multi-category Discriminator D

However, the above adversarial mechanism alone is insufficient to train a reliable G because it could arbitrarily manipulate the feature representation F with no suitable constraints. For example, G could simply output random vectors to achieve a lower value of $\mathcal{L}_{G,tri}$, which was useless for training a better F. Thus, to properly constrain the triplet generator G, we require its output features should not change the label of its input features $F(x)$.

Consider a discriminator D. Given a feature vector, D categories it into $(K + 1)$ categories, where the first K categories represent real classes of examples and the last one denotes a *fake* class. For a triplet $<a, p, n>$ and their labels $<l_a, l_p, l_n>$, we have $l_a = l_p$ for the positive pair and $l_a \neq l_n$ for the negative pair. Then, we minimize the following loss function to train D

$$\mathcal{L}_D = \mathcal{L}_{D,real} + \beta\mathcal{L}_{D,fake} \tag{4}$$

Here, the first term enforces D to correctly classify the feature vectors in the triplet,

$$\mathcal{L}_{D,real} = \frac{1}{3}(\mathcal{L}_{sm}(D(F(a)), l_a) + \mathcal{L}_{sm}(D(F(p)), l_p) + \mathcal{L}_{sm}(D(F(n)), l_n)) \tag{5}$$

where $\mathcal{L}_{sm}$ denotes the softmax loss. Meanwhile, the second term enables D to distinguish generated features from real ones,

$$\mathcal{L}_{D,fake} = \frac{1}{3}(\mathcal{L}_{sm}(D(G(F(a))), l_{fake}) \\ + \mathcal{L}_{sm}(D(G(F(p))), l_{fake}) + \mathcal{L}_{sm}(D(G(F(n))), l_{fake})) \tag{6}$$

where l_{fake} represents the fake class.

Once we have D, as aforementioned, G ought to preserve the label of its input features. Thus we have the following loss to enforce this label preservation assumption,

$$\mathcal{L}_{G,cls} = \frac{1}{3}(\mathcal{L}_{sm}(D(G(F(a))), l_a) \\ + \mathcal{L}_{sm}(D(G(F(p))), l_p) + \mathcal{L}_{sm}(D(G(F(n))), l_n)) \tag{7}$$

Putting together with (2), now we will minimize the following loss to train the hard triplet generator G,

$$\mathcal{L}_G = \mathcal{L}_{G,tri} + \gamma \mathcal{L}_{G,cls} \tag{8}$$

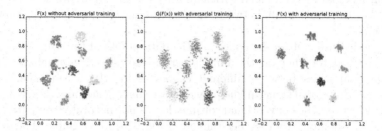

Fig. 2. Visualization of feature embedding on MNIST dataset.

3.3 Summary

Figure 1 illustrates the architecture of the proposed adversarial method. In summary, the proposed method contains an alternate optimization problem to train

(i) the feature embedding network F by minimizing the triplet loss (3) combined with the classification loss (5):

$$\mathcal{L}_{F,tri} + \mu \mathcal{L}_{D,real} \tag{9}$$

where the classification loss ensures the learned features F can correctly classify different categories of real examples.

(ii) the discriminator D in (4), and

(iii) the hard triplet generator G in (8).

It is not hard to see that G and F form a pair of adversarial players who compete to learn feature representation resilient against hard triplets. On the other hand, D and G is another adversarial pair playing the similar role as the discriminator and generator in the classic GAN, except that G is trained to preserve labels of given examples.

Figure 2 visualizes the feature space with and without adversarial training on MNIST dataset by t-SNE [19]. It demonstrates that G pushes $F(x)$ away from the middle of the cluster, while F learns a tighter distribution of feature with the effect of G. More details will be further discussed in the next section.

4   Algorithm Details

We will discuss more details about our method in this section. First, a basic model that jointly minimizes the softmax loss and the triplet loss is presented. Then the adversarial triplet generator is added to the basic model. Finally, we also elaborate on the network details.

4.1   Basic Model

The basic model of learning the feature embedding network is illustrated in Fig. 3. The output (embedded) feature layer is followed by one fully-connected layer for the softmax loss and one l_2-normalization layer for the similarity loss. The softmax loss was combined with similarity loss in several previous works [21, 34,45], but the relationship between softmax loss and similarity loss has not been well studied.

In the feature embedding space, all the data points of the same class ought to be grouped together on the unit hyper sphere after l_2-normalization. The decision boundaries between different classes divide the feature space for K classes and this global structure helps accelerate convergence and achieve optimal results. However, the conventional softmax loss is not naturally compatible with distance-based similarity loss. See the left of Fig. 3(b) for example. The decision boundaries by minimizing conventional softmax loss may not pass through the origin due to the existence of a bias b. Thus, the data points from different classes may overlap each other after l_2-normalization. This results in a short inter-class distance that impacts the performance of feature embedding. Hence, we propose to use softmax loss without a bias. As shown in the right of Fig. 3(b), all the decision boundaries from such no-bias softmax loss pass through the origin and the decision area for a class is cone-shaped with its vertex located at the origin. Thus, a class of examples have a separate projection on the unit hyper sphere, which ensures a long inter-class distance between examples from different classes.

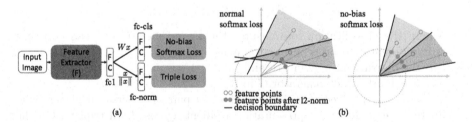

Fig. 3. (a) Architecture of the basic model with joint no-bias softmax loss and triplet loss. (b) Illustration of the feature space in 2-dimensional with conventional softmax loss and no-bias softmax loss. Hollow dots denote the feature points and filled dots denote the points projected to the unit circle after l2-norm. The solid line represent the decision boundary of softmax. The embedded feature points with no-bias softmax loss have longer inter-class distance than those with conventional softmax loss.

Given a training tuple $<a, p, n, l>$, where the anchor image a is labeled as class l, the no-bias softmax loss is defined as

$$\mathcal{L}_{F,cls} = -\log \frac{e^{W_l F(a)}}{\sum_{k=1}^{K} e^{W_k F(a)}} \tag{10}$$

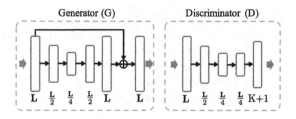

Fig. 4. Architecture of the generator (G) and discriminator (D).

where $F(\cdot)$ denotes the output feature of a CNN model. Then the network F is trained by minimizing $\mathcal{L}_F = \mathcal{L}_{F,cls} + \lambda \mathcal{L}'_{F,tri}$ by stochastic gradient descent, and λ is the weight to control the trade-off between the no-bias softmax loss and the original triplet loss (1).

4.2 Adversarial Training

The above basic model trains a benchmark feature extractor F, and here we will show that it can benefit from the hard triplets generated by an adversarial generator. In the basic model, F is trained by randomly sampling triplets from a training set without considering their hardness. Now we attempt to train a hard triplet generator at the feature level.

As shown in the left dotted box in Fig. 4, the generator denoted by G takes an input feature vector $F(x) \in \mathbb{R}^L$ output from F and produces a generated feature vector of the same dimension. The generator G consists of 4 fully-connected layers, first two of which reduce the input feature dimension by half as a bottleneck and then the last two layers redouble it to the original dimension. Each layer is followed with BatchNormalization [10] and ReLU [18], and the output vector is calculated by performing an element-wise addition between the output fully-connected layer and the input vector. Such residual structure enforces G to learn the offset of the input vector, which yields faster convergence of G in the training phase. In this fashion, G only needs to learn how to move a feature vector in the feature space instead of generating features from scratch.

On the other hand, the discriminator D also takes an input feature vector $F(x) \in \mathbb{R}^L$ from F and classifies it into one of $K + 1$ classes. D also has four fully-connected layers, where the first three are followed with BatchNormalization and ReLU and the last one is a softmax layer.

We use mini-batch SGD with the learning rate α to train the networks F, D, and G step by step with the loss functions introduced in Sect. 3.

(i) Update the feature embedding network F with $\mathcal{L}_F = \mathcal{L}_{F,tri} + \mu \mathcal{L}_{D,real}$, where F is trained by ensuring the distance of a positive pair should be smaller than that of the negative pair by at least a margin m in a hard triplet generated by G; meanwhile, all feature vectors of F should be correctly classified by D.

(ii) Update the discriminator D with $\mathcal{L}_D = \mathcal{L}_{D,real} + \beta\mathcal{L}_{D,fake}$, where D is learned by distinguishing real vectors F from the fake counterparts generated by G, and $\mathcal{L}_{D,real}$ is also used to train D to classify the labeled examples.

(iii) Update the hard triplet generator G with $\mathcal{L}_G = \mathcal{L}_{G,tri} + \gamma\mathcal{L}_{G,cls}$, where G is trained to produce hard triplets that can challenge F while it is regularized by preserving the labels of training examples.

4.3   Harder Triplet Generation from Local Details

Furthermore, we attempt to build a more powerful extractor F allowing the HTG to create harder triplets from fine-grained local details, thus a visual recognition model can be challenged with harder triplet examples to become more robust.

Indeed, local features play a critical role in many fine-grained visual recognition tasks. Typical deep neural networks designed for image classification are good at extracting high-level global features, but the features of local details are often missing. This could limit the HTG in exploring local details to create harder triplets. For example, without local details, the HTG could not generate such hard triplets that could force a model to focus on most discriminative parts such as logos, lights and sunroof in identifying different cars.

To address this problem, we introduce keypoint maps for training HTG by focusing on local details. For example ResNet-18 consists of four sequential convolution blocks, and the output of the fully-connected (FC) layer following the last convolution block is used as the global feature f_{global}. The output feature map of a convolution block-l is denoted by $X^l \in \mathbb{R}^{C \times W \times H}$. Then we add a local branch called keypoint block, which has an architecture similar to a convolution block, to localize the distribution of keypoints that could focus on the most discriminative parts to create harder triplets. The high-level semantic feature maps are sparse and we assume that each channel of a keypoint layer corresponds to a particular type of keypoint, thus we apply channel-wise softmax on the output feature map of the keypoint layer to estimate the density of a keypoint over different image locations:

$$M^l_{cij} = \frac{e^{P^l_{cij}}}{\sum_{w=1}^{W} \sum_{h=1}^{H} e^{P^l_{cwh}}} \tag{11}$$

with P^l_{cij} being the output feature of channel c at (i,j) in keypoint block-l.

This softmax output is used as a channel-wise keypoint mask, which allows us to perform element-wise product of X^l and M^l. The resulting local feature f^l of block-l is calculated by a channel-wise summation over locations: $f^l_c = \sum_{i=1}^{W} \sum_{j=1}^{H} X^l_{cij} M^l_{cij}$.

In experiments, we will extract such local features at block-3 and block-4, which are then concatenated with the global feature to form the final output feature $f_{out} = [f_{global}; f^3; f^4]$.

5   Experiments

We evaluate the proposed method on four real-world datasets in two performance metrics, i.e., Recall@K [12] and mAP. For the network architecture, we choose ResNet-18 [8] pre-trained on ImageNet ILSVRC-2012 [25]. The keypoint blocks described in Sect. 4.3 are initialized with the same weights as the ResNet-18 convolution blocks. We use the same hyper parameters in all experiments without tuning them. Input images are first resized to 256×256 and cropped at 224×224. For the data augmentation, we use random crops with random horizontal mirroring for training and a single center crop for testing.

For training basic model in Sect. 4.1, mini-batch size is 128, triplet margin is $m = 0.1$, and $\lambda = 1$. The learning rate α starts from 0.01 and is divided by 10 every 5 epochs to train the model for 15 epochs.

For training adversarial triplet generator in Sect. 4.2, mini-batch size is 64, and $\mu = \beta = \gamma = 1$. The generator network is trained for 10 epochs with the learning rate α being initialized to 0.001 and divided by 10 every 5 epochs.

5.1   Datasets

We use four datasets in our experiments which are commonly used in many fine-grained visual recognition tasks. We follow the standard experiment protocol to split train and test sets for a fair comparison with existing methods.

- **CUB200** [36] dataset has 200 classes of birds with $11,788$ images, in which the first 100 classes (5,864 images) are used for training and the rest 100 classes (5,924 images) are used for testing. Both query and gallery sets are from the test set.
- **CARS196** [13] dataset has 196 classes of cars with 16,185 images, where the first 98 classes (8,054 images) are used for training and the rest 98 classes (8,131 images) are used for testing. Also, both query and gallery sets are from the test set.
- **In-Shop Clothes Retrieval** is one of the three benchmarks used in [17], which has 7,982 classes of clothes with 52,712 images. Among them, 3,997 classes (25,882 images) are used for training and the other 3,985 classes (28,760 images) are used for testing. The test images are partitioned to a query set and a gallery set. The query set contains 14,218 images and the gallery set has 12,612 images.
- **VehicleID** [16] dataset contains 221,763 images of 26,267 vehicles, where the training set contains 110,178 images of 13,134 vehicles and the test set contains 111,585 images of 13,133 vehicles. It is more challenging than CARS196 because different identities of vehicles are considered as different classes, even though they share the same car model. Following the protocol in [16], there are three test sets of different sizes. The smallest test set contains 7,332 images of 800 vehicles. The medium test set contains 12,995 images of 1600 vehicles. The largest test set contains 20,038 images of 2,400 vehicles.

5.2   Generation-Based Method v.s. Mining-Based Method

We start by demonstrating the improvements of our proposed HTG method. We focus on the CARS196 dataset and evaluate models with different settings on training strategy. The network architecture is ResNet-18 without any additional branch. Results are presented in Table 1. We compare random sampling and online hard example mining (OHEM) [29] to our hard triplet generation (HTG). For training OHEM, we sample 32 identities with 4 images for each identity to form a mini-batch, and mine the nearest negative sample and longest positive sample for each anchor data to constitute a triplet. The experimental results show that OHEM improves the recall scores by learning from hard triplets and our HTG method outperforms OHEM further with an absolute 2.4% improvement on Recall@1 score. The results of A/D, B/E and C/F prove that removing the bias of softmax loss offers notable boost on varied training strategies, which means the no-bias softmax loss is more compatible with distance-based similarity loss.

Table 1. Recall@K(%) on CARS196 with different model settings

Model	Training	Softmax	1	2	4	8
A	Random	Bias	65.4	76.5	84.7	91.0
B	OHEM	Bias	67.1	78.1	86.2	91.7
C	HTG	Bias	69.3	79.2	86.7	92.0
D	Random	No-bias	66.6	77.0	85.2	91.3
E	OHEM	No-bias	68.2	78.7	86.5	92.0
F	HTG	No-bias	**70.6**	**79.9**	**87.3**	**92.9**

5.3   Hard Triplet Generation from Local Attentions

In the last section, we showed the HTG with global ResNet-18 features outperformed the other compared methods. We also consider to add a local keypoint branch to maximize the ability of the HTG in generating hard triplets. This could allow the HTG to explore local details so that harder triplets with fine-grained details can be produced to further imporve the recognition accuracy. Below we will demonstrate more competitive performance can be achieved by the HTG with various local attentions models.

To this end, we compare the global vanilla model without any modification, K-branch [46] and ResAttention [37] with our keypoint maps (KPM). These methods are all based on ResNet-18 backbone for fair comparison. K-branch designs 8 branch to detect discriminative regions and align local parts. ResAttention extracts local feature with attention-aware masks. All the architectures are tested with three training strategies and the results are shown in Table 2. The attention models outperform the base model with different training strategies.

Table 2. Recall@1(%) score on CARS196

	Vanilla	K-Branch	ResAttention	KPM
Random	66.6	71.9	72.3	72.7
OHEM	68.2	72.2	72.6	72.5
HTG	70.6	72.7	73.9	76.5

It is worth nothing that on attention models, OHEM does not significantly outperform random sampling of triplets as on the vanilla model. We attribute this performance degeneration to the bad local optimum of OHEM. On the contrary, the proposed HTG successfully boosts the performance on attention models, especially on KPM model. This demonstrates the competency of HTG in exploring local details to generate harder triplet examples for training more competitive recognition models.

In order to demonstrate that KPM is able to find keypoints, we intuitively illustrate detected keypoints by taking the maximum response over C channels at different locations:

$$V_{i,j} = \max_{c \in 1, \cdots, C} \{M_{c,i,j}\} \tag{12}$$

The keypoint maps are superimposed on their input images in Fig. 5. On VehicleID dataset, there are high responses on logo, lights, sunroof and antenna on the car roof. These are the most discriminative parts to classify car models. To tell the differences between distinct vehicles of the same model, the model further localizes more customized landmarks, such as the stickers on the car window and the small objects put on the car dashboard. It shows that this model is able to find these subtle keypoints effectively.

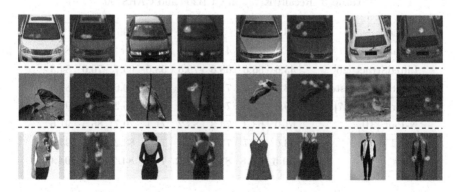

Fig. 5. Visualization of keypoint maps on VehicleID, CUB200 and In-Shop Clothes datasets respectively.

Local features play an important role in fine-grained image recognition tasks. Although the local branch of keypoint blocks does not need any manual annotations, it is expected to localize discriminative parts by learning from the generated hard triplets to distinguish subtle differences between fine-grained image classes.

On CUB200 dataset, the detected keypoints often locate in eyes, beaks, wings and tails, which are useful to classify different species of birds. On In-Shop Clothes dataset, collar ends, sleeve ends and hem parts are detected. These examples demonstrate that the proposed model trained from the generated hard triplets successfully localizes the most discriminative part in classifying or identifying images at a very fine-grained level.

5.4   Comparison with the State-of-the-Art Methods

On the CUB200 and CARS196 datasets, the proposed model is compared with five state-of-the-art methods. LiftedStruct [20] uses an algorithm taking full advantage of the training batches by lifting the vector of pairwise distances within the batch to the matrix of pairwise distance. StructuredCluster [32] uses structured prediction that is aware of the global structure of an embedding space. SmartMining [7] proposes an adaptive controller that automatically adjusts the smart mining hyper-parameters and speeds up the convergence. N-Pair [31] proposes multi-class N-pair loss to leverage more than one negative examples for each anchor. HDC [44] ensembles a set of models with increasing complexities in a cascaded manner to mine hard samples at different levels. Table 3 shows the Recall@K results on these two datasets. Our proposed method successfully boosts the Recall@K upon the existing methods and gets an absolute 5.9% improvement on Recall@1 compared with HDC on CUB200 dataset, and 2.8% improvement on CARS196 dataset.

Table 3. Recall@K(%) on CUB200 and CARS196

Dataset	CUB200				CARS196			
Recall@K	1	2	4	8	1	2	4	8
LiftedStruct [20]	43.6	56.6	68.6	79.6	53.0	65.7	76.0	84.3
StructuredCluster [32]	48.2	61.4	71.8	81.9	58.1	70.6	80.3	87.8
SmartMining [7]	49.8	62.3	74.1	83.3	64.7	76.2	84.2	90.2
N-Pair [31]	51.0	63.3	74.3	83.2	71.1	79.7	86.5	91.6
HDC [44]	53.6	65.7	77.0	85.6	73.7	83.2	89.5	93.8
Ours	**59.5**	**71.8**	**81.3**	**88.2**	**76.5**	**84.7**	**90.4**	**94.0**

On In-Shop Clothes dataset, FashionNet [17] is a novel deep model that learns clothing features by jointly predicting landmark locations and massive attributes. HDC is also included in comparison on this dataset. Table 4 reports the results. Compared methods suffer from the problem with a large number of classes and limited images in each class. The proposed method significantly improves the

Recall@1 score from 62.1% to 80.3%. It is worth noting that the proposed method does not use any manually annotated landmarks and attributes. FashionNet did not report the numeric results on this task, and the results of FashionNet are referred to [44].

Table 4. Recall@K(%) on In-Shop Clothes Retrieval, FN is short for FashionNet.

K	1	10	20	30	40
FN+Joints [17]	41.0	64.0	68.0	71.0	73.0
FN+Poselets [17]	42.0	65.0	70.0	72.0	72.0
FN [17]	53.0	73.0	76.0	77.0	79.0
HDC [44]	62.1	84.9	89.0	91.2	92.3
Ours	**80.3**	**93.9**	**95.8**	**96.6**	**97.1**

On VehicleID dataset, Mixed Diff + CCL [16] uses coupled cluster loss and the mixed difference network structure. Table 5 reports the results on VehicleID. This dataset contains many hard negative examples that are different vehicles with the same model, and it is an ideal example showing the advantage of learning from hard triplets. Compared with HDC, our model achieves an absolute 7.7%/7.5%/9.0% improvement on Small/Medium/Large test set in mAP, respectively. The results on these four datasets show the proposed method outperforms the existing state-of-the-art methods.

Table 5. mAP(%) on VehicleID

Method	Small	Medium	Large
VGG+Triple Loss [16]	44.4	39.1	37.1
VGG+CCL [16]	49.2	44.8	38.6
Mixed Diff + CCL [16]	54.6	48.1	45.5
HDC [44]	65.5	63.1	57.5
Ours	**73.2**	**70.6**	**66.5**

6   Conclusion

In this paper, we propose a novel algorithm, Hard Triplet Generation via Adversarial training for learning an optimal embedding of images. A feature extractor is pushed to distinguish relevant examples from irrelevant ones even for the most challenging queries in the generated hard triplets. This generation-based method avoids the problem of being trapped to a bad local optimum by a greedy mining-based method. Experimental results on four real-world datasets demonstrate the advantage of the proposed model over the compared state-of-the-art methods.

Acknowledgements. This paper is partially supported by NSFC (No. 61772330, 61533012, 61472075), the Basic Research Project of Innovation Action Plan (16JC1402800), the Major Basic Research Program (15JC1400103) of Shanghai Science and Technology Committee, NSF under award #1704309 and IARPA under grant #D17PC00345.

References

1. Cheng, D., Gong, Y., Zhou, S., Wang, J., Zheng, N.: Person re-identification by multi-channel parts-based CNN with improved triplet loss function. In: Proceedings of the IEEE Conference on Computer Vision and Pattern Recognition, pp. 1335–1344 (2016)
2. Cui, Y., Zhou, F., Lin, Y., Belongie, S.: Fine-grained categorization and dataset bootstrapping using deep metric learning with humans in the loop. In: Proceedings of the IEEE Conference on Computer Vision and Pattern Recognition, pp. 1153–1162 (2016)
3. Denton, E.L., Chintala, S., Fergus, R., et al.: Deep generative image models using a Laplacian pyramid of adversarial networks. In: Advances in Neural Information Processing Systems, pp. 1486–1494 (2015)
4. Edraki, M., Qi, G.J.: Generalized loss-sensitive adversarial learning with manifold margins. In: Proceedings of European Conference on Computer Vision (ECCV 2018) (2018)
5. Goodfellow, I., et al.: Generative adversarial nets. In: Advances in Neural Information Processing Systems, pp. 2672–2680 (2014)
6. Hadsell, R., Chopra, S., LeCun, Y.: Dimensionality reduction by learning an invariant mapping. In: 2006 IEEE Computer Society Conference on Computer Vision and Pattern Recognition, vol. 2, pp. 1735–1742. IEEE (2006)
7. Harwood, B., Kumar, B., Carneiro, G., Reid, I., Drummond, T., et al.: Smart mining for deep metric learning. In: IEEE International Conference on Computer Vision (2017)
8. He, K., Zhang, X., Ren, S., Sun, J.: Deep residual learning for image recognition. In: Proceedings of the IEEE Conference on Computer Vision and Pattern Recognition, pp. 770–778 (2016)
9. Hu, J., Lu, J., Tan, Y.P.: Discriminative deep metric learning for face verification in the wild. In: Proceedings of the IEEE Conference on Computer Vision and Pattern Recognition, pp. 1875–1882 (2014)
10. Ioffe, S., Szegedy, C.: Batch normalization: accelerating deep network training by reducing internal covariate shift. In: International Conference on Machine Learning, pp. 448–456 (2015)
11. Isola, P., Zhu, J.Y., Zhou, T., Efros, A.A.: Image-to-image translation with conditional adversarial networks. In: IEEE Conference on Computer Vision and Pattern Recognition (2017)
12. Jegou, H., Douze, M., Schmid, C.: Product quantization for nearest neighbor search. IEEE Trans. Pattern Anal. Mach. Intell. **33**(1), 117–128 (2011)
13. Krause, J., Stark, M., Deng, J., Fei-Fei, L.: 3D object representations for fine-grained categorization. In: Proceedings of the IEEE International Conference on Computer Vision Workshops, pp. 554–561 (2013)
14. Krizhevsky, A., Sutskever, I., Hinton, G.E.: Imagenet classification with deep convolutional neural networks. In: Advances in Neural Information Processing Systems, pp. 1097–1105 (2012)

15. Li, J., Liang, X., Wei, Y., Xu, T., Feng, J., Yan, S.: Perceptual generative adversarial networks for small object detection. In: IEEE Conference on Computer Vision and Pattern Recognition (2017)
16. Liu, H., Tian, Y., Yang, Y., Pang, L., Huang, T.: Deep relative distance learning: tell the difference between similar vehicles. In: Proceedings of the IEEE Conference on Computer Vision and Pattern Recognition, pp. 2167–2175 (2016)
17. Liu, Z., Luo, P., Qiu, S., Wang, X., Tang, X.: Deepfashion: powering robust clothes recognition and retrieval with rich annotations. In: Proceedings of the IEEE Conference on Computer Vision and Pattern Recognition, pp. 1096–1104 (2016)
18. Maas, A.L., Hannun, A.Y., Ng, A.Y.: Rectifier nonlinearities improve neural network acoustic models. In: Proceedings of the ICML, vol. 30 (2013)
19. van der Maaten, L., Hinton, G.: Visualizing data using t-SNE. J. Mach. Learn. Res. 9(Nov), 2579–2605 (2008)
20. Oh Song, H., Xiang, Y., Jegelka, S., Savarese, S.: Deep metric learning via lifted structured feature embedding. In: Proceedings of the IEEE Conference on Computer Vision and Pattern Recognition, pp. 4004–4012 (2016)
21. Parkhi, O.M., Vedaldi, A., Zisserman, A.: Deep face recognition. In: BMVC, vol. 1, p. 6 (2015)
22. Qi, G.J.: Loss-sensitive generative adversarial networks on Lipschitz densities. arXiv preprint arXiv:1701.06264 (2017)
23. Qi, G.J., Zhang, L., Hu, H., Edraki, M., Wang, J., Hua, X.S.: Global versus localized generative adversarial nets. In: Proceedings of IEEE Conference on Computer Vision and Pattern Recognition (CVPR) (2018)
24. Radford, A., Metz, L., Chintala, S.: Unsupervised representation learning with deep convolutional generative adversarial networks. arXiv preprint arXiv:1511.06434 (2015)
25. Russakovsky, O., et al.: Imagenet large scale visual recognition challenge. Int. J. Comput. Vis. 115(3), 211–252 (2015)
26. Schroff, F., Kalenichenko, D., Philbin, J.: Facenet: a unified embedding for face recognition and clustering. In: Proceedings of the IEEE Conference on Computer Vision and Pattern Recognition, pp. 815–823 (2015)
27. Schultz, M., Joachims, T.: Learning a distance metric from relative comparisons. In: Advances in Neural Information Processing Systems, pp. 41–48 (2004)
28. Shi, H., et al.: Embedding deep metric for person re-identification: a study against large variations. In: Leibe, B., Matas, J., Sebe, N., Welling, M. (eds.) ECCV 2016. LNCS, vol. 9905, pp. 732–748. Springer, Cham (2016). https://doi.org/10.1007/978-3-319-46448-0_44
29. Simo-Serra, E., Trulls, E., Ferraz, L., Kokkinos, I., Fua, P., Moreno-Noguer, F.: Discriminative learning of deep convolutional feature point descriptors. In: Proceedings of the IEEE International Conference on Computer Vision, pp. 118–126 (2015)
30. Simonyan, K., Zisserman, A.: Very deep convolutional networks for large-scale image recognition. arXiv preprint arXiv:1409.1556 (2014)
31. Sohn, K.: Improved deep metric learning with multi-class N-pair loss objective. In: Advances in Neural Information Processing Systems, pp. 1857–1865 (2016)
32. Song, H.O., Jegelka, S., Rathod, V., Murphy, K.: Learnable structured clustering framework for deep metric learning. In: IEEE Conference on Computer Vision and Pattern Recognition (2017)
33. Springenberg, J.T.: Unsupervised and semi-supervised learning with categorical generative adversarial networks. In: International Conference on Learning Representations (ICLR) (2016)

34. Sun, Y., Chen, Y., Wang, X., Tang, X.: Deep learning face representation by joint identification-verification. In: Advances in Neural Information Processing Systems, pp. 1988–1996 (2014)
35. Szegedy, C., et al.: Going deeper with convolutions. In: Proceedings of the IEEE Conference on Computer Vision and Pattern Recognition, pp. 1–9 (2015)
36. Wah, C., Branson, S., Welinder, P., Perona, P., Belongie, S.: The Caltech-UCSD birds-200-2011 dataset (2011)
37. Wang, F., et al.: Residual attention network for image classification. In: Proceedings of the IEEE Conference on Computer Vision and Pattern Recognition, pp. 3156–3164 (2017)
38. Wang, X., Shrivastava, A., Gupta, A.: A-fast-RCNN: hard positive generation via adversary for object detection. In: IEEE Conference on Computer Vision and Pattern Recognition (2017)
39. Weinberger, K.Q., Blitzer, J., Saul, L.K.: Distance metric learning for large margin nearest neighbor classification. In: Advances in Neural Information Processing Systems, pp. 1473–1480 (2006)
40. Wen, Y., Zhang, K., Li, Z., Qiao, Y.: A discriminative feature learning approach for deep face recognition. In: Leibe, B., Matas, J., Sebe, N., Welling, M. (eds.) ECCV 2016. LNCS, vol. 9911, pp. 499–515. Springer, Cham (2016). https://doi.org/10.1007/978-3-319-46478-7_31
41. Xing, E.P., Jordan, M.I., Russell, S.J., Ng, A.Y.: Distance metric learning with application to clustering with side-information. In: Advances in Neural Information Processing Systems, pp. 521–528 (2003)
42. Yi, D., Lei, Z., Liao, S., Li, S.Z.: Deep metric learning for person re-identification. In: 2014 22nd International Conference on Pattern Recognition (ICPR), pp. 34–39. IEEE (2014)
43. Yi, Z., Zhang, H., Tan, P., Gong, M.: DualGAN: unsupervised dual learning for image-to-image translation. In: IEEE International Conference on Computer Vision (2017)
44. Yuan, Y., Yang, K., Zhang, C.: Hard-aware deeply cascaded embedding. In: ICCV (2017)
45. Zhang, X., Zhou, F., Lin, Y., Zhang, S.: Embedding label structures for fine-grained feature representation. In: Proceedings of the IEEE Conference on Computer Vision and Pattern Recognition, pp. 1114–1123 (2016)
46. Zhao, L., Li, X., Wang, J., Zhuang, Y.: Deeply-learned part-aligned representations for person re-identification. In: IEEE Conference on Computer Vision and Pattern Recognition (2017)
47. Zhu, J.Y., Park, T., Isola, P., Efros, A.A.: Unpaired image-to-image translation using cycle-consistent adversarial networks. In: IEEE International Conference on Computer Vision (2017)

SphereNet: Learning Spherical Representations for Detection and Classification in Omnidirectional Images

Benjamin Coors[1,3]([✉]), Alexandru Paul Condurache[2,3], and Andreas Geiger[1]

[1] Autonomous Vision Group, MPI for Intelligent Systems and University
of Tübingen, Tübingen, Germany
benjamin.coors@tue.mpg.de
[2] Institute for Signal Processing, University of Lübeck, Lübeck, Germany
[3] Robert Bosch GmbH, Stuttgart, Germany

Abstract. Omnidirectional cameras offer great benefits over classical cameras wherever a wide field of view is essential, such as in virtual reality applications or in autonomous robots. Unfortunately, standard convolutional neural networks are not well suited for this scenario as the natural projection surface is a sphere which cannot be unwrapped to a plane without introducing significant distortions, particularly in the polar regions. In this work, we present SphereNet, a novel deep learning framework which encodes invariance against such distortions explicitly into convolutional neural networks. Towards this goal, SphereNet adapts the sampling locations of the convolutional filters, effectively reversing distortions, and wraps the filters around the sphere. By building on regular convolutions, SphereNet enables the transfer of existing perspective convolutional neural network models to the omnidirectional case. We demonstrate the effectiveness of our method on the tasks of image classification and object detection, exploiting two newly created semi-synthetic and real-world omnidirectional datasets.

1 Introduction

Over the last years, omnidirectional imaging devices have gained in popularity due to their wide field of view and their widespread applications ranging from virtual reality to robotics [10,16,21,27,28]. Today, omnidirectional action cameras are available at an affordable price and 360° viewers are integrated into social media platforms. Given the growing amount of spherical imagery, there is an increasing interest in computer vision models which are optimized for this kind of data.

The most popular representation of 360° images is the equirectangular projection where latitude and longitude of the spherical image are mapped to horizontal

Electronic supplementary material The online version of this chapter (https://doi.org/10.1007/978-3-030-01240-3_32) contains supplementary material, which is available to authorized users.

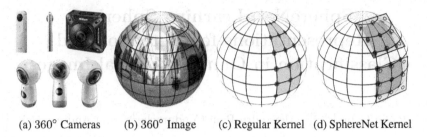

(a) 360° Cameras   (b) 360° Image   (c) Regular Kernel   (d) SphereNet Kernel

Fig. 1. Overview. (a+b) Capturing images with fisheye or 360° action camera results in images which are best represented on the sphere. (c) Using regular convolutions (e.g., with 3 × 3 filter kernels) on the rectified equirectangular representation (see Fig. 2b) suffers from distortions of the sampling locations (red) close to the poles. (d) In contrast, our SphereNet kernel exploits projections (red) of the sampling pattern on the tangent plane (blue), yielding filter outputs which are invariant to latitudinal rotations. (Color figure online)

and vertical grid coordinates, see Figs. 1 and 2 for an illustration. However, the equirectangular image representation suffers from heavy distortions in the polar regions which implies that an object will appear differently depending on its latitudinal position. This presents a challenge to modern computer vision algorithms, such as convolutional neural networks (CNNs) which are the state-of-the-art solution to many computer vision tasks.

While CNNs are capable of learning invariances to common object transformations and intra-class variations, they would require significantly more parameters, training samples and training time to learn invariance to these distortions from data. This is undesirable as data annotation is time-consuming and annotated omnidirectional datasets are scarce and smaller in size than those collected for the perspective case. An attractive alternative is therefore to encode invariance to geometric transformations directly into a CNN, which has been proven highly efficient in reducing the number of model parameters as well as the required number of training samples [4,29].

In this work, we present *SphereNet*, a novel framework for processing omnidirectional images with convolutional neural networks by encoding distortion invariance into the architecture of CNNs. SphereNet adjusts the sampling grid locations of the convolutional filters based on the geometry of the spherical image representation, thus avoiding distortions as illustrated in Figs. 1 and 2. The SphereNet framework applies to a large number of projection models including perspective, wide-angle, fisheye and omnidirectional projection. As SphereNet builds on regular convolutional filters, it naturally enables the transfer of CNNs between different image representations by adapting the sampling locations of the convolution kernels. We demonstrate this by training object detectors on perspective images and transferring them to omnidirectional inputs. We provide extensive experiments on semi-synthetic as well as real-world datasets which demonstrate the effectiveness of the proposed approach for image classification and object detection.

In summary, this paper makes the following **contributions**:

- We introduce SphereNet, a framework for learning spherical image representations by encoding distortion invariance into convolutional filters. SphereNet retains the original spherical image connectivity and, by building on regular convolutions, enables the transfer of perspective CNN models to omnidirectional inputs.
- We improve the computational efficiency of SphereNet using an approximately uniform sampling of the sphere which avoids oversampling in the polar regions.
- We create two novel semi-synthetic and real-world datasets for object detection in omnidirectional images.
- We demonstrate improved performance as well as SphereNet's transfer learning capabilities on the tasks of image classification and object detection and compare our results to several state-of-the-art baselines.

2 Related Work

There are few deep neural network architectures specifically designed to operate on omnidirectional inputs. In this section, we review the most related approaches.

Khasanova et al. [14] propose a graph-based approach for omnidirectional image classification. They represent equirectangular images using a weighted graph, where each image pixel is a vertex and the weights are designed to minimize the difference between filter responses at different image locations. This graph structure is processed by a graph convolutional network, which is invariant to rotations and translations [15]. While a graph representation solves the problem of discontinuities at the borders of an equirectangular image, graph convolutional networks are limited to small graphs and image resolutions (50×50 pixels in [15]) and have not yet demonstrated recognition performance comparable to regular CNNs on more challenging datasets. In contrast, our method builds on regular convolutions, which offer state-of-the-art performance for many computer vision tasks, while also retaining the spherical image connectivity.

In concurrent work, Cohen et al. [3] propose to use spherical CNNs for classification and encode rotation equivariance into the network. However, often full rotation invariance is not desirable: similar to regular images, 360° images are mostly captured in one dominant orientation (i.e., it is rare that the camera is flipped upside-down). Incorporating full rotation invariance in such scenarios reduces discriminative power as evidenced by our experiments. Furthermore, unlike our work which builds on regular convolutions and is compatible with modern CNN architectures, it is non-trivial to integrate either graph or spherical convolutions into network architectures for more complex computer vision tasks like object detection. In fact, no results beyond image classification are provided in the literature. In contrast, our framework readily allows for adapting existing CNN architectures for object detection or other higher-level vision tasks to the omnidirectional case. While currently only few large omnidirectional datasets exist, there are many trained perspective CNN models available, which our method enables to transfer to any omnidirectional vision task.

Su et al. [30] propose to process equirectangular images with regular convolutions by increasing the kernel size towards the polar regions. However, this adaptation of the convolutional filters is a simplistic approximation of distortions in the equirectangular representation and implies that weights can only be shared along each row, resulting in a significant increase in model parameters. Thus, this model is hard to train from scratch and kernel-wise pre-training against a trained perspective model is required. In contrast, we retain weight sharing across all rows and columns so that our model can be trained directly end-to-end. At the same time, our method better approximates the distortions in equirectangular images and allows for perspective-to-omnidirectional representation transfer.

One way of mitigating the problem of learning spherical representations are cube map projections as considered in [19,22]. Here, the image is mapped to the six faces of a cube which are considered as image planes of six virtual perspective cameras and processed with a regular CNN. However, this approach does not remove distortions but only minimizes their effect. Besides, additional discontinuities at the patch boundaries are introduced and post-processing may be required to combine the individual outputs of each patch. We avoid these problems by providing a suitable representation for spherical signals which can be directly trained end-to-end.

Besides works on distortion invariance, several works focus on invariances to geometric transformations such as rotations or flips. Jaderberg et al. [11], introduce a separate network which learns to predict the parameters of a spatial transformation of an input feature map. Scattering convolution networks [1,25] use predefined wavelet filters to encode stable geometric invariants into networks while other recent works encode invariances into learned convolutional filters [4,9,29,31]. These works are orthogonal to the presented framework and can be advantageously combined.

Several recent works also consider adapting the sampling locations of convolutional networks, either dynamically [5] or statically [12,18]. Unlike our work, these methods need to learn the sampling locations during training, which requires additional model parameters and training steps. In contrast, we take advantage of the geometric properties of the camera to inject this knowledge explicitly into the network architecture.

3   Method

This section introduces the proposed SphereNet framework. First, we describe the adaptation of the sampling pattern to achieve distortion invariance on the surface of the sphere (Sect. 3.1). Second, we propose an approximation which uniformly samples the sphere to improve the computational efficiency of our method (Sect. 3.2). Finally, we present details on how to incorporate SphereNet into a classification model (Sect. 3.3) as well as how to perform object detection on spherical inputs (Sect. 3.4).

3.1   Kernel Sampling Pattern

The central idea of SphereNet is to lift local CNN operations (e.g. convolution, pooling) from the regular image domain to the sphere surface where fisheye or omnidirectional images can be represented without distortions. This is achieved by representing the kernel as a small patch tangent to the sphere as illustrated in Fig. 1d. Our model focuses on distortion invariance and not rotation invariance, as in practice 360° images are mostly captured in one dominant orientation. Thus, we consider upright patches which are aligned with the great circles of the sphere.

More formally, let S be the unit sphere with S^2 its surface. Every point $\mathbf{s} = (\phi, \theta) \in S^2$ is uniquely defined by its latitude $\phi \in [-\frac{\pi}{2}, \frac{\pi}{2}]$ and longitude $\theta \in [-\pi, \pi]$. Let further Π denote the tangent plane located at $\mathbf{s}_\Pi = (\phi_\Pi, \theta_\Pi)$. We denote a point on Π by its coordinates $\mathbf{x} \in \mathbb{R}^2$. The local coordinate system of Π is hereby centered at $\mathbf{s}$ and oriented upright. Let Π_0 denote the tangent plane located at $\mathbf{s} = (0,0)$. A point $\mathbf{s}$ on the sphere is related to its tangent plane coordinates $\mathbf{x}$ via a gnomonic projection [20].

While the proposed approach is compatible with convolutions of all sizes, in the following we consider a 3×3 kernel, which is most common in state-of-the-art architectures [8,26]. We assume that the input image is provided in equirectangular format which is the de facto standard representation for omnidirectional cameras of all form factors (e.g. catadioptric, dioptric or polydioptric). In Sect. 3.2 we consider a more efficient representation that improves the computational efficiency of our method.

The kernel shape is defined so that its sampling locations $\mathbf{s}_{(j,k)}$, with $j, k \in \{-1, 0, 1\}$ for a 3×3 kernel, align with the step sizes Δ_θ and Δ_ϕ of

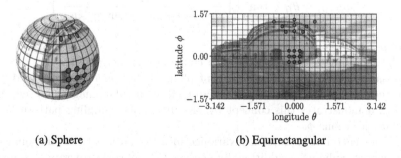

(a) Sphere   (b) Equirectangular

Fig. 2. Kernel sampling pattern at $\phi = 0$ (blue) and $\phi = 1.2$ (red) in spherical (a) and equirectangular (b) representation. Note the distortion of the kernel at $\phi = 1.2$ in (c). (Color figure online)

the equirectangular image at the equator. This ensures that the image can be sampled at Π_0 without interpolation:

$$\mathbf{s}_{(0,0)} = (0,0) \tag{1}$$

$$\mathbf{s}_{(\pm1,0)} = (\pm\Delta_\phi, 0) \tag{2}$$

$$\mathbf{s}_{(0,\pm1)} = (0, \pm\Delta_\theta) \tag{3}$$

$$\mathbf{s}_{(\pm1,\pm1)} = (\pm\Delta_\phi, \pm\Delta_\theta) \tag{4}$$

The position of these filter locations on the tangent plane Π_0 can be calculated via the gnomonic projection [20]:

$$x(\phi, \theta) = \frac{\cos\phi \sin(\theta - \theta_{\Pi_0})}{\sin\phi_{\Pi_0} \sin\phi + \cos\phi_{\Pi_0} \cos\phi \cos(\theta - \theta_{\Pi_0})} \tag{5}$$

$$y(\phi, \theta) = \frac{\cos\phi_{\Pi_0} \sin\phi - \sin\phi_{\Pi_0} \cos\phi \cos(\theta - \theta_{\Pi_0})}{\sin\phi_{\Pi_0} \sin\phi + \cos\phi_{\Pi_0} \cos\phi \cos(\theta - \theta_{\Pi_0})} \tag{6}$$

For the sampling pattern $\mathbf{s}_{(j,k)}$, this yields the following kernel pattern $\mathbf{x}_{(j,k)}$ on Π_0:

$$\mathbf{x}_{(0,0)} = (0,0) \tag{7}$$

$$\mathbf{x}_{(\pm1,0)} = (\pm\tan\Delta_\theta, 0) \tag{8}$$

$$\mathbf{x}_{(0,\pm1)} = (0, \pm\tan\Delta_\phi) \tag{9}$$

$$\mathbf{x}_{(\pm1,\pm1)} = (\pm\tan\Delta_\theta, \pm\sec\Delta_\theta \tan\Delta_\phi) \tag{10}$$

We keep the kernel shape on the tangent fixed. When applying the filter at a different location $\mathbf{s}_\Pi = (\phi_\Pi, \theta_\Pi)$ of the sphere, the inverse gnomonic projection is applied

$$\phi(x, y) = \sin^{-1}\left(\cos\nu \sin\phi_\Pi + \frac{y \sin\nu \cos\phi_\Pi}{\rho}\right) \tag{11}$$

$$\theta(x, y) = \theta_\Pi + \tan^{-1}\left(\frac{x \sin\nu}{\rho \cos\phi_\Pi \cos\nu - y \sin\phi_\Pi \sin\nu}\right)$$

where $\rho = \sqrt{x^2 + y^2}$ and $\nu = \tan^{-1}\rho$.

The sampling grid locations of the convolutional kernels thus get distorted in the same way as objects on a tangent plane of the sphere get distorted when projected from different elevations to an equirectangular image representation. Figure 2 demonstrates this concept by visualizing the sampling pattern at two different elevations ϕ.

Besides encoding distortion invariance into the filters of convolutional neural networks, SphereNet additionally enables the network to wrap its sampling locations around the sphere. As SphereNet uses custom sampling locations for sampling inputs or intermediary feature maps, it is straightforward to allow a filter to sample data across the image boundary. This eliminates any discontinuities which are present when processing omnidirectional images with a regular

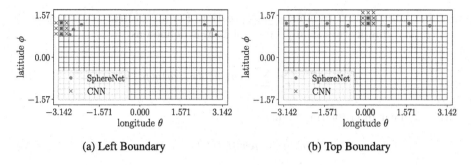

(a) Left Boundary   (b) Top Boundary

Fig. 3. Sampling locations. This figure compares the sampling locations of SphereNet (red) to the sampling locations of a regular CNN (blue) at the boundaries of the equirectangular image. Note how the SphereNet kernel automatically wraps at the left image boundary (a) while correctly representing the discontinuities and distortions at the pole (b). SphereNet thereby retains the original spherical image connectivity which is discarded in a regular convolutional neural network that utilizes zero-padding along the image boundaries. (Color figure online)

convolutional neural network and improves recognition of objects which are split at the sides of an equirectangular image representation or which are positioned very close to the poles, see Fig. 3.

By changing the sampling locations of the convolutional kernels while keeping their size unchanged, our model additionally enables the transfer of CNN models between different image representations. In our experimental evaluation, we demonstrate how an object detector trained on perspective images can be successfully applied to the omnidirectional case. Note that our method can be used for adapting almost any existing deep learning architecture from perspective images to the omnidirectional setup. In general, our SphereNet framework can be applied as long as the image can be mapped to the unit sphere. This is true for many imaging models, ranging from perspective over fisheye[1] to omnidirectional models. Thus, SphereNet can be seen as a generalization of regular CNNs which encodes the camera geometry into the network architecture.

Implementation: As the sampling locations are fixed according to the geometry of the spherical image representation, they can be precomputed for each kernel location at every layer of the network. Further, their relative positioning is constant in each image row. Therefore, it is sufficient to calculate and store the sampling locations once per row and then translate them. We store the sampling locations in look-up tables. These look-up tables are used in a customized convolution operation which is based on highly optimized general matrix multiply (GEMM) functions [13]. As the sampling locations are real-valued, interpolation of the input feature maps is required. In our experiments, we compare nearest

---

[1] While in some cases the single viewpoint assumption is violated, the deviations are often small in practice and can be neglected at larger distances.

neighbor interpolation to bilinear interpolation. For an arbitrary sampling location (p_x, p_y) in a feature map f, interpolation is defined as:

$$f(p_x, p_y) = \sum_n^H \sum_m^W f(m, n) g(p_x, m) g(p_y, n) \qquad (12)$$

with a bilinear interpolation kernel:

$$g(a, b) = max(0, 1 - |a - b|) \qquad (13)$$

or a nearest neighbor kernel:

$$g(a, b) = \delta(\lfloor a + 0.5 \rfloor - b) \qquad (14)$$

where $\delta(\cdot)$ is the Kronecker delta function.

3.2   Uniform Sphere Sampling

In order to improve the computational efficiency of our method, we investigate a more efficient sampling of the spherical image. The equirectangular representation oversamples the spherical image in the polar regions (see Fig. 4a), which results in near duplicate image processing operations in this area. We can avoid unnecessary computation in the polar regions by applying our method to a representation where data is stored uniformly on the sphere, in contrast to considering the pixels of the equirectangular image.

To sample points evenly from a sphere, we leverage the method of Saff and Kuijlaars [24] as it is fast to compute and works with an arbitrary number of sampling points N, including large values of N. More specifically, we obtain points along a spiral that encircles the sphere in a way that the distance between adjacent points along the spiral is approximately equal to the distance between successive coils of the spiral. As visualized in Fig. 4 for an equirectangular image with $N_e = 20 \times 10 = 200$ sampling points, this results in a sampling grid of $N = 127$ points with a similar sampling density to the equirectangular representation at the equator, while significantly reducing the number of sampling points at the poles.

To minimize the loss of information when sampling the equirectangular image we use bilinear interpolation. Afterwards, the image is represented by an $N \times c$ matrix, where c is the number of image channels. Unlike the equirectangular format, this representation no longer encodes the spatial position of each data point. Thus, we save this information in a separate matrix. This location matrix is used to compute the look-up tables for the kernel sampling locations as described in Sect. 3.1. Downsampling of the image is implemented by recalculating a reduced set of sampling points. For applying the kernels and downsampling the image nearest neighbor interpolation is used.

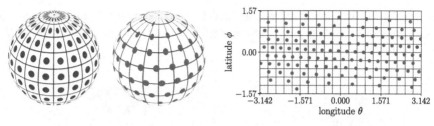

(a) Equirectangular   (b) Uniform Sphere   (c) Uniform Sampling in the Image Plane
Sphere Sampling   Sampling

Fig. 4. Uniform sphere sampling. Comparison of an equirectangular sampling grid on the sphere with $N = 200$ points (a) to an approximation of evenly distributing $N = 127$ sampling points on a sphere with the method of Saff and Kuijlaars [24] (b and c). Note that the sampling points at the poles are much more evenly spaced in the uniform sphere sampling (b) compared to the equirectangular representation (a) which oversamples the image in these regions.

3.3   Spherical Image Classification

SphereNet can be integrated into a convolutional neural network for image classification by adapting the sampling locations of the convolution and pooling kernels as described in Sect. 3.1. Furthermore, it is straightforward to additionally utilize a uniform sphere sampling (see Sect. 3.2), which we will compare to nearest neighbor and bilinear interpolation on an equirectangular representation in the experiments. The integration of SphereNet into an image classification network does not introduce novel model parameters and no changes to the training of the network are required.

3.4   Spherical Object Detection

In order to perform object detection on the sphere, we propose the *Spherical Single Shot MultiBox Detector (Sphere-SSD)*, which adapts the popular Single Shot MultiBox Detector (SSD) [17] to objects located on tangent planes of a sphere. SSD exploits a fully convolutional architecture, predicting category scores and box offsets for a set of default anchor boxes of different scales and aspect ratios. We refer the reader to [17] for details. As in the regular SSD, Sphere-SSD uses a weighted sum between a localization loss and confidence loss. However, in contrast to the original SSD, anchor boxes are now placed on tangent planes of the sphere and are defined in terms of spherical coordinates of their respective tangent plane, the width/height of the box on the tangent plane as well as an in-plane rotation. An illustration of anchor boxes at different scales and aspect ratios is provided in Fig. 5.

In order to match anchor boxes to ground truth detections, we select the anchor box closest to each ground truth box. During inference, we perform non-maximum suppression. For evaluation, we use the Jaccard index computed as the overlap of two polygonal regions which are constructed from the gnomonic projections of evenly spaced points along the rectangular bounding box on the tangent plane.

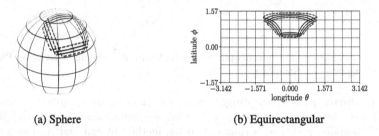

(a) Sphere   (b) Equirectangular

Fig. 5. Spherical anchor boxes are gnomonic projections of 2D bounding boxes of various scales, aspect ratios and orientations on tangent planes of the sphere. The above figure visualizes anchors of the same orientation at different scales and aspect ratios on a 16×8 feature map on a sphere (a) and an equirectangular grid (b).

4 Experimental Evaluation

While the main focus of this paper is on the detection task, we first validate our model with respect to several existing state-of-the-art methods using a simple omnidirectional MNIST classification task.

4.1 Classification: Omni-MNIST

For the classification task, we create an omnidirectional MNIST dataset (*Omni-MNIST*), where MNIST digits are placed on tangent planes of the image sphere and an equirectangular image of the scene is rendered at a resolution of 60×60 pixels.

We compare the performance of our method to several baselines. First, we trained a regular convolutional network operating on the equirectangular images (EquirectCNN) as well as one operating on a cube map representation of the input (CubeMapCNN). We further improved the EquirectCNN model by combining it with a Spherical Transformer Network (SphereTN) which learns to undistort parts of the image by performing a global rotation of the sphere. A more in-depth description of the Spherical Transformer Network is provided in the supplemental. Finally, we also trained the graph convolutional network of Khasanova et al. [14] and the spherical convolutional model of Cohen et al. [3]. For [3] we use the code published by the authors[2]. As [14] does not provide code, we reimplemented their model based on the code of Defferrard et al. [6][3].

---

[2] https://github.com/jonas-koehler/s2cnn.
[3] https://github.com/mdeff/cnn_graph.

Table 1. Classification results on Omni-MNIST. Performance comparison on the omnidirectional MNIST dataset.

Method	Test error (%)	# of Parameters
GCNN [14]	17.21	282K
S2CNN [3]	11.86	149K
CubeMapCNN	10.03	167K
EquirectCNN	9.61	196K
EquirectCNN+SphereTN	8.22	291K
SphereNet (Uniform)	7.16	144K
SphereNet (NN)	7.03	196K
SphereNet (BI)	**5.59**	196K

The network architecture for all models consist of two blocks of convolution and max-pooling, followed by a fully-connected layer. We use 32 filters in the first and 64 filters in the second layer and each layer is followed by a ReLU activation. The fully connected layer has 10 output neurons and uses a softmax activation function. In the CNN and SphereNet models, the convolutional filter kernels are of size 5×5 and are applied with stride 1. Max pooling is performed with kernels of size 3×3 and a stride of 2. The Spherical Transformer Network uses an identical network architecture but replaces the fully-connected output layer with a convolutional layer that outputs the parameters of the rotation. After applying the predicted transformation of the Spherical Transformer the transformed output is then used as input to the EquirectCNN model.

Similarly, the graph convolutional baseline (GCNN) uses graph-conv layers with 32 and 64 filters of polynomial order 25 each, while the spherical CNN baseline (S2CNN) uses an S^2-conv layer with 32 filters and a $SO(3)$-conv layer with 64 filters. Downsampling in the S2CNN model is implemented with bandwidths of $30, 10, 6$ as suggested in [3]. Thus, all models have a comparable number of trainable model parameters (see Table 1). In addition, all models are trained with identical training parameters using Adam, a base learning rate of 0.0001 and batches of size 100 for 100 epochs.

Results on Omni-MNIST: Table 1 compares the performance of SphereNet with uniform sphere sampling (Uniform), nearest neighbor interpolation in the equirectangular image (NN) and bilinear interpolation in the equirectangular image (BI) to the baseline methods. Our results show that all three variants of SphereNet outperform all baselines.

Despite its high number of model parameters, the graph convolutional (GCNN) model struggles to solve the Omni-MNIST classification task. The spherical convolutional (S2CNN) model performs better but is outperformed by all CNN-based models. For the CNN-based models, the CubeMapCNN has a higher test error than EquirectCNN, most likely du to the discontinuities at cube borders and varying digit orientation in the top and bottom faces. The performance of the EquirectCNN is improved when combined with a Spherical Transformer Network (EquirectCNN+SphereTN), demonstrating that the SphereTN is able to support the classification task. However, it does not reach the performance of SphereNet, thus confirming the effectiveness of encoding distortion invariance into the network architecture itself compared to learning it from data.

For SphereNet, the uniform sphere sampling (Uniform) variant performs similar to the nearest neighbor (NN) variant, which demonstrates that the loss of information by uniformly sampling the sphere is negligible. SphereNet with bilinear interpolation (BI) overall performs best, improving upon all baselines by a significant margin.

Please consult the supplemental for further analysis on the impact of varying object scale, object elevation and choice of interpolation on the performance of each model.

Fig. 6. Detection results on FlyingCars dataset. The ground truth is shown in green, our SphereNet (NN) results in red. (Color figure online)

Table 2. Detection results on FlyingCars dataset. All models are trained and tested on the FlyingCars dataset.

Method	Test mAP (%)	Training speed	Inference speed
EquirectCNN+SphereTN	38.91	3.0 s/step	0.232 s/step
EquirectCNN	41.57	1.7 s/step	0.091 s/step
EquirectCNN++	45.65	3.1 s/step	0.175 s/step
CubeMapCNN	48.42	1.8 s/step	0.095 s/step
SphereNet (NN)	**50.18**	2.1 s/step	0.101 s/step

4.2   Object Detection: FlyingCars

We now consider the object detection task. Due to a lack of suitable existing omnidirectional image benchmarks, we create the novel *FlyingCars* dataset.

FlyingCars combines real-world background images of an omnidirectional 360° action camera with rendered 3D car models. For the 3D car models we select a subset of 50 car models from the popular ShapeNet dataset [2], which are rendered onto the background images at different elevations, distances and orientations.

The scenes are rendered using an equirectangular projection to images of dimension 512×256, covering a complete 360° field of view around the camera. Each rendered scene contains between one to three cars, which may be partially occluded. Object bounding boxes are automatically extracted and represented by the lat/lon coordinates (ϕ_i, θ_i) of the object's tangent plane as well as the object width w and height h on the tangent plane and its in-plane rotation α. All groundtruth coordinates are normalized to a range of $[-1.0, 1.0]$. In total, the dataset comprises $1,000$ test and $5,000$ training images with multiple objects each, out of which a subset of $1,000$ images is used as validation set.

For this task, we integrate the nearest neighbor variant (NN) of SphereNet into the Sphere-SSD framework (see Sect. 3.4) as it strikes a balance between computational efficiency and ease of integration into an object detection model. Because the graph and spherical convolution baselines are not applicable to the object detection task, we compare the performance of SphereNet to a CNN operating on the cube map (CubeMapCNN) and equirectangular representation (EquirectCNN). The latter is again tested in combination with a Spherical Transformer Network (EquirectCNN+SphereTN).

Following [30] we evaluate a version of EquirectCNN where the size of the convolutional kernels is enlarged towards the poles to approximate the object distortion in equirectangular images (EquirectCNN++). Like [30] we limit the maximum kernel dimension to 7×7. However, unlike [30] we keep weight tying in place for image rows with filters of the same dimension, thus reducing the number of model parameters. We thereby enable regular training of the network without kernel-wise knowledge distillation as in [30]. In addition, we utilize pre-trained weights when kernel dimensions match with the kernels in a pre-trained network architecture so that not all model parameters need to be trained from scratch.

As feature extractor all models use a VGG-16 network [26], which is initialized with weights pre-trained on the ILSVRC-2012-CLS dataset [23]. We change the max-pooling kernels to size 3×3 and use ReLU activations, L_2 regularization with weight $4e^{-5}$ and batch normalization in all layers of the network. Additional convolutional box prediction layers of depth $256, 128, 128, 128$ are attached to layer *conv5_3*. Anchors of scale 0.2 to 0.95 are generated for layer *conv4_3*, *conv5_3* and the box prediction layers. The aspect ratio for all anchor boxes is fixed to the aspect ratio of the side view of the rendered cars $(2 : 1)$. The full network is trained end-to-end in the Sphere-SSD framework with the RMSProp optimizer, batches of size 5 and a learning rate of 0.004.

Results on FlyingCars: Table 2 presents the results for the object detection task on the FlyingCars dataset after $50,000$ steps of training. Following common practice, we use an intersection-over-union (IoU) threshold of 0.5 for evaluation.

Again, our results demonstrate that SphereNet outperforms the baseline methods. Qualitative results of the SphereNet model are shown in Fig. 6.

Compared to the classification experiments, the Spherical Transformer Network (SphereTN) demonstrates less competitive performance as no transformation is able to account for undistorting all objects in the image at the same time. It is thus outperformed by the EquirectCNN. The performance of the EquirectCNN model is improved when the kernel size is enlarged towards the poles (EquirectCNN++), but all EquirectCNN models perform worse than the CNN operating on a cube map representation (CubeMapCNN). The reason for the improved performance of the CubeMapCNN compared to the classification task is most likely that discontinuities at the patch boundaries are less often present in the FlyingCars dataset due to the smaller relative size of the objects.

Besides accuracy, another important property of an object detector is its training and inference speed. Table 2 therefore additionally lists the training time per batch and inference time per image on an NVIDIA Tesla K20. The numbers show similar runtimes for EquirectCNN and CubeMapCNN. SphereNet has a small runtime overhead of factor 1.1 to 1.2, while the EquirectCNN++ and EquirectCNN+SphereTN models have a larger runtime overhead of factor 1.8 for training and 1.9 to 2.5 for inference.

Fig. 7. Detection results on OmPaCa dataset. The ground truth is shown in green, our SphereNet (NN) results in red. (Color figure online)

Table 3. Transfer learning results on OmPaCa dataset. We transfer detection models trained on perspective images from the KITTI dataset [7] to an omnidirectional representation and finetune the models on the OmPaCa dataset.

Method	Test mAP (%)
CubeMapCNN	34.19
EquirectCNN	43.43
SphereNet (NN)	**49.73**

4.3 Transfer Learning: OmPaCa

Finally, we consider the transfer learning task, where a model trained on a perspective dataset is transferred to handle omnidirectional imagery. For this task we record a new real-world dataset of omnidirectional images of real cars with a handheld action camera. The images are recorded at different heights and orientations. The *omnidirectional parked cars (OmPaCa)* dataset consists of 1,200 labeled images of size 512×256 with more than 50 different car models in total. The dataset is split into 200 test and 1,000 training instances, out of which a subset of 200 is used for validation.

We use the same detection architecture and training parameters as in Sect. 4.2 but now start from a perspective SSD model trained on the KITTI dataset [7], convert it to our Sphere-SSD framework and fine-tune for 20,000 iterations on the OmPaCa dataset. For this experiment we only compare against the EquirectCNN and CubeMapCNN baselines. Both the EquirectCNN+SphereTN as well as the EquirectCNN++ are not well suited for the transfer learning task due to the introduction of new model parameters, which are not present in the perspective detection model and which would thus require training from scratch.

Results on OmPaCa: Our results for the transfer learning task on the OmPaCa dataset are shown in Table 3 and demonstrate that SphereNet outperforms both baselines. Unlike in the object detection experiments on the FlyingCars dataset, the CubeMapCNN performs worse than the EquirectCNN by a large margin of nearly 10%, indicating that the cube map representation is not well suited for the transfer of perspective models to omnidirectional images. On the other hand, SphereNet performs better than the EquirectCNN by more than 5%, which confirms that the SphereNet approach is better suited for transferring perspective models to the omnidirectional case.

A selection of qualitative results for the SphereNet model is visualized in Fig. 7. As evidenced by our experiments, the SphereNet model is able to detect cars at different elevations on the sphere including the polar regions where regular convolutional object detectors fail due to the heavy distortions present in the input images. Several additional qualitative comparisons between SphereNet and the EquirectCNN model for objects located in the polar regions are provided in the supplementary material.

5 Conclusion and Future Work

We presented SphereNet, a framework for deep learning with 360° cameras. SphereNet lifts 2D convolutional neural networks to the surface of the unit sphere. By applying 2D convolution and pooling filters directly on the sphere's surface, our model effectively encodes distortion invariance into the filters of convolutional neural networks. Wrapping the convolutional filters around the sphere further avoids discontinuities at the borders or poles of the equirectangular projection. By updating the sampling locations of the convolutional filters we allow for easily transferring perspective CNN models to handle omnidirectional inputs. Our experiments show that the proposed method improves upon a variety of strong baselines in both omnidirectional image classification and object detection.

We expect that with the increasing availability and popularity of omnidirectional sensors in both the consumer market (e.g., action cameras) as well as in industry (e.g., autonomous cars, virtual reality), the demand for specialized models for omnidirectional images such as SphereNet will increase in the near future. We therefore plan to exploit the flexibility of our framework by applying it to other related computer vision tasks, including semantic (instance) segmentation, optical flow and scene flow estimation, single image depth prediction and multi-view 3D reconstruction in the future.

References

1. Bruna, J., Mallat, S.: Invariant scattering convolution networks. IEEE Trans. Pattern Anal. Mach. Intell. (PAMI) **35**(8), 1872–1886 (2013)
2. Chang, A.X., et al.: ShapeNet: an information-rich 3D model repository. arXiv.org 1512.03012 (2015)
3. Cohen, T.S., Geiger, M., Köhler, J., Welling, M.: Spherical CNNs. In: International Conference on Learning Representations (2018)
4. Cohen, T.S., Welling, M.: Group equivariant convolutional networks. In: Proceedings of the International Conference on Machine learning (ICML) (2016)
5. Dai, J., Qi, H., Xiong, Y., Li, Y., Zhang, G., Hu, H., Wei, Y.: Deformable convolutional networks. In: Proceedings of the IEEE International Conference on Computer Vision (ICCV). arXiv.org abs/ 1703.06211 (2017)
6. Defferrard, M., Bresson, X., Vandergheynst, P.: Convolutional neural networks on graphs with fast localized spectral filtering. In: Advances in Neural Information Processing Systems (NIPS) (2016)
7. Geiger, A., Lenz, P., Urtasun, R.: Are we ready for autonomous driving? The KITTI vision benchmark suite. In: Proceedings of IEEE Conference on Computer Vision and Pattern Recognition (CVPR) (2012)
8. He, K., Zhang, X., Ren, S., Sun, J.: Deep residual learning for image recognition. In: Proceedings of IEEE Conference on Computer Vision and Pattern Recognition (CVPR) (2016)
9. Henriques, J.F., Vedaldi, A.: Warped convolutions: efficient invariance to spatial transformations. In: Proceedings of the International Conference on Machine learning (ICML) (2017)
10. Hu, H.N., Lin, Y.C., Liu, M.Y., Cheng, H.T., Chang, Y.J., Sun, M.: Deep 360 pilot: learning a deep agent for piloting through 360° sports video. In: Proceedings of IEEE Conference on Computer Vision and Pattern Recognition (CVPR) (2017)
11. Jaderberg, M., Simonyan, K., Zisserman, A., Kavukcuoglu, K.: Spatial transformer networks. In: Advances in Neural Information Processing Systems (NIPS) (2015)
12. Jeon, Y., Kim, J.: Active convolution: learning the shape of convolution for image classification. In: Proceedings of IEEE Conference on Computer Vision and Pattern Recognition (CVPR) (2017)
13. Jia, Y.: Learning semantic image representations at a large scale. Ph.D. thesis, EECS Department, University of California, Berkeley, May 2014. http://www2.eecs.berkeley.edu/Pubs/TechRpts/2014/EECS-2014-93.html

14. Khasanova, R., Frossard, P.: Graph-based classification of omnidirectional images. In: Proceedings of the IEEE International Conference on Computer Vision (ICCV) Workshops (2017)
15. Khasanova, R., Frossard, P.: Graph-based isometry invariant representation learning. In: Proceedings of the International Conference on Machine learning (ICML) (2017)
16. Lai, W., Huang, Y., Joshi, N., Buehler, C., Yang, M., Kang, S.B.: Semantic-driven generation of hyperlapse from 360° video (2017)
17. Liu, W.: SSD: single shot multiBox detector. In: Leibe, B., Matas, J., Sebe, N., Welling, M. (eds.) ECCV 2016. LNCS, vol. 9905, pp. 21–37. Springer, Cham (2016). https://doi.org/10.1007/978-3-319-46448-0_2
18. Ma, J., Wang, W., Wang, L.: Irregular convolutional neural networks (2017)
19. Monroy, R., Lutz, S., Chalasani, T., Smolic, A.: SalNet360: saliency maps for omnidirectional images with CNN. In: ICME (2017)
20. Pearson, F.: Map Projections: Theory and Applications. Taylor & Francis, London (1990)
21. Ran, L., Zhang, Y., Zhang, Q., Yang, T.: Convolutional neural network-based robot navigation using uncalibrated spherical images. Sensors **17**(6), 1341 (2017)
22. Ruder, M., Dosovitskiy, A., Brox, T.: Artistic style transfer for videos and spherical images. arXiv.org abs/1708.04538 (2017)
23. Russakovsky, O.: ImageNet large scale visual recognition challenge. Int. J. Comput. Vis. (IJCV) **115**, 211–252 (2015)
24. Saff, E.B., Kuijlaars, A.B.J.: Distributing many points on a sphere. Math. Intell. **19**(1), 5–11 (1997)
25. Sifre, L., Mallat, S.: Rotation, scaling and deformation invariant scattering for texture discrimination. In: Proceedings of IEEE Conference on Computer Vision and Pattern Recognition (CVPR) (2013)
26. Simonyan, K., Zisserman, A.: Very deep convolutional networks for large-scale image recognition. In: Proceedings of the International Conference on Learning Representations (ICLR) (2015)
27. Su, Y.C., Grauman, K.: Making 360° video watchable in 2D: learning videography for click free viewing. In: Proceedings of IEEE Conference on Computer Vision and Pattern Recognition (CVPR) (2017)
28. Su, Y.C., Jayaraman, D., Grauman, K.: Pano2Vid: automatic cinematography for watching 360° videos. In: Proceedings of the Asian Conference on Computer Vision (ACCV) (2016)
29. Worrall, D.E., Garbin, S.J., Turmukhambetov, D., Brostow, G.J.: Harmonic networks: deep translation and rotation equivariance. In: Proceedings of IEEE Conference on Computer Vision and Pattern Recognition (CVPR) (2017)
30. Yu-Chuan Su, K.G.: Flat2sphere: learning spherical convolution for fast features from 360° imagery. In: Advances in Neural Information Processing Systems (NIPS) (2017)
31. Zhou, Y., Ye, Q., Qiu, Q., Jiao, J.: Oriented response networks. In: Proceedings of IEEE Conference on Computer Vision and Pattern Recognition (CVPR) (2017)

Deep Directional Statistics: Pose Estimation with Uncertainty Quantification

Sergey Prokudin[1]([✉]) [iD], Peter Gehler[2] [iD], and Sebastian Nowozin[3] [iD]

[1] Max Planck Institute for Intelligent Systems, Tübingen, Germany
sergey.prokudin@tuebingen.mpg.de
[2] Amazon, Tübingen, Germany
[3] Microsoft Research, Cambridge, UK

Abstract. Modern deep learning systems successfully solve many perception tasks such as object pose estimation when the input image is of high quality. However, in challenging imaging conditions such as on low resolution images or when the image is corrupted by imaging artifacts, current systems degrade considerably in accuracy. While a loss in performance is unavoidable, we would like our models to quantify their uncertainty to achieve robustness against images of varying quality. Probabilistic deep learning models combine the expressive power of deep learning with uncertainty quantification. In this paper we propose a novel probabilistic deep learning model for the task of angular regression. Our model uses *von Mises* distributions to predict a distribution over object pose angle. Whereas a single von Mises distribution is making strong assumptions about the shape of the distribution, we extend the basic model to predict a mixture of von Mises distributions. We show how to learn a mixture model using a finite and *infinite* number of mixture components. Our model allows for likelihood-based training and efficient inference at test time. We demonstrate on a number of challenging pose estimation datasets that our model produces calibrated probability predictions and competitive or superior point estimates compared to the current state-of-the-art.

Keywords: Pose estimation · Deep probabilistic models
Uncertainty quantification · Directional statistics

1 Introduction

Estimating object pose is an important building block in systems aiming to understand complex scenes and has a long history in computer vision [1,2].

P. Gehler—This work has been done prior to Peter Gehler joining Amazon.

Electronic supplementary material The online version of this chapter (https://doi.org/10.1007/978-3-030-01240-3_33) contains supplementary material, which is available to authorized users.

V. Ferrari et al. (Eds.): ECCV 2018, LNCS 11213, pp. 542–559, 2018.
https://doi.org/10.1007/978-3-030-01240-3_33

Whereas early systems achieved low accuracy, recent advances in deep learning and the collection of extensive data sets have led to high performing systems that can be deployed in useful applications [3–5].

However, the reliability of object pose regression depends on the quality of the image provided to the system. Key challenges are low-resolution due to distance of an object to the camera, blur due to motion of the camera or the object, and sensor noise in case of poorly lit scenes (see Fig. 1).

We would like to predict object pose in a way that captures uncertainty. *Probability* is the right way to capture the uncertainty [6] and in this paper we therefore propose a novel model for object pose regression whose predictions are fully probabilistic. Figure 1 depicts an output of the proposed system. Moreover, instead of assuming a fixed form for the predictive density we allow for flexible multimodal distributions, specified by a deep neural network.

The value of quantified uncertainty in the form of probabilistic predictions is two-fold: *first*, a high prediction uncertainty is a robust way to diagnose poor inputs to the system; *second*, given accurate probabilities we can summarize them to improved point estimates using Bayesian decision theory.

More generally, accurate representation of uncertainty is especially important in case a computer vision system becomes part of a larger system, such as when providing an input signal for an autonomous control system. If uncertainty is not well-calibrated, or—even worse—is not taken into account at all, then the consequences of decisions made by the system cannot be accurately assessed, resulting in poor decisions at best, and dangerous actions at worst.

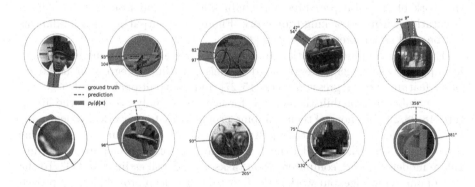

Fig. 1. Our model predicts complex multimodal distributions on the circle (truncated by the outer circle for better viewing). For difficult and ambiguous images our model report high uncertainty (bottom row). Pose estimation predictions (pan angle) on images from IDIAP, TownCentre and PASCAL3D+ datasets.

In the following we present our method and make the following contributions:

- We demonstrate the importance of probabilistic regression on the application of object pose estimation;

- We propose a novel efficient probabilistic deep learning model for the task of circular regression;
- We show on a number of challenging pose estimation datasets (including PASCAL 3D+ benchmark [7]) that the proposed probabilistic method outperforms purely discriminative approaches in terms of predictive likelihood and show competitive performance in terms of angular deviation losses classically used for the tasks.

2   Related Work

Estimation of object orientation arises in different applications and in this paper we focus on the two most prominent tasks: head pose estimation and object class orientation estimation. Although those tasks are closely related, they have been studied mostly in separation, with methods applied to exclusively one of them. We will therefore discuss them separately, despite the fact that our model applies to both tasks.

Head pose estimation has been a subject of extensive research in computer vision for a long time [2,8] and the existing systems vary greatly in terms of feature representation and proposed classifiers. The input to pose estimation systems typically consists of 2D head images [9–11], and often one has to cope with low resolution images [8,12–14]. Additional modalities such as depth [15] and motion [14,16] information has been exploited and provides useful cues. However, these are not always available. Also, information about the full body image could be used for joint head and body pose prediction [17–19]. Notably the work of [18] also promotes a probabilistic view and fuse body and head orientation within a tracking framework. Finally, the output of facial landmarks can be used as an intermediate step [20,21].

Existing head pose estimation models are diverse and include manifold learning approaches [22–25], energy-based models [19], linear regression based on HOG features [26], regression trees [15,27] and convolutional neural networks [5]. A number of probabilistic methods for head pose analysis exist in the literature [18,28,29], but none of them combine probabilistic framework with learnable hierarchical feature representations from deep CNN architectures. At the same time, deep probabilistic models have shown an advantage over purely discriminative models in other computer vision tasks, e.g., depth estimation [30]. To the best of our knowledge, our work is the first to utilize deep probabilistic approach to angular orientation regression task.

An early dataset for estimating the *object rotation for general object classes* was proposed in [31] along with an early benchmark set. Over the years the complexity of data increased, from object rotation [31] and images of cars in different orientations [32] to Pascal3D [33]. The work of [33] then assigned a separate Deformable Part Model (DPM) component to a discrete set of viewpoints. The work of [34,35] then proposed different 3D DPM extensions which allowed viewpoint estimation as integral part of the model. However, both [34] and [35] and do not predict a continuous angular estimate but only a discrete number of bins.

More recent versions make use of CNN models but still do not take a probabilistic approach [3,4]. The work of [36] investigates the use of a synthetic rendering pipeline to overcome the scarcity of detailed training data. The addition of synthetic and real examples allows them to outperform previous results. The model in [36] predicts angles, and constructs a loss function that penalizes geodesic and ℓ_1 distance. Closest to our approach, [37] also utilizes the von Mises distribution to build the regression objective. However, similarly to [5], the shape of the predicted distribution remains fixed with only mean value of single von Mises density being predicted. In contrary, in this work we advocate the use of complete likelihood estimation as a principled probabilistic training objective.

The recent work of [38] draws a connection between viewpoints and object keypoints. The viewpoint estimation is however again framed as a classification problem in terms of Euler angles to obtain a rotation matrix from a canonical viewpoint. Another substitution of angular regression problem was proposed in a series of work [39–41], where CNN is trained to predict the 2D image locations of virtual 3D control points and the actual 3D pose is then computed by solving a perspective-n-point (PnP) problem that recovers rotations from 2D–3D correspondences. Additionally, many works phrase angular prediction as a classification problem [3,36,38] which always limits the granularity of the prediction and also requires the design of a loss function and a means to select the number of discrete labels. A benefit of a classification model is that components like softmax loss can be re-used and also interpreted as an uncertainty estimate. In contrast, our model mitigate this problem: the likelihood principle suggests a direct way to train parameters, moreover ours is the only model in this class that conveys an uncertainty estimate.

3   Review of Biternion Networks

We build on the Biternion networks method for pose estimation from [5] and briefly review the basic ideas here. Biternion networks regress angular data and currently define the state-of-the-art model for a number of challenging head pose estimation datasets.

A key problem is to regress angular orientations which is periodic and prevents a straight-forward application of standard regression methods, including CNN models with common loss functions. Consider a ground truth value of $0°$, then both predictions $1°$ and $359°$ should result in the same absolute loss. Applying the mod operator is no simple fix to this problem, since it results in a discontinuous loss function that complicates the optimization. A loss function needs to be defined to cope with this discontinuity of the target value. Biternion networks overcome this difficulty by using a different parameterization of angles and the cosine loss function between angles.

3.1   Biternion Representation

Beyer et al. [5] propose an alternative representation of an angle ϕ using the two-dimensional sine and cosine components $\boldsymbol{y} = (\cos \phi, \sin \phi)$.

This *biternion representation* is inspired by quaternions, which are popular in computer graphics systems. It is easy to predict a (cos, sin) pair with a fully-connected layer followed by a normalization layer, that is,

$$f_{BT}(x; W, b) = \frac{Wx + b}{||Wx + b||} = (\cos \phi, \sin \phi) = y_{pred}, \tag{1}$$

where $x \in \mathbb{R}^n$ is an input, $W \in \mathbb{R}^{2 \times n}$, $b \in \mathbb{R}^2$. A Biternion network is then a convolutional neural network with a layer (1) as the final operation, outputting a two-dimensional vector y_{pred}. We use VGG-style network [42] and InceptionRes-Net [43] networks in our experiments and provide a detailed description of the network architecture in Sect. 6.1. Given recent developments in network architectures it is likely that different network topologies may perform better than selected backbones. We leave this for future work, our contributions are orthogonal to the choice of the basis model.

3.2 Cosine Loss Function

The cosine distance is chosen in [5] as a natural candidate to measure the difference between the predicted and ground truth Biternion vectors. It reads

$$L_{cos}(y_{pred}, y_{true}) = 1 - \frac{y_{pred} \cdot y_{true}}{||y_{pred}|| \cdot ||y_{true}||} = 1 - y_{pred} \cdot y_{true}, \tag{2}$$

where the last equality is due to $||y|| = \cos^2 \phi + \sin^2 \phi = 1$.

The combination of a Biternion angle representation and a cosine loss solves the problems of regressing angular values, allowing for a flexible deep network with angular output. We take this state-of-the-art model and generalize it into a family of probabilistic models of gradually more flexibility.

4   Probabilistic Models of Circular Data

We utilize the von Mises (vM) distribution as the basic building block of our probabilistic framework, which is a canonical choice for a distribution on the unit circle [44]. Compared to standard Gaussian, the benefit is that it have as a support any interval of length 2π, which allow it to truthfully models the domain of the data, that is angles on a circle.

We continue with a brief formal definition and in Sect. 4.1 describe a simple way to convert the output of Biternion networks into a $\mathcal{VM}$ density, that does not require any network architecture change or re-training as it requires only selection of the model variance. We will then use this approach as a baseline for more advanced probabilistic models. Section 4.2 slightly extends the original Biternion network by introducing an additional network output unit that models uncertainty of our angle estimation and allows optimization for the log-likelihood of the $\mathcal{VM}$ distribution.

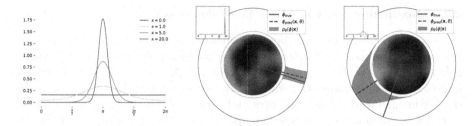

Fig. 2. Left: examples of the von Mises probability density function for different concentration parameters κ. Center, right: predicted $\mathcal{VM}$ distributions for two images from the CAVIAR dataset. We plot the predicted density on the viewing circle. For comparison we also include the 2D plot (better visible in zoomed pdf version). The distribution on the center image is very certain, the one on the right more uncertain about the viewing angle.

The von Mises distribution $\mathcal{VM}(\mu, \kappa)$ is a close approximation of a normal distribution on the unit circle. Its probability density function is

$$p(\phi; \mu, \kappa) = \frac{\exp\left(\kappa \cos\left(\phi - \mu\right)\right)}{2\pi I_0(\kappa)}, \tag{3}$$

where $\mu \in [0, 2\pi)$ is the mean value, $\kappa \in \mathbb{R}_+$ is a measure of concentration (a reciprocal measure of dispersion, so $1/\kappa$ is analogous to σ^2 in a normal distribution), and $I_0(\kappa)$ is the modified Bessel function of order 0. We show examples of $\mathcal{VM}$-distributions with $\mu = \pi$ and varying κ values in Fig. 2 (left).

4.1   Von Mises Biternion Networks

A conceptually simple way to turn the Biternion networks from Sect. 3 into a probabilistic model is to take its predicted value as the center value of the $\mathcal{VM}$ distribution,

$$p_\theta(\phi|\boldsymbol{x}; \kappa) = \frac{\exp\left(\kappa \cos\left(\phi - \mu_\theta(\boldsymbol{x})\right)\right)}{2\pi I_0(\kappa)}, \tag{4}$$

where $\boldsymbol{x}$ is an input image, θ are parameters of the network, and $\mu_\theta(\boldsymbol{x})$ is the network output. To arrive at a probability distribution, we may regard $\kappa > 0$ as a hyper-parameter. For fixed network parameters θ we can select κ by maximizing the log-likelihood of the observed data,

$$\kappa^* = \underset{\kappa}{\operatorname{argmax}} \sum_{i=1}^{N} \log p_\theta(\phi^{(i)}|\boldsymbol{x}^{(i)}; \kappa), \tag{5}$$

where N is the number of training samples. The model (4) with κ^* will serve as the simplest probabilistic baseline in our comparisons, referred as *fixed* κ model in the experiments.

4.2   Maximizing the von Mises Log-Likelihood

Using a single scalar κ for every possible input in the model (4) is clearly a restrictive assumption: model certainty should depend on factors such as image quality, light conditions, etc. For example, Fig. 2 (center, right) depicts two low resolution images from a surveillance camera that are part of the CAVIAR dataset [13]. In the left image facial features like eyes and ears are distinguishable which allows a model to be more certain when compared to the more blurry image on the right (Fig. 3).

We therefore extend the simple model by replacing the single constant κ with a function $\kappa_\theta(\boldsymbol{x})$, predicted by the Biternion network,

$$p_\theta(\phi|\boldsymbol{x}) = \frac{\exp\left(\kappa_\theta(\boldsymbol{x})\cos\left(\phi - \mu_\theta(\boldsymbol{x})\right)\right)}{2\pi I_0(\kappa_\theta(\boldsymbol{x}))}. \tag{6}$$

We train (6) by maximizing the log-likelihood of the data,

$$\log \mathcal{L}(\theta|\boldsymbol{X},\Phi) = \sum_{i=1}^{N} \kappa_\theta(\boldsymbol{x}^{(i)})\cos\left(\phi^{(i)} - \mu_\theta(\boldsymbol{x}^{(i)})\right) - \sum_{i=1}^{N} \log 2\pi I_0(\kappa_\theta(\boldsymbol{x}^{(i)})). \tag{7}$$

Note that when κ is held constant in (7), the second sum in $\log \mathcal{L}(\theta|\boldsymbol{X},\Phi)$ is constant and therefore we recover the Biternion cosine objective (2) up to constants C_1, C_2,

$$\log \mathcal{L}(\theta|\boldsymbol{X},\Phi,\kappa) = C_1 \sum_{i=1}^{N} \cos\left(\phi^{(i)} - \mu_\theta(\boldsymbol{x}^{(i)})\right) + C_2.$$

The sum has the equivalent form,

$$\sum_{i=1}^{N} \cos\left(\phi^{(i)} - \mu_\theta(\boldsymbol{x}^{(i)})\right) = \sum_{i=1}^{N} \left[\cos\phi^{(i)}\cos\mu_\theta(\boldsymbol{x}^{(i)}) + \sin\phi^{(i)}\sin\mu_\theta(\boldsymbol{x}^{(i)})\right] \tag{8}$$

$$= \sum_{i=1}^{N} \boldsymbol{y}_{\phi^{(i)}} \cdot \boldsymbol{y}_{\mu_\theta(\boldsymbol{x}^{(i)})}, \tag{9}$$

where $\boldsymbol{y}_\phi = (\cos\phi, \sin\phi)$ is a Biternion representation of an angle. Note, that the above derivation shows that the loss function in [5] corresponds to optimizing the von Mises log-likelihood for the fixed value of $\kappa = 1$. This offers an interpretation of Biternion networks as a probabilistic model.

The additional degree of freedom to learn $\kappa_\theta(\boldsymbol{x})$ as a function of $\boldsymbol{x}$ allows us to capture the desired image-dependent uncertainty as can be seen in Fig. 2.

However, like the Gaussian distribution the von Mises distribution makes a specific assumption regarding the shape of the density. We now show how to overcome this limitation by using a mixture of von Mises distributions.

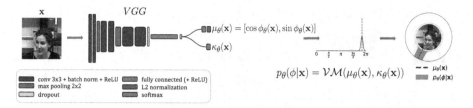

Fig. 3. The single mode von Mises model (VGG backbone variation). A BiternionVGG network regresses both mean and concentration parameter of a single vM distribution.

5   Mixture of von Mises Distributions

The model described in Sect. 4.2 is only unimodal and can not capture ambiguities in the image. However, in case of blurry images like the ones in Fig. 2 we could be interested in distributing the mass around a few potential high probability hypotheses, for example, the model could predict that a person is looking sideways, but could not determine the direction, left or right, with certainty. In this section we present two models that are able to capture multimodal beliefs while retaining a calibrated uncertainty measure.

5.1   Finite Mixture of von Mises Distributions

One common way to generate complex distributions is to sum multiple distributions into a *mixture distribution*. We introduce K different component distributions and a K-dimensional probability vector representing the mixture weights. Each component is a simple von Mises distribution. We can then represent our density function as

$$p_\theta(\phi|\boldsymbol{x}) = \sum_{j=1}^{K} \pi_j(\boldsymbol{x},\theta)\, p_j(\phi|\boldsymbol{x},\theta), \tag{10}$$

where $p_j(\phi|\boldsymbol{x},\theta) = \mathcal{VM}(\phi|\mu_j,\kappa_j)$ for $j = 1,\ldots,K$ are the K component distributions and the mixture weights are $\pi_j(\boldsymbol{x},\theta)$ so that $\sum_j \pi_j(\boldsymbol{x},\theta) = 1$. We denote all parameters with the vector θ, it contains component-specific parameters as well as parameters shared across all components.

To predict the mixture in a neural network framework, we need $K \times 3$ output units for modeling all von Mises component parameters (two for modeling the Biternion representation of the mean, $\mu_j(\boldsymbol{x},\theta)$ and one for the $\kappa_j(\boldsymbol{x},\theta)$ value), as well as K units for the probability vector $\pi_j(\boldsymbol{x},\theta)$, defined by taking the `softmax` operation to get a positive mixture weights.

The finite von Mises density model then takes form

$$p_\theta(\phi|\boldsymbol{x}) = \sum_{j=1}^{K} \pi_j(\boldsymbol{x},\theta)\, \frac{\exp\left(\kappa_j(\boldsymbol{x},\theta)\cos\left(\phi - \mu_j(\boldsymbol{x},\theta)\right)\right)}{2\pi I_0\left(\kappa_j(\boldsymbol{x},\theta)\right)}. \tag{11}$$

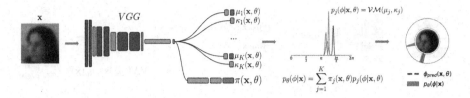

Fig. 4. The finite $\mathcal{VM}$ mixture model. A VGG network predicts K mean and concentration values and the mixture coefficients π. This allows to capture multimodality in the output.

Similarly to the single von Mises model, we can train by directly maximizing the log-likelihood of the observed data, $\sum_{i=1}^{N} \log p_\theta(\phi^{(i)}|\boldsymbol{x}^{(i)})$. No specific training schemes or architectural tweaks were done to avoid redundancy in mixture components. However, empirically we observe that model learns to set mixture weights π_j of the redundant components close to zero, as well as to learn the ordering of the components (e.g. it learns that some output component j should correspond to the component with high mixture weight).

We show an overview of the model in Fig. 4.

5.2   Infinite Mixture (CVAE)

To extend the model from a finite to an infinite mixture model, we follow the variational autoencoder (VAE) approach [45,46], and introduce a vector-valued latent variable $\boldsymbol{z}$. The resulting model is depicted in Fig. 5. The continuous latent variable becomes the input to a decoder network $p(\phi|\boldsymbol{x}, \boldsymbol{z})$ which predicts the parameters—mean and concentration—of a single von Mises component. We define our density function as the infinite sum (integral) over all latent variable choices, weighted by a learned distribution $p(\boldsymbol{z}|\boldsymbol{x})$,

$$p_\theta(\phi|\boldsymbol{x}) = \int p(\phi|\boldsymbol{x}, \boldsymbol{z})\, p(\boldsymbol{z}|\boldsymbol{x}) dz, \tag{12}$$

where $p_\theta(\phi|\boldsymbol{x}, \boldsymbol{z}) = \mathcal{VM}(\mu(\boldsymbol{x}, \theta), \kappa(\boldsymbol{x}, \theta))$, and $p_\theta(\boldsymbol{z}|\boldsymbol{x}) = \mathcal{N}(\mu_1(\boldsymbol{x}, \theta), \sigma_1^2(\boldsymbol{x}, \theta))$. The log-likelihood $\log p_\theta(\phi|\boldsymbol{x})$ for this model is not longer tractable, preventing simple maximum likelihood training. Instead we use the variational autoencoder framework of [45,46] in the form of the conditional VAE (CVAE) [47]. The CVAE formulation uses an auxiliary *variational* density $q_\theta(\boldsymbol{z}|\boldsymbol{x}, \phi) = \mathcal{N}(\mu_2(\boldsymbol{x}, \phi, \theta), \sigma_2^2(\boldsymbol{x}, \phi, \theta))$ and instead of the log-likelihood optimizes a *variational lower bound*,

$$\log p_\theta(\phi|\boldsymbol{x}) = \log \int p_\theta(\phi|\boldsymbol{x}, \boldsymbol{z})\, p_\theta(\boldsymbol{z}|\boldsymbol{x}) dz \tag{13}$$

$$\geq \mathbb{E}_{z \sim q_\theta(z|x,\phi)} \left[\log \frac{p_\theta(\phi|\boldsymbol{x}, \boldsymbol{z})\, p_\theta(\boldsymbol{z}|\boldsymbol{x})}{q_\theta(\boldsymbol{z}|\boldsymbol{x}, \phi)} \right] =: \mathcal{L}_{\text{ELBO}}(\theta|\boldsymbol{x}, \phi). \tag{14}$$

We refer to [45–48] for more details on VAEs.

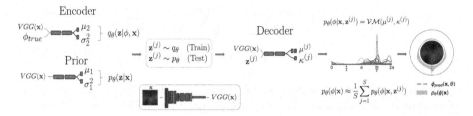

Fig. 5. The infinite mixture model (CVAE). An encoder network predicts a distribution $q(z|x)$ over latent variables z, and a decoder network $p(\phi|x, z)$ defines individual mixture components. Integrating over z yields an infinite mixture of von Mises distributions. In practice we approximate this integration using a finite number of Monte Carlo samples $z^{(j)} \sim q(z|x)$.

The CVAE model is composed of multiple deep neural networks: an *encoder network* $q_\theta(z|x, \phi)$, a *conditional prior network* $p_\theta(z|x)$, and a *decoder network* $p_\theta(\phi|x, z)$. Like before, we use θ to denote the entirety of trainable parameters of all three model components. We show an overview of the model in Fig. 5. The model is trained by maximizing the variational lower bound (14) over the training set (X, Φ), where $X = (x^{(1)}, \ldots, x^{(N)})$ are the images and $\Phi = (\phi^{(1)}, \ldots, \phi^{(N)})$ are the ground truth angles. We maximize

$$\hat{\mathcal{L}}_{\text{CVAE}}(\theta|X, \Phi) = \frac{1}{N} \sum_{i=1}^{N} \hat{\mathcal{L}}_{\text{ELBO}}(\theta|x^{(i)}, \phi^{(i)}), \tag{15}$$

where we use $\hat{\mathcal{L}}_{\text{ELBO}}$ to denote the Monte Carlo approximation to (14) using S samples. We can optimize (15) efficiently using stochastic gradient descent.

To evaluate the log-likelihood during testing, we use the importance-weighted sampling technique proposed in [49] to derive a stronger bound on the marginal likelihood,

$$\log p_\theta(\phi|x) \geq \log \frac{1}{S} \sum_{j=1}^{S} \frac{p_\theta(\phi|x, z^{(j)}) \, p_\theta(z^{(j)}|x)}{q_\theta(z^{(j)}|x, \phi)}, \tag{16}$$

$$z^{(j)} \sim q_\theta(z^{(j)}|x, \phi) \qquad j = 1, \ldots, S. \tag{17}$$

Simplified CVAE. In our experiments we also investigate a variant of the aforementioned model where $p_\theta(z|x) = q_\theta(z|x, \phi) = p(z) = \mathcal{N}(0, I)$. Compared to the full CVAE framework, this model, which we refer to as *simplified CVAE* (sCVAE) in the experiments, sacrifices the adaptive input-dependent density of the hidden variable z for faster training and test inference as well as optimization stability. In that case the KL-divergence $KL(q_\theta \parallel p_\theta)$ term in $\hat{\mathcal{L}}_{\text{ELBO}}$ becomes zero, and we train for a Monte Carlo estimated log-likelihood of the data:

$$\hat{\mathcal{L}}_{\text{sCVAE}}(\theta|\boldsymbol{X}, \varPhi) = \frac{1}{N} \sum_{i=1}^{N} \log \left(\frac{1}{S} \sum_{j=1}^{S} p_\theta(\phi^{(i)}|\boldsymbol{x}^{(i)}, \boldsymbol{z}^{(j)}) \right), \quad (18)$$

$$\boldsymbol{z}^{(j)} \sim p(\boldsymbol{z}) = \mathcal{N}(0, I), j = 1, \dots, S. \quad (19)$$

In some applications it is necessary to make a single best guess about the pose, that is, to summarize the posterior $p(\phi|\boldsymbol{x})$ to a single point prediction $\hat{\phi}$. We now discuss an efficient way to do that.

5.3 Point Prediction

To obtain an optimal single point prediction we utilize Bayesian decision theory [6,50,51] and minimize the expected loss,

$$\hat{\phi}_\varDelta = \underset{\phi \in [0, 2\pi)}{\arg\min} \, \mathbb{E}_{\phi' \sim p(\phi|\boldsymbol{x})} \left[\varDelta(\phi, \phi') \right], \quad (20)$$

where $\varDelta : [0, 2\pi) \times [0, 2\pi) \to \mathbb{R}_+$ is a loss function. We will use the $\varDelta_{\text{AAD}}(\phi, \phi')$ loss which measures the absolute angular deviation (AAD). To approximate (20) we use the empirical approximation of [50] and draw S samples $\{\phi_j\}$ from $p_\theta(\phi|\boldsymbol{x})$. We then use the empirical approximation

$$\hat{\phi}_\varDelta = \underset{j=1,\dots,S}{\arg\min} \, \frac{1}{S} \sum_{k=1}^{S} \varDelta(\phi_j, \phi_k). \quad (21)$$

We now evaluate our models both in terms of uncertainty as well as in terms of point prediction quality.

6 Experiments

This section presents the experimental results on several challenging head and object pose regression tasks. Section 6.1 introduces the experimental setup including used datasets, network architecture and training setup. In Sect. 6.2 we present and discuss qualitative and quantitative results on the datasets of interest.

6.1 Experimental Setup

Network Architecture and Training. We use two types of network architectures [42,43] during our experiments and Adam optimizer [52], performing random search [53] for the best values of hyper-parameters. We refer to supplementary and corresponding project repository for more details[1].

Head Pose Datasets. We evaluate all methods together with the non-probabilistic BiternionVGG baseline on three diverse (in terms of image quality

---

[1] https://github.com/sergeyprokudin/deep_direct_stat.

and precision of provided ground truth information) headpose datasets: IDIAP head pose [9], TownCentre [54] and CAVIAR [13] coarse gaze estimation. The IDIAP head pose dataset contains 66295 head images stemmed from a video recording of a few people in a meeting room. Each image has a complete annotation of a head pose orientation in form of pan, tilt and roll angles. We take 42304, 11995 and 11996 images for training, validation, and testing, respectively. The TownCentre and CAVIAR datasets present a challenging task of a coarse gaze estimation of pedestrians based on low resolution images from surveillance camera videos. In case of the CAVIAR dataset, we focus on the part of the dataset containing occluded head instances (hence referred to as CAVIAR-o in the literature).

PASCAL3D+ Object Pose Dataset. The Pascal 3D+ dataset [33] consists of images from the Pascal [55] and ImageNet [56] datasets that have been labeled with both detection and continuous pose annotations for the 12 rigid object categories that appear in Pascal VOC12 [55] train and validation set. With nearly 3000 object instances per category, this dataset provide a rich testbed to study general object pose estimation. In our experiments on this dataset we follow the same protocol as in [36,38] for viewpoint estimation: we use ground truth detections for both training and testing, and use Pascal validation set to evaluate and compare the quality of our predictions.

Table 1. Quantitative results on the IDIAP head pose estimation dataset [9] for the three head rotations pan, roll and tilt. In the situation of fixed camera pose, lightning conditions and image quality, all methods show similar performance (methods are considered to perform on par when the difference in performance is less than *standard error of the mean*).

Estimated pose component	Pan		Tilt		Roll	
	MAAD	Log-likelihood	MAAD	Log-likelihood	MAAD	Log-likelihood
Beyer et al. ([5]), fixed κ	$5.8° \pm 0.1*$	0.37 ± 0.01	$2.4° \pm 0.1$	1.31 ± 0.01	$3.1° \pm 0.1$	1.13 ± 0.01
Ours (single von Mises)	$6.3° \pm 0.1$	0.56 ± 0.01	$2.3° \pm 0.1$	1.56 ± 0.01	$3.4° \pm 0.1$	1.13 ± 0.01
Ours (mixture-CVAE)	$6.4° \pm 0.1$	$\approx 0.52 \pm 0.02$	$2.9° \pm 0.1$	$\approx 1.35 \pm 0.01$	$3.5° \pm 0.1$	$\approx 1.05 \pm 0.02$

*standard error of the mean (SEM).

6.2 Results and Discussion

Quantitative Results. We evaluate our methods using both discriminative and probabilistic metrics. We use discriminative metrics that are standard for the dataset of interest to be able to compare our methods with previous work. For headpose tasks we use the mean absolute angular deviation (MAAD), a widely used metric for angular regression tasks. For PASCAL3D+ we use the metrics advocated in [38]. Probabilistic predictions are measured in terms of log-likelihood [57,58], a widely accepted scoring rule for assessing the quality of probabilistic predictions. We summarize the results in Tables 1, 2 and 3. It can be seen from results on IDIAP dataset presented in Table 1 that when camera pose,

Table 2. Quantitative results on the CAVIAR-o [13] and TownCentre [54] coarse gaze estimation datasets. We see clear improvement in terms of quality of probabilistic predictions for both datasets when switching to mixture models that allow to output multiple hypotheses for gaze direction.

	CAVIAR-o		TownCentre	
	MAAD	Log-likelihood	MAAD	Log-likelihood
Beyer et al. [5], fixed κ	$5.74° \pm 0.13$	0.262 ± 0.031	$22.8° \pm 1.0$	-0.89 ± 0.06
Ours (single von Mises)	$5.53° \pm 0.13$	0.700 ± 0.043	$22.9° \pm 1.1$	-0.57 ± 0.05
Ours (mixture-finite)	$\mathbf{4.21° \pm 0.16}$	$\mathbf{1.87 \pm 0.04}$	$23.5° \pm 1.1$	$\mathbf{-0.50 \pm 0.04}$

Table 3. Results on PASCAL3D+ viewpoint estimation with ground truth bounding boxes. First two evaluation metrics are defined in [38], where $Acc_{\frac{\pi}{6}}$ measures accuracy (the higher the better) and $MedErr$ measures error (the lower the better). Additionally, we report the log-likelihood estimation $\log \mathcal{L}$ of the predicted angles (the higher the better). We can see clear improvement on all metrics when switching to probabilistic setting compared to training for a purely discriminative loss (fixed κ case).

	aero	bike	boat	bottle	bus	car	chair	table	mbike	sofa	train	tv	mean
$Acc_{\frac{\pi}{6}}$ (Tulsiani et al.[38])	0.81	0.77	0.59	0.93	**0.98**	0.89	**0.80**	0.62	0.88	0.82	0.80	0.80	0.81
$Acc_{\frac{\pi}{6}}$ (Su et al.[36])	0.80	0.82	0.62	0.95	0.93	0.83	0.75	**0.86**	0.86	0.85	0.82	0.89	0.83
$Acc_{\frac{\pi}{6}}$ (Grabner et al.[41])	0.83	0.82	**0.64**	0.95	0.97	0.94	**0.80**	0.71	0.88	0.87	0.80	0.86	**0.84**
$Acc_{\frac{\pi}{6}}$ (Ours, fixed κ)	0.83	0.75	0.54	0.95	0.92	0.90	0.77	0.71	**0.90**	0.82	0.80	0.86	0.81
$Acc_{\frac{\pi}{6}}$ (Ours, single v.Mises)	0.87	0.78	0.55	**0.97**	0.95	**0.91**	0.78	0.76	**0.90**	0.87	**0.84**	**0.91**	**0.84**
$Acc_{\frac{\pi}{6}}$ (Ours, mixture-sCVAE)	**0.89**	**0.83**	0.46	0.96	0.93	0.90	**0.80**	0.76	**0.90**	**0.90**	0.82	**0.91**	**0.84**
$MedErr$ (Tulsiani et al.[38])	13.8	17.7	21.3	12.9	5.8	9.1	14.8	15.2	14.7	13.7	8.7	15.4	13.6
$MedErr$ (Su et al.[36])	10.0	**12.5**	20.0	6.7	4.5	6.7	12.3	8.6	13.1	11.0	5.8	13.3	10.4
$MedErr$ (Grabner et al.[41])	10.0	15.6	**19.1**	8.6	3.3	5.1	13.7	11.8	12.2	13.5	6.7	11.0	10.9
$MedErr$ (Ours, fixed κ)	11.4	18.1	28.1	6.9	4.0	6.6	14.6	12.1	12.9	16.4	7.0	12.9	12.6
$MedErr$ (Ours, single v.Mises)	**9.7**	17.7	26.9	**6.7**	**2.7**	4.9	12.5	8.7	13.2	10.0	4.7	**10.6**	10.7
$MedErr$ (Ours, mixture-sCVAE)	**9.7**	15.5	45.6	**5.4**	2.9	**4.5**	13.1	12.6	**11.8**	**9.1**	**4.3**	12.0	12.2
$\log \mathcal{L}$(Ours, fixed κ)	-0.89	**-0.73**	-1.21	0.18	2.09	1.43	-0.08	0.69	**-0.50**	-0.75	0.06	-1.02	-0.07 ± 0.15
$\log \mathcal{L}$(Ours, single v.Mises)	0.19	-1.12	-0.30	2.40	**4.87**	**2.85**	**0.42**	**0.79**	-0.72	**-0.54**	**2.52**	0.52	$\mathbf{1.17 \pm 0.07}$
$\log \mathcal{L}$(Ours, mixture-sCVAE)	**0.60**	**-0.73**	**-0.26**	**2.71**	4.45	2.52	-0.58	0.08	-0.62	-0.64	2.05	**1.14**	1.15 ± 0.07

lightning conditions and image quality are fixed, all methods perform similarly. In contrast, for the coarse gaze estimation task on CAVIAR we can see a clear improvement in terms of quality of probabilistic predictions for both datasets when switching to mixture models that allow to output multiple hypotheses for gaze direction. Here low resolution, pure light conditions and presence of occlusions create large diversity in the level of head pose expressions. Finally, on a challenging PASCAL3D+ dataset we can see clear improvement on all metrics and classes when switching to a probabilistic setting compared to training for a purely discriminative loss (fixed κ case). Our methods also show competitive or superior performance compared to state-of-the-art methods on disriminative metrics advocated in [38]. Method of [36] uses large amounts of synthesized images in addition to the standard training set that was used by our method. Using this data augmentation technique can also lead to an improved performance of our method and we consider this future work.

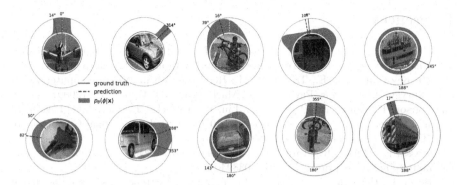

Fig. 6. Qualitative results of our simpified CVAE model on the PASCAL3D+ dataset. Our model correctly quantifies the uncertainty of pose predictions and is able to model ambiguous cases by predicting complex multimodal densities. Lower right images are failure cases (confusing head and tail of the object with high confidence).

Qualitative Results. Examples of probabilistic predictions for PASCAL3D+ dataset are shown in Fig. 6. Upper left images highlight the effect we set out to achieve: to correctly quantify the level of uncertainty of the estimated pose. For easier examples we observe sharp peaks and a highly confident detection, and more spread-out densities otherwise. Other examples highlight the advantage of mixture models, which allow to model complex densities with multiple peaks corresponding to more than one potential pose angle. Failure scenarios are highlighted in the lower right: high confidence predictions in case if the model confuses head and tail.

7   Conclusion

We demonstrated a new probabilistic model for object pose estimation that is robust to variations in input image quality and accurately quantifies its uncertainty. More generally our results confirm that our approach is flexible enough to accommodate different output domains such as angular data and enables rich and efficient probabilistic deep learning models. We train all models by maximum likelihood but still find it to be competitive with other works from the literature that explicitly optimize for point estimates even under point estimate loss functions. In the future, to improve our predictive performance and robustness, we would also like to handle uncertainty of model parameters [30] and to use the Fisher-von Mises distribution to jointly predict a distribution of azimuth-elevation-tilt [44].

We hope that as intelligent systems increasingly rely on perception abilities, future models in computer vision will be robust and probabilistic.

Acknowledgments. This work was supported by Microsoft Research through its PhD Scholarship Programme.

References

1. Marchand, E., Uchiyama, H., Spindler, F.: Pose estimation for augmented reality: a hands-on survey. IEEE Trans. Vis. Comput. Graph. **22**(12), 2633–2651 (2016)
2. Murphy-Chutorian, E., Trivedi, M.M.: Head pose estimation in computer vision: a survey. IEEE Trans. Pattern Anal. Mach. Intell. **31**(4), 607–626 (2009)
3. Poirson, P., Ammirato, P., Fu, C.Y., Liu, W., Kosecka, J., Berg, A.C.: Fast single shot detection and pose estimation. In: 2016 Fourth International Conference on 3D Vision (3DV), pp. 676–684. IEEE (2016)
4. Massa, F., Marlet, R., Aubry, M.: Crafting a multi-task CNN for viewpoint estimation. arXiv preprint arXiv:1609.03894 (2016)
5. Beyer, L., Hermans, A., Leibe, B.: Biternion nets: continuous head pose regression from discrete training labels. In: Gall, J., Gehler, P., Leibe, B. (eds.) GCPR 2015. LNCS, vol. 9358, pp. 157–168. Springer, Cham (2015). https://doi.org/10.1007/978-3-319-24947-6_13
6. Berger, J.O.: Statistical Decision Theory and Bayesian Analysis. Springer, Heidelberg (1980). https://doi.org/10.1007/978-1-4757-4286-2
7. Xiang, Y., Mottaghi, R., Savarese, S.: Beyond PASCAL: a benchmark for 3D object detection in the wild. In: 2014 IEEE Winter Conference on Applications of Computer Vision (WACV), pp. 75–82. IEEE (2014)
8. Siriteerakul, T.: Advance in head pose estimation from low resolution images: a review. Int. J. Comput. Sci. Issues **9**(2) (2012)
9. Odobez, J.M.: IDIAP Head Pose Database. https://www.idiap.ch/dataset/headpose
10. Gourier, N., Hall, D., Crowley, J.L.: Estimating face orientation from robust detection of salient facial structures. In: FG Net Workshop on Visual Observation of Deictic Gestures, vol. 6 (2004)
11. Demirkus, M., Clark, J.J., Arbel, T.: Robust semi-automatic head pose labeling for real-world face video sequences. Multimedia Tools Appl. **70**(1), 495–523 (2014)
12. Murphy-Chutorian, E., Doshi, A., Trivedi, M.M.: Head pose estimation for driver assistance systems: a robust algorithm and experimental evaluation. In: IEEE Intelligent Transportation Systems Conference, ITSC 2007, pp. 709–714. IEEE (2007)
13. Fisher, R., Santos-Victor, J., Crowley, J.: Caviar: context aware vision using image-based active recognition (2005)
14. Benfold, B., Reid, I.: Unsupervised learning of a scene-specific coarse gaze estimator. In: 2011 IEEE International Conference on Computer Vision (ICCV), pp. 2344–2351. IEEE (2011)
15. Fanelli, G., Gall, J., Van Gool, L.: Real time head pose estimation with random regression forests. In: 2011 IEEE Conference on Computer Vision and Pattern Recognition (CVPR), pp. 617–624. IEEE (2011)
16. Chamveha, I., et al.: Head direction estimation from low resolution images with scene adaptation. Comput. Vis. Image Underst. **117**(10), 1502–1511 (2013)
17. Chen, C., Odobez, J.M.: We are not contortionists: coupled adaptive learning for head and body orientation estimation in surveillance video. In: 2012 IEEE Conference on Computer Vision and Pattern Recognition (CVPR), pp. 1544–1551. IEEE (2012)
18. Flohr, F., Dumitru-Guzu, M., Kooij, J.F.P., Gavrila, D.: A probabilistic framework for joint pedestrian head and body orientation estimation. IEEE Trans. Intell. Transp. Syst. **16**, 1872–1882 (2015)

19. Osadchy, M., Cun, Y.L., Miller, M.L.: Synergistic face detection and pose estimation with energy-based models. J. Mach. Learn. Res. **8**(May), 1197–1215 (2007)
20. Dantone, M., Gall, J., Fanelli, G., Van Gool, L.: Real-time facial feature detection using conditional regression forests. In: 2012 IEEE Conference on Computer Vision and Pattern Recognition (CVPR), pp. 2578–2585. IEEE (2012)
21. Zhu, X., Ramanan, D.: Face detection, pose estimation, and landmark localization in the wild. In: 2012 IEEE Conference on Computer Vision and Pattern Recognition (CVPR), pp. 2879–2886. IEEE (2012)
22. Lu, J., Tan, Y.P.: Ordinary preserving manifold analysis for human age and head pose estimation. IEEE Trans. Hum.-Mach. Syst. **43**(2), 249–258 (2013)
23. Huang, D., Storer, M., De la Torre, F., Bischof, H.: Supervised local subspace learning for continuous head pose estimation. In: 2011 IEEE Conference on Computer Vision and Pattern Recognition (CVPR), pp. 2921–2928. IEEE (2011)
24. Tosato, D., Spera, M., Cristani, M., Murino, V.: Characterizing humans on riemannian manifolds. IEEE Trans. Pattern Anal. Mach. Intell. **35**(8), 1972–1984 (2013)
25. BenAbdelkader, C.: Robust head pose estimation using supervised manifold learning. In: Daniilidis, K., Maragos, P., Paragios, N. (eds.) ECCV 2010. LNCS, vol. 6316, pp. 518–531. Springer, Heidelberg (2010). https://doi.org/10.1007/978-3-642-15567-3_38
26. Geng, X., Xia, Y.: Head pose estimation based on multivariate label distribution. In: Proceedings of the IEEE Conference on Computer Vision and Pattern Recognition, pp. 1837–1842 (2014)
27. Kazemi, V., Sullivan, J.: One millisecond face alignment with an ensemble of regression trees. In: Proceedings of the IEEE Conference on Computer Vision and Pattern Recognition, pp. 1867–1874 (2014)
28. Ba, S.O., Odobez, J.M.: A probabilistic framework for joint head tracking and pose estimation. In: Proceedings of the 17th International Conference on Pattern Recognition, ICPR 2004, vol. 4, pp. 264–267. IEEE (2004)
29. Demirkus, M., Precup, D., Clark, J.J., Arbel, T.: Probabilistic temporal head pose estimation using a hierarchical graphical model. In: Fleet, D., Pajdla, T., Schiele, B., Tuytelaars, T. (eds.) ECCV 2014. LNCS, vol. 8689, pp. 328–344. Springer, Cham (2014). https://doi.org/10.1007/978-3-319-10590-1_22
30. Kendall, A., Gal, Y.: What uncertainties do we need in Bayesian deep learning for computer vision? arXiv preprint arXiv:1703.04977 (2017)
31. Savarese, S., Fei-Fei, L.: 3D generic object categorization, localization and pose estimation. In: IEEE 11th International Conference on Computer Vision, ICCV 2007, pp. 1–8. IEEE (2007)
32. Ozuysal, M., Lepetit, V., Fua, P.: Pose estimation for category specific multiview object localization. In: 2009 IEEE Conference on Computer Vision and Pattern Recognition, pp. 778–785 (2009)
33. Xiang, Y., Mottaghi, R., Savarese, S.: Beyond PASCAL: a benchmark for 3D object detection in the wild. In: IEEE Winter Conference on Applications of Computer Vision (WACV) (2014)
34. Pepik, B., Gehler, P., Stark, M., Schiele, B.: 3D^{2}PM – 3D deformable part models. In: Fitzgibbon, A., Lazebnik, S., Perona, P., Sato, Y., Schmid, C. (eds.) ECCV 2012. LNCS, vol. 7577, pp. 356–370. Springer, Heidelberg (2012). https://doi.org/10.1007/978-3-642-33783-3_26
35. Pepik, B., Stark, M., Gehler, P., Schiele, B.: Teaching 3D geometry to deformable part models. In: IEEE Conference on Computer Vision and Pattern Recognition (CVPR), pp. 3362–3369. IEEE, Providence, June 2012. Oral Presentation

36. Su, H., Qi, C.R., Li, Y., Guibas, L.J.: Render for CNN: viewpoint estimation in images using CNNs trained with rendered 3D model views. In: Proceedings of the IEEE International Conference on Computer Vision, pp. 2686–2694 (2015)

37. Braun, M., Rao, Q., Wang, Y., Flohr, F.: Pose-RCNN: joint object detection and pose estimation using 3D object proposals. In: 2016 IEEE 19th International Conference on Intelligent Transportation Systems (ITSC), pp. 1546–1551. IEEE (2016)

38. Tulsiani, S., Malik, J.: Viewpoints and keypoints. In: Proceedings of the IEEE Conference on Computer Vision and Pattern Recognition, pp. 1510–1519 (2015)

39. Crivellaro, A., Rad, M., Verdie, Y., Moo Yi, K., Fua, P., Lepetit, V.: A novel representation of parts for accurate 3D object detection and tracking in monocular images. In: Proceedings of the IEEE International Conference on Computer Vision, pp. 4391–4399 (2015)

40. Rad, M., Lepetit, V.: BB8: a scalable, accurate, robust to partial occlusion method for predicting the 3D poses of challenging objects without using depth. In: International Conference on Computer Vision, vol. 1, p. 5 (2017)

41. Grabner, A., Roth, P.M., Lepetit, V.: 3D pose estimation and 3D model retrieval for objects in the wild. In: Proceedings of the IEEE Conference on Computer Vision and Pattern Recognition, pp. 3022–3031 (2018)

42. Simonyan, K., Zisserman, A.: Very deep convolutional networks for large-scale image recognition. arXiv preprint arXiv:1409.1556 (2014)

43. Szegedy, C., Ioffe, S., Vanhoucke, V., Alemi, A.A.: Inception-v4, inception-resnet and the impact of residual connections on learning. In: AAAI, vol. 4 (2012)

44. Mardia, K.V., Jupp, P.E.: Directional Statistics, vol. 494. Wiley, Hoboken (2009)

45. Kingma, D.P., Welling, M.: Auto-encoding variational Bayes. arXiv preprint arXiv:1312.6114 (2013)

46. Rezende, D.J., Mohamed, S., Wierstra, D.: Stochastic backpropagation and approximate inference in deep generative models. arXiv preprint arXiv:1401.4082 (2014)

47. Sohn, K., Lee, H., Yan, X.: Learning structured output representation using deep conditional generative models. In: Advances in Neural Information Processing Systems, pp. 3483–3491 (2015)

48. Doersch, C.: Tutorial on variational autoencoders. arXiv preprint arXiv:1606.05908 (2016)

49. Burda, Y., Grosse, R., Salakhutdinov, R.: Importance weighted autoencoders. arXiv preprint arXiv:1509.00519 (2015)

50. Premachandran, V., Tarlow, D., Batra, D.: Empirical minimum Bayes risk prediction: how to extract an extra few % performance from vision models with just three more parameters. In: Proceedings of the IEEE Conference on Computer Vision and Pattern Recognition, pp. 1043–1050 (2014)

51. Bouchacourt, D., Mudigonda, P.K., Nowozin, S.: DISCO nets: DISsimilarity COefficients networks. In: Advances in Neural Information Processing Systems, pp. 352–360 (2016)

52. Kingma, D., Ba, J.: Adam: a method for stochastic optimization. arXiv preprint arXiv:1412.6980 (2014)

53. Bergstra, J., Bengio, Y.: Random search for hyper-parameter optimization. J. Mach. Learn. Res. 13(Feb), 281–305 (2012)

54. Benfold, B., Reid, I.: Stable multi-target tracking in real-time surveillance video. In: 2011 IEEE Conference on Computer Vision and Pattern Recognition (CVPR), pp. 3457–3464. IEEE (2011)

55. Everingham, M., Van Gool, L., Williams, C.K., Winn, J., Zisserman, A.: The PASCAL visual object classes (VOC) challenge. Int. J. Comput. Vis. **88**(2), 303–338 (2010)
56. Deng, J., Dong, W., Socher, R., Li, L.J., Li, K., Fei-Fei, L.: ImageNet: a large-scale hierarchical image database. In: IEEE Conference on Computer Vision and Pattern Recognition, CVPR 2009, pp. 248–255. IEEE (2009)
57. Good, I.J.: Rational decisions. J. R. Stat. Soc. Ser. B (Methodol.) 107–114 (1952)
58. Gneiting, T., Raftery, A.E.: Strictly proper scoring rules, prediction, and estimation. J. Am. Stat. Assoc. **102**(477), 359–378 (2007)

Joint Representation and Truncated Inference Learning for Correlation Filter Based Tracking

Yingjie Yao[1], Xiaohe Wu[1], Lei Zhang[2], Shiguang Shan[3],
and Wangmeng Zuo[1(✉)]

[1] Harbin Institute of Technology, Harbin 150001, China
yaoyoyogurt@gmail.com, xhwu.cpsl.hit@gmail.com, wmzuo@hit.edu.cn
[2] University of Pittsburgh, 3362 Fifth Avenue, Pittsburgh, PA 15213, USA
cszhanglei@gmail.com
[3] Institute of Computing Technology, CAS, Beijing 100049, China
sgshan@ict.ac.cn

Abstract. Correlation filter (CF) based trackers generally include two modules, i.e., feature representation and on-line model adaptation. In existing off-line deep learning models for CF trackers, the model adaptation usually is either abandoned or has closed-form solution to make it feasible to learn deep representation in an end-to-end manner. However, such solutions fail to exploit the advances in CF models, and cannot achieve competitive accuracy in comparison with the state-of-the-art CF trackers. In this paper, we investigate the joint learning of deep representation and model adaptation, where an updater network is introduced for better tracking on future frame by taking current frame representation, tracking result, and last CF tracker as input. By modeling the representor as convolutional neural network (CNN), we truncate the alternating direction method of multipliers (ADMM) and interpret it as a deep network of updater, resulting in our model for learning representation and truncated inference (RTINet). Experiments demonstrate that our RTINet tracker achieves favorable tracking accuracy against the state-of-the-art trackers and its rapid version can run at a real-time speed of 24 fps. The code and pre-trained models will be publicly available at https://github.com/tourmaline612/RTINet.

Keywords: Visual tracking · Correlation filters
Convolutional neural networks · Unrolled optimization

1 Introduction

In recent years, correlation filters (CFs) have achieved noteworthy advances as well as state-of-the-art performance in visual tracking. Generally, the CF-based

Electronic supplementary material The online version of this chapter (https://doi.org/10.1007/978-3-030-01240-3_34) contains supplementary material, which is available to authorized users.

© Springer Nature Switzerland AG 2018
V. Ferrari et al. (Eds.): ECCV 2018, LNCS 11213, pp. 560–575, 2018.
https://doi.org/10.1007/978-3-030-01240-3_34

approaches learn CFs on feature representation for model adaptation along with an image sequence. Therefore, the advancement of CF-based tracking performance is mainly driven by the improvement on both feature representation and CF learning model. The development of feature representation has witnessed the evolution from handcrafted HOG [16] and ColorNames (CN) [11] to deep convolutional neural network (CNN) features [7,22,26]. And their combination has also been adopted [6,10]. Meanwhile, the learning models have also been continuously improved with the introduction of spatial regularization [7–9], continuous convolution [10], target response adaptation [2], context regularization [23], temporal regularization [20], and other sophisticated learning models [6,17,34].

Motivated by the unprecedented success of CNNs [14,19,27,28] in computer vision, it is encouraging to study the off-line training of deep CNNs for feature representation and model adaptation in CF trackers. Unfortunately, model adaptation in CF tracking usually requires to solve a complex optimization problem, and is not trivial to be off-line trained together with deep representation. To enable off-line training of deep representation specified for visual tracking, the Siamese network solutions [1,4,29] are suggested to bypass the model adaptation by learning a matcher to discriminate whether a patch is matched with the exemplar image annotated in the first frame. In [1,4,29], the tracker is fixed since the first frame, and cannot adapt to the appearance temporal variation of target. For joint off-training of deep representation and model adaptation, Valmadre et al. [30] adopt the original CF form due to its model adaptation has the closed-form solution and can be interpreted as a differentiable CNN layer. Instead of directly taking model adaptation into account, Guo et al. [13] suggest a dynamic Siamese network for modeling temporal variation, while Choi et al. [5] exploit the forward-pass of meta-learner network to provide new appearance information to Siamese network. These approaches, however, fail to exploit the continuous improvement on CF models [7,8,10,17], and even may not achieve comparable tracking accuracy with the deployment of advanced CF models on deep features pre-trained for classification and detection tasks.

In response to the aforementioned issues, this paper presents a bi-level optimization formulation as well as a RTINet architecture for joint off-line learning of deep representation and model adaptation in CF-based tracking. To exploit the advances in CF tracking, the lower-level task adopts a more sophisticated CF model [17] by incorporating background-aware modeling, which can learn CFs with limited boundary effect from large spatial supports. And we define the upper-level objective on future frame for task-driven learning and improving the tracking accuracy. With unrolled optimization, we truncate the alternating direction method of multipliers (ADMM) for solving the lower-level task to form our RTINet, which can be interpreted as an updater network based on the deep representation provided by another representor network. Therefore, our RTINet model enables the end-to-end off-line training of both deep representation and truncated inference. Furthermore, task-driven learning of truncated inference is also helpful in improving the effectiveness of the baseline CF tracker [30]. Experiments show that combining CNN with advanced CF tracker can benefit tracking performance, and the joint learning of deep representation and truncated inference also improves tracking accuracy. In comparison with state-of-the-art trackers, our RTINet tracker achieves favorable tracking accuracy, and its rapid version can achieve a real time speed of 24 fps.

To sum up, the contribution of this work is three-fold:

1. We present a framework, i.e., RTINet, for off-line training of deep representation and model adaptation. Instead of combining CNN with the standard CF tracker [30], we show that the combination with the advanced CF tracker (i.e., BACF [17]) can improve the tracking performance with a large margin.
2. The model adaptation of the advanced CFs generally requires to solve a complex optimization problem, making it difficult to jointly train the representor and updater networks. To tackle this issue, we design the updater network by unrolling the ADMM algorithm, and define the loss on future frame to guide the model learning.
3. Experiments show that our RTINet achieves favorable accuracy against state-of-the-art trackers, while its rapid version can perform at real time speed.

2   Related Work

Deep CNNs have demonstrated excellent performance in many challenging vision tasks [12,27], and inspire numerous works to adopt deep features in CF based trackers [6,7,22]. These methods simply use the feature representation generated by CNNs pre-trained for image classification, which, however, are not tailored to visual tracking. Several Siamese networks, e.g., SINT [29], GOTURN [15], and SiameseFC [1], have been exploited for the off-line learning of CNN feature extractor for tracking, but both the feature extractor and tracker are fixed for the first frame, making them generally perform inferior to state-of-the-arts.

As a remedy, Guo et al. [13] and Choi et al. [5] learn to on-line update the feature extractor for adapting to appearance variation during tracking. Instead of learning to update the feature extractor, Valmadre et al. [30] adopt the simple CF model to off-line learn deep representation. Due to that the original CF has the closed-form solution, it can be interpreted as a differentiable CNN layer and enables the joint learning of deep representation and model adaptation. These aforementioned approaches fail to exploit the continuous improvement on CF models [7,8,10,17], and cannot compete with the advanced CF models based on deep features.

Another related work is the meta-tracker by Park et al. [25] which automatically learns fast gradient directions for online model adaptation of an existing tracker (e.g., MDNet [24]). In contrast, our RTINet focuses on the joint off-line learning of deep representation and model adaptation in CF-based tracking. Moreover, most advanced CF trackers are formulated as constrained optimization, which cannot be readily solved by gradient descent as meta-tracker [25] does. Therefore, we truncate the ADMM algorithm for solving BACF [10,17] to design the updater network, and then present our RTINet that enables the end-to-end off-line training of both deep representation and truncated inference.

Furthermore, off-line learning of truncated inference also benefits the improvement on effectiveness of the baseline optimization algorithm [32,33].

3 Proposed Method

In this section, we present our RTINet approach for joint off-line training of deep representation and model adaptation in CF trackers. To this end, we first briefly revisit a recent CF tracker, i.e., BACF [17], to deliver some insights, and then introduce the formulation, network architecture, and learning of our RTINet.

3.1 Revisiting BACF

Let $\mathbf{z}_t \in \mathbb{R}^{m \times n \times L}$ and $\mathbf{f}_t$ denote the feature representation of the current frame $\mathbf{x}_t$, and the CFs adopted at frame t, respectively. In CF based trackers, tracking can be performed by first computing the response map $\sum_{l=1}^{L} \mathbf{z}_{t,l} \star \mathbf{f}_{t,l}$ as the cross-correlation between $\mathbf{z}_t$ and $\mathbf{f}_t$, and then locating the target based on the maximum of the response map. Here, $\star$ denotes the convolution operator, and the cross-correlation can be efficiently performed with the Fast Fourier Transform (FFT), making CFs very encouraging and intensively studied in visual tracking. The original CF model updates the CFs by solving the following problem,

$$\min_{\mathbf{f}} \frac{1}{2} \left\| \mathbf{y}_t - \sum_{l=1}^{L} \mathbf{z}_{t,l} \star \mathbf{f}_l \right\|^2 + \frac{\lambda}{2} \sum_{l=1}^{L} \|\mathbf{f}_l\|^2, \tag{1}$$

where $\mathbf{y}_t$ is a Gaussian shaped function based on the tracking result at frame t, and λ is the regularization parameter.

Recently, many advanced CF models have been suggested to improve the original CF, resulting in continuous performance improvement on visual tracking. Here we take BACF [17] as an example, which learns CFs by better exploiting real negative samples via background-aware modeling. The BACF model can be equivalently formulated as,

$$\min_{\mathbf{f},\mathbf{h}} \frac{1}{2} \left\| \mathbf{y}_t - \sum_{l=1}^{L} \mathbf{z}_{t,l} \star \mathbf{f}_l \right\|^2 + \frac{\lambda}{2} \|\mathbf{h}\|^2, \text{ s.t. } \mathbf{f}_l = \mathbf{M}^\top \mathbf{h}_l, \tag{2}$$

where $\mathbf{M}$ is a binary selection matrix to crop the center patch of an image. The BACF model can be efficiently solved using the Alternating Direction Method of Multipliers (ADMM). Accordingly, the augmented Lagrangian function of Eq. (2) can be expressed as,

$$L(\mathbf{f},\mathbf{h},\boldsymbol{\mu}) = \frac{1}{2} \left\| \mathbf{y}_t - \sum_{l=1}^{L} \mathbf{z}_{t,l} \star \mathbf{f}_l \right\|^2 + \frac{\lambda}{2} \|\mathbf{h}\|^2 + \sum_{l=1}^{L} \boldsymbol{\mu}_l^\top (\mathbf{f}_l - \mathbf{M}^\top \mathbf{h}_l) + \frac{\rho}{2} \sum_{l=1}^{L} \|\mathbf{f}_l - \mathbf{M}^\top \mathbf{h}_l\|^2, \tag{3}$$

where $\boldsymbol{\mu}$ denotes the Lagrange multiplier, and ρ is the penalty parameter. By introducing $\mathbf{g} = \frac{1}{\rho}\boldsymbol{\mu}$, the optimization on $\{\mathbf{f}, \mathbf{h}\}$ of Eq. (3) can be equivalently formed as,

$$L(\mathbf{f}, \mathbf{h}, \mathbf{g}) = \frac{1}{2}\left\|\mathbf{y}_t - \sum_{l=1}^{L} \mathbf{z}_{t,l} \star \mathbf{f}_l\right\|^2 + \frac{\lambda}{2}\|\mathbf{h}\|^2 + \frac{\rho}{2}\sum_{l=1}^{L}\|\mathbf{f}_l - \mathbf{M}^{\top}\mathbf{h}_l + \mathbf{g}_l\|^2. \quad (4)$$

The ADMM algorithm can then be applied to alternatingly update $\mathbf{h}$, $\mathbf{g}$ and $\mathbf{f}$,

$$\begin{cases} \mathbf{h}^{(k+1)} = \arg\min_{\mathbf{h}} \frac{\lambda}{2}\|\mathbf{h}\|^2 + \frac{\rho}{2}\sum_{l=1}^{L}\|\mathbf{f}_l^{(k)} - \mathbf{M}^{\top}\mathbf{h}_l + \mathbf{g}_l^{(k)}\|^2 \\ \mathbf{g}_l^{(k+1)} = \mathbf{g}_l^{(k)} + \mathbf{f}_l^{(k)} - \mathbf{M}^{\top}\mathbf{h}_l^{(k+1)} \\ \mathbf{f}^{(k+1)} = \arg\min_{\mathbf{f}} \frac{1}{2}\left\|\mathbf{y}_t - \sum_{l=1}^{L}\mathbf{z}_{t,l} \star \mathbf{f}_l\right\|^2 + \frac{\rho}{2}\sum_{l=1}^{L}\|\mathbf{f}_l - \mathbf{M}^{\top}\mathbf{h}_l^{(k+1)} + \mathbf{g}_l^{(k+1)}\|^2 \end{cases} \quad (5)$$

We note that the subproblems on $\mathbf{f}^{(k+1)}$ and $\mathbf{h}^{(k+1)}$ have closed-form solutions. Once the solution $\mathbf{f}^*$ to Eq. (2) is obtained, the CFs adopted at frame $t + 1$ can then be attained with the linear interpolation updating rule defined as,

$$\mathbf{f}_{t+1} = (1 - \eta)\mathbf{f}_t + \eta\mathbf{f}^* \quad (6)$$

where η denotes the on-line adaptation rate.

Based on the formulation and optimization of BACF [17], we further explain its motivations to the extension of CFNet [30] and the joint off-line learning of deep representation and model adaptation:

1. In CFNet, the deep representation is integrated with the simplest CF tracker [16] for offline training. Note that many advanced CF models, e.g., BACF [17], can significantly outperform the simple CF in terms of tracking accuracy. Thus, it is natural to conjecture that the combination of deep representation and BACF can result in improved tracking performance.
2. One reason that CFNet only considers the conventional CF is that it has closed-form solution and can be interpreted as a differentiable CNN layer. As for BACF, the solution to Eq. (2) defines an implicit function of the feature representation $\mathbf{z}_t$ and model parameter λ, restricting its integration with CNN representation. Fortunately, when the number of iterations is fixed (i.e., truncated inference [32,33]), the $\mathbf{f}_{t+1}$ from Eqs. (5) and (6) can then be represented as an explicit function of the feature representation and model parameter. Therefore, by unrolling the ADMM optimization of BACF, it is feasible to facilitate the end-to-end off-line learning of truncated inference for visual tracking.
3. Moreover, BACF is performed on the handcrafted features in [17]. Denote by $\psi(\cdot; \mathbf{W}_F)$, a fully convolutional network with parameters $\mathbf{W}_F$. Thus, by letting $\mathbf{z}_t = \psi(\mathbf{x}_t; \mathbf{W}_F)$, both deep representation and truncated inference can be jointly off-line learned from annotated sequences.

Motivated by the above discussions, we in the following first introduce a bi-level optimization framework for joint learning of deep representation and truncated inference, and then present the architecture and learning of our RTINet.

3.2   Model Formulation

Suppose $\mathbf{z}_t = \psi(\mathbf{x}_t; \mathbf{W}_F)$ is the deep representation of $\mathbf{x}_t$, where $\mathbf{W}_F$ denotes the parameters of the representor network $\psi(\cdot; \mathbf{W}_F)$. Naturally, we require that the learned CFs $\mathbf{f}_{t+1} = \eta\mathbf{f}^* + (1 - \eta)\mathbf{f}_t$ should be effective in tracking the target of the future frame. Thus, the integration of BACF and deep representation can be formulated as a bi-level optimization problem,

$$\min_{\lambda,\rho,\mathbf{M},\eta} \left\| \mathbf{y}_{t+1} - \sum_{l=1}^{L} \mathbf{z}_{t+1,l} \star (\eta\mathbf{f}_l^* + (1-\eta)\mathbf{f}_{t,l}) \right\|^2,$$

$$\text{s.t. } \mathbf{f}^* = \arg\min_{\mathbf{f}} \left\| \mathbf{y}_t - \sum_{l=1}^{L} \mathbf{z}_{t,l} \star \mathbf{f}_l \right\|^2 + \lambda\|\mathbf{h}\|^2, \qquad (7)$$

$$\text{s.t. } \mathbf{f}_l = \mathbf{M}^\top \mathbf{h}_l$$

However, $\mathbf{f}^*$ defines an implicit function of $\mathbf{z}_t$, and $\mathbf{f}_{t+1}$, making it difficult to compute the gradient.

With the unrolled ADMM optimization, when the number of iterations K is fixed, all the $\mathbf{f}^{(1)}, \ldots, \mathbf{f}^{(K)}$, and $\mathbf{f}_{t+1}$ can be represented as the functions of $\mathbf{z}_t$, $\mathbf{y}_t$, and $\mathbf{f}_t$. For joint learning of deep representation and truncated inference, we also slightly modify the BACF model and ADMM algorithm to make that the model parameters λ and $\mathbf{M}$, algorithm parameters ρ and η are both iteration-wise and learnable, i.e., $\Theta = \{\Theta^{(1)}, \ldots, \Theta^{(K)}\}$ with $\Theta^{(k)} = \{\lambda^{(k)}, \mathbf{M}^{(k)}, \rho^{(k)}, \eta^{(k)}\}$. To improve the robustness of the learned tracker, we require that $\mathbf{f}_{t+1}$ can also be applied to the $(t + 1)$-th frame. To ease the training, we further introduce $\mathbf{f}_{t+1}^{(k)} = \eta^{(k)}\mathbf{f}^{(k)} + (1 - \eta^{(k)})\mathbf{f}_t$, and require that $\mathbf{f}_{t+1}^{(k)}$ also performs well. Taking all the aforementioned factors into account, we present the whole RTINet model for joint learning of representation and truncated inference as

$$\min \mathcal{L}(\mathbf{W}_F, \Theta) = \sum_{k=1}^{K} \left\| \mathbf{y}_{t+1} - \sum_{l=1}^{L} \psi_l(\mathbf{x}_{t+1}; \mathbf{W}_F) \star \mathbf{f}_{t+1,l}^{(k)} \right\|^2 \qquad (8)$$

where

$$\mathbf{f}_{t+1}^{(k)} = F_{Int}(\mathbf{f}^{(k)}, \mathbf{f}_t; \eta^{(k)}) = \eta^{(k)}\mathbf{f}^{(k)} + (1 - \eta^{(k)})\mathbf{f}_t, \qquad (9)$$

$$\begin{cases} \mathbf{h}^{(k)} = F_{\mathbf{h}}(\mathbf{f}^{(k-1)}, \mathbf{g}^{(k-1)}; \lambda^{(k)}, \rho^{(k)}, \mathbf{M}^{(k)}) & (10a) \\ \quad = \left(\lambda^{(k)}\mathbf{I} + \rho^{(k)}\left(\mathbf{M}^{(k)}\mathbf{M}^{(k)^\top} \otimes \mathbf{I}_L\right)\right)^{-1}\rho^{(k)}\left(\mathbf{M}^{(k)} \otimes \mathbf{I}_L\right)\left(\mathbf{f}^{(k-1)} + \mathbf{g}^{(k-1)}\right) \\ \mathbf{g}_l^{(k)} = F_{\mathbf{g}}(\mathbf{g}^{(k-1)}, \mathbf{f}^{(k-1)}, \mathbf{h}^{(k)}; \mathbf{M}^{(k)}) & (10b) \\ \quad = \mathbf{g}_l^{(k-1)} + \mathbf{f}_l^{(k-1)} - \mathbf{M}^{(k)\top}\mathbf{h}_l^{(k)} \\ \hat{\mathbf{f}}_l^{(k)} = F_{\mathbf{f}}(\mathbf{z}_t, \mathbf{y}_t, \mathbf{g}^{(k)}, \mathbf{h}^{(k)}; \rho^{(k)}, \mathbf{M}^{(k)}) & (10c) \\ \quad = \dfrac{\hat{\mathbf{z}}_{t,l}^* \circ \hat{\mathbf{q}}}{\rho^{(k)} + \sum_{l=1}^{L} \hat{\mathbf{z}}_{t,l}^* \circ \hat{\mathbf{z}}_{t,l}}, \quad \hat{\mathbf{q}} = \rho^{(k)}\hat{\mathbf{h}}_l^{(k)} - \rho^{(k)}\hat{\mathbf{g}}_l^{(k)} + \hat{\mathbf{z}}_{t,l} \circ \hat{\mathbf{y}}_t \end{cases}$$

where $\hat{\cdot} = \mathcal{F}(\cdot)$ denotes the FFT of a signal, $\otimes$ indicates the Kronecker product, $\mathbf{I}_L$ is an identity matrix of size $L \times L$ and $\hat{\mathbf{h}}_l^{(k)} = \mathcal{F}(\mathbf{M}^{(k)\top}\mathbf{h}_l^{(k)})$. $\mathbf{f}^{(k)}$ can be further obtained by the inverse FFT of $\hat{\mathbf{f}}^{(k)}$. In the first iteration, $\mathbf{f}^{(0)}$ and $\mathbf{g}^{(0)}$ are initialized as zeros.

To sum up, our RTINet consists of two subnetworks: (i) a representor network to generate deep representation $\mathbf{z}_t = \psi(\mathbf{x}_t; \mathbf{W}_F)$, and (ii) an updater network to update the CF model $\mathbf{f}_{t+1} = \mathbf{f}_{t+1}^{(K)} = \phi(\mathbf{z}_t, \mathbf{y}_t, \mathbf{f}_t; \Theta)$. While the representor network adopts the architecture of fully convolutional network, the updater network is recursively defined based on Eqs. (9)–(10c). More detailed explanation on the representor and updater architecture will be given in the next subsection.

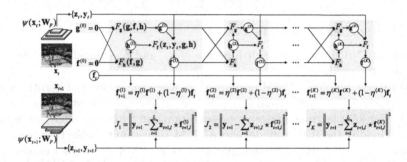

Fig. 1. Overview of the RTINet architecture, which includes a representor network and an updater network. In the inference learning, we compute $\mathbf{h}$, $\mathbf{g}$ and $\mathbf{f}$ recursively following Eqs. (9)–(10c) in each stage.

3.3   Architecture of RTINet

Figure 1 provides an overview of the RTINet architecture, which includes a representor network and a updater network. For the representor network $\psi(\cdot; \mathbf{W}_F)$, we adopt the first three convolution (conv) layers of the VGG-M [3]. ReLU nonlinearity and local response normalization are employed after each convolution operation, and the pooling operation is deployed for the first two conv layers. To handle different sizes of targets, we resize the patches to 224×224 as inputs and produce the feature map with the size of $13 \times 13 \times 512$.

As for the updater network $\phi(\mathbf{z}_t, \mathbf{y}_t, \mathbf{f}_t; \Theta)$, we follow the unrolled ADMM optimization to design the network architecture. As shown in Fig. 1, given $\{\mathbf{z}_t, \mathbf{y}_t\}$, we initialize $\mathbf{f}^{(0)} = \mathbf{0}$ and $\mathbf{g}^{(0)} = \mathbf{0}$. In the first stage of the updater network, (i) the node $F_{\mathbf{h}}(\mathbf{f}, \mathbf{g})$ takes $\mathbf{f}^{(0)}$ and $\mathbf{g}^{(0)}$ as input to generate $\mathbf{h}^{(1)}$, (ii) the node $F_{\mathbf{g}}(\mathbf{g}, \mathbf{f}, \mathbf{h})$ takes $\mathbf{g}^{(0)}$, $\mathbf{f}^{(0)}$, and $\mathbf{h}^{(1)}$ as input to generate $\mathbf{g}^{(1)}$, and finally (iii) the node $F_{\mathbf{f}}(\mathbf{z}, \mathbf{y}, \mathbf{g}, \mathbf{h})$ takes $\mathbf{z}_t$, $\mathbf{y}_t$, $\mathbf{g}^{(1)}$ and $\mathbf{h}^{(1)}$ as input to generate $\mathbf{f}^{(1)}$. By repeating K stages, we can obtain $\mathbf{f}^{(K)}$, and then the node $F_{Int}(\mathbf{f}, \mathbf{f}_t)$ takes $\mathbf{f}^{(K)}$ and $\mathbf{f}_t$ as input to generate $\mathbf{f}_{t+1}$. Note that all the nodes $F_{\mathbf{g}}$, $F_{\mathbf{h}}$, $F_{\mathbf{f}}$, and F_{Int} are differentiable. Thus, with the annotated video sequences, both the updater network and the representor network can be end-to-end trained by minimizing the model objective in Eq. (8).

3.4 Model Learning

In this subsection, we present a stage-wise learning scheme to learn the model parameters $\mathbf{W}_F$ and $\Theta = \{\Theta^{(k)}\}_{k=1,2,\cdots,K}$. After the first $(k'-1)$ stages of learning, we can obtain the current model parameters $\mathbf{W}_F$ and $\{\Theta^{(k)}\}_{k=1,2,\cdots,(k'-1)}$. Denote by $\Theta^{(k')} = \{\lambda^{(k')}, \mathbf{M}^{(k')}, \rho^{(k')}, \eta^{(k')}\}$. To guide the model learning, we define the stage-wise loss function as,

$$J_{k'} = \left\| \mathbf{y}_{t+1} - \sum_{l=1}^{L} \mathbf{z}_{t+1,l} \star \mathbf{f}_{t+1,l}^{(k')} \right\|^2. \tag{11}$$

Then we introduce the gradient computation which is used to update model parameters with the stochastic gradient descent (SGD) algorithm.

According to Eqs. (9)–(10c), we have the following observations:

(a) $\mathbf{f}_{t+1}^{(k')}$ is a function of $\mathbf{f}^{(k')}$, $\mathbf{f}_t$ and $\eta^{(k')}$;
(b) $\mathbf{h}^{(k')}$ is a function of $\mathbf{f}^{(k'-1)}$, $\mathbf{g}^{(k'-1)}$, $\lambda^{(k')}$, $\rho^{(k')}$ and $\mathbf{M}^{(k')}$;
(c) $\mathbf{g}^{(k')}$ is a function of $\mathbf{g}^{(k'-1)}$, $\mathbf{f}^{(k'-1)}$, $\mathbf{h}^{(k')}$ and $\mathbf{M}^{(k')}$;
(d) $\mathbf{f}^{(k')}$ is a function of $\mathbf{z}_t$, $\mathbf{y}_t$, $\mathbf{h}^{(k')}$, $\mathbf{g}^{(k')}$, $\rho^{(k')}$ and $\mathbf{M}^{(k')}$.

Combined these observations with Eq. (11), we can obtain the gradient of $J_{k'}$ w.r.t. $\Theta^{(k')}$ in the k'-th stage, i.e., $\nabla_{\Theta^{(k')}} J_{k'} = \left(\nabla_{\eta^{(k')}} J_{k'}, \nabla_{\rho^{(k')}} J_{k'}, \nabla_{\mathbf{M}^{(k')}} J_{k'}, \nabla_{\lambda^{(k')}} J_{k'} \right)$.

Specifically, for each parameter in $\Theta^{(k')}$, we have,

$$
\begin{cases}
\nabla_{\eta^{(k')}} J_{k'} = \nabla_{\mathbf{f}_{t+1}^{(k')}} J_{k'} \nabla_{\eta^{(k')}} \mathbf{f}_{t+1}^{(k')} \\
\nabla_{\rho^{(k')}} J_{k'} = \nabla_{\mathbf{f}^{(k')}} J_{k'} \nabla_{\rho^{(k')}} \mathbf{f}^{(k')} + \nabla_{\mathbf{h}^{(k')}} J_{k'} \nabla_{\rho^{(k')}} \mathbf{h}^{(k')} \\
\nabla_{\mathbf{M}^{(k')}} J_{k'} = \nabla_{\mathbf{f}^{(k')}} J_{k'} \nabla_{\mathbf{M}^{(k')}} \mathbf{f}^{(k')} + \nabla_{\mathbf{g}^{(k')}} J_{k'} \nabla_{\mathbf{M}^{(k')}} \mathbf{g}^{(k')} + \nabla_{\mathbf{h}^{(k')}} J_{k'} \nabla_{\mathbf{M}^{(k')}} \mathbf{h}^{(k')} \\
\nabla_{\lambda^{(k')}} J_{k'} = \nabla_{\mathbf{h}_{t+1}^{(k')}} J_{k'} \cdot \nabla_{\lambda^{(k')}} \mathbf{h}_{t+1}^{(k')}
\end{cases} \tag{12}
$$

The derivations of $\nabla_{\mathbf{f}^{(k')}} J_{k'}$, $\nabla_{\mathbf{g}^{(k')}} J_{k'}$ and $\nabla_{\mathbf{h}^{(k')}} J_{k'}$ are presented in the supplementary materials.

Furthermore, $J_{k'}$ should also be used to update the model parameters $\mathbf{W}_F$ and $\{\Theta^{(k)}\}_{k=1,2,\cdots,(k'-1)}$ for the sake of joint representation and truncated inference learning. Thus, we also give the gradient of $J_{k'}$ w.r.t. $\mathbf{h}^{(k'-1)}$, $\mathbf{g}^{(k'-1)}$, and $\mathbf{f}^{(k'-1)}$ as follows,

$$
\begin{cases}
\nabla_{\mathbf{h}^{(k'-1)}} J_{k'} = \nabla_{\mathbf{g}^{(k'-1)}} J_{k'} \nabla_{\mathbf{h}^{(k'-1)}} \mathbf{g}^{(k'-1)} + \nabla_{\mathbf{f}^{(k'-1)}} J_{k'} \nabla_{\mathbf{g}^{(k'-1)}} \mathbf{f}^{(k'-1)} \\
\nabla_{\mathbf{g}^{(k'-1)}} J_{k'} = \nabla_{\mathbf{g}^{(k')}} J_{k'} \nabla_{\mathbf{g}^{(k'-1)}} \mathbf{g}^{(k')} + \nabla_{\mathbf{h}^{(k')}} J_{k'} \nabla_{\mathbf{g}^{(k'-1)}} \mathbf{h}^{(k')} \\
\nabla_{\mathbf{f}^{(k'-1)}} J_{k'} = \nabla_{\mathbf{g}^{(k')}} J_{k'} \nabla_{\mathbf{f}^{(k'-1)}} \mathbf{g}^{(k')} + \nabla_{\mathbf{h}^{(k')}} J_{k'} \nabla_{\mathbf{f}^{(k'-1)}} \mathbf{h}^{(k')}
\end{cases} \tag{13}
$$

Please refer to the supplementary material for the detail of the derivation. Therefore, we can back-propagate the gradient to the $(k'-1), \ldots, 1$ layers and the representor network $\psi(\cdot; \mathbf{W}_F)$. After the learning of the k'-th stage, we can further conduct the $(k'+1)$-th stage-wise training by learning $\Theta^{(k'+1)}$ and fine-tuning $\mathbf{W}_F$ and $\{\Theta^{(k)}\}_{k=1,2,\cdots,k'}$ until the ending of the K-th stage-wise training. Finally, all the model parameters $\mathbf{W}_F$ and Θ are adopted for target localization and model adaptation during the on-line tracking process.

4   Experiments

In this section, we first describe the implementation details, then compare with the baseline trackers highly relevant to our approach. For comprehensive analysis, ablation studies are conducted to investigate the effect of the joint feature representation learning and stage-wise training scheme. Finally, we compare the proposed RTINet with state-of-the-art trackers on the OTB-2015 [31], TB-50 [31] (i.e., the 50 more challenging sequences from OTB-2015), TempleColor-128 [21] and VOT2016 [18] datasets. Our approach is implemented in MATLAB 2017a using MatConvNet library, and all the experiments are run on a PC equipped with an Intel i7 CPU 4.0 GHz, 32 GB and a single NVIDIA GTX 1080 GPU.

4.1   Implementation Details

Training Set. To train the RTINet, we employ the 2015 edition of ImageNet Large Scale Visual Recognition Challenge (ILSVRC2015) dataset, which consists of more than 4,500 videos from 30 different object categories. For each video, we pick up 20 successive frames in which the target sizes are not larger than 50% of the image size. Then, 2,000 sequences are randomly chosen for training and the rest are used as the validation set. To avoid the influence of target distortion, we crop the square region centered at the target with the size of $5\sqrt{WH} \times 5\sqrt{WH}$, where W and H represent the width and height of the target, respectively. And the cropped regions are further resized to 224×224 as the input of the RTINet.

Training Details. Since it is not trivial to train the RTINet with all the parameters directly, we decouple the training of the representor network and updater network into two steps: (1) We firstly keep the representor network fixed and train the updater network in a greedily stage-wise manner. As for the stage k, we initialize the hyper-parameters of the updater network (i.e., $\lambda^{(k)}$, $\rho^{(k)}$, $\eta^{(k)}$ and $\mathbf{M}^{(k)}$) with the trained parameters in the previous stage $k-1$. Then the updater network is trained with 50 epochs with all the parameters in the previous stages fixed. (2) After the stage-wise training of the updater network, we apply another 50 epochs to jointly train the representor network and updater network.

During training, we initialize the convolution layers of the representor network with the pre-trained VGG-M model [3]. As for the model parameters, we set $\lambda^{(0)}$, $\rho^{(0)}$, $\eta^{(0)}$ and $\mathbf{M}^{(0)}$ in the first stage of the updater network as 1, 1, 0.013 and the binary selection matrix, respectively. We use the stochastic gradient descent (SGD) as the optimizer with the mini-batch size of 16, and the learning rate is exponentially decayed from 10^{-2} to 10^{-5}.

Table 1. Comparison with the baseline CFNet variants on OTB-2015.

Trackers	CFNet-conv1	CFNet	CFNet-conv1-Rep	CFNet-Rep	RTINet-conv1	RTINet
AUC	53.6	56.8	54.8	58.0	64.3	68.2
FPS	84	75	82.7	68	23.3	9.0

Table 2. Comparison with the baseline BACF variants on OTB-2015.

Trackers	BACF	BACF-VGGM	BACF-Rep	RTINet-VGGM	stdBACF-Rep	RTINet
AUC	61.5	63.1	64.0	66.5	64.2	68.2
FPS	35.3	6.1	6.5	8.9	7.0	9.0

4.2 Comparison with CFNet

The most relevant methods to our RTINet is CFNet [30], which is also proposed for the joint learning of deep representation and CF tracker. In comparison, the updater network of our RTINet is designed based on the unrolled optimization of BACF [17]. Here, we evaluate two variants of the proposed method: RTINet with three convolution layers and its rapid version, i.e., RTINet-conv1 with one convolution layer, and compare them with CFNet, CFNet-conv1, and their two variants with features extracted by RTINet representor, i.e., CFNet-conv1-Rep and CFNet-Rep on OTB-2015. Following the protocols in [31], we report the results in terms of area under curve (AUC) and tracking speed in Table 1. And we have two observations. (1) The CFNet variants with RTINet features perform better than CFNet-conv1 and CFNet with an AUC gain of 1.2% and 1.2%, respectively, thereby showing the effectiveness and generalization of the deep features learned by RTINet. (2) In terms of AUC, both RTINet variants perform favorably against their counterparts, indicating that RTINet is effective in learning feature representation and truncated inference. In particular, RTINet brings an AUC gain of 11.4% over CFNet on the OTB-2015 dataset. As for the rapid version, RTINet-conv1 also outperforms its baseline CFNet-conv1 by a gain of 10.7%. RTINet even achieves an AUC of 68.2% on OTB-2015, outperforming other trackers with a large margin. We owe the improvements to both the introduction of the advanced BACF tracker and truncated inference into the RTINet framework.

We also report the average FPS of different trackers. While the best speed belongs to the CFNet-conv1 (84 fps) and CFNet-conv1-Rep (82.7 fps), RTINet runs at 9 fps and achieves the state-of-the-art tracking accuracy. Actually, a large part of computational cost in RTINet comes from the deeper CNN feature extraction. When conv1 feature is adopted, and RTINet-conv1 achieves a real time speed of 24 fps while still performing favorably against CFNet.

Table 3. The AUC scores of RTINet by training with different number of stages.

Number of stages	1	2	3	4	5	6	7	8	9	10
Basketball	62.0	75.9	69.1	64.3	69.4	69.1	68.9	68.9	68.8	68.8
BlurCar1	77.1	83.0	81.2	81.1	80.6	80.7	80.5	80.4	80.3	80.3
CarDark	76.2	85.7	83.3	82.9	82.2	82.1	81.6	81.7	82.2	82.3
Human4	44.1	57.0	55.6	57.7	61.5	51.0	52.2	51.5	52.0	52.3
Toy	60.1	61.1	63.1	62.8	62.1	61.9	62.8	62.8	62.7	63.0
OTB-2015	59.6	68.2	67.2	67.2	66.3	66.0	65.6	66.3	66.0	66.2

4.3   Ablation Studies

In this section, we analyze in depth the effect of joint feature representation and truncated inference learning as well as stage-wise training.

Joint Learning. To investigate the effect of joint learning, we decouple the feature representation and truncated inference learning, which results in four variants of RTINet: BACF-VGGM (BACF with the fixed convolutional feature from pre-trained VGG-M), BACF-Rep (BACF with the learned RTINet representation), RTINet-VGGM (RTINet with the fixed convolution feature from pre-trained VGG-M) and the full RTINet model. Besides, we also apply the learned RTINet representation and model parameters λ, η and M to the standard BACF, resulting in stdBACF-Rep. Table 2 shows the AUC scores of the default BACF with HOG features, and the BACF variants on OTB-2015.

From Table 2, it can be seen that RTINet and RTINet-VGGM improve the AUC scores significantly in comparison with the corresponding BACF variants. This can be attributed to that the truncated inference learning in updater network does benefit the tracking performance. Moreover, RTINet also improves the performance of RTINet-VGGM by an AUC gain of 1.7%, and BACF-Rep obtains a gain of 0.9% over BACF-VGGM, validating the effectiveness of representation learning. It is worth noting that, in our RTINet the inference learning improves the performance more than the feature learning, implying that pre-trained VGG-M does have good representation and generalization ability. To sum up, both the learned feature representation and truncated inference are helpful in improving tracking accuracy, which together explain the favorable performance of our RTINet.

Stage-Wise Learning. In Sect. 3, we present a stage-wise training scheme to learn model parameters. In particular, we solve the BACF [17] formulation using the truncated ADMM optimization. Thus, we analyse the effect of stage number on tracking performance. Table 3 gives the average AUC score of RTINet on all sequences as well as several representative ones by setting different number of stages on the OTB-2015 dataset. RTINet with one stage performs poorly with the AUC of 59.6%, even lower than the BACF (61.5%). This is reasonable due to that RTINet only with one stage is similar to the simple CF rather than the advanced BACF model. Benefited from the advanced BACF, RTINet achieves significantly better performance within 2–5 iterations for most sequences. The best AUC score of 68.2% of RTINet is attained with two stages on OTB-2015, indicating that efficient solver can be learned. It can also be found that increasing number of stages causes moderate decrease on AUC. One possible reason is that for smaller number of stages, RTINet focuses on minimizing upper loss in Eq. (7) and benefits accuracy. For larger number of stages, RTINet may begin to minimize lower loss in Eq. (7) instead of accuracy.

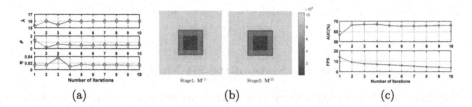

Fig. 2. (a) The learned λ, ρ, η for each stage. (b) Visualization of **M** for the first two stages. (c) Evaluation on the number of stages used for testing with an off-line trained 10-stage RTINet.

Visualization of Learned Parameters. Parameters at all stages are off-line trained and then keep fixed during tracking. Figure 2(a) shows the plots of the learned stage-wise λ, ρ, η used in Table 3. It can be noted that the values of λ, ρ, η become stable from the fourth stage. From Table 3, the best tracking accuracy is attained when the stage number is two. Thus, we present the visualization of the learned **M**s for the first two stages in Fig. 2(b). From Fig. 2(a) and (b), we have two observations: (1) each stage has its specific parameter values, (2) the learned **M**s relax the binary cropping operation which is slightly different with the **M** adopted in BACF. We also note that both the **M** in BACF and our learned **M**s are resized to the feature map size in tracking.

Effects of Convergence on Tracking. Generally, the ADMM algorithms are adopted to resolve the constrained convex optimization problem with a guarantee of convergence. Thus, it is interesting to discuss the effect of iteration numbers after training RTINet with a fixed number of stages. To this end, we train a 10-stage RTINet and test it on the OTB-2015 by using different number of iterations in tracking. From Fig. 2(c), the best tracking accuracy is obtained after 4 iterations. Then RTINet may focus on minimizing the lower loss and more iterations does not bring any increase on accuracy. Figure 2(c) also shows the plot of tracking speed. Comparing Table 3 and Fig. 2(c), it can be seen that direct training RTINet with small K is better than first training a 10-stage RTINet and then testing it with small iterations.

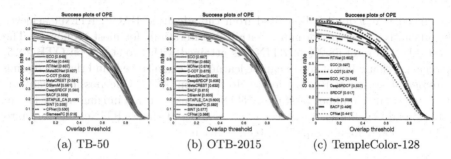

(a) TB-50   (b) OTB-2015   (c) TempleColor-128

Fig. 3. Overlap success plots of different trackers on the TB-50, OTB-2015 and TempleColor-128 datasets.

4.4   Comparison with the State-of-the-art Methods

We compare RTINet with several state-of-the-art trackers, including CF-based trackers (i.e., ECO [6], C-COT [10], DeepSRDCF [7], BACF [17], STAPLE-CA [23]) and learning-based CNN trackers (i.e., MDNet [24], MetaSDNet [25], MetaCREST [25], SiameseFC [1], DSiamM [13] and SINT [29]). Note that all the results are obtained by using either the publicly available codes or the results provided by the authors for fair comparison. Experiments are conducted on TB-50 [31], OTB-2015 [31], TempleColor-128 [21] and VOT-2016 [18]. On the first three datasets, we follow the OPE protocol provided in [31] and present the success plots ranked by the AUC scores. On VOT-2016, we evaluate the trackers in terms of accuracy, robustness and expected average overlap (EAO).

OTB-2015 and TB-50. Figure 3(a) and (b) shows the success plots of the competing trackers the OTB-2015 and TB-50 benchmarks. And the proposed RTINet is ranked in top-3 on the two datasets, achieves comparable performance with the top trackers such as ECO and MDNet [24]. Moreover, RTINet obtains an AUC score of 68.2% on OTB-2015, outperforming its counterparts CFNet and BACF by a margin of 11.4% and 6.7%, respectively. In Fig. 3, we also compare RTINet with the recently proposed Meta-Trackers [25] (i.e., MetaSDNet and MetaCREST). Again our RTINet performs better than both MetaSDNet and MetaCREST by the AUC score. And even the rapid version RTINet-conv1 outperforms MetaCREST, and is comparable to MetaSDNet. On the more challenging sequences in TB-50, our RTINet is still on par with the state-of-the-art ECO and ranks the second among the competing trackers. Specifically, RTINet performs better than the other learning-based trackers, including SiameseFC [1], DSiamM [13] and SINT [29], and surpasses its baseline CFNet [30] by 10.7%. In comparison to CFNet and BACF, the superiority of RTINet can be ascribed to the incorporation of the advanced BACF model, and the joint learning of deep representation and truncated inference. Finally, we analyze the performance with respect to attributes. RTINet performs in top-3 on 6 of the 11 attributes and is on par with the state-of-the-arts on the other attributes. Detailed results are given

Table 4. Comparison with the state-of-the-art trackers in terms of EAO, Robustness, and Accuracy on VOT-2016 dataset

Trackers	ECO	C-COT	DeepSRDCF	SRDCF	HCFT	Staple	BACF	RTINet
EAO	0.374	0.331	0.276	0.247	0.220	0.295	0.233	0.298
Accuracy	0.54	0.52	0.51	0.52	0.47	0.54	0.56	0.57
Robustness	0.72	0.85	1.17	1.50	1.38	1.35	1.88	1.07

in the supplementary materials. The results further validates the effectiveness of our proposed RTINet.

TempleColor-128. Figure 3(c) shows the success plots on TempleColor-128. RTINet performs favorably against ECO with an AUC score of 60.2%, and achieves significant improvements over BACF and C-COT, by a gain of 10.4% and 2.8%, respectively. In particular, compared with its counterpart CFNet, RTINet improves the performance with a large margin of 16.1%. The results further demonstrate the effectiveness of joint representation and truncated inference learning.

VOT2016. Quantitative results on VOT2016 are also be presented in terms of accuracy, robustness and EAO in Table 4. RTINet achieves promising performance and performs much better than the BACF, SRDCF and DeepSRDCF both in terms of accuracy and robustness. In particular, it obtains the best result on accuracy with a value of 0.57, and performs the third-best on robustness and EAO. It is worth noting that, RTINet performs favorably to ECO by accuracy but is inferior by robustness, which may be ascribed to that only the accuracy is considered in the training loss in Eq. (8) of RTINet.

5   Conclusion

This paper presents a RTINet framework for joint learning of deep representation and model adaptation in visual tracking. We adopt the deep convolutional network for feature representation and integrate the CNN with advanced BACF tracker. To solve the BACF in the CNN architecture, we design the model adaptation network as truncated inference by unrolling the ADMM optimization of the BACF model. Moreover, a greedily stage-wise learning scheme is introduced for the joint learning of deep representation and truncated inference from the annotated video sequences. Experimental results on three tracking benchmarks show that our RTINet tracker achieves favorable performance in comparison with the state-of-the-art trackers. Besides, our rapid version of RTINet can run in real-time (24 fps) at a moderate sacrifice of accuracy. By taken BACF as an example, our RTINet sheds some light on incorporating the advances in CF modeling for improving the performance of learning-based trackers, and thus deserves in-depth investigation in future work.

Acknowledgments. This work was supported in part by the National Natural Science Foundation of China under Grant Nos. 61671182 and 61471146.

References

1. Bertinetto, L., Valmadre, J., Henriques, J.F., Vedaldi, A., Torr, P.H.S.: Fully-convolutional siamese networks for object tracking. In: Hua, G., Jégou, H. (eds.) ECCV 2016. LNCS, vol. 9914, pp. 850–865. Springer, Cham (2016). https://doi.org/10.1007/978-3-319-48881-3_56
2. Bibi, A., Mueller, M., Ghanem, B.: Target response adaptation for correlation filter tracking. In: Leibe, B., Matas, J., Sebe, N., Welling, M. (eds.) ECCV 2016. LNCS, vol. 9910, pp. 419–433. Springer, Cham (2016). https://doi.org/10.1007/978-3-319-46466-4_25
3. Chatfield, K., Simonyan, K., Vedaldi, A., Zisserman, A.: Return of the devil in the details: delving deep into convolutional nets. In: BMVC (2014)
4. Chen, K., Tao, W.: Once for all: a two-flow convolutional neural network for visual tracking. TCSVT **PP**, 1 (2017)
5. Choi, J., Kwon, J., Lee, K.M.: Deep meta learning for real-time visual tracking based on target-specific feature space. arXiv:1712.09153 (2017)
6. Danelljan, M., Bhat, G., Khan, F.S., Felsberg, M.: ECO: efficient convolution operators for tracking. In: CVPR, pp. 21–26 (2017)
7. Danelljan, M., Hager, G., Shahbaz Khan, F., Felsberg, M.: Convolutional features for correlation filter based visual tracking. In: ICCV Workshop, pp. 58–66 (2015)
8. Danelljan, M., Hager, G., Shahbaz Khan, F., Felsberg, M.: Learning spatially regularized correlation filters for visual tracking. In: ICCV, pp. 4310–4318 (2015)
9. Danelljan, M., Hager, G., Shahbaz Khan, F., Felsberg, M.: Adaptive decontamination of the training set: a unified formulation for discriminative visual tracking. In: CVPR, pp. 1430–1438 (2016)
10. Danelljan, M., Robinson, A., Shahbaz Khan, F., Felsberg, M.: Beyond correlation filters: learning continuous convolution operators for visual tracking. In: Leibe, B., Matas, J., Sebe, N., Welling, M. (eds.) ECCV 2016. LNCS, vol. 9909, pp. 472–488. Springer, Cham (2016). https://doi.org/10.1007/978-3-319-46454-1_29
11. Danelljan, M., Shahbaz Khan, F., Felsberg, M., Van de Weijer, J.: Adaptive color attributes for real-time visual tracking. In: CVPR, pp. 1090–1097 (2014)
12. Dong, C., Loy, C.C., He, K., Tang, X.: Learning a deep convolutional network for image super-resolution. In: Fleet, D., Pajdla, T., Schiele, B., Tuytelaars, T. (eds.) ECCV 2014. LNCS, vol. 8692, pp. 184–199. Springer, Cham (2014). https://doi.org/10.1007/978-3-319-10593-2_13
13. Guo, Q., Feng, W., Zhou, C., Huang, R., Wan, L., Wang, S.: Learning dynamic siamese network for visual object tracking. In: ICCV, pp. 1–9 (2017)
14. He, K., Zhang, X., Ren, S., Sun, J.: Deep residual learning for image recognition. In: CVPR, pp. 770–778 (2016)
15. Held, D., Thrun, S., Savarese, S.: Learning to track at 100 FPS with deep regression networks. In: Leibe, B., Matas, J., Sebe, N., Welling, M. (eds.) ECCV 2016. LNCS, vol. 9905, pp. 749–765. Springer, Cham (2016). https://doi.org/10.1007/978-3-319-46448-0_45
16. Henriques, J.F., Caseiro, R., Martins, P., Batista, J.: High-speed tracking with kernelized correlation filters. TPAMI **37**(3), 583–596 (2015)
17. Kiani Galoogahi, H., Fagg, A., Lucey, S.: Learning background-aware correlation filters for visual tracking. In: CVPR, pp. 1135–1143 (2017)

18. Kristan, M., et al.: The visual object tracking VOT2016 challenge results. In: Hua, G., Jégou, H. (eds.) ECCV 2016. LNCS, vol. 9914, pp. 777–823. Springer, Cham (2016). https://doi.org/10.1007/978-3-319-48881-3_54
19. Krizhevsky, A., Sutskever, I., Hinton, G.E.: ImageNet classification with deep convolutional neural networks. In: NIPS, pp. 1097–1105 (2012)
20. Li, F., Tian, C., Zuo, W., Zhang, L., Yang, M.H.: Learning spatial-temporal regularized correlation filters for visual tracking. In: CVPR (2018)
21. Liang, P., Blasch, E., Ling, H.: Encoding color information for visual tracking: algorithms and benchmark. TIP **24**(12), 5630–5644 (2015)
22. Ma, C., Huang, J.B., Yang, X., Yang, M.H.: Hierarchical convolutional features for visual tracking. In: ICCV, pp. 3074–3082 (2015)
23. Mueller, M., Smith, N., Ghanem, B.: Context-aware correlation filter tracking. In: CVPR, pp. 1396–1404 (2017)
24. Nam, H., Han, B.: Learning multi-domain convolutional neural networks for visual tracking. In: CVPR, pp. 4293–4302 (2015)
25. Park, E., Berg, A.C.: Meta-tracker: fast and robust online adaptation for visual object trackers. arXiv:1801.03049 (2018)
26. Qi, Y., et al.: Hedged deep tracking. In: CVPR, pp. 4303–4311 (2016)
27. Ren, S., He, K., Girshick, R., Sun, J.: Faster R-CNN: towards real-time object detection with region proposal networks. In: NIPS, pp. 91–99 (2015)
28. Simonyan, K., Zisserman, A.: Very deep convolutional networks for large-scale image recognition. arXiv:1409.1556 (2014)
29. Tao, R., Gavves, E., Smeulders, A.W.: Siamese instance search for tracking. In: CVPR, pp. 1420–1429 (2016)
30. Valmadre, J., Bertinetto, L., Henriques, J., Vedaldi, A., Torr, P.H.: End-to-End representation learning for correlation filter based tracking. In: CVPR, pp. 5000–5008 (2017)
31. Wu, Y., Lim, J., Yang, M.H.: Object Tracking Benchmark. TPAMI **37**(9), 1834–1848 (2015)
32. Yang, Y., Sun, J., Li, H., Xu, Z.: Deep ADMM-Net for compressive sensing MRI. In: NIPS, pp. 10–18 (2016)
33. Zuo, W., Ren, D., Gu, S., Lin, L., Zhang, L., et al.: Discriminative learning of iteration-wise priors for blind deconvolution. In: CVPR, pp. 3232–3240 (2015)
34. Zuo, W., Wu, X., Lin, L., Zhang, L., Yang, M.H.: Learning support correlation filters for visual tracking. TPAMI (2018)

Consensus-Driven Propagation in Massive Unlabeled Data for Face Recognition

Xiaohang Zhan[1](✉)[iD], Ziwei Liu[1][iD], Junjie Yan[2], Dahua Lin[1][iD],
and Chen Change Loy[3][iD]

[1] CUHK - SenseTime Joint Lab, The Chinese University of Hong Kong,
Shatin, Hong Kong
{zx017,zwliu,dhlin}@ie.cuhk.edu.hk
[2] SenseTime Group Limited, Beijing, China
yanjunjie@sensetime.com
[3] Nanyang Technological University, Singapore, Singapore
ccloy@ieee.org

Abstract. Face recognition has witnessed great progress in recent years, mainly attributed to the high-capacity model designed and the abundant labeled data collected. However, it becomes more and more prohibitive to scale up the current million-level identity annotations. In this work, we show that unlabeled face data can be as effective as the labeled ones. Here, we consider a setting closely mimicking the real-world scenario, where the unlabeled data are collected from unconstrained environments and their identities are exclusive from the labeled ones. Our main insight is that although the class information is not available, we can still faithfully approximate these semantic relationships by constructing a relational graph in a bottom-up manner. We propose Consensus-Driven Propagation (CDP) to tackle this challenging problem with two modules, the "committee" and the "mediator", which select positive face pairs robustly by carefully aggregating multi-view information. Extensive experiments validate the effectiveness of both modules to discard outliers and mine hard positives. With CDP, we achieve a compelling accuracy of 78.18% on MegaFace identification challenge by using only 9% of the labels, comparing to 61.78% when no unlabeled data are used and 78.52% when all labels are employed.

1 Introduction

Modern face recognition system mainly relies on the power of high-capacity deep neural network coupled with massive annotated data for learning effective face representations [3,11,14,21,26,29,32]. From CelebFaces [25] ($200K$ images) to MegaFace [13] ($4.7M$ images) and MS-Celeb-1M [9] ($10M$ images), face databases of increasingly larger scale are collected and labeled. Though

Electronic supplementary material The online version of this chapter (https://doi.org/10.1007/978-3-030-01240-3_35) contains supplementary material, which is available to authorized users.

V. Ferrari et al. (Eds.): ECCV 2018, LNCS 11213, pp. 576–592, 2018.
https://doi.org/10.1007/978-3-030-01240-3_35

impressive results have been achieved, we are now trapped in a dilemma where there are hundreds of thousands manually labeling hours consumed behind each percentage of accuracy gains. To make things worse, it becomes harder and harder to scale up the current annotation size to even more identities. In reality, nearly all existing large-scale face databases suffer from a certain level of annotation noises [5]; it leads us to question how reliable human annotation would be.

To alleviate the aforementioned challenges, we shift the focus from obtaining more manually labels to leveraging more unlabeled data. Unlike large-scale identity annotations, unlabeled face images are extremely easy to obtain. For example, using a web crawler facilitated by an off-the-shelf face detector would produce abundant in-the-wild face images or videos [24]. Now the critical question becomes how to leverage the huge existing unlabeled data to boost the performance of large-scale face recognition. This problem is reminiscent of the conventional semi-supervised learning (SSL) [34], but significantly differs from SSL in two aspects: First, the unlabeled data are collected from unconstrained environments, where pose, illumination, occlusion variations are extremely large. It is non-trivial to reliably compute the similarity between different unlabeled samples in this in-the-wild scenario. Second, there is usually no identity overlapping between the collected unlabeled data and the existing labeled data. Thus, the popular label propagation paradigm [35] is no longer feasible here.

In this work, we study this challenging yet meaningful semi-supervised face recognition problem, which can be formally described as follows. In addition to some labeled data with known face identities, we also have access to a massive number of in-the-wild unlabeled samples whose identities are exclusive from the labeled ones. Our goal is to maximize the utility of the unlabeled data so that the final performance can closely match the performance when all the samples are labeled. One key insight here is that although unlabeled data do not provide us with the straightforward semantic classes, its inner structure, which can be represented by a graph, actually reflects the distribution of high-dimensional face representations. The idea of using a graph to reflect structures is also adopted in cross-task tuning [31]. With the graph, we can sample instances and their relations to establish an auxiliary loss for training our model.

Finding a reliable inner structure from noisy face data is non-trivial. It is well-known that the representation induced by a single model is usually prone to bias and sensitive to noise. To address the aforementioned challenge, we take a bottom-up approach to construct the graph by first identifying positive pairs reliably. Specifically, we propose a novel **Consensus-Driven Propagation** (CDP)[1] approach for graph construction in massive unlabeled data. It consists of two modules: a "committee" that provides multi-view information on the proposal pair, and a "mediator" that aggregates all the information for a final decision.

The "**committee**" module is inspired by query-by-committee (QBC) [22] that was originally proposed for active learning. Different from QBC that

---

[1] Project page: http://mmlab.ie.cuhk.edu.hk/projects/CDP/.

measures disagreement, we collect consents from a committee, which comprises a base model and several auxiliary models. The heterogeneity of the committee reveals different views on the structure of the unlabeled data. Then positive pairs are selected as the pair instances that the committee members most agree upon, rather than the base model is most confident of. Hence the committee module is capable of selecting meaningful and hard positive pairs from the unlabeled data besides just easy pairs, complementing the model trained from just labeled data. Beyond the simple voting scheme, as practiced by most QBC methods, we formulate a novel and more effective "**mediator**" to aggregate opinions from the committee. The mediator is a binary classifier that produces the final decision as to select a pair or not. We carefully design the inputs to the mediator so that it covers distributional information about the inner structure. The inputs include (1) voting results of the committee, (2) similarity between the pair, and (3) local density between the pair. The last two inputs are measured across all members of the committee and the base model. Thanks to the "committee" module and the "mediator" module, we construct a robust consensus-driven graph on the unlabeled data. Finally, we propagate pseudo-labels on the graph to form an auxiliary task for training our base model with unlabeled data.

To summarize, we investigate the usage of massive unlabeled data (over 6M images) for large-scale face recognition. Our setting closely resembles real-world scenarios where the unlabeled data are collected from unconstrained environments and their identities are exclusive from the labeled ones. We propose consensus-driven propagation (CDP) to tackle this challenging problem with two carefully-designed modules, the "committee" and the "mediator", which select positive face pairs robustly by aggregating multi-view information. We show that a wise usage of unlabeled data can complement scarce manual labels to achieve compelling results. With consensus-driven propagation, we can achieve comparable results by only using 9% of the labels when compared to its fully-supervised counterpart.

2   Related Work

Semi-supervised Face Recognition. Semi-supervised learning [4,34] is proposed to leverage large-scale unlabeled data, given a handful of labeled data. It typically aims at propagating labels to the whole dataset from limited labels, by various ways, including self-training [19,30], co-training [2,16], multi-view learning [20], expectation-maximization [6] and graph-based methods [36]. For face recognition, Roli and Marcialis [18] adopt a self-training strategy with PCA-based classifiers. In this work, the labels of unlabeled data are inferred with an initial classifier and are added to augment the labeled dataset. Zhao et al. [33] employ Linear Discriminant Analysis (LDA) as the classifier and similarly use self-training to infer labels. Gao et al. [8] propose a semi-supervised sparse representation based method to handle the problem in few-shot learning that labeled examples are typically corrupted by nuisance variables such as bad lighting, wearing glasses. All the aforementioned methods are based on the assumption that the set of categories are shared between labeled data and unlabeled data. However, as mentioned before, this assumption is impractical when the quantity of face identities goes massive.

Query-by-Committee. Query By Committee (QBC) [22] is a strategy relying on multiple discriminant models to explore disagreements, thus mining meaningful examples for machine learning tasks. Argamon-Engelson *et al.* [1] extend the QBC paradigm to the context of probabilistic classification and apply it to natural language processing tasks. Loy *et al.* [15] extend QBC to discover unknown classes via a framework for joint exploration-exploitation active learning. These previous works make use of the disagreements of the committee for threshold-free selection. On the contrary, we exploit the consensus of the committee and extend it to the semi-supervised learning scenario.

3   Methodology

We first provide an overview of the proposed approach. Our approach consists of three stages:

(1) **Supervised initialization** - Given a small portion of labeled data, we separately train the base model and committee members in a fully-supervised manner. More precisely, the base model B and all the N committee members $\{C_i | i = 1, 2, \ldots, N\}$ learn a mapping from image space to feature space $\mathcal{Z}$ using labeled data D_l. For the base model, this process can be denoted as the mapping: $\mathcal{F}_B : D_l \mapsto \mathcal{Z}$, and as for committee members: $\mathcal{F}_{C_i} : D_l \mapsto \mathcal{Z}$, $i = 1, 2, \ldots, N$.

(2) **Consensus-driven propagation** - CDP is applied on unlabeled data to select valuable samples and conjecture labels thereon. The framework is shown in Fig. 1. We use the trained models from the first stage to extract deep features for unlabeled data and create k-NN graphs. The "committee" ensures the diversity of the graphs. Then a "mediator" network is designed to aggregate diverse opinions in the local structure of k-NN graphs to select meaningful pairs. With the selected pairs, a consensus-driven graph is created on the unlabeled data and nodes are assigned with pseudo labels via our label propagation algorithm.

(3) **Joint training using labeled and unlabeled data** - Finally, we re-train the base model with labeled data, and unlabeled data with pseudo labels, in a multi-task learning framework.

3.1   Consensus-Driven Propagation

In this section, we formally introduce the detailed steps of CDP.

i. Building k-NN Graphs. For the base model and all committee members, we feed them with unlabeled data D_u as input and extract deep features $\mathcal{F}_B(D_u)$

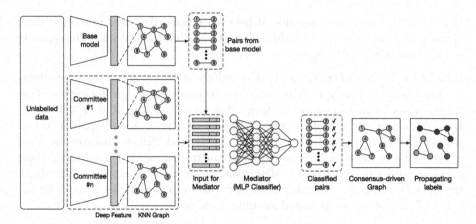

Fig. 1. Consensus-driven propagation. We use a base model and committee models to extract features from unlabeled data and create k-NN graphs. The input to the mediator is constructed by various local statistics of the k-NN graphs of the base model and committee. Pairs that are selected by the mediator compose the "consensus-driven graph". Finally, we propagate labels in the graph, and the propagation for each category ends by recursively eliminating low-confidence edges.

and $\mathcal{F}_{C_i}(D_u)$. With the features, we find k nearest neighbors for each sample in D_u by cosine similarity. This results in different versions of k-NN graphs, $\mathcal{G}_B$ for the base model and $\mathcal{G}_{C_i}$ for each committee member, totally $N+1$ graphs. The nodes in the graphs are examples of the unlabeled data. Each edge in the k-NN graph defines a pair, and all the pairs from the base model's graph $\mathcal{G}_B$ form candidates for the subsequent selection, as shown in Fig. 1.

ii. Collecting Opinions from Committee. Committee members map the unlabeled data to the feature space via different mapping functions $\{\mathcal{F}_{C_i}|i = 1, 2, \ldots, N\}$. Assume two arbitrary connected nodes n_0 and n_1 in the graph created by the base model, and they are represented by different versions of deep features $\{\mathcal{F}_{C_i}(n_0)|i = 1, 2, \ldots, N\}$ and $\{\mathcal{F}_{C_i}(n_1)|i = 1, 2, \ldots, N\}$. The committee provides the following factors:

(1) The *relationship*, R, between the two nodes. Intuitively, it can be understood as whether two nodes are neighbors in the view of each committee member.

$$R_{C_i}^{(n_0, n_1)} = \begin{cases} 1 & \text{if } (n_0, n_1) \in \mathcal{E}(\mathcal{G}_{c_i}) \\ 0 & \text{otherwise.} \end{cases}, \quad i = 1, 2, \ldots, N, \quad (1)$$

where $\mathcal{G}_{c_i}$ is the k-NN graph of i-th committee model and $\mathcal{E}$ denotes all edges of a graph.

(2) The *affinity*, A, between the two nodes. It can be computed as the similarity measured in the feature space with the mapping functions defined by the committee members. Assume that we use cosine similarity as a metric,

$$A_{C_i}^{(n_0, n_1)} = \cos\left(\langle \mathcal{F}_{C_i}(n_0), \mathcal{F}_{C_i}(n_1) \rangle\right), \quad i = 1, 2, \ldots, N. \quad (2)$$

(3) The *local structures* w.r.t each node. This notion can refer to the distribution of a node's first-order, second-order, and even higher-order neighbors. Among them the first-order neighbors play the most important role to represent the "local structures" w.r.t a node. And such distribution can be approximated as the distribution of similarities between the node x and all of its neighbors x_k, where $k = 1, 2, ..., K$.

$$D_{C_i}^x = \{\cos\left(\langle \mathcal{F}_{C_i}(x), \mathcal{F}_{C_i}(x_k) \rangle\right), k = 1, 2, \ldots, K\}, \quad i = 1, 2, \ldots, N. \quad (3)$$

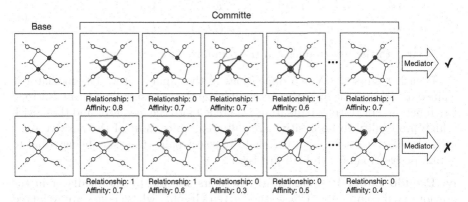

Fig. 2. Committee and mediator. This figure illustrates the mechanisms of committee and mediator. The figure shows some sampled nodes in different versions of graphs brought by the base model and the committee. In each row, the two red nodes are candidate pairs. The pair in the first row is classified as positive by the mediator, while the pair in the second row is considered as negative. The committee provides diverse opinions on "relationship", "affinity", and "local structure". The "local structure" is represented as the distribution of first-order (red edges) and second-order (orange edges) neighbors. Note that the figure only shows the "local structure" centered on one of the two nodes (the node with double circles). (Color figure online)

As illustrated in Fig. 2, given a pair of nodes extracted from the base model's graph, the committee members provide diverse opinions to the *relationships*, the *affinity* and the *local structures*, due to their nature of heterogeneity. From these diverse opinions, we seek to find a consent through a mediator in the next step.

iii. Aggregate Opinions via Mediator. The role of a mediator is to aggregate and convey committee members' opinions for pair selection. We formulate the mediator as a Multi-Layer Perceptron (MLP) classifier albeit other types of classifier are applicable. Recall that all pairs extracted from the base model's graph constitute the candidates. The mediator shall re-weight the opinions of the committee members and make a final decision by assigning a probability to each pair to indicate if a pair shares the same identity, *i.e.*, positive, or have different identities, *i.e.*, negative.

The input to the mediator for each pair (n_0, n_1) is a concatenated vector containing three parts (here we denote B as C_0 for simplicity of notation):

(1) "relationship vector" $I_R \in \mathbb{R}^N$: $I_R = \left(\dots R_{C_i}^{(n_0, n_1)} \dots \right), i = 1, 2, \dots, N$, from the committee.
(2) "affinity vector" $I_A \in \mathbb{R}^{N+1}$: $I_A = \left(\dots A_{C_i}^{(n_0, n_1)} \dots \right), i = 0, 1, 2, \dots, N$, from both the base model and the committee.
(3) "neighbors distribution vector" including "mean vector" $I_{D_{mean}} \in \mathbb{R}^{2(N+1)}$ and "variance vector" $I_{D_{var}} \in \mathbb{R}^{2(N+1)}$:

$$
\begin{aligned}
I_{D_{mean}} &= \left(\dots E\left(D_{C_i}^{n_0} \right) \dots , \ \dots E\left(D_{C_i}^{n_1} \right) \dots \right), i = 0, 1, 2, \dots, N, \\
I_{D_{var}} &= \left(\dots \sigma\left(D_{C_i}^{n_0} \right) \dots , \ \dots \sigma\left(D_{C_i}^{n_1} \right) \dots \right), i = 0, 1, 2, \dots, N,
\end{aligned}
\tag{4}
$$

from both the base model and the committee for each node.

Then it results in $6N + 5$ dimensions of the input vector. The mediator is trained on D_l, and the objective is to minimize the corresponding Cross-Entropy loss function. For testing, pairs from D_u are fed into the mediator and those with a high probability to be positive are collected. Since most of the positive pairs are redundant, we set a high threshold to select pairs, thus sacrificing recall to obtain positive pairs with high precision.

iv. Pseudo Label Propagation. The pairs selected by the mediator in the previous step compose a "Consensus-Driven Graph", whose edges are weighted by pairs' probability to be positive. Note that the graph does not need to be a connected graph. Unlike conventional label propagation algorithms, we do not assume labeled nodes on the graph. To prepare for subsequent model training, we propagate pseudo labels based on the connectivity of nodes. To propagate pseudo labels, we devise a simple yet effective algorithm to identify connected components. At first, we find connected components based on the current edges in the graph and add it to a queue. For each identified component, if its node number is larger than a pre-defined value, we eliminate low-score edges in the component, find connected components from it, and add the new disjoint components to the queue. If the node number of a component is below the pre-defined value, we annotate all nodes in the component with a new pseudo label. We iterate this process until the queue is empty when all the eligible components are labeled.

3.2 Joint Training Using Labeled and Unlabeled Data

Once the unlabeled data are assigned with pseudo labels, we can use them to augment the labeled data and update the base model. Since the identity intersection of two data sets is unknown, we formulate the learning in a multi-task training fashion, as shown in Fig. 3. The CNN architectures for the two tasks are exactly the same as the base model, and the weights are shared. Both CNNs are followed by a fully-connected layer to map deep features into the respective label space. The overall optimization objective is

$\mathcal{L} = \lambda \sum_{x_l, y_l} \ell\left(x_l, y_l\right) + (1 - \lambda) \sum_{x_u, y_a} \ell\left(x_u, y_a\right)$, where the loss, $\ell(\cdot)$, is the same as the one for training the base model and committee members. In the following experiments, we employ *softmax* as our loss function. But note that there is no restriction to which loss is equipped with CDP. In Sect. 4.3, we show that CDP still helps considerably despite with advanced loss functions. In this equation, $\{x_l, y_l\}$ denotes labeled data, while $\{x_u, y_a\}$ denotes unlabeled data and the assigned labels. $\lambda \in (0, 1)$ is the weight to balance the two components. Its value is fixed following the proportion of images in the labeled and unlabeled set. The model is trained from scratch.

4   Experiments

Training Set. MS-Celeb-1M [9] is a large-scale face recognition dataset containing $10M$ training examples with $100K$ identities. To address the original annotation noises, we clean up the official training set and crawl images of more identities, producing about $7M$ images with $385K$ identities. We split the cleaned dataset into 11 balanced parts randomly by identities, so as to ensures that there is no identity overlapping between different parts. Note that though our experiments adopt this harder setting, our approach can be readily applied to identity-overlapping settings since it makes no assumptions on the identities. Among the different parts, one part is regarded as labeled and the other ten parts are regarded as unlabeled. We also use one of the unlabeled parts as a validation set to adjust hyper-parameters and perform ablation study. The labeled part contains $634K$ images with $35,012$ identities. The model trained only on the labeled part is regarded as the lower bound performance. The fully-supervised version is trained with full labels from all the 11 parts. To investigate the utility of the unlabeled data, we compare different methods with 2, 4, 6, 8, and 10 parts of unlabeled data included, respectively.

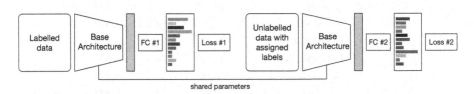

Fig. 3. Model updating in multi-task fashion. The weights of two CNNs are shared. "FC" denotes fully-connected classifier. In our experiments we use weighted Cross-Entropy loss as the objective.

Testing Sets. MegaFace [13] is currently the largest public benchmark for face identification. It includes a gallery set containing $1M$ images, and a probe set from FaceScrub [17] with 3,530 images. However, there are some noisy images from FaceScrub, hence we use the noises list proposed by InsightFace[2] to clean it. We adopt rank-1 identification rate in MegaFace benchmark, which is to select the top-1 image from the $1M$ gallery and average the top-1 hit rate. IJB-A [17] is a face verification benchmark contains 5,712 images from 500 identities. We report the *true positive rate* under the condition that the *false positive rate* is 0.001 for evaluation.

Committee Setup. To create a "committee" with high heterogeneity, we employ popular CNN architectures including *ResNet18* [10], *ResNet34*, *ResNet50*, *ResNet101*, *DenseNet121* [12], *VGG16* [23], *Inception V3* [28], *Inception-ResNet V2* [27] and a smaller variant of *NASNet-A* [37]. The number of committee members is eight in our experiments, but we also explore the choice of the number of committee member from 0 to 8. We trained all the architectures with the labeled part of data and the performance is listed in Table 1. The numbers of parameters are also listed. *Tiny NASNet-A* shows the best performance among all the architectures but uses the smallest number of parameters. Model ensemble results are also presented. Empirically, the best ensemble combination is to assemble the four top-performing models, i.e., *Tiny NASNet-A*, *Inception-Resnet V2*, *DenseNet121*, *ResNet101*, yielding 68.86% and 76.97% on two benchmarks. We select *Tiny NASNet-A* as our base architecture and the other 8 models as committee members. The following experiments demonstrate that the "committee" helps even though its members are weaker than the base architecture. In Sect. 4.3 we also show that our approach is widely applicable by switching the base architecture.

Table 1. Performance and the number of parameters of the base model and the committee members.

	Architecture	MegaFace	IJB-A	Parameters
Base	Tiny NASNet-A	**61.78**	**75.87**	20.1M
Committee	VGG16	50.22	70.75	75.6M
	ResNet18	51.48	69.23	23.5M
	ResNet34	52.44	72.52	33.6M
	Inception V3	52.82	75.53	33.0M
	ResNet50	56.16	73.21	36.3M
	ResNet101	57.87	74.52	55.3M
	Inception-ResNet V2	58.68	75.13	66.1M
	DesNet121	60.77	69.78	28.9M
Ensemble	(multiple)	69.86	76.97	-

Implementation Details. The "mediator" is an MLP classifier with 2 hidden layers, each of which containing 50 nodes. It uses ReLU as the activation

---

[2] InsightFace: https://github.com/deepinsight/insightface/tree/master/src/megaface.

function. At test time, we set the probability threshold as 0.96 to select high-confident pairs. More details can be found in the supplementary material.

4.1   Comparisons and Results

Competing Methods. (1) *Supervised deep feature extractor + Hierarchical Clustering*: We prepare a strong baseline by hierarchical clustering with supervised deep feature extractor. Hierarchical clustering is a practical way to deal with massive data comparing to other clustering methods. The clusters are assigned pseudo labels and augment the training set. For best performance, we carefully adjust the threshold of hierarchical clustering using the validation set and discard clusters with just a single image. (2) *Pair selection by naive committee voting*: A pair is selected if this pair is voted by all the committee members (best setting empirically). A vote is counted if there is an edge in the k-NN graph of a committee member.

Benchmarking. As shown in Fig. 4, the proposed CDP method achieves impressive results on both benchmarks. From the results, we observe that:

(1) Comparing to the lower bound (ratio of unlabeled:labeled is 0:1) with no unlabeled data, CDP obtains significant and steady improvements given different quantities of unlabeled data.
(2) CDP surpasses the baseline "Hierarchical Clustering" by a large margin, obtaining competitive or even better results over the fully-supervised counterpart. In the MegaFace benchmark, with 10 fold unlabeled data added, CDP yields 78.18% of identification rate. Comparing to the lower bound without unlabeled data that yields 61.78%, CDP obtains 16.4% of improvement. Notably, there are only 0.34% gap between CDP and the fully-supervised setting that reaches 78.52%. The results suggest that CDP is capable of maximizing the utility of the unlabeled data.
(3) CDP by the "mediator" performs better than by naive voting, indicating that the "mediator" is more capable in aggregating committee opinions.
(4) In the IJB-A face verification task, both settings of CDP surpass the fully-supervised counterpart. The poorer results observed on the fully-supervised baseline suggest the vulnerability of this task against noisy annotations in the training set, as discussed in Sect. 1. By contrast, our method is more resilient to noise. We will discuss this next based on Fig. 6.

Visual Results. We visualize the results of CDP in Fig. 6. It can be observed that CDP is highly precise in identity label assignment, regardless the diverse backgrounds, expressions, poses and illuminations. It is also observed that CDP behaves to be selective in choosing samples for pair candidates, as it automatically discards (1) wrongly-annotated faces not belonging to any identity; (2) samples with extremely low quality, including heavily blurred and cartoon images. This explains why CDP outperforms the fully-supervised baseline in the IJB-A face verification task (Fig. 4).

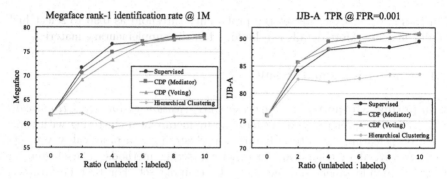

Fig. 4. Performance comparison on MegaFace identification task and IJB-A verification task with different ratios of unlabeled data added to one portion of labeled data. CDP is proven to (1) obtain large improvements over the lower bound (ratio of unlabeled:labeled is 0:1); (2) surpass the clustering method by a large margin; (3) obtain competitive or even higher results over the fully-supervised counterpart.

4.2   Ablation Study

We perform ablation study on the validation set to show the gain of each component, as shown in Table 2. Several indicators are included for comparison. Higher recall and precision of selected pairs will result in better consensus-driven graph, hence improves the quality of assigned labels. For assigned labels, pairwise recall and precision reflect the quality of the labels, and directly correlate the final performance on two benchmarks. Higher pairwise recall indicates more true examples in a category, which is important for the subsequent training. Higher pairwise precision indicates less noises in a category.

The Effectiveness of "Committee". When we vary the number of committee members, we adjust pair similarity threshold to obtain fixed recall for convenience. With increasing committee number, an interesting observation is that, the peak of precision occurs where the number is 4. However, it does not bring the best quality of assigned labels, which occurs where the number is 6–8. This shows that more committee members will bring more meaningful pairs rather than just correct pairs. This conclusion is consistent with our assumption that the committee is able to select more hard positive pairs relative to the base model.

The Effectiveness of "Mediator". For the "mediator", we study the influence of different input settings. With only the "relationship vector" I_R as input, the values of those indicators are close to that of direct voting. Then the "affinity vector" I_A remarkably improves recall and precision of selected pairs, and also improves both pairwise recall and precision of assigned labels. The "neighbors distribution vector" $I_{D_{mean}}$ and $I_{D_{var}}$ further boost the quality of the assigned labels. The improvements originate in the effect brought by these aspects of information, and hence the "mediator" performs better than naive voting.

Table 2. Ablation study on validation set. I_R: "relationship vector", I_A: "affinity vector", I_D: "neighbors distribution vector". Among the indicators pairwise recall and precision for assigned labels directly correlate the benchmarking results. It is concluded that more committee members bring more meaningful pairs rather than just correct pairs, and the "mediator" is capable in aggregating multiple aspects of consensus information.

Methods	Committee number	Mediator inputs	Pair selection			Assigned labels	
			Pair number	Recall	Precision	Pairwise recall	Pairwise precision
Clustering	-	-	-	-	-	0.558	0.950
Voting	0	-	1.4M	0.313	0.966	0.680	0.829
	2	-	1.4M	0.313	0.986	0.783	0.849
	4	-	1.4M	0.313	**0.987**	0.791	0.862
	6	-	1.4M	0.313	0.984	0.801	**0.877**
	8	-	1.4M	0.313	0.979	**0.807**	0.876
Mediator	8	I_R	1.4M	0.318	0.975	0.825	0.822
		I_R+I_A	2.5M	**0.561**	0.982	**0.832**	0.888
		$I_R+I_A+I_D$	2.4M	0.527	**0.983**	0.825	**0.912**

4.3 Further Analysis

Different Base Architectures. In previous experiments we have chosen *Tiny NASNet-A* as the base model and other architecture as committee members. To investigate the influence of the base model, here we switch the base model to *ResNet18, ResNet50, Inception-ResNet V2* respectively and list their performance in Table 3. We observe consistent and large improvements from the lower bound on all the base architectures. Specifically, with high-capacity *Inception-ResNet V2*, our CDP achieves 81.88% and 92.07% on MegaFace and IJB-A benchmarks, with 23.20% and 16.94% improvements. It is significant considering that CDP uses the same amount of labeled data as the lower bound (9% of all the labels). Our performance is also much higher than the ensemble of base model and committee, indicating that CDP actually exploits the intrinsic structure of the unlabeled data to learn effective representations.

Table 3. The comparison of different base architectures. Lower bound: the models trained on 1-fold labeled data only; CDP: our semi-supervised models with 1-fold labeled data and 10-fold unlabeled data; Supervised: the models trained on all the 11-fold data with labels. With higher-capacity architectures, CDP achieves even larger improvements.

Base	ResNet18		ResNet50		Tiny NASNet-A		Inception-ResNet V2	
	MegaFace	IJB-A	MegaFace	IJB-A	MegaFace	IJB-A	MegaFace	IJB-A
Lower bound	51.48	69.23	56.16	73.12	61.78	75.87	58.68	75.13
CDP	72.75	86.23	75.66	88.34	78.18	90.64	81.88	92.07
Supervised	73.88	85.08	77.13	87.92	78.52	89.40	84.74	91.90

Different k in k-NN. Here we inspect the effect of k in k-NN. In this comparable study, the probability threshold of a pair to be positive is fixed to 0.96. As shown in Table 4, higher k results in more selected pairs and thus a denser consensus-driven graph, but the precision is almost unchanged. Note that the recall drops because the cardinal true pair number increases faster than the that of selected pairs. Actually, it is unnecessary to pursue high recall rate if the selected pairs are enough. For assigned labels, denser graph brings higher pairwise recall and lower precision. Hence it is a trade-off between pairwise recall and precision of the assigned labels via varying k.

Table 4. The influence of k in k-NN. Varying k provides a trade-off between pairwise recall and precision of the assined labels.

k	Pair selection			Assigned labels	
	Pair number	Recall	Precision	Pairwise recall	Pairwise precision
10	1.61M	**0.601**	**0.985**	0.810	**0.940**
20	2.54M	0.527	0.983	0.825	0.912
30	2.96M	0.507	0.982	0.834	0.886
40	**3.17M**	0.464	0.982	**0.837**	0.874

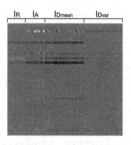

Fig. 5. Mediator weights.

Committee Heterogeneity. To study the influence of committee heterogeneity, we conduct experiments with homogeneous committee architectures. The homogeneous committee consists of eight *ResNet50* models that are trained with different data feeding orders, and the base model is the identical one as the heterogeneous setting. The model capacity of *ResNet50* is at the median of the heterogeneous committee, for a fair comparison. As shown in Table 5, heterogeneous committee performs better than the homogeneous one via either voting or the "mediator". The study verifies that committee heterogeneity is helpful.

Table 5. The influence of committee heterogeneity. As a comparison, the heterogeneous committee performs better than the homogeneous committee.

Committee	Methods	Pair selection			Assigned labels	
		Pair number	Recall	Precision	Pairwise recall	Pairwise precision
Homogeneous	Voting	1.93M	0.368	0.648	0.746	0.681
	Mediator	2.46M	0.508	0.853	0.798	0.831
Heterogeneous	Voting	1.41M	0.313	0.979	0.807	0.876
	Mediator	2.54M	**0.527**	**0.983**	**0.825**	**0.912**

Inside Mediator. To evaluate the participation of each input, we visualize the first layer's weights in the "mediator", as shown in Fig. 5. It is the 50×53

Table 6. Comparisons of the gain brought by CDP with 2-folds unlabeled data between the previous baseline (Softmax) and the new baseline (ArcFace [7] with a cleaner training set). The performances are reported on MegaFace test set.

	Softmax	ArcFace [7]
Baseline	61.78%	76.93%
CDP (Ratio=2)	70.51%	83.68%

Fig. 6. This figure shows two groups of faces in the unlabeled data. All faces in a group has the same identity according to the original annotations. The number on the top-left conner of each face is the label assigned by our proposed method, and the faces in red boxes are discarded by our method. The results suggest the high precision of our method in identifying persons of the same identity. Interestingly, our method is robust in pinpointing wrongly annotated faces (group 1), extremely low-quality faces (e.g., heavily blurred face, cartoon in group 2), which do not help training. See supplementary materials for more visual results. (Color figure online)

weights of the first layer in the "mediator", where the number of input and output channels is 53 and 50. Hence each column represents the weights of each input. The values in green is close to 0, and blue less than 0, yellow greater than 0. Both values in yellow and blue indicate high response to the corresponding inputs. We conclude that the committee's "affinity vector" (I_A) and the mean vector of "neighbors distribution" ($I_{D_{mean}}$) contribute higher to the response, than "relationship vector" (I_R) and the variance vector of "neighbors distribution" ($I_{D_{var}}$). The result is reasonable since similarities contain more information than voting results, and the mean of neighbors' distribution directly reflects the local density.

Incorporating Advanced Loss Functions. Our CDP framework is compatible with various forms of loss functions. Apart from *softmax*, we also equip CDP with an advanced loss function, ArcFace [7], the current top entry on MegaFace benchmark. For parameters related to ArcFace, we set the margin $m = 0.5$ and adopt the output setting "E", that is "BN-Dropout-FC-BN". We also use a cleaner training set aiming to obtain a higher baseline. As shown in Table 6, we observe that CDP still brings large improvements over this much higher baseline.

Efficiency and Scalability. The step-by-step runtime of CDP is listed as follows: for million-level data, graph construction (k-NN search) takes 4 min to perform on a CPU with 48 processors, the "committee"+"mediator" network inference takes 2 min to perform on eight GPUs, and the propagation takes another 2 min on a single CPU. Since our approach constructs graphs in a bottom-up manner and the "committee"+"mediator" only operate on local structures, the runtime of CDP grows linearly with the number of unlabeled data. Therefore, CDP is both efficient and scalable.

5 Conclusion

We have proposed a novel approach, Consensus-Driven Propagation (CDP), to exploit massive unlabeled data for improving large-scale recognition. We achieve highly competitive results against fully-supervised counterpart by using only 9% of the labels. Extensive analysis on different aspects of CDP is conducted, including influences of the number of committee members, inputs to the mediator, base architecture, and committee heterogeneity. The problem is well-solved for the first time in the literature, considering the practical and non-trivial challenges it brings.

Acknowledgement. This work is partially supported by the Big Data Collaboration Research grant from SenseTime Group (CUHK Agreement No. TS1610626), the General Research Fund (GRF) of Hong Kong (No. 14236516, 14241716).

References

1. Argamon-Engelson, S., Dagan, I.: Committee-based sample selection for probabilistic classifiers. J. Artif. Intell. Res. **11**, 335–360 (1999)
2. Blum, A., Mitchell, T.: Combining labeled and unlabeled data with co-training. In: Proceedings of the Eleventh Annual Conference on Computational Learning Theory (1998)
3. Cao, K., Rong, Y., Li, C., Tang, X., Loy, C.C.: Pose-robust face recognition via deep residual equivariant mapping. In: CVPR (2018)
4. Chapelle, O., Scholkopf, B., Zien, A.: Semi-supervised learning. IEEE Trans. Neural Netw. **20**(3), 542 (2009). Chapelle, o. et al. (eds.) (2006) [book reviews]
5. Chen, L., et al.: The devil of face recognition is in the noise. In: ECCV (2018)
6. Dempster, A.P., Laird, N.M., Rubin, D.B.: Maximum likelihood from incomplete data via the EM algorithm. J. Roy. Stat. Soc. Ser. B (methodol.) **39**, 1–38 (1977)

7. Deng, J., Guo, J., Zafeiriou, S.: Arcface: additive angular margin loss for deep face recognition. arXiv preprint arXiv:1801.07698 (2018)
8. Gao, Y., Ma, J., Yuille, A.L.: Semi-supervised sparse representation based classification for face recognition with insufficient labeled samples. TIP **26**(5), 2545–2560 (2017)
9. Guo, Y., Zhang, L., Hu, Y., He, X., Gao, J.: MS-Celeb-1M: a dataset and benchmark for large-scale face recognition. In: Leibe, B., Matas, J., Sebe, N., Welling, M. (eds.) ECCV 2016. LNCS, vol. 9907, pp. 87–102. Springer, Cham (2016). https://doi.org/10.1007/978-3-319-46487-9_6
10. He, K., Zhang, X., Ren, S., Sun, J.: Deep residual learning for image recognition. In: CVPR (2016)
11. Huang, C., Li, Y., Loy, C.C., Tang, X.: Deep imbalanced learning for face recognition and attribute prediction. arXiv preprint arXiv:1806.00194 (2018)
12. Iandola, F., Moskewicz, M., Karayev, S., Girshick, R., Darrell, T., Keutzer, K.: DenseNet: implementing efficient convnet descriptor pyramids. arXiv preprint arXiv:1404.1869 (2014)
13. Kemelmacher-Shlizerman, I., Seitz, S.M., Miller, D., Brossard, E.: The MegaFace benchmark: 1 million faces for recognition at scale. In: CVPR (2016)
14. Liu, Z., Luo, P., Wang, X., Tang, X.: Deep learning face attributes in the wild. In: ICCV (2015)
15. Loy, C.C., Hospedales, T.M., Xiang, T., Gong, S.: Stream-based joint exploration-exploitation active learning. In: CVPR (2012)
16. Mitchell, T.M.: The role of unlabeled data in supervised learning. In: Larrazabal, J.M., Miranda, L.A.P. (eds.) Language, Knowledge, and Representation. PSSP, vol. 99, pp. 103–111. Springer, Dordrecht (2004). https://doi.org/10.1007/978-1-4020-2783-3_7
17. Ng, H.W., Winkler, S.: A data-driven approach to cleaning large face datasets. In: ICIP (2014)
18. Roli, F., Marcialis, G.L.: Semi-supervised PCA-based face recognition using self-training. In: Yeung, D.-Y., Kwok, J.T., Fred, A., Roli, F., de Ridder, D. (eds.) SSPR /SPR 2006. LNCS, vol. 4109, pp. 560–568. Springer, Heidelberg (2006). https://doi.org/10.1007/11815921_61
19. Rosenberg, C., Hebert, M., Schneiderman, H.: Semi-supervised self-training of object detection models (2005)
20. de Sa, V.R.: Learning classification with unlabeled data. In: NIPS (1994)
21. Schroff, F., Kalenichenko, D., Philbin, J.: FaceNet: a unified embedding for face recognition and clustering. In: CVPR (2015)
22. Seung, H.S., Opper, M., Sompolinsky, H.: Query by committee. In: Proceedings of the Fifth Annual Workshop on Computational Learning Theory (1992)
23. Simonyan, K., Zisserman, A.: Very deep convolutional networks for large-scale image recognition. arXiv preprint arXiv:1409.1556 (2014)
24. Sohn, K., Liu, S., Zhong, G., Yu, X., Yang, M.H., Chandraker, M.: Unsupervised domain adaptation for face recognition in unlabeled videos. In: Proceedings of the IEEE Conference on Computer Vision and Pattern Recognition, pp. 3210–3218 (2017)
25. Sun, Y., Chen, Y., Wang, X., Tang, X.: Deep learning face representation by joint identification-verification. In: NIPS (2014)
26. Sun, Y., Wang, X., Tang, X.: Deep learning face representation from predicting 10,000 classes. In: CVPR (2014)
27. Szegedy, C., Ioffe, S., Vanhoucke, V., Alemi, A.A.: Inception-v4, inception-ResNet and the impact of residual connections on learning. In: AAAI, vol. 4 (2017)

28. Szegedy, C., Vanhoucke, V., Ioffe, S., Shlens, J., Wojna, Z.: Rethinking the inception architecture for computer vision. In: CVPR (2016)
29. Wen, Y., Zhang, K., Li, Z., Qiao, Y.: A discriminative feature learning approach for deep face recognition. In: Leibe, B., Matas, J., Sebe, N., Welling, M. (eds.) ECCV 2016. LNCS, vol. 9911, pp. 499–515. Springer, Cham (2016). https://doi.org/10.1007/978-3-319-46478-7_31
30. Yarowsky, D.: Unsupervised word sense disambiguation rivaling supervised methods. In: ACL (1995)
31. Zhan, X., Liu, Z., Luo, P., Tang, X., Loy, C.C.: Mix-and-match tuning for self-supervised semantic segmentation. In: AAAI (2018)
32. Zhang, X., Yang, L., Yan, J., Lin, D.: Accelerated training for massive classification via dynamic class selection. In: AAAI (2018)
33. Zhao, X., Evans, N., Dugelay, J.L.: Semi-supervised face recognition with LDA self-training. In: ICIP (2011)
34. Zhu, X.: Semi-supervised learning literature survey. Comput. Sci. Univ. Wisconsin-Madison 2(3), 4 (2006)
35. Zhu, X., Ghahramani, Z.: Learning from labeled and unlabeled data with label propagation (2002)
36. Zhu, X., Lafferty, J., Rosenfeld, R.: Semi-supervised learning with graphs. Ph.D. thesis, Carnegie Mellon University, Language Technologies Institute, School Of Computer Science (2005)
37. Zoph, B., Vasudevan, V., Shlens, J., Le, Q.V.: Learning transferable architectures for scalable image recognition. arXiv preprint arXiv:1707.07012 (2017)

Predicting Future Instance Segmentation by Forecasting Convolutional Features

Pauline Luc[1,2]([✉]), Camille Couprie[1], Yann LeCun[3,4], and Jakob Verbeek[2]

[1] Facebook AI Research, Paris, France
{paulineluc,coupriec}@fb.com
[2] Univ. Grenoble Alpes, Inria, CNRS, Grenoble INP (Institute of Engineering
Univ. Grenoble Alpes), LJK, 38000 Grenoble, France
jakob.verbeek@inria.fr
[3] New York University, New York, USA
[4] Facebook AI Research, New York, USA
yann@fb.com

Abstract. Anticipating future events is an important prerequisite towards intelligent behavior. Video forecasting has been studied as a proxy task towards this goal. Recent work has shown that to predict semantic segmentation of future frames, forecasting at the semantic level is more effective than forecasting RGB frames and then segmenting these. In this paper we consider the more challenging problem of future instance segmentation, which additionally segments out individual objects. To deal with a varying number of output labels per image, we develop a predictive model in the space of fixed-sized convolutional features of the Mask R-CNN instance segmentation model. We apply the "detection head" of Mask R-CNN on the predicted features to produce the instance segmentation of future frames. Experiments show that this approach significantly improves over strong baselines based on optical flow and repurposed instance segmentation architectures.

Keywords: Video prediction · Instance segmentation
Deep learning · Convolutional neural networks

1 Introduction

The ability to anticipate future events is a key factor towards developing intelligent behavior [2]. Video prediction has been studied as a proxy task towards pursuing this ability, which can capitalize on the huge amount of available unlabeled video to learn visual representations that account for object interactions and interactions between objects and the environment [3]. Most work in video prediction has focused on predicting the RGB values of future video frames [3–6].

Electronic supplementary material The online version of this chapter (https://doi.org/10.1007/978-3-030-01240-3_36) contains supplementary material, which is available to authorized users.

ⓒ Springer Nature Switzerland AG 2018
V. Ferrari et al. (Eds.): ECCV 2018, LNCS 11213, pp. 593–608, 2018.
https://doi.org/10.1007/978-3-030-01240-3_36

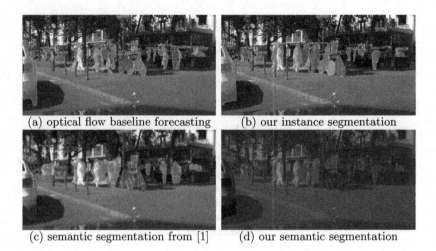

(a) optical flow baseline forecasting   (b) our instance segmentation

(c) semantic segmentation from [1]   (d) our semantic segmentation

Fig. 1. Predicting 0.5 s. into the future. Instance modeling significantly improves the segmentation accuracy of the individual pedestrians.

Predictive models have important applications in decision-making contexts, such as autonomous driving, where rapid control decisions can be of vital importance [7,8]. In such contexts, however, the goal is not to predict the raw RGB values of future video frames, but to make predictions about future video frames at a semantically meaningful level, *e.g.* in terms of presence and location of object categories in a scene. Luc *et al.* [1] recently showed that for prediction of future semantic segmentation, modeling at the semantic level is much more effective than predicting raw RGB values of future frames, and then feeding these to a semantic segmentation model.

Although spatially detailed, semantic segmentation does not account for individual objects, but rather lumps them together by assigning them to the same category label, *e.g.* the pedestrians in Fig. 1(c). Instance segmentation overcomes this shortcoming by additionally associating with each pixel an instance label, as show in Fig. 1(b). This additional level of detail is crucial for down-stream tasks that rely on instance-level trajectories, such as encountered in control for autonomous driving. Moreover, ignoring the notion of object instances prohibits by construction any reasoning about object motion, deformation, *etc.* Including it in the model can therefore greatly improve its predictive performance, by keeping track of individual object properties, *c.f.* Fig. 1(c) and (d).

Since the instance labels vary in number across frames, and do not have a consistent interpretation across videos, the approach of Luc *et al.* [1] does not apply to this task. Instead, we build upon Mask R-CNN [9], a recent state-of-the-art instance segmentation model that extends an object detection system by predicting with each object bounding box a binary segmentation mask of the object. In order to forecast the instance-level labels in a coherent manner, we predict the fixed-sized high level convolutional features used by Mask R-CNN.

We obtain the future object instance segmentation by applying the Mask R-CNN "detection head" to the predicted features.

Our approach offers several advantages: (i) we handle cases in which the model output has a variable size, as in object detection and instance segmentation, (ii) we do not require labeled video sequences for training, as the intermediate CNN feature maps can be computed directly from unlabeled data, and (iii) we support models that are able to produce multiple scene interpretations, such as surface normals, object bounding boxes, and human part labels [10], without having to design appropriate encoders and loss functions for all these tasks to drive the future prediction. Our contributions are the following:

- the introduction of the new task of future instance segmentation, which is semantically richer than previously studied anticipated recognition tasks,
- a self-supervised approach based on predicting high dimensional CNN features of future frames, which can support many anticipated recognition tasks,
- experimental results that show that our feature learning approach improves over strong baselines, relying on optical flow and repurposed instance segmentation architectures.

2   Related Work

Future Video Prediction. Predictive modeling of future RGB video frames has recently been studied using a variety of techniques, including autoregressive models [6], adversarial training [3], and recurrent networks [4,5,11]. Villegas *et al.* [12] predict future human poses as a proxy to guide the prediction of future RGB video frames. Instead of predicting RGB values, Walker *et al.* [13] predict future pixel trajectories from static images.

Future prediction of more abstract representations has been considered in a variety of contexts in the past. Lan *et al.* [14] predict future human actions from automatically detected atomic actions. Kitani *et al.* [15] predict future trajectories of people from semantic segmentation of an observed video frame, modeling potential destinations and transitory areas that are preferred or avoided. Lee *et al.* predict future object trajectories from past object tracks and object interactions [16]. Dosovitskiy and Koltun [17] learn control models by predicting future high-level measurements in which the goal of an agent can be expressed from past video frames and measurements.

Vondrick *et al.* [18] were the first to predict high level CNN features of future video frames to anticipate actions and object appearances in video. Their work is similar in spirit to ours, but while they only predict image-level labels, we consider the more complex task of predicting future instance segmentation, requiring fine spatial detail. To this end, we forecast spatially dense convolutional features, where Vondrick *et al.* were predicting the activations of much more compact fully connected CNN layers. Our work demonstrates the scalability of CNN feature prediction, from 4K-dimensional to 32M-dimensional features, and yields results with a surprising level of accuracy and spatial detail.

Luc *et al.* [1] predicted future semantic segmentation in video by taking the softmax pre-activations of past frames as input, and predicting the softmax pre-activations of future frames. While their approach is relevant for future semantic segmentation, where the softmax pre-activations provide a natural fixed-sized representation, it does not extend to instance segmentation since the instance-level labels vary in number between frames and are not consistent across video sequences. To overcome this limitation, we develop predictive models for fixed-sized convolutional features, instead of making predictions directly in the label space. Our feature-based approach has many advantages over [1]: segmenting individual instances, working at a higher resolution and providing a framework that generalizes to other dense prediction tasks. In a direction orthogonal to our work, Jin *et al.* [19] jointly predict semantic segmentation and optical flow of future frames, leveraging the complementarity between the two tasks.

Instance Segmentation Approaches. Our approach can be used in conjunction with any deep network to perform instance segmentation. A variety of approaches for instance segmentation has been explored in the past, including iterative object segmentation using recurrent networks [20], watershed transformation [21], and object proposals [22]. In our work we build upon Mask R-CNN [9], which recently established a new state-of-the-art for instance segmentation. This method extends the Faster R-CNN object detector [23] by adding a network branch to predict segmentation masks and extracting features for prediction in a way that allows precise alignment of the masks when they are stitched together to form the final output.

3   Predicting Features for Future Instance Segmentation

In this section we briefly review the Mask R-CNN instance segmentation framework, and then present how we can use it for anticipated recognition by predicting internal CNN features of future frames.

3.1   Instance Segmentation with Mask R-CNN

The Mask R-CNN model [9] consists of three main stages. First, a convolutional neural network (CNN) "backbone" architecture is used to extract high level feature maps. Second, a region proposal network (RPN) takes these features to produce regions of interest (ROIs), in the form of coordinates of bounding boxes susceptible of containing instances. The bounding box proposals are used as input to a *RoIAlign* layer, which interpolates the high level features in each bounding box to extract a fixed-sized representation for each box. Third, the features of each RoI are input to the detection branches, which produce refined bounding box coordinates, a class prediction, and a fixed-sized binary mask for the predicted class. Finally, the mask is interpolated back to full image resolution within the predicted bounding box and reported as an instance segmentation for the predicted class. We refer to the combination of the second and third stages as the "detection head".

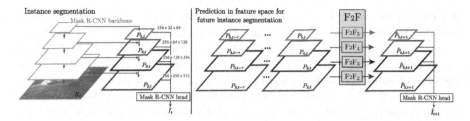

Fig. 2. Left: Features in the FPN backbone are obtained by upsampling features in the top-down path, and combining them with features from the bottom-up path at the same resolution. Right: For future instance segmentation, we extract FPN features from frames $t - \tau$ to t, and predict the FPN features for frame $t + 1$. We learn separate feature-to-feature prediction models for each FPN level: F2F$_l$ denotes the model for level l.

He *et al.* [9] use a Feature Pyramid Network (FPN) [24] as backbone architecture, which extracts a set of features at several spatial resolutions from an input image. The feature pyramid is then used in the instance segmentation pipeline to detect objects at multiple scales, by running the detection head on each level of the pyramid. Following [24], we denote the feature pyramid levels extracted from an RGB image X by P_2 through P_5, which are of decreasing resolution $(H/2^l \times W/2^l)$ for P_l, where H and W are respectively the height and width of X. The features in P_l are computed in a top-down stream by up-sampling those in P_{l+1} and adding the result of a 1×1 convolution of features in a layer with matching resolution in a bottom-up ResNet stream. We refer the reader to the left panel of Fig. 2 for a schematic illustration, and to [9,24] for more details.

3.2   Forecasting Convolutional Features

Given a video sequence, our goal is to predict instance-level object segmentations for one or more future frames, *i.e.* for frames where we cannot access the RGB pixel values. Similar to previous work that predicts future RGB frames [3–6] and future semantic segmentations [1], we are interested in models where the input and output of the predictive model live in the same space, so that the model can be applied recursively to produce predictions for more than one frame ahead. The instance segmentations themselves, however, do not provide a suitable representation for prediction, since the instance-level labels vary in number between frames, and are not consistent across video sequences. To overcome this issue, we instead resort to predicting the highest level features in the Mask R-CNN architecture that are of fixed size. In particular, using the FPN backbone in Mask R-CNN, we want to learn a model that given the feature pyramids extracted from frames $X_{t-\tau}$ to X_t, predicts the feature pyramid for the unobserved RGB frame X_{t+1}.

Architecture. The features at the different FPN levels are trained to be input to a shared detection head, and are thus of similar nature. However, since the resolution changes across levels, the spatio-temporal dynamics are distinct from one level to another. Therefore, we propose a multi-scale approach, employing a separate network to predict the features at each level, of which we demonstrate the benefits in Sect. 4.1. The per-level networks are trained and function completely independently from each other. This allows us to parallelize the training across multiple GPUs. Alternative architectures in which prediction across different resolutions is tied are interesting, but beyond the scope of this paper. For each level, we concatenate the features of the input sequence along the feature dimension. We refer to the "feature to feature" predictive model for level l as $F2F_l$. The overall architecture is summarized in the right panel of Fig. 2.

Each of the $F2F_l$ networks is implemented by a resolution-preserving CNN. Each network is itself multi-scale as in [1,3], to efficiently enlarge the field of view while preserving high-resolution details. More precisely, for a given level l, $F2F_l$ consists of s_l subnetworks $F2F_l^s$, where $s \in \{1, ..., s_l\}$. The network $F2F_l^{s_l}$ first processes the input downsampled by a factor of 2^{s_l-1}. Its output is upsampled by a factor of 2, and concatenated to the input downsampled by a factor of 2^{s_l-2}. This concatenation constitutes the input of $F2F_l^{s_l-1}$ which predicts a refinement of the initial coarse prediction. The same procedure is repeated until the final scale subnetwork $F2F_l^1$. The design of subnetworks $F2F_l^s$ is inspired by [1], leveraging dilated convolutions to further enlarge the field of view. Our architecture differs in the number of feature maps per layer, the convolution kernel sizes and dilation parameters, to make it more suited for the larger input dimension. We detail these design choices in the supplementary material.

Training. We first train the $F2F_5$ model to predict the coarsest features P_5, precomputed offline. Since the features of the different FPN levels are fed to the same recognition head network, the next levels are similar to the P_5 features. Hence, we initialize the weights of $F2F_4$, $F2F_3$, and $F2F_2$ with the ones learned by $F2F_5$, before fine-tuning them. For this, we compute features on the fly, due to memory constraints. Each of the $F2F_l$ networks is trained using an ℓ_2 loss.

For multiple time step prediction, we can fine-tune each subnetwork $F2F_l$ autoregressively using backpropagation through time, similar to [1] to take into account error accumulation over time. In this case, given a single sequence of input feature maps, we train with a separate ℓ_2 loss on each predicted future frame. In our experiments, all models are trained in this autoregressive manner, unless specified otherwise.

4   Experimental Evaluation

In this section we first present our experimental setup and baseline models, and then proceed with quantitative and qualitative results, that demonstrate the strengths of our F2F approach.

4.1   Experimental Setup: Dataset and Evaluation Metrics

Dataset. In our experiments, we use the Cityscapes dataset [25] which contains 2,975 train, 500 validation and 1,525 test video sequences of 1.8 s each, recorded from a car driving in urban environments. Each sequence consists of 30 frames of resolution 1024×2048. Ground truth semantic and instance segmentation annotations are available for the 20-th frame of each sequence.

We employ a Mask R-CNN model pre-trained on the MS-COCO dataset [26] and fine-tune it in an end-to-end fashion on the Cityscapes dataset, using a ResNet-50-FPN backbone. The coarsest FPN level P5 has resolution 32×64, and the finest level P2 has resolution 256×512.

Following [1], we temporally subsample the videos by a factor three, and take four frames as input. That is, the input sequence consists of feature pyramids for frames $\{X_{t-9}, X_{t-6}, X_{t-3}, X_t\}$. We denote by *short-term* and *mid-term* prediction respectively predicting X_{t+3} only (0.17 s) and through X_{t+9} (0.5 s). We additionally evaluate *long-term* predictions, corresponding to X_{t+27} and 1.6 s ahead on the two long Frankfurt sequences of the Cityscapes validation set.

Conversion to Semantic Segmentation. For direct comparison to previous work, we also convert our instance segmentation predictions to semantic segmentation. To this end, we first assign to all pixels the *background* label. Then, we iterate over the detected object instances in order of ascending confidence score. For each instance, consisting of a confidence score c, a class k, and a binary mask m, we either reject it if it is lower than a threshold θ and accept it otherwise, where in our experiments we set $\theta = 0.5$. For accepted instances, we update the spatial positions corresponding to mask m with label k. This step potentially replaces labels set by instances with lower confidence, and resolves competing class predictions.

Evaluation Metrics. To measure the instance segmentation performance, we use the standard Cityscapes metrics. The average precision metric AP50 counts an instance as correct if it has at least 50% of intersection-over-union (IoU) with the ground truth instance it has been matched with. The summary AP metric is given by average AP obtained with ten equally spaced IoU thresholds from 50% to 95%. Performance is measured across the eight classes with available instance-level ground truth: *person, rider, car, truck, bus, train, motorcycle,* and *bicycle.*

We measure semantic segmentation performance across the same eight classes. In addition to the IoU metric, computed w.r.t. the ground truth segmentation of the 20-th frame in each sequence, we also quantify the segmentation accuracy using three standard segmentation measures used in [27], namely the Probabilistic Rand Index (RI) [28], Global Consistency Error (GCE) [29], and Variation of Information (VoI) [30]. Good segmentation results are associated with high RI, low GCE and low VoI.

Implementation Details and Ablation Study. We cross-validate the number of scales, the optimization algorithm and hyperparameters per level of the pyramid. For each level of the pyramid a single scale network was selected, except for $F2F_2$, where we employ 3 scales. The $F2F_5$ network is trained for 60 K iterations of SGD with Nesterov Momentum of 0.9, learning rate 0.01, and batch size of 4 images. It is used to initialize the other networks, which are trained for 80 K iterations of SGD with Nesterov Momentum of 0.9, batch size of 1 image

Table 1. Ablation study: short-term prediction on the Cityscapes val. set.

Levels	P_5	P_4–P_5	P_3–P_5	P_2–P_5	P_5 //
IoU	15.5	38.5	54.7	**60.7**	38.7
AP50	2.2	10.2	24.8	**40.2**	16.7

and learning rates of 5×10^{-3} for F2F$_4$ and 0.01 for F2F$_3$. For F2F$_2$, which is much deeper, we used Adam with learning rate 5×10^{-5} and default parameters. Table 1 shows the positive impact of using each additional feature level, denoted by $P_i - P_5$ for $i = 2, 3, 4$. We also report performance when using all features levels, predicted by a model trained on the coarsest P_5 features, shared across levels, denoted by P_5 //. The drop in performance w.r.t. the column P_2–P_5 underlines the importance of training specific networks for each feature level.

4.2   Baseline Models

As a performance upper bound, we report the accuracy of a Mask R-CNN oracle that has access to the future RGB frame. As a lower bound, we also use a trivial copy baseline that returns the segmentation of the last input RGB frame. Besides the following baselines, we also experiment with two weaker baselines, based on nearest neighbor search and on predicting the future RGB frames, and then segmenting them. We detail both baselines in the supplementary material.

Optical Flow Baselines. We designed two baselines using the optical flow field computed from the last input RGB frame to the second last, as well as the instance segmentation predicted at the last input frame. The *Warp* approach consists in warping each instance mask independently using the flow field inside this mask. We initialize a separate flow field for each instance, equal to the flow field inside the instance mask and zero elsewhere. For a given instance, the corresponding flow field is used to project the values of the instance mask in the opposite direction of the flow vectors, yielding a new binary mask. To this predicted mask, we associate the class and confidence score of the input instance it was obtained from. To predict more than one time-step ahead, we also update the instance's flow field in the same fashion, to take into account the previously predicted displacement of physical points composing the instance. The predicted mask and flow field are used to make the next prediction, and so on. Maintaining separate flow fields allows competing flow values to coexist for the same spatial position, when they belong to different instances whose predicted trajectories lead them to overlap. To smoothen the results of this baseline, we perform post-processing operations at each time step, which significantly improve the results and which we detail in the supplementary material.

Warping the flow field when predicting multiple steps ahead suffers from error accumulation. To avoid this, we test another baseline, *Shift*, which shifts each mask with the average flow vector computed across the mask. To predict T time steps ahead, we simply shift the instance T times. This approach, however, is

Table 2. Instance segmentation accuracy on the Cityscapes validation set.

	Short-term		Mid-term	
	AP50	AP	AP50	AP
Mask R-CNN oracle	65.8	37.3	65.8	37.3
Copy last segmentation	24.1	10.1	6.6	1.8
Optical flow – *Shift*	37.0	16.0	9.7	2.9
Optical flow – *Warp*	36.8	16.5	11.1	4.1
Mask H2F*	25.5	11.8	14.2	5.1
F2F w/o ar. fine tuning	**40.2**	19.0	17.5	6.2
F2F	39.9	**19.4**	**19.4**	**7.7**

* Separate models were trained for short-term and mid-term predictions.

unable to scale the objects, and is therefore unsuitable for long-term prediction when objects significantly change in scale as their distance to the camera changes.

Future Semantic Segmentation Using Discrete Label Maps. For comparison with the future semantic segmentation approach of [1], which ignores instance-level labels, we train their S2S model on the label maps produced by Mask R-CNN. Following their approach, we down-sample the Mask R-CNN label maps to 128 × 256. Unlike the soft label maps from the Dilated-10 network [31] used in [1], our converted Mask R-CNN label maps are discrete. For autoregressive prediction, we discretize the output by replacing the softmax network output with a one-hot encoding of the most likely class at each position. For autoregressive fine-tuning, we use a softmax activation with a low temperature parameter at the output of the S2S model, to produce near-one-hot probability maps in a differentiable way, enabling backpropagation through time.

Future Segmentation Using the Mask R-CNN Architecture. As another baseline, we fine-tune Mask R-CNN to predict mid-term future segmentation given the last 4 observed frames, denoted as the Mask H2F baseline. As initialization, we replicate the weights of the first layer learned on the COCO dataset across the 4 frames, and divide them by 4 to keep the features at the same scale.

4.3   Quantitative Results

Future Instance Segmentation. In Table 2 we present instance segmentation results of our future feature prediction approach (F2F) and compare it to the performance of the oracle, copy, optical flow and Mask H2F baselines. The copy baseline performs very poorly (24.1% in terms of AP50 *vs.* 65.8% for the oracle), which underlines the difficulty of the task. The two optical flow baselines perform comparably for short-term prediction, and are both much better than the copy baseline. For mid-term prediction, the *Warp* approach outperforms *Shift*. The Mask H2F baseline performs poorly for short-term prediction, but its results degrade slower with the number of time steps predicted, and it outperforms the *Warp* baseline for mid-term prediction. As Mask H2Foutputs a single time step prediction, either for short or mid-term predictions, it is not subject to accumulation of errors, but each prediction setting requires training a specific model. Our F2F approach gives the best results overall, reaching more than 37% of relative improvement over our best mid-term baseline. While our F2F autoregressive fine-tuning makes little difference in case of short-term prediction (40.2% *vs.* 39.9% AP50 respectively), it gives a significant improvement for mid-term prediction (17.5% *vs.* 19.4% AP50 respectively).

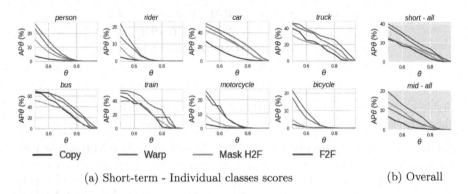

(a) Short-term - Individual classes scores   (b) Overall

Fig. 3. Instance segmentation APθ across different IoU thresholds θ. (a) Short-term prediction per class; (b) Average across all classes for short-term (top) and mid-term prediction (bottom).

In Fig. 3(a), we show how the AP metric varies with the IoU threshold, for short-term prediction across the different classes and for each method. For individual classes, F2F gives the best results across thresholds, except for very few exceptions. In Fig. 3(b), we show average results over all classes for short-term and mid-term prediction. We see that F2F consistently improves over the baselines across all thresholds, particularly for mid-term prediction.

Future Semantic Segmentation. We additionally provide a comparative evaluation on semantic segmentation in Table 3. First, we observe that our discrete implementation of the S2S model performs slightly better than the best results obtained by [1], thanks to our better underlying segmentation model (Mask R-CNN *vs.* the Dilation-10 model [31]). Second, we see that the Mask H2F baseline performs weakly in terms of semantic segmentation metrics for both short and mid-term prediction, especially in terms of IoU. This may be due to frequently duplicated predictions for a given instance, see Sect. 4.4. Third, the advantage of *Warp* over *Shift* appears clearly again, with a 5% boost in mid-term IoU. Finally, we find that F2F obtains clear improvements in IoU over all methods for short-term segmentation, ranking first with an IoU of 61.2%. Our F2F mid-term IoU is comparable to those of the S2S and *Warp* baseline, while being much more accurate in depicting contours of the objects as shown by consistently better RI, VoI and GCE segmentation scores.

Table 3. Short and mid-term semantic segmentation of moving objects (8 classes) performance on the Cityscapes validation set.

	Short-term				Mid-term			
	IoU	RI	VoI	GCE	IoU	RI	VoI	GCE
Oracle [1]	64.7	–	–	–	64.7	–	–	–
S2S [1]	55.3	–	–	–	40.8	–	–	–
Oracle	73.3	94.0	20.8	2.3	73.3	94.0	20.8	2.3
Copy	45.7	92.2	29.0	3.5	29.1	90.6	33.8	4.2
Shift	56.7	92.9	25.5	2.9	36.7	91.1	30.5	3.3
Warp	58.8	**93.1**	25.2	3.0	41.4	91.5	31.0	3.8
Mask H2F*	46.2	92.5	27.3	3.2	30.5	91.2	31.9	3.7
S2S	55.4	92.8	25.8	2.9	**42.4**	91.8	29.7	3.4
F2F	**61.2**	**93.1**	**24.8**	**2.8**	41.2	**91.9**	**28.8**	**3.1**

* Separate models were trained for short-term and mid-term predictions.

4.4 Qualitative Results

Figures 4 and 5 show representative results of our approach, both in terms of instance and semantic segmentation prediction, as well as results from the *Warp* and Mask H2F baselines for instance segmentation and S2S for semantic segmentation. We visualize predictions with a threshold of 0.5 on the confidence of masks. The Mask H2F baseline frequently predicts several masks around objects, especially for objects with ambiguous trajectories, like pedestrians, and less so for more predictable categories like cars. We speculate that this is due to the loss that the network is optimizing, which does not discourage this behavior, and due to which the network is learning to predict several plausible future positions, as long as they overlap sufficiently with the ground-truth position. This does not occur with the other methods, which are either optimizing a per-pixel loss or are not learned at all. F2F results are often better aligned with the actual layouts of the objects than the *Warp* baseline, showing that our approach has learned to model dynamics of the scene and objects more accurately than the baseline. As expected, the predicted masks are also much more precise than those of the S2S model, which is not instance-aware.

In Fig. 6 we provide additional examples to better understand why the difference between F2F and the *Warp* baseline is smaller for semantic segmentation metrics than for instance segmentation metrics. When several instances of the same class are close together, inaccurate estimation of the instance masks may still give acceptable semantic segmentation. This typically happens for groups of pedestrians and rows of parked cars. If an instance mask is split across multiple objects, this will further affect the AP measure than the IoU metric. The same example also illustrates common artifacts of the *Warp* baseline that are due to error accumulation in the propagation of the flow field.

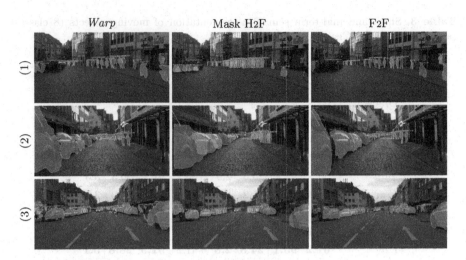

Fig. 4. Mid-term instance segmentation predictions (0.5 s future) for 3 sequences, from left to right: *Warp* baseline, Mask H2F baseline and F2F.

4.5   Discussion

Failure Cases. To illustrate some of the remaining challenges in predicting future instance segmentation we present several failure cases of our F2F model in Fig. 7. In Fig. 7(a), the masks predicted for the truck and the person are incoherent, both in shape and location. More consistent predictions might be obtained with a mechanism for explicitly modeling occlusions. Certain motions and shape transformations are hard to predict accurately due to the inherent ambiguity in the problem. This is, *e.g.*, the case for the legs of pedestrians in Fig. 7(b), for which there is a high degree of uncertainty on the exact pose. Since the model is deterministic, it predicts a rough mask due to averaging over several possibilities. This may be addressed by modeling the intrinsic variability using GANs, VAEs, or autoregressive models [6,32,33].

Long Term Prediction. In Fig. 8 we show a prediction of F2F up to 1.5 s. in the future in a sequence of the long Frankfurt video of the Cityscapes validation set, where frames were extracted with an interval of 3 as before. To allow more temporal consistency between predicted objects, we apply an adapted version of the method of Gkioxari *et al.* [34] as a post-processing step. We define the linking score as the sum of confidence scores of subsequent instances and of their IoU. We then greedily compute the paths between instances which maximize these scores using the Viterbi algorithm. We thereby obtain object tracks along the (unseen) future video frames. Some object trajectories are forecasted reasonably well up to a second, such as the rider, while others are lost by that time such as the motorbike. We also compute the AP with the ground truth of the long Frankfurt video. For each method, we give the best result of either predicting 9 frames with a frame interval of 3, or the opposite. For Mask H2F, only the latter

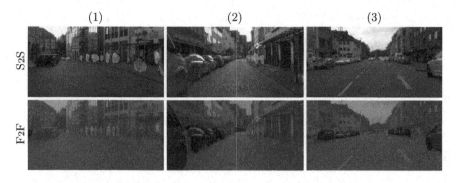

Fig. 5. Mid-term semantic segmentation predictions (0.5 s) for 3 sequences. For each case we show from top to bottom: S2S model and F2F model.

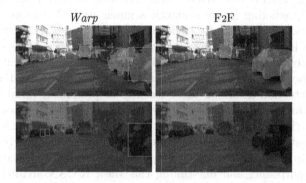

Fig. 6. Mid-term predictions of instance and semantic segmentation with the *Warp* baseline and our F2F model. Inaccurate instance segmentations can result in accurate semantic segmentation areas; see orange rectangle highlights. (Color figure online)

is possible, as there are no such long sequences available for training. We obtain an AP of 0.5 for the flow and copy baseline, 0.7 for F2F and 1.5 for Mask H2F. All methods lead to very low scores, highlighting the severe challenges posed by this problem.

Fig. 7. Failure modes of mid-term prediction with the F2F model, highlighted with the red boxes: incoherent masks (a), lack of detail in highly deformable object regions, such as legs of pedestrians (b). (Color figure online)

0.5 sec   1 sec   1.5 sec

Fig. 8. Long-term predictions (1.5 s) from our F2F model.

5   Conclusion

We introduced a new anticipated recognition task: predicting instance segmentation of future video frames. This task is defined at a semantically meaningful level rather the level of raw RGB values, and adds instance-level information as compared to predicting future semantic segmentation. We proposed a generic and self-supervised approach for anticipated recognition based on predicting the convolutional features of future video frames. In our experiments we apply this approach in combination with the Mask R-CNN instance segmentation model. We predict the internal "backbone" features which are of fixed dimension, and apply the "detection head" on these features to produce a variable number of predictions. Our results show that future instance segmentation can be predicted much better than naively copying the segmentations from the last observed frame, and that our future feature prediction approach significantly outperforms two strong baselines, the first one relying on optical-flow-based warping and the second on repurposing and fine-tuning the Mask R-CNN architecture for the task. When evaluated on the more basic task of semantic segmentation without instance-level detail, our approach yields performance quantitatively comparable to earlier approaches, while having qualitative advantages.

Our work shows that with a feed-forward network we are able to obtain surprisingly accurate results. More sophisticated architectures have the potential to further improve performance. Predictions may be also improved by explicitly modeling the temporal consistency of instance segmentation, and predicting multiple possible futures rather than a single one.

We invite the reader to watch videos of our predictions at http://thoth. inrialpes.fr/people/pluc/instpred2018.

Acknowledgment. This work has been partially supported by the grant ANR-16-CE23-0006 "Deep in France" and LabEx PERSYVAL-Lab (ANR-11-LABX-0025-01). We thank Matthijs Douze, Xavier Martin, Ilija Radosavovic and Thomas Lucas for their precious comments.

References

1. Luc, P., Neverova, N., Couprie, C., Verbeek, J., LeCun, Y.: Predicting deeper into the future of semantic segmentation. In: ICCV (2017)
2. Sutton, R., Barto, A.: Reinforcement Learning: An Introduction. MIT Press, Cambridge (1998)

3. Mathieu, M., Couprie, C., LeCun, Y.: Deep multi-scale video prediction beyond mean square error. In: ICLR (2016)
4. Ranzato, M., Szlam, A., Bruna, J., Mathieu, M., Collobert, R., Chopra, S.: Video (language) modeling: a baseline for generative models of natural videos. arXiv 1412.6604 (2014)
5. Srivastava, N., Mansimov, E., Salakhutdinov, R.: Unsupervised learning of video representations using LSTMs. In: ICML (2015)
6. Kalchbrenner, N., et al.: Video pixel networks. In: ICML (2017)
7. Shalev-Shwartz, S., Ben-Zrihem, N., Cohen, A., Shashua, A.: Long-term planning by short-term prediction. arXiv 1602.01580 (2016)
8. Shalev-Shwartz, S., Shashua, A.: On the sample complexity of end-to-end training vs. semantic abstraction training. arXiv 1604.06915 (2016)
9. He, K., Gkioxari, G., Dollár, P., Girshick, R.: Mask R-CNN. In: ICCV (2017)
10. Kokkinos, I.: UberNet: training a universal convolutional neural network for low-, mid-, and high-level vision using diverse datasets and limited memory. In: CVPR (2017)
11. Villegas, R., Yang, J., Hong, S., Lin, X., Lee, H.: Decomposing motion and content for natural video sequence prediction. In: ICLR (2017)
12. Villegas, R., Yang, J., Zou, Y., Sohn, S., Lin, X., Lee, H.: Learning to generate long-term future via hierarchical prediction. In: ICML (2017)
13. Walker, J., Doersch, C., Gupta, A., Hebert, M.: An uncertain future: forecasting from static images using variational autoencoders. In: Leibe, B., Matas, J., Sebe, N., Welling, M. (eds.) ECCV 2016. LNCS, vol. 9911, pp. 835–851. Springer, Cham (2016). https://doi.org/10.1007/978-3-319-46478-7_51
14. Lan, T., Chen, T.-C., Savarese, S.: A hierarchical representation for future action prediction. In: Fleet, D., Pajdla, T., Schiele, B., Tuytelaars, T. (eds.) ECCV 2014. LNCS, vol. 8691, pp. 689–704. Springer, Cham (2014). https://doi.org/10.1007/978-3-319-10578-9_45
15. Kitani, K.M., Ziebart, B.D., Bagnell, J.A., Hebert, M.: Activity forecasting. In: Fitzgibbon, A., Lazebnik, S., Perona, P., Sato, Y., Schmid, C. (eds.) ECCV 2012. LNCS, vol. 7575, pp. 201–214. Springer, Heidelberg (2012). https://doi.org/10.1007/978-3-642-33765-9_15
16. Lee, N., Choi, W., Vernaza, P., Choy, C., Torr, P., Chandraker, M.: DESIRE: distant future prediction in dynamic scenes with interacting agents. In: CVPR (2017)
17. Dosovitskiy, A., Koltun, V.: Learning to act by predicting the future. In: ICLR (2017)
18. Vondrick, C., Pirsiavash, H., Torralba, A.: Anticipating the future by watching unlabeled video. In: CVPR (2016)
19. Jin, X., et al.: Predicting scene parsing and motion dynamics in the future. In: NIPS (2017)
20. Romera-Paredes, B., Torr, P.H.S.: Recurrent instance segmentation. In: Leibe, B., Matas, J., Sebe, N., Welling, M. (eds.) ECCV 2016. LNCS, vol. 9910, pp. 312–329. Springer, Cham (2016). https://doi.org/10.1007/978-3-319-46466-4_19
21. Bai, M., Urtasun, R.: Deep watershed transform for instance segmentation. In: CVPR (2017)
22. Pinheiro, P.O., Lin, T.-Y., Collobert, R., Dollár, P.: Learning to refine object segments. In: Leibe, B., Matas, J., Sebe, N., Welling, M. (eds.) ECCV 2016. LNCS, vol. 9905, pp. 75–91. Springer, Cham (2016). https://doi.org/10.1007/978-3-319-46448-0_5

23. Ren, S., He, K., Girshick, R., Sun, J.: Faster R-CNN: towards real-time object detection with region proposal networks. In: NIPS (2015)
24. Lin, T.Y., Dollár, P., Girshick, R., He, K., Hariharan, B., Belongie, S.: Feature pyramid networks for object detection. In: CVPR (2017)
25. Cordts, M., et al.: The Cityscapes dataset for semantic urban scene understanding. In: CVPR (2016)
26. Lin, T.-Y., et al.: Microsoft COCO: common objects in context. In: Fleet, D., Pajdla, T., Schiele, B., Tuytelaars, T. (eds.) ECCV 2014. LNCS, vol. 8693, pp. 740–755. Springer, Cham (2014). https://doi.org/10.1007/978-3-319-10602-1_48
27. Yang, A., Wright, J., Ma, Y., Sastry, S.: Unsupervised segmentation of natural images via lossy data compression. CVIU $110(2)$, 212–225 (2008)
28. Parntofaru, C., Hebert, M.: A comparison of image segmentation algorithms. Technical report CMU-RI-TR-05-40, Carnegie Mellon University (2005)
29. Martin, D., Fowlkes, C., Tal, D., Malik, J.: A database of human segmented natural images and its application to evaluating segmentation algorithms and measuring ecological statistics. In: ICCV (2001)
30. Meilă, M.: Comparing clusterings: An axiomatic view. In: ICML (2005)
31. Yu, F., Koltun, V.: Multi-scale context aggregation by dilated convolutions. In: ICLR (2016)
32. Goodfellow, I., et al.: Generative adversarial nets. In: NIPS (2014)
33. Kingma, D., Welling, M.: Auto-encoding variational Bayes. In: ICLR (2014)
34. Gkioxari, G., Malik, J.: Finding action tubes. In: CVPR (2015)

Flow-Grounded Spatial-Temporal Video Prediction from Still Images

Yijun Li[1(✉)], Chen Fang[2], Jimei Yang[2], Zhaowen Wang[2], Xin Lu[2], and Ming-Hsuan Yang[1,3]

[1] University of California, Merced, Merced, USA
{yli62,mhyang}@ucmerced.edu
[2] Adobe Research, San Jose, USA
{cfang,jimyang,zhawang,xinl}@adobe.com
[3] Google, Mountain View, USA

Abstract. Existing video prediction methods mainly rely on observing multiple historical frames or focus on predicting the next one-frame. In this work, we study the problem of generating consecutive multiple future frames by observing one single still image only. We formulate the multi-frame prediction task as a multiple time step flow (multi-flow) prediction phase followed by a flow-to-frame synthesis phase. The multi-flow prediction is modeled in a variational probabilistic manner with spatial-temporal relationships learned through 3D convolutions. The flow-to-frame synthesis is modeled as a generative process in order to keep the predicted results lying closer to the manifold shape of real video sequence. Such a two-phase design prevents the model from directly looking at the high-dimensional pixel space of the frame sequence and is demonstrated to be more effective in predicting better and diverse results. Extensive experimental results on videos with different types of motion show that the proposed algorithm performs favorably against existing methods in terms of quality, diversity and human perceptual evaluation.

Keywords: Future prediction · Conditional variational autoencoder
3D convolutions

1 Introduction

Part of our visual world constantly experiences situations that require us to forecast what will happen over time by observing one still image from a single moment. Studies in neuroscience show that this *preplay* activity might constitute an automatic prediction mechanism in human visual cortex [1]. Given the great progress in artificial intelligence, researchers also begin to let machines learn to perform such a predictive activity for various applications. For example in Fig. 1(top), from a snapshot by the surveillance camera, the system is expected to predict the man's next action which could be used for safety precautions. Another application in computational photography is turning still images into vivid cinemagraphs for aesthetic effects, as shown in Fig. 1(bottom).

© Springer Nature Switzerland AG 2018
V. Ferrari et al. (Eds.): ECCV 2018, LNCS 11213, pp. 609–625, 2018.
https://doi.org/10.1007/978-3-030-01240-3_37

In this work, we mainly study how to generate pixel-level future frames in multiple time steps given one still image. A number of existing prediction models [2–5] are under the assumption of observing a short video sequence (>1 frame). Since multiple historical frames explicitly exhibit obvious motion cues, most of them use deterministic models to render a fixed future sequence. In contrast, our single-image based prediction task, without any motion information provided, implies that there are obvious uncertainties existed in both spatial and temporal domains. Therefore we propose a probabilistic model based on a conditional variational autoencoder (cVAE) to model the uncertainty. Our probabilistic model has two unique features. First, it is a 3D-cVAE model, i.e., the autoencoder is designed in a spatial-temporal architecture with 3D convolution layers. The 3D convolutional layer [6], which takes a volume as input, is able to capture correlations between the spatial and temporal dimension of signals, thereby rendering distinctive spatial-temporal features for better predictions. Second, the output of our model is optical flows which characterize the spatial layout of how pixels are going to move step by step. Different from other methods that predict trajectories [7], frame differences [8] or frame pixels [5], the flow is a more natural and general representation of motions. It serves as a relatively low-dimensional reflection of high-level structures and can be obtained in an unsupervised manner.

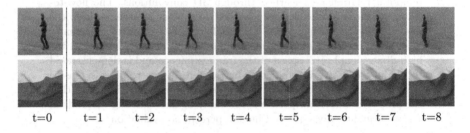

Fig. 1. Multi-step future sequences generated by our algorithm (t = 1 – 8) conditioned on one single still image (t = 0). Images are of size 128 × 128.

With the predicted flows, we next formulate the full frame synthesis as a generation problem. Due to the existence of occlusions, flow-based pixel-copying operations (e.g., warping) are obviously ineffective here. The model should be capable of "imagining" the appearance of future frames and removing the unnecessary parts in the previous frame at the same time. Therefore we propose a generative model *Flow2rgb* to generate pixel-level future frames. Such a model is non-trivial and is demonstrated to be effective in keeping the generated sequence staying close to the manifold of real sequences (Fig. 5). Overall, we formulate the multi-frame prediction task as a multiple time step flow prediction phase followed by a flow-to-frame generation phase. Such a two-phase design prevents the model from directly looking at the high-dimensional pixel space of the frame sequence and is demonstrated to be more effective in predicting better results. During the testing, by drawing different samples from the learned latent distribution, our approach can also predict diverse future sequences.

The main contributions of this work are summarized as follows:

- We propose a spatial-temporal conditional VAE model (3D-cVAE) to predict future flows in multiple time steps. The diversity in predictions is realized by drawing different samples from the learned distribution.
- We present a generative model that learns to generate the pixel-level appearance of future frames based on predicted flows.
- We demonstrate the effectiveness of our method for predicting sequences that contain both articulated (e.g., humans) objects and dynamic textures (e.g., clouds).

2   Related Work

Action Prediction. The macroscopic analysis of prediction based on the given frame(s) can be predicting what event is going to happen [9–11], trajectory paths [12], or recognizing the type of human activities [13,14]. Some of early methods are supervised, requiring labels (e.g., bounding boxes) of the moving object. Later approaches [14] realize the unsupervised way of prediction by relying on the context of scenes. However, these approaches usually only provide coarse predictions of how the future will evolve and are unable to tell richer information except for a action (or event) label.

Pixel-Level Frame Prediction. Recent prediction methods move to the microcosmic analysis of more detailed information in the future. This is directly reflected by requiring the pixel-level generation of future frames in multiple time steps. With the development of deep neural networks, especially when recursive modules are extensively used, predicting realistic future frames has being dominated. Much progress has been made in the generated quality of future outputs by designing different network structures [2,15–18] or using different learning techniques, including adversarial loss [19,20], motion/content separation [4,5,21], and transformation parameters [22,23].

Our work also aims at accurate frame predictions but the specific setting is to model the uncertainties of multi-frame prediction given a single still image as input. In terms of multi-frame predictions conditioning on still images, closest work to ours are [24,25]. However, [24] only predicts the pose information and the proposed model is deterministic. The work in [25] also estimates poses first and then use an image-analogy strategy to generate frames. But their pose generation step relies on observing multiple frames. Moreover, both approaches employ the recursive module (e.g., recurrent neural networks) for consecutive predictions which may overemphasize on learning the temporal information only. Instead, we use the 3D convolutional layer [6] which takes a volume as input. Since both spatial and temporal information are encoded together, the 3D convolution can generally capture correlations between the spatial and temporal dimension of signals, thereby rendering distinctive spatial-temporal features [6]. In addition, both [24,25] focus on human dynamics while our work targets on both articulated objects and dynamic textures.

In terms of modeling future uncertainties, two methods [7,8] are closely related. However, Xue et al. [8] only model the uncertainty in the next one-step prediction. If we iteratively run the one-step prediction model for multi-step predictions, the frame quality will degrade fast through error accumulations, due to the lack of temporal relationships modeling between frames. Though Walker et al. [7] could keep forecasting over the course of one second, instead of predicting real future frames, it only predicts the dense trajectory of pixels. Also such a trajectory-supervised modeling requires laborious human labeling. Different from these methods, our approach integrates the multi-frame prediction and uncertainty modeling in one model.

Dynamic Textures. The above-mentioned methods mainly focus on the movement of articulated objects (e.g., human). In contrast, dynamic textures often exhibit more randomness in the movement of texture elements. Both traditional methods based on linear dynamical systems [26,27] and neural network based methods [28] require learning a model for each sequence example. Different from those methods, we collect a large number of dynamic texture video data and aims at modeling the general distribution of their motions. Such a model can immediately serve as an editing tool when animating static texture examples.

3   Proposed Algorithm

We formulate the video prediction as two phases: flow prediction and flow-to-frame generation. The flow prediction phase, triggered by a noise, directly predicts a set of consecutive flow maps conditioned on the observed first frame. Then the flow-to-frame phase iteratively synthesizes future frames with the previous frame and the corresponding predicted flow map, starting from the first given frame and first predicted flow map.

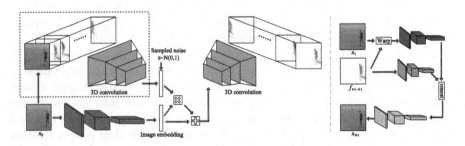

Fig. 2. Architecture of the proposed multi-step prediction network. It consists of a 3D-cVAE (left) for predicting consecutive flows and a *Flow2rgb* model to generate future frame pixels (right). During the testing, the encoder (blue rectangle) of 3D-cVAE is no longer used and we directly sample points from the distribution for predictions. (Color figure online)

3.1 Flow Prediction

Figure 2(left) illustrates the architecture of our proposed model for predicting consecutive optical flows. Formally, our model is a conditional variational autoencoder [29,30] with a spatial-temporal convolutional architecture (3D-cVAE). Given a sequence $X = \{x_i\}_0^M$ with x_0 as the starting frame, we denote the set of consecutive optical flows between adjacent frames in X as $F = \{f_i\}_0^{M-1}$. The network is trained to map the observation F (conditioned on x_0) to the latent variable z which are likely to reproduce the F. In order to avoid training a deterministic model, we produces a distribution over z values, which we sample from before the decoding. Such a variational distribution $q_\phi(z|x_0, F)$, known as the recognition model in [30], is assumed to be trained to follow a Gaussian distribution $p_z(z)$. Given a sampled z, the decoder decodes the flow F from the conditional distribution $p_\theta(F|x_0, z)$. Therefore the whole objective of network training is to maximize the variational lower-bound [29] of the following negative log-likelihood function:

$$\mathcal{L}(x_0, F; \theta, \phi) \approx -\mathcal{D}_{KL}(q_\phi(z|x_0, F)\|p_z(z)) + \frac{1}{L}\sum_1^L \log p_\theta(F|x_0, z), \quad (1)$$

where $\mathcal{D}_{KL}$ is the Kullback-Leibler (K-L) divergence and L is the number of samples. Maximizing the term at rightmost in (1) is equivalent to minimizing the L1 distance between the predicted flow and the observed flow. Hence the loss $\mathcal{L}$ consists of a flow reconstruction loss and a K-L divergence loss.

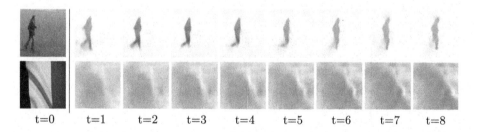

$t=0 \qquad t=1 \qquad t=2 \qquad t=3 \qquad t=4 \qquad t=5 \qquad t=6 \qquad t=7 \qquad t=8$

Fig. 3. Examples of our multi-step flow prediction. During the testing, by simply sampling a noise from $N \sim (0, 1)$, we obtain a set of consecutive flows that describe the future motion field in multiple time steps. Note that since we have a warp operation in the later flow-to-frame step (Sect. 3.2) and the backward warping will not result in *holes* in results, we predict the backward flow in this step, i.e., the motion from x_{t+1} to x_t. This is just for convenience and we empirically do not find obvious difference between predicting forward and backward flows.

Different from traditional cVAE models [7,8,30], our 3D-cVAE model employs the 3D convolution (purple blocks in Fig. 2) which is demonstrated to be well-suited for spatial-temporal feature learning [6,19]. In terms of network architecture, the 3D convolutional network outputs multiple (a volume of) flow maps instead of one, which can be used to predict multiple future frames. More importantly, the spatial-temporal relationship between adjacent flows are implicitly modeled during the training due to the 3D convolution operations, ensuring that the predicted motions are continuous and reasonable over time. In order to let the variational distribution $q_\phi(z|x_0, F)$ conditioned on the starting frame, we stack x_0 with each flow map f_i in F as the encoder input. Meanwhile, learning the conditional distribution $p_\theta(F|x_0, z)$ for flow reconstruction also needs to be conditioned on x_0 in the latent space. Therefore, we propose an image encoder (pink blocks in Fig. 2) to first map x_0 to a latent vector that has the same dimension as z. Inspired by the image analogy work [31], we use a conditioning strategy of combining the multiplication and addition operation, as shown in Fig. 2(left). After we obtain the flow sequence for the future, we proceed to generate the pixel-level full frames.

3.2 Frame Generation

Given the flow information, a common way to obtain the next frame is warping or pixel copying [32]. However, due to the existence of occlusions, the result is often left with unnecessary pixels inherited from the previous frame. The frame interpolation work [33] predicts a mask indicating where to copy pixels from previous and next frame. But they require at least two frames to infer the occluded parts. Since we only observe one image, it is straightforward to formulate this step as a generation process, meaning that this model can "imagine" the appearance of next frame according to the flow and starting frame. The similar idea is also applied in the task of novel view synthesis [34].

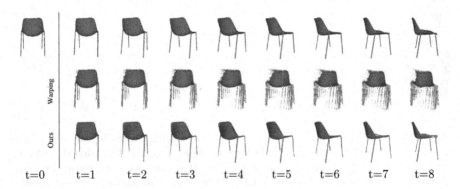

Fig. 4. Comparisons between our *Flow2rgb* model and warping operation, given the first frame and all precomputed flows (between adjacent ground truth frames). Starting from the first frame and first flow, we iteratively run warping or the proposed *Flow2rgb* model based on the previous result and next flow to obtain the sequence. Top: ground truth, Middle: warping results, Bottom: our results.

The architecture of the proposed frame generation model *Flow2rgb* is shown in Fig. 2(right). Given the input x_t and its optical flow f_t that represents the motion of next time step, the network is trained to generate the next frame x_{t+1}. Since two adjacent frames often share similar information (especially in the static background regions), in order to let the network focus on learning the difference of two frames, we first warp the x_t based on the flow to get a coarse estimation $\tilde{x}_{t+1}$. Then we design a Siamese-like [35] network with the warped frame and the flow as two streams of input. The frame and flow encoders (blue and green blocks) borrow the same architecture of the VGG-19 up to the Relu_4_1 layer, and the decoder (yellow blocks) is designed as being symmetrical to the encoder with the nearest neighbor upsampling layer used for enlarging feature maps. We train the model using a pixel reconstruction loss and a feature loss [36,37] as shown below:

$$\mathcal{L} = \|\hat{x}_{t+1} - x_{t+1}\|_2 + \sum_{K=1}^{5} \lambda \|\Phi_K(\hat{x}_{t+1}) - \Phi_K(x_{t+1})\|_2 , \qquad (2)$$

where $\hat{x}_{t+1}$, x_{t+1} are the network output and ground truth (GT), and Φ_K is the VGG-19 [38] encoder that extracts the Relu_K_1 features. λ is the weight to balance the two losses. This model is learned in an unsupervised manner without human labels. Note that this is a one-step flow-to-frame model. Since we predict multi-step flows in the flow prediction stage, starting with the first given frame, we iteratively run this model to generate the following frame based on the next flow and previous generated frame.

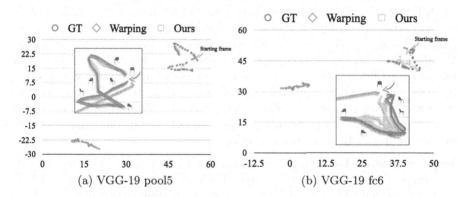

(a) VGG-19 pool5   (b) VGG-19 fc6

Fig. 5. Visualization of sequence (a chair turning around) manifold in deep feature space. Staring from the same frame, each predicted frame of three sequences is visualized as a 2-D point by applying t-SNE [39] on its deep features. The moving average is shown as lines to imply the shape (or trending) of the manifold. For example in (a), the GT rotating chair (blue) follows a "8" like manifold in pool5 feature space, which our predicted sequence (yellow) follows closely but the warping sequence (green) deviates much further. (Color figure online)

We show the effectiveness of our *Flow2rgb* model in Fig. 4 with an example of chair rotating sequence [40]. To verify the frame generation phase alone, we assume that the flows are already available (computed by [41]). Then given the first frame and future flows, the second row of Fig. 4 shows the iterative warping results where the chair legs are repeatedly copied in future frames as the warping is unable to depict the right appearance of chair in difference views. In contrast, our model iteratively generates the occluded parts and removed unnecessary parts in the previous frame according to the flow at each time step. As claimed in [40], the deep embeddings of objects under consecutively changing views often follow certain manifold in feature space. If we interpret this changing view as a type of rotating motion, our predicted results for different views also needs to stay close to the manifold shape of the GT sequence. We demonstrate this by extracting the VGG-19 [38] features of each predicted frame, mapping it to a 2-D point through t-SNE [39], and visualizing it in Fig. 5. It clearly shows that our predictions follows closely with the manifold of the GT sequence, while the warping drives the predictions to deviate from the GT further and further.

4   Experimental Results

In this section, we first discuss the experimental settings and implementation details. We then present qualitative and quantitative comparisons between the proposed algorithm and several competing algorithms. Finally, we analyze the diversity issue in uncertainty modeling.

Datasets. We mainly evaluate our algorithm on three datasets. The first one is the KTH dataset [42] which is a human action video dataset that consists of six types of action and totally 600 videos. It represents the movement of articulated objects. Same as in [4,5], we use person 1–16 for training and 17–25 for testing. We also collect another two datasets from online websites, i.e., the *WavingFlag* and *FloatingCloud*. These two datasets represents dynamic texture videos where motions may bring the shape changes on dynamic patterns. The *WavingFlag* dataset contains 341 videos of 80K+ frames and the *FloatingCloud* dataset has 415 videos of 150K+ frames in total. In each dataset, we randomly split all videos into the training (4/5) and testing (1/5) set.

Implementation Details. Given the starting frame x_0, our algorithm predicts the future in next $M = 16$ time steps. Each frame is resized to 128×128 in experiments. Similar to [14,43], we employ an existing optical flow estimator SPyNet [41] to obtain flows between GT frames for training the 3D-cVAE. As described in Sect. 3.1, we stack x_0 with each flow map f_i in F. Thus during the training, the input cube to the 3D-cVAE is of size $16 \times 5 \times 128 \times 128$ where $5 = 2 + 3$ (2-channel flow and 3-channel RGB). The dimension of the latent variable z in the bottle neck is set as 2000. Another important factor for a successful network training is to normalize the flow roughly to $(0, 1)$ before feeding it into the network, ensuring pixel values of both flows and RGB frames are within the similar range. Since the *Flow2rgb* model can be an independent module for motion transfer with known flows, we train the 3D-cVAE and *Flow2rgb* model separately in experiments.

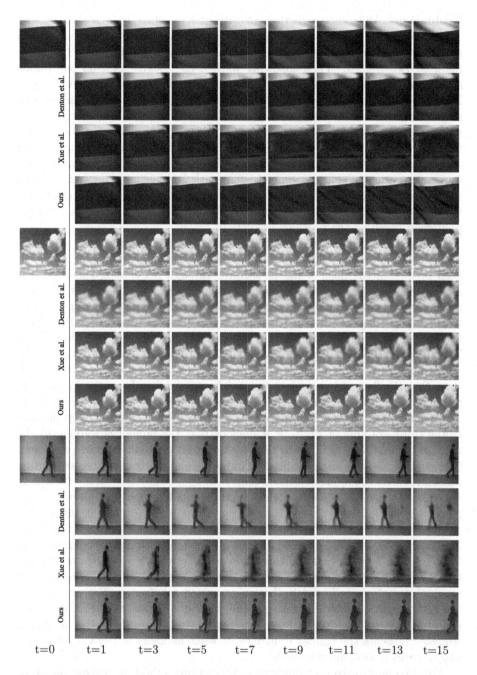

Fig. 6. Visual comparisons of different prediction algorithms. Top left: the starting frame. From top to bottom in example: GT, Denton et al. [5], Xue et al. [8], Ours. The GT sequence provides a sense of motion rightness, while the predicted sequence is unnecessary to be exactly the same with GT.

Evaluations. Different prediction algorithms have their unique settings and assumptions. For example, Mathieu et al. [2] requires four frames stacked together as the input. Villegas et al. [4] ask for feeding the image difference (at least two frames). Their following work [25], though based on one frame, additionally needs multiple historical human pose maps to start the prediction. For fair comparisons, we mainly select prediction methods [5,8] that accept one single image as the only input to compare. The work of [5] represents the typical recursive prediction pipeline, which builds upon a fully-connected long short-term memory (FC-LSTM) layer for predictions. Their model is originally trained and tested by observing multiple frames. Here we change their setting to one-frame observance in order to be consistent with our setting. The work of [8] is the typical one-step prediction method based on one given frame. To get multi-frame predictions, we train their model and iteratively test it to get the next prediction based on the previous prediction.

In Fig. 6, we provide a visual comparison between the proposed algorithm and [5,8]. In [5], a pre-trained and disentangled *pose* embedding is employed to keep predicting the pose of the next frame through a FC-LSTM module. For articulated objects, the pose is often compact and in low dimensions, which is relatively easier to handle with a single LSTM module. However, for dynamic textures (e.g., flag, cloud) where all pixels are likely to move, the global pose becomes complex and is no longer a low-dimensional structure representation. Therefore the capacity of recursive models is not enough to capture the spatial and temporal variation trend at the same time. The first two examples in Fig. 6 show that the flag and cloud in predicted frames are nearly static. Meanwhile, the pose only describes the static structure of the object in the current frame and cannot tell as much information as the flow about the next-step motion. In the third example of Fig. 6, it is obvious that the human is walking to the right. But the results of [5] show that the human is going in a reverse direction. Moreover, since they directly predict frame pixels and use the reconstruction loss only, their results are relatively blurry. In [8], as they only predict the next one frame, the motion is often clear in the second frame. But after we keep predicting the following frame using the previous predicted frame, the motion gradually disappears and the quality of results degrades fast during a few steps. Moreover, they choose to predict the image difference which only shows global image changes but does not capture how each pixel will move to its correspond-ing one in the next frame. In contrast, our results show more continuous and reasonable motion, reflected by better generated full frames. For example, in the first flag example, the starting frame indicates that the fold on top right will disappear and the fold at bottom left will bring bigger folds. Our predicted sequence presents the similar dynamics as what happens in the GT sequence, which makes it look more realistic.

We also quantitatively evaluate these prediction methods using three different metrics, i.e., the root-mean-square error (RMSE), perceptual similarity [44], and user preference. The RMSE is the classic per-pixel metric which measures the spatial correspondence without considering any high-level semantics and is often

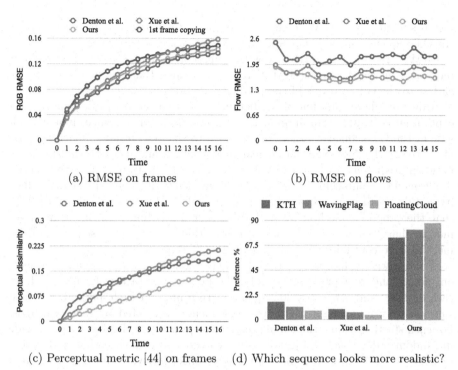

(a) RMSE on frames

(b) RMSE on flows

(c) Perceptual metric [44] on frames   (d) Which sequence looks more realistic?

Fig. 7. Quantitative evaluations of different prediction algorithms. We start from the per-pixel metrics (e.g., RMSE) and gradually take human perception into consideration. Our method achieves the best performance under metrics (b)–(d).

easily favored by smooth results. Based on this observation, the recent work of [44] proposes a perceptual similarity metric by using deep network embeddings. It is demonstrated to agree with human perceptions better. Lastly, we directly ask the feedback from users by conducting user studies to understand their preference towards the predicted results by different algorithms.

We start with the traditional RMSE to compute the difference between predicted sequence and GT sequence frame-by-frame and show the result in Fig. 7(a). To understand how effective these prediction methods are, we design a simple baseline by copying the given frame as multi-step predictions. However, we do not observe obvious difference among all these methods. While the prediction from one single image is originally ambiguous, the GT sequence can be regarded as just one possibility of the future. The trending of motion may be similar but the resulted images can be significantly different in pixel-level. But the RMSE metric is actually very sensitive to the pixel spatial mismatch. Similar observations are also found in [5,44]. That is why all these methods, when comparing with the GT sequence, shows the similar RMSE results. Therefore, instead of measuring the RMSE on frames, we turn to measure the RMSE on optical flows because the optical flow represents whether the motion field is pre-

dicted similarly or not. We compute the flow maps between adjacent frames of
the GT sequence and other predicted sequences using the SPyNet [41] and show
the RMSE results in Fig. 7(b). Now the difference becomes more clear and our
method achieves the lowest RMSE results, meaning that our prediction is the
closest to the GT in terms of the predicted motions.

However, the evaluation of prediction results still need to take human perception into consideration in order to determine whether sequences look as realistic as the GT sequence. Therefore we turn to the perceptual similarity metric
[44]. We use the Alex-Net [45] for feature extraction and measure the similarity
between predicted sequence and GT sequence frame-by-frame. Since this metric
is obtained by computing feature distances, we denote it as perceptual dissimilarity so that small values means being more similar. The results in Fig. 7(c) show
that the proposed method outperforms other algorithms with an even larger
margin than that in Fig. 7(b), which means that the predicted sequence of our
method is perceptually more similar to the GT sequence.

Finally, we conduct the user study to get the feedback from human subjects
on judging different predicted results. We prepare 30 starting frames (10 from
each dataset) and generated 30 sequences (16-frame) for each method. For each
subject, we randomly select 15 sets of sequences predicted by three methods.
For each starting frame, the three predicted sequences are displayed side-by-side
in random order. Each subject is asked to vote one sequence that looks most
realistic for each starting frame. We finally collect 900 votes from 60 users and
report the results (in percentage) in Fig. 7(d). The study results clearly show
that the proposed method receives the most votes for more realistic predictions
among all three categories. Both Fig. 7(c) and (d) indicate that the proposed
method performs favorably against [5, 8] in terms of perceptual quality.

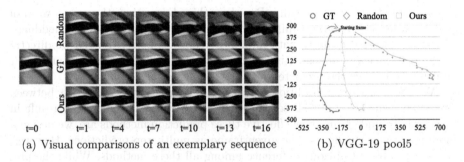

(a) Visual comparisons of an exemplary sequence   (b) VGG-19 pool5

Fig. 8. Comparison with a naive baseline which transfers a random motion field. (b)
The GT sequence follows a "C" like manifold in pool5 feature space, which our prediction follows closely but the random prediction deviates much further.

Random Motion. We also compare with a naive approach which uses random
flow maps (e.g., sampling from the Gaussian distribution $N(0, 2)$ for each pixel).
We apply the proposed *flow2rgb* model to both random and the learned motions

by our method to generate frames. Figure 8(a) shows one example. In Fig. 8(b), we visualize the manifold of predicted sequences in the deep feature space using the t-SNE scheme (as did in Fig. 5). Both demonstrate that the learned motion generates much better results than those by the random motion, as the naive approach neither models the motion distribution nor considers the temporal relationship between frames.

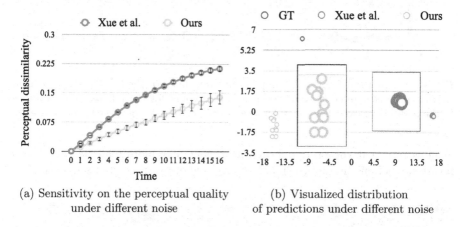

(a) Sensitivity on the perceptual quality under different noise

(b) Visualized distribution of predictions under different noise

Fig. 9. Comparisons between [8] and the proposed algorithm on uncertainty modeling given the same starting frame. By drawing different samples, the generated predictions by our method exhibits more diversities while still being more similar to GT.

Diversity. Both [8] and the proposed method model the uncertainty in predictions, but are different in one-step [8] or multi-step uncertainties. By drawing different samples, we evaluate how the quality of predictions is affected by the noise input and how diverse the predicted sequences are. While [8] uses a noise vector of 3200 dimensions and we use that of 2000 dimensions, the noise inputs of two models are not exactly the same but they are all sampled from $N(0, 1)$. We sample 10 noise inputs for each method, while ensuring that the two sets of noise inputs have the similar mean and standard deviation. Then we obtain 10 sequences for each method, and compare them with the GT sequence. Figure 9(a) shows the mean and standard deviation of the perceptual metric over each method's 10 predictions when compared with the GT frame-by-frame. Under different noise inputs, our method keeps generating better sequences that are more similar to the GT. Meanwhile, the results of our algorithm show larger deviation, which implies that there are more diversities in our predictions. To further verify this, we show the embeddings of generated sequences in Fig. 9(b). For each sequence, we extract the VGG-19 [38] features (e.g., fc6 layer) of each frame, stack them as one vector, and map it to a 2-D point through t-SNE [39]. Figure 9(b) shows that our 10 predictions are much closer to the GT sequence while being scattered to be different from each other. In contrast, the 10 predictions of [8] huddle together and are far from the GT. Those comparisons

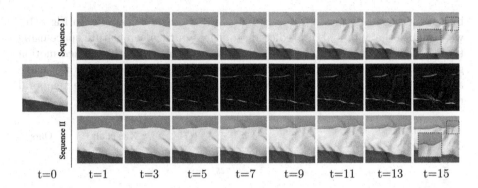

t=0   t=1   t=3   t=5   t=7   t=9   t=11   t=13   t=15

Fig. 10. Given a still image, by sampling different noise in the latent space, our algorithm synthesizes different future outcomes to account for the intrinsic uncertainties. In the middle row, we show the difference of two generated sequences frame-by-frame.

demonstrate that the proposed algorithm generates more realistic and diverse future predictions. Figure 10 shows an example of two predicted sequences.

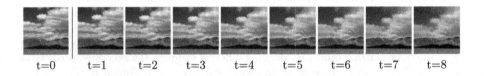

t=0   t=1   t=2   t=3   t=4   t=5   t=6   t=7   t=8

Fig. 11. Potential application of our algorithm in video editing.

Bringing Still Images to Life. Unlike previous video prediction methods [4,7,25] that mainly focus on humans for action recognition, our algorithm is more general towards bringing elements in the still image to life, i.e., turning a still image into a vivid GIF for aesthetic effects. It can be an effective tool for video editing.

In Fig. 11, we show a example of turning a photo into a vivid sequence. We mask out the sky region, apply our model trained on the *FloatingCloud* dataset and generate the effect of clouds floating in the sky. This could further benefit existing sky editing methods [46]. Moreover, if we replace our flow prediction with known flows from a reference sequence, our flow-to-frame model *Flow2rgb* becomes a global motion style transfer model. As the current random sampling strategy for flow predictions is uncontrollable, future work may include introducing more interactions from users to control detailed motions.

5   Conclusions

In this work, we propose a video prediction algorithm that synthesizes a set of likely future frames in multiple time steps from one single still image.

Instead of directly estimating the high-dimensional future frame space, we choose to decompose this task into a flow prediction phase and a flow-grounded frame generation phase. The flow prediction models the future uncertainty and spatial-temporal relationship in a 3D-cVAE model. The frame generation step helps prevent the manifold shape of predicted sequences from straying off the manifold of real sequences. We demonstrate the effectiveness of the proposed algorithm on both human action videos and dynamic texture videos.

Acknowledgement. This work is supported in part by the NSF CAREER Grant #1149783, gifts from Adobe and NVIDIA. YJL is supported by Adobe and Snap Inc. Research Fellowship.

References

1. Ekman, M., Kok, P., de Lange, F.P.: Time-compressed preplay of anticipated events in human primary visual cortex. Nat. Commun. **8**, 15276 (2017)
2. Mathieu, M., Couprie, C., LeCun, Y.: Deep multi-scale video prediction beyond mean square error. In: ICLR (2016)
3. Xingjian, S., Chen, Z., Wang, H., Yeung, D.Y., Wong, W.K., Woo, W.C.: Convolutional LSTM network: a machine learning approach for precipitation nowcasting. In: NIPS (2015)
4. Villegas, R., Yang, J., Hong, S., Lin, X., Lee, H.: Decomposing motion and content for natural video sequence prediction. In: ICLR (2017)
5. Denton, E., Birodkar, V.: Unsupervised learning of disentangled representations from video. In: NIPS (2017)
6. Tran, D., Bourdev, L., Fergus, R., Torresani, L., Paluri, M.: Learning spatiotemporal features with 3D convolutional networks. In: ICCV (2015)
7. Walker, J., Doersch, C., Gupta, A., Hebert, M.: An uncertain future: forecasting from static images using variational autoencoders. In: Leibe, B., Matas, J., Sebe, N., Welling, M. (eds.) ECCV 2016. LNCS, vol. 9911, pp. 835–851. Springer, Cham (2016). https://doi.org/10.1007/978-3-319-46478-7_51
8. Xue, T., Wu, J., Bouman, K., Freeman, B.: Visual dynamics: probabilistic future frame synthesis via cross convolutional networks. In: NIPS (2016)
9. Yuen, J., Torralba, A.: A data-driven approach for event prediction. In: Daniilidis, K., Maragos, P., Paragios, N. (eds.) ECCV 2010. LNCS, vol. 6312, pp. 707–720. Springer, Heidelberg (2010). https://doi.org/10.1007/978-3-642-15552-9_51
10. Lan, T., Chen, T.-C., Savarese, S.: A hierarchical representation for future action prediction. In: Fleet, D., Pajdla, T., Schiele, B., Tuytelaars, T. (eds.) ECCV 2014. LNCS, vol. 8691, pp. 689–704. Springer, Cham (2014). https://doi.org/10.1007/978-3-319-10578-9_45
11. Hoai, M., De la Torre, F.: Max-margin early event detectors. IJCV **107**(2), 191–202 (2014)
12. Kitani, K.M., Ziebart, B.D., Bagnell, J.A., Hebert, M.: Activity forecasting. In: Fitzgibbon, A., Lazebnik, S., Perona, P., Sato, Y., Schmid, C. (eds.) ECCV 2012. LNCS, vol. 7575, pp. 201–214. Springer, Heidelberg (2012). https://doi.org/10.1007/978-3-642-33765-9_15
13. Vondrick, C., Pirsiavash, H., Torralba, A.: Anticipating visual representations from unlabeled video. In: CVPR (2016)

14. Walker, J., Gupta, A., Hebert, M.: Dense optical flow prediction from a static image. In: ICCV (2015)
15. Srivastava, N., Mansimov, E., Salakhudinov, R.: Unsupervised learning of video representations using LSTMS. In: ICML (2015)
16. Oh, J., Guo, X., Lee, H., Lewis, R.L., Singh, S.: Action-conditional video prediction using deep networks in atari games. In: NIPS (2015)
17. Babaeizadeh, M., Finn, C., Erhan, D., Campbell, R.H., Levine, S.: Stochastic variational video prediction. In: ICLR (2018)
18. Finn, C., Levine, S.: Deep visual foresight for planning robot motion. In: ICRA (2017)
19. Vondrick, C., Pirsiavash, H., Torralba, A.: Generating videos with scene dynamics. In: NIPS (2016)
20. Liang, X., Lee, L., Dai, W., Xing, E.P.: Dual motion GAN for future-flow embedded video prediction. In: ICCV (2017)
21. Tulyakov, S., Liu, M.Y., Yang, X., Kautz, J.: Mocogan: decomposing motion and content for video generation. arXiv preprint arXiv:1707.04993 (2017)
22. Finn, C., Goodfellow, I., Levine, S.: Unsupervised learning for physical interaction through video prediction. In: NIPS (2016)
23. Vondrick, C., Torralba, A.: Generating the future with adversarial transformers. In: CVPR (2017)
24. Chao, Y.W., Yang, J., Price, B., Cohen, S., Deng, J.: Forecasting human dynamics from static images. In: CVPR (2017)
25. Villegas, R., Yang, J., Zou, Y., Sohn, S., Lin, X., Lee, H.: Learning to generate long-term future via hierarchical prediction. In: ICML (2017)
26. Doretto, G., Chiuso, A., Wu, Y.N., Soatto, S.: Dynamic textures. IJCV **51**(2), 91–109 (2003)
27. Yuan, L., Wen, F., Liu, C., Shum, H.-Y.: Synthesizing dynamic texture with closed-loop linear dynamic system. In: Pajdla, T., Matas, J. (eds.) ECCV 2004. LNCS, vol. 3022, pp. 603–616. Springer, Heidelberg (2004). https://doi.org/10.1007/978-3-540-24671-8_48
28. Xie, J., Zhu, S.C., Wu, Y.N.: Synthesizing dynamic patterns by spatial-temporal generative convnet. In: CVPR (2017)
29. Kingma, D.P., Welling, M.: Auto-encoding variational bayes. In: ICLR (2014)
30. Sohn, K., Lee, H., Yan, X.: Learning structured output representation using deep conditional generative models. In: NIPS (2015)
31. Reed, S.E., Zhang, Y., Zhang, Y., Lee, H.: Deep visual analogy-making. In: NIPS (2015)
32. Zhou, T., Tulsiani, S., Sun, W., Malik, J., Efros, A.A.: View synthesis by appearance flow. In: Leibe, B., Matas, J., Sebe, N., Welling, M. (eds.) ECCV 2016. LNCS, vol. 9908, pp. 286–301. Springer, Cham (2016). https://doi.org/10.1007/978-3-319-46493-0_18
33. Liu, Z., Yeh, R., Tang, X., Liu, Y., Agarwala, A.: Video frame synthesis using deep voxel flow. In: ICCV (2017)
34. Park, E., Yang, J., Yumer, E., Ceylan, D., Berg, A.C.: Transformation-grounded image generation network for novel 3D view synthesis. In: CVPR (2017)
35. Chopra, S., Hadsell, R., LeCun, Y.: Learning a similarity metric discriminatively, with application to face verification. In: CVPR (2005)
36. Johnson, J., Alahi, A., Fei-Fei, L.: Perceptual losses for real-time style transfer and super-resolution. In: Leibe, B., Matas, J., Sebe, N., Welling, M. (eds.) ECCV 2016. LNCS, vol. 9906, pp. 694–711. Springer, Cham (2016). https://doi.org/10.1007/978-3-319-46475-6_43

37. Dosovitskiy, A., Brox, T.: Generating images with perceptual similarity metrics based on deep networks. In: NIPS (2016)
38. Simonyan, K., Zisserman, A.: Very deep convolutional networks for large-scale image recognition. In: ICLR (2015)
39. van der Maaten, L., Hinton, G.: Visualizing data using t-SNE. JMLR **9**(Nov), 2579–2605 (2008)
40. Wu, Z., et al.: 3D shapenets: a deep representation for volumetric shapes. In: CVPR (2015)
41. Ranjan, A., Black, M.J.: Optical flow estimation using a spatial pyramid network. In: CVPR (2017)
42. Schuldt, C., Laptev, I., Caputo, B.: Recognizing human actions: a local SVM approach. In: ICPR (2004)
43. Gao, R., Xiong, B., Grauman, K.: Im2Flow: motion hallucination from static images for action recognition. arXiv preprint arXiv:1712.04109 (2017)
44. Zhang, R., Isola, P., Efros, A.A., Shechtman, E., Wang, O.: The unreasonable effectiveness of deep networks as a perceptual metric. In: CVPR (2018)
45. Krizhevsky, A., Sutskever, I., Hinton, G.E.: Imagenet classification with deep convolutional neural networks. In: NIPS (2012)
46. Tsai, Y.H., Shen, X., Lin, Z., Sunkavalli, K., Yang, M.H.: Sky is not the limit: semantic-aware sky replacement. ACM Trans. Graph. **35**(4), 149–159 (2016)

Learning to Reconstruct High-Quality 3D Shapes with Cascaded Fully Convolutional Networks

Yan-Pei Cao[1,2(✉)], Zheng-Ning Liu[1], Zheng-Fei Kuang[1], Leif Kobbelt[3], and Shi-Min Hu[1]

[1] Tsinghua University, Beijing, China
caoyanpei@gmail.com, lzhengning@gmail.com, kzf15@mails.tsinghua.edu.cn,
shimin@tsinghua.edu.cn
[2] Owlii Inc., Beijing, China
[3] RWTH Aachen University, Aachen, Germany
kobbelt@cs.rwth-aachen.de

Abstract. We present a data-driven approach to reconstructing high-resolution and detailed volumetric representations of 3D shapes. Although well studied, algorithms for volumetric fusion from multi-view depth scans are still prone to scanning noise and occlusions, making it hard to obtain high-fidelity 3D reconstructions. In this paper, inspired by recent advances in efficient 3D deep learning techniques, we introduce a novel cascaded 3D convolutional network architecture, which learns to reconstruct implicit surface representations from noisy and incomplete depth maps in a progressive, coarse-to-fine manner. To this end, we also develop an algorithm for end-to-end training of the proposed cascaded structure. Qualitative and quantitative experimental results on both simulated and real-world datasets demonstrate that the presented approach outperforms existing state-of-the-art work in terms of quality and fidelity of reconstructed models.

Keywords: High-fidelity 3D reconstruction · Cascaded architecture

1 Introduction

High-quality reconstruction of 3D objects and scenes is key to 3D environment understanding, mixed reality applications, as well as the next generation of robotics, and has been one of the major frontiers of computer vision and computer graphics research for years [13,18,30,39,42]. Meanwhile, the availability of consumer-grade RGB-D sensors, such as the *Microsoft Kinect* and the *Intel*

Y.-P. Cao and Z.-N. Liu—Equal contribution.

Electronic supplementary material The online version of this chapter (https://doi.org/10.1007/978-3-030-01240-3_38) contains supplementary material, which is available to authorized users.

RealSense, involves more novice users to the process of scanning surrounding 3D environments, opening up the need for robust reconstruction algorithms which are resilient to errors in the input data (e.g., noise, distortion, and missing areas).

In spite of recent advances in 3D environment reconstruction, acquiring high-fidelity 3D shapes with imperfect data from casual scanning procedures and consumer-level RGB-D sensors is still a particularly challenging problem. Since the pioneering *KinectFusion* work [39], many 3D reconstruction systems, both real-time [18,29,32,52,59] and offline [13], have been proposed, which often use a volumetric representation of the scene geometry, i.e., the truncated signed distance function (TSDF) [17]. However, depth measurement acquired by consumer depth cameras contains a significant amount of noise, plus limited scanning angles lead to missing areas, making vanilla depth fusion suffer from blurring surface details and incomplete geometry. Another line of research [30,40,46] focuses on reconstructing complete geometry from noisy and sparsely-sampled point clouds, but cannot process point clouds with a large percentage of missing data and may produce bulging artifacts.

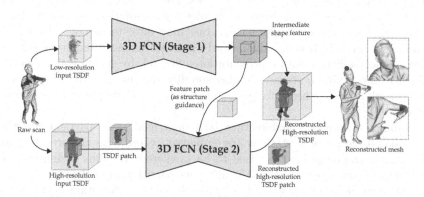

Fig. 1. Illustration of a two-stage 3D-CFCN architecture. Given partial and noisy raw depth scans as input, a fused low-resolution TSDF volume is fed to the stage-1 3D fully convolutional network (3D-FCN), producing an intermediate representation. Exploiting this intermediate feature, the network then (1) regresses a low-resolution but complete TSDF and (2) predicts which TSDF patches should be further refined. For each patch that needs further refinements, the corresponding block is cropped from a fused high-resolution input TSDF, and the stage-2 3D-FCN uses it to infer a detailed high-resolution local TSDF volume, which substitutes the corresponding region in the aforementioned regressed TSDF and thus improves the output's resolution. Note a patch of the global intermediate representation also flows into stage 2 to provide structure guidance. The rightmost column shows the high-quality reconstruction. Close-ups show accurately reconstructed details, e.g., facial details, fingers, and wrinkles on clothes. Note the input scan is fused from 4 viewpoints.

The wider availability of large-scale 3D model repositories [6,61] stimulates the development of data-driven approaches for shape reconstruction and completion. Assembly-based methods, such as [10,49], require carefully *segmented*

3D databases as input, operate on a few specific classes of objects, and can only generate shapes with limited variety. On the other hand, recent deep learning-based approaches [14,22,28,48,50,51,54,55,60,63,64] mostly focus on inferring 3D geometry from single-view images [22,50,51,54,55,63,64] or high-level information [48,60] and often get stuck at low resolutions (typically 32^3 voxel resolution) due to high memory consumption, which is far too low for recovering geometric details.

In this work, we present a coarse-to-fine approach to high-fidelity volumetric reconstruction of 3D shapes from noisy and incomplete inputs using a 3D cascaded fully convolutional network (3D-CFCN) architecture, which outperforms state-of-the-art alternatives regarding the resolution and accuracy of reconstructed models. Our approach chooses recently introduced octree-based efficient 3D deep learning data structures [43,53,56] as the basic building block, however, instead of employing a standard single-stage convolutional neural network (CNN), we propose to use multi-stage network cascades for detailed shape information reconstruction, where the object geometry is predicted and refined progressively via a sequence of sub-networks. The rationale for choosing the cascaded structure is two-fold. First, to predict high-resolution (e.g., 512^3, 1024^3, or even higher) geometry information, one may have to deploy a deeper 3D neural network, which could significantly increase memory requirements even using memory-efficient data representations. Second, by splitting the geometry inference into multiple stages, we also simplify the learning tasks, since each sub-network now only needs to learn to reconstruct 3D shapes at a certain resolution.

Training a cascaded architecture is a nontrivial task, particularly when octree-based data representations are employed, where both the *structure* and the *value* of the output octree need to be predicted. We thus design the sub-networks to learn where to refine the 3D space partitioning of the input volume, and the same information is used to guide the data propagation between consecutive stages as well, which makes end-to-end training feasible by avoiding exhaustively propagating every volume block.

The primary contribution of our work is a novel learning-based, progressive approach for high-fidelity 3D shape reconstruction from imperfect data. To train and quantitatively evaluate our model on real-world 3D shapes, we also contribute a dataset containing both detailed full body reconstructions and raw depth scans of 10 subjects. We then conduct careful experiments on both simulated and real-world datasets, comparing the proposed framework to a variety of state-of-the-art alternatives. These experiments show that, when dealing with noisy and incomplete inputs, our approach produces 3D shapes with significantly higher accuracy and quality than other existing methods.[1]

---

[1] We will make our 3D-CFCN implementation publicly available.

2   Related Work

There has been a large body of work focused on 3D reconstruction over the past a few decades. We refer the reader to [2] and [9] for detailed surveys of methods for reconstructing 3D objects from point clouds and RGB-D streams, respectively. Here we only summarize the most relevant previous approaches and categorize them as geometric, assembly-based, and learning-based approaches.

Geometric Approaches. In the presence of sample noise and missing data, many choose to exploit the smoothness assumption, which constrains the reconstructed geometry to satisfy a certain level of smoothness. Gradient-domain methods [1,4,30] require that the input point clouds be equipped with (oriented) normals and utilize them to estimate an implicit soft indicator function which discriminates the interior region from the exterior of a 3D shape. Similarly, [5,36] use globally supported radial basis functions (RBFs) to interpolate the surface. On the other hand, a series of moving least squares (MLS) -based methods [25,41] attack 3D reconstruction by fitting the input point clouds to a spatially varying low-degree polynomial. By assuming local or global surface smoothness, these approaches, to a certain extent, are robust to noise, outliers, and missing data.

Sensor visibility is another widely used prior in scan integration for object and scene reconstruction [17,23], which acts as an effective regularizer for structured noise [65] and can be used to infer empty spaces. For large-scale indoor scene reconstruction, since the prominent KinectFusion, plenty of systems [13,18,29] have been proposed. However, they are mostly focused on improving the accuracy and robustness of camera tracking in order to obtain a globally consistent model.

Compared to these methods, we propose to learn natural 3D shape priors from massive training samples for shape completion and reconstruction, which better explores the 3D shape space and avoids undesired reconstructed geometries resulted from hand-crafted priors.

Assembly-Based Approaches. Another line of work assumes that a target object can be described as a composition of primitive shapes (e.g., planes, cuboids, spheres, etc.) or known object parts. [8,45] detect primitives in input point clouds of CAD models and optimize their placement as well as the spatial relationship between them via graph cuts. The method introduced in [47] first interactively segments the input point cloud and then retrieves a complete and similar 3D model to replace each segment, while [10] extends this idea by exploiting the contextual knowledge learned from a scene database to automate the segmentation as well as improve the accuracy of shape retrieval. To increase the granularity of the reconstruction to the object component level, [49] proposes to reassemble parts from different models, aiming to find the combination of candidates which conforms the input RGB-D scan best. Although these approaches can deal with partial input data and bring in semantic information, 3D models obtained by them still suffer from the lack of geometric diversity.

Learning-Based Approaches. 3D deep neural networks have achieved impressive results on various tasks [7,15,61], such as 3D shape classification, retrieval, and segmentation. As for generative tasks, previous research mostly focuses on inferring 3D shapes from (single-view) 2D images, either with only RGB channels [14,28,50,54,55,60,63], or with depth information [22,51,64]. While showing promising advances, these techniques are only capable of generating rough 3D shapes at low resolutions. Similarly, in [48,57], shape completion is also performed on low-resolution voxel grids due to the high demand of computational resources.

Aiming to complete and reconstruct 3D shapes at higher resolutions, [19] proposes a 3D Encoder-Predictor Network (3D-EPN) to firstly predict a coarse but complete shape volume and then refine it via an iterative volumetric patch synthesis process, which copy-pastes voxels from k-nearest-neighbors to improve the resolution of each predicted patch. [26] extends 3D-EPN by introducing a local 3D CNN to perform patch-level surface refinement. However, these methods both need separate and time-consuming steps before local inference, either nearest neighbor queries [19], or 3D boundary detection [26]. By contrast, our approach only requires a single forward pass for 3D shape reconstruction and produces higher-resolution results (e.g., 512^3 vs. 128^3 or 256^3). On the other hand, [27,53] propose efficient 3D convolutional architectures by using octree representations, which are designed to decode high-resolution geometry information from dense intermediate features; nevertheless, no volumetric convolutional encoders and corresponding shape reconstruction architectures are provided. While [42] presents an OctNet-based [43] end-to-end deep learning framework for depth fusion, it refines the intermediate volumetric output globally, which makes it infeasible for producing reconstruction results at higher resolutions even with memory-efficient data structures. Instead, our 3D-CFCN learns to refine output volumes at the level of local patches, and thus significantly reduces the memory and computational cost.

3   Method

This section introduces our 3D-CFCN model. We first give a condensed review of relevant concepts and techniques in Sect. 3.1. Then we present the proposed architecture and its corresponding training pipeline in Sects. 3.2 and 3.3. Section 3.4 summaries the procedure of collecting and generating the data which we used for training our model.

3.1   Preliminaries

Volumetric Representation and Integration. The choice of underlying data representation for fusing depth measurements is key to high-quality 3D reconstruction. Approaches varies from point-based representations [31,58], 2.5D fields [24,38], to volumetric methods based on occupancy maps [62] or implicit surfaces [17,18]. Among them, TSDF-based volumetric representations have become the preferred method due to their ability to model continuous surfaces, efficiency for incremental updates in parallel, and simplicity for extracting surface interfaces. In this work, we adopt the definition of TSDF from [39]:

$$V(\mathbf{p}) = \Psi(S(\mathbf{p})), \tag{1}$$

$$S(\mathbf{p}) = \begin{cases} \|\mathbf{p} - \partial\Omega\|_2, & if\ \mathbf{p} \in \Omega \\ -\|\mathbf{p} - \partial\Omega\|_2, & if\ \mathbf{p} \in \Omega^c \end{cases}, \tag{2}$$

$$\Psi(\eta) = \begin{cases} \min(1, \frac{\eta}{\mu})\operatorname{sgn}(\eta), & if\ \eta \geq -\mu \\ invalid, & otherwise \end{cases}, \tag{3}$$

where S is the standard signed distance function (SDF) with Ω being the object volume, and Ψ denotes the truncation function with μ being the corresponding truncation threshold. The truncation is performed to avoid surface interference, since in practice during scan fusion, the depth measurement is only locally reliable due to surface occlusions. In essence, a TSDF obliviously encodes free space, uncertain measurements, and unknown areas.

Given a set of depth scans at hand, we follow the approach in [17] to integrate them into a TSDF volume:

$$V(\mathbf{p}) = \frac{\sum w_i(\mathbf{p})\,V_i(\mathbf{p})}{\sum w_i(\mathbf{p})}, \tag{4}$$

where $V_i(\mathbf{p})$ and $w_i(\mathbf{p})$ are the TSDFs and weight functions from the i-th depth scan, respectively.

OctNet. 3D CNNs are a natural choice for operating TSDF volumes under the end-to-end learning framework. However, the cubic growth of computational and memory requirements becomes a fundamental obstacle for training and deploying 3D neural networks at high resolution. Recently, there emerges several work [43,53,56] that propose to exploit the sparsity in 3D data and employ octree-based data structures to reduce the memory consumption, among which we take OctNet [43] as our basic building block.

In OctNet, features and data are organized in the *grid-octree* data structure, which consists of a grid of shallow octrees with maximum depth 3. The structure of shallow octrees are encoded as bit strings so that the features and data of sparse octants can be packed into continuous arrays. Common operations in convolutional networks (e.g., convolution, pooling and unpooling) are defined on the grid-octree structure correspondingly. Therefore, the computational and memory cost are significantly reduced, while the OctNet itself, as a processing module, can be plugged into most existing 3D CNN architectures transparently. However, one major limitation of OctNet is that the structure of grid-octrees is determined by the input data and keeps fixed during training and inference, which is undesirable for reconstruction tasks where hole filling and detail refinement need to be performed. We thus propose an approach to eliminate this drawback in Sect. 3.2.

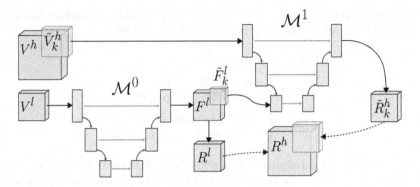

Fig. 2. Architecture of a two-stage 3D-CFCN. In this case, the network takes a pair of low- and high-resolution (i.e., 128^3 and 512^3) noisy TSDF volume $\{V_l, V_h\}$ as input, and produces a refined TSDF at 512^3 voxel resolution.

3.2 Architecture

Our 3D-CFCN is a cascade of volumetric reconstruction modules, which are OctNet-based fully convolutional sub-networks aiming to infer missing surface areas and refine geometric details. Each module $\mathcal{M}^i$ operates at a given voxel resolution and spatial extent. We find 512^3 *voxel resolution* and a corresponding *two-stage* architecture suffice to common daily 3D scanning tasks in our experiments, and thus will concentrate on this architecture in the rest of the paper; nevertheless, the proposed 3D-CFCN framework can be easily extended to support arbitrary resolutions and number of stages.

In our implementation, for both sub-networks, we adopt the U-net architecture [44] while substituting convolution and pooling layers with the corresponding operations from OctNet. Skip connections are also employed between corresponding encoder and decoder layers to make sure the structures of input volumes are preserved in the inferred output predictions. To complete the partial input data and refine its grid-octree structure, we refrain from using OctNet's unpooling operation and propose a *structure refinement module*, which learns to predict whether an octant needs to be split for recovering finer geometric details.

The first sub-network, $\mathcal{M}^0$, receives the encoded low-resolution (i.e., 128^3) TSDF volume V^l (see Sect. 3.4), which is fused from raw depth scans $\{\mathcal{D}_i\}$ of an 3D object $\mathcal{S}$, as input and produces a feature map F^l as well as a reconstructed TSDF volume R^l at the same resolution. Then for each 16^3 patch $\tilde{F}^l_k$ of F^l, we use a modified structure refinement module to predict if its corresponding block in R^l needs further improvement.

If a TSDF patch $\tilde{R}^l_k$ is predicted to be further refined, we then crop its corresponding 64^3 patch $\tilde{V}^h_k$ from V^h, which is an encoded TSDF volume fused from the same depth scans $\{\mathcal{D}_i\}$, but at a higher voxel resolution, i.e., 512^3. $\tilde{V}^h_k$ is next fed to the second stage $\mathcal{M}^1$ to produce a local feature map $\tilde{F}^h_k$ with increased *spatial* resolution and reconstruct a more detailed local 3D patch $\tilde{R}^h_k$

of $\mathcal{S}$. Meanwhile, since input local TSDF patches $\{\tilde{V}_k^h\}$ may suffer from a large portion of missing data, we also propagate $\{\tilde{F}_k^l\}$ to incorporate global guidance. More specifically, a propagated $\tilde{F}_k^l$ is concatenated with the high-level 3D feature map after the second pooling layer in $\mathcal{M}^1$ (see Fig. 2). Note this extra path, in return, also helps to refine F^l during back propagation. Finally, the regressed local TSDF patch $\{\tilde{R}_k^h\}$ is substituted back into the global TSDF, which can be further used to extract surfaces.

To avoid inconsistency across TSDF patch boundaries, we add interval overlaps when cropping feature maps and TSDF volumes. When cropping $\{\tilde{F}_k^l\}$, we expand two more voxels on each side of the 3D patch, making the actual resolution of $\{\tilde{F}_k^l\}$ grow to 20^3; similarly, for $\{\tilde{V}_k^h\}$ and $\{\tilde{F}_k^h\}$, we apply 8-voxel overlapping and increase their resolution to 80^3. However, when substituting back $\{\tilde{R}_k^h\}$, overlapping regions are discarded. So in its essence, this cropping approach acts as a smart padding scheme. Note that all local patches are still organized in grid-octrees.

Structure Refinement Module. Since the unpooling operation of OctNet restrains the possibility of refining the octree structure on-the-fly, inspired by [42, 53], we propose to replace unpooling layers with a structure refinement module. Instead of inferring new octree structures implicitly from reconstructions as in [42], we use 3^3 convolutional filters to directly predict from feature maps whether an octant should be further split. In contrast, OGN [53] predicts three-state masks using 1^3 filters followed by three-way softmax. To determine if a 3D local patch needs to be fed to $\mathcal{M}^1$, we take the average "split score" of all the octants in this patch and compare it with a confidence threshold $\rho \ (= 0.5)$. By employing this adaptive partitioning and propagation scheme, we achieve high-resolution volumetric reconstruction while keeping the computational and memory cost to a minimum level.

3.3 Training

The 3D-CFCN is trained in a supervised fashion on a TSDF dataset $\{\mathcal{F}_n = \{V^l, V^h, G^l, G^h\}\}$ in two phases, where V^l and V^h denote the incomplete input TSDFs at low and high voxel resolution, while G^l and G^h are low- and high-resolution ground-truth TSDFs, respectively.

In the first phase, $\mathcal{M}^0$ is trained alone with a hybrid of ℓ_1, binary cross entropy, and structure loss:

$$\mathcal{L}(\theta; V^l, G^l) = \mathcal{L}_{\ell_1} + \lambda_1 \mathcal{L}_{bce} + \lambda_2 \mathcal{L}_s. \tag{5}$$

The ℓ_1 term is designed for TSDF denoising and reconstruction, and we employ the auxiliary binary cross entropy loss $\mathcal{L}_{bce}$ to provide the network more guidance for learning shape completion; while in our experiments, we find $\mathcal{L}_{bce}$ also leads to faster convergence. Our structure refinement module is learned with $\mathcal{L}_s$, where

$$\mathcal{L}_s = \frac{1}{|\mathcal{O}|} \sum_{o \in \mathcal{O}} BCE \left(1 - f(o', T_{gt}), p(o) \right). \tag{6}$$

Here, $\mathcal{O}$ represents the set of octants in the current grid-octree, and BCE denotes the binary cross entropy. $p(o)$ is the prediction of whether the octant o should to be split, while o' is the corresponding octant of o in the ground-truth grid-octree structure T_{gt} (in this case, the structure of G_l). We define $f(o', T_{gt})$ as an indicator function that identifies whether o' exists in T_{gt}:

$$f(o', T_{gt}) = \begin{cases} 1, \exists \, \tilde{o}', \; such \; that \; h(\tilde{o}') \leq h(o') \\ 0, otherwise \end{cases}, \tag{7}$$

where h denotes the height of an octant in the octree.

Furthermore, we employ multi-scale supervision [15,20] to alleviate potential gradient vanishing. Specifically, after each pooling operation, the feature map is concatenated with a downsampled input TSDF volume at the corresponding resolution, and we evaluate the downscaled hybrid loss at each structure refinement layer.

In the second phase, $\mathcal{M}^1$ is trained; at the same time, $\mathcal{M}^0$ is being fine-tuned. To alleviate over-fitting and speed up the training process, among all the local patches that are predicted to be fed to $\mathcal{M}^1$, we keep only K of them randomly and discard the rest (we set $K = 2$ across our experiments). At this stage, the inferred global structure $\tilde{F}_k^l$ flows into $\mathcal{M}^1$ to guide the shape completion, while the refined local features also provide feedbacks and improves $\mathcal{M}^0$. The same strategy, i.e., hybrid loss (see Eq. 5) and multi-scale supervision, is adopted here when training $\mathcal{M}^1$ together with $\mathcal{M}^0$.

3.4   Training Data Generation

Synthetic Dataset. Our first dataset is built upon the synthetic 3D shape repository ModelNet40 [61]. We choose a subset of 10 categories, with 4051 shape instances in total (3245 for training, 806 for testing). Similar to existing approaches, we set up virtual cameras around the objects[2] and render depth maps, then simulate the volumetric fusion process [17] to generate ground-truth TSDFs. To produce noisy and partial training samples, previous methods [18,26,42] add random noise and holes to the depth maps to mimic sensor noise. However, synthetic noise reproduced by this approach usually does not conform real noise distributions. Thus, we instead implement a synthetic stereo depth camera [21]. Specifically, we virtually illuminate 3D shapes with a structured light pattern, which is extracted from *Asus XTion* sensors using [12,37], and apply the PatchMatch Stereo algorithm [3] to estimate disparities (and hence depth maps) across stereo speckle images. In this way, the distribution of noise and missing area in synthesized depth images behaves much closer to real ones, thus makes the trained network generalize better on real-world data. In our experiments, we pick 2 or 4 virtual viewpoints randomly when generating training samples.

In essence, apart from shape completion, learning volumetric depth fusion is to seek a function $g(\{\mathcal{D}_1, \ldots, \mathcal{D}_n\})$ that maps raw depth scans to a noise free

---

[2] We place virtual cameras at the vertices of a icosahedron.

TSDF. Therefore, to retain information from all input depth scans, we adopt the histogram-based TSDF representation (TSDF-Hist) proposed in [42] as the encoding of our input training samples. A 10D smoothed-histogram, which uses 5 bins for negative and 5 bins for positive distances, with the first and the last bin reserved for truncated distances, is allocated for each voxel. The contribution of a depth observation is distributed linearly between the two closest bins. For outputs, we simply choose plain 1-dimensional TSDFs as the representation.

Since we employ a cascaded architecture and use multi-scale supervision during network training, we need to generate training and ground-truth sample pairs at multiple resolutions. Specifically, TSDFs at 32^3, 64^3, 128^3, 256^3, and 512^3 voxel resolutions are simultaneously generated in our experiments.

Real-World Dataset. We construct a high-quality dynamic 3D reconstruction (or, free-viewpoint video, FVV) system similar to [16] and collect 10 4D sequences of human actions, each capturing a different subject. Then a total of 9746 frames are randomly sampled from the sequences and split into training and test set by the ratio of 4:1. We name this dataset as *Human10*. For each frame, we fuse 2 or 4 randomly picked *raw depth scans* and obtain the TSDF-Hist encodings of the training sample; while the ground-truth TSDFs is produced by virtually scanning (see the previous section) the corresponding output triangle mesh of our FVV system. The sophisticated pipeline of our FVV system guarantees the quality and accuracy of the output mesh, however, the design and details of the FFV system is beyond the scope of this paper.

4   Experiments

We have evaluated our 3D-CFCN architecture on both ModelNet40 and Human10 and compared different aspects of our approach with other state-of-the-art alternatives.[3]

4.1   High-Resolution Shape Reconstruction

In our experiments, we train the 3D-CFCN separately on each dataset for 20 epochs (12 for stage 1, 8 for two stages jointly), using the ADAM optimizer [33] with 0.0001 learning rate, which takes ≈80 h to converge. Balancing weights in Eq. 5 are set to: $\lambda_1 = 0.5$ and $\lambda_2 = 0.1$. During inference, it takes ≈3.5 s on average to perform a forward pass through both stages on a NVIDIA GeForce GTX 1080 Ti. The Marching Cubes algorithm [35] is used to extract surfaces from output TSDFs. Figs. 1, 3, and 4 illustrate the high-quality reconstruction results achieved with our 3D-CFCN architecture.

In Fig. 3 we show a variety of test cases from both Human10 and ModelNet40 dataset. All the input TSDF-Hists were fused using depth maps from 2 viewpoints, and the same TSDF truncation threshold were applied. Despite the presence of substantial noise and missing data, our approach was able to reduce the noise and

---

[3] Please find more experiment results in the supplementary material.

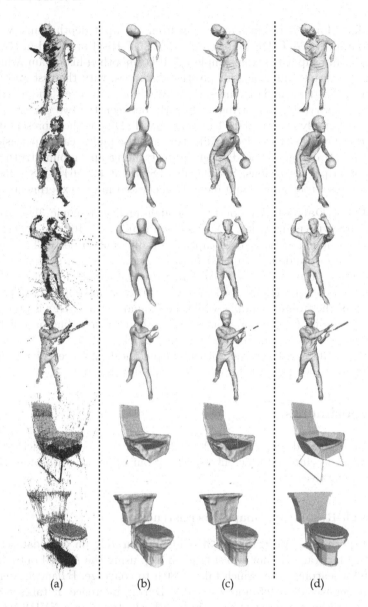

(a)   (b)   (c)   (d)

Fig. 3. Results gallery. (a): Input scans fused from 2 randomly picked viewpoints. (b): Reconstruction results of the first stage of our 3D-CFCN. (c): Full-resolution reconstruction results of the two-stage 3D-CFCN architecture. (d): Ground-truth references.

infer the missing structures, producing clean and detailed reconstructions. Comparing the second and the third column, for Human10 models, stage 2 of our 3D-CFCN significantly improved the quality by bringing more geometric details to output meshes; on the other hand, 128^3 voxel resolution suffices to ModelNet40, thus stage 2 does not show significant improves in these cases.

Auxiliary Visual Hull Information. In practice, most depth sensors can also capture synchronized color images, which opens up the possibility of getting auxiliary segmentation masks [11]. Given the segmentation masks from each view, a corresponding visual hull [34], which is essentially an occupancy volume, can be extracted. Visual hulls provide additional information about the distribution of occupied and empty spaces, which is important for shape completion. We thus evaluated the performance of our 3D-CFCN when visual hull information is available. Towards this goal, we added corresponding visual hull input branches to both two stages, which are concatenated with intermediate features after two 3^3 convolutional layers. Table 1 reports the average Hausdorff RMS distance between predicted and ground-truth 3D meshes, showing that using additional visual hull volumes as input brought a performance gain around 11%. Both TSDF-Hists and visual hull volumes in this experiment were generated using 2 viewpoints. Note that we also scaled the models in Human10 to fit into a 3^3 bounding box.

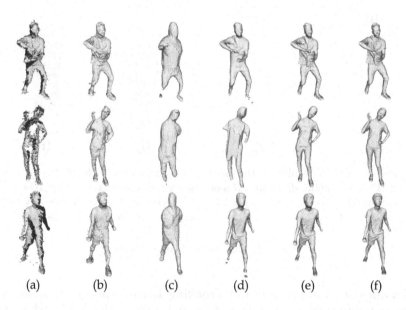

(a)   (b)   (c)   (d)   (e)   (f)

Fig. 4. Comparison of our reconstruction results with other state-of-the-art alternatives. (a): Input scans. (b): PSR [30]. (c): 3D-EPN [19]. (d): OctNetFusion [42]. (e): Ours. (f): Ground-truth references. Note the bulging artifacts on PSR's results.

Number of Viewpoints. Here we evaluated the impact of the completeness of input TSDF-Hists, i.e., the number of viewpoints used for fusing raw depth scans, on reconstruction quality. We trained and tested the 3D-CFCN architecture using TSDF-Hists fused from 2 and 4 viewpoints, listing the results in Table 1. As expected, using more depth scans led to increasing accuracy of output meshes, since input TSDF-Hists were less incomplete.

Table 1. Quantitative comparisons of shape reconstruction techniques. Relative Hausdorff RMS distance with respect to the diagonals of bounding boxes are measured against the ground-truth triangle meshes. All baseline methods use input data fused from 2 views.

	PSR	3D-EPN	OctNet-Fusion	3D-CFCN (2 views)	3D-CFCN (2 views w/visual hull)	3D-CFCN (4 views)
Human10	0.0092	0.0263	0.0040	0.0035	0.0031	0.0021
ModelNet40	0.0620	0.0178	0.0035	0.0032	0.0019	0.0010

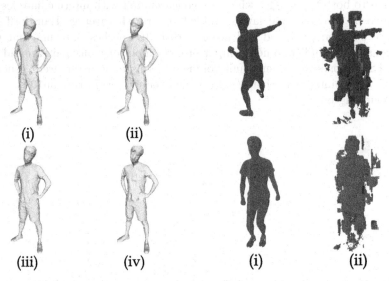

(a) Reconstruction results of the proposed 3D-CFCN under different levels of calibration error. (i): No error. (ii): 2.5%. (iii): 5%. (iv): 10%.

(b) Comparison with OGN. (i): Occupancy maps reconstructed by 3D-CFCN. (ii): Occupancy maps decoded by OGN, using features learned by 3D-CFCN.

Fig. 5. Evaluation and comparisons.

Robustness to Calibration and Tracking Error. Apart from sensor noise, calibration and tracking error is another major factor that can crack scanned models. To evaluate the robustness of the proposed approach to calibration and tracking error, we added random perturbations (from 2.5% to 10%) to ground-truth camera poses, generated corresponding test samples, and predicted the reconstruction results using 3D-CFCN. As shown in Fig. 5(a), although the network has not been trained on samples with calibration error, it can still infers geometric structures reasonably.

4.2   Comparison with Existing Approaches

Figure 4 and Table 1 compare our 3D-CFCN architecture with three learning-based state-of-the-art alternatives for 3D shape reconstruction, i.e., OctNetFusion [42], 3D-EPN [19], and OGN [53], as well as the widely used geometric method Poisson surface reconstruction (PSR) [30].

OctNetFusion. Similar to our approach, OctNetFusion adopts OctNet as the building block and learns to denoise and complete input TSDFs in a multi-stage manner. However, each stage in OctNetFusion is designed to take an up-sampled TSDF and refine it globally (i.e., each stage needs to process *all* the octants in the grid-octree at the current resolution), making it infeasible to reconstruct 3D shape at higher resolutions, as learning at higher resolutions (e.g., 512^3) not only increases the memory cost at input and output layers, but also requires deeper network structures, which further challenges the limited computational resource. Figure 4 and Table 1 summarize the comparison of our reconstruction results at 512^3 voxel resolution with OctNetFusion's results at 256^3.

3D-EPN. Without using octree-based data structures, 3D-EPN employs a hybrid approach, which first completes the input model at a low resolution (32^3) via a 3D CNN and then uses voxels from similar high-resolution models in the database to produce output distance volumes at 128^3 voxel resolution. However, as shown in Fig. 4, while being able to infer the overall shape of input models, this approach fails to recover fine geometric details due to the limited resolution.

OGN. As another relevant work to our 3D-CFCN architecture, OGN is a octree-based convolutional decoder. Although scales well to high resolution outputs, it remains challenging to recover accurate and detailed geometry information from encoded shape features via only deconvolution operations. To compare our approach with OGN, we trained the proposed 3D-CFCN on Human10 dataset to predict occupancy volumes, extracted 32^3 intermediate feature from the stage-1 3D FCN of our architecture, and used these feature maps to train an OGN. Figure 5(b) compares the occupancy maps decoded by OGN with the corresponding occupancy volumes predicted by the proposed 3D-CFCN (both at 512^3 resolution), showing that our method performs significantly better than OGN with respect to fidelity and accuracy.

5   Conclusions

We have presented a cascaded 3D convolutional network architecture for efficient and high-fidelity shape reconstruction at high resolutions. Our approach refines the volumetric representations of partial and noisy input models in a progressive and adaptive manner, which substantially simplifies the learning task and reduces computational cost. Experimental results demonstrate that the proposed method can produce high-quality reconstructions with accurate geometric details. We also believe that extending the proposed approach to reconstructing sequences is a promising direction.

Acknowledgement. This work was supported by the Joint NSFC-DFG Research Program (project number 61761136018), and the Natural Science Foundation of China (Project Number 61521002).

References

1. Alliez, P., Cohen-Steiner, D., Tong, Y., Desbrun, M.: Voronoi-based variational reconstruction of unoriented point sets. In: Symposium on Geometry Processing, vol. 7, pp. 39–48 (2007)
2. Berger, M., et al.: A survey of surface reconstruction from point clouds. In: Computer Graphics Forum, vol. 36, pp. 301–329. Wiley Online Library (2017)
3. Bleyer, M., Rhemann, C., Rother, C.: Patchmatch stereo - stereo matching with slanted support windows. In: BMVC, January 2011. https://www.microsoft.com/en-us/research/publication/patchmatch-stereo-stereo-matching-with-slanted-support-windows/
4. Calakli, F., Taubin, G.: SSD: smooth signed distance surface reconstruction. In: Computer Graphics Forum, vol. 30, pp. 1993–2002. Wiley Online Library (2011)
5. Carr, J.C., et al.: Reconstruction and representation of 3D objects with radial basis functions. In: Proceedings of the 28th Annual Conference on Computer Graphics and Interactive Techniques, pp. 67–76. ACM (2001)
6. Chang, A.X., et al.: Shapenet: an information-rich 3D model repository. arXiv preprint arXiv:1512.03012 (2015)
7. Charles, R.Q., Su, H., Kaichun, M., Guibas, L.J.: PointNet: deep learning on point sets for 3D classification and segmentation. In: 2017 IEEE Conference on Computer Vision and Pattern Recognition (CVPR), pp. 77–85. IEEE (2017)
8. Chauve, A.L., Labatut, P., Pons, J.P.: Robust piecewise-planar 3D reconstruction and completion from large-scale unstructured point data. In: 2010 IEEE Conference on Computer Vision and Pattern Recognition (CVPR), pp. 1261–1268. IEEE (2010)
9. Chen, K., Lai, Y.K., Hu, S.M.: 3D indoor scene modeling from RGB-D data: a survey. Comput. Vis. Media **1**(4), 267–278 (2015)
10. Chen, K., Lai, Y., Wu, Y.X., Martin, R.R., Hu, S.M.: Automatic semantic modeling of indoor scenes from low-quality RGB-D data using contextual information. ACM Trans. Graph. **33**(6) (2014)
11. Chen, L.C., Papandreou, G., Kokkinos, I., Murphy, K., Yuille, A.L.: DeepLab: semantic image segmentation with deep convolutional nets, atrous convolution, and fully connected CRFs. arXiv preprint arXiv:1606.00915 (2016)
12. Chen, Q., Koltun, V.: Fast MRF optimization with application to depth reconstruction. In: Proceedings of the IEEE Conference on Computer Vision and Pattern Recognition, pp. 3914–3921 (2014)
13. Choi, S., Zhou, Q.Y., Koltun, V.: Robust reconstruction of indoor scenes. In: 2015 IEEE Conference on Computer Vision and Pattern Recognition (CVPR), pp. 5556–5565, June 2015
14. Choy, C.B., Xu, D., Gwak, J.Y., Chen, K., Savarese, S.: 3D-R2N2: a unified approach for single and multi-view 3D object reconstruction. In: Leibe, B., Matas, J., Sebe, N., Welling, M. (eds.) ECCV 2016. LNCS, vol. 9912, pp. 628–644. Springer, Cham (2016). https://doi.org/10.1007/978-3-319-46484-8_38

15. Çiçek, Ö., Abdulkadir, A., Lienkamp, S.S., Brox, T., Ronneberger, O.: 3D U-net: learning dense volumetric segmentation from sparse annotation. In: Ourselin, S., Joskowicz, L., Sabuncu, M.R., Unal, G., Wells, W. (eds.) MICCAI 2016. LNCS, vol. 9901, pp. 424–432. Springer, Cham (2016). https://doi.org/10.1007/978-3-319-46723-8_49

16. Collet, A., et al.: High-quality streamable free-viewpoint video. ACM Trans. Graph. **34**(4), 69:1–69:13 (2015). https://doi.org/10.1145/2766945

17. Curless, B., Levoy, M.: A volumetric method for building complex models from range images. In: Proceedings of the 23rd Annual Conference on Computer Graphics and Interactive Techniques, SIGGRAPH 1996, pp. 303–312. ACM, New York (1996). https://doi.org/10.1145/237170.237269

18. Dai, A., Nießner, M., Zollhöfer, M., Izadi, S., Theobalt, C.: Bundlefusion: real-time globally consistent 3D reconstruction using on-the-fly surface reintegration. ACM Trans. Graph. **36**(3), 24:1–24:18 (2017). https://doi.org/10.1145/3054739

19. Dai, A., Qi, C.R., Nießner, M.: Shape completion using 3D-encoder-predictor CNNs and shape synthesis. In: Proceedings of IEEE Conference on Computer Vision and Pattern Recognition (CVPR), vol. 3 (2017)

20. Dou, Q., et al.: 3D deeply supervised network for automated segmentation of volumetric medical images. Med. Image Anal. **41**, 40–54 (2017)

21. Fanello, S.R., et al.: Ultrastereo: efficient learning-based matching for active stereo systems. In: 2017 IEEE Conference on Computer Vision and Pattern Recognition (CVPR), pp. 6535–6544. IEEE (2017)

22. Firman, M., Mac Aodha, O., Julier, S., Brostow, G.J.: Structured prediction of unobserved voxels from a single depth image. In: Proceedings of the IEEE Conference on Computer Vision and Pattern Recognition, pp. 5431–5440 (2016)

23. Fuhrmann, S., Goesele, M.: Fusion of depth maps with multiple scales. In: ACM Transactions on Graphics (TOG), vol. 30, p. 148. ACM (2011)

24. Gallup, D., Pollefeys, M., Frahm, J.-M.: 3D reconstruction using an n-layer heightmap. In: Goesele, M., Roth, S., Kuijper, A., Schiele, B., Schindler, K. (eds.) DAGM 2010. LNCS, vol. 6376, pp. 1–10. Springer, Heidelberg (2010). https://doi.org/10.1007/978-3-642-15986-2_1

25. Guennebaud, G., Gross, M.: Algebraic point set surfaces. In: ACM Transactions on Graphics (TOG), vol. 26, p. 23. ACM (2007)

26. Han, X., Li, Z., Huang, H., Kalogerakis, E., Yu, Y.: High-resolution shape completion using deep neural networks for global structure and local geometry inference. In: IEEE International Conference on Computer Vision (ICCV), October 2017

27. Häne, C., Tulsiani, S., Malik, J.: Hierarchical surface prediction for 3D object reconstruction. arXiv preprint arXiv:1704.00710 (2017)

28. Ji, M., Gall, J., Zheng, H., Liu, Y., Fang, L.: SurfaceNet: an end-to-end 3D neural network for multiview stereopsis. arXiv preprint arXiv:1708.01749 (2017)

29. Kähler, O., Prisacariu, V.A., Murray, D.W.: Real-time large-scale dense 3D reconstruction with loop closure. In: Leibe, B., Matas, J., Sebe, N., Welling, M. (eds.) ECCV 2016. LNCS, vol. 9912, pp. 500–516. Springer, Cham (2016). https://doi.org/10.1007/978-3-319-46484-8_30

30. Kazhdan, M., Hoppe, H.: Screened poisson surface reconstruction. ACM Trans. Graph. **32**(3), 29:1–29:13 (2013). https://doi.org/10.1145/2487228.2487237

31. Keller, M., Lefloch, D., Lambers, M., Izadi, S., Weyrich, T., Kolb, A.: Real-time 3D reconstruction in dynamic scenes using point-based fusion. In: 2013 International Conference on 3D Vision-3DV 2013, pp. 1–8. IEEE (2013)

32. Kerl, C., Sturm, J., Cremers, D.: Robust odometry estimation for RGB-D cameras. In: 2013 IEEE International Conference on Robotics and Automation, pp. 3748–3754, May 2013. https://doi.org/10.1109/ICRA.2013.6631104
33. Kingma, D.P., Ba, J.: Adam: a method for stochastic optimization. arXiv preprint arXiv:1412.6980 (2014)
34. Kutulakos, K.N., Seitz, S.M.: A theory of shape by space carving. Int. J. Comput. Vis. **38**(3), 199–218 (2000)
35. Lorensen, W.E., Cline, H.E.: Marching cubes: a high resolution 3D surface construction algorithm. In: ACM SIGGRAPH Computer Graphics, vol. 21, pp. 163–169. ACM (1987)
36. Macedo, I., Gois, J.P., Velho, L.: Hermite radial basis functions implicits. In: Computer Graphics Forum, vol. 30, pp. 27–42. Wiley Online Library (2011)
37. McIlroy, P., Izadi, S., Fitzgibbon, A.: Kinectrack: 3D pose estimation using a projected dense dot pattern. IEEE Trans. Vis. Comput. Graph. **20**(6), 839–851 (2014)
38. Meilland, M., Comport, A.I.: On unifying key-frame and voxel-based dense visual slam at large scales. In: 2013 IEEE/RSJ International Conference on Intelligent Robots and Systems (IROS), pp. 3677–3683. IEEE (2013)
39. Newcombe, R.A., et al.: KinectFusion: real-time dense surface mapping and tracking. In: 2011 10th IEEE International Symposium on Mixed and Augmented Reality, pp. 127–136, October 2011
40. Oeztireli, A.C., Guennebaud, G., Gross, M.: Feature preserving point set surfaces based on non-linear kernel regression. Comput. Graph. Forum (2009). https://doi.org/10.1111/j.1467-8659.2009.01388.x
41. Öztireli, A.C., Guennebaud, G., Gross, M.: Feature preserving point set surfaces based on non-linear kernel regression. In: Computer Graphics Forum, vol. 28, pp. 493–501. Wiley Online Library (2009)
42. Riegler, G., Ulusoy, A.O., Bischof, H., Geiger, A.: OctNetFusion: learning depth fusion from data. In: Proceedings of the International Conference on 3D Vision (2017)
43. Riegler, G., Ulusoy, A.O., Geiger, A.: OctNet: learning deep 3D representations at high resolutions. In: Proceedings of the IEEE Conference on Computer Vision and Pattern Recognition, vol. 3 (2017)
44. Ronneberger, O., Fischer, P., Brox, T.: U-net: convolutional networks for biomedical image segmentation. In: Navab, N., Hornegger, J., Wells, W.M., Frangi, A.F. (eds.) MICCAI 2015. LNCS, vol. 9351, pp. 234–241. Springer, Cham (2015). https://doi.org/10.1007/978-3-319-24574-4_28
45. Schnabel, R., Degener, P., Klein, R.: Completion and reconstruction with primitive shapes. In: Computer Graphics Forum, vol. 28, pp. 503–512. Wiley Online Library (2009)
46. Shan, Q., Curless, B., Furukawa, Y., Hernandez, C., Seitz, S.M.: Occluding contours for multi-view stereo. In: 2014 IEEE Conference on Computer Vision and Pattern Recognition, pp. 4002–4009, June 2014
47. Shao, T., Xu, W., Zhou, K., Wang, J., Li, D., Guo, B.: An interactive approach to semantic modeling of indoor scenes with an RGBD camera. ACM Trans. Graph. (TOG) **31**(6), 136 (2012)
48. Sharma, A., Grau, O., Fritz, M.: VConv-DAE: deep volumetric shape learning without object labels. In: Hua, G., Jégou, H. (eds.) ECCV 2016. LNCS, vol. 9915, pp. 236–250. Springer, Cham (2016). https://doi.org/10.1007/978-3-319-49409-8_20
49. Shen, C.H., Fu, H., Chen, K., Hu, S.M.: Structure recovery by part assembly. ACM Trans. Graph. **31**(6), 180:1–180:11 (2012). https://doi.org/10.1145/2366145.2366199

50. Sinha, A., Unmesh, A., Huang, Q., Ramani, K.: SurfNet: generating 3D shape surfaces using deep residual networks. In: Proceedings of CVPR (2017)
51. Song, S., Yu, F., Zeng, A., Chang, A.X., Savva, M., Funkhouser, T.: Semantic scene completion from a single depth image. In: 2017 IEEE Conference on Computer Vision and Pattern Recognition (CVPR), pp. 190–198. IEEE (2017)
52. Steinbrcker, F., Sturm, J., Cremers, D.: Real-time visual odometry from dense RGB-D images. In: 2011 IEEE International Conference on Computer Vision Workshops (ICCV Workshops), pp. 719–722, November 2011. https://doi.org/10.1109/ICCVW.2011.6130321
53. Tatarchenko, M., Dosovitskiy, A., Brox, T.: Octree generating networks: efficient convolutional architectures for high-resolution 3D outputs. In: IEEE International Conference on Computer Vision (ICCV) (2017). http://lmb.informatik.uni-freiburg.de/Publications/2017/TDB17b
54. Tatarchenko, M., Dosovitskiy, A., Brox, T.: Multi-view 3D models from single images with a convolutional network. In: Leibe, B., Matas, J., Sebe, N., Welling, M. (eds.) ECCV 2016. LNCS, vol. 9911, pp. 322–337. Springer, Cham (2016). https://doi.org/10.1007/978-3-319-46478-7_20
55. Tulsiani, S., Zhou, T., Efros, A.A., Malik, J.: Multi-view supervision for single-view reconstruction via differentiable ray consistency. In: CVPR, vol. 1, p. 3 (2017)
56. Wang, P.S., Liu, Y., Guo, Y.X., Sun, C.Y., Tong, X.: O-CNN: octree-based convolutional neural networks for 3D shape analysis. ACM Trans. Graph. (SIGGRAPH) **36**(4) (2017)
57. Wang, W., Huang, Q., You, S., Yang, C., Neumann, U.: Shape inpainting using 3D generative adversarial network and recurrent convolutional networks. arXiv preprint arXiv:1711.06375 (2017)
58. Whelan, T., Leutenegger, S., Salas-Moreno, R.F., Glocker, B., Davison, A.J.: Elasticfusion: dense slam without a pose graph. Robot.: Sci. Syst. (2015)
59. Whelan, T., Salas-Moreno, R.F., Glocker, B., Davison, A.J., Leutenegger, S.: ElasticFusion: real-time dense slam and light source estimation. Int. J. Robot. Res. **35**(14), 1697–1716 (2016). https://doi.org/10.1177/0278364916669237
60. Wu, J., Zhang, C., Xue, T., Freeman, B., Tenenbaum, J.: Learning a probabilistic latent space of object shapes via 3D generative-adversarial modeling. In: Advances in Neural Information Processing Systems, pp. 82–90 (2016)
61. Wu, Z., et al.: 3D shapenets: a deep representation for volumetric shapes. In: Proceedings of the IEEE Conference on Computer Vision and Pattern Recognition, pp. 1912–1920 (2015)
62. Wurm, K.M., Hornung, A., Bennewitz, M., Stachniss, C., Burgard, W.: Octomap: A probabilistic, flexible, and compact 3D map representation for robotic systems. In: Proceedings of the ICRA 2010 Workshop on Best Practice in 3D Perception and Modeling for Mobile Manipulation, vol. 2 (2010)
63. Yan, X., Yang, J., Yumer, E., Guo, Y., Lee, H.: Perspective transformer nets: learning single-view 3D object reconstruction without 3D supervision. In: Advances in Neural Information Processing Systems, pp. 1696–1704 (2016)
64. Yang, B., Wen, H., Wang, S., Clark, R., Markham, A., Trigoni, N.: 3D object reconstruction from a single depth view with adversarial learning. arXiv preprint arXiv:1708.07969 (2017)
65. Zach, C., Pock, T., Bischof, H.: A globally optimal algorithm for robust TV-L 1 range image integration. In: IEEE 11th International Conference on Computer Vision, ICCV 2007, pp. 1–8. IEEE (2007)

A Dataset of Flash and Ambient Illumination Pairs from the Crowd

Yağız Aksoy[1,2]([⊠]), Changil Kim[1], Petr Kellnhofer[1], Sylvain Paris[3],
Mohamed Elgharib[4], Marc Pollefeys[2,5], and Wojciech Matusik[1]

[1] MIT CSAIL, Cambridge, MA, USA
[2] ETH Zürich, Zürich, Switzerland
`ya@inf.ethz.ch`
[3] Adobe Research, Cambridge, MA, USA
[4] QCRI, Doha, Qatar
[5] Microsoft, Redmond, WA, USA

Abstract. Illumination is a critical element of photography and is essential for many computer vision tasks. Flash light is unique in the sense that it is a widely available tool for easily manipulating the scene illumination. We present a dataset of thousands of ambient and flash illumination pairs to enable studying flash photography and other applications that can benefit from having separate illuminations. Different than the typical use of crowdsourcing in generating computer vision datasets, we make use of the crowd to directly take the photographs that make up our dataset. As a result, our dataset covers a wide variety of scenes captured by many casual photographers. We detail the advantages and challenges of our approach to crowdsourcing as well as the computational effort to generate completely separate flash illuminations from the ambient light in an uncontrolled setup. We present a brief examination of illumination decomposition, a challenging and underconstrained problem in flash photography, to demonstrate the use of our dataset in a data-driven approach.

Keywords: Flash photography · Dataset collection
Crowdsourcing · Illumination decomposition

1 Introduction

Crowdsourcing has been a driving force for computer vision datasets especially with the rise of data-driven approaches. The typical use of crowdsourcing in this field has been obtaining answers to high-level questions about photographs [7] or obtaining ground truth annotations [21] for simple tasks such as segmentation in a scalable and economical manner. However, commonplace strategies that rely on

---

Electronic supplementary material The online version of this chapter (https://doi.org/10.1007/978-3-030-01240-3_39) contains supplementary material, which is available to authorized users.

V. Ferrari et al. (Eds.): ECCV 2018, LNCS 11213, pp. 644–660, 2018.
https://doi.org/10.1007/978-3-030-01240-3_39

user interaction do not apply to scenarios where complex physical processes are involved, such as flash/no-flash, short/long exposure, high/low dynamic range, or shallow/deep depth of field. With the wide availability and high quality of current mobile cameras, crowdsourcing has a larger potential that includes the collection of photographs directly. With the motivation of scalability and diversity, we tackle the challenge of crowdsourcing a computational photography dataset. We introduce a new approach where the crowd *captures* the images that make up the dataset directly, and illustrate our strategy on the flash/no-flash task.

Fig. 1. We introduce a diverse dataset of thousands of photograph pairs with flash-only and ambient-only illuminations, collected via crowdsourcing.

Illumination is one of the most critical aspects of photography. The scene illumination determines the dominant aesthetic aspect of a photograph, as well as control of the visibility of and attention drawn to the objects in the scene. Furthermore, it is an important subject in visual computing and the availability of different illuminations of the same scene allows studying many different aspects of the photograph such as relighting, white balancing and illumination separation. However, capturing the same scenes under different illuminations is challenging, as the illumination is not easily controllable without photographic studio conditions. With its wide availability, flash is the easiest way for a casual photographer to alter the scene illumination. Thus, we focus on collecting a flash/no-flash dataset for demonstrating our crowdsourcing strategy. Similar to the Frankencamera [1], we use burst photography to capture several images in quick succession. This allows us to obtain pairs of nearly aligned images under different conditions; in our case, one is a flash photograph and the other is one only lit by the ambient light sources existing in the scene.

We present a dataset of thousands of images under ambient illumination and matching pairs that capture the same scene under *only* flash illumination. Figure 1 shows several examples of illumination pairs from our dataset. We have crowdsourced the collection of photograph pairs that result in a wide variety of scenes. This would not have been possible under fully controlled studios. We detail our approach, the challenges of crowdsourcing the photograph collection, and the processing pipeline to provide flash and ambient illumination pairs.

We envision that having two separate illuminations can aid in high-level tasks such as semantic segmentation or single-image depth estimation, as such high-level information is illumination-invariant. The dataset with image pairs identical up to illumination can also help with illumination analysis [13] or intrinsic image decomposition. Additionally, as one of the images in each pair is flash illumination, we hope that our dataset will encourage development of automatic image enhancement and lighting manipulation methods for mobile devices such as [8,27] or support computer vision applications similar to [31].

Illumination analysis has been an important problem in visual computing, e.g. the classical research problem of intrinsic image decomposition [4,5,20,23] where an image is decomposed into albedo and shading layers. Our dataset with two separate illuminations enables a new and related problem, single-image illumination decomposition. We present a brief study of illumination decomposition to see our dataset in action, where we train a network to decompose a flash photograph into corresponding ambient and flash illuminations and list the challenges that arise with this underconstrained problem. We show that although it is still an unsolved problem, a network trained with our dataset can generalize to substantially different images.

2   Related Work

Datasets of Separate Illuminations. Capturing the same scene under different illuminations is a challenging task that typically requires specialized setups and controlled environments. He and Lau [11] provide a dataset of 120 flash/no-flash photograph pairs captured with a DSLR camera and a tripod for the application of saliency detection. The dataset includes several objects, which define the salient regions in the image. Hui et al. [12] also provide a small set of 5 flash/no-flash photograph pairs. Murmann et al. [24] present 14 image sets captured using their specialized setup, each set consisting of 4 photographs taken under different flash directions. Krishnan and Fergus [18] also provide flash images taken with their hardware setup for 5 scenes. Our new dataset is significantly larger than the previously available examples, which allows its use for more data-demanding machine learning methods.

Another major difference is that we provide the ambient and flash illuminations separately, while flash photos in most of the previous work are indeed flash-dominant photos including ambient illumination as well. Weyrich et al. [33] provided a large dataset of facial images under different illuminations that were collected using a lighting dome in studio conditions. Separate illuminations have been provided for outdoor scenes with changing daylight and weather conditions [25]. Vonikakis et al. [32] captured 15 scenes under two separate illuminations in studio conditions. In contrast, we have collected our photographs via crowdsourcing in the wild, which allows for a larger dataset with a high variety of scenes.

Crowdsourced Datasets. Crowdsourcing has been an important tool for generating large-scale computer vision datasets. The crowd is typically utilized for tasks like labeling images [7], annotating images for interactive tasks [4,15,17], or drawing detailed object segmentations [21]. These datasets and many others use the crowd to conduct higher-level tasks for a given set of images. In our data collection setup, however, the crowd takes the photographs themselves. The main advantage of this approach is the wide variety of the input images that can be collected. We discuss the challenges that arise with direct data collection via crowdsourcing further in this paper.

Flash Photography. Previous work processing flash photographs mainly focuses on the joint processing of flash and no-flash pairs. Petschnigg et al. [27] and Eisemann and Durand [8] independently proposed the use of a flash photograph to denoise and improve the corresponding no-flash photograph taken in low-light conditions. Agrawal et al. [2] similarly use a flash/no-flash pair to remove the highlights from the flash photograph. In addition to image processing, flash/no-flash pairs have been used to improve image matting [31], automatic object segmentation [30], image deblurring [35], saliency detection [11], and stereo matching [34]. Recently, such pairs have been shown to be useful for white-balancing scenes with multiple ambient illuminations [12], and separation of such distinct light sources [13]. These works point to a wide set of use cases of flash/no-flash image pairs. By providing a large set of flash/ambient illumination pairs, the presented dataset enables further studies in these and other areas, as well as enabling data-driven approaches.

3   A Dataset of Flash and Ambient Illumination Pairs

We introduce a dataset of flash and ambient illumination pairs. Specifically, each pair consists of a photograph with only ambient illumination in a well-lit indoor environment, accompanied by the same scene illuminated *only* with the flash light.

The illuminations are provided as linear images at 1440×1080 resolution and 12-bit depth. Utilizing the superposition of light when there are multiple light sources in the scene, the pairs can be used to generate multiple versions of the same scene with varying lighting. For instance, to simulate a regular flash photograph taken in a dark environment, the typical use case of flash, a portion of the ambient illumination can be added to the flash illumination. Figure 3 shows several such variations. The white balance of the two illuminations can also be altered separately to create more alternatives.

Our dataset consists of more than 2700 illumination pairs of a wide variety of scenes. We have divided the dataset into 6 loosely defined categories, and several examples of each category are shown in Fig. 2. Roughly, 12% of the image pairs are in the category *People*, 15% in *Shelves* and *Toys* categories each, 10% in *Plants*, 30% in *Rooms* and the rest in the generic *Objects* category.

Previous work in flash photography presents flash/no-flash photograph pairs taken in dark environments [8,27], and hence the flash photograph contains a

People   Shelves   Toys   Plants   Rooms   Objects

Fig. 2. We present a dataset of flash-only illumination with corresponding ambient illumination. The dataset consists of thousands photograph pairs collected via crowd-sourcing. The wide variety of images cover loosely-defined categories as listed at the top of the figure.

Fig. 3. The flash and ambient illumination pairs can be linearly combined with varying contributions (α) to simulate a flash photograph taken in darker environments.

portion of the ambient light. One important advantage of our dataset is that the flash pair does not contain any ambient illumination, making the two illuminations completely separate.

Ideally, obtaining such separate illumination pairs requires a controlled setup where the ambient illumination can be turned on and off. However, such a controlled setting makes it very challenging to scale the dataset size and limits the variety of the photographs that can be captured. Instead of a controlled setup, we use a dedicated mobile application to capture flash/no-flash photograph pairs and then computationally generate the flash-only illumination. Our setup also enables crowdsourcing of the collection process which in turn increases the variety of the scenes that are included in our dataset. We detail our collection procedure in Sect. 4.

We will open our dataset to the public to facilitate further research. Previous literature in flash photography shows that our dataset can be utilized for studying white balance, enhancement of flash photographs, saliency and more. The availability of such a dataset enables studying these problems in a data-driven manner. In addition, the availability of separate illuminations can be utilized for studying illumination-invariance in a variety of scenarios, as well as opening up the study of new problems such as illumination decomposition. We provide a brief examination of illumination decomposition, i.e. estimating the flash illumination from a single flash photograph, as an example use case of our dataset in Sect. 5.

4 Dataset Collection

We compute flash-only illumination from a pair of photographs, one taken with flash and one without. Using the superposition of different illuminants as seen by the camera, the difference between the flash photograph and the no-flash one contains the information for the flash illuminant under certain conditions. First of all, the raw values from the camera are required to correctly estimate the flash light. The camera parameters such as exposure and white balance must also match for the two photographs. In addition, the photographs, especially the no-flash photograph, should not contain saturated pixels. Finally, the two photographs must be well-aligned.

In order to allow for crowdsourcing, we needed to devise an easy and uncontrolled capture setup. We achieved this with a dedicated mobile application that takes the photograph pair with a single click. The application saves the raw image files and allows the user to upload them to a server. We match the image camera parameters using the photo metadata before computing the flash illumination. Handheld capture of two consecutive photographs inevitably results in small misalignments. We computationally align the two photographs before subtracting the no-flash photograph from the flash one. We detail these procedures and our crowdsourcing framework in the rest of this section.

Illumination Conditions. Unlike the previous work on flash photography where the photographs were typically taken in dark environments, we would like to have sufficient ambient lighting in the environment to generate varying illumination conditions as shown in Fig. 3 as well as to enable a larger set of possible uses for our dataset. In addition, we would like to reliably estimate the flash illumination and hence the flash light should be bright enough relative to the ambient light. This prevents us from taking photographs under daylight, where the flash light is much weaker compared to the sunlight. Hence, we restrict the scenes we capture to be indoor environments with sufficient ambient illumination, and free of directly visible light sources to avoid saturation.

Alignment. The flash and no-flash photographs are sequentially captured by our mobile app with a half to one second delay between the two exposures. This results in a small misalignment that must be corrected. However, accurate and reliable alignment of two images with different illuminations is a challenging task, as the image features that alignment methods rely on can be quite different in the presence of the flash light. One particular challenge is the hard shadows cast by the flash light, which results in strong gradients in one of the images. Hence, we limit our alignment to be rigid and estimate a homography between the two images using two different methods. We then review the two alignments and select the successful one by visual inspection, or remove the pair from the dataset if both methods fail.

The first method we utilize is the dual inverse compositional alignment algorithm (DIC) [3] from the image alignment toolbox [9]. DIC estimates geometric and photometric transformations simultaneously and is known for its robustness against illumination changes. DIC is effective when the ambient illumination is strong but fails in the presence of hard shadows.

We complement DIC by generating a shadow-free gradient map for both photographs and using Lucas-Kanade image registration [22] between these representations. We observed that the edges of the shadows cast by the flash light appear colorless when the white balance matches the flash color. We take advantage of this fact to remove the shadow edges, as shown in Fig. 4. We generate RGB gradient images for the two photographs and convert them to the HSV color space. We then multiply the saturation and value channels in this representation, which effectively diminishes the colorless edges including those of

Flash / no-flash pair   RGB edges   Shadow-free   Only flash

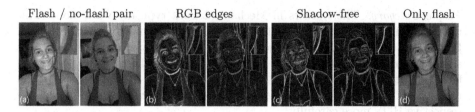

Fig. 4. For an unaligned flash and no-flash photograph pair (a), we compute the shadow-free edge representations (c) from the RGB image gradients (b). Inset shows the edge of the shadow in the flash image (b) disappearing in our representation (c). We estimate the alignment using the shadow-free representations and subtract the no-flash image from flash image after alignment to get the flash-only illumination (d).

flash shadows. Although some naturally colorless edges are lost, we are able to properly align the two photographs using this representation.

Collecting Photograph Pairs via Crowdsourcing. Diversifying images is important to generate a representative and generalizable dataset. This was a major advantage that drove us to crowdsource our dataset collection. We used Amazon's Mechanical Turk platform to recruit a large and diverse group of casual photographers. Using the crowdsourcing terminology, we will refer to the assignments as *human intelligence tasks (HITs)* and the photographers as *workers*. We list the major considerations we had to devise to enable the collection of our dataset in this part.

Framework. One essential component of our crowdsourcing effort was the mobile application we use to capture the dataset. The mobile application, developed for iOS devices, enables many casual photographers to participate in our collection effort from their home. Our HIT definition details our previously listed illumination expectations, provides a link and instructions for our application, and assigns a unique identifier per HIT. The worker is asked to install the application and enter the HIT identifier in the application. After taking the photographs, the worker uploads them to our server via the application. We then match the identifiers from Mechanical Turk and our servers to confirm the uploads. An example HIT definition is provided in the supplementary material.

Scene Categories. After initial trials, we observed that specifying scene categories guides the workers to find suitable scenes and increases the participation and the quality of the photographs. This lead us to define the first five categories shown in Fig. 2. These categories are loosely defined to allow the workers to easily find matching scenes around them, typically in their homes or workplaces. For most categories, we request the workers to take ten pictures per HIT. We give more details for the people category below. Not all workers strictly followed the category definitions, hence, we added the last category *objects* for the photographs that do not fit elsewhere.

People Category. The workers in Mechanical Turk typically work alone. This makes the HITs that require photographing other people much more challenging. In addition, the movement of subjects between the two photographs makes the alignment procedure even harder. Nevertheless, as one of the main use-cases of flash is portrait photography and facial image editing is an important topic in research, it is an important category to cover and, therefore, we defined the respective HITs more carefully.

A unique instruction is that instead of asking for ten photographs of different people, we ask the workers to take *five* photographs of the *same* person from different angles. This makes the worker complete each HIT much more quickly and makes the HIT more attractive. We ask the worker to instruct their subject to be still during capture, but subjects often fail to do so especially due to the flash light. This makes the percentage of portrait photographs we have to discard higher than average. Having five pictures of the same person increases the chance of using at least one of the poses and hence does not waste the worker's effort to recruit subjects. We also ask the worker to explain our dataset collection effort and get an explicit confirmation from the subject to participate in the study, as well as to avoid photographing minors.

Compensation and Noise. Not all the photographs we received were included in our dataset. Some common issues were photographs in very dark or very bright environments, non-static scenes and motion-blurred images. Other than such issues, there were cases of workers not uploading any photographs or uploading the same scenes many times. In such cases, we contacted the workers directly and usually got a positive response. We retained about a third of the images we received from the workers. We set the compensation as one U.S. dollar per HIT.

5   The Dataset in Action: Illumination Decomposition

Previous work in flash photography focuses on improving the low ambient lighting using a matching flash pair [8,27] or combining multiple flash images [24]. While these methods focus on estimating one high-quality image by combining multiple images, data-driven approaches allow tackling more difficult, but also more general problems.

To test our dataset, we present a data-driven approach to illumination decomposition as a baseline for future work. The goal of illumination decomposition is to estimate and separate the ambient and flash illuminations from a single flash photograph. We define the application scenario to include typical flash photographs that are taken in dark environments. We generate the input images by combining the illumination pairs in our dataset to simulate such dark environments as shown in Fig. 3. The ambient and flash illuminations then serve as the ground truth.

Illumination decomposition is an underconstrained problem, even when one of the illuminations is coming from the flash. We present several strategies we found to be useful in tackling this problem and present the challenges that arise.

We use a standard architecture to test our dataset and show that although the decomposition problem is far from being solved, a network trained with our dataset can be helpful in editing legacy photographs.

Network Structure and Implementation Details. We adopt the architecture proposed by Isola et al. [14] for generic image-to-image translation and experiment with several alternatives for the loss function and the estimation on ratio images as detailed in the rest of this section. The generator part of the network utilizes the U-net 256 network scheme [28] with eight convolution-deconvolution layer pairs and skip connections to pass full-resolution information to the next stage. It predicts

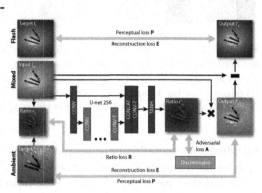

Fig. 5. The network structure with the losses shown in orange. (Color figure online)

the ratio image $\hat{r}_a$, which is used to reconstruct the estimated ambient illumination $\hat{I}_a$. We use Adam solver [16] with an initial learning rate of $2 \cdot 10^{-4}$ to train the main network and a lower rate of $2 \cdot 10^{-6}$ to train the discriminator. We decrease the learning rate by a factor of 10 every 30 epochs and we terminate the training after 150 epochs which takes approximately 2 h on our setup. The forward pass including all other processing is fast enough for interactive applications (Fig. 5).

Ratio Images. We observed that directly estimating the ambient or flash illuminations results in loss of high-frequency details and periodic noise structures. Trying to correct such artifacts via joint filtering such as the domain transform [10] either does not remove such artifacts, or oversmooths the image. Instead of a direct estimation of the illuminations, we chose to first estimate the ratio image an intermediate representation. Inspired by the use of *ratio images* in facial relighting literature [6,26], we define the output of our network as the ratio between the input image I_m and the ambient illumination I_a. Although the exact definition of how this ratio is computed does not have a substantial effect on the network, we define the ratio to be in range $[0, 1]$ and compute the estimated ambient illumination accordingly:

$$r_a = \frac{2 \cdot (I_a + 1)}{3 \cdot (I_m + 1)} - \frac{1}{3} \qquad I_a = \frac{3 \cdot (r_a + I_m \, r_a) + I_m - 1}{2} \qquad (1)$$

The artifacts mentioned above also appear in the ratio images, but when the domain transform is applied, we are able to remove them without the loss of

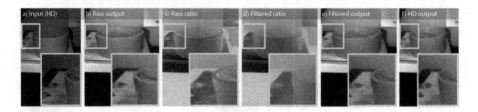

Fig. 6. High resolution input image (a) is downsampled and fed into the network. The ambient illumination image output may contain a residual noise (b) which would stand out in an otherwise smooth ratio image (c). We filter the ratio image while preserving its edges using the input image as a guide (d). The reconstructed image is free of noise (e). Same approach is used to upsample the output to the original high resolution (f).

high-frequency details in the output ambient illumination. Another advantage of using ratio images is the ease of upscaling. The network works on a downscaled version of the image and we upscale the ratio image before the domain filtering. This way, we are able to generate high-resolution outputs without the need of feeding the image at full resolution to the network. Figure 6 shows our workflow.

Dataset Augmentation. At each epoch, we generate the input images by randomly sampling α (Fig. 3) to determine how dark the ambient illumination is compared to the flash light. This makes the learning process more robust against different illumination conditions. We also randomly crop, rotate, flip and scale the images at each epoch before feeding them into the network.

Loss Functions. The original Pix2Pix [14] combines an adversarial loss **A** and an L_1 loss **R**:

$$\mathbf{R} = \|\hat{r}_a - r_a\|_1, \qquad (2)$$

which we refer to as the ratio loss, as the output of the network is the ratio image in our approach. In addition to these, we also define an L_2 loss that applies to both the estimated ambient illumination and the flash illumination $\hat{I}_f = I_m - \hat{I}_a$:

$$\mathbf{E} = \|\hat{I}_a - I_a\|_2^2 + \|\hat{I}_f - I_f\|_2^2. \qquad (3)$$

We observed that, while the two terms of Eq. 3 are correlated, including the losses on both flash and ambient illuminations leads to better performance.

We have also tested a perceptual loss **P** proposed by Sajjadi et al. [29] that preserves the perceived image quality:

$$\mathbf{P} = \|\mathcal{P}(\hat{I}_a, I_a)\|_2^2 + \|\mathcal{P}(\hat{I}_f, I_f)\|_2^2 \qquad (4)$$

where $\mathcal{P}$ extracts the features from a pre-trained network [19].

We combine a subset of these losses in our experiments with empirically determined weights $100 \cdot \mathbf{R} + 1000 \cdot \mathbf{E} + 1000 \cdot \mathbf{P} + \mathbf{A}$. We have tested the quantitative results for several combinations of these loss functions and the results are summarized in Table 1. We observed that the use of adversarial loss **A** leads to a strong high-frequency noise. Using the perceptual loss **P**, on the other hand, results in a color shift for some image regions. Removing loss **R** or **E** generally led to a result similar to the baseline **RE** as they are correlated metrics. However, we got best visual as well as quantitative results using both losses.

Table 1. Test errors for the estimated ambient illuminations

α	PSNR (dB)					SSIM				
	RE	R	E	REP	REA	RE	R	E	REP	REA
0.1	**15.220**	14.801	14.708	15.163	14.099	**0.583**	0.516	0.505	0.567	0.334
0.3	**18.046**	17.338	17.288	17.676	16.431	**0.720**	0.638	0.634	0.694	0.427
0.5	**20.261**	19.199	19.333	19.568	18.116	**0.804**	0.707	0.716	0.773	0.495

Qualitative Evaluation. Figure 7 shows several examples that demonstrate the strengths and shortcomings of the presented illumination decomposition method. For instance, the network estimates a uniform illumination for the ambient illumination, and a dark background and bright foreground for the flash illumination (green highlights in the figure). Even when the ambient illumination in the input image is very dim, such as in (1, 2, 5), the estimated ambient illumination is uniform and bright. The highlights from the flash light are typically well-detected by the network, as seen in examples (3, 4).

However, there are several limitations. The flash highlights may bleed into the estimated ambient illumination (2, 5) or the flash (1) and ambient (4) shadows cannot be reliably separated. After analyzing our results, we believe that a more dedicated approach to facial images would be useful. In some images, our network is better at identifying the highlights on the face but misses more subtle ambient lighting details (3). In others, it may fail to generate a satisfactory ambient light, especially if the environment is dark (5). With the wide variety of images, some unusual examples also arise. For example, our network works well in decomposition in (6) but gets confused around the mirror image of the flower.

These examples demonstrate the difficulty of illumination decomposition. We argue that its underconstrained nature underscores the need for data-driven approaches, as they can potentially learn the strong priors for the flash illumination from many examples to better constrain the problem.

Generalization. We present illumination decomposition examples in old photographs that were scanned from film to test if our dataset can train the network for a generalizable decomposition. We apply inverse gamma mapping to linearize the input images before feeding them into the network. In Fig. 8, from a single image, we recreate the photographs with varying ambient illumination we showed in Fig. 3 using the actual flash and ambient illuminations. This way,

Input image   Flash illum.   Estimated flash   Ambient illum.   Est. ambient

Fig. 7. Several illumination decomposition examples using our dataset. The highlighted areas, red squares demonstrating the limitations, are discussed further in the text. (Color figure online)

Fig. 8. The estimated ambient and flash illuminations can be used to generate a wide range of possible combination of two illuminations.

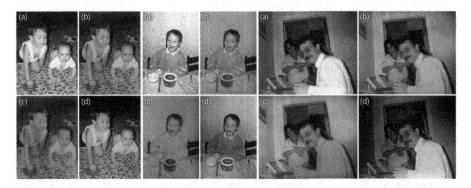

Fig. 9. Input images that were originally taken on film (a) are decomposed into ambient (c) and flash (d) illuminations. The decomposed illuminations can be edited separately and then combined for a more pleasant look (b).

using illumination decomposition, an artist can change the ambient illumination as desired. The decomposed illuminations can also be used to create more pleasant photographs by softening the flash light. Figure 9 shows such examples, where the decomposed flash illuminations are edited to match the color of the ambient illumination, and the ambient illuminations are made stronger to give the photographs a more natural look.

These examples demonstrate that, even with a modest size of several thousands of pairs, by allowing a wide range of augmentations such as varying ambient contribution to the image, our dataset can be used to train a network that can generalize to previously unseen images.

6   Conclusion

We presented a large-scale collection of crowdsourced flash and ambient illumination pairs using smartphone cameras. Our dataset is unique in that it provides complete separation of flash and ambient illuminations in its photo collection unlike previous datasets, and consists of a significantly larger number of photographs. We provide the details of our data collection pipeline, which leverages crowdsourcing and the increasing capabilities of current smartphones, that is designed to be used in unconstrained environments. We demonstrate the use of our dataset in the problem of single-image illumination decomposition and provide considerations for further research in this avenue.

Acknowledgements. We would like to thank Alexandre Kaspar for his support on crowdsourcing, James Minor and Valentin Deschaintre for their feedback on the text, and Michaël Gharbi for our discussions. Y. Aksoy was supported by QCRI-CSAIL Computer Science Research Program at MIT, and C. Kim was supported by Swiss National Science Foundation fellowship P2EZP2 168785.

References

1. Adams, A., et al.: The frankencamera: an experimental platform for computational photography. Commun. ACM **55**(11), 90–98 (2012)
2. Agrawal, A., Raskar, R., Nayar, S.K., Li, Y.: Removing photography artifacts using gradient projection and flash-exposure sampling. ACM Trans. Graph. **24**(3), 828–835 (2005)
3. Bartoli, A.: Groupwise geometric and photometric direct image registration. IEEE Trans. Pattern Anal. Mach. Intell. **30**(12), 2098–2108 (2008)
4. Bell, S., Bala, K., Snavely, N.: Intrinsic images in the wild. ACM Trans. Graph. **33**(4) (2014)
5. Bonneel, N., Kovacs, B., Paris, S., Bala, K.: Intrinsic decompositions for image editing. Comput. Graph. Forum **36**(2), 593–609 (2017)
6. Chen, J., Su, G., He, J., Ben, S.: Face image relighting using locally constrained global optimization. In: Daniilidis, K., Maragos, P., Paragios, N. (eds.) ECCV 2010. LNCS, vol. 6314, pp. 44–57. Springer, Heidelberg (2010). https://doi.org/10.1007/978-3-642-15561-1_4
7. Deng, J., Dong, W., Socher, R., Li, L.J., Li, K., Fei-Fei, L.: ImageNet: a large-scale hierarchical image database. In: Conference on Computer Vision and Pattern Recognition (CVPR) (2009)
8. Eisemann, E., Durand, F.: Flash photography enhancement via intrinsic relighting. ACM Trans. Graph. **23**(3), 673–678 (2004)
9. Evangelidis, G.: IAT: a Matlab toolbox for image alignment (2013). http://www.iatool.net
10. Gastal, E.S.L., Oliveira, M.M.: Domain transform for edge-aware image and video processing. ACM Trans. Graph. **30**(4), 69:1–69:12 (2011)
11. He, S., Lau, R.W.H.: Saliency detection with flash and no-flash image pairs. In: Fleet, D., Pajdla, T., Schiele, B., Tuytelaars, T. (eds.) ECCV 2014. LNCS, vol. 8691, pp. 110–124. Springer, Cham (2014). https://doi.org/10.1007/978-3-319-10578-9_8
12. Hui, Z., Sankaranarayanan, A.C., Sunkavalli, K., Hadap, S.: White balance under mixed illumination using flash photography. In: International Conference on Computational Photography (ICCP) (2016)
13. Hui, Z., Sunkavalli, K., Hadap, S., Sankaranarayanan, A.C.: Illuminant spectra-based source separation using flash photography. In: Conference on Computer Vision and Pattern Recognition (CVPR) (2018)
14. Isola, P., Zhu, J., Zhou, T., Efros, A.A.: Image-to-image translation with conditional adversarial networks. In: Conference on Computer Vision and Pattern Recognition (CVPR) (2017)

15. Kaspar, A., Patterson, G., Kim, C., Aksoy, Y., Matusik, W., Elgharib, M.: Crowd-Guided ensembles: how can we choreograph crowd workers for video segmentation? In: ACM CHI Conference on Human Factors in Computing Systems (2018)
16. Kingma, D., Ba, J.: Adam: a method for stochastic optimization. In: International Conference on Learning Representations (ICLR) (2014)
17. Kovacs, B., Bell, S., Snavely, N., Bala, K.: Shading annotations in the wild. In: Conference on Computer Vision and Pattern Recognition (CVPR) (2017)
18. Krishnan, D., Fergus, R.: Dark flash photography. ACM Trans. Graph. **28**(3), 96:1–96:11 (2009)
19. Krizhevsky, A., Sutskever, I., Hinton, G.E.: ImageNet classification with deep convolutional neural networks. In: Neural Information Processing Systems Conference (NIPS) (2012)
20. Lettry, L., Vanhoey, K., Van Gool, L.: DARN: a deep adversarial residual network for intrinsic image decomposition. In: Winter Conference on Applications of Computer Vision (WACV) (2018)
21. Lin, T.-Y., et al.: Microsoft COCO: common objects in context. In: Fleet, D., Pajdla, T., Schiele, B., Tuytelaars, T. (eds.) ECCV 2014. LNCS, vol. 8693, pp. 740–755. Springer, Cham (2014). https://doi.org/10.1007/978-3-319-10602-1_48
22. Lucas, B.D., Kanade, T.: An iterative image registration technique with an application to stereo vision. In: International Joint Conference on Artificial Intelligence (IJCAI) (1981)
23. Meka, A., Zollhöfer, M., Richardt, C., Theobalt, C.: Live intrinsic video. ACM Trans. Graph. **35**(4), 109:1–109:14 (2016)
24. Murmann, L., Davis, A., Kautz, J., Durand, F.: Computational bounce flash for indoor portraits. ACM Trans. Graph. **35**(6), 190:1–190:9 (2016)
25. Narasimhan, S.G., Wang, C., Nayar, S.K.: All the images of an outdoor scene. In: Heyden, A., Sparr, G., Nielsen, M., Johansen, P. (eds.) ECCV 2002. LNCS, vol. 2352, pp. 148–162. Springer, Heidelberg (2002). https://doi.org/10.1007/3-540-47977-5_10
26. Peers, P., Tamura, N., Matusik, W., Debevec, P.: Post-production facial performance relighting using reflectance transfer. ACM Trans. Graph. **26**(3) (2007)
27. Petschnigg, G., Szeliski, R., Agrawala, M., Cohen, M., Hoppe, H., Toyama, K.: Digital photography with flash and no-flash image pairs. ACM Trans. Graph. **23**(3), 664–672 (2004)
28. Ronneberger, O., Fischer, P., Brox, T.: U-Net: convolutional networks for biomedical image segmentation. In: Navab, N., Hornegger, J., Wells, W.M., Frangi, A.F. (eds.) MICCAI 2015. LNCS, vol. 9351, pp. 234–241. Springer, Cham (2015). https://doi.org/10.1007/978-3-319-24574-4_28
29. Sajjadi, M.S., Schölkopf, B., Hirsch, M.: EnhanceNet: single image super-resolution through automated texture synthesis. In: International Conference on Computer Vision (ICCV) (2017)
30. Sun, J., Sun, J., Kang, S.B., Xu, Z.B., Tang, X., Shum, H.Y.: Flash cut: foreground extraction with flash and no-flash image pairs. In: Conference on Computer Vision and Pattern Recognition (CVPR) (2007)
31. Sun, J., Li, Y., Kang, S.B., Shum, H.Y.: Flash matting. ACM Trans. Graph. **25**(3), 772–778 (2006)
32. Vonikakis, V., Chrysostomou, D., Kouskouridas, R., Gasteratos, A.: Improving the robustness in feature detection by local contrast enhancement. In: International Conference on Imaging Systems and Techniques (IST) (2012)
33. Weyrich, T., et al.: Analysis of human faces using a measurement-based skin reflectance model. ACM Trans. Graph. **25**(3), 1013–1024 (2006)

34. Zhou, C., Troccoli, A., Pulli, K.: Robust stereo with flash and no-flash image pairs. In: Conference on Computer Vision and Pattern Recognition (CVPR) (2012)
35. Zhuo, S., Guo, D., Sim, T.: Robust flash deblurring. In: Conference on Computer Vision and Pattern Recognition (CVPR) (2010)

Pose-Normalized Image Generation
for Person Re-identification

Xuelin Qian[1], Yanwei Fu[2,3], Tao Xiang[4], Wenxuan Wang[1], Jie Qiu[5],
Yang Wu[5], Yu-Gang Jiang[1(✉)], and Xiangyang Xue[1,2]

[1] Shanghai Key Lab of Intelligent Information Processing,
School of Computer Science, Fudan University, Shanghai, China
{15110240002,17210240045,ygj,xyxue}@fudan.edu.cn
[2] School of Data Science, Fudan University, Shanghai, China
yanweifu@fudan.edu.cn
[3] Tencent AI Lab, Bellevue, USA
[4] Queen Mary University of London, London, UK
t.xiang@qmul.ac.uk
[5] Nara Institute of Science and Technology, Ikoma, Japan
qiu.jie.qf3@is.naist.jp, yangwu@rsc.naist.jp

Abstract. Person Re-identification (re-id) faces two major challenges:
the lack of cross-view paired training data and learning discriminative
identity-sensitive and view-invariant features in the presence of large
pose variations. In this work, we address both problems by proposing a
novel deep person image generation model for synthesizing realistic person images conditional on the pose. The model is based on a generative
adversarial network (GAN) designed specifically for pose normalization
in re-id, thus termed pose-normalization GAN (PN-GAN). With the synthesized images, we can learn a new type of deep re-id features free of
the influence of pose variations. We show that these features are complementary to features learned with the original images. Importantly, a
more realistic unsupervised learning setting is considered in this work,
and our model is shown to have the potential to be generalizable to a
new re-id dataset without any fine-tuning. The codes will be released at
https://github.com/naiq/PN_GAN.

Keywords: Person re-id · GAN · Pose normalization

1 Introduction

Person Re-identification (re-id) aims to match a person across multiple non-
overlapping camera views [14]. It is a very challenging problem because a person's appearance can change drastically across views, due to the changes in

---

X. Qian and Y. Fu—Equal contributions.

Electronic supplementary material The online version of this chapter (https://
doi.org/10.1007/978-3-030-01240-3_40) contains supplementary material, which is
available to authorized users.

© Springer Nature Switzerland AG 2018
V. Ferrari et al. (Eds.): ECCV 2018, LNCS 11213, pp. 661–678, 2018.
https://doi.org/10.1007/978-3-030-01240-3_40

Fig. 1. The same person's appearance can be very different across camera views, due to the presence of large pose variations.

various covariate factors independent of the person's identity. These factors include viewpoint, body configuration, lighting, and occlusion (see Fig. 1). Among these factors, pose plays an important role in causing a person's appearance changes. Here pose is defined as a combination of viewpoint and body configuration. It is thus also a cause of self-occlusion. For instance, in the bottom row examples in Fig. 1, the big backpacks carried by the three persons are in full display from the back, but reduced to mostly the straps from the front.

Most existing re-id approaches [2,9,25,34,40,47,51,63] are based on learning identity-sensitive and view-insensitive features using deep neural networks (DNNs). To learn the features, a large number of persons' images need to be collected in each camera view with variable poses. With the collected images, the model can have a chance to learn what features are discriminative and invariant to the camera view and pose changes. These approaches thus have a number of limitations. The first limitation is **lack of scalability** to large camera networks. Existing models require sufficient identities and sufficient images per identity to be collected from each camera view. However, manually annotating persons across views in the camera networks is tedious and difficult even for humans. Importantly, in a real-world application, a camera network can easily consist of hundreds of cameras (i.e. those in an airport or shopping mall); annotating enough training identities from all camera views are infeasible. The second limitation is **lack of generalizability** to new camera networks. Specifically, when an existing deep re-id model is deployed to a new camera network, view points and body poses are often different across the networks; additional data thus need to be collected for model fine-tuning, which severely limits its generalization ability. As a result of both limitations, although deep re-id models are far superior for large re-id benchmarks such as Market-1501 [61] and CUHK03 [25], they still struggle to beat hand-crafted feature based models on smaller datasets such as CUHK01 [24], even when they are pre-trained on the larger re-id datasets.

Even with sufficient labeled training data, existing deep re-id models face the challenge of learning identity-sensitive and view-insensitive features in the presence of large pose variations. This is because a person's appearance is determined by a combination of identity-sensitive but view-insensitive factors and identity-insensitive but view-sensitive ones, which are inter-connected. The former correspond to semantic related identity properties, such as gender, carrying, color, and texture. The latter are the covariates mentioned earlier including poses. Existing models aim to keep the former and remove the latter in the learned feature representations. However, these two aspects of the appearance are not independent, e.g., the appearance of the carrying depends on the pose. Making the learned features pose-insensitive means that the features supposed to represent the backpacks in the bottom row examples in Fig. 1 are reduced to those representing only the straps – a much harder type of features to learn.

In this paper, we argue that the key to learning an effective, scalable and generalizable re-id model is to remove the influence of pose on the person's appearance. Without the pose variation, we can learn a model with much less data thus making the model scalable to large camera networks. Furthermore, without the need to worry about the pose variation, the model can concentrate on learning identity-sensitive features and coping with other covariates such as different lighting conditions and backgrounds. The model is thus far more likely to generalize to a new dataset from a new camera network. Moreover, with the different focus, the features learned without the presence of pose variation would be different and complementary to those learned with pose variation.

To this end, a novel deep re-id framework is proposed. Key to the framework is a deep person image generation model. The model is based on a generative adversarial network (GAN) designed specifically for pose normalization in re-id. It is thus termed pose-normalization GAN (PN-GAN). Given any person's image and a desirable pose as input, the model will output a synthesized image of the same identity with the original pose replaced with the new one. In practice, we define a set of eight canonical poses, and synthesize eight new images for any given image, resulting in a 8-fold increase in the training data size. The pose-normalized images are used to train a pose-normalized re-id model which produces a set of features that are complementary to the feature learned with the original images. The two sets of feature are thus fused as the final feature.

Contributions. Our contributions are as follows. (1) We identify pose as the chief culprit for preventing a deep re-id model from learning effective identity-sensitive and view-insensitive features, and propose a novel solution based on generating pose-normalized images. This also addresses the scalability and generalizability issues of existing models. (2) A novel person image generation model PN-GAN is proposed to generate pose-normalized images, which are realistic, identity-preserving and pose controllable. With the synthesized images of canonical poses, strong and complementary features are learned to be combined with features learned with the original images. Extensive experiments on several benchmarks show the efficacy of our proposed model. (3) A more realistic unsupervised transfer learning is considered in this paper. Under this setting, no data from the target dataset is used for model updating: the model trained from labeled source domain is applied to the target domain without any modification.

2   Related Work

Deep Re-id Models. Most recently proposed re-id models employ a DNN to learn discriminative view-invariant features [2,9,25,34,40,47,51,63]. They differ in the DNN architectures – some adopt a standard DNN developed for other tasks, whilst others have architectures tailor-made. They differ also in the training objectives. Different models use different training losses including identity classification, pairwise verification, and triplet ranking losses. A comprehensive study on the effectiveness of different losses and their combinations on re-id can be found in [12]. The focus of this paper is not on designing new re-id deep model architecture or loss – we use an off-the-shelf ResNet architecture [16] and the standard identity classification loss. We show that once the pose variation problem is solved, it could help to improve the performance of re-id.

Pose-Guided Deep Re-id. The negative effects of pose variation on deep re-id models have been recognised recently. A number of models [23,39,45,50, 57,58,62] are proposed to address this problem. Most of them are pose-guided based on body part detection. For example, [39,57] first detect normalized part regions from a person image, and then fuse the features extracted from the original images and the part region images. These body part regions are predefined and the region detectors are trained beforehand. Differently, [58] combine region selection and detection with deep re-id in one model. Our model differs significantly from these models in that we synthesize realistic whole-body images using the proposed PN-GAN, rather than only focusing on body parts for pose normalization. Note that body parts are related to semantic attributes which are often specific to different body parts. A number of attributes based re-id models [11,37,44,52] have been proposed. They use attributes to provide additional supervision for learning identity-sensitive features. In contrast, without using the additional attribute information, our PN-GAN is learned as a conditional image generation model for the re-id problem.

Deep Image Generation. Generating realistic images of objects using DNNs has received much interest recently, thanks largely to the development of GAN [15]. GAN is designed to find the optimal discriminator network D between training data and generated samples using a min-max game and simultaneously enhance the performance of an image generator network G. It is formulated to optimize the following objective functions:

$$\min_{G}\max_{D}\mathcal{L}_{GAN} = \mathbb{E}_{x \sim p_{data}(x)}\left[\log D\left(x\right)\right]$$
$$+ \mathbb{E}_{z \sim p_{prior}(z)}\left[\log\left(1 - D\left(G\left(z\right)\right)\right)\right] \tag{1}$$

where $p_{data}\left(x\right)$ and $p_{prior}\left(z\right)$ are the distributions of real data x and Gaussian prior $z \sim \mathcal{N}\left(0, 1\right)$. The training process iteratively updates the parameters of G and D with the loss functions $\mathcal{L}_D = -\mathcal{L}_{GAN}$ and $\mathcal{L}_G = \mathcal{L}_{GAN}$ for the generator and discriminator respectively. The generator can draw a sample $z \sim p_{prior}\left(z\right) = \mathcal{N}\left(0, 1\right)$ and utilize the generator network G, i.e., $G(z)$ to generate an image.

Among all the variants of GAN, our pose normalization GAN is built upon deep convolutional generative adversarial networks (DCGANs) [35]. Based on a standard convolutional decoder, DCGAN scales up GAN using Convolutional Neural Networks (CNNs) and it results in stable training across various datasets. Many other variants of GAN, such as VAEGAN [21], Conditional GAN [18], stackGAN [53] also exist. However, most of them are designed for training with high-quality images of objects such as celebrity faces, instead of low-quality surveillance video frames of pedestrians. This problem is tackled in a very recent work [22,30]. Their objective is to synthesize person images in different poses, whilst our work aims to solve the re-id problem with the synthesized images. Besides, both of them utilized two generators/parts from coarse to fine to generate images. As a result, their models are more complicated and not easy to train.

Overall, our model differs from the existing variants of GAN. In particular, built upon the residual blocks, our PN-GAN is learned to change the poses and yet keeps the identity of input person. Note that the only work so far that uses deep image generator for re-id is [65]. However, their model is not a conditional GAN and thus cannot control either identity or pose in the generated person images. As a result, the generated images can only be used as unlabeled or weakly labeled data. In contrast, our model generate strongly labeled data with its ability to preserve the identity and remove the influence of pose variation.

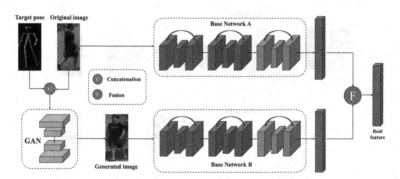

Fig. 2. Overview of our framework. Given an person image, we utilize PN-GAN to synthesize auxiliary images with different poses. Base Networks A and B are then deployed to extract features of original image and synthesized images, respectively. Finally, two types of features are merged for final re-identification task. (Color figure online)

3   Methodology

3.1   Problem Definition and Overview

Problem Definition. Assume we have a training dataset of N persons $\mathcal{D}_{Tr} = \{\mathbf{I}_k, y_k\}_{k=1}^{N}$, where $\mathbf{I}_k$ and y_k are the person image and person id of the k-th person. In the training stage we learn a feature extraction function ϕ so that a given image $\mathbf{I}$ can be represented by a feature vector $\mathbf{f_I} = \phi(\mathbf{I})$. In the testing stage, given a pair of person images $\{\mathbf{I}_i, \mathbf{I}_j\}$ in the testing dataset $\mathcal{D}_{Te}$, we need to judge whether $y_i = y_j$ or $y_i \neq y_j$. This is done by simply computing the Euclidean distance between $\mathbf{f_{I}}_i$ and $\mathbf{f_{I}}_j$ as the identity-similarity measure.

Framework Overview. As shown in Fig. 2, our framework has two key components, *i.e.*, a GAN based person image generation model (Sect. 3.2) and a person re-id feature learning model (Sect. 3.3).

3.2 Deep Image Generator

Our image generator aims at producing the same person's images under different poses. Particularly, given an input person image $\mathbf{I}_i$ and a desired pose image $\mathbf{I}_{\mathcal{P}_j}$, our image generator aims to synthesize a new person image $\hat{\mathbf{I}}_j$, which contains the same person but with a different pose defined by $\mathbf{I}_{\mathcal{P}_j}$. As in any GAN model, the image generator has two components, a Generator G_P and a Discriminator D_P. The generator is learned to edit the person image conditional on a given pose; the discriminator discriminates real data samples from the generated samples and help to improve the quality of generated images.

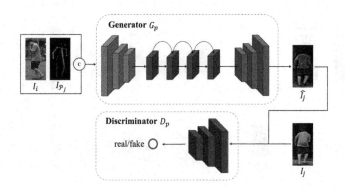

Fig. 3. Schematic of our PN-GAN model

Pose Estimation. The image generation process is conditional on the input image and one factor: the desired pose represented by a skeleton pose image. Pose estimation is obtained by a pretrained off-the-shelf model. More concretely, the off-the-shelf pose detection toolkit – OpenPose [4] is deployed, which is trained without using any re-id benchmark data. Given an input person image $\mathbf{I}_i$, the pose estimator can produce a pose image $\mathbf{I}_{\mathcal{P}_i}$, which localizes and detects 18 anatomical key-points as well as their connections. In the pose images, the orientation of limbs is encoded by color (see Fig. 2, target pose). In theory, any pose from any person image can be used as a condition to control the pose of another person's generated image. In this work, we focus on pose normalization so we stick to eight canonical poses as shown in Fig. 4(a), to be detailed later.

Generator. As shown in Fig. 3, given an input person image $\mathbf{I}_i$, and a target person image $\mathbf{I}_j$ which contains the same person as $\mathbf{I}_i$ but a different pose $\mathbf{I}_{\mathcal{P}_j}$, our generator will learn to replace pose information in $\mathbf{I}_i$ with the target pose $\mathbf{I}_{\mathcal{P}_j}$ and generate the new pose $\hat{\mathbf{I}}_j$. The input to the generator is the concatenation of the input person image $\mathbf{I}_i$ and target pose image $\mathbf{I}_{\mathcal{P}_j}$. Specifically, we treat the target body pose image $\mathbf{I}_{\mathcal{P}_j}$ as a three-channel image and directly concatenate it with the three-channel source person image as the input of the generator. The generator G_P is designed based on the "ResNet" architecture and is an encoder-decoder network [17]. The encoder-decoder network progressively down-samples $\mathbf{I}_i$ to a bottleneck layer, and then reverse the process to generate $\hat{\mathbf{I}}_j$. The encoder contains 9 ResNet basic blocks[1].

The motivation of designing such a generator is to take advantage of learning residual information in generating new images. The general shape of "ResNet" is learning $y = f(x) + x$ which can be used to pass invariable information from the bottom layers of the encoder to the decoder, and change the variable information of pose. To this end, the other features (e.g., clothing, and the background) will also be reserved and passed to the decoder in order to generate $\hat{\mathbf{I}}_j$. With this architecture (see Fig. 3), we have the best of both worlds: the encoder-decoder network can help learn to extract the semantic information, stored in the bottleneck layer, while the ResNet blocks can pass rich invariable information of person identity to help synthesize more realistic images, and change variable information of poses to realize pose normalization at the same time.

Formally, let $G_P(\cdot)$ be the generator network which is composed of an encoder subnet $G_{Enc}(\cdot)$ and a decoder subnet $G_{Dec}(\cdot)$, the objective of the generator network can be expressed as

$$\mathcal{L}_{G_P} = \mathcal{L}_{GAN} + \lambda_1 \cdot \mathcal{L}_{L_1}, \tag{2}$$

where $\mathcal{L}_{GAN}$ is the loss of the generator in Eq. (1) with the generator $G_P(\cdot)$ and discriminator $D_P(\cdot)$ respectively,

$$\mathcal{L}_{GAN} = \mathbb{E}_{\mathbf{I}_j \sim p_{data}(\mathbf{I}_j)} \{\log D_P(\mathbf{I}_j) + \log(1 - D_P(G_P(\mathbf{I}_i, \mathbf{I}_{\mathcal{P}_j})))\} \tag{3}$$

and $\mathcal{L}_{L_1} = \mathbb{E}_{\mathbf{I}_j \sim p_{data}(\mathbf{I}_j)} \left[\left\| \mathbf{I}_j - \hat{\mathbf{I}}_j \right\|_1 \right]$, and $\hat{\mathbf{I}}_j = G_{Dec}(G_{Enc}(\mathbf{I}_i, \mathbf{I}_{\mathcal{P}_j}))$ is the reconstructed image for $\mathbf{I}_j$ from the input image $\mathbf{I}_i$ with the body pose $\mathbf{I}_{\mathcal{P}_j}$. Here the L_1−norm is used to yield sharper and cleaner images. λ_1 is the weighting coefficient to balance the importance of each term.

Discriminator. The discriminator $D_P(\cdot)$ aims at learning to differentiate the input images as real or fake (i.e., a binary classification task). Given the input

---

[1] Details of structure are in the Supplementary.

image $\mathbf{I}_i$ and target output image $\mathbf{I}_j$, the objective of the discriminator network can be formulated as

$$\mathcal{L}_{D_P} = -\mathcal{L}_{GAN}, \tag{4}$$

Since our final goal is to obtain the best generator G_P, the optimization step would be to iteratively minimize the loss function $\mathcal{L}_{G_P}$ and $\mathcal{L}_{D_P}$ until convergence. Please refer to the Supplementary Material for the detailed structures and parameters of the generator and discriminator.

3.3   Person Re-id with Pose Normalization

As shown in Fig. 2, we train two re-id models. One model is trained using the original images in a training set to extract identity-invariant features in the presence of pose variation. The other is trained using the synthesized images with normalized poses using our PN-GAN to compute re-id features free of pose variation. They are then fused as the final feature representation.

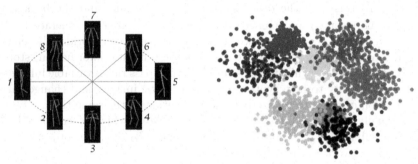

(a) Eight canonical poses on Market-1501 (b) t-SNE visualization of different poses.

Fig. 4. Visualization of canonical poses. Note that red crosses in (b) indicates the canonical pose obtained as the cluster means. (Color figure online)

Pose Normalization. We need to obtain a set of canonical poses, which are representative of the typical viewpoint and body-configurations exhibited by people in public captured by surveillance cameras. To this end, we predict the poses of all training images in a dataset and then group the poses into eight clusters $\{\mathbf{I}_{\mathcal{P}_C}\}_{c=1}^8$. We use VGG-19 [5] pre-trained on the ImageNet ILSVRC-2012 dataset to extract the features of each pose images, and K-means algorithm is used to cluster the training pose images into canonical poses. The mean pose images of these clusters are then used as the canonical poses. The eight poses obtained on Market-1501 [61] is shown in Fig. 4(a). With these poses, given each image $\mathbf{I}_i$, our generator will synthesize eight images $\left\{\hat{\mathbf{I}}_{i,\mathcal{P}_C}\right\}_{C=1}^8$ by replacing the original pose with these poses.

Re-id Feature with Pose Variation. We train one re-id model with the original training images to extract re-id features with pose variation. The ResNet-50 model [16] is used as the base network. It is pre-trained on the ILSVRC-2012 dataset, and fine-tuned on the training set of a given re-id dataset to classify the training identities. We name this network ResNet-50-A (Base Network A), as shown in Fig. 2. Given an input image $\mathbf{I}_i$, ResNet-50-A produces a feature set $\{\mathbf{f}_{\mathbf{I}_i, layer}\}$, where $layer$ indicates from which layer of the network, the re-id features are extracted. Note that, in most existing deep re-id models, features are computed from the final convolutional layer. Inspired by [29] which shows that layers before the final layer in a DNN often contain useful mid-level identity-sensitive information. We thus merge the $5a$, $5b$ and $5c$ convolutional layers of ResNet-50 structures into a 1024-d feature vector after an FC layer.

Re-id Feature Without Pose Variation. The second model called ResNet-50-B has the same architecture as ResNet-50-A, but performs feature learning using the pose-normalized synthetic images. We thus obtain eight sets of features for the eight poses $\mathbf{f}_{\hat{\mathbf{I}}_{i,\mathcal{P}_C}} = \left\{ \mathbf{f}_{\hat{\mathbf{I}}_{i,\mathcal{P}_C}} \right\}_{C=1}^{8}$.

Testing Stage. Once ResNet-50-A and ResNet-50-B are trained, during testing, for each gallery image, we feed it into ResNet-50-A to obtain one feature vector; as for synthesize eight images of the canonical poses, in consideration of confidence, we feed them into ResNet-50-B to obtain 8 pose-free features and one extra FC layer for the fusion of original feature and each pose feature. This can be done offline. Then given a query image $\mathbf{I}_q$, we do the same to obtain nine feature vectors $\left\{ \mathbf{f}_{\mathbf{I}_q}, \mathbf{f}_{\hat{\mathbf{I}}_{q,\mathcal{P}_C}} \right\}$. Since Maxout and Max-pooling have been widely used in multi-query video re-id, we thus obtain one final feature vector by fusing the nine feature vectors by element-wise maximum operation. We then calculate the Euclidean distance between the final feature vectors of the query and gallery images and use the distance to rank the gallery images.

4   Experiments

4.1   Datasets and Settings

Experiments are carried out on four benchmark datasets:

Market-1501. [61] is collected from 6 different camera views. It has 32,668 bounding boxes of 1,501 identities obtained using a Deformable Part Model (DPM) person detector. Following the standard split [61], we use 751 identities with 12,936 images as training and the rest 750 identities with 19,732 images for testing. The training set is used to train our PN-GAN model.

CUHK03. [25] contains 14,096 images of 1,467 identities, captured by six camera views with 4.8 images for each identity in each camera on average. We utilize the more realistic yet harder detected person images setting. The training and testing sets consist of 1,367 identities and 100 identities respectively. The testing process is repeated with 20 random splits following [25].

Table 1. Results on Market-1501. '-' indicates not reported. Note that *: on [65], we report the results of using both Basel. + LSRO and Verif.-Identif. + LSRO. Our model only uses the identification loss, so should be compared with Basel. + LSRO which uses the same ResNet-50 base network and the same loss.

Methods	Single-query		Multi-query	
	R-1	mAP	R-1	mAP
TMA [31]	47.90	22.3	–	–
SCSP [6]	51.90	26.40	–	–
DNS [54]	61.02	35.68	71.56	46.03
LSTM Siamese [41]	–	–	61.60	35.31
Gated_Sia [42]	65.88	39.55	76.50	48.50
HP-net [29]	76.90	–	–	–
Spindle [57]	76.90	–	–	–
Basel. + LSRO [65]*	78.06	56.23	85.12	68.52
PIE [62]	79.33	55.95	–	–
Verif.-Identif. [64]	79.51	59.87	85.84	70.33
DLPAR [58]	81.00	63.40	–	–
DeepTransfer [12]	83.70	65.50	89.60	73.80
Verif-Identif. + LSRO [65]*	83.97	66.07	88.42	76.10
PDC [39]	84.14	63.41	–	–
DML [56]	87.7	68.8	–	–
SSM [3]	82.2	68.8	88.2	76.2
JLML [26]	85.10	65.50	89.70	74.50
ResNet-50-A	87.26	69.32	91.81	77.85
Ours (SL)	**89.43**	**72.58**	**92.93**	**80.19**

DukeMTMC-reID. [36] is constructed from the multi-camera tracking dataset – DukeMTMC. It contains 1,812 identities. Following the evaluation protocol [65], 702 identities are used as the training set and the remaining 1,110 identities as the testing set. During testing, one query image for each identity in each camera is used for query and the remaining as the gallery set.

CUHK01. [24] has 971 identities with 2 images per person captured in two disjoint camera views respectively. As in [24], we use as probe the images of camera A and utilize those from camera B as gallery. 486 identities are randomly selected for testing and the remaining are used for training. The experiments are repeated for 10 times with the average results reported.

Evaluation Metrics. Two evaluation metrics are used to quantitatively measure the re-id performance. The first one is Rank-1, Rank-5 and Rank-10 accuracy. For Market-1501 and DukeMTMC-reID datasets, the mean Average Precision (mAP) is also used.

Table 2. Results on CUHK01 and CUHK03 datasets. Note that both Spindle [57] and HP-net [29] reported higher results on CUHK03. But their results are obtained using a very different setting: six auxiliary re-id datasets are used and both labeled and detected bounding boxes are used for both training and testing. So their results are not comparable to those in this table.

Method	R-1	R-5	R-10
DeepReid [25]	19.89	50.00	64.00
Imp-Deep [2]	44.96	76.01	83.47
EMD [38]	52.09	82.87	91.78
SI-CI [43]	52.17	84.30	92.30
LSTM Siamese [41]	57.30	80.10	88.30
PIE [62]	67.10	92.20	96.60
Gated_Sia [42]	68.10	88.10	94.60
Basel. + LSRO [65]	73.10	92.70	96.70
DGD [46]	75.30	–	–
OIM [48]	77.50	–	–
PDC [39]	78.92	94.83	97.15
DLPAR[58]	**81.60**	**97.30**	98.40
ResNet-50-A (SL)	76.83	93.79	97.27
Ours (SL)	79.76	96.24	**98.56**
ResNet-50-A (TL)	16.50	38.60	52.84
Ours (TL)	16.85	39.05	53.32

(a) Results on CUHK03

Method	R-1	R-5	R-10
eSDC [59]	19.76	32.72	40.29
kLFDA [49]	32.76	59.01	69.63
mFilter [60]	34.30	55.00	65.30
Imp-Deep [2]	47.53	71.50	80.00
DeepRanking [7]	50.41	75.93	84.07
Ensembles [33]	53.40	76.30	84.40
ImpTrpLoss [10]	53.70	84.30	91.00
GOG [32]	57.80	79.10	86.20
Quadruplet [8]	62.55	83.44	89.71
NullReid [55]	64.98	84.96	89.92
ResNet-50-A (SL)	64.56	83.66	89.74
Ours (SL)	**67.65**	**86.64**	**91.82**
ResNet-50-A (TL)	27.20	48.60	59.20
Ours (TL)	27.58	49.17	59.57

(b) Results on CUHK01

Implementation Details. Our model is implemented on Tensorflow [1] (PN-GAN part) and Caffe [19] (re-id feature learning part) framework. The λ_1 in Eq. (2) is empirically set as 10 in all experiments. We utilize the two-stepped fine-tuning strategy in [13] to fine-tune re-id networks. The input images are resized into 256×128. Adam [20] is used to train both the PN-GAN model and re-id networks with a learning rate of 0.0002, $\beta_1 = 0.5$, a batch size of 32, and a learning rate of 0.00035, $\beta_1 = 0.9$, a batch size of 16, respectively. The dropout ratio is set as 0.5. PN-GAN models and re-id networks are converged in 19 h and 8 h individually on Market-1501 with one NVIDIA 1080Ti GPU card.

Experimental Settings. Experiments are conducted under two settings. The first is the standard **Supervised Learning** (SL) setting on all datasets: the models are trained on the training set of the dataset, and evaluated on the testing set. The other one is the **Transfer Learning** (TL) setting only for the datasets, CUHK03, CUHK01, and DukeMTMC-reID. Specifically, the re-id model is trained on Market-1501 dataset. We then directly utilize the trained single model to do the testing (i.e., to synthesize images with canonical poses and to extract the nine feature vectors) on the test set of CUHK03, CUHK01, and DukeMTMC-reID. That is, no model updating is done using any data from these three datasets. The TL setting is especially useful in real-world scenarios, where a pre-trained model needs to be deployed to a new camera network without any model fine-tuning. This setting thus tests how generalizable a re-id model is.

Table 3. Results on DukeMTMC-reID.

Methods	R-1	R-10	mAP
LOMO + XQDA [27]	30.80	–	17.00
ResNet50 [16]	65.20	–	45.00
Basel. + LSRO [65]	67.70	–	47.10
AttIDNet [28]	70.69	–	51.88
ResNet-50-A (SL)	72.80	87.90	52.48
Ours (SL)	**73.58**	**88.75**	**53.20**
ResNet-50-A (TL)	27.87	51.12	13.94
Ours (TL)	29.94	51.62	15.77

4.2 Supervised Learning Results

Results on Large-Scale Datasets. Tables 1, 3 and 2(a) compare our model with the best performing alternative models. We can make the following observations:

(1) On all three datasets, the results clearly show that, in the supervised learning settings, our results are improved over those of ResNet-50-A baselines by a clear margin. This validates that the synthetic person images generated by PN-GAN can indeed help the person re-id tasks.
(2) Compared with the existing pose-guided re-id models [39,57,62], our model is clearly better, indicating that synthesizing multiple normalized poses is a more effective way to deal with the large pose variation problem.
(3) Compared with the other re-id model that uses synthesized images for re-id model training [65], our model yields better performance for all datasets, the gap on Market-1501 and DukeMTCM-reID being particularly clear. This is because our model can synthesize images with different poses, which can thus be used for supervised training. In contrast, the synthesized images in [65] do not correspond to any particular person identities or poses, so can only be used as unlabeled or weakly-labeled data.

Results on Small-Scale Dataset. On the smaller dataset – CUHK01, Table 2(b) shows that, again our ResNet-50-A is a pretty strong baseline which can beat almost all the other methods. And by using the normalized pose images generated by PN-GAN, our framework further boosts the performance of ResNet-50-A by more than 3% in the supervised setting. This demonstrates the efficacy of our framework. Note that on the small dataset CUHK01, the handcrafted feature + metric learning based models (e.g., NullReid [55]) are still quite competitive, often beating the more recent deep models. This reveals the limitations of the existing deep models on scalability and generalizability. In particular, previous deep re-id models are pre-trained on some large-scale training datasets, such as CUHK03 and Market-1501. But the models still struggle

Table 4. The Ablation study of Rank-1 and Rank-5 on benchmarks.

Dataset	Market-1501		DukeMTMC-reID		CUHK03		CUHK01	
Methods	R-1	mAP	R-1	mAP	R-1	R-5	R-1	R-5
ResNet-50-A	87.26	69.32	72.80	52.48	76.83	93.79	64.56	83.66
ResNet-50-B	63.75	41.29	26.62	14.30	32.54	55.12	36.18	51.17
Ours	**89.43**	**72.58**	**73.58**	**53.20**	**79.76**	**96.24**	**67.65**	**86.64**

Table 5. The Ablation study of Market-1501 on 1 pose feature and 8 pose features.

Feature(s)	1 pose		8 poses	
Methods	R-1	mAP	R-1	mAP
ResNet-50-A	87.26	69.32	87.26	69.32
ResNet-50-B	58.70	36.69	63.75	41.29
Ours (SL)	87.65	69.60	89.43	72.58

Table 6. The Rank-1/mAP results of ensembling two networks and ours. 'A+B' means training one ResNet-50-A and one ResNet-50-B model.

Methods	ResNet-50-A	ResNet-50-A	ResNet-50-B	Fusion
Ensemble (A+A)	87.26/69.32	87.29/69.36	–	87.38/69.57
Ours (A+B)	87.26/69.32	–	63.75/41.29	89.43/72.58

to fine-tune on the small datasets such as CUHK01 due to the covariate condition differences between them. With the pose normalization, our model is more adaptive to the small datasets and the model pre-trained on only Market-1501 can be easily fine-tuned on the small datasets, achieving much better result than existing models.

4.3 Transfer Learning Results

We report our results obtained under the TL settings on the three datasets – CUHK03, CUHK01, and DukeMTMC-reID in Tables 2(b) and 3 respectively. On CUHK01 dataset, we can achieve 27.58% Rank-1 accuracy in Table 2(b) which is comparable to some models trained under the supervised learning setting, such as eSDC [59]. These results thus show that our model has the potential to be generalizable to a new re-id data from new camera networks – when operating in a 'plug-and-play' mode. Our results are also compared against those of ResNet-50-A (TL) baseline. On all three datasets, we can observe that our model gets improved over those of ResNet-50-A (TL) baseline. Again, this demonstrates that our pose normalized person images can also help the person re-id in the transfer learning settings. Note that due to the intrinsic difficulty of transfer setting, the results are still much lower than those in supervised setting.

Fig. 5. Visualization of different poses generated by PN-GAN model. (Color figure online)

4.4 Further Evaluations

Ablation Studies. (1) We first evaluate the contributions from the two types of features computed using ResNet-50-A and ResNet-50-B respectively towards the final performance. Table 4 shows that although ResNet-50-B alone performs poorly compared to other methods, when the two types of features are combined, there is an improvement in the final results on all four datasets. This clearly indicates that the two types of features are complementary to each other. (2) In a second study, we compare the result obtained when features are merged with 8 poses and that obtained with only one pose, in Table 5. The result drops from 72.58 to 69.60 on Market-1501 on mAP. This suggests that having eight canonical poses is beneficial – the quality of generated image under one particular pose may be poor; using all eight poses thus reduces the sensitivity to the quality of the generated images for specific poses. (3) In order to prove that the performance gain comes from synthesized images instead of ensembling 2 networks, we conducted experiments on ensembling two ResNet-50-A models. As shown in Table 6, the gain from ensembling two ResNet-50-A is clearly less than that of ensembling one ResNet-50-A and one ResNet-50-B, despite the fact that the ResNet-50-B is much weaker than the second ResNet-50-A. These results thus suggest that our approaches performance gain is not due to ensembling but complementary features extracted from the ResNet-50-B model.

Examples of the Synthesized Images. Figure 5 gives some examples of the synthesized image poses. Given one input image, our image generator can produce realistic images under different poses, while keeping the similar visual appearance as the input person image. We find that, (1) Even though we did not explicitly use the attributes to guide the PN-GAN, the generated images of different poses have roughly the same visual attributes as the original images. (2) Our model can help alleviate the problems caused by occlusion as shown in the last row of Fig. 5: a man with yellow shirt and grey trousers is blocked by a bicycle, while our image generator can generate synthesized images to keep his key attributes whilst removing the occlusion.

5 Conclusion

We have proposed a novel deep person image generation model by synthesizing pose-normalized person images for re-id. In contrast to previous re-id approaches that try to extract discriminative features which are identity-sensitive but view-insensitive, the proposed method learns complementary features from both original images and pose-normalized synthetic images. Extensive experiments on four benchmarks showed that our model achieves state-of-the-art performance. More importantly, we demonstrated that our model has the potential to be generalized to new re-id datasets collected from new camera networks without any additional data collection and model fine-tuning.

Acknowledgments. This work was supported in part by National Key R&D Program of China (#2017YFC0803700), three projects from NSFC (#U1611461, #U1509206 and #61572138), two projects from STCSM (#16JC1420400 and #16JC1420401), two JSPS KAKENHI projects (#15K16024 and #16K12421), Eastern Scholar (TP2017006), and The Thousand Talents Plan of China (for young professionals, D1410009).

References

1. Abadi, M., et al.: TensorFlow: a system for large-scale machine learning. In: OSDI, vol. 16, pp. 265–283 (2016)
2. Ahmed, E., Jones, M., Marks, T.K.: An improved deep learning architecture for person re-identification. In: CVPR (2015)
3. Bai, S., Bai, X., Tian, Q.: Scalable person re-identification on supervised smoothed manifold. In: CVPR, vol. 6, p. 7 (2017)
4. Cao, Z., Simon, T., Wei, S.E., Sheikh, Y.: Realtime multi-person 2D pose estimation using part affinity fields. In: CVPR (2017)
5. Chatfield, K., Simonyan, K., Vedaldi, A., Zisserman, A.: Return of the devil in the details: delving deep into convolutional nets. In: BMVC (2014)
6. Chen, D., Yuan, Z., Chen, B., Zheng, N.: Similarity learning with spatial constraints for person re-identification. In: CVPR (2016)
7. Chen, S.Z., Guo, C.C., Lai, J.H.: Deep ranking for person re-identification via joint representation learning. IEEE TIP **25**, 2353–2367 (2016)
8. Chen, W., Chen, X., Zhang, J., Huang, K.: Beyond triplet loss: a deep quadruplet network for person re-identification. In: CVPR (2017)

9. Cheng, D., Gong, Y., Zhou, S., Wang, J., Zheng, N.: Person re-identification by multi-channel parts-based cnn with improved triplet loss function. In: CVPR (2016)

10. Cheng, D., Gong, Y., Zhou, S., Wang, J., Zheng, N.: Person re-identification by multi-channel parts-based CNN with improved triplet loss function. In: Proceedings of the IEEE Conference on Computer Vision and Pattern Recognition, pp. 1335–1344 (2016)

11. Deng, Y., Luo, P., Loy, C.C., Tang, X.: Learning to recognize pedestrian attribute. arXiv preprint arXiv:1501.00901 (2015)

12. Geng, M., Wang, Y., Xiang, T., Tian, Y.: Deep transfer learning for person re-identification. arXiv:1611.0524 (2016)

13. Geng, M., Wang, Y., Xiang, T., Tian, Y.: Deep transfer learning for person re-identification. arXiv preprint arXiv:1611.05244 (2016)

14. Gong, S., Xiang, T.: Person re-identification. In: Visual Analysis of Behaviour, pp. 301–313. Springer, London (2011). https://doi.org/10.1007/978-0-85729-670-2_14

15. Goodfellow, I., et al.: Generative adversarial nets. In: Advances in Neural Information Processing Systems, pp. 2672–2680 (2014)

16. He, K., Zhang, X., Ren, S., Sun, J.: Deep residual learning for image recognition. In: CVPR (2015)

17. Hinton, G.E., Salakhutdinov, R.R.: Reducing the dimensionality of data with neural networks. Science 313, 504–507 (2006)

18. Isola, P., Zhu, J.Y., Zhou, T., Efros, A.A.: Image-to-image translation with conditional adversarial networks. In: CVPR (2017)

19. Jia, Y., et al.: Caffe: convolutional architecture for fast feature embedding. arXiv (2014)

20. Kingma, D., Ba, J.: Adam: a method for stochastic optimization. arXiv preprint arXiv:1412.6980 (2014)

21. Larsen, A.B.L., Sønderby, S.K., Larochelle, H., Winther, O.: Autoencoding beyond pixels using a learned similarity metric. arXiv preprint arXiv:1512.09300 (2015)

22. Lassner, C., Pons-Moll, G., Gehler, P.V.: A generative model of people in clothing. In: Proceedings of the IEEE International Conference on Computer Vision, vol. 6 (2017)

23. Li, D., Chen, X., Zhang, Z., Huang, K.: Learning deep context-aware features over body and latent parts for person re-identification. In: Proceedings of the IEEE Conference on Computer Vision and Pattern Recognition, pp. 384–393 (2017)

24. Li, W., Zhao, R., Wang, X.: Human reidentification with transferred metric learning. In: Lee, K.M., Matsushita, Y., Rehg, J.M., Hu, Z. (eds.) ACCV 2012. LNCS, vol. 7724, pp. 31–44. Springer, Heidelberg (2013). https://doi.org/10.1007/978-3-642-37331-2_3

25. Li, W., Zhao, R., Xiao, T., Wang, X.: DeepReID: deep filter pairing neural network for person re-identification. In: CVPR (2014)

26. Li, W., Zhu, X., Gong, S.: Person re-identification by deep joint learning of multi-loss classification. In: IJCAI (2017)

27. Liao, S., Hu, Y., Zhu, X., Li., S.Z.: Person re-identification by local maximal occurrence representation and metric learning. In: CVPR (2015)

28. Lin, Y., Zheng, L., Zheng, Z., Wu, Y., Yang, Y.: Improving person re-identification by attribute and identity learning. arXiv preprint arXiv:1703.07220 (2017)

29. Liu, X., et al.: HydraPlus-Net: attentive deep features for pedestrian analysis. In: ICCV (2017)

30. Ma, L., Sun, Q., Jia, X., Schiele, B., Tuytelaars, T., Gool, L.V.: Pose guided person image generation. In: NIPS (2017)

31. Martinel, N., Das, A., Micheloni, C., Roy-Chowdhury, A.K.: Temporal model adaptation for person re-identification. In: Leibe, B., Matas, J., Sebe, N., Welling, M. (eds.) ECCV 2016. LNCS, vol. 9908, pp. 858–877. Springer, Cham (2016). https:// doi.org/10.1007/978-3-319-46493-0_52

32. Matsukawa, T., Okabe, T., Suzuki, E., Sato, Y.: Hierarchical Gaussian descriptor for person re-identification. In: Proceedings of the IEEE Conference on Computer Vision and Pattern Recognition, pp. 1363–1372 (2016)

33. Paisitkriangkrai, S., Shen, C., van den Hengel, A.: Learning to rank in person re-identification with metric ensembles. In: Proceedings of the IEEE Conference on Computer Vision and Pattern Recognition, pp. 1846–1855 (2015)

34. Qian, X., Fu, Y., Jiang, Y.G., Xiang, T., Xue, X.: Multi-scale deep learning architecture for person re-identification. In: ICCV (2017)

35. Radford, A., Metz, L., Chintala, S.: Unsupervised representation learning with deep convolutional generative adversarial networks. In: ICLR (2016)

36. Ristani, E., Solera, F., Zou, R., Cucchiara, R., Tomasi, C.: Performance measures and a data set for multi-target, multi-camera tracking. In: Hua, G., Jégou, H. (eds.) ECCV 2016. LNCS, vol. 9914, pp. 17–35. Springer, Cham (2016). https://doi.org/ 10.1007/978-3-319-48881-3_2

37. Sarfraz, M.S., Schumann, A., Wang, Y., Stiefelhagen, R.: Deep view-sensitive pedestrian attribute inference in an end-to-end model. arXiv preprint arXiv:1707.06089 (2017)

38. Shi, H., et al.: Embedding deep metric for person re-identification: a study against large variations. In: Leibe, B., Matas, J., Sebe, N., Welling, M. (eds.) ECCV 2016. LNCS, vol. 9905, pp. 732–748. Springer, Cham (2016). https://doi.org/10.1007/ 978-3-319-46448-0_44

39. Su, C., Li, J., Zhang, S., Xing, J., Gao, W., Tian, Q.: Pose-driven deep convolutional model for person re-identification. In: ICCV (2017)

40. Sun, Y., Zheng, L., Weijian, D., Shengjin, W.: SVDNet for pedestrian retrieval. In: ICCV (2017)

41. Varior, R.R., Shuai, B., Lu, J., Xu, D., Wang, G.: A Siamese long short-term memory architecture for human re-identification. In: Leibe, B., Matas, J., Sebe, N., Welling, M. (eds.) ECCV 2016. LNCS, vol. 9911, pp. 135–153. Springer, Cham (2016). https://doi.org/10.1007/978-3-319-46478-7_9

42. Varior, R.R., Haloi, M., Wang, G.: Gated Siamese convolutional neural network architecture for human re-identification. In: Leibe, B., Matas, J., Sebe, N., Welling, M. (eds.) ECCV 2016. LNCS, vol. 9912, pp. 791–808. Springer, Cham (2016). https://doi.org/10.1007/978-3-319-46484-8_48

43. Wang, F., Zuo, W., Lin, L., Zhang, D., Zhang, L.: Joint learning of single-image and cross-image representations for person re-identification. In: CVPR (2016)

44. Wang, J., Zhu, X., Gong, S., Li, W.: Attribute recognition by joint recurrent learning of context and correlation. In: ICCV (2017)

45. Wei, L., Zhang, S., Yao, H., Gao, W., Tian, Q.: GLAD: global-local-alignment descriptor for pedestrian retrieval. arXiv preprint arXiv:1709.04329 (2017)

46. Xiao, T., Li, H., Ouyang, W., Wang, X.: Learning deep feature representations with domain guided dropout for person re-identification. In: 2016 IEEE Conference on Computer Vision and Pattern Recognition, CVPR, pp. 1249–1258. IEEE (2016)

47. Xiao, T., Li, S., Wang, B., Lin, L., Wang, X.: Joint detection and identification feature learning for person search. In: CVPR (2017)

48. Xiao, T., Li, S., Wang, B., Lin, L., Wang, X.: Joint detection and identification feature learning for person search. In: 2017 IEEE Conference on Computer Vision and Pattern Recognition, CVPR, pp. 3376–3385. IEEE (2017)

49. Xiong, F., Gou, M., Camps, O., Sznaier, M.: Person re-identification using kernel-based metric learning methods. In: Fleet, D., Pajdla, T., Schiele, B., Tuytelaars, T. (eds.) ECCV 2014. LNCS, vol. 8695, pp. 1–16. Springer, Cham (2014). https://doi.org/10.1007/978-3-319-10584-0_1
50. Yao, H., Zhang, S., Zhang, Y., Li, J., Tian, Q.: Deep representation learning with part loss for person re-identification. arXiv preprint arXiv:1707.00798 (2017)
51. Yu, H.X., Wu, A., Zheng, W.S.: Cross-view asymmetric metric learning for unsupervised person re-identification. In: ICCV (2017)
52. Yu, K., Leng, B., Zhang, Z., Li, D., Huang, K.: Weakly-supervised learning of mid-level features for pedestrian attribute recognition and localization. arXiv preprint arXiv:1611.05603 (2016)
53. Zhang, H., et al.: StackGAN: text to photo-realistic image synthesis with stacked generative adversarial networks. In: ICCV (2017)
54. Zhang, L., Gong, T.X.S.: Learning a discriminative null space for person re-identification. In: CVPR (2016)
55. Zhang, L., Xiang, T., Gong, S.: Learning a discriminative null space for person re-identification. In: Proceedings of the IEEE Conference on Computer Vision and Pattern Recognition, pp. 1239–1248 (2016)
56. Zhang, Y., Xiang, T., Hospedales, T.M., Lu, H.: Deep mutual learning. arXiv preprint arXiv:1706.00384 (2017)
57. Zhao, H., et al.: Spindle net: person re-identification with human body region guided feature decomposition and fusion. In: Proceedings of the IEEE Conference on Computer Vision and Pattern Recognition, pp. 1077–1085 (2017)
58. Zhao, L., Li, X., Wang, J., Zhuang, Y.: Deeply-learned part-aligned representations for person re-identification. In: ICCV (2017)
59. Zhao, R., Ouyang, W., Wang, X.: Unsupervised salience learning for person re-identification. In: CVPR (2013)
60. Zhao, R., Ouyang, W., Wang, X.: Learning mid-level filters for person re-identification. In: Proceedings of the IEEE Conference on Computer Vision and Pattern Recognition, pp. 144–151 (2014)
61. Zheng, L., Shen, L., Tian, L., Wang, S., Wang, J., Tian, Q.: Scalable person re-identification: a benchmark. In: ICCV (2015)
62. Zheng, L., Huang, Y., Lu, H., Yang, Y.: Pose invariant embedding for deep person re-identification. arXiv preprint arXiv:1701.07732 (2017)
63. Zheng, L., Zhang, H., Sun, S., Chandraker, M., Tian, Q.: Person re-identification in the wild. arXiv preprint arXiv:1604.02531 (2016)
64. Zheng, Z., Zheng, L., Yang, Y.: A discriminatively learned CNN embedding for person re-identification. arXiv:1611.05666 (2016)
65. Zheng, Z., Zheng, L., Yang, Y.: Unlabeled samples generated by GAN improve the person re-identification baseline in vitro. In: ICCV (2017)

Learning 3D Human Pose from Structure and Motion

Rishabh Dabral[1(✉)], Anurag Mundhada[1], Uday Kusupati[1], Safeer Afaque[1],
Abhishek Sharma[2], and Arjun Jain[1]

[1] Indian Institute of Technology Bombay, Mumbai, India
{rdabral,ajain}@cse.iitb.ac.in, {anuragmundhada,udaykusupati}@iitb.ac.in
[2] Gobasco AI Labs, Lucknow, India
abhsharayiya@gmail.com

Abstract. 3D human pose estimation from a single image is a challenging problem, especially for in-the-wild settings due to the lack of 3D annotated data. We propose two anatomically inspired loss functions and use them with a weakly-supervised learning framework to jointly learn from large-scale in-the-wild 2D and indoor/synthetic 3D data. We also present a simple temporal network that exploits temporal and structural cues present in predicted pose sequences to temporally harmonize the pose estimations. We carefully analyze the proposed contributions through loss surface visualizations and sensitivity analysis to facilitate deeper understanding of their working mechanism. Jointly, the two networks capture the anatomical constraints in static and kinetic states of the human body. Our complete pipeline improves the state-of-the-art by 11.8% and 12% on Human3.6M and MPI-INF-3DHP, respectively, and runs at 30 FPS on a commodity graphics card.

1 Introduction

Accurate 3D human pose estimation from monocular images and videos is the key to unlock several applications in robotics, human computer interaction, surveillance, animation and virtual reality. These applications require *accurate* and *real-time* 3D pose estimation from monocular image or video under challenging variations of clothing, lighting, view-point, self-occlusions, activities, background clutter etc. [32,33]. With the advent of recent advances in deep learning, compute hardwares and, most importantly, large-scale *real-world* datasets (ImageNet [31], MS COCO [20], CityScapes [10] etc.), computer vision systems have witnessed dramatic improvements in performance. Human-pose estimation has also benefited from synthetic and real-world datasets such as MS COCO [20], MPII Pose [3], Human3.6M [6,14], MPI-INF-3DHP [22], and SURREAL [37]. Especially, 2D pose prediction has witnessed tremendous improvement due to

---

Electronic supplementary material The online version of this chapter (https://doi.org/10.1007/978-3-030-01240-3_41) contains supplementary material, which is available to authorized users.

V. Ferrari et al. (Eds.): ECCV 2018, LNCS 11213, pp. 679–696, 2018.
https://doi.org/10.1007/978-3-030-01240-3_41

large-scale in-the-wild datasets [3,20]. However, 3D pose estimation still remains challenging due to severely under-constrained nature of the problem and absence of any real-world 3D annotated dataset.

A large body of prior art either directly regresses for 3D joint coordinates [17, 18,34] or infers 3D from 2D joint-locations in a two-stage approach [19,22,24,41, 43]. These approaches perform well on synthetic 3D benchmark datasets, but lack generalization to the real-world setting due to the lack of 3D annotated in-the-wild datasets. To mitigate this issue, some approaches use synthetic datasets [9, 37], green-screen composition [22,23], domain adaptation [9], transfer learning from intermediate 2D pose estimation tasks [17,22], and joint learning from 2D and 3D data [34,41]. Notably, joint learning with 2D and 3D data has shown promising performance in-the-wild owing to large-scale real-world 2D datasets. We seek motivation from the recently published joint learning framework of Zhou et al. [41] and present a novel structure-aware loss function to facilitate training of Deep ConvNet architectures using both 2D and 3D data to accurately predict the 3D pose from a single RGB image. The proposed loss function is applicable to 2D images during training and ensures that the predicted 3D pose does not violate anatomical constraints, namely joint-angle limits and left-right symmetry of the human body. We also present a simple learnable temporal pose model for pose-estimation from videos. The resulting system is capable of jointly exploiting the structural cues evident in the static and kinetic states of human body.

Our proposed structure-aware loss is inspired by anatomical constraints that govern the human body structure and motion. We exploit the fact that certain body-joints cannot bend beyond an angular range; e.g. the knee (elbow) joints cannot bend forward (backward). We also make use of left-right symmetry of human body and penalize unequal corresponding pairs of left-right bone lengths. Lastly, we also use the bone-length ratio priors from [41] that enforce certain pairs of bone-lengths to be constant. It is important to note that the illegal-angle and left-right symmetry constraints are complementary to the bone-length ratio prior, and we show that they perform better too. We present the visualization of the loss surfaces of the proposed losses to facilitate a deeper understanding of their workings. The three aforementioned structure losses are used to train our *Structure-Aware PoseNet*. Joint-angle limits and left-right symmetry have been used previously in the form of optimization functions [1,4,13]. To the best of our knowledge we are the first ones to exploit these two constraints, in the form of differentiable and tractable loss functions, to train ConvNets directly. Our structure-aware loss function outperforms the published state-of-the-art in terms of Mean-Per-Joint-Position-Error (MPJPE) by 7% and 2% on Human3.6M and MPI-INF-3DHP, respectively.

We further propose to learn a temporal motion model to exploit cues from sequential frames of a video to obtain anatomically coherent and smoothly varying poses, while preserving the realism across different activities. We show that a moving-window fully-connected network that takes previous N poses performs extremely well at capturing temporal as well as anatomical cues from pose sequences. With the help of carefully designed controlled experiments we show the temporal and anatomical cues learned by the model to facilitate better understanding. We report an additional 7% improvement on Human3.6M with the use of our temporal model and demonstrate real-time performance of the full pipeline at 30 fps. Our final model improves the published state-of-the-art on Human3.6M [14] and MPI-INF-3DHP [22] by 11.8% and 12%, respectively.

2 Related Work

This section presents a brief summary of the past work related to human pose estimation from three viewpoints: (1) ConvNet architectures and training strategies, (2) Utilizing structural constraints of human bodies, and (3) 3D pose estimation from video. The reader is referred to [32] for a detailed review of the literature.

ConvNet Architectures: Most existing ConvNet based approaches either directly regress 3D poses from the input image [17,34,42,43] or infer 3D from 2D pose in a two-stage approach [19,23,24,35,41]. Some approaches make use of volumetric-heatmaps [27], some define a pose using bones instead of joints [34], while the approach in [23] directly regresses for 3D location maps. The use of 2D-to-3D pipeline enables training with large-scale in-the-wild 2D pose datasets [3,20]. A few approaches use statistical priors [1,43] to lift 2D poses to 3D. Chen et al. [7] and Yasin et al. [40] use a pose library to retrieve the nearest 3D pose given the corresponding 2D pose prediction. Recent ConvNet based approaches [23,27,30,34,41,43] have reported substantial improvements in real-world setting by pre-training or joint training of their 2D prediction modules, but it still remains an open problem.

Utilizing Structural Information: The structure of the human skeleton is constrained by fixed bone lengths, joint angle limits, and limb inter-penetration constraints. Some approaches use these constraints to infer 3D from 2D joint locations. Akhter and Black [1] learn pose-dependent joint angle limits for lifting 2D poses to 3D via an optimization problem. Ramakrishna et al. [28] solve for anthropometric constraints in an activity-dependent manner. Recently, Moreno [24] proposed to estimate the 3D inter-joint distance matrix from 2D inter-joint distance matrix using a simple neural network architecture. These approaches do not make use of rich visual cues present in images and rely on the predicted 2D pose that leads to sub-optimal results. Sun et al. [34] reparameterize the pose presentation to use bones instead of joints and propose a structure-aware loss. But, they do not explicitly seek to penalize the feasibility of inferred 3D pose in the absence of 3D ground-truth data. Zhou et al. [41] introduce a weakly-supervised framework for joint training with 2D and 3D data with the help of a geometric loss function to exploit the consistency of bone-length ratios in human body. We further strengthen this weakly-supervised setup with the help of joint-angle limits and left-right symmetry based loss functions for better training. Lastly, there are methods that recover both shape and pose from a 2D image via a mesh-fitting strategy. Bogo et al. [4] penalize body-part inter-penetration and illegal joint angles in their objective function for finding SMPL [21] based shape and pose parameters. These approaches are mostly offline in nature due to their computational requirements, while our approach runs at 30 fps.

Utilizing Temporal Information: Direct estimation of 3D pose from disjointed images leads to temporally incoherent output with visible jitters and varying bone lengths. 3D pose estimates from a video can be improved by using simple filters or temporal priors. Mehta et al. [23] propose a real-time approach which penalizes acceleration and depth velocity in an optimization step after generating 3D pose proposals using a ConvNet. They also smooth the output poses with the use of a tunable low-pass filter [5] optimized for interactive systems. Zhou et al. [43] introduce a first order smoothing prior in their temporal optimization step. Alldieck et al. [2] exploit 2D optical flow features to predict 3D poses from videos. Wei et al. [38] exploit physics-based constraints to realistically interpolate 3D motion between video keyframes. There have also been attempts to learn motion models. Urtasun et al. [36] learn activity specific motion priors using linear models while Park et al. [26] use a motion library to find the nearest motion given a set of 2D pose predictions followed by iterative fine-tuning. The motion models are activity-specific whereas our approach is generic. Recently, Lin et al. [19] used recurrent neural networks to learn temporal dependencies from the intermediate features of their ConvNet based architecture. In a similar attempt, Coskun et al. [11] use LSTMs to design a Kalman filter that learns human motion model. In contrast with the aforementioned approaches, our temporal model is simple yet effectively captures short-term interplay of past poses and predicts the pose of the current frame in a temporally and anatomically consistent manner. It is generic and does not need to be trained for activity-specific settings. We show that it learns complex, non-linear inter-joint dependencies over time; e.g. it learns to refine wrist position, for which the tracking is least accurate, based on the past motion of elbow and shoulder joints.

3   Background and Notations

This section introduces the notations used in this article and also provides the required details about the weakly-supervised framework of Zhou et al. [41] for joint learning from 2D and 3D data.

A 3D human pose $P = \{p_1, p_2, \ldots, p_k\}$ is defined by the positions of $k = 16$ body joints in Euclidean space. These joint positions are defined relative to a root joint, which is fixed as the pelvis. The input to the pose estimation system could be a single RGB image or a continuous stream of RGB images $I = \{\ldots, I_{i-1}, I_i\}$. The ith joint p_i is the coordinate of the joint in a 3D Euclidean space i.e. $p_i = (p_i^x, p_i^y, p_i^z)$. Throughout this article inferred variables are denoted with a $\tilde{*}$ and ground-truth is denoted with a $\hat{*}$, therefore, an inferred joint will be denoted as $\tilde{p}$ and ground-truth as $\hat{p}$. The 2D pose can be expressed with only the x, y-coordinates and denoted as $p^{xy} = (p^x, p^y)$; the depth-only joint location is denoted as $p^z = (p^z)$. The ith training data from a 3D annotated dataset consists of an image I_i and corresponding joint locations in 3D, $\hat{P}_i$. On the other hand, the 2D data has only the 2D joint locations, $\hat{P}_i^{xy}$. Armed with these notations, below we describe the weakly-supervised framework for joint learning from [41].

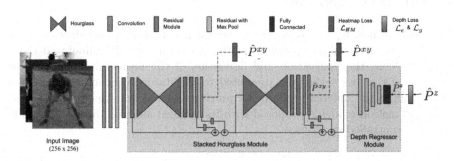

Fig. 1. A schematic of the network architecture. The stacked hourglass module is trained using the standard Euclidean loss $\mathcal{L}_{HM}$ against ground truth heatmaps. Whereas, the depth regressor module is trained on either $\mathcal{L}_{3D}^z$ or $\mathcal{L}_{2D}^z$ depending on whether the ground truth depth $\hat{P}^z$ is available or not.

Due to the absence of in-the-wild 3D data, the pose estimation systems learned using the controlled or synthetic 3D data fail to generalize well to in-the-wild settings. Therefore, Zhou et al. [41] proposed a weakly-supervised framework for joint learning from both 2D and 3D annotated data. Joint learning exploits the 3D data for depth prediction and the in-the-wild 2D data for better generalization to real-world scenario. The overall schematic of this framework is shown in Fig. 1. It builds upon the stacked hourglass architecture [25] for 2D pose estimation and adds a depth-regression sub-network on top of it. The stacked hourglass is trained to output the 2D joint locations, $\tilde{P}^{xy}$ in the image coordinate with the use of standard Euclidean loss between the predicted and the ground-truth joint-location heatmaps, please refer to [25] for more details. The depth-regression sub-network, a series of four residual modules [12] followed by a fully connected layer, takes a combination of different feature maps from stacked hourglass and outputs the depth of each joint i.e. $\tilde{P}^z$. Standard Euclidean loss $\mathcal{L}_e(\tilde{P}^z, \hat{P}^z)$ is used for the 3D annotated data-sample. On the other hand, a weak-supervision in the form of a geometric loss function, $\mathcal{L}_g(\tilde{P}^z, \hat{P}^{xy})$, is used to train with a 2D-only annotated data-sample. The geometric loss acts as a regularizer and penalizes the pose configurations that violate the consistency of bone-length ratio priors. Please note that the ground-truth xy-coordinates, $\hat{P}^{xy}$, with inferred depth, $\tilde{P}^z$ are used in $\mathcal{L}_g$ to make the training simple.

The geometric loss acts as an effective regularizer for the joint training and improves the accuracy of 3D pose estimation under controlled and in-the-wild test conditions, but it ignores certain other *strong* anatomical constraints of the human body. In the next section, we build upon the discussed weakly-supervised framework and propose a novel structure-aware loss that captures richer anatomical constraints and provides stronger weakly-supervised regularization than the geometric loss.

4 Proposed Approach

This section introduces two novel anatomical loss functions and shows how to use them in the weakly-supervised setting to train with 2D annotated data-samples. Next, the motivation and derivation of the proposed losses and the analyses of the loss surfaces is presented to facilitate a deeper understanding and highlight the differences from the previous approaches. Lastly, a learnable temporal motion model is proposed with its detailed analysis through carefully designed controlled experiments.

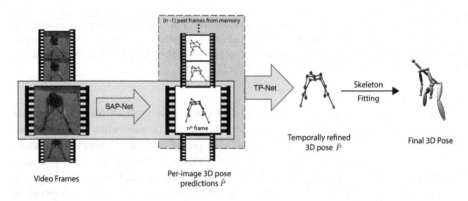

Fig. 2. Overall pipeline of our method: We sequentially pass the video frames to a ConvNet that produces 3D pose outputs (one at a time). Next, the prediction is temporally refined by passing a context of past N frames along with the current frame to a temporal model. Finally, skeleton fitting may be performed as an optional step depending upon the application requirement.

Figure 2 shows our complete pipeline for 3D pose estimation. It consists of

1. **Structure-Aware PoseNet or SAP-Net:** A single-frame based 3D pose-estimation system that takes a single RGB image I_i and outputs the inferred 3D pose $\tilde{P}_i$.
2. **Temporal PoseNet or TP-Net:** A learned temporal motion model that can take a continuous sequence of inferred 3D poses $\{\ldots, \tilde{P}_{i-2}, \tilde{P}_{i-1}\}$ and outputs a temporally harmonized 3D pose $\bar{P}_i$.
3. **Skeleton fitting:** Optionally, if the actual skeleton information of the subject is also available, we can carry out a simple skeleton fitting step which preserves the directions of the bone vectors.

4.1 Structure-Aware PoseNet or SAP-Net

SAP-Net uses the network architecture shown in Fig. 2, which is taken from [41]. This network choice allows joint learning with both 2D and 3D data in weakly-supervised fashion as described in Sect. 3. A 3D annotated data-sample provides strong supervision signal and drives the inferred depth towards a unique solution. On the other hand, weak-supervision, in the form of anatomical constraints, imposes penalty on invalid solutions, therefore, restricts the set of solutions. Hence, the stronger and more comprehensive the set of constraints, the smaller and better the set of solutions. We seek motivation from the discussion above and propose to use loss functions derived from joint-angle limits and left-right symmetry of human body in addition to bone-length ratio priors [41] for weak-supervision. Together, these three constraints are stronger than the bone-length ratio prior only and lead to better 3D pose configurations. For example, bone-length ratio prior will consider an elbow bent backwards as valid, if the bone ratios are not violated, but the joint-angle limits will invalidate it. Similarly, the symmetry loss eliminates the configurations with asymmetric left-right halves in the inferred pose. Next we describe and derive differentiable loss functions for the proposed constraints.

Illegal Angle Loss ($\mathcal{L}_a$): Most body joints are constrained to move within a certain angular limits only. Our illegal angle loss, $\mathcal{L}_a$, encapsulates this constraint for the knee and elbow joints and restricts their bending beyond $180°$. For a given 2D pose P^{xy}, there exist multiple possible 3D poses and $\mathcal{L}_a$ penalizes the 3D poses that violate the knee or elbow joint-angle limits. To exploit such constraints, some methods [1,8,13] use non-differentiable functions to infer the legality of a pose. Unfortunately, the non-differentiability restricts their direct use in training a neural network. Other methods resort to representing a pose in terms of rotation matrices or quaternions for imposing joint-angle limits [1,38] that affords differentiability, but, makes it difficult to use in-the-wild 2D data (MPII). Therefore, this formulation is non-trivial when representing poses in terms of joint-positions, which are a more natural representation for ConvNets.

Our novel formulation of illegal-angle discovery resolves the ambiguity involved in differentiating between the internal and external angle of a joint for a 3D joint-location based pose representation. Using our formulation and keeping in mind our the requirement of differentiability, we formulate $\mathcal{L}_a$ to be used directly as a loss function. We illustrate our formulation with the help of Fig. 3, and explain its derivation for the right elbow joint. Subscripts n, s, e, w, k denote neck, shoulder, elbow, wrist and knee joints in that order, and superscripts l and r represent left and right body side, respectively. We define $\mathbf{v_{sn}^r} = P_s^r - P_n$, $\mathbf{v_{es}^r} = P_e^r - P_s^r$ and $\mathbf{v_{we}^r} = P_w^r - P_e^r$ as the collar-bone, upper-arm and the lower-arm, respectively (See Fig. 3). Now, $\mathbf{n_s^r} = \mathbf{v_{sn}^r} \times \mathbf{v_{es}^r}$ is the normal to the plane defined by the collar-bone and the upper-arm. For the elbow joint to be legal, $\mathbf{v_{we}^r}$ must have a positive component in the direction of $\mathbf{n_s^r}$, i.e. $\mathbf{n_s^r} \cdot \mathbf{v_{we}^r}$ must be positive. We do not incur any penalty when the joint angle is legal and define $E_e^r = \min(\mathbf{n_s^r} \cdot \mathbf{v_{we}^r}, 0)$ as a measure of implausibility. Note that this case is opposite for the right knee and left elbow joints (as shown by the right hand rule)

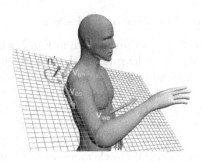

Fig. 3. Illustration of Illegal Angle loss: For the elbow joint angle to be legal, the lower-arm must project a positive component along $\mathbf{n_s^r}$ (normal to collarbone-upper arm plane), i.e. $\mathbf{n_s^r} \cdot \mathbf{v_{we}} \geq 0$. Note that we only need 2D annotated data to train our model using this formulation.

and requires E_k^r and E_e^l to be positive for the illegal case. We exponentiate E to strongly penalize large deviations beyond legality. $\mathcal{L}_a$ can now be defined as:

$$\mathcal{L}_a = -E_e^r e^{-E_e^r} + E_e^l e^{E_e^l} + E_k^r e^{E_k^r} - E_k^l e^{-E_k^l} \tag{1}$$

All the terms in the loss are functions of bone vectors which are, in turn, defined in terms of the inferred pose. Therefore, $\mathcal{L}_a$ is differentiable. Please refer to the supplementary material for more details.

Symmetry Loss ($\mathcal{L}_s$): It is simple yet heavily constrains the joint depths, especially when the inferred depth is ambiguous due to occlusions. $\mathcal{L}_s$ is defined as the difference in lengths of left/right bone pairs. Let $\mathcal{B}$ be the set of all the bones on right half of the body except torso and head bones. Also, let BL_b represent the bone-length of bone b. We define L_s as

$$\mathcal{L}_s = \sum_{b \in \mathcal{B}} \|BL_b - BL_{C(b)}\|_2 \tag{2}$$

where $C(.)$ indicates the corresponding left side bone.

Finally, our structure-aware loss $\mathcal{L}_{SA}^z$ is defined as weighted sum of illegal-angle loss $\mathcal{L}_a^z$, symmetry-loss $\mathcal{L}_s^z$ and geometric loss $\mathcal{L}_g^z$ from [41] -

$$\mathcal{L}_{SA}^z(\tilde{P}^z, \hat{P}^{xy}) = \lambda_a \mathcal{L}_a(\tilde{P}^z, \hat{P}^{xy}) + \lambda_s \mathcal{L}_s(\tilde{P}^z, \hat{P}^{xy}) + \lambda_g \mathcal{L}_g(\tilde{P}^z, \hat{P}^{xy}) \tag{3}$$

Loss Surface Visualization: Here we take help of local loss surface visualization to appreciate how the proposed losses are pushing invalid configurations towards their valid counterparts. In order to obtain the loss surfaces we take a random pose P and vary the (x_{le}, z_{le}) coordinates of left elbow over an XZ grid while keeping all other joint locations fixed. Then, we evaluate $\mathcal{L}_{SA}^z$ at different (x, z) locations in the XZ grid to obtain the loss, which is plotted as surfaces in Fig. 4. We plot loss surfaces with only 2D-location loss,

2D-location+symmetry loss, 2D-location+symmetry+illegal angle loss and 3D-annotation based Euclidean loss to show the evolution of the loss surfaces under different anatomical constraints. From the figure it is clear that both the symmetry loss and illegal angle loss morph the loss surface to facilitate moving away from illegal joint configurations.

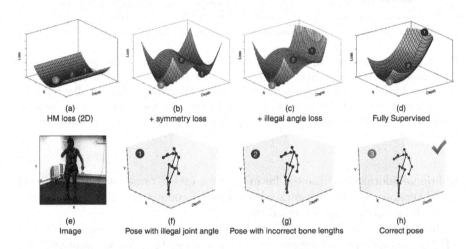

Fig. 4. Loss Surface Evolution: Plots (a) to (d) show the local loss surfaces for (a) 2D-location loss. (b) 2D-location+symmetry loss (c) 2D-location+symmetry+illegal angle loss and (d) full 3D-annotation Euclidean loss. The points (1), (2) and (3) highlighted on the plots are the corresponding 3D poses shown in (f), (g) and (h), with (3) being the ground-truth depth. The illegal angle penalty increases the loss for pose (1), which has the elbow bent backwards. Pose (2) has a legal joint angle, but the symmetry is lost. Pose (3) is correct. We can see that without the angle loss, the loss at (1) and (3) are equal and we cannot discern between the two points.

4.2 Temporal PoseNet or TP-Net

In this section we propose to learn a temporal pose model, referred as Temporal PoseNet, to exploit the temporal consistency and motion cues present in video sequences. Given independent pose estimates from SAP-Net, we seek to exploit the information from a set of adjacent pose-estimates $\mathbf{P}_{adj}$ to improve the inference for the required pose P. We propose to use a simple two-layer, 4096 hidden neurons, fully-connected network with ReLU non-linearity that takes a fixed number, $N = 20$, of adjacent poses as inputs and outputs the required pose $\bar{P}$. The adjacent pose vectors are simply flattened and concatenated in order to make a single vector that goes into the TP-Net and it is trained using standard L_2 loss from the ground-truth pose. Despite being extremely simple in nature, we show that it outperforms a more complex variant such as RNNs, see Table 4. Why? We believe it happens because intricate human motion has increasing variations possible with increasing time window, which perhaps makes

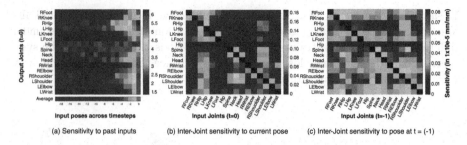

(a) Sensitivity to past inputs   (b) Inter-Joint sensitivity to current pose   (c) Inter-Joint sensitivity to pose at t = (-1)

Fig. 5. (a) The variation of sensitivity in output pose w.r.t to the perturbations in input poses of TP-Net for from $t = 0$ to $t = -19$. (b) Strong structural correlations are learned from the pose input at $t = 0$ frame. (c) Past frames show smaller but more complex structural correlations. The self correlations (diagonal elements) are an order of magnitude larger and the colormap range has been capped to better display. (Color figure online)

additional information from too far in the time useless or at least difficult to utilize. Therefore, a dense network with a limited context can effectively capture the useful consistency and motion cues.

In order to visualize the temporal and structural information exploited by TP-Net we carried out a simple sensitivity analysis in which we randomly perturbed the joint locations of P_t that is t time-steps away from the output of TP-Net $\bar{P}$ and plot the sensitivity for time-steps $t = -1$ to $t = -19$ for all joints in Fig. 5(a). We can observe that poses beyond 5 time-steps (or 200 ms time-window) does not have much impact on the predicted pose. Similarly, Fig. 5(b) shows the structural correlations the model has learned just within the current frame. TP-Net learns to rely on the locations of hips and shoulders to refine almost all the other joints. We can also observe that the child joints are correlated with parent joints, for e.g. the wrists are strongly correlated with elbows, and the shoulders are strongly correlated with the neck. Figure 5(c) shows the sensitivity to the input pose at $t = -1$. Here, the correlations learned from the past are weak, but exhibit a richer pattern. The sensitivity of the child joints extends further upwards into the kinematic chain, e.g., the wrist shows higher correlations with elbow, shoulder and neck, for the $t = -1$ frame. Therefore, we can safely conclude that TP-Net learns complex structural and motion cues despite being so simple in nature. We hope this finding would be useful for future research in this direction.

Since TP-Net takes as input a fixed number of adjacent poses, we can choose to take all the adjacent poses before the required pose, referred to as *online* setting, or we can choose to have $N/2 = 10$ adjacent poses on either side of required pose, referred to as *semi-online* setting. Since our entire pipeline runs at 30 fps, even semi-online setting will run at a lag of 10 fps only. From Fig. 5 we observe that TP-Net can learn complex, non-linear inter-joint dependencies over time - for e.g. it learns to refine wrist position, for which the tracking is least accurate, based on the past motion of elbow and shoulder joints.

4.3   Training and Implementation Details

While training the SAP-Net, both 2D samples, from MPII2D, and 3D samples, from either of the 3D datasets, were consumed in equal proportion in each iteration with a minibatch size of 6. In the *first stage* we obtain a strong 2D pose estimation network by pre-training the hourglass modules of SAP-Net on MPII and Human3.6 using SGD as in [25]. Training with weakly-supervised losses require a warm start [44], therefore, in the *second stage* we train the 3D depth module with only 3D annotated data-samples for 240k iterations so that it learns to output reasonable poses before switching on weak-supervision. In the *third stage* we train SAP-Net with $\mathcal{L}_g$ and $\mathcal{L}_a$ for 160k iterations with $\lambda_a = 0.03$, $\lambda_g = 0.03$ with a learning-rate of $2.5e{-}4$. Finally, in the *fourth stage* we introduce the symmetry loss, $\mathcal{L}_f$ with $\lambda_s = 0.05$ and learning-rate $2.5e{-}5$.

TP-Net was trained using Adam optimizer [16] for 30 epochs using the pose predictions generated by fully-trained SAP-Net. In our experiments, we found that a context of $N = 20$ frames yields the best improvement on MPJPE (Fig. 5) and we use that in all our experiments. It took approximately two days to train SAP-Net and one hour to train TP-Net using one NVIDIA 1080 Ti GPU. SAP-Net runs at an average testing time of 20 ms per image while TP-Net adds negligible delay ($<$1 ms).

5   Experiments

In this section, we present ablation studies, quantitative results on Human3.6M and MPI-INF-3DHP datasets and comparisons with previous art, and qualitative results on MPII 2D and MS COCO datasets. We start by describing the datasets used in our experiments.

Human3.6M has 11 subjects performing different indoor actions with ground-truth annotations captured using a marker-based MoCap system. We follow [35] and evaluate our results under (1) *Protocol 1* that uses Mean Per Joint Position Error (MPJPE) as the evaluation metric w.r.t. root relative poses and (2) *Protocol 2* that uses Procrustes Aligned MPJPE (PAMPJPE) which is MPJPE calculated after rigid alignment of predicted pose with the ground truth. As is common, we evaluate the results on every fifth frame.

MPI-INF-3DHP (test) dataset is a recently released dataset of 6 test subjects with different indoor settings (green screen and normal background) and 2 subjects performing in-the-wild that makes it more challenging than Human3.6M, which only has a single indoor setting. We follow the evaluation metric proposed in [22] and report Percentage of Correct Keypoints (PCK) within *150* mm range and Area Under Curve (AUC). Like [41], we assume that the global scale is known and perform skeleton retargeting while training to account for the difference of joint definitions between Human3.6M and MPI-INF-3DHP datasets. Finally, skeleton fitting is done as an optional step to fit the pose into a skeleton of known bone lengths.

Table 1. Comparative evaluation of our model on Human 3.6 following Protocol 1. The evaluations were performed on subjects 9 and 11 using ground truth bounding box crops and the models were trained only on Human3.6 and MPII 2D pose datasets.

Method	Direction	Discuss	Eat	Greet	Phone	Pose	Purchase	Sit
Zhou [43]	68.7	74.8	67.8	76.4	76.3	84.0	70.2	88.0
Jahangiri [15]	74.4	66.7	67.9	75.2	77.3	70.6	64.5	95.6
Lin [19]	58.0	68.2	63.2	65.8	75.3	61.2	65.7	98.6
Mehta [22]	57.5	68.6	59.6	67.3	78.1	56.9	69.1	98.0
Pavlakos [27]	58.6	64.6	63.7	62.4	66.9	57.7	62.5	76.8
Zhou [41]	54.8	60.7	58.2	71.4	62.0	53.8	55.6	75.2
Sun [34]	52.8	54.8	54.2	54.3	61.8	53.1	53.6	71.7
Ours (SAP-Net)	46.9	53.8	47.0	52.8	56.9	45.2	48.2	68.0
Ours (TP-Net)	**44.8**	**50.4**	**44.7**	**49.0**	**52.9**	**43.5**	**45.5**	**63.1**
Method	SitDown	Smoke	Photo	Wait	Walk	WalkDog	WalkPair	Avg
Zhou [43]	113.8	78.0	78.4	89.1	62.6	75.1	73.6	79.9
Jahangiri [15]	127.3	79.6	79.1	73.4	67.4	71.8	72.8	77.6
Lin [19]	127.7	70.4	93.0	68.2	50.6	72.9	57.7	73.1
Mehta [22]	117.5	69.5	82.4	68.0	55.3	76.5	61.4	72.9
Pavlakos [27]	103.5	65.7	70.7	61.6	56.4	69.0	59.5	66.9
Zhou [41]	111.6	64.1	65.5	66.0	51.4	63.2	55.3	64.9
Sun [34]	**86.7**	61.5	67.2	53.4	47.1	61.6	53.4	59.1
Ours (SAP-Net)	94.0	55.7	63.6	51.6	40.3	55.4	44.3	55.5
Ours (TP-Net)	87.3	**51.7**	**61.4**	**48.5**	**37.6**	**52.2**	**41.9**	**52.1**

Table 2. Comparative evaluation of our model on Human 3.6M using Protocol 2. The models were trained only on Human3.6M and MPII 2D datasets.

Method	Direct.	Discuss	Eat	Greet	Phone	Pose	Purch.	Sit	Sit Down	Smoke	Photo	Wait	Walk	Walk Dog	Walk Pair	Avg
Yasin [40]	88.4	72.5	108.5	110.2	97.1	91.6	107.2	119.0	170.8	108.2	142.5	86.9	92.1	165.7	102.0	108.3
Rogez [29]	-	-	-	-	-	-	-	-	-	-	-	-	-	-	-	88.1
Chen [7]	71.6	66.6	74.7	79.1	70.1	67.6	89.3	90.7	195.6	83.5	93.3	71.2	55.7	85.9	62.5	82.7
Nie [39]	62.8	69.2	79.6	78.8	80.8	72.5	73.9	96.1	106.9	88.0	86.9	70.7	71.9	76.5	73.2	79.5
Moreno [24]	67.4	63.8	87.2	73.9	71.5	69.9	65.1	71.7	98.6	81.3	93.3	74.6	76.5	77.7	74.6	76.5
Zhou [43]	47.9	48.8	52.7	55.0	56.8	49.0	45.5	60.8	81.1	53.7	65.5	51.6	50.4	54.8	55.9	55.3
Sun [34]	42.1	44.3	45.0	45.4	51.5	43.2	41.3	59.3	73.3	51.0	53.0	44.0	38.3	48.0	44.8	48.3
Ours(SAP-Net)	32.8	36.8	42.5	38.5	42.4	35.4	34.3	53.6	66.2	46.5	49.0	34.1	30.0	42.3	39.7	42.2
Ours (TP-Net)	**28.0**	**30.7**	**39.1**	**34.4**	**37.1**	**28.9**	**31.2**	**39.3**	**60.6**	**39.3**	**44.8**	**31.1**	**25.3**	**37.8**	**28.4**	**36.3**

2D Datasets: MS-COCO and MPII are in-the-wild 2D pose datasets with no 3D ground truth annotations. Therefore, we show qualitative results for both of them in Fig. 6. Despite lack of depth annotation, our approach generalizes well and predicts valid 3D poses under background clutter and significant occlusion.

Table 3. Ablation of different loss terms on Human3.6M using Protocol 1.

Method	MPJE
Zhou w/o $\mathcal{L}_g$ [41]	65.69
+ Geometry loss	64.90
Baseline	58.50
Baseline + $\mathcal{L}_s$	58.30
Baseline + $\mathcal{L}_a$	57.70
Baseline + $\mathcal{L}_g$	58.30
Baseline + $\mathcal{L}_g + \mathcal{L}_a$	56.20
Baseline + $\mathcal{L}_g + \mathcal{L}_a + \mathcal{L}_s$	55.51
Baseline + $\mathcal{L}_g + \mathcal{L}_a + \mathcal{L}_s$ + TP-Net	**52.10**
Baseline + $\mathcal{L}_g + \mathcal{L}_a + \mathcal{L}_s$ + Bi-TP-Net	**51.10**

Table 4. Comparison of different temporal models considered with varying context sizes. LSTM nets model the entire past context till time t. Bidirectional networks take half contextual frames from the future and half from the past.

Model	Number of input frames		
	4	10	20
LSTM	-	-	54.05
Bi-LSTM	53.86	53.72	53.65
TP-Net	53.0	52.24	52.1
Bi-TP-Net	52.4	51.36	**51.1**

5.1 Quantitative Evaluations

We evaluate the outputs of the three stages of our pipeline and show improvements at each stage.

1. **Baseline:** We train the same network architecture as SAP-Net but with only the fully supervised losses i.e. 2D heatmap supervision and $\mathcal{L}^e$ for 3D data only.
2. **SAP-Net:** Trained with the proposed structure-aware loss following Sect. 4.3.
3. **TP-Net:** Trained on the outputs of SAP-Net from video sequences (see Sect. 4.3).
4. **Skeleton Fitting (optional):** We fit a skeleton based on the subject's bone lengths while preserving the bone vector directions obtained from the 3D pose estimates.

Below, we conduct ablation study on SAP-Net and report results on the two datasets.

SAP-Net Ablation Study: In order to understand the effect of individual anatomical losses, we train SAP-Net with successive addition of geometry $\mathcal{L}_g^z$, illegal-angle $\mathcal{L}_a^z$ and symmetry $\mathcal{L}_s^z$ losses and report their performance on Human3.6M under *Protocol 1* in Table 3. We can observe that the incorporation of illegal-angle and symmetry losses to geometry loss significantly improves the performance while geometry loss does not offer much improvement even over the baseline. Similarly, TP-Net offers significant improvements over SAP-Net and the *semi-online* variant of TP-Net (Bi-TP-Net) does even better than TP-Net.

Evaluations on Human3.6M: We show significant improvement over the state-of-the-art and achieve an MPJPE of 55.5 mm with SAP-Net which is further improved by TP-Net to 52.1 mm. Tables 1 and 2 present a comparative analysis of our results under *Protocol 1* and *Protocol 2*, respectively. We outperform

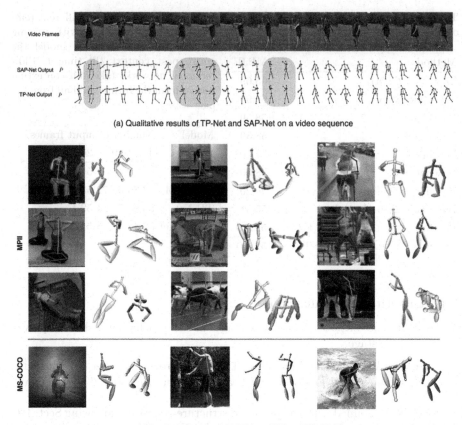

(a) Qualitative results of TP-Net and SAP-Net on a video sequence

(b) Qualitative results of SAP-Net on MPII and MS-COCO

Fig. 6. (a) Comparison of our temporal model TP-Net with SAP-Net on a video. The highlighted poses demonstrate the ability of TP-Net to learn temporal correlations, and smoothen and refine pose estimates from SAP-Net. (b) Qualitative results of SAP-Net on some images from MPII and MS-COCO datasets, from multiple viewpoints.

other competitive approaches by significant margins leading to an improvement of 12%.

Evaluations on MPI-INF-3DHP: The results from Table 5 show that we achieve slightly worse performance in terms of PCK and AUC but much better performance in terms of MPJPE, improvement of 12%, as compared to the current state-of-the-art. It is despite the lack of data augmentation through green-screen compositing during training.

5.2   Structural Validity Analysis

This section analyzes the validity of the predicted 3D poses in terms of the anatomical constraints, namely left-right symmetry and joint-angle limits. Ide-

Table 5. Results on MPI-INF-3DHP dataset. Higher PCK and AUC are desired while a lower MPJPE is better. Note that unlike [22,23], the MPI-INF-3DHP training dataset was not augmented.

Method	PCK	AUC	MPJPE
Mehta [22]	75.7	39.3	117.6
Mehta [23]	76.6	**40.4**	124.7
Ours	**76.7**	39.1	**103.8**

Table 6. Evaluating our models on (i) symmetry - mean L_1 distance in mm between left/right bone pairs (upper half), and (ii) the standard deviation (in mm) of bone lengths across all video frames (lower half) on MPI-INF-3DHP dataset.

Bone	Zhou [41]	SAP-Net	TP-Net
Upper arm	37.8	$25.8_{\downarrow 31.7\%}$	$\mathbf{23.9}_{\downarrow 36.7\%}$
Lower arm	50.7	$\mathbf{32.1}_{\downarrow 36.7\%}$	$33.9_{\downarrow 33.1\%}$
Upper leg	43.4	$27.8_{\downarrow 35.9\%}$	$\mathbf{24.8}_{\downarrow 42.8\%}$
Lower leg	47.8	$38.2_{\downarrow 20.1\%}$	$\mathbf{29.2}_{\downarrow 38.9\%}$
Upper arm	–	49.6	**39.8**
Lower arm	–	66.0	**48.3**
Upper leg	–	61.3	**48.8**
Lower leg	–	68.8	**48.3**

ally, the corresponding left-right bone pairs should be of similar length; therefore, we compute the mean L_1 distance in mm between the corresponding left-right bone pairs on MPI-INF-3DHP dataset and present the results in the upper half of Table 6. For fairness of comparison, we evaluate on model trained only on Human3.6M. We can see that SAP-Net, trained with symmetry loss, significantly improves the symmetry as compared to the system in [41] which uses bone-length ratio priors and TP-Net offers further improvements by exploiting the temporal cues from adjacent frames. It shows the importance of explicit enforcement of symmetry. Moreover, it clearly demonstrates the effectiveness of TP-Net in implicitly learning the symmetry constraint. The joint-angle validity of the predicted poses is evaluated using [1] and we observe only 0.8% illegal non-torso joint angles as compared to 1.4% for [41].

The lower-half of Table 6 tabulates the standard deviation of bone lengths in mm across frames for SAP-Net and TP-Net. We can observe that TP-Net reduces the standard deviation of bone-length across the frames by 28.7%. It is also worth noting that we do not use any additional filter (moving average, 1 Euro, etc.) which introduces lag and makes the motion look *uncanny*. Finally, we present some qualitative results in Fig. 6 and in the supplementary material to show that TP-Net effectively corrects the jerks in the poses predicted by SAP-Net.

6 Conclusion

We proposed two anatomically inspired loss functions, namely illegal-angle and symmetry loss. We showed them to be highly effective for training weakly-supervised ConvNet architectures for predicting valid 3D pose configurations from a single RGB image in-the-wild setting. We analyzed the evolution of local loss surfaces to clearly demonstrate the benefits of the proposed losses. We also proposed a simple, yet surprisingly effective, sliding-window fully-connected network for temporal pose modeling from a sequence of adjacent poses. We showed that it is capable of learning semantically meaningful short-term temporal and structure correlations. Temporal model was shown to significantly reduce jitters and noise from pose prediction for video sequences while taking <1 ms per inference. Our complete pipeline improved the published state-of-the-art by 11.8% and 12% on Human3.6M and MPI-INF-3DHP, respectively while running at 30 fps on NVIDIA Titan 1080Ti GPU.

Acknowledgement. This work is supported by Mercedes-Benz Research & Development India (RD/0117-MBRDI00-001).

References

1. Akhter, I., Black, M.J.: Pose-conditioned joint angle limits for 3D human pose reconstruction. In: CVPR (2015)
2. Alldieck, T., Kassubeck, M., Wandt, B., Rosenhahn, B., Magnor, M.: Optical flow-based 3D human motion estimation from monocular video. In: Roth, V., Vetter, T. (eds.) GCPR 2017. LNCS, vol. 10496, pp. 347–360. Springer, Cham (2017). https://doi.org/10.1007/978-3-319-66709-6_28
3. Andriluka, M., Pishchulin, L., Gehler, P., Schiele, B.: 2D human pose estimation: New benchmark and state of the art analysis. In: CVPR (2014)
4. Bogo, F., Kanazawa, A., Lassner, C., Gehler, P., Romero, J., Black, M.J.: Keep it SMPL: automatic estimation of 3D human pose and shape from a single image. In: Leibe, B., Matas, J., Sebe, N., Welling, M. (eds.) ECCV 2016. LNCS, vol. 9909, pp. 561–578. Springer, Cham (2016). https://doi.org/10.1007/978-3-319-46454-1_34
5. Casiez, G., Roussel, N., Vogel. D.: 1 filter: a simple speed-based low-pass filter for noisy input in interactive systems. In: SIGCHI (2012)
6. Sminchisescu, C., Ionescu, C., Li, F.: Latent structured models for human pose estimation. In: ICCV (2011)
7. Chen, C.-H., Ramanan, D.: 3D human pose estimation = 2D pose estimation + matching. In: CVPR (2017)
8. Chen, J., Nie, S., Ji, Q.: Data-free prior model for upper body pose estimation and tracking. IEEE Trans. Image Process. **22**, 4627–4639 (2013)
9. Chen, W., et al.: Synthesizing training images for boosting human 3D pose estimation. In: 3DV (2016)
10. Cordts, M., et al.: The cityscapes dataset for semantic urban scene understanding. In: CVPR (2016)
11. Coskun, H., Achilles, F., DiPietro, R., Navab, N., Tombari, F.: Long short-term memory Kalman filters: recurrent neural estimators for pose regularization. In: ICCV (2017)
12. He, K., Zhang, X., Ren, S., Sun, J.: Deep residual learning for image recognition. In: CVPR (2016)
13. Herda, L., Urtasun, R., Fua, P.: Hierarchical implicit surface joint limits for human body tracking. Comput. Vis. Image Underst. **99**, 189–209 (2005)

14. Ionescu, C., Papava, D., Olaru, V., Sminchisescu, C.: Human3.6M: large scale datasets and predictive methods for 3D human sensing in natural environments. IEEE TPAMI **36**, 1325–1339 (2014)
15. Jahangiri, E., Yuille, A.L.: Generating multiple diverse hypotheses for human 3D pose consistent with 2D joint detections. In: ICCV (2017)
16. Kingma, D.P., Ba, J.: Adam: a method for stochastic optimization. In: ICLR (2015)
17. Li, S., Chan, A.B.: 3D human pose estimation from monocular images with deep convolutional neural network. In: Cremers, D., Reid, I., Saito, H., Yang, M.-H. (eds.) ACCV 2014. LNCS, vol. 9004, pp. 332–347. Springer, Cham (2015). https://doi.org/10.1007/978-3-319-16808-1_23
18. Li, S., Zhang, W., Chan, A.B.: Maximum-margin structured learning with deep networks for 3D human pose estimation. In: ICCV (2015)
19. Lin, M., Lin, L., Liang, X., Wang, K., Cheng, H.: Recurrent 3D pose sequence machines. In: CVPR (2017)
20. Lin, T., et al.: Microsoft COCO: common objects in context. arXiv preprint arXiv:1405.0312 (2014)
21. Loper, M., Mahmood, N., Romero, J., Pons-Moll, G., Black, M.J.: SMPL: a skinned multi-person linear model. ACM Trans. Graph. **34**, 248 (2015)
22. Mehta, D., et al.: Monocular 3D human pose estimation in the wild using improved CNN supervision. In: 3DV (2017)
23. Mehta, D.: VNect: real-time 3D human pose estimation with a single RGB camera. ACM ToG **36**, 44 (2017)
24. Moreno-Noguer, F.: 3D human pose estimation from a single image via distance matrix regression. In: CVPR (2017)
25. Newell, A., Yang, K., Deng, J.: Stacked hourglass networks for human pose estimation. In: Leibe, B., Matas, J., Sebe, N., Welling, M. (eds.) ECCV 2016. LNCS, vol. 9912, pp. 483–499. Springer, Cham (2016). https://doi.org/10.1007/978-3-319-46484-8_29
26. Park, M.J., Choi, M.G., Shinagawa, Y., Shin, S.Y.: Video-guided motion synthesis using example motions. ACM ToG **25**, 1327–1359 (2006)
27. Pavlakos, G., Zhou, X., Derpanis, K.G., Daniilidis, K.: Coarse-to-fine volumetric prediction for single-image 3D human pose. In: CVPR (2017)
28. Ramakrishna, V., Kanade, T., Sheikh, Y.: Reconstructing 3D human pose from 2D image landmarks. In: Fitzgibbon, A., Lazebnik, S., Perona, P., Sato, Y., Schmid, C. (eds.) ECCV 2012. LNCS, vol. 7575, pp. 573–586. Springer, Heidelberg (2012). https://doi.org/10.1007/978-3-642-33765-9_41
29. Rogez, G., Schmid, C.: MoCap-guided data augmentation for 3D pose estimation in the wild. In: NIPS (2016)
30. Rogez, G., Weinzaepfel, P., Schmid, C.: LCR-Net: localization-classification-regression for human pose. In: CVPR (2017)
31. Russakovsky, O., et al.: ImageNet large scale visual recognition challenge. ArXiv e-prints (2014)
32. Sarafianos, N., Boteanu, B., Ionescu, B., Kakadiaris, I.A.: 3D human pose estimation: a review of the literature and analysis of covariates. Comput. Vis. Image Underst. **152**, 1–20 (2016)
33. Sminchisescu, C., Triggs, B.: Estimating articulated human motion with covariance scaled sampling. Int. J. Robot. Res. **22**, 371–391 (2003)
34. Sun, X., Shang, J., Liang, S., Wei, Y.: Compositional human pose regression. In: ICCV (2017)
35. Tome, D., Russell, C., Agapito, L.: Lifting from the deep: convolutional 3D pose estimation from a single image. In: CVPR (2017)

36. Urtasun, R., Fleet, D.J., Fua, P.: Temporal motion models for monocular and multiview 3D human body tracking. Comput. Vis. Image Underst. **104**, 157–177 (2006)
37. Varol, G., et al.: Learning from synthetic humans. In: CVPR (2017)
38. Wei, X., Chai, J.: VideoMocap: modeling physically realistic human motion from monocular video sequences. ACM ToG **29**, 42 (2010)
39. Nie, B.X., Wei, P., Zhu, S.-C.: Monocular 3D human pose estimation by predicting depth on joints. In: ICCV, October 2017
40. Yasin, H., Iqbal, U., Kruger, B., Weber, A., Gall, J.: A dual-source approach for 3D pose estimation from a single image. In: CVPR (2016)
41. Zhou, X., Huang, Q., Sun, X., Xue, X., Wei, Y.: Towards 3D human pose estimation in the wild: a weakly-supervised approach. In: ICCV (2017)
42. Zhou, X., Sun, X., Zhang, W., Liang, S., Wei, Y.: Deep kinematic pose regression. In: Hua, G., Jégou, H. (eds.) ECCV 2016. LNCS, vol. 9915, pp. 186–201. Springer, Cham (2016). https://doi.org/10.1007/978-3-319-49409-8_17
43. Zhou, X., Zhu, M., Derpanis, K., Daniilidis, K.: Sparseness meets deepness: 3D human pose estimation from monocular video. In: CVPR (2016)
44. Zhou, Z.-H.: A brief introduction to weakly supervised learning. Natl. Sci. Rev. **5**, 44–53 (2017)

Deep Reinforcement Learning
with Iterative Shift for Visual Tracking

Liangliang Ren[1], Xin Yuan[1], Jiwen Lu[1(✉)], Ming Yang[2], and Jie Zhou[1]

[1] Tsinghua University, Beijing, China
{renll16,yuanx16}@mails.tsinghua.edu.cn, {lujiwen,jzhou}@tsinghua.edu.cn
[2] Horizon Robotics, Inc., Beijing, China
ming.yang@horizon-robotics.com

Abstract. Visual tracking is confronted by the dilemma to locate a target *both* accurately and efficiently, and make decisions *online* whether and how to adapt the appearance model or even restart tracking. In this paper, we propose a deep reinforcement learning with iterative shift (DRL-IS) method for single object tracking, where an actor-critic network is introduced to predict the iterative shifts of object bounding boxes, and evaluate the shifts to take actions on whether to update object models or re-initialize tracking. Since locating an object is achieved by an iterative shift process, rather than online classification on many sampled locations, the proposed method is robust to cope with large deformations and abrupt motion, and computationally efficient since finding a target takes up to 10 shifts. In offline training, the critic network guides to learn how to make decisions jointly on motion estimation and tracking status in an end-to-end manner. Experimental results on the OTB benchmarks with large deformation improve the tracking precision by 1.7% and runs about 5 times faster than the competing state-of-the-art methods.

Keywords: Visual object tracking · Reinforcement learning
Actor-critic algorithm

1 Introduction

Visual object tracking (VOT) aims at locating a target efficiently in a video sequence, which remains a challenging problem in unconstrained applications due to deformation, abrupt motion, occlusions and illumination, after several decades of intensive research [5,10,20,36,41,42,51]. Essentially VOT needs to address 3 key issues: (1) How to represent a target, *i.e.*, the observation model; (2) How to *efficiently* leverage the motion smoothness assumption to locate a target in the next frame; (3) How to update tracking models online, if necessary, to handle dynamic scenarios.

L. Ren and X. Yuan—Equal contribution.

Electronic supplementary material The online version of this chapter (https:// doi.org/10.1007/978-3-030-01240-3_42) contains supplementary material, which is available to authorized users.

© Springer Nature Switzerland AG 2018
V. Ferrari et al. (Eds.): ECCV 2018, LNCS 11213, pp. 697–713, 2018.
https://doi.org/10.1007/978-3-030-01240-3_42

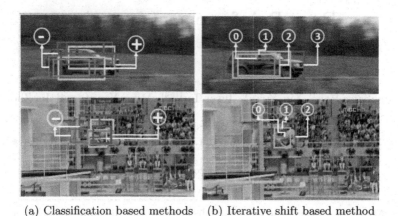

(a) Classification based methods   (b) Iterative shift based method

Fig. 1. Illustration of tracking using classification (left column) vs. iterative shift (right column): tracking a fast moving vehicle (first row) and tracking a diving athlete with large deformation (second row). Given the initial box (green), classification based methods sample many proposals, select the box (red) with the highest classification score, and collect positive (yellow and red) and negative samples (blue) to fine-tune the classifiers online. There may not be enough good samples for online learning in these hard scenarios. In contrast, the proposed iterative shift tracking adjusts the bounding box step by step to locate the target (*e.g.*, 3 steps for the vehicle and 2 steps for the athlete), and makes decisions formally when and how to update object models by reinforcement learning. The shift process generally tends to be more efficient since less candidate regions are evaluated than in classification based methods (Color figure online)

The appearance models have evolved from intensity templates [19], color histograms [14], and sparse features [4], to the dominating *deep features* [47] extracted by CNN models. Thus, naturally tracking may be formulated as a classification or detection-and-association problem [35] using CNN classifiers. Even a strong observation model may not capture all possible variations of targets and need to be updated on-the-fly during tracking. Nevertheless, online classifier learning may be vulnerable to samples with ambiguous labels in hard scenarios, such as deformation, quick motion and occlusions,*etc.*, leading to *model drift*. The tracker needs to make decisions simultaneously on target's motion status and on tracking status, *i.e.*, whether and how to update observation models or even restart tracking if necessary. These are indeed tough decisions to make during online tracing.

To tackle the aforementioned issue 2 and 3, we introduce a deep reinforcement learning process to make decisions jointly on a target's motion status and a tracker's status in VOT. The motion status, *i.e.*, the displacement and scaling of an object's bounding box, is estimated in an efficient iterative shift process by a *prediction* network. The tracker's status, referring to whether or how to update the observation model and whether stop and restart tracking, is determined by an *actor* network. The proposed method, coined as deep reinforcement learning with iterative shift (DRL-IS), exploits the correlation between object's motion estimation and current tracking status. The prediction and actor networks are learned offline from a large number of training video sequences guided by a *critic* network, on how to take actions given the current frame and the previous target location and representations.

This method utilizes reinforcement learning as a principled way to learn how to make decisions during tracking, therefore, it is especially robust to deal with hard cases such as deformation or abrupt motion, where either updating the model or stop-and-restart may be a sensible action. In contrast, existing methods ADNet [52], EAST [21] and POMDP [44] which employed reinforcement learning to either estimate motion or make decisions on tracking status separately. Moreover, as shown in Fig. 1, the tracking result is estimated iteratively, instead of performing CNN classification on many candidate locations, thus leading to an efficient computation.

The main contributions of our paper are on two-fold: (1) We propose an Actor-Critic network to predict the object motion parameters and select actions on the tracking status, where the rewards for different actions are dedicatedly designed according to their impacts; (2) We formulate object tracking as an iterative shift problem, rather than CNN classification on possible bounding boxes, thus locates a target efficiently and precisely. The proposed DRL-IS is particularly capable of dealing with objects with large deformations and abrupt motion, since the motion parameters are iteratively estimated and accumulated by the prediction network, and in such hard cases the tracker is kind of self-aware to update the target feature and model or resort to detection to restart tracking. Our tracker achieves 0.909 distance precision, 0.671 overlap success on the OTB2015 benchmark and 0.812 distance precision and 0.590 overlap success on the Temple-Color128 benchmark, on a par with the best performance, and runs about 5 times faster than competing state-of-the-art methods.

2   Related Work

Visual tracking has undergone extensive study over several decades on how to represent and locate a target in video sequences, and adapt the observation model online if necessary. Deep neural networks, pre-trained for recognition tasks, tend to be also effective in delineating an object appearance in tracking, *e.g.*, as in the MDNet [35], FCNT [46], and CREST [42] trackers, and [10,18,32,47]. To find a target in current frame, a motion model is assumed to sample some candidate locations, as in the Kalman filter [1] or particle filter [22,38]. Then, the observation model may be evaluated on hundreds of these locations, as a correlation filtering in MOSSE [5] and KCF [20], or as a discriminative classification [11] or regression problem [16], which is demanding in computation. Alternatively, an observation model may allow to calculate or search the candidate locations gradually and iteratively, as in the optical flow [14] or mean-shift tracking [9], which is generally efficient since only a few locations examined. This motivates us to propose the iterative shift process, where a prediction network adjusts target locations in an iterative manner and evaluates the neural net much less times.

The observation model may need to be updated during tracking to follow the changing appearance of an target, for instance, by collecting positive and negative samples [24] or bags [3] to conduct online learning [50]. A tracker has to make very tough decisions on when and how to update the observation model. For some difficult scenarios, such as deformation, occlusion and abrupt motion, on one hand, without any model update, the tracker may lost the target, on the other hand, due to some ambiguous or wrong labels, the tracker may drift to clutter background after the online update. In these hard but not rare cases, a sensible decision might be to stop tracking and resort to object detection or other means to reinitialize, rather than drifting blindly and silently. This fundamental issue demands for a formal decision making procedure in tracking.

Deep reinforcement learning [2,6,7,23,26,29,33,34,40] is a principled paradigm to learn how to make decisions and select actions online, which has achieved great successes in Atari games [34], search of attention patches [7], and finding objects [29] and visual relations [40]. Recently, reinforcement learning has been adopted for tracking [21,25,44,52,53], *e.g.*, an action-decision network [52] to generate actions to seek the locations and the sizes of a target object, or a decision policy tracker [44] by using reinforcement learning to decide where to look in the upcoming frames, and when to re-initialize and update its appearance model for the tracked object. In this paper, we extend to learn how to jointly derive the target motion and make decisions on the tracker status, by a new and unified actor-critic network.

3   Approach

The proposed deep reinforcement learning with iterative shift (DRL-IS) approach involves three sub-networks: (1) the actor network, (2) the prediction network, and (3) the critic network, which *share* the convolutional layers and one fully connected layer (fc4), as shown in Fig. 2. We elaborate the formulation of DRL-IS for tracking and the learning procedure of these networks, in the following subsections.

3.1   Iterative Shift for Visual Tracking

We formulate visual object tracking as an iterative shift problem. Given current frame and previous tracking results, the prediction network ψ iteratively shifts the candidate bounding box to locate the target, meanwhile, the actor network θ makes decisions on the tracking status, whether or not to update the target representation and the prediction network, or even restart tracking.

Formally, given a video $V = \{I_1, I_2, \cdots, I_N\}$, where I_t is the tth frame. The tracker is initialized by cropping a target with $l_1 = \{x_1, y_1, w_1, h_1\}$ in the first frame and its appearance is represented by the feature f_1 , *i.e.*, the fc4 layer's outputs in the shared network. With the tracking results of

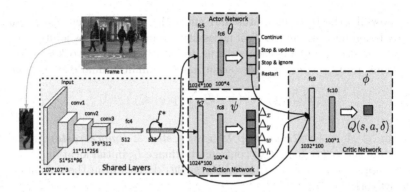

Fig. 2. The overview of the DRL-IS tracking method. Given the initial bounding box of a target, we first extract deep feature $f \in \mathbb{R}^{1*512}$ from fc4 layer. Then we concatenate the feature of a candidate box f and the current target feature $f^* \in \mathbb{R}^{1*512}$. We generate shift δ using the prediction network ψ and employ the actor network θ. For action *continue*, we adjust the bounding box of the target according to the output δ of ψ. For action *stop* and *update*, we stop the iteration and update the appearance features of the target and the parameters of ψ, while we skip the update for action *stop* and *ignore*. When taking action *restart*, the target may be lost, so we re-sample for the initial bounding box. In the training stage, we use a deep critic network to estimate the Q-value of current actions with δ, and fine-tune the prediction network ψ and actor network θ

$l_{t-1}^* = \{x_{t-1}, y_{t-1}, w_{t-1}, h_{t-1}\}$ and f_{t-1}^*, we first extract f_t of I_t cropped by l_{t-1}^*, and exploit the prediction network ψ to predict the movement δ of the target between frames, which takes f_t and f_{t-1}^* as input:

$$\delta = \psi(f_t, f_{t-1}^*). \tag{1}$$

We denote the outputs of the prediction network as $\delta = \{\Delta_x, \Delta_y, \Delta_w, \Delta_h\}$:

$$\begin{aligned}
\Delta_x &= (x_t - x_{t-1})/w_{t-1}, \\
\Delta_y &= (y_t - y_{t-1})/h_{t-1}, \\
\Delta_w &= log(w_t/w_{t-1}), \\
\Delta_h &= log(h_t/h_{t-1}),
\end{aligned} \tag{2}$$

where Δ_x and Δ_y specify a scale-invariant translation of the bounding box, Δ_w and Δ_h specify log-space translations of the width and height of bounding box against the previous frame [17]. It is hard to estimate the movement and shape change of the target accurately in one step when the object moves rapidly or deforms. Hence, the prediction network outputs the adjustments of the bounding box iteratively and accumulate them to obtain the tracking result. Thus, the neural network is evaluated in K_t iterations at I_t and δ_k of each step in Eq. 2 are accumulated. This iterative shift process is considerably faster than running a classification network on hundreds of bounding boxes.

Meanwhile, the tracking status may affect the results as well, *e.g.*, updating the prediction network on the fly if necessary. To make decisions jointly on a target's motion status and a tracker's status, we use the actor network θ to generate the actions $a_1, a_2, \cdots, a_k, \cdots, a_{K_t}$ according to a multinomial distribution:

$$p(a|s_{t,k}) = \pi(s_{t,k}|\theta), \sum_i p(a_i|s_{t,k}) = 1, \tag{3}$$

where $a_k \in \mathcal{A} = \{continue, stop~\&~update, stop~\&~ignore, restart\}$, and the initial state $s_{t,0} = \{I_t, l_{t,0}, f_{t-1}^*\}$ contains the image I_t, initial location $l_{t,0} = l_{t-1}^*$, and the appearance feature f_{t-1}^*, and $\pi(s_{t,k}|\theta)$ derives from the outputs of the actor network θ.

For the action *continue* (continue shifting without updating the model) in step k, the shift $\delta_k = \psi(f_{t,k}, f_{t-1}^*)$ is generated by the prediction networks ψ. $f_{t,k}$ is extracted from the crop $l_{t,k}$. The position, $l_{t,k}$, of the target is updated iteratively according to δ_k with $l_{t,k-1}$.

For the action *stop & update* (stop shifting and update the model), we stop the iterations and take $l_t^* = l_{t,K_t}$ as the location for object and update the feature of the target and the parameters of the prediction network ψ,

$$f_t^* = \rho f_{t,K_t} + (1 - \rho) f_{t-1}^*, \tag{4}$$

$$\psi_t = \psi_{t-1} + \mu \mathbb{E}_{s,a} \frac{\partial Q(s, a, \delta|\phi)}{\partial \delta} \frac{\partial \delta}{\partial \psi}, \tag{5}$$

where ρ is a weight coefficient since Eq. (5) is a common practice in tracking allowing the target feature evolve as a weighted sum of current and previous representations. Equation (6) is an online learning rule to update the prediction network, so μ is an adequate learning rate. $Q(s, a, \delta)$ is the output of critic network ϕ and defined in Eq. 11. This action indicates a reliable tracking, confident enough to update the target representation and the model.

For the action *stop & ignore* (stop shifting without updating the object feature), we stop the iteration and take $l_t^* = l_{t,k}$ as the location for object and move on to track the target in the next frame, where the appearance feature f_t^* and the prediction network ψ are not updated. This action indicates that the target is found, yet the tracker is not confident to update the model, *e.g.*, if motion blur or occlusions present.

For the action *restart* (restart tracking), we restart the iteration by resampling a random set of candidate patches L_t around l_{t-1}^* in I_t, and select the patch which has the highest Q-values, which is defined in Eq. 12 according to the IoU objective, as the initial location:

$$l_{t,0} = \arg \max_{s=\{I_t, l, f_{t-1}^*\}, l \in L_t} Q(s, a = stop~\&~update, \delta = 0|\phi). \tag{6}$$

This action represents the cases that the tracker loses the target temporarily and resorts to an extensive search to re-initialize tracking.

Figure 3 presents a sample action sequence in tracking. The prediction and actor networks formulate the motion estimation and tracking status change in a unified way as taking actions in reinforcement learning. Nevertheless, learning these neural networks requires dedicatedly designed rewards for each type of actions.

3.2 Training the Neural Networks in DRL-IS

In this subsection, we detail the training procedure of the prediction, actor, and critic networks by deep reinforcement learning, from a large number of labeled video sequences. Note that the prediction network is pre-trained offline while during online tracking, both the prediction and actor networks are jointly updated by the actor-critic approach.

Learning of the Prediction Network: The prediction network estimates the iterative shift of the object in a given frame, from the object location and features in consecutive frames. We pre-train a convolutional neural network in an end-to-end manner to predict the shift of the target object between frames or iteration steps.

Network Architecture: As illustrated in Fig. 2, the prediction network uses three convolutional layers to extract features from the target patch and the current candidate box during pre-training. Then the features are concatenated and fed into two fully connected layers to produce the parameters which estimate the location translation and scaling changes.

Network Inputs: We sample pairs of crops from the sequences between every two frames to feed the network. The first crop is the object location in the previous frame and the second crop is in the current frame at the same location. The crops are padded with a fixed ratio to the object scale, which is empirically determined in our experiments. The network receives a pair of crops which are warped into 107×107 pixels and estimates the motion δ between two adjacent frames.

Network Pretraining: Instead of extracting the feature of the region proposals and performing regression on the bounding box, we train a fully end-to-end network to learn location translations and deformations directly. We perform data augmentation by sampling multiple examples with scale variations which are near the target bounding box and then create crops in the current frame. Using labeled video frames and these augmented samples, the training of prediction network promotes to locate a target with less iteration steps.

DRL-IS with Actor-Critic: We exploit the actor-critic algorithm [28] to jointly train the three sub-networks, θ, ψ, ϕ. Firstly, we define the rewards according to the tracking performance. The reward of the action *continue* with $\delta_{t,k}$ is defined by ΔIoU rather than the IoU to adjust bounding boxes.

$$r_{t,k} = \begin{cases} 1 & \Delta_{IoU} \geq \epsilon \\ 0 & -\epsilon < \Delta_{IoU} < \epsilon \\ -1 & \Delta_{IoU} \leq -\epsilon \end{cases}, \tag{7}$$

where $\epsilon > 0$ and Δ_{IoU} is computed as:

$$\Delta_{IoU} = g(l_t^*, l_{t,k}) - g(l_t^*, l_{t,k-1}), g(l_i, l_j) = \frac{l_i \cap l_j}{l_i \cup l_j}. \tag{8}$$

For the action *stop & update* and *stop & ignore*, the rewards are defined by the IoU of the final prediction and the ground truth. To encourage tracking stop with less iterations, the positive reward is related to the the iteration times K_t. We take l_t^* as the location for object and the rewards are computed as:

$$r_{t,K_t} = \begin{cases} 10/K_t & g(l_t^*, l_{t,K_t}) \geq 0.7 \\ 0 & 0.4 \leq g(l_t^*, l_{t,K_t}) \leq 0.7 \\ -5 & else \end{cases} . \tag{9}$$

For the action *restart*, the reward is positive when the IoU of the final prediction and the ground truth is less than 0.4 considering the high computational costs of *restart*.

$$r_{t,K_t} = \begin{cases} -1 & g(l_t^*, l_{t,K_t}) \geq 0.7 \\ 0 & 0.4 \leq g(l_t^*, l_{t,K_t}) \leq 0.7 \\ 1 & else \end{cases} . \tag{10}$$

Then we define the calculation of Q-values of each action. The Q value of the action *continue* and other actions are quite different, since the reward of *continue* is based on the increment of IoU while others are based on the tracking performance evaluated by IoU. The Q value of action *continue* with $\delta_{t,k}$ is computed as follows:

$$Q(s, a, \delta_{t,k}) = \sum_{i=k}^{K_t} \gamma^{(i-k)} r_{t,i}. \tag{11}$$

The Q values of actions *stop & update, stop & ignore, restart* are computed as:

$$Q(s, a, \delta_{t,k} = 0) = \sum_{j=t}^{N} \gamma^{j-t} r_{j,k_j}. \tag{12}$$

Equation (12) sums the rewards upon the step k in the current frame while Eq. (13) sums the rewards upon the time step t. The reason for the different calculations of Q-values in Eqs. (12) and (13) is that the action *continue* locates the target with the current models in frame t while other actions involve the decision whether to stop tracking based on previous tracking performance.

Finally, we formulate the optimization problem of ϕ and θ as follows:

$$\phi = \arg\min_{\phi} L(\phi) = \mathbb{E}_{s,a}(Q(s, a|\phi) - r - \gamma Q(s', a', |\phi^-))^2, \tag{13}$$

$$\theta = \arg\min_{\theta} J(\theta) = -\mathbb{E}_{s,a} \log(\pi(a, s|\theta)) \hat{A}(s, a). \tag{14}$$

s' is the next state and $a' = \arg\max_a Q(s', a|\phi^-)$. Action-value $\hat{A}(s, a)$ and value function $V(s)$ is calculated as follows:

$$\hat{A}(s, a) = Q(s, a|\phi) - V(s), \tag{15}$$

$$V(s) = \mathbb{E}_s \pi(s, a|\theta^-) Q(s, a|\phi^-), \tag{16}$$

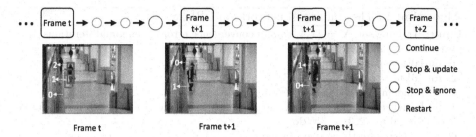

Fig. 3. An illustrative example of the actions on tracking status change by the actor network: (1) at I_t, the target is readily located by two *continue* actions and a *stop & update* action updates the target feature $f*_t$ and the prediction network ϕ accordingly; (2) at I_{t+1}, at first, a *continue* action tracks to a distractor person nearby, than the tracker spots this and take a *restart* action to re-initialize the tracking; (3) the shift process is restarted at I_{t+1}, with a *continue* action, the target is found yet the scale is not reliable, and then a *stop & ignore* action return the results but does not update the target feature f_t^*

where ϕ^- is the target network, which has the same architecture with ϕ but is only updated in each 10 iterations. Please refer to [37] for the details of reinforcement learning. We update the parameters of the critic network ϕ and actor network θ as follows:

$$\phi = \phi - \mu_\phi \frac{\partial L(\phi)}{\partial \phi},\tag{17}$$

$$\theta = \theta - \mu_\theta \frac{\partial J(\theta)}{\partial \theta}.\tag{18}$$

Algorithm 1 summarizes the learning of proposed method.

4   Experiments

To validate the proposed approach, we conducted experiments on the popular Object Tracking Benchmark [48,49], Temple-Color128 [31] and VOT-2016 [30], and compared with recent state-of-the-art trackers.

4.1   Datasets and Settings

We conducted experiments on the standard benchmarks: OTB-2015, Temple-Color128 and VOT-2016. OTB-2015 [49] contains 100 video sequences, where each video was fully annotated with ground truth bounding boxes. Temple-Color128 contains 128 color sequences. The challenging attributes for visual object tracking on these two datasets include illumination variation (IV), scale variation (SV), occlusion (OCC), deformation (DEF), motion blur (MB), fast motion (FM), in-plane rotation (IPR), out-of-plane rotation (OPR), out-of-view

Algorithm 1. The training of networks in DRL-IS

Input: Training set: $\mathbf{V} = \{V_i\}$, ψ, and convergence error ϵ_1, maximal iterations M.
Output: ϕ, θ and ψ
 1: Initialize ϕ and θ;
 2: **for all** $m = 1, 2, \ldots, M$ **do**
 3:    Randomly select a video V;
 4:    Initialize the appearance feature f and l_1 using the ground truth in 1-st frame
 5:    **for all** $t = 2, 3, \ldots, N$ **do**
 6:       Generate the action a using θ;
 7:       **while** $a == continue$ **do**
 8:          compute δ using ψ;
 9:          Adjust $l_t = l_t + \delta$
10:          Generate an action a using θ;
11:       **end while**
12:       Update ψ, f_t^* or restart according to a;
13:    **end for**
14:    Calculate $J_t(\theta)$ and L_ϕ;
15:    Update actor network θ and critic network ϕ;
16:    **if** $l > 1$ and $|J_t(\theta) - J_{t-1}((\theta))| + |L_t(\phi) - L_{t-1}((\phi))| < \epsilon_1$ **then**
17:       Go to **return**
18:    **end if**
19: **end for**
20: **return** θ, ψ and ϕ;

(OV), background clutters (BC), and low resolution (LR). We followed the standard evaluation metrics on these benchmarks. We used the one-pass evaluation (OPE) with the distance precision metric and overlap success plots metrics, where each tracker was initialized with the ground truth location until the end of each sequence. Specifically, the overlap success rate measures the overlap between predicted bounding boxes and ground truth bounding boxes, and the distance precision metric is the percentage of frames where the estimated location center error from the ground truth is smaller than a given distance threshold. In our experiments, we set the threshold distance as 20 pixels for all trackers. The VOT-2016 dataset consists 60 challenging videos from a set of more than 300 videos. The performance in terms of both accuracy (overlap with the ground-truth) and robustness (failure rate) is evaluated in our experiments. Noting that on VOT-2016 dataset, a tracker is restarted by the ground-truth in the case of a failure.

4.2   Implementation Details

We implemented our tracker in Python using the Pytorch library. The implementation was conducted on a PC with an Intel Core i7 3.4 GHz CPU with 24 GB RAM and the deep neural networks were trained on GeForce GTX 1080 Ti GPU with 11 GB VRAM. In our settings, the proposed tracker runs about 10 frames per second on these two benchmarks [48,49].

Prediction Network: The prediction network has three convolutional layers which are initialized by the VGG-M [8] network which was pretrained on ImageNet [15]. The next two fully connected layers has 512 and 100 output units with ReLU activations. The output fully connected layer has 4 output units combined with the *tanh* activation.

Actor-Critic Network: The actor network has two fully connected layers of 100 and 4 output units with the *ReLU* activation. The critic network is similar to the actor network but the final layer has only one output unit. The current and candidate features are concatenated as the input to these two networks. We use the Adam optimizer [27] with a learning rate of 0.0001 and a discount of β (set as 0.95) to train the actor-critic network. We trained our actor-critic network by using sequences which were randomly sampled from the VOT-2013, VOT-2014, and VOT-2015 [30] in which videos overlapping with OTB and Temple-Color were excluded. The maximal number of actions is set to 10 for each frame and the starting frame for each episode is randomly selected. The end operation is determined by the mean IoU ratio of the last 5 predicted bounding boxes compared to the ground truth bounding boxes of the total frames of one sequence. If the mean IoU is under 0.2 or at the end of a sequence, we terminate the episode and update the models. We trained the network for a total num of 50,000 episodes until convergence. On VOT-2016 dataset, we conducted experiments using ImageNet as the training set for our tacker. Since each object on the training set has only one frame (static image), we set γ as 0 in Eq. 12, and removed the action *stop & ignore*.

4.3   Results and Analysis

Quantitative Evaluation: We conducted quantitative evaluations on the OTB-2015 Dataset, Temple-Color Dataset and VOT-2016 Dataset.

OBT-2015 Dataset. We compared our approach with the state-of-the-art trackers including CREST [43], ADNet [52], MDNet [36], HCFT [32], SINT [45], DeepSRDCF [12], and HDT [39]. Figure 4 shows the performance of different trackers in terms of precision and success rate based on center location error and overlap ratio on OTB-2015. We also evaluated the performance of different tracking methods and the processing speed (fps) on OTB-2015 dataset. Overall, our tracker performs favorably on both the precision and the success rate, meanwhile runs at 10.2 fps which is 5 times faster than the state-of-the-art tracker MDNet (2.1 fps in Pytorch implementation). One variant of our tracker with only two action types shown later runs even faster with an acceptable trade-off of accuracy.

We also analyzed the performance of our tracker for three different challenge attributes labeled for each sequence including fast motion, deformation, scale variations. We compute the OPE on the distance precision metric under 8 main video attributes. As shown in Fig. 5, our tracker shows competitive results on all the attributes. Specifically, the effectiveness in deformation attributes to the prediction network update according to the policy to capture target appearance

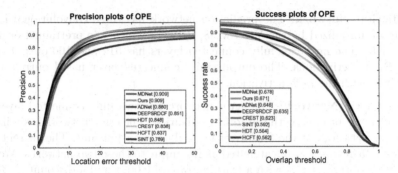

Fig. 4. The precision and success rate over all sequences by using one-pass evaluation on the OTB-2015 Dataset [49]. The legend includes the area-under-the-curve score and the average distance precision score at 20 pixels for each tracker

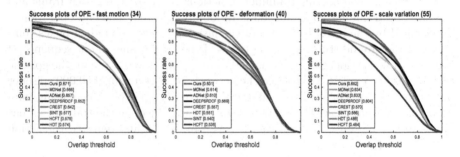

Fig. 5. The success plots over three tracking challenges, including fast motion, deformation, scale variations, for all the compared trackers on OTB-2015

changes. For scale variation, our tracker still performs well which demonstrates that our prediction network is robust to the scale change of the target object. Our tracker performs better on all three challenges than ADNet [52], which is also a deep reinforcement learning based tracker. The main reason is that our prediction network can be adjusted according to the action learned by the policy network. Meanwhile, the action *stop & ignore* and *stop & update* can guide our tracker whether to update the target feature, which avoids inadequate model update in long-term tracking. We have also obtained similar performance in fast motion, where MDNet [36] and our tracker both benefit from the convolutional features and the re-detection process. However, the percentage of the frames using re-detection to the total frames of MDNet [36] is high, resulting in more computation.

Temple-Color Dataset. We evaluate our approach on the Temple-Color dataset containing 128 videos. Figure 7 shows the performance of different trackers in terms of precision and success rate based on center location error and overlap ratio. The C-COT tracker [13] and MEEM [54] reach the average distance precision score of 0.781 and 0.706. Our approach improves by a significant

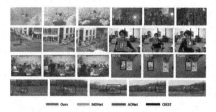

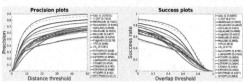

Fig. 6. Qualitative evaluation of our tracker, MDNet [36], ADNet [52] and CREST [43] on 7 challenging sequences

Fig. 7. The precision and success plots over all sequences by using one-pass evaluation on the Temple-Color Dataset. The legend contains the average distance precision score and the area-under-the-curve score for each tracker

Table 1. Comparison with state-of-the-art methods in terms of robustness and accuracy ranking on the VOT-2016 dataset(the lower the better)

Baseline	MDNet_N	DeepSRDCF	Staple	MLDF	SSAT	TCNN	C-COT	DRL-IS
Robustness	5.75	5.92	5.70	4.23	4.60	4.18	2.92	**2.70**
Accuracy	4.63	4.88	4.23	6.17	**3.42**	4.22	4.85	3.60

margin, achieving a score of 0.818. In the success plot in Fig. 7, our method also achieves a notable absolute gain of 1.2% in area-under-the-curve score compared to state-of-the-art method C-COT.

VOT-2016 Dataset. Table 1 shows the comparison of our approach with the top 5 competing trackers in the VOT-2016 challenge. As shown in Table 1, we obtain competitive accuracy and robustness ranking with state-of-the-art methods on the VOT-2016 Dataset. Our method achieves favorable results in terms of accuracy while keeping a low failure rate, which attributes to the decision making on motion estimation and tracking status guided by reinforcement learning. Noting that MDNet_N is a variation of MDNet, which does not pre-train CNNs with other tracking datasets. MDNet_N is also initialized using the ImageNet like our method. Our DRL-IS improves the performance of MDNet_N by a significant margin, which shows that our tracker has good generality without using the tracking sequences as training data.

Qualitative Evaluation: Figure 6 shows qualitative comparisons of top performing visual tracking methods including MDNet [36], ADNet [52], CREST [43] and our method on 7 challenging sequences. Our tracker performs well against the compared these methods in all sequences. Moreover, none of the other methods is able to track targets for the *CarScale* sequence whereas our tracker successfully locates the target as well as estimates the scale changes. There are two reasons: (1) Our method accounts for the appearance changes caused by deformation and background clutters (*Bird1*, *Soccer* and *Freeman4*) by adjusting the bounding box of the object iteratively; (2) The feature of objects and the models are updated adaptively with deep reinforcement learning to account for appearance variations.

Table 2. The comparisons of different ablation variants of DRL-IS over the distance precision and overlap success plots on the OTB-2015 dataset

Variants	Shift (22 fps)	Shift+IS (15 fps)	DRL-IS (10.2 fps)
Prec.(20px)	0.822	0.887	0.909
IOU(AUC)	0.593	0.651	0.671

Ablation Study of Different Components: To show the impacts of different components of our tracker, we developed three variants of our tracker by integrating the prediction network with different types of policies combination and evaluated them using OTB-2015. These three variants are: (1) "Shift" is a baseline tracker which contains only one module based on the pre-trained prediction network; (2) "Shift + IS" is a pre-trained prediction model which was guided with only two action types: *continue* and *stop & update*; and (3) "DRL-IS" is our final model which was guided with full action types: *continue, restart, stop & ignore* and *stop & update*. Table 2 shows the distance precision and overlap success plots of these variations on the OTB-2015 dataset. The "Shift" tracker can only obtain the one-step shift based on deep convolutional features, which dose not perform well because the model is not updated during tracking and may fail when the target object changes fast. The "Shift + IS" tracker enables iterative shift and updates the model according to the policy learned by the actor network, which outperforms the baseline tracker by 6.5% and 5.7% in terms of the precision and overlap success, respectively. Moreover, "DRL-IS" incorporates all actions with the prediction network and achieves 8.7% and 2.2% performance gains of in terms of the precision over the "Shift" and "Shift + IS" variations, respectively.

5   Conclusion

In this paper, we have proposed a DRL-IS method for visual tracking, which has demonstrated reinforcement learning is an effective way to model the tough decision making process for tracking, *i.e.*, performing motion estimation and changing tracking status at the same time. The new iterative shift by deep nets locates targets efficiently than online classification and copes well with the cases that deformation or motion blur present in video. Extensive experiments on 3 public datasets have validated the advantages on tracking robustness and efficiency of the proposed method.

Acknowledgements. This work was supported in part by the National Key Research and Development Program of China under Grant 2017YFA0700802, in part by the National Natural Science Foundation of China under Grant 61672306, Grant U1713214, Grant 61572271, and in part by the Shenzhen Fundamental Research Fund (Subject Arrangement) under Grant JCYJ20170412170602564.

References

1. Ali, N.H., Hassan, G.M.: Kalman filter tracking. Int. J. Comput. Appl. (0975–8887) **89**(9) (March 2014)
2. Ammar, H.B., Eaton, E., Ruvolo, P., Taylor, M.: Online multi-task learning for policy gradient methods. In: ICML, pp. 1206–1214 (2014)
3. Babenko, B., Yang, M.H., Belongie, S.: Visual tracking with online multiple instance learning. In: CVPR, pp. 983–990 (2009)
4. Bao, C., Wu, Y., Ling, H., Ji, H.: Real time robust L1 tracker using accelerated proximal gradient approach. In: CVPR, pp. 1830–1837 (2012)
5. Bolme, D.S., Beveridge, J.R., Draper, B.A., Lui, Y.M.: Visual object tracking using adaptive correlation filters. In: CVPR, pp. 2544–2550 (2010)
6. Caicedo, J.C., Lazebnik, S.: Active object localization with deep reinforcement learning. In: ICCV, pp. 2488–2496 (2015)
7. Cao, Q., Lin, L., Shi, Y., Liang, X., Li, G.: Attention-aware face hallucination via deep reinforcement learning. In: CVPR, pp. 690–698 (2017)
8. Chatfield, K., Simonyan, K., Vedaldi, A., Zisserman, A.: Return of the devil in the details: delving deep into convolutional nets. arXiv (2014)
9. Comaniciu, D., Ramesh, V., Meer, P.: Real-time tracking of non-rigid objects using mean shift. In: CVPR, pp. 142–149 (2000)
10. Cui, Z., Xiao, S., Feng, J., Yan, S.: Recurrently target-attending tracking. In: CVPR, pp. 1449–1458 (2016)
11. Danelljan, M., Häger, G., Khan, F.S., Felsberg, M.: Discriminative scale space tracking. TPAMI **39**(8), 1561–1575 (2017)
12. Danelljan, M., Hager, G., Shahbaz Khan, F., Felsberg, M.: Learning spatially regularized correlation filters for visual tracking. In: ICCV, pp. 4310–4318 (2015)
13. Danelljan, M., Robinson, A., Shahbaz Khan, F., Felsberg, M.: Beyond correlation filters: learning continuous convolution operators for visual tracking. In: Leibe, B., Matas, J., Sebe, N., Welling, M. (eds.) ECCV 2016. LNCS, vol. 9909, pp. 472–488. Springer, Cham (2016). https://doi.org/10.1007/978-3-319-46454-1_29
14. Decarlo, D., Metaxas, D.: Optical flow constraints on deformable models with applications to face tracking. In: IJCV **38**(2), 99–127 (2000)
15. Deng, J., Dong, W., Socher, R., Li, L., Li, K., Li, F.: ImageNet: a large-scale hierarchical image database. In: CVPR, pp. 248–255 (2009)
16. Gao, J., Ling, H., Hu, W., Xing, J.: Transfer learning based visual tracking with gaussian processes regression. In: Fleet, D., Pajdla, T., Schiele, B., Tuytelaars, T. (eds.) ECCV 2014. LNCS, vol. 8691, pp. 188–203. Springer, Cham (2014). https://doi.org/10.1007/978-3-319-10578-9_13
17. Girshick, R.B., Donahue, J., Darrell, T., Malik, J.: Rich feature hierarchies for accurate object detection and semantic segmentation. In: CVPR, pp. 580–587 (2014)
18. Gordon, D., Farhadi, A., Fox, D.: Re3 : Real-time recurrent regression networks for object tracking. CoRR (2017)
19. Hager, G.D., Belhumeur, P.N.: Efficient region tracking with parametric models of geometry and illumination. TPAMI **20**(10), 1025–1039 (1998)
20. Henriques, J.F., Caseiro, R., Martins, P., Batista, J.: High-speed tracking with kernelized correlation filters. TPAMI **37**(3), 583–596 (2015)
21. Huang, C., Lucey, S., Ramanan, D.: Learning policies for adaptive tracking with deep feature cascades. In: ICCV, pp. 105–114 (2017)
22. Isard, M., Blake, A.: Condensation-conditional density propagation for visual tracking. In: IJCV, pp. 5–28 (1998)

23. Jie, Z., Liang, X., Feng, J., Jin, X., Lu, W., Yan, S.: Tree-structured reinforcement learning for sequential object localization. In: NIPS, pp. 127–135 (2016)
24. Kalal, Z., Mikolajczyk, K., Matas, J.: Tracking-learning-detection. TPAMI **34**(7), 1409–1422 (2012)
25. Kamalapurkar, R., Andrews, L., Walters, P., Dixon, W.E.: Model-based reinforcement learning for infinite-horizon approximate optimal tracking. TNNLS **28**(3), 753–758 (2017)
26. Karayev, S., Baumgartner, T., Fritz, M., Darrell, T.: Timely object recognition. In: NIPS, pp. 899–907 (2012)
27. Kingma, D.P., Ba, J.: Adam: a method for stochastic optimization. CoRR (2014)
28. Konda, V.R., Tsitsiklis, J.N.: Actor-critic algorithms. In: NIPS, pp. 1008–1014 (2000)
29. Kong, X., Xin, B., Wang, Y., Hua, G.: Collaborative deep reinforcement learning for joint object search. In: CVPR (2017)
30. Kristan, M.: A novel performance evaluation methodology for single-target trackers. TPAMI **38**(11), 2137–2155 (2016)
31. Liang, P., Blasch, E., Ling, H.: Encoding color information for visual tracking: algorithms and benchmark. TIP **24**(12), 5630–5644 (2015)
32. Ma, C., Huang, J.B., Yang, X., Yang, M.H.: Hierarchical convolutional features for visual tracking. In: ICCV, pp. 3074–3082 (2015)
33. Mathe, S., Pirinen, A., Sminchisescu, C.: Reinforcement learning for visual object detection. In: CVPR, pp. 2894–2902 (2016)
34. Mnih, V.: Human-level control through deep reinforcement learning. Nature (7540) **518**, 529–533 (2015)
35. Nam, H., Han, B.: Learning multi-domain convolutional neural networks for visual tracking. CoRR (2015)
36. Nam, H., Han, B.: Learning multi-domain convolutional neural networks for visual tracking. In: CVPR, pp. 4293–4302 (2016)
37. O'Donoghue, B., Munos, R., Kavukcuoglu, K., Mnih, V.: PGQ: combining policy gradient and q-learning. arXiv preprint arXiv:1611.01626 (2016)
38. Okuma, K., Taleghani, A., de Freitas, N., Little, J.J., Lowe, D.G.: A boosted particle filter: multitarget detection and tracking. In: Pajdla, T., Matas, J. (eds.) ECCV 2004. LNCS, vol. 3021, pp. 28–39. Springer, Heidelberg (2004). https://doi.org/10.1007/978-3-540-24670-1_3
39. Qi, Y., et al.: Hedged deep tracking. In: CVPR, pp. 4303–4311 (2016)
40. Rao, Y., Lu, J., Zhou, J.: Attention-aware deep reinforcement learning for video face recognition. In: ICCV, pp. 3931–3940 (2017)
41. Smeulders, A.W., Chu, D.M., Cucchiara, R., Calderara, S., Dehghan, A., Shah, M.: Visual tracking: an experimental survey. TPAMI **36**(7), 1442–1468 (2014)
42. Song, Y., Ma, C., Gong, L., Zhang, J., Lau, R.W.H., Yang, M.: CREST: convolutional residual learning for visual tracking. CoRR (2017)
43. Song, Y., Ma, C., Gong, L., Zhang, J., Lau, R.W.H., Yang, M.H.: Crest: convolutional residual learning for visual tracking. In: ICCV, pp. 2555–2564 (2017)
44. Supancic III, J., Ramanan, D.: Tracking as online decision-making: learning a policy from streaming videos with reinforcement learning. In: ICCV, pp. 322–331 (2017)
45. Tao, R., Gavves, E., Smeulders, A.W.: Siamese instance search for tracking. In: CVPR, pp. 1420–1429 (2016)
46. Wang, L., Ouyang, W., Wang, X., Lu, H.: STCT: sequentially training convolutional networks for visual tracking. In: CVPR, pp. 1373–1381 (2016)

47. Wang, N., Yeung, D.Y.: Learning a deep compact image representation for visual tracking. In: NIPS, pp. 809–817 (2013)
48. Wu, Y., Lim, J., Yang, M.H.: Online object tracking: a benchmark. In: CVPR, pp. 2411–2418 (2013)
49. Wu, Y., Lim, J., Yang, M.H.: Object tracking benchmark. TPAMI 37(9), 1834–1848 (2015)
50. Yang, B., Nevatia, R.: Multi-target tracking by online learning of non-linear motion patterns and robust appearance models. In: CVPR, pp. 1918–1925 (2012)
51. Yang, H., Shao, L., Zheng, F., Wang, L., Song, Z.: Recent advances and trends in visual tracking: a review. Neurocomputing (18), 3823–3831 (2011)
52. Yun, S., Choi, J., Yoo, Y., Yun, K., Young Choi, J.: Action-decision networks for visual tracking with deep reinforcement learning. In: CVPR, pp. 2711–2720 (2017)
53. Zhang, D., Maei, H., Wang, X., Wang, Y.F.: Deep reinforcement learning for visual object tracking in videos. arXiv preprint arXiv:1701.08936 (2017)
54. Zhang, J., Ma, S., Sclaroff, S.: MEEM: robust tracking via multiple experts using entropy minimization. In: Fleet, D., Pajdla, T., Schiele, B., Tuytelaars, T. (eds.) ECCV 2014. LNCS, vol. 8694, pp. 188–203. Springer, Cham (2014). https://doi.org/10.1007/978-3-319-10599-4_13

PSDF Fusion: Probabilistic Signed Distance Function for On-the-fly 3D Data Fusion and Scene Reconstruction

Wei Dong[1,2（✉）], Qiuyuan Wang[1,2], Xin Wang[1,2], and Hongbin Zha[1,2（✉）]

[1] Key Laboratory of Machine Perception (MOE), School of EECS,
Peking University, Beijing, China
{w.dong,qiuyuanwang,xinwang_cis}@pku.edu.cn, zha@cis.pku.edu.cn
[2] Cooperative Medianet Innovation Center, Shanghai Jiao Tong University,
Shanghai, China

Abstract. We propose a novel 3D spatial representation for data fusion and scene reconstruction. *Probabilistic Signed Distance Function* (Probabilistic SDF, PSDF) is proposed to depict uncertainties in the 3D space. It is modeled by a joint distribution describing SDF value and its inlier probability, reflecting input data quality and surface geometry. A *hybrid data structure* involving voxel, surfel, and mesh is designed to fully exploit the advantages of various prevalent 3D representations. Connected by PSDF, these components reasonably cooperate in a consistent framework. Given sequential depth measurements, PSDF can be incrementally refined with less ad hoc parametric Bayesian updating. Supported by PSDF and the efficient 3D data representation, high-quality surfaces can be extracted on-the-fly, and in return contribute to reliable data fusion using the geometry information. Experiments demonstrate that our system reconstructs scenes with higher model quality and lower redundancy, and runs faster than existing online mesh generation systems.

Keywords: Signed Distance Function · Bayesian updating

1 Introduction

In recent years, we have witnessed the appearance of consumer-level depth sensors and the increasing demand of real-time 3D geometry information in next-generation applications. Therefore, online dense scene reconstruction has been a popular research topic. The essence of the problem is to fuse noisy depth data stream into a reliable 3D representation where clean models can be extracted. It is necessary to consider uncertainty in terms of sampling density, measurement accuracy, and surface complexity so as to better understand the 3D space.

Electronic supplementary material The online version of this chapter (https://doi.org/10.1007/978-3-030-01240-3_43) contains supplementary material, which is available to authorized users.

© Springer Nature Switzerland AG 2018
V. Ferrari et al. (Eds.): ECCV 2018, LNCS 11213, pp. 714–730, 2018.
https://doi.org/10.1007/978-3-030-01240-3_43

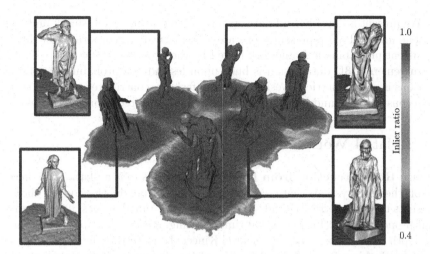

Fig. 1. Reconstructed mesh of *burghers*. The heatmap denotes the SDF inlier ratio (SDF confidence). Note details are preserved and outliers have been all removed without any post-processing. Inlier-ratio heatmaps in Figs. 4, 5 and 6 also conform to this colorbar. (Color figure online)

Many representations built upon appropriate mathematical models are designed for robust data fusion in such a context. To handle uncertainties, *surfel* and *point* based approaches [13,15,29] adopt filtering-based probabilistic models that explicitly manipulate input data. *Volume* based methods [5,12,20,27], on the other hand, maximize spatial probabilistic distributions and output discretized 3D properties such as SDF and occupancy state. With fixed topologies, *mesh* based methods [35] may also involve parametric minimization of error functions.

While such representations have been proven effective by various applications, their underlying data structures endure more or less drawbacks. Surfels and points are often loosely managed without topology connections, requiring additional modules for efficient indexing and rendering [1], and is relatively prone to noisy input. Volumetric grids lack flexibility to some extent, hence corresponding data fusion can be either oversimplified using weighted average [20], or much time-consuming in order to maximize joint distributions [27]. In addition, ray-casting based volume rendering is also non-trivial. Usually storing vertices with strong topological constraints, mesh is similarly hard to manipulate and is less applicable to many situations. There have been studies incorporating aforementioned data structures [14,18,23,24], yet most of these pipelines are loosely organized without fully taking the advantages of each representation.

In this paper, we design a novel framework to fully exploit the power of existing 3D representations, supported by PSDF-based probabilistic computations. Our framework is able to perform reliable depth data fusion and reconstruct high-quality surfaces in real-time with more details and less noise, as depicted in Fig. 1. Our contributions can be concluded as:

1. We present a novel hybrid data structure integrating voxel, surfel, and mesh;
2. The involved 3D representations are systematically incorporated in the consistent probabilistic framework linked by the proposed PSDF;
3. Incremental 3D data fusion is built upon less ad-hoc probabilistic computations in a parametric Bayesian updating fashion, contributes to online surface reconstruction, and benefits from iteratively recovered geometry in return.

2   Related Work

Dense Reconstruction from Depth Images. There is a plethora of successful off-the-shelf systems that reconstruct 3D scenes from depth scanners' data. [4] presents the volumetric 3D grids to fuse multi-view range images. [20] extends [4] and proposes KinectFusion, a real-time tracking and dense mapping system fed by depth stream from a consumer-level Kinect. KinectFusion has been improved by VoxelHashing [22], InfiniTAM [12], and BundleFusion [5] that leverage more memory-efficient volumetric representations. While these systems perform online depth fusion, they usually require offline MarchingCubes [17] to output final mesh models; [6,14,24] incorporates online meshing modules in such systems. Instead of utilizing volumetric spatial representations, [13] proposes point-based fusion that maintains light-weight dense point cloud or surfels as 3D maps. ElasticFusion [31] and InfiniTAM_v3 [23] are efficient implementations of [13] with several extensions; [16] further improves [13] by introducing surface curvatures. The point-based methods are unable to output mesh online, hence may not be suitable for physics-based applications. [2,34] split scenes into fragments and register partially reconstructed mesh to build comprehensive models, but their offline property limits their usages.

3D Scene Representations. Dense 3D map requires efficient data structures to support high resolution reconstructions. For volumetric systems, plain 3D arrays [20] are unsuitable for large scale scenes due to spatial redundancies. In view of this, moving volumes method [30] is introduced to maintain spatial properties only in active areas. Octree is used to ensure a complete yet adaptive coverage of model points [10,24,33]. As the tree might be unbalanced causing long traversing time, hierarchical spatial hashing is utilized [12,22] supporting O(1) 3D indexing, and is further extended to be adaptive to local surface complexities [11].

There are also studies that directly represent scenes as point clouds or mesh during reconstruction. In [13,31] point clouds or surfels are simply arranged in an 1D array. Considering topologies in mesh, [18] manages point clouds with inefficient KD-Tress for spatial resampling. [35] maintains a 2.5D map with fixed structured triangles which will fail to capture occlusions. Hybrid data structures are also used to combine volumes and mesh. [24] builds an octree-based structure where boundary conditions have to be carefully considered in term of mesh triangles. [14] uses spatial hashed blocks and stores mesh triangles in the block level, but ignores vertex sharing between triangles. [6] reveals the correspondences between mesh vertices and voxel edges, reducing the redundancy in the aspect of data structure. Yet improvement is required to remove false surfaces generated from noisy input data.

Uncertainty-Aware Data Fusion. Uncertainty is one of the core problems remain in 3D reconstruction, which may come from imperfect inputs or complex environments. In volumetric representations that split the space into grids, probability distributions are usually utilized to model spatial properties. Binary occupancy is an intuitive variable configuration, denoting whether a voxel is physically occupied. [32] proposes a joint distribution of point occupancy state and inlier ratio over the entire volume with visual constraints and achieves competitive results. [27,28] similarly emphasize ray-consistency to reconstruct global-consistent surfaces, whose inferences are too sophisticated to run in real-time. Although surface extraction can be performed on occupancy grids via thresholding or ray-casting, it is usually very sensitive to parameters. Instead of maintaining a $\{0,1\}$ field, [4] introduces SDF which holds signed projective distances from voxels to their closest surfaces sampled by input depth measurements. [19,20] use weight average of Truncated SDF in the data fusion stage by considering a per-voxel Gaussian distribution regarding SDF as a random variable. While Gaussian noise can be smoothed by weight average, outliers have to be carefully filtered out with ad hoc operations. [22] uses a temporal recycling strategy by periodically subtracting weight in volumes; [14] directly carves out noisy inputs; [5] proposes a weighted subtraction to de-integrate data which are assumed to be incorrectly registered. As a non-local prior, [7] refines SDF value on-the-go using plane fitting, which performs well mainly in flat scenes with relatively low voxel resolutions. We find a lack of systematic probabilistic solution for SDF dealing both Gaussian noise and possible outliers.

For point-based representations, [29] proposes an elegant math model treating inlier ratio and depth of a point as random variables subject to a special distribution. The parameters of such distributions are updated in a Bayesian fashion. This approach is adopted by [8] in SLAM systems for inverse depths, achieving competitive results. An alternative is to select ad hoc weights involving geometry and photometric properties of estimated points and computing weighted average [15,26]. This simple strategy shares some similarity to the fusion of SDF values, and is also used in RGB-D systems where depths are more reliable [13,23]. Despite the solid math formulations, point-based methods are comparatively prone to noise due to their discrete representations.

3 Overview

Our framework is based on the *hybrid data structure* involving three *3D representations* linked by *PSDF*. The pipeline consists of iterative operations of data fusion and surface generation.

3.1 Hybrid Data Structure

We follow [6,14,22] and use a spatial hashing based structure to efficiently manage the space. A hash entry would point to a block, which is the smallest unit to

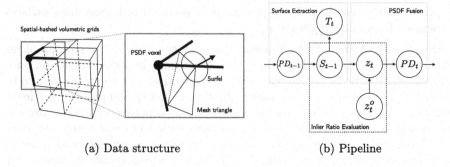

(a) Data structure   (b) Pipeline

Fig. 2. A basic hybrid unit, and the system pipeline.

allocate and free. A block is further divided into $8 \times 8 \times 8$ small voxels. Following [6] we consider a voxel as a 3-edge structure instead of merely a cube, as depicted in Fig. 2(a), which will avoid ambiguity when we refer to shared edges. PSDF values are stored at the corners of these structures. In addition, we maintain surfels on the volumetric grids by limiting their degree of freedom on the edges of voxels; within a voxel at most 3 surfels on edges could be allocated. This constraint would regularize the distribution of surfels, guarantee easier access, and avoid duplicate allocation. Triangles are loosely organized in the level of blocks, linking adjacent surfels. In the context of mesh, a surfel could be also interpreted as a triangle vertex.

3.2 3D Representations

Voxel and PSDF. In most volumetric reconstruction systems SDF or truncated SDF (TSDF) (denoted by D) of a voxel is updated when observed 3D points fall in its neighbor region. Projective signed distances from measurements, which could be explained as SDF observations, are integrated by computing weight average. Newcombe [19] suggests that it can be regarded as the solution of a maximum likelihood estimate of a joint Gaussian distribution taking SDF as a random variable. While Gaussian distribution could depict the uncertainty of data noise, it might fail to handle outlier inputs which are common in reconstruction tasks using consumer-level sensors. Moreover, SDF should depict the projective distance from a voxel to its *closest* surface. During integration, however, it is likely that *non-closest* surface points are taken into account, which should also be regarded as outlier SDF observations. In view of this, we introduce another random variable π to denote the inlier ratio of SDF, initially used in [29] to model the inlier ratio of 3D points:

$$p(D_i^o \mid D, \tau_i, \pi) = \pi \mathcal{N}(D_i^o; D, \tau_i^2) + (1 - \pi)\mathcal{U}(D_i^o; D_{min}, D_{max}), \qquad (1)$$

where D_i^o reads an SDF observation computed with depth measurements, τ_i is the variance of the SDF observation, $\mathcal{N}$ and $\mathcal{U}$ are Gaussian and Uniform distributions.

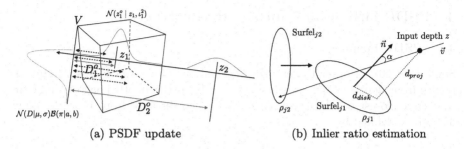

(a) PSDF update   (b) Inlier ratio estimation

Fig. 3. Left, illustration of PSDF distribution with multiple SDF observations (D_1^o is likely to be an inlier observation, D_2^o is possibly an outlier). The red curves show Gaussian distributions per observation. The blue curve depicts a Beta distribution which intuitively suggests that inlier observations should be around D_1^o. Right, estimation of SDF inlier ratio ρ involving observed input 3D point and already known surfels. (Color figure online)

Following [29], the posterior of PSDF can be parameterized by a Beta distribution multiplying a Gaussian distribution $\mathcal{B}(a,b)\mathcal{N}(\mu;\sigma^2)$, given a series of observed input SDF measurements. The details will be discussed in Sect. 4.1. The parameters a, b, μ, σ of the parameterized distribution are maintained per voxel.

Surfel. A surfel in our pipeline is formally defined by a position x, a normal n, and a radius r. Since a certain surfel is constrained on an edge in the volume, x is generally an interpolation of 2 adjacent voxel corners.

Triangle. A triangle consists of 3 edges, each linking two adjacent surfels. These surfels can be located in different voxels, even different blocks. In our framework triangles are mainly extracted for rendering; the contained topology information may be further utilized in extensions.

Depth Input. We receive depth measurements from sensors as input, while sensor poses are assumed known. Each observed input depth z^o is modeled as a random variable subject to a simple Gaussian distribution:

$$p(z^o \mid z, \iota) = \mathcal{N}(z^o; z, \iota^2), \tag{2}$$

where ι can be estimated from a precomputed sensor error model.

3.3 Pipeline

In general, our system will first generate a set of surfels S_{t-1} in the volumetric PSDF field PD_{t-1}. Meanwhile, mesh triangle set T_t is also determined by linking reliable surfels in S_{t-1}. S_{t-1} explicitly defines the surfaces of the scene, hence can be treated as a trustworthy geometry cue to estimate outlier ratio of the input depth data z_t^o. PD_{t-1} is then updated to PD_t by fusing evaluated depth data distribution z_t via Bayesian updating. The process will be performed iteratively every time input data come, as depicted in Fig. 2(b). We assume the poses of the sensors are known and all the computations are in the world coordinate system.

4   PSDF Fusion and Surface Reconstruction

4.1   PSDF Fusion

Similar to [20], in order to get SDF observations of a voxel V given input 3D points from depth images, we first project V to the depth image to find the projective closest depth measurement z_i. Signed distance from V to the input 3D data is defined by

$$D_i = z_i - z^V, \tag{3}$$

where z^V is a constant value, the projective depth of V along the scanning ray.

The observed D_i^o is affected by the variance ι_i of z_i in Eq. 2 contributing to the Gaussian distribution component in Eq. 1, provided D_i is an inlier. Otherwise, D_i would be counted in the uniform distribution part. Figure 3(a) illustrates the possible observations of SDF in one voxel.

Variance ι_i can be directly estimated by pre-measured sensor priors such as proposed in [21]. In this case, due to the simple linear form in Eq. 3, we can directly set $D_i^o = z_i^o - z^V$ and $\tau_i = \iota_i$ in Eq. 1.

Given a series of independent observations D_i^o, we can derive the posterior

$$p(D, \pi \mid D_1^o, \tau_1 \cdots D_n^o, \tau_n) \propto p(D, \pi) \prod_i p(D_i^o \mid D, \tau_i^2, \pi), \tag{4}$$

where $p(D, \pi)$ is a prior and $p(D_i^o \mid D, \tau_i^2, \pi)$ is defined by Eq. 1. It would be intractable to evaluate the production of such distributions with additions. Fortunately, [29] proved that the posterior could be approximated by a parametric joint distribution:

$$p(D, \pi \mid D_1^o, \tau_1 \cdots D_n^o, \tau_n) \propto \mathcal{B}(\pi \mid a_n, b_n)\mathcal{N}(D \mid \mu_n, \sigma_n^2), \tag{5}$$

therefore the problem could be simplified as a parameter estimation in an incremental fashion:

$$\mathcal{B}(\pi \mid a_n, b_n)\mathcal{N}(D \mid \mu_n, \sigma_n^2) \propto p(D_n^o|D, \tau_n^2, \pi)\mathcal{B}(\pi \mid a_{n-1}, b_{n-1})\mathcal{N}(D \mid \mu_{n-1}, \sigma_{n-1}^2). \tag{6}$$

In [29] by equating first and second moments of the random variables π and D, the parameters could be easily updated, in our case evoking the change of SDF distribution and its inlier probability:

$$\mu_n = \frac{C_1}{C_1 + C_2}m + \frac{C_2}{C_1 + C_2}\mu_{n-1}, \tag{7}$$

$$\mu_n^2 + \sigma_n^2 = \frac{C_1}{C_1 + C_2}(s^2 + m^2) + \frac{C_2}{C_1 + C_2}(\sigma_{n-1}^2 + \mu_{n-1}^2), \tag{8}$$

$$s^2 = 1/(\frac{1}{\sigma_{n-1}^2} + \frac{1}{\tau_n^2}), \tag{9}$$

$$m = s^2(\frac{\mu_{n-1}}{\sigma_{n-1}^2} + \frac{D_i^o}{\tau_n^2}), \tag{10}$$

$$C_1 = \frac{a_{n-1}}{a_{n-1} + b_{n-1}} \mathcal{N}(D_i^o; \mu_{n-1}, \sigma_{n-1}^2 + \tau_n^2), \tag{11}$$

$$C_2 = \frac{b_{n-1}}{a_{n-1} + b_{n-1}} \mathcal{U}(D_i^o; D_{min}, D_{max}), \tag{12}$$

the computation of a and b are the same as [29] hence ignored here. In our experiments we find that a truncated D_i^o leads to better results, as it directly rejects distant outliers. SDF observations from non-closest surfaces are left to be handled by PSDF.

4.2   Inlier Ratio Evaluation

In Eqs. 11–12, the expectation of $\mathcal{B}(\pi \mid a, b)$ is used to update the coefficients, failing to make full use of known geometry properties in scenes. In our pipeline, available surface geometry is considered to evaluate the inlier ratio ρ_n of D_n^o, replacing the simple $\frac{a_{n-1}}{a_{n-1}+b_{n-1}}$. Note ρ_n is computed per-frame in order to update C_1, C_2; π is still parameterized by a and b.

ρ_n can be determined by whether an input point z is near the closest surface of a voxel and results in an inlier SDF observation. We first cast the scanning ray into the volume and collect the surfels maintained on the voxels hit by the ray. Given the surfels, 3 heuristics are used, as illustrated in Fig. 3(b).

Projective Distance. This factor is used to measure whether a sampled point is close enough to a surfel which is assumed the nearest surface to the voxel:

$$w_{dist} = \exp(\frac{-|n^T(x - zv)|^2}{2\theta^2}), \tag{13}$$

where v is the normalized direction of the ray in world coordinate system and θ is a preset parameter proportional to the voxel resolution.

Angle. Apart from projective distance, we consider angle as another factor, delineating the possibility that a scanning ray will hit a surfel. We use the empirical angle weight in [15]:

$$w_{angle} = \begin{cases} \frac{\cos(\alpha) - \cos(\alpha_{max})}{1 - \cos(\alpha_{max})}, \text{if } \alpha < \alpha_{max}, \\ w_{angle}^0, \qquad\qquad \text{else}, \end{cases} \tag{14}$$

where $\alpha = \langle n, v \rangle$, α_{max} is set to $80°$ and w_{angle}^0 assigned to 0.1.

Radius. The area that surfels could influence vary, due to the local shape of the surface. The further a point is away from the center of a surfel, the less possible it would be supported. A sigmoid-like function is used to encourage a smooth transition of the weight:

$$w_{radius} = \gamma + \frac{2(1 - \gamma)}{1 + \exp(\frac{-d_{disk}}{r})}, \tag{15}$$

$$d_{disk} = \sqrt{(zv - x)^T(I - nn^T)(zv - x)}, \tag{16}$$

where parameter $\gamma \in [0, 1)$ and is set to 0.5 in our case.

Putting all the factors together, we now have

$$\rho = w_{dist} \cdot w_{radius} \cdot w_{angle}. \tag{17}$$

To compute the ρ predicted by all the surfels, one may consider either summations or multiplications. However, we choose the highest ρ instead – intuitively a depth measurement is a sample on a surface, corresponding to exactly one surfel. A more sophisticated selection might include a ray consistency evaluation [27,28,32] where occlusion is handled. When a new area is explored where no surfels have been extracted, we use a constant value $\rho_{pr} = 0.1$ to represent a simple occupancy prior in space, hence we have

$$\rho = \max_j \{\rho_{pr}, \rho_1, \cdots, \rho_j, \cdots\}. \tag{18}$$

4.3 Surface Extraction

PSDF implicitly defines zero crossing surfaces and decides whether they are true surfaces. The surface extraction is divided into two steps.

Surfel Generation. In this stage we enumerate zero-crossing points upon 3 edges of each voxel and generate surfels when condition

$$\mu^{i1} \cdot \mu^{i2} < 0,$$
$$\frac{a^{i1}}{a^{i1} + b^{i1}} > \pi_{thr} \text{ and } \frac{a^{i2}}{a^{i2} + b^{i2}} > \pi_{thr}, \tag{19}$$

are satisfied, where $i1$ and $i2$ are indices of adjacent voxels and π_{thr} is a confidence threshold. Supported by the reliable update of the PSDF, false surfaces could be rejected and duplicates could be removed. According to our experiments, our framework is not sensitive to π_{thr}; 0.4 would work for all the testing scenes. A surfel's position x would be the linear interpolation of corresponding voxels' positions x^i indexed by i, and the radius would be determined by σ of adjacent voxels, simulating its affecting area. Normal is set to normalized gradient of the SDF field, as mentioned in [20].

$$x = \frac{|\mu^{i2}|}{|\mu^{i1}| + |\mu^{i2}|} x^{i1} + \frac{|\mu^{i1}|}{|\mu^{i1}| + |\mu^{i2}|} x^{i2}, \tag{20}$$

$$r = \frac{|\mu^{i2}|}{|\mu^{i1}| + |\mu^{i2}|} \sigma^{i1} + \frac{|\mu^{i1}|}{|\mu^{i1}| + |\mu^{i2}|} \sigma^{i2}, \tag{21}$$

$$n = \nabla\mu / ||\nabla\mu||. \tag{22}$$

Triangle Generation. Having sufficient geometry information within surfels, there is only one more step to go for rendering-ready mesh. The connections between adjacent surfels are determined by the classical MarchingCubes [17] method. As a simple modification, we reject edges in the voxel whose σ is larger than a preset parameter σ_{thr}. This operation will improve the visual quality of reconstructed model while preserving surfels for the prediction stage.

5   Experiments

We test our framework (denoted by *PSDF*) on three RGB-D datasets: TUM [25], ICL-NUIM [9], and dataset from Zhou and Koltun [34]. Our method is compared against [6] (denoted by *TSDF*) which incrementally extracts mesh in spatial-hashed TSDF volumes. The sensors' poses are assumed known for these datasets, therefore the results of *TSDF* should be similar to other state-of-the-art methods such as [22,23] where TSDF integration strategies are the same. We demonstrate that our method reconstructs high quality surfaces by both qualitative and quantitative results. Details are preserved while noise is removed in the output models. The running speed for online mesh extraction is also improved by avoiding computations on false surfel candidates.

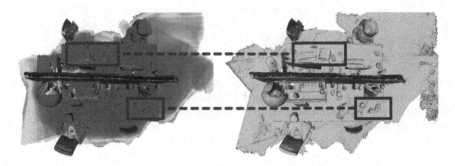

Fig. 4. Comparison of output mesh of *frei3_long_office* scene. Left, *PSDF*. Right, *TSDF*. Our method generates smooth surfaces and clean edges of objects, especially in blue boxes. (Color figure online)

For [25,34] we choose a voxel size of 8 mm and $\sigma_{thr} = 16$ mm; for [9] voxel size is set to 12 mm and $\sigma_{thr} = 48$ mm. The truncation distance is set to $3\times$ voxel size plus $3 \times \tau$; with a smaller truncation distance we found strides and holes in meshes. Kinect's error model [21] was adopted to get ι where the factor of angle was removed, which we think might cause double counting considering w_{angle} in the inlier prediction stage. The program is written in C++/CUDA 8.0 and runs on a laptop with an Intel i7-6700 CPU and an NVIDIA 1070 graphics card.

5.1   Qualitative Results

We first show that *PSDF* accompanied by the related mesh extraction algorithm produces higher quality surfaces than *TSDF*. Our results are displayed with shaded heatmap whose color indicates the inlier ratio of related SDF. Both geometry and probability properties can be viewed in such a representation.

Figure 4 shows that *PSDF* outperforms *TSDF* by generating clean boundaries of small objects and rejecting noisy areas on the ground. In Fig. 5, in addition to the results of *TSDF*, we also display the reconstructed mesh from offline

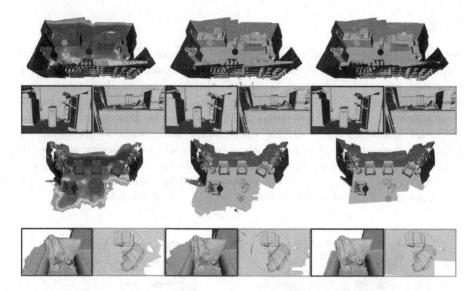

Fig. 5. Output mesh of the *copyroom* and *lounge* scenes. From left to right, *PSDF*, *TSDF*, mesh provided by [34]. Zoomed in regions show that our method is able to filter outliers while maintaining complete models and preserving details. Best viewed in color. (Color figure online)

methods provided by [34] as references. It appears that our method produces results very similar to [34]. While guaranteeing well-covered reconstruction of scenes, we filter outliers and preserve details. In *copyroom*, the wires are completely reconstructed, one of which above PC is smoothed out in [34] and only partially recovered by *TSDF*. In *lounge*, we can observe a complete shape of table, and de-noised details in the clothes.

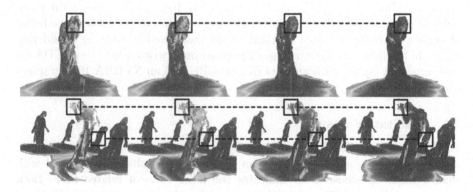

Fig. 6. Incremental reconstruction of the *burghers* dataset. Fluctuation of probability could be observed at error-prone regions as an indication of uncertainty propagation. (Color figure online)

We also visualize the incremental update of π by rendering $\mathbb{E}(\beta(\pi|a,b)) = a/(a+b)$ as the inlier ratio of reconstructed mesh in sequence using colored heatmap. Figure 6 shows the fluctuation of confidence around surfaces. The complex regions such as fingers and wrinkles on statues are more prone to noise, therefore apparent change of shape along with color can be observed.

5.2   Quantitative Results

Reconstruction Accuracy. We reconstruct mesh of the synthetic dataset *livingroom2* with added noise whose error model is presented in [9]. Gaussian noise

Table 1. Statistics of the point-to-point distances from the reconstructed model vertices to the ground truth point cloud. *PSDF* yields better reconstruction accuracy.

Method	MEAN (m)	STD (m)
PSDF	**0.011692**	**0.015702**
TSDF	0.022556	0.076120

(a) Point-to-point distance heatmap. Left, *PSDF*. Right, *TSDF*.

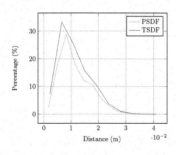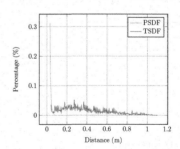

(b) Histogram head: 0 to 4*cm*   (c) Histogram tail: 4*cm* to ∞

Fig. 7. Comparison of output mesh quality of *PSDF* and *TSDF*. First row: heatmap of the point-to-point distance from the reconstructed model to the ground truth. Notice the outliers in the red box. Second row, the distance histogram divided into two parts to emphasize the existence of outliers. As shown in the histogram tail, *TSDF* generates many outliers, while *PSDF* avoids such problems. Best viewed in color. (Color figure online)

on inverse depth plus local offsets is too complicated for our error model, therefore we simplify it by assigning inverse sigma at certain inverse depths to ι_i. The mesh vertices are compared with the ground truth point cloud using the free software *CloudCompare* [3].

Table 1 indicates that *PSDF* reconstructs better models than *TSDF*. Further details in Fig. 7 suggest that less outliers appear in the model reconstructed by *PSDF*, leading to cleaner surfaces.

Mesh Size. Our method maintains the simplicity of mesh by reducing false surface candidates caused by noise and outliers. As shown in Fig. 8 and Table 2, *PSDF* in most cases generates less vertices (% 20) than *TSDF*, most of which are outliers and boundaries with low confidence. Figure 8 shows that the vertex count remains approximately constant when a loop closure occurred in *frei3_long_office*, while the increasing rate is strictly constrained in the *lounge* sequence where there is no loop closure.

Time. To make a running time analysis, we take real world *lounge* as a typical sequence where noise is common while the camera trajectory fits scanning behavior of humans. As we have discussed, evaluation of inlier ratio was performed, increasing total time of the fusion stage. However we find on a GPU,

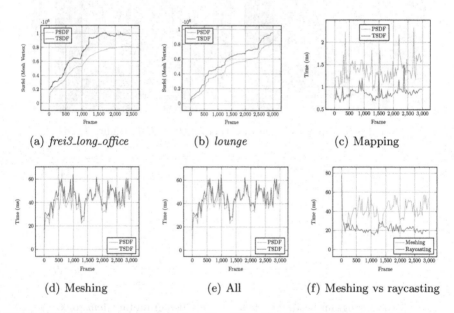

Fig. 8. (a)–(b), increasing trend of mesh vertices (surfels). (a), *frei3_long_office* scene in which a loop closure occurs at around 1500 frames. (b), *lounge* scene without loop closures. Mesh generated by *PSDF* consumes approximately 80% the memory of *TSDF*. (c)–(f), running time analysis of our approaches and compared methods on *lounge* scene. *PSDF* is 1ms slower on GPU due to additional inlier prediction stage, but will save more time for surface extraction, causing a faster speed in general. The speed of online meshing is slower than raycasting but comparable.

Table 2. Evaluation of memory and time cost on various datasets. PSDF reduces model's redundancy by rejecting false surfaces and noise. The mapping stage of TSDF is faster, but in general PSDF spends less time considering both mapping and meshing stages.

Dataset	Frames	MEMORY (vertex count)		TIME (ms)				
		PSDF	TSDF	PSDF		TSDF		Ray-casting
				Mapping	Meshing	Mapping	Meshing	
burghers	11230	**1362303**	1438818	1.053	39.691	**0.771**	**38.907**	27.761
copyroom	5490	**1222196**	1328397	1.329	**39.090**	0.909	41.595	21.292
garden	6152	**922534**	978206	1.473	68.224	**0.907**	**66.680**	25.479
lounge	3000	**821360**	955218	1.331	**41.270**	0.881	45.248	22.097
livingroom1	965	529305	**518885**	1.255	33.090	**0.743**	**32.865**	27.248
livingroom2	880	**609421**	683008	1.407	**33.446**	0.759	40.230	29.069
office1	965	**667614**	674034	1.264	**24.933**	0.799	27.654	26.957
office2	880	**712685**	883138	1.322	**35.029**	0.767	45.923	29.981
frei1_xyz	790	**212840**	352444	1.193	**45.163**	1.149	71.670	19.796
frei3_long_office	2486	**811092**	963875	2.424	**159.417**	1.375	161.485	26.545

even with a relatively high resolution, the average increased time is at the scale of ms (see Fig. 8(c) and Table 2) and can be accepted.

When we come to meshing, we find that by taking the advantage of PSDF fusion and inlier ratio evaluation, unnecessary computations can be avoided and *PSDF* method runs faster than *TSDF*, as plotted in Fig. 8(d). The meshing stage is the runtime bottleneck of the approach, in general the saved time compensate for the cost in fusion stage, see Fig. 8(e) and Table 2.

We also compare the time of meshing to the widely used ray-casting that renders surfaces in real-time. According to Table 2, in some scenes where sensor is close to the surfaces performing scanning, less blocks are allocated in viewing frustum and the meshing speed could be comparative to ray-casting, as illustrated in Fig. 8(f). As for other scenes requiring a large scanning range, especially *frei3_long_office* where more blocks in frustum have to be processed, ray-casting shows its advantage. We argue that in applications that only require visualization, ray-casting can be adopted; otherwise meshing offers more information and is still preferable.

6   Conclusions

We propose PSDF, a joint probabilistic distribution to model the 3D geometries and spatial uncertainties. With the help of Bayesian updating, parameters of the distribution could be incrementally estimated. Built upon a hybrid data structure, our framework can iteratively generate surfaces from the volumetric PSDF field and update PSDF values through reliable probabilistic data fusion supported by reconstructed surfaces. As an output, high-quality mesh can be generated in real-time with duplicates removed and noise cleared.

In the future, we seek to improve our framework by employing more priors to enrich the PSDF distribution. Localization modules will also be integrated in the probabilistic framework for a complete SLAM system.

Acknowledgments. This work is supported by the National Natural Science Foundation of China (61632003, 61771026), and National Key Research and Development Program of China (2017YFB1002601).

References

1. Botsch, M., Kobbelt, L.: High-quality point-based rendering on modern GPUs. In: Proceedings of Pacific Conference on Computer Graphics and Applications, pp. 335–343 (2003)
2. Choi, S., Zhou, Q.Y., Koltun, V.: Robust reconstruction of indoor scenes. In: Proceedings of IEEE Conference on Computer Vision and Pattern Recognition (2015)
3. CloudCompare-project: CloudCompare. http://www.cloudcompare.org/
4. Curless, B., Levoy, M.: A volumetric method for building complex models from range images. In: Proceedings of ACM SIGGRAPH, pp. 303–312 (1996)
5. Dai, A., Nießner, M., Zollhöfer, M., Izadi, S., Theobalt, C.: BundleFusion: real-time globally consistent 3D reconstruction using on-the-fly surface reintegration. ACM Trans. Graph. **36**(3), 24 (2017)
6. Dong, W., Shi, J., Tang, W., Wang, X., Zha, H.: An efficient volumetric mesh representation for real-time scene reconstruction using spatial hashing. In: Proceedings of IEEE International Conference on Robotics and Automation (2018)
7. Dzitsiuk, M., Sturm, J., Maier, R., Ma, L., Cremers, D.: De-noising, stabilizing and completing 3D reconstructions on-the-go using plane priors. In: Proceedings of IEEE International Conference on Robotics and Automation, pp. 3976–3983 (2017)
8. Forster, C., Pizzoli, M., Scaramuzza, D.: SVO: fast semi-direct monocular visual odometry. In: Proceedings of IEEE International Conference on Robotics and Automation, pp. 15–22 (2014)
9. Handa, A., Whelan, T., Mcdonald, J., Davison, A.J.: A benchmark for RGB-D visual odometry, 3D reconstruction and SLAM. In: Proceedings of IEEE International Conference on Robotics and Automation, pp. 1524–1531 (2014)
10. Hornung, A., Wurm, K.M., Bennewitz, M., Stachniss, C., Burgard, W.: OctoMap: an efficient probabilistic 3D mapping framework based on octrees. Auton. Rob. **34**(3), 189–206 (2013)
11. Kähler, O., Prisacariu, V., Valentin, J., Murray, D.: Hierarchical voxel block hashing for efficient integration of depth images. IEEE Rob. Autom. Lett. **1**(1), 192–197 (2016)
12. Kähler, O., Prisacariu, V.A., Ren, C.Y., Sun, X., Torr, P., Murray, D.: Very high frame rate volumetric integration of depth images on mobile devices. IEEE Trans. Vis. Comput. Graph. **21**(11), 1241–1250 (2015)
13. Keller, M., Lefloch, D., Lambers, M., Weyrich, T., Kolb, A.: Real-time 3D reconstruction in dynamic scenes using point-based fusion. In: Proceedings of International Conference on 3DTV, pp. 1–8 (2013)
14. Klingensmith, M., Dryanovski, I., Srinivasa, S.S., Xiao, J.: CHISEL: real time large scale 3D reconstruction onboard a mobile device using spatially-hashed signed distance fields. In: Proceedings of Robotics: Science and Systems, pp. 1–8 (2015)

15. Kolev, K., Tanskanen, P., Speciale, P., Pollefeys, M.: Turning mobile phones into 3D scanners. In: Proceedings of IEEE Conference on Computer Vision and Pattern Recognition, pp. 3946–3953 (2014)
16. Lefloch, D., Kluge, M., Sarbolandi, H., Weyrich, T., Kolb, A.: Comprehensive use of curvature for robust and accurate online surface reconstruction. IEEE Trans. Pattern Anal. Mach. Intell. **39**(12), 2349–2365 (2017)
17. Lorensen, W.E., Cline, H.E.: Marching cubes: a high resolution 3D surface construction algorithm. In: Proceedings of ACM SIGGRAPH, vol. 6, pp. 7–9 (1987)
18. Marton, Z.C., Rusu, R.B., Beetz, M.: On fast surface reconstruction methods for large and noisy point clouds. In: Proceedings of IEEE International Conference on Robotics and Automation, pp. 3218–3223 (2009)
19. Newcombe, R.: Dense visual SLAM. Ph.D. thesis, Imperial College London, UK (2012)
20. Newcombe, R.A., et al.: KinectFusion: real-time dense surface mapping and tracking. In: Proceedings of IEEE and ACM International Symposium on Mixed and Augmented Reality, pp. 127–136 (2011)
21. Nguyen, C.V., Izadi, S., Lovell, D.: Modeling kinect sensor noise for improved 3D reconstruction and tracking. In: Proceedings of IEEE International Conference on 3D Imaging, Modeling, Processing, Visualization and Transmission, pp. 524–530 (2012)
22. Nießner, M., Zollhöfer, M., Izadi, S., Stamminger, M.: Real-time 3D reconstruction at scale using voxel hashing. ACM Trans. Graph. **32**(6), 169 (2013)
23. Prisacariu, V.A., et al.: InfiniTAM v3: a framework for large-scale 3D reconstruction with loop closure. arXiv e-prints, August 2017
24. Steinbrücker, F., Sturm, J., Cremers, D.: Volumetric 3D mapping in real-time on a CPU. In: Proceedings of IEEE International Conference on Robotics and Automation, pp. 2021–2028 (2014)
25. Sturm, J., Engelhard, N., Endres, F., Burgard, W., Cremers, D.: A benchmark for the evaluation of RGB-D SLAM systems. In: Proceedings of International Conference on Intelligent Robot Systems, pp. 573–580 (2012)
26. Tanskanen, P., Kolev, K., Meier, L., Camposeco, F., Saurer, O., Pollefeys, M.: Live metric 3D reconstruction on mobile phones. In: Proceedings of the IEEE International Conference on Computer Vision, pp. 65–72 (2013)
27. Ulusoy, A.O., Black, M.J., Geiger, A.: Patches, planes and probabilities: a nonlocal prior for volumetric 3D reconstruction. In: Proceedings of IEEE Conference on Computer Vision and Pattern Recognition, pp. 3280–3289 (2016)
28. Ulusoy, A.O., Geiger, A., Black, M.J.: Towards probabilistic volumetric reconstruction using ray potentials. In: Proceedings of International Conference on 3D Vision, pp. 10–18 (2015)
29. Vogiatzis, G., Hernández, C.: Video-based, real-time multi-view stereo. Image Vis. Comput. **29**(7), 434–441 (2011)
30. Whelan, T., Kaess, M., Fallon, M., Johannsson, H., Leonard, J., Mcdonald, J.: Kintinuous: spatially extended KinectFusion. Rob. Auton. Syst. **69**(C), 3–14 (2012)
31. Whelan, T., Kaess, M., Johannsson, H., Fallon, M., Leonard, J.J., McDonald, J.: Real-time large-scale dense RGB-D SLAM with volumetric fusion. Int. J. Robot. Res. **34**(4–5), 598–626 (2015)
32. Woodford, O.J., Vogiatzis, G.: A generative model for online depth fusion. In: Fitzgibbon, A., Lazebnik, S., Perona, P., Sato, Y., Schmid, C. (eds.) ECCV 2012. LNCS, vol. 7576, pp. 144–157. Springer, Heidelberg (2012). https://doi.org/10.1007/978-3-642-33715-4_11

33. Zeng, M., Zhao, F., Zheng, J., Liu, X.: Octree-based fusion for realtime 3D reconstruction. Graph. Models **75**(3), 126–136 (2013)
34. Zhou, Q., Koltun, V.: Dense scene reconstruction with points of interest. ACM Trans. Graph. **32**(4), 112 (2013)
35. Zienkiewicz, J., Tsiotsios, A., Davison, A., Leutenegger, S.: Monocular, real-time surface reconstruction using dynamic level of detail. In: Proceedings of International Conference on 3D Vision, pp. 37–46 (2016)

AugGAN: Cross Domain Adaptation with GAN-Based Data Augmentation

Sheng-Wei Huang[1]([✉]), Che-Tsung Lin[1,2][iD], Shu-Ping Chen[1], Yen-Yi Wu[1],
Po-Hao Hsu[1], and Shang-Hong Lai[1]

[1] Department of Computer Science, National Tsing Hua University, Hsinchu, Taiwan
shengwei@mx.nthu.edu.tw, lai@cs.nthu.edu.tw
[2] Intelligent Mobility Division, Mechanical and Mechatronics Systems Research
Laboratories, Industrial Technology Research Institute, Zhudong, Taiwan
AlexLin@itri.org.tw

Abstract. Deep learning based image-to-image translation methods
aim at learning the joint distribution of the two domains and finding
transformations between them. Despite recent GAN (Generative Adversarial Network) based methods have shown compelling results, they are
prone to fail at preserving image-objects and maintaining translation
consistency, which reduces their practicality on tasks such as generating
large-scale training data for different domains. To address this problem,
we purpose a structure-aware image-to-image translation network, which
is composed of encoders, generators, discriminators and parsing nets for
the two domains, respectively, in a unified framework. The purposed network generates more visually plausible images compared to competing
methods on different image-translation tasks. In addition, we quantitatively evaluate different methods by training Faster-RCNN and YOLO
with datasets generated from the image-translation results and demonstrate significant improvement on the detection accuracies by using the
proposed image-object preserving network.

Keywords: Generative adversarial network
Image-to-image translation · Semantic segmentation
Object detection · Domain adaptation

1 Introduction

Deep learning pipelines have stimulated substantial progress for general object
detection. Detectors kept pushing the boundaries on several detection datasets.

S.-W. Huang and C.-T. Lin—Indicates equal contribution.

Electronic supplementary material The online version of this chapter (https://
doi.org/10.1007/978-3-030-01240-3_44) contains supplementary material, which is
available to authorized users.

© Springer Nature Switzerland AG 2018
V. Ferrari et al. (Eds.): ECCV 2018, LNCS 11213, pp. 731–744, 2018.
https://doi.org/10.1007/978-3-030-01240-3_44

However, despite being able to efficiently detect objects seen by arbitrary viewing angles, CNN-based detectors are still limited in a way that they could not function properly when faced with domains significantly different from those in the original training dataset. The most common way to obtain performance gain is to go through the troublesome data collection/annotation process. Nevertheless, the recent successes of Generative Adversarial Networks (GANs) on image-to-image translation have opened up possibilities in generating large-scale detection training data without the need for object annotation.

Generative adversarial networks [1], which put two networks (i.e., a generator and a discriminator) competing against each other, have emerged as a powerful framework for learning generative models of random data distributions. While expecting GANs to produce an RGB image and its associated bounding boxes from a random noise vector still sounds like a fantasy, training GANs to translate images from one scenario to another could help skip the tedious data annotation process. In the past, GAN-based image-to-image translation methods, such as Pix2Pix [2], were considered to have limited applications due to the requirement for pairwise training data. Although these methods yielded impressive results, the fact that they require pairwise training images largely reduces their practicality for the problem that we aim to solve.

Recently, unpaired image-to-image translation methods have achieved astonishing results on various domain adaptation challenges. Having almost identical architectures, CycleGAN [3], DiscoGAN [4], and DualGAN [5] made unpaired image-to-image translation possible through introducing the cycle consistency constraint. CoGAN [6] is a model which also works on unpaired images, using two shared-weight generators to generate images of two domains with one random noise. UNIT [7] is an extension of CoGAN. Aside from having similar hard weight-sharing constraints as CoGAN, Liu et al. further implemented the latent space assumption by encouraging two encoders to map images from two domains into the same latent space, which largely increases the translation consistency. These methods all demonstrate compelling visual results on several image-to-image translation tasks; however, what hinders the capability of these methods for providing large-scale detection training data, specifically when faced with translation tasks with a large domain shift, is the fact that these networks often arrive at solutions where the translation results are indistinguishable from the the target domain in terms of style, and usually contain corrupted image-objects.

In this paper we propose a structure-aware image-to-image translation network, which allows us to directly benefit object detection by translating existing detection RGB data from its original domain other scenarios. The contribution of this work is three-fold: (1) We train the encoder networks to extract structure-aware information through the supervision of a segmentation subtask, (2) we experiment on different weight sharing strategy to ensure the preservation of image-objects during image-translations, and (3) our object-preserving network provides significant performance gain on the night-time vehicle detection.

We stress particularly on day-to-night image translation not only for the importance of night-time detection, but also for the fact that day/night image translation is one of the most difficult domain transformations. However, our method is also capable of handling various domain pairs. We train our network on synthetic (i.e., SYNTHIA [8], GTA dataset [9]) Compared to the competing methods, the domain translation results of our network significantly enhance the capability of the object detector for application on both synthetic (i.e., SYNTHIA, GTA) and real-world (i.e., KITTI [10], ITRI) data. In addition, we welcome those who are interested in the ITRI dataset to email us for provision.

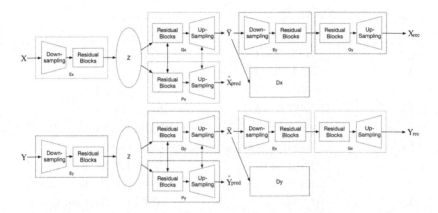

Fig. 1. Overall structure of the proposed image-to-image translation network. X, Y: image domain X and Y; Z: feature domain; $\hat{X}_{pred}$, $\hat{Y}_{pred}$: predicted segmentation masks; $\bar{X}$, $\bar{Y}$: translated results; dotted line implicates soft-sharing, solid line implicates hard-sharing.

2   Proposed Framework

In unsupervised image-to-image translation, models learn joint distribution where the network encodes images from the two domains into a shared feature space. We assume that, for an image to be properly translated to the other domain, the encoded information is required to contain (1) mutual style information between domain A and B, and (2) structural information of the given input image, as illustrated in Fig. 1. Based on the assumption we design our network to jointly optimize image-translation and semantic segmentation. Through our weight-sharing strategy, the segmentation subtask serves as an auxiliary regularization for image-translation.

Let X and Y denote the two image domains, $\hat{X}$ and $\hat{Y}$ denote the corresponding segmentation masks, and Z represent the encoded feature space. Our network, as depicted in Fig. 1, consists of two encoders $E_x : X \rightarrow Z$ and $E_y : Y \rightarrow Z$, two generators, $G_x : Z \rightarrow \bar{Y}$ and $G_y : Z \rightarrow \bar{X}$, two segmentation generators, $P_x : Z \rightarrow \hat{X}_{pred}$, and $P_y : Z \rightarrow \hat{Y}_{pred}$, and two discriminators D_x and D_y for the two image domains, respectively. Our network learns image domain translation in both directions and the segmentation sub-tasks simultaneously. For an input

$x \in X$, E_x first encodes x into the latent space, and the 256-channel feature vector is then processed to produce (1) the translated output $\bar{y}$ via G_x, and (2) the semantic representation $\hat{x}_{pred}$ via P_x. The translated output $\bar{y}$ is then fed through the inverse encoder-generator pair $\{E_y, G_y\}$ to yield the reconstructed image x_{rec}. Detailed architecture of our network is given in Table 1.

Table 1. Network architecture for the image-to-image translation experiments. N, K, and S denote the number of convolution filters, kernel size, and stride, respectively

Layer	Encoders	Layer info
1	CONV	N64, K7, S1
2	CONV, ReLU	N128, K3, S2
3	CONV, ReLU	N256, K3, S2
4	RESBLK, ELU	N512, K3, S1
5	RESBLK, ELU	N512, K3, S1
5	RESBLK, ELU	N512, K3, S1
Layer	Generators/parsing networks	Layer info
1	RESBLK, ELU	N512, K3, S1, hard shared
2	RESBLK, ELU	N512, K3, S1, hard shared
3	RESBLK, ELU	N512, K3, S1, hard shared
4	RESBLK, ELU	N512, K3, S1, hard shared
5	RESBLK, ELU	N512, K3, S1, hard shared
6	RESBLK, ELU	N512, K3, S1, hard shared
7	DCONV, ReLU	N128, K3, S2, soft shared
8	DCONV, ReLU	N64, K3, S2, soft shared
9 (generator)	CONV, Tanh	N3, K7, S1
9 (parsing net)	CONV, ReLU	N (task specific), K7, S1
10 (parsing net)	CONV, Softmax	N6 (task specific), K1, S0
Layer	Discriminator	Layer info
1	CONV, LeakyReLU	N64, K4, S2
2	CONV, LeakyReLU	N128, K4, S2
3	CONV, LeakyReLU	N256, K4, S2
3	CONV, LeakyReLU	N512, K4, S2
3	CONV, LeakyReLU	N512, K4, S1
3	CONV, Sigmoid	N1, K4, S1

2.1 Structure-Aware Encoding and Segmentation Subtask

We actively guide the encoder networks to extract context-aware features by regularizing them via segmentation subtask so that the extracted 256-channel feature vector contains not only mutual style information between X and Y domains, but also the intricate low-level semantic features of the input image that are valuable in the preservation of image-objects during translation. The segmentation loss is formulated as:

$$\mathcal{L}_{seg-x}(P_x, E_x, X, \hat{X}) = \lambda_{seg-L1}\mathbb{E}_{x \sim p_{data(x)}}[\|\|P_x(E_x(x)) - \hat{x}\|_1]$$
$$+ \lambda_{seg-crossentropy}\mathbb{E}_{x \sim p_{data(x)}}[\|\| \log(P_x(E_x(x)) - \hat{x})\|_1] \quad (1)$$

$$\mathcal{L}_{seg-y}(P_y, E_y, Y, \hat{Y}) = \lambda_{seg-L1}\mathbb{E}_{y \sim p_{data(y)}}[\|\|P_y(E_y(y)) - \hat{y}\|_1]$$
$$+ \lambda_{seg-crossentropy}\mathbb{E}_{y \sim p_{data(y)}}[\|\| \log(P_y(E_y(y)) - \hat{y})\|_1] \quad (2)$$

2.2 Weight Sharing for Multi-task Network

Sharing weights between the generator and parsing network allows the generator to fully take advantage of the context-aware feature vector. We hard-share the first 6 residual blocks and soft-share the subsequent two deconvolution blocks for generators and parsing networks. We experiment on different weight-sharing strategies, as illustrated in Sect. 3.2, such as hard-share, not sharing the deconvolution blocks, and not sharing the residual blocks, and come to the best sharing strategy. We calculate the weight difference between deconvolution layers of the two networks and model the difference as a loss function through mean square error with target as a zero matrix. The mathematical expression for the soft weight sharing loss function is given by

$$\mathcal{L}_\omega(\omega_G, \omega_P) = -\log((\omega_{G_x} \cdot \omega_{P_x} / \|\omega_{G_x}\|_2 \|\omega_{P_x}\|_2)^2) \quad (3)$$

where ω_G and ω_P denote the weight vectors formed by the deconvolution layers of the generator and parsing networks, respectively.

2.3 Cycle Consistency

The cycle consistency loss has been proven quite effective in preventing network from generating random images in the target domain. We also enforce the cycle-consistency constraint in the proposed framework to further regularize the ill-posed unsupervised image-to-image translation problem. The loss function is given by

$$\mathcal{L}_{cyc}(E_x, G_x, E_y, G_y, X, Y) = \mathbb{E}_{x \sim p_{data(x)}}[\|\|G_y(E_y(G_x(E_x(x)))) - x\|_1]$$
$$+ \mathbb{E}_{y \sim p_{data(y)}}[\|\|G_x(E_x(G_y(E_y(y)))) - y\|_1]. \quad (4)$$

2.4 Adversarial Learning

Our network contains two Generative Adversarial Networks: GAN_1: $\{E_x, G_x, D_x\}$, and GAN_2: $\{E_y, G_y, D_y\}$. We apply adversarial losses to both GANs, and formulate the objective loss functions as:

$$\mathcal{L}_{GAN_1}(E_x, G_x, D_x, X, Y) = \mathbb{E}_{y \sim p_{data(y)}}[\log D_x(y)]$$
$$+ \mathbb{E}_{x \sim p_{data(x)}}[\log(1 - D_x(G_x(E_x(x))))] \quad (5)$$

$$\mathcal{L}_{GAN_2}(E_y, G_y, D_y, Y, X) = \mathbb{E}_{x \sim p_{data(x)}}[\log D_y(x)]$$
$$+ \mathbb{E}_{y \sim p_{data(y)}}[\log(1 - D_y(G_y(E_y(y))))] \quad (6)$$

2.5   Network Learning

We jointly solve the learning problems for the image-translation streams: $\{E_1, G_1\}$ and $\{E_2, G_2\}$, the image-parsing streams: $\{E_1, P_1\}$ and $\{E_2, P_2\}$, and two GAN networks: GAN_1 and GAN_2, for training the proposed network. The integrated objective function is given as follows:

$$
\begin{aligned}
\mathcal{L}_{full} = {} & \mathcal{L}_{GAN}(E_x, G_x, D_x, X, Y) + \mathcal{L}_{GAN}(E_y, G_y, D_y, Y, X) \\
& + \lambda_{cyc} * \mathcal{L}_{cyc}(E_x, G_x, E_y, G_y, X, Y) \\
& + \lambda_{seg} * (\mathcal{L}_{seg}(E_x, P_x, X, \hat{X}) + \mathcal{L}_{seg}(E_y, P_y, Y, \hat{Y})) \\
& + \lambda_\omega * (\mathcal{L}_{\omega_x}(\omega_{G_x}, \omega_{P_x}) + \mathcal{L}_{\omega_y}(\omega_{G_y}, \omega_{P_y}))
\end{aligned}
\tag{7}
$$

3   Experimental Results

Though many works were dedicated on providing large-scale vehicle datasets for the research community [11–15], most public are collected in daytime. Considering that CNN-based detectors highly rely data augmentation techniques to stimulate performance, training detectors with both day and night images is necessary so as to make them more general. Synthetic dataset, such as SYNTHIA or GTA dataset, provides diverse on-road synthetic sequences as well as segmentation masks in scenarios such as day, night, snow, etc. As our network requires both segmentation mask and nighttime image, we conducted the training of our network with SYNTHIA and GTA datasets. For evaluation purpose, however, we utilize real-world data such as KITTI and our ITRI datasets.

The performance of the network was further analyzed through training YOLO [16] and Faster R-CNN (VGG 16-based) [17] detectors with generated image sets. Aside from revising both detectors to perform 1-class vehicle detection, all hyper-parameters were the same as those used for training on PASCAL VOC challenge. The IOU threshold for objects to be considered true-positives is 0.5, where we follow the standard for common object detection datasets. In the transformation of segmentation Ground-Truth to its counterpart in detection, we exclude the bounding boxes whose heights lower than 40 pixels or occluded for more than 75% in the subsequent AP estimation.

3.1   Synthetic Datasets

We first assess the effectiveness of training detectors with transformed images in both day and night scenarios. We evaluated our network, which is trained with SYNTHIA, by training detectors with transformed images produced by our network. As shown in Table 2, AugGAN outperforms competing methods in both day and night scenarios. AugGAN also surpasses its competitors when trained with GTA dataset, see Table 3. Visually, the transformation results of AugGAN is clearly better in terms of image-object preservation and preventing the appearance of artifacts as shown in Figs. 2 and 3.

Fig. 2. SYNTHIA day-to-night transformation results - GANs trained with SYNTHIA: first row: SYNTHIA daytime testing images; second row: results of Cycle-GAN; 3rd row: results of UNIT; 4th row: results of AugGAN

Fig. 3. GTA day-to-night transformation results - GANs trained with GTA: first row: GTA daytime testing images; second row: outputs of CycleGAN; 3rd row: outputs of UNIT; 4th row: outputs of AugGAN.

Table 2. Detection accuracy comparison (AP) - GANs trained with SYNTHIA. SDTrain/SNTrain: SYNTHIA daytime/nightime training set; SDTest/SNTest: SYNTHIA daytime/nighttime testing set.

Training	Testing	CycleGAN	UNIT	AugGAN	Detector
SDTrain	SNTest	36.1	35.2	39.0	YOLO
SNTrain	SDTest	33.8	32.6	38.0	YOLO
SDTrain	SNTest	65.9	57.2	72.2	Faster RCNN
SNTrain	SDTest	65.7	62.7	70.1	Faster RCNN

Table 3. Detection accuracy comparison (AP) - detectors trained with transformed images produced by GANs (trained with GTA dataset), and tested with real images. GTA-D-Train: transformed data with GTA training daytime images as input; GTA-N-Test: GTA testing nighttime data.

Training	Testing	CycleGAN	UNIT	AugGAN	Detector
GTA-D-Train	GTA-N-Test	20.5	23.6	25.3	YOLO
GTA-D-Train	GTA-N-Test	54.4	62.5	67.4	Faster-RCNN

3.2 KITTI and ITRI-Night Datasets

Aside from testing on SYNTHIA and GTA datasets, we also assess the capability of our network on real world data, such as KITTI, which has been widely used in assessing the performance of on-road object detectors used in autonomous driving systems. With the previously trained AugGAN, be it trained with SYNTHIA or GTA dataset, we transformed the KITTI dataset (7481 images with 6686 of which contains vehicle instances) [18] to its nighttime version and evaluate the translation results via detector training. We trained vehicle detectors with the translated KITTI dataset and tested on our ITRI-Night testing set (9366 images with 20833 vehicle instances). As experimental result indicates, real-world data transformed by AugGAN quantitatively and visually achieves better result even though AugGAN was trained with synthetic dataset, see Table 4, Figs. 4 and 5.

Table 4. Detection accuracy comparison (AP) - detectors trained with transformed images produced by GANs (trained with GTA dataset and SYNTHIA), and tested with real images. KITTI-D2N-S/KITTI-D2N-G: KITTI day-to-night training data generated by GANs; ITRIN: ITRI-Night dataset.

Training	Testing	CycleGAN	UNIT	AugGAN	Detector
KITTI-D2N-S	ITRIN	20.2	19.0	31.5	YOLO
KITTI-D2N-G	ITRIN	28.5	20.5	46.0	YOLO
KITTI-D2N-S	ITRIN	59.6	49.2	65.6	Faster RCNN
KITTI-D2N-G	ITRIN	72.0	64.0	79.3	Faster RCNN

3.3 ITRI Daytime and Nighttime Datasets

We collected a set of real-driving daytime (25104 images/87374 vehicle instances) dataset, captured mostly in the same scenario as its our nighttime dataset (9366 images with 20833 vehicle instances). In Table 5, the experiments demonstrate similar results as in other datasets. The transformed day-to-night training images

Table 5. Detection accuracy comparison (AP) - detectors trained with transformed images produced by GANs (trained with SYNTHIA/GTA dataset). ITRID-D2N-S/ITRID-D2N-G: ITRI-day day-to-night training data generated by GANs trained with SYNTHIA/GTA datasets; ITRIN: ITRI-Night dataset.

Training	Testing	CycleGAN	UNIT	AugGAN	Detector
ITRID-D2N-S	ITRIN	35.5	41.3	45.3	YOLO
ITRID-D2N-G	ITRIN	37.9	42.6	44.1	YOLO
ITRID-D2N-S	ITRIN	72.4	74.5	81.2	Faster RCNN
ITRID-D2N-G	ITRIN	86.2	85.9	86.1	Faster RCNN

Fig. 4. KITTI day-to-night transformation results - GANs trained with SYNTHIA: first row: KITTI images; second row: result of CycleGAN; 3rd row: result of UNIT; 4th row: result of AugGAN.

Fig. 5. KITTI dataset day-to-night transformation results - GANs trained with GTA dataset: first row: input images from KITTI dataset; second row: outputs of CycleGAN; 3rd row: outputs of UNIT; 4th row: outputs of AugGAN

Fig. 6. ITRI-Day dataset day-to-night transformation results - GANs trained with **SYNTHIA:** First row: input images from ITRI-Day dataset; Second row: outputs of cycleGAN; 3rd row: outputs of UNIT; 4th row: outputs of AugGAN

Fig. 7. ITRI-Day dataset day-to-night transformation results - GANs trained with **GTA dataset:** first row: input images from ITRI-Day dataset; second row: outputs of cycleGAN; 3rd row: outputs of UNIT; 4th row: outputs of AugGAN

are proved to be helpful in vehicle detector training. Training images generated by AugGAN outperforms those by competing methods due to its preservation in image-objects, with some examples shown in Figs. 6 and 7.

3.4 Transformations Other Than Daytime and Nighttime

AugGAN is capable of learning transformation across unpaired synthetic and real domains and only segmentation supervision in domain-A is required. This increases the flexibility of learning cross-domain adaptation for subsequent detector training. As shown in Fig. 8: 2nd row, our method could learn image translation from not only synthetic-synthetic, but also synthetic-real domain pairs.

Fig. 8. More image translation cases: 1st column: GTA-day to SYNTHIA; 2nd column: GTA-day to GTA-sunset; 3rd column: GTA-day to GTA-rain; 4th column: SYNTHIA-day to ITRI-night

4 Model Analysis

4.1 Segmentation Subtask

In our initial experiment on introducing the segmentation subtask, the parsing network was only utilized in the forward cycle (e.g., only day-to-night). We later on discovered that our results are improved by utilizing the parsing network to regularize both forward and inverse cycles. As can be seen in Table 6, it is quite obvious that adding regularization to the inverse cycle leads to better transformation results which make detectors more accurate. Although using only single-sided segmentation has already outperformed the previous works, introducing segmentation in both forward and backward cycles brings further accuracy improvement for object detection.

Table 6. Detection accuracy comparison (AP) - detectors trained with transformed data produced by GANs (trained with SYNTHIA). SDTrain: SYNTHIA daytime training set, transformed into nighttime; SNTest: SYNTHIA nighttime testing set.

Training	Testing	CycleGAN	UNIT	AugGAN-1	AugGAN-2	Detector
SDTrain	SNTest	36.1	35.2	38.1	39.0	YOLO
SDTrain	SNTest	65.9	57.2	68.7	72.2	Faster RCNN

4.2 Weight-Sharing Strategy

Our network design is based on the assumption that extracted semantic segmentation features of individual layers, through proper weight sharing, can serve as auxiliary regularization for image-to-image translation. Thus finding the proper weight sharing policy came to be the most important factor in our design. Weighting sharing mechanism in neural networks can be roughly categorized into soft weight-sharing and hard weight-sharing. Soft weight-sharing [19] was originally proposed for regularization and could be applied to network

Table 7. Weight-sharing strategy comparison: λ_w denotes the cosine similarity loss multiplier, with $\lambda_w = 0.02$ yielded best result. The matrix in this table is the average precision of Faster RCNN

Training	Testing	Weight-sharing strategy	AP - AugGAN
SDTrain	SNTest	Encoder: hard	39.9
SDTrain	SNTest	Encoder: hard; Decoder: hard	57.2
SDTrain	SNTest	Encoder: hard; Decoder: soft ($\lambda_w = 0.02$)	68.7

Fig. 9. Style transfer and segmentation results for different weight-sharing strategies: 1st row: input images; 2nd row: style transfer and segmentation results of hard weight sharing, hard-weighting on encoder only ($\lambda_w = 0$), and hard weighting sharing in encoder with soft-weight sharing ($\lambda_w = 0.02$) in decoder.

compression [20]. Recently, hard weight-sharing has been proven useful in generating images with similar high-level semantics [6]. The policy that we currently adopt is two-folded: (1) hard-share encoders and residual blocks of the generator-parsing net pairs, (2) soft-share deconvolution layers of the generator-parsing net pairs. We came to this setting based on extensive trial and error, and during the process we realized that both policies are integral for the optimization of our network. Without hard-sharing the said layers in (1), image-objects tends to be distorted; Without (2), the network tends to only optimize one of the tasks, see Table 7 and Fig. 9. In short, our network surpasses competing methods because our multi-task network can maintain realistic transformation style as well as preserving image-objects with the help of segmentation subtask.

5   Conclusion and Future Work

In this work, we proposed an image-to-image translation network for generating large-scale trainable data for vehicle detection algorithms. Our network is especially adept in preserving image-objects, thanks to the extra guidance of the segmentation subtask. Our method, though far from perfect, quantitatively surpasses competing methods for stimulating vehicle detection accuracy. In the future, we will continue to experiment on different tasks based on this framework, and our pursuit for creating innovative solutions for the world will continue to stride.

References

1. Goodfellow, I., et al.: Generative adversarial nets. In: NIPS (2014)
2. Isola, P., Zhu, J.Y., Zhou, T., Efros, A.A.: Image-to-image translation with conditional adversarial networks. CVPR (2017)
3. Zhu, J.Y., Park, T., Isola, P., Efros, A.A.: Unpaired image-to-image translation using cycle-consistent adversarial networks. In: ICCV (2017)
4. Kim, T., Cha, M., Kim, H., Lee, J., Kim, J.: Learning to discover cross-domain relations with generative adversarial networks. arXiv preprint arXiv:1703.05192 (2017)
5. Yi, Z., Zhang, H., Tan, P., Gong, M.: Dualgan: unsupervised dual learning for image-to-image translation. arXiv preprint (2017)
6. Liu, M.Y., Tuzel, O.: Coupled generative adversarial networks. In: NIPS (2016)
7. Liu, M.Y., Breuel, T., Kautz, J.: Unsupervised image-to-image translation networks. In: NIPS (2017)
8. Ros, G., Sellart, L., Materzynska, J., Vazquez, D., Lopez, A.M.: The synthia dataset: a large collection of synthetic images for semantic segmentation of urban scenes. In: CVPR (2016)
9. Richter, S.R., Vineet, V., Roth, S., Koltun, V.: Playing for data: ground truth from computer games. In: Leibe, B., Matas, J., Sebe, N., Welling, M. (eds.) ECCV 2016. LNCS, vol. 9906, pp. 102–118. Springer, Cham (2016). https://doi.org/10.1007/978-3-319-46475-6_7
10. Geiger, A., Lenz, P., Urtasun, R.: Are we ready for autonomous driving? The KITTI vision benchmark suite. In: CVPR (2012)

11. Sivaraman, S., Trivedi, M.M.: A general active-learning framework for on-road vehicle recognition and tracking. IEEE Trans. Intell. Transp. Syst. **11**(2), 267–276 (2010)
12. Zhou, Y., Liu, L., Shao, L., Mellor, M.: DAVE: a unified framework for fast vehicle detection and annotation. In: Leibe, B., Matas, J., Sebe, N., Welling, M. (eds.) ECCV 2016. LNCS, vol. 9906, pp. 278–293. Springer, Cham (2016). https://doi.org/10.1007/978-3-319-46475-6_18
13. Yang, L., Luo, P., Change Loy, C., Tang, X.: A large-scale car dataset for fine-grained categorization and verification. In: CVPR (2015)
14. Krause, J., Stark, M., Deng, J., Fei-Fei, L.: 3D object representations for fine-grained categorization. In: ICCV Workshops (2013)
15. Everingham, M., Van Gool, L., Williams, C.K., Winn, J., Zisserman, A.: The Pascal visual object classes (VOC) challenge. IJCV **88**, 303 (2010)
16. Redmon, J., Divvala, S., Girshick, R., Farhadi, A.: You only look once: unified, real-time object detection. In: CVPR (2016)
17. Ren, S., He, K., Girshick, R., Sun, J.: Faster R-CNN: towards real-time object detection with region proposal networks. In: NIPS (2015)
18. Xiang, Y., Choi, W., Lin, Y., Savarese, S.: Subcategory-aware convolutional neural networks for object proposals and detection. In: WACV (2017)
19. Nowlan, S.J., Hinton, G.E.: Simplifying neural networks by soft weight-sharing. Neural Comput. **4**(4), 473–493 (1992)
20. Ullrich, K., Meeds, E., Welling, M.: Soft weight-sharing for neural network compression. arXiv preprint arXiv:1702.04008 (2017)

Graininess-Aware Deep Feature Learning for Pedestrian Detection

Chunze Lin[1], Jiwen Lu[1]($\boxtimes$), Gang Wang[2], and Jie Zhou[1]

[1] Tsinghua University, Beijing, China
lcz16@mails.tsinghua.edu.cn, {lujiwen,jzhou}@tsinghua.edu.cn
[2] Alibaba AI Labs, Hangzhou, China
wg134231@alibaba-inc.com

Abstract. In this paper, we propose a graininess-aware deep feature learning method for pedestrian detection. Unlike most existing pedestrian detection methods which only consider low resolution feature maps, we incorporate fine-grained information into convolutional features to make them more discriminative for human body parts. Specifically, we propose a pedestrian attention mechanism which efficiently identifies pedestrian regions. Our method encodes fine-grained attention masks into convolutional feature maps, which significantly suppresses background interference and highlights pedestrians. Hence, our graininess-aware features become more focused on pedestrians, in particular those of small size and with occlusion. We further introduce a zoom-in-zoom-out module, which enhances the features by incorporating local details and context information. We integrate these two modules into a deep neural network, forming an end-to-end trainable pedestrian detector. Comprehensive experimental results on four challenging pedestrian benchmarks demonstrate the effectiveness of the proposed approach.

Keywords: Pedestrian detection · Attention · Deep learning Graininess

1 Introduction

Pedestrian detection is an important research topic in computer vision and has attracted a considerable attention over past few years [4,7,9,11,18,32,37,39,43, 45,48]. It plays a key role in several applications such as autonomous driving, robotics and intelligent video surveillance. Despite the recent progress, pedestrian detection task still remains a challenging problem because of large variations, low resolution and occlusion issues.

Existing methods for pedestrian detection can mainly be grouped into two categories: hand-crafted features based [7,9,40,44] and deep learning features based [4,11,18,48]. In the first category, human shape based features such as Haar [39] and HOG [7] are extracted to train SVM [7] or boosting classifiers [9]. While these methods are sufficient for simple applications, these hand-crafted

© Springer Nature Switzerland AG 2018
V. Ferrari et al. (Eds.): ECCV 2018, LNCS 11213, pp. 745–761, 2018.
https://doi.org/10.1007/978-3-030-01240-3_45

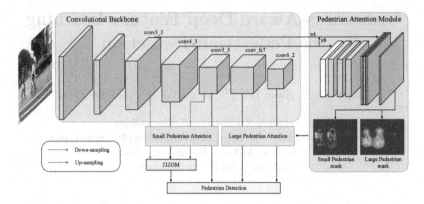

Fig. 1. Overview of our proposed framework. The model includes three key parts: convolutional backbone, pedestrian attention module and zoom-in-zoom-out module (ZIZOM). Given an image, the backbone generates multiple features representing pedestrians of different scales. The attention masks are encoded into backbone feature maps to highlight pedestrians and suppress background interference. ZIZOM incorporates local details and context information to further enhance the feature maps.

feature representations are not robust enough for detecting pedestrian in complex scenes. In the second category, deep convolutional neural network (CNN) learns high-level semantic features from raw pixels, which shows more discriminative capability to recognize pedestrian with complex poses from noisy background. Deep learning features have considerably improved pedestrian detection performance. While many CNN based methods have been proposed [4,11,18,26,48], there are still some shortcomings for methods in this category. On one hand, most methods employ heavy deep network and need refinement stage to boost the detection results. The inference time is scarified to ensure accuracy, making these methods unsuitable for real-time application. On the other hand, feature maps of coarse resolution and fixed receptive field are often used for prediction, which is inefficient for distinguishing targets of small size from background.

In this paper, we propose a graininess-aware deep feature learning (GDFL) based detector for pedestrian detection. We exploit fine-grained details into deep convolutional features for robust pedestrian detection. Specifically, we propose a scale-aware pedestrian attention module to guide the detector to focus on pedestrian regions. It generates pedestrian attentional masks which indicate the probability of human at each pixel location. With its fine-grained property, the attention module has high capability to recognize small size target and human body parts. By encoding these masks into the convolutional feature maps, they significantly eliminate background interference while highlight pedestrians. The resulting graininess-aware deep features have much more discriminative capability to distinguish pedestrians, especially the small-size and occluded ones from complex background. In addition, we introduce a zoom-in-zoom-out module to further alleviate the detection of targets at small size. It mimics our intuitive zoom in and zoom out processes, when we aim to locate an object in an image.

The module incorporates local details and context information in a convolutional manner to enhance the graininess-aware deep features for small size target detection. Figure 1 illustrates the overview of our proposed framework. The proposed two modules can be easily integrated into a basic deep network, leading to an end-to-end trainable model. This results in a fast and robust single stage pedestrian detector, without any extra refinement steps. Extensive experimental results on four widely used pedestrian detection benchmarks demonstrate the effectiveness of the proposed method. Our GDFL approach achieves competitive performance on Caltech [10], INRIA [7], KITTI [14] and MOT17Det [29] datasets and executes about 4 times faster than competitive methods.

2 Related Work

Pedestrian Detection: With the prevalence of deep convolutional neural network, which has achieved impressive results in various domains, most recent pedestrian detection methods are CNN-based. Many methods were variations of Faster R-CNN [35] which has shown great accuracy in general object detection. RPN+BF [43] replaced the downstream classifier of Faster R-CNN with a boosted forest and used aggregated features with a hard mining strategy to boost the small size pedestrian detection performance. SA-FastRCNN [19] and MS-CNN [5] extended Fast and Faster R-CNN [15,35] with a multi-scale network to deal with the scale variations problem, respectively. Instead of a single downstream classifier, F-DNN [11] employed multiple deep classifiers in parallel to post verify each region proposal using a soft-reject strategy. Different from these two stages methods, our proposed approach directly outputs detection results without post-processing [23,34]. Apart the above full-body detectors, several human part based methods [12,31,32,37,47,48] have been introduced to handle occlusion issues. These occlusion-specific methods learned a set of part-detector, where each one was responsive to detect a human part. The results from these part detections were then fused properly for locating partially occluded pedestrians. The occlusion-specific detectors were able to give a high confidence score based on the visible parts when the full-body detector was confused by the presence of background. Instead of part-level classification, we explore pixel-level masks which guide the detector to pay more attention to human body parts.

Segmentation in Detection: Since our pedestrian attention masks are generated in a segmentation manner [17,25], we present here some methods that have also exploited semantic segmentation information. Tian *et al.* [38] optimized pedestrian detection with semantic tasks, including pedestrian attributes and scene attributes. Instead of simple binary detection, this method considered multiple classes according to the attributes to handle pedestrian variations and discarded hard negative samples with scene attributes. Mao *et al.* [27] have demonstrated that fusing semantic segmentation features with detection features improves the performance. Du *et al.* [11] exploited segmentation as a strong cue in their F-DNN+SS framework. The segmentation mask was used in

Fig. 2. Visualization of feature maps from different convolutional layers. Shallow layers have strong activation for small size targets but are unable to recognize large size instances. While deep layers tend to encode pedestrians of large size and ignore small ones. For clarity, only one channel of feature maps is shown here. Best viewed in color.

a post-processing manner to suppress prediction bounding boxes without any pedestrian. Brazil *et al.* [4] extended Faster R-CNN [35] by replacing the downstream classifier with an independent deep CNN and added a segmentation loss to implicitly supervise the detection, which made the features be more semantically meaningful. Instead of exploiting segmentation mask for post-processing or implicit supervision, our attention mechanism directly encodes into feature maps and explicitly highlights pedestrians.

3   Approach

In this section, we present the proposed GDFL method for pedestrian detection in detail. Our framework is composed of three key parts: a convolutional backbone, a scale-aware pedestrian attention module and a zoom-in-zoom-out module. The convolutional backbone generates multiple feature maps for representing pedestrian at different scales. The scale-aware pedestrian attention module generates several attention masks which are encoded into these convolutional feature maps. This forms graininess-aware feature maps which have more capability to distinguish pedestrians and body parts from background. The zoom-in-zoom-out module incorporates extra local details and context information to further enhance the features. We then slide two sibling 3 × 3 convolutional layers over the resulting feature maps to output a detection score and a shape offset relative to the default box at each location [23].

3.1   Multi-layer Pedestrian Representation

Pedestrians have a large variance of scales, which is a critical problem for an accurate detection due to the difference of features between small and large instances. We exploit the hierarchical architecture of the deep convolutional network to address this multi-scale issue. The network computes feature maps of different spatial resolutions with successive sub-sampling layers, which forms naturally a feature pyramid [22]. We use multiple feature maps to detect pedestrians at different scales. Specifically, we tailor the VGG16 network [36] for detection, by removing all classification layers and converting the fully connected layers into

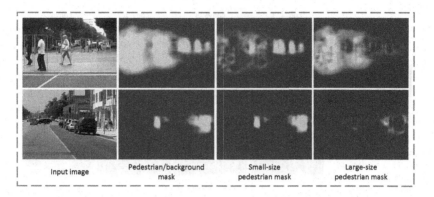

Fig. 3. Visualization of pedestrian attention masks generated from Caltech test images. From left to right are illustrated: images with the ground truth bounding boxes, pedestrian v.s. background mask, small-size pedestrian mask, and large-size pedestrian mask. The pedestrian/background mask corresponds to the sum of the last two masks and can be seen as a single scale pedestrian mask. Best viewed in color.

convolutional layers. Two extra convolutional layers are added on the end of the converted-VGG16 in order to cover large scale targets. The architecture of the network is presented on the top of Fig. 1. Given an input image, the network generates multiple convolutional feature layers with increasing sizes of receptive field. We select four intermediate convolutional layers {conv4_3, conv5_3, conv_fc7, conv6_2} as detection layers for multi-scale detection. As illustrated in Fig. 2, shallower convolutional layers with high resolution feature maps have strong activation for small size targets, while large-size pedestrians emerge at deeper layers. We regularly place a series of default boxes [23] with different scales on top of the detection layers according to their representation capability. The detection bounding boxes are predicted based on the offsets with respect to these default boxes, as well as the pedestrian probability in each of those boxes. The high resolution feature maps from layers conv4_3 and conv5_3 are associated with default boxes of small scales for detecting small target, while those from layers conv_fc7 and conv6_2 are designed for large pedestrian detection.

3.2 Pedestrian Attention Module

Despite the multi-layer representation, the feature maps from the backbone are still too coarse, e.g., stride 8 on conv4_3, to effectively locate small size pedestrians and recognize human body parts. In addition, even if each detection layer tends to represent pedestrian of particular size, it would also consider target of other scales, which is undesirable and may lead to box-in-box detection. We propose a scale-aware pedestrian attention module to make our detector pay more attention to pedestrians, especially small size ones, and guide feature maps to focus on target of specific scale via pixel-wise attentional maps. By encoding the fine-grained attention masks into the convolutional feature maps, the features

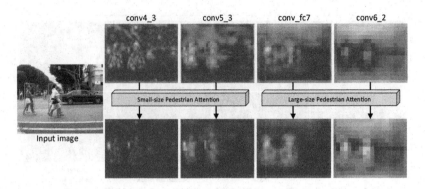

Fig. 4. Visualization of feature maps from detection layers of the backbone network (top), and visualization of feature maps with pedestrian attention (bottom). With our attention mechanism, the background interference is significantly attenuated and each detection layer is more focused on pedestrians of specific size. Best viewed in color.

representing pedestrian are enhanced, while the background interference is significantly reduced. The resulting graininess-aware features have more powerful capability to recognize human body parts and are able to infer occluded pedestrian based on the visible parts.

The attention module is built on the layers conv3_3 and conv4_3 of the backbone network. It generates multiple masks that indicate the probability of pedestrian of specific size at each pixel location. The architecture of the attention module is illustrated in Fig. 1. We construct a max-pooling layer and three atrous convolutional layers [20] on top of conv4_3 to get conv_*mask* layer which has high resolution and large receptive field. Each of conv3_3, conv4_3 and conv_*mask* layers is first reduced into $(S_c + 1)$-channel maps and spatially up-sampled into the image size. They are then concatenated and followed by a 1×1 convolution and softmax layer to output attention maps. Where S_c corresponds to the number of scale-class. In default, we distinguish small and large pedestrians according to a height threshold of 120 pixels and set $S_c = 2$. Figure 3 illustrates some examples of pedestrian masks, which effectively highlight pedestrian regions.

Once the attention masks $M \in \mathcal{R}^{W \times H \times 3}$ are generated, we encode them into the feature maps from the convolutional backbone to obtain our graininess-aware feature maps by resizing the spatial size and element-wise product:

$$\tilde{F}_i = F_i \odot R(M_S, i), \quad i \in \{\text{conv4}, \text{conv5}\} \tag{1}$$

$$\tilde{F}_j = F_j \odot R(M_L, j), \quad j \in \{\text{conv\_fc7}, \text{conv6}\} \tag{2}$$

where $M_S \in \mathcal{R}^{W \times H \times 1}$ and $M_L \in \mathcal{R}^{W \times H \times 1}$ correspond to attention masks highlighting small and large pedestrians, respectively. W and H are the size of input image. $R(\cdot, i)$ is the function that resizes the input into the size of ith layer. $\odot$ is the channel element-wise dot product operator. F_i represents the feature maps from backbone network while $\tilde{F}_i$ is the graininess-aware feature maps with pedestrian attention. The mask $R(M_S, i)$ is encoded into the feature maps from

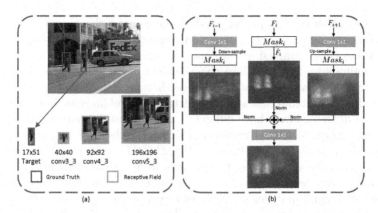

Fig. 5. Zoom-in-zoom-out module. (a) According to their receptive fields, the layer conv5_3 has more capability to get context information while the layer conv3_3 is able to get more local details. (b) Architecture of the module. Features from adjacent detection layers are re-sampled and encoded with the corresponding attention mask before to be fused with current detection features.

layers conv4_3 and conv5_3, which are responsive for small pedestrian detection. While the mask $R(M_L, i)$ is encoded into the feature maps from conv_fc7 and conv6_2, which are used for large pedestrian detection. The feature maps with and without attention masks are shown in Fig. 4, where pedestrian information is highlighted while background is smoothed with masks.

3.3   Zoom-In-Zoom-Out Module

When our human annotators try to find and recognize a small object in an image, we often zoom in and zoom out several times to correctly locate the target. The zoom-in process allows to get details information and improve the location precision. While the zoom-out process permits to import context information, which is a key factor when reasoning the probability of a target in the region, *e.g.*, pedestrians tend to appear on the ground or next to cars than on sky. Inspired by these intuitive operations, we introduce a zoom-in-zoom-out module (ZIZOM) to further enhance the features. It explores rich context information and local details to facilitate detection.

We implement the zoom-in-zoom-out module in a convolutional manner by exploiting the feature maps of different receptive fields and resolutions. Feature maps with smaller receptive fields provide rich local details, while feature maps with larger receptive fields import context information. Figure 5(b) depicts the architecture of the zoom-in-zoom-out module. Specifically, given the graininess-aware feature maps $\tilde{F}_i$, we incorporate the features from directly adjacent layers F_{i-1} and F_{i+1} to mimic zoom-in and zoom-out processes. Each adjacent layer is followed by an 1×1 kernel convolution to select features and an up- and down-sampling operation to harmonize the spatial size of feature maps. The sampling operations consist of max-pooling and bi-linear interpolation without learning parameters for simplicity. The attention mask of the current layer, $Mask_i$, is encoded into these sampled feature maps, making them focus on targets of the corresponding size. We then fuse these feature maps along their channel axis and generate the feature maps for final prediction with an 1×1 convolutional layer for dimension reduction as well as features recombination. Since the feature maps from different layers have different scales, we use L2-normalization [24] to rescale their norm to 10 and learn the scale during the back propagation.

Figure 5(a) analyzes the effects of the ZIZOM in terms of receptive field with some convolutional layers. The features from conv5_3 enhance the context information with the presence of a car and another pedestrian. Since the receptive field of conv3_3 matches with size of target, its features are able to import more local details about the pedestrian. The concatenation of these two adjacent features with conv4_3 results in more powerful feature maps as illustrated in Fig. 5(b).

3.4   Objective Function

All the three components form a unified framework which is trained end-to-end. We formulate the following multi-task loss function L to supervise our model:

$$L = L_{\text{conf}} + \lambda_l L_{\text{loc}} + \lambda_m L_{\text{mask}} \tag{3}$$

where L_{conf} is the confidence loss, L_{loc} corresponds to the localization loss and L_{mask} is the loss function of pedestrian attention masks. λ_l and λ_m are two parameters to balance the importance of different tasks. In our experiments we empirically set λ_l to 2 and λ_m to 1.

The confidence score branch is supervised by a Softmax loss over two classes (pedestrian vs. background). The box regression loss L_{loc} targets at minimizing the Smooth L1 loss [15], between the predicted bounding-box regression offsets and the ground truth box regression targets. We develop a weighted Softmax loss to supervise our pedestrian attention module. There are two main motivations for this weighting policy: (1) Most regions are background, but only few pixels correspond to pedestrians. This imbalance makes the training inefficient; (2) The large size instance occupies naturally larger area compared to the small ones. This size inequality pushes the classifier to ignore small pedestrians. To address the above imbalances, we introduce a instance-sensitive weight $\omega_i = \alpha + \beta \frac{1}{h_i}$ and define the attention mask loss L_{mask} as a weighted Softmax loss:

$$L_{\text{mask}} = -\frac{1}{N_s} \sum_{i=1}^{N_s} \sum_{l_s=0}^{S_c} \mathbb{1}\{y_i = l_s\} \omega_i^{\mathbb{1}\{l_s \neq 0\}} \log(c_i^{l_s}) \tag{4}$$

where N_s is the number of pixels in mask, S_c is the number of scale-class, and h_i is the height of the target representing by the ith pixel. $\mathbb{1}\{\cdot\}$ is the indicator function. y_i is the ground truth label, $l_s = 0$ corresponds to the background label and $c_i^{l_s}$ is the predicted score of ith pixel for l_s class. The constants α and β are set to 3 and 10 by cross validation.

4   Experiments and Analysis

4.1   Datasets and Evaluation Protocols

We comprehensively evaluated our proposed method on 3 benchmarks: Caltech [10], INRIA [7] and KITTI [14]. Here we give a brief description of these benchmarks.

The Caltech dataset [10] consists of ~10 h of urban driving video with $350K$ labeled bounding boxes. It results in 42,782 training images and 4,024 test images. The log-average miss rate is used to evaluate the detection performance and is calculated by averaging miss rate on false positive per-image (FPPI) points sampled within the range of $[10^{-2}, 10^0]$. As the purpose of our approach is to alleviate occlusion and small-size issues, we evaluated our GDFL on three subsets: *Heavy Occlusion, Medium* and *Reasonable*. In the *Heavy Occlusion* subset, pedestrians are taller than 50 pixels and 36 to 80% occluded. In the *Medium* subset, people are between 30 and 80 pixels tall, with partial occlusion. The *Reasonable* subset consists of pedestrians taller than 50 pixels with partial occlusion.

The INRIA dataset [7] includes 614 positive and 1,218 negative training images. There are 288 test images available for evaluating pedestrian detection methods. The evaluation metric is the log-average miss rate on FPPI. Due to limited available annotations, we only considered the *Reasonable* subset for comparison with state-of-the-art methods.

The KITTI dataset [14] consists of 7,481 training images and 7,518 test images, comprising about 80K annotations of cars, pedestrians and cyclists. KITTI evaluates the PASCAL-style mean Average Precision (mAP) with three metrics: *easy, moderate* and *hard*. The difficulties are defined based on minimum pedestrian height, occlusion and truncation level.

The MOT17Det dataset [29] consists of 14 video sequences in unconstrained environments, which results in 11,235 images. The dataset is split into two parts for training and testing, which are composed of 7 video sequences respectively. The Average Precision (AP) is used for evaluating different methods.

4.2   Implementation Details

Weakly Supervised Training for Attention Module: To train the pedestrian attention module, we only use the bounding box annotations in order to be independent of any pixel-wise annotation. To achieve this, we explore a weakly supervised strategy by creating artificial foreground segmentation using bounding box information. In practice, we consider pixels within the bounding box as foreground while the rest are labeled as background. We assign the pixels that belong to multiple bounding boxes to the one that has the smallest area. As illustrated in Fig. 3, despite the weak supervised training, our generated pedestrian masks carry significant semantic segmentation information.

Training: Our network is trained end-to-end using stochastic gradient descent algorithm (SGD). We partially initialize our model with the pre-trained model

Table 1. Comparison with the state-of-the-art methods on the Caltech heavy occlusion subset in terms of speed and miss rate.

Method	Miss rate (%)	Computing time (s)
FPDW [8]	95.56	0.2
DeepCascade+ [1]	82.19	0.06
RPN+BF [43]	74.36	0.36
SA-FastRCNN [19]	64.35	0.59
DeepParts [37]	60.42	1
MS-CNN [5]	59.94	0.10
SDS-RCNN [4]	58.55	0.26
F-DNN+SS [11]	53.76	2.48
JL-TopS [48]	49.20	0.6
Our GDFL	43.18	0.05

in [23], and all new additional layers are randomly initialized with the "xavier" method [16]. We adopt the data augmentation strategies as in [23] to make our model more robust to scale and illumination variations. Besides, during the training phase, negative samples largely over-dominate positive samples, and most are easy samples. For more stable training, instead of using all negative samples, we sort them by the highest loss values and keep the top ones so that the ratio between the negatives and positives is at most 3:1.

Inference: We use the initial size of input image to avoid loss of information and save inference time: 480 × 640 for Caltech and INRIA, and 384 × 1280 for KITTI. In inference stage, a large number of bounding boxes are generated by our detector. We perform non-maximum suppression (NMS) with a Intersection over Union (IoU) threshold of 0.45 to filter redundant detection. We use a single GeForce GTX 1080 Ti GPU for computation and our detector executes about 20 frames per second with inputs of size 480 × 640 pixels.

4.3 Results and Analysis

Comparison with State-of-the-Art Methods: We evaluated our proposed GDFL method on four challenging pedestrian detection benchmarks, Caltech [10], INRIA [7], KITTI [14] and MOT17Det [29].

Caltech: We trained our model on the Caltech training set and evaluated on the Caltech testing set. Table 1 lists the comparison with state-of-the-art methods on Caltech heavy occlusion subset in terms of execution time and miss rate. Figure 6 illustrates the ROC plot of miss rate against FPPI for the available top performing methods reported on Caltech medium and reasonable subsets [1,4–6,8,11,19,37,43]. In heavy occlusion case, our GDFL achieves 43.18% miss rate, which is significantly better than the existing occlusion-specific detectors.

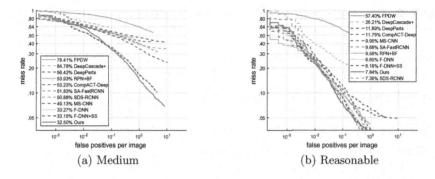

(a) Medium   (b) Reasonable

Fig. 6. Comparison with state-of-the-art methods on the Caltech dataset.

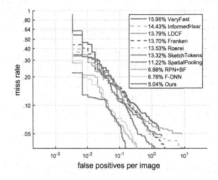

Fig. 7. Comparison with state-of-the-art methods on the INRIA dataset using the *reasonable* setting.

This performance suggests that our detector, guided by fine-grained information, has better capability to identify human body parts and thus to locate occluded pedestrians. In Caltech medium subset, our method has a miss rate of 32.50% which is slightly better than the previous best method [11]. In more reasonable scenarios, our approach achieves comparable performance with the method that achieves best results on Caltech reasonable subset [4].

Since our goal is to propose a fast and accurate pedestrian detector, we have also examined the efficiency of our method. Table 1 compares the running time on Caltech dataset. Our GDFL method is much faster than F-DNN+SS [11] and is about 10× faster than the previous best method on Caltech heavy occlusion subset, JL-TopS [48]. While SDS-RCNN [4] performs slightly better than our method on Caltech reasonable subset (7.36% vs. 7.84%), it needs 4× more inference times than our approach. The comparison shows that our pedestrian detector achieves a favorable trade-off between speed and accuracy.

INRIA: We trained our model with 614 positive images by excluding the negative images and evaluated on the test set. Figure 7 illustrates the results of our approach and the methods that perform best on the INRIA set [2,3,21,28,30,33,44].

Table 2. Comparison with published pedestrian detection methods on the KITTI dataset. The mAP (%) and running time are collected from the KITTI leaderboard.

Method	mAP on easy	mAP on moderate	mAP on hard	Time (s)
FilteredICF [46]	69.05	57.12	51.46	2
DeepParts [37]	70.49	58.68	52.73	1
CompACT-deep [6]	69.70	58.73	52.73	1
RPN+BF [43]	77.12	61.15	55.12	0.6
SDS-RCNN [4]	-	63.05	-	0.21
CFM [18]	74.21	63.26	56.44	2
MS-CNN [5]	83.70	73.62	68.28	0.4
Ours (384 × 1280)	83.78	67.73	60.07	0.15
Ours (576 × 1920)	84.61	68.62	66.86	0.27

Table 3. Comparison with published state-of-the-art methods on MOT17Det benchmark. The symbol * means that external data are used for training.

Method	KDNT* [42]	Our GDFL	SDP [41]	FRCNN [35]	DPM [13]
Average precision	0.89	0.81	0.81	0.72	0.61

Our detector yields the state-of-the-art performance with 5.04% miss rate, outperforming the competitive methods by more than 1%. It proves that our method can achieve great results even if the training set is limited.

KITTI: We trained our model on the KITTI training set and evaluated on the designated test set. We compared our proposed GDFL approach with the current pedestrian detection methods on KITTI [4–6,18,37,43,46]. The results are listed in Table 2. Our detector achieves competitive performance with MS-CNN [5] yet executes about 3× faster with the original input size. Apart its scale-specific property, MS-CNN [5] has explored input and feature up-sampling strategies which are crucial for improving the small objects detection performance. Following this process, we up-sampled the inputs by 1.5 times and we observed a significant improvement on the hard subset but with more execution time. Note that in the KITTI evaluation protocol, cyclists are regarded as false detections while people-sitting are ignored. With this setting, our pedestrian attention mechanism is less helpful since it tends to highlight all human-shape targets including person riding a bicycle. This explains the reason our model does not perform as well as on KITTI than that on Caltech or INRIA.

MOT17Det: We trained and evaluated our detector on the designated training and testing sets, respectively and compared with existing methods. Table 3 tabulates the detection results of our method and the state-of-the-art approaches. Our proposed detector achieves competitive 0.81 average precision without using

Table 4. Ablation experiments evaluated on the Caltech test set. Analysis show the effects of various components and design choices on detection performance.

Component	Choice							
Single-layer detection	✓							
Multi-layer detection		✓	✓	✓	✓	✓	✓	✓
Instance-sensitive weight			✓	✓		✓	✓	
Single scale attention			✓					
Scale-aware attention				✓	✓	✓	✓	
ZIZOM on $\tilde{F}_{conv4\_3}$						✓	✓	
ZIZOM on $\tilde{F}_{conv5\_3}$						✓		
ZIZOM on F_{conv4_3}								✓
Miss rate on reasonable	16.86	9.44	9.16	8.44	9.59	**7.36**	8.01	8.86
Miss rate on medium	42.96	36.49	34.36	33.45	34.40	**32.50**	32.99	35.74
Miss rate on heavy occlusion	53.44	50.21	47.60	44.68	47.69	43.18	**42.86**	45.73

external datasets for training. This performance demonstrates the generalization capability of our model.

Ablation Experiments: To better understand our model, we conducted ablation experiments using the Caltech dataset. We considered our convolutional backbone as baseline and successively added different key components to examine their contributions on performance. Table 4 summarizes our comprehensive ablation experiments.

Multi-layer Detection: We first analyzed the advantages of using multiple detection layers. To this end, instead of multi-layer representation, we only used conv_fc7 layer to predict pedestrians of all scales. The experimental results of these two architectures demonstrate the superiority of multi-layer detection with a notable gain of 7% on Caltech Reasonable subset.

Attention Mechanism: We analyzed the effects of our attention mechanism, in particular the difference between single scale attention mask and multiple scale-aware attention masks. To control this, we compared two models with these two attention designs. From Table 4, we can see that both models improve the results, but the model with scale-aware attention has clearly better results. The confusions, such as box-in-box detection, are suppressed with our scale-aware attention masks. We observe an impressive improvement on the Caltech heavy occlusion subset, which demonstrates that the fine-grained masks better capture body parts. Some examples of occlusion cases are depicted in Fig. 8. We can see that the features without attention are unable to recognize human parts and tend to ignore occluded pedestrians. When we encode the pedestrian masks into these feature maps, human body parts are considerably highlighted. The detector

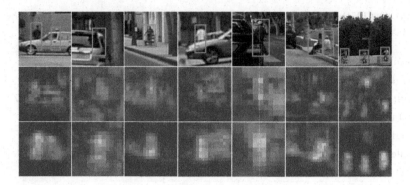

Fig. 8. Hard detection samples where box-based detector is often fooled due to noisy representation. The first row illustrates the images with pedestrians located by green bounding boxes. The second and third rows show the feature maps without attention masks and the graininess-aware feature maps, respectively. Best viewed in color.

becomes able to deduce the occluded parts by considering visible parts, which makes plausible the detection of occluded targets.

Instance-Sensitive Weight in Softmax Loss: During the training stage, our attention module was supervised by a weighted Softmax loss and we examined how the instance-sensitive weight contributed to the performance. We compared two models trained with and without the weight term. As listed in the 5th column of Table 4, the performance drops on all three subsets of Caltech with the conventional Softmax loss. In particular, the miss rate increases from 44.68% to 47.69% in heavy occlusion case. The results point out that the instance-sensitive weight term is a key component for accurate attention masks generation.

ZIZOM: We further built the zoom-in-zoom-out module on our model with attention masks. Table 4 shows that with the ZIZOM on top of the graininess-aware features $\tilde{F}_{conv4\_3}$, the performance is ameliorated by 1% on all subsets of Caltech. However, when we further constructed a ZIZOM on $\tilde{F}_{conv5\_3}$, the results were nearly the same. Since the feature maps $\tilde{F}_{conv5\_3}$ represent pedestrians with about 100 pixels tall, these results confirm our intuition that context information and local details are important for small targets but are less helpful for large ones. To better control the effectiveness of this module, we disabled the attention mechanism and considered a convolutional backbone with the ZIZOM on F_{conv4_3} model. The comparison with the baseline shows a gain of 4% on the Caltech heavy occlusion subset. The results prove the effectiveness of the proposed zoom-in-zoom-out module.

5   Conclusion

In this paper, we have proposed a framework which incorporates pixel-wise information into deep convolutional feature maps for pedestrian detection. We have introduced scale-aware pedestrian attention masks and a zoom-in-zoom-out module to improve the capability of the feature maps to identify small and occluded pedestrians. Experimental results on three widely used pedestrian benchmarks have validated the advantages on detection robustness and efficiency of the proposed method.

Acknowledgment. This work was supported in part by the National Key Research and Development Program of China under Grant 2017YFA0700802, in part by the National Natural Science Foundation of China under Grant 61822603, Grant U1713214, Grant 61672306, Grant 61572271, and in part by the Shenzhen Fundamental Research Fund (Subject Arrangement) under Grant JCYJ20170412170602564.

References

1. Angelova, A., Krizhevsky, A., Vanhoucke, V., Ogale, A.S., Ferguson, D.: Real-time pedestrian detection with deep network cascades. In: BMVC, vol. 2, p. 4 (2015)
2. Benenson, R., Mathias, M., Timofte, R., Van Gool, L.: Pedestrian detection at 100 frames per second. In: CVPR, pp. 2903–2910 (2012)
3. Benenson, R., Mathias, M., Tuytelaars, T., Van Gool, L.: Seeking the strongest rigid detector. In: CVPR, pp. 3666–3673 (2013)
4. Brazil, G., Yin, X., Liu, X.: Illuminating pedestrians via simultaneous detection and segmentation. In: ICCV, pp. 4950–4959 (2017)
5. Cai, Z., Fan, Q., Feris, R.S., Vasconcelos, N.: A unified multi-scale deep convolutional neural network for fast object detection. In: Leibe, B., Matas, J., Sebe, N., Welling, M. (eds.) ECCV 2016. LNCS, vol. 9908, pp. 354–370. Springer, Cham (2016). https://doi.org/10.1007/978-3-319-46493-0_22
6. Cai, Z., Saberian, M., Vasconcelos, N.: Learning complexity-aware cascades for deep pedestrian detection. In: ICCV, pp. 3361–3369 (2015)
7. Dalal, N., Triggs, B.: Histograms of oriented gradients for human detection. In: CVPR, pp. 886–893 (2005)
8. Dollár, P., Belongie, S.J., Perona, P.: The fastest pedestrian detector in the west. In: BMVC, vol. 2, p. 7 (2010)
9. Dollár, P., Tu, Z., Perona, P., Belongie, S.: Integral channel features. In: BMVC, pp. 91.1–91.11 (2009)
10. Dollár, P., Wojek, C., Schiele, B., Perona, P.: Pedestrian detection: a benchmark. In: CVPR, pp. 304–311 (2009)
11. Du, X., El-Khamy, M., Lee, J., Davis, L.: Fused DNN: a deep neural network fusion approach to fast and robust pedestrian detection. In: WACV, pp. 953–961 (2017)
12. Enzweiler, M., Eigenstetter, A., Schiele, B., Gavrila, D.M.: Multi-cue pedestrian classification with partial occlusion handling. In: CVPR, pp. 990–997 (2010)
13. Felzenszwalb, P.F., Girshick, R.B., McAllester, D., Ramanan, D.: Object detection with discriminatively trained part-based models. TPAMI **32**(9), 1627–1645 (2010)
14. Geiger, A., Lenz, P., Urtasun, R.: Are we ready for autonomous driving? The KITTI vision benchmark suite. In: CVPR, pp. 3354–3361 (2012)
15. Girshick, R.: Fast R-CNN. In: ICCV, pp. 1440–1448 (2015)
16. Glorot, X., Bengio, Y.: Understanding the difficulty of training deep feedforward neural networks. In: AISTATS, pp. 249–256 (2010)
17. Hariharan, B., Arbeláez, P., Girshick, R., Malik, J.: Hypercolumns for object segmentation and fine-grained localization. In: CVPR, pp. 447–456 (2015)

18. Hu, Q., Wang, P., Shen, C., van den Hengel, A., Porikli, F.: Pushing the limits of deep CNNs for pedestrian detection. TCSVT **28**, 1358–1368 (2017)
19. Li, J., Liang, X., Shen, S., Xu, T., Feng, J., Yan, S.: Scale-aware fast R-CNN for pedestrian detection. TMM **20**, 985–996 (2017)
20. Liang-Chieh, C., Papandreou, G., Kokkinos, I., Murphy, K., Yuille, A.: Semantic image segmentation with deep convolutional nets and fully connected CRFs. In: ICLR (2015)
21. Lim, J.J., Zitnick, C.L., Dollár, P.: Sketch tokens: a learned mid-level representation for contour and object detection. In: CVPR, pp. 3158–3165 (2013)
22. Lin, T.Y., Dollár, P., Girshick, R., He, K., Hariharan, B., Belongie, S.: Feature pyramid networks for object detection. In: CVPR, p. 4 (2017)
23. Liu, W., et al.: SSD: single shot multibox detector. In: Leibe, B., Matas, J., Sebe, N., Welling, M. (eds.) ECCV 2016. LNCS, vol. 9905, pp. 21–37. Springer, Cham (2016). https://doi.org/10.1007/978-3-319-46448-0_2
24. Liu, W., Rabinovich, A., Berg, A.C.: Parsenet: looking wider to see better. In: ICLR, p. 3 (2016)
25. Long, J., Shelhamer, E., Darrell, T.: Fully convolutional networks for semantic segmentation. In: CVPR, pp. 3431–3440 (2015)
26. Luo, P., Tian, Y., Wang, X., Tang, X.: Switchable deep network for pedestrian detection. In: CVPR, pp. 899–906 (2014)
27. Mao, J., Xiao, T., Jiang, Y., Cao, Z.: What can help pedestrian detection? In: CVPR, pp. 3127–3136 (2017)
28. Mathias, M., Benenson, R., Timofte, R., Van Gool, L.: Handling occlusions with franken-classifiers. In: ICCV, pp. 1505–1512 (2013)
29. Milan, A., Leal-Taixé, L., Reid, I., Roth, S., Schindler, K.: Mot16: a benchmark for multi-object tracking. arXiv preprint arXiv:1603.00831 (2016)
30. Nam, W., Dollár, P., Han, J.H.: Local decorrelation for improved pedestrian detection. In: NIPS, pp. 424–432 (2014)
31. Ouyang, W., Wang, X.: A discriminative deep model for pedestrian detection with occlusion handling. In: CVPR, pp. 3258–3265 (2012)
32. Ouyang, W., Zhou, H., Li, H., Li, Q., Yan, J., Wang, X.: Jointly learning deep features, deformable parts, occlusion and classification for pedestrian detection. TPAMI **40**, 1874–1887 (2017)
33. Paisitkriangkrai, S., Shen, C., van den Hengel, A.: Strengthening the effectiveness of pedestrian detection with spatially pooled features. In: Fleet, D., Pajdla, T., Schiele, B., Tuytelaars, T. (eds.) ECCV 2014. LNCS, vol. 8692, pp. 546–561. Springer, Cham (2014). https://doi.org/10.1007/978-3-319-10593-2_36
34. Redmon, J., Divvala, S., Girshick, R., Farhadi, A.: You only look once: unified, real-time object detection. In: CVPR, pp. 779–788 (2016)
35. Ren, S., He, K., Girshick, R., Sun, J.: Faster R-CNN: towards real-time object detection with region proposal networks. In: NIPS, pp. 91–99 (2015)
36. Simonyan, K., Zisserman, A.: Very deep convolutional networks for large-scale image recognition. In: ICLR (2015)
37. Tian, Y., Luo, P., Wang, X., Tang, X.: Deep learning strong parts for pedestrian detection. In: CVPR, pp. 1904–1912 (2015)
38. Tian, Y., Luo, P., Wang, X., Tang, X.: Pedestrian detection aided by deep learning semantic tasks. In: CVPR, pp. 5079–5087 (2015)
39. Viola, P., Jones, M.J., Snow, D.: Detecting pedestrians using patterns of motion and appearance. In: IJCV, p. 734 (2003)
40. Wang, X., Han, T.X., Yan, S.: An HOG-LBP human detector with partial occlusion handling. In: ICCV, pp. 32–39 (2009)

41. Yang, F., Choi, W., Lin, Y.: Exploit all the layers: fast and accurate CNN object detector with scale dependent pooling and cascaded rejection classifiers. In: CVPR, pp. 2129–2137 (2016)
42. Yu, F., Li, W., Li, Q., Liu, Y., Shi, X., Yan, J.: POI: multiple object tracking with high performance detection and appearance feature. In: Hua, G., Jégou, H. (eds.) ECCV 2016. LNCS, vol. 9914, pp. 36–42. Springer, Cham (2016). https://doi.org/10.1007/978-3-319-48881-3_3
43. Zhang, L., Lin, L., Liang, X., He, K.: Is faster R-CNN doing well for pedestrian detection? In: Leibe, B., Matas, J., Sebe, N., Welling, M. (eds.) ECCV 2016. LNCS, vol. 9906, pp. 443–457. Springer, Cham (2016). https://doi.org/10.1007/978-3-319-46475-6_28
44. Zhang, S., Bauckhage, C., Cremers, A.B.: Informed Haar-like features improve pedestrian detection. In: CVPR, pp. 947–954 (2014)
45. Zhang, S., Benenson, R., Omran, M., Hosang, J., Schiele, B.: How far are we from solving pedestrian detection? In: CVPR, pp. 1259–1267 (2016)
46. Zhang, S., Benenson, R., Schiele, B.: Filtered channel features for pedestrian detection. In: CVPR, p. 4 (2015)
47. Zhou, C., Yuan, J.: Learning to integrate occlusion-specific detectors for heavily occluded pedestrian detection. In: Lai, S.-H., Lepetit, V., Nishino, K., Sato, Y. (eds.) ACCV 2016. LNCS, vol. 10112, pp. 305–320. Springer, Cham (2017). https://doi.org/10.1007/978-3-319-54184-6_19
48. Zhou, C., Yuan, J.: Multi-label learning of part detectors for heavily occluded pedestrian detection. In: ICCV, pp. 3486–3495 (2017)

Seeing Tree Structure from Vibration

Tianfan Xue[1]($\boxtimes$), Jiajun Wu[2], Zhoutong Zhang[2], Chengkai Zhang[2],
Joshua B. Tenenbaum[2], and William T. Freeman[2,3]

[1] Google Research, Mountain View, USA
tianfan.xue@gmail.com
[2] MIT CSAIL, Cambridge, USA
[3] Google Research, Cambridge, USA

Abstract. Humans recognize object structure from both their appearance and motion; often, motion helps to resolve ambiguities in object structure that arise when we observe object appearance only. There are particular scenarios, however, where neither appearance nor spatial-temporal motion signals are informative: occluding twigs may look connected and have almost identical movements, though they belong to different, possibly disconnected branches. We propose to tackle this problem through spectrum analysis of motion signals, because vibrations of disconnected branches, though visually similar, often have distinctive natural frequencies. We propose a novel formulation of tree structure based on a physics-based link model, and validate its effectiveness by theoretical analysis, numerical simulation, and empirical experiments. With this formulation, we use nonparametric Bayesian inference to reconstruct tree structure from both spectral vibration signals and appearance cues. Our model performs well in recognizing hierarchical tree structure from real-world videos of trees and vessels.

Keywords: Vibration · Tree structure · Hierarchical Bayesian model

1 Introduction

In visual perception, motion information often helps to resolve appearance ambiguities. Animals may conceal themselves with camouflaged clothing, but they are unlikely to match their motion with that in the background, such as foliage waving in the breeze [6]. In medical imaging, it might be hard to separate blood vessels (or fibers) purely from their appearance, but the distinction becomes clear once the vessels start to vibrate. Extensive studies in cognitive science also suggest that humans, including young children, recognize objects from both appearance and motion cues [37].

T. Xue and J. Wu—Contributed equally to this work.

Electronic supplementary material The online version of this chapter (https://doi.org/10.1007/978-3-030-01240-3_46) contains supplementary material, which is available to authorized users.

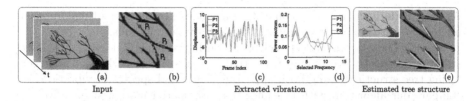

(a)   (b)   (c)   (d)   (e)
Input   Extracted vibration   Estimated tree structure

Fig. 1. We want to infer the hierarchical structure of the tree in video (a). Inference based on a single frame has inherent ambiguities: figure (b) shows an example, where it is hard to tell from appearance whether point P_1 is connected to P_2 (orange curve) or to P_3 (blue curve). Time domain motion signals do not help much, as these branches have almost identical movements (c). We observe that the difference is significant in the frequency domain (d), from which we can see P_1 is more likely to connect to P_2 due to their similar spectra. We therefore develop an algorithm that infers tree structure based on both vibration spectra and appearance cues. The results are shown in (e). (Color figure online)

Computer vision researchers have combined motion and appearance information to solve a range of tasks [1,34]. Bouman *et al.* proposed to estimate physical object properties based on their appearance and vibration [3]. Wang *et al.* proposed a layered motion representation [42], which has been widely employed in object segmentation and structural prediction [23,38].

In this paper, we focus on tree structure estimation. This problem is even more challenging, as both motion and appearance cues can fail to discriminate pixels of disjoint branches. We show an example in Fig. 1. The three points $\{P_i\}$ in Fig. 1 are on two occluding branches. There are two plausible explanations: either P_1 and P_2, or P_1 and P_3 may be on the same branch. Due to self-occlusion, it is hard to infer the underlying connection just from their appearance. It is also challenging to resolve this ambiguity using only temporal motion information: the movement of these three nodes are dominated by the vibration of the root branch, so they share almost the same trajectories (Fig. 1c).

We propose to incorporate spectral analysis to deal with this problem. This is inspired by our observation that pixels of different branches often have distinctive modes in their spectra of frequency responses, despite their similar spatial trajectories. As shown in Fig. 1d, P_3 has distinct amplitude at certain frequencies compared with P_1 and P_2; intuitively and theoretically (discussed in Sect. 3), P_3 is more likely to be on a separate branch.

Our formulation of tree vibration builds upon and extends a physics-based link model from the field of botany [33]. Here, we deduce a key property of tree structure: each branch is a linear time-invariant (LTI) system with respect to the vibration of root. With this property, we can infer the natural frequencies of each sub-branch in a tree from its frequency response, and group nodes based on the inferred natural frequencies. We also provide justifications of this property through theoretical analysis, numerical simulation, and empirical experiments.

Based on our tree formulation, we develop a hierarchical grouping algorithm to infer tree structure, using both spectral motion signals and appearance cues.

As each node in a tree may connect to an indefinite number of children, our inference algorithm employs nonparametric Bayesian methods.

For evaluation, we collect videos of both artificial and real-world tree-structured objects. We demonstrate that our algorithm works well in recognizing tree structure, using both appearance cues and spectra of vibration. We compare our algorithm with baselines that use spatial motion signals; we also conduct ablation studies to reveal how each component contributes to the algorithm's final performance. Our model has wide applications, as tree structure exists extensively in real life. Here we show two of them: seeing shape from shadow, and connecting blood vessels from retinal videos.

Our contributions are three-fold. Our main contribution is to show that tiny, barely visible object motion can reveal object structure. Our model can resolve the ambiguity in tree structure estimation using spectral information. Second, we propose a novel, physics-based tree formulation, with which we may estimate the natural frequencies of each sub-branch. Third, we design a hierarchical inference algorithm, using nonparametric Bayesian methods to predict tree structure. Our algorithm achieves good performance on real-world videos.

2   Related Work

Motion for Structured Prediction. Researchers in computer vision have been using motion signals for various tasks [1, 34, 39, 47]. For structured prediction in particular, the layered motion representations [42] have been studied and applied extensively [23, 38]. These papers model motion signals in the temporal domain; they are not for scenarios where objects may only have subtle motion differences.

Regarding spectral analysis of motion, the pioneer work of Fleet and Jepson [10] discussed how phase signals could help to estimate object velocity. Gautama and Van Hulle [14] extended the work, proposing a phase-based approach for optical flow estimation. Zhou et al. [48] also discussed how phase information helps recognizing object motion. Recently, there have also been a number of works on visualizing and magnifying subtle motion signals from video [7, 46], and Rubinstein et al. did a thorough review in [35].

The problem of tree structure estimation has been widely studied in computer vision, especially in medical imaging [11, 40, 41, 43], mostly from a static image. In this paper, we explore how motion signals in a video could help in structured prediction, in addition to appearance cues. Though we currently employ a simple and intuitive appearance model, it is straightforward to incorporate more sophisticated appearance models into our approach.

Modeling Tree Vibration. Tree vibration is an important research area in the field of botany [20, 31]. Moore and Maguire [31] reviewed the concepts and dynamic studies by examining the natural frequencies and damping ratios of trees in winds. Recently, James et al. [20] reviewed tree bio-mechanics studies using dynamic methods of analysis.

Our formulation of tree vibration is based on the lumped-mass procedure. Related literature include spring-mass-damper models for trees as a single mass point [30], or as a complex system of coupled masses that represent the trunk and branches [21,33]. Our formulation also considers a tree as a system of coupled masses, but different from Murphy *et al.* [33] which studied only one-layer structure, we explore hierarchical tree structure of multiple layers.

Bayesian Theory of Perception. Researchers have developed Bayesian theories for human visual perception in general [24,26,32], and for object motion perception in particular [4,44]. Our inference algorithm draws inspirations from the recent hierarchical Bayesian model for object motion from Gershman *et al.* [16], which employs the nested Chinese restaurant process (nCRP) [2] as a prior of object structure.

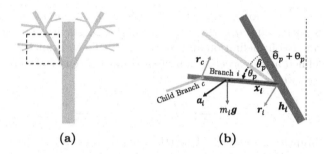

(a)   **(b)**

Fig. 2. (a) Hierarchical beam structure. (b) Force analysis for one of the branches (the one marked by dashed rectangle in (a)).

3   Formulation

We here present our formulation that recovers tree structure from the temporal complex spectra of vertices. We start by introducing a physics-based, hierarchical link model, representing a tree as a set of beams with certain mass and stiffness (Fig. 2a). Using this model, we derive a set of ordinary differential equations (ODEs) of node vibrations (Sect. 3.2) and prove an important property (Sect. 3.3): each sub-branch of a tree is a linear time-invariant system under certain assumptions. A Bayesian inference algorithm exploits the property for structure estimation (Sects. 4.1 and 4.2).

3.1   A Physics-Based Link Model

We use a rigid link model to describe the vibration of a tree, as shown in Fig. 2a. In this model, each branch i of the tree is modeled as a rigid beam with a certain mass m_i and length l_i. Under the uniform mass assumption, the center of mass of a branch is at $\frac{l_i}{2}$. Each branch connects to its parent through a torsional spring with stiffness k_i. Our model relates to the simpler, one-layer physical model from

Murphy *et al.* [33], where they attempted to compute the mass and stiffness of all the beams. We observe this to be impractical in real data given the presence of noise and occlusion. Instead, we derive a set of non-linear ordinary derivative equations (ODEs) that describe the relationship between the vibration of a tree and its structure and physical properties.

We describe the vibration of a tree by the deviation angles $\{\theta_i\}$ of branches. As shown in Fig. 2b, let $\hat{\theta}_i$ be the directional angle from vertical line to a branch when the tree is static (no external forces except gravity), and let θ_i be the deviation angle from its static location when the tree is vibrating (θ_i changes over time). To derive the governing equations for θ_i, we start by applying the Newton's law to each branch i, which gives[1]

$$m\boldsymbol{a}_i = -\boldsymbol{r}_i + \sum_{c \in C_i} \boldsymbol{r}_c + m\boldsymbol{g}, \tag{1}$$

where $\boldsymbol{r}_c \in \mathbb{R}^2$ is the force exerted by branch c on its parent, C_i is the set of children of branch i, and $\boldsymbol{g}$ is the acceleration due to gravity. The negative sign before $\boldsymbol{r}_i$ is due to our definition and Newton's third law. Branch i's acceleration $\boldsymbol{a}_i \in \mathbb{R}^2$ is defined as the acceleration of the branch's center of mass.

In addition, we have the rotation equation,

$$I_i\dot{\omega}_i = -k_i\theta_i + \sum_{c \in C_i} k_c\theta_c + \boldsymbol{r}_i \times \boldsymbol{x}_i + \sum_{c \in C_i} \boldsymbol{r}_c \times \boldsymbol{x}_i, \tag{2}$$

where I_i is branch i's moment of inertia when it rotates around its center, $\dot{\omega}_i$ is its angular acceleration, θ_c is branch c's deviation angle, $\boldsymbol{x}_i$ is its movement, and k_i is the stiffness of the torsional spring it connects to. Also, the branch acceleration $\boldsymbol{a}_i$ relates to the acceleration of its endpoint $\boldsymbol{a}_{i_o}$ via

$$\boldsymbol{a}_i = \boldsymbol{a}_{i_o} + \dot{\omega}_i \times \boldsymbol{x}_i + \omega_i \times (\omega_i \times \boldsymbol{x}_i), \tag{3}$$

where $\boldsymbol{a}_{i_o} \in \mathbb{R}^2$ is the acceleration of the junction point.

Therefore, the angular velocity and angular acceleration of branch i are

$$\omega_i = \dot{\theta}_i + \sum_{p \in P_i} \dot{\theta}_p \quad \text{and} \quad \dot{\omega}_i = \ddot{\theta}_i + \sum_{p \in P_i} \ddot{\theta}_p, \tag{4}$$

where P_i is the set of ancestors of branch i. These equations do not include fictitious forces. All quantities are global values under the reference frame.

At last, replacing the branch acceleration ($\boldsymbol{a}_i$ and $\boldsymbol{a}_{i_o}$) and angular acceleration $\dot{\omega}_i$ in Eqs. 1 and 2 using Eqs. 3 and 4, and eliminating forces between branches r_i, we get the ODE with respect to all deviation angles $\{\theta_i\}$,

$$I_if_i(\ddot{\theta}) = -k_i\theta_i + \sum_{c \in C_i} k_c\theta_c + \boldsymbol{r}_i(\theta, \dot{\theta}, \ddot{\theta}) \times \boldsymbol{x}_i + \sum_{c \in C_i} \boldsymbol{r}_c(\theta, \dot{\theta}, \ddot{\theta}) \times \boldsymbol{x}_i, \tag{5}$$

where $\boldsymbol{r}_i(\theta, \dot{\theta}, \ddot{\theta})$ is a vector functions of θ, $\dot{\theta}$, and $\ddot{\theta}$. Please see our supplementary material for its definition in detail.

---

[1] In this chapter, we use a lower-case letter a to denote a scalar, a bold lower-case letter $\boldsymbol{a}$ to denote a vector, and a capital letter A to denote a matrix. We denote the matrix product as $A\boldsymbol{b}$, where $A \in \mathbb{R}^{n \times m}$ and $\boldsymbol{b} \in \mathbb{R}^m$.

3.2   ODE of Node Vibration

The ODE (Eq. 5) is highly nonlinear due to sinusoidal and quadratic terms. To solve it, we first linearize the equation around its stable solution. We assume that the deviation angle θ_i of each branch i is small and ignore all $O(\theta_i^2)$ terms. Under this assumption, the quadratic term of angular velocity $O(\dot{\theta}^2)$ can also be ignored, because according to the conservation of energy, the potential energy $\frac{1}{2}k\theta^2$ of a branch is on the same scale of its kinetic energy $\frac{1}{2}I_i\dot{\theta}^2$.

We can now derive a fully linear system under the above assumption as

$$M\ddot{\boldsymbol{\theta}} + K\boldsymbol{\theta} = \mathbf{0}, \tag{6}$$

where M and K are two matrices depending on the structure of a tree and its physical properties, including the moment of inertia (I), mass (m), and stiffness (k) of all branches.

In practice, from an input video, it is easier to measure the 2D shift of each node, rather than the rotation of each branch. To derive the ODE of 2D shifts of all nodes from Eq. 6, we denote node i's 2D location in a stable tree as $\hat{\boldsymbol{y}}_i$, and the 2D shifts from its stable location as $\boldsymbol{y}_i$. We have

$$\boldsymbol{y}_i + \hat{\boldsymbol{y}}_i = \sum_{j \in P_i} l_j \boldsymbol{n}(\theta_j + \hat{\theta}_j), \tag{7}$$

where $\boldsymbol{n}(\theta) = (\cos\theta, \sin\theta)$ and l_j is the length of branch j (recall that P_i is the set of ancestors of branch i). Let $\boldsymbol{y}$ be the concatenation of 2D shifts of all the nodes. Plugging Eqs. 7 to 6, we have

$$N\ddot{\boldsymbol{y}} + L\boldsymbol{y} = \mathbf{0}, \tag{8}$$

where N and L are matrices depending on M, K, l_j, and θ_j. The constant term must be zero, as $\boldsymbol{y} = \ddot{\boldsymbol{y}} = \mathbf{0}$ when the tree is stable. Please see our supplementary material for a detailed derivation.

3.3   Inferring Modes of Each Sub-branch

Based on the second order ODE, we can infer the modes of each sub-branch and use them to group nodes into branches using the following property.

Property 1 (Each sub-branch is a LTI-system). *Imagine a branch undergoes a forced vibration. Let $y_{root}^i(t)$ and $y_{leaf}^i(t)$ be the displacements of the root and one of its leaf node respectively at time t ($i = 1, 2$). Then, if the displacement of the root is $\alpha_1 \cdot y_{root}^1(t) + \alpha_2 \cdot y_{root}^2(t)$, where $\alpha_1, \alpha_2 \in \mathbb{R}$, the vibration of the leaf is $\alpha_1 \cdot y_{leaf}^1(t) + \alpha_2 \cdot y_{leaf}^2(t)$.*

This is a corollary of Eq. 8, which shows that the displacement of a node satisfies a linear, second order ODE. The system is also time-invariant, as all matrices in Eq. 8 do not change in time.

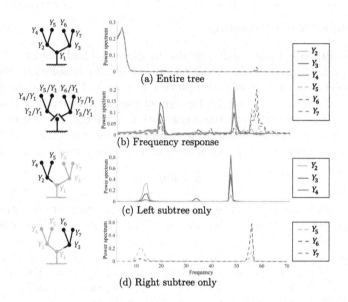

Fig. 3. Spectrum analysis on a synthetic tree. Directly calculating the power spectrum of the vibration of each nodes does not help to infer the tree structure, as all the nodes have similar power spectrum (a). By dividing the spectrum of each node by the spectrum of the root node, we obtain the frequency response of each node. We now clearly see the difference between the two subtrees (b). The modes of each frequency response also match the modes of the free vibration of each subtree (c) and (d).

The key observation of our work is that we can infer the mode of free vibration of each sub-branch as if that sub-branch is disconnected from the rest of the tree, as suggested by Property 1. Let S be a set of nodes in a sub-branch; let $Y_i(\eta)$ be the temporal spectrum of the displacement of the i-th node in that branch ($i \in S$), where η is the frequency index; let Y_{root} be the temporal spectrum of the root displacement. Because each sub-branch is a LTI-system, the frequency response of the sub-branch is

$$\overline{Y}_i(\eta) = \frac{Y_i(\eta)}{Y_{root}(\eta)}, \quad \forall \eta. \tag{9}$$

It is well known that when there is no damping, the natural frequencies of an oscillating system coincide with its resonance frequency [12, Chap. 4]. In our case, this suggests that the natural frequencies of a sub-branch are the same as the modes of the frequency response of that branch[2].

As an illustration, Fig. 3a shows a tree with two sub-branches (Y_{2-4} and Y_{5-7}). All nodes have similar power spectra as their vibrations are dominated by the vibration of the root (Y_1). To distinguish the spectra of the two sub-branches, we calculate the frequency response of each node, *i.e.*, the ratio between the

---

[2] In the presence of small damping, the difference between the modes of frequency response and the modes of free vibration is also small.

spectrum of the root and the spectrum of each branch. As shown in Fig. 3b, there is a clear difference between the frequency responses of two branches. The modes of each frequency response also match the modes of free vibrations of each sub-branch, as if they are detached from the root (see Fig. 3c and d).

We can then group nodes into different sub-branches based on their spectrum response, because the natural frequencies of each sub-branch depend on its inherent physical properties like mass and stiffness. In practice, the modes of frequency responses are not a robust measure in the presence of noise and damping. Therefore, we group nodes based on their the normalized power spectra and phases instead, with the help of the appearance information described in Sect. 4.1.

4 Algorithm

We now introduce our structure estimation algorithm based on the tree formulation. Our algorithm has two major components: a recognition module that extracts motion and appearance cues from visual input, and an inference module that predicts tree structure.

4.1 Extracting Motion and Appearance Cues

We use an bottom-up recognition algorithm to obtain motion and appearance cues from input videos (Fig. 4a) with a given set of interest points (Fig. 4b).

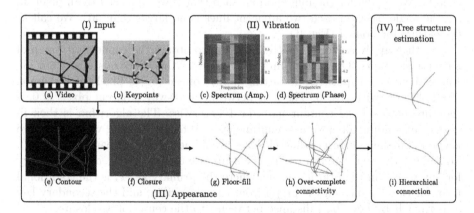

Fig. 4. Overview of our framework. We take a video (a) and a set of keypoints (b) as input (I). We use normalized amplitudes (c) and phases (d) of keypoints as our vibration signals (II); we also obtain appearance cues (III) through several intermediate steps (Sect. 4.1). Finally, we apply our inference algorithm (Sect. 4.2) for tree structure estimation.

Motion. Given an input video, we first manually label all nodes in the first frame and then track them over time using optical flow. There are many tracking algorithms that can extract trajectories of sparse keypoints [18,19,28,36], but we choose to calculate the dense motion field for two reasons. First, most of vibrations are small, and optical flow is known to perform well on capturing the small motion with subpixel accuracy. Second, sparse tracking algorithms, like the KLT tracker [28], might suffer the aperture problem, as most of branches only contain one-dimensional local structure. On the other hand, dense optical flow algorithms aggregate the information from other locations, so it would be more robust to the aperture problem.

Specifically, we first compute a dense flow field from the first frame to one of the frame t in the sequence [27]. We then get trajectory of each node in the sequences from dense motion fields through interpolation. We further apply Fourier transform to the trajectory of each node independently to get its complex spectrum Y (Fig. 4-II), and extract its modes from the fifth order spectral envelope [13]. We use the normalized amplitude (Fig. 4c) and phase (Fig. 4d) of these modes for inference, as discussed in Sect. 4.2.

Appearance. We use an over-complete connectivity matrix as our appearance cues. As shown in Fig. 4-III, we compute the matrix via the following steps: obtaining a contour map, computing the closure of each interest point, flood-filling the contour map from all closures, and adding edges to junctions.

Given the first frame from an input video, we first use Canny edge detector [5] with threshold 0.5 to obtain an initial contour map (Fig. 4e). Then, for each interest point i, we consider all contour pixels S_i whose distance to i is no larger than r_i. We search for the minimum r_i, such that if we connect i to all pixels in S_i, the angle between each two adjacent lines is no larger than $30°$. We call S_i the closure for point i (Fig. 4f).

We then apply a shortest-path algorithm to obtain the connectivity map of all interest points. Our algorithm is a variant of the Dijkstra's algorithm [8], where there is a hypothetical starting point connecting to pixels in the union of all closures with cost 0. The cost between two 8-way adjacent pixels is 0, if they are both on the contour map, or 1 otherwise. The algorithm is then in essence expanding all closures simultaneously. When it finishes, we connect two keypoints if their corresponding closures are adjacent after expansion (Fig. 4g). To balance the expansion rate of each closure, we use a tuple (c_i, d_i) as the entry for any pixel i in the priority queue, where the primary key c_i is the traditional term for the distance on the graph from i to the origin, and the secondary key d_i is the Chebyshev (L_∞) distance between i to the center of its closure.

Finally, an observed junction in a 2D image may be an actual tree fork, or may be just two disconnected, overlapping branches. To deal with the case, for all points that have 4 or more neighbors, we add an edge between each pair of its neighbors whose angle is no smaller than $135°$. This leads to an over-complete connectivity matrix E (Fig. 4h), which we use as our appearance cues.

Algorithm *cluster*($\boldsymbol{Y}$, r)
Data: Nodes with complex spectra $\boldsymbol{Y} = \{Y_i\}$ and the root's index r

1 Calculate the free vibration of each node in this tree
2 **for** *each node i* **do**
3 $\quad\mid\quad Y_i \leftarrow Y_i ./ Y_r$
4 **end**
5 Cluster nodes based on their appearance and frequency
6 Let $\{S_j\}_{j=1,\cdots,k}$ be all k clusters
7 **for** $j = 1, \cdots, k$ **do**
8 $\quad\mid\quad$ Select subroot r_j
9 $\quad\mid\quad$ Call *cluster*($\boldsymbol{Y}_{S_j}, r_j$) recursively
10 **end**

Algorithm 1. Our hierarchical clustering algorithm

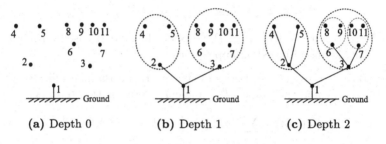

(a) Depth 0   (b) Depth 1   (c) Depth 2

Fig. 5. Illustration of our hierarchical clustering algorithm. See Sect. 4.2 for details.

4.2   Inference

Overview with a Toy Example. We start with a high-level overview of our hierarchical inference algorithm along with a toy tree with three levels of hierarchy (Fig. 5). As shown in Algorithm 1, given the root, our algorithm first computes the free vibration of the rest of nodes (Step I), groups them into several clusters (Step II), and then recursively finds tree structure for each cluster (Step III).

In this toy tree with v_1 as the root, the algorithm groups the other nodes into two clusters: (v_2, v_4, v_5) and $(v_3, v_6, v_7, \ldots, v_{11})$, as shown in Fig. 5b. For each subtree, the algorithm recursively applies itself for finer-level tree structure. Here in the right branch, we get two level-2 subtrees (v_6, v_8, v_9) and (v_7, v_{10}, v_{11}).

Step I: Computing Free Vibration. We first compute the vibration of each node given the root. Based on Eq. 9, we divide the complex spectrum of each leaf node by the complex spectrum of the root. Note that under certain frequency, the complex spectrum of the root might be close to zero. Therefore, a direct division might magnify the noise. To deal with this, we calculate the spectrum of each node i after removing the root r via $Y_i \cdot Y_r^* / \left(|Y_r|^2 + \epsilon^2\right)$, where Y_r^* is the complex conjugate of Y_r, and ϵ controls the noise level. This is similar to the Weinner filter [45]. When $\epsilon = 0$, We have the normal division as

$$\frac{Y_i \cdot Y_r^*}{|Y_r|^2} = \frac{Y_i \cdot Y_r^*}{Y_r \cdot Y_r^*} = \frac{Y_i}{Y_r}. \tag{10}$$

Step II: Grouping Nodes. We group nodes into clusters $\{S_j\}$ under the assumption that nodes in each cluster share similar vibration patterns (complex frequencies) and appearance cues. Each node has an unknown number of children, we use a Chinese Restaurant Process (CRP) prior [2] over the tree structure. Let z_i be the index of cluster that node i is assigned to, and let $Z = \{z_i\}$ be the assignment of all nodes. The joint probability of assignment is

$$P(Z|E, Y) \propto P_{\mathrm{CRP}}(Z) \cdot P_m(Y|Z) \cdot P_a(E|Z), \tag{11}$$

where $P_{\mathrm{CRP}}(\cdot)$ is the CRP prior, $P_m(\cdot)$ is the likelihood based on motion, and $P_a(\cdot)$ is the likelihood based on appearance.

Motion Term: we use two statistics of the spectrum: the normalized amplitude $Y_i^n = |Y_i|/\|Y_i\|_2$ and the phase $Y_i^p = \mathrm{angle}(Y_i)$. Our motion term is

$$\log P_m(Y|Z) = \sum_i -\sigma_n^{-2} \|Y_i^n - C_{z_i}^n\|_2^2 - \sigma_p^{-2} \|Y_i^p - C_{z_i}^p\|_2^2. \tag{12}$$

C_k^n and C_k^p are the mean normalized amplitudes and phases of nodes in cluster k.

Appearance Term: nodes in the same sub-branch are expected to be connected to each other and to the root. To this end, we define the appearance term as

$$\log P_a(E|Z) = \sum_{z_i = z_j} \alpha \cdot \mathbf{1}(i, j|Z, E) + \sum_i \beta \cdot \mathbf{1}(i, r|Z, E), \tag{13}$$

where $\mathbf{1}(i, j)$ is the indicator function of whether there exists a path between nodes i and j given the current assignment Z and the estimated connectivity matrix E (see Sect. 4.1). Given the joint probability in Eq. 11, we run Gibbs sampling [15] for 20 iterations over each assignment z_i.

Step III: Recursion. As shown in the toy example (Fig. 5), for each cluster S_j, our algorithm selects the node closest to the root r in the Euclidean space as the subroot r_j. It then infers subtree structure for S_j recursively. The whole inference algorithm takes 3–5 s for a tree of 50 vertices on a Desktop CPU.

5   Evaluations

We now present how we use simulation to verify our formulation (Sect. 3), and show qualitative and quantitative results on videos of artificial and real trees.

5.1   Simulation

Based on formulation described in Sect. 3.1, we implemented a tree simulator by solving Eq. 5 using the Euler Method [9]. As shown in Sect. 4.1, the analytic form of ODE is very complicated. Therefore, we do not eliminate all the redundant variables, including the acceleration of the branch (a_i and a_{i_o}), forces between branches (r_i), and angular velocity of each branch (ω_i). Instead, we directly solve Eqs. 1 and 2 numerically. Also, to increase the stability of Euler method in presence of numerical error, we force the system to have constant total energy for every time-stepping update. If the system's energy increases during an update, we rescale the kinetic and potential energy of each branch to ensure that the total energy of the system is constant. This makes our simulation robust and stable. See the supplementary material for the detailed derivation.

Figure 6 shows the vibration modes of a simulated tree (left) with three mode shapes (right). Here we manually specify the structure of the tree and physical property of each branch, including mass, stiffness, and length, and numerically solve for the rotation angle of each branch. The mode of power spectra (the natural frequencies) of the trunk and two branches matches the three mode shapes of the tree, which is consistent with the theory in Sect. 3.

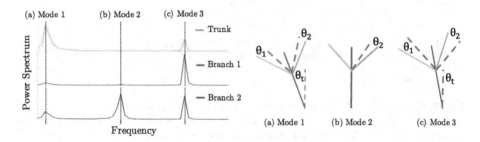

Fig. 6. Mode shapes. The left three curves show the power spectra of the trunk and the two branches. The three mode shapes extracted from vibration are shown on the right.

5.2   Real, Normal Speed Videos

Data. We record videos of both artificial and real trees. For artificial trees, we take 3 videos in an indoor lab environment, where wind is generated by a fan. We take 8 videos of outdoor real trees. All videos are taken at 24 frames per second by a Canon EOS 6D DSLR camera, with a resolution of 1920 × 1080.

Methods. We compare our full model, which makes use of appearance and vibration cues jointly (appearance + motion), with a simplified variant, which uses only appearance information, but ignores all motion signals during inference. We also compare with three alternative approaches for hierarchical structure recovery from spatial-temporal motion signals.

- **Appearance + Flow/Tracking:** We replace the spatial-temporal feature in our algorithm by motion recovered by either optical flow or a KLT tracker.
- **Hierarchical motion segmentation:** We use the popular hierarchical video segmentation algorithm [17] to obtain image segments and their structure. We then derive the tree structure from the segment hierarchy.

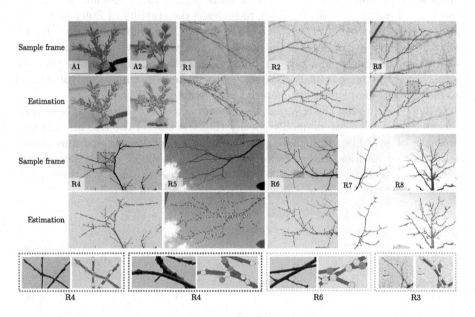

Fig. 7. Estimated tree structure on real videos. A1–A2: on artificial trees; R1–R8: on real trees. At bottom, we show cases where appearance is insufficient for inferring the correct structure. Using vibration signals, our algorithm works well in these cases.

Results. Figure 7 shows that our algorithm works well on real videos. Results in the bottom row suggest that our algorithm can deal with challenging cases. Using motion signals, it correctly recovers the structure of occluded twigs, which is indistinguishable from pure visual appearance.

For quantitative evaluations, we manually label the parents of each node and use it as ground truth. We use two metrics. In Table 1, we evaluate different methods in (a) the percentage of nodes whose parents are correctly recovered and (b) minimum edit distance—the minimum edges that need to be displaced to make the predicted tree and the ground truth identical. Our algorithm achieves good performance in general. Including motion cues consistently improves the accuracy of the inference on videos of all types, and spatial feature significantly out-performs the raw motion signal.

Table 1. Results evaluated by the percentage of nodes whose parents are correctly recovered (top) and the edit distance between reconstruction and ground truth (bottom). Our method outperforms the alternatives in most cases.

Metrics	Methods	Artificial			Real trees								High-speed videos						Avg.
		A1	A2	A3	R1	R2	R3	R4	R5	R6	R7	R8	H1	H2	H3	H4	H5	H6	
Acc. (%)	MoSeg	33	37	73	50	65	84	56	56	68	70	74	47	57	46	47	43	51	56.3
	Appear.	40	31	90	67	59	83	70	66	71	89	85	55	56	62	66	61	69	65.7
	A+Flow	43	32	92	79	69	83	85	75	84	95	**94**	64	58	69	69	72	**76**	73.5
	A+Track	38	**46**	88	79	63	83	84	**83**	**88**	89	93	67	64	66	76	71	**76**	73.8
	Ours	**54**	45	**100**	**81**	**76**	**94**	**95**	**83**	**88**	**97**	**94**	**69**	**69**	**72**	**77**	**74**	70	**79.3**
Edit Dis.	MoSeg	26	16	7	25	22	8	16	20	13	8	15	20	21	24	22	17	15	17.4
	Appear.	20	21	3	12	19	5	5	30	9	4	8	16	16	16	16	16	16	13.7
	A+Flow	19	13	2	**7**	13	5	3	12	11	**1**	6	13	18	11	12	**8**	8	9.5
	A+Track	24	**10**	2	10	16	6	4	12	8	4	7	13	15	12	10	10	8	10.1
	Ours	**14**	12	**0**	8	**12**	**2**	**0**	**6**	**4**	**1**	6	**10**	12	**9**	**6**	9	8	**7.0**

5.3 Real, High-Speed Videos

Experimental Setup. To understand and analyze motion, we take high-speed videos of trees using an Edgertronic high-speed camera. We captured 1 normal-speed video (30 FPS) and 5 high-speed videos with a frame rate varying from 60 to 500 FPS, each of which contains 1,000 frames. For each video, we manually label around 100 interest points and their connections. Intuitively, the root branches should have higher stiffness and lower natural frequencies. Therefore, low-frame-rate videos should provide more information about the tree's main structure, whose natural frequency is low, and high-frame-rate videos should provide more information of fast vibrating thin structure.

Evaluation. For evaluation, we first pick two points (P_1 and P_2 in Fig. 8c) on two major branches of the tree and compare their power spectra as shown in

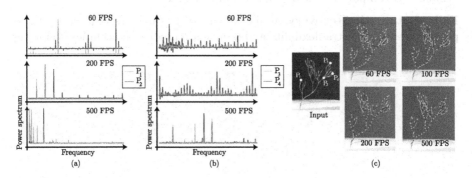

Fig. 8. Evaluation of the algorithm on videos with different frame rates. (a) and (b) shows the power spectra of selected nodes in the input videos captured at different frame rates, and (c) shows the estimated tree structures. See Sect. 5.2 for more details.

Fig. 8a. At 60 FPS, the power spectra of these two nodes are different for a wide range of frequencies; at 500 FPS, they are only different at lower frequencies, as the natural frequencies of the main branches are low. We then pick two points (P_3 and P_4 in Fig. 8c) on two small branches of the tree and compare their power spectra (see Fig. 8b). Now in both 60 FPS and 200 FPS videos, their spectra are similar, and the difference in modes only become significant at 500 FPS. Figure 8c shows that the estimation errors from low-frame videos (60 or 100 FPS) on the top-right corner no longer exist when the input is at 500 FPS, indicating high-speed videos are better for estimating fine structure. All these results are consistent with our theory. H1 to H6 in Tables 1 refer to videos captured at 30, 60, 100, 200, 400, 500 FPS, respectively.

6   Applications

Our model has wide applications in inferring tree-shaped structure in real-life scenarios. To demonstrate this, we show two applications: seeing object structure from shadows, and inferring blood vessels from retinal videos.

Shapes from Shadows. In circumstances like video surveillance, often the only available data is videos of projections of an object, but not the object itself. For example, we can see the shadows of trees in the video, but not the trees themselves. In these cases, it would be of strong interests to reconstruct the actual shape of the object. Our algorithm deals with these cases well. Among the eight real videos in Fig. 7, R2 and R3 are videos of tree shadows. Our algorithm successfully reconstructs the underlying tree structure, as shown in Fig. 7 and Table 1.

Vessels from Retinal Videos. Our model can contribute to biomedical research. We apply our model on a retinal video from OcuScience LLC. As shown in Fig. 9a–b, our algorithm performs well, reconstructing the connection among retinal vessels despite limited video quality. It achieves a smaller edit distance (4) compared with A+Flow (7) and A+Track (6).

Fully Automatic Recovery. While we choose to take keypoints as input to provide users with extra flexibility and to increase prediction accuracy, following

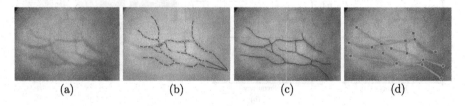

(a)   (b)   (c)   (d)

Fig. 9. Our result on a retinal video. (a) A frame from the input video. (b) Our model reconstructs the structure of blood vessels despite low video quality. (c–d) Results on fully automatic structure inference, where (c) shows the estimated object skeleton and (d) shows the object structure inferred by our model.

the convention in the literature [40], our system can be easily extended to become fully automatic. Here we provide an additional experiment on the retinal video. We first apply the segmentation method from Maninis *et al.* [29] on the first frame to obtain a segmentation of vessels. We then employ the classical skeletonization algorithm from Lee *et al.* [25] (Fig. 9c), and use the endpoints and junctions of the obtained skeleton as input keypoints to our model. As shown in Fig. 9d, our system works well without manual labels.

7   Discussion

In this paper, we have demonstrated that vibration signals in the spectral domain, in addition to appearance cues, can help to resolve the ambiguity in tree structure estimation. We designed a novel formulation of trees from physics-based link models, from which we distilled physical properties of vibration signals, and verified them both theoretically and experimentally. We also proposed a hierarchical inference algorithm, using nonparametric Bayesian methods to infer tree structure. The algorithm works well on real-world videos.

Our derivation makes four assumptions: passive motion, small vibration, no damping, and a known root. While real trees often satisfy the first two, they do not have zero damping (damping ratio ranging from 1.2% to 15.4% [22]). In these cases, our algorithm still successfully recovers their geometry from vibration. When the root is unknown, our method can discover multiple subtrees from a virtual root with a uniform motion spectrum. On the other hand, our model performs less well when assumptions are significantly violated (*e.g.*, large vibration or an incorrect root).

We see our work as an initial exploration on how spectral knowledge may help structured inference, and look forward to its potential applications in fields even outside computer science, *e.g.*, fiber structure estimation.

Acknowledgements. This work is supported by NSF #1231216, #1212849, and #1447476, ONR MURI N00014-16-1-2007, Toyota Research Institute, Shell Research, and Facebook. We thank Xiuming Zhang for helpful discussions.

References

1. Bascle, B., Blake, A., Zisserman, A.: Motion deblurring and super-resolution from an image sequence. In: Buxton, B., Cipolla, R. (eds.) ECCV 1996. LNCS, vol. 1065, pp. 571–582. Springer, Heidelberg (1996). https://doi.org/10.1007/3-540-61123-1_171

2. Blei, D.M., Griffiths, T.L., Jordan, M.I.: The nested chinese restaurant process and bayesian nonparametric inference of topic hierarchies. JACM **57**(2), 7 (2010)

3. Bouman, K.L., Xiao, B., Battaglia, P., Freeman, W.T.: Estimating the material properties of fabric from video. In: ICCV (2013)

4. Braddick, O.: Segmentation versus integration in visual motion processing. Trends Neurosci. **16**(7), 263–268 (1993)

5. Canny, J.: A computational approach to edge detection. IEEE TPAMI **8**(6), 679–698 (1986)
6. Davies, M.N., Green, P.R.: Perception and Motor Control in Birds: an Ecological Approach. Springer, Heidelberg (2012)
7. Davis, A., Bouman, K.L., Chen, J.G., Rubinstein, M., Durand, F., Freeman, W.T.: Visual vibrometry: estimating material properties from small motion in video. In: CVPR (2015)
8. Dijkstra, E.W.: A note on two problems in connexion with graphs. Numer. Math. **1**(1), 269–271 (1959)
9. Farlow, S.J.: Partial Differential Equations for Scientists and Engineers. Courier Corporation, North Chelmsford (1993)
10. Fleet, D.J., Jepson, A.D.: Computation of component image velocity from local phase information. IJCV **5**(1), 77–104 (1990)
11. Fraz, M.M., et al.: Blood vessel segmentation methodologies in retinal images-a survey. Comput. Methods Programs Biomed. **108**(1), 407–433 (2012)
12. French, A.: Vibrations and Waves. WW Norton, New York (1971)
13. Furoh, T., Fukumori, T., Nakayama, M., Nishiura, T.: Detection for lombard speech with second-order mel-frequency cepstral coefficient and spectral envelope in beginning of talking-speech. J. Acoust. Soc. Am. **133**(5), 3246 (2013)
14. Gautama, T., Van Hulle, M.: A phase-based approach to the estimation of the optical flow field using spatial filtering. IEEE TNN **13**(5), 1127–1136 (2002)
15. Geman, S., Geman, D.: Stochastic relaxation, Gibbs distributions, and the Bayesian restoration of images. IEEE TPAMI **6**(6), 721–741 (1984)
16. Gershman, S.J., Tenenbaum, J.B., Jäkel, F.: Discovering hierarchical motion structure. Vis. Res. **126**, 232–241 (2016)
17. Grundmann, M., Kwatra, V., Han, M., Essa, I.: Efficient hierarchical graph-based video segmentation. In: CVPR (2010)
18. Hare, S., et al.: Struck: structured output tracking with kernels. IEEE TPAMI **38**(10), 2096–2109 (2016)
19. Henriques, J.F., Caseiro, R., Martins, P., Batista, J.: High-speed tracking with kernelized correlation filters. IEEE TPAMI **37**(3), 583–596 (2015)
20. James, K.R., Dahle, G.A., Grabosky, J., Kane, B., Detter, A.: Tree biomechanics literature review: dynamics. J. Arboric. Urban For. **40**, 1–15 (2014)
21. James, K.R., Haritos, N., Ades, P.K.: Mechanical stability of trees under dynamic loads. Am. J. Bot. **93**(10), 1522–1530 (2006)
22. James, K., Haritos, N.: Branches and damping on trees in winds. In: Australasian Conference on the Mechanics of Structures and Materials (2014)
23. Jepson, A.D., Fleet, D.J., Black, M.J.: A layered motion representation with occlusion and compact spatial support. In: Heyden, A., Sparr, G., Nielsen, M., Johansen, P. (eds.) ECCV 2002. LNCS, vol. 2350, pp. 692–706. Springer, Heidelberg (2002). https://doi.org/10.1007/3-540-47969-4_46
24. Knill, D.C., Richards, W.: Perception as Bayesian inference. Cambridge University Press, Cambridge (1996)
25. Lee, T.C.: Building skeleton models via 3-D medial surface axis thinning algorithms. CVGIP **56**(6), 462–478 (1994)
26. Lee, T.S., Mumford, D.: Hierarchical bayesian inference in the visual cortex. JOSA A **20**(7), 1434–1448 (2003)
27. Liu, C.: Beyond pixels: exploring new representations and applications for motion analysis. Ph.D. thesis, Citeseer (2009)
28. Lucas, B.D., Kanade, T.: An iterative image registration technique with an application to stereo vision. In: IJCAI (1981)

29. Maninis, K.-K., Pont-Tuset, J., Arbeláez, P., Van Gool, L.: Deep retinal image understanding. In: Ourselin, S., Joskowicz, L., Sabuncu, M.R., Unal, G., Wells, W. (eds.) MICCAI 2016. LNCS, vol. 9901, pp. 140–148. Springer, Cham (2016). https://doi.org/10.1007/978-3-319-46723-8_17

30. Miller, L.A.: Structural dynamics and resonance in plants with nonlinear stiffness. J. Theor. Biol. **234**(4), 511–524 (2005)

31. Moore, J.R., Maguire, D.A.: Natural sway frequencies and damping ratios of trees: concepts, review and synthesis of previous studies. Trees **18**(2), 195–203 (2004)

32. Moreno-Bote, R., Knill, D.C., Pouget, A.: Bayesian sampling in visual perception. PNAS **108**(30), 12491–12496 (2011)

33. Murphy, K.D., Rudnicki, M.: A physics-based link model for tree vibrations. Am. J. Bot. **99**(12), 1918–1929 (2012)

34. Pathak, D., Girshick, R., Dollár, P., Darrell, T., Hariharan, B.: Learning features by watching objects move. In: CVPR (2017)

35. Rubinstein, M.: Analysis and visualization of temporal variations in video. Ph.D. thesis, MIT (2013)

36. Rubinstein, M., Liu, C., Freeman, W.T.: Towards longer long-range motion trajectories. In: BMVC (2012)

37. Spelke, E.S., Breinlinger, K., Macomber, J., Jacobson, K.: Origins of knowledge. Psychol. Rev. **99**(4), 605 (1992)

38. Sun, D., Liu, C., Pfister, H.: Local layering for joint motion estimation and occlusion detection. In: CVPR (2014)

39. Sun, D., Sudderth, E.B., Black, M.J.: Layered segmentation and optical flow estimation over time. In: CVPR (2012)

40. Türetken, E., Benmansour, F., Andres, B., Głowacki, P., et al.: Reconstructing curvilinear networks using path classifiers and integer programming. IEEE TPAMI **38**(12), 2515–2530 (2016)

41. Türetken, E., González, G., Blum, C., Fua, P.: Automated reconstruction of dendritic and axonal trees by global optimization with geometric priors. Neuroinformatics **9**(2–3), 279–302 (2011)

42. Wang, J.Y., Adelson, E.H.: Layered representation for motion analysis. In: CVPR (1993)

43. Wang, Y., Narayanaswamy, A., Roysam, B.: Novel 4-D open-curve active contour and curve completion approach for automated tree structure extraction. In: CVPR (2011)

44. Weiss, Y., Adelson, E.H.: Slow and smooth: a Bayesian theory for the combination of local motion signals in human vision. Technical report, MIT (1998)

45. Wiener, N.: Extrapolation, Interpolation, and Smoothing of Stationary Time Series: with Engineering Applications. MIT Press, Cambridge (1949)

46. Wu, H.Y., Rubinstein, M., Shih, E., Guttag, J., Durand, F., Freeman, W.: Eulerian video magnification for revealing subtle changes in the world. ACM TOG **31**(4), 65 (2012)

47. Xue, T., Rubinstein, M., Liu, C., Freeman, W.T.: A computational approach for obstruction-free photography. ACM TOG **34**(4), 79 (2015)

48. Zhou, B., Hou, X., Zhang, L.: A phase discrepancy analysis of object motion. In: Kimmel, R., Klette, R., Sugimoto, A. (eds.) ACCV 2010. LNCS, vol. 6494, pp. 225–238. Springer, Heidelberg (2011). https://doi.org/10.1007/978-3-642-19318-7_18

The Devil of Face Recognition
Is in the Noise

Fei Wang[1]([✉])[iD], Liren Chen[2][iD], Cheng Li[1][iD], Shiyao Huang[1][iD],
Yanjie Chen[1][iD], Chen Qian[1][iD], and Chen Change Loy[3][iD]

[1] SenseTime Research, Beijing, China
{wangfei,chengli,huangshiyao,chenyanjie,qianchen}@sensetime.com
[2] University of California San Diego, San Diego, USA
lic002@eng.ucsd.edu
[3] Nanyang Technological University, Singapore, Singapore
ccloy@ieee.org

Abstract. The growing scale of face recognition datasets empowers us
to train strong convolutional networks for face recognition. While a variety of architectures and loss functions have been devised, we still have
a limited understanding of the source and consequence of label noise
inherent in existing datasets. We make the following contributions: (1)
We contribute cleaned subsets of popular face databases, *i.e.*, MegaFace
and MS-Celeb-1M datasets, and build a new large-scale noise-controlled
IMDb-Face dataset. (2) With the original datasets and cleaned subsets,
we profile and analyze label noise properties of MegaFace and MS-Celeb-
1M. We show that a few orders more samples are needed to achieve the
same accuracy yielded by a clean subset. (3) We study the association
between different types of noise, *i.e.*, label flips and outliers, with the
accuracy of face recognition models. (4) We investigate ways to improve
data cleanliness, including a comprehensive user study on the influence of
data labeling strategies to annotation accuracy. The IMDb-Face dataset
has been released on https://github.com/fwang91/IMDb-Face.

1 Introduction

Datasets are pivotal to the development of face recognition. From the early
FERET dataset [16] to the more recent LFW [7], MegaFace [8,13], and MS-
Celeb-1M [5], face recognition datasets play a main role in driving the development of new techniques. The datasets not only become more diverse, the scale
of data is also growing tremendously. For instance, MS-Celeb-1M [5] contains
around 10M images for 100 K celebrities, far exceeding FERET [16] that only
has 14,126 images from 1,199 individuals. Large-scale datasets together with the
emergence of deep learning have led to the immense success of face recognition
in recent years.

F. Wang and L. Chen—Equal contribution.

V. Ferrari et al. (Eds.): ECCV 2018, LNCS 11213, pp. 780–795, 2018.
https://doi.org/10.1007/978-3-030-01240-3_47

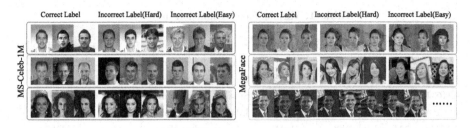

Fig. 1. Label noises in MegaFace [13] and MS-Celeb-1M [5]. Each row depicts images that are labeled with the same identity. Some incorrect labels are easy while many of them are hard.

Large-scale datasets are inevitably affected by label noise. The problem is pervasive since well-annotated datasets in large-scale are prohibitively expensive and time-consuming to collect. That motivates researchers to resort to cheap but imperfect alternatives. A common method is to query celebrities' images by their names on search engines, and subsequently clean the labels with automatic or semi-automatic approaches [4,11,15]. Other methods introduce clustering with constraints on social photo sharing sites. The aforementioned methods offer a viable way to scale the training samples conveniently but also bring label noises that adversely affect the training and performance of a model. We show some samples with label noises in Fig. 1. As can be seen, MegaFace [13] and MS-Celeb-1M [5] consist considerable incorrect identity labels. Some noisy labels are easy to remove while many of them are hard to be cleaned. In MegaFace, there are a number of redundant images too (shown in the last row).

The first goal of this paper is to develop an understanding of the source of label noise and its consequences towards face recognition by deep convolutional neural networks (CNN) [1,6,18,19,23,26]. We seek answers to questions like: How many noisy samples are needed to achieve an effect tantamount to clean data? What is the relationship between noise and final performance? What is the best strategy to annotate face identities? A better understanding of the aforementioned questions would help us to design a better data collection and cleaning strategy, avoid pitfalls in training, and formulate stronger algorithms to cope with real-world problems. To facilitate our research, we manually clean subsets of two most popular face recognition databases, namely, MegaFace [13] and MS-Celeb-1M [5]. We observe that a model trained with only 32% of MegaFace or 20% of MS-Celeb-1M cleaned subsets, can already achieve comparable performance with models that are trained on the respective full dataset. The experiments suggest that a few orders more samples are needed for face recognition model training if noisy samples are used.

The second goal of our study is to build a clean face recognition dataset for the community. The dataset could help training better models and facilitate further understanding of the relationship between noise and face recognition performance. To this end, we build a clean dataset called **IMDb-Face**. The dataset consists of 1.7M images of 59 K celebrities collected from movie

Table 1. Various face recognition datasets.

Dataset	#Identities	#Images	Source	Cleaned?	Availablity
LFW [7]	5K	13K	Search engine	Automatic detection	Public
CelebFaces [19,20]	10K	202K	Search engine	Manually cleaned	Public
VGG-Face [15]	2.6K	2.5M	Search engine	Semi-automated clean	Public
CASIA-WebFace [25]	10k	0.5M	IMDb	Automatic clean	Public
MS-Celeb-1M(v1) [5]	100k	10M	Search engine	None	Public
MegaFace [13]	670K	4.7M	Flickr	Automatic cleaned	Public
Facebook [21]	4k	4.4M	–	–	Private
Google [18]	8M	200M	–	–	Private
IMDb-Face	**59K**	**1.7M**	**IMDb**	**Manually cleaned**	**Public**

screenshots and posters from the IMDb website[1]. Due to the nature of the data source, the images exhibit large variations in scale, pose, lighting, and occlusion. We carefully clean the dataset and simulate corruption by injecting noise on the training labels. The experiments show that the accuracy of face recognition decreases rapidly and nonlinearly with the increase of label noises. In particular, we confirm the common belief that the performance of face recognition is more sensitive towards label flips (example has erroneously been given the label of another class within the dataset) than outliers (image does not belong to any of the classes under consideration, but mistakenly has one of their labels). We also conduct an interesting experiment to analyze the reliability of different ways of annotating a face recognition dataset. We found that label accuracy correlates with time spent on annotation. The study helps us to find the source of erroneous labels and thereafter design better strategies to balance annotation cost and accuracy.

We hope that this paper could shed lights on the influences of data noise to the face recognition task, and point to potential labelling strategies to mitigate some of the problems. We contribute the new data **IMDb-Face** with the community. It could serve as a relatively clean data to facilitate future studies of noises in large-scale face recognition. It can also be used as a training data source to boost the performance of existing methods, as we will show in the experiments.

2   How Noisy Is Existing Data?

We first introduce some popular datasets used in face recognition study and then approximate their respective signal-to-noise ratio.

2.1   Face Recognition Datasets

Table 1 provides a summary of representative datasets used in face recognition research.

---

[1] www.IMDb.com.

LFW: Labeled Faces in the Wild (LFW) [7] is perhaps the most popular dataset to date for benchmarking face recognition approaches. The database consists of 13,000 facial images of 1,680 celebrities. Images are collected from Yahoo News by running the Viola-Jones face detector. Limited by the detector, most of the faces in LFW is frontal. The dataset is considered sufficiently clean despite some incorrectly labeled matched pairs are reported. Errata of LFW are provided in http://vis-www.cs.umass.edu/lfw/.

CelebFaces: CelebFaces [19,20] is one of the early face recognition training databases that are made publicly available. Its first version contains 5,436 celebrities and 87,628 images, and it was upgraded to 10,177 identities and 202,599 images in a year later. Images in CelebFaces were collected from search engines and manually cleaned by workers.

VGG-Face: VGG-Face [15] contains 2,622 identities and 2.6M photos. More than 2,000 images per celebrity were downloaded from search engines. The authors treat the top 50 images as positive samples and train a linear SVM to select the top 1,000 faces. To avoid extensive manual annotation, the dataset was 'block-wise' verified, *i.e.*, ranked images of each identity are displayed in blocks and annotators are asked to validate blocks as a whole. In this study we did not focus on VGG-Face [15] since it should have the similar 'search-engine bias' problem with MS-Celeb-1M [5].

CASIA-WebFace: The images in CASIA-WebFace [25] were collected from IMDb website. The dataset contains 500 K photos of 10 K celebrities and it is semi-automatically cleaned via tag-constrained similarity clustering. The authors start with each celebrity's main photo and those photos that contain only one face. Then faces are gradually added to the dataset constrained by feature similarity and name tag. CASIA-WebFace uses the same source as the proposed IMDb-Face dataset. However, limited by the feature and clustering steps, CASIA-WebFace may fail to recall many challenging faces.

MS-Celeb-1M: MS-Celeb-1M [5] contains 100 K celebrities who are selected from the 1M celebrity list in terms of their popularities. Public search engines are then leveraged to provide approximately 100 images for each celebrity, resulting in about 10M web images. The data is deliberately left uncleaned for several reasons. Specifically, collecting a dataset of this scale requires tremendous efforts in cleaning the dataset. Perhaps more importantly, leaving the data in this form encourages researchers to devise new learning methods that can naturally deal with the inherent noises.

MegaFace: Kemelmacher-Shlizerman *et al.* [13] clean massive number of images published on Flickr by proposing algorithms to cluster and filter face data from the YFCC100M dataset. For each user's albums, the authors merge face pairs with a distance closer than β times of average distance. Clusters that contain more than three faces are kept. Then they drop 'garbage' groups and clean potential outliers in each group. A total of 672 K identities and 4.7M images were collected. MegaFace2 avoids 'search-engine' bias as in VGG-Face [15] and

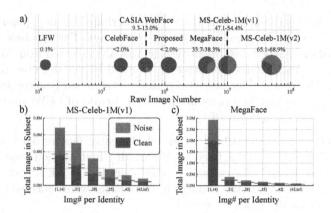

Fig. 2. (a) A visualization of size and estimated noise percentage of datasets. (b) Noise distribution of MS-Celeb-1M(v1) [5]. (c) Noise distribution of MegaFace [13]. The two horizontal lines in each bar represent the lower- and upper-bounds of noise, respectively. See Sect. 2.2 for details.

MS-Celeb-1M [5]. However, we found this cluster-based approach introduces new bias. MegaFace prefers small groups with highly duplicated images, *e.g.*, face captured from the same video. Limited by the base model for clustering, considerable groups in MegaFace contain noises, or sometimes mess up multiple people in the same group.

2.2 An Approximation of Signal-to-Noise Ratio

Owing to the source of data and cleaning strategies, existing large-scale datasets invariably contain label noises. In this study, we aim to profile the noise distribution in existing datasets. Our analysis may provide a hint to future research on how one should exploit the distribution of these data.

It is infeasible to obtain the exact number of these noises due to the scale of the datasets. We bypass this difficulty by randomly selecting a subset of a dataset and manually categorize them into three groups – 'correct identity assigned', 'doubtful', and 'wrong identity assigned'. We select a subset of 2.7M images from MegaFace [13] and 3.7M images from MS-Celeb-1M [5]. For CASIA-WebFace [25] and CelebFaces [19,20], we sampled 30 identities to estimate their signal-to-noise ratio. The final statistics are visualized in Fig. 2(a). Due to the difficulty in estimating the exact ratio, we approximate an upper and a lower bound of noisy data during the estimation. The lower-bound is more optimistic considering doubtful labels as clean data. The upper-bound is more pessimistic considering all doubtful cases as badly labeled. As observed in Fig. 2(a), the noise percentage increases dramatically along the scale of data. This is not surprising given the difficulty in data annotation. It is noteworthy that the proposed IMDb-Face pushes the envelope of large-scale data with a very high signal-to-noise ratio (noise is under 10% of the full data).

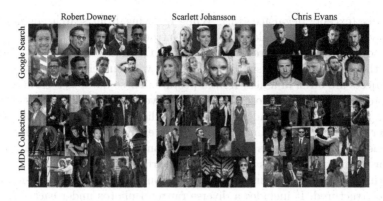

Fig. 3. The second row depicts the raw data from the IMDb website. As a comparison, we show the images of the same identity queried from the Google search engine in the first row.

We investigate further the noise distribution of the two largest public datasets to date, MS-Celeb-1M [5] and MegaFace [13]. We first categorize identities in a dataset based on their number of images. A total of six groups/bins are established. We then plot a histogram showing the signal-to-noise ratio of each bin along the noise lower- and upper-bounds. As can be seen in Fig. 2(b and c), both datasets exhibit a long-tailed distribution, *i.e.*, most identities have very few images. This phenomenon is especially obvious on the MegaFace [13] dataset since it uses automatically formed clusters for determining identities, therefore, the same identity may be distributed in different clusters. Noises across all groups in MegaFace [13] are less in comparison to MS-Celeb-1M [5]. However, we found that many images in the clean portion of MegaFace [13] are duplicated images. In Sect. 4.2, we will perform experiments on the MegaFace and MS-Celeb-1M datasets to quantify the effect of noise on the face recognition task.

3   Building a Noise-Controlled Face Dataset

As shown in the previous section, face recognition datasets that are more than a million scale typically have a noise ratio higher than 30%. How about building a large scale noise controlled face dataset? It can be used to train better face recognition algorithms. More importantly, it can be used to further understand the relationship between noise and face recognition performance. To this end, we seek not only a cleaner and more diverse source to collect face data, but also an effective way to label the data.

3.1   Celebrity Faces from IMDb

Search engines are important sources from which we can quickly construct a large-scale dataset. The widely used ImageNet [3] was built by querying images from Google Image. Most of the face recognition datasets were built in the same way (except MegaFace [13]). While querying from search engines offers the convenience of data collection, it also introduces data bias. Search engines usually operate in a high-precision regime [2]. Observing the queried images in Fig. 3, they tend to have a simple background with sufficient illumination, and the subjects are often in a near frontal posture. These data, to a certain extent, are more restricted than those we could observe in reality, *e.g.*, faces in videos (IJB-A [9] and YTF [24]) and selfie photos (millions of distractors in MegaFace). Another pitfall in crawling images from search engines is the low recall rate. We performed a simple analysis and found that on average the recall rate is only 40% for the first 200 photos we query for a particular name.

In this study, we turn our data collection source to the IMDb website. IMDb is more structured. It includes a diverse range of photos under each celebrity's profile, including official photos, lifestyle photos, and movie snapshots. Movie snapshots, we believe, provide essential data samples for training a robust face recognition model. Those screenshots are rarely returned by querying a search engine. In addition, the recall rate is much higher (90% on average) when we query a name on IMDb. This is much higher than 40% from search engines. The IMDb website lists about 300 K celebrities who have official and gallery photos. By clawing IMDb dataset, we finally collected and cleaned 1.7M raw images from 59 K celebrities.

3.2   Data Distribution

Figure 4a presents the distribution of yaw angle in our dataset compared with MS-Celeb-1M and MegaFace. Figures 4c, d and e present the age, gender and race distributions. As can be observed, images in IMDb-Face exhibit larger pose variations, and they also show diversity in age, gender and race.

3.3   How Good Can Human Label Identity?

The data downloaded from IMDb are noisy as multiple celebrities may co-exist on the same image. We still need to clean the dataset before it can be used for training. We take this opportunity to study how human annotators would clean a face data. The study will help us to identify the source of noise during annotation and design a better data cleaning strategy for the full dataset.

For the purpose of the user study, we extract a small subset of 30 identities from the IMDb raw data. We carefully select three images with confirmed identity serving as gallery images. The remaining images of these 30 identities are treated as query images. To make the user study more challenging and statistically more meaningful, we inject 20% outliers to the query set. Next, we prepare three annotation schemes as follows. The interface of each scheme is depicted in Fig. 5.

Scheme I - Draw the Box: We present the target person to a volunteer by showing the three gallery faces. We then show a query image selected from the query set. The image may contain multiple persons. If the target appears in the

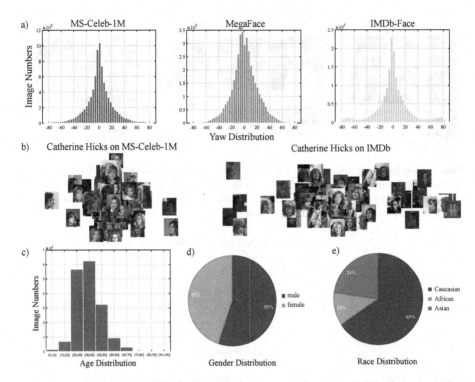

Fig. 4. (a) Comparing the distribution of yaw angle of images in the proposed dataset against MS-Celeb-1M and MegaFace. (b) A qualitative sample from the proposed IMDb-Face and MS-Celeb-1M. (c) Age distribution of images in IMDb-Face. (d) Gender distribution of identities in IMDb-Face. (e) Race distribution of identities in IMDb-Face.

query image, the volunteer is asked to draw a bounding box on the target. The volunteer can either confirm the selection or assign a 'doubt' flag on the box if he/she is not confident about the choice. 'No target' is selected when he/she cannot find the target person.

Scheme II - Choose 1 in 3: Similar to Scheme I, we present the target person to a volunteer by showing the gallery images. We then randomly sample three faces detected from the query set, from which the volunteer will select a single image as the target face. We ensure that all query faces have the same gender as the target person. Again, the volunteer can choose a 'doubt' flag if he/she is not confident about the selection or choose 'no target' at all.

Scheme III - Yes or No: Binary query is perhaps be the most natural and popular way to clean a face recognition set. We first rank all faces based on their similarity to probe faces in the gallery, and then ask a volunteer to make a choice if each belongs to the target person. The volunteer is allowed to answer 'doubt'.

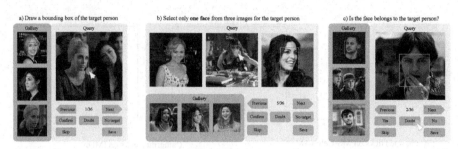

Fig. 5. Interfaces for user study: (a) Scheme I - volunteers were asked to draw a box on the target's face. (b) Scheme II - given three query faces, volunteers were asked to select the face that belongs to the target person. (c) Scheme III - volunteers were asked to select the face that belongs to the target.

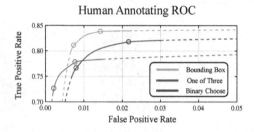

Fig. 6. A ROC comparison between three different annotating schemes; volunteers were allowed to select 'doubt' so two data points can be obtained depending if we count doubt data as positive or negative.

Which Scheme to Choose?: Before we can quantify the effectiveness of different schemes, we first need to generate the ground truth of these 30 identities. We use a 'consensus' approach. Specifically, each of the aforementioned schemes was conducted on three different volunteers. We ensure that each query face was annotated nine times across the three schemes. If four of the annotations consistently point to the same identity, we assign the query face to the targeted identity. With this ground truth, we can measure the effectiveness of each annotation scheme.

Figure 6 shows the Receiver operating characteristic (ROC) curve of each of the three schemes[2]. Scheme I achieves the highest F_1 score. It recalls more than 90% faces with under 10% false positive samples. Finding a face and drawing a box seems to make annotators more focused on finding the right face. Scheme II provides a high true positive rate when the false positive is low. The existence of distractors forces annotators to work harder to match the faces. Scheme III yields

---

[2] We should emphasize that the curves in Fig. 6 are different from actual human's performance on verifying arbitrary face pairs. This is because in our study the faces from a query set are very likely to belong to the same person. The ROC thus represents human's accuracy on 'verifying face pairs that likely belong to the same identity'.

the worse true positive rate when the false positive is low. This is not surprising since this task is much easier than Schemes I and II. The annotators tend to make mistakes given this relaxing task, especially after a prolonged annotation process. We observe an interesting phenomenon: *the longer a volunteer spends on annotating a sample, the more accurate the annotation is.* With full speed in one hour, each volunteer can draw 180-300 faces in Scheme I, or finish around 600 selections in Scheme II, or answer over 1000 binary questions in Scheme III. We believe the most reliable way to clean a face recognition dataset is to leverage both Schemes I and II to achieve a high precision and recall. Limited by our budget, we only conducted Scheme I to clean the IMDb-Face dataset.

During the cleaning of the IMDb-Face, since multiple identities may co-exist on the same image, first we annotated gallery images to make sure the queried identity. The gallery images come from the official gallery provided by the IMDb website, which most of these official gallery images contain the true identity. We ask volunteers to look through the 10 gallery images back and forth and draw bounding box of the face that occurs most frequently. Then, annotators label the rest of the queried images guided by the three largest labeled faces as galleries. For identities having fewer than three gallery images, their queried images may have too much noise. To save labor, we did not annotate their images.

It took 50 annotators one month to clean the IMDb-Face dataset. Finally, we obtained 1.7M clean facial images from 2M raw images. We believe that the cleaning is of high quality. We estimate the noise level of IMBb-Face as the product of approximated noise level in the IMDb raw data ($2.7 \pm 4.5\%$) and the false positive rate (8.7%) of Scheme I. The noise level is controlled under 2%. The quality of IMDb-Face is validated in our experiments.

4   Experiments

We divide our experiments into a few sections. First, we conduct ablation studies by simulating noise on our proposed dataset. The studies help us to observe the deterioration of performance in the presence of increasing noise, or when a fixed amount of clean data is diluted with noise. Second, we perform experiments on two existing datasets to further demonstrate the effect of noise. Third, we examine the effectiveness of our dataset by comparing it to other datasets with the same training condition. Finally, we compare the model trained on our dataset with other state-of-the-arts. Next, we describe the experimental setting.

Evaluation Metric: We report rank-1 identification accuracy on the Megaface benchmark [8]. It is a very challenging task to evaluate the performance of face recognition methods at the million scale of distractors. The MegaFace benchmark consists of one gallery set and one probe set. The gallery set contains more than 1 million images and the probe set consists of two existing datasets: Facescrub [14] and FGNet. We use Facescrub [14] as MegaFace probe dataset in our experiments. We also test LFW [7] and YTF [24] in Sect. 4.4.

Architecture: To better examine the effect of noise, we use the same architecture in all experiments. After a comparison among ResNet-50, ResNet-101 and Attention-56 [22], we finally choose Attention-56 that achieves a good balance between computation and accuracy. As a reference, the model converges on a database with 80 h on an 8-GPU server with a batch-size of 256. The output of Attention-56 is a 256-dimensional feature for each input image. We use cosine similarity to compute scores between image pairs.

Pre-processing: We cropped and aligned faces, then rigidly transferred them onto a mean shape. Then we resized the cropped image into 224 × 256, and subtracted them with the mean value in each RGB channel.

Loss: We apply three losses: SoftMax [20], Center Loss [23] and A-Softmax [12]. Our implementation is based on the public implementation of these losses:

Softmax: Softmax loss is the most commonly used loss, either for model initialization or establishing a baseline.

Center Loss: Wen *et al.* [23] propose center loss, which minimizes the intra-class distance to enhance features' discriminative power. The authors jointly trained CNN with the center loss and the softmax loss.

A-Softmax: Liu *et al.* [12] formulate A-Softmax to explicitly enforce the angle margin between different identities. The weight vector of each category was restricted on a hypersphere.

4.1   Investigating the Effect of Noise on IMDb-Face

The proposed IMDb-Face dataset enables us to investigate the effect of noise. There are two common types of noise in large-scale face recognition datasets: (1) *label flips:* example has erroneously been given the label of another class within the dataset (2) *outliers:* image does not belong to any of the classes under consideration, but mistakenly has one of their labels. Sometimes even non-faces may be mistakenly included. To simulate the first type of noise, we randomly perturb faces into incorrect categories. For the second type, we randomly replace faces in IMDb-Face with images from MegaFace.

Here we perform two experiments: (1) We gradually contaminate our dataset with different types of noise. We gradually increase the noise in our dataset by 10%, 20% and 50%. (2) We fix the size of clean data and 'dilute' it with label flips. We do not use ensemble models in these experiments.

Figure 7(a) and (b) summarize the results of our first experiment. (1) Label flips severely deteriorate the performance of a model, more so than outliers. (2) A-Softmax, which used to achieve a better result on a clean dataset, becomes worse than Center loss and Softmax in the high-noise region. (3) Outliers seem to have a less abrupt effect on the performance across all losses, matching the observation in [10] and [17].

The second experiment was inspired by a recent work from Rolnick *et al.* [17]. They found that if a dataset contains sufficient clean data, a deep learning

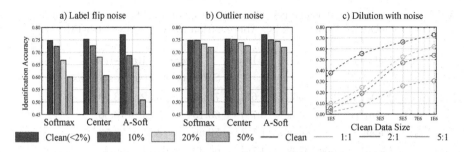

Fig. 7. 1:1M rank-1 identification results on MegaFace benchmark: (a) introducing label flips to IMDb-Face, (b) introducing outliers to IMDb-Face, and (c) fixing the size of clean data and dilute it with different ratios of label flips.

model can still be properly trained on it when the data is diluted by a large amount of noise. They show that a model can still achieve a feasible accuracy on CIFAR-10, even the ratio of noise to clean data is increased to 20:1. Can we transfer their conclusion to face recognition? Here we sample four subsets from IMDb-Face with $1E5$, $2E5$, $5E5$ and $1E6$ images. And we dilute them with an equal number, double, and five times of label flip noise. Figure 7(c) shows that a large performance gap still exists against the completely clean baseline, even we maintain the same number of clean data. We conjecture two reasons that cleanliness of data still plays a key role in face recognition: (1) current dataset, even it is clean, still far from sufficient to address the challenging face recognition problem thus noise matters. (2) Noise is more lethal on a 10,000-class problem than on a 10-class problem.

4.2   The Effect of Noise on MegaFace and MS-Celeb-1M

To further demonstrate the effect of noise, we perform experiments on two public datasets: MegaFace and MS-Celeb-1M. In order to quantify the effect of noise on the face recognition, we sampled subsets from the two datasets and manually cleaned them. This provides us with a noisy sampled subset and a clean subset for each dataset. For a fair comparison, the noisy subset was sampled to have the same distribution of image numbers to identities as the original dataset. Also, we control the scale of noisy subsets to make sure the scales for each clean subset are nearly the same. Because of the large size of the sampled subsets, we have chosen the third labeling method mentioned in Sect. 3.3, which is the fastest.

Three different losses, namely, SoftMax, Center Loss and A-Softmax, are respectively applied to the original datasets, sampled, and cleaned subsets. Table 2 summarizes the results on the MegaFace recognition challenge [8]. The effect of clean datasets is tremendous. By comparing the results between cleaned datasets and sampled datasets, the average improvement of accuracy is as large as 4.14%. The accuracies on clean subsets even surpass those on raw datasets, which are 4 times larger on average. The results suggest the effectiveness of

Table 2. Noisy data vs. Clean data. The results are obtained from rank-1 identification test on the MegaFace benchmark [8]. Abbreviation MSV1 = MS-Celeb-1M(v1).

Dataset	#Iden.	#Imgs.	MegaFace Rank-1(%)		
			Softmax	Center	A-softmax
MSV1-raw	96k	8.6M	71.70	73.82	73.99
-sampled	46k	3.7M	66.15	69.81	70.56
-clean	46k	1.76M	70.66	73.15	73.53
MegaFace-raw	670k	4.7M	64.32	64.71	66.95
-sampled	270k	2.7M	59.68	62.55	63.12
-clean	270k	1.5M	62.86	67.64	68.88

reducing noise for large-scale datasets. As the mater of fact, the result of this experiment is part of our motivation to collect IMDb-Face dataset.

It is worth pointing out that recent metric learning based methods such as A-Softmax [12] and Center-loss [23] also benefit from learning on clean datasets, although they already perform much better than Softmax [20]. As shown in Table 2, the improvements of accuracy on MegaFace using A-Softmax and Center-loss are over 5%. The results suggest that reducing dataset noise is still helpful, especially when metric learning is performed. Reducing noisy samples could help an algorithm focuses more on hard examples learning, rather than picking up meaningless noises.

4.3   Comparing IMDb-Face with Other Face Datasets

In the third experiment, we wish to show the competitiveness of IMDb-Face against several well-established face recognition training datasets including: (1) CelebFaces [19,20], (2) CASIA-WebFace [25], (3) MS-Celeb-1M(v1) [5], and (4) MegaFace [13]. The data size of the two latter datasets is a few times larger than the proposed IMDb-Face. Note that MS-Celeb-1M has a larger subset(v2), containing 900,000 identities. Limited by our computational resources we did not conduct experiments on it. We do not use ensemble models in this experiment. Table 3 summarizes the results of using different datasets as the training source across three losses. We observed that the proposed noise-controlled IMDb-Face dataset is competitive as a training source despite its smaller size, validating the effectiveness of the IMDb data source and the cleanliness of IMDb-Face.

4.4   Comparisons with State-of-the-Arts

We are interested to compare the performance of model trained on IMDb-Face with state-of-the-arts. Evaluation is conducted on MegaFace [8], LFW [7], and YTF [24] following the standard protocol. For LFW [7] we compute equals error rate (EER). For YTF [24] we report accuracy for recognition. To highlight the effect of training data, we do not adopt model ensemble. The comparative results

Table 3. Comparative results on using different face recognition datasets for training. Rank-1 identification accuracy on MegaFace benchmark is reported.

Dataset	#Iden.	#Imgs.	Rank-1 (%)		
			Softmax	Center Loss	A-Softmax
CelebFaces	10k	0.20M	36.15	42.54	43.72
CASIA-WebFace	10.5k	0.49M	65.17	68.09	70.89
MS-Celeb-1M(V1)	96k	8.6M	71.70	73.82	73.99
MegaFace	670k	4.7M	64.32	64.71	66.95
IMDbFace	59k	1.7M	**74.75**	**79.41**	**84.06**

Table 4. Comparisons with state-of-the-arts methods on LFW, MegaFace and YTF benchmarks.

Method, Dataset	LFW	Mega (Ident.)	YTF
Vocord-deep V3[†], Private	-	**91.76**	-
YouTu Lab[†], Private	-	83.29	-
DeepSense V2[†], Private	-	81.23	-
Marginal Loss[♯] [4] MS-Celeb-1M	99.48	80.278	95.98
SphereFace [12],CASIA-WebFace	99.42	75.77	95.00
Center Loss [23],CASIA-WebFace	99.28	65.24	94.90
A-Softmax[♯], MS-Celeb-1M	99.58	73.99	97.45
A-Softmax[♯], IMDb-Face	**99.79**	**84.06**	**97.67**

† Commercial, have not been published
♯ Single Model

are shown in Table 4. Our single model trained on IMDb-Face (A-Softmax[♯], IMDb-Face) achieves a state-of-the-art performance on LFW, MegaFace, and YTF against published methods. It is noteworthy that the performance of our final model is also comparable to a few private methods on MegaFace.

5   Conclusion

Beyond existing efforts of developing sophisticated losses and CNN architectures, our study has investigated the problem of face recognition from the data perspective. Specifically, we developed an understanding of the source of label noise and its consequences. We also collected a new large-scale data from IMDb website, which is naturally a cleaner and wilder source than search engines. Through user studies, we have discovered an effective yet accurate way to clean our data. Extensive experiments have demonstrated that both data source and cleaning effectively improve the accuracy of face recognition. As a result of our study, we have presented a noise-controlled IMDb-Face dataset, and a state-of-the-art model trained on it. A clean dataset is important as the face recognition community has been looking for large-scale clean datasets for two practical reasons: (1) to better study the training performance of contemporary deep networks as a function of noise level in data. Without a clean dataset, one cannot induce controllable noise to support a systematic study. (2) to benchmark large-scale automatic data cleaning methods. Although one can use the final performance of a deep network as a yardstick, this measure can be affected by many uncontrollable factors, *e.g.*, network hyperparameters setting. A clean and large-scale dataset enables unbiased analysis.

References

1. Cao, K., Rong, Y., Li, C., Tang, X., Loy, C.C.: Pose-robust face recognition via deep residual equivariant mapping. In: CVPR (2018)
2. Chen, X., Shrivastava, A., Gupta, A.: Enriching visual knowledge bases via object discovery and segmentation. In: CVPR (2014)
3. Deng, J., Dong, W., Socher, R., Li, L.J., Li, K., Fei-Fei, L.: ImageNet: a large-scale hierarchical image database. In: CVPR (2009)
4. Deng, J., Zhou, Y., Zafeiriou, S.: Marginal loss for deep face recognition. In: CVPRW (2017)
5. Guo, Y., Zhang, L., Hu, Y., He, X., Gao, J.: MS-Celeb-1M: a dataset and benchmark for large-scale face recognition. In: Leibe, B., Matas, J., Sebe, N., Welling, M. (eds.) ECCV 2016. LNCS, vol. 9907. Springer, Cham (2016). https://doi.org/10.1007/978-3-319-46487-9
6. Huang, C., Li, Y., Loy, C.C., Tang, X.: Deep imbalanced learning for face recognition and attribute prediction. arXiv preprint arXiv:1806.00194 (2018)
7. Huang, G.B., Ramesh, M., Berg, T., Learned-Miller, E.: Labeled faces in the wild: a database for studying face recognition in unconstrained environments. Technical report 07–49, University of Massachusetts, Amherst (2007)
8. Kemelmacher-Shlizerman, I., Seitz, S.M., Miller, D., Brossard, E.: The MegaFace benchmark: 1 million faces for recognition at scale. In: CVPR (2016)
9. Klare, B.F., et al.: Pushing the frontiers of unconstrained face detection and recognition: IARPA Janus benchmark A. In: CVPR (2015)
10. Krause, J., et al.: The unreasonable effectiveness of noisy data for fine-grained recognition. In: Leibe, B., Matas, J., Sebe, N., Welling, M. (eds.) ECCV 2016. LNCS, vol. 9907, pp. 301–320. Springer, Cham (2016). https://doi.org/10.1007/978-3-319-46487-9_19
11. Li, J., et al.: Robust face recognition with deep multi-view representation learning. In: ACMMM (2016)
12. Liu, W., Wen, Y., Yu, Z., Li, M., Raj, B., Song, L.: SphereFace: deep hypersphere embedding for face recognition. In: CVPR (2017)
13. Nech, A., Kemelmacher-Shlizerman, I.: Level playing field for million scale face recognition. In: CVPR (2017)
14. Ng, H.W., Winkler, S.: A data-driven approach to cleaning large face datasets. In: ICIP (2014)
15. Parkhi, O.M., Vedaldi, A., Zisserman, A., et al.: Deep face recognition. In: BMVC (2015)

16. Phillips, P.J., Wechsler, H., Huang, J., Rauss, P.J.: The FERET database and evaluation procedure for face-recognition algorithms. Image Vis. Comput. **16**, 295–306 (1998)
17. Rolnick, D., Veit, A., Belongie, S., Shavit, N.: Deep learning is robust to massive label noise. arXiv preprint arXiv:1705.10694 (2017)
18. Schroff, F., Kalenichenko, D., Philbin, J.: FaceNet: a unified embedding for face recognition and clustering. In: CVPR (2015)
19. Sun, Y., Chen, Y., Wang, X., Tang, X.: Deep learning face representation by joint identification-verification. In: NIPS (2014)
20. Sun, Y., Wang, X., Tang, X.: Deep learning face representation from predicting 10,000 classes. In: CVPR (2014)
21. Taigman, Y., Yang, M., Ranzato, M., Wolf, L.: DeepFace: closing the gap to human-level performance in face verification. In: CVPR (2014)
22. Wang, F., et al.: Residual attention network for image classification. In: CVPR (2017)
23. Wen, Y., Zhang, K., Li, Z., Qiao, Y.: A discriminative feature learning approach for deep face recognition. In: Leibe, B., Matas, J., Sebe, N., Welling, M. (eds.) ECCV 2016. LNCS, vol. 9911, pp. 499–515. Springer, Cham (2016)
24. Wolf, L., Hassner, T., Maoz, I.: Face recognition in unconstrained videos with matched background similarity. In: CVPR (2011)
25. Yi, D., Lei, Z., Liao, S., Li, S.Z.: Learning face representation from scratch. arXiv preprint arXiv:1411.7923 (2014)
26. Zhan, X., Liu, Z., Yan, J., Lin, D., Loy, C.C.: Consensus-driven propagation in massive unlabeled data for face recognition. In: Ferrari, V., et al. (eds.) ECCV 2018, Part IX. LNCS 11213, pp. 576–592. Springer, Cham (2018)

Shape Reconstruction Using Volume Sweeping and Learned Photoconsistency

Vincent Leroy$^{(\boxtimes)}$, Jean-Sébastien Franco, and Edmond Boyer

Univ. Grenoble Alpes, Inria, CNRS, Grenoble INP (Institute of Engineering Univ. Grenoble Alpes), LJK, 38000 Grenoble, France
{vincent.leroy,jean-sebastien.franco,edmond.boyer}@inria.fr

Abstract. The rise of virtual and augmented reality fuels an increased need for content suitable to these new technologies including 3D contents obtained from real scenes. We consider in this paper the problem of 3D shape reconstruction from multi-view RGB images. We investigate the ability of learning-based strategies to effectively benefit the reconstruction of arbitrary shapes with improved precision and robustness. We especially target real life performance capture, containing complex surface details that are difficult to recover with existing approaches. A key step in the multi-view reconstruction pipeline lies in the search for matching features between viewpoints in order to infer depth information. We propose to cast the matching on a 3D receptive field along viewing lines and to learn a multi-view photoconsistency measure for that purpose. The intuition is that deep networks have the ability to learn local photometric configurations in a broad way, even with respect to different orientations along various viewing lines of the same surface point. Our results demonstrate this ability, showing that a CNN, trained on a standard static dataset, can help recover surface details on dynamic scenes that are not perceived by traditional 2D feature based methods. Our evaluation also shows that our solution compares on par to state-of-the-art-reconstruction pipelines on standard evaluation datasets, while yielding significantly better results and generalization with realistic performance capture data.

Keywords: Multi view · Stereo reconstruction
Learned photoconsistency · Performance capture · Volume sweeping

1 Introduction

In this paper, we examine the problem of multi-view shape reconstruction of real-life performance sequences, in other words with realistic clothing, motions, and corresponding capture set assumptions. 3D reconstruction is a popular and mature field with numerous applications related to the ability to record and replay 3D dynamic scenes, as with for instance the growing domain of virtual and augmented reality. An essential and still improvable aspect in this matter,

© Springer Nature Switzerland AG 2018
V. Ferrari et al. (Eds.): ECCV 2018, LNCS 11213, pp. 796–811, 2018.
https://doi.org/10.1007/978-3-030-01240-3_48

Fig. 1. Challenging scene captured with a passive RGB multi-camera setup [1]. (*left*) one input image, (*center*) reconstructions obtained with classical 2D features [22], (*right*) proposed solution. Our results validate the key improvement of a CNN-learned disparity to MVS for performance capture scenarios. Results particularly improve in noisy, very low contrast and low textured regions such as the arm, the leg or even the black skirt folds, which can be better seen in a brightened version of the picture in Fig. 8.

in particular with performance capture setups, is the fidelity and quality of the recovered shapes, our goal in this work.

Multi-view stereo (MVS) based methods have attained a good level of quality with pipelines that typically comprise feature extraction, matching stages and 3D shape inference. Interestingly, very recent works have re-examined stereo and MVS by introducing features and similarity functions automatically inferred using deep learning. The main promise of this type of method, is to include better data-driven priors, either in 2D [24,39–41] as improvement over classic 2D features, or in 3D to account for relative view placement and local or global shape priors [5,17,18]. These novel MVS methods have been tested on static scene benchmarks with promising results, offering the prospect of outperforming standard feature pipelines thanks to these data-aware feature measures.

Our main goal is to examine whether these improvements transfer to the more general and complex case of live performance capture, where a diverse set of additional difficulties arise. Typical challenges for these capture situations include smaller visual projection areas of objects of interest due to wider necessary fields of view for capturing motion; occlusion and self-occlusion of several subjects interacting together; lack of texture content typical of real-life subject appearance and clothing; or motion blur with fast moving subjects such as sport action scenes (see Fig. 7). To the best of our knowledge, existing learning-based MVS schemes report results on static datasets such as DTU [16] or ShapeNet [4] but have not yet been demonstrated on performance capture data with the aforementioned typical issues.

With the aim to generalize to this type of data we propose a novel framework that takes advantage of recent learning methods while keeping the precision advantage of a per view depth map extraction, as applied in many successful MVS algorithms [28]. Our approach performs multi-view matching within local volumetric units of inference. Contrary to previous methods, our volumetric unit is defined in a given view's own reference, so as to capture camera inherent 3D dependencies, specifically for the purpose of per-view decision. Instead of inferring occupancies, we infer disparity scores to ease training and to focus the method more on photometric configurations than local shape patterns. We sweep viewing rays with this volumetric receptive field, a process we coin *volume sweeping*, and embed the algorithm in a multi-view depth-map extraction and fusion pipeline followed by a geometric surface reconstruction. With this strategy, we are able to validate that CNN-based MVS outperforms classical MVS approaches in dynamic performance scenarios. We obtain high precision geometric results on complex sequences, outperforming both existing CNN-based and classic non-learning methods. We verify this improvement on available benchmarks with static objects. These results on diverse data situations are obtained using only a DTU subset as training data, which evidences the generalization capabilities of our network.

2   Related Work

Multi-view stereo reconstruction is a longstanding active vision problem [32]. Initially applied on static scenes, the extension to performance capture of dynamic scenes has become increasingly popular. Stereo and MVS-based approaches are a modality of choice for high fidelity capture applications [12,13,16,27,29,31,34], possibly complementing other strategies such as depth-based reconstruction [6, 10,15,28] by addressing shortcomings that include limited range, sensitivity to high contrast lighting, and interference when increasing the number of viewpoints.

While considering various shape representations, for instance point clouds [12], fused depth maps [25], meshes [21,33], or volumetric discretizations [8,20,38], most MVS methods infer 3D shape information by relying on the photoconsistency principle that rays observing the same scene point should convey similar photometric information.

In its simplest form, such similarity can be measured by considering projected color variances among views, as used in early works [20] with limited robustness. In stereo and short baseline situations, simple normalized forms of 2D window correlation are sufficient to characterize similarity under simple lighting and contrast changes, using *e.g.,* ZNCC, SSD, SHD. For broader geometric and photometric resilience, various features based on scale-invariant gradient characterizations [2,23,26] have been designed, some specialized for the dense matching required for the MVS problem [36]. More recently, image features have been successfully applied to moving sequences in *e.g.,* [22,27]. Generally, MVS methods characterize photoconsistency either with a symmetric, viewpoint agnostic, combination of all pairwise similarities [30], or with a per image depth map determination through sweeping strategies [7,25]. Our approach employs also a sweeping strategy, which proves generally simpler and still significantly more robust to occlusion than view-agnostic methods, an issue that quite often occurs in practice with multiple moving shapes or through limb self-occlusion.

While classic MVS approaches have been generally successful, recent works aimed at learning stereo photoconsistency have underlined that additional priors and more subtle variability co-dependencies are still discoverable in real world data. Several works leverage this by learning how to match 2D patch pairs for short baseline stereo, letting deep networks infer what features are relevant [24, 39–41]. Very recent works extend this principle to wide baseline MVS, with symmetric combination of 2D learned features [14].

The common limitation of such methods with 2D receptive fields is the difficulty to correctly capture 3D correlations with hence both false positive and false negative correlations arising from the 2D projection. Consequently, a number of learned MVS methods resort to full volumetric 3D receptive fields instead, to broaden the capability to any form of data 3D correlation [5,17,18]. While casting correlations in 3D as well, our approach proposes several key differences: our volumetric receptive field is a back-projected image region, similar to some binocular stereo [19] or image-based rendering [11] works, where the latter only uses the grid as proxy without explicitly extracting 3D information. This enables a sweeping search strategy along viewing rays, which proves a robust search strategy as plane sweeping in stereo reconstruction. This scheme also avoids decorrelating camera resolution and 3D receptive field resolution, as with *e.g.,* voxels, the volumetric receptive field being defined as a backprojection along pixel rays. Additionally, this volumetric receptive field learns local pairwise correlations, a lower level and easier task than learning occupancy grid patterns. Our evaluation on practical performance capture scenes, beyond traditional static datasets, validates the benefit of such a learning strategy over traditional approaches.

3   Method Overview

As for many recent multi-view stereo reconstruction methods, ours estimates per camera depth maps, followed by depth fusion, allowing therefore each camera to provide local details on the observed surface with local estimations. We take this strategy a step further by replacing the traditional photoconsistency measure used to estimate depths with a learned version. This version is based on CNNs and exploits their ability to learn local photometric configurations near surfaces observed from multiple viewpoints. As depicted in Fig. 2, our approach takes as input a set of calibrated images and outputs a 3D mesh obtained by fusing depth maps. Depths along pixel viewing rays are obtained using a volume sweeping strategy that samples multi-view photoconsistency along rays and identifies the maxima. For a point along a viewing ray, the photoconsistency is estimated using a discretized 3D volumetric patch around that point. In such a 3D patch, at each point within, color information from the primary camera ray incident to that point is paired to the color information of the incident ray of another camera.

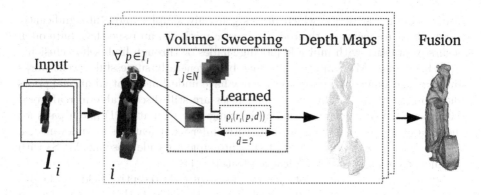

Fig. 2. Method pipeline and notations.

We collect these paired color volumes for every other camera than the primary. A trained CNN is used to recognize the photoconsistent configurations given pairs of color samples within the 3D patch. The key aspects of this strategy are:

- The per camera approach, which, by construction, samples the photoconsistency at a given location as captured and thus enables more local details to be revealed compared to global approaches, as shown in Fig. 8.
- The 3D receptive field for the photoconsistency evaluation, which resolves some 2D projection ambiguities that hindered 2D based strategies.
- The learning based strategy using a convolutional neural network, which outperforms traditional photometric features when evaluating the photoconsistency in dynamic captured scenes, as demonstrated by our experiments.

The following sections focus on our main contributions, namely the 3D volume sampling and the learning based approach for the photoconsistency evaluation. Note that for the final step, without loss of generality, we use the TSDF to fuse depth information and [22] to get a 3D mesh from the fused depths.

4   Depth Map Estimation by Volume Sweeping

Our reconstruction approach takes as input N images $\{I_i\}_{i=1}^N$, along with their projection operators $\{\pi_i\}_{i=1}^N$, and computes depth maps, for the input images, that are subsequently fused into a 3D implicit form. This section explains how these maps are estimated. Given a pixel p in an input image i, the problem is therefore to find the depth d along its viewing ray of its intersection with the observed surface. The point along the ray of pixel p at depth d is noted $r_i(p, d)$. Our approach searches along viewing rays using a likelihood function for a point to be on the surface given the input color pairs in the evaluation volume. In contrast to traditional methods that consider hand-crafted photoconsistency measures, we learn this function from multiview datasets with ground-truth surfaces. To this purpose we build a convolutional neural network which, given a reference camera i and a query point $x \in \mathbb{R}^3$, maps a local volume of color pair samples around x to a scalar photoconsistency score $\rho_i(x) \in [0 \ldots 1]$. The photoconsistency score accounts in practice for color information from camera i at native resolution, and for other camera colors and their relative orientation implicitly encoded in the volume color pair construction. These important features allow our method to adapt to specific ray incidences. Its intentionally asymmetric nature also allows subsequent inferences to automatically build visibility decisions, e.g., deciding for occlusion when the primary camera i's color is not confirmed by other view's colors. This would not have been possible with a symmetric function such as [14].

We thus cast the photoconsistency estimation as a binary classification problem from these color pairs around x, with respect to the reference image i and the other images. In the following, we first provide details about the 3D sampling regions before describing the CNN architecture used for the classification and its training. We then explain the volume sweeping strategy that is subsequently applied to find depths along rays.

4.1   Volume Sampling

In order to estimate photoconsistency along a viewing ray, a 3D sampling region is moved along that ray at regular distances. Within this region, pairs of colors backprojected from the images are sampled. Each pair contains a color from the reference image and its corresponding color in another image. Samples within the 3D region are taken at regular depths along viewing rays in the reference image (see Fig. 3). The corresponding volume is a truncated pyramid that projects onto a 2D region of constant and given dimension in the reference image. This allows the 3D sampling to adapt to the camera perception properties, e.g., resolution and focal length.

More precisely, consider the back-projection $r_i(p, d)$ at depth d of pixel p from the reference image i. The k^3 input sample grid used to compare pairs of colors from images $\{i, j\}_{j \neq i}$ is then the set of back-projected pixels in a k^2 window centered on p, regularly sampled from depth $d - k\lambda/2$ to $d + k\lambda/2$, with λ chosen s.t. spacing in the depth direction is equal to inter-pixel distance from the reference camera at that depth. Every sample contains the reference color of the originating pixel in image i and the color of the point projected on camera j.

Volume sampling is always performed with the same orientation and ordering with respect to the reference camera. Convolutions are thus consistently oriented relative to the camera depth direction.

Volume Size. In our experiments and with no loss of generality, $k = 8$. Our strategy is to learn pairwise photoconsistent configurations along rays, in order to detect the surface presence. This is in contrast with previous works that try to infer directly shape within regular voxel grids, e.g., [17] with 32^3 or 64^3 grids. By considering the surface detection problem alone, and letting the subsequent step of fusion integrate depth in a robust and consistent way, we simplify the problem and require little spatial coherence, hence allowing for small grids.

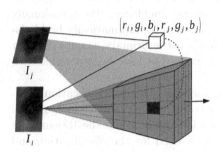

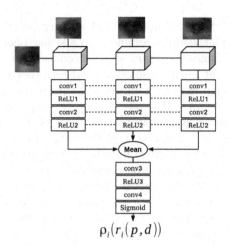

Fig. 3. The 3D volume used to estimate photoconsistency along rays from the reference image i. k^3 samples within the volume are regularly distributed along viewing rays and contain color pairs as back-projected from images i and j. At a given depth along a ray from i each image $j \neq i$ defines a pairwise comparison volume.

Fig. 4. CNN architecture. Each cube is a pairwise comparison volume with k^3 samples that contain 6 valued vectors of RGB pairs and over which 3D convolutions are applied. The output score $\rho_i(r_i(p,d)) \in [0 \dots 1]$ encodes the photoconsistency at depth d along the ray from pixel p in image i.

4.2 Multi-view Neural Network

As explained in the previous section, at a given point x along a viewing ray we are given $N-1$ volumes colored by pairs of views, i.e., $(N-1) \times k^3$ pairs of colors, and we want to detect whether the surface is going through x. To this aim, we build siamese encoders similarly to [14], with however 3D volumes instead of 2D patches. Each encoder builds a feature given a pairwise volume. These features are then averaged and fed into a final decision layer. Weight sharing and averaging are chosen to achieve camera order invariance.

The network is depicted in Fig. 4. The inputs are $N-1$ colored volumes of size $k^3 \times 6$ where RGB pairs are concatenated at each sample within the volume. Convolutions are performed in 3D over the 6 valued vectors of RGB pairs. The first layers (encoders) of the network process every volume in parallel, with shared weights. Every encoder is a sequence of two convolutions followed by non-linearities, and max-pooling with stride. Both convolutional layers consist of respectively 16 and 32 filters of kernel $4 \times 4 \times 4$, followed by a Rectified Linear Unit (ReLU) and a max-pooling with kernel $2 \times 2 \times 2$ with stride 2. We then average the obtained $2 \times 2 \times 2 \times 32$ features and feed the result to a 128 filter $1 \times 1 \times 1$ convolutional layer, followed by a ReLU and a final $1 \times 1 \times 1$ decision layer, for a total of $72K$ parameters. The network provides a score $\rho_i(r_i(p,d)) \in [0 \dots 1]$ for the photoconsistency at depth d along the ray from pixel p in image i.

We experimented with this network using different configurations. In particular, instead of averaging pairwise comparison features, we tried max-pooling which did not yield better results. Compared to the volumetric solution proposed by [17], the number of parameters is an order of magnitude less. As mentioned earlier, we believe that photoconsistency is a local property that requires less spatial coherence than shape properties.

4.3 Network Training

The network was implemented using TensorFlow and trained from scratch using the DTU Robot Image Dataset [16], which provides multiview data equipped with *ground-truth* surfaces that present an accuracy up to 0.5 mm. From this dataset 11 million k^3 sample volumes were generated, from which we randomly chose 80% for training, and the remaining part for evaluation. Both positive and negative samples were equally generated by randomly sampling volumes up to 20 cm away from ground truth points, where a volume is considered as positive when it contains at least μ ground truth points. In theory, the network could be trained with any number of camera pairs, however, in practice, we randomly choose from one up to 40 pairs. Training was performed with the binary cross entropy function as loss. Model weights are optimized by performing a Stochastic Gradient Descent, using Adaptive Moment Estimation on 560,000 iterations with batch size of 50 comparisons, and with a random number of compared cameras (from 2 up to 40). Since our sampling grids are relatively small and camera dependent, we are able to generate enough sample variability for training, without the need for data augmentation.

4.4 Volume Sweeping

In order to estimate the depth along viewing rays, our volumetric solution is integrated in an existing standard plane sweeping algorithm, replacing the plane with a volume and computing the N-way photoconsistency score using our network. For every camera, we sample therefore along viewing rays, test possible depth values, and choose the most photoconsistent candidate with respect to the network score. In practice, a reference view i is only compared to the cameras such that $\cos(\theta_{ij}) > 0.5$, where θ_{ij} is the angle between the optical axes of camera i and j. Then, we sample rays from camera i through every pixel p and build colored volumes at every candidate depth. We define the estimated depth d_i^p as:

$$d_i^p = \operatorname*{argmax}_{d \in [d_{min}, d_{max}]} (\rho_i(r_i(p, d))), \tag{1}$$

where $\rho_i(r_i(p, d))$ is the consistency measure along the ray from p in image i, as estimated by the network, and $[d_{min}, d_{max}]$ defines the range of search that can be limited using for instance the visual hull when available. Depths for all pixels and from all images are further fused using a volumetric truncated signed distance function [9].

5   Results

We perform various evaluations to verify and quantify the benefit of our learned multi-view similarity. First, we study different classifiers performances, with an emphasis on comparing planar or volumetric receptive fields. We next apply our approach in the static case using the [16] benchmark and compare it to state-of-the-art MVS methods, both classic and learning based. Finally, we build experiments to test the main claim of improvement with real life performance data. To this goal we use several captured dynamic sequences which exhibit typical difficulties of such data, with very significant qualitative improvements compared to the state-of-the-art approaches [17], and [22].

5.1   Surface Detection

Surface detection along viewing rays can be formulated as a binary classification problem. In order to assess the benefit of our volumetric strategy, we compare performances of classifiers based on various receptive fields.

1. Deterministic Zero-Mean Normalized Cross Correlation (*ZNCC*): ZNCC is applied over the samples within the volumetric receptive field.
2. Learning (CNN) with a planar receptive field: a planar equivalent of our volumetric solution, with the same architecture and number of weights, in a fronto-facing plane sweeping fashion.
3. Learning (CNN) with a volumetric receptive field: our solution described in the previous sections.

To speed up computations, we limit the search along a viewing ray to 5 mm around a coarse depth estimation based on image descriptors [35]. Depths are sampled every 0.5 mm. As a post processing step, we simply add a soft bilateral filter, similarly to [14], accounting for color, spatial neighborhood, and probability of the detection. Figure 5 shows, with the classifiers' ROC curves, that the most accurate results are obtained with a volumetric receptive field and learning. Intuitively, a volumetric sampling region better accounts for the local non-planar geometry of the surface than planar sampling regions. This graph also emphasizes the significantly higher discriminative ability of learned correlations compared to deterministic ones.

We also evaluate the robustness to baseline variability by testing classification with more further apart cameras. Table 2 shows the accuracy of the classifiers with a varying number of cameras and for the optimal threshold values in Fig. 5. As already noticed in the litterature, *e.g.,* [12,29], a planar receptive field gives better results with a narrow baseline and the accuracy consistently decreases when the inter-camera space grows with additional cameras. In contrast the classifier based on a volumetric receptive field exhibits more robustness to the variety in the camera baselines. This appears to be an advantage with large multi-camera setup as it enables more cameras to contribute and hence reduces occlusion issues.

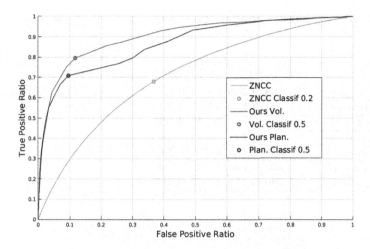

Fig. 5. ROC Curves of three different classifiers, ZNCC, planar and volumetric receptive fields, on the DTU Dataset [16]. Circles represent thresholds that optimize sensitivity + specificity with the values 0.2, 0.5 and 0.5 respectively.

5.2   Quantitative Evaluation

In this section, we compare our solution to various state-of-the-art methods using the DTU Robot Image Dataset [16]. We use the standard accuracy and completeness metrics to quantify the quality of the estimated surface. We compare to Furukawa et al. [12], Campbell et al. [3] and Tola et al. [36], as well as to additional learning-based results from Ji et al. [17] and Hartmann et al. [14]. To conduct a fair comparison with [14], which is a patch based approach building a depthmap with a network comparable to ours, we use the result of our volume sweeping approach on only one depth map.

Reconstructions results are depicted in Table 1. We obtain quality on par with other methods, with a median accuracy and completeness in the range of the ground truth accuracy that we measured around 0.5 mm. It should be noticed that the best accuracy is obtained by Tola et al. [37] which tend to favor accuracy over completeness whereas Campbell et al. [3], in a symetric manner, tend to favor completeness over accuracy. We obtain more balanced results on the 2 criteria, similarly to the widely used approach by Furukawa et al. [12], with however better performances. We also outperform the recent learning based method Surfacenet [17] on most measures in this experiment.

Compared to Hartmann et al. [14], and under similar experimental conditions, our approach obtains better results with 2 orders of magnitude less parameters, thereby confirming the benefit of volumetric receptive fields over planar ones. Compared to Surfacenet [17] (cube size 64 × 64 × 64, sample step 0.4 mm) we obtain reconstructions of slightly better quality with an order of magnitude less parameters.

Table 1. Reconstruction accuracy and completeness (in mm).

Measure	Acc.		Compl.	
	Mean	Med.	Mean	Med.
Tola et al. [37]	**0.448**	**0.205**	0.754	0.425
Furukawa et al. [12]	0.678	0.325	0.597	0.375
Campbell et al. [3]	1.286	0.532	**0.279**	**0.155**
Ji et al. [17]	0.530	0.260	0.892	0.254
Ours (*fused*)	0.490	0.220	0.532	0.296
Hartmann et al. [14]	1.563	0.496	1.540	0.710
Ours (*depthmap*)	**0.599**	**0.272**	**1.037**	**0.387**

Table 2. Classifier accuracy (%).

Camera #	5	20	49
ZNCC	64.98	65.46	65.58
Ours Plan.	80.67	77.87	75.92
Ours Vol.	**82.95**	**84.84**	**83.45**

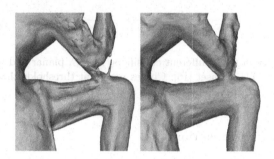

Fig. 6. Close up view of the arm region in Fig. 1. (*Left*) Results from [22], (*right*) our reconstruction

5.3   Qualitative Evaluation and Generalization

One of our main goals is to verify whether a learning based strategy generalizes to the performance capture scenario and how it compares to state-of-the-art deterministic approaches in this case. To this purpose, we perform reconstructions of dynamic RGB sequences captured by a setup largely different from the training one, *i.e.*, a hemispherical setup with 68 cameras of $4M$ resolution with various focal lengths, as provided in [22] along with reconstructions obtained with a deterministic approach. In this scenario, standard MVS assumptions are often violated, *e.g.*, specular surfaces, motion blur and occlusions, challenging therefore the reconstruction methods.

We adapted our volume sweeping algorithm to limit depth search, along viewing rays, inside visual hulls. No other modification was applied, in particular the network previously trained was kept as such without any fine tuning. Figure 1 shows a reconstruction using our method compared to [22], which is a patch based sweeping method using traditional image features and specifically designed for this scenario. Even though [22] performs well in contrasted regions, the patch based descriptors reach their limits in image regions with low contrast or low resolution. Figures 6 and 7 give such examples. They show that our solution helps recover finer surface details, while strongly decreasing noise in low contrast

Fig. 7. (*Top*) input images, (*middle*) result with [22], (*bottom*) result with our method. Motion blur and low contrast are visible in the input images. Best viewed magnified.

regions. The results obtained also demonstrate strong improvements in surface details, such as dress folds, that were undetected by the deterministic approach. In addition, they demonstrate lower levels of noise, particularly in self-occluded regions, and more robustness to motion blur as with the toes or tongue-in-cheek details that appear in Fig. 7-bottom.

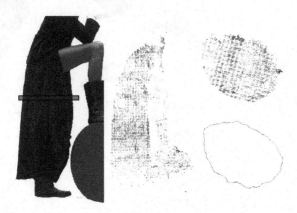

Fig. 8. Qualitative comparison with [17]. (*Left*) input image with the horizontal section in *red*, (*middle*) point cloud with [17], (*right-top*) point cloud horizontal section with [17] (*right-bottom*) point cloud horizontal section with our approach. (Color figure online)

We also compared with a recent learning based approach [17] using the code available online (see Fig. 8). Reconstructions with this approach were limited to a tight bounding box and different values for the volume sampling step were tested. The best results were obtained with a 2 mm step. To conduct a fair comparison with our method, all points falling outside the visual hull were removed from the reconstruction. In this scenario, the point cloud obtained using [17] appeared to be very noisy and incomplete (see Fig. 8-middle), plaguing the subsequent surface extraction step. Figure 8-left also shows a horizontal section of the model in a poorly contrasted image region of the dress. The global strategy used in [17] wrongly reconstruct many surface points inside the shape volume (top figure), as a result of the ambiguous appearance of the dress. In contrast, our approach (bottom figure) correctly identifies surface points by maximizing learned correlations along viewing rays.

The final qualitative experiment studies the impact of a volumetric receptive field compared to the equivalent planar one (see Sect. 5.1) in Fig. 9. The volume allows a sharp reconstruction of finer details of the belt, where a plane cannot handle finer geometry details. A video demonstrating results on dynamic sequences is available online: https://hal.archives-ouvertes.fr/hal-01849286.

Fig. 9. (*Left*) 3 input images, (*middle*) plane based classifier, (*right*) volumetric classifier. The face is highly occluded (*left*) yielding noisier and less accurate reconstructions when using a planar receptive field, whereas the volume counterpart yields smoother and more accurate details.

6   Conclusion

We presented a learning framework for surface reconstruction in passive multi-view scenarios. Our solution consists in a N-view volume sweeping, trained on static scenes from a small scale dataset equipped with ground truth. Thanks to this new model, we validate the improvement of CNN-learned MVS similarity in the case of complex moving sequence captures, with significant challenges typical of these datasets such as low light areas and low texture content and perceived resolution. This result is achieved with an order of magnitude less training parameters than previous comparable learned MVS works, showing significant network generalization from a training performed only on static DTU inputs, and fully leverages the high quality ground truth now available with these datasets. Our method achieved significantly improved detail recovery and noise reduction in complex real life scenarios, outperforming all existing approaches in this case, and consequently offers very interesting prospects for even more challenging capture scenarios or even better ground truth datasets in the future.

Acknowledgements. Funded by France National Research grant ANR-14-CE24-0030 ACHMOV. Images 1-2-6-8 courtesy of Anja Rubik.

References

1. Kinovis INRIA Platform. https://kinovis.inria.fr/inria-platform/
2. Bay, H., Tuytelaars, T., Van Gool, L.: SURF: speeded up robust features. In: Leonardis, A., Bischof, H., Pinz, A. (eds.) ECCV 2006. LNCS, vol. 3951, pp. 404–417. Springer, Heidelberg (2006). https://doi.org/10.1007/11744023_32

3. Campbell, N.D.F., Vogiatzis, G., Hernández, C., Cipolla, R.: Using multiple hypotheses to improve depth-maps for multi-view stereo. In: Forsyth, D., Torr, P., Zisserman, A. (eds.) ECCV 2008. LNCS, vol. 5302, pp. 766–779. Springer, Heidelberg (2008). https://doi.org/10.1007/978-3-540-88682-2_58

4. Chang, A.X., et al.: ShapeNet: an information-rich 3D model repository. Technical report. arXiv:1512.03012 [cs.GR] (2015)

5. Choy, C.B., Xu, D., Gwak, J.Y., Chen, K., Savarese, S.: 3D-R2N2: a unified approach for single and multi-view 3D object reconstruction. In: Leibe, B., Matas, J., Sebe, N., Welling, M. (eds.) ECCV 2016. LNCS, vol. 9912, pp. 628–644. Springer, Cham (2016). https://doi.org/10.1007/978-3-319-46484-8_38

6. Collet, A., et al.: High-quality streamable free-viewpoint video. ACM Trans. Graph. (2015)

7. Collins, R.T.: A space-sweep approach to true multi-image matching. In: CVPR (1996)

8. Cremers, D., Kolev, K.: Multiview stereo and silhouette consistency via convex functionals over convex domains. IEEE Trans. Pattern Anal. Mach. Intell. (2011)

9. Curless, B., Levoy, M.: A volumetric method for building complex models from range images. In: SIGGRAPH (1996)

10. Dou, M., et al.: Fusion4D: real-time performance capture of challenging scenes. ACM Trans. Graph. (2016)

11. Flynn, J., Neulander, I., Philbin, J., Snavely, N.: DeepStereo: learning to predict new views from the world's imagery. In: CVPR (2016)

12. Furukawa, Y., Ponce, J.: Accurate, dense, and robust multi-view stereopsis. In: CVPR (2007)

13. Gall, J., Stoll, C., Aguiar, E.D., Theobalt, C., Rosenhahn, B., Seidel, H.-P.: Motion capture using joint skeleton tracking and surface estimation. In: CVPR (2009)

14. Hartmann, W., Galliani, S., Havlena, M., Van Gool, L., Schindler, K.: Learned multi-patch similarity. In: ICCV (2017)

15. Innmann, M., Zollhöfer, M., Nießner, M., Theobalt, C., Stamminger, M.: VolumeDeform: real-time volumetric non-rigid reconstruction. In: Leibe, B., Matas, J., Sebe, N., Welling, M. (eds.) ECCV 2016. LNCS, vol. 9912, pp. 362–379. Springer, Cham (2016). https://doi.org/10.1007/978-3-319-46484-8_22

16. Jensen, R.R., Dahl, A.L., Vogiatzis, G., Tola, E., Aanæs, H.: Large scale multi-view stereopsis evaluation. In: CVPR (2014)

17. Ji, M., Gall, J., Zheng, H., Liu, Y., Fang, L.: SurfaceNet: an end-to-end 3D neural network for multiview stereopsis. In: ICCV (2017)

18. Kar, A., Häne, C., Malik, J.: Learning a multi-view stereo machine. In: NIPS (2017)

19. Kendall, A., et al.: End-to-end learning of geometry and context for deep stereo regression. In: ICCV (2017)

20. Kutulakos, K.N., Seitz, S.M.: A theory of shape by space carving. IJCV 38, 199–218 (2000)

21. Labatut, P., Pons, J., Keriven, R.: Efficient multi-view reconstruction of large-scale scenes using interest points, delaunay triangulation and graph cuts. In: ICCV (2007)

22. Leroy, V., Franco, J.S., Boyer, E.: Multi-view dynamic shape refinement using local temporal integration. In: ICCV (2017)

23. Lowe, D.G.: Distinctive image features from scale-invariant keypoints. IJCV 60, 91–110 (2004)

24. Luo, W., Schwing, A.G., Urtasun, R.: Efficient deep learning for stereo matching. In: CVPR (2016)

25. Merrell, P., et al.: Real-time visibility-based fusion of depth maps. In: CVPR (2007)
26. Mikolajczyk, K., Schmid, C.: A performance evaluation of local descriptors. In: CVPR (2003)
27. Mustafa, A., Kim, H., Guillemaut, J., Hilton, A.: Temporally coherent 4D reconstruction of complex dynamic scenes. In: CVPR (2016)
28. Newcombe, R.A., Fox, D., Seitz, S.M.: DynamicFusion: reconstruction and tracking of non-rigid scenes in real-time. In: CVPR (2015)
29. Oswald, M.R., Cremers, D.: A convex relaxation approach to space time multi-view 3D reconstruction. In: ICCV Workshop on Dynamic Shape Capture and Analysis (4DMOD) (2013)
30. Pons, J.P., Keriven, R., Faugeras, O.: Multi-view stereo reconstruction and scene flow estimation with a global image-based matching score. IJCV **72**, 179–193 (2007)
31. Schöps, T., et al.: A multi-view stereo benchmark with high-resolution images and multi-camera videos. In: CVPR (2017)
32. Seitz, S.M., Curless, B., Diebel, J., Scharstein, D., Szeliski, R.: A comparison and evaluation of multi-view stereo reconstruction algorithms. In: CVPR (2006)
33. Starck, J., Hilton, A.: Surface capture for performance-based animation. IEEE Comput. Graph. Appl. **27**, 21–31 (2007)
34. Strecha, C., von Hansen, W., Gool, L.V., Fua, P., Thoennessen, U.: On benchmarking camera calibration and multi-view stereo for high resolution imagery. In: CVPR (2008)
35. Tola, E., Lepetit, V., Fua, P.: A fast local descriptor for dense matching. In: CVPR (2008)
36. Tola, E., Lepetit, V., Fua, P.: DAISY: an efficient dense descriptor applied to wide-baseline stereo. IEEE Trans. Pattern Anal. Mach. Intell. **32**, 815–830 (2010)
37. Tola, E., Strecha, C., Fua, P.: Efficient large-scale multi-view stereo for ultra high-resolution image sets. Mach. Vis. Appl. **23**, 903–920 (2012)
38. Ulusoy, A.O., Geiger, A., Black, M.J.: Towards probabilistic volumetric reconstruction using ray potentials. In: 3DV (2015)
39. Ummenhofer, B., et al.: Demon: depth and motion network for learning monocular stereo. In: CVPR (2017)
40. Žbontar, J., LeCun, Y.: Stereo matching by training a convolutional neural network to compare image patches. J. Mach. Learn. Res. **17**, 2287–2318 (2016)
41. Zagoruyko, S., Komodakis, N.: Learning to compare image patches via convolutional neural networks. In: CVPR (2015)

PyramidBox: A Context-Assisted Single Shot Face Detector

Xu Tang◉, Daniel K. Du◉, Zeqiang He◉, and Jingtuo Liu(✉)◉

Baidu Inc., Beijing, China
{tangxu02,hezeqiang,liujingtuo}@baidu.com, daniel.kang.du@gmail.com

Abstract. Face detection has been well studied for many years and one of remaining challenges is to detect small, blurred and partially occluded faces in uncontrolled environment. This paper proposes a novel context-assisted single shot face detector, named *PyramidBox* to handle the hard face detection problem. Observing the importance of the context, we improve the utilization of contextual information in the following three aspects. First, we design a novel context anchor to supervise high-level contextual feature learning by a semi-supervised method, which we call it PyramidAnchors. Second, we propose the Low-level Feature Pyramid Network to combine adequate high-level context semantic feature and Low-level facial feature together, which also allows the Pyramid-Box to predict faces of all scales in a single shot. Third, we introduce a context-sensitive structure to increase the capacity of prediction network to improve the final accuracy of output. In addition, we use the method of Data-anchor-sampling to augment the training samples across different scales, which increases the diversity of training data for smaller faces. By exploiting the value of context, PyramidBox achieves superior performance among the state-of-the-art over the two common face detection benchmarks, FDDB and WIDER FACE. Our code is available in PaddlePaddle: https://github.com/PaddlePaddle/models/tree/develop/fluid/face_detection.

Keywords: Face detection · Context · Single shot · PyramidBox

1 Introduction

Face detection is a fundamental and essential task in various face applications. The breakthrough work by Viola-Jones [1] utilizes AdaBoost algorithm with Haar-Like features to train a cascade of face vs. non-face classifiers. Since that, numerous of subsequent works [2–7] are proposed for improving the cascade

---

X. Tang and D. K. Du—Equal contribution.

Electronic supplementary material The online version of this chapter (https://doi.org/10.1007/978-3-030-01240-3_49) contains supplementary material, which is available to authorized users.

V. Ferrari et al. (Eds.): ECCV 2018, LNCS 11213, pp. 812–828, 2018.
https://doi.org/10.1007/978-3-030-01240-3_49

detectors. Then, [8–10] introduce deformable part models (DPM) into face detection tasks by modeling the relationship of deformable facial parts. These methods are mainly based on designed features which are less representable and trained by separated steps.

With the great breakthrough of convolutional neural networks(CNN), a lot of progress for face detection has been made in recent years due to utilizing modern CNN-based object detectors, including R-CNN [11–14], SSD [15], YOLO [16], FocalLoss [17] and their extensions [18]. Benefiting from the powerful deep learning approach and end-to-end optimization, the CNN-based face detectors have achieved much better performance and provided a new baseline for later methods.

Recent anchor-based detection frameworks aim at detecting hard faces in uncontrolled environment such as WIDER FACE [19]. SSH [20] and S^3FD [21] develop scale-invariant networks to detect faces with different scales from different layers in a single network. Face R-FCN [22] re-weights embedding responses on score maps and eliminates the effect of non-uniformed contribution in each facial part using a position-sensitive average pooling. FAN [23] proposes an anchor-level attention by highlighting the features from the face region to detect the occluded faces.

Though these works give an effective way to design anchors and related networks to detect faces with different scales, how to use the contextual information in face detection has not been paid enough attention, which should play a significant role in detection of hard faces. Actually, as shown in Fig. 1, it is clear that faces never occur isolated in the real world, usually with shoulders or bodies, providing a rich source of contextual associations to be exploited especially when the facial texture is not distinguishable for the sake of low-resolution, blur and occlusion. We address this issue by introducing a novel framework of context assisted network to make full use of contextual signals as the following steps.

Fig. 1. Hard faces are difficult to be located and classified due to the lack of visual consistency, while the larger regions which give hints to the position of face are easier to be located and classified, such as head and body.

Firstly, the network should be able to learn features for not only faces, but also contextual parts such as heads and bodies. To achieve this goal, extra labels are needed and the anchors matched to these parts should be designed. In this work, we use a semi-supervised solution to generate approximate labels for contextual parts related to faces and a series of anchors called PyramidAnchors are invented to be easily added to general anchor-based architectures.

Secondly, high-level contextual features should be adequately combined with the low-level ones. The appearances of hard and easy faces can be quite different, which implies that not all high-level semantic features are really helpful to smaller targets. We investigate the performance of Feature Pyramid Networks (FPN) [24] and modify it into a *Low-level Feature Pyramid Network (LFPN)* to join mutually helpful features together.

Thirdly, the predict branch network should make full use of the joint feature. We introduce the *Context-sensitive prediction module (CPM)* to incorporate context information around the target face with a wider and deeper network. Meanwhile, we propose a max-in-out layer for the prediction module to further improve the capability of classification network.

In addition, we propose a training strategy named as *Data-anchor-sampling* to make an adjustment on the distribution of the training dataset. In order to learn more representable features, the diversity of hard-set samples is important and can be gained by data augmentation across samples.

For clarity, the main contributions of this work can be summarized as five-fold:

1. We propose an anchor-based context assisted method, called PyramidAnchors, to introduce supervised information on learning contextual features for small, blurred and partially occluded faces.
2. We design the Low-level Feature Pyramid Networks (LFPN) to merge contextual features and facial features better. Meanwhile, the proposed method can handle faces with different scales well in a single shot.
3. We introduce a context-sensitive prediction module, consisting of a mixed network structure and max-in-out layer to learn accurate location and classification from the merged features.
4. We propose the scale aware Data-anchor-sampling strategy to change the distribution of training samples to put emphasis on smaller faces.
5. We achieve superior performance over state-of-the-art on the common face detection benchmarks FDDB and WIDER FACE.

The rest of the paper is organized as follows. Section 2 provides an overview of the related works. Section 3 introduces the proposed method. Section 4 presents the experiments and Sect. 5 concludes the paper.

2 Related Work

Anchor-Based Face Detectors. Anchor was first proposed by Faster R-CNN [14], and then it was widely used in both two-stage and one single shot object detectors. Then anchor-based object detectors [15, 16] have achieved remarkable progress in recent years. Similar to FPN [24], Lin [17] uses translation-invariant anchor boxes, and Zhang [21] designs scales of anchors to ensure that the detector can handle various scales of faces well. FaceBoxes [25] introduces anchor densification to ensure different types of anchors have the same density on the image. S^3FD [21] proposed anchor matching strategy to improve the recall rate of tiny faces.

Scale-Invariant Face Detectors. To improve the performance of face detector to handle faces of different scales, many state-of-the-art works [20,21,23,26] construct different structures in the same framework to detect faces with variant size, where the high-level features are designed to detect large faces while low-level features for small faces. In order to integrate high-level semantic feature into low-level layers with higher resolution, FPN [24] proposed a top-down architecture to use high-level semantic feature maps at all scales. Recently, FPN-style framework achieves great performance on both objection detection [17] and face detection [23].

Context-Associated Face Detectors. Recently, some works show the importance of contextual information for face detection, especially for finding small, blurred and occluded faces. CMS-RCNN [27] used Faster R-CNN in face detection with body contextual information. Hu et al. [28] trained separate detectors for different scales. SSH [20] modeled the context information by large filters on each prediction module. FAN [23] proposed an anchor-level attention, by highlighting the features from the face region, to detect the occluded faces.

3 PyramidBox

This section introduces the context-assisted single shot face detector, *Pyramid-Box*. We first briefly introduce the network architecture in Sect. 3.1. Then we present a context-sensitive prediction module in Sect. 3.2, and propose a novel anchor method, named *PyramidAnchors*, in Sect. 3.3. Finally, Sect. 3.4 presents the associated training methodology including data-anchor-sampling and max-in-out.

3.1 Network Architecture

Anchor-based object detection frameworks with sophisticated design of anchors have been proved effective to handle faces of variable scales when predictions are made at different levels of feature map [14,15,20,21,23]. Meanwhile, FPN structures showed strength on merging high-level features with the lower ones. The architecture of PyramidBox (Fig. 2) uses the same extended VGG16 backbone and anchor scale design as S^3FD [21], which can generate feature maps at different levels and anchors with equal-proportion interval. Low-level FPN is added on this backbone and a Context-sensitive Predict Module is used as a branch network from each pyramid detection layer to get the final output. The key is that we design a novel pyramid anchor method which generates a series of anchors for each face at different levels. The details of each component in the architecture are as follows:

Scale-Equitable Backbone Layers. We use the base convolution layers and extra convolutional layers in S^3FD [21] as our backbone layers, which keep layers

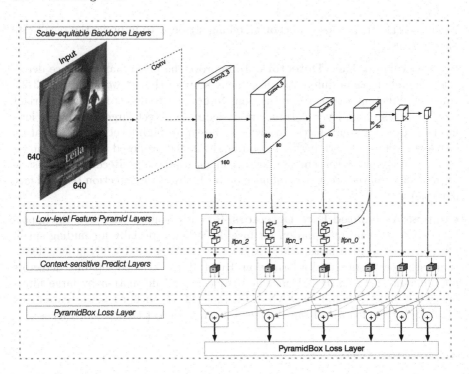

Fig. 2. Architecture of PyramidBox. It consists of **Scale-equitable Backbone Layers**, **Low-level Feature Pyramid Layers (LFPN)**, **Context-sensitive Predict Layers** and **PyramidBox Loss Layer**.

of VGG16 from $conv1\_1$ to $pool5$, then convert $fc6$ and $fc7$ of VGG16 to $conv\_fc$ layers, and then add more convolutional layers to make it deeper.

Low-Level Feature Pyramid Layers. To improve the performance of face detector to handle faces of different scales, the low-level feature with high-resolution plays a key role. Hence, many state-of-the-art works [20,21,23,26] construct different structures in the same framework to detect faces with variant size, where the high-level features are designed to detect large faces while low-level features for small faces. In order to integrate high-level semantic feature into low-level layers with higher resolution, FPN [24] proposed a top-down architecture to use high-level semantic feature maps at all scales. Recently, FPN-style framework achieves great performance on both objection detection [17] and face detection [23].

As we know, all of these works build FPN start from the top layer, which should be argued that not all high-level features are undoubtedly helpful to small faces. First, faces that are small, blurred and occluded have different texture feature from the large, clear and complete ones. So it is rude to directly use all high-level features to enhance the performance on small faces. Second, high-level features are extracted from regions with little face texture and may introduce

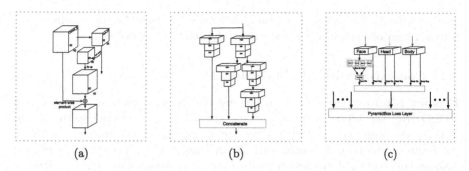

(a)   (b)   (c)

Fig. 3. (a) Feature Pyramid Net. (b) Context-sensitive Prediction Module. (c) PyramidBox Loss.

noise information. For example, in the backbone layers of our PyramidBox, the receptive field [21] of the top two layers $conv7\_2$ and $conv6\_2$ are 724 and 468, respectively. Notice that the input size of training image is 640, which means that the top two layers contain too much noisy context features, so they may not contribute to detecting medium and small faces.

Alternatively, we build the *Low-level Feature Pyramid Network (LFPN)* starting a top-down structure from a middle layer, whose receptive field should be close to the half of the input size, instead of the top layer. Also, the structure of each block of LFPN, as same as FPN [24], one can see Fig. 3(a) for details.

Pyramid Detection Layers. We select $lfpn\_2$, $lfpn\_1$, $lfpn\_0$, $conv\_fc7$, $conv6\_2$ and $conv7\_2$ as detection layers with anchor size of 16, 32, 64, 128, 256 and 512, respectively. Here $lfpn\_2$, $lfpn\_1$ and $lfpn\_0$ are output layer of LFPN based on $conv3\_3$, $conv4\_3$ and $conv5\_3$, respectively. Moreover, similar to other SSD-style methods, we use L2 normalization [29] to rescale the norm of LFPN layers.

Predict Layers. Each detection layer is followed by a *Context-sensitive Predict Module (CPM)*, see Sect. 3.2. Notice that the outputs of CPM are used for supervising pyramid anchors, see Sect. 3.3, which approximately cover face, head and body region in our experiments. The output size of the l-th CPM is $w_l \times h_l \times c_l$, where $w_l = h_l = 640/2^{2+l}$ is the corresponding feature size and the channel size c_l equals to 20 for $l = 0, 1, \ldots, 5$. Here the features of each channels are used for classification and regression of faces, heads and bodies, respectively, in which the classification of face need 4 $(= cp_l + cn_l)$ channels, where cp_l and cn_l are max-in-out of foreground and background label respectively, satisfying

$$cp_l = \begin{cases} 1, & \text{if } l = 0, \\ 3, & \text{otherwise.} \end{cases}$$

Moreover, the classification of both head and body need two channels, while each of face, head and body have four channels to localize.

PyramidBox Loss Layers. For each target face, see in Sect. 3.3, we have a series of pyramid anchors to supervise the task of classification and regression simultaneously. We design a *PyramidBox Loss.* see Sect. 3.4, in which we use softmax loss for classification and smooth L1 loss for regression.

3.2 Context-Sensitive Predict Module

Predict Module. In original anchor-based detectors, such as SSD [15] and YOLO [16], the objective functions are applied to the selected feature maps directly. As proposed in MS-CNN [30], enlarging the sub-network of each task can improve accuracy. Recently, SSH [20] increases the receptive field by placing a wider convolutional prediction module on top of layers with different strides, and DSSD [31] adds residual blocks for each prediction module. Indeed, both SSH and DSSD make the prediction module deeper and wider separately, so that the prediction module get the better feature to classify and localize.

Inspired by the Inception-ResNet [32], it is quite clear that we can jointly enjoy the gain of wider and deeper network. We design the *Context-sensitive Predict Module (CPM)*, see Fig. 3(b), in which we replace the convolution layers of context module in SSH by the residual-free prediction module of DSSD. This would allow our CPM to reap all the benefits of the DSSD module approach while remaining rich contextual information from SSH context module.

Max-in-Out. The conception of Maxout was first proposed by Goodfellow et al. [33]. Recently, S^3FD [21] applied max-out background label to reduce the false positive rate of small negatives. In this work, we use this strategy on both positive and negative samples. Denote it as max-in-out, see Fig. 3(c). We first predict $c_p + c_n$ scores for each prediction module, and then select max c_p as the positive score. Similarly, we choose the max score of c_n to be the negative score. In our experiment, we set $c_p = 1$ and $c_n = 3$ for the first prediction module since that small anchors have more complicated background [25], while $c_p = 3$ and $c_n = 1$ for other prediction modules to recall more faces.

3.3 PyramidAnchors

Recently anchor-based object detectors [15–17,24] and face detectors [21,25] have achieved remarkable progress. It has been proved that balanced anchors for each scale are necessary to detect small faces [21]. But it still ignored the context feature at each scale because the anchors are all designed for face regions. To address this problem, we propose a novel alternatively anchor method, named *PyramidAnchors*.

For each target face, PyramidAnchors generate a series of anchors corresponding to larger regions related to a face that contains more contextual information, such as head, shoulder and body. We choose the layers to set such anchors by matching the region size to the anchor size, which will supervise higher-level layers to learn more representable features for lower-level scale faces. Given extra labels of head, shoulder or body, we can accurately match the anchors to ground truth to generate the loss. As it's unfair to add additional labels, we implement it in a semi-supervised way under the assumption that

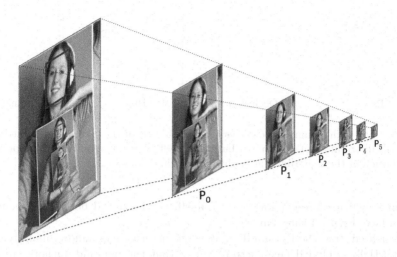

Fig. 4. Illustration of PyramidAnchors. For example, the largest purple face with size of 128 have pyramid-anchors at P_3, P_4 and P_5, where P_3 are anchors generated from $conv\_fc7$ labeled by the face-self, P_4 are anchors generated from $conv6\_2$ labeled by the head (of size about 256) of the target face, and P_5 are anchors generated from $conv7\_2$ labeled by the body (of size about 512) of the target face. Similarly, to detect the smallest cyan face with the size of 16, one can get a supervised feature from pyramid-anchors on P_0 which labeled by the original face, pyramid-anchors on P_1 which labeled by the corresponding head with size of 32, and pyramid-anchors on P_2 labeled by the corresponding body with size of 64.

regions with the same ratio and offset to different faces own similar contextual feature. Namely, we can use a set of uniform boxes to approximate the actual regions of head, shoulder and body, as long as features from these boxes are similar among different faces. For a target face localized at $region_{target}$ at original image, considering the $anchor_{i,j}$, which means the j-th anchor at the i-th feature layer with stride size s_i, we define the label of k-th pyramid-anchor by

$$label_k(anchor_{i,j}) = \begin{cases} 1, \text{ if } iou(anchor_{i,j} \cdot s_i/s_{pa}^k, region_{target}) > threshold, \\ 0, otherwise, \end{cases}$$

(1)

for $k = 0, 1, \ldots, K$, respectively, where s_{pa} is the stride of pyramid anchors. $anchor_{i,j} \cdot s_i$ denotes the corresponding region in the original image of $anchor_{i,j}$, and $anchor_{i,j} \cdot s_i/s_{pa}^k$ represents the corresponding down-sampled region by stride s_{pa}^k. The $threshold$ is the same as other anchor-based detectors. Besides, a Pyramid-Box Loss will be demonstrated in Sect. 3.4.

In our experiments, we set the hyper parameter $s_{pa} = 2$ since the stride of adjacent prediction modules is 2. Furthermore, let $threshold = 0.35$ and $K = 2$. Then $label_0$, $label_1$ and $label_2$ are labels of face, head and body respectively. One can see that a face would generate 3 targets in three continuous prediction

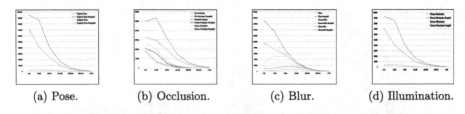

| (a) Pose. | (b) Occlusion. | (c) Blur. | (d) Illumination. |

Fig. 5. Data-anchor-sampling changes the distribution of the train data. Dotted lines show the distribution of certain attribute, while solid lines represent the corresponding distribution of those attribute after the data-anchor-sampling.

modules, which represent for the face itself, the head and body corresponding to the face. Figure 4 shows an example.

Benefited from the PyramidBox, our face detector can handle small, blurred and partially occluded faces better. Notice that the pyramid anchors are generated automatically without any extra label and this semi-supervised learning help PyramidAnchors extract approximate contextual features. In prediction process, we only use output of the face branch, so no additional computational cost is incurred at runtime, compared to standard anchor-based face detectors.

3.4 Training

In this section, we introduce the training dataset, data augmentation, loss function and other implementation details.

Train Dataset. We trained PyramidBox on $12,880$ images of the WIDER FACE training set with color distort, random crop and horizontal flip.

Data-Anchor-Sampling. Data sampling [34] is a classical subject in statistics, machine learning and pattern recognition, it achieves great development in recent years. For the task of objection detection, Focus Loss [17] address the class imbalance by reshaping the standard cross entropy loss.

Here we utilize a data augment sample method named Data-anchor-sampling. In short, data-anchor-sampling resizes train images by reshaping a random face in this image to a random smaller anchor size. More specifically, we first randomly select a face of size s_{face} in a sample. As previously mentioned that the scales of anchors in our PyramidBox, as shown in Sect. 3.1, are

$$s_i = 2^{4+i}, \text{ for } i = 0, 1, \ldots, 5,$$

let

$$i_{anchor} = \mathrm{argmin}_i \mathrm{abs}(s_{anchor_i} - s_{face})$$

be the index of the nearest anchor scale from the selected face, then we choose a random index i_{target} in the set

$$\{0, 1, \ldots, \min(5, i_{anchor} + 1)\},$$

finally, we resize the face of size of s_{face} to the size of

$$s_{target} = random(s_{i_{target}}/2, s_{i_{target}} * 2).$$

Thus, we got the image resize scale

$$s^* = s_{target}/s_{face}.$$

By resizing the original image with the scale s^* and cropping a standard size of 640×640 containing the selected face randomly, we get the anchor-sampled train data. For example, we first select a face randomly, suppose its size is 140, then its nearest anchor-size is 128, then we need to choose a target size from $16, 32, 64, 128$ and 256. In general, assume that we select 32, then we resize the original image by scale of $32/140 = 0.2285$. Finally, by cropping a 640×640 sub-image from the last resized image containing the originally selected face, we get the sampled train data.

As shown in Fig. 5, data-anchor-sampling changes the distribution of the train data as follows: (1) the proportion of small faces is larger than the large ones. (2) generate smaller face samples through larger ones to increase the diversity of face samples of smaller scales.

PyramidBox Loss. As a generalization of the multi-box loss in [13], we employ the *PyramidBox Loss* function for an image is defined as

$$L(\{p_{k,i}\}, \{t_{k,i}\}) = \sum_k \lambda_k L_k(\{p_{k,i}\}, \{t_{k,i}\}), \tag{2}$$

where the k-th pyramid-anchor loss is given by

$$L_k(\{p_{k,i}\}, \{t_{k,i}\}) = \frac{\lambda}{N_{k,cls}} \sum_{i_k} L_{k,cls}(p_{k,i}, p^*_{k,i}) + \frac{1}{N_{k,reg}} \sum_{i_k} p^*_{k,i} L_{k,reg}(t_{k,i}, t^*_{k,i}). \tag{3}$$

Here k is the index of pyramid-anchors ($k = 0, 1$, and 2 represents for face, head and body, respectively, in our experiments), and i is the index of an anchor and $p_{k,i}$ is the predicted probability of anchor i being the k-th object (face, head or body). The ground-truth label defined by

$$p^*_{k,i} = \begin{cases} 1, & \text{if the anchor down-sampled by stride } s^k_{pa} \text{ is positive,} \\ 0, & otherwise. \end{cases} \tag{4}$$

For example, when $k = 0$, the ground-truth label is equal to the label in Fast R-CNN [13], otherwise, when $k \geq 1$, one can determine the corresponding label by matching between the down-sampled anchors and ground-truth faces. Moreover, $t_{k,i}$ is a vector representing the 4 parameterized coordinates of the predicted bounding box, and $t^*_{k,i}$ is that of ground-truth box associated with a positive anchor, we can define it by

$$t^*_{k,i} = \left(t^*_x + \frac{1 - s^k_{pa}}{2} t^*_w s_{w,k} + \Delta_{x,k}, t^*_y + \frac{1 - s^k_{pa}}{2} t^*_h s_{h,k} + \Delta_{y,k}, \right.$$
$$\left. s^k_{pa} t^*_w s_{w,k} - 2\Delta_{x,k}, s^k_{pa} t^*_h s_{h,k} - 2\Delta_{y,k} \right), \tag{5}$$

where $\Delta_{x,k}$ and $\Delta_{y,k}$ denote offset of shifts, $s_{w,k}$ and $s_{h,k}$ are scale factors respect to width and height respectively. In our experiments, we set $\Delta_{x,k} = \Delta_{y,k} = 0$, $s_{w,k} = s_{h,k} = 1$ for $k < 2$ and $\Delta_{x,2} = 0, \Delta_{y,2} = t_h^*, s_{w,2} = \frac{7}{8}, s_{h,2} = 1$ for $k = 2$. The classification loss $L_{k,cls}$ is log loss over two classes (face vs. not face) and the regression loss $L_{k,reg}$ is the smooth L_1 loss defined in [13]. The term $p_{k,i}^* L_{k,reg}$ means the regression loss is activated only for positive anchors and disabled otherwise. The two terms are normalized with $N_{k,cls}$, $N_{k,reg}$, and balancing weights λ and λ_k for $k = 0, 1, 2$.

Optimization. As for the parameter initialization, our PyramidBox use the pre-trained parameters from VGG16 [35]. The parameters of *conv_fc* 67 and *conv_fc* 7 are initialized by sub-sampling parameters from *fc* 6 and *fc* 7 of VGG16 and the other additional layers are randomly initialized with "xavier" in [36]. We use a learning rate of 10^{-3} for 80k iterations, and 10^{-4} for the next 20k iterations, and 10^{-5} for the last 20k iterations on the WIDER FACE training set with batch size 16. We also use a momentum of 0.9 and a weight decay of 0.0005 [37].

4   Experiments

In this section, we firstly analyze the effectiveness of our PyramidBox through a set of experiments, and then evaluate the final model on WIDER FACE and FDDB face detection benchmarks.

4.1   Model Analysis

We analyze our model on the WIDER FACE validation set by contrast experiments.

Baseline. Our PyramidBox shares the same architecture of S^3FD, so we directly use it as a baseline.

Contrast Study. To better understand PyramidBox, we conduct contrast experiments to evaluate the contributions of each proposed component, from which we can get the following conclusions.

Low-Level Feature Pyramid Network (LFPN) Is Crucial for Detecting Hard Faces. The results listed in Table 1 prove that LFPN started from a middle layer, using *conv_fc* 7 in our PyramidBox, is more powerful, which implies that features with large gap in scale may not help each other. The comparison between the first and forth column of Table 1 indicates that LFPN increases the mAP by 1.9% on hard subset. This significant improvement demonstrates the effectiveness of joining high-level semantic features with the low-level ones.

Data-Anchor-Sampling Makes Detector Easier to Train. We employ Data-anchor-sampling based on LFPN network and the result shows that our data-anchor-sampling effectively improves the performance. The mAP is

Table 1. Performances of LFPN starting from different layers.

Start layer		Baseline	$conv7\_2$(FPN)	$conv6\_2$	$conv\_fc7$(LFPN)	$conv5\_3$	$conv4\_3$
RF/InputSize			1.13125	0.73125	0.53125	0.35625	0.16875
mAP	Easy	94.0	93.9	94.1	**94.3**	94.1	93.6
	Medium	92.7	92.9	93.1	**93.3**	93.1	92.5
	Hard	84.2	85.9	85.9	**86.1**	85.7	84.8

Table 2. The parameters of PyramidAnchors.

Method		Baseline	(K, s_{pa}) $(1, 1.5)$	(K, s_{pa}) $(1, 2.0)$	(K, s_{pa}) $(1, 3.0)$	(K, s_{pa}) $(2, 2.0)$
mAP	Easy	94.0	93.8	94.2	94.3	**94.7**
	Medium	92.7	92.7	93.0	93.1	**93.3**
	Hard	84.2	84.8	84.9	85.0	**85.1**

increased by 0.4%, 0.4% and 0.6% on easy, medium and hard subset, respectively. One can see that Data-anchor-sampling works well not only for small hard faces, but also for easy and medium faces.

PyramidAnchor and PyramidBox Loss Is Promising. By comparing the first and last column in Table 2, one can see that PyamidAnchor effectively improves the performance, i.e., 0.7%, 0.6% and 0.9% on easy, medium and hard, respectively. This dramatical improvement shows that learning contextual information is helpful to the task of detection, especially for hard faces.

Wider and Deeper Context Prediction Module Is Better. Table 3 shows that the performance of CPM is better than both DSSD module and SSH context module. Notice that the combination of SSH and DSSD gains very little compared to SSH alone, which indicates that large receptive field is more important to predict the accurate location and classification. In addition, by comparing the last two column of Table 4, one can find that the method of Max-in-out improves the mAP on WIDER FACE validation set about +0.2%(Easy), +0.3%(Medium) and +0.1%(Hard), respectively.

Table 3. Context-sensitive Predict Module.

Method		DSSD prediction module	SSH context module	CPM
mAP	Easy	95.3	95.5	**95.6**
	Medium	94.3	94.3	**94.5**
	Hard	88.2	88.4	**88.5**

To conclude this section, we summarize our results in Table 4, from which one can see that mAP increase 2.1%, 2.3% and **4.7%** on easy, medium and

Table 4. Contrast results of the PyramidBox on WIDER FACE validation subset.

Contribution		Baseline					PyramidBox
lfpn?			√	√	√	√	√
data-anchor-sampling?				√	√	√	√
pyramid-anchors?					√	√	√
context-prediect-module?						√	√
max-in-out?							√
mAP	Easy	94.0	94.3	94.7	95.5	95.9	**96.1**
	Medium	92.7	93.3	93.7	94.3	94.7	**95.0**
	Hard	84.2	86.1	86.7	88.3	88.8	**88.9**

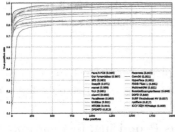
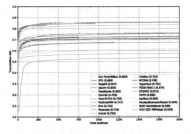

(a) Discontinous ROC curves   (b) Continous ROC curves

Fig. 6. Evaluation on the FDDB dataset.

hard subset, respectively. This sharp increase demonstrates the effectiveness of proposed PyramidBox, especially for hard faces.

4.2   Evaluation on Benchmark

We evaluate our PyramidBox on the most popular face detection benchmarks, including Face Detection Data Set and Benchmark (FDDB) [38] and WIDER FACE [39].

FDDB Dataset. It has $5,171$ faces in $2,845$ images collected from the Yahoo! news website. We evaluate our face detector on FDDB against the other state-of-art methods $[4,19,21,25,30,40-54]$. The PyramidBox achieves state-of-art performance and the result is shown in Fig. 6(a) and (b).

WIDER FACE Dataset. It contains $32,203$ images and $393,703$ annotated faces with a high degree of variability in scale, pose and occlusion. The database is split into training (40%), validation (10%) and testing (50%) set, where both validation and test set are divided into "easy", "medium" and "hard" subsets, regarding the difficulties of the detection. Our PyramidBox is trained only on the training set and evaluated on both validation set and testing

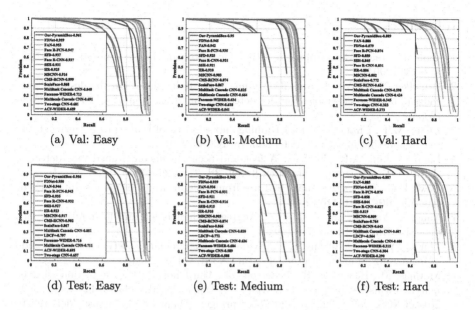

(a) Val: Easy   (b) Val: Medium   (c) Val: Hard

(d) Test: Easy   (e) Test: Medium   (f) Test: Hard

Fig. 7. Precision-recall curves on WIDER FACE validation and test sets.

set comparing with the state-of-the-art face detectors, such as [6, 20–23, 25–28, 30, 39, 40, 43, 51, 55, 56]. Figure 7 presents the precision-recall curves and mAP values. Our PyramidBox outperforms others across all three subsets, i.e. 0.961 (easy), 0.950 (medium), 0.889 (hard) for validation set, and 0.956 (easy), 0.946 (medium), 0.887 (hard) for testing set.

5   Conclusion

This paper proposed a novel context-assisted single shot face detector, denoted as PyramidBox, to handle the unconstrained face detection problem. We designed a novel context anchor, named PyramidAnchor, to supervise face detector to learn features from contextual parts around faces. Besides, we modified feature pyramid network into a low-level feature pyramid network to combine features from high-level and high-resolution, which are effective for finding small faces. We also proposed a wider and deeper prediction module to make full use of joint feature. In addition, we introduced Data-anchor-sampling to augment the train data to increase the diversity of train data for small faces. The experiments demonstrate that our contributions lead PyramidBox to the state-of-the-art performance on the common face detection benchmarks, especially for hard faces.

Acknowledgments. We wish to thank Dr. Shifeng Zhang and Dr. Yuguang Liu for many helpful discussions.

References

1. Viola, P., Jones, M.J.: Robust real-time face detection. Int. J. Comput. Vis. **57**(2), 137–154 (2004)
2. Brubaker, S.C., Wu, J., Sun, J., Mullin, M.D., Rehg, J.M.: On the design of cascades of boosted ensembles for face detection. Int. J. Comput. Vis. **77**(1–3), 65–86 (2008)
3. Pham, M.T., Cham, T.J.: Fast training and selection of Haar features using statistics in boosting-based face detection. In: ICCV (2007)
4. Liao, S., Jain, A.K., Li, S.Z.: A fast and accurate unconstrained face detector. IEEE Trans. Parttern Anal. Mach. Intell. **38**, 211–223 (2016)
5. Lowe, D.G.: Distinctive image features from scale-invariant keypoints. Int. J. Comput. Vis. **60**(2), 91–110 (2004)
6. Yang, B., Yan, J., Lei, Z., Li, S.Z.: Aggregate channel features for multi-view face detection. In: IJCB, pp. 1–8 (2014)
7. Zhu, Q., Yeh, M.C., Cheng, K.T., Avidan, S.: Fast human detection using a cascade of histograms of oriented gradients. In: CVPR, vol. 2 (2006)
8. Mathias, M., Benenson, R., Pedersoli, M., Van Gool, L.: Face detection without bells and whistles. In: Fleet, D., Pajdla, T., Schiele, B., Tuytelaars, T. (eds.) ECCV 2014. LNCS, vol. 8692, pp. 720–735. Springer, Cham (2014). https://doi.org/10.1007/978-3-319-10593-2_47
9. Yan, J., Lei, Z., Wen, L., Li, S.Z.: The fastest deformable part model for object detection. In: CVPR (2014)
10. Zhu, X., Ramanan, D.: Face detection, pose estimation, and landmark localization in the wild. In: CVPR (2012)
11. Girshick, R., Donahue, J., Darrell, T., Malik, J.: Rich feature hierarchies for accurate object detection and semantic segmentation. In: CVPR (2014)
12. Girshick, R., Donahue, J., Darrell, T., Malik, J.: Region-based convolutional networks for accurate object detection and segmentation. TIEEE Trans. Parttern Anal. Mach. Intell. **38**(3), 142–158 (2016)
13. Girshick, R.: Fast R-CNN. In: ICCV (2015)
14. Ren, S., Girshick, K.H.R., Sun, J.: Faster R-CNN: towards real-time object detection with region proposal networks. In: NIPS (2015)
15. Liu, W., et al.: SSD: single shot multibox detector. In: Leibe, B., Matas, J., Sebe, N., Welling, M. (eds.) ECCV 2016. LNCS, vol. 9905, pp. 21–37. Springer, Cham (2016). https://doi.org/10.1007/978-3-319-46448-0_2
16. Redmon, J., Divvala, S., Girshick, R., Farhadi, A.: You only look once: unified, real-time object detection. In: CVPR (2016)
17. Lin, T.Y., Goyal, P., Girshick, R., He, K., Dollár, P.: Focal loss for dense object detection. In: ICCV (2017)
18. Zhang, S., Wen, L., Bian, X., Lei, Z., Li, S.Z.: Single-shot refinement neural network for object detection. arXiv preprint (2017)
19. Barbu, A., Gramajo, G.: Face detection with a 3D model. arXiv preprint arXiv:1404.3596 (2014)
20. Najibi, M., Samangouei, P., Chellappa, R., Davis, L.S.: SSH: single stage headless face detector. In: ICCV (2017)
21. Zhang, S., Zhu, X., Lei, X., Shi, H., Wang, X., Li, S.Z.: S^{3}FD: single shot scale-invariant face detector. In: ICCV (2017)
22. Wang, Y., Ji, X., Zhou, Z., Wang, H., Li, Z.: Detecting faces using region-based fully convolutional networs. arXiv preprint arXiv:1709.05256 (2017)

23. Wang, J., Yuan, Y., Yu, G.: Face attention network: an effective face detector for the occluded faces. arXiv preprint arXiv:1711.07246 (2017)
24. Lin, T.Y., Dollár, P., Girshick, R.: Feature pyramid networks for object detection. In: CVPR (2017)
25. Zhang, S., Zhu, X., Lei, X., Shi, H., Wang, X., Li, S.Z.: FaceBoxes: a CPU real-time face detector with high accuracy. arXiv preprint arXiv:1708.05234 (2017)
26. Yang, S., Xiong, Y., Loy, C.C., Tang, X.: Face detection through scale-friendly deep convolutional networks. arXiv preprint arXiv:1706.02863 (2017)
27. Zhu, C., Zheng, Y., Luu, K., Savvides, M.: CMS-RCNN: contextual multi-scale region-based CNN for unconstrained face detection. arXiv preprint arXiv:1606.05413 (2016)
28. Hu, P., Ramanan, D.: Finding tiny faces. In: CVPR (2017)
29. Liu, W., Rabinovich, A., Berg, A.C.: ParseNet: looking wider to see better. ICLR (2016)
30. Cai, Z., Fan, Q., Feris, R.S., Vasconcelos, N.: A unified multi-scale deep convolutional neural network for fast object detection. In: Leibe, B., Matas, J., Sebe, N., Welling, M. (eds.) ECCV 2016. LNCS, vol. 9908, pp. 354–370. Springer, Cham (2016). https://doi.org/10.1007/978-3-319-46493-0_22
31. Fu, C.Y., Liu, W., Ranga, A., Tyagi, A., Berg, A.C.: DSSD: deconvolutional single shot detector. arXiv preprint arXiv:1701.06659
32. Szegedy, C., Ioffe, S., Vanhoucke, V.: Inception-v4, inception-resnet and the impact of residual connections on learning. arXiv preprint arXiv:1602.07261 (2016)
33. Goodfellow, I.J., Farley, D.W., Mirza, M., Courville, A., Bengio, Y.: Maxout networks (2013)
34. Thompson, S.K.: Sampling. Wiley, Hoboken (2012)
35. Russakovsky, O., et al.: Imagenet large scale visual recognition challenge. Int. J. Comput. Vis. **115**(3), 211–252 (2015)
36. Glorot, X., Bengio, Y.: Understanding the difficulty of training deep feedforward neural networks. In: AISTATS, vol. 9 (2010)
37. Krizhevsky, A., Sutskever, I., Hinton, G.: ImageNet classification with deep convolutional neural networks. In: NIPS (2012)
38. Jain, V., Learned-Miller, E.G.: FDDB: a benchmark for face detection in unconstrained settings. UMass Amherst Technical report (2010)
39. Yang, S., Luo, P., Loy, C.C., Tang, X.: Wider face: a face detection benchmark. In: CVPR (2016)
40. Zhang, K., Zhang, Z., Li, Z., Qiao, Y.: Joint face detection and alignment using multitask cascaded convolutional networks. In: SPL, vol. 23, no. 10 (2016)
41. Yu, J., Jiang, Y., Wang, Z., Cao, Z., Huang, T.: UnitBox: an advanced object detection network. In: MM. ACM (2016)
42. Triantafyllidou, D., Tefas, A.: A fast deep convolutional neural network for face detection in big visual data. In: INNS Conference on Big Data (2016)
43. Yang, S., Luo, P., Loy, C.C., Tang, X: From facial parts responses to face detection: a deep learning approach. In: ICCV (2015)
44. Li, Y., Sun, B., Wu, T., Wang, Y.: Face detection with end-to-end integration of a convnet and a 3D model (2016)
45. Farfade, S.S., Saberian, M.J., Li, L.J.: Multi-view face detection using deep convolutional neural networks
46. Ghiasi, G., Fowlkes, C.: Occlusion coherence: detecting and localizing occluded faces (2015)
47. Kumar, V., Namboodiri, A., Jawahar, C.: Visual phrases for exemplar face detection. In: ICCV (2015)

48. Li, H., Hua, G., Lin, Z., Brandt, J., Yang, J.: Probabilistic elastic part model for unsupervised face detector adaptation. In: ICCV (2013)
49. Li, J., Zhang, Y.: Learning surf cascade for fast and accurate object detection. In: CVPR (2013)
50. Li, H., Lin, Z., Brandt, J., Shen, X., Hua, G.: Efficient boosted exemplar-based face detection. In: CVPR (2014)
51. Ohn-Bar, E., Trivedi, M.M.: To boost or not to boost? On the limits of boosted trees for object detection. In: ICPR (2016)
52. Ranjan, R., Patel, V.M., Chellappa, R.: A deep pyramid deformable part model for face detection. In: BTAS (2015)
53. Ranjan, R., Patel, V.M., Chellappa, R.: HyperFace: a deep multi-task learning framework for face detection, landmark localization, pose estimation, and gender recognition. arXiv preprint arXiv:1603.01249 (2016)
54. Wan, S., Chen, Z., Zhang, T., Zhang, B., Wong, K.K.: Bootstrapping face detection with hard negative examples. arXiv preprint arXiv:1608.02236 (2016)
55. Zhang, C., Xu, X., Tu, D.: Face detection using improved faster RCNN. arXiv preprint arXiv:1802.02142 (2018)
56. Wang, H., Li, Z., Ji, X., Wang, Y.: Face R-CNN. arXiv preprint arXiv:1706.01061, vol. 7 (2017)

Author Index

Author Index

Printed in the United States
By Bookmasters